Nineteenth-Century Literature Criticism

Guide to Gale Literary Criticism Series

When you need to review criticism of literary works, these are the Gale series to use:

If the author's death date is: **You should turn to:**

After Dec. 31, 1959
(or author is still living)

CONTEMPORARY LITERARY CRITICISM

for example: Jorge Luis Borges, Anthony Burgess,
William Faulkner, Mary Gordon,
Ernest Hemingway, Iris Murdoch

1900 through 1959

TWENTIETH-CENTURY LITERARY CRITICISM

for example: Willa Cather, F. Scott Fitzgerald,
Henry James, Mark Twain, Virginia Woolf

1800 through 1899

NINETEENTH-CENTURY LITERATURE CRITICISM

for example: Fyodor Dostoevsky, Nathaniel Hawthorne,
George Sand, William Wordsworth

1400 through 1799

LITERATURE CRITICISM FROM 1400 TO 1800 *(excluding Shakespeare)*

for example: Anne Bradstreet, Daniel Defoe,
Alexander Pope, François Rabelais,
Jonathan Swift, Phillis Wheatley

SHAKESPEAREAN CRITICISM

Shakespeare's plays and poetry

Antiquity through 1399

CLASSICAL AND MEDIEVAL LITERATURE CRITICISM

for example: Dante, Homer, Plato, Sophocles, Vergil,
the Beowulf Poet

Gale also publishes related criticism series:

CHILDREN'S LITERATURE REVIEW

This series covers authors of all eras who have written for the
preschool through high school audience.

SHORT STORY CRITICISM

This series covers the major short fiction writers of all
nationalities and periods of literary history.

ISSN 0732-1864

Volume 30

Nineteenth-Century Literature Criticism

Excerpts from Criticism of the
Works of Novelists, Poets, Playwrights,
Short Story Writers, Philosophers, and Other
Creative Writers Who Died between 1800
and 1899, from the First Published Critical
Appraisals to Current Evaluations

**Laurie DiMauro
Paula Kepos**
Editors

**David Kmenta
Marie Lazzari
Thomas Ligotti
Michelle L. McClellan
Joann Prosyniuk**
Associate Editors

 Gale Research Inc. · DETROIT · LONDON

Contents

Preface   vii

Acknowledgments   xi

Preface

Since its inception in 1981, *Nineteenth-Century Literature Criticism* has been a valuable resource for students and librarians seeking critical commentary on writers of this transitional period in world history. Designated an "Outstanding Reference Source" by the American Library Association with the publication of its first volume, *NCLC* has since been purchased by over 6,000 school, public, and university libraries. The series has covered more than 300 authors representing 22 nationalities and over 15,000 titles. No other reference source has surveyed the critical reaction to nineteenth-century authors and literature as thoroughly as *NCLC*.

Scope of the Series

NCLC is designed to serve as an introduction for students and advanced readers to the authors of the nineteenth century, and to the most significant interpretations of these authors' works. The great poets, novelists, short story writers, dramatists, and philosophers of this period are frequently studied in high school and college literature courses. By organizing and reprinting the enormous amount of commentary written on these authors, *NCLC* helps students develop valuable insight into literary history, promotes a better understanding of the texts, and sparks ideas for papers and assignments. Each entry in *NCLC* presents a comprehensive survey of an author's career or an individual work of literature and provides the user with a multiplicity of interpretations and assessments. Such variety allows students to pursue their own interests; furthermore, it fosters an awareness that literature is dynamic and responsive to many different opinions.

Every fourth volume of *NCLC* is devoted to literary topics that cannot be covered under the author approach used in the rest of the series. Such topics include literary movements, prominent themes in nineteenth-century literature, literary reaction to political and historical events, significant eras in literary history, prominent literary anniversaries, and the literatures of cultures that are often overlooked by English-speaking readers.

NCLC continues the survey of criticism of world literature begun by Gale's *Contemporary Literary Criticism (CLC)* and *Twentieth-Century Literary Criticism (TCLC)*, both of which excerpt and reprint commentary on authors of the twentieth century. For additional information about *TCLC, CLC,* and Gale's other criticism series, users should consult the Guide to Gale Literary Criticism Series preceding the title page in this volume.

Coverage

Each volume of *NCLC* is carefully compiled to present:
- criticism of authors, or literary topics, representing a variety of genres and nationalities
- both major and lesser-known writers and literary works of the period
- 8-12 authors or 4-6 topics per volume
- individual entries that survey critical response to each author's work or each topic in literary history, including early criticism to reflect initial reactions; later criticism to represent any rise or decline in reputation; and current retrospective analyses.

Organization of This Book

An author entry consists of the following elements: author heading, biographical and critical introduction, list of principal works, excerpts of criticism (each preceded by an annotation and followed by a bibliographic citation), and a bibliography of further reading.

- The **author heading** consists of the name under which the author most commonly wrote, followed by birth and death dates. If an author wrote consistently under a pseudonym, the pseudonym will be listed in the author heading and the real name given in parentheses on the first line of the biographical and critical introduction. Also located at the beginning of the introduction to the author entry are any name variations under which an author wrote, including transliterated forms for authors whose languages use nonroman alphabets.

- The **biographical and critical introduction** outlines the author's life and career, as well as the critical issues surrounding his or her work. References are provided to past volumes of *NCLC* and to other biographical and critical reference series published by Gale, including *Short Story Criticism, Poetry Criticism, Children's Literature Review, Contemporary Authors, Dictionary of Literary Biography,* and *Something about the Author.*

• Most *NCLC* entries include **portraits** of the author. Many entries also contain reproductions of materials pertinent to an author's career, including manuscript pages, title pages, dust jackets, letters, and drawings, as well as photographs of important people, places, and events in an author's life.

• The **list of principal works** is chronological by date of first book publication and identifies the genre of each work. In the case of foreign authors with both foreign-language publications and English translations, the title and date of the first English-language edition are given in brackets. Unless otherwise indicated, dramas are dated by first performance, not first publication.

• **Criticism** is arranged chronologically in each author entry to provide a perspective on changes in critical evaluation over the years. All titles of works by the author featured in the entry are printed in boldface type to enable the user to easily locate discussion of particular works. Also for purposes of easier identification, the critic's name and the publication date of the essay are given at the beginning of each piece of criticism. Unsigned criticism is preceded by the title of the journal in which it appeared. Some of the excerpts in *NCLC* also contain translated material. Unless otherwise noted, translations in brackets are by the editors; translations in parentheses or continuous with the text are by the critic. Publication information (such as publisher names and book prices) and parenthetical numerical references (such as footnotes or page and line references to specific editions of works) have been deleted at the editors' discretion to provide smoother reading of the text.

• Critical excerpts are prefaced by **annotations** providing the reader with information about both the critic and the criticism that follows. Included are the critic's reputation, individual approach to literary criticism, and particular expertise in an author's works. Also noted are the relative importance of a work of criticism, the scope of the excerpt, and the growth of critical controversy or changes in critical trends regarding an author. In some cases, these annotations cross-reference excerpts by critics who discuss each other's commentary.

• A complete **bibliographic citation** designed to facilitate location of the original essay or book follows each piece of criticism.

• An annotated list of **further reading** appearing at the end of each author entry suggests secondary sources on the author. In some cases it includes essays for which the editors could not obtain reprint rights.

Cumulative Indexes

• Each volume of *NCLC* contains a cumulative **author index** listing all authors who have appeared in the following Gale series: *Contemporary Literary Criticism, Twentieth-Century Literary Criticism, Nineteenth-Century Literature Criticism, Literature Criticism from 1400 to 1800,* and *Classical and Medieval Literature Criticism.* Topic entries devoted to a single author, such as the entry on James Joyce's *Ulysses* in *TCLC* 26, are listed in this index. Also included are cross-references to the Gale series *Poetry Criticism, Short Story Criticism, Children's Literature Review, Authors in the News, Contemporary Authors, Contemporary Authors Autobiography Series, Dictionary of Literary Biography, Concise Dictionary of American Literary Biography, Something about the Author, Something about the Author Autobiography Series,* and *Yesterday's Authors of Books for Children.* Useful for locating authors within the various series, this index is particularly valuable for those authors who are identified by a certain period but who, because of their death dates, are placed in another, or for those authors whose careers span two periods. For example, Fyodor Dostoevsky is found in *NCLC,* yet Leo Tolstoy, another major nineteenth-century Russian novelist, is found in *TCLC* because he died after 1899.

• Each *NCLC* volume includes a cumulative **nationality index** which lists all authors who have appeared in *NCLC* volumes, arranged alphabetically under their respective nationalities, as well as Topics volume entries devoted to particular national literatures.

• Each new volume in Gale's Literary Criticism Series includes a cumulative **topic index,** which lists all literary topics treated in *NCLC, TCLC, LC 1400-1800,* and the *CLC* Yearbook.

• Each new volume of *NCLC,* with the exception of the Topics volumes, contains a **title index** listing the titles of all literary works discussed in the volume. The first volume of *NCLC* published each year contains an index listing all titles discussed in the series since its inception. Titles discussed in the Topics volume entries are not included in the *NCLC* cumulative index.

A Note to the Reader

When writing papers, students who quote directly from any volume in Gale's Literary Criticism Series may use the following general forms to footnote reprinted criticism. The first example pertains to material drawn from periodicals, the second to material reprinted from books.

[1] T. S. Eliot, "John Donne," *The Nation and the Athenaeum,* 33 (9 June 1923), 321-32; excerpted and reprinted in *Literature Criticism from 1400 to 1800,* Vol. 10, ed. James E. Person, Jr. (Detroit: Gale Research, 1989), pp. 28-9.

[2] Clara G. Stillman, *Samuel Butler: A Mid-Victorian Modern* (Viking Press, 1932); excerpted and reprinted in *Twentieth-Century Literary Criticism,* Vol. 33, ed. Paula Kepos (Detroit: Gale Research, 1989), pp. 43-5.

Suggestions Are Welcome

In response to suggestions, several features have been added to *NCLC* since the series began, including annotations to excerpted criticism, a cumulative index to authors in all Gale literary criticism series, entries devoted to criticism on a single work by a major author, more extensive illustrations, and a title index listing all literary works discussed in the series since its inception.

Readers who wish to suggest authors or topics to appear in future volumes, or who have other suggestions, are cordially invited to write the editors.

Acknowledgments

The editors wish to thank the copyright holders of the excerpted criticism included in this volume, the permissions managers of many book and magazine publishing companies for assisting us in securing reprint rights, and Anthony Bogucki for assistance with copyright research. We are also grateful to the staffs of the Detroit Public Library Complex, and University of Michigan Libraries for making their resources available to us. Following is a list of copyright holders who have granted us permission to reprint material in this volume of *NCLC*. Every effort has been made to trace copyright, but if omissions have been made, please let us know.

COPYRIGHTED EXCERPTS IN *NCLC*, VOLUME 30, WERE REPRINTED FROM THE FOLLOWING PERIODICALS:

American Quarterly, v. XXVIII, Fall, 1976. Copyright © 1976 by American Studies Association./ v. 37, Spring, 1985 for "English Satire and Connecticut Wit" by Peter M. Briggs. Copyright © 1985 by American Studies Association. Reprinted by permission of the publisher and the author.—*The American-Scandinavian Review,* v. L, December, 1962. Reprinted by permission of the publisher.—*American Speech,* v. XXXVII, May, 1962; v. 54, Spring, 1979. Copyright © 1962, 1979 by the University of Alabama Press. Both reprinted by permission of the publisher.—*Ariel: A Review of International English Literature,* v. 8, January, 1977 for "Mrs. Trollope's Artistic Dilemma in Michael Armstrong" by Roger P. Wallins. Copyright © 1977 The Board of Governors, The University of Calgary. Reprinted by permission of the publisher and the author.—*Books from Finland,* v. XVIII, 1984 for "Seven Brothers in Germany" by Pertti Lassila, translated by Hildi Hawkins; v. XVIII, 1984 for "The Stages of Aleksis Kivi" by Pekka Lounela, translated by Hildi Hawkins. Both reprinted by permission of the respective authors.—*Early American Literature,* v. X, Winter, 1975-76 for "John Trumbull: Essayist" by Bruce Granger. Copyrighted, 1976, by the University of Massachusetts. Reprinted by permission of the publisher and the author.—*Mosaic: A Journal for the Interdisciplinary Study of Literature,* v. XIV, Spring, 1981; v. XVIII, Summer, 1985. © Mosaic 1981, 1985. Both acknowledgment of previous publication is herewith made.—*The Nation,* New York, v. 178, April 24, 1954. Copyright 1954, renewed 1982 by *The Nation* magazine/The Nation Company, Inc. Reprinted by permission of the publisher.—*The New England Quarterly,* v. XI, December, 1938 for "John Trumbull as a Critic of Poetry," by Alexander Cowie. Copyright 1938 by *The New England Quarterly*. Reprinted by permission of the publisher and author.—*The New York Times Book Review,* May 10, 1942. Copyright 1942 by the New York Times Company. Reprinted by permission of the publisher.—*PMLA,* v. 98, January, 1983; v. 102, October, 1987. Copyright © 1983, 1987 by the Modern Language Association of America. Both reprinted by permission of the Modern Language Association of America.—*The Saturday Review of Literature,* v. V, February 2, 1929. Copyright 1929 *Saturday Review* magazine.—*Scandinavian Studies,* v. 50, Summer, 1978 for "Aleksis Kivi's 'Kullervo': A Historical Drama of Ideas" by K. Börje Vähämäki. Reprinted by permission of the publisher and the author.—*Slavic and East European Journal,* v. VI, Winter, 1962; v. XIV, 1970. © 1962, 1970 by AATSEEL of U.S., Inc. Both reprinted by permission of the publisher.—*A Yearbook of Studies in English Language and Literature,* v. 80, 1985-86. © 1986 by Wilhelm Braumüller. Reprinted by permission of the publisher.

COPYRIGHTED EXCERPTS IN *NCLC*, VOLUME 30, WERE REPRINTED FROM THE FOLLOWING BOOKS:

Ahokas, Jaakko. From *A History of Finnish Literature.* Indiana University Uralic and Altaic Series, Volume 72. Research Center for the Language Sciences, 1973. Copyright © 1973 by Indiana University. All rights reserved. Reprinted by permission of Denis Sinor.—Arner, Robert D. From Atheneum, 1971. "The Connecticut Wits," in *American Literature: 1764-1789, The Revolutionary Years.* Edited by Everett Emerson. The University of Wisconsin Press, 1977. Copyright © 1977 by The Regents of the University of Wisconsin System. All rights reserved. Reprinted by permission of the publisher.—Auden, W. H. From *Forewords and Afterwords.* Edited by Edward Mendelson. Random House, 1973. Copyright © 1973 by W. H. Auden. Reprinted by permission of Random House, Inc.—Babbidge, Homer D., Jr. From an introduction to *On Being American: Selected Writings, 1783-1828.* By Noah Webster, edited by Homer D. Babbidge, Jr. Frederick A. Praeger, Publishers, 1967. © 1967 by Homer D. Babbidge, Jr. All rights reserved. Reprinted by permission of the Literary Estate of Homer D. Babbidge, Jr.—Barbier, Carl Paul. From *William Gilpin: His Drawings, Teaching, and Theory of the Picturesque.* Oxford at the Clarendon Press, 1963. © Oxford University Press 1963. Reprinted by permission of the publisher.—Benz, Ernst. From "Theogony and the Transformation of Man in Friedrich Wilhelm Joseph Schelling," in *Man and Transformation: Papers from the Eranos Yearbooks.* Edited by Joseph Campbell, translated by Ralph Manheim. Bollingen Series XXX. Pantheon Books, 1964. Copyright © 1964 by Bollingen Foundation. Reprinted with permission of

PHOTOGRAPHS AND ILLUSTRATIONS APPEARING IN *NCLC,* VOLUME 30, WERE RECEIVED FROM THE FOLLOWING SOURCES:

Catharine Beecher

1800-1878

American essayist.

A member of one of the most prominent families in nineteenth-century America, Beecher is best known for her efforts to promote education for women and to improve their status in society. She published numerous works to explain and advance her causes, the most renowned being her *Treatise on Domestic Economy for the Use of Young Ladies at Home and at School,* which contains both practical advice and general ideas about women's roles. Although Beecher's achievements have been largely overshadowed by those of her siblings Harriet Beecher Stowe, the author of *Uncle Tom's Cabin* (1852), and Henry Ward Beecher, a well-known preacher and reformer, she was one of the most famous women in the United States at the height of her career and is credited with effecting significant changes in nineteenth-century domestic life as well as contributing to the developing ideology about the importance of women in American society.

Born in East Hampton, New York, Beecher was the oldest child of Lyman Beecher, a noted clergyman, and Roxanna Foote Beecher, his first wife. When Beecher was nine, the family moved to Litchfield, Connecticut, where her father became the minister of a prestigious church. There she attended Miss Pierce's school, one of the few institutions in the United States then providing education for girls, and in 1821 she left home to teach school in New London, Connecticut. The death of her fiancé, Yale University professor Alexander Metcalf Fisher, the following year, caused Beecher to reevaluate her religious beliefs and her plans for her life. According to the Calvinist doctrine propounded by Beecher's father, Fisher was denied salvation despite leading a virtuous life because he had never experienced conversion. Unwilling to accept the idea that an ostensibly benevolent deity would condemn her fiancé's soul to eternal torment on these grounds, Beecher sought to construct an alternative system of belief, emphasizing the redeeming value of character and behavior rather than the Calvinist conversion experience. Her revised Protestant theology was outlined in several volumes, most notably *Letters on the Difficulties of Religion* and *Common Sense Applied to Religion; or, The Bible and the People.*

Considering education to be the only profession open to her, Beecher opened a girls' school in Hartford with her sister Mary in 1823. Determined that their institution, the Hartford Female Seminary, would be more than a finishing school, the Beecher sisters sought to provide a solid moral and intellectual education for their students. While the number of students and teachers grew rapidly, Beecher was unable to raise sufficient funds to run the school, and she resigned her position as headmistress in 1831. The next year she accompanied her father to Cincinnati, where she founded the Western Female Institute. While in Cincinnati, Beecher became convinced of the need for teachers in the western United States; believing that the education of American children was essential to the future of the country and that the need for teachers provided unparal-

leled opportunities for women to support themselves and live independently, Beecher devoted most of the rest of her life to this issue. She set up several associations to organize the training and placement of teachers, including the Central Committee for Promoting National Education and the American Women's Educational Association; traveled through the eastern states to raise money and recruit teachers, lecturing and publishing pamphlets and essays; and established institutions in Minnesota, Wisconsin, Illinois, and Iowa to train teachers. Although a number of Beecher's goals were realized, she faced a constant shortage of funds, and the training institutions she founded were not as successful as she had hoped. Near the end of her life, Beecher returned to New England to be closer to her family, and she died at her brother's home in 1878.

Most of Beecher's writings reflect her concerns regarding women's participation in society. In the *Treatise on Domestic Economy for the Use of Young Ladies at Home and at School,* she defined a new role for women in the household, asserting that as managers of their households women bore the responsibility for shaping both the domestic environment and the character of their children and should therefore be supplied with the information necessary to perform those tasks well. In this volume and

1

others she related scientific and technical knowledge in an accessible manner, covering a wide range of topics that included women's and children's health, home design, clothing, and nutrition. Beecher further believed that although women should confine themselves to such traditional roles as wife, mother, teacher, and nurse, the work they did should be recognized as both important and challenging, and she sought to professionalize those roles in order to improve women's status in society. However, Beecher did not argue for full equality for women. For example, she was against women's suffrage, an issue on which her opinion differed from most of her family, especially her brother Henry Ward Beecher and her sister Isabella Beecher Hooker, and she believed that women should not be involved in the antislavery movement, asserting that they should exert their moral influence through example rather than through advocacy. Nevertheless, Beecher remains an important figure in American history for her efforts to improve both the quality of women's lives and the perception of their importance to society.

(See also *Dictionary of Literary Biography,* Vol. 1.)

PRINCIPAL WORKS

Suggestions Respecting Improvements in Education (essay) 1829

An Essay on the Education of Female Teachers (essay) 1835

Letters on the Difficulties of Religion (essays) 1836

An Essay on Slavery and Abolitionism with Reference to the Duty of American Females (essay) 1837

A Treatise on Domestic Economy for the Use of Young Ladies at Home and at School (manual) 1841

Letters to Persons Who Are Engaged in Domestic Service (essays) 1842

The Duty of American Women to Their Country (essay) 1845

The Evils Suffered by American Women and American Children: The Causes and the Remedy (essay) 1846

Miss Beecher's Domestic Receipt Book (cookbook) 1846

Truth Stranger Than Fiction: A Narrative of Recent Transactions Involving Inquiries in Regard to the Principles of Honor, Truth and Justice Which Obtain in a Distinguished American University (essay) 1850

The True Remedy for the Wrongs of Woman (essay) 1851

Letters to the People on Health and Happiness (essays) 1855

Physiology and Calisthenics (essays) 1856

Common Sense Applied to Religion; or, The Bible and the People (essay) 1857

An Appeal to the People on Behalf of Their Rights as Authorized Interpreters of the Bible (essay) 1860

Religious Training of Children in the School, the Family, and the Church (essay) 1864

The American Woman's Home; or, Principles of Domestic Science [with Harriet Beecher Stowe] (manual) 1869

Woman's Profession as Mother and Educator: With Views in Opposition to Woman Suffrage (essay) 1872

Miss Beecher's Housekeeper and Healthkeeper (manual) 1873

Educational Reminiscences and Suggestions (essay) 1874

The North American Review   (essay date 1830)

[*In the following excerpt, the critic offers a positive assessment of* Suggestions Respecting Improvements in Education.]

Much of the existing evil in the world may be removed or lessened by human agency. What now is, and always has been, regarded as the most powerful means for improving the condition of our race, is education. This being so well understood, it is sometimes asked, Why, then, are the hopes of careful and conscientious parents so often defeated in the future character of their offspring? Why is it, that the wealth lavished on education, and the unremitted labors of friends and teachers, so often yield but miserable and unsatisfactory returns; that where the good seed is sown, the harvest is nothing but weeds? We do not now inquire, as to the causes of crime and wretchedness among individuals who are borne down by poverty and ignorance; or of the low and sensual morality of nations on which the light of Christianity has not yet shone; or of those which have been for ages oppressed under absurd political systems. But why is it, that, in a country like our own, whose political institutions are wise, in which education is made an object of chief importance, it should so often prove unsuccessful in its influence on the character even of those who are most fortunately situated? (pp. 323-24)

[We] cannot but confess, that education is as yet a very imperfect instrument, compared with what it might be rendered. The object of [*Suggestions Respecting Improvements in Education*] appears to be to show some of the causes of this imperfection, and to suggest improvements. The author is the Principal of the Hartford Female Seminary, an institution for the education of females, which has acquired a high reputation under her direction. It appears from the title-page, that it was presented to the trustees of the Seminary, and that it is published at their request. The author, after pointing out the defects in school education, states some of the modes of instruction which are pursued in her own establishment, and finally proposes certain changes in it for the consideration of the trustees.

We can truly say, that we have read this little volume with great pleasure. Not that we give our entire assent to all that the author advances, for we shall have occasion, before we finish, to controvert some of her positions; but her book exhibits great good sense, a thorough practical knowledge of the business of instruction, and a deep and lively interest in the subject. It is evidently the work of patient reflection and careful observation; and written in a very animated and forcible manner. Her suggestions do not all merit the praise of absolute novelty, but many of them have the higher merit of truth and correctness; and, indeed, when we consider that, as far back as the time of Lycurgus, the science of education was, in some respects, as well understood and thoroughly practised as at present, and recollect the attention which such minds as Quinctilian and Locke, to mention no others, have devoted to the subject, we shall readily believe, that what the public requires is not always to have new paths pointed out, but to be recalled to the old. We believe that few parents and few instructers can read this little volume without deriving from it something useful. And perhaps that heavy mass, the public, which is oftentimes so difficult to move, but whose momentum is so irresistible when it is once set in motion, may be forced into action by this and similar publications. (pp. 325-26)

> *"Suggestions on Education," in* The North American Review, *n.s. Vol. XXX, No. XLII, April, 1830, pp. 323-37.*

The Biblical Repertory (essay date 1836)

[*In the following excerpt, the critic assesses the strengths and weaknesses of the system of theology Beecher outlined in* Letters on the Difficulties of Religion.]

Female writers have been so few in this country, that we have never before had occasion to review a work from the pen of one of the softer sex. Miss Beecher, however, is not a stranger to the American public. She has produced already some works on education which have met with no small approbation. And whether her strong good sense, the versatility of her talents, or the ease and energy of her style be considered, it must be admitted, that as a writer she has no need of any peculiar indulgence from reviewers. Indeed there is nothing feminine in the productions of this lady: if the work had been anonymous we should never have suspected that it proceeded from the hand of a lady. As this praise may possibly be misapprehended, we distinctly avow, that there is nothing masculine in this performance, but its strength. The spirit of [*Letters on the Difficulties of Religion*] is throughout amiable. A love of truth and a heart of kindness and good will to men, are manifestly the characteristics of the writer. If there should be detected by the severe critic some appearance of self-complacency, and an unshrinking confidence in her knowledge and abilities in grappling with the most abstruse subjects of philosophy and theology, the discussion is generally so well sustained, and so much perspicacity and ingenuity are displayed, that some indications of literary vanity,—as the temptation to it was great,—may well be pardoned in so clever a writer. We doubt whether any of the celebrated female authors of the present age, excel Miss Beecher in intellectual strength; and we are pleased to observe the general sobriety and correctness of her opinions. We had been led to expect some degree of eccentricity or extravagance. We were led to believe that she entertained many opinions in theology, which, if not new, are in our day peculiar. We were therefore agreeably disappointed, in finding her, generally, the able advocate of doctrines which we consider sound. In some cases, it is true, she slides over difficulties instead of removing them; and seems to think that she has placed a point in a satisfactory light, when in fact she has not appreciated the difficulty, or has dexterously kept it out of view.

The first letter in this series contains a just view of the New England character, and a fair vindication of the mass of the inhabitants of that enlightened region from the aspersions which have been cast on them through prejudice; or

rather from observing the moral defects of certain itinerant traders who annually come forth from this hive of our population, and spread themselves through the southern country. Miss Beecher shows how unreasonable it is to characterize a whole people from a few, who while they partake of the intelligence so general among their countrymen, are destitute of the virtues by which they are distinguished. We are persuaded that this vindication of the people of New England is just; for before we visited that region, we acknowledge that we partook of the prejudices mentioned above; but a free intercourse with the people in the whole extent of the country, convinced us, that for simplicity and moral honesty and integrity, there are no people superior to those of this land of the pilgrims. That they do not exhibit so conspicuously, as some of the southern people, the virtues of generosity and hospitality, arises out of their peculiar situation. Profusion, or even the want of frugality in domestic economy, would be ruinous to a country so little productive in some of those things most useful for the subsistence of man. Most of the people are under the necessity not only of hard labour, but of exercising a sharp wit in contriving means to enable them to bring up and educate their children. (pp. 515-16)

In the second letter Miss Beecher attacks the doctrine of the fatalist and atheist, who maintain that man is a necessary being and not accountable for his actions. This she does, not by entering into the labyrinth of metaphysical reasoning about cause and effect, motives and volitions, but by an appeal to common sense, and to the conduct of these very persons in what relates to their bodily welfare. In the next letter the same subject is continued, with a particular application of the principles laid down to the theory of Robert Owen and Fanny Wright, which they have endeavoured to propagate in this country with a zeal and industry which would have been laudable in a good cause. Respecting Robert Owen's enterprize at New Harmony, Miss B. expresses herself with energy.

"I have never seen or heard of any thing," says she,

> attempted by persons who have claims to rationality and to an enlightened education, that to me seemed more like the wild vagaries of lunacy than the establishment of Robert Owen at New Harmony. To collect together a company of persons of all varieties of age, taste, habits, and preconceived opinions, and teach them that there is no God, no future state, no retributions after death, no revealed standard of right and wrong, and no free agency: that the laws that secure private property are a nuisance, that religion is a curse, that marriage is a vexatious restraint, and the family state needless and unwise; and then to expect such a community to dwell together in harmony, and practise upon the rules of benevolence, what can be conceived more childish or improbable by any person who has seen the world, or known any thing of human nature? And yet such is the plan and expectation of the leaders of practical atheism. Their experiment, will probably prove one of the best antidotes to their wild theories.

This letter is concluded with some just remarks in favour of religion, as compared with the unnatural and comfortless system of atheism.

The fourth and fifth letters are addressed to a deist, and contain sound principles of evidence and just rules of investigation; and in the latter the perspicacious writer makes some excellent remarks on the grounds of objection to revelation, assumed by skeptical writers, and shows that judicious men are not governed by principles of this kind in their common affairs. Miss B. is wise in attempting to bring every class of opposers of religion to the principles of common sense; that is, to those maxims and rules by which sensible men are regulated in the management of their worldly concerns.

In the two following letters, though addressed to another person, the same subject is continued; and with much clearness and force of reasoning. In the sixth letter, the objections, derived from the numerous discordant opinions of Christians, are attempted to be answered. Miss B. undertakes to show that these discrepancies commonly relate to things not essential to salvation. And to confirm this view of the subject, she states a single proposition which includes every thing absolutely necessary to secure eternal happiness, in which all Protestants would readily unite. The proposition is, that *"Any man who sincerely and habitually loves his Maker, so as to make it the chief object of interest and effort, to discover his will and obey it, will secure eternal happiness."* Now we do not believe, that all Protestants will be contented to have all fundamental articles of religion reduced to this one. It is true, indeed, that the man who sincerely and habitually loves God must be in a safe state; but if he has been a sinner, his love to God will not expiate his former sins, and cannot secure for him exemption from deserved punishment; nor can his imperfect love, however sincere, procure for him a title to that heavenly inheritance which by sin has been forfeited. This article is much more suited to the deistical than the Christian system. The deist with whom Miss B. is reasoning, might turn upon her and say, what you have stated as the only thing essential, is believed by sober deists as firmly as it can be by any sect of Christians. We hold that there is a God of infinite perfection, whom it is our duty "to love sincerely and habitually, so as to make it the chief object of interest and effort to discover his will and obey it." He might justly say that there is nothing peculiar to Christianity in this creed: it is the very doctrine which deists holding natural religion have always inculcated. And if this is all that Protestants agree in, there is evidently no need of a revelation. It was a fundamental article in the creed of the Theophilanthropists of France, that there was one God, and that it was the duty of all rational creatures to love him supremely and do what was pleasing to him. Lord Herbert, the father of the English deists, maintained the same. We must say, therefore, that this method of answering the objection of deists, is not only unsatisfactory but dangerous.

Another objection very commonly urged by deists is, that the Bible teaches what is contrary to reason. With this our authoress grapples with no despicable skill; and upon the whole her answer appears to be solid. There are, however, some sentiments here advanced, which do not appear to us correct. On the 87th page we find the following: "I deny that you have any right to claim that there is a God, almighty in power, and infinite in wisdom, when you deny the authority of revelation, and I challenge you to bring me a single proof, by the aid of reason and nature, to show that the wisdom and power of the Creator are not limited." Now against this method of defending revelation, by denying the first principles of natural religion, we protest.

It is the preposterous method of exhibiting the strength of a building, by tearing away the foundation on which it rests. If it cannot be proved by reason that God is infinite in knowledge, how can we depend upon any revelations which he may make? What sort of evidence of omnipotence and of infinite wisdom can be demanded, which does not exist in the creation? Can a limited power bring something out of nothing, existence out of non-existence? Can any stronger evidence of almighty power be conceived, than the creation of a world? The conviction would not be stronger if we could believe that the creation was infinite. And in this argument there is no right to assume, without proof, that the creation is finite. Many philosophers have believed the contrary. If the evidence of infinite wisdom from the works of God is not complete, it is incumbent on those who deny it to show how greater wisdom could have been manifested. But we will argue the question on another principle. To deny that there exists proof of infinite wisdom and almighty power in creation, supposes that we have some conception of that which is infinite. If we have, whence was it derived? It must be answered, either from a survey of the works of God, which exceed all our powers of conception, or from the constitution of our own minds, by which we are able to transcend the limits of creation and conceive of a perfection not observed in the works of God. Take it either way and the conclusion follows, that all perfection of which we can conceive must be in the Great First Cause. For a greater perfection cannot be in the effect than in the cause, and whatever perfection we see in the creation, must exist *eminently* in the Creator. And again, as he is the author of our minds, whatever perfection we can conceive, must have its archetype somewhere, and if it be not in the works of God it must be in himself; for to suppose the conception of a perfection which has no existence any where is an absurdity; it is to conceive a nonentity, and call it perfection.

Our honest belief is, that when we have arrived at the knowledge of a first cause, whether by reason or tradition, we intuitively believe that all possible perfection belongs to him. This is evident, because all men, whether Christians or deists, agree in arguing on this principle as certain. Any theological proposition is considered as disproved, or reduced to an absurdity, if from it may be derived a conclusion inconsistent with the absolute and infinite perfection of God. If this foundation were taken away, we believe it would be found very difficult to re-establish it by revelation, however clearly it might be there inculcated; for a revelation from an imperfect being, limited in power and knowledge, and of course in every other attribute, could never be satisfactorily established.

Miss B. is not one of your timid and cautious writers, who go round difficult questions and shun the *cross*. She comes up boldly, we had almost said *manfully*, and looks them in the face. Whether in this she is always as wise as she is bold, it is unnecessary to determine. In her seventh letter, she enters on the difficult subject of *the existence of natural and moral evil*. And we confess that in her way of reasoning she has come to a conclusion, which seems to vindicate the benevolence of God; but it is at the expense of his wisdom and power. It is, that God saves from all the evil and does all the good within his power. Whether this "gordian knot of theology," as she terms it, is solved or only cut, by this explanation, we leave the discriminating reader to judge. But we are pained to read such expressions as that "God does the best he possibly can do—He has not the power of doing any thing better than he has done. All agree in saying that there is one thing that God has not the power to do, that is, the power to do more wisely or benevolently than he has done."—"And saves from evil to the full extent of his wisdom and power." This really appears to us to be darkening counsel by words without knowledge. We would ask Miss B., whence she derives the principles on which these conclusions are founded—from reason or revelation? It is taken for granted all along, that God can have nothing else in view than the promotion of the greatest possible degree of happiness. This principle is denied by many, and should have been demonstrated. Is not the whole of our reasoning here, on a subject entirely beyond our depth? And upon this principle, how can it be reconciled with infinite benevolence, that such systems as the one now existing were not brought into being from eternity; and that the work of creation is not continued every moment? We wish not to enter into this abyss which cannot be fathomed by human intellect. God has not authorized feeble mortals to lay down principles for the regulation of his conduct. It is best to put our hand upon our mouth, and to cry with Paul: "O the depth of the riches both of the wisdom and of the knowledge of God! How unsearchable are his judgments, and his ways past finding out. For who hath known the mind of the Lord, or who hath been his counsellor?" May not the reason of the permission of evil be far beyond the reach of our feeble intellect? May there not be reasons and principles of the divine conduct, of which in the present state, we are totally incapable of conceiving? God has not required it of any mortal to explain this difficulty, and most of those who have dared to explore this *terra incognita,* have rather given evidence of their presumption than of their humility.

Miss B. brings into view the two theories on this subject which now divide New England theologians. The first is the *beltistian* or *optimian* scheme of Leibnitz, adopted by President Edwards and his followers, which is the key-stone of the Hopkinsian system, namely, that evil, natural and moral, is the means of the greatest possible good. According to this, there never has been, nor ever will be, one pain or one sin which could be spared. The deduction of the least quantity of natural or moral evil would render the system of the universe less perfect. "The only difficulty" says our author, "is to conceive of any amount of good that would be sufficient to repay the evils of everlasting suffering; but though we cannot do it, the infinite mind of Jehovah may perceive that the amount of evil in the universe will be as a drop to the ocean, compared with the good; and that in the nature of things there was as much contradiction in making all the good without any evil, as there is in making a hill without a valley, or machinery without friction." The difference between the two theories is, that the one supposes that God could not accomplish the greatest possible good without employing natural and moral evil as a means; the other supposes that moral evil never can be the means of good; but that in accomplishing the greatest good it could not be avoided. The one represents God as choosing and bringing about evil as a means of good; the other as hating the evil and endeavouring by every means to avoid it, but as unable to bring into being the good which he desired, without the accompaniment of evil. Miss B. seems to be inclined to the latter theory and we do not blame her for leaning to the theory which seems

most favourable to just views of the evil of sin. But when this theory is extended so far as to represent God as exerting his utmost power to prevent sin, without effect, we are obliged strongly to dissent from all such views of the divine character and government. That God could have prevented the sin of angels and men, we have no more doubt than that he exists. The permission of their sins was necessary not as a means, but as an occasion of accomplishing that good which he will accomplish. This is the good old doctrine of the Christian church, which is marred and not improved by either of the new-divinity theories. As to there being any thing in the nature of *free agency* which would render evil necessary, as Miss B. intimates, it is to our view an unreasonable supposition; except on the principle of a self-determining power in the human will, which is an absurdity. If it were so, it would be impossible for God to govern the world, or even to forsee what would be the ultimate event of things.

Upon the whole we regret that Miss B. ventured on this difficult subject. It argues rather too much confidence in her own strength; and in our opinion the result has not been favourable. The objections of no infidel will be removed or diminished, by this discussion.

The following nine letters, beginning with the eighth, are addressed to a person, who is represented to be a believer in Christianity, and a supporter of the institutions of the gospel; but who is so far from being a practical Christian, that he seriously doubts whether the Bible furnishes any authority for those views and principles which are considered evangelical, and pleads for liberality and charity as the prime Christian virtues. Though a professed believer in Christianity, this correspondent seems disposed to shelter himself under the great uncertainty which attends all religious opinions, and especially pleads as an apology for a neglect of the requirements of religion, the exceeding great variety of sects, and diversity of religious faith; so that amid the conflicting tenets it is next to impossible to ascertain what the Bible does teach. Miss Beecher assails the inconsistency of her friend with much smartness and good sense, and shows that his position is even more unfavourable than that of the infidel. She argues from the very nature of a *revelation,* that something must be *made known;* and insists that every thing necessary to salvation is so clear that every person who desires to discover the right way, may find "the method by which we are to secure future happiness after death." To demonstrate this, Miss B. goes to work very methodically and scientifically. She goes back to first principles, and lays down the position, that all systems of religion which ever existed, require either *"character, or external performances* irrespective of character." The former she asserts is not required by Pagans, Mohammedans, or the Romish church; but only certain external rites, while most Protestants require *character,* as that which decides the condition of men after death. The next step is to ascertain what is meant by *character,* or to use her own words, "what constitutes human character." The subject is first considered negatively; or some things are specified which are not taken into the account when we estimate moral character; among which are mentioned, "mere external actions without regard to motives," and "the *relative proportion* of good and bad actions." But the following are the particulars which are always objects of regard in judging of human character. "First, *Natural disposition and constitutional peculiari-*

ties." Now, as the writer was so exact in defining what kind of character she meant, and was careful to exclude from the account "all intellectual and physical considerations," we were more than a little astonished to find the very first trait in moral character to be *natural disposition and constitutional peculiarities.* But these, she assures us, always come into consideration in estimating human character. Here, indeed, we have what is so abhorrent to some minds, physical and constitutional morality.

The next test of character is, *"a man's moral principles in resisting temptation, as learned by experience and testimony."* To inform us what constitutes moral character is one thing, but to tell us what is the *test* of moral character is another. The first was what Miss B. set out to perform; but she seems to have forgotten her own purpose before she had proceeded through a single page. Moral character might exist in perfection, as it does in heaven, where there is no temptation.

The third thing laid down is "the nature of *a man's principles, or his intellectual views of what is right and wrong."*

This again is very astonishing. Miss B., not two pages before, informed us that "intellectual and physical characteristics" are left out of view, and here we have as a principal characteristic of the moral kind, "a man's principles," which are explained to mean his *"intellectual views" of what is right and wrong.* And even if Miss B. had not thus palpably contradicted herself, we are sure she would not deliberately inculcate the opinion, that mere "intellectual views" constitute moral character in the view of mankind. Some of the wickedest men that ever lived had clear intellectual views of the difference between right and wrong. But perhaps we do not apprehend her meaning. Upon a perusal of her explanation and amplification of this principle, we suspect that what she intended to express was, not that mere intellectual views *constitute* moral character, (which, according to her own plan, ought to have been her purpose,) but that mankind, in judging of human character take into consideration the opinions which a person has adopted concerning right and wrong. As if one believes that no peculiar sacredness attaches to the sabbath, such an one should not be censured for its violation, as we would one who believed in its sacred obligation. There may be some truth in this representation; but there are many other things entirely omitted in this enumeration of particulars, which are far more essential in the constitution of moral character than this difference of opinion. To judge how far erroneous belief justifies or excuses, it would be necessary to ascertain its origin and cause. In general, practical errors are the result of evil passions or habits, and do not exculpate the person who acts wrong under their influence.

The last thing which Miss B. mentions, as entering into the estimate of human character, is *"the predominant interest or ruling passion."* The further we advance in this survey of the constituent parts of human character, the more are we bewildered. If we did not know that Miss Beecher's knowledge of the meaning of terms in the English language was precise, we should have supposed that she did not understand what she was writing. Or, if she had not so formally stated that she was about to lay down the principles which go to *constitute moral character,* we might have supposed, that she was merely mentioning some circumstances which had a tendency to modify

human character. But in the close of this letter she says: "These four particulars, I believe, include all that is ever regarded as constituting moral character, viz.: constitutional peculiarities; strength and extent of principles as learned by experience; the nature of a man's principles, or his intellectual views of what is right and wrong; and the leading interest or governing purpose of the mind." Now we maintain, that of all these particulars, which are laid down as the only things that *constitute moral character,* there is not one which possesses any moral quality, except the second, and perhaps the fourth. A more obscure and defective analysis of moral character, we venture to say, cannot be found in print. But it seems from the opening paragraph, that her correspondent fully acquiesced in all her views and statements respecting the constituents of moral character; and admitted that those specified include all that ever are regarded in forming an estimate of character among mankind, and all that can be made a subject of divine legislation. It is evident, therefore, that Miss B. did not lay down these particulars without deliberation, but considered herself as laying the foundation of a system, to be constructed in her future reasonings. We would, therefore, pause a moment, to inquire what moral character is. We suppose that to be moral character which is conformable to some moral law; taking the word *moral* in its broadest sense, as referring to qualities both good and bad, moral character is the character as measured by a moral rule. The next question is, what is the moral standard by which character must be judged? We know of no perfect moral rule, but the law of God. What are the requisitions of this law? Those things in human beings which are conformable to the law constitute a good moral character; those disconformed to this standard constitute a bad moral character. Now, supreme love to God, including all right affections towards him as our Creator, Preserver, and Redeemer, and sincere and intense love to our fellow men, is what the law requires. Under these two heads all moral virtues are comprehended. But what does this lady tell us? That all moral character consists in constitutional peculiarities; in power of resisting temptation; in intellectual views of right and wrong; and in the ruling passion. How she could hope with such elements, to pour light into the mind of a *liberal Christian,* we know not. Her correspondent, however, as we have seen, is represented as coming fully into these preliminary views. But we suspect, that the acquiescence is fictitious, and that no human being ever expressed a consent to these radical principles of her system of moral philosophy. Upon a careful perusal of the ninth letter, it may be thought that we have, through ignorance of the real design of the author, done her some injustice in our criticisms; for here we observe that the whole of these preliminaries about the constitution of moral character are intended to pave the way for establishing the principle, that the only thing required of men, in order to secure eternal happiness, is that the ruling passion be right; and the result is, that unless our ruling passion be a desire to please God, it cannot be right. Accordingly, all the other particulars laid down as constituting moral character are here examined, and found to be of no account in the character which is certainly connected with future happiness; and after digging so deep for a foundation, and so scientifically ascertaining the elements of moral character, it turns out, that only one of these, namely, the ruling passion, has any necessary connexion with eternal life. Thus we have caught our author in the act of refuting her own errors; for after having mentioned constitutional peculiarities as the first constituent of a moral character, and of course a proper subject for the requisitions of a moral law; she now speaks of these constitutional traits in a way which shows that she considers them as having no moral quality whatever; which is a correct view of the subject. Hear her own words: "To which of these four particulars does divine legislation refer, in teaching us how to gain eternal life? Will you take the Bible and examine for yourself? In the first place, does it teach that any particular trait or combination of traits, in the original mental constitution, is made the term of salvation? Is it any where taught that a man must have a naturally amiable disposition, or a calm temperament, or a pliant disposition, or any thing which depends solely on the original formation of the mind, and *for which we are no more responsible* (except for its proper regulation) than we are for the colour of the eyes or of the hair, &c." Here the inconsistency—and it is a glaring one—is, that one of the four grand elements of a moral character is a thing, for which we are no more responsible than for the colour of our eyes or hair!

If there be four constituent parts or elements of moral character, how does it happen that only one of them is necessary to future happiness? We might reason thus— either all these ingredients are necessary to the formation of a good moral character, or they are not. If the former, then as a good moral character is requisite to entitle us to eternal life, all these must be found in the character to which eternal life is promised in the Bible; if they are not necessary to a good moral character, why are they brought forward as the only things taken into consideration in estimating moral character? This whole discussion exhibits one of the strangest moral *disquisitions* we have ever met with. But that which we consider as by far the most censurable in these letters is, that in undertaking to point out what the Bible teaches as necessary to the acquisition of eternal life, there does not appear a solitary ray of evangelical light. There is no more notice taken of the mediation of Jesus Christ, than if he had never appeared in the world. If these letters, which professedly undertake to point out the way to future happiness, had been put into our hands without any information of their author, we should have judged that they must have proceeded from the pen of a deist or Unitarian, except that the words Christ and Bible are occasionally introduced, as if by accident.

Miss Beecher's system of religion may be reduced to a single point. The Bible requires many duties, a conformity to which is not necessary to obtain salvation; an internal character of piety, which may consist with many imperfections, is all that is essential to that religion which is connected with future happiness; and this character of piety consists in the governing purpose or passion of the mind. When this is a desire to please God, the person may be said to possess true religion. Thus eternal life is made to depend entirely on a man's own goodness. To be justified by faith, is to be justified by a good principle or disposition within us. No intimation is any where given in these letters, that our acceptance with God is through the merits of another. According to her theory it is our own inherent righteousness or moral goodness by which we are rendered acceptable to God, and not by the merit or righteousness of Christ, which is never once mentioned or referred to. That this is her notion of the plan of salvation,

is evident from the whole tenor of these letters. . . . (pp. 517-28)

We know not what to call Miss Beecher's system of religion. It is far below any of the *isms* which divide the Christian world. Here is laid down a method of acceptance with God, having no reference to a Mediator; and a change of heart without the least aid from the Holy Spirit. In this whole concern the need of such grace is never hinted. "He puts himself in the way of duty; turns his mind to think on the folly of his ways; repents and resolves to do no more wickedly; studies the works and the word of his Maker; daily seeks to commune with Him; consecrate his time, property, and influence to his service, and in the course of obedience, emotions of affection soon glow in his bosom, and cheer and invigorate all his efforts." Here you have Miss Beecher's *recipe* for the conversion of a sinner; for changing enmity into love. One defect we cannot but notice. The sinner must be a well-disposed good man before he is converted, or he will never be disposed to do what she requires of him; unless he plays the hypocrite. Perhaps, too, the wicked heart, instead of breaking and yielding, and glowing with affection, might remain hard, and the person be conscious of unsubdued pride and enmity. We have witnessed many such cases, in which all external means had been used; and Miss B. does not prescribe for such a case. She might say, indeed, if the appropriate means were used in a proper manner, the effect would certainly follow. That is, if the sinner will believingly and piously read, pray, &c. he will be sure to be converted; love to God will soon glow in his heart. This much resembles the promises and prescriptions of empirical venders of catholicons and nostrums. There is just as much quackery in religion as in medicine.

In our review of Miss Beecher's **Letters,** our plan is to go straight on, and to remark on what we find, without looking forward to see if she may not have said something in a subsequent part to supply the defects or correct the errors which may be apparent. The consequence is, that in our progress, we find it necessary to give her credit sometimes for sounder opinions, than from her previous matter, we thought she entertained. Thus in her fourteenth letter, she avows her belief in the supernatural agency of the Holy Spirit in producing a change of heart; of which, however, we heard not a word in the preceding letter, where she gave explicit directions for effecting this change. Her correspondent seems to have remarked the same deficiency in this respect, and to have brought to view the doctrine of our entire dependence on divine agency, as inconsistent with the account which she had given of conversion. She here attempts to reconcile this doctrine with the views which she had already exhibited. The method of reconciliation, as far as we apprehend her meaning, is, that in many cases men have *ability* to perform a certain thing, but the motives to it are not strong enough to excite them to vigorous action, when if by some foreign influence the strength of these motives is increased, we perform what we before had power to do, but which we never would have done had not this increase of the power of the motives taken place. And this is the office of the Holy Spirit, to give this increased energy to the motives which should influence the mind. This part of the subject, however, is treated very concisely, and we are left much in the dark, as to the precise nature of the efficiency ascribed to this supernatural agency. And upon a review of the sentiments of the former letter, on which we have remarked, we cannot see any necessity for such supernatural influence, any more in the case of producing in our own hearts love to God, than in the case of the reformed husband. No doubt, the great defect is the want of a prevailing motive to turn from sin unto God,—but what is the requisite motive? It is no other than love to God, and this is the very thing which she says any man may produce in himself by the use of appropriate means. We readily admit that, in a carnal mind which is enmity against God, this motive is not strong enough, because it has no existence. From what has been said, the reader will perceive how much light has been shed by this female theologian on the subject of human ability, concerning which there has been so much unprofitable controversy in our day.

The fifteenth letter is intended to show the reasonableness of our being required to love God supremely, by showing that his character is lovely. In order to make this clear, Miss B., who delights to go up to ultimate principles, undertakes to inform us what those particulars are which can be the causes of affection; and the reader will be surprized to learn that they are, *personal beauty, physical strength, intellectual superiority, the power of sympathy, the power of giving and appreciating benevolence and affection.* Each of these she dwells upon at some length, and we are beginning to grow weary of this species of philosophizing, and cannot consent to follow her through the details; especially, as we find nothing which it would be profitable to make the subject of remark.

The seventeenth and eighteenth letters, in this volume, are addressed to a Unitarian; and in them the writer displays no small intellectual acumen. She takes up and answers the objections commonly made by Unitarians to the doctrine of Trinitarians, with admirable adroitness. No one can impartially read the first of these letters without being convinced that Miss B. possesses a penetrating and discriminating mind. We have observed only one thing objectionable in these letters. We regret to find in this volume the old exploded heresy of the Apollinarists, stated as one of the opinions now entertained by some Trinitarians. We hope there are very few in the present day who are inclined to this untenable, and we must think, very absurd opinion. We believe that Miss Beecher herself has a leaning towards this long exploded heresy, and we cannot but feel astonished that a mind so perspicacious and penetrating, should become entangled in an error fraught with consequences so manifestly unreasonable. The very statement of the doctrine involves what is as impossible as that God should cease to exist. It implies that the Son of God, while incarnate, was limited in the exercise of his divine attributes, and that the divine nature was subject to all the infirmities of human appetite and passion, and suffered all the pains which were endured by the man Christ Jesus. This subject was so fully canvassed when the heresy was condemned in the ancient church, that we need only refer our readers to the writers of that age. If any one can embrace the opinion that the eternal God can suffer so as to be overwhelmed with distress, so as to pour out strong cries and tears, and to complain of being forsaken, we should deem it a useless labour to attempt to reason with such a person. If the great God can be the subject of such sufferings, instead of being blessed for evermore, he is probably the most miserable of beings. But all such opinions border on the blasphemous; we have no patience to consider them.

What Miss B. says in the twentieth and twenty-first letters, respecting the refusal of the orthodox to recognize Unitarians as fellow Christians, is good: the Jews and Mohammedans have just as much claim to be admitted to the communion of the Christian church. Among the Unitarians in England, it became a question whether some members who had adopted deistical sentiments should be excluded from fellowship. It was a hard question: and determine it as they might, it ought to stop their mouths from complaining of the want of charity in the orthodox. Miss B. properly denies, that Unitarians have manifested more meekness and charity than the orthodox church. She also has some sensible remarks in answer to those who are for ever declaiming against "creeds." (pp. 537-40)

We trust that we have in no instance departed from Christian courtesy in this review. As reviewers, we have been placed in a new attitude, and if we have in any respect violated the laws of politeness, we are very sorry; for although we differ widely from Miss B. on many points, we entertain a high respect for her talents and her amiable temper. But we hope she will consent to leave theological and ecclesiastical contention to male polemics, who delight in such warfare; or, who feel that it is a work which they are bound in duty to perform; and if our advice should have any influence in inducing her to adopt a course so well suited to her sex and her profession, our end will be attained; for as to converting her to our opinions, we are not so presumptuous as to cherish such a hope. (p. 545)

A review of "Letters on the Difficulties of Religion," in The Biblical Repertory, *Vol. VIII, No. IV, October, 1836, pp. 515-45.*

The North American Review   (essay date 1855)

[*In the following excerpt, the critic asserts the value of* Letters to the People on Health and Happiness.]

The *perfervidum ingenium* of the Beecher family renders it hardly necessary that its members should prefix their names to their books. We certainly could have guessed the parentage of [*Letters to the People on Health and Happiness*] had it been anonymous. It relates mainly to the prevalence of what, by a Hibernianism almost Anglicized, we are wont to term "ill health" among American women, its causes, its concomitant evils, its ominous import for coming generations, and its remedies. We cannot but trust that Miss Beecher unconsciously exaggerates the evils she laments and deprecates; for, as an invalid, and as an *habituée* of divers hydropathic and other sanitary establishments, she must, within the last few years, have been in peculiarly intimate conversance with what of disease and infirmity exists. But if a tithe of her estimate on this head does not exceed the truth,—nay, if the facts within her own personal knowledge on which she grounds her inductions are not overstated, (and we cannot for a moment believe that they are,)—it is time that the alarm were sounded, and we are thankful that it issues from a voice that will make itself heard. The book ought to be in the hands of every mother in the country, and some of its suggestions certainly merit the grave heed of the medical profession.

A review of "Letters to the People on Health

and Happiness," in The North American Review, *Vol. LXXXI, No. CLXIX, October, 1855, p. 555.*

The Christian Examiner   (essay date 1864)

[*In the following excerpt, the critic discusses Beecher's approach to religious issues as demonstrated in several of her works, objecting to her affirmation of the innate goodness of human beings.*]

We are glad to find a writer who is not an ecclesiastic discussing theological questions with earnestness and vigor. We are glad all the more that the writer is a woman. It is some guaranty that the discussion will not proceed in the ruts of tradition, and that the theology of the pulpit, the divinity schools and ministerial conventions, is to be ventilated and humanized. Miss Beecher comes to her subject with rare qualifications at least for negative criticism. With a nature of ardent aspirations and clear intellectual activity, she endured for years the perplexities and agonies which are inflicted upon keenly susceptible minds under Calvinistic theories of conversion and regeneration. As an educator of the young, and especially of young women, she has watched the effect of these doctrines upon them, causing the same perplexing dread, and stifling the most generous uprisings of the spiritual nature. She lived under the influence of this theology during years of sorrow and trial, joined a Calvinistic Church under mental protest that "there was a dreadful mistake somewhere," and after long struggle and difficulty rejected the Calvinistic system as false and baneful, and now finds shelter in the broader toleration and hospitality of the Episcopal Church. In her **Common Sense Applied to Religion, Appeal to the People** and the work now published on the **Religious Training of Children,** she develops very fully her views of theology. With great moral earnestness, in a style perfectly free from all scholasticism, appealing with boldness and vigor to the plain sense and understanding of common minds, she deals a most destructive criticism against the theories that had troubled her so long, and presents ideas of Christianity which she deems accordant with the character of God, with the plain meaning of the New Testament, with the wants of the soul and the common sense of mankind.

The negative, or more properly the destructive portion of her work, is admirably done. Sometimes by invincible logic, sometimes by apt illustration more telling than argument, sometimes by personal narrative calculated to touch the pity and indignation even of theologians who have any dregs of manhood left in them, she succeeds in making Calvinism not only absurd, but utterly hateful. The eleventh, twelfth, and thirteenth chapters, entitled "Puritan Church Training," in her last work, are made up mainly of extracts from the personal experience of a daughter of the late Dr. Payson, written, we suppose, by the daughter herself, and not designed, of course, to blacken the memory of that good man. It is only paralleled by the cross-examinations of the "Holy Office" in the exquisite refinements of cruelty. A little girl, of quick perceptions, acute conscientiousness, and tender feelings, is taken when three years of age, and in the ten long years that followed put through the tortures of a Calvinistic conversion. She is made to believe that her whole nature is depraved, and that she can do nothing to change it; that even

her prayers are hateful to God; that she cannot love him without a change of heart, which he only can bestow; and that for not loving him she is exposed to eternal fire. One would suppose that a parent who believed in such a theory of conversion would at least leave his children alone till God chose to take them in hand. But no: this good man thought it his duty to ply his child constantly with the theological pincers and thumbscrews, and her innocent girlhood, which should have been bright and joyous, is a continuous night of terror and anguish under the brooding wrath of God.

In the constructive portion of her work, Miss Beecher is less successful, because this work is vastly more difficult. She reproduces in its main features the theology of Pelagius. She denies with emphasis, not merely the "total depravity" of human nature, but any depravity of nature whatsoever. The infant mind is the creation of God, and we impeach his wisdom or goodness when we deny that it is rightly constructed. To suppose that new-created minds are brought into being corrupt and sinful and incapable of obedience, and yet responsible and guilty for disobedience, is to represent the Divine character in such light that no child can love him, nor is even bound to love him. Sin arises not from depraved nature, but from depraved action, and there is no sin previous to voluntary transgression. Vindicating the native ability and free-agency of man, she makes "a controlling purpose of obedience," manifested in good works and an unselfish life, the condition of salvation. She believes fully in the Deity of Christ, in his atoning sacrifice as a means of saving the sinner, in the influence of the Holy Spirit in human culture and regeneration, and the endless misery after death of those who have had their probation here, and become confirmed in their wickedness. She does not accept, however, the Puritan doctrine of immediate salvation or damnation at death of all mankind, but brings out very distinctly the belief of the primitive Church, still retained in a modified form by the Episcopal, of a threefold state after death,— Heaven and Hell and *Hades;* which last is not the final abode, but the passage-way thereto. The notion of imputed righteousness is rejected as absurd, and the atonement of Christ evidently is not conceived as penal and vicarious.

We select the following illustration from many others designed to uncover the hideous absurdity of the received orthodox doctrine of depravity.

> Suppose a colony by some mischance settles on an [isolated] island which is found covered with the tobacco-plant. They clear their plantations, but find, by a remarkable and unintelligible arrangement, after every shower there is a fall of tobacco-seeds, disseminated from an inaccessible height by a machine erected for the purpose and constantly supplied. After some years they receive a mission from the king to whom the island belongs, in which he informs them that tobacco is the chief object of his detestation; that it is doing incalculable mischief to his subjects; that it is the chief end of his life, and he wishes it to be of theirs, to exterminate the plant and thus its use.
>
> He at the same time states that he is the author of the contrivance for scattering the seed, and that he keeps it constantly supplied, and claims that he has a right 'to do what he will with his own' without being questioned by his subjects.

He then enacts that any person who is found to use tobacco, or even to have a single seed or plant on his premises, shall be burned alive in a caldron of fire and brimstone.

If, in addition to this, that king were to command supreme love to him and perfect confidence in his wisdom, justice, and goodness, all this would but faintly illustrate that awful system under consideration whose penalties are *eternal.—Common Sense Applied to Religion*

The articles of faith, as Miss Beecher holds them, are thus summed up by herself:—

That at the *first birth* of a child it is "impossible in the nature of things" for it to feel and act for the happiness of others, till it has learned to know what gives pleasure and pain to *self,* and that there are other beings who can enjoy and suffer; so that a child by its very nature is at first obliged to be *selfish* in the *exercise* of faculties which *in reference to the great whole* are perfect.

That the "second birth" is the sudden or gradual entrance into a life in which the will of the Creator is to control the self-will of the creature; while under the influence of love and gratitude to him and guided by faith in his teachings, *living chiefly for the great commandment* takes the place of *living chiefly for self.* For this the supernatural aid of the Holy Spirit is promised to all who seek it; and without this aid success is hopeless. But the grand instrumentality is the *right training* of parents and teachers.

Then in reference to that great change of character which wrongly educated minds must pass, in order to gain eternal life, there are three modes of expression in the Bible in regard to that, viz. "love to God," "faith in Jesus Christ," and "repentance."

According to all uses of these terms in *practical* matters, *love* is nothing which does not include obedience or conformity of will and action to the being loved. Faith or belief is nothing unless it includes its fruits of obedience. *Repentance* is nothing unless it includes ceasing to do evil. *Obedience* to the laws of God, physical, social, moral, and religious, is the grand indispensable requisite. Now when any person is so engaged in striving to obey all these laws that it is the *first interest* of the mind, then there is a "new heart"; and so great is the change from one of self-indulgence and disobedience to one of such earnest desire and efforts to obey God, that it is properly expressed by the terms "born again" and "created anew."

That the grand decisive change in becoming a Christian is stated here very inadequately, resolving itself, as it must in Miss Beecher's system, into a change of external conduct and relations, and not change of nature, we think it would be very easy to show. Indeed, we do not see that, with Pelagian theories, "being born again" or "created anew" has any vital significance. Those words imply changes deeper and more radical than changes of the external man; and as to the internal man, that needs no changing, if Miss Beecher is right, except by way of development, since it was perfect at the first creation. Ceasing to *do* evil, not ceasing to *be* evil, is the whole work of repentance; and education, not regeneration, is the whole work of Christian nurture.

As opposed to Calvinism, Miss Beecher's system is vastly to be preferred, for any one might rejoice to escape from the gloom of a dungeon, though he emerged into the cold air beneath a wintry sky. Most heartily, then, do we sympathize with her in the good work she is doing, and the vigorous strokes which break open the prison-doors. But how she can rest in her present belief, we do not see. Pelagianism may be a good resting-place, even as many Unitarians have found it, where we may stop and take breath after struggling out of the darkness and the galling chains of spiritual bondage. But as a system adequate to solve the hard problems of existence, to satisfy either the heart or the intellect, and bring man into God's profound and sufficing peace, as it has always been found wanting, so it will always continue to be.

First of all, we say it discharges the fundamental facts of the Gospel of their vital import. If man needed only development, and not radical change,—if sin comes only from diseased action, and not from diseased constitution,— what need was there of anything more than educators and prophets to show us the way? Why the Divine Incarnation to redeem the race, when they only needed teachers to enlighten and guide them? All but a small fraction of Christendom, who rest in the sheerest Ebionism, have been profoundly convinced that Christ was more than a teacher,— even a Redeemer and Saviour; and that his incarnation, sufferings, death, resurrection, ascension, and second coming in the Paraclete, were not merely to move on the surface of human nature, and lead to right action, but down among its native springs and elements, there to heal and cleanse, to readjust, inspire, and energize, and evolve a new creation out of chaos. Surely, this uniform testimony points to something in the nature itself of the religious life. True enough, Miss Beecher holds fast to the Orthodox Trinity, and, in her way, believes in the Deity of Christ. But these doctrines hang loose in her system, without use and without coherence; for as human nature in every newborn child from the days of Adam downward has been whole and perfect, and its native motions heavenward, why could not prophets and angels have guided it? and what mean the wonderful events which took place in Palestine eighteen hundred years ago, and around which the whole history of the race, before and after, becomes organized?

Moreover, Pelagianism, though less revolting to our moral sentiments than Calvinism, succeeds no better in clearing the Divine justice. A part of the race are to be saved through education and persuasion. So far the Divine plan is successful. But how is it with that vast portion who are lost forever in consequence of wrong training and unpropitious circumstance? Starting with natures perfectly pure and well directed, how easily, by a wise adjustment of circumstance, might all this native goodness have been wooed forth and set free! And yet, brought here by no act of their own, they are plunged into such external evil and corruption, that their goodness is repressed and deflected to everlasting ruin. It helps the matter very little to say that the sinner chooses evil rather than good. If he chooses it to his eternal destruction, why was he put in the way of it? or why was he created at all, when the Creator foresaw that existence was to turn out a failure and a curse for ever and ever? If the grand system of Providence is one of education only, and this is the dismal result of it, then we say, too, "There is a dreadful mistake somewhere," and the mistake lies plainly in the Divine arrangements. Suppose fifty young women have been committed to Miss Beecher to educate. They are given to her care in their unspotted innocence, their faculties all perfect, their affections and aspirations all pure. She has the entire control of place and circumstance in locating her seminary. She can place it amid the sweetest charms of art and nature, and amid society of the selectest and holiest influence. And yet, with all these appliances at her command, she gives them bad books to read, and admits evil tempters among them, and returns twenty-five of these once innocent girls to their parents corrupted and ruined, and fit only for dens of infamy. And suppose the teacher should put forward the plea that the young women were free agents, and chose the ruin themselves, would the parents think the plea a valid one, and not rather a cruel and insulting aggravation of the wrong? And yet what else does Pelagianism make of the whole scheme of creation and providence, plunging pure and new-created souls, generation after generation, amid seductions and temptations which the Creator foreknows will turn them downward among the fiends, and not amid persuasions that will win them upward among his angels? You gain nothing by removing evil from the nature *in* man to the nature *about* him, which dominates and schools him through the most tender and susceptible period of his endless existence,—you gain nothing, that is to say, for the Divine character and justice,—unless you can show that evil has some better use and economy than this in the universe of God. (pp. 301-07)

> *"Miss Beecher's Pelagianism,"* in The Christian Examiner, *Vol. LXXVII, No. III, November, 1864, pp. 301-14.*

Mae Elizabeth Harveson   (essay date 1931)

[*In the following excerpt, Harveson provides a survey of Beecher's writings.*]

Between 1827 and 1874, Catharine Beecher's literary output comprised more than two dozen books, besides numerous written addresses, circulars, and magazine articles. During this period of almost half a century, there was a remarkable consistency in her writings, for while, at first glance, the titles seem to show considerable variety of subject-matter, a closer analysis proves them nearly all directed toward one end. One may roughly separate Miss Beecher's works into two groups: those dealing with religion and those concerned with education. We shall learn, however, that the two are related in her mind and that it is with the teacher's eye that she views and attempts to solve religious problems. (p. 149)

It seems natural that Catharine Beecher's pen should be active on religious questions, with a father and seven brothers in the ministry. Accustomed, as she was all her life, to hear the perplexing knots of theology dexterously untied to the satisfaction of her father and brothers, it was inevitable that her mind should have formed a bent in this direction. That it was expressed in a form unlike the more glamorous mode of her novelist sister was due to the fact that she was Catharine and not Harriet, and therefore possessed of a markedly different set of reactions to external stimuli. A famous suffragist has written in her autobiography: "As well wonder why lilies and lilacs in the same latitude are not all alike in color and equally fragrant. Chil-

dren differ as widely as these in the primal elements of their physical and psychical life." In Catharine, these primal elements ordained that she should attack her problems with a sincerity and directness which eschewed the more circuitous route of the romance-maker, and though her language was sometimes delicately beautiful, it was more often plain, unfrilled, and even blunt. (pp. 149-50)

Catharine's awakening to the many vexing questions involved in the theology of Calvinism was brought about suddenly by the tragic death of her lover, Alexander Metcalf Fisher, in April of 1822, under circumstances which, according to the accepted beliefs of the Congregational Church, consigned his soul to an eternity of torment. During the following half-dozen years, Catharine's mind was torn with conflict over the apparent inconsistency of the tenets of her father's religion and life as she saw it. Eventually, though she presented an unrippled surface of acceptance to these unreconcilable conditions, there lay beneath a turmoil of fear, anger and doubt. (p. 150)

Catharine Beecher's first attempt to put her scattered thoughts into form was forced upon her in the exercise of her duties at the Hartford Female Seminary. Upon joining her father's church, she had determined to assume that God was wise, just, and good and that she would seek to ascertain all that was required of her and then strive to do it. She imitated the methods of "Christian worthies": kept a religious diary, read religious books, went to religious meetings, prayed in her school and taught religion to her pupils as it had been taught to her. But when these earnest young pupils came to her with the same problems with which she, herself, had struggled, she was sorely perplexed and could scarcely nerve herself to instruct them along the accepted lines. At the same time that Catharine was unhappily submerged in this sea of doubt, she was teaching a class in mental philosophy and from the intermingling of the elements of this science with those of theology was evolved a new compound, in the form of her *Elements of Mental and Moral Philosophy* of 1831. The Catharine of this day was far less certain of her ability to solve efficiently the world's problems than was the authoress of a decade later, so this little book carries such apologies as "It is in too imperfect a form to be presented to the public" and "Of course it is expected that defects and mistakes, will be discovered, and it is hoped that due allowance will be made, for what the writer knows is a hasty and imperfect attempt to remedy some difficulties in education, which for a long time have been daily subjects of regret." The little book was printed, but never published, distributed, or sold. After submitting it to the criticism of men of various schools and sects, it was found to contain so much that might result in theological controversy, that it was thought modest and wise for Catharine to wait until age, experience and farther examination had lent their maturing influence. (p. 151)

In 1836, Catharine made her next attempt to untie the Gordian knots of theology in her *Letters on the Difficulties of Religion.* This expression of her thoughts was not made in the half-apologetic tone of her 1831 production, but with that self-assurance which came to be characteristic of her later pronouncements. (p. 153)

Catharine's exposition . . . is of a practical nature, espousing Presbyterianism to be sure, in name at least, but concerning itself little with the more depressing doctrines.

Her points are made in a series of letters supposed to be written to particular atheists, Unitarians and other sceptics, answering questions or objections raised by them. She speaks not only of right views of truth and duty, but also of the right state of heart which will lead men to practice what they know to be right; of virtue and moral excellence and of happiness. She defines them as "those principles of action that regulate men in the common business of life, principles, which, though not drawn out into axioms, are as well understood, as if they were formally propounded, like the vulgar and sententious principles of science." The five principles she lists are these:

> 1. Nothing is to be considered as true, which has no positive evidence in its favor.
>
> 2. Whatever has the balance of evidence in its favor, is to be considered as true, even when there is some opposing evidence.
>
> 3. Men have the control of their belief; that they are to blame for believing wrong; and that their guilt for wrong belief, is proportional to the importance of the interests involved, and the amount of evidence within reach.
>
> 4. A man's actions in certain cases, are the proof of what is his belief.
>
> 5. Where there are two alternatives, and one of them involves danger, and the other is equally promising as to benefit, and is also perfectly safe, we are obliged to choose the safe course.

With these weapons, Catharine slays the looming enemies—atheism and Unitarianism—and solves such practical difficulties as discovering "what is and what is not demanded in the Bible as a condition of eternal safety"; "Difficulties occasioned by the inconsistent lives and characters of the professers of religion"; "Objection that man has not the control of his emotions"; and, "certain unpleasant associations in regard to the character of God." In explaining the last, Catharine shows a richness of imagery that is not expected, for while her language is always well-chosen, it is rarely effusive. "The exterior of nature," she writes, "is the clothing of the Almighty Mind, where in visible forms of beauty, dignity and grace, he still communes with those children of his love, that lift the adoring eye to him, who smiles in the landscape, and breathes in the gale. The heavings of the ocean, the rush of the tornado, the sheeted lightning, and the talking of fierce thunderbolts, are majestic expressions of his dignity and power. The whispers of evening, the low murmur of waters, the soft melodies of nature, are the breathings of his love. In the graceful movements of vegetable life, in gliding shadows and curling vapors, in the delicately blending colors, and in the soft harmonies of animated existence, may be discovered his gentleness, purity and grace. The sighing of the wind, the moaning of the wood, the beaming of some lonely star, the pensive gleam of moonlight, recall his tenderness and pitying sympathy. Man cannot turn his eye abroad, without beholding in the thousand mirrors of nature, the glories and perfect form of him who filleth all in all."

This is not the stern God of Calvinism, who rules by fear alone, but a milder, more paternal one. Catharine dared to interpret according to her own standards, and that trumpet of Presbyterianism, the *Biblical Repertory and*

Princeton Review, devoted thirty pages to a review of her book [see excerpt dated 1836], starting with lavish praise and ending with insulting abuse. The condescension of the male toward the "dependent sex" is exhibited in both phases of his "Indeed, there is nothing feminine in the productions of the lady: if the work had been anonymous we should never have suspected that it proceeded from the hand of a lady" to his "we cease to expect accurate statements from Miss B. We suspect that she is inclined to meddle with too many things, and with things out of her reach." As a final touch of authority, he quoted Saint Paul and his "I suffer not a woman to speak in the church." Elaborating this, he continues: "and although he has not prohibited them from teaching by writing for the public, yet we cannot but think, if he were now on earth, he would discourage the female sex, however gifted or learned, from giving themselves in theological and ecclesiastical controversies." (pp. 154-56)

In 1857 [Beecher's] *Common Sense Applied to Religion* came from the press, four years after her brother Edward had published his *Conflict of Ages.* (p. 157)

In Catharine's case, the cause of this book of hers is given in her introduction: "This work is the result of thirty years of devotion to the training of the human mind for the great end for which it was created. Early in that period it was felt that at the very foundation of such efforts were opposing theological theories that seemed at war with both the common sense and the moral sense of mankind." We begin to understand her point of view when we recall that the much-praised Hannah More wrote of the "Natural Depravity of Children" these blighting words: "Is it not a fundamental error to consider children as innocent beings, whose little weaknesses may perhaps want some correction, rather than as beings who bring into the world a corrupt nature and evil dispositions, which it should be the great end of education to rectify?" The belief of orthodoxy in man's depravity was about like this:

> 1. His deep innate depravity as an individual.
>
> 2. His subjection to the power of depraved social organizations called, taken collectively, the world.
>
> 3. His subjection to the power of unseen malignant spirits, who are centralized and controlled by Satan, the leader and head.

Catharine says: "The real difficulty at the root of all is the indifference to the training of the habits of childhood resulting from its long-established dogma of a misformed mind, whose propagated incapacity is not within the reach of educational training." In a word, Catharine attributes the failure of her educational plans to these abhorred beliefs.

It is therefore her purpose in this book to present a new and better system of Christian Ethics. To this end, she first sets out to prove that the doctrine of natural depravity is a fiction of theology unsupported by the Word of God and opposed to the intuitive convictions of reason. She states that it was unknown to the early Christians, being invented by St. Augustine and that, once adopted as a part of the Faith, it gradually fortified itself by tradition, custom and prejudice. To arrive at these conclusions, she uses the criteria of reason and common sense,—tools, the excellence of which has been attested by their use from the time of the Greeks to the present day. (pp. 157-58)

The conclusion at which she arrives is this: that every human being is born with a perfect mental constitution, that sin is to be found only in voluntary action and that by proper education, proper habits, proper social influence and proper circumstances generally, voluntary action may be so controlled as to be perfect. (p. 159)

Three years after the appearance of *Common Sense Applied to Religion* came another exposition in similar vein. In 1860, Harper published Miss Beecher's *An Appeal to the People in Behalf of Their Rights as Authorized Interpreters of the Bible.* This book, contains practically nothing in the way of theology, psychology or pedagogy that is not in the preceding volume although the principles involved are newly illustrated. With a flourish, Miss Beecher dedicates this work to "The Editors of the Secular Press, The True Tribunes of the People, Called of God in Behalf of the Commonwealth to Defend Liberty of Conscience, Freedom of Speech, and the Right of all to Interpret the Bible for Themselves, unrestrained by any Ecclesiastical Power."

Miss Beecher states that the religious world is on the verge of a great impending change, which has been preceded by a long course of unobserved preparation. The great question is "What must we do to be saved"? It is important to each individual and to every parent and educator of children. She then assigns as the object of her book: "to show that the answer to this great question has, for ages, been involved in mystery and difficulty by means of a philosophical theory, . . . which is so contrary to the moral sense of humanity, that theologians have failed to render it consistent and satisfactory even to themselves and that the people are endowed with principles of common sense by which they can educe from the works of God a system of natural religion far superior." In the course of her explanation to "the People" of the line of reasoning they are to follow, Catharine is, now and then, what one writer has called her—"the arid authoress" for the discussions partake of the flavor of dictionary citations and encyclopedia information. On the other hand, there are many spots in the book where a point is so well made or a view so clearly expressed that interest is aroused and held. Catharine contrasts at length what she calls "the two systems of theology"—the Augustinian (orthodox) and the Common Sense (hers) and elaborates the latter on all controversial points. In brief, her system teaches that all mankind must, in order to have eternal happiness, be trained by human agencies to choose what is best, guided by the laws of God, as learned by experience or by revelation.

Four years later, 1864, Catharine Beecher made her last public exposition of her system of common sense, this time applied to the *Religious Training of Children in the School, the Family and the Church.* In the introduction she says that her observations over a long period of time in the families of her former pupils and relatives have resulted in the "deep conviction that the right training of children is the most difficult of all human pursuits; that success is invariably proportioned to the wisdom and fitness of the methods pursued; that the best modes are to be obtained only by a wide experience, involving many failures and, as yet, offering no perfect examples; that the records of experience are indispensable to future success,

and that educators like medical men are bound to make such records for the benefit of the profession."

Following this expressed intention, the author explains that a child is trained to be religious just as far as he is educated to obey the laws of God in regard to self, to others, and to his maker. She then describes the method by which this obedience is to be produced, advising the insurance of the prompt obedience of faith with small children rather than that of reasoning and persuasion. The infant is to learn self-sacrifice when it first must give up its place in the mother's arms to the next infant and when it must share playthings and help amuse. The child is to get his ideas of God from his own parents; the characteristics of love, patience, meekness, gentleness, sympathy, self-denying labors and care, united with firm and steady government can readily be transferred in conception to the Heavenly Father. Most emphatic is she in advising against the use of fear as a motive, though this was the one predominantly employed in her own generation among the orthodox. When the child passes from the nursery to the schoolroom, the teacher should explain that the great end of school education is to train him to a loving and prompt obedience to the laws of God as the best and only sure way of being happy. Thus, according to her view, an infant begins to be a Christian as soon as it begins to act intelligently in conforming to the laws of God, with the intention to act right; and it grows in Christian life just as fast as its impulses and desires are controlled by a voluntary submission to the laws of true rectitude, which are none other than the laws of God. An infant begins its Christian life long before it has any knowledge of God, while it is forming habits of loving obedience to its earthly parents, who are the agents, and should be the representatives, to the child, of its heavenly father. This, of course, was quite contrary to the common theory, which contended that until a child's mind was new created or "healed," in its constitutional powers, no true love and obedience to God could occur. Having definitely and finally rejected this "soul-withering system" and its organ, the Presbyterian Church, Catharine advocates the Episcopal Church, which she had recently joined. According to this faith, instead of "joining the church" in the Congregational sense, which means being examined and voted into a close corporation as already true Christians and fitted for heaven, all children are in the church and confirmation is a public acknowledgment of their obligations and their desire and purpose to fulfill them in future by God's help. (pp. 160-62)

The *Christian Examiner,* which had spoken well of her *Common Sense* of 1857, was now equally congratulatory in discussing all three of her most recent publications on this theme [see excerpt dated 1864]. "We are glad," it said, "to find a writer who is not an ecclesiastic discussing theological questions with earnestness and vigor. We are glad all the more that the writer is a woman. It is some guarantee that the discussion will not proceed in the ruts of tradition, and that the theology of the pulpit, the divinity schools and ministerial conventions, is to be ventilated and humanized." The reviewer points out, to be sure, Miss Beecher's errors, stating among other things that her system is not original, but displays rather many features of Pelagianism, but on the whole he is quite commendatory.

Whether Catharine's theories were original or not does not detract from the importance of her pronouncement of them. She of all the Beechers, original and independent though they were, dared publicly defy the religion of her fathers, and with her, in her exodus from the orthodox church, went her sister Harriet. Catharine was fired with the zeal of the reformer, hence no fear of censure, ridicule or opposition stayed her hand. Moreover, behind these writings, as behind all her actions of the last half century of her life, was the single purpose of training woman for her profession. In the way of effectively performing this were the doctrines of Calvinistic theology. They were, then, simply one more obstacle to be removed before the attainment of her purpose was possible.

Catharine Beecher's writings on educational topics were voluminous, and varied as to subject-matter, but a unity of purpose threads them all like pearls on a single string. According to her often reiterated statement and belief, *woman has a distinctive profession, embracing the three departments of teaching, health and domestic economy,* and Miss Beecher's life history was one systematic and comprehensive effort, absorbing all her thoughts, her time and her income, toward rendering this profession honorable and remunerative. To this end her books, articles and addresses were written: on female education, that the intellectual training to fit woman to teach might be bettered; on physiology and health, to fit her to be a nurse of infancy and the sick; and on domestic economy, to train her to be a good housekeeper. Although 1829 was the year of Miss Beecher's first widely-noticed expression of her views, as early as 1827, in an article on **"Female Education,"** written for the *American Journal of Education,* she indicates her leaning toward professional education of girls. At this time she quoted approvingly Hannah More's statement: "the chief end to be pursued in cultivating the understanding of women is to fit them for the practical purposes of life." Miss Beecher added to the statement however, another: "Knowledge, when it can be obtained without the sacrifice of higher duties, is as valuable to a woman as to a man." She then followed it with this suggestion: "If the public sentiment has advanced so much on the subject of female culture that a course of study very similar to that pursued by young men in our public institutions, is demanded for young ladies of the higher circles, should not the public afford facilities somewhat similar for accomplishing it?" By this she meant endowed institutions, well supplied with the necessary facilities for instruction, regular courses of study and division of labor among the faculty members.

In 1829, Catharine Beecher published her *Suggestions Respecting Improvements in Education* which announced clearly for the first time her conception of the practical education for girls referred to in her article of 1827. (pp. 164-66)

[The *Treatise on Domestic Economy*] touched on all the phases of the housekeeper's never-ending round of duties, guiding her footsteps from sunrise to bedtime, from the Monday washing to the Saturday baking, setting out to mold her mind as well as her manners, for we find a chapter entitled: "On the Preservation of a good Temper in a Housekeeper." The prospective young wife and mother is instructed on health, food, clothing, cleanliness, exercise, manners, charity, economy, care of domestics and of infants, construction of houses and their care, dressmaking and gardening. Much of the content, though written in

1841 and contrary to the accepted custom of that day, is common knowledge in 1931. Miss Beecher advised against "the abundant variety . . . usually met at the tables of almost all classes," against excessive use of condiments, and tea and coffee. Applying her favorite "Common Sense" she wrote: "But there is little probability that the present generation will make so decided a change in their habits as to give up these beverages; and the subject is presented rather in reference to forming habits of children." (p. 173)

In the matter of dress, Miss Beecher decried the prevailing styles as did many others. . . . Her standard was: "Any mode of dress, not suited to the employment, the age, the season, or the means of the wearer, is in bad taste." She derided the foolish women who risked their health and lives to secure some resemblance to the deformities of the human frame, represented by the wasp-like figures held up as models of excellence. "The folly of the Chinese belle," she stated, "who totters on two useless deformities, is nothing compared to that of the American belle, who impedes all the internal organs in the discharge of their functions, that she may have a slender waist." She deplored the want of exercise, "Inducing softness in the bones, weakness in the muscles, inactivity in the digestive organs, and general debility in the nervous system."

Miss Beecher recommended allowances for young girls, that they might learn systematic economy, believing that "the art of system and economy can no more come by intuition, than the art of watchmaking or bookkeeping." The economical housewife, however, was warned of making "penurious savings," by "getting the poor to work as cheap as possible." An invariable maxim, in dealing with the poor, Miss Beecher believed, was, "liberal prices and prompt payment."

The question of mental hygiene . . . was considered by Catharine Beecher in her **Domestic Economy.** She did not, however, talk of complexes or psychoses, but named as the "first cause" of much of the mental disease and suffering a want of proper supply of duly oxygenized blood. The deficiency was due, obviously to sleeping in close rooms, and remaining in crowded or badly ventilated apartments. While Catharine's assignment of cause and effect in this particular might not stand in the light of more recent data, the lesson was well timed, for the era was that of the sub-

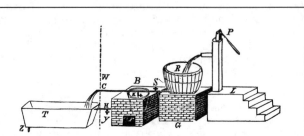

P, Pump. *L*, Steps to use when pumping. *R*, Reservoir. *G*, Brickwork to raise the Reservoir. *B*, A large Boiler. *F*, Furnace, beneath the Boiler. *C*, Conductor of cold water. *H*, Conductor of hot water. *K*, Cock for letting cold water into the Boiler. *S*, Pipe to conduct cold water to a cock over the kitchen sink. *T*, Bathing-tub, which receives cold water from the Conductor, *C*, and hot water from the Conductor, *H*. *W*, Partition separating the Bathing-room from the Wash-room. *Y*, Cock to draw off hot water. *Z*, Plug to let off the water from the Bathing-tub into a drain.

Illustration from A Treatise on Domestic Economy.

stitution of closed stoves for the open fire-place,—a substitution which combined an absence of ventilation with an increase of heat. This matter of the necessity of pure air was a favorite subject with Miss Beecher for many years.

At the time Catharine was writing her *Domestic Economy,* she was developing her plans for the transfer of teachers from the east to the west. It is not surprising, therefore, to find her referring to the project which was beginning to absorb all her thoughts. And, of course, no book of Catharine Beecher's would be complete without a plea for equality of educational opportunity for her sex. Like the regular blows of a hammer, come her repeated appeals for woman's right to an adequate preparation for her profession. (pp. 173-74)

The *Domestic Economy* was such a success that in 1870 Catharine and her sister, Harriet Beecher Stowe, published *The American Woman's Home; or, Principles of Domestic Science,* which was practically an enlarged edition of the earlier book with some quotations from Mrs. Stowe's *House and Home Papers* and some material that was entirely new. The same topics were discussed as in the first *Domestic Economy,* with additional evidence gleaned through the intervening years. Again, in 1873, J. B. Ford and Company published *The New Housekeeper's Manual* and *The Handy Cook Book* bound together and Harper and Brothers brought out *Miss Beecher's Housekeeper and Healthkeeper,* both of which were practically identical with the 1870 publication.

Miss Beecher's aim, and it was well met, we feel, was to design a complete encyclopedia of all that relates to a woman's duties as housekeeper, wife, mother and nurse. At the end of the *Principles of Domestic Science* of 1870 is an "Address of the Senior Author to the Female Teachers of her Country" which begins: "My Honored and Dear Friends: I address you somewhat as did 'Paul the aged,' when, near the close of a life of toil and suffering, he wrote exultingly to his younger co-laborers, 'I have fought a good fight.' It is now nearly half a century since I entered the field where you are now toiling, and the more I have labored the more have I rejoiced in the grandeur of our calling and its glorious rewards." She proceeded then to deplore the lack of training of woman for her profession; the persistence with which women of wealth endowed colleges for men instead of those for their own sex and the activities of those who would thrust on woman the ballot. She described her ideal of a Woman's University and emphasized nursing as a profession for women.

In 1842, following closely on the heels of her *Domestic Economy,* and somewhat related to it in spirit, came Catharine Beecher's *Letters to Persons Engaged in Domestic Service.* This was, indeed, a novel field and no one more than Catharine realized the difficulty involved in addressing a class who were probably not qualified to read and profit by her well-considered counsel. (pp. 176-77)

The eighteen letters of which the book is composed contain advice on the various topics of manners, visiting, company, religion, meetings, trials of domestics and their remedies, economy, health, care of children, dress and language, together with the importance of raising the character of this useful sphere of necessary service. The language is simple and direct and general principles are made clear by the use of illustrative stories. One of Miss Beecher's

firmly-held ideas is illustrated in the seventh and eighth letters in which she presents "Reasons why the station of a domestic is a desirable one, and superior to that of a seamstress, a shop girl, or a factory girl" and "The importance of raising the respectability of the station of a domestic in public estimation and the mode by which it can be done." Commendable as was this attempt of Miss Beecher's, it was probably not productive of much good, for she continues for some years to complain of the incompetency of the only available domestics. . . .

In 1835 came her *Essay on the Education of Female Teachers,* written at the solicitation of the American Lyceum. (p. 178)

Nowhere in her writings does Catharine Beecher better justify her position among the most advanced thinkers of her age than in this essay. Against the memoriter philosophy most commonly exemplified, she protests in no uncertain tones:

> School is generally considered as a place where children are sent, not to form their habits, opinions, and character, but simply to learn from books. And yet, whatever may be the opinion of teachers and parents, children do, to a very great extent, form their character under the influences bearing upon them at school. . . . The mere committing to memory of the facts contained in books, is but a small portion of education.

In behalf of moral education, she is equally emphatic: "it may be set down as one of the current truisms of society, that the formation of the moral and religious principles and habits is the most important part of education, even in reference to this life alone." (p. 179)

In her essay of 1835, Catharine made her first public presentation of her budding plans for the ignorant children of the west. She told her appalling story of a million and a half children without schools and the ninety thousand teachers who would immediately be required to save them from permanent ignorance and vice and set forth her plans for the establishment of institutions for the education of female teachers. (p. 180)

In 1845, came Catharine Beecher's address entitled *American Women: Will You Save Your Country* which appeared shortly in book form as *The Duty of American Women to Their Country.* This was a powerful appeal to American women to save the country from impending devastations due to the increasing number of children who were growing up destitute of the influence of schools or teachers. In vehement language, Miss Beecher describes in detail the horrors of mob-ridden France during the Reign of Terror. In case her readers should quiet their aroused fear with the sedative thought that such cruelty and rage could never appear among them, she called before their mind's eye recent mob-activities in Baltimore, New York, Philadelphia, Cincinnati. The country had only been saved from such widesweeping horrors as had desolated France, because we had such a large body of educated citizens. "Nothing," she wrote, impressively, "can preserve this nation from such scenes but perpetuating this preponderance of intelligence and virtue. This is our only safeguard." More specifically, of course, the women appealed to were to volunteer for teaching service in the west or to aid others who wished to do so by gifts of money to the cause. (pp. 181-82)

We have reviewed Catharine Beecher's literary efforts in two fields of the three assigned by her to women: teaching and home-making. The third related to woman's duty in procuring and guarding health. To assist in the preparation for this duty, Catharine wrote her *Letters to the People on Health and Happiness* (1855) and her *Physiology and Calisthenics* (1856). In the former, the plan was outlined as follows: first, a description of certain organs of the human body most important to health and happiness, and which are most injured and abused by the American people; second, the proper treatment of these organs in order to secure the most perfect health and physical happiness; third, various methods in which these organs are most frequently injured; fourth, the many evil results of such abuse and mismanagement; and fifth, the remedies for these evils.

In the first letter Miss Beecher says: "It is a very small book; it will not take over two or three hours to read it. I beseech you, for your own sake, for the sake of all you love best, to read the whole." In the same part, which treats of "Laws of Health and Happiness" Miss Beecher displays her favorite attribute—"Common Sense"—. One wonders at the necessity for stating such self-evident truths and then recalls that the prevailing ill-health was indisputable proof that they were not "self-evident." Such laws as "Take care that the stomach has food of a proper kind and quality, and that the lungs are fully supplied with cool and pure air"; "Take care that the body has sufficient exercise in pure air every day"; "Take care that the spine shall never habitually be kept out of its natural position either when awake or asleep" were some of the admonitions. In discussing food values and uses, Miss Beecher did not, it is true, speak of "calories" or "diets" but she did distinguish "heat-forming" from "flesh-forming" and "stimulating" from "nourishing" foods. She suggested variety, so that all the elements needed to nourish the body might be furnished; she advised change of food with temperature and season and with age, temperament and occupation. These are modern criteria for choosing a diet.

In Part Third where abuses of the bodily organs are laid down for inspection, Miss Beecher names a lengthy list of causes of the inferior health of the generation of the day,—wrong food, lack of sufficient air and exercise, foolish dress, wrong posture, being the principle ones described. In each case, her point is excellently made with illustration and scientific fact. To give strength to her arguments, she tells the story of her own search for health and to still further prove the necessity for immediate remedial and preventive measures, she quotes statistics of female health gathered through personal contact and through facts contributed by friends. The method she adopted was to ask each lady she met to write the initials of ten of the married ladies with whom she was best acquainted in her place of residence and to write beside each her impression of the lady's health.

The result of much inquiry in this fashion left Miss Beecher with the conclusion that a perfectly sound, healthy, vigorous woman was the rarest of all human specimens. "What is to be done"? she asks in Letter Twenty-Third, and answers: pure air and ventilation as the first and most important requisite, healthful exercise and amusement,

and the correct selection of diet and drink. She knew well her fellow-citizens. "To change essentially," she writes, "the habits, customs, and daily practices of a whole nation, in regard to exercise, ventilation, food, drink, amusements, medical treatment, and modes of training the young, certainly is a most Herculean undertaking; and yet nothing less than this will at all meet the case. But then the American people never fail in any thing they choose to undertake, and they would feel a pride and pleasure in accomplishing a wonderful and beneficient change, and one, too, that would in all respects set them at the head of the human race." Obviously, she was entirely correct.

The *Letters to the People on Health and Happiness* were followed by the *Physiology and Calisthenics.* This book differed little from its predecessor except that the physiology was discussed in more detail and questions in the text were placed at the bottom of each page. The "Laws of Health and Happiness" and the "Abuses and Remedies" were presented in nearly identical fashion with the earlier book. In the 1856 book, however, was included a system of calisthenic exercises suitable for schools, families and health establishments. To give force to her arguments in favor of these exercises, Miss Beecher quotes Galen, the celebrated ancient physician, Lord Bacon, Montaigne, Plato, and Rousseau. (pp. 183-85)

Among Catharine Beecher's educational writings, we find two books which are almost purely narrative in form. The first of these is her *True Remedy for the Wrongs of Woman, With a History of an Enterprise Having That for Its Object,* published in 1851, and her *Educational Reminiscences* of 1874. . . . [The former book] describes in considerable detail her educational activities from 1823 until 1851, including the period of the schools at Hartford, Cincinnati, Burlington, Milwaukee and Quincy. It is written in the form of letters to Mrs. Stowe, so that the style may be familiar and the same easy flow of thought and language be preserved as would be natural in private, unrestrained and earnest conversation.

The *Reminiscences* of 1874 are much milder in tone than the *True Remedy* of twenty years before, or of any of Miss Beecher's writings, for that matter. Accustomed, as one has become, to emphatic, decided, keen-edged phrases, so characteristic of her, one is surprised at their absence, until the explanation offers itself that at seventy-four the world is viewed with a greater measure of placidity and interpreted by an increasingly gentle philosophy. (pp. 187-88)

Thus the pen of Catharine Beecher, making its trail of firm strokes through nearly fifty years, leaves a remarkably clear picture of the woman,—of her life, of her hopes and fears for herself and others, in both this world and the next. One does not need to read between the lines, for all is written in clear black upon white. One reads of a woman who walked with unhesitating step along a well planned path, with eyes upon a distant vision of a justice which should be truly blind and cease to tip the scales in favor of the "stronger sex." (p. 192)

Mae Elizabeth Harveson, in her Catharine Esther Beecher: Pioneer Educator, *n.p., 1932, 295 p.*

Kathryn Kish Sklar   (essay date 1973)

[*In the following excerpt from her biography of Beecher, Sklar analyzes the* Treatise on Domestic Economy *for the Use of Young Ladies at Home and at School as an example of the nineteenth-century ideology of domesticity.*]

Insofar as Catharine Beecher's career can be said to have had a widespread and immediate impact on her society, that effect was achieved through the publication of her **Treatise on Domestic Economy**. . . . Together with her supplementary receipt book, first published in 1846 and reprinted fourteen times before the publication of her enlarged compendium **The American Woman's Home** in 1869, Catharine Beecher's **Treatise** established her as a national authority on the psychological state and the physical well-being of the American home. This reputation was fortified by her **Letters to Persons Who Are Engaged in Domestic Service** (1842) and her **Letters to the People on Health and Happiness** (1855).

Catharine's **Treatise** explained every aspect of domestic life from the building of a house to the setting of a table. Students of technology have noted its crisp and effective designs, such as that for the plumbing system of a kitchen. Describing the first servantless household, she supplied designs for the ingenious labor-saving devices she believed more pertinent to a democratic and "improving" age. In 1840, women who relied on written rather than oral instruction in domestic arts had to read separate books on health, child care, housebuilding, and cooking, or else rely on English compendiums that drew these topics together but were, in their extensive use of servants, inappropriate for American readers. Catharine's was the first American volume to pull all the disparate domestic employments together and to describe their functions in the American environment.

In addition to its functional utility, the book devoted careful attention to the psychology of domesticity. This duality of purpose made her book unique when it was published and renders it historically significant for the twentieth century. Here for the first time was a text that standardized American domestic practices—prescribing one system that integrated psychological, physiological, economic, religious, social, and political factors, and in addition demonstrating how the specifics of the system should work. In the next three decades Catharine Beecher could enter virtually any community in the United States and expect to be received as the heroine who had simplified and made understandable the mysterious arts of household maintenance, child rearing, gardening, cooking, cleaning, doctoring, and the dozen other responsibilities middle class women assumed to keep their children and husbands alive and well. Her **Treatise,** well worth its price of fifty cents, conveyed a sense of shared experience, but its purposeful tone prevented it from lapsing into sentimental intimacy. Catharine took her constituency seriously, and they rewarded her with their patronage.

A Treatise on Domestic Economy appeared at a time when there was a great need for such a standardized text. Many cultural indicators point to the heightened concern over the quality of domestic life in the 1840s—a concern that grew more emphatic when increasing geographic mobility removed many families from traditional sources of domestic knowledge. Just when Americans began to expect more from their domestic lives than ever before, the ability of the average American woman to meet this expectation diminished as she moved away from communal and familial ties that might have fortified her skills. Scholars of the history of technology have confirmed the technological rigor of Catharine Beecher's household designs, and have credited her with the beginning of household automation. Her innovations were meant to fill the gap she perceived between the society's expectations of women and the resources at their disposal for fulfilling those expectations. She more than anyone else may have made domesticity workable.

Catharine was acutely conscious of the trials to which women were put by being unprepared to assume their domestic burdens. Conditions were so bad, Catharine said, that "it would seem as if the primeval curse, which has written the doom of pain and sorrow on one period of a young mother's life, in this country had been extended over all." This was due to a lack of adequate information about how to fulfill domestic responsibilities. Tocqueville also noted the pioneer woman whose "delicate limbs appear shrunken; her features are drawn in; her eye is mild and melancholy; her whole physiognomy bears marks of a degree of religious resignation, a deep quiet of all passion," Catharine quoted him. "To look at [her children's] strength, and her languor, one might imagine that the life she had given them had exhausted her own."

Even settled communities desired new definitions of and attributed greater importance to domestic duties. In Hartford, a young preacher named Horace Bushnell agonized over his inability to arouse the interest of his congregation in the early 1840s, but in 1845 his career was rescued by a series of sermons declaring the careful nurture of children in the home as more important than conversion in shaping a Christian character. His parishioners eagerly adopted this doctrine, for it condoned the distinctive meanings they had already begun to attribute to the family group as an oasis of innocence amid the commercial acquisitiveness of American society. To this emerging ideology of domesticity, Catharine Beecher's **Treatise** contributed both practical details and some basic building blocks of social theory.

Its major contribution was to define a new role for women within the household. Of her four major predecessors, three were men, and all assumed male control of the domestic environment. In *The Father's Book* (1834), Theodore Dwight assumed male hegemony in the household, as did Amherst College's President, Herman Humphrey in his *Domestic Education* (1840). William Alcott advocated a more open and mutual relationship between men and women in his *Young Housekeeper* (1838), but he, like Lydia Maria Child in *The American Frugal Housewife* (1832), assumed the continuance of traditional gender roles inherited from the eighteenth century. While overtly acknowledging male dominance, Catharine Beecher's **Treatise** also exaggerated and heightened gender differences and thereby altered and romanticized the emphasis given to women's domestic role. Subsequent domestic manuals described a significantly different role for women from that anticipated by Dwight, Humphrey, Alcott, and Child. Horace Bushnell and Sarah Josepha Hale, the two chief representatives of this later style, diverged from

Catharine Beecher on many points, as we shall see, but they shared essentially the same universe—one bifurcated into masculine and feminine dichotomies.

Quite apart from its ability to elucidate the new American ideology of the family, Catharine's book was, on a more utilitarian level, a badly needed modern compendium of the domestic arts relating to health, diet, hygiene, and general well-being. As a postrevolutionary generation bent on extracting practical benefits from their theoretical innovations, many Americans believed that elementary matters like diet and health should be as susceptible to improvement as anything else in the new age, and that wherever possible they should be made perfect. These expectations outreached the still rather crude abilities of professional medicine, however, and men and women turned to a variety of popular nostrums ranging from patent medicines to phrenology in their search for physiological betterment. In this context Catharine Beecher offered to new and settled communities alike a scientific but personal guide to improved health and well-being. The contrast between Catharine's *Treatise* and its best-selling predecessor, Lydia Maria Child's *The American Frugal Housewife* (1832), was as great as that between medieval and modern medicine. Child's volume passed on traditional home remedies for a wide variety of ailments and injuries, but gave no causal explanation for the link between illness and treatment. Catharine, however, explained such physiological differences as that between arteries and veins, and she described the fundamentals of modern first aid.

She provided a solid basis for understanding how the body functioned and how to keep it functioning well. Complete with illustrations describing the bone, muscle, nerve, circulation, digestive, and respiratory systems, her discussions of the bodily functions were straightforward and informative, presenting the topic in ways that engendered self-confidence and self-understanding. Catharine did not reserve the role of expert for herself but readily acknowledged the medical sources she had used and implied that anyone could easily learn as much as she by mastering these basic physiological facts. Like Dr. Benjamin Spock's *Baby and Child Care* of a century later, Catharine's manual provided simple rules to enable the reader to judge for herself how best to deal with an inevitably more complicated reality. Thus in a typical discussion of a point of infant care she explained:

> Take particular care of the food of an infant. If it is nourished by the mother, her own diet should be simple, nourishing, and temperate. If the child be brought up by hand, the milk of a new-milch cow, mixed with one third water, and sweetened a little with *white* sugar, should be the only food given, until the teeth come. . . . If the food appear to distress the child, after eating, first ascertain if the milk be really from a new-milch cow, as it may otherwise be too old. Learn also whether the cow lives on proper food.

Perhaps as important as the simple rules were the frequent exceptions her manual pointed out. After a discussion of "the management of young children," in which she recommended government "by rewards more than penalties" and advised an intermediate path between too stern parental control and too weak, she concluded with a discussion of exceptions to that rule, the sensitivity of which was worthy of a twentieth-century child psychiatrist:

> Children of active, heedless temperament, or those who are odd, awkward, or unsuitable, in their remarks and deportment, are often essentially injured by a want of patience and self-control in those who govern them. Such children often possess a morbid sensibility, which they strive to conceal, or a desire of love and approbation, which preys like a famine on the soul. And yet, they become objects of ridicule and rebuke, to almost every member of the family, until their sensibilities are tortured into obtuseness or misanthropy. Such children, above all others, need tenderness and sympathy. A thousand instances of mistake or forgetfulness should be passed over, in silence, while opportunities for commendation and encouragement should be diligently sought.

The volume was like a good companion—knowledgeable but unpretentious, supportive without being intrusive, and above all, able to resolve self-doubts. Designed to reduce the anxiety of the reader, Catharine's discussions commiserated with her about the difficulties of her duties and supplied convincing resolutions of the ambiguities and contradictions involved in her everyday tasks.

The major ambiguity faced by American women in the 1830s and 1840s was not, however, whether they should govern their children with a light or heavy hand, but how, in an egalitarian society, the submission of one sex to the other could be justified. Women in America had always experienced such inequity, but they had never before needed to reconcile it with a growing ideology of popular democracy and equal rights. Furthermore, this contradiction was heightened as the increased options available to white males in the first decades of the nineteenth century seemed to accompany a more sharply limited sphere designated for white women during the same period. Catharine Beecher did not believe that the connection between these two phenomena was accidental. Like other writers of the period, most notably Sarah Josepha Hale and Horace Bushnell, Catharine Beecher tried to reconcile the inequality of women with an egalitarian democracy by emphasizing the importance of woman's sphere of domesticity. But unlike Bushnell and Hale, Catharine Beecher did not try to obscure the fundamental assumption of inequality upon which this separation of spheres rested. Bushnell and Hale believed that women were "naturally" suited to domesticity, but Catharine Beecher explained to her readers that women were restricted to the domestic sphere as a political expedient necessary to the maintenance of democracy in America.

The greater the social, political, and economic expansiveness in the country at large, the greater the tensions, and the keener the need to discover ways to reduce conflict, Catharine believed. Otherwise the system might generate more self-destruction than coherence. In a democracy as agitated and tension-filled as the United States in the 1840s, some form of hierarchy was needed to avoid a war of all against all, she said. She led her readers to conclude that by removing half the population from the arena of competition and making it subservient to the other half, the amount of antagonism the society had to bear would be reduced to a tolerable limit. Moreover, by defining gender identity as more important than class, regional, or religious identity, and by ignoring altogether the imponderables of American racial divisions, she promoted the belief that the society's only basic division was that between men and women.

Catharine Beecher drew most of these ideas from her reading of Tocqueville's *Democracy in America,* and she frequently quoted at length from his study. "The Americans have applied to the sexes the great principle of political economy which governs the manufactories of our age," Catharine explained, "by carefully dividing the duties of man from those of woman, in order that the great work of society may be the better carried on." To support her remarks she cited Tocqueville's belief that "in no country has such constant care been taken, as in America, to trace two clearly distinct lines of action for the two sexes." Tocqueville noted, Catharine continued, that the American woman's centrality in the home did not subvert the power of the man in the family. Americans believe, Tocqueville concluded,

> that the natural head of the conjugal association is man. [Americans] do not, therefore, deny him the right of directing his partner; and they maintain, that, in the smaller association of husband and wife, as well as in the great social community, the object of democracy is, to regulate and legalize the powers which are necessary, not to subvert all power.

Elaborating on Tocqueville's analysis, Catharine explained that this sharp division of sex roles arose from the tensions generated by democratic conditions. Unlike the females of "monarchical and aristocratic lands," where "all ranks and classes are fixed in a given position, and each person is educated for a particular sphere and style of living," Catharine wrote, American women live in a society where "every thing is moving and changing." The flow of wealth is constantly shifting, she added, and since the society lacks permanent definitions of status, it is in a constant state of agitation.

> Persons in poverty, are rising to opulence, and persons of wealth, are sinking to poverty. The children of common laborers, by their talents and enterprise, are becoming nobles in intellect, or wealth, or office; while the children of the wealthy, enervated by indulgence, are sinking to humbler stations. The sons of the wealthy are leaving the rich mansions of their fathers, to dwell in the log cabins of the forest, where very soon they shall bear away the daughters of ease and refinement, to share the privations of a new settlement. Meantime, even in the more stationary portions of the community, there is a mingling of all grades of wealth, intellect, and education. . . . Thus, persons of humble means are brought into contact with those of vast wealth, while all intervening grades are placed side by side. Thus too, there is a constant comparison of conditions, among equals, and a constant temptation presented to imitate the customs, and to strive for the enjoyments, of those who possess larger means.

In this democratic turmoil, Catharine said, in order to decrease hostilities and tensions, "a system of laws must be established, which sustain certain relations and dependencies in social and civil life." Chief among these was the subordination of the wife to the husband. Like the subordination of children to parents, employees to employers, and citizens to magistrates, the subordination of women to men was necessary if society was to "go forward harmoniously."

The position of women in American culture was therefore an example of how "superior and subordinate relations" contribute to "the general good of all." Women "take a subordinate station" not because they are naturally subordinate, or even because subordination suits them, but because it promotes the general good of the society. Catharine believed it was essential to tell women that their submissive role had a social importance transcending their own personal interests, for she thought that they would thereby be better reconciled to it and more effective in implementing the grander purposes of their role.

This was only one example, however, of the ways in which the American domestic experience could promote the national good, but it and other potential contributions to the general weal could not be fully utilized as long as Americans remained confused about the link between domesticity and nationality. In her *Treatise* Catharine Beecher proceeded, often by indirection and implication, to shape a coherent ideology of domesticity that would answer the needs of American democracy.

Catharine began with the premise that the home was a perfect vehicle for national unity because it was a universally experienced institution recognizing no economic, political, or regional boundaries. Even girls who worked in the mills made a small home for themselves, Catharine said, and adopting Tocqueville's thesis that the conditions of mobility and equality in America engendered a loss of traditional social identities, she pointed to the domestic experience as a focus around which a new and unified national identity could be built. For the language of domesticity could more easily be universalized than any single dialect of class or region or age. At the beginning of the 1850s Harriet Beecher Stowe did much to persuade Americans that white and black Americans obeyed the same domestic impulses, and through *Uncle Tom's Cabin* she helped unify a theretofore divided northern opinion. At the beginning of the decade Catharine Beecher set out to transcend social divisions by emphasizing the universality and standardizing the contours of domestic values. Her task was lightened by the fact that she could build on the traditional American distinction between sex roles and the contemporary eagerness to reinforce them.

To this principle of universality, Catharine added four corollary concepts to round out her domestic ideology. By the end of her *Treatise* the domestic sphere seemed not so much removed from as central to the national life.

Catharine first paid ample homage to the role of women in shaping the future of the American experiment. After a long quotation from Tocqueville testifying to the significance of the "social revolution" in America, Catharine agreed that the millennium seemed to be coming in a social rather than a strictly religious form. "Startled kings and sages, philosophers and statesmen, are watching us with that interest which a career so illustrious, and so involving their own destiny, is calculated to excite," Catharine wrote. "They are studying our institutions, scrutinizing our experience, and watching for our mistakes," she said, "that they may learn whether 'a social revolution, so irresistible, be advantageous or prejudicial to mankind.'" The future of the United States was a global, not just a national concern. "This is the Country," Catharine continued, which the Disposer of events designs shall go forth as the cynosure of nations, to guide them to the light and blessedness of that [millennial] day. To us is committed the grand, the responsible privilege, of exhibiting to the world, the beneficent influences of Christianity, when carried into every social, civil, and political institution. . . .

Since the future of the world depended on the United States, and the future of the United States depended on "the intellectual and moral character of the mass of the people," and the shaping of that character was in turn "committed mainly to the female hand," Catharine concluded that "to American women, more than to any others on earth, is committed the exalted privilege of extending over the world those blessed influences, which are to renovate degraded man."

Catharine insisted all American women were equally important to the achievement of this task. Their class or regional differences did not matter since they all worked within a shared system of values and toward the same goal. "No American woman then has any occasion for feeling that hers is an humble or insignificant lot," Catharine continued, for "the value of what an individual accomplishes, is to be estimated by the importance of the enterprise achieved, and not by the particular position of the laborer." Women should not see themselves as "isolated" laborers, Catharine said, but should be "invigorated and cheered" by the fact that they are "indispensable portions of a grand result." The end of the first section of her *Treatise* rose to the pinnacle of rhetorical heights to extol the unified purposes of American womanhood:

> The woman who is rearing a family of children; the woman, who labors in the schoolroom; the woman who, in her retired chamber, earns, with her needle, the mite, which contributes to the intellectual and moral elevation of her Country; even the humble domestic, whose example and influence may be moulding and forming young minds, while her faithful services sustain a prosperous domestic state;—each and all may be animated by the consciousness, that they are agents in accomplishing the greatest work that ever was committed to human responsibility. It is the building of a glorious temple, whose base shall be coextensive with the bounds of the earth, whose summit shall pierce the skies, whose splendor shall beam on all lands; and those who hew the lowliest stone, as much as those who carve the highest capital, will be equally honored, when its top-stone shall be laid, with new rejoicings of the morning stars, and shoutings of the sons of God.

This apotheosis of American national development was to be achieved by the united efforts of American women—exemplary in their ability to conform to the needs of their nation on the basis of their gender alone and to disregard their secondary identities of class and locale. Thus through their nurturing role women were bound to a common purpose and form. In contrast to most of American society, they formed a homogeneous group.

Employing Tocqueville again, Catharine noted further that most of American society acknowledged the homogeneous identity of women by generalizing the domestic relationship between men and women throughout the culture. Thus the whole culture was in a sense made "safe" for women, so that wherever they moved in it, the ideology

of male protection and female dependence would be maintained. Thus, Tocqueville saw that "in America, a young unmarried woman may, alone, and without fear, undertake a long journey." For whatever her status all women are assumed by American men "to be virtuous and refined." "As if in compensation for [their subordination]," Catharine said, women "universally in this country, through every class of society [are given] precedence . . . in all the comforts, conveniences and courtesies, of life." Catharine did not articulate this argument fully, but she implied that since a woman's gender defined her completely, the culture could, by adding a middle-class bias to female identity, significantly enlarge the scope of middle-class values and behavior. For every woman then became a purveyor of middle-class culture. Thus what some historians have called the feminization of American culture can be seen as a means of promoting nationally homogeneous cultural forms, and the emphasis given to gender identity can be viewed as an attempt by a society laden with class and regional anxieties to compensate for these divisive factors.

Besides the creation and extension of a homogeneous ethic, domesticity contributed two other stabilizing pillars to American democracy. These were, according to Catharine Beecher, the example women provided of voluntary and self-initiated submission to authority, and the compensatory role women played in counteracting commercial and acquisitive values. In their submission to men American women acted as an archetypal example of how to achieve social order in a democracy, Catharine said, for their marriage partner, being of their own choosing, is legitimized in his authority over her, just as the American government, being of the people's choosing, is justified in the assertion of its authority. Again quoting Tocqueville, Catharine's *Treatise* concluded that women deem it an honor to act in this exemplary manner: "They attach a sort of pride to the voluntary surrender of their own will, and make it their boast to bend themselves to the yoke, not to shake it off." A more far-reaching and immediately effective consequence of American domesticity, however, was to define an oasis of noncommercial values in an otherwise acquisitive society.

Like other writers of the period, including Sarah Josepha Hale and Horace Bushnell, Catharine Beecher believed that the values of the home stood in opposition to some other American values, but unlike Bushnell and Hale, she wanted the same set of values to apply to both spheres, and she was far more aggressive in applying domestic values to the rest of society. The success of Catharine Beecher's *Treatise* may have been due to its ability to combine a convincing domestic ideology with practical advice demonstrating how these ideals could be realized. Recognizing the practical fact that American women lived in a society as well as a home, she frequently noted the ways in which the values of the society necessarily impinged on the home. "The practice of early rising has a relation to the general interests of the social community, as well as to that of each distinct family," Catharine wrote in a typical passage. "Now if a small portion of the community establish very different hours," she continued, decrying the practices of some families, "it makes a kind of jostling, in all the concerns and interests of society." In both theory and practice, Catharine's *Treatise* promoted congruence between domestic and social values. That goal remained unchanged by the fact that the spheres were not yet completely in harmony.

Horace Bushnell and Sarah Hale, however, described a basic and enduring opposition between the values of domesticity and much of American society. In *Christian Nurture* Bushnell described the home as a source of "permanent, consistent, singleness of aim," set apart from a too mobile and confusing outside world. In contrast to "the extreme individualism of our modern philosophy," Bushnell said, the family operated by an "organic law" by "associating children with the character and destiny of their parents." In what was perhaps the beginnings of the feminine mystique, Bushnell attributed to the mother powers of intuition and sentiment that play on the child's "emotions and sentiments, and work a character in him by virtue of an organic power." Nevertheless, Bushnell admonished the women who acted by this mystical romantic formula to recognize the occasions when "common sense and solid reality" are needed, when "no rhapsodies are wanted, or flights of feeling."

While the mother was thus encouraged to use her powers of intuition, she was denied their full employment, and required to recognize the greater authority of the common sense world her sons were destined to enter after their character had been properly molded. Bushnell could more easily ignore the contradictions of this policy than could the women who tried to implement it. They were left to discover for themselves when to employ their "organic" powers and when to use their common sense. *Christian Nurture* may have closed the gap between parent and child, but it enlarged the gulf between the home and the outside world, and placing women firmly inside the walls of domesticity, it asked them to perform a kind of penance for the sins of a society they were not fully allowed to enter. Catharine Beecher's readers labored under no such handicap, for they were asked to eliminate rather than to endure the contradictions between general and domestic values.

Sarah Hale, editor for half a century of the influential magazine, *Godey's Lady's Book,* also adopted and promoted the ideology of domesticity as a compensating set of values in "a society given over without reservation to the pursuit of wealth." The male and female spheres were separated to allow men to continue their acquisitive pursuits and to enable women to concentrate on their moral role. Without one the growth of the society would stop, and

The Hartford Female Seminary.

without the other the course of that growth might be morally objectionable. Together they gave the society an energized labor force and a free conscience. So long as women's labor was unsullied by the business mentality, so long as it was a labor of love and not for gain, the culture might retain its contact with primitive virtue and goodness.

Catharine's analysis of domesticity does not differ in purpose from that of Bushnell or Hale. All agreed that the isolation of women in the home and away from full participation in the society decreased the tensions and anxieties that characterized American life. They agreed, moreover, that this was done "in order that the great work of society may be the better carried on." But rather than seeing the home as a haven set apart from society to compensate for or counteract certain characteristics of American life, Catharine saw the home as an integral part of a national system, reflecting and promoting mainstream American values. The only requirement for a place on this cultural dais was that women reject aggression and embrace deference as a style of social interaction.

Three lifelong concerns of Catharine Beecher's were resolved in her ideology of domesticity. First, domesticity revived the Puritan notion of the subjection of the individual to the larger social welfare, yet it presented this notion in a form acceptable to the nineteenth century. In this democratic context the home was a much more effective agency of social authority than the clergy or aristocracy. For in the delineation of its own lines of authority the family relied on "natural" relationships of superiority and subordination. As a society in miniature, the family could therefore be used as a model for the extension of such relationships elsewhere in the society. Although the family located authority at a personal level, domesticity, as Catharine Beecher described it, confirmed the individual's obligation to recognize and conform to "a system of laws" that sustained "superior and subordinate relations" in the society as a whole.

Second, domesticity answered the dilemma over piety and morality that Catharine inherited from her father. Bushnell, a clergyman like Lyman Beecher, superimposed a romantic epistemology on a common-sense culture in order to maintain the importance of piety over morality. Catharine overcame this dichotomy by using the concept of self-denial to show how the impulses of the heart were related to external behavior. Self-denial was built into the very identity Catharine Beecher defined for women in the United States. Submission to the will and needs of others was, Catharine believed, automatically required of American women. Therefore their own personal promptings of the heart were necessarily related to their behavior since sacrifice was by definition an act that linked selflessness of heart with an external deed.

In her *Treatise* Catharine called on businessmen to imitate the self-denying ethic of the home and use their wealth "for the greatest good of those around them," rather than for "mere selfish indulgences." Fighting the spread of undomestic and "aristocratic" habits in the wealthy, Catharine decried the "great portion of the rich [who] seem to be acting on the principle, that the more God bestows on them, the less are they under obligation to practice any self-denial, in fulfilling his benevolent plan of raising our race to intelligence and holiness."

In addition to treating the two important problems of leadership and morality, Catharine's brand of domesticity also addressed the problem of national unity—a concern Catharine inherited from her father but recast in a mold that gave centrality to women. Her *Treatise* promoted a practical as well as theoretical base for national unity, however, for throughout her rules for health care, her receipts, her formulas for household management, her description of proper manners, her prescriptions for infant care, Catharine sought above all to standardize and systematize American domestic practices.

This urge for regularity that marked nearly every page of Catharine's *Treatise* had both a personal and a social dimension. On a private level it tried to lift women out of the confusing morass of contradictory demands on their time and energies by establishing priorities or precise timetables and by adopting efficient work methods. "Without attempting any such systematic employment of time, and carrying it out, so far as they can control circumstances, most women are rather driven along, by the daily occurrences of life," Catharine wrote, "so that, instead of being the intelligent regulators of their own time, they are the mere sport of circumstances." There was nothing, she said, "which so distinctly marks the difference between weak and strong minds, as the fact, whether they control circumstances, or circumstances control them." This private psychological regimen was further enhanced by the belief that these same priorities and practices were adopted by families throughout the country.

Deeming the standardization of public manners and attitudes as important as standardization of household routine, Catharine Beecher said that just as one set of management rules could apply to all households, so one code of manners applied to all Americans. "Now the principles of democracy require, that the same courtesy, which we accord to our own circle, shall be extended to every class and condition; and that distinction, of superiority and subordination, shall depend, not on accidents of birth, fortune, or occupation, but solely on those relations, which the good of all classes equally require," Catharine wrote. "The distinctions demanded, in a democratic state, are simply those, which result from relations, that are common to every class, and are for the benefit of all." Thus although class differences do admittedly exist, Catharine said that American manners should not reflect these differences, but rather acknowledge differences of status only where these are "common to every class." Manners may therefore recognize only differences such as those between men and women, children and elders, feeble and healthy. "The rules of good breeding, in a democratic state must be founded on these principles," Catharine concluded. "Otherwise there would be constant scrambling, among those of equal claims, and brute force must be the final resort."

In a similar way she provided rules standardizing diet, food preparation, meal hours, health care, house and kitchen furnishings, size and number of rooms, charitable responsibilities, and recreation—here even suggesting that "serious and intelligent persons" patronize horseraces "in order to regulate them."

In the history of writings on domestic management, *A Treatise on Domestic Economy* stood between traditional guides like Lydia Maria Child's *The American Frugal Housewife* of 1832 (for many years its chief competitor) and professional writings like Helen Campbell's *Household Economics* of 1898. Catharine Beecher marked the midpoint between Child's "general maxims" and Campbell's highly specialized lectures. This progression is perhaps best described by their respective attitudes toward the rooms of a house. Child nowhere mentioned differentiated rooms within the home; Catharine Beecher provided detailed drawings and instructions for the construction of an eight-room house, each room designed for an explicit use as a parlor, kitchen, bedroom, or nursery; and Helen Campbell further elaborated on these distinctions to claim that "a separate room is the right of every human being; a place where one can lock the door, be safe from intrusion, and in silence and freedom gather strength for the next thing to be done." Catharine Beecher's concern was to subsume individual diversity in order to build a commonality of culture. By the end of the century this culture had passed through the crucible in which its identity was forged and had elaborated so ubiquitous a structure that isolation was more to be desired than heightened participation.

Catharine's several writings on domestic economy in the 1870s and her enlarged and partially revised *The American Woman's Home,* co-authored with Harriet Beecher Stowe in 1869, presented essentially the same ideology linking domestic life with the life of the nation, but two pairs of tensions that Catharine had tried to resolve in the 1840s appear by the 1870s to have stretched beyond the possibility of mutual accommodation. Neither the relationship between men and women nor that between upper and lower classes were by 1869 so easily resolved for Catharine. For each of these new problems Catharine devised new domestic forms.

Articulating a more complex argument in defense of "the unequal distribution of property," generally more conscious of the gulf between rich and poor, and citing Herbert Spencer rather than Tocqueville to justify the importance of the domestic sphere, Catharine advocated in 1869 the creation of settlement houses wherein "several ladies" should take up residence in areas of urban poverty and "from the vast accumulation of misery and sin at hand on every side, should select the orphans, the aged, the sick, and the sinful, and spend time and money for their temporal and spiritual elevation." The last paragraph of *Miss Beecher's Housekeeper and Healthkeeper* of 1873 rejoiced "in the increasingly open avenues to useful and remunerating occupations for women, enabling them to establish *homes of their own,* where, if not as the natural mother, yet as a Christ-mother, they may take in neglected ones, and train future mothers, teachers, and missionaries for the world." The family, although still a source of morality and virtue, seemed no longer a society in miniature to Catharine. It seemed to embody rather than to meliorate the tensions between social classes and between men and women. In her later works Catharine appended to the usual domestic forms an entirely female domesticity, in which a woman "who earns her own livelihood can institute the family state" by adopting children. "Then to her will appertain the authority and rights that belong to man as the head of a family," Catharine pointed out. She also reminded her readers "that the distinctive duty of obedience to man does not rest on women who do not enter the relations of married life." Between 1841 and 1869 Catharine Beecher not only witnessed the development of an urban industrial society, but she also committed herself to the creation of a more autonomous female culture.

Thus her *Treatise* paradoxically provided Catharine with the framework whereby she could begin to explore alternatives to the American ethic of domesticity. Nevertheless she was too deeply immersed in its rituals to break away completely from domestic forms. In her *Treatise* she had articulated concepts central to her own life as well as to the life of her nation. For her the *Treatise* was both a summary and an exorcising of the domestic impulses she had known since childhood. It cleared the way for new personal and professional concerns. For the nation, domesticity may have been equally effective in easing the passage from turbulent youth to regulated maturity. (pp. 151-67)

> *Kathryn Kish Sklar, in her* Catharine Beecher: A Study in American Domesticity, *Yale University Press, 1973, 356 p.*

Jeanne Boydston, Mary Kelley, and Anne Margolis (essay date 1988)

[*In the following excerpt, the authors discuss Beecher's writings as they exemplify her evolving attitudes towards women's roles in society.*]

In 1829 . . . Beecher published *Suggestions Respecting Improvements in Education.* Offered as a treatise on education, *Suggestions* was also Beecher's first full-scale statement of the social philosophy to which—with strikingly few alterations—she would remain committed for the rest of her life. In it, she attempted to pull together the threads of her experience. She identified her chosen career as teacher with women's traditional domestic work; at the same time, and undoubtedly remembering her struggle to find her own voice in her religious debates with Lyman [her father] and Edward [her brother], she recast both the teacher and the mother as female counterparts of the minister, charged, not only with the education of the mind, but with the perfection of the soul. But the soul as it concerned Catharine in *Suggestions* was changed from the one for which Lyman struggled: rather than in spiritual redemption, she looked for salvation in social conduct. . . . (pp. 19-20)

[In *The Elements of Mental and Moral Philosophy,* Beecher] returned to the religious themes raised in her *Suggestions Regarding Improvements in Education,* now binding morality even more securely to behavior and to the pursuit of "a course of conscious rectitude." God's purpose in creating humans, she wrote, "was *the production of happiness.*" Because humans were social beings, "the purest and highest kind of happiness" was found, not in individual pleasure, but in "the mutual relations of minds," in seeking "the *greatest amount of general happiness,* irrespective of [one's] own particular share." That general happiness, Beecher believed, consisted in each person's pursuit of "a perfect and infallible standard of rectitude"—"rules of *neatness,* of *order,* of *regularity,* and of *taste* or *fitness*" found in the Bible. Since "the mind is a free and independent agent . . . influenced by *motives,*" those rules—and thus virtue itself—could be *taught,* developed in habits of self-sacrifice and proper social conduct. (p. 115)

In 1837, [Beecher] published *An Essay on Slavery and Abolitionism,* a response to the efforts of Sarah and Angelina Grimké to enlist women in the abolitionist cause. Averring that she abhorred slavery, Beecher nonetheless denounced abolitionism as unchristian and inappropriate for women. In an early exposition of her concept of female influence, she argued that women's power must never be exerted directly (as active abolitionism would have required), for to do so would associate women with self-interest and deprive them of the high moral ground of self-sacrifice she had envisioned in *Mental and Moral Philosophy:* "Woman is to win every thing by peace and love," she insisted, "by making herself so much respected, esteemed and loved, that to yield to her opinions and to gratify her wishes, will be the free-will offering of the heart." She called on "every female instantly to relinquish the attitude of a partisan, in every matter of clashing interests" and to assume her role as gentle moral exemplar to her nation.

In the *Essay,* too, Catharine returned to the association that had been at the heart of her earlier *Suggestions*—that of teaching with mothering. Having determined that woman's influence was to be confined to "the domestic and social circle," Beecher went on to suggest that, among other reasons for eschewing abolition work, women were needed in more "appropriate" tasks—especially that of educating themselves to work as teachers in the West. Because many Americans still considered education incompatible with "true womanhood," in 1837 Beecher added that "the more intelligent a woman becomes, the more she can appreciate the wisdom of that ordinance that appointed her subordinate station, and the more her taste will conform to the graceful and dignified retirement and submission it involves." Later (in part as a result of her own efforts), Beecher would feel less compelled to defend women's professional training per se; indeed, she would eventually argue that it was in supporting women's education that society showed its true esteem for womanhood. (p. 116)

As well as compendia of useful household information, [*A Treatise on Domestic Economy for the Use of Young Ladies at Home and at School*] and *The American Woman's Home* comprised an extended paean to American womanhood and to woman's special role in determining the character of American society. Those views began, as did the *Treatise* with its dedication to "American Mothers," with the equation of womanhood with motherhood, and of motherhood with the success or failure of society: "The mother writes the character of the future man," Beecher warned, " . . . whose energies may turn for good or for evil the destinies of a nation." Beecher's emphasis on motherhood derived directly from her conclusions in the *Mental and Moral Philosophy.* In that work, she had cautioned that apparently altruistic behavior might in fact spring from essentially selfish motives—"a desire for notoriety, and the praise of men," for example. Such temptations assailed one at every turn in public life, tainting the impulse to true virtue.

In both the *Treatise* and *The American Woman's Home,* Beecher argued that a reliable model of virtue existed only in the privacy and self-sacrifice of the family, and there, only in the role of the mother. Focused constantly on the welfare of others, mothers embodied that selflessness which lay at the heart of true morality: their "great mission is self-denial, in training [the family] members to self-sacrificing labors for the ignorant and weak." As *women,* mothers were unenfranchised, and therefore could not become competitors in the political sphere. As *married* women, they were subordinate in the relations of civic and domestic life. Thus, their position in society and the family set mothers apart from the self-aggrandizement that might underlay the actions of others. To them alone might American society entrust "the formation of the moral and intellectual character" of others.

As she had in the *Essay on Slavery and Abolitionism,* Beecher insisted that the nature of female influence was to be indirect. Like the "drops of heaven," woman would "freshen the earth," "extending over the world those blessed influences, that are to renovate degraded man, and 'clothe all climes with beauty.'" Should women feel a grievance, they had but to express it: "in all cases, in which [women] do feel a concern," Beecher insisted, "their opinions and feelings have a consideration, equal, or even superior, to that of the other sex." Presumably, a grateful society would always listen.

The *Treatise* and *The American Woman's Home* both focused primarily on the family, and on woman as wife and mother. But as Beecher knew all too well, unmarried women, like herself, remained marginal to that definition of womanhood. Indeed, on at least one occasion her unmarried status called into question her credentials for even writing about family life: observing Catharine's progress on the *Treatise,* her cousin Elizabeth Elliot Foote had commented acidly, "If it were not for these maiden ladies instructing the married ones how to keep house and take

Beecher at age 57.

care of children I don't know what would become of us." Alert to the criticism, Beecher explained in the volume's preface that she had been trained as a young girl "to the care of children, and to the performance of most domestic duties" and had lived "most of her life, in the families of exemplary and accomplished housekeepers." In another respect, Beecher's status as an unmarried woman made it appropriate that she should write the book. Like most unmarried women in the antebellum period, she faced recurrent financial hardship: she needed the money. Aware of the numbers of women, like herself, for whom "womanhood" must include money-making, she was determined to expand the rhetoric to fit her own circumstances.

Perhaps for this reason, although Beecher based woman's power on the model of motherhood, she did not recognize as "mothers" only those women who actually bore children. While the *Essay* had focused on the influence of women in families, the *Treatise* also specifically included women in paid employment:

> the woman who labors in the schoolroom; the woman who, in her retired chamber, earns, with her needle, the mite to contribute to the intellectual and moral elevation of her country; even the humble domestic . . . ;—each and all . . . are agents in accomplishing the greatest work that ever was committed to human responsibility.

In the *Treatise,* broadening the definition of motherhood remained a minor theme. In 1851, however, in response to the new women's rights movement, which sought protection for women in expanded legal rights, Beecher published *True Remedy for the Wrongs of Woman.* As [Beecher's sister Harriet Beecher Stowe] observed, it was in *True Remedy* that Catharine's work at last became a "great *whole.*" There she fused the two elements of her thinking, creating a domestic utopia based on woman's position in the home but encompassing women's professional work beyond the home. Beecher accomplished this, in part, by explicitly designating "motherhood" a profession, not a biological relationship; specifically, it was the profession of acting "as the conservators of the domestic state, the nurses of the sick, the guardians and developers of the human body in infancy, and the educators of the human mind." In all of its contexts, the work of mothering was undervalued, Beecher insisted, but "the grand source of the heaviest wrong that oppresses our sex is found in the fact that they are so extensively cut off from honorable and rumunerative employ in their professional vocation." What women suffered from most was the general disdain of their work as nurses, domestic servants, and, most especially, teachers. In that "perfected state of society" toward which humanity progressed, Beecher prophesied, "the office now filled by the domestic, the nurse, and the teacher, will become the most honorable"—and, not incidentally, profitable. Although throughout the work Beecher conflated the "mother" and the "teacher," she had made an important modification in the domestic ideal: it was not wives, but teachers, "who really are rendering the most service to society," and it was by their status that the status of womanhood must be measured.

Beecher pursued this linkage of the domestic female ideal with a new professional female ideal in *The American Woman's Home,* which took as its purpose "to elevate both the honor and the remuneration of all employments that sustain . . . the family state." In this work, Beecher emphasized the increased autonomy for women implicit in her redefinition of motherhood: "The blessed privileges of the family state are not confined to those who rear children of their own." Any woman, married or single, became a mother simply through her ministrations to others—and not necessarily children: "the orphan, the sick, the homeless, and the sinful," husband, brothers, and friends were all potential objects of her aid. Indeed, other than as recipients of women's care, men were virtually expendable in the creation of motherhood, since, "Any woman who can earn a livelihood, as every woman should be trained to do, can take a properly qualified female associate, and institute a family of her own."

Her interest in defining motherhood as a profession helps to account for an interesting inconsistency in Beecher's thought. Although she variously ascribed woman's role as mother to Nature, the principles of democracy, and the tenets of Christianity, she also viewed motherhood as a socially constructed role. In *Mental and Moral Philosophy,* she had concluded that self-sacrifice—the core of motherhood—was itself *learned* behavior. She returned to this theme in her *Educational Reminiscences and Suggestions,* recalling that her father took that delight in childrearing "which is generally deemed a distinctive element of the woman." Thinking of her parents, she concluded that "much that passes for natural talent is mainly the result of culture." Determined to elevate the importance of trained female teachers as agents of moral development, Beecher would leave to another age the belief that woman's destiny lay entirely in her anatomy.

Beecher had based her argument for female selflessness on women's social subordination and close association with domestic life. But, as she made clear in *True Remedy,* submission did not mean subservience. She was adamant that those women who "write and talk as if the great end and aim of woman was to conform to the will and wishes of husbands" utterly misunderstood the relationship. "The true attitude to be assumed by woman," she insisted, "not only in the domestic but in all our social relations, is that of an intelligent, immortal being, whose interests and rights are *every* way equal in value to that of the other sex." Women were to exercise power; they merely were not to be *perceived* as exercising it. Moreover, far from diminishing woman's role in social affairs, subordination was its base.

In each of these works, Beecher was attempting to shape the social order even as she accepted it, selecting those elements that validated her view of America and of the power of women within it. (pp. 117-21)

> *Jeanne Boydston, Mary Kelley and Anne Margolis, in their* The Limits of Sisterhood: The Beecher Sisters on Women's Rights and Woman's Sphere, *The University of North Carolina Press, 1988, 369 p.*

FURTHER READING

Bacon, Martha. "Miss Beecher in Hell." In her *Puritan Promenade,* pp. 73-93. Boston: Houghton Mifflin Co., 1964.

Describes the crisis in religious belief Beecher experienced following the death of her fiancé Alexander Metcalf Fisher.

Burstyn, Joan N. "Catharine Beecher and the Education of American Women." *New England Quarterly* XLVII, No. 3 (September 1974): 386-403.
Discusses Beecher's beliefs about women's place in society and her career as an educator and reformer. Burstyn concludes: "Men and women today cannot subscribe to Catharine Beecher's belief in equal but separate spheres for the sexes, but they can appreciate the importance of her attempts to ensure to women their share of top jobs in an occupational hierarchy."

Cross, Barbara M. Introduction to *The Educated Woman in America: Selected Writings of Catharine Beecher, Margaret Fuller, and M. Carey Thomas,* pp. 1-48. New York: Columbia University Teacher's College, 1965.
Includes biographical material on Beecher emphasizing her role in promoting the education of women.

Goodsell, Willystine. "Catharine Beecher." In her *Pioneers of Women's Education in the United States: Emma Willard, Catharine Beecher, and Mary Lyon,* pp. 115-228. 1931. Reprint. AMS Press, 1970.
Contains a brief biography of Beecher and annotated excerpts from some of her major writings, including *Suggestions Regarding Improvements in Education, An Address on Female Suffrage,* and *Letters to the People on Health and Happiness.*

Grimké, A. E. *Letters to Catharine E. Beecher: In Reply to "An Essay on Slavery and Abolitionism."* Boston: Isaac Knapp, 1838, 130 p.
Collection of letters written by prominent abolitionist Angelina Grimké in response to Beecher's *An Essay on Slavery and Abolitionism with Reference to the Duty of American Females,* in which Beecher asserted that women should not participate in the abolitionist movement but should confine themselves to the domestic sphere, exerting their moral influence on society through example rather than through advocacy.

Martin, Jane Roland. "Beecher's Homemakers." In her *Reclaiming a Conversation: The Ideal of the Educated Woman,* pp. 103-38. New Haven, Conn.: Yale University Press, 1985.
Compares Beecher's views regarding women's role in the family and in society, particularly her ideas on female education and the professionalization of domestic work, with those of Mary Wollstonecraft and Jean-Jacques Rousseau.

Rose, Willie Lee. "Reforming Women." *The New York Review of Books* XXIX, No. 15 (7 October 1982): 45-9.
Explores the relationship between the "cult of domesticity" and reform movements in nineteenth-century America, comparing the approaches of Catharine Beecher and Angelina Grimké.

Stowe, Lyman Beecher. "Catharine Beecher, 1800-1878." In his *Saints, Sinners, and Beechers,* pp. 73-137. Indianapolis: Bobbs-Merrill Co., 1934.
Biographical sketch.

William Gilpin

1724-1804

English travel writer, essayist, and biographer.

Gilpin is best known for his series of travel books detailing his pursuit of the "picturesque" in British landscape. These works are credited with establishing the picturesque as an aesthetic fashion in England, promoting an awareness of the artistic in nature which presaged Romantic literature.

Gilpin was born near Carlisle, Cumberland, to a family of distinguished lineage. He entered Queen's College, Oxford, at the age of fifteen and received his bachelor of arts degree in 1744. According to his *Memoirs,* Gilpin considered his education at Oxford "no better than solemn trifling" and maintained that "all he gained was from *reading books,* which he might have read any where, as well as at college; & without the loss of that time he had squandered on the appearance of doing something more." His disillusionment caused him to abandon graduate studies and return to Carlisle, where he engaged in private study and practiced the art of sketching. When he reached the age of twenty-two, Gilpin was ordained a minister and appointed curate of Irthington, a small town near Carlisle. He was soon persuaded by his family, however, to accept an invitation from Queen's College to resume his studies. Receiving his master's degree in 1748, Gilpin accepted a curacy in London and began work on a biography of his ancestor, clergyman Bernard Gilpin. Following two unsuccessful petitions for ecclesiastical preferment, Gilpin accepted a position as assistant to Rev. James Sanxay in conducting his boys' school at Cheam, a village near London. Assuming control of the school at Sanxay's urging in 1852, Gilpin remained there more than two decades, during which he composed biographical sketches of the lives of religious reformers, including Hugh Latimer, John Wycliffe, and Jan Hus, and completed his *Essay upon Prints,* in which he elaborated his theory of the picturesque, defining it as "a term expressive of that peculiar kind of beauty, which is agreeable in a picture." Gilpin began sketching British landscape extensively during summer tours beginning in 1770, at which time he wrote his *Observations on the River Wye, and Several Parts of South Wales,* the first of several works articulating his concept of picturesque travel. Gilpin left Cheam in 1777 and accepted the offer of a vicarage at Boldre, remaining there and continuing his prolific production of sketches, essays, biographies, and sermons until his death in 1804.

In his series of *Observations* Gilpin highlights the appeal of picturesque travel, describing the thrilling expectancy in seeking picturesque scenery, the intellectual satisfaction in its discernment, and the emotional pleasure which results when "some grand scene . . . strikes [the traveler] beyond the power of thought." Gilpin's *Three Essays* differentiates between the beautiful and the picturesque by emphasizing "roughness" as the distinguishing feature of the latter. Concluding a summary of the principle of Gil-

pin's theory, William D. Templeman writes: "Roughness is essential to picturesque beauty because when certain elements (execution, composition, variety, contrast, effect of light and shade, and coloring) are properly pleasing in a picture they of necessity make use of rough objects." As Gilpin asserted in his *Observations,* ruins are thus more agreeable to pictorial representation than the "solid, square" form of undecayed structure because ruins receive "the richest decorations from the various colours . . . the stains of weather; the incrustations of moss; and the varied tints of flowering weeds." Gilpin's treatment of the picturesque insists upon a direct observation of nature for objects or scenery suitable for depiction in art, necessitating the viewer's development of a pictorial perception of nature which attends only to a select combination of elements in a landscape. By further advocating the use of the imagination both to modify the relationship between the components of a scene, thus accentuating picturesque qualities, and to contemplate the vistas beyond it, Gilpin established his influence in what Christopher Hussey describes as "the picturesque interregnum between classic and romantic art necessary in order to enable the imagination to form the habit of feeling through the eyes."

PRINCIPAL WORKS

Life of Bernard Gilpin (biography) 1753

Life of Hugh Latimer, Bishop of Worcester (biography) 1755

The Lives of John Wicliff; and the Most Eminent of His Disciples; Lord Cobham, John Huss, Jerome of Prague, and Zisca (biography) 1765

An Essay upon Prints (nonfiction) 1768

Lectures on the Church Catechisms (addresses) 1779

Observations on the River Wye, and Several Parts of South Wales (nonfiction) 1782

The Life of Thomas Cranmer, Archbishop of Canterbury (biography) 1784

Observations, on Several Parts of England, Particularly the Mountains and Lakes of Cumberland and Westmoreland, Relative Chiefly to Picturesque Beauty (nonfiction) 1786

Observations, on Several Parts of Great Britain, Particularly the High-lands of Scotland, Relative Chiefly to Picturesque Beauty (nonfiction) 1789

Remarks on Forest Scenery, and Other Woodland Views (nonfiction) 1791

Three Essays: On Picturesque Beauty; On Picturesque Travel; and On Sketching Landscape (essays) 1794

Observations on the Western Parts of England, Relative Chiefly to Picturesque Beauty. To Which Are Added, a Few Remarks on the Picturesque Beauties of the Isle of Wight (nonfiction) 1798

Observations on the Coasts of Hampshire, Sussex, and Kent, Relative Chiefly to Picturesque Beauty (nonfiction) 1804

Observations on Several Parts of the Counties of Cambridge, Norfolk, Suffolk, and Essex. Also on Several Parts of North Wales (nonfiction) 1809

Memoirs of Dr. Richard Gilpin, of Scaleby Castle in Cumberland; and of His Posterity in the Two Succeeding Generations (biography) 1879

William Combe (essay date 1817)

[*Combe was a satirical poet and fiction writer who also wrote and edited numerous essays, histories, and letters. Employed by publisher Rudolph Ackermann in 1812 to provide text for Thomas Rowlandson's series of plates portraying a traveling schoolmaster, Combe composed his satire* The Tour of Doctor Syntax, In Search of the Picturesque, *a parody of Gilpin's travel books which was successful enough to merit two sequels and remains Combe's most popular work. In the following excerpt, Combe parodies Gilpin's theories of picturesque landscape.*]

"I find that I have lost my way.
Oh what a wide expanse I see,
Without a wood, without a tree;
No one at hand, no house is near,
To tell the way, or give good cheer;
For now a sign would be a treat,
To tell us we might drink and eat;
But sure there is not in my sight

The sign of any living wight;
And all around upon this common
I see not either man or woman;
Nor dogs to bark, nor cocks to crow,
Nor sheep to bleat, nor herds to low:
Nay, if these asses did not bray,
And thus some signs of life betray,
I well might think that I were hurl'd
Into some sad, unpeopled world.
How could I come, misguided wretch!
To where I cannot make a sketch?"

Thus as he ponder'd what to do,
A guide post rose within his view:
And, when the pleasing shape he spied,
He prick'd his steed and thither hied;
But some unheeding, senseless wight,
Who to fair learning ow'd a spite,
Had ev'ry letter'd mark defac'd,
Which once its several pointers grac'd.
The mangled post thus long had stood,
An uninforming piece of wood;
Like other guides, as some folks say,
Who neither lead, nor tell the way.
The Sun, as hot as he was bright,
Had got to his meridian height:
'Twas sultry noon—for not a breath
Of cooling zephyr fann'd the heath;
When Syntax cried—" 'Tis all in vain
To find my way across the plain;
So here my fortune I will try,
And wait till some one passes by:
Upon that bank awhile I'll sit,
And let poor Grizzle graze a bit;
But, as my time shall not be lost,
I'll make a drawing of the post;
And, tho' a flimsy taste may flout it,
There's something *picturesque* about it:
'Tis rude and rough, without a gloss,
And is well cover'd o'er with moss;
And I've a right—(who dares deny it?)
To place yon group of asses by it.
Aye! this will do: and now I'm thinking,
That self-same pond where Grizzle's drinking
If hither brought 'twould better seem,
And faith I'll turn it to a stream:
I'll make this flat a shaggy ridge,
And o'er the water throw a bridge:
I'll do as other sketchers do—
Put any thing into the view;
And any object recollect,
To add a grace, and give effect.
Thus, though from truth I haply err,
The scene preserves its character.
What man of taste my right will doubt,
To put things in, or leave them out?
'Tis more than right, it is a duty,
If we consider landscape beauty:
He ne'er will as an artist shine,
Who copies Nature line by line:
Whoe'er from Nature takes a view,
Must copy and improve it too.
To heighten every work of art,
Fancy should take an active part:
Thus I (which few I think can boast)
Have made a Landscape of a Post.

(pp. 9-11)

William Combe, *"Losing His Way,"* in his The Tour of Doctor Syntax, In Search of the Picturesque: A Poem, *Methuen & Co., 1903, pp. 9-11.*

Christopher Hussey   (essay date 1927)

[*In the following excerpt, Hussey comments on Gilpin's criteria for discerning the picturesque.*]

In the Scottish Tour [Gilpin] revealed himself as the romantic that he was at heart. In Scotland he found the limitless, a land in the state of nature, still enjoying "the reign of picturesque beauty." Agriculture, like clothes, he believed, hid the form of nature. Wherever man appeared with his tools, deformity followed his steps. He reprimanded Dr. [Samuel] Johnson for his sentence on the Scottish scene, where the sage observed that "the appearance is that of matter, incapable of form or usefulness, dismissed by nature from her care and left in its original elemental state." "It is true," replied Gilpin, "that an eye like Doctor Johnson's, which he himself acknowledged was accustomed only to see the beauties of landscape in 'flowery pastures' and 'waving harvests,' cannot be attracted by the great and sublime in nature. As for a Scotch mountain being incapable of form, he can only mean that it cannot be formed into meadows. Its form as a mountain is grand and sublime in the highest degree." (p. 112)

Gilpin, the romantic, believed nature could do no wrong. She was the Ideal. Only man had deformed her. To the classical Johnson the process was the exact reverse. Nature in her primitive state was chaotic. Only with the assistance of art and intellect could she be made beautiful, regular, fruitful. In practice, however, Gilpin could not throw off the aesthetic habit of his age. Though wild nature "is always great in design," she is "unequal in composition." "She is an admirable colourist and can harmonize her tints with infinite variety and inimitable beauty: but is seldom so correct in composition as to produce a harmonious whole. . . . The case is, the immensity of nature is beyond human comprehension. She works on a *vast scale;* and, no doubt, harmoniously, if her scheme could be comprehended. The artist, in the mean time, is confined to *space.* He lays down his little rules, therefore, which he calls the *principles of picturesque beauty,* merely to adapt such diminutive parts of nature's surfaces to his own eye, as comes within its scope."

Had Gilpin been a poet, he might have consistently apprehended the existence of this mighty force, nature, and have united it to his own spirit. He saw her vastness, and knew that he could not comprehend it. But he was a painter, in mind if not in execution, and a painter trained in the same art principles as was Johnson. He was thus involved in a perpetual compromise, adapting nature, which he understood only vaguely, to art, which he understood (in his generation) well. He tried to mould what he knew to be above reason, to a rational system. Thus we get perpetually the comical vision of the kindly parson, first abasing himself before nature as the source of all beauty and emotion; then getting up and giving her a lesson in deportment. He saw romantic scenery, and analysed and bottled it into the picturesque.

Gilpin's sketches, reproduced in his books in aquatint, exactly embody Johnson's requirements of pictures. They exhibit "the prominent and striking features" and "neglect the minute descriptions." In the *Tour to the Lakes* Gilpin explained their object. They made, he said, no attempt to be portraits, for "Mr. Farington's prints render any other portraits unnecessary." On the other hand they were intended "to illustrate and explain picturesque ideas—one of the most useful aids of the pencil," and to characterize the general face of the country which, as Johnson put it, "are alike obvious to attention and neglect." They were glimpses of the ideal—showing what nature would have liked to produce, according to man's idea of picturesque beauty. They generalized in order, as [Sir Joshua] Reynolds would have said, to express the particular. "Exact copies," Gilpin felt, "can scarcely ever be entirely beautiful, whilst he who works from imagination, culling a distance here, and there a foreground, will probably make a much better landscape."

Nevertheless he laid down certain bounds beyond which the imagination should not pass. Since only the picturesque features in any scene were admired, the artist might be allowed some liberty with the ground he stood upon. Trees might be moved or altered; withered stumps be substituted for spreading oaks and *vice versa*. But the insertion of a magnificent castle or a river in a scene was forbidden. The artist might, however, break an ill-formed hillock, or pull up an awkward piece of paling, or throw down a cottage, and alter the line of a road or river a few yards. Such events might, in fact, take place to-morrow.

There is something of the same beauty in Gilpin's little plates, as aquatinted, that is usually confined to Chinese landscape painting. Both illustrate, not an actual scene but an idea, everything unessential to which is eliminated. Gilpin gives us the essence of picturesque beauty. It is thus to mistake their intention to look for detail, and to call them "poor in character" [S. T. Prideaux, *Aquatint Engraving*]. Most of his plates, some of which he engraved himself, have a tinted ground, generally of yellow ochre. He considered that a yellowish or reddish stain took off the glare of the paper and added also "a degree of harmony to the rawness of black and white."

The picturesque method of composing a landscape by selecting and combining objects necessitated clear ideas as to what was and was not picturesque. So in his *Tour to the Lakes* Gilpin made an *Analysis of Romantic Scenery* or, in other words, a collector's list of features suitable for inclusion in a picture. For this purpose he divided every view into three parts: *Background,* containing Mountains and Lakes; *Off-skip,* comprising Valleys, Woods, Rivers; *Foreground,* comprising Rocks, Cascades, Broken Ground, and Ruins. Of the whole collection of these objects only certain specimens were picturesque—adapted to form part of a picture. In the case of mountains, for instance, "the pyramidical shape and easy flow of an irregular line will be found the truest source of beauty." The majority of mountains erred one way or another into ugliness of outline—saddlebacks, alps, and all such forms, suggested lumpishness, heaviness, and were disgusting. Gilpin was happier when he was appreciating, not attempting to criticize. Thus, in writing of the colours on a distant mountain side he anticipated to some extent the vision of Turner:

> They are rarely permanent; but seem to be a sort of floating silky colours—alway in motion—always in harmony—and playing with a thousand changeable varieties into each other. They are literally colours dipped in heaven.

The picturesque function of mountain and lake was to provide the background and middle distance. Gilpin then went on to analyse the most fitting kinds of foregrounds, which consisted in broken ground, trees, rocks, cascades, and valleys. Whereas the ruling character of the distance was tenderness, in the foreground this must give way "to what the painter calls force and richness, variety of parts and glowing tints." "The painter will easily find broken ground, a rough knoll, the sloping corner of a hill, perhaps worn by a mountain torrent, or a rugged road winding through the chasm of a rifted promontory—or some other part of nature equally grand and picturesque." A true remark, for the painters of the time were singularly apt at discovering such appropriate foregrounds. Then, too, we may "call for an ancient oak to give the foreground grandeur when we want the magnificence of its shadowing form to mantle over a vacant corner of a landscape, or to scatter a few loose branches over some ill-shaped line." How many sketchers, professional and amateur, have successfully "called on" this invaluable tree! Rocks, too, were well adapted to receiving "smart catching light," but "happy the pencil that can seize the spirit, agitation, and brilliancy of a broken cascade."

So closely did he consider rivers to be associated with the picturesque that he recommended the student to place before him a map of England and to settle in his head the course of all the chief rivers, making of them the "great directing lines of his excursions. On their banks he would be sure, not only to find the most beautiful views; but also obtain a compleat system of every kind of landscape."

Valleys were particularly valuable to the picturesque artist, as providing ready-made "side screens" for his compositions, and Gilpin's sketches make copious use of them.

Ruins, an integral part of landscape, came excellently into foregrounds. His view of them was naturally not architectural. At Tintern he found that to the beauty of the architecture

> are superadded the ornaments of Time. Ivy, in masses uncommonly large, has taken possession of many parts of the walls; and gives a happy contrast to the grey-coloured stone. . . . Nor is this undecorated. Mosses of various hues, with lychens, maiden hair, penny-leaf, and other humble plants, overspread the surface . . . all together they give those full-blown tints which add the richest finishing to a ruin.

An even richer finishing, of grouted concrete, has now "overspread the surface" of many parts of Tintern.

Figures were, of course, invaluable in carrying out the "idea" of a scene. Between Grasmere and Rydal he found a view "entirely of the horrid kind, not a tree appearing to add cheerfulness. With regard to the adorning of such a scene with figures nothing could suit it better than a group of banditti. Of all scenes I ever saw, this was the most adapted to the perpetration of some dreadful deed."

The subject of figures involved him in a difficulty. "Moral and picturesque ideas do not always coincide."

> In a moral view, the industrious mechanic is a more pleasing object than the loitering peasant. But in a picturesque light, it is otherwise. The arts of industry are rejected; and even idleness, if I may so speak, adds dignity to a character. Thus the lazy cowherd resting on his pole; or the peasant lolling

on a rock, may be allowed in the grandest scenes. . . .

> The characters that are most *suited to these scenes* of grandeur, are such as impress us with some idea of greatness, wildness or ferocity; all which touch on the sublime.

> Figures in long, folding draperies; gypsies; banditti; and soldiers—not in modern regimentals; but as Virgil paints them.—

> —*longis adnixi hastis, et scuta tenentes*

> are all marked with one or other of these characters, and mixing with the magnificence, wildness or horror of the place, they properly coalesce.

In corroboration he appealed to Salvator Rosa, "who seems to have thoroughly studied propriety in figures . . . his grand scenes being inhabited chiefly by banditti." He also referred to his book of figures. Many years later W. H. Pyne took a different view of the function of "figures." In his great collection of suitable groups [*Picturesque Groups for the Embellishment of Landscape*] only one page of "banditti" was given, as against several devoted to such avocations as Rustics, Travellers, and Brickmakers. The reason was that sublimity had gone out of fashion and the picturesque had become respectable, responsible. The "encyclopaedia," it was hoped, "opens a new field to the student of the picturesque. It may be useful even to the advanced artist." Note the distinction.

From human figures Gilpin went on to consider animals. "In a picturesque light no ornament is more adapted to a mountainous or rocky country than an animal. . . . The actions of a goat are still more pleasing than the shagginess of his coat." Then, in a remark reminiscent of the goat that petrified Gray, "it would add new terror to a scene, to see an animal browsing on the steep of a perpendicular rock." The lines of the cow are more picturesque than those of the horse, her lines being varied here and there by a squareness which is very picturesque. The tints of cows he would have us know, are broken and warm, and that "cows are commonly the most picturesque in the months of April and May, when the old hair is coming off."

So Sidney Smith summed up the difference between the two great categories: "The Vicar's horse is *beautiful,* the Curate's *picturesque.*"

From the picturesque point of view the grouping of figures and animals was at least as important as the animals themselves. Various directions are given, one of the more important of which is that two cows will not group well. "With three you are sure of a good group, except indeed they all stand in the same attitude at equal distances." Presumably the gentleman mentioned by Price was a disciple of Gilpin, who, when his economical wife suggested that for their domestic needs two of their three cows would suffice, answered, "Lord, my dear, *two* cows you know can never group."

In the accounts of his excursions, it is evident that Gilpin made every effort to approach each "scene" in an appropriate frame of mind. He saw clearly the necessity of the mind's being educated to appreciate scenery, or else that would be called picturesque which in reality was merely fruitful or pleasant. Similarly wild, natural country re-

A pen and wash drawing of Tintern Abbey by Gilpin.

pelled the generality of people who could not view it abstractly.

> The spectator should investigate the *sources of beauty,* and evince that a scene, though replete with every circumstance of *horror,* may be very picturesque. I have an instance at hand to my purpose. One of the voyagers in the Northern seas [Captain King, who succeeded Captain Cook] in sailing up a river thus describes the scene:—
>
> "The country," says he, "on each side was very romantic, but unvaried; the river running between mountains of the most craggy and barren aspect, where there was nothing to diversify the scene, but now and then the sight of a bear, or a flight of wild fowl. So uninteresting a passage leaves me nothing further to add."
>
> It is hardly possible, in so few words, to present more picturesque ideas of the horrid and savage kind. We have a river running up a country broken on both sides with wild romantic rocks, which we know nature never constructs in a uniform manner. We naturally conclude, therefore, that they ran out in some parts into vast diagonal strata, on the ledges of which a bear or two appeared, sitting on their hams or howling at the boat. In other parts, the rocks would form lofty promontories, hanging over the river and inhabited by numerous wild-fowl screaming round them. This is copied from Captain King's sketch, and yet he has no idea that a scene so savage could present any other ideas than such as were disgusting.

This instructive passage, in which we see a sketch worked up into a picture by what Gilpin called "high colouring," shows the essential contribution of the picturesque to literature, and appreciation. "It is the aim of picturesque description," he says, "to bring the images of nature as forcibly and as closely to the eye as it can, by high colouring." This process "is not a string of rapturous epithets, but *an attempt to analyse the views of nature,* and to express all the detail in terms as appropriate and vivid as possible."

This was the task he set himself in his books. They were to be preparations for the ceremony of visiting the scenes themselves. But not only was the visitor to be prepared for appreciating. His critical faculty was to be stimulated and instructed as well. (pp. 113-21)

> *Christopher Hussey, "Picturesque Travel," in his* The Picturesque: Studies in a Point of View, *Frank Cass & Co., Ltd., 1967, pp. 83-127.*

John Harrington Smith   (essay date 1934)

[*In the following excerpt, Smith argues that Gilpin's* Observations, on Several Parts of England; Particularly the Mountains, and Lakes of Cumberland, and Westmoreland *influenced the style and content of William Wordsworth's play* The Borderers.]

Some [of the features of Wordsworth's play *The Borderers*] remain unexplained. Prominent among these is its

Gothicism. The country of *The Borderers* is the Wordsworth country, yet it is here made to present an aspect of wildness and terror not met with elsewhere in Wordsworth's work. It is in the hope of accounting for this atmosphere and of throwing further light upon the origins of the play that I venture to present what seems to me evidence that Wordsworth, in its composition, drew upon a hitherto unnoticed printed source. (p. 922)

[Gilpin's *Observations, Relative Chiefly to Picturesque Beauty, Made in the Year 1772*] records the reactions of its author-illustrator to the scenery of Wordsworth's own lake-district; and it will be obvious from the samples which follow that his feeling about it was very different from Wordsworth's usual feeling and at the same time strikingly suggestive of *The Borderers*.

Consider, for example, the impression which Gilpin (looking toward Grasmere from the road leading from Grasmere to Keswick) forms of the fields and hills which were to Michael

> A pleasurable feeling of blind love,
> The pleasure which there is in life itself:

> The whole view is entirely of the horrid kind. Not a tree appeared to add the least cheerfulness to it.

> With regard to the adorning of such a landscape with figures, nothing could suit it better than a group of banditti. Of all the scenes I ever saw, this was the most adapted to the perpetration of some dreadful deed. The imagination can hardly avoid conceiving a band of robbers lurking under the shelter of some projecting rock; and expecting the traveller, as he approaches along the valley below.

There are here three features worthy of remark. The first is Gilpin's talent for wringing a pleasurable terror from natural surroundings about which we know Wordsworth normally felt very differently. Gilpin's tastes in scenery were thoroughly Gothic. He writes:

> In a moral light, cultivation, in all it's parts, is pleasing; the hedge, and the furrow; the waving corn field, and rows of ripened sheaves. But all these, the picturesque eye, in quest of scenes of grandeur, and beauty, looks at with disgust: It ranges after nature, untamed by art, and bursting wildly into all its irregular forms.

Through the book, he returns to the terror-motif whenever possible—as in this passage descriptive of the country north of Dunmail-Raise.

> Of all the rude scenery we had yet visited, none equalled this in *desolation*. The whole is one immensity of barrenness. The mountains are universally overspread with craggs, and stones . . . These vast regions . . . have the strongest effect upon the imagination.

>   . . . . .

> We now approached the lake of Wyburn [Thirlmere]—an object every way suited to the ideas of desolation, which surround it. No tufted verdure graces its banks . . . but every form, which it suggests, is savage, and desolate.

In the second place, one should note Gilpin's strong insistence upon the appropriateness of the scene for "the per-

petration of some dreadful deed," linked with (thirdly) his feeling that it needed to be peopled with a group of banditti or robbers. He returns to this idea later, in the course of an exposition on the picturesque, when laying down rules for the use of figures in landscape composition:

> The characters, which are most suited to these scenes of grandeur, are such as impress us with some idea of greatness, wildness, or ferocity; all which touch on the sublime.

> Figures in long, folding draperies; gypsies; banditti; and soldiers . . . are all marked with one or other of these characters: and mixing with the magnificence, wildness, or horror of the place, they properly coalesce; and reflecting the same image, add a deeper tinge to the character of the scene.

> For the truth of all these remarks I might appeal to the decisive judgment of Salvator Rosa . . . His works are a model on this head . . . All his figures are either of (what I have called) the *negative* kind; or marked with some trait of greatness, wildness, or ferocity. Of this last species his figures generally partook: his grand scenes being inhabited chiefly by banditti.

To these three features should be added a fourth—Gilpin's references to the romantic border past. Thus of Dunmail-Raise he writes:

> The history of this rude monument . . . is little known. It was probably intended to mark a division, not between these two northern counties; but rather between the two kingdoms of England, and Scotland, in elder times, when the Scottish border extended beyond its present bounds.

The Domain of Netherby, near Carlisle, was known, he says, as

> The Debateable Land, and was the great rendezvous of those crews of outlawed banditti, who, under the denomination of Moss-troopers, plundered the country. We have already had occasion to mention them.

The beacon at Penrith reminds him of

> those tumultuous times which preceded the union . . . those turbulent times, when no man could sleep in safety unless secured by a fortress. In war he feared the invasion of an open enemy: and in peace a mischief still more formidable, the ravages of banditti, with whom the country was always at that time infested. These wretches were composed of the outlaws from both nations; and inhabiting the fastnesses of bogs, and mountains, used to sally out, and plunder in all directions.

To these Gilpin more than once applies the term borderers.

The book presents, then, certain general features which encourage the presumption that it had something to do with Wordsworth's play. Better proof, as well as illustration, is furnished by what seems to me the fact that a combination of passages in it determined the character of the most striking scene in *The Borderers*—the ruined-castle scene in Act II. Wordsworth, apparently, was thinking of the Brougham castle ruin in the vicinity of Penrith. At least it and the ruin in the play are alike in several respects. Each is connected with the name Clifford; each offers access to a dungeon, useful in the play as a convenient means of getting Herbert off the stage; each has subsidiary masses of ruin at a little distance from the main mass. And yet, when one turns from the ruin of Brougham to what it has become in *The Borderers,* what a change is here! The original,

> that monastic castle, mid tall trees,
> Low standing by the margin of the stream

from whose towers, during Wordsworth's second summer's vacation from Cambridge the poet and Dorothy often

> in safety looked
> Forth, through some Gothic window's open space,
> And gathered with one mind a rich reward
> From the far-stretching landscape, by the light
> Of morning beautified, or purple eve;
> Or, not less pleased, lay on some turret's head,
> Catching from tufts of grass and harebell flowers
> Their faintest whisper to the passing breeze

has been transferred (as its name in the play, "Stone-Arthur Castle," implies) to precisely that region which seemed to Gilpin so perfectly adapted to "the perpetration of some dreadful deed" ("nowhere upon earth is place so fit To look upon the deed" Oswald assures Marmaduke); Stone-Arthur itself, that Eminence above Grasmere which, when Wordsworth saw it with his own eyes, seemed—in spite of its loneliness—to send "its own deep quiet" to restore his heart and Dorothy's, has become the "beetling rock" from which hangs

> The shattered Castle in which Clifford oft
> Has held infernal orgies;

the Emont, smooth-flowing before Brougham Castle, has been replaced by the terrific plank-crossed torrent of Wordsworth's scene; and the whole has been loaded with devices intended to build up its terror-affect. Gilpin furnishes most of these.

Chief among them is the torrent, which I take to have come from the following passage in the **Observations** (Gilpin is skirting Derwent Water):

> As we proceeded in our rout along the lake, the road grew wilder, and more romantic. There is not an idea more tremendous than that of riding along the edge of a precipice, unguarded by any parapet, under the impending rocks, which threaten above; while the ravages of a flood, or the whirlpools of a rapid river, terrify below.
>
> Many such roads there are in various parts of the world; particularly among the mountains of Norway and Sweden; where they are carried along precipices of such frightful height, that the trees at the bottom assume the azure tint of distance; and the cataracts which roar among them, cannot even be heard, unless the air be perfectly still. These tremendous roads are often not only without rail, or parapet of any kind; but so narrow, that travellers in opposite directions cannot pass, unless one of them draw himself to the rock. In some places, where the precipice does not afford footing even for this narrow shelf, or where it may have foundered, a cleft pine is thrown across the chasm. The appalled traveller arriving at this spot, surveys it with dismay.—Return, he dare not—for he knows what a variety of terrors he has already crossed. Yet if

his foot slip, or the plank, on which he rests, give way; he will find his death, and his grave together, and never more be heard of.

> But here we have the miniature of these dreadful ideas . . . for in the steepest part, we were scarcely thirty or forty feet above the water.

A later descriptive passage supplies other hints for the scene:

> The storm gathers on the tops of the mountains; and spreads its black mantle before the moon. It comes along in the majesty of darkness . . . The lightning from the rifted cloud flashes before it: the thunder rolls along the mountain in its rear . . .
>
> For now the whole storm descends. The mountain torrents join their impetuous streams. The growing river swells.
>
> The benighted traveller pauses as he enters the gloomy dell. The glaring sky discovers the terrors of the scene. With a face of wild despair he looks around. He recollects neither the rock above, nor the precipice below. Still he urges his bewildered way. His steed trembles at the frequent flash. The thunder bursts over his head.—The torrents roar aloud.—He attempts the rapid ford.—Heard you that scream?—It was the shriek of death.

We have here the effect of night and elemental tumult, plus certain specific details grouped in *The Borderers:* the "clap of thunder" which "Burst on the mountains with hell-rousing force" and for which Herbert found such apropos comment; "That horseman, who at full speed swept by us where the Wood Roared in the tempest," and who would have had no excuse for appearing in the tragedy had not Wordsworth read about him in Gilpin; and the "piercing outcry" which Marmaduke's taut nerves drew out of him when the dog Leader plunged into the abyss.

I am aware that the foregoing is open to the objection that Wordsworth need not have gone to Gilpin for these things. Gilpin's taste in landscape was, of course, thoroughly conventional, as the Salvator Rosa excerpt cited above sufficiently indicates. The combination of wild mountainous scenery and brigands was of course not new. Again, Wordsworth had probably read that appendage to *Ossian* known as "The Six Bards," parts of which Gilpin is paraphrasing in the night scene just quoted. Again, although one searches in vain in *The Prelude* and in *Descriptive Sketches* for a plank-crossed torrent comparable to that in *The Borderers,* and although Gilpin found "only the miniature of these dreadful ideas" in the country about which Wordsworth was writing, it is difficult to insist that the torrent could not have come from Wordsworth's own experience. But its behavior in the play makes such a derivation unlikely. In the ruined-castle scene it is sufficient to dash an oak into splinters; in the next, the poet absent-mindedly makes Oswald call it a brook. A real torrent in Wordsworth's poetry would certainly have held its character better than this—unless it too, like the ruin of Brougham, had been inflated, tuned up to terror pitch, by the same foreign influence, at its strongest in the ruin-and-torrent scene.

The features of the play which we have been considering might have been assembled piecemeal from a variety of sources. But all—torrent and plank, night tempest, benighted horseman, outcry, dreadful deed, borderers, Gothic atmosphere—are to be found in the *Observations,* under a high emotional charge which would bring them out together in Wordsworth's writing, and this fact, linked with the high probability that Wordsworth would have had Gilpin's book in his hands at a time not long before that at which—according to Dorothy—he was actually at work on the composition of the play, is to me sufficient to establish it as one of his materials. (pp. 923-28)

> *John Harrington Smith, "Genesis of 'The Bor-*
> *derers' ", in PMLA, Vol. XLIX, No. 3, Sep-*
> *tember, 1934, pp. 922-30.*

William D. Templeman   (essay date 1939)

[*Templeman is an American educator and critic. In the following excerpt, he offers a favorable assessment of Gilpin's biographical works.*]

In writing [his first biography, *The Life of Bernard Gilpin*], Gilpin used as chief source the biography written in Latin by one of Bernard's own students and protegées, George Carleton, Bishop of Chicester. He amplified this by his own research in other records and letters of Bernard. His work is far from being merely a translation. It is a new utilization of old material, plus additional information. It provides a sympathetic, interpretative account.

This first signed work of any consequence sounds the personal note that characterizes everything which Gilpin's pen has left. The author clearly purposed to observe the truth: he wished to satisfy the scholars. But to affect the general reading public was his primary purpose in handling the truth. His style, therefore, is simple and plain; yet it is never mean nor paltry; its simple dignity bears an earnest personal appeal, always on a high plane. Although some of his sentences in this early work are long, they are never cumbersome. Most of these are not complex, but compound. The ideas in sentences and in paragraphs are developed not in a tangled but always in a direct, straightforward manner. Variety he achieves, but with it he always maintains his simple clarity. Dignity never fails; yet along with dignity Gilpin sends as constant companion a personal, respectful intimacy with the reader. His style in his biographies is not colorful; but it is striking, poised, and pleasing.

The two quoted paragraphs which follow are, it must be remarked, the concluding paragraphs of the biography of Bernard Gilpin. But even so, summarizing as they do, they well exemplify the structure and effect of Gilpin's style:

> Such was the life and character of this excellent man. A conduct so agreeable to the strictest rules of morality and religion gained him among his contemporaries the title of the *Northern Apostle.* And indeed the parallel was striking: his quitting the corrupt doctrines, in the utmost reverence of which he had been educated; the persecutions he met with for the sake of his integrity; the danger he often ran of martyrdom; his contempt of the world; his unwearied application to the business of his calling; and the boldness and freedom with which he reproved the guilty, whatever their fortunes or stations were, might justly characterize him a truly apostolical person.

> Viewed with such a life, how mean and contemptible do the idle amusements of the great appear! how trifling that uninterrupted succession of serious folly, which engages so great a part of mankind, crouding into so small a compass each real concern of life! How much more nobly doth that person act, who, unmoved by all that the world calls great and happy, can separate appearances from realities, attending only to what is just and right; who, not content with the closet-attainment of speculative virtue, maintains each worthy resolution that he forms, persevering steadily, like this excellent man, in the conscientious discharge of the duties of that station, whatever that station is, in which providence hath placed him!

The primary reason, however, for quoting the above two paragraphs is that they indicate the general tone of this biography. Clearly it is moralizing. Yet clearly also the story is told with concrete incidents. And this is its dominant note: Learn of the past, by all means, *but only that you, Mr. Reader, may better know how to express in daily action your own integrity, your own noblest conscience (in reform if you think best)!*

In numerous places throughout this biography the note of reform is emphasized—always fearless reform, yet always reform accompanied by intelligent conservatism. For example, pages 241-311 present a reprint of a sermon preached by Bernard Gilpin in 1552, and in an introductory paragraph by William Gilpin this sermon is referred to as "a remarkable instance of that commendable zeal and noble freedom which the illustrious reformers of our church then exerted in the cause of virtue and religion."

This implies that Gilpin had become interested in the lives of other men concerned in the Reformation in England. Before long the publication of another biography bore out this implication. His *The Life of Hugh Latimer, Bishop of Worcester,* appeared in 1755. Here also, as he had done in his first biography, Gilpin presents a noble character with the addition of few new facts, but with an interpretation new and different from that given by previous biographers.

Gilpin here shows a distinct advance over his earlier technique. Not sacrificing the personal, intimate note, his style is terser, and his didacticism is of a far more indirect type. For comparison's sake, let the illustration be the final part of the concluding summary:

> And as danger could not daunt, so neither could ambition allure him. Though conversant in courts, and intimate with princes, he preserved to the last, a rare instance of moderation, his primeval plainness.

> In his profession he was indefatigable: and that he might bestow as much time as possible on the active part of it, he allowed himself only those hours for his private studies, when the busy world is at rest; constantly rising, at all seasons of the year, by two in the morning.

> How conscientious he was in the discharge of the public parts of his office, we have many examples. No man could persuade more forcibly: no man could exert, on proper occasions, a more commanding severity. The wicked, in whatever station, he rebuked with censorian dignity; and awed vice more than the penal laws. He was not esteemed a

very learned man; for he cultivated only useful learning; and that, he thought, laid in a very narrow compass. He never engaged in worldly affairs, thinking that a clergyman ought to employ himself only in his profession. Thus he lived rather a good, than what the world calls a great man. He had not those commanding talents, which give superiority in business: but for honesty and sincerity of heart, for true simplicity of manners, for apostolic zeal in the cause of religion, and for every virtue both of a public and private kind, that should adorn the life of a christian, he was eminent and exemplary beyond most men of his own, or of any other time; well deserving that evangelical commendation, "With the testimony of a good conscience, in simplicity and godly sincerity, not with fleshly wisdom, but by the grace of God, he had his conversation in the world."

Besides indicating Gilpin's style, the above paragraphs show that the *Life of Hugh Latimer* carries along in its substance that emphasis on reform which appeared in the earlier biography. (pp. 39-42)

In 1765 appeared in one volume a series of biographies. A second edition was published in the following year, its title page reading:

> The / Lives / of / John Wicliff; / And of the most Eminent of his / Disciples; / Lord Cobham, / John Huss, / Jerome of Prague, / and / Zisca. / After the way, which they call Heresy, so worship *we* the / God of *our* Fathers. / Acts XXIV. 14. / By William Gilpin, M.A. / The Second Edition, corrected and improved. / *London:* / Printed for J. Robson, Bookseller to her Royal / Highness the Princess Dowager of Wales, in *New- / Bond-Street.* / M.DCC.LXVI.

(pp. 43-4)

The men whose biographies are given in this book were, for a time at least, contemporaries. The three last named were Bohemian Protestant reformers. When Richard II in 1381 married Anne of Bohemia, the union brought about a great increase in the traffic between the two countries. Among the Bohemian students who went to study at Oxford were Huss and Jerome. There they became strong Wiclifites. On their return they proved aggressive leaders of reform in Bohemia. Zisca was a Hussite, who after Huss and Jerome had been burned at the stake, brought religious reform to Bohemia by his military valor. These biographies are shorter than Gilpin's two earlier ones. They have the same characteristics, however. Again there is clarity and unified harmony in presenting the facts. The result is effective interpretation. The accounts are short; but convey an impression of succinct totality. In a postscript, Gilpin writes that he used the materials brought together by others, but used them critically, rejecting and rearranging, and at times adding to them by his own research into manuscripts. The reader cannot fail to recognize Gilpin's visual power (evident also in his other works). He feels not only that Gilpin was present during the action or scene described, but also that he, the reader, was there in person, observing with his own eyes. Many illuminating examples of this quality could be extracted. As an instance here is Gilpin's account of a great battle and its consequences:

> On the thirteenth of January, 1422, the two armies met, on a spacious plain, near Kamnitz. Zisca ap-

peared in the centre of his front line; guarded, or rather conducted by a horseman on each side, armed with a poll-ax. His troops having sung an hymn, with a determined coolness drew their swords, and waited for the signal.

> Zisca stood not long in view of the enemy; when his officers had informed him, that the ranks were all well closed, he waved his sabre round his head, which was the sign of battle.

> Historians speak of the onset of Zisca's troops, as a shock beyond credibility; and it appears to have been such on this occasion. The imperial infantry hardly made a stand. In the space of a few minutes they were disordered beyond a possibility of being rallied. The cavalry made a feeble effort; but seeing themselves unsupported, they wheeled round, and fled upon the spur.—Thus suddenly was the extent of the plain, as far as the eye could reach, spread with disorder; the pursuers and the pursued mixed together, the whole one indistinct mass of moving confusion. Here and there might be seen, interspersed, a few parties endeavouring to unite; but they were broken as soon as formed.

> The routed army fled towards the confines of Moravia; the Taborites, without intermission, galling their rear. The river Igla, which was then frozen, opposed their flight. Here new disasters befell them. The bridge being immediately choked, and the enemy pressing furiously on, many of the infantry, and in a manner the whole body of the cavalry attempted the river. The ice gave way; and not fewer than 2000 were swallowed up in the water.

> Here Zisca sheathed his sword, which had been sufficiently glutted with blood; and returned in triumph to Tabor, laden with all the spoils, and all the trophies, which the most compleat victory could give.

Although never bitter nor intense, Gilpin throughout strongly emphasizes the value of an energetic reform controlled by intelligence.

Before the last-mentioned book appeared, Gilpin had begun work definitely on the biography of another early reformer, Thomas Cranmer. The book finally appeared twenty years later: *The Life of Thomas Cranmer, Archbishop of Canterbury.* In his preface Gilpin states that his account is practically a digest and condensation of the works of other biographers, mostly those in easily accessibly printed versions. Some manuscript aid he had, from a gentleman who had planned to write a life of Cranmer, and had gathered considerable material. Of this man's work Gilpin remarks: "Our plans too rather differed. His was chiefly to explain the opinions of the archbishop: mine attempts rather to illustrate his character." Here, then, is Gilpin's own declaration of purpose—to illustrate character. His work is to progress toward the portrayal of character, of human nature. The accumulation of facts about a man is merely a means to a larger purpose—the interpretation of his life as a living personality. And in Cranmer, as in his other biographical subjects, he chose for interpretation a figure whose character, shown by his life, could carry to the ordinary reader an effective and a practical inspiration. (pp. 44-6)

In 1808 was published posthumously [Gilpin's] book-length biography of a naval hero, formerly a member of

Gilpin's own parish, who had lived from 1755 to 1795: ***Memoirs of Fosias Rogers, Esq. Commander of His Majesty's Ship Quebec.*** The work had been composed by May 18, 1803. On that day William Gilpin signed his dedication of it to Sir Andrew Snape Hammond, Comptroller of the Navy. This gentleman had been the early commander and patron of Rogers. From the dedication it appears that Gilpin's materials were "a variety of letters, journals, and verbal accounts from persons acquainted with the facts." Gilpin had known Rogers personally. His attitude toward the biography is best expressed in his own words at the close of the dedication:

> . . . a life so full of incidents, and noble actions, ought not to lie hid in journals, and log-books, but should be produced into public, as an example of acting, and suffering with the magnanimity of a hero. A long and cruel war hath opened the characters of many gallant men, and given birth to many gallant actions. Many, who have survived their gallant exploits, have been gratified by their country with honours, and rewards—but many, who might equally deserve them were cut off in the midst of their glory. Among them was the subject of these memoirs; and as he cannot receive the honours of his country, let us at least pay his memory the tribute it deserves. And as the minister of his parish, it appeared to me, that I was a proper person to bring such an example forward.

By that statement the reader is prepared for what he finds: a narrative of adventures, of glory and hardship in war, and death in service. Rogers, a native of Lymington, had entered the navy from his own enthusiastic inclination. He became commander of a vessel through his own merit. In the war with America he distinguished himself for bravery and intelligence. Afterward he was doing a notable work against insurrectionists in the West Indies, when he succumbed to a sudden attack of yellow fever. Gilpin maintains interest throughout. He sketches the incidents with a few clear strokes, drawn with apparent artlessness, effecting a memorable vividness of character and of action. This life-story of a contemporary person recalls the stories of the early Reformers: here, too, Gilpin has made himself master of all the generally available facts, has sifted them, and (here in a different phase of activity) marshalled them in such style as to stimulate energetic action controlled by intelligence, for the good of the world.

Gilpin comments on Rogers' complete technical knowledge and skill; his devotion to friends and family and to sailors under him; his broad interests; his high moral principles. And in a beautifully climactic paragraph, Gilpin, with characteristic restraint, presents the spirit of the man. This paragraph exemplifies in an effective fashion several qualities characteristic of Gilpin: easy restraint, power of visual suggestion, rhetorical simplicity, and an element of universality in scope!

> No man ever indulged himself less. When he was engaged in any enterprize, himself was never in his thoughts. The business before him wholly ingrossed him. Eating, sleeping, every thing that related to himself, was considered merely as a matter of necessity. Many a time he would roll himself up in his boat-cloak, and with a shot-box for his pillow, take the little rest he allowed himself to take. He was actuated therefore with something more than a mere sense of duty. A mere sense of duty is a cold, inanimate principle. It suffers nothing wrong; but it leads to nothing great. His sense of duty was fired with a zeal, which pushed him to be always first in every exertion. It is this noble zeal, which turns soldiers into heroes—statesmen into patriots—and churchmen into saints.

In the latest of Gilpin's works to appear in print there is a combination of the past and of the contemporary. This work is a series of family biographies, which was excellently edited, and published for the Cumberland and Westmoreland Antiquarian and Archaeological Society: ***Memoirs of Dr. Richard Gilpin, of Scaleby Castle in Cumberland; and of His Posterity in the Two Succeeding Generations; Written, in the Year 1791, by the Rev. Wm. Gilpin, Vicar of Boldre; together with an Account of the Author, by Himself; and a Pedigree of the Gilpin Family.*** Edited by William Jackson, F.S.A. Gilpin had drawn up these memoirs (except the one of himself) by the summer of 1791. From the little note which he prefixed to the manuscript, it is obvious that he himself had been influenced by the example of the past in his own family. In order to preserve knowledge of past generations for the interest and guidance of future members of the family, he wrote these memoirs. "Such a family-monument might both preserve many amiable characters, w. ͪ might otherwise be lost; & also raise a kind of emulation in succeeding generations."

The memoirs begin with an account of Gilpin's great-grandfather, Dr. Richard Gilpin. There follow accounts of descendants, insofar as the author knew of them, for two generations. Chiefly the space is given over to William Gilpin and John Bernard Gilpin, Gilpin's grandfather and father. The accounts are supplemented by a number of letters. The chief value of this material is in providing evidence of the best sort for such a study of Gilpin's family background as is presented in the first chapter of the present book.

Ten years later (in 1801) Gilpin wrote an account of himself, to be inserted in the family record. Even though he, along with others, had always considered autobiographical writing an affectation, he was convinced that a man could write of his own life better than any one else could, if he wrote truly and candidly. Moreover, he had been practically forced to it, he said, in order to prevent his son's writing for him, and overstating matters. This autobiography is of course invaluable for the student of Gilpin. It is primary source material that is frequently unique. Gilpin purposely made it terse and concise. He wished to avoid prolixity and the appearance of vanity. The account accordingly has many omissions. He dwelt on those activities which he thought possessed the greatest possibilities for moral influence; he excluded many that were valuable. Even his works of purely religious import he dwelt on rather lightly. He chiefly discussed his educational and philanthropic activities. In the account practically no mention occurs regarding his connection with prints, and with the development of public interest in picturesque beauty; and there is but a scant reference to his drawing and painting, and to his artistic and literary associations. Gilpin himself has written that his sketch of his own life is little more than an account of his management of the School at Cheam, and his manner of endowing his parish school at Boldre.

These family memoirs, composed for the entertainment

and edification of his own family, lack the colorful vigor of incident possessed by his other biographical writings. Jackson proclaims their general historical value as great; he is doubtless correct. They have in addition a literary interest (a "fascination," Jackson calls it) for the individual reader. Aside from thus being a supply-house of facts and atmosphere, the memoirs show that the simple dignity of Gilpin's style appears in his private as well as in his public compositions, and that as a biographer Gilpin was avowedly concerned with the future as well as with the past and the contemporary. A concluding note about the memoirs may be struck in Gilpin's own words, written regarding his mother and father. They might well be addressed to posterity in general, and might refer to the subjects of all his biographical writings:

> Lives only like theirs, their posterity may be well assured, *will bring them peace at the last;* and ought to shew them early (what they will all find out in the end) that every human enjoyment is insignificant, in comparison of a well-spent life.

In all his biographies Gilpin has dealt with characters and deeds which not only are worthy, but also incite to emulation. The stories are told succinctly. They carry a strong power of suggestion. He has written the lives of scholar, prelate, nobleman, soldier, physician, business man, clergyman, and naval officer. Moral they are, but never offensively didactic: they make absolutely no parade of pious verbiage. One light shines through them all. It is the value of energetic reform controlled by intelligence. (pp. 47-50)

> *William D. Templeman, "Biographer," in* Illinois Studies in Language and Literature, *Vol. XXIV, Nos. 3-4, 1939, pp. 39-57.*

Walter John Hipple, Jr.   (essay date 1957)

> [*Hipple is an American educator and critic. In the following excerpt, he discusses a paradox inherent in Gilpin's conception of picturesque landscape.*]

[William Gilpin made "picturesque"] the key term of the new aesthetic attitude of which he was himself the earliest exponent. The "venerable founder and master of the picturesque school," Gilpin exerted a profound and lasting influence upon the taste not only of England but of Europe, though his analysis of the picturesque was soon superseded by the more subtle and philosophical studies of Uvedale Price and Payne Knight.

In the youthful and anonymous *Dialogue at Stow,* Gilpin uses the term "picturesque" conventionally: the picturesque is that which is suited to pictorial representation. There is already apparent, however, the tendency to consider rough and irregular scenes of nature especially picturesque, to find in landscape the peculiar locus of the picturesque. In the later and more widely influential *Essay on Prints,* to be sure, the subject itself demanded that Gilpin avoid the appropriation of the picturesque to wild and intricate scenes exclusively, and the term is employed, accordingly, in its more general acceptation. The definition given in the preliminary "Explanation of Terms" is simply this: "a term expressive of that peculiar kind of beauty, which is agreeable in a picture." The entire *Essay on Prints* is implicitly a discussion of picturesque beauty in this traditional sense, in its various aspects of composition,

lighting, drawing, expression, execution, and so forth. The *word* "picturesque," however, is very sparingly employed. The landscapes of Ridinger are praised for being "picturesque and romantic," a phrase applied also to the landscapes of Sadler; and this is the use of the word which Gilpin was to make conventional. But when Ridinger's scenes of hunting are said to be didactic and "least picturesque of any of his works," the application is the older and broader—suitable for a picture.

It was in Gilpin's picturesque travels, which began to appear in 1782, that the picturesque of roughness and intricacy was defined and popularized; the extension of the term was pretty well fixed by Gilpin, though philosophical dispute over its intension was later to engross aestheticians, gardeners, painters, and amateurs. The most theoretical of these works of Gilpin is his *Three Essays: On Picturesque Beauty; On Picturesque Travel; and On Sketching Landscape: to Which Is Added a Poem, On Landscape Painting.* The general principles developed in these essays are reduced to principles of landscape in the *Remarks on Forest Scenery, and Other Woodland Views, Relative Chiefly to Picturesque Beauty Illustrated by the Scenes of New Forest in Hampshire. In Three Books.* This work, then, is of an intermediate degree of abstraction, and the middle principles devised in it are applied in the six volumes of tours—all which bear titles of the form, *Observations* [*upon some part of Great Britain*] *Relative Chiefly to Picturesque Beauty.* All of these volumes, illustrated by Gilpin's fine aquatints, were immensely popular and greatly affected British taste in natural and artificial scenery.

In this study, however, attention must be confined to the theoretical essays, in which, unhappily, Gilpin is least impressive. The first of the *Three Essays,* **"On Picturesque Beauty,"** attempts to dispel the confusion (which all philosophers lament, and which each claims the honor of terminating) about the nature of beauty: "Disputes about beauty," Gilpin declares, "might perhaps be involved in less confusion, if a distinction were established, which certainly exists, between such objects as are *beautiful* [merely], and such as are *picturesque*—between those, which please the eye in their *natural state;* and those, which please from some quality, capable of being *illustrated by painting.*" Gilpin is careful to emphasize that the picturesque is a species of beauty, not a distinct character, and in his dedicatory letter defends himself against the charge of "supposing, *all beauty* to consist in *picturesque beauty*—and the face of nature to be examined *only by the rules of painting.*" The pleasures of imagination are various, and the picturesque is only one additional mode. The problem of Gilpin's essay is to define the causes of that mode: *"What is that quality in objects, which particularly marks them as picturesque?"*

When Gilpin remarks that "in examining the *real object,* we shall find, one source of beauty arises from that species of elegance, which we call *smoothness,* or *neatness,*" the phrase, "the *real object,*" suggests that his theory deals not with art itself but with nature considered as a subject for art; and this is, indeed, an obvious consequence of the general sense Gilpin assigns to the "picturesque." But in picturesque representation, neatness and smoothness, "instead of being picturesque, in reality strip the object, in which they reside, of all pretensions to *picturesque beau-*

ty." In fact, Gilpin continues, "*roughness* forms the most essential point of difference between the *beautiful,* and the *picturesque;* as it seems to be that particular quality, which makes objects chiefly pleasing in painting.—I use the general term *roughness;* but properly speaking roughness relates only to the surfaces of bodies: when we speak of their delineation, we use the word *ruggedness.* Both ideas however equally enter into the picturesque; and both are observable in the smaller, as well as in the larger parts of nature. . . ." A quick induction supports this principle: the painter prefers ruins to perfect architecture, an overgrown cart track to a finished garden, an aged face with dishevelled locks to the smoother beauty of youth, a human figure in action to one in repose, a cart horse or an ass to a polished Arabian. (Sydney Smith summed up the difference between beautiful and picturesque in remarking that "the Vicar's horse is *beautiful,* the Curate's *picturesque.*") Price and others urge that the induction is imperfect; but Gilpin casts about anxiously to discover reasons for what he conceives to be this general preference.

The painter's love of the shaggy stems partly from the encouragement a rough subject gives to a sketchy facility of execution. It is not only that a rougher touch is easier to master than a smoother and more elegant style—Gilpin does not stress this point, which is not likely to appeal to the spectator expecting skill in the artist; rather, "a free, bold touch is in itself pleasing." Gilpin gives no reason for this effect, though it is pretty clear that associations with ideas of unconstrained ease underlie it. But "it is not merely for the sake of his *execution,* that the painter prefers *rough* objects to *smooth.* The very essence of his art requires it." Picturesque composition, in the first place, "consists in uniting in one whole a variety of parts; and these parts can only be obtained from rough objects." Rough objects, again, alone yield what Gilpin terms "effect of light and shade"—massed and graduated lights and shades, with richness of minute variations, and "catching lights" on prominences. In coloring, too, roughness affords greater variation. In sum, roughness is more various; the taste for the picturesque is a taste for a greater measure of complexity and intricacy than either beautiful or sublime affords. Gilpin supports his reasons with an experiment. One of his aquatints exhibits "a smooth knoll coming forward on one side, intersected by a smooth knoll on the other; with a smooth plain perhaps in the middle, and a smooth mountain in the distance," while a companion aquatint shows the same general scene broken into irregular and jutting forms, marked by rugged rocks, clothed with shaggy boskage, and enlivened by two figures and a ruined castle. This experiment can not, however, quite pretend to be an instance of the Method of Difference: the second print is not merely rougher; it brings with it all the interest of complicated imitation and all the charms of manifold associations. Gilpin passes over the crucial question, how much of the effect is to be attributed to these causes?

He does, however, pause to explain away apparent exceptions to the principle that roughness is the ideal subject for art. Those really smooth objects which may have a good effect in a picture, he argues, are apparently rough or highly varied: the lake seems rough from the broken light on its surface undulations, or from the reflection of rough objects; the horse's smooth coat displays the play of muscle beneath; the smoothness of plumage is only the ground for

its breaking coloration; the polish of the column only displays the irregularity of the veining. Or (if the preceding does not convince) smoothness may be picturesque by contrast, adding piquancy to roughness. These explanations are specious, but it is clear that there is a difficulty, and that it has not been met so adequately as to remove all doubt; Price was subsequently to direct a part of his criticism of Gilpin to this vulnerable point.

This difficulty set aside, however, Gilpin seems to have solved his problem. But instead, he resumes the analysis: "Having thus from a variety of examples endeavoured to shew, that *roughness* either *real,* or *apparent,* forms an essential difference between the *beautiful,* and the *picturesque;* it may be expected, that we should point out the reason of this difference. It is obvious enough, why the painter prefers *rough* objects to *smooth:* but it is not so obvious, why the quality of *roughness* should make an *essential difference* between objects of *beauty,* and objects suited to *artificial representation.*" This is a subtle distinction. The question is, why do we come to approve *in nature* of things which would look well *in pictures?* Implicit in the very question is the recognition that our liking for the real objects is not merely from an association with painting, but has an independent basis (although, perhaps, a basis so concealed and obscured that a knowledge of painting is usually requisite to cultivate the natural aptitude). If this *is* Gilpin's point, he should be led here into the kind of inquiry in which Price later engaged; if it is *not,* his inquiry should have terminated with the determination of the reasons why the rough and rugged pleases in painting.

In any event, Gilpin fails to discover the natural basis of the "essential difference" between objects of natural beauty and those suited to artificial representation. Four hypotheses are tested and rejected: (1) That "the picturesque eye abhors art; and delights solely in nature: and that as art abounds with *regularity,* which is only another name for *smoothness;* and the images of nature with *irregularity,* which is only another name for *roughness,* we have here a solution of our question." But art is not invariably regular; and many art objects—drapery, shipping, ruined castles, et cetera—are excellent subjects in painting. (2) That the picturesque is based upon the "*happy union of simplicity and variety,* to which the *rough* ideas essentially contribute." But the beautiful in general equally with that species of its denominated picturesque is characterized by this happy union. (3) That the imitative art of painting can more readily imitate rough objects. This, however, is false in fact. (Gilpin had, to be sure, asserted something like this in treating facility of execution; the present point, however, concerns *fidelity,* not mechanical facility, of imitation.) (4) That painting is not strictly imitative, but *deceptive;* that the rough touches of the painter permit concealment of the deception; and that rough objects permit rough touches. But rough objects may be executed by smooth touches and these last are then picturesque.

It is interesting to observe that, the second excepted, these conjectures are drawn from considerations involving art. Now, the question to which they are addressed has meaning only if we suppose that the reason of the essential difference of picturesque and beautiful is found in nature and *not* in art; for, if the delight in the picturesque is based only on some kind of association with art, the reasons already given for the painter's preference of it are sufficient, and no problem exists. Gilpin's conjectures, then, are an *ignoratio elenchi. . . .* Thwarted by his methodological error, Gilpin throws up his hands in despair: "Thus foiled, should we in the true spirit of inquiry, persist; or honestly give up the cause, and own we cannot search out the source of this difference? I am afraid this is the truth, whatever airs of dogmatizing we may assume. Inquiries into *principles* rarely end in satisfaction. Could we even gain satisfaction in our present question, new doubts would arise. The very first principles of our art would be questioned. . . . We should be asked, What is beauty? What is taste?" To clinch his argument, Gilpin pretends to examine the debates of the learned on taste; he hears authors contend for the cultivation of innate talents, for utility, common sense, a special sense of beauty, proportion generally, and particular canons of proportion. "Thus," he concludes, "in our inquiries into *first principles,* we go on without end, and without satisfaction. The human understanding is unequal to the search. In philosophy we inquire for them in vain—in physics—in metaphysics—in morals. Even in the polite arts, where the subject, one should imagine, is less recondite, the inquiry, we find, is equally vague. We are puzzled, and bewildered; but not informed, all is uncertainty; a strife of words. . . ."

Such a disclaimer can not be expected to satisfy the pride of philosophers; Gilpin leaves an opening here for re-examination of the entire question. Before advancing to such re-examination, however, I shall describe briefly the other essays of the present volume. Baffled in his search for causes, Gilpin turns, in the second essay, **"On Picturesque Travel,"** to closer examination of the effects. Picturesque travel has for its object natural and artificial beauty of every kind, but especially, of course, the picturesque. The distinction between beauty and sublimity might be expected to afford a corresponding division of the picturesque; but since Gilpin has defined "picturesque" to denote *"such objects, as are proper subjects for painting,"* it must be granted that *"sublimity alone* cannot make an object *picturesque."* Mere vastness, the merely terrific, does not lend itself to depiction; only an admixture of the beautiful can render sublimity picturesque. Granted this proviso, Gilpin is ready to admit the sublime, too, as an object of picturesque travel, and even descants on scenes of *"picturesque horror." . . .* [The] picturesque eye is not attracted to the curious and fantastic, but "is fond of the simplicity of nature; and sees most beauty in her *most usual* forms." These usual forms are not, however, insipid; the strongly marked, the "characteristic," is most picturesque. So essential, indeed, is the characteristic to the picturesque that Gilpin even remarks of a scene beautiful as a whole but with no strongly characteristic parts, that "it exhibits such a specimen of the picturesque (if I may speak in terms seemingly contradictory) as is not well calculated to make a picture."

"After the *objects* of picturesque travel," says Gilpin (with a little flourish of organizational skill), "we consider it's *sources of amusement. . . .*" These consist in the pursuit itself and the attainment. In the attainment we are sometimes so happy as to come upon an agreeable whole, but are usually reduced to admiring parts. Our pleasure may be "scientifical," conjecturing amendments and forming comparisons with scenes of nature or works of art; but the great pleasure from natural scenes is enthusiastic: "We are most delighted, when some grand scene, tho perhaps of in-

correct composition, rising before the eye, strikes us beyond the power of thought. . . . In this pause of intellect; this *deliquium* of the soul, an enthusiastic sensation of pleasure overspreads it, previous to any examination by the rules of art. The general idea of the scene makes an impression, before any appeal is made to the judgment." But beyond contemplation of the object itself, new vistas of delight open before us: our general ideas are formed, and from these we learn to sketch, first by way of rememberance, then as a free exercise of fancy, an exercise which can be indulged even without the pencil. "There may be more pleasure," Gilpin declares,

> in recollecting, and recording, from a few transient lines, the scenes we have admired, than in the present enjoyment of them. If the scenes indeed have *peculiar greatness,* this secondary pleasure cannot be attended with those enthusiastic feelings, which accompanied the real exhibition. But, in general, tho it may be a calmer species of pleasure, it is more uniform, and uninterrupted. It flatters us too with the idea of a sort of creation of our own. . . .

It is noteworthy that Gilpin finds objects of art less capable of arousing enthusiasm than the works of nature. The picturesque traveler, in fact, is apt to acquire some contempt for the haunts of men, which have so often a poor effect on landscape. The unnaturalness of the garden, the limitations of painting become more obvious to the enthusiast of the picturesque. "The more refined our taste grows from the *study of nature,*" Gilpin generalizes, "the more insipid are the *works of art.* Few of it's efforts please. The idea of the great original is so strong, that the copy must be pure, if it do not disgust. But the varieties of nature's charts are such, that, study them as we can, new varieties will always arise: and let our taste be ever so refined, her works, on which it is formed (at least when we consider them as *objects,*) must always go beyond it; and furnish fresh sources both of pleasure and amusement." There is a paradox here: a system which isolates a certain property of nature for admiration, a property defined by its excellence as a subject for art, comes at last to reject the art for the nature which was at first only its subject. I have observed above that Gilpin is led to the point of redefining the picturesque as a universal complex of properties pervading both nature and art, and acting upon our physical organism or our mental associations to produce an effect peculiar to itself. Here again a picturesque with a basis independent of art is needed to resolve the paradox of setting out to find the qualities of pictures in nature and returning with a preference of nature to pictures.

Gilpin's third essay deals with one of the "sources of amusement" afforded by picturesque travel: sketching landscape. His precepts have a practical bent, yet they rest upon the aesthetic ideas of the first essay. The subject is handled in a natural order: composition (both *design* in the selection of subject and its parts, and *disposition* in arrangement of them), chiaroscuro, coloring—the order of execution. Sketching is based upon general ideas picked up in picturesque travel; even more than in finished drawings and pictures, in sketches "general ideas only must be looked for; not the peculiarities of portrait." (pp. 192-99)

Vague as are the indications which Gilpin gives of a causal analysis of the picturesque, it is possible to conjecture that he would have been more sympathetic to an associational than a physiological account. He is decisive in proclaiming that the picturesque eye sees through the imagination—that "the picturesque eye has nothing to do with tunics, irises, and retinas." At times, Gilpin's picturesque appears to depend upon association with concrete wholes, as in his repeated resentment at the intrusion of art into natural scenes. But this kind of association is not prominent in Gilpin; his picturesque depends chiefly upon associations with abstract qualities—with roughness of texture, with irregularity of outline, with contrasting lights and shades, with variegated and graduated colors. These associations he does not attempt to trace, and this omission invites further exploration of the picturesque. (p. 201)

Walter John Hipple, Jr., "William Gilpin," in his The Beautiful, the Sublime, and the Picturesque in Eighteenth-Century British Aesthetic Theory, *The Southern Illinois University Press, 1957, pp. 192-201.*

Carl Paul Barbier (essay date 1963)

[*In the following excerpt, Barbier summarizes Gilpin's conception of the role of the imagination in perceiving picturesque landscape.*]

[The] impact Gilpin made on his contemporaries stemmed from the *practical* uses to which the word picturesque was put. The word was taken from the realm of abstraction, was tested against reality, was made to work, to describe real things, real objects in nature, and thereby acquired many meanings, so much so that by 1801 George Mason, in his *Supplement* to Johnson, gave no less than six meanings to the word: what pleases the eye; remarkable for singularity; striking the imagination with the force of painting; to be expressed in painting; affording a good subject for a landscape; proper to take a landscape from. With all these Gilpin would have agreed. This multiplicity of meanings testifies to the success of the word once Gilpin transferred it from the realm of art criticism and made it available as an instrument—admittedly a pictorial instrument—for the analysis, the description, and finally the representation and recording of natural scenery. But the Picturesque is much more than that. It is a frame of mind, an aesthetic attitude involving man in a direct and active relationship with the natural scenery through which he travels.

This active and creative aspect of the Picturesque is all important, for the theory's validity lay in its practice. Here Gilpin, by precept and example, gave the lead. He was able to describe what constituted a picturesque landscape and to show by his writings and drawings what enjoyment could be derived from picturesque practice, that, once the eye had been trained to recognize a picturesque 'object', many pleasures would become accessible through a wide range of associations between individual sensibility and the ever changing panorama of the countryside—for instance the pleasures of seeking, anticipating, finding, examining, comparing, recording, re-creating.

It is very doubtful whether the word Picturesque can be encompassed in a single definition. If we restrict its application to landscape in the latter half of the eighteenth century, we observe that for the term to have any meaning three quite distinct elements are required: art, nature, and a man of sensibility and culture to link the first two in the

One of many "picturesque" vistas painted by Gilpin during his travels.

perennial debate of art versus nature; and according to the way we focus our attention, either on man with his personal aptitudes and inclinations, on nature as seen through art, or on the artistic representation of landscape, we grapple with only one side of the Picturesque. Each of the three elements influences the other two in some degree, and so the various aspects which the Picturesque has assumed depend on the character of these component parts. Thus the way of looking at landscape in the eighteenth century was largely determined by the use of criteria derived from an analysis of landscape painting of the previous century—change these criteria, these standards, and the landscape composes itself in quite a different way. The essential factor without which the Picturesque can find no general acceptance is a society, or at least an effective element in society, which is *actively* interested in art and nature.

The scenery of Britain afforded many varied landscapes, a few of which were 'capable of being illustrated by painting'. The rules of painting, in particular those governing composition and effect, guided the eye to make a choice but were not sufficient in themselves to account for the wide range of subjects which the picturesque school imprisoned within its formula. There was also a large element of personal choice dictated by temperament, predilections, and the physical appearance of the countries one had visited—thus, . . . for Gilpin the topography of his native Cumberland cast a dominant shadow over all his thoughts. . . . (pp. 98-100)

The various qualities which in Gilpin's eyes made a landscape picturesque consisted of an amalgam of personal preferences and aesthetic qualities—roughness or ruggedness of texture, singularity, variety and irregularity, chiaroscuro, and the power to stimulate the imagination. None of these qualities in isolation was picturesque, but where all, or the majority of them, were present in a landscape (real or imaginary), the landscape was said to be picturesque. Contrarywise, a landscape which lacked these qualities—for example, a flat stretch of country devoid of distinctive features—might be termed 'simply beautiful' but certainly not picturesque. (p. 100)

Gilpin . . . fully realized that 'the chief end of landscape is to please', and that 'in a drama something more is required to give it success, than the bare observance of the unities' (or basic principles applied to landscape composition). The painter should 'endeavour to please the eye. He should aim to make the country he carries us through, such as we should wish to inhabit, or at least to examine.' But what is equally important is to stimulate, to arouse the imagination of the spectator. This Gilpin explains as follows:

> When we see a pleasing landscape in *nature,* we not only wish to enjoy it; but we are incited by the beauty of what we see, to proceed in the same direction in search of scenes of the same kind, which we suppose it may lead to. It should be thus in artificial landscape. When we see a pleasing scene, we cannot help supposing, there are other beautiful appendages connected with it, tho' concealed from our view. If therefore we can interest the imagination of the spectator, so as to create in him an idea of some beautiful scenery beyond such a hill, or such a promontory, which intercepts the view, we give a scope to a very pleasing deception. *It is like the landscape of a dream.* The mind naturally runs on with an idea, which had long possessed it. When slumber shuts the senses, after seeing a fine view, the idea often continues—somewhat faded indeed, but strong enough to preserve a very amusing picture.

Here surely by the role he assigns to the imagination Gilpin parts company with a very large group of picturesque artists, in particular with those whom [Christopher] Hussey considers as representatives of the painter's ideal of the Picturesque, artists such as George Morland or [George] Barret. By interpreting the Picturesque in purely painterly terms they seek only to please the eye, to evoke a pleasing sensation in the onlooker—all is stated, obvious, and at times anecdotal or sentimental. Gilpin goes further by achieving effects which result in ambiguity and mystery: 'Some people must account for all they see, and hear; they allow mystery in nothing. Now I suppose mystery in every thing; and think that a certain degree of faith, where we *cannot have* compleat knowledge, is as necessary in reading nature, as scripture.'

He also adds an implicit or hidden element to his landscapes, which, while carefully related to the explicit or visible parts, allows the spectator's imagination to run on. In this way he suggests large vistas (often bathed in light) hidden from the spectator's view by intersecting slopes in the middle distance; yet on the crest of those slopes small figures are silhouetted, who, from their privileged viewpoint, contemplate a prospect that must be left to the spectator's imagination. As Gilpin said to William Lock, 'the spectator both in scenical, and picturesque representation, must allow himself to be imposed on in *every* thing'. The spectator is impelled to identify himself with the only figures in the landscape, and thus the artist, by stimulating the imagination, succeeds in opening up his landscape, in suggesting more than he can actually depict within the compass of his frame. It is one way of solving the dilemma of trying to render within a small compass material garnered from the whole of nature. Furthermore, by hinting at vistas seen from a high vantage-point by his banditti, Gilpin solves another problem: he can hint at scenes which may be impressive and even beautiful, but which are not in themselves picturesque, and which cannot be picturesquely represented. As Gray had agreed before him, the picturesque artist nearly always chooses a low vantage-point. (pp. 136-37)

In other compositions containing only a foreground, Gilpin suggests the chasm that lies just beyond. Figures are made to point at what cannot be seen or at what is only dimly suggested. Others proceed into a cave, the depth of which remains unfathomable to the spectator. And 'even when a figure cannot be supposed to be placed in a situation proper for viewing a scene, yet considering it as a person travelling through a country, we may go along with him, & conceive the view he will have, when he arrives at such a point, or in such a direction'. 'The grey atmosphere, which gives such picturesque indistinctness to objects, . . . the grey, misty air, which rubs off the harsh lines, & corners of objects, softening every thing, into one general tint', these are all effects which may give us repose but which also incite the imagination and the chance to dream.

Gilpin not only gave form to his conception of the Picturesque by means of drawings, he also did so in a number of purely imaginary journeys and descriptions. These little known and unpublished pieces epitomize even better than his drawings the ideal landscape of mountain and lake scenery which haunted his thoughts. . . . They are necessarily short and fragmentary, for a sustained account of perfection would soon lead to satiety. The first, probably written in the late 1760's, in an imaginary piece of landscape-gardening, entitled **"Situation of the House."** The house, ideally placed, is surrounded by a perfect panorama which partakes in turn of lake, woodland, river, and mountain scenery. (pp. 137-38)

The second manuscript dates from his last years. In the guise of **"A Fragment,"** all that remains of a lost work, Gilpin gives us a picturesque tour of an imaginary country built up from twenty-four of his own drawings, which are made to illustrate the journey like so many chosen 'stills' from a film sequence. He invents place-names and a local history, and fosters a sense of reality by a number of devices. For example, on mentioning the ruins of Groinseg-castle he adds 'I believe I spell the name right', and he decides to gloss over Rocktingen Castle, 'as the gazettes of Europe have been so full of the honour it lately received from an imperial visit'.

He projects himself into this topography and we follow him on his way round Lake Venlis, with its island of Ulmar, its promontory and castle of Bilvers. Around are the mountains of Ooust and Ovedon. Interest is maintained as the scenery unfolds, as features at first only dimly perceived in the distance come more clearly into view. Occasionally the eye is unable to see a distant object, the imagination must then feed on an anecdote:

> In a peaceful valley, at the bottom of this mountain, lies a small monastery. It was pointed out to us; but as the eyes of a person acquainted with a spot, see clearer, I suppose, than those of a stranger, we could not even pretend to see it, tho the day was sufficiently bright. In this monastery, we were told, a very extraordinary pennance exists, tho for what particular offences we were not informed. The offender is sentenced to ascend the pinnacle of the mountain; where he waves the flag of St. Anthony, to give notice of his arrival. . . .

At this juncture we may ask ourselves what exactly was

Gilpin's conception of the imagination: was his attitude so different from the general trend of eighteenth-century thought on the subject, and if so, how near did he come to that sincerity of poetic insight we associate with the 'romantic' poets?

If we take our definition of imagination as being that function of the mind which calls up images, having on the one hand the power of recalling in detail experiences already undergone, and, on the other, the power of creating images not previously experienced or merely suggested or hinted at, we find that the eighteenth century did not advance much beyond Hobbes's conception of imagination as 'decaying sense'. We have to wait till Wordsworth before imagination is conceived as a 'power of interpreting the world'. By imagination 'Wordsworth attains something like a mystical vision of the whole world as a living thing, every fragment of the world alive with the life of the whole'. This the picturesque mind could not conceive of, by the very nature of the single-minded inquiry it was engaged upon; in his considerations of landscape the picturesque observer rarely allows ideas which are not pictorial to intrude upon his contemplation of the scene before his eyes or that in his imagination. However, if the picturesque artist's imagination appears limited compared with the all-embracing one of the romantic poets, his grasp of landscape is often all the more profound. As W. P. Ker rightly observed:

> Landscape was, on the whole, better understood in the eighteenth century than it was after the appearance of the 'romantic' authors, because the 'romantic' authors took the mind away from pure landscape to other allied interests, such as the interests of historical association.

> Both Cowper and Wordsworth tried to render life. Usually it is life from which the natural landscape is inseparable, life in which landscape has a large share; but what they are interested in is not the scene by itself, not the people by themselves, but the scene as animated by the people, the whole life in which the different elements are inextricable.

The eighteenth-century man of taste tended to remain detached and objective in the pursuit of the several subjects that interested him; each subject studied for its own sake, remaining in its water-tight compartment. Such a person was Gilpin. But what distinguishes him from the majority of his picturesque friends is that he makes much greater use of imagination than they dared to call upon. In fact, one can say that the development shown in his sketches represents a gradual release of imagination from the shackles of objective reason, so that by the time Gilpin settled down at Vicar's Hill in 1777 the last concessions to topographical accuracy had been discarded, and the creative imagination became free to convey the 'spirit' of lake and mountain scenery. How often we find his artist friends saying to him that his drawings are more 'imaginative', while theirs are more 'natural', more closely wedded to actual observation. Gilpin writing to Mary Hartley recognized this difference: 'You work best with nature before you; and I from imagination. . . . You work from the original archetype, I only from its reflected images.'

His rational attitude, sound common sense, and liking of what appeared normal and natural—all these restricted the field of play of his imagination. The picturesque ideal

rejected those weird and curious appearances in nature which could act as such a powerful stimulus: 'Every thing, both here, & among the mountains, was wild, & romantic in the highest degree; *but not fantastic.* The shapes were all grand, natural, & noble, & *borrowed no affected beauties from odd forms, & lawless singularity.*'

And even where he has deliberately sought to awaken the interest of his reader, Gilpin only allows the fancy to be stirred so far. A good example occurs in the **"Fragment."** In a sequestered bay we come upon a strange building, which from the shore appears 'to rise out of the lake'. We take a boat to get a nearer view. The edifice is now seen to stand on an island; it is shaped like an immense roofless church, which however 'seems never to have had any windows'. What can it have been?

> The common opinion is, that it was built for a prison; & we heard a romantic story of a prince, who had been confined there, 30 years, with his daughter, a beautiful princess, lest there should be any children to disturb the succession of the usurper. The prince however gave her in marriage to the keeper of the prison, by whom she had a son, who afterwards became a man of great prowess, & cut off the usurper's head.

At this juncture Gilpin calls a halt to what has been for him an enjoyable game of make-believe, and invents a rational explanation: 'I rather believe this strange edifice . . . was built as a repository for . . . goods. . . . On the north side is the appearance of a vast gate, now walled up, opening into the water; which could have been intended, I should think, only to receive barges, & crane up goods.' (pp. 138-40)

In conclusion, 'though the slender confines of art cannot rouse the imagination like the scenes of nature', it is the function of art so to stimulate the imagination of the spectator that by looking at the landscape depicted, he should thereby recall scenes in nature which have had an even greater effect upon him. For this impressionistic technique to succeed, one must assume that the spectator is like Gilpin, an adept at picturesque travel with many delightful scenes stored in his memory. 'The picture is not so much the *ultimate end,* as it is the *medium,* through which the ravishing scenes of nature are excited in the imagination.' (p. 143)

> *Carl Paul Barbier, in his* William Gilpin: His Drawings, Teaching, and Theory of the Picturesque, *Oxford at the Clarendon Press, 1963, 212 p.*

Sue E. Coffman (essay date 1982)

[*In the following excerpt, Coffman comments on Gilpin's depiction of mountainous landscape.*]

More than any other individual, William Gilpin popularized picturesque touring, primarily in the Lake District. Others had written tourist guides, but Gilpin's outshone them all. The rules for picturesque viewing of the scenery, which he propagated through **Observations on the River Wye, Observations, Relative Chiefly to Picturesque Beauty made in the Year 1772, in Several Parts of England, Particularly the Mountains and Lakes of Cumberland and Westmoreland,** and **Three Essays on Picturesque**

Beauty, guided the sensibilities of tourists who poured into the Lake District. But Gilpin never became a fell-walker; he was an observer who filled his eyes with the region's beauties but ever sought to rearrange what he saw to make the scenes more correctly picturesque. His flights of praise seem artificial and superficial to the twentieth-century mind, and he apparently never felt Coleridge's passion for mountains. Nevertheless, Gilpin riveted England's eyes upon its choicest natural beauties and catalyzed the attraction to the region that became the mountain and rock climbing center of England in the nineteenth century.

A standard feature of picturesque reaction to mountains may be seen in Gilpin's views on Derwent and its surrounding cluster of peaks: "Here is beauty indeed—Beauty lying in the lap of Horrour!" "Horrour" refers to the mountains, "Beauty" to Derwent. . . . Gilpin often commented on mountains' irregular features, a preeminent feature of picturesque scenes. Thus of Ullswater he writes, "the road carried us to the higher grounds, from whence we had a view of the whole lake, and all it's [sic] vast accompaniments together—a troubled sea of mountains; a broken scene." But brokenness and irregularities sometimes disturbed the picturesque eye, as Gilpin indicates in *Cumberland and Westmoreland:* "In such immense bodies of rough-hewn matter, many irregularities, and even many deformities, must exist, which a practiced eye would wish to correct. . . . In all these cases the imagination is apt to whisper, what glorious scenes might here be made, if these stubborn materials could yield to the judicious hand of art!—and, to say the truth, we are sometimes tempted to let the imagination loose among them." Unlike Wordsworth, Coleridge, and the later climbers who operated with different perspectives and from different motives, Gilpin rarely felt satisfied with what he saw. He was never interested in mountains for their own sake; instead he superimposed his picturesque theories upon the mountains he viewed. This weakness perhaps prevented the picturesque method from being anything but a passing fad, but even in its dwindling glory it paved the way for a truer, more authentic admiration of the mountains. (pp. 13-14)

[Gilpin] often seemed physically uncomfortable during his picturesque tours. Recalling the ascent of one mountain, Gilpin remarks that "after a painful perpendicular march of near 2 miles, and many a breathing pause, which our horses required, we gained the top." He fails to indicate whether the horses were being led or ridden; thus we do not know whether to sympathize with him or the horses, or both. Gilpin adds the postscript that the view from the top had not been worth the effort. Just before this ascent, as Gilpin and his party are asking directions, he reports that the path:

> [was] up a lofty mountain, steeper than the tilting of a house. . . . To those, who are accustomed to mountains, these perpendicular motions may be amusing: but to us, whose ideas were less elevated [a pun?], they seemed rather peculiar. . . . To move upwards, keeping a steady eye on the objects before us, was no great exercise to the brain: but it rather gave it a rotation to look back on what was past—and to see our companions below clinging, as it appeared, to the mountain's side; and the rising breasts and bellies of their horses, straining up a

path so steep, that it seemed, as if the least false step would have carried them rolling many hundred yards to the bottom.

A novice indeed was he in the art of mountain climbing, and it is difficult for those accustomed to steep mountain paths to sympathize with Gilpin's misgivings.

As Gilpin traveled, he remained on the perimeter of experience, as we in the twentieth century would appraise his journeys. He was everywhere accompanied by a guide or "conductor," of whose choices he did not always approve. Touring the environs of Derwent, he laments the fact that "the inexperienced conductor, showing you the lake, carries you to some garish stand, where the eye may range far and wide." His concern lies with just the right angle for viewing, and he objects to viewpoints which command a breathtaking sweep of scenery. How alien to those who have scaled the peaks and reflected on the magnificence of what lies beneath and around them and far into the purple distance.

With his conductor shielding him from the reality of the mountains, Gilpin traveled by coach or horseback. Sometimes his method of travel is unclear: at Ullswater, for example, he mentions "our evening's ride, [in which] we had skirted only one side of the lake." In his account of a tour near the fall of Lodore, he reveals that conditions sometimes force him to dismount (this time from his horse) and take a precarious walk: ". . . dismounting, we continued, by winding round the thickets, and clinging to the projections of the rocks, to get a dangerous peep down the abyss." There is more dread here than exhilaration, and one may surmise that Gilpin admired the mountains most often from the safety of a chaise. His fears and his modes of transportation kept him . . . an outsider whose baggage of preconceived notions about the mountains weighted him down everywhere he traveled. (pp. 14-15)

> *Sue E. Coffman, "Early English Climbers in the Lake District," in* Essays on the Literature of Mountaineering, *edited by Armand E. Singer, West Virginia University Press, 1982, pp. 11-25.*

Charles Kostelnick   (essay date 1985)

[*In the following excerpt, Kostelnick focuses on the interaction of emotion and imagination in Gilpin's writings on picturesque landscape.*]

[William Gilpin's] tours and treatises explore the interworking of a range of faculties—intuitive, intellectual and moral—exercised by nature enthusiasts, primarily through the medium of "picturesque travel." (p. 31)

The first principle of Gilpin's concept of picturesque beauty, which he delineates in various tours (most notably the Wye River and Lakes tours) and subsequently formulates into a rudimentary theory in *Three Essays,* is that it "please from some quality, capable of being *illustrated by painting.*" Although at the outset of *Three Essays* picturesque beauty may appear to be a derivative only of the beautiful (those objects that "please the eye in their *natural state*"), it actually requires an interaction between both of Burke's categories explicated in [*A Philosophical Enquiry into the Sublime and Beautiful*] and is established neither as a category independent of the sublime and the beautiful nor as a simple adjunct to one or the other. For example, objects of beauty that are too regular—a smooth hill, a straight hedgerow, an elegant piece of Palladian architecture—will not be pleasing in a picturesque composition. On the other hand, objects that are rough and irregular, cast in obscurity, or heightened by sharp contrast—in short, objects associated with Burke's sublime—are essential to picturesque beauty, though sublime objects alone will not function well in a picturesque scene:

> That we may examine picturesque objects with more ease, it may be useful to class them into the *sublime,* and the *beautiful;* tho, in fact, this distinction is rather inaccurate. *Sublimity alone* cannot make an object *picturesque.* However grand the mountain, or the rock may be, it has no claim to this epithet, unless it's form, it's colour, or it's [*sic*] accompaniments have *some degree of beauty.* . . . When we talk therefore of a sublime object, we always understand, that it is also beautiful: and we call it sublime, or beautiful, only as the idea of sublimity, or of simple beauty prevail.

In picturesque landscapes, therefore, where sublime and beautiful objects are combined in the same composition, the prevailing element in Burke's dichotomy will be assisted by its counterpart. . . . (p. 32)

Although the methodology employed by Gilpin . . . for composing picturesque scenes violates Burke's dictum in the *Enquiry* regarding the diminished effects of mingling the sublime and the beautiful, it scarcely represents a break with Burke's esthetics (unlike Uvedale Price's scheme, which establishes the picturesque as a separate category, or Richard Payne Knight's, which dissolves all categories) but is rather an assimilation of the *Enquiry*'s rich, seminal vocabulary as a lexicon for rendering natural and artificial objects.

If Gilpin is unable to articulate a precise theory of picturesque beauty—a task undertaken more scrupulously by his successors Price and Knight—his role in popularizing picturesque travel and hence of viewing nature picturesquely is much more certain. In one of the *Three Essays,* entitled **"Picturesque Travel,"** Gilpin forwards several reasons for engaging in this type of amusement. The first concerns the pleasure of pursuing the object: the traveler, like a hunter, is kept under a constantly "agreeable suspense" in searching tirelessly for the quintessential view. Polyphton, one of the commentators in Gilpin's first treatise on the picturesque, **A Dialogue upon the Gardens at Stow,** reveals this appetite when he remarks how he "rode the Northern Circuit," presumably among the Lakes, "hunting after beautiful Objects." (p. 33)

The first amusement of picturesque travel appeals to the appetite, the second to the intellectual capacity of the tourist to judge landscape according to its visual qualities or deficiencies. Mountains, lakes, valleys, hillocks, trees, shrubs—all are the raw materials that the picturesque traveler, armed with Gilpin's tours and treatises, can appraise for their picturesqueness, their suitability for composing pleasing pictures. Where nature or art has failed to measure up to the standard, the critical eye can isolate the shortcoming and dictate the necessary adjustments: the bend in the river needs to be sharpened, the "side-screens" of the valley adjusted to frame the view, the gables of Tin-

tern Abbey fractured into an appropriate state of ruin. (p. 34)

The arousal of emotion is . . . one of the primary pleasures of picturesque travel, even superceding the exercise of the critical faculty: "But it is not from this *scientifical* employment, that we derive our chief pleasure. We are most delighted, when some grand scene, tho perhaps of incorrect composition, rising before the eye, strikes us beyond the power of thought . . . and every mental operation is suspended. In this pause of the intellect; this *deliquium* of the soul, an enthusiastic sensation of pleasure overspreads it, previous to any examination by the rules of art. The general idea of the scene makes an impression, before any appeal is made to the judgment. We rather *feel,* than *survey* it."

Feeling is fundamental to the intuitive perception impelled by the visual stimuli of picturesque travel and is complemented by another subjective operation of the viewer—the exercise of the imagination. Gilpin intimates the interworking of emotion and imagination as early as **A Dialogue upon the Gardens at Stow,** where in a tour through the improved grounds of Lord Cobham two commentators are "exceedingly taken with" views of various objects—artificial ruins, grottoes and temples—that are "pleasing to the Imagination" and indeed improved upon by its assistance. In **Tour to the Lakes** Gilpin prescribes methods for constructing artificial ruins which, through a carefully orchestrated deception, can stimulate the emotions and trigger the imagination of the viewer. Under the more liberal conditions of picturesque travel the imagination enjoys the freedom to transform the scenes that the eye beholds. Among the "*grand scenery* of nature" where sublimity prevails, feeling and imagination are the most active, but even when the eye encounters more mundane views, the synthesizing power of the imagination continues to respond: "The imagination can plant hills; can form rivers, and lakes in vallies; can build castles, and abbeys; and if it find no other amusement, can dilate itself in vast ideas of space." The engagement of the imagination may even be prolonged after the objects upon which it has been operating have been removed from the eye: "Often, when slumber has half-closed the eye, and shut out all the objects of sense, especially after the enjoyment of some splendid scene; the imagination, active, and alert, collects its scattered ideas, transposes, combines, and shifts them into a thousand forms, producing such exquisite scenes, such sublime arrangements, such glow, and harmony of colouring, such brilliant lights, such depth, and clearness of shadow, as equally foil description, and every attempt of artificial colouring."

The acts of exercising the imagination and of feeling through the eyes are the basic subjective operations of the mind in Gilpin's picturesque perception. Whether the medium be the garden or landscape, the composition of objects contrived or natural, Gilpin's purpose is essentially to set up a succession of views—spatial matrices of picturesque raw materials like ruins, woods and topographical variations—and to narrate how diverse combinations of such objects arouse the viewer's curiosity and excitement, and the imagination, as Gilpin puts it, "transposes, combines, and shifts them into a thousand forms." (pp. 34-6)

Charles Kostelnick, "From Picturesque View to Picturesque Vision: William Gilpin and Ann

Radcliffe," *in* Mosaic: A Journal for the Inter-disciplinary Study of Literature, *Vol. XVIII, No. 3, Summer, 1985, pp. 31-48.*

FURTHER READING

"The World of Books." *The Athenaeum* 32, No. 4836 (6 January 1923): 549.
> Review focusing on Gilpin's conception of the picturesque. Concludes that he was "a unique figure in the relation of literature and landscape."

Boudreau, Gordon V. "H. D. Thoreau, William Gilpin, and the Metaphysical Ground of the Picturesque." *American Literature* 45, No. 3 (November 1973): 357-69.
> Analyzes Gilpin's "brief, two-year period of influence" on Thoreau which ends with Thoreau's "rejection of the picturesque as expounded by Gilpin, on account of its superficiality and lack of a moral basis."

Brown, W. E. M. "William Gilpin: Student of the Picturesque." In his *The Polished Shaft: Studies in the Purpose and Influence of the Christian Writer in the Eighteenth Century,* pp. 89-108. London: S. P. C. K., 1950.
> Biographical account of Gilpin's literary career.

Review of *Observations on the River Wye,* by William Gilpin. *The Monthly Review* LXIX (November 1783): 361-63.
> Praises Gilpin for having "employed his cultivated judgment and taste, in a manner which may point out to future travellers new sources of elegant entertainment."

Review of *Observations on the Western Parts of England,* by William Gilpin. *The Monthly Review* XXVIII (April 1799): 394-400.
> Favorable review calling Gilpin "the venerable founder and master of the picturesque school."

Williams, Iolo A. "The Reverend William Gilpin." *The Bookman,* London LXXXV, No. 506 (November 1933): 120-21.
> Overview of Gilpin's life and works.

Aleksis Kivi

1834-1872

(Born Aleksis Stenvall) Finnish novelist, dramatist, and poet.

Considered Finland's greatest nineteenth-century author, Kivi was the first to use the Finnish language to write in modern literary forms. He is best known for the novel *Seitsemän veljestä* (*Seven Brothers*), the tale of a peasant family's adventures in the wilderness. While Kivi wrote a number of other works which were similarly inspired by peasant life and which also contributed to the development of Finnish literature, *Seven Brothers* is generally regarded as his masterpiece.

Born in the village of Palojoki in the parish of Nurmijärvi, Kivi was the eldest son of an impoverished tailor. He received his early education at the village school, where he exhibited great promise. With financial assistance from relatives, Kivi was able to matriculate at the university in Helsinki in 1857, taking courses in literature, folklore, and history. There he came under the influence of several scholars, most notably Elias Lönnrot, a Finnish linguist and folklorist who had compiled the *Kalevala,* the Finnish national epic, from traditional folk songs. Kivi was also strongly influenced by his reading of classical and European authors, including Homer, Dante, Miguel de Cervantes, and William Shakespeare, and during these years he began to write his first literary works.

Although Swedish was the language used by Finnish authors of the time, and had been for centuries due to Sweden's political domination of Finland from the twelfth to the early nineteenth centuries, Kivi was encouraged by his mentors to write in Finnish. In 1860 his play *Kullervo,* based on the exploits of a hero from the *Kalevala,* won a prize from the Finnish Literary Society. Kivi left school after this success, intent on devoting all his time to writing. Extreme poverty, however, hampered his efforts. In 1863 a sympathetic friend, Charlotta Lönnqvist, invited him to stay at her home outside Helsinki, where he lived until 1870. Kivi produced his best works under Lönnqvist's patronage: thirteen plays, including two peasant comedies on the failure of marriage plans, *Nummisuutarit* and *Kihlaus* (*The Betrothal, or Eva*), and *Karkurit,* a tragedy on the divisive nature of unrequited love; *Kanervala,* a collection of poems on religion, love, and death; and the novel *Seven Brothers.* None of these works was well received, however, and only one of his plays, *Lea,* a biblical drama, was produced during his lifetime. Some biographers speculate that this lack of acceptance combined with monetary difficulties contributed to the deterioration of Kivi's mental health. Institutionalized in 1870, he was released in 1872 and died the same year.

Seven Brothers is a picaresque adventure novel that blends a realistic depiction of Finnish peasants with elements of folklore and fantasy. After their father's death, seven unruly brothers refuse to comply with the efforts of their vil-

lage to educate and civilize them. They flee to the woods in defiance, experiencing both the pleasures and dangers of a wilderness existence: while they have unlimited opportunities to indulge in hunting, eating, and drinking, they are also forced to defend themselves against a horde of oxen and are menaced by wolves. Dream sequences and visions induced by alcohol reveal the brothers' moral and intellectual growth as a result of their adventures. At the end of ten years, after having realized the value of cultivating the forest and educating themselves, they return to their village, marry, and live out their lives as civilized men. The primary theme of the novel is the coming of age of the brothers, although the work has also been read as a symbolic portrait of the Finnish race in which the brothers exhibit characteristics traditionally associated with Finns, such as stubbornness, individualism, and love of liberty. An especially noteworthy aspect of the novel, according to commentators, is Kivi's unusual narrative technique, which employs long sections set in dialogue form without authorial commentary. While *Seven Brothers* and Kivi's other works were largely overlooked during his lifetime, they slowly gained critical acknowledgment, and his reputation in Finland grew steadily after his death.

PRINCIPAL WORKS

Kullervo [first publication] (drama) 1864
  [*Kullervo* (partial translation) published in journal
    Books from Finland, 1989]
Nummisuutarit [first publication] (drama) 1864
Kanervala (poetry) 1866
Kihlaus [first publication] (drama) 1866
  [*The Betrothal, or Eva* published in journal *Dublin Re-
    view,* 1926]
Olviretki Schleusingenissä [first publication] (drama)
  1866
Karkurit [first publication] (drama) 1867
Yö ja päivä [first publication] (drama) 1867
Canzio [first publication] (drama) 1868
Lea (drama) 1869
Margareta [first publication] (drama) 1871
Seitsemän veljestä (novel) 1873
  [*Seven Brothers,* 1929]
Kootut teokset. 4 vols. (dramas, poetry, novel, and let-
    ters) 1984

Phillips D. Carleton   (essay date 1929)

[*In the following excerpt, Carleton praises* Seven Brothers.]

Seven Brothers is a tale of the revolt of seven lawless
brothers against a civilization which they cannot understand. They leave their ancestral farm, erect their own hut
in the woods, and live for the better part of ten years in
a barbaric rhythm—working or hunting furiously, eating
enormously, and sleeping days at a time after strenuous
feasting or drinking. Finally, to avoid the just processes of
law, they have to set to work, and they carve a great farm
out of the wilderness, conquer their own wildness of soul,
and, at the end of the ten years, they settle down as married men in a countryside that they have tamed as effectively as they have their own bursting exuberance. Great
scenes stand out unforgettably in this forest life: the four-
days' siege that they stand, on a rock surrounded by thir-
ty-three wild bulls, the whole-hearted drinking scenes, the
wild chase back to their farm when their cabin burns and
the wolves pursue, and the strenuous and sweating efforts
that they make to comply with the law and learn their a,
b, c's.

In form the book is as unusual as it is in content: lyric passages of tremendous vehemence between pages of dialogue
printed as if they were part of a play; folk tales told by the
brothers to each other. And all these discordant elements
are held in firm unity by a style that reminds one of that
"impassioned poem of the sea, *Moby Dick,*" that has the
swing and vigor of a Shakespearian play, and epithets and
oaths that belong to Homer.

The significance and the value of the book lie in the new
point of view that it presents. It is no modern tale of old
times with a conscientiously unrolled background, nor yet
a saga, bare and pithy. It does not resemble the strange,
spiritual struggles of Hamsun or Undset or Lagerlöf; the
struggle of the brothers is a physical one: sweat oozes from
their fingertips as they grip their primers; they wrestle
against flesh and blood, and not against principalities and
powers of darkness. It presents a revolt against the decorum of civilization, depicts a hearty animal life with no
law save that of satiety, a side of the peasant and farmer
too little dwelt upon, evident in an ordered community
only in sporadic outbursts but always present. Alexis Kivi
(Stenvall) was near enough to his source to make his touch
authentic, and sufficiently imbued with the spirit of his
models—Shakespeare and Cervantes—to give flame and
color to what he felt and saw. This passage illustrates, as
well as a brief illustration can, the virtues of his writing:

> . . . Soon the wolves halted in their flight, and re-
> turning, again flitted swiftly towards the nocturnal
> wayfarers. The snow foamed around them and Kil-
> java's naked heath drummed as they came on in a
> body. At fiery speed they drew level with their com-
> rade who squirmed in his blood; they charged al-
> ready past him, but turned quickly round as the
> tempting smell of blood was borne to their nostrils.
> Round they spun: tails wagged, the snow boiled
> and fire flashed in the night from eyes of lust and
> greed. Then, grinning fearfully, the whole pack
> sprang at their wounded brother; and on the heath
> arose a grim struggle and a din such that one might
> have believed the pillars of the earth would collapse
> crashing down. The ground quaked and the snow
> was turned to a grisly pulp as former comrades tore
> the son of the woods into pieces, the wolf whose
> blood Tuomas's and Lauri's well-aimed bullets had
> set flowing. Then silence reigned again on the
> night-clad heath. Only a soft panting and the snap-
> ping of bones was heard, as with bloody faces and
> flashing eyes the brutes rent and devoured their vic-
> tim.

*Phillips D. Carleton, "Revolt against Deco-
rum," in* The Saturday Review of Literature,
Vol. V, No. 28, February 2, 1929, p. 639.

Edna Kenton   (essay date 1929)

[*In the following essay, Kenton favorably reviews* Seven
Brothers.]

Sixty years ago Alexis Kivi's **Seven Brothers** burgeoned
on the Finnish branch of the great world tree of letters,
but only recently has it been offered as Finland's ambassa-
dorial gift to the nations. Within the last few years it has
been published in Swedish, German, French, and, finally,
English translations, and I have no doubt that before long
these seven lusty brothers of Finland will be known to
other readers of other languages. A book thoroughly native to its soil, steeped to richness in native folk-lore and
legend and customs, which at the same time strikes the native note in other soils, makes for racial understanding and
a sense of racial kinship of which we cannot have too
much, and of which we have unfortunately all too little.
It is at once a child's book and a man's book—best test
of all for a good book; it is a rollicking, lusty tale which,
oddly enough, reads at times like the adventures of seven
herculean gods engaged not only in the task of building a
new world but in the vaster effort of achieving a modicum
of understanding during the process of creation. So, as we
reckon time, it is a "timeless" book. It might have been
written yesterday or tomorrow or a thousand years ago.
And, like all true folk romance made thick with old tradi-

tion, it will be fresh and "modern" a thousand years
hence. It is not too soon, in this first paragraph, to speak
of the virile English translation of this Finnish classic.
Poured into the channel of another language, the tale
flows free and strong. Vigorous idiom matches vigorous,
idiom unimpeded by stilted, unclever recasting of vernacular.

> Like the Great Bear up in heaven,
> Jukola has brothers seven.

and these brothers seven had a wise forbear. Far, far away,
"at the first great settlement of boundaries," he had accepted as his share of land a forest ravaged by fire, and had
therefore received seven times the area of his neighbors.
He called this mighty holding Jukola Farm, and by the
time the sons of his sons of his sons came into their inheritance, the dense forests had grown again over most of the
ancestral land.

Bereft of their father, one of the great "long hunters," the
brothers had tumbled up to maturity, unlettered and un-
disciplined, until, at their mother's death, they faced the
forbidding world, which was for them the village rector
with his rigid law that all the youth of the village must
read or sit in the stocks and die unwed. They faced, too,
among themselves a "headless body" and reluctantly
vowed obedience to their eldest, Juhani. This involved, as
it developed, disobedience to outer authority, for Juhani
provoked their common revolt against the laws of their little world. Two days' struggle with their A B C books settled that affair. "In the matter of reading," said Juhani,
"we have God's own laws and regulations on our side,
which rise against any attempt. Look you, already in our
mother's womb He gave us such hard heads that it is impossible for us to learn to read." And on the third morning, taking inventory of the results of revolt, they decided,
as one, on flight. Insulted and injured by the men of
Toukola, they had retaliated in horrid kind; they had been
refused, all seven, by Venla, daughter of Mother Pine-
wood; by negligence their great bathhouse had burned
down while they tended their wounds; and the stocks waited for them on the coming Sunday. They, therefore, rent-
ed Jukola Farm to the village tanner for ten long years,
and set out for the furthermost edge of their holdings, to
Ilvesjärvi Lake on the side of Impivaara, to build a new
world. They took with them Killi and Kiiski, the fierce
Jukola dogs, their one-eyed horse Valko, the doughty
Jukola cock, an iron cauldron, seven spoons, and the old
farm cat.

These are the seven "world builders," in the order of their
ages from twenty-five to eighteen: Hot-tempered Juhani
with no reason to guide him in the exercise of authority;
Tuomas the wonderer of the seven, "grave, manly, and
strong"; Aapo his twin, called the just, who "holds up a
mirror to us"; Simeoni the moralist, who "fluttered the
wings of his soul a bit too much," who nagged the most
and slept the least; Timo, fire-maker, proverb-quoter, and
cook; Lauri his twin, molder of clay, who first of all the
brothers realized one day that "God had once created him
a thinking human being"; and Eero, youngest of the seven,
at once the petted and the picked on, "small as a dwarf
and swift and keen as lightning." Diverse temperaments
from which might spring a new and lawless world.

But law, inner or outer, is never to be evaded, and the mad

young Titans discover this cosmic fact at Impivaara, as
adventure follows on adventure, and of wisdom tiny seed
on seed, until they succumb at last to the necessity of ham-
mering in on their unfurrowed brains the alphabet.
"What," breathed Aapo, "if we were to start this great
work together, without resting until it is done!" Not only
do the thick-skulled rascals decide on this all but impossible undertaking, but the consent, as final discipline, to sit
under the teaching of their little Eero, youngest, but, alas,
brightest of the seven. And finally, at the end of ten years,
learned men all, they set out from Impivaara to take possession once again of the old Jukola Farm.

No wonder **Seven Brothers** is a Finnish classic; it has all
the qualities to make it that. But Kivi caught more than
the local racial note; beneath—and not too far beneath—
the local color of lore and legend and merely native custom pulses the absurdity, the comedy, the tragedy, of the
race itself, which the reader may find for himself, and so
double the bubbling humor of the story.

> *Edna Kenton, "Seven against the Law," in*
> The Nation, *New York, Vol. CXXVIII, No.*
> *3319, February 13, 1929, p. 196.*

Alex Matson   (essay date 1959)

[*In the following foreword to his translation of* Seven
Brothers, *Matson provides an overview of Kivi's works,
focusing on the structure of* Seven Brothers.]

Seven Brothers, for three quarters of a century the most
widely circulated book in Finland next to the Bible, can
be read as a simple tale of adventure and humour, as it is
read and enjoyed by Finns of all ages who ask of a book
solely that it shall engross and entertain them. For the
non-Finnish reader it can be something more. Entertainment certainly, but at the same time a key to the Finnish
national character and the country by which that character was moulded.

The face of Finland has of course altered greatly since
Kivi wrote his novel in the 1860's, drawing even then on
his memories of earlier times. It might be difficult to recognize in the Finnish farmer of to-day the children of nature
Kivi drew. Yet for all that, national character does not
easily change, and Kivi's "brothers" are still typical of the
nation. The traits of character that determined the course
of their lives—stubbornness, hardy individualism, endurance, independence, love of liberty—are those which have
determined the course of Finland's history in our times.

Nor has the character of the Finnish landscape changed
for all the local transformations brought about by industrialization and a growing population. If it is the spirit of
the nation a stranger to Finland wishes to know, there is
still no better introduction than Kivi's novel.

Aleksis Kivi, to-day Finland's best-known author, unani-
mously acclaimed as the greatest genius in the history of
Finnish literature, suffered the fate of most original artists.
His gifts did not go unrecognized in his lifetime, but his
greatness was divined only by a slow process of discovery
that still continues as successive generations of critics
study his work. The farther back he recedes in time, the
higher he is seen to tower not only over his contemporaries, but over those who came after him.

The son of a poor village tailor, he was able with the fitful aid of a brother and at the cost of privations that now seem almost incredible to prepare himself for the university, only to find systematic study made impossible by extreme poverty. And even in the country, to which he was forced to retire, his existence was dependent largely on charity. A successful literary career seemed to open for him when his first major work *Kullervo,* a tragedy on a theme from the Kalevala, was awarded a State prize. Later, too, his full-length comedy *The Heath Cobblers* and a shorter comedy *The Betrothal,* the first works in which he gave expression to his profound love and understanding of the unspoiled Finnish rustic, were highly praised by a discerning critic of authority. His short lyrical drama *Lea* was the first serious play ever to be staged in Finnish. The public, however, for a writer in Finnish was small in those days, when as a result of the long connection with Sweden the Swedish language still dominated in cultural matters, and Kivi never earned enough by his pen even for the merest subsistence.

The wonder is that there is no taint of bitterness in his work, no railing against fate, only joy in the richness and beauty of the universe: the illumined idealism of a Shelley coupled with warm human feeling and a delicious humour. Even his melancholy is the unearthly melancholy that is sister to rapture. A heroic soul, if ever there was one. Only, no human frame could long endure the combination of physical suffering and the intense concentration of the inspired poet. The strain was too great, and in 1871 Kivi, born in 1834 and thus only 38, died, the mental collapse that preceded his death hastened on by a cruel criticism of *The Seven Brothers* accusing him of coarseness and of dishonouring the calling of an author. He himself never saw his belief in his "brothers" vindicated.

Kivi began his *Seven Brothers* with no further intention than that of narrating in a humorous vein the adventures of seven brothers in the Finnish wilds. The theme, however, aroused the artist in him so thoroughly that instead of carrying out his plan of publishing the work in serial parts—that he might earn as he wrote—he toiled at it for nine years.

This genesis of the work accounts in part for its unusual character, but not altogether. Thus, the original plan is evident in the absence of a central plot beyond that provided by the brothers' revolt against civilization and their ultimate return to its fold, and in a certain outward picaresque quality. This aspect of the novel doubtless also owes something to the fact that instead of studying the works of contemporary novelists, Kivi derived his conception of literary art from Cervantes and Shakespeare. The influence of both of these can be traced in his work, that of Shakespeare in Aapo's speeches and the stories he tells, in which the language rises on occasion to a poetry exceeding the speaker's own powers of expression as in the Shakespearen monologue. Kivi was however an original genius, and in the novel there is something else that is peculiarly his own: an instinctive feeling for form in the strictest sense of the word.

It is to this instinct, to a powerful striving for balanced architectural form, that every element in the structure of his novel can ultimately be traced back. Close study of the structure of *The Seven Brothers* reveals the work to be something more than narrative; it is seen to be an ordered work of art, perfectly integrated, a composition in which each word plays the part of a note in a symphony—hence Kivi's economical old-fashioned notation of dialogue. Behind the outward irregularity, the shapelessness characteristic of the true novel-form, structural principles can be discerned too consequently applied to be accidental. Thus, each important event grows out of a previous similar theme in miniature. The flight of the brothers into the wilds on which the main action hangs, is a development on a grand scale of the incident from the brothers' childhood Kivi describes in his opening pages, and similar parallels can be detected all along. No turn occurs in the narrative that is not heralded by words or sentences sounding at first unobtrusively, then ever more insistently, so that when the new theme opens, the reader's ear is prepared for a change in key, tempo and mood.

The equivalent of modulation and variation can be seen in the manner in which the legends in which Kivi gives rein to his poetical imagination are followed by a burlesque version, either action or direct parody. Here, the swing from poetry and romance to the comic restores the balance of the novel on that plane of naturalism, of truth to everyday life, from which the novelist departs at his peril. Musical structure is apparent also in the manner in which Kivi alternates solo passages with a full orchestra working up to a crescendo. Kivi's stage-setting, too, his grouping of stars and chorus and manipulation of sound effects, can be curiously reminiscent of opera. Even his choice of words, the construction of his sentences, his prose rhythms, are analogous to music, though for this the reader must take the translator's word, for a translator, compelled to stick to an author's meaning, can but rarely reproduce the cadences and beats of the original sentences in which sound, stress and meaning were created simultaneously.

In all this there is nothing deliberate, no laboured theory; the structure never obtrudes as it does when an author works consciously to a theory of form. Indeed, the form of Kivi's novel is doubly interesting for the very reason that it was arrived at unconsciously in the course of a search for perfection in what Kivi to the end regarded as a story, for it points to hidden affinities between the novel and the other arts, to the element of art in the novel-form that aesthetic research has so far failed to pin down. Kivi knew nothing of the theory of music and his opportunities for hearing good music were few, yet led solely by feeling, by his sense of the beautiful, he arrived through endless rewriting, recasting, adding and eliminating at thematic, or better still, symphonic structure. By sheer natural genius he anticipated findings in regard to the novel only diffidently expressed by Henry James and E. M. Forster.

And not for a moment did he forget the claims of the realistic story that was his material. That provided the stuff which the artist in him moulded into a form that was to become the complete expression of his own personality, yet a picture to be looked at and judged on its own merits as a composition. Ever in the forefront of his mind was his desire to communicate his own intense delight in the simple country people among whom most of his life was spent, and to open the eyes of his fellow-Finns to the beauty of the country it was their privilege to inhabit. Hence, partly, the care with which he modelled his characters until each of the brothers stands out in the round, all individualized, yet each a facet of a larger personality, that of a race. Hence, also, the lovingness with which he depicts landscape.

For appreciation of Kivi's novel, it is by no means necessary that the reader should pay attention to its structural merits. Such matters are for the professional student of literature. Like all other novels, Kivi's novel was written to be read as a story. It was to that end that Kivi's art was directed, and the layman is advised to ignore all that has been said herein about thematic structure and simply to read.

The effect at which an artist aims is the main thing, and the struggles of the artist to achieve the desired effect are no matter for the public. Yet one remark should perhaps still be added on the subject of structure. The result of Kivi's labours to satisfy his sense of form is an unusual solidity that becomes apparent only after repeated re-readings in an increased vividness and reality in the scenes depicted. As for perfect pleasure in great music some acquaintance with its pattern is necessary, so too Kivi's novel reads best after its contents have become familiar. Experience has shown this to be the case in Finland, where people talk not of having read the book, but of the number of times they have read it. Indeed, there are Kivi-enthusiasts who know the novel by heart and can at any time summon to memory favorite pages precisely as a music-lover will recall to mind passages from a musical composition. One might say that what drives them to re-read to the point of memorizing need not be so much any excellence the book may possess, as their own pleasure in it. But how many novels will bear memorizing and still continue to enchant? (pp. 5-10)

> *Alex Matson, "Translator's Foreword," in* Seven Brothers: A Novel *by Aleksis Kivi, translated by Alex Matson, The American-Scandinavian Foundation, 1962, pp. 5-10.*

Kai Laitinen   (essay date 1962)

[*In the following excerpt, Laitinen emphasizes the importance of* Seven Brothers *in the history of Finnish literature.*]

The *Kalevala,* the national epic of Finland, has indeed played an important role in Finnish cultural history. But there is another classic in Finnish literature, whose influence has been equally powerful, even if less obvious, and which, today, is a far more vigorous book than the *Kalevala.* It is Aleksis Kivi's novel **Seven Brothers** (**Seitsemän veljestä**), the best known and the most beloved book in Finland. Its sentences have become part and parcel of the common tongue. Its events are often cited as historical happenings, its characters and their vicissitudes are now permanent national property just as the characters of Shakespeare are so for the English, those of Molière for the French, or those of Cervantes for the Spaniards. (p. 373)

The position of **Seven Brothers** as Kivi's central work has not been shaken. . . . The book is unique for its period and, indeed, in all Finnish literature. The chief characters are seven adolescent, stubborn brothers who, some time in the early 1800s flee from society and its obligations (including the necessity of learning to read) into deep woods,

build a house there, clearing land for tilling and, as if unnoticed, grow into socially-minded responsible citizens in the hard school of solitude and the forest. The book combines realism and romanticism, humor and lyricism, so that even today it can be approached from many different angles. Kivi had not in vain read the writers of the Renaissance; something of the spirit and conception of art inherent in the works of Shakespeare and Cervantes can be detected in his novel. Because of other qualities, too, it can be characterized as a "Renaissance novel": it was born at the dawn of Finnish literature, during the years of the awakening of Finnish culture, when conscious cultural work in Finland underwent a sudden expansion gaining dimensions far larger than ever before. Its language is archaic, patinated Finnish, the like of which is no longer written and which for a modern Finnish reader is almost as distant as Shakespearean English is for a modern American reader. For this reason, the genuine tone of **Seven Brothers** hardly comes through in translation. This is especially true of its humor.

A foreign reader of **Seven Brothers** is probably mostly impressed by the environment. The entity formed by the great woods and the seven stubborn brothers is distant and strange, wild and "exotic". A Finnish reader, however, values the book, not because of its ethnographical and historical qualities, but for its artistic merits. The hand of a deliberate, careful artist can be traced everywhere in its structure: the environmental description and the portraiture and juxtaposition of its characters. Kivi rewrote his novel three times, a sign of unusually vigilant and purposeful artistic self-criticism. For example, the characters of the brothers are outlined by the dialogues without explanations: they introduce themselves to the readers through their words and deeds; no background comments by the author are audible. In his narrative Kivi is surprisingly "modern". Scene by scene, the action of the novel advances with careful deliberation; humorous situations, exciting adventures, and lyrical, fantastic stories are interwoven into a balanced, harmonious, and thoroughly original pattern.

There is one contemporary of Kivi's, whose themes are a far cry from his, but who can be viewed as his distant counterpart: Herman Melville. Kivi springs from an equally unsullied literary scene; his work is as independent and fresh, and he received as little understanding from his contemporaries. The distance from Melville's vast oceans to Kivi's vast forests is great, and Kivi's lyrical imagination and Melville's symbolism have hardly anything in common. But each writer demonstrates that an exceptional talent is capable of freeing himself in an astounding manner from his own time and from its conventional standards, and of creating in his art a world of his own which cannot be understood without a knowledge of its hidden laws. (pp. 376-77)

> *Kai Laitinen, "Aleksis Kivi: The Man and His Work," in* The American-Scandinavian Review, *Vol. L, No. 4, December, 1962, pp. 373-77.*

Jaakko Ahokas   (essay date 1973)

[*Ahokas is a Finnish educator, translator, and critic. In the following excerpt from his* History of Finnish Literature, *he examines Kivi's major themes and provides a survey of his works.*]

In spite of all that has been written about artistic genius, there is no general definition of this term; a literary genius seems to be a figure read in several countries and considered a genius by his readers. Thus, an author of a small nation not widely read outside his native country cannot be proved a genius. Consequently the efforts of Finnish critics and scholars in that direction on behalf of Aleksis Kivi (officially Aleksis Stenvall) have been useless, and we must simply state, with certainty, that he was one of the greatest Finnish authors, if not the greatest, not only in his lifetime (only Runeberg can be compared to him) but up to the present. He was also the first real author to write in Finnish (that is, author only by profession and not author and something else). By a mere reading of his works, one should be convinced of his strength of vision and depth of feeling, of his need to communicate with his fellow men through writing. His biography confirms his inner compulsion to write, for writing cost him whatever fortune he had, his physical and mental health, and his life—he died at the age of thirty-eight, insane.

In spite of the romantic impression these facts give, of misunderstood genius and proud spirit conquered in an unequal struggle with a prosaic world, Kivi remained until the last years of his life a strong, healthy, genial country boy who liked to roam the forests with his rifle on his shoulder, to swim, and to fish. He once wrote that he considered man's highest quality humor, "And, when I mention humor," he said, "I mean a fresh and natural one, not such as springs from a shipwreck suffered on the sea of life. I mean a sense for the comic, the ultimate foundation of which, after all, is a good but strong and healthy heart," but he often found that the only source of mirth in life's difficulties was alcohol, which hastened his death. He seems most like Robert Burns; both came from the country, were of modest origin but acquired education, were accepted, then rejected by society, could not find a stable position, drank too much, and died at almost the same age. More important is their attachment to their native soil, its traditions and its speech, less conspicuous, however, in Kivi than in Burns as far as the form of the language is concerned. (p. 73)

[Kivi] never married, though it is certain that he was in love at least twice. Even before he was a student, he asked for the first girl's hand, but her father, a well-to-do craftsman, disapproved. He wrote the second girl, an innkeeper's daughter, several letters, but the relationship never progressed further. Other letters hint bitterly at the cheap kind of sexual adventures he had. Significantly, we find in his works characters who are at odds with their neighbors and surroundings, find adjusting to society difficult, and have unhappy love affairs. He liked to describe simple country people realistically and wished to have an optimistic or, as he said, humorous philosophy. Some of his works are broad comedies or farces, such as *Kihlaus* (*The Betrothal,* 1866) or *Nummisuutarit* (*The Cobblers on the Heath,* 1864), and there are many comic elements in *Seitsemän veljestä* (*Seven Brothers,* 1870) as well. But, in spite of the slapstick humor in *The Betrothal* and *Cobblers,* one finds in them a message that is, if not tragic, at least pathetic; in each play the main character seems ridiculous because he wants to marry a woman who will not

have him and has to accommodate himself to the situation in the best possible way, to remain a bachelor. A similar incident occurs near the beginning of *Seven Brothers.* A purely humorous, almost nonsensical comedy is *Olviretki Schleusingenissä* (*The Beer Expedition at Schleusingen,* 1866), whose subject was suggested by an actual incident of the Austro-Prussian War in the same year. A Bavarian detachment occupied the small town of Schleusingen and drank an unbelievable quantity of beer in a few days. Kivi turned the event into an uproarious farce with a humorous effect underlined by the characters' ludicrously serious remarks about the state of the world and life. It was not published in his lifetime (it would have been perhaps more damaging to his reputation than *Seven Brothers* was) and was not presented until after 1920.

Kivi experienced, however, deep emotions and considered love a dark, destructive force or a dreamy feeling which could not be fulfilled in this life; many of his love stories end in death and destruction. An early work, *Kullervo,* which won the prize of the Society for Finnish Literature in 1860, is a five-act tragedy based on a canto from the *Kalevala,* one of the most coherent in the book although Lönnrot composed it from different folk poems. It deals with the fate of a man who feels he must avenge the death of his parents but, in doing so, brings death and destruction to the innocent. Eventually his parents are discovered, not dead, but hiding from their enemies. However, he has previously committed unwitting incest with his sister, who kills herself when she discovers their sin; when his parents die of the sorrows he has brought upon them, he takes his own life. The action closely follows that of the original poem, which centers on hate and revenge, although it might be said that it is the criminal relationship with the sister which prevents the hero from finding a place in society. *Karkurit* (*The Fugitives,* 1865, printed in 1867), another full-length tragedy often said to have been inspired by Shakespeare's *Romeo and Juliet,* actually has little in common with the English play besides the circumstances of young lovers whose families are feuding and who die at the play's end. In *Karkurit* the tragic ending seems contrived, for the enemies are near reconciliation and the couple near marriage when the unmasked, dying villain shoots the hero fatally and the bride dies of sorrow. *Canzio* (1868), set in Italy, has an improbable and complicated plot although its core is simple: Canzio, a young nobleman returning home to his family and fiancée after a long absence, falls in love with an adventuress (who is respectable insofar as her late husband's and her own republican ideals have brought her to that position) and thus sets off a series of incidents ending in his killing his best friend, driving his sister insane and his fiancée to a cloister. Despite the artificial mechanics of the end, poison and a duel, obviously inspired by *Hamlet,* the play is not inadequate in its analysis of the destructive force of love. His characters also discuss the problem of atonement and the soul's immortality, concerns which reappear in other works, e.g., *Lea.*

Although the major part of *Seven Brothers* deals with the main characters' free and adventurous life in the forests, love is treated in both the beginning and the end and appears in two tales or legends told by one of the brothers. These stories, unrelated to the action, are introduced only to relate events which occurred at the place where the characters are at that point. The first is about a father who murders his stepdaughter and her beloved, whom he has forbidden her to see, when he surprises them together, then kills himself; the second, entirely supernatural, concerns a maid carried away and imprisoned by a monster, but ultimately rescued by the young man she loved in life—both appear at the end in the form of radiant, heavenly spirits. The tales are built on motifs from the folklore of various nations—the first is most reminiscent, perhaps, of the Greek myth of Acis and Galatea, the second of the many legends of virgins threatened or abducted by monsters and rescued by young heroes, beginning with Perseus and Andromeda—but their style and incidents are far too literary and refined for the circumstances in which they are told. This discrepancy is emphasized by the contrast to other stories of a popular nature, about ghosts, giants and memorable hunting expeditions to Lapland, for example. They obviously reflect problems which were so vital to the author that he had to express them even in an inappropriate context.

He speaks of unhappy, destructive love in two poems, one exclusively devoted to it, **'Nuori karhunampuja'('The Young Bear Hunter,'** in the collection *Kanervala,* 1866; also called **'Ensimmäinen lempi' 'First Love'**.) Kivi produced several works about hunting bears, the largest and most dangerous game in Finland. This poem opens with a brief description of the beast's killing, then tells that the young man, coming home, finds that the girl to whom he was engaged is celebrating her marriage to another man and kills himself, a tragic version of the situation treated humorously in *The Cobblers on the Heath.* The other poem, **'Mies'('The Man,'** same collection), describes a man who loses his property, crops, and house, but is comforted by the thought of his faithful beloved. When she proves untrue, he momentarily considers suicide, but eventually submits to his destiny and lives thenceforth as a pious hermit.

Other poems of his deal with love as a dreamy, almost mystic feeling he does not even attempt to fulfill. Not even a kiss is described. We see only the lovers standing on a mountain, united in a pure embrace, watching the scenery before their eyes. This motif of a mountain and its view recurs many times in Kivi's works, for example, in the poems **'Onnelliset' ('The Blissful'**) and **'Sunnuntai' ('Sunday'**), both written before the publication of *Kanervala.* Two often quoted are **'Keinu' ('The Swing'**) and **'Anianpelto'** (place), both in *Kanervala.* The typical opening in which the narrator stands on a high hill or walks in smiling valleys is followed by the description of a noisy, merry market at Anianpelto and a beautiful maid who stands in the crowd with "an earnest brow, with smiling lips" but then disappears, leaving her image forever in the viewer's mind. **'The Swing,'** which repeats the lines *Heilahda korkeelle, keinu, / Ja liehukoon impeni liina / Illalla lempeäl.* ('Swing high, swing, / Wave, my maid's kerchief / In the mild evening.'), at the end of each stanza, is like a folksong of the West European type, also known in Finland, and the "maid with the white kerchief" has become proverbial in mentioning Kivi. A strong erotic undercurrent, however, is expressed in the swing's movement, in the image of flying together to a faraway country (fourth stanza), and in the last lines of the poem, *Seisahda, heiluva keinu, / jo kelmenee impeni poski / Illalla lempeäl.* ('Stop swinging, swing, My maid is growing pale / In the mild evening'). **'Helavalkea' ('The Whitsuntide Fire')** and **'Ruususolmu'**

(**'A Knot of Roses')**, both from *Kanervala,* are even more like folksongs. The first is a description of folk life, showing without further dramatization young men and girls dancing at a country feast. The second centers on a universal symbol of love, the rose, used by a young woman to mark her affection toward her suitor.

Another frequent motif in Kivi's poems is the mother-child relationship, often with tragic undertones. Many times this motif is blended with that of wandering, lost but found again. **'Lapsi' ('The Child')** is the simple description of a child's coming home to his loving mother, but in **'Hannan laulu' ('Hanna's Song')**, a three-stanza poem from *Karkurit,* the child is briefly lost, then finds his mother, who has a "waving kerchief," and sleeps happily in her lap. The image of the road of golden sand frequent in Kivi's works also appears in this poem; it is not an imaginary road in fairyland, but a simple road along which walking in the sunshine is pleasant. Even his visions of another world are constructed of elements from daily life and Finnish nature. Kivi ultimately followed the development initiated by Creutz and Franzén by creating a dreamworld that is completely Finnish. **'Kaunisnummella' ('On Kaunisnummi'**; the name means 'the beautiful heath,' 'Fairheath') is a further development of the same subject, a child lost in a forest and found by his mother. **'Paimentyttö' ('The Shepherd Girl')** describes a small girl sent to watch cows, who is lost in the forest but in the end finds her way home again. **'Äiti ja lapsi' ('The Mother and the Child')** is the most tragic poem; a dying mother is forced to send her child to beg and, hearing the wolves' howling outside, prays for God to protect him—her prayer is answered, for the child freezes before the beasts reach him.

'The Song of My Heart' . . . is close to folksongs having the same motif found in Finland, Estonia, Ingria, and Russia. The contents of both Kivi's poem and the songs may seem startling: a description of the land of death (not paradise) as a beautiful, quiet place to which the mother says she is sending, or would like to send, her child. The names for death and the land of death used by Kivi and in some of the folk poems, *Tuoni, Tuonela,* are (at least today) poetic and unusual, leaving a different impression than does the usual word, *kuolema.* Kivi's poem is sung by an exalted, visionary woman at the end of *Seven Brothers,* but the motif is found in a wide area.

A more conventional yearning for death appears in the poem **'Ikävyys'** ('spleen,' 'sadness,' or 'dejection,' not the present translation **'Boredom'**; 1866), although its form is personal. It reveals that Kivi was already capable of deep depression although he was in his best creative period and two years later was still explaining his philosophy of humor to Bergbom; perhaps his many writings in those years were an attempt to ward off the impending doom he sensed. In the poem he expresses a wish to escape from the "pain of knowledge" to the "silent emptiness" and asks his friends to build him a house of death (*Tuoni*) and leave him forever under the "dim willow tree" in an unmarked grave so that no one might know his resting place.

One of his most original poetic creations is his vision of another world, a dreamland or Isle of the Blessed, somewhat like the age-old myth in Homer, Hesiod, Pindar, or the life of St. Brendan, though still very personal and Finnish. It appears in **'Kesäyö' ('A Summer Night')**, **'Lintukoto'** (name), and **'Kaukametsä' ('The Faraway For-**

est'), for which Kivi perhaps found inspiration in contemporary Swedish poets like Atterbom and Stagnelius, although he includes motifs from Finnish folklore. Influence from world literature is perhaps most clearly seen in **'A Summer Night,'** in which the poet sees a rocky island or mountain floating in the air over a meadow on a summer night. It is reminiscent of both Virgil's "pleasant greenery of the fortunate forests and blissful seats" and Dante's Limbo; the voice of an angel explains to the poet that it is the "island of peace of the pious heroes whose lives' morning was lit, whose day, pure of the clouds of sin, was spent before the rise of the star in Bethlehem, before they heard the joyful message," where they "wait for the great day on which the voice of the trumpet shall call them to their home." Kivi, less rigorous than Dante, admits thus that the souls of great men born before Christ's coming will be redeemed at the Last Judgment; he adds that this island is an abode of joy, whereas Dante says that Limbo's inhabitants had a countenance "neither sad nor gay." The Finnish description reminds us more of Virgil's heroes, who dance in choirs and recite poems.

To understand fully the poem **'Lintukoto'** (lit. **'The Home of the Birds,'** but no birds appear), one must have a knowledge of Finnish folklore, although the same motif appears in many other parts of the world. It is actually a combination of two myths: according to the first, somewhere in the ocean is an island on which migratory birds spend the winter which they find by following the Milky Way, called *Linnunrata,* 'Track of the Birds'; according to the second, people living near the edge of the world, where heaven and earth meet and there is, consequently, little space, are dwarfs like the pygmies in Greek mythology. The story of their wars with the birds, especially cranes, told, e.g., in the third canto of the *Iliad,* appears in Finnish folklore. Kivi expects his readers to know the Greek myth; he says at the beginning of the poem that the inhabitants of Lintukoto are beautiful, innocent small beings, not ugly trolls "as in many tales." He describes their abode and life, which have no reference to a Christian heaven and simply represent a dreamland of eternal bliss. The island is not, however, ethereal: it has forests, meadows, fields, and a flowery mound on which there is a castle made of the wood of birdsongtree, taken from Finnish fairytales. The island people engage in real activities: men plow the fields, women weave cloth, they have meals together and sometimes sail around their home. Still, at times a vague sadness overcomes them, and they remain gazing at the grass, not knowing why, for "they do not seek and do not find the answer," but the sadness is without pain and soon fades away like the morning dew. The poem ends with a few lines again describing their life, underlining its perennial character.

Without literary reminiscences, **'Kaukametsä'** is the simplest of the three poems, an unadorned description of a child's dreamland. The poet seems to say that he wishes to go to a country reminding him of his native place instead of a resplendent, glorious heaven:

> Alas kalliolta lapsi riensi,
> Äitins luoksi riensi hän,
> Lausui loistavalla katsannolla:
> Nähnyt olen taivaan maan.
>
> "Mitä haastelet, mun pienoseni,
> Mitä taivaan kaukamaast'?

> Missä näit sä autuitten mailman?
> Sano, kulta-omenain."
>
> Vuoren harjanteella kauan seisoin,
> Katsahdellen koilliseen,
> Siellä näin mä nummen sinertävän,
> Honkametsän kaukasen.
>
> Puitten kärjill' näin mä kunnaan kauniin,
> Armas päivä paistoi siell'
> Ylös kunnaan kiirehelle juoksi
> Kultasannotettu tie.
>
> Tämän näin ja sydämmeni riutui,
> Kyynel juoksi poskellein,
> Enkä ymmärtänyt miksi itkin,
> Mutta näinhän taivaan maan.
>
> "Ei, mun lapsein; sineydess' ylhääll'
> Taivaan korkee sali on,
> Siellä lamput, kultakruunut loistaa,
> Siell' on istuin Jumalan."
>
> Ei, vaan siellä, missä ilmanrannall'
> Kaukametsä haamottaa,
> Siellä ompi onnellisten mailma,
> Siellä autuitten maa.

> The child came from the slopes of the high hill
> To his mother came he, saying,
> Turning blissful eyes toward her:
> I have seen the land of heaven.
>
> "What say'st thou, my beloved,
> What about a country far away?
> Where didst thou see the bless'd and their land?
> Say, golden apple mine."
>
> On the rock near our own fields
> I was, the northeast watching
> There I saw a pale blue heath
> And pine trees, all so wonderful.
>
> A hill rose from among the trees,
> The sun shone bright upon the hill,
> And to the highest summit went
> A road with golden sand bestrewn.
>
> This I saw, and felt my heart a-burning,
> Tears a-running on my cheeks
> Could not understand my crying,
> But Heaven it was I saw.
>
> "No, my child! In the blue, high up,
> Is the lofty hall of Heaven
> There the lamps and golden crowns are shining,
> There the Lord had raised his seat."
>
> No, but where the skies are ending,
> Where the forest faraway is looming,
> There the blissful have their home,
> There the holy have their land.

Kivi seldom speaks of formal religion or of man's relation to God. He never experienced a religious crisis, but he doubted the truth of certain dogmas, especially the immortality of the soul; these doubts appear in some of his letters. He seems to have accepted in general the traditional views of the church, but even in 1870 he wrote to Bergbom, "Could I believe with certainty in something about life beyond the grave. . . ." Canzio is an agnostic who discusses with his friend Claudio the soul's immortality; Claudio, who defends the religious ideas, has the better arguments. Kivi usually gave his characters his own straightforward, quiet attitude toward an acceptance of religion, but he could also depict religious ecstacy. A typical character in the second respect is a young girl or woman who proclaims eternal truths with a force and exaltation not of this world. Anna Seunala, wife of one of the seven brothers, Selma of *Karkurit,* Liisa in *Yö ja päivä* (**Night and Day,** 1867), and Margareta in the play with the same name (1870) are such characters.

Lea is built entirely on a subject from the New Testament, although Kivi expanded it far beyond the few words of the Gospel. Of all the characters, only one appears in St. Luke (19:1-8), Zacchaeus, the publican who climbed up into a sycamore tree to see Jesus and promised to give half of his goods to the poor. Insofar that almost no outer action takes place onstage, and only the changes in the minds and hearts of the characters are shown, the play follows closely the rules of classical French tragedy. The play has been and is admired greatly in Finland, more, possibly, for sentimental and religious reasons than for artistic merits. The language is beautiful, and Kivi inserted a few half-humorous interludes, which are irrelevant to the plot; but the play is like an oratorio in which each character sings about his rapture at the sight of Christ and about his conversion. These conversions, however, are brought about through supernatural intervention of the Savior, not by inner struggle. Some action is introduced by the secondary plot, in which Zacchaeus first wants to marry his daughter Lea to a Pharisee, Joas, who is later revealed a hypocrite interested in Zacchaeus's money, then gives her to Aram, a young Sadducee (agnostic), who is converted by Lea after she is converted by Jesus.

The most often translated work of Kivi, *Seven Brothers,* is also the work for which he is best known in Finland, with *The Cobblers on the Heath* and *The Betrothal.* Its dialogue is play-like, without explanatory remarks such as "he said" or "answered the other"; the speaker's name merely precedes each line. Consequently, it was easily adapted to the stage, a version which added to its popularity. (pp. 75-82)

Kivi described the book as a "merry tale," and almost none of its scenes, no matter how tragic, are without comic elements. Several later Finnish authors, e.g., Lehtonen, Kianto, Sillanpää, and Haanpää, have also sympathetically described people struggling with hardship while seeing that suffering does not necessarily ennoble man and that pity does not require blindness to its object's defects. Kivi described the seven brothers as sturdy country boys like his childhood friends and himself. They occasionally quarrel and fight with their neighbors . . . , drink more than they should, make unrefined jokes and indulge in boisterous fun and games. They are represented almost free of superstition; Simeoni says, when listening to a horned owl's hooting in the forest: "It announces fires, bloody fights, and murders," but adds "as old people say," and Tuomas retorts, "It's his job to hoot in the forests, and it doesn't mean a thing." Kivi never introduced folk customs, beliefs, or practices in his works to make them more thrilling or attractive, and he never acquired the city dweller's interest in the quaint manners of the country people. What violence, terror and brutality he depicted were unadorned. The Finns have been accused occasionally of lengthy brooding over real or imaginary wrongs ending in sudden eruptions of destructive violence; Kivi describes this temperament in his characters. A long-standing hostility between the brothers and boys of the neighboring village leads to three neither gentlemanly nor heroic fights of senseless brutality which almost result in murder. Among themselves some of the brothers also have fits of sudden anger, and they experience the surrounding world as hostile. They react with hate and near panic, but their most destructive actions make them see the dangers in their way of life and help them to become law-abiding citizens. A central episode, combining realism and fantasy in a way typical of Kivi, concerns the brothers' adventure on the Devil's Stone, a rock on which they are besieged by forty oxen from a neighboring manor. After three days and three nights without food, they shoot their way to freedom with the rifles they have with them as they were originally on a hunt. The scene is described from the point of view of the characters, and, to underline its importance as a turning-point in their lives, the author builds the noise and smoke of the rifle fire, the bellowing and rushing of the stampeding animals and a breaking thunderstorm into a terrifying cataclysm. Next they must face the owner of the oxen, and, though they first spurn his threats, they eventually agree to pay a reparation, for which they must cultivate the ground to find the necessary means, the first step on their road toward an orderly life. They meet difficulties due to their own character, and Kivi gives a simple but penetrating description of their mental struggles, both conscious and unconscious, in reaching a well-balanced attitude toward the world, which some of them never achieve. Their psychological development is motivated partially by external factors, partially by the workings of their subconscious, expressed in dreams and delirious visions, which are attributed to excess drink. Kivi projects in the brothers, especially with the vision, many of his own mental sufferings, but his mastery in combining realism and fantasy is evident in the presentation of the difficult motifs of dream and vision. They are not too literary, beautiful, or romantic, but are composed of realistic and even humorous details; nevertheless, they produce an unreal impression of sadness, dejection, and wild terror. In the dream one brother sees himself transformed into a mole; in this form he forces his way through the rotten core of a pine tree to its top for a look at the world. There he sees "the steep mountain of Impivaara, but at an immeasurable, heart-breaking distance, he sees there, in the midst of the forests, in the evening, the melancholy little house, and (he sees also) his dear brothers . . . on the misty, resounding heath." Eventually the brothers are carried away in a cloud by a whirlwind raised by the rector of their parish, who has warned them in vain against their ungodly lives; then the dreamer wakes. In the vision one brother sees himself carried by the devil to the moon and there taken to a tower made of boot leather, from which he can see the whole world and its ultimate destruction, which he takes as a warning for his brothers and himself to better their ways.

By far Kivi's most popular work besides his comedies, *Seven Brothers* has been printed in many editions illustrated by well-known Finnish artists. It alone does not give an altogether one-sided picture of his work, for it does not reflect only the optimistic side of his creations. Nevertheless, as often happens when a book is "officially" recommended for general admiration, an official idea about it is easily accepted; in this case, the book is considered an edifying, optimistic, and humorous tale, a view which obscures its tragic conflicts, lyrical beauties, and psychological depth. The many descriptions of nature, hunting expeditions, and the farmer's work are realistic, but they contain something of an epic majesty and breadth, which give an impression of a remote, almost mythological past, although the scenes are composed of familiar, everyday elements. Kivi's language . . . gives the same impression; it seems age-old, archaic, and solemn, though it is used to tell the most ordinary incidents in a way understandable even today. We might compare Carlyle's English to it, but Kivi had none of Carlyle's conscious oddities; he simply wrote in a manner influenced by the speech of his native region and old literary Finnish (especially the Bible translation) at a time when other writers and linguists were developing a different form, which Kivi could not accept. His thoughts and their expression are so intertwined that whether the subject matter or the style makes his works cannot be judged; perhaps it is this total equation of form and content that best marks a great writer. His works give a full and vivid picture of the Finnish man in his Finnish surroundings, but also of Man in human surroundings, and, as such, should be foreign to no member of the human race. (pp. 83-5)

> *Jaakko Ahokas, "Literature in Finnish from the Beginning of the Nineteenth Century through Kivi," in his* A History of Finnish Literature, *Indiana University, 1973, pp. 63-85.*

K. Börje Vähämäki   (essay date 1978)

[*In the following excerpt, Vähämäki offers a detailed analysis of the themes and structure of* Kullervo.]

Even before it was published in 1864, Aleksis Kivi's *Kullervo* was subject to critical debate. The tragedy was Kivi's entry in a literary contest in 1860. Pronouncements by the committee of this contest gave birth to several opinions concerning Kivi which have been influential and long lasting.

One of these is the notion that *Kullervo* is not a genuine tragedy, since it is not built upon any conflict of ideas between which the hero would be caught. *Kullervo* was seen merely as a story about one man, his hard destiny and deep suffering. Another persistent notion is that *Kullervo* is too episodic and its language too lyrical, i.e., that the dramatic structure is loose and disconnected. Kivi seems to digress frequently from his "subject matter," Kullervo's vengeance on Untamo. Since *Kullervo* is built upon the Kullervo myth of the *Kalevala* (1849), critics tend to see the merits of the drama as those of the *Kalevala* and on the other hand they view the defects as merely technical problems deriving from Kivi's still undeveloped literary competence. *Kullervo* in other words, is usually seen as a stage version of the Kalevala myth. Another complicating factor is F. Cygnaeus's psychological-aesthetic analysis of the *Kalevala*'s Kullerva character, *Det tragiska elementet i Kalevala* (1853). Since Kivi was known to be well acquainted with both the *Kalevala* and the publication by Cygnaeus, both works came to exert an influence on the evaluation of the drama.

The result was that Kivi was considered not to have mastered drama as a genre. The evaluation committee of 1860 included A. Ahlqvist, perhaps Kivi's most implacable an-

Charlotta Lönnqvist's house.

tagonist in aesthetic matters. In later years, writing in his own name, Ahlqvist minced no words in his denigration of Kivi, both as an author and as a person.

Since the time of Ahlqvist and of the contest committee, many studies of *Kullervo* have been undertaken, based on the 1864 version of the play—no copy of the original version has been found—but the general line of interpretation has remained constant. The unanimous contention, again, is that *Kullervo* lacks a conflict of ideas, that the tragedy is merely a play about one individual whose harsh fate causes him extreme suffering: he is born a free man, but is degraded by fate to the status of a slave.

The story in *Kullervo* is as follows:

> The brothers Kalervo and Untamo have for some reason become involved in a feud with each other. Untamo and his men assailed and killed Kalervo and his people. Only Kalervo's son, Kullervo, a little boy, and Kalervo's hired man, Kimmo, survived, but were enslaved by Untamo, both with a mark branded on their foreheads. When the play begins, Kullervo has sworn to take revenge on his father's murderer, Untamo, but his vengeance is deferred when Kullervo is sold to Ilmarinen. Now a series of dramatic incidents follows: Kullervo kills Ilmarinen's wife, flees from the farm, arrives at the hiding place of his parents, who turn out to be alive after all, does not thrive there, and, in the woods, unknowingly commits incest with his sister Ainikki, who commits suicide upon discovering Kullervo's identity. Kullervo turns toward home, gives a brutal account of what has happened, decides to take his own life, but remembers that Untamo still is not punished. Total destruction is the result of Kullervo's vengeance, everyone is killed and everything burnt, but still he finds no peace of mind. He strays, driven by voices demanding expiation, back to his parents' cottage, and finds everyone dead except Kimmo, who has become insane. Summoned by his deceased mother's voice, Kullervo goes to the forest; reaching the scene of the incest, he takes his life in the presence of Väinämöinen, Ilmarinen, and Lemminkäinen. These heroes of the *Kalevala* bury Kullervo on the shore of the rapids in which Ainikki ended her life.

V. Tarkiainen, one of the most prominent Kivi experts, expresses in his biography of Kivi views which by and large coincide with traditional criticisms of the play, even though Tarkiainen recognizes many merits in **Kullervo,** particularly in its character description and its language. In still another biography of Kivi, again from 1934, V. A. Koskenniemi offers quite similar opinions of **Kullervo.** Kullervo's very last words: "Eikö tuo ole päivän kajastus idässä tuolla?" ("Isn't that the light of dawn, there in the east?") are interpreted by Koskenniemi as a promise of reconciliation for Kullervo after death. R. Koskimies, too, sides with this traditional view of **Kullervo** in his monograph on Kivi (1974). He agrees with Ahlqvist in the judgment that Kivi, being a nonreflective, intuitive, and untheoretical writer, lacked the ability to create a perfect tragedy in the classical sense. L. Viljanen detects a superficial influence from Hegel's philosophy of history in **Kullervo,** but is otherwise in agreement with the above critics.

One scholar who has made a specific effort to interpret **Kullervo** solely on the basis of the text is Aarne Kinnunen. He too states that the drama lacks a conflict of ideas and that the hero does not have an antagonist in the classical sense. Kinnunen attempts to solve "the problem of the fourth act" by interpreting the relevance of the act as emerging from the necessity of letting Kullervo for once function as a leader of a group.

According to Kinnunen there are three factors determining Kullervo's development—that Kullervo believes himself to have lost his humanity; that, as a result, the world has become evil; and that he has broken with the gods—which, he says, are totally inexplicable and unmotivated in the text. In this, Kinnunen's view partially coincides with Tarkiainen's. Kinnunen diverges from Koskenniemi's interpretation of Kullervo's last words and contends that they have mainly practical relevance; Kullervo wanted the men who were present to look away. In support of this Kinnunen provides two arguments: that the stage direction in parentheses states that the men looked to the east, and the assumption that the men otherwise might have tried to prevent Kullervo's suicide.

Still another analysis of **Kullervo** should be mentioned, L. Valkama's interesting study of the imagery and its function in **Kullervo.** He concludes that the imagery does not form any connected whole, and sees the recurrent storm as accidental. He thereby supports the view that **Kullervo**'s composition is loose. Valkama furthermore claims that the imagery at times is hyperbolic and psychologically not sufficiently motivated.

A notable tendency in the study of **Kullervo** is to see the drama as a preparatory phase in Aleksis Kivi's literary career, the peaks of which are the epic-novel **Seven Brothers** and the comedy **Cobblers on the Heath. Kullervo** is used as a source in which to look for "signs of the talent" which, however, manifested itself only later.

The purpose of my study is to show that Kivi's **Kullervo** in its thematic structure is a historical drama of ideas in the sense in which the term (and genre) was used by Schiller. The hero is traditionally in a period of transition between an old and a new era, between outdated ethical standards and a new moral. [The critic adds in a footnote, "Kivi's **Kullervo** seems, in principle, to correspond to the basic criteria of a historical drama of ideas as it was introduced by Schiller, e.g., in *Wallenstein*. The essence was not in history as such, but in the moral conflict of the era. There is a conflict between conventional morality and instinctive morality, between old, established values and new ideas, which emerge out of idealism. In **Kullervo** we find the ancient ingredients revived by Schiller: family guilt, nemesis, hubris, and peripeteia. Kivi seems to have been very familiar with tragedy as genre; his admiration of Shakespeare has been strongly evidenced. He also was familiar with works by Schiller, probably even *Wallenstein.*"]

Kivi has chosen as motif of his tragedy a myth which is represented in the *Kalevala,* the Kullervo myth. Kivi, of course, has adapted this myth to suit his own purposes. The historical era to which the play refers is the one of transition from paganism to Christianity. Kivi thus stages the conflict of ideas inherent in the confrontation between these two sets of values.

It is interesting to note that by building on old traditional materials from folklore, Kivi joins an eminent group of Scandinavian dramatists. Adam Oehlenschläger wrote his Schiller drama, *Haakon Jarl,* on Eddic materials, actually developing much the same theme as Kivi does in **Kullervo,** that of the conflict between pagan and Christian philosophies. Henrik Ibsen's early dramas were national historical plays based on traditional materials, especially *Hærmændene på Helgeland* (1858) comes to mind. Even August Strindberg started in the genre of historical drama. In Kivi's case, as in Ibsen's case as well, the choice of motifs is related to nationalistic aspirations of creating a truly national theater in Finland and Norway, respectively.

In the grouping of the characters Kivi shows various weaknesses of the declining pagan culture. Untamo and Kiili are cynics; they embody the social values of a decadent society. Amorality is another consequence of the outdated ethical norms and is represented in Nyyrikki and Tiera and his men. Kalervo, Kullervo's father, reacts to the conflicts of the transition with an attitude of escapism; he flees to a hidden, anonymous existence outside society.

Several of the minor characters in the drama lack an intellectual understanding of their position. Some of them are ardent proponents of outdated codes of conduct, especially the code of vengeance. Characters in this category are, e.g., Untamo's wife and Ilmarinen's servant. Other subordinate characters function as uncomprehending spectators, as do the two shepherds.

In Kimmo as well as in Kullervo one finds inner conflicts which emerge from a conflict between two outlooks on life, the outdated pagan and the arriving Christian one. Kimmo's reaction is resignation, a kind of passive idealism which comes from a feeling of guilt. Kullervo on the other hand is possessed by a strong idealism, which demands action.

The three Kalevala heroes who appear at the very end of the final act are advocates of the new ethic. (Even Ilmarinen's wife is actually a representative of the newer ideas.)

Kivi has thus in his character portrayal covered a whole range of attitudes toward the era's conflict of ideas. He has set up the tragic conflict by having Kullervo swear vengeance against Untamo before the play begins and by making Kullervo a slave under Untamo, his father's murderer, with a slave mark on his forehead. Vengeance and slavery are the prerequisites for the tragic conflict to follow.

What does vengeance mean in the drama? Society is relatively unorganized in **Kullervo**'s era. Vengeance is the main, perhaps the only means of obtaining justice. In the absence of an organized judicial system it was left to the individual to exact justice. Vengeance was a punishment, and the severity of the punishment was to correspond to the seriousness of the offence, according to the ancient principle of "an eye for an eye, a tooth for a tooth." Since the victim himself (or his family) was to measure and execute the punishment, it was also his own decision whether to do it or not.

Consequently, vengeance was a socially accepted institution of the time depicted. It was one that was both complicated and reinforced by the prevalent ideal of manliness, since a person was esteemed and valued primarily on the basis of his acts. This was the case particularly with offences which required blood vengeance. Such an offence was murder, which was to be avenged by the victim's family. In such cases vengeance was a duty, reinforced by the ideal of manliness. It was particularly crucial for a young man if his father or his whole family had been killed. Then vengeance came to function as a test of manliness, which had to be carried out successfully before the son could obtain respect from others or from himself.

Another aspect of this ideal reflected in the text was to die gloriously. Mercy or forgiveness were not contained in the old ethical system of the drama; they were not part of the morality of the ancient period. (Untamo, for example, refuses to beg for mercy when he is to be killed.) For Kullervo, vengeance according to the old philosophy was a categorical duty.

Kullervo exposes many different attitudes toward vengeance. Kimmo, Kullervo's brother in misfortune, has exacted vengeance long before the play begins. He has shot an arrow into the back of one of Untamo's men in revenge for damage Untamo and his men had done to Kalervo's property and cattle. Kimmo considers himself a murderer; he suffers remorse. His revenge was not ethically acceptable. He had reached the conviction that vengeance as an institution was inadequate; he was himself a victim of the abuse inherent in the code of vengeance. Kimmo becomes an exponent of the Christian philosophy.

Tiera and his men also become avengers. When they meet Kullervo in the fourth act, they decide to join him on his vengeance raid. They suddenly recall that they had reason to take revenge on Untamo:

> TIERA: . . . Tiedä, että eräs kumppanimme, Korventaustan Kinnu, karhunampuja hyvä, Untolan peikkoin pesässä surmansa sai. Hänen murhasit he ja viskasit kurjan kujalle kuin koiran, saaliiksi korpeille; mutta meidänpä surmansa kostaa tulee. Mies, eikö asiamme ole yhteinen?
>
> KÄPSÄ: Meitä ankara velvollisuus vaatii.
>
> TIERA: Miehet, jos tallustaisimme tästä Untolaan?
>
> VIKSARI: Minä valmis olen.
>
> KÄPSÄ: Samoin minä kumppanimme kuolemata kostamaan.
>
> TIIMANEN: Käymmepä oivalliseen partioret-

keen. Oltta Untolassa kylliksi löytyy ja ehkä kultaa ja hopeata myös.

> TIERA: . . . You should know that a companion of ours, Kinnu from Korventausta, a fine bear hunter, was killed in the den of the Untola monsters. They murdered him and threw the poor wretch into the path like a dog, as a prey for vultures; but we are to avenge his death. Man, is not our cause the same?
>
> KÄPSÄ: Grim duty calls us.
>
> TIERA: Men, how about heading for Untola?
>
> VIKSARI: I am ready.
>
> KÄPSÄ: So am I, to avenge our companion's death.
>
> TIIMANEN: We are going on an excellent raiding trip. There is plenty of beer at Untola and perhaps gold and silver, too.)

The contrast between Kullervo's motive and that of the Tiera gang is distinct. Not even the thought of possibly innocent people at Untamo's farm bothers them, even though they realize that Kullervo's vengeance will be total. For them the code of vengeance becomes a means of pursuing selfish gain. Here Kivi shows the degeneration of an old idea in a newer time, a point typical of dramas of ideas in general.

Another example of vengeance occurs when Ilmarinen's wife bakes a stone into Kullervo's bread as a lesson to him for his disrespectful remarks of the evening before. Kullervo sees this as vengeance. Kalervo, Kullervo's father, wants to take revenge on Kullervo on two occasions—first for the murder of Ilmarinen's wife, second for the incest with Ainikki. He claims, however, that he does not want to besmirch his hands with his own blood.

The main avenger in the tragedy is Kullervo. He has sworn even before the play begins to take revenge on Untamo for the murder of Kalervo and his clan. For Kullervo, vegeance is an obligation. His attitude toward vengeance as an institution is, however, not as clear as earlier research has indicated. Kullervo already in the first act discloses doubts in regard to vengeance in his reaction to Kimmo's confession of his murder:

> KULLERVO: Oi Kimmo, mitä ilmoitat!—Mutta mille tuntuu murhamiehenä olla?
>
> KIMMO: Kullervo! kuumasti sydän povessa tytkyy, muisto riutuu ja elon kirkas päivä ehtooksi käynyt on.
>
> KULLERVO: Jotain tämänkaltaista siinä tilassa kuvaillut olen ja arvellut mitä tekisin.
>
> (KULLERVO: Oh Kimmo, what are you telling me!—But how does it feel to be a murderer?
>
> KIMMO: Kullervo! my heart is pounding like fire in my breast, my memory grows dull and life's bright day has turned into night.
>
> KULLERVO: Something of that nature I have been picturing in that situation and I have pondered over what to do.)

Kullervo's question shows that he thinks of himself as a future murderer. In Kullervo a conflict between the old and the new philosophy is present. He ponders what he should do. Here the basic conflict of ideas in the drama is exemplified. If Kullervo does take revenge, he becomes a murderer by the ethical standards of the new morality, and if he does not, he is not a man according to the old ideal.

Throughout the first act Kullervo feels that the moral of the society is wrong. In the initial soliloquy of the second act this feeling becomes knowledge, insight. Kullervo's ethical development provides the peripeteia of the drama:

> Tässä lakeus, jota jo kiivaasti nähdä himosin, tunkeissani läpi tiuhan metsän. Äärettömäksi sen luulin, mutta vapaasti hengitän taas ja lepään kunnes jähtyy otsani; sillä olihan metsässä kuumempi kuin tässä paistavan auringon alla.—Aurinko, pyöri kiireesti lännen alamäkeä ja päivästä päätös tee! Tätä pyytää paimen, joka loimostas ja kääntelevästä varjosta ajan kulkua mittailee. Varjo lännestä itään kiertyy, päinvastoin sinun tarhas juoksua, joka koillisesta alkaa ja päättyy luoteiseen, piirtäen avaruuteen ankaran kaaren. Heleä loimo, sinä kultaisia säteitäs . . . Oi Kullervo! käytkö polkuja kurjan paimenen?

> (Here is the plain which I ardently desired to see, as I pushed my way through the dense forest. I thought it to be infinite, but I breathe freely again and rest until my brow cools; for it was hotter in the forest than here under the shining sun.—O Sun, roll quickly in your western descent and make an end to the day! This asks a shepherd, who measures the passing of time by your brightness and the changing shadow. The shadow turns from west to east, contrary to your course, which starts in the northeast and ends in the northwest, forming a merciless arch in space. Oh bright flame, your golden beams . . . O Kullervo! Do you walk the paths of a wretched shepherd?)

Here Kullervo for the first time sees society from a distance and his own situation in a new perspective. He brushes by a deeper insight. He starts with a request directed to the sun, but he is still a captive of his concrete, enslaved situation. The impulse which releases Kullervo's action is the episode with the knife. His only inheritance from his father is a knife, which he always carries with him, and which is also, of course, a reminder of the vengeance obligation. When the knife is broken on the stone in his bread, Kullervo's obligation is also broken:

> Tyhmästi kostit [I:n emäntä], mutta paha oli tahtos toki mua kohtaan, sinä Hiien portto; mutta koston vannon kostoa vastaan.

> (Unwise was your revenge [Ilmarinen's wife], and evil was your intention toward me, your whore of the Devil; but I swear vengeance against vengeance.)

This is a manifestation of a new insight. He is going to settle with vengeance as an institution, and this will be accomplished on society's terms, i.e., realized through vengeance.

Kullervo's insight requires total confrontation with no consideration of the consequences. The distinction between good and evil in the prevailing ethical norm system was distorted. This insight gives him relief, even joy:

> Tämänmoista jotain toivoin, ja olkoon niin, kuin vaan ilman äärtä on. Hyvä tahi paha, yhtä kaikki!

> (Something of this sort I have been hoping for, and so be it, to the full extent. Good or evil, all the same!)

Kullervo's joy is further expressed with the appearance of Sinipiika, the good fairy:

> KULLERVO: . . . Ken tulee tuossa? Ken olet sinä houru, joka kannat muotoa niin armasta ja hymyelet niin makeasti mailmalle, jonka menoa viisaan kirota täytyy?—Pois tämä muoto, tyttöseni! se ei maksa vaivaa, usko minua, ei maksa se vaivaa.

> SINIPIIKA: Murhetta nähdessäni, sen muodon kannan; mutta iloitsenpa koska täällä iloa havaitsen.

> (KULLERVO: . . . Who is coming there? Who are you, ghostly one, who carry an appearance so dear and who smile so sweetly to the world, the ways of which the wise must curse?—Away with this appearance, my girl! It is futile, believe me, it is futile.

> SINIPIIKA: When I see grief, I carry the shape of grief; but I rejoice when I see joy here.)

The clearly exhibited peripeteia of the tragedy brings about a classical hubris in Kullervo. He feels superior to others; he is the only one who has this insight. He lets Ajatar, the evil fairy, understand that she exerts no influence whatsoever over him; only because it happens to suit Kullervo's purposes is she employed to destroy the cattle. In the next scene with Nyyrikki the insight theme is again emphasized. Kullervo watches the slaughter of the cattle, thus gathering wisdom. He also claims to know how such evil is to be prevented in the future. He expresses a superficially banal proverb "Vahingosta viisastuu" (in Swedish "Av skadan blir man vis"; in English "Once bitten, twice shy"). This refers both to Ilmarinen's misfortune and to his own misadventure, especially the knife episode, which had led him to his own insight.

Kullervo's hubris makes him unsusceptible to any new considerations. He does not want to believe Sinipiika's message about his parents' existence:

> Jätä meidät, tyttöseni, ja elä tarinoillasi kostoani pilaa! Mene tiehes, valheen neito ihanassa haamussa!

> (Leave us, my girl, and do not spoil my revenge with your stories! Go away, you maiden of lies in a shape so lovely.)

In solitude after this episode Kullervo meditates why he still vacillates, but concludes instantly that the confrontation with the social morality is more important to him than possible individual happiness:

> Ei kelpaa enään tämä maa päivänpaisteelle sille, se pimeyttä, sadetta ja myrskyä tahtoo, koston myrskyä, ja sade olkoon verenvuodatus, koska metsästä käyn.

(This land is no longer good enough for that sunshine. It wants darkness, rain and storm, the storm
of revenge, and let bloodshed be the rain when I appear from the darkness of the forest as a villain.)

From the standpoint of the play's idea, it is interesting to
study the relevance of unexecuted vengeance in **Kullervo.**
The one who, next to Kullervo, has the most pressing motive for revenge is Ilmarinen, who should have avenged his
wife's murder. The drama, however, does not mention any
plans of revenge in Ilmarinen before these two men meet
by accident after Kullervo's final vengeance in the fifth
act. Kullervo is then totally crushed by feelings of guilt
and has made the decision to take his life. Ilmarinen's
grief breaks forth during this meeting, and in his bitterness
he wants to kill Kullervo. He is easily restrained, however,
by Väinämöinen's argument that he would suffer remorse
for his act and that he should note that Kullervo's appearance showed extreme despair. On the level of allegory, Ilmarinen is a figure of the future society's leaders. This is
so although he does not exact vengeance, perhaps even
thanks to his not doing so; the new social ethic did not include vengeance.

Another character in the drama who abstains from bloodshed is Kullervo's father, who did have strong motives for
taking vengeance on Untamo and his clan. However, he
chooses the less honorable alternative, flight. He flees to
solitude with his family, lives a quiet life under an adopted
name, but is unable to achieve happiness for himself or his
family. From the perspective of historical ideas this was
no solution.

Kullervo's bloody confrontation with the conventions of
the time emerges as more valuable than Kalervo's choice.
Kullervo's situation was from the very beginning complicated by his being a slave under the man whom he had to
attack. As long as he was a slave specifically under Untamo, his vengeance could never become ethically acceptable because it would only be interpreted as revolt. The
values and norms were not the same for slaves as for free
men. Society was in this respect far from equal. To this extent **Kullervo** can be considered "a play about an individual who was born free, but by fate degraded to slave."

Kullervo's slavery thus formed a crucial element in his development towards an evaluation of the values of the era.
These put strong pressure upon him, and he is forced to
weigh available alternatives. In the first act he sees only
three equally unacceptable possibilities: to continue serving Untamo, to escape, or to become a robber. Staying to
serve his enemy would be intolerable, escaping would only
result in capture, and the life of a robber appears unsatisfactory.

The infeasability of these three courses leads Kullervo to
total hopelessness. His despondency is depicted in the famous parable about the prisoner in the mountain:

> On teräsvuori, joka tuhansia penikulmia korkeut-
> een kohoaa, tuhansia tunkee syvyyteen ja sama on
> sen levyys ja pituus. Keskellä tätä vuorta, sen sy-
> dämmessä löytyy komero, niin pieni, että vanki,
> joka siellä nääntyy, tuskin kymeröissä mahtuu siinä
> istumaan, eikä läpeä niin suurta, että hyttyinen
> hengittää taitaisi, juokse tästä ulos raikkaaseen il-
> maan. Tähän kuumaan ahtauteen vanki ainiaksi
> tuomittiin, sillä kuolla ei hän saa, vaan tukahtua ik-
> uisesti täytyy, ja ikuisesti enenee kolossaan tulinen

kuumuus. Niin hän kauvas kätketyssä kammios-
saan asua saa vuosituhansien kuluessa; mutta tämä
on tuska.

(There is a mountain of steel, which rises thousands
of miles to the heights, thousands of miles it penetrates to the depths, and its width and length are
the same. In the midst of this mountain, in its heart,
there is a space so small that the prisoner who is
languishing in there can hardly sit doubled up, and
no opening, not even so big that a mosquito could
breathe, runs from there into the fresh air. To this
tight space the prisoner was sentenced forever, for
he is not allowed to die, he must suffer eternally;
and constantly in his hole the heat increases. He
must also live so in his hidden space while thousands of years pass; and this is anguish.)

In his deep despair Kullervo grabs Kimmo's throat in
order to strangle him for having committed murder, but
calms down in time. This desperate act is crucial in the development that leads Kullervo to insight about the inherent destructiveness of vengeance.

Kullervo is still a slave after being sold for practically
nothing to Ilmarinen in the first act. Kullervo's obsession
with his price as a slave emphasizes the degrading nature
of slavery. In Ilmarinen's possession Kullervo is given the
possibility of analyzing slavery as an institution without
the personal conflicts which shaped his relationship with
Untamo. Kullervo's insight in the second act came to include the injustice of slavery. This insight provided the alternative Kullervo had been seeking.

The murder of Ilmarinen's wife is irrevocably decisive for
the rest of Kullervo's life. He had decided to punish her,
but not kill her. Still, he murders her because she reacts
to his defiant manner in telling about the disaster with the
cattle by repeatedly calling him a slave:

> I:N EMÄNTÄ: Orjako näin korskailee?
>
> KULLERVO: Orja! Ellös mainittako sitä sanaa.
>
> I:N EMÄNTÄ: Miksi en, koska orjaksi merkitty
> olet ja orjana ostettu?
>
> KULLERVO: Puhees taitaa sokeaksi, hurjaksi
> mun saattaa. Vaikene, vaimo!
>
> I:N EMÄNTÄ: Minä edessäsi vaijeta? Hävytön!
> Miksi karjani menetit, sinä villisusi, peto?
>
> KULLERVO: Niin; kuin ei vaan orja.
>
> I:N EMÄNTÄ: Orja, viheliäinen orja!
>
> KULLERVO: Tuli ja leimaus! (*Lyö veitsellänsä
> I:n emäntää rintaan*) Veitseni pystyy vielä.
>
> (ILMARINEN'S WIFE: Does a slave brag like this?
>
> KULLERVO: Slave! Don't mention that word.
>
> ILMARINEN'S WIFE: Why not, since you are
> branded a slave and bought as a slave?
>
> KULLERVO: Your speech makes me blind and
> wild. Silent, woman!
>
> ILMARINEN'S WIFE: I be silent before you?
> Shameless! Why did you destroy my cattle, you
> wild wolf, beast?

KULLERVO: Yes, just as long as not a slave.

ILMARINEN'S WIFE: Slave, wretched slave!

KULLERVO: Thunder and lightning! [*Strikes Ilmarinen's wife in her breast with his knife*] My knife is still good.)

Kullervo loses control over himself upon hearing the word slave. He has not reacted to this word prior to this scene in the drama. He had as a result of his insight declared himself no longer a slave; he had decided to put himself outside society, above society. In regard to this, Kullervo's fierce reaction does not seem to have a sufficient psychological motivation. His unrepressed rage becomes more understandable in relation to the struggle of ideas in the play: he senses that she is right, that he is still a slave according to the old social norms. He lacks all other means in his struggle with the values of society than the very course he had decided to thwart, i.e., vengeance.

Another slave in **Kullervo** is Kimmo, whose destiny forms a parallel to Kullervo's. Previous research has generally considered Kimmo to be a weak character with the spirit of a slave. It is true that he accepts his slavery without struggle. He is weighed down by remorse for his murder and he is haunted by "the one buried in the marsh." When Kimmo in the first act learns from Nyyrikki that Kullervo's parents are still alive, Kimmo exacts a vow of silence from him under a threat of death. Kimmo's impetuosity in this scene has been considered to lack sufficient psychological motivation. For Kimmo, however, this is a question of "life and death," perhaps something even more important. Kimmo, who has felt his slavery to be a rightful punishment for the murder he has committed, now sees a chance to atone for his wrongdoing. By returning Kullervo to his parents, Kimmo is enabled to bring back "the one buried in the marsh." (Kimmo expresses this explicitly in the second act. The thought of "the one buried in the marsh" recurs later in the reaction of Kullervo's mother to the son's homecoming.) One of the best examples of tragic error in the drama is represented in Kimmo's necessity to confirm the accuracy of Nyyrikki's message; while Kimmo is delayed, Kullervo becomes a murderer. Kimmo grieves bitterly over this. Mistrust, which was concomitant to the degenerate morality of the time, spoiled his prospects of reconciliation.

In the fifth act Kimmo has become insane. This is a consequence of his unsuccessful mission and the destructiveness of the moral system of the old society. Kullervo's life's work is a manifestation of the nature of that destructiveness. Kalervo and his family are dead; vengeance can never be undone. The outdated ideas crush Kimmo. When one sees how destructive the norm system was, one understands the necessity of Kullervo's mission; passivity and individual withdrawal are not enough. Kimmo's words, when he believes that Kullervo is going to burn him at the stake, exhibit how fixed he is in the old ideal of the time:

KIMMO: Tapahtukoon mitä jumalissa päätetty on; mutta saata tänne tuohta sata pihtiä ja tervaksia tuhatta rekeä, sillä olenpa sitkeätä juurta enkä juuri leikin menehdy.

KULLERVO: (*Itseks*) Häntä turhaan manaan.

KIMMO: Et toki mua teurasta kuin karitsaa;

käyppäs ensin vähän rinnusteloon. (*Astuu uhaten K:voa kohden*)

KULLERVO: Mikä aikomukses?

KIMMO: (*Astuu takaisin ja sieppaa käteensä rahin, jolla uhkaa K:voa*) Sanoman ihmisten pitää: kalliisti henkensä Kimmo myi.

(KIMMO: May it be as is determined by the gods; but bring here kindling by the hundreds and logs by the thousands, for I am of tough roots and do not perish easily.

KULLERVO: (*To himself*) In vain do I call out to him.

KIMMO: You are not going to slaughter me like a lamb; let us first have a little fight. (*Steps threateningly toward K:vo*)

KULLERVO: What is your intention?

KIMMO: (*Steps back and grabs a stool and threatens K:vo with it*) People will say: in unyielding struggle Kimmo gave up his life.)

A third character in **Kullervo,** Nyyrikki, turns out to have also been a slave. He does not, however, see slavery as any problem:

Orja tahi vapaa, yhtä kaikki, kuin onnemme osaan tydymme vaan; ja suruton on orjan elo.

(Slave or free, all the same, as long as you are content with your share of luck; and carefree is the life of a slave.)

Throughout the play Nyyrikki is depicted as being totally characterless. He is cowardly, cajoling, and dishonest, indeed amoral. Nyyrikki is blind and deaf to the world of ideas.

Thus in the three slaves in the drama Kivi has shown diverse aspects of slavery. After his physical liberation, i.e., after the murder of Ilmarinen's wife, Kullervo's slavery becomes a slavery under the outdated norms and values which he is combatting. This kind of slavery drives him to despair. When Kalervo, upon learning of Ainikki's death, calls Kullervo a branded beast, Kullervo reacts very strongly:

Tänne mustat pilvet joka ilmasta ja kauhistuksen yö, jossa huhkaimena Kullervo kuolon sanomia huutelee! Kuulkaat, kuulkaat mitä teille ilmoitan: Tyttärenne Ainikki, joka eksynyt oli, itsensä vihasen kosken kuohuun viskasi, ja nieli hänen ahne pyörre. . . . Taiten juuri hän itsensä pyörteen kitaan syöksi, ja kuin viattomuutensa hän kadotetuksi, näki, sentähden läksi hän, hourupäinen, Ahden jyrisevään kartanoon. . . . Pimeys tulkoon pimeyden päälle! Loppuun asti teille asian kertoa tahdon, ja kuulu se näin: Hän, joka immen päälle iski niinkuin kotka ja väkisten neitsyyttänsä kunniankruunun vei, ken oli hän? Kalervon ainoa poika hän oli. Juuri niin; miksi tuijottelette minua noin?

(Come, dark clouds from all directions and the night of horror, where Kullervo as an owl howls the message of death! Listen to this, listen to what I tell you: Your daughter Ainikki, who had gone astray, threw herself into the raging rapids, and was swallowed by the greedy whirlpool. . . . Knowingly indeed she rushed into the throat of the rapids, and when she saw herself deprived of her innocence, this is why she left, the mad one, for the turbulent domains of Ahti. . . . May darkness come upon darkness! I will tell the story to its end, and this is how it goes: The one who attacked the virgin like an eagle and took her virginity by force, who was he? The only son of Kalervo was he. Yes, that is right; why are you staring at me like that?)

The tragedy in this scene touches Kalervo as well as Kullervo. Kalervo sees the consequence of vengeance carried to the second generation; he realizes that he is to blame for Kullervo's tragic fate. Even Kullervo has realized this. He fully understands that he is a victim of the conflict for which the previous generation is responsible. This insight brings about the fierce outbursts in these two men. In a sense, Kullervo's revelation is a revenge against his father.

Still, in the very last scene of the tragedy Kullervo motivates his killing of Ilmarinen's wife by the fact that she has called him a wretched slave. Kullervo dies with the insight that during his whole life he has been a victim of the old philosophy of life, especially of the code of vengeance. His only consolation is that his idealism will result in a new era with other ideas.

Kullervo perceives in the end that the duty of vengeance now is laid upon him, the last representative of the outdated moral system. Since he is a victim, the only course left to him is to remain a victim and sacrifice his own life.

If *Kullervo* is seen as a historical drama of ideas, concepts of time become important in the structure of the play. Time is experienced as something magical in *Kullervo.* Kullervo's soliloquy in the beginning of the second act is crucial in relation to the concept of time: he speaks of the sun as measuring time and as tracing a merciless arch in the universe. The sun drives away the shadows with its power, in the direction opposite to its own course. The shadows are thus thrust into the past. Kullervo's incomplete request to the sun is quoted above. After his insight he once again directs a request to the sun, to the day, quickly to leap to evening, i.e., quickly to complete its task.

Unfortunate events are often referred to as dark memories from days long past, e.g., Kullervo's recollection of his murder of Ilmarinen's wife the following night and Kimmo's line at the end of the play: ". . . sumea on tämä tarina, mutta kaukaisimpia aikoja se kertoilee" (". . . dark is this story, but it tells about the most ancient times").

Reactions of this nature most frequently consist of a wish to make certain acts undone by reversing time, e.g., Kullervo in the first act believes that he could have prevented the development which the social ethic has taken:

> Voimallinen aika, lievitä sun kankaastas se verinen kude, joka kahdesta veljestä siihen revittiin! Käännä pyöräs ympäri ja kiiritä se entisyyteen takaisin, kunnes lapsena, mutta tällä tiedolla, kotovuoren harjanteella seisoisin ja ravistelisi kihariani pohjatuuli! Siinä pyöräs pysähtyä saisi ja kääntyä taasen pyörimään ääretöntä avaruutta; mutta tietäisinpä silloin kuinka häntä seuraisin.

> (Powerful Time, loosen from your fabric that bloody cloth left there by two brothers. Turn your

wheel back to the past to a moment when, still a child but with this knowledge, I would be standing on the slope of my home-hill with the North Wind rustling my curls! Then your wheel could stop and begin turning again through infinity; but at least then I should know how to follow him.)

Even Untamo goes back in time. He does not accept any guilt, but reacts in the first act only by thinking of the past and the vengeance which awaits him:

> Kahdenpuolin riehui vaino veljesten välillä ja rauhaa toinen toiselle ei suonut. Ne ajat ja riidat veriset muistan ja tahtoisinpa kaikki nyt toisin päättyneeksi.

> (On both sides did the discord rage between the brothers and one did not leave the other in peace. Those times and bloody quarrels I remember and now I wish that everything had ended differently.)

When Kullervo in the fourth act already is on his way to his final vengeance, Untamo utters:

> Voi, että synnyin tänne minä, minä Untamoinen, joka heimoni veren vuodattanut olen ja paljon verta vierasta vielä!—Miksi en sovinnon äänelle korviani kallistanut, ennenkuin riitamme sai tuon verisen muodon!—Mutta eteenpäin kulkee kaikkivaltias aika.

> (Oh, that I was born to this earth, I Untamo, who have shed the blood of my family and much foreign blood too!—Why did I not lend my ears to the voice of peace before our feud became bloody!—But forward goes almighty time.)

These quotes imply that Untamo knows that the old time soon has to yield to a new time. Even Kiili, Untamo's servant and intimate friend, realizes this. He therefore suggests that they make the most of the old values:

> KILLI: Jonakuna pimeänä yönä saa Ruotus [eräs naapuri] ja pöyhkeä ämmänsä meiltä näpsäyksen, joka heidät ainiaksi nukuttaa, mutta aarteensa ovat meidän. . . .

> UNTAMO: Suuri, Kiili, siinä kohdassa, jo velkani on.

> KIILI: Velat uudet vanhat mielestämme saattakoot.

> UNTAMO: Tunnenpa puheen lahjasi.

> KIILI: Tosin elonpyörämme alesmäkeä jo kiiriskelee, mutta ehtooseen on vielä matkaa. Taidammehan elää vuosia vielä, hyvin huikeasti viisi ja kaksikymmentä, joka on aika kappale ajan tiellä.

> UNTAMO: Sanotpa jotain.

> KIILI: Mutta jos nyt viisaita olemme, niin hauskasti kuljemme tämän matkan.

> (KIILI: Some dark night Ruotus [a neighbor] and his arrogant wife will get a lesson from us, which will put them to sleep forever, but their treasures will be ours. . . .

> UNTAMO: Large, Kiili, is my debt in this.

KIILI: Let new debts put old ones out of our minds.

UNTAMO: I know your eloquence.

KIILI: It is true that the wheel of our lives is turning downwards, but there is still some distance to evening. We may still have years left, quite possibly five and twenty, which is a considerable distance on the path of time.

UNTAMO: There is something to that.

KIILI: But if we now are wise, then we will walk this journey joyfully.)

Untamo's reservations concerning his own debt can be cancelled by new debts, a series which shows the increasing evil of a vendetta: vengeance contains an inherent tendency to accumulate.

The antipodes of the sun image are darkness and night. The night after the murder Kullervo claims that he no longer measures time according to the previous criteria; Kullervo is no longer led by the sun, by the right. *Kullervo* is full of references to mist, dusk, darkness, and night. Interestingly enough Kullervo emphasizes the bright sunshine in the crucial soliloquy in the second act, while the home people mention the same day as being so cloudy and gloomy that one can hardly tell day from night.

Dawn, the time when darkness yields to light, symbolizes to Kullervo the new time and the perishing of the old. He makes four explicit references to dawn in the drama. Remembering his victim, Ilmarinen's wife, Kullervo says that her forehead beamed like dawn. Kullervo realized only afterwards that she was more a proponent of new than old ideas, and that her behavior was caused by him. During his first arrival at his parents' home Kullervo erroneously takes the rising moon for morning dawn; the utopia Kalervo had built was merely an illusion. Some moments later Kullervo interprets his mother's loving eyes as the dawn, which surprises him. He very soon concludes, however, that his personal happiness no longer meant anything to him, but that the main thing was a higher mission. There, dawn was still far away.

Kullervo's last words agree with the dawn as an image of a new time. He now sees the true dawn arriving in the east, which he, however, will not live to see himself, but which is his achievement, the very fulfillment of the purpose of his life. The dawn is the symbol of his true insight. The following line by Väinämöinen confirms this:

> Kas lempeätä muotoa luonnon: hymyen nousee aurinkoinen ja hongat kankaalla punertavat; kaikki hengittävi rauhaa.
>
> (Look at the mild form of nature: smilingly the sun rises and the trees on the heath turn red; everything breathes peace.)

Dawn, though in the form of reflected evening light, is mentioned by Kullervo at the time of his murder of Ilmarinen's wife:

> Naisen kauniin murhasin ja tapahtui tämä illan ikävässä hämärässä, ja ehtooruskosta silloin paistoivat idän vuorien tutkaimet. Sen hetken muistan.
>
> (This beautiful woman I murdered and it happened in the dreary dusk of evening, and from the evening sunset the hilltops in the east were shining. That moment I will remember.)

Additional references to time and what it symbolizes are, e.g., Kullervo's statement when he learns that his family is still alive that this world is not worthy of such happiness, Kullervo's referring to his father's dress armor as being rusty, and Tiera's and Nyyrikki's mutual opinion that this world is full of deception.

Perhaps the most explicit reference in the play to the transition from the old to the new outlook on life are the words Väinämöinen utters in the final scene, when he first sees Kullervo:

> VÄINÄMÖINEN: Mies, miksi seisot siinä niinkuin jäätynyt, kuin ales pilvistä viskattu ja ensi kerran näkisit, kuinka eletään alhaalla täällä? Onko henkeä sinussa?
>
> KULLERVO: Pilvistä.
>
> (VÄINÄMÖINEN: Man, why are you standing there as if frozen, like one thrown down from the clouds and who for the first time sees how people live down here? Is there life in you?
>
> KULLERVO: From the clouds, yes.)

Kullervo is at this time the only representative left of the outdated society in the new era which is beginning.

The play *Kullervo* does not give clear definitions of the ideas it employs, particularly the new ones. We learn that vengeance, slavery, deception, and distrust are elements of the old social morality. Some indications of new ideas are, however, given in the text. The ideal of manliness changes. For instance, Ilmarinen's wish of peace to Kullervo's memory is mentioned as manly by Väinämöinen, i.e., a kind of Christian forgiveness is included. This also implies that a person is not judged solely on the grounds of his actions, but that the mind is the decisive factor. This criterion was already employed by Ilmarinen's wife, who gave Kullervo a chance to say that the devastation of her cattle was an accident, in which case the punishment would have been milder. Ilmarinen's refraining from taking vengeance on Kullervo in the end is a sign of a similar judgment. The new ideal of manliness is based on equality, as is indicated by Väinämöinen's remark that all his men be helpful in burying Kullervo. The need for organized justice and respect for human life is also shown by Väinämöinen's saying that he does not want to proclaim Kullervo an outlaw.

Another sign of change is the fact that the only crime Kullervo is concerned about at the end of the play is the incest he had committed, a crime against nature, even in the moral system of the new society.

The attitudes of the characters thus form a pattern illustrating diverse ways of responding to the transitional problems of the era. An interpretation of *Kullervo* as a historical drama of ideas proves justified. It also casts new light on certain assertions in previous *Kullervo* studies. *Kullervo* turns out to be a tragedy with a dominant conflict of ideas. Both the protagonist and the antagonist are represented within Kullervo's character. Because of family loyalty and traditional ties Kullervo becomes a victim of two struggling powers, which were manifested in the fued between Untamo and Kalervo. Kullervo is forced to choose between the old and the new moral in this time of transition. Kullervo and Untamo are not protagonist and antagonist respectively in the correct sense of the words.

Kullervo realizes that the ideas of the old value system are antiquated and corrupt. The necessity of a confrontation provides Kullervo with insight into the evil of vengeance. This necessity is further accentuated after Kullervo had found Kalervo's escapist solution unacceptable. The tragic conflict involves Kullervo as a human being whose suffering and feeling of guilt assume enormous proportions. It is hardly just to say that Kullervo departs from his main objective.

Charges of a loose and disorganized composition in *Kullervo* have generally been based on Kivi's introducing Tiera and his men in the fourth act and Väinämöinen and his men in the final act. As illustrations of the conflict of ideas, however, these characters show on the one hand the inadequacy of the old norm system and on the other the advent and content of the new value system. "The problem of the fourth act" ceases to be a problem.

Väinämöinen is referred to in the first act as representing a positive factor. The historical idea structure of the play is reenforced in a natural way in the last act by letting Väinämöinen and his men show the meaningfulness of Kullervo's work. They are forerunners of a new time with new ideas. This is the factor of reconciliation in the tragedy. For Kullervo there is no atonement, he is the reconciliatory victim. This is emphasized in his dialogue with Kimmo in the fourth act:

> Kimmo, elä mua härsyttele.—Taitaisinpa sanoa, että kaiken tämän saatoit matkaan sinä. . . . Asioja toki kertoilit, jotka väkisinkin synnyttävät koston himon. . . . Enhän päälles tahdo vierittää, vaan tänne kaikki virratkoon.
>
> (Kimmo, do not arouse my temper.—I could say that all this was brought about by you. . . . You did tell me things which cannot but arouse the lust to avenge. . . . Yet I do not wish to evade anything, but let everything flow to me.)

Kimmo has functioned as a transmitter of the information which, according to the old norm system, required vengeance, but Kullervo now appreciates that neither Kimmo nor other persons were to blame, and that his mission is to be the redeeming victim.

This analysis is based solely on the text of Kivi's *Kullervo.* It becomes obvious that the *Kalevala* and Cygnaeus's analysis have had considerable influence on previous study. Both the *Kalevala* and Cygnaeus do exhibit a Kullervo whose deliberations are dictated by purely individualistic emotions and ambitions; a Kullervo, born free, but by fate degraded to slave, who pursues a struggle for personal liberation. Kivi has from the Kullervo myth created a historical drama of ideas of notable originality. (pp. 269-88)

Kivi presents his hero as a basically social human being. The concepts of right and wrong, good and evil appear in the Aristotelian sense as values in a given era, in a given society; ethical norms, ideas of good and evil are anchored in the community.

In Kivi's main work, *Seven Brothers,* the brothers feel their society to be hostile and unjust. They mature during their ten years outside society to the insight that the problem lay not in society, but in themselves, in their egocentricity and failing sense of responsibility. The brothers grow into socially mature members of society. In a similar way Kullervo felt, in the first act, that his society was unjust and inadequate. In *Kullervo,* however, society is revealed as wrong. Kullervo also overcomes his strong egocentricity and sees the degenerate elements of the norm system of that society. Kullervo's idealism is founded on a sense of social and moral responsibility, which requires a definitive confrontation with the old philosophy. This sense of responsibility in Kullervo leads to the social paradox: the stronger the social sense of responsibility, the deeper his isolation from society. It is this idealism in Kullervo which makes the tragic conflict possible in the drama, and makes of him a true tragic hero. (p. 288)

> *K. Börje Vähämäki, "Aleksis Kivi's 'Kullervo': A Historical Drama of Ideas," in* Scandinavian Studies, *Vol. 50, No. 3, Summer, 1978, pp. 269-91.*

Pertti Lassila   (essay date 1984)

[*In the following essay, Lassila traces the critical reception of* Seven Brothers *in Finland and Germany.*]

Manfred Peter Hein, a German poet, translator and literary scholar, who has lived in Finland for many years, looks at *Seitsemän veljestä* from an angle rare in Finnish literary criticism. His new study, *Die Kanonisierung eines Romans. Alexis Kivis 'Sieben Brüder' 1870-1980* traces the reception of *Seitsemän veljestä* and the growth of its fame from its publication, when contemporary critics awarded it a booby prize, to its inviolable status as the universally acclaimed great Finnish novel. Hein's theoretical and methodological model in his approach to his subject is the work of Hans Robert Jauss, particularly *Literaturgeschichte als Provokation der Literaturwissenschaft.*

The reception of *Seitsemän veljestä* in the German-speaking countries forms an essential part of Hein's study. Outside Finland, the novel is best-known in Germany; no less than five more or less abridged translations were published there between 1921 and 1961, and there were in addition a number [of] reprintings of which the latest appeared in 1982. This German interest in *Seitsemän veljestä* is a reflection of the strength of wider political and cultural links between Germany and Finland. An important phase in this relationship was the Finnish civil war of 1918, when the White army was supported by soldiers of the German regular army. And during the 1920s and 1930s, the ties were strengthened by the open alignment with Germany of certain key figures of the Finnish literary world.

Public reaction to *Seitsemän veljestä* was coloured for decades after its publication by the view first put forward by the philosopher J. V. Snellman in the early nineteenth century, that a Finnish literature—whose representative Kivi was—was one of the prerequisites for the birth and development of the Finnish nation state. On the novel's publication Professor August Ahlqvist, himself a poet who wrote in Finnish, gave it a damning review. His motives were complex: partly tactical, they had to do with in-

Scene from Kihlaus *staged by the summer theater of Viborg, 1920.*

ternal disagreements within the Fennomane party to which he belonged. But his central argument was that the novel gave a false picture of the Finnish nation, painting it blacker than it really was. For years all discussion of the novel and its merits centred on this question—was the book fit for its proper purpose, that is to say, was it fit to be used in the construction of the Finnish nation state?

As the new tide of national romanticism rose at the turn of the century, a new attitude to the novel began to make itself felt: the novel's great value and meaning lay in its unique Finnishness. A complete denial of value became unqualified praise. Now the novel demonstrated the innate qualities of the Finnish race, its power, its humour, its poetry and its profundity, in a way that found its equal only in the *Kalevala*. Indeed, *Seitsemän veljestä* took its place alongside the *Kalevala* as a classic of Finnish literature and as a foundation stone of Finnish culture. It was now a part of the national mythology. A work that had once been derided by critics who did not understand it was now being smothered with love. The novel was adopted as a kind of touchstone of Finnishness: in the civil war, the White army of farmers and landowners was seen to be exemplifying the virtues and power of the brothers, while the defeated Reds could be seen as characteristically Finnish personifications of the raw strength and social rebellion

also found in the seven men. In the Second World War, too, the tenacity and courage of the Finnish soldiers was compared to the same qualities as they appeared in the brothers.

Academic literary scholarship took a positivist, biographical approach, centring on the analysis of sources, and the novel's unique Finnishness appears again and again as an unquestioned aesthetic tenet. Such aspects as the novel's nature as a work of art, as a piece of world literature that rose above its national origins, were left aside. Hein, who has a profound knowledge of Finnish cultural history and of Kivi's work, has an extra advantage: he is a foreigner, and the distance this gives him from his subject allows him to take a detached look at the way in which Finnish scholars and critics have wrestled with their changeling over the years.

This emphasis of the Finnishness of the novel has had some long-term repercussions on its reception in Germany. The affinity between Finland and the Germanic races, felt so keenly on both sides, was the source of German interest in Kivi. This interest was allied to the 'Heimat' movement in literature and the approval with which the Nazis viewed anything 'völkisch'. That *Seitsemän veljestä* was seen in this light has since become burdensome; one consequence was that any possibility of seeing it as a universal work of art was lost. Finland and its literature were one, in the eyes of the novel's German readers, and Finnish literature was *Seitsemän veljestä.* The book was put to work to proclaim health, strength and closeness to the land as an antidote to the canker of Western civilisation that was being spread by the new literature. The Germans were not entirely to blame for this interpretation; in Finland the same sentiments were enthusiastically taken up by, among others, the influential academic and poet V. A. Koskenniemi, who was well known for his Nazi sympathies. The most important of the German scholars of Kivi's novel was Oskar Loerke, who alone among his colleagues recognised its universal nature.

It is perhaps not surprising that neither the examination of the social criticism contained in *Seitsemän veljestä* nor its liberation from the national mythology took place before the end of the Second World War. Study of the novel advanced quickly once the old-fashioned tradition of biographical analysis was abandoned. All the same, Manfred Peter Hein's study shows that the results achieved by Kivi scholarship so far are only the first fruits of the disengagement from the positivist, biographical and nationalist research tradition. Hein's *Die Kanonisierung eines Romans* is a valuable and timely challenge to all those engaged in study of *Seitsemän veljestä.* (pp. 105-06)

> *Pertti Lassila, "Seven Brothers in Germany," in* Books from Finland, *Vol. XVIII, No. 3, 1984, pp. 105-06.*

Pekka Lounela   (essay date 1984)

[*In the following excerpt, Lounela discusses Kivi's career as a dramatist.*]

The organic unity of written and performed drama is today considered an unarguable truth especially in acting circles. The work of Aleksis Kivi appears, on this view, anachronistic to say the least: he created the basis of Finnish drama at a time when the indigenous Swedish-language theatre was taking its first faltering steps and theatre in Finnish was not even dreamed of. And more: his most important works still inspire interpretation after interpretation, and audiences continue to flock to see his plays. (p. 107)

Kivi drew his education as a dramatist from Aristophanes, Shakespeare, Molière, Holberg, Schiller, Lessing and some lesser playwrights among his own contemporaries. It appears, to judge by the results, that he had the capacity to distil from them what was dramatically essential, and to reject the rest. His technical abilities developed to span an impressive range from the wildest farce to the deepest tragedy or the most tender lyricism.

In writing plays Kivi was consciously creating drama. He realised the importance of a gripping plot and its development through characters and incidents. All the same, he often left the structure relatively open and permitted himself to diverge from formal unity, allowing the plot, for instance, to evolve naturally into a many-layered tangle.

Stage directions and dramatic hints in the manuscripts indicate that Kivi was in the habit of imagining the staging and direction of his plays as he wrote. He had formed his own independent concept of drama: he grasped the freedom offered by the example of Shakespeare, but often contented himself, particularly in his miniature plays, with a strict and disciplined form that, in the best of them—plays such as *Kihlaus* (*The Engagement*) and *Leo ja Liina* (*Leo and Liina*)—recalls the short story.

It is known that Kivi wrote fourteen plays, of which two are no longer extant and two are unfinished. *Seitsemän veljestä* itself contains a great deal of dramatic material; it could almost be called a dialogue novel, since the characters and the situations in which they find themselves are developed almost exclusively through dialogue. Kivi's artistic interests, therefore, lay principally in drama, although in his poetry and epic, just as in his drama, he transcended the traditional divisions between the genres; one of his best stories, 'Härkä-Tuomo' ('Bull-Thomas') is an extended poem, and in his plays one encounters jewels of poetry.

The bitterest disappointment of Kivi's literary career occurred at the publication of *Seitsemän veljestä,* when a number of his former supporters appeared uncertain of the novel's literary merit, and were reluctant to defend it against the rough treatment it received at the hands of August Ahlqvist. By this stage he was no stranger to such disappointments; his career as a dramatist had already suffered a number of setbacks.

His star had begun to rise with a critical award for *Kullervo* in 1864, and it reached its zenith when his *Nummisuutarit* (*Heath Cobblers,* 1866) beat *Salamiin kuninkaat* (*The Kings of Salamis*) by J. L. Runeberg—an established writer, later to be hailed as Finland's national poet, who wrote in Swedish—in competition for a government prize in 1864. But his third full-length play, *Karkurit* (*The Fugitives,* 1867), was disparaged by his own circle of friends: surely, they felt, it was impossible for the ill-educated son of a country tailor to write a play concerning the lives of the aristocracy?

Why did Kivi attempt such a thing? He must surely have been aware of his own limitations where such a subject was concerned, and of the risks involved. Perhaps, conscious that he was at the height of his creative powers, he wanted to overstep the bounds of the category in which his previous plays had placed him, 'the country realist'. Certainly he was in danger of being classified as such after the success of *Kullervo,* in which his choice of subject—a retelling of one of the major tales of the *Kalevala*—was very much in the prevalent spirit of Finnish nationalism; both *Nummisuutarit* and the irreproachable masterpiece of the one-act *Kihlaus* were cast in the same mode of Finnishness. Kivi wanted to demonstrate that he could handle with equal sovereignty a more universal theme.

His friends, however, continued to disagree; though here the fact that many of them had attempted similar subjects, and failed, is perhaps to the point. The author of *Nummisuutarit* was not, however, content to take their advice. He was shown his proper place when his text was allocated to the German-born philologist Julius Krohn—and this at a time when Kivi was single-handedly raising the expressive power of the Finnish language to unprecedented heights.

There was also an incident that humiliated Kivi both as a writer and as a man. Happening upon a newspaper account of an incident in the war between Bavaria and Prussia, he set to work enthusiastically and produced a didactic farce on the consequences of excessive drinking in the army, called *Olviretki Schleusingenissä* (*Beer-Drinking Trip in Schleusingen*). He invited his friends to a reading; but unfortunately he had drunk a great deal of beer before they arrived, and the reading came to nothing. It is only recently that the play itself has been recognized as unsurpassed in its genre.

The only one of Kivi's plays performed during his lifetime was a biblical drama by the title of *Lea.* It was a great success—but the credit was claimed by its producer, Kaarlo Bergbom, whose ambition was to become the founder of Finnish theatre, and his star, the Swedish actress Charlotte Raa. It seems likely that Kivi himself was not present at his play's opening on 10 May 1869.

Kivi spent his last years completing *Seitsemän veljestä.* After *Karkurit* he wrote a number of plays, mainly in the hope that by doing so he might earn some money from having them printed for the use of amateur dramatic groups. He was disappointed. The only more extended piece he produced during this period was a play set in Italy, entitled *Canzio;* and it met with an even more ignominious fate than had *Karkurit*—it was buried among the papers of the very same theatrical expert and impresario, Bergbom.

To complete his humiliation, Kivi was forced to spend his last days struggling with what was in effect a commission: a 'small but noble tragedy' called *Margareta,* which had been suggested to him by his friends Bergbom and Emil Nervander. He was, in short, required to rework someone else's material. It was a task that he found both foreign and repugnant.

Despite the amendments suggested by Bergbom, nothing came of the play. As he worked on, Kivi asked repeatedly whether it was likely to be staged, without—judging from his letters—ever receiving a clear reply. Thus, even after the success of *Lea,* he was made to feel the precariousness of his position; Bergbom, if anyone, after all, should have been able to promote a specially commissioned work from his protégé.

Even in such extremity, however, Kivi's dramatic instinct did not desert him. For the end of *Margareta* he composed a poetic farewell that remains among the best that Finnish drama has produced. (pp. 108-12)

Pekka Lounela, "The Stages of Aleksis Kivi,"
in Books from Finland, *Vol. XVIII, No. 3,*
1984, pp. 107-12.

FURTHER READING

Review of *Seven Brothers,* by Alexis Kivi. *The Bookman* LXIX, No. 3 (May 1929): 311.

    Positive review of Alex Matson's translation of *Seven Brothers.*

Kronenberger, Louis. "A Finnish Classic of Elemental Quality." *New York Times Book Review* (10 February 1929): 7.

    Reviews Alex Matson's translation of *Seven Brothers* and describes the plot and characters of the novel.

Laitinen, Kai. "From the Forest to the City: Great Tradition in Finnish Prose." In *Snow in May: An Anthology of Finnish Writing, 1945-1972,* edited and translated by Richard Dauenhauer and Philip Binham, pp. 21-8. Rutherford, N. J.: Associated University Presses, 1978.

    Discusses Finnish prose, demonstrating how *Seven Brothers* influenced later Finnish novels in "choice of setting, handling of character, and style."

———. "Aleksis Kivi, 1834-1872: The Man and His Work" and "Kivi the Poet: Introduction." *Books from Finland* XVIII, No. 3 (1984): 100-04, 114-17.

    Biographical and critical introduction to Kivi's works and an introduction to Kivi's poetry that includes a French translation of "Sydämeni laulu" ("Chanson de mon coeur") and an English translation of "Karhunpyynti" ("The Bear Hunt").

Review of *Seven Brothers,* by Alexis Kivi. *The New Republic* LVIII, No. 745 (13 March 1929): 106.

    Praises Alex Matson's translation of *Seven Brothers.*

Rubulis, Aleksis. "Aleksis Kivi: *Seven Brothers.*" In his *Baltic Literature: A Survey of Finnish, Estonian, Latvian, and Lithuanian Literatures,* pp. 20-3. Notre Dame, Ind.: University of Notre Dame Press, 1970.

    Discusses *Seven Brothers* and Kivi's other works in relation to Romanticism in Finland.

Strunsky, Rose. "Play Boys of the North." *New York Herald Tribune Books* 5, No. 21 (10 February 1929): 3-4.

    Favorable review of Alex Matson's translation of *Seven Brothers.*

José Joaquín Fernández de Lizardi

1776-1827

Mexican novelist, essayist, poet, pamphleteer, and dramatist.

Esteemed as his country's first novelist, Lizardi was a popular writer and notorious political activist in Mexico during the early nineteenth century. While once famous for numerous hortatory essays and pamphlets, he is best remembered today for his picaresque novel *El periquillo Sarniento* (*The Itching Parrot*), which couches his deep concern for the moral and political stability of Mexico in a spirited account of a young man's misadventures.

Lizardi was born in Mexico City into a proud but impoverished Creole family. Encouraged by his parents to become a man of letters, a pursuit they deemed commensurate with his Spanish heritage, Lizardi received an education typical of that of the upper classes of Mexico. In 1793 he entered the University of Mexico, where he studied physics, philosophy, and rhetoric. Unable to finance the remainder of his education after his father's death, Lizardi left the university in 1798 without completing a degree. Lizardi's university studies coincided with the onset of the French Revolution, a time during which Mexican scholars were reacting to the European Enlightenment. This philosophical movement, in championing science, reason, and humankind's ability to control its destiny, inspired Mexico's desire for independence from Spain. Lizardi's espousal of these new ideas is evident in the liberal political beliefs that formed an integral part of his life and writings. Katherine Anne Porter, in her introduction to *The Itching Parrot,* remarked that Lizardi's career "was quite literally created by a movement of history."

Little is known about the next decade of Lizardi's life, but by 1811 he had begun publishing poetry and pamphlets in Mexico City. One year later he founded the periodical *El pensador mexicano* ("The Mexican Thinker"), a name which became Lizardi's pseudonym. In didactic articles addressed to Mexico's working class, "The Mexican Thinker" strongly protested Spanish control of the Mexican government, accused its officials of corruptness, and advocated insurrection. In December of 1812, Lizardi was incarcerated for publishing these "incendiary pamphlets." After a seven-month prison term, he agreed to refrain from writing attacks on the government, and his next publications advised his readership on civic improvements and social reform. During this time, Lizardi also began to write fiction, and his 1816 novel *The Itching Parrot,* although replete with social commentary, became popular for its entertaining plot and characterizations. As revolution against Spain became imminent, Lizardi returned to writing insurgent pamphlets. In 1821 he joined the forces of the military leader Augustin de Iturbide as the publisher of literature propagandizing Mexican independence. He and his press followed Iturbide's troops to Mexico City, where, on September 21, independence was won and Iturbide was made head of a provisional government before assuming the title of emperor in 1822. Characteristic of Lizardi's reformist nature, his next pamphlets questioned the legitimacy of Iturbide's leadership. Lizardi's controversial essays covered such topics as his skepticism of papal infallibility and his defense of freemasonry. He continued to publish pamphlets on religious, political, and social topics until he died in 1827 of tuberculosis.

Although Lizardi was known to his contemporaries primarily as a pamphleteer, subsequent critical recognition of his works centers on *The Itching Parrot,* his only work to be published in English translation. In addition to its importance as the first Mexican novel, *The Itching Parrot* is often commended as a successful example of the Spanish picaresque, as an expression of concern for the political and moral condition of the Mexican middle class, and as a portrayal of common life that anticipated the realist fiction that flourished in the late nineteenth century. *The Itching Parrot* is an episodic chronicle that relates in plain language and vivid detail the misadventures of a young rogue (or "picaro") while satirizing social conventions and the caste system. The protagonist, who is known as the "Parrot," wanders without direction: he attends and then quits the university, joins a monastery, is thrown into prison and is later released, apprentices himself to a succession of trades, and, finally, in an act not typical of the picaresque hero, repents his purposeless wandering and becomes a model citizen. The Parrot's mishaps are the humorous element in Lizardi's satire of an economic class of Mexican people that he considered lazy and hypocritical and an educational system that he saw as ineffective. The novel's criticisms, however, are not always tempered with humor and appear in digressive, moralizing passages which many critics maintain diminish the artistic aspects of the novel. At the same time, critics recognize that Lizardi never intended to achieve artistry in the novel form, but rather sought to advance his reformist principles in a more entertaining and less controversial manner than that of his political pamphlets. Moreover, *The Itching Parrot* is considered a significant precursor of literary realism, and Lizardi is often praised for his vivid and revealing descriptions of Mexican culture. Summarizing Lizardi's strengths as a novelist, Carlos González Peña has stated that "He is quick to see the depths as well as the surfaces of things: he reproduces atmosphere, creates types, describes episodes pleasingly; and, though he does not stir the reader deeply, he is interesting, convincing, and humorous. For this reason, [*The Itching Parrot*] is incomparable as a picture of that epoch. It is the best museum of Mexican customs during the decline of the viceregal period."

PRINCIPAL WORKS

El periquillo Sarniento (novel) 1816
  [*The Itching Parrot,* 1942]
Fabulas del pensador mexicano (fables) 1817
Noches tristes y día alegre (novel) 1818
La Quixotita y su prima (novel) 1818-19

+*Don Catrín de la fachenda* (novel) 1820
Obras. 10 vols. (fables, poetry, essays, and novels) 1963

*These works were not published in their entirety until 1831.

+This work was not published in its entirety until 1832.

Jefferson Rea Spell   (essay date 1931)

[*Spell was an American educator and critic noted for introducing Mexican literature as a scholarly concern to American universities. In the following excerpt, reprinted from his 1931 dissertation,* The Life and Works of José Joaquín Fernández de Lizardi, *he offers an analysis of Lizardi's poetry, drama, and fiction.*]

In relation to the whole output of his pen, the literary work of Fernández de Lizardi is limited in extent; yet it includes poetry, drama, and fiction, some of which has attained more than national fame. All of his verse would not fill more than one fair-sized volume; less than a half dozen of his poems are cast in dramatic form; and his novels are limited to four, even including *Noches tristes,* which scarcely merits such a classification. Yet it is this small contribution which must be studied, carefully and impartially, if the work of the man is to be understood, or his literary importance determined.

Lizardi's career as a poet probably began in 1808 with the commonplace poem written in celebration of the accession of Ferdinand VII to the throne; it reached its zenith in 1811 and 1812 while he was attracting much attention by issuing his poetic contributions in pamphlets to be sold on the streets; but he continued to write incidental poetry until his death. Some of this appeared in the many periodicals and prose pamphlets that he published, and some is to be found in his novels, especially in *El periquillo* and *La Quixotita.* His other poetical work known today includes a *pastorela* and an *auto;* a collection of fables; a volume of verse entitled *Ratos entretenidos,* in which he republished many of the poems that he had written in 1811 and 1812; a second part which he added to *El negro sensible,* a melodrama by Comella; and several monologues written to be recited on the stage.

In Lizardi's poetical contribution as a whole, there is great variety both in theme and in the verse form employed. A classification of his poetical works according to themes treated reduces them more or less to the seven following divisions: (1) poems in which types of society are satirized; (2) fables; (3) light or jocose verse; (4) poems on various political issues of the day; (5) dramatic attempts; (6) religious poems; and (7) translations from classical writers. Among the verse forms used are sonnets, *romances, romancillos, romances heroicos, décimas, letrillas, silvas, quintillas, redondillas, seguidillas, endechas reales, cuartetas,* and octaves.

Of Lizardi's satiric verse, most of which was written in 1811 and 1812, one of the most striking features is his keen observation of the life then existent in the Mexican capital. He derived, it is true, much inspiration from [the seven-

teenth-century Mexican poet] Quevedo; but the abuses, errors, vices and follies that he reproves or ridicules were characteristic of the society that he saw about him. . . . In **"Busque Vd. quien cargue el saco, que yo no he de ser el loco,"** men are warned concerning all the vices and folly that characterize womankind. A lazy woman who spends all day in bed will not make a good wife; nor will the one who marries for money; nor the coquette; nor the *trotaconventos* ["procuress"] type; nor the widow who is constantly extolling the virtues of her deceased husband. Two poems, **"Hay muertos que no hacen ruido"** and **"Hacen las cosas tan claras que hasta los ciegos ven,"** present other types that existed in the life of the capital—the girl, with a lover, who passes for a virgin; the wife who pretends to be a widow; the girl who lives with a discreet mother, without property or income, who has all the comforts of the rich; and the husband who, without an occupation, profits by the gifts which his pretty wife receives from her gentlemen friends. **"Ninguna diga quién es, que sus obras lo dirán,"** which reveals further Lizardi's hatred for all sham and pretense, ridicules those who attempt to pass for what they are not. Among such is the man of low birth who poses as a Spaniard after he has acquired wealth; the ignorant man who pretends to be learned; and the *currutaco* ["dandy"] who, without a shirt underneath, presents a bold front in his dress suit and angles for an invitation to dinner. The dishonesty that characterized certain trades and professions came in, too for its share of scorn and contempt. In **"Hacen las cosas . . . "** the merchant cheats with false weights and measures, and the notary condemns the criminal unable to bribe him with money; in **"El médico y su mula,"** a charlatan doctor prescribes for patients without looking at them as he passes through a hospital; and in **"El bando de Lucifer"** as well as in other poems, we are told how the apothecaries deceive with useless drugs. This dishonesty, which characterized every walk in life, had its source, the poet states, in the lust for money. . . . While the general purpose of his poetry won for him a few admirers, the satiric verse of Lizardi as a whole was treated unmercifully by most of the critics of the day, perhaps because they themselves were not spared the shafts he aimed at the foolish and the ignorant. When Lizardi asked one who had referred to his poetry as a disgrace to the country to criticize his work and show wherein it was so inferior, the self-appointed critic, who was probably José María Lacunza, characterized Lizardi as an unworthy imitator of Quevedo, and objected to his poetry on account of the truncated verses and rimes which required the pronunciation used in Mexico; he cited, too, instances of what he considered faulty and monotonous meter, vulgarisms, obscure words and false assertions. His later criticism of Lizardi in a fable in verse, "El piojo y las hormigas," in which a louse deceives some ants by selling them poems with sensational titles, led the budding poet to return the compliment with another fable, **"La abeja y el zángano."**

It was probably Lacunza's fable which introduced Lizardi to a form in which he soon became an adept. Some scattering fables appeared in *El pensador Mexicano* in 1813 and 1814, but not until 1817 did he publish the volume of fables which has since made his name known to all Mexican school children. Written with more care than his earlier satiric verse, these fables continue to express poignantly the author's hatred for the evil, the injustice, and moral laxity that he saw about him. There appears in a few, however, a fatalistic and hopeless attitude. For example, the improvident must suffer the consequences of their thriftlessness; the weak always lose when they contend with the strong; troubles are as numerous in this life as fleas, and painstaking work often is without its reward. In **"El herrador y el zapatero,"** the prevailing prejudice against certain trades is derided; while in **"El perro en barrio ageno"** the fact that a newcomer or a foreigner suffers the fate of a dog that wanders from his locality is lamented. As in his satiric verse, certain types are scorned or ridiculed: the talkative fool; the hypocritical skinflint who pretends compassion for a fellow-man in want; the rich man who considers himself of superior clay; the flatterer; the poor but proud boaster; and the ignorant doctor. In **"El novillo y el toro viejo"** an old bull teaches a young one worldly wisdom; in **"La paloma celosa"** the dire result of foolish jealousy is taught; and in **"La mula y el macho"** lack of harmony between man and wife is likened to that of a span of mules that do not pull well together. On the whole, moral admonition predominates. For example, young girls should guard their virtue as the rose protects itself with its thorns; if they fail to heed sound advice they are lost like butterflies that are caught in a net; the headstrong who follow a foolish caprice perish; the evildoer attempts in vain to reprove evil in others; and evil companions bring certain destruction.

Although Lizardi uses in his fables a great variety of verse forms, of which the irregular mixture of seven- and eleven-syllable lines predominates, it must be admitted that artistic finish is lacking. As a fabulist, as in much of his other work, he is primarily a moralist. The connection between the story and the precept, which in his fables, as in those of his master Samaniego, comes at the end, is often forced or slight; but as a story-teller Lizardi displays no mean ability. Many of the fables smack of originality and freshness, which is increased by local color often secured by employing Indian words. Even when Lizardi draws from Iriarte and Samaniego, he takes only a thought from which, by varying the story, by drawing a different precept or moral, or by using different animals, he sometimes evolves something new and distinctive. Such variations are, at other times, exceedingly disappointing, as, for example, in his **"La tortuga y la hormiga,"** which is the fable of the Grasshopper and the Ant. Lizardi took the fable from Samaniego, but his substitution of the Turtle for the Grasshopper is unhappy, for the latter, and not the former, has become, since La Fontaine's "La cigale et la fourmi," symbolic of improvidence. (pp. 213-19)

Aside from his fables and satiric poetry, Lizardi wrote also light, jocose verse in which the moralizing tone is less pronounced. Such is the sonnet in which he renounces the profession of writing after running afoul of the governmental authorities in 1812. Typical of this kind of poetry, but even more amusing, are some verses—two sonnets, four *octavas,* four *décimas,* and four *endechas*—in *La Quixotita y su prima,* extolling in mock-heroic style the virtues of the deceased Pamela, a little lap dog, and thereby satirizing flippantly the elaborate funeral customs of the times. In another facetious poem, **"Epitalamio,"** a mock marriage song which sounds a more personal and slightly vindictive note, Lizardi ridicules a former landlady and a conniving judge.

But this Mexican poet had no interest in light satiric verse

during those brief intervals when freedom of the press made it possible for him to devote his attention to political issues; the small amount of verse he wrote then was entirely devoted to propaganda. . . .

In a sonnet that begins, "No me digas tu patria . . . ," he expresses his belief in the universal brotherhood of man, it being, apparently, his purpose to fight the distinction that was being made in Mexico between the creoles and the Spaniards. After the absolute government was reestablished, he wrote a long satiric poem in *octavas,* praising Ferdinand VII and his newly appointed viceroy, Apodaca, and rejoicing that the revolutionists were surrendering and beseeching amnesty. In 1820 he was defending, in verse as well as in numerous prose articles, the Constitution, and again ridiculing the Inquisition. (p. 221)

Of the few attempts that Lizardi made at writing for the stage, the one that most succinctly expresses certain views that he held is the *Segunda parte* that he added to Comella's *El negro sensible,* a melodrama written against slavery, an echo, probably, of some of the French ideas that had filtered into Spain. In his *Segunda parte,* written also in *romance heroico,* and even more melodramatic than the original, he added two new characters, Enrique, a dealer in slaves, and Bunga, the wife of the slave Catul, who is the protagonist of the play. Catul expresses the sentiments of a highly civilized European; the slave owners are treacherous and inhumanly cruel and vindictive; and Doña Martina, the rich and noble Spanish lady who buys slaves only to free them, is the soul of charity and sentiment. . . . On the whole, the characters are overdrawn; the tragic situations are characterized by an overseriousness that renders them comic; and the play presents a few inane attempts at humor.

Much more poetic and imaginative than *El negro sensible* is the *Auto Mariano para recordar la milagrosa aparición de Nuestra Madre y señora de Guadalupe.* In this Lizardi makes use of one of the most famous of Mexican legends—the story of the incidents that led to the founding of the Church of Guadalupe, a few miles from Mexico City. (pp. 222-24)

In this little work, utterly different in tone and style from Lizardi's moralizing verse, there appears a small spark of true poetic and dramatic ability. The narrative, which contains elements of suspense as well as a climax, moves swiftly forward; the characters are presented with skill and understanding. (p. 225)

Two other poems—**"La gloria de México en María Santísima de Guadalupe"** (1811) and **"La muralla de México en la protección de María Santísima Nuestra Señora"** (1811)—reveal further Lizardi's devotion to the Virgin of Guadalupe. The former, in octaves, was written in celebration of the day sacred to her, while the latter, in *silvas,* likens her to a wall that gave protection to the capital when it miraculously escaped capture in 1810 at the hands of the insurgent mob under the leadership of Hidalgo. Another poem, **"Canto al glorioso protomártir San Felipe de Jesús,"** gives evidence of his pride in a saint reputed to have been born in Mexico. It recounts in octaves the parentage, early life, education, and final martyrdom in Japan, in 1597, of San Felipe de Jesús, an account of whose life, Lizardi states, he had read in the works of Fray Baltasar de Medina. It happens, too, that Lizardi's best known poem, the one taught to all Mexican children, **"Himno a la divina providencia,"** is religious in theme. This poem not only bespeaks a nature that was deeply and sincerely religious, but it contains some verse, especially the opening lines, that reach a height and grandeur seldom attained by Lizardi. . . . (p. 226)

A comparison of Lizardi's verse with that of his contemporaries reveals that it is rather typical of his age. Like much of that produced both in Spain and Mexico during the second half of the eighteenth century, it is, in the main, satiric, moralizing, and didactic. Even that which is apparently jocular in tone carries with it a seriousness of purpose from which it was impossible for the author to escape. He was ever objective, and utterly unable, as a true poet, to depict subjective ideas and impressions. A few lines, it is true, are sublime; but these are lost in a prosaic mass of verse hastily composed and entirely lacking in the euphonic and flowing qualities of true poetry. Able critics who have studied Lizardi's poetry have justly condemned it. (p. 229)

And yet, while not a real poet, Lizardi gave evidence, even in his early poems, of a peculiar ability to portray life, to sketch in picturesque fashion the figures which flitted across the Plaza Mayor of Mexico City. That ability he was to turn to more effective use in his novels, which, although limited in number, have a far greater appeal. The main interest of two of these, *El periquillo Sarniento* and *Don Catrín de la fachenda,* which are picaresque, lies in the realistic portrayal of the life of two rogues, Periquillo and Don Catrín; while the third, *La Quixotita y su prima,* portrays, in equally realistic fashion, the intimate home life of two well-to-do Mexican families. In spite of the fact that the continuity of each narrative is marred by many moralizing passages and by many criticisms of all phases of social life, especially the rearing and education of children, the popularity of the stories has been immense in Mexico ever since their publication.

All three novels present pictures of middle class life in Mexico in the early part of the 19th century—the life of Lizardi's own day; and the main theme which runs through both *El periquillo* and *Don Catrín* is the foolish pride, characteristic of that class, which refuses to regard labor as respectable or honorable. *El periquillo* has an added interest for any serious student of Lizardi, for many of the incidents recounted are unquestionably drawn from the writer's own experience. The early life of Lizardi, particularly, is recorded in detail in the life of Periquillo; here are his father and mother, his early schools and schoolmasters, his university courses, and his observation of student life. Don Catrín is a later development of Periquillo. Both these boys are represented as sons of parents in very moderate circumstances; but while the father of the former had sufficient common sense to realize that his son ought to be trained for a trade, his mother, who boasted that the blood of the Ponces, Tagles, Pintas, and Velascos ran in her veins, could not endure that her son should demean himself by engaging in such an occupation. Consequently he was sent, as a gentleman's son, to the university although he had neither an inclination for study nor any real desire to engage in a learned profession. After obtaining the degree of *bachiller,* Periquillo cast about for the profession requiring the least amount of preparation. As theology best met his requirement, he began to prepare for

the priesthood; but he wasted his time, and evil companions diverted him from his studies. The threat of his father to apprentice him to a trade drove him in desperation to entering a monastery, for anything, he thought, was preferable to tarnishing his honor by engaging in a trade. But accustomed as he was to the pleasures of the world, the rigorous life held few charms, and his stay within the walls was brief. A small inheritance left on the death of his father a few months later was quickly squandered. An escapade followed which led to his imprisonment. His release was obtained by an unscrupulous notary whose only purpose was to secure Periquillo's services as a clerk. After freeing himself from this master, our hero passed from one adventure to another, suffered dire poverty, enjoyed to the fullest such wealth as came through occasional turns of fortune, and, with it all, ran the whole gamut of masters usually found in the picaresque novel. Among these was a barber, an apothecary, a charlatan doctor, a sexton, a dishonest *subdelegado,* an upright army captain, a noble Chinese, and a rich property owner. He was really a coward at heart; he could engage in petty pilfering and stealing from a man while he was asleep; but nerve failed him in more daring undertakings. In the end, in contrast to the typical Spanish *pícaro,* he mended his ways and died a respected citizen.

Not so with Don Catrín. Unlike Periquillo, he never entered the service of any master or engaged in any honest occupation, for, to use his own words, it was against his birth and breeding to serve anyone unless it was the king himself in person. After receiving his university degree, finding himself incapable of pursuing the higher studies leading to a profession, he entered the army. Evil companions and dissolute living brought about his dismissal; after this he became an *alcahuete,* a servant in a house of ill-fame, a comic actor, and then a thief. As a result of the latter career, he was sentenced to serve a term in Morro Castle. But through it all, both his pride and cowardice are evident. Once, on being beaten by an old man whose rich but homely daughter he had tried to steal, D. Catrín threatened to come next day and show his family pedigree. As a gambler's assistant, it was his practice to steal part of the winnings. When this was discovered and a severe drubbing was his reward, he consoled himself with the thought that the gambler was of low birth and did not know how to treat those of higher rank. He did not return, however, to the gambling house; for, he observed, *catrines* have no fear of sword thrusts, but they do have a fear of drubbings. After complaining, while a convict, of the harsh treatment from which a person of his birth might rightfully expect to be exempted, and having received no further consolation than the governor's reply that a thief is never a noble and has no right to expect the privileges of one, he tore up, in disgust, his *ejecutorias,* vowing he would never depend on them again for anything. After his return to Mexico, the loss of a leg in a love affair admitted him to the ranks of the beggars—a gainful occupation he followed until his premature death as the result of intemperance.

The dominant note—false pride—which characterizes Don Catrín is also emphasized in *La Quixotita y su prima.* In the former the author lays bare the evil effects of a false system of education in the life of a boy; *La Quixotita,* on the other hand, deals with the education of girls. It, however, is more positive than either *Don Catrín* or *El per-*

iquillo; for, in addition to the destructive criticisms of the prevailing educational system that characterizes the other two works, it outlines clearly the author's notion of an ideal system to be followed in the rearing of girls. To give interest to facts that might otherwise be dry and uninteresting, Lizardi contrasts the rearing and education of two cousins, Pomposa and Pudenciana, who are daughters respectively of Dionisio Langaruta and Eufrosina Contreras, and of Rodrigo Linares and Matilde, who is the sister of Eufrosina. Dionisio, who is somewhat young, is rich, lacks force of character, is easily ruled by his wife, and given to a life of pleasure, luxury, and diversions. On the other hand, Rodrigo, the author's mouthpiece, who is a retired army officer somewhat past middle life and in moderate circumstances, is serious-minded, wise, and given to the reading of good books. The wives, young and recently married at the beginning of the story, reflect the views and inclinations of their husbands. Matilde, who follows her husband's injunctions, finds her pleasures, for the most part, at home; while Eufrosina, who is interested only in the latest styles and is a constant attendant at balls, theatres, and like diversions, lives the life of the typical society lady of the day. To each of these families a girl is born about the same time, but how different is the education given to each! Like other society women of her day, Eufrosina has a wet nurse for Pomposa, and later a nursemaid whose influence is injuries in various ways. The child is permitted to associate and become familiar with servants; they frighten her and make her superstitious with their tales of hobgoblins and ghosts. Although she is sent at a very early age to the *amiga,* or kindergarten, to memorize the catechism, her later education is limited to instruction which prepared her to embroider, to dance, to conduct herself properly in polite society, and to dress in the latest styles. Not so with Pudenciana, whose mother nurses her when she is young, whose nursemaid is chosen judiciously, whose father teaches her at home until she is five, and then sends her to an *amiga* taught by a good teacher. But her best teacher continues to be her father, who instills in her, first, a desire to read and write, and then, before permitting her to memorize the catechism, teaches her by ingenious devices its meaning. Later, still under her father's direction, she learns to read, write, and cipher correctly, becomes familiar with the main points of law that deal with inheritance and property rights, receives a training that will enable her to rear children correctly and to manage a household efficiently, and even learns a trade, that of repairing watches. The colonel advises her to confide in her parents, that men are ever ready to rob young girls of their virtue, that it is folly to rely on *alcahuetas* that lovers may send; and he gives her to understand that he will not oppose her marrying a poor man provided he be honorable and industrious. Just such a man, in time, becomes her husband; and not until she is settled in her own household, bringing up her own children as she herself had been reared, does her father die, contented with his life's work. How different is the fate of the other family! Pomposa, called "La Quixotita" as the result of her extravagances, and her mother bring financial ruin upon the weak Dionisio, who, after abandoning them for a while, is able to recoup somewhat his fortunes, and returns only to die shortly thereafter. The little money that he leaves is quickly squandered; and Pomposa, after spurning good offers of marriage in hopes of marrying a nobleman, is seduced and then marries an impostor, who is soon after arrested and imprisoned for his many crimes. Both mother and daughter then become public prostitutes, suffer imprisonment, and, in the end, die horrible deaths.

Lizardi's other novel—if it may be so called—*Noches tristes,* recounts, in realistic fashion, the trials and tribulations suffered by Teófilo, an upright and God-fearing man, on four successive nights. On the first, he is taken for a criminal and thrown into prison. Next morning, when the error is discovered, he is released only to find that his wife, on being told that her husband had been sent to Acapulco, had started for that place; he, then, in turn, sets out to overtake her. The second night finds him lost in a deep forest, in a raging storm, and with no other guide than his servant, an atheist and murderer, who meets death by falling over a precipice. The next morning Teófilo comes upon a couple who had been bound to a tree by robbers; he releases them, and aids the poor man to carry his wife, who is worn out by the exposure, to their humble home. Owing to their poverty, neither a doctor nor a priest will come to her aid; and the following night Teófilo witnesses the death of the poor woman and the despair of the husband. On the fourth night, when Teófilo enters a church for shelter, he discovers a sexton disinterring, for the purpose of robbing it, a body that had that day been buried. Fearing that the body is that of his wife, Teófilo urges the sexton to continue the work, but falls unconscious when he sees the corpse. He is then taken to the home of the sexton, and there finds not only his wife safe and well, but a kinsman, a well-to-do priest, who invites the couple to live with him and share his wealth. The last section of the work, entitled "Día alegre," recounts the happiness of Teófilo and his wife on being reunited, the sterling qualities of the good priest and various acts of charity performed by him.

Such is the action of Lizardi's four novels, all of which, if analyzed from the standpoint of the various elements that constitute narrative art, reveal many technical flaws. The plots, which are loose, consist of a series of more or less skilfully connected incidents, so entertaining in character that the reader forgets at times the injected moralizing passages whose number and length are such as to destroy the proportion and the unity of the whole. The plot structure in *El periquillo* and *Don Catrín* is that characteristic of the picaresque novel—the simplest known to fiction; each concerns itself in the main with the experiences of a single individual. In Lizardi's novels, however, is found a more complete working out of the plot than is typical of the picaresque, which as a rule ends abruptly. The regeneration of the protagonist marks a definite climax in *El periquillo,* as does the one incident that leads to the complete abandon to rascality of the main character in *Don Catrín.* The death of the protagonist, which gives in each case a sense of finality to the whole, is recounted in a final chapter written by one of his friends—a device that has not been used in any other Spanish picaresque novel known to the writer. The period embraced by the incidents recounted in these novels differs widely: *Noches tristes,* in its four or five incidents told in dialogue, covers but a short interval in the life of Teófilo; while *Don Catrín* and *El periquillo,* autobiographic in form, each trace the career of the chief character from birth to death.

A plot more complicated in structure than that of either of the foregoing novels is found in *La Quixotita y su prima,* in which two families, instead of two individuals as in many novels, are contrasted with each other. Although these families are bound to each other by close ties of blood, they hold views toward life that are as far apart as the poles of the earth. One is guided by what the author considers a sane and admirable philosophy of life, while the other is the victim of false views. In the development of this plot the author brings these two families into close contact with each other, makes clear the reactions of each to the problems confronted, contrasts the training given to the two daughters, and notes the struggles of each family to impose its views on the other. A climax is reached when the father of "La Quixotita," finding himself financially ruined by the extravagance of his wife and daughter, abandons them to seek his fortune elsewhere. From this point the action sweeps rapidly to a close. Breach after breach occurs, which makes intercourse between the two families impossible; and, in the end, peace and happiness are accorded the one whose conduct the author approves, while complete annihilation is meted out to the others; each of whom sees and acknowledges, when it is too late to mend, the error of his way. To relieve the monotony of the rather long story, the author introduces into the plot, as he does also in *El periquillo,* extraneous episodes, which he attempts to harmonize with the main thread of the story. Some of the more outstanding of these in *La Quixotita y su prima* are the description of a country wedding, a story concerning a "viejo verde," and two romantic novelettes, **"Carlota y Welster"** and **"Jacobo e Irene."**

From the standpoint of plot building, Lizardi's work is open to much criticism. His incidents, well chosen and not always unskillfully joined, would in themselves have served as the basis for an artistic production; but into what might have been a well-knit plot, he injected extraneous material which did not lend itself to artistic effects. In the midst of a description of the wedding festivities of Periquillo, he introduced a sermon four pages in length on dancing. (pp. 229-35)

It is this persistent insertion of unrelated material which prevented Lizardi's work from approaching that of a master of fiction. The didactic portion—strongly suggestive of his pamphlets in both style and content—is too extensive, too unskilfully introduced, and too loosely and inartistically connected with the incidents of the main story to permit the whole to approach the proportion, the smoothness, or the finish of a work of art.

Even less did Lizardi interest himself in the artistic details of character portrayal. The figures that he presents were those familiar to him in daily life; they belong to low and middle class society of the early 19th century rather than to the aristocracy; and they speak as those about him in Mexico City spoke. He has modified them in some cases, it is true; but this modification is due more to his reading, notably in picaresque fiction, than to his imagination. In three of the novels—*Noches tristes, El periquillo* and *Don Catrín*—the story is woven about one central character, but in *La Quixotita* there are three—the colonel, Eufrosina, and Quixotita—which stand out above the rest. Concerning the personal appearance of all of these the author leaves much to the imagination; for, if we except the excellent description of the Indian bride in *La Quixotita,* he concerns himself little with such details. The reader comes to know each character through his actions, words, or thoughts, especially when moralizing on his own or others' behavior. To some extent, character is emphasized through dominant traits. In Teófilo, it is forbearance; in Periquillo, it is laziness; in Don Catrín, it is pride of birth; in Eufrosina and Quixotita, it is love for outward show; and, in the colonel, it is wisdom. There is little trace of character development; it is generally only when the evil ones are on their deathbeds that they become introspective and regret the error of their ways. Even the regeneration of Periquillo comes late in life. The many incidents in which each of the main characters figures serve only to emphasize their dominant traits, not to leave any impress upon the characters themselves. Indeed, after the point is reached at which a change of heart becomes evident, the characters cease to be themselves—they reflect only the views of the author. In almost every instance, the immoral characters, Quixotita, Eufrosina, and Don Catrín, are much more human, more nearly living and breathing creatures, than those which personify moral perfection. Into these the author injects too much of his own idealism. The wise colonel speaks for Lizardi, as does the noble Chinese whom Periquillo meets in the Ladrone Islands. In the many moralizing discourses of Periquillo, Don Catrín, and those with whom they come in contact, Lizardi's own views are repeatedly finding expression. (pp. 236-37)

On the whole, Lizardi's characters are not individuals but types; and to such an extent are the good and bad qualities emphasized in some of these that they are merely exaggerated figures bearing suggestive titles, such as Taravilla, Tremendo, Tronera, Constante, Pudenciana, or Pomposa. All of his characters, both moral and immoral, exhibit typical Mexican traits—thus some of the follies of his compatriots are satirized. But psychological depth is entirely lacking.

The background on which these characters appear is Mexico City and its environs. Periquillo, it is true, goes to the Philippine and Ladrone Islands, and Don Catrín is sent to Morro Castle in Havana, but there is no attempt on the part of the author to describe either of these places or to suggest their atmosphere. He assumes, too, to a large degree, that his reader is already familiar with the capital; for, although he alludes to many public buildings, parks, streets, and districts nearby, such as the Cathedral, the Parián, the Volador, the Coliseo, the university, and the *barrio* of San Lázaro, he makes no attempt to describe them minutely, as to a stranger. Few are the passages descriptive of nature; but many interiors are pictured in detail, as, for example, a room inhabited by a company of beggars. . . . Catalogues of concrete things, such as the long list of articles left in the house after the death of Periquillo's mother, lend themselves to the realistic portrayal of the wretchedness of the poor.

Realism is further attained by the abundant use of local color in the skillful depiction of the manners and customs of the various elements which composed the society of the time. Lizardi's novels make clear the great social gulfs separating the different classes which then constituted Mexican society: the wealthy few; the poverty-stricken Spaniards, lazy both by birth and breeding yet proud as Lucifer; and the Indians, naturally industrious, but ignorant and indigent as the result of injustice. The natives are always treated by Lizardi with a sympathetic touch; in his work they appear, whether as laborers on the haciendas or as vendors on the streets of the capital, as simple, submissive, yet industrious folk, who lack the vices which characterize the other two classes. Such a figure is Pascual in *La Quixotita* and also his daughter Marantona, whose marriage gives the author an opportunity to describe in detail some Indian weddings customs. Periquillo tells us of the Indians living near Tula, who came with their native musical instruments and gifts in the form of hens, pigs, and lambs to do honor to their governor. He recounts, too, that the Indians of this same town who were his patients, never came emptyhanded, but, to pay their fee, brought "hens, fruits, eggs, vegetables, cheese, and whatever they found at hand." In the same story are minute descriptions of the superstitious practices of the Indians of Tixtla on Good Friday and All Souls' Day, all of which were encouraged by the priest because they contributed to his personal profit.

But it is the life of the second class that Lizardi paints most vividly. . . . With the daily life of [this class], . . . Lizardi's novels teem. In them we see the knavery of a village mayor; the venality of a notary in his public acts and the immorality of his private life; the ignorance, avarice, vanity, and worldly ambitions of certain members of the clergy; the false show of learning made by Doctor Purgante; the ignorance and laxity of teachers and of overindulgent and extravagant parents; the intolerable conditions that exist in jails and hospitals; life in the gambling halls; and the tricks employed by beggars to obtain alms. (pp. 237-39)

In his presentation of the various levels that composed Mexican society, the author does not fail to catch the language peculiar to each, especially of the trades and professions, both honest and dishonest, and to record it accurately. He is familiar with the slang of the students, with the cant of the lawyers and doctors, with the jargon of gamblers, with the argot of thieves and the habitués of the underworld, and with the dialect of the Indian. The utterance of each is in keeping with the character—whether it is the Indian Pascual, who speaks the language of the hacienda; Doctor Purgante, who uses terms unintelligible except to the initiated; or Periquillo's friend, Juan Largo, who reveals to him the art of marking the cards.

As a realist Lizardi has far more commendable virtues than as a stylist. For his diction, even when he is not writing popular dialogue, includes many barbarisms and words peculiar to Mexico; his sentence structure is occasionally faulty; and many of the paragraphs show haste and lack of careful planning. It is clearly evident, from the want of finish that characterizes each and every one of his novels, that his natural endowment and the facility with which he wrote led him to do hasty and careless work. (p. 241)

In spite of this lack of finish which prevented Lizardi from attaining a polished style, he recognized and responded to what he considered good stylistic qualities in the works of others. His admiration for the style of Cadalso in *Noches lúgubres* led him to attempt an imitation in *Noches tristes,* which was not a success. For the qualities of style which distinguish him as a novelist are to be found in the other novels rather than in this deliberate attempt to attain style. It is in his ability to adapt his form of expression to the demands of the narrative that Lizardi excels. He can write, as he seldom does, in a florid, grandiloquent style, as in

the funeral oration in *La Quixotita;* or he can write, as he generally does, in an intimate, chatty, gossipy vein, as when he records the conversation of the "chata" in the same work. Along with its many defects, there are certain admirable qualities in his style. It is realistic in its simplicity; it is fresh; it is spontaneous; and it is not lacking in harmony and rhythm. It was just these qualities that served to endear Lizardi to the common people; and to win for him, at the same time, the hatred of the pedants of his day who were attempting to produce literature. There is, too, in his style, an element which reveals something of his own personality. He is ironic and satiric, but too over-serious to be witty; he can move us to laughter, for he has a keen sense of the ludicrous, but he lacks the ability to move us to tears; he is sometimes coarse and vulgar, but he is never indecent; and while he is a moralist, he is generous to a fault, and not without sympathy for his weak and shallow compatriots.

The extent to which Lizardi borrowed from other writers must be taken into consideration in estimating his originality. He was, beyond a doubt, well read in Spanish picaresque fiction, and from it derived the plan for *El periquillo* and *Don Catrín.* His indebtedness to picaresque literature has been recognized by all of the competent critics who have considered his work. . . . Lizardi himself refers to certain writers and works with which he was familiar: Quevedo, Torres Villarroel, Montengón's *Eusebio, Gil Blas,* and repeatedly to *Don Quixote.* From a few other Spanish works of fiction, to which he makes no reference, he may have derived suggestions or incidents. The title of "Periquillo" may have been drawn from *Periquillo el de las Gallineras;* and either from this same work or from the *Varia fortuna del soldado Píndaro* Lizardi may have borrowed the general scheme for *El periquillo* or *Don Catrín.* Similarities of incident are not difficult to find. A device employed in *Don Quixote,* by which the fight between the hero and the Biscayan is broken off at the moment each had his weapon drawn, is employed in the incident of the brawl in *Don Catrín.* Periquillo's marriage with Mariana, his extravagance, and the exchange swindle he perpetrated are similar to that portrayed in *Guzmán de Alfarache.* The portrayal of the *leperaje* in Mexico recalls *Rinconete y Cortadillo,* the *Buscón, Guzmán,* and *Día y noche de Madrid* of Santos. There are also incidents suggestive of *Vida y hechos de Estebanillo González.*

In the didactic passages which embody Lizardi's views on science, political economy, pedagogy, and popular superstitions, the sources from which he drew are even more definite. Particularly is he indebted to Feijóo's *Teatro crítico universal* (1726-1739) and *Cartas eruditas y curiosas* (1753-1760). The opinions he expresses in *El periquillo* in regard to what constitutes real patriotism, the neglect of agriculture, prejudices of those who on account of birth or riches regard themselves as above common labor, the shortcomings of the university course of study, doctors and medicine, the eulogy of Chinese doctors, superstitions in regard to eclipses and comets, and premature burials seem to have come directly from Feijóo. He touches again upon some of these same matters in *La Quixotita,* but here the similarity of opinions expressed by the two writers is especially to be noted in their statements regarding miracles and in the arguments adduced to prove that woman is not mentally inferior to man. (pp. 242-44)

From a careful examination of his sources, then, it can be seen that from earlier writers, particularly the Spanish picaresque novelists, Lizardi unquestionably drew the inspiration for many of the best features of his novels—the picaresque type, the general framework or plan, the series of interesting incidents, the pictures of life of the lower class, and the language of the people. From the picaresque novelists he also derived the idea of introducing moralizing passages—the feature which above all else mars his work; for while some of the Spanish writers were able to make these portions piquant and to link them with the narrative with some degree of art, the Mexican writer was not capable of doing so. The substance of the didactic portions, however, is drawn largely from Feijóo and French sources.

But, in spite of the extent of his borrowing, Lizardi is not guilty of anything that can fairly be called plagiarism. While he follows the plan of the picaresque novels, the subject matter is indisputably his own. His contribution was that which no other picaresque writer attempted—pen pictures of Mexican life. Doctor Sangredo in *Gil Blas* is, no doubt, the prototype of Doctor Purgante in *El periquillo,* but the two exaggerated portraits are, after all, by no means similar. Periquillo, like Gil Blas, falls in with a band of robbers, but how different from Gil's are his experiences with them! Neither Periquillo nor Don Catrín spring from Spanish soil. Both are Mexicans par excellence, with all the characteristics of the poor Spaniard who has grown up under colonial conditions. The life that is sketched in the novels of Lizardi is that of colonial Mexico; and in them are to be found the best existing pictures of manners and customs of the people among whom he lived and to whose best interests he devoted his life. (pp. 244-45)

> *Jefferson Rea Spell, "The Literary Work of Lizardi," in his* Bridging the Gap: Articles on Mexican Literature, *Editorial Libros de México, 1971, pp. 213-45.*

J. Lloyd Read   (essay date 1939)

[*In the following excerpt, Read offers a brief overview of Lizardi's principal works, noting their significance in the history of the Mexican novel.*]

For purposes of literary criticism Fernández de Lizardi must be considered the first Mexican novelist, and his *Periquillo Sarniento,* 1816, the first Mexican novel.

El periquillo Sarniento follows rather closely the technique and procedure of the better known Spanish picaresque novels and adds thereto an almost constant moralizing didacticism. Written in a journalistic tone, without formal refinements of any kind, and full of annoying digressions that destroy its unity, the work nevertheless has substantial merits, especially for the student of origins in Mexican literature. It is the product of the aroused spirit of revolt and ferments of change that characterized the epoch in which it appeared. Its author has rightly been called the pamphleteer of the revolution, and in this novel and others he is still to some extent a campaigning pamphleteer. Not until the time of Manuel Payno did Mexico produce another author who painted so realistically the life of the Mexican people. *El periquillo* is more than a pic-

ture, however; it is a protest of a new sense of national identity against the regime that held sway in the revolutionary period. It is also an attack on social vices that had their roots in the moral decadence of the times.

La Quixotita y su prima (1818), essentially picaresque, shows the influence of Rousseau's *Emile* in its preoccupation with the education of women as a determining factor in their character. Its primary interest for us in this connection is its spirit of social criticism that was a part of the movement toward liberalism and reform.

Vida y hechos del famoso caballero D. Catrín de la fachenda brings under severe scrutiny the parasitic dandy of the colonial regime. It is not essentially different from *El periquillo* except in the matter of the class to which the protagonist belonged.

In the partially autobiographical *Noches tristes y día alegre* (1818) there is visible a rather marked influence emanating from the pre-romantic *Noches lúgubres* (about 1771) of Cadalso, who in turn had found inspiration in the *Night Thoughts* of Edward Young. González Peña said of this work:

> . . . es la primera manifestación de la influencia del pre-romanticismo europeo en las letras mexicanas.
>
> [". . . it is the first manifestation of the influence of European pre-romanticism in Mexican letters."]

The vogue of Lizardi in literary circles was surprisingly great. Until well beyond the middle of the nineteenth century he was the most popular Mexican author. Whether that was because he had no competition at first does not alter the fact that his popularity encouraged imitation even in his more unfortunate trends. Much of the weakness of Mexican fiction can be traced to the example set by Lizardi in the first stages of the novel's development in Mexico.

But the critic will recognize the fact that many of his weaknesses were quite natural in the period of transition in which Lizardi lived. He must be considered a projection of the eighteenth century with a superimposed spirit of renovation and change. His works are a curious combination of the two. From the old he took his procedure; from the contemporary, his spirit. And precisely that is one of the major characteristics of early Mexican fiction. (pp. 69-72)

> *J. Lloyd Read, "Introduction," in his* The Mexican Historical Novel, 1826-1910, *Instituto de las Españas, 1939, pp. 1-79.*

Lionel Trilling   (essay date 1942)

[*Trilling was one of the twentieth century's most significant and influential American literary and social critics, and he is often called the single most important American critic to apply Freudian psychological theories to literature. In the following excerpt, he reviews the 1942 English translation of Lizardi's* El periquillo Sarniento, *finding the novel an imperfect example of the picaresque.*]

We have in English no book of equal appeal [to *El per-*

iquillo Sarniento]; beside such popularity, our best-loved classics—*Robinson Crusoe, Tom Jones, Pickwick Papers, Huckleberry Finn*—are almost esoteric. *Uncle Tom's Cabin* was once universally read in our North, but it had a narrower reference and a shorter day; up to a few years ago *Ben Hur* was still selling enormously, but it was probably never very important in its readers' lives; even *Pilgrim's Progress,* which was once to be found in every simple English home, never attained an influence like this.

And so we approach *The Itching Parrot* with a respect amounting nearly to awe. A book with such a history is almost more than a work of literature. It must contain, we feel, the "secret" of a people. But if it does, the reader of the work in translation can only leave it with the secret undisclosed, even deepened. Its charm will remain a mystery; to him it will seem an extraordinarily dull book. Because its genre, the picaresque, is not at present in general esteem, I ought perhaps to say that I have a special affection for the type, from Lazarillo of Tormes, the primitive ancestor, to Pickwick. But I found *The Itching Parrot* a bore, and I can only hope that, to balance the account of international misunderstanding, Spanish readers are puzzled by what it is we enjoy in *Moll Flanders* and *Tom Jones.*

The Itching Parrot is all the more disappointing because the story of its author, as told in Miss Porter's admirable introduction [see Further Reading], is so very interesting. Lizardi—he wrote under the engaging name of the Mexican Thinker—combined in his character elements of Defoe, Voltaire, Rousseau, and Figaro. It would be impossible to claim for him any great original powers of intellect, but in Mexico at the beginning of the nineteenth century—he was born in 1771, and his literary career seems to have begun in 1811—he was the agent of the Enlightenment. He had a winning touch of the poltroon about him; he confessed to great physical cowardice, and when he was in danger he could not always be relied on to keep his head or hold his tongue. But if he could not and then be bent, he could not be broken. He fought endlessly against political and ecclesiastical oppression; the anonymous and voiceless masses loved him, and church and state hated him. He was always being silenced and always managing to speak out; he was forbidden to publish and he published; he was excommunicated and still he published. To the naivete which marks so much of eighteenth-century liberalism, Lizardi seems to have added a certain provincialism, perhaps not to be avoided by a Mexican intellectual isolated amid the ignorance and obscurantism of the time, but his limitations no doubt made him only the more useful in his time and place. For a short period he was petted by a quasi-liberal government, but through most of his life he lived in dire poverty, and he died in penury.

But the hero of Lizardi's novel is a lesser man than his author. With Lizardi's heroism there is, indeed, mingled, as Miss Porter points out, an element of commonness; it is a peculiarly eighteenth-century mixture and it is rather endearing: the cliché forces itself upon us that Lizardi was Don Quixote and Sancho Panza in one. But the Parrot, the hero of his novel, is all Panza, all belly, all poltroon, yet without the great saving grace of the intellect of the belly. There is no philosophy in the rogue; he is not witty himself nor the cause of wit in others. He cannot justify the life of the belly, as of course we want him to; he cannot defend

the pure pleasure of scratching in the sun. The great bellymen—Sancho himself, Falstaff, Diderot's fine creation, Rameau's Nephew—make us laugh at pomp and respectability. But it is worth noting that the Parrot never gets involved with pomp or with true respectability. Of the paraphernalia of the picaresque tale Lizardi gives us only the literal and the petty matters, the filthy jail but not the ceremonious courtroom, the gambling hell but not the elegant drawing-room, the grasping parish priest but not the portly bishop, the village quack but not the successful physician; he has no sensitivity to affectation, from which, according to Fielding, all humor comes.

Then, too, a good picaresque story ought to have a social and moral ambivalence: we ought to condemn the rogue but we ought to be tempted into an alliance with him, and the great rogues—Jonathan Wild, Captain Macheath, Moll Flanders—make us revise our notions of morality. But Lizardi seems to want to involve us in a simple rather than an ambivalent judgment; the prime moral error of the Parrot, in which his parents abetted him, was that he did not bind himself to a middling way of life and learn an honest trade. Well, all picaresque heroes are likely to lament their departure from virtuous industry, but the Parrot seems to mean it. Lizardi, like so many European moralists of the eighteenth century, found the norm of conduct in the tradesman and the merchant; perhaps the sociological point of the picaresque novel is that the life it represents in its ambivalent way is simply the degeneration of the aristocratic ideal, for the picaresque hero wants to live and enjoy himself without work or duties. And no doubt in the history of the Spanish peoples the illusions and compulsions of aristocracy—both Lizardi and his hero sprang from the impoverished gentry—created a crucial social and moral difficulty. But as Miss Porter herself points out, faith in the middling people is not enough; certainly it is not enough for a novel. It makes a dull hero, and Miss Porter, feeling the Parrot's inadequacy, tells us that the "real heroes" are his comrades, Juan Largo, who gets hanged, and the Eaglet, who is killed leading a bandit raid; but it seems to me that these characters are quite as much without moral and intellectual salt as the Parrot himself.

It is disquieting to be unable to respond to a book that has meant so much to so many people—so much, too, to such judges as Ford Madox Ford and Miss Porter. Perhaps I feel as I do because I have not read the same book they read. Miss Porter's translation is a model of firm, simple prose in the manner of the eighteenth-century masters of realism; but she tells us that the allusive and obscene language of the original will not submit to translation. Perhaps in the verbal play of that incommunicable Spanish lies the power of mind which I feel so sadly absent from the translated book. Or perhaps that power of mind lies in the many moral and political tracts which have been cut out of this version. These, to a foreign public, would of course be dull, if comprehensible at all; yet I cannot help wondering whether their inclusion isn't just what endears the book to its native readers, who, it seems to me, might well be charmed by the exposition of serious matters in the setting of a picaresque novel's low actuality. (pp. 373-74)

Lionel Trilling, "Mexican Classic," in The Nation, *New York, Vol. 154, No. 13, March 28, 1942, pp. 373-74.*

Edith H. Walton (essay date 1942)

[*In the following excerpt from a review of* The Itching Parrot, *Walton praises the novel's vivid depictions of Mexican culture.*]

When a book has had a sale of 100,000,000 copies, and when that sale has stretched over a period of nearly a century and a quarter, it is obvious that it has a claim to attention irrespective of its merits and that it must rank as one of the great best sellers of all time. Apart, however, from its popular success, **The Itching Parrot,** or *El periquillo Sarniento,* is generally considered to be a true Mexican classic—as well as the most important novel which was produced in the past century by the Spanish-speaking world. So, at least, says Katherine Anne Porter, who has cut, revised and edited an earlier translation and who has written an introduction concerning **The Itching Parrot**'s author [see Further Reading]. Having stripped from the narrative most of the moralizing and philosophizing which it originally contained, the resulting product, says Miss Porter, is a picaresque novel of a very high order—worthy to be classed with *Tom Jones, Roderick Random* or *Gil Blas.*

Whatever one thinks of this verdict—which I shall put aside for the moment—there can be no doubt as to the excellence of Miss Porter's introduction. . . .

El periquillo Sarniento—which was not published in full until after Lizárdi's death in 1827—was an attempt on the part of the author to outwit his enemy, the censor, who nevertheless clamped down on it promptly when the opening chapters first appeared. He thought of it as a vehicle for his political ideas, which he hoped would escape attention if concealed in fictional form. Actually, of course, **The Itching Parrot** has survived for far different reasons, and it is likely that the millions who have followed the adventures of its hero skipped or ignored Lizárdi's moral preachments. For the truth is that **El periquillo** is, first of all, a rip-roaring tale, set against a superbly vivid background of the common people's life as it once existed in Mexico City. It is a tale straight from the heart of that city's lower depths—its brothels, its inns, its flop houses and its prisons. As such, it has a persisting vitality which is certainly responsible for its survival and success. . . .

To detail the plot of **The Itching Parrot** would, however, be an unprofitable undertaking, as well as a very nearly impossible one. It is sufficient to say that one exploit follows another, laughably and dizzily, and that Poll [El periquillo] in his lifetime plays an infinity of roles, from quack doctor and barber to sacristan and soldier. Always, however, he is the same high-hearted buffoon, with a tendency to moralize smugly about his own sins and to warn the reader against his example. So pronounced, indeed, is this comic streak of sententiousness that one is hardly surprised when Poll in the end is converted and dies in an odor of domesticity and sanctity. El Periquillo, in short, is the perfect picaresque hero, just as this novel, with its ribaldry and gusto, conforms to a time-honored pattern. What is exceptional about it is its background and the vividness with which it pictures the dregs of a bygone world.

> *Edith H. Walton, "Bygone World," in* The New York Times Book Review, *May 10, 1942, p. 22.*

John M. Fein (essay date 1958)

[*In the following excerpt, Fein points out inconsistencies in the characterization of Periquillo in* The Itching Parrot.]

If Lizardi's intention in writing the **Periquillo** was in fact the twofold one of both entertaining and instructing the reader, the construction of the work as a whole reflects the duality of purpose: a section of narrative is followed or interrupted by a section of moralizing commentary, forming a series of alternating blocks. The lessons to be gained, instead of being implied in the telling of the incidents, are thus developed separately in numerous lengthy digressions, which reiterate the faults of Periquillo and serve as a reminder that virtue and sin infallibly reap their own rewards. Consciously violating the precept of action and morality intertwined, as he himself points out in the "Apología" of the work, Lizardi follows the pattern of the *Guzmán de Alfarache* in this clear-cut separation of the two. It is interesting to note, however, that the part of the moralist in the case of the **Periquillo** is taken by the *pícaro* himself after he has made a radical transformation in his way of life and in his ethical standards. Reviewing the previous actions of his entire career, supposedly for the edification of his children, he serves as the mouthpiece for the author in passing moral judgment upon the person he was in the past. But this moral judgment is not available to the protagonist of the narrative, who was not designed by the author to analyze the ways of his fellow men on anything but a very subjective and self-centered level, the *pícaro*'s traditional unilateral view of life, at the time of the action of the story. The effect of such a pattern is to give the unreformed Periquillo the maximum of liberty with regard to the ethics of his deeds; in fact, Periquillo is not so much immoral as amoral, lacking completely the higher standard of values so amply supplied by his conscience as it surveys his former life after the reformation of his character takes place.

Yet there are several instances in which the author, probably through carelessness, puzzles the reader by allowing his protagonist to adopt a moral attitude contemporaneous with the occurrence of the incident being criticized. The result of the introduction of this attitude is to combine moralizing and action into one indivisible unit, which constitutes a temporary abandonment of the division of the two previously established by Lizardi. One such inconsistency occurs when Periquillo becomes acquainted with the fraudulent beggars. Although only curious and surprised when first informed of the methods used to swindle the charitable public, his mood immediately changes to one of indignation when he discovers that an innocent child is being mistreated in order to spur the generous impulses of potential donors:

> Supe con el mayor dolor que aquella indigna madre y despiadada mujer, pellizcaba al pobre inocente cuando pedía limosna, a fin de conmover a los fieles y excitar su caridad con la vehemencia de sus gritos. No me escandalicé poco con semejante inhumanidad.

> ["I knew with the greatest pain that that undeserving mother and merciless woman pinched the poor innocent when he asked for alms, in order to disturb the faithful and to stir up their charity with the

vehemence of his cries. I was not a little shocked
by similar inhumanity."]

The remark taken by itself might be overlooked as an example of a value judgment (although Periquillo is sufficiently impressed by this cruelty to make a major point of
it when he informs upon the beggars later on in the same
chapter) if it were not the introduction to an eloquent passage in which Periquillo denounces the evil ways of beggars, the stupidity and superstition of the ones who support them, and the pseudo-religious falsities the beggars
tell. What is needed, we are told, is the careful examination and reform of such practices.

One cannot help but feel that these ideas and the sentiment
which they convey are inappropriate to the character of
the protagonist as developed in the book up to this point.
Carried away by his own, not Periquillo's, protest, Lizardi
has overlooked his previous method of putting commentary upon the action in the guise of advice which the reformed Periquillo gives to his children. The error could
have been corrected partially by rewriting a single sentence, which, as it stands, introduces the lengthy passage
of moralizing into the time of the incident:

> Aturdido me quedé al escuchar tantos despropósi-
> tos juntos, *y decía entre mí: ¿* cómo es posible que
> no haya quien contenga estos abusos, y quien les
> ponga una mordaza a estos locos?

> ["Stunned, I stayed to listen to all of these absurdi-
> ties, and I would say to myself: How is it possible
> that no one is able to contain such abuses, and who
> can put a muzzle on these madmen?"]

Another lapse of characterization occurs in the episode of
the egoist, whose debate with Periquillo on the subject of
human relationships temporarily casts the protagonist in
the role of a preacher. When the egoist points out that one
should be concerned only with what he himself suffers,
Periquillo replies that even if he does not suffer, he is
moved to pity by the sufferings of his fellow men, whom
he must consider his brothers or parts of his own person.
He continues in the same vein, declaring that one does not
seek friends for what one can obtain from them, aside
from their esteem and advice. When the egoist retorts that
he will seek only friends that can help him attain material
wealth, Periquillo is unable to go on:

> Escandalizado al escuchar tan inefables máximas,
> mudé de conversación y a poco rato me separé de
> su lado.

> ["Scandalized by listening to so many ineffable
> maxims, I changed the subject and after a while
> separated myself from his side."]

Nor is he able to dismiss the matter lightly, for he feels
compelled to tell the incident to his master, the colonel,
on the following day, in the hope of receiving an explanation of such unusual views. What is curious about Periquillo's reaction, naturally, is that he has committed
deeds that are far worse than the egoist's theory. If the cultivation of friendships only for selfish and material ends
were the least of Periquillo's sins, he could almost be
proud of his conduct. The history of his life before the incident dealing with the egoist, indeed, includes such pecca-
dillos as swindling, theft, outrageous misappropriation of
public funds, murder, and plundering a grave. The same

Periquillo who is repelled by the idea of self-centered associations has stolen and squandered the small legacy left his
mother, seduced the mistress of the man who freed him
from jail and gave him a home, had his own mistress seduced by a friend so that he would have an excuse to get
rid of her, and treated his wife to beatings and starvation
after he tired of her. In short, the Periquillo of the story
acted frequently out of the same motives which he denounces here. By assigning ethical sentiments to him during the progress of the action, the author causes him to
usurp the function of the reformed and moralizing Periquillo.

There are other passages also, which although they are not
apparent violations of the novel's dual structure, create an
atmosphere of inconsistency and contribute to a feeling of
mistrust on the part of the reader. In this connection one
thinks particularly of Periquillo's compassion for a patient
in the hospital, his shock at the idea of being a common
thief, and his remarkably idealistic concealment from the
authorities of the identity of his tormenter, Aguilucho,
whom he did not want to harm since the poor fellow already had the burden of his crimes to bear. If it is stated
in defense of the author here that Periquillo is meant to
have a little kindness and sentiment in his nature even
when he is doing wrong, then one must take the opposite
side of the argument to classify as an inconsistency the absolute lack of such feelings in the incident in which Periquillo refuses a loan to a supplicant and needy relative,
allows him to be beaten by his servants, and laughs at the
injuries that have been inflicted.

The faults of the characterization of Periquillo noted may
be considered as part of a more general carelessness which
pervades the entire work and which, as critics such as Jefferson Rea Spell [see excerpt dated 1931] have noted, is
apparent not only in the choice of words, but also in sentence and paragraph structure. Lizardi himself admits to
a lack of literary discipline at the conclusion of the *Periquillo,* and confesses that he does not have the patience
to reread his work, much less to correct it:

> Yo mismo me avergüenzo de ver impresos errores
> que no advertí al tiempo de escribirlos. La facilidad
> con que escribo no prueba acierto. Escribo mil
> veces en medio de la distracción de mi familia y de
> mis amigos; pero esto no justifica mis errores, pues
> debía escribir con sosiego y sujetar mis escritos a la
> lima.

> ["I myself am embarrassed to see printed errors
> that I did not notice at the time I wrote them. The
> ease with which I write does not always prove to
> be accurate. I write a thousand times between the
> distraction of my family and my friends; but that
> does not justify my errors, well I should write when
> it is quiet and keep my writings in the file."]

This honest acknowledgment of defects suggests that the
inconsistencies in portrayal of character are simply oversights on the part of Lizardi and that he might have noted
and corrected them if he had taken the pains to do so.

Even though their presence in the story tends to obscure
a valid estimate of the character of the protagonist, however, there is some compensating advantage in what they
have to tell us of the author's personality. It is not exagger-
ating to say that Lizardi was more of a pamphleteer than
a novelist, and that the creation of the *Periquillo* was due

in part to the author's desire to avoid the effects of censorship. Writing in an era of revolution and social upheaval, it was natural for an intellectual of liberal tendencies to protest against the injustices of his time. The fact that Lizardi could not confine his feelings to the moralizing passages and that they spilled over to color the presentation of his principal character, should be interpreted as evidence of the extent to which the author was reflecting his personal reactions, perhaps his own experiences. As such, they must be judged as an indication of the warmth and sincerity of Lizardi's humanitarian sentiments. (pp. 428-431)

> John M. Fein, "Inconsistencies of Characterization in the 'Periquillo'," in Modern Language Notes, *Vol. LXXIII, No. 6, June, 1958, pp. 428-31.*

John S. Brushwood   (essay date 1966)

[*An American translator and critic, Brushwood has written extensively on the Spanish-American novel. In the following excerpt, he comments on Lizardi's best-known works.*]

The best known of [Mexico's nineteenth-century] pamphleteers was José Joaquín Fernández de Lizardi, the perfect human representation of the movement from ideas to action [in Mexican literary society]. He had faith in the new ideas and defended them bravely; he also had faith in the common people, understood them, and considered it his mission to communicate to the masses the ideas that he cherished. His great sensitivity to the popular enabled him to capture the speech of the ordinary people, and he used it, to the disgust of many, for the propagation of liberalism. Whenever he wrote in the popular vein, he was a successful writer; when he deserted it, he failed. Like Hidalgo, his vision incorporated the whole society.

The best known of the several periodicals that Lizardi published was *El pensador Mexicano (The Mexican Thinker)* which lasted from 1812 to 1814. Its name was Lizardi's pseudonym, and appropriately so, because it is typical of the writer at his best. His ideas are firmly rooted in the academic security of the eighteenth century, but his manner of expression belongs to the people. Without regard for correctness, he captured the flavor of their speech with their own informalities and imagery. His range of subject matter is wide, and it varied according to what the particular time demanded or allowed. With the same aplomb, he wrote of the natural rights of man, or the nuisance of dogs wandering in the streets of the city. He was critical of the power of the Church, he found the education of the time totally inadequate, he deplored poor sanitation. His topics are sometimes humble, sometimes elevated, but they are always dealt with honorably and sharply.

Lizardi wrote in all genres, but it is only in the political essay and in the novel that he cultivated his popular touch. *El periquillo Sarniento* (1816) is generally considered to be the first novel published in the New World. Censorship made the 1816 edition incomplete—it is surprising what the censors didn't see—and the first complete edition was published in 1830-1831. In all there have been more than fifteen editions.

El periquillo Sarniento is a picaresque novel, a develop-

Title page to Lizardi's collection of fables, Fabulas del pensador Mexicano.

ment of the characteristics already apparent in *El pensador Mexicano.* It is also full of moralizing digressions that all but destroy it. But we have to remember that the author was first of all a reformer. The character of Periquillo is fairly typical of the Spanish *pícaro* with the important difference that Periquillo mends his ways and hopes that his life will serve as an example of what not to do. Throughout his many adventures, he is properly opportunistic and cynical, regularly punished and just as regularly deserving of punishment. Some of the types with whom he comes in contact are standard, like the well-known but still amusing Dr. Purgante (Dr. Purgative) who is professionally inadequate and personally ridiculous. Other types are more characteristic of the time, and all of them together present a fascinating picture of Mexico City at the beginning of the last century.

Over and above the plethora of opinion and advice offered throughout the novel, Lizardi does have an overall judgment which is apparent to the reader. It is that society is hypocritical in that men are dishonest with themselves and with other men. This conviction is apparent without taking into account the author's moralization, and we are inclined to say that Lizardi would have done well to have left out his digressions. Indeed, it is possible to edit the novel so that the digressions are cut to a minimum and we are left with an excellent picaresque story. Given an edition of this kind, the reader's reaction will depend on his acceptance of picaresque humor. If we cringe at the cruelty of every trick of the *pícaro,* we will surely be miserable. If, on the other hand, we suspend our reluctance to view cruelty and enter into the cynicism of the *pícaro,* the story is uproariously funny. But to read only the story of *pícaro* is not to read Lizardi, because his teaching, his desire to improve the world, his wish to make men reasonable, constitute an essential part of his effort.

Lizardi's second novel, *La Quixotita y su prima* (1818), loses the sprightliness of the *Periquillo* and becomes overbearingly didactic. Probably inspired by [Rousseau's] *Emile,* and certainly encouraged by his own dim view of education, Lizardi undertook to show the horrible consequences of the frivolous education of women, and to demonstrate how they ought to be taught. Since the presentation of the argument involves the treatment of two families who are related to each other, the structure of the novel is somewhat more complicated than the picaresque. Pomposita, the victim of an education that has taught her to write social notes, dance, and eat bonbons, is the epitome of frivolity. And so are her parents. She marries imprudently and is deserted by the man who was not what he pretended to be. The death of Pomposita's improvident father leaves mother and daughter with no recourse short of prostitution. Cousin Pudenciana, on the other hand, is given a sound education, knows how to run the house, and even learns watch-making, a trade which can provide a living in the absence of her husband. But Pudenciana and her good parents take no chances on the husband either— they have as many recourses as we have fringe benefits— and select a serious, older man whose lack of glamor is his greatest attraction. Pudenciana's life is secure, if boring. The trouble with Lizardi's moral lesson is that the reader finds Pomposita and her devil-may-care father a lot more attractive than their opposite numbers. And there are times when we may ask whether the author's advice concerns the nature of education, or the proper standards for choosing a husband.

The truth of the matter is that *La Quixotita y su prima* will not stand by itself. It is an interesting part of Lizardi's work, but interest in it depends upon interest in the author's total production. No one would read the book for pleasure in our time, a fact that makes it entirely different from *El periquillo Sarniento.* Happily, Lizardi returned to the kind of novel that was most suited to his talents in *Don Catrín de la fachenda,* which was published-posthumously in 1832.

The second picaresque novel is traditionally considered inferior to the *Periquillo,* probably with good cause, but it does not deserve the relative oblivion into which it has been cast. Don Catrín is not the same kind of *pícaro* as Periquillo. He lacks his forerunner's conscience, and his antisocial attitudes are less justifiable. His model is the "dandy" of the period who thinks the world owes him a living and who is willing to do anything to avoid legitimate work. This character does not attract the sympathy that Periquillo attracts, but enjoyment of the novel depends only on the reader's ability to take one further step into the world of *pícaro.* If our judgment is controlled by the attractive qualities of the character, the book will not pro-

vide a pleasant experience; if we accept Don Catrín as an instrument of satire, the novel is funny.

Whatever the reader's personal reaction to Lizardi's novels, there is no doubt that they show a great deal of the world in which he lived. (pp. 64-8)

> *John S. Brushwood, "The Colonial Temperament (1521-1831)," in his* Mexico in Its Novel: A Nation's Search for Identity, *University of Texas Press, 1966, pp. 55-68.*

Walter M. Langford   (essay date 1971)

[In the following excerpt, Langford praises Lizardi for his contributions as Mexico's first novelist.]

Although Mexico City was firmly in Spanish hands when the first Spanish-American novel was published in 1816, it was a period of confusion and transition. There had been a change of viceroys, the Cádiz decree of 1810 was finally made public in Mexico, despite the fact that this was largely neutralized by a viceregal edict decreeing the death penalty for any author of incendiary pamphlets or other writings. Amid all this uncertainty a most unusual person named José Joaquín Fernández de Lizardi (1776-1827), who thrived on confusion and spent a lifetime creating more and more of it, seized upon the idea of producing a novel as a means of sneaking past the censors many of his reform notions about social conditions, education, and political evils. He persuaded a printer to risk printing it, and thus was born the first real Spanish-American novel, *El periquillo Sarniento (The Itching Parrot).*

While the purist might profess disappointment that the novel came into being in those countries in such a backhanded manner, playing second fiddle to the reform intentions of a social critic, it seems to me fortunate that the novel was propelled on stage by such a lively figure as Lizardi, who knew the social reality around him as few others did and who had devoted his life to writing about it. As a result, we have a work which is steeped in the reality of the Mexican populace of its time.

It was probably Fernández de Lizardi's social instinct which urged him to tell his story in the form of a picaresque novel, a near-perfect vehicle for the purposes he had in mind. A major characteristic of the picaresque works, always founded in satire, is that they contrast the social mores of the affluent class with the oppressed existence of the lower class. The *pícaro* or rogue, who in his poverty must attach himself to one upper-class master after another, discovers and exposes the sham, the shallowness, the insensitivity and crassness, the selfishness and arrogance and false values of the masters he serves.

The sprightly *El periquillo Sarniento* commands attention and respect both for what it says and how it says it. The one trouble with the book is that Lizardi didn't really want to write a novel. He simply wanted to get before the reading public his biting attacks on the system and his ideas for reforming it. Interlarded throughout the narrative are nearly all the pamphlets he had written over the course of some years, many of which he had failed to get past the baleful eye of the censor. (pp. 4-5)

Fernández de Lizardi, who often used the pen name of

"The Mexican Thinker," reserved much of his choicest satire for doctors, hospitals, funeral customs, politicians, and religions. In one chapter [of *El periquillo Sarniento*] the *pícaro* Perico serves for a time a pedantic old medico called Doctor Purgative. After observing closely his manner and his practices and reading all the medical and anatomical books in his library, Perico departs one night with the doctor's mule, books, money, medical diploma, and assorted other items, with the intention of passing himself off as a doctor in other parts. This sort of gambit is commonplace in the Spanish picaresque novels.

Having established himself in Tula (with an assistant, no less), Perico is called to the home of a tax collector who seems on the brink of death. The scene develops in the following manner:

> Affecting a great serenity of spirit and with the confidence of a prophet, I told them: "Calm yourselves, ladies, why should he die? This is only the effervescence of sanguinary humor which, oppressing the ventricles of his heart, stifle his cerebrum, because it presses with all the *pondus* or weight of the blood upon the medular and the trachea; but all of this will be ended at once, for if *evaquatio fit, recedet pletora,* that is, by evacuation we will free ourselves of the plethora."
>
> The ladies listened to me astonished and the priest kept looking me up and down, no doubt scoffing at my nonsense, which he interrupted by saying:
>
> "Ladies, spiritual remedies never do harm, nor are they opposed to temporal aid. It will be well to absolve my friend and annoint him, and let God's will be done."

After this has been accomplished, Perico takes over:

> At once I approached the bed, took his pulse, and gazed at the beams of the ceiling for some time; then I took his pulse again, all the time putting on an act by arching my eyebrows, wrinkling my nose, staring at the floor, biting my lips, moving my head from side to side, and going through every pantomime I could think of to stupefy those poor people who, never taking their eyes off me, remained in deep silence, taking me for a second Hippocrates; at least, that was my intention. . . .

Finally the point is reached when he can stall no longer, and so he addresses his assistant, Andrés:

> "You, as a good phlebotomist, will give him without delay a pair of bleedings of the cava vein."
>
> Andrés, although frightened and knowing as little as I about cava veins, tied his arms and gave him two slashes that looked like dagger wounds. After he had bled enough to shock all those present, the sick man opened his eyes and began to recognize and speak to the people surrounding him.

This success and another "cure" shortly after make Perico's fame as a doctor, so that he and Andrés prosper mightily for a time.

> In spite of my ignorance, some sick people were cured by accident, although the ones who perished from my mortal remedies were much more numerous. Despite this, my fame did not diminish, for three reasons: first, most of the ones who died were poor, and neither their life nor their death was

much noticed; second, I had already gained renown and so I could sleep without worry, even if I killed more Toltecs than the Cid did with the Saracens; third, and this is what most favors the doctors, because those who were cured lauded my skill and those who died couldn't complain about my ignorance. . . .

Some time later a plague puts an end to Perico's medical career, and he returns to the life of a *pícaro*. One significant difference to be noted between the Spanish *pícaro* and Lizardi's rogue is that in the end the latter repents of his misdeeds and settles down to a normal and decent existence, something no self-respecting *pícaro* of the Spanish breed would be caught dead at.

Having created Spanish America's first novel, Fernández de Lizardi went on to write a couple of others. *La Quixotita y su prima* (1818) is too pedantic and moralizing and does not convince. But *Don Catrín de la fachenda* (published posthumously in 1832), another picaresque effort, has some of the same qualities found in *El periquillo Sarniento.* Thus, the first novelist gave us not just one novel but three, an output which not many nineteenth-century Spanish-American novelists would surpass.

Yet the significance of José Joaquín Fernández de Lizardi rests not merely on his role as the first to use the novel form in the New World. The enduring popularity of *El periquillo Sarniento* over more than a century and a half is but one evidence that this work possesses extraordinary qualities. This outsized picaresque effort ranks well up among the leaders of all the novels of its century. In fact, some critics regard it definitely as the foremost novel of the 1800s [see Porter entry in Further Reading]. And it has still other distinctions. Always ahead of his time, Lizardi gave us in this work a novel of social protest and a novel expressed in the language of the people. (pp. 5-7)

> *Walter M. Langford, "The Mexican Novel before Mariano Azuela," in his* The Mexican Novel Comes of Age, *University of Notre Dame Press, 1971, pp. 1-13.*

Nancy Vogeley   (essay date 1987)

[*In the following excerpt, Vogeley examines the "colonial reader," a phrase she uses to refer to the reading public in early nineteenth-century Mexico. Concerned with the interaction between reader and text and the political and social effects of a literary work on its audience, Vogeley explores the ways in which Lizardi's* The Itching Parrot *was read and understood by his contemporaries.*]

El periquillo Sarniento, published in 1816 in Nueva España by José Joaquín Fernández de Lizardi, poses important questions for critics attempting to arrive at broad theories of reader response. A construct such as the "virtual reader" or the "ideal reader" is rendered useless in the colonial context, where choice of language was politicized; whether one wrote using Peninsular or Mexican Spanish loudly proclaimed one's political sympathies and automatically divided one's readership. The "colonial reader," a term used in the singular for consistency with other critical expressions, stands for a composite of many readers who would have responded variously to this early effort by Lizardi to create indigenous fiction. One category of colonial readers, culturally dominated by the metropolis and aware of European literary models, would have decried any deviation. Another, also familiar with Continental tradition but conscious of the need for linguistic reform as well as for political change, would have applauded Lizardi's Mexicanizing innovations. Still another, literate but less educated according to European expectations, might have accepted Lizardi's popular novel in its serial from in the same way they read the many newspapers published in Nueva España in those years.

The various members of this interpretive community, however, generally shared an awareness of print as power. Normally only powerful voices were permitted access to the medium; thus *El periquillo Sarniento,* in which characters representative of the lower classes were made to command the readers' attention, redefined the reading interlude. Lizardi's colonial readers, even those who belonged to the viceregal elite, mostly felt themselves deprived of real power because of their derivative political status. Instead of simply regarding their experience with this book as an encounter with a higher authority, they would see it as contact with degraded compatriots, shunned by most respectable readers among the literate sectors. Therefore, the assimilative process of these colonial readers must be understood as a mixed response to the prestigious medium and the novel's realistically drawn characters. In focusing on the fantasy of the imaginative moment, the work of psychoanalytic critics studying the affective dimensions of the literary process has often neglected such sociological aspects of reading.

Lizardi's story of a middle-class youth, irresponsibly fallen into poverty after his parents' death, recorded contemporary realities; the portrayal of corruption in high places and nastiness among the lower classes forced Mexican readers to recognize the book's pertinence to their world. Mexican readers were accustomed to finding disreputable characters in Spanish picaresque novels, but they could dismiss these types in the same way they distanced themselves from the imported book and that foreign land. Now, however, in Lizardi's novel, Mexicans recognized their own world; they became literarily conscious that racial differences, ignorance, and political disunion characterized the colony. The Mexican version of the picaresque story, while retaining some of the slapstick of some European forms, made a comic tradition serious.

As psychoanalytic criticism has usefully emphasized, one re-creates in the reading process mechanisms that, in general, one uses in coping with the world; this critical discovery underscores not only the potential for varied responses that the notion of the colonial reader points to but also the way such responses reflect political, religious, and economic concerns. For example, if Lizardi's readers owed their loyalty to the governing class, their response to the fiction and its often broken or plain idiom might have ranged from curious involvement to anxious consideration to hostile dismissal; if, however, they sympathized with the insurgent movement, they might have welcomed the book's fresh points of view as a weapon in the struggle and found gratification, if not pleasure, in the shared perspective. The situation of the colonial reader presents psychoanalytic critics with the problem of explaining how identity may be realized in literature if the language is inherited, if it is regarded as imposed or borrowed.

Finally, the notion of "literary competence" is challenged by the historical example of a society that viewed the book with ambivalence. While for many the book had an aura of sacredness, an attitude the church and powerful interests encouraged, others associated the book with the hated authority and empty rhetoric of official language. Thus "literary competence"—which suggests a high regard at least for a book tradition, if not also for a common cultural past, and a sense of the shared meaning of the literary work—must have different value in a colonial society.

The example of Lizardi's work is important to students of Spanish American literature, for whom *El periquillo Sarniento* stands as the first Spanish American novel; however, it should also interest those who see in colonial discourse not just the record of a minority group but the struggle implicit in any effort to employ official language and channels of communication while at the same time challenging their control.

Lizardi had available as readers a small group of literate, Spanish-speaking individuals, who were greatly outnumbered by the illiterate and semiliterate Indians, blacks, and persons of mixed caste who either had no access to Spanish at all or else spoke and wrote it imperfectly. The elite—members of the military, ecclesiastical, administrative, and commercial classes in Mexico City and in the provincial capitals—largely depended for recreational literature on books printed in Spain. Since a printing monopoly forbade the publishing of everything except church-related materials and official documents such as edicts, speeches, and a gazette, other reading matter had to be imported. Although there are records of private libraries that had liberal French books and although ecclesiastical censors in positions of cultural prominence knew of works such as *Tom Jones,* importation controls generally limited Mexican readers to the literary production of Spain. A work such as Padre José Francisco de Isla's *Fray Gerundio de Campazas* (1758) reached Mexico in many editions; there its satire of the pompous language in sermons would have particularly appealed to readers. Isla's translation of *Gil Blas,* which also circulated in Mexico, was probably an important model for Lizardi's picaresque novel.

Literary production in eighteenth-century Spain, however, can be shown to be more open and enlightened than has been thought. I offer as an example a work selected at random from the library of the Mexican Abadiano family, inheritors of the printing press and bookstore of Alejandro Valdés, an important figure in Mexico City in the first decades of the nineteenth century. In *Origen, progresos y estado actual de la literatura* (Madrid, 1784), the Abate D. Juan Andrés argues that literature possesses universal characteristics such as eloquence. In addition to citing the literatures of Greece and Rome, he mentions that of the Arabs. The translator comments:

> . . . que la literatura moderna reconoce por su madre á la arábiga, no solo en las ciencias, sino tambien en las buenas letras.
>
> [". . . modern literature recognizes as its mother Arab literature, not only in the sciences but also in letters."]

It is not known when this book entered Mexico or in what numbers, but its presence in the Abadiano collection suggests that unorthodoxy spread to colonial areas. The secular literature of this collection reflects the strong Bourbon influence, that is, a neoclassical aesthetic of truth and utility. Histories, biographies, philosophical treatises, military studies, science books—as well as the collections of poetry and the women's novels more normally thought of as literature—constitute the main part of this colonial repository.

By the first decades of the nineteenth century, however, many Mexicans seem to have become critical of books. Evidence suggests that books were suspect because they symbolized church and governmental power, which was increasingly regarded as corrupt. Historically, books had been accessible only to the privileged few; and as the message of the European Enlightenment spread, its emphasis on practical knowledge and socializing skills contributed to the development of the newspaper as the colony's preferred literary medium. From 1805 to 1812 the *Diario de México,* though subject to government censorship, had great currency as a privately owned source of information. . . . Typical of this shifting view of the printed word is the plea contained in a letter written to this newspaper.

> No espere V. de mí nada bueno. Soy un pobre labrador, que no entiendo latines, teologias, ni nada de aquello que hace sabios á los hombres. Leo muy medianamente el castellano, y eso en unos quantos libros de doctrina christiana, que me sirven de instruccion, aciendome capaz de enseñar á mis hijos. Furera de estos libros no tengo otro que el gran libro del universo. . . . Carezco asta de las luces que puede comunicarme la compañia de las gentes; pues encerrado siempre en el recinto de mi rancho, para atender á su cultivo, no gozo de otra sociedad que la que tuvieron los primeros patriarcas, la de mi esposa, de mis hijos, y domesticos. . . .
>
> Un sabio extrangero á quien tuve la satisfaccion de hospedar una noche en mi casa, hablandome de la agricultura de los Olandeses me dijo que ellos habian usurpado al mar sus dominios, plantando verdes praderías y jardines hermosísimos sobre el terreno que antes ocupaban las aguas salobres del oceano. Y ¿no sería para nosotros casi de igual gloria convertir en una llanura de doradas espigas el fondo *tequezquitoso* que hemos ido quitando poco á poco á la laguna de Tezcoco? La cosa es tan importante y gloriosa que para conseguirla me parece poco emplear todos los analysis de la química, todos los principios de la botánica, las reglas todas de la fisica, y la constancia de muchos años.

> Don't expect anything good of me. I am a poor worker, who does not understand Latin, theology, or anything of that which makes men wise. I read Castilian at a very average level from a few books of Christian doctrine, which instruct me so that I may teach my children. Apart from these books I have no other than the great good book of the universe. . . . I lack even the education that the company of other people could provide me with; because always isolated on my ranch, I enjoy no other society than that which the first patriarchs had—their wives, their children, and their servants. . . .
>
> A learned foreigner whom I had the pleasure of entertaining one night in my home, speaking to me of

agriculture in Holland, told me that there they had found land formerly claimed by the sea, planting green meadows and gardens in areas previously covered by the salt waters of the ocean. Would it not be equally glorious for us to convert into a plain of golden grain the rocky bottom of Lake Tezcoco . . . ? The thing is so important and glorious that, to accomplish it, it seems to me a small [investment] to employ all the analyses of chemistry, all the principles of botany, all the rules of physics, and the constancy of many years.

(24-25 Nov. 1805)

Although he does not say so, this provincial of obvious means and respectable education clearly also read the *Diario*; the newspaper, doctrinal books, and scientific literature were the only printed forms he deemed necessary for his country life. It is significant that he learned of foreign advances through personal contact, the spoken word.

Books, commonly associated with law and medicine, were viewed as part of the ostentatious display of learning the members of these professions required to maintain their often fraudulent power and privilege. Many colonials considered the ancient history told by books irrelevant for purposes of present-day instruction. For example, an advertiser wrote to the editor of the *Diario* complaining that a series on pre-Columbian Mexico was running too long:

> Esas son unas vejeces, que para nada sirven, sino para conciliar el sueño á unos, y fastidiar á otros; los que quieran saber esas cosas, tienen libros en donde verlas: ya es otro mundo, otros tiempos: los hombres de ahora no son como los de antaño: ni la guerra, ni la paz se hacen como se hacian, y todo es diferente.

> These are only old stories that don't serve for anything but to put some men to sleep and to irritate others; those who want to know these things have books in which to find them. Now it is another world, another time. The men of today are not like those of long ago; neither war nor peace is like it used to be, and everything is different.

(22 Dec. 1809)

The editor's response, which argues that lessons can be learned by reading accounts of earlier periods, reveals much about the difficulties of printing longer works separately. In pre-independence Mexico, paper was scarce, printers were few, and the small number of potential buyers did not warrant the publishing costs. The only local writing in demand was that found in inexpensive newspapers and in pamphlets with short, entertaining pieces.

In 1809 the *Diario* printed an allegory, by "Mr. Klopstock," in which "Arts" and "Letters" argue to determine which is superior. Although "Letters" finally take precedence, the exchange sets out additional criticism of books:

> LAS BELLAS ARTES: el aspecto de un almacen de libros, ¿puede acaso proporcionar al aficionado de lo bello, placeres tan deliciosos? Entre ellos se ven obras cubiertas de polvo, y que pretendieron los honores de la inmortalidad, ahora tristes movimientos de los . . . esfuerzos inùtiles del entendimiento humano. . . . no hallarian compradores, si el grabado no se dignase adornarlos con las producciones de su buril. Por otra parte, ¿qué cosa mas comun que un libro? Lo poco que cuesta, es causa

de que todo el mundo le tenga, y de que puede ser-
vir, á no ser para deleytar al ocioso, y para presen-
tar ideas muchas veces falsas al lector, que con sus
propias reflexîones, llegaria con mas seguridad á
descubrir la verdad. . . .

LAS BELLAS LETRAS: La ventaja que tenemos de
dirigir el espiritu, y el corazon del hombre . . . de
hacerle amar sus obligaciones, y de dirigirle sin
cesar hàcia la felicidad . . . es la ùnica de que ten-
gamos derecho de ensobervecernos. . . . Consenti-
mos con gusto en que las bellas artes tambien pue-
den hacer deliciosa la virtud; pero nos atrevemos á
sostener . . . que sus medios son insuficientes para
extender su imperio. Por su naturaleza, parece que
es objeto de sus producciones, mas bien la belleza,
que la utilidad . . . y es incapaz de producir aquel
enlace de ideas y sensaciones, que deben excitarse
en el corazon del hombre, para que conozca la virtud.

ARTS: The appearance of a book warehouse, can it
perchance afford the enthusiast delicious pleasures?
There are to be found works covered with dust,
which pretended to the honor of immortality and
are now sad tracings . . . of the futile efforts at
human understanding. . . . [T]hey would not find
buyers if they were not adorned with engravings.
On the other hand, what is more common than a
book? It costs so little that everyone can buy it; it
entertains the lazy man and presents ideas that are
often false to the reader who, on his own reflection,
would more surely arrive at the truth. . . .

LETTERS: The advantage that we have of directing
the spirit and the heart of man . . . of making him
fond of his obligations and of guiding him unceas-
ingly toward happiness . . . is the only one of
which we have the right to be proud. We grant with
pleasure that Arts can also make virtue attractive;
but we dare to assert . . . that its means are insufficient to extend its dominion. By its very nature it
seems that beauty, rather than utility, is the object
of its production . . . and it is incapable of producing that mixture of ideas and sensations that must
be stirred in the heart of man so that he may know
virtue.

(1, 3-4 Mar.)

The discussion, born of European neoclassical concern to
legitimate secular and pagan art forms, had special resonance in the colonial world. Amid the vast numbers of illiterates, the visual arts such as sculpture and architecture
could achieve what books could not; indeed the *Diario*
printed an extended discussion on the "language" of architecture. Sermons were also a topic of much interest in
the newspaper because they spread their message broadly
by means of the spoken word.

It is clear, then, that a new national writer, entering this
linguistic arena for the purpose of creating imaginative literature, had a difficult task. The challenge, as Umberto
Eco describes Manzoni's, was not to please an audience
but to "create a public who could not help liking his
novel." Therefore, in producing the first Mexican novel
José Joaquín Fernández de Lizardi had to overcome several problems. The book was a much discredited medium,
his market was undefined, and his use of the written word
had to take into account Mexicans' awareness of competing orality. The letters appearing in the *Diario* suggest

great diversity in the audience's ability to appreciate and
understand a literary text. For example, some wrote that
Latin grammar and usage should still be observed, suggesting political loyalty to Spain and her empire; others,
whose spelling, use of accents, and punctuation reveal
their uncertainty about rules, argued that Mexican speech
should determine writing forms. There must have been
still other colonials who did not deign to write in the
straightforward style of the newspaper and to participate
in the vulgarizing process that the newspaper represented.

Evidence that Lizardi was aware of the special character
of the colonial reader survives in the text of *El periquillo
Sarniento* and in statements he made about the novel. Significantly, he pluralizes his readers at all times; his readers
are his "children," whom he addresses in a fatherly way
through the voice of his narrator, Pedro Sarmiento, a reformed *pícaro*. In his dedication to the novel, Lizardi in
his own voice enumerates his readers' identities and emphasizes their diversity:

> Muy bien sé que descendéis de un ingrato, y que
> tenéis relaciones de parentesco con los Caínes
> fratricidas, con los idólatras Nabucos, con las pros-
> titutas Dalilas, con los sacrílegos Baltasares, con
> los malditos Canes, con los traidores Judas, con los
> pérfidos Sinones, con los Cacos ladrones, con los
> herejes Arrios, y con una multitud de pícaros y pí-
> caras que han vivido y aún viven en el mismo
> mundo que nosotros.
>
> Sé que acaso seréis, algunos, plebeyos, indios, mula-
> tos, negros, viciosos, tontos y majaderos.

> I know very well that you are descended from an
> ingrate, that you are related to fratricidal Cains,
> idolatrous Nebuchadnezzars, prostituting Delilahs,
> sacrilegious Balthazars, cursed *Canes*, traitorous
> Judases, perfidious Sinons, thieving Cacuses, heret-
> ical Ariuses, and a multitude of *pícaros* and *pícaras*
> who have lived and who still inhabit the same
> world as we.
>
> I know that perhaps you are, some of you, common
> men, Indians, mulattoes, blacks, addicted to vice,
> foolish and a nuisance.

His insulting tone comically parodies the recognition former novelists accorded their patrons; however, the language of sinfulness also disguises the sense of shame and
self-hatred afflicting many colonials. Inferior in the eyes
of Peninsular Spaniards, American Spaniards, as they
were called, were now criminals as a result of their rebellion against God and king.

Plebeian and fratricidal, Lizardi's readers were also, by his
account, "ignorant." The novelist felt they needed an explicit restatement of the moral hidden in the story. Thus
the fatherly Pedro constantly interjects preaching asides
into the story of delinquency the youthful Periquillo is telling, and Lizardi himself intervenes in the narrative with
lengthy moral and erudite digressions on law, history, ethics, theology, philosophy, and the emerging natural sciences. In this mixture of drama and didactic commentary,
Lizardi's novel is like those Mexican votive paintings that
depict a miracle and then also spell out the alleged facts
through the written word. Although the visual dimension
remains intact in both parts of the painting, the literate
viewer understands two messages, one from the illustra-

tion and one from its explanation. Perhaps Mariano Az-uela perceived something similar when he wrote

> Como obra de arte equiparo *El periquillo* a esos re-tablos que suelen encontrarse en las sacristías y en los camerinos de nuestros santuarios más famosos por sus milagros, pintados con mano torpe e in-genua, pero pujantes de verdad y vida.

> I compare *El periquillo* as a work of art to those al-tars that are commonly to be found in the sacristies and chambers of our sanctuaries most famous for their miracles—painted with an awkward and in-genuous hand but charged with truth and life.

Azuela probably compared Lizardi's art with folk crafts because he thought Lizardi's original reader

> de inteligencia rudimentaria, ignorancia supina e ingenuidad infantil, no más aventajado segura-mente que el que aplaudía los autos y coloquios en tiempos de la Colonia.

> Of rudimentary intelligence, supine ignorance, and infantile ingenuousness—surely no more advan-taged than he who applauded the *autos* and *colo-quios* in colonial times.

Azuela's criticism of Lizardi's technique largely rests on his objections to the "pamphleteering" passages; Azuela shows he is judging the novel by latter-day realist stan-dards when he writes that because of these passages

> se ve la mano que mueve los hilos, se oye la voz monótona y cansada del que impulsa a los muñe-cos.

> the hand that controls the strings is revealed, the monotonous and tired voice of the one who moves the puppets is heard.

If it is true, as Azuela proclaims, that the colonial reader did not have the refined taste of Azuela's model reader in the twentieth century—and even Lizardi acknowledged his reader's "ignorance"—it becomes critical to ask just what this "ignorance" was and whether something in the colonial experience fostered it. Azuela's comment that Lizardi's reader was like the faithful viewer of a church play, uncritically accepting its dogmatic statement, asso-ciates naive acceptance with illiteracy and the colonial past. Lizardi's readers, though necessarily literate, were in Azuela's view undiscriminating in their blind approval of Lizardi's obvious preaching.

Lizardi's concern for the reading process—his insistence on how his book was to be read and his thoughtful analysis of his reader's special requirements—makes central the question of the textual interpretation and acceptance of his novel. Writing at a moment when press censorship lim-ited direct statement, Lizardi saw in the novel an imagina-tive form that allowed him to disguise his criticism while continuing his writing career. In fact, censors did prohibit the publication of the last part of the *Periquillo* during Lizardi's lifetime; in these chapters (vols. 4 and 5 of the projected book), Lizardi arranged a dialogue in which the premises underlying colonialism and slavery were explicit-ly examined and debated.

Lizardi's novel, however, is much more than a potboiler produced when his primary interest in journalism was frustrated. It is also an experiment in adapting a European

literary form to indigenous needs, an effort to incorporate into a work pretending to be serious literature the colony's many linguistic forms—oral and written, upper-class and vulgar. Scrutinized, therefore, are not only the prestigious literary traditions and near-sacred utterances of the upper classes but also the reviled speech of the lower classes that Lizardi recorded as part of this Mexican world. At the end of the novel he somewhat apologetically describes the plain style with which he corrects these language varieties in the framing story and in the authorial passages and brings these two worlds together:

> Escribió su vida en un estilo ni rastrero ni finchado; huye de hacer del sabio, usa un estilo casero y fa-miliar, que es el que usamos todos comúnmente y con el que nos entendemos y damos a entender con más facilidad.

> He wrote his life in a style neither base nor high-flown; he avoided sounding learned; he used a homely, common style, that which we use every day and with which we understand each other most easily.

In this way, the literary work and its example of a com-mon language—made up of Lizardi's plain style as well as the bits and pieces of snobbish usage, garbled speech, argot, and jargon of the *Periquillo*'s characters—symbolically reconcile the colony's warring elements. In this historical novel documenting contemporary events, Lizardi describes Mexico in 1813:

> . . . la guerra es el mayor de todos los males para cualquiera nación o reino; pero incomparablemente son más perjudiciales las conmociones sangrientas dentro de un mismo país, pues la ira, la venganza y la crueldad . . . se ceban en los mismos ciuda-danos que se arman para destruirse mutuamente.

> . . . war is the greatest of all evils of any nation or kingdom; but incomparably more harmful is bloody unrest within the country itself, for anger, vengeance, and cruelty . . . rage unchecked in the citizens who arm to destroy one another.

In presenting his reader with a kind of linguistic union in the body of the text, Lizardi offers psychosocial solace in the suggestion that political harmony may also be possi-ble.

The deathbed speech that Periquillo Sarniento, now the rehabilitated *pícaro* Pedro Sarmiento, delivers toward the novel's end is a good example of Lizardi's use of several voices to indicate Mexico's diverse population. Pedro is speaking to a priest friend whose experience as a *pícaro* in his youth ratifies the friend as wise and honest.

> No te apartes de mí hasta que expire, no sea que entre aquí algún devoto o devota que con el *Rami-llete* u otro formulario semejante me empiece a je-susear, machacándome el alma con su frialdad y sonsonete, y quebrándome la cabeza con sus gritos desaforados. No quiero decir que no me digan Jesús, ni Dios permita que yo hablara tal idioma. Sé muy bien que este dulce nombre es sobre todo nombre; que a su invocación el cielo se goza, la tie-rra se humilla y el infierno tiembla; pero lo que no quiero es que se me plante a la cabecera algún buen hombre con un librito de los que te digo; que tal vez empiece a deletrear, y no pudiendo, tome la ordi-naria cantinela de *Jesús te ayude, Jesús te ampare,*

Jesús te favorezca, no saliendo de eso para nada, y
que conociendo él mismo su frialdad quiera inspi-
rarme fervor a fuerza de gritos. . . . Tú sabes que
en estos momentos lo que importa es mover al en-
fermo a contrición y confianza en la divina miseri-
cordia; hacerlo que repita en su corazón los actos
de fe, esperanza y caridad; ensancharle el espíritu
con la memoria de la bondad divina, acordándole
que Jesucristo derramó por él su sangre y es su
medianero, y por fin ejercitándolo en actos de amor
de Dios y avivándole los deseos de ver a Su Maj-
estad en la gloria. . . .

También te ruego que no consientas que las señoras
viejas me acaben de despachar con buena intención
echándome en la boca, y en estado agonizante,
caldo de sustancia ni agua de la palata.

Don't leave me until I die, lest some devout man
or woman with the Flowery Prayer or some other
such rigamarole begin to be-Jesus me, crushing my
soul with cold singsong, breaking my head with
wild crying. I know very well that this sweet name
is above all names; that at its invocation heaven delights, earth humbles itself, and hell trembles; but
what I don't want is some good soul to stand at the
head of my bed with one of those foolish books such
as I described; then when he starts to try to read it
and finds he's not able to, he sets up the chant he
does know of "May Jesus aid you, may Jesus solace
you, may Jesus bless you," sticking with this forever and, in recognizing its coldness, trying to inspire
fervor by shouting. . . . You know that in these
moments what matters is moving a sick man to
contrition and confidence in divine mercy; to make
him repeat in his heart the articles of faith, hope,
and charity; to open up his spirit with the memory
of divine goodness, reminding him that Jesus shed
his blood for him and is his intercessor and, finally,
exercising him in acts of love of God and kindling
in him the desire to see his Lord in glory. . . .

I also beg you not to allow the old women to finish
me off with their good intentions, choking me with
thick soup or water out of a dipper when I am agonizing.

Pedro's lengthy description of what language and behavior are proper conveys the narrator's faith in an appropriate language to console a dying man. He rejects as unsatisfactory the mechanical litany of the ignorant priest and
the pieties of books. The old ladies are present, though
they say nothing; their misguided actions provoke the
dying Pedro into giving a learned-sounding lecture on
anatomy and the dangers of suffocating. What seem to be
several voices are here a single voice that dramatically operates at several levels of discourse; an ignorant priest
never, in fact, speaks, but instead Pedro parodies such
speech in his own. Not only has Lizardi written a picaresque tale that contrasts folly and wisdom, but within his
story he makes the same point by ironic shifts of language.
As [M. N.] Bakhtin notes, style is to be found in the very
combination of styles.

Early in the novel Pedro, in recounting his life to his children, stresses the importance of knowing how to read.
This advice, drawn from childhood experience, is more
necessary to Lizardi's text than critics have thought. In
addition to indicating the educational system of the day,
the passage instructs Lizardi's readers, most of whom
were probably adult, in the skills required for understand-

ing the work at hand: "el que lee debe saber distinguir los
estilos en que se escribe. . . . " 'he who reads ought to
know how to distinguish the various styles in which the
book is written. . . .' Although the story at this point
centers on the classroom and specifically on the singsong
way in which Periquillo's teacher read aloud to the students, Lizardi is emphasizing to his own readers that to
understand the meaning of words one must recognize
their context. If, as Lizardi believed, his colonial readers
needed explicit advice to look for high and low styles ("No
se han de leer las oraciones de Cicerón como los anales de
Tácito, ni el panegírico de Plinio como las comedias de
Moreto" 'The orations of Cicero are not to be read like the
annals of Tacitus, nor the panegyric of Pliny like the comedies of Moreto'), this inability to perceive differences—to
maintain a critical perspective on the use of language so
as constantly to alter one's relations to the text—becomes
important in identifying the colonial reader.

This failure, if indeed it was that, may have been due to
several factors. Colonial readers often were poorly educated. As Lizardi shows, many colonials were unfamiliar
with the written language because in many schools "las es-
critura [es] . . . como mera curiosidad" 'writing [is] . . .
a mere curiosity.' Encouraged to speak well, they had little
knowledge of such concerns as punctuation and spelling.
Lizardi editorializes:

> . . . es una lástime ver que este defecto de orto-
> grafía se extiende a muchas personas de fina
> educacíon . . . de manera que no es muy raro oír
> un bello discurso a un orador, y notar en este
> mismo discurso escrito por su mano sesenta mil de-
> fectos ortográficos. . . .

> . . . it is a shame to see how common this igno-
> rance of spelling is among many persons of fine
> education . . . it is not rare to hear an orator deliv-
> er a beautiful speech and then to find in the same
> speech, written by his own hand, sixty thousand er-
> rors in spelling. . . .

Nuns and priests, representatives of a Latin cultural tradition, were frequently mentioned in the literature of the period as corrupters of this tradition because their aural
knowledge of Latin often caused them to mouth sounds
without understanding meanings. Although Lizardi generally does not mock the ignorance of these religious, his
novel exposes the knowledge of many other representatives of the colonial order, such as doctors and lawyers,
as the mere flaunting of jargon.

Lizardi's mouthpiece, Periquillo, describes how in his philosophy class he memorized words and phrases in the
same way a child learns the parts of a catechism lesson,
orally and by rote:

> se oía discutir sobre el *ente de razón, las cualidades
> ocultas y la materia prima,* y esta misma se definía
> con la explicación de la nada, *nec est quid,* etc.

> one heard argument over a "rational being," "oc-
> cult qualities," and "primary matter," and this last
> was defined with the explanation of nothingness,
> *nec est quid,* etc.

In his transcription of this oral material Lizardi humorously shows how Periquillo and his fellow students played
with this language, which had no meaning for them:

. . . en el estudio de la gramática aprendí varios equivoquillos impertinentes . . . como *Caracoles comes; pastorcito come adobes; non est peccatum mortale occidere patrem suum* y otras simplezas . . . así también, en el estudio de las súmulas, aprendí luego luego mil sofismos ridículos, de los que hacía mucho alarde con los condiscípulos más cándidos, como por ejemplo: *besar la tierra es acto de humildad: la mujer es tierra, luego* . . . . cuidado, que echaba yo un *ergo* con más garbo que el mejor doctor de la Academia de París. . . .

. . . in my grammar studies, I learned nothing but impertinent puns . . . such as *Caracoles comes; pastorcito come adobes; non est peccatum mortale occidere patrem suum;* and other nonsense . . . and in my study of logic, also, I learned immediately a thousand ridiculous sophisms, which I bawled in chorus with my simple fellow students. For example: To kiss the earth is an act of humility; woman is earth; therefore, etc. . . . Rest assured I threw in my *ergo* with more knack than the best doctor of the Paris Academy. . . .

In what follows, the colloquial phrase "I didn't understand a word of that" registers a growing Mexican disillusionment with such language:

. . . mi buen preceptor nos enseñó algunos principios de geometría, de cálculo y de física moderna; . . . pero . . . yo no entendí palabra de esto; y, sin embargo, decía al concluir este curso, que era *físico,* y no era más que un ignorante patarato; pues después que sustenté un actillo de física, de memoria, y después que hablaba de esta enorme ciencia con tanta satisfacción en cualquiera concurrencia, temo que me mochen si hubiera sabido explicar en qué consiste que el chocolate dé espuma, mediante el movimiento del molinillo . . . ni otras cosillas de éstas que traemos todos los días entre manos.

. . . my good preceptor taught us some principles of geometry, calculus, and modern physics; . . . but . . . I didn't understand a word of it; nevertheless, when the course was finished, I said I was a *physicist,* although I was really a humbug. I devoured a simple little physics experiment by memory and then I spoke of this enormous science with great satisfaction in any gathering. However, I'm afraid you may lop off my head if I knew how to explain why chocolate foams when the beater is whirled . . . or any of the other simple little things that we do every day.

Periquillo's educational experience is representative of the colonial's. Indeed, the title of the novel, *El periquillo Sarniento (The Itching Parrot)*—a derogatory play on the name Pedro Sarmiento, which his schoolmates provided—suggests that his linguistic parroting is a key to the colonial's identity.

For Lizardi mastery of the written language meant overcoming an aspect of colonial inferiority; it meant acquiring the body of knowledge behind the erudite terms; and it also meant using language to help rather than harm one's fellows. The critical skills that allow a reader to judge style, to perceive falsity in language, were especially important in a society where a literate minority bore the responsibility, as the Enlightenment taught, for opening up the lessons of a book culture to many uncivilized illiterates.

Homi Bhabha, who has written on colonials' fetishistic regard for the book, shows ambivalence to be typical of colonial discourse. In the colonial writer's repetition of dominant strategies to achieve authority, Bhabha finds a mimicry that makes the text ironic. Although Bhabha chiefly grounds his analysis in the example of nineteenth-century English writers writing either in or about India and focuses his conclusions on the way the colonial subject is denied identity by this failure of representation, his observations are valuable in helping us understand how Lizardi, an indigenous writer, attacks a book tradition so as to reconstitute it in Mexico.

Lizardi begins by distancing himself from earlier writers, the titles of whose works, as he describes in the prospectus for the *Periquillo,* promised "puntos menos que la ciencia general, y la llave de los arcanos de Dios y la Naturaleza" 'no less than total knowledge and the key to the secrets of God and Nature.' In setting his own work against the writing of these authors, many of whom pretended to new secular truths, Lizardi paradoxically links his novel to an established tradition, thus borrowing some of the earlier writers' respectability. In criticizing the pompous language of many books' titles, he challenges their claims to authority and then humorously compares these books to a Mexican phenomenon:

Ni faltan entre nosotros, quiero decir, en nuestro tiempo, semejantes libros que llevan al frente estos títulos altos, sonoros y significativos; . . . estas obras suelen ser como unos animalitos que hay en algunos lugares de este reino, que llaman Punches, los cuales son del tamaño de un sapo mediano, y cuando están en sus charcos se inflan, y empujan el aire con tal fuerza, que el que no los conoce . . . al oírlos gritar le parece que son, por lo menos unos becerros. . . .

Así, pues, suelen ser estos libros de que hablamos: títulos pomposos en la carátula, y en el centro aire y más aire.

There's not lacking among us, I mean in our time, similar books that carry on their exterior these exalted, sonorous, significant titles; . . . these works are usually like those little critters that are to be found in some places in this land. They are called *Punches* and are about the size of an average toad. When they are in their ponds, they blow themselves up and then expel the air with such force that the person who isn't familiar with them . . . upon hearing them thinks that they are the cries of two-year-old calves. . . .

The books we talked about are the same: pompous titles on the title page and inside air and more air.

Here Lizardi's metaphor, drawn from the nonbook context of animal life in "this land," deflates the puffed promise of the earlier books. Lizardi's title for his own work is simple: *Vida de Periquillo Sarniento, escrita por él para sus hijos, y publicada para los que la quieran leer, por D. J. F. de L. autor del periódico titulado* **El pensador mexicano** 'Life of Periquillo Sarniento, written by him for his children, and published for those who wish to read it, by D. J. F. de L., author of the periodical titled *The Mexican Thinker*.'

By making himself and his readers part of the book's title, Lizardi emphasizes the new relationship he would establish. He identifies himself as one who has already written for a newspaper, a genre colonial readers had learned to trust; and he loosely collects his potential readers into the category "those who wish to read [Sarniento's life]." In using "life" rather than either "novel" or "history" to characterize his book, Lizardi establishes the immediate value of this story. The following passage from the *Periquillo* contrasts a "life" with a "novel":

> Ninguno *diga quien es, que sus obras lo dirán.* Este proloquio es tan antiguo como cierto; todo el mundo está convencido de su infalibilidad; y así ,qué tengo yo que ponderar mis malos procederes cuando con referirlos se ponderan? Lo que apeteciera, hijos míos, sería que no leyerais mi vida como quien lee una novela, sino que pararais la consideración más allá de la cáscara de los hechos, advirtiendo los tristes resultados de la holgazanería . . . ; haciendo análisis de los extraviados sucesos de mi vida, indagando sus causas, temiendo sus consecuencias y desechando los errores vulgares que veis adoptados por mí y por otros, empapándoos en las sólidas máximas de la sana y crisitiana moral que os presentan a la vista mis reflexiones, . . . desearía que penetrárais en todas sus partes la sustancia de la obra; que os divirtiérais con lo ridículo, que conociérais el error y el abuso para no imitar el uno ni abrazar el otro, y que donde hallárais algún hecho virtuoso os enamorárais de su dulce fuerze y procurárais imitarlo. Esto es deciros . . . que deseara que de la lectura de mi vida sacárais tres frutos, dos principales y uno accesorio. Amor a la virtud, aborrecimiento al vicio y diversión. . . .

> Let no *one say who he is, for his works will say it for him.* This maxim is as ancient as it is certain. Everyone is convinced of its infallibility; thus, why do I need to ponder my bad actions when, in telling them, the pondering is accomplished? What I should like, my children, is not that you read my life as one reads a novel but that you stop your consideration beyond the shell of the deeds, noticing the sad results of shiftlessness . . . analyzing the wayward events of my life . . . soaking up the solid maxims of healthy, Christian morality that my reflections show you. . . . I should like you to penetrate to the substance of the work . . . enjoy the ridiculous, become familiar with error and abuse so as not to imitate the one or embrace the other, and . . . wherever you find some virtuous act, you become enamored of its sweet force and strive to imitate it. . . . I should wish that from the reading of my life you extract three fruits, two principal and one secondary. Love of virtue, abhorrence of vice, and entertainment. . . .

Lizardi's explicit instructions on how to read ("the reading of my life") suggest that the colonial reader has in hand a genre not seen before.

A narrative as a "life" was not new in Nueva España. Saints' lives served as a model for storytelling; thus in this Catholic society a "life" did not assume the comic character an individual's perhaps eccentric history might have had elsewhere. In addition, the *Life* of Diego de Torres y Villarroel with its manifestly autobiographical story was widely known in the colony; Lizardi recalls Torres by using a quotation from another of Torres's works to introduce the *Periquillo.* Lizardi's use of the term *life,* however, carries with it a greater sense of the person whose experiences give rise to the recounting; in constantly admon-

ishing his readers that his "life" shows, rather than tells about, a person, Lizardi exhibits an American effort to rethink the relation between life and art. The emphasis on the novel as deeds, rather than as words about deeds, suggests that Lizardi expected his work to elicit something akin to a visual response in the reader, a fresh reaction to a flesh-and-blood individual, which is not linguistically mediated for purposes of indoctrination. In the last chapter Lizardi introduces himself as the editor of Pedro Sarmiento's notebooks; in summing up Pedro's story he contrasts it with those openly moralistic works whose sermons often bored the reader:

> Los libros morales es cierto que enseñan, pero sólo por los oídos, y por eso se olvidan sus lecciones fácilmente. Estos [la vida de Pedro Sarmiento] instruyen por los oídos y por los ojos. Pintan al hombre como él es, y pintan los estragos del vicio y los premios de la virtud en acaecimientos que todos los días suceden. Cuando leemos estos hechos nos parece que los estamos mirando, los retenemos en la memoria; . . . nos acordamos de este o del otro individuo de la historia luego que vemos a otro que se le parece, y de consiguiente no podemos aprovechar de la instrucción que nos ministró la anécdota. . . .

> It is true that moral books teach but only through one's ears; that's why their lessons are easily forgotten. These [books such as the life of Pedro Sarmiento] instruct through the ears and through the eyes. They paint man as he is, and they paint the ravages of vice and the rewards of virtue in events that happen every day. When we read these happenings it seems to us that we are looking at them, we hold them in our memories; . . . we remember one individual or another from the story when we see someone who resembles him, and then we can benefit from the instruction that the anecdote provided us. . . .

Although Lizardi in using the metaphor of painting is talking about the power of anecdote in the novel, his language reflects his awareness of both the visual and the auditory, the written and the spoken, in the reading process. Yet in another episode, when Pedro is speaking to his children, Lizardi affirms the superior value of print over oral exchanges between persons that his concept of "life" has implied:

> El buen ejemplo mueve más que los consejos, las insinuaciones, los sermones y los libros. Todo esto es bueno, pero, por fin, son palabras, que casi siempre se las lleva el viento. La doctrina que entra por los ojos se imprime mejor que la que entra por los oídos.

> The good example moves [us] more than advice, hints, sermons, and books. All these are good, but finally they are only works that the wind usually blows away. Doctrine that enters through the eyes is impressed [on us] better than that which enters through our ears.

Here Lizardi shows how the written word not only prolongs the life of the spoken word but also allows for extended contemplation and thought.

Thus Lizardi's sense of orality in the making of his text can be seen to be as important as previous criticism has shown, although somewhat richer and qualitatively different. Although critics have compared Lizardi's technique to the mechanical facilities of recording machines such as the camera and the tape recorder—and the critics' continued use of the nineteenth-century term *cuadros de costumbre* 'genre scenes' hints at the incorporation of visual data into the literary medium—academic readers of the **Periquillo** have generally failed to recognize the unique way in which Lizardi combines verbal and visual elements so as to reach the colonial reader. They have noted his use of peculiarly Mexican lexical items and remarked on the way his dialogue orthographically imitates low-class speech. They have also studied his use of proverbs. But critics have usually passed lightly over the professional mumbo jumbo. And they have generally ignored the earnest plainness of Lizardi's style in the long passages in which the author preaches or restates the wisdom of the ancients or the discoveries of modern science and contemporary ideas. Most have wished these passages away as extraneous to the picaresque tale.

Lizardi's heavy reliance on the language of speech in the making of his literary language results not only from his consciousness that peculiar Mexican speech patterns underscore the Americanness of his picaresque tale but also from his desire to enhance the visual experience of reading with more familiar auditory resonances. Recent theories of orality and literacy by critics such as Walter Ong shed light on Lizardi's complex style. Although many of these theories on orality derive from studies of primitive societies, they are useful for viewing an artifact produced in the semiliterate context of colonial Mexico. Like many in the theoretical structure, the colonial world represents both orality and literacy. Readers in such a situation—generally estranged from books—are caught between feeling their colonial inferiority because they are denied the chance to participate in print production and recognizing that their speech has already empowered them to produce an independent communication system. Seeing that books often intimidated or bored colonial readers, Lizardi responded by infusing his own book with as much untraditional, nonbook material as possible—both linguistic and narrative.

Clearly, Lizardi means to shatter his readers' expectations that a literary work should follow European models and have an elevated style removed from quotidian concerns. Depicting Mexico's ugly realities in the social satire of his story could be justified on the rhetorical grounds of the need for a believable setting; recording the life of a sinner could be rationalized by the moral argument that exemplary punishment was more effective than exhortation to virtue. While it is true that verisimilitude was a concern of many eighteenth-century European writers and that Lizardi was considerably affected by the imported aesthetic doctrine that art be utilitarian, his concern for readers' acceptance of his innovative text exceeded that of most European writers. In addition to legitimizing a new genre that writers in the eighteenth century preferred to call "letters," "history," "biography," "life," or "confessions" rather than the "novel," Lizardi as a colonial writer needed to carve out a space for his literature in order to win a readership. The picaresque form he borrowed had respectable antecedents in the Spanish Golden Age, but he deviated from these in abandoning the intellectual wordplay with which the baroque authors often told their stories. Therefore, as the writer of the first Latin American

novel, Lizardi had not only to convince colonial readers of the novel's worth but also to persuade them that verisimilitude, translated into Mexican terms, called for a different language.

The plain style Lizardi claimed for himself—language that was inclusive in revealing its meaning to many, rather than exclusive in addressing the few—was obviously patterned after colonial newspaper usage. Out of a desire to communicate to large numbers of readers, newspaper editors and contributors had adopted a serviceable style, one that abandoned preciousness and elitist display. Although a plain style is sometimes thought to be a manipulative tool whereby a state exercises social control, in Lizardi's hands it was subversive. It was the linguistic equivalent of egalitarianism, an indictment of colonial rank and privilege. A style that authorized Mexican speech habits in a non-comic way and linked levels of society in a common discourse was a cry for American independence from the tyranny of imposed structures. The idea of informality, of equals addressing equals, implicit in the concept of plainness, would have had special appeal among those lesser colonials, the criollos customarily passed over for high position.

Plainness results from the impression of several language styles brought together and subjected to colonial standards of utility and morality. For example, the reformed *pícaro* contrasts two vocabularies as Lizardi criticizes imported urbanity:

> Estos amigos pícaros que me perdieron y que pierden a tantos 'en el mundo, saben el arte maldito de disfrazar los vicios con nombres de virtudes. A la disipación llaman liberalidad; al juego diversión honesta, por más que por modo de diversión se pierdan los caudales; a la lubricidad, cortesanía; a la embriaguez, placer; a la soberbia, autoridad; a la vanidad, circunspección. . . .

> These devilish friends who led me astray and who lead so many astray in this world are expert in the cursed art of cloaking vices with the names of virtues. They call dissipation liberality; gambling honest entertainment, no matter how many savings are lost; lewdness, courtliness; drunkenness, pleasure; arrogance, authority; shallowness, dignity. . . .

By such juxtapositions readers are recurrently made aware of language as a tool whereby powerful, immoral interests misrepresented reality and erroneously persuaded colonials of the truth of the language code. The Indian population in Mexico, often set off from the Spanish-speaking sector because of a perceived language deficiency, is characterized in Lizardi's text as truly worthy if one looks at the work of their hands. A wise friend lectures Periquillo:

> . . . esa dureza e idiotismo que adviertes en los indios, mulatos y demás castas, no es por defecto de su entendimiento, sino por su ninguna cultura y educación. Ya habrás visto que muchos de esos mismos que no saben hablar, hacen mil curiosidades con las manos. . . . Esto prueba bien que tienen más talento del que tú les concedes. . . .

> . . . that coarseness and ignorance that you notice in the Indians, mulattoes, and the other castes are not on account of some defect in their intellect but rather the result of no training or education. You

must have noticed that many of those who don't know how to talk perform thousands of intricate tasks with their hands. . . . This proves conclusively that they are smarter than you have granted. . . .

At another point, when he has Periquillo comment on the unlearned way in which a lower-class friend expresses himself, Lizardi shows his readers how skill at speaking is often an invalid index for measuring a person's real wisdom: "Tú hablas mal . . . pero dices bien" 'You talk badly . . . but you speak truly.'

However, it is in the change of discourse represented by the moral and erudite digressions that Lizardi most frequently advises his readers that the text requires an attitudinal shift. More than ordinary transitions the markers introducing a digression ("Tal vez no os digustará saberlas [demostraciones hechas en Grecia y en Roma por sus muertos]" 'Perhaps it wouldn't displease you to learn about them [ceremonies conducted in Greece and Rome for their dead]') or signaling a return to the story line ("Volviendo a mis adelantamientos en la escuela" 'Returning to my progress in school') call attention to Lizardi's voice directing the reader. Wolfgang Iser's studies of gaps in the text [in his *Implied Reader*], particularly in serialized eighteenth- and nineteenth-century literary works, show these moments of discontinuity to be opportunities for readers to participate in creating the text. In the colonial text it is clear that these gaps or textual discontinuities mark the readers' identity; readers are defined in that space between the traditional, codified knowledge of the ancients and the rational abstractions of the European Enlightenment. Theirs is the story of Periquillo, the representative of empirical thought, whose tale of suffering while he learns through trial and error duplicates the colonial experience. The readers' task, then, is to try to join those segments in which they recognize a portrayal of their own world to those passages in which they perceive a civilization from which they feel culturally and linguistically estranged. In bridging these gaps the readers would seem to be guided by the narrative voice, the surviving *pícaro*, whose morality is the result of tested virtue. Early nineteenth-century colonial readers, however, had not yet learned to base their acceptance of the text on uninterrupted illusion as later realist practice taught. It is more likely that to reconcile the novel's parts and to think through the relation ideated between the work of literature and its host world, colonial readers relied on their own judgment. These readers were probably as skeptical of a writer's authority as they were of other claims to authority, and the degree to which they accepted this indigenous text would more logically seem to have been determined by political commitments.

The "ignorance" Lizardi saw as characterizing his colonial readers was arguably a blindness to changing political realities and a stubborn resistance to allowing an indigenous literature that in any way departed from prestigious European models. Trained to a baroque taste, colonial readers were conditioned to expect literary artifice; they were simply unaccustomed to Lizardi's plain style. Indeed, the evidence of contemporary journalism proves that colonial readers were considerably sophisticated in understanding indirect political statement, where they seem unskilled was in finding their own, honest level of expression among the range of discourses available to them.

That such an endeavor may have been practically impossible is suggested by Roberto Fernández Retamar's description of the American as Caliban. Brutalized by the conquest and stripped of languages, the colonials were forced into mental slavery by the imposition of another tongue. Lacking educational institutions, libraries, and books that might have transmitted to them whole the European culture of the powerful classes, colonials had become expert in imitating that culture's external signs. Because they feared being judged inferior by civilized people throughout the world, many of them preferred the half-understood language of the colonizer. A salient characteristic of the American character, Lizardi had written in an earlier essay, is its capacity for imitating foreign modes.

El periquillo Sarniento, which was meant to be read as a primer of how to read, may have failed in its design to teach criticism, to show literature against itself, so as to subvert established norms. From surviving documents pertaining to the novel's initial reception, the literary historian learns that Lizardi's book offended many academic critics, probably among the colony's elite. While a number seem to have read the first installments and some recognized the novel's merit when compared with European models of the picaresque, these upper-class readers distanced themselves from the work by labeling it "popular" (Reyes summarizes early reactions to the *Periquillo*). They fastened on its low-life scenes and vulgar language and said that Lizardi was the first to write novels in the style of the *canalla* 'rabble.' That these readers did not seem sure whether he was writing in one style or three obviously concerned Lizardi, for later in the apologia for the novel, which he composed to respond especially to the criticism of a Sr. Terán, he amusingly pointed out this reader's contradictory charges that the book lacked "una variedad de locución" 'a variety of locution' while at the same time "Desde una sencillez muy mediana pasa su estilo a la bajeza y con harta frecuencia a la grosería del de la taberna" 'Its style passes from a very average simplicity to lowness and with excessive frequency to the grossness of the tavern.' Less amused, he answered Terán's criticism that there was no portrayal of ranking officials to redeem the book (i.e., "[el retrato] de un embajador, de un príncipe, de un cardenal, de un soberano" '[the portrait] of an ambassador, a prince, a cardinal, a sovereign'): "¿Cómo había de ser eso si en este Reino no hay esta clase de señores?" 'How could there be if in this land this class of person doesn't exist?' Terán's inability to recognize colonial powerlessness and deprivation in Lizardi's choice of style and subject matter was typical of many colonial readers who, for one reason or another, resisted Lizardi's message. (pp. 784-96)

Nancy Vogeley, "Defining the 'Colonial Reader': 'El periquillo Sarniento'," in PMLA, *Vol. 102, No. 5, October, 1987, pp. 784-800.*

FURTHER READING

Bancroft, Robert L. "*El periquillo Sarniento* and *Don Catrín de la fachenda:* Which Is the Masterpiece?" *Revista Hispania Moderna* 34, No. 3-4 (July-October 1968): 533-38.

>Contends that while most critics recognize *El periquillo Sarniento* as Lizardi's best novel, the narration and characterization are superior in *Don Catrín.*

Knowlton, Edgar C. "China and the Philippines in *El periquillo Sarniento.*" *Hispanic Review* XXXI, No. 4 (October 1963): 336-47.

>Studies Lizardi's use of Filipino and Chinese language in *El periquillo Sarniento,* concluding that the novel was, in part, inspired by Lizardi's interest in the Far East.

Pawlowski, John. "*Periquillo* and *Catrín:* Comparison and Contrast." *Hispania* 58, No. 4 (December 1975): 830-42.

>Praises the protagonists, secondary characters, parallel passages, and novelistic techniques of both *El periquillo Sarniento* and *Don Catrín.*

Peña, Carlos González. "The Epoch of Independence: Prose." In his *History of Mexican Literature,* translated by Gusta Barfield Nance and Florene Johnson Dunstan, pp. 153-90. Dallas: Southern Methodist University Press, 1968.

>Overview of Lizardi's works, judging *The Itching Parrot* to be his primary contribution to Mexican literature.

Porter, Katherine Anne. Introduction to *The Itching Parrot,* by José Joaquín Fernández de Lizardi, translated by Katherine Anne Porter, pp. xiii-xliii. New York: Doubleday, Doran, and Co., 1942.

>Biographical material on Lizardi focusing on the historical context of *The Itching Parrot,* which Porter refers to as "The Novel of the past century, not only for Mexico but for all Spanish-speaking countries."

Radin, Paul. "An Annotated Bibliography of the Poems and Pamphlets of Fernández de Lizardi." *Hispanic American Historical Review* 26, No. 2 (May 1946): 284-91.

>Bibliography with annotations in English.

Reynolds, Winston A. "The Clergy in the Novels of Fernández de Lizardi." *Modern Language Forum* XL, No. 2 (1955): 105-12.

>Catalogs the clerical characters and identifies their didactic function in Lizardi's novels, concluding that his criticism of the church is constructive in its emphasis on "the ideal priest, the Lizardi clergyman."

Rugoff, Milton. Review of *The Itching Parrot,* by José Joaquín Fernández de Lizardi. *New York Herald Tribune Books* 18, No. 30 (22 March 1942): 12.

>Describes *The Itching Parrot* as "the rash and racy chronicles of a knave" in a generally favorable review.

Yancey, Myra L. "Fernández de Lizardi and His Foreign Sources for *Las noches tristes.*" *Hispanic Review* 9, No. 3 (July 1941): 394-97.

>Suggests that Edward Young's *Night Thoughts on Life, Death, and Immortality* was the primary influence on Lizardi's novel *Noches tristes y día alegre.*

Young, Carol M. "Lizardi's *El negro sensible.*" *College Language Association Journal* 24, No. 3 (March 1981): 369-75.

>Regards Lizardi's version of the drama *El negro sensible* as one of Mexico's "earliest calls for racial freedom and equality."

Alexander Ostrovsky

1823-1886

(Full name Alexander Nikolaevich Ostrovsky; also trans-literated as Ostrovski, Ostrovskii, Ostrovskij, Ostróvsky) Russian dramatist, translator, and essayist.

Considered one of the most important Russian play-wrights of the nineteenth century, Ostrovsky is credited with bringing dramatic realism to the Russian stage. In his best-known plays, he meticulously portrayed the Russian society of his time, focusing in particular on the morals and manners of the newly emerging merchant class. Ex-tremely popular during his lifetime, Ostrovsky's works re-main an integral part of the Russian repertoire and are es-teemed for their skillful characterization and use of dia-lect.

Born in Moscow, Ostrovsky was the oldest of nine chil-dren of an ambitious lawyer who frequently represented members of the merchant class. Ostrovsky developed an interest in literature from reading in his father's library and frequently attended performances at the Maly The-ater, where many of his own plays were later produced. He was admitted to the University of Moscow in 1840, and although he preferred to study literature, he reluctant-ly complied with his father's wish that he enter law school. Unsuccessful in his law studies, Ostrovsky withdrew from the University in 1843 to work as a clerk in the Court of Conscience, which settled family disputes, and later in the Moscow Commercial Court, where he observed many cases arising from the unscrupulous business dealings that had become common among Russian merchants.

In 1847 Ostrovsky finished his first drama, *Semeynaya kartina* (*A Domestic Picture*), a one-act play about a Rus-sian family of the mercantile class. Two years later he completed *Svoi lyudi—sochtemsya!* (*It's a Family Affair—We'll Settle It Ourselves*), a four-act satirical comedy that exposed the use of fraudulent bankruptcies to hide assets from creditors. Objecting to Ostrovsky's negative portray-al of the powerful commercial class, government censors prohibited production of both plays. Ostrovsky appealed the decision, but the censors' judgment was upheld by Czar Nicholas I, who ordered police surveillance of Ostrovsky. In 1851 Ostrovsky was dismissed from his po-sition in the civil service.

For the next two years, Ostrovsky continued to write and often gave readings of his plays in private homes. In 1853 his play *Ne v svoi sani ne sadis!*, a comedy considered inof-fensive by the censors, was staged in an extremely popular production at the Maly Theater. Although he continued to have frequent disagreements with censors, throughout the next three decades Ostrovsky wrote a long series of successful plays. He also organized associations for actors and dramatists, and wrote several essays on the rights of dramatists and the effects of censorship. He was placed in charge of the Moscow Imperial Theaters and Drama School shortly before his death in 1886.

Ostrovsky wrote nearly fifty plays and translated approxi-mately twenty plays into Russian, including several works

by William Shakespeare. With the exception of *Snegurochka,* a fantasy based on Russian folklore, critics usually divide Ostrovsky's works into two categories: his-torical plays and social dramas. Believed to have been in-fluenced by Shakespeare's chronicle plays, Ostrovsky's six historical plays were written in blank verse and are noted for incorporating Russian legends and folklore, as well as for their use of dialects from the Volga region. These plays are considered inferior to his social and satirical dramas, which portray a world described by Nikolai Dobrolyubov as a "realm of darkness," an oppressive social environ-ment dominated by *samodurs,* or "petty tyrants," whose demands for obedience and conformity terrorize family members and employees, stripping them of their will to think or feel for themselves. For example, in Ostrovsky's most famous tragedy, *Groza* (*The Storm*), Marfa Ka-banova's domineering abuse of her family eventually drives her daughter-in-law to commit suicide. Although Ostrovsky's plays frequently present a negative portrayal of Russian life, some critics note that they also celebrate those aspects of his culture Ostrovsky admired, most nota-bly the rugged endurance of the Russian peasantry. Others contend, however, that the "realm of darkness" dominates Ostrovsky's works. His frank discussion of the social prob-lems resulting from the autocratic and patriarchal features of Russian culture provoked the censorship of his works. In banning *It's a Family Affair,* the censor noted: "All the characters in the play . . . are first-rate villains. The dialogue is filthy. The entire play is an insult to the Russian merchant class." While Ostrovsky agreed with the government's position that drama should serve a moral purpose, he believed that, rather than limiting the theater to presentations of virtuous behavior as a means for public edification, immoral conduct should be exposed to provoke public outrage. Some critics have suggested that early censorship of his works affected Ostrovsky's style, noting that many of his plays were banned until he agreed to substantial alterations and that his later works usually contain at least one character evincing a readily recognizable virtue.

Ostrovsky is today considered a master of the realistic drama. He is praised in particular for his insight into the psychology of the Russian people, and many of his well-drawn characters are favorites among Russian actors and audiences. While international recognition of his talent has been limited by the difficulties of translating his heavily idiomatic dialogue, his contributions remain central to the development of modern Russian drama.

PRINCIPAL WORKS

Bednaya nevesta (drama) 1853
 [*The Poor Bride* published in *Masterpieces of the Russian Drama,* 1933]
Ne v svoi sani ne sadis! (drama) 1853
Utro molodogo cheloveka (drama) 1853
Bednost ne porok (drama) 1854
 [*Poverty Is No Crime* published in *Plays by Alexander Ostrovsky,* 1917]
Ne tak zhivi, kak khochetsya (drama) 1854
Semeynaya kartina (drama) 1855
 [*A Domestic Picture* published in *A Treasury of Classic Russian Literature,* 1961]
V chuzhom piru pokhmelye (drama) 1856
Prazdnichny son—do obeda (drama) 1857
Groza (drama) 1859
 [*The Storm,* 1899; also published as *The Thunderstorm,* 1927]
Svoi lyudi—sochtemsya! (drama) 1860
 [*It's a Family Affair—We'll Settle It Ourselves* published in *Plays by Alexander Ostrovsky,* 1917]
Dokhodnoye mesto (drama) 1863
Grekh da beda na kogo ne zhivyot (drama) 1863
 [*Sin and Sorrow Are Common to All* published in *Plays by Alexander Ostrovsky,* 1917]
Tyazhelye dni (drama) 1863
Vospitannitsa (drama) 1863
 [*A Protégée of the Mistress* published in *Plays by Alexander Ostrovsky,* 1917]
Shutniki (drama) 1864
Na boykom meste (drama) 1865
 [*At the Jolly Spot* published in journal *Poet Lore,* 1925]
Voevoda: Son na Volge (drama) 1865
Kozma Zakharich Minin, Sukhoruk (drama) 1866
Dmitry Samozvanets i Vasily Shuysky (drama) 1867
Tushino (drama) 1867
Na vsyakogo mudretsa dovolno prostoty (drama) 1868
 [*Even A Wise Man Stumbles* published in *Easy Money and Two Other Plays,* 1944; also published as *The Scoundrel* in *Five Plays of Alexander Ostrovsky,*

1969; and *Even the Wise Can Err* in *Plays by Alexander Ostrovsky,* 1974]
Goryachee serdtse (drama) 1869
Beshenye dengi (drama) 1870
 [*Easy Money* published in *Easy Money, and Two Other Plays,* 1944]
Les (drama) 1871
 [*The Forest,* 1926]
Ne vse kotu maslenitsa (drama) 1871
 [*A Cat Has Not Always Carnival* published in journal *Poet Lore,* 1929]
Komik XVII stoletiya (drama) 1872
Ne bylo ni grosha, da vdrug altyn (drama) 1872
Pozdnyaya lyubov (drama) 1873
Snegurochka (drama) 1873
Trudovoy khleb (drama) 1874
Bogatye nevesty (drama) 1875
Volki i ovtsy (drama) 1875
 [*Wolves and Sheep* published in journal *Poet Lore,* 1926]
Pravda—khorosho, a schastye luchshe (drama) 1876
Poslednyaya zhertva (drama) 1877
 [*A Last Sacrifice* published in journal *Poet Lore,* 1928]
Bespridannitsa (drama) 1878
Serdtse ne kamen (drama) 1879
Nevolnitsy (drama) 1880
 [*Bondwomen* published in journal *Poet Lore,* 1925]
Talanty i poklonniki (drama) 1881
 [*Artistes and Admirers,* 1970]
Krasavets-muzhchina (drama) 1882
Bez viny vinovatye (drama) 1884
 [*More Sinned against Than Sinning* published in *Plays by Alexander Ostrovsky,* 1974]
Ne ot mira sego (drama) 1885
Polnoye sobraniye sochineny. 16 vols. (dramas) 1949-58
Stikhotvornye dramy (dramas) 1961

Vasily Sleptsov (essay date 1863)

[*In the following essay, which was written in 1863, Sleptsov discusses Ostrovsky's play* Dokhodnoye mesto (A Suitable Place), *focusing on its central character.*]

Ostrovsky's main talent as a dramatist lies in the extraordinary faithfulness with which he reproduces Russian life, in his ability to catch it, so to speak, in the very act of the crime and reproduce it in its entirety with all its minute facets and its peculiar scent. Most of his plays are concerned with resolving some particular question of the time. This is certainly true of Ostrovsky's play **A Suitable Place,** which depicts the struggle of the so-called "new generation" with the one that is passing away. He chose the civil service as his arena for this conflict. The unavoidable bribes of that time play an important role, extortion is punished, and altruism triumphs. Matters of honor and other civic virtues are resolved on the basis of standards existing then, and, since Ostrovsky is always faithful to reality, his solution emerges as it should. But we should not forget that, after all, these proceedings take place in the sphere of the theater, and not in life. In life questions once decided do not always remain decided and things very often can end up inside out.

But we need not be concerned with things in life. We are speaking about Ostrovsky's presentation of life, about the banning of the play when it was first written, and about the fact that the play hasn't ever been staged entirely successfully; that is to say, the play itself is successful, and yet it has failed to produce any important effect upon the public. In this case the public has reacted correctly: the play is somewhat outmoded. The author, of course, is not at fault in this, and the comedy has lost nothing. So both the author and the public are correct, and the fact merely remains that the play is irrelevant. What is the cause of this? The cause is very simple. One must only ask who in 1863 can find it interesting to observe how bribetakers are confounded and subjected to social condemnation in 1855. For who does not know that in our times, thanks to a reduction in the size of staff and an increase in the official salaries, it is no longer necessary to take bribes? Why, then, expose what does not exist? Why rail against bribes when no one takes them any more?

Quietly, modestly, in proper fashion, with the aid of certain administrative measures, by means of cutting some red tape, the reform passed hardly noticed, and extortion, that old, deeply rooted evil, which had so thoroughly debilitated the morale of our civil service, was amputated like a bad limb. But one result is that social opinion suddenly found itself in approximately the same position as pepper served after dinner: one no longer has any need of it. This is why it is strange to see the play's hero, Zhadov, try to frighten his superior with the specter of social opinion.

And Zhadov would, in any case, be incapable of dealing with corruption. Zhadov is a kind of Hamlet, a Russian Hamlet, and he serves as a contemporary representative of the very type to which Griboedov's Chatsky also belongs. If one compares the three men—Hamlet, Chatsky, and Zhadov—the similarity is truly striking. All three are young men who have found themselves in opposition to the life that surrounds them; all three are weak-willed in the same way; all three are in love with unintelligent but beautiful girls; and all three are considered demented. The real Hamlet struggles with life and with himself, although in both these struggles he is inclined toward rhetoric. However that may be, in the end he cannot avoid physical struggle, and as a consequence of this Shakespeare's hero perishes. Our fellow countrymen Chatsky and Zhadov, although they both also struggle and show a propensity to rhetoric, do not enter into hand-to-hand fighting with anyone—probably because they live in a more civilized society, where such debauches are not permitted. God only knows what they would have done if they had found themselves in the place of the Danish Prince! But, fortunately, both our heroes are Muscovites and, moreover, Russian gentlemen, both are noted for their good manners, and although they do not act entirely respectfully toward their elders, even in this they express themselves more or less literarily and phrase their abuse evasively, without calling anyone a scoundrel to his face but, rather, putting the indictment in a broader context, abusing Moscow, social evil, the ignorant majority, etc.

No, the crux of it is that for our heroes everything is words. This constitutes the sole source of their weakness, and also of their strength. "Words, words, words!" These immortal words spoken by the prototype of all our Hamlets have been branded across their foreheads: Unfortunates! Life has treated you badly! Your nerves are somehow weak, and your desire to master life is small. One must grant that you are intelligent, but not overly so. Beautiful phrases, beautiful suffering, and beautiful women have always been dearer to Russians than accomplishments. You didn't know what to do, that is true; but that just makes it the worse for you, my friends, just the worse for you! What kind of heroes can you be after this, not knowing what you should do, not knowing how you should demonstrate your heroism!? For there is one solution to your moaning and curses: words, words! The best and most gifted of you long racked his brain and was in no way able to decide on a course of action. He was, you see, very taken with the question

> Whether 'tis nobler in the mind to suffer
> The slings and arrows of outrageous fortune,
> Or to take arms against a sea of troubles,
> And by opposing end them?

Chatsky, the first Russian Hamlet, goes

> To search the world over
> To find a corner for offended feeling . . .

The third, our contemporary Zhadov, after his fourth glass in a tavern, makes an openhearted confession to a complete stranger: "What sort of man am I? I am a child, I haven't the slightest comprehension of life. All of this is new to me. . . . So hard for me! I don't know if I can bear it! Everything is debauchery around one, one has so little strength! What was the purpose of education?!"

Little by little we come to see that our hero is not a very important bird. He submitted himself easily to the influence of "rules of honor," and he submits himself just as easily to the charms of his sweet spouse. (Unless we assume a lack of firm character and taste in Zhadov, it is impossible to explain his passion for a woman whom he considers stupid and does not esteem and who, for her part, also considers him stupid and does not esteem him.) Zhadov submits himself to her influence to such a degree that he spits on his "rules of honor" and goes to ask a "suitable place" from a man whom he knows to be dishonorable. From all of this it is evident that Zhadov's convictions are slippery and that he will turn out to be made of dubious material in all respects. If he has fallen in among heroes, this somehow happened inadvertently, through lack of calculation.

What is the conclusion to be drawn from all this? The conclusion is that although the comedy is indisputedly a good one it does not please very much, because its theme is outdated and its hero is not a hero. Correct? Possibly I am not correct, but, well, there is nothing to be done about it. (pp. 152-55)

Vasily Sleptsov, "Vasily Sleptsov on Alexandr Ostrovsky," in The Complection of Russian Literature: A Cento, *edited by Andrew Field, Atheneum, 1971, pp. 152-55.*

Edward Garnett   (essay date 1898)

[Garnett was a prominent editor for several London publishing houses, and discovered or greatly influenced the work of many important English writers, including Jo-

seph Conrad, John Galsworthy, and D. H. Lawrence. He also published several volumes of criticism. In the following essay, originally published as the introduction to The Storm, *Garnett discusses the play, praising the depth of Ostrovsky's insights into the psychology of the Russian people.*]

Up to the years of the Crimean War Russia was always a strange, uncouth riddle to the European consciousness. It would be an interesting study to trace back through the last three centuries the evidence of the historical documents that our forefathers have left us when they were brought face to face, through missions, and commerce, with the fantastic life, as it seemed to them, led by the Muscovite. But in any chance record we may pick up, from the reports of a seventeenth century embassy down to the narrative of an early nineteenth century traveller, the note always insisted on is that of all the outlandish civilizations, queer manners and customs of Europeans, the Russians' were the queerest and those which stood furthest removed from the other nations'. And this sentiment has prevailed today, side by side with the better understanding we have gained of Russia. Nor can this conception, generally held among us, which is a half truth, be removed by personal contact or mere objective study; for example, of the innumerable memoirs published on the Crimean War, it is rare to find one that gives us any real insight into the nature of the Russian. And the conception itself can only be amended and enlarged by the study of the Russian mind as it expresses itself in its own literature. The mind of the great artist, of whatever race he springs, cannot lie. From the works of Thackeray and George Eliot in England and Turgenev and Tolstoy in Russia, a critic penetrates into the secret places of the national life, where all the clever objective pictures of foreign critics must lead him astray. Ostrovsky's drama, ***The Storm,*** . . . is a good instance of this truth. It is a revelation of the old-fashioned Muscovite life *from the inside,* and Ostrovsky thereby brings us in closer relation to that primitive life than was in the power of Tolstoy or Goncharov, or even Gogol to bring us. These great writers have given us admirable pictures of the people's life as it appeared to them at the angle of the educated Westernized Russian mind; but here in ***The Storm*** is the atmosphere of the little Russian town, with its primitive inhabitants, merchants, and workpeople, an atmosphere untouched, unadulterated by the *ideas* of any exterior European influence. It is the Russia of Peter the Great and Catherine's time, the Russian patriarchal family life that has existed for hundreds of years through all the towns and villages of Great Russia, that lingers indeed today in out-of-the-way corners of the Empire, though now invaded and much broken up by modern influences. It is, in fact, the very Muscovite life that so puzzled our forefathers, and that no doubt will seem strange to many English readers. But the special triumph of ***The Storm*** is that although it is a realistic picture of old-fashioned Russian patriarchal life, it is one of the deepest and simplest psychological analyses of the Russian soul ever made. It is a very deep though a very narrow analysis. Katerina, the heroine, to the English will seem weak, and crushed through her weakness; but to a Russian she typifies revolt, freedom, a refusal to be bound by the cruelty of life. And her attitude, despairing though it seems to us, is indeed the revolt of the spirit in a land where Tolstoy's doctrine of non-resistance is the logical outcome of centuries of serfdom in a people's history. The

merchant Dikoy, the bully, the soft characterless lover Boris, the idealistic religious Katerina, Kuligin the artisan, and Madame Kabanova, the tyrannical mother, all these are true national types, true Russians of the changing ages, and the counterparts of these people may be met today, if the reader takes up Tchehov's tales. English people no doubt will find it difficult to believe that Madame Kabanova could so have crushed Katerina's life, as Ostrovsky depicts. Nothing indeed is so antagonistic to English individualism and independence as is the passivity of some of the characters in ***The Storm.*** But the English reader's very difficulty in this respect should give him a clue to much that has puzzled Europeans, should help him to penetrate into the strangeness of Russian political life, the strangeness of her love of despotism. Only in the country that produces such types of weakness and tyranny is possible the fettering of freedom of thought and act that we have in Russia today. Ostrovsky's striking analysis of this fatalism in the Russian soul will help the reader to understand the unending struggle in Russia between the enlightened Europeanized intelligence of the few, and the apathy of the vast majority of Russians who are disinclined to rebel against the crystallized conditions of their lives. Whatever may be strange and puzzling in ***The Storm*** to the English mind, there is no doubt that the Russians hail the picture as essentially true. The violence of such characters as Madame Kabanova and Dikoy may be weakened today everywhere by the gradual undermining of the patriarchal family system now in progress throughout Russia, but the picture is in essentials a criticism of the national life. On this point the Russian critic Dobroliubov, criticizing ***The Storm*** [see Further Reading], says:

> The need for justice, for respect for personal rights, this is the cry . . . that rises up to the ear of every attentive reader. Well, can we deny the wide application of this need in Russia? Can we fail to recognize that such a dramatic background corresponds with the true condition of Russian society? Take history, think of our life, look about you, everywhere you will find justification of our words. This is not the place to launch out into historical investigation; it is enough to point out that our history up to the most recent times has not fostered among us the development of a respect for equity, has not created any solid guarantees for personal rights and has left a wide field to arbitrary tyranny and caprice.

This criticism of Dobroliubov's was written in 1860, the date of the play; but we have only to look back at the internal history of Russia for the last thirty years to see that it too "Has not created any solid guarantees for personal rights, and has left a wide field to arbitrary tyranny and caprice." And here is Ostrovsky's peculiar merit, that he has in his various dramas penetrated deeper than any other of the great Russian authors into one of the most fundamental qualities of the Russian nature—its innate fondness for arbitrary power, oppression, despotism. Nobody has drawn so powerfully, so truly, so incisively as he, the type of the "samodour" or "bully," a type that plays a leading part in every stratum of Russian life. From Turgenev we learn more of the reverse side of the Russian character, its lack of will, tendency to weakness, dreaminess and passivity; and it is this aspect that the English find so hard to understand, when they compare the characters in the great Russian novels with their own idea of

Russia's formidable power. The people and the nation do not seem to correspond. But the riddle may be read in the co-existence of Russia's internal weakness and misery along with her huge force, and the immense rôle she fills as a civilizing power. In *The Storm* we have all the contradictory elements: a life strongly organized, yet weak within; strength and passivity, despotism and fatalism side by side.

The author of the *Storm,* Alexander Ostrovsky, is acknowledged to be the greatest of the Russian dramatists. He has been called "a specialist in the natural history of the Russian merchant," and his birth, upbringing, family connections and vocations gave him exceptional facilities for penetrating into the life of that class which he was the first to put into Russian literature. His best period was from 1850 to 1860, but all his work received prompt and universal recognition from his countrymen. In 1859 Dobroliubov's famous article, "The Realm of Darkness," appeared, analysing the contents of all Ostrovsky's dramas, and on the publication of *The Storm* in 1860, it was followed by another article from the same critic, "A Ray of Light in the Realm of Darkness." These articles were practically a brief for the case of the Liberals, or party of Progress, against the official and Slavophil party. Ostrovsky's dramas in general are marked by intense sombreness, biting humour and merciless realism. *The Storm* is the most poetical of his works, but all his leading plays still hold the stage.

The Storm will repay a minute examination by all who recognize that in England today we have a stage without art, truth to life, or national significance. There is not a single superfluous line in the play: all is drama, natural, simple, deep. There is no *falsity,* no forced situations, no sensational effects, none of the shallow or flashy caricatures of daily life that our heterogeneous public demands. All the reproach that lives for us in the word *theatrical* is worlds removed from *The Storm.* The people who like "farcical comedy" and social melodrama, and "musical sketches" will find *The Storm* deep, forbidding and gloomy. The critic will find it an abiding analysis of a people's temperament. The reader will find it literature. (pp. 135-42)

> Edward Garnett, "Ostrovsky's 'The Storm',"
> *in his* Friday Nights: Literary Criticisms and
> Appreciations, *first series, Alfred A. Knopf,*
> *1922, pp. 135-42.*

The Bookman   (essay date 1899)

[*In the following review, the critic discusses* The Storm, *disagreeing with Edward Garnett's assessment of the play's merits. For Garnett's comments, see the excerpt above.*]

Those who read Mr. Garnett's preface after they have read [*The Storm*], may be troubled that they cannot echo the warm eulogy therein. We hesitate, and then feel we cannot. It is one of the things that must lose force when they cross their native frontiers. A great part of its interest, at least to us, is not merely human or artistic, but directly instructive, as telling us of some awful possibilities in the Russian domestic life of a past generation. We do not think it is so poetical or so sublimely stormy as do Mr.

Garnett and the Russian critics. But it is striking and very pathetic—simple even to baldness, quite unforced, perfectly natural, we feel, even amid the strangeness of its circumstances. It is a play made for the stage, not for reading by the fireside, where it strikes one as too frugal of literary effect. "An abiding analysis of a people's temperament," Mr. Garnett calls it. Well, it does suggest darkly and gloomily the national types; and perhaps there was direct intention of so doing, else why are Kuligin, the dreamer, and Feklusha, the pilgrim woman, neither having any essential connection with the story, introduced? Kuligin is, of course, useful as mouthing the wrongs that cling about and hide in the little provincial town, but these are sufficiently evident in the conduct and conversation of the chief personages. In his words, however, are the easiest key to the general situation.

> "But what are the rich about? You'd wonder why they shouldn't walk about and enjoy the fresh air. But not a bit of it! They've all had their gates, sir, locked up long ago, and their dogs let loose. . . . Do you suppose they are at work at their business, or praying to God? No, sir! And it's not for fear of thieves they lock themselves up; it's that folks shouldn't see the way they ill-treat their household, and bully their families. And the tears that flow behind those bolts, unseen, unheard of ! . . . And the sordid, sodden vice within those barred gates, sir! And all hidden and buried—no one sees or knows anything of it, God alone beholds it!"

The Storm is a protest against the monstrous patriarchal system; and the revelation of a sensitive, delicate, joy-loving nature wrecked and killed by household tyranny, while her natural protector, her husband, as well as her lover, stay placid and helpless before domestic bullies in the shape of mother and uncle. Here in the West the conditions of tragedy would not be fulfilled by this story, where the world is divided into the bullies and the feeble. Here we demand, at least, some resisting struggle against brute force. But the conditions of tragedy in Russia, in old Russia, are different, and non-resistance is evidently one of them.

> *"A Russian Drama," in* The Bookman, *London, Vol. XV, No. 89, February, 1899, p. 150.*

The Critic   (essay date 1899)

[*In the following review, the critic faults* The Storm *for its lack of literary and dramatic interest.*]

The Storm by the Russian dramatist, Ostrovsky, . . . is not likely to excite much enthusiasm on the part of the ordinary reader either by its literary or dramatic qualities. The former, indeed, are scarcely discernible, or only very dimly, through the English medium, while the latter, so far as actual representation is concerned, are practically non-existent. The interminable narrations, explanations, discussions, and soliloquies would be intolerable on the modern stage. But as a study of Russian life in a country town, half a century or more ago, while primitive conditions were still unaffected by any contact with the spirit of modern progress, it is extraordinarily interesting. The veracity of it is self-evident. Strange as are the personages and the social conditions presented the whole picture carries with it the conviction of utter truthfulness. It is a most

Scene from the 1935 Moscow Art Theatre production of Groza.

striking, even terrible demonstration of the effect upon a community, and individuals, of long generations of tyranny, ignorance, and superstition. . . . [The] unconscionable despotism of the superior, and the patient, unrepining endurance of the lower classes in the play, are emblematic of the state of the nation at large. It is only of late that revolt has seemed possible to a people trained to submission. The heroine of the story is meant to represent a "revolting daughter"; having no instinct of resistance, her only resource is suicide. Driven into the arms of a lover by the tyranny of her mother-in-law and the cowardly neglect of her husband, she drowns herself rather than face the consequences. This is the whole plot, told with a minimum of dramatic artifice or adornment, but with a wealth of sordid illuminative detail. The selfish, pusillanimous husband; the sanctimonious, shrewish, exacting mother-in-law and her wayward unmarried daughter; the hypocritical female religious mendicant; the coarse, grasping, bullying merchant, Dikoy; the flabby, selfish lover; the semi-intelligent artisan, Kuligin, are all endowed with an extraordinary vitality. As for the unhappy young wife, she is a poor, hysterical creature, but she exacts sympathy by the very hopelessness of her struggle against relentless circumstance, although her fate is scarcely intelligible to those who live in a freer atmosphere. A gloomier or more depressing play than this has seldom been written. There is not a ray of humor in it from first to last, but it throws a flood of light upon some of the mysteries of darker Russia. (pp. 840-41)

> *A review of "The Storm," in* The Critic, New York, *Vol. XXXV, No. 867, September, 1899, pp. 840-41.*

K. Waliszewski   (essay date 1910)

[*In the following excerpt, Waliszewski assesses Ostrovsky's works, objecting to his realism while praising his characterizations.*]

I feel some embarrassment when I come to speak of the great playwright, Ostrovski. His pieces have held the Russian stage for half a century, and their reputation still stands high. In his own country he is currently accepted, not only as the creator of the national drama, but as the renewer of the scenic art from a more general point of view; and I clearly see that, even in the West, his theory is in course of acceptation. But in this theory, which consists in knocking down a corner of the famous "wall of private life," and revealing what lies behind it, in all the natural complexity and apparent disorder which go to make up this life, I recognise an absolute negation of theatrical art, and of Nature herself. And this, because it is founded on *an appearance* which is false, the impression of disorder in Nature being merely a mistaken estimate on our part. Ostrovski's characters come and go, talk on indifferent subjects, until the moment when, all of a sudden—for on the stage things must happen suddenly—the commonplaceness of their behaviour or of their conversation reveals the comic or dramatic elements of the "object of the scene." And I am told that this is the process of real life! Yes, indeed, of real life extending over a space of several years. But the playwright reduces this real period to one of a few hours. By so doing, he disturbs the natural balance of circumstance, and the only method of reestablishing it, and escaping a false presentment, is the use of art—that is to say, of interpretation. The drama lives by synthesis, and it is going against its nature (for it has a nature of its own) to attempt to introduce analytical methods, which belong to a different order of creation, into its system.

The son of a general business agent at Moscow, [Ostrovski] was still devoid of even elementary education when he published his first dramatic efforts in 1847. He filled up this void by studying and adapting foreign models, and did not always choose the best. Living in the *Zamoskvoriétchié,* and mixed up, in consequence of his father's profession, in the life of the small Muscovite tradesmen, he set himself to study and reproduce the manners and customs of that class, and succeeded in attaining a point of realism similar to that of Gogol in another sphere. The subject of his first great comedy, **Between Ourselves, We Shall Settle It (Svoï lioudi sotchtiémsia),** published in 1850, but not performed till ten years later, was, like that of *Dead Souls,* the story of a swindle as mean as it was improbable. A shopkeeper, a kind of comic King Lear, takes it into his head to make over his fortune to his clerk, and to marry him to his own daughter—all to cheat his creditors by means of a sham bankruptcy. He arranges with his son-in-law to pay them 25 per cent., or more, if necessary. But the rascal, once in possession of the funds, refuses to pay anything at all, and allows his miserable father-in-law to be hauled to prison. The elder man had no reason for committing the fraud; his business was a prosperous one; and the author, to make us realise the corruption of thought, the absence of principle, and the demoralisation touched with despotic fancy reigning in that sphere of underhand dealing, draws him as, on the whole, a worthy fellow.

Ostrovski's second great success, **Every One in His Own Place (Nié v svoï sani nié sadis),** played in 1853, gave rise to a great deal of controversy. It also is concerned with a *samodour* shopkeeper, that is to say, one who has preserved the features of originality and despotic fancifulness peculiar to the old Muscovite type—whose daughter elopes with a nobly-born fortune-hunter. The gentleman, learning that her father has disinherited her, leaves her to her fate, and the poor creature returns to the parental hearth, covered with confusion and disappointment. The subject, it will be perceived, is by no means novel, and the author's development of it is not over-clear. Some critics have taken it to be an apology for the patriarchal régime; others regard it as a condemnation of that system.

The treatment of a subject will not always atone for its commonplace nature. Ostrovski, in pursuance of a theory dear to Biélinski, depended on his actors for the development of his characters, which he sketched very lightly. He left them a great deal to do.

The most celebrated, and certainly the best of all his plays, is **The Storm.** This brings us into the upper commercial class in the provinces. During the absence of her husband, who, both on account of business matters and to avoid the tedium of life in a home rendered odious by the presence of a severe and quarrelsome mother, leaves his wife far too much alone, Catherine, a young woman full of dreams and enthusiasms, is false to her marriage vow. Ostrovski makes her public avowal of her sin, under the influence of the nervous agitation caused by a thunderstorm, which stirs all her religious terrors and alarms, the culminating point and dramatic moment of his piece. This idea was to be repeated by Tolstoï in his *Anna Karénine.* The unhappy wife, cursed by her mother-in-law and beaten by her husband, as is the custom in that class, goes out and drowns herself. In this play, Ostrovski's object was to depict the miserable condition of the Russian woman of the middle class, in which, in his day, the traditions of the *Domostroï* still held good, and the corruption existing in this class, due, in part, to a latent process of decomposition, under the action of the new ideas which were beginning to percolate from without. Catherine is a romantic, with leanings towards mysticism. She sins, and curses her love and her lover even as she yields to them. Her husband is a brute,

with coarse instincts and some good feeling. His mother is a domestic tyrant, brought up in the school of Pope Sylvester. When, at the moment of her indifferent husband's departure, Catherine, with a presentiment of her impending fate, casts herself on his breast, beseeching him to stay, or to take her with him, the old woman interferes:—

> "What is the meaning of this? Do you take him for a lover? At his feet, wretched creature! cast yourself at his feet!"

And so Catherine seeks in another man's arms the caress, the loving words, the tender clasp for which her soul—the soul of a modern woman—hungers.

Dobrolioubov [see Further Reading] claimed to see other things, and many more, in this play. According to him—he has covered seventy pages with the demonstration of his idea—the author has hugely advanced the literature of his country by realising what all his predecessors, from Tourguéniev to Gontcharov, had vainly attempted, responding to the universal and pressing demand of the national conscience, and filling the void in the national existence caused by its repudiation of the ideas, customs, and traditions of the past. He has created the ideal character and type of the future. Which is it? A woman's figure, of course. A wonderful conception, according to Dobrolioubov, because woman has had to suffer most from the past; because woman has been the first and the greatest victim; because it was above all for woman that the state of things had become impossible. But who is this woman? My readers will hardly guess her to be Catherine. Dobrolioubov was only four-and-twenty when he formulated this theory—a somewhat disturbing one for the possessors of romantic wives and disagreeable mothers-in-law. His youth is his excuse. And here is another. Dostoïevski was to follow suit, and apply the same theory to Pouchkine's *Tatiana,* after a fashion yet more far-fetched.

After 1860, Ostrovski conceived the idea of walking in Pouchkine's footsteps, and attempting historical drama in the style of Shakespeare. He had already borrowed much from the foreign stage. In his **Lost Sheep** we recognise Cicconi's *Pecorelle smarrite;* in **A Café,** Goldoni's *Bottega del caffé;* in **The Slavery of Husbands,** A. de Léris's *Les maris sont esclaves.* His imitations of the English dramatist were less successful. Two years before his death, having early quitted an administrative career which brought him nothing but disappointment, he undertook the management of the Moscow Theatre. He was no *blagonadiojnyï* (a man possessing the confidence of the Government). Though not directly concerned in the events of his day, he shared in the general ferment of reforming ideas. He followed the same course as Gogol—the Gogol of *The Examiner* and the first part of *Dead Souls.* His earlier plays, until 1854, seem to be systematically devoted to the representation of types of perverted morality. After that date, and influenced by the Slavophil movement, he betrays a budding sympathy for certain phases of the national life, the idealisation of which was henceforth to be his endeavour. In **Every One in His Own Place** he allots the most sympathetic parts to persons belonging to the old intellectual and moral régime, such as Roussakov, the unpretentious and upright shopkeeper, and Avdotia Maksimovna, the austere and simple-minded middle-class woman. All the rest—Vikhorev, Barantchevski, Arina Fiodorovna—have been poisoned by Western culture, and have carried the elements of disorder and corruption into their own circle. When the reforms of 1861 drew near, the author's point of view underwent another change, and he strove to bring out the backwardness and excessive folly, the obstinate *samodourstro* of the *pamiéchtchiki* (rural proprietors), as compared with the enlightened spirit of the younger generation.

His plays, as a rule, are neither comedies nor dramas. Dobrolioubov called them "representations of life." The audience is not given anything to laugh at, nor yet anything to cry over. The general setting of the piece is some social sphere which has little or no connection with the characters we see moving in it. These characters themselves are neutral in tint—neither heroes nor malefactors. Not one of them rouses direct sympathy. They are all overwhelmed by a condition of things the weight of which they might shake off, the danger of which would vanish, if they showed some little energy. But of this they have not a spark. And the struggle is not between them, but between the facts, the fatal influence of which they undergo, for the most part, unconsciously. A sort of gloomy fatalism presides over this conception of mundane matters, an idea that any man belonging to a particular moral type must act in a particular manner. The natural deduction from this theory is, that actions are not good or bad in themselves. They are merely life. And so life itself is neither good nor evil. It is as it is, and has no account to give to anybody. Ostrovski's pieces have generally no *dénouement,* or, if they have one, it is always of an uncertain nature. The dramatic action never really closes, it is broken off; the author cutting it short, not by an effective scene or phrase, but frequently, and deliberately, at the most commonplace point, or in the middle of a rejoinder. He seems to avoid effect just where it naturally would occur in the situation. Ostrovski's admirers hold this to be his manner of typifying real life, which, in Nature, has neither beginning nor end. I have already made my reservations on this head; and I am glad indeed to affirm that no other Russian writer, save Tolstoï, has painted so great a number of types and circles corresponding with almost every group in Russian society. His language, full of power and fancy, constitutes, with that of Krylov, the richest treasure-house of picturesque and original expressions to be found in Russia. Pouchkine had already declared that the way to learn Russian was by talking to the Moscow *Prosvirnié* (the women who make the sacred bread, *prosfora*). They taught Ostrovski precious lessons. (pp. 271-77)

K. Waliszewski, "Lermontov, Gogol, and Tourguéniev," in his A History of Russian Literature, *D. Appleton and Company, 1910, pp. 227-98.*

George Rapall Noyes   (essay date 1917)

[*In the following excerpt, Noyes offers a favorable assessment of Ostrovsky's works, noting that their greatest strength lies in their realistic characters and dialogue.*]

Alexander Nikoláyevich Ostróvsky is the great Russian dramatist of the central decades of the nineteenth century, of the years when the realistic school was all-powerful in Russian literature, of the period when Turgénev, Dostoyévsky, and Tolstóy created a literature of prose fiction that has had no superior in the world's history. His work

in the drama takes its place beside theirs in the novel. Obviously inferior as it is in certain ways, it yet sheds light on an important side of Russian life that they left practically untouched. Turgénev and Tolstóy were gentlemen by birth, and wrote of the fortunes of the Russian nobility or of the peasants whose villages bordered on the nobles' estates. Dostoyévsky, though not of this landed-proprietor school, still dealt with the nobility, albeit with its waifs and strays. None of these masters more than touched the Russian merchants, that homespun moneyed class, crude and coarse, grasping and mean, without the idealism of their educated neighbors in the cities or the homely charm of the peasants from whom they themselves sprang, yet gifted with a rough force and determination not often found among the cultivated aristocracy. This was the field that Ostróvsky made peculiarly his own. (p. 3)

As a boy of seventeen Ostróvsky had already developed a passion for the theatre. His literary career began in the year 1847, when he read to a group of Moscow men of letters his first experiments in dramatic composition. In this same year he printed one scene of *A Family Affair,* which appeared in complete form three years later, in 1850, and established its author's reputation as a dramatist of undoubted talent. Unfortunately, by its mordant but true picture of commercial morals, it aroused against him the most bitter feelings among the Moscow merchants. Discussion of the play in the press was prohibited, and representation of it on the stage was out of the question. It was reprinted only in 1859, and then, at the instance of the censorship, in an altered form, in which a police officer appears at the end of the play as a *deus ex machina,* arrests Podkhalyúzin, and announces that he will be sent to Siberia. In this mangled version the play was acted in 1861; in its original text it did not appear on the stage until 1881. Besides all this, the drama was the cause of the dismissal of Ostróvsky from the civil service, in 1851. The whole episode illustrates the difficulties under which the great writers of Russia have constantly labored under a despotic government. (p. 4)

The plays of Ostróvsky are of varied character, including dramatic chronicles based on early Russian history, and a fairy drama, ***Little Snowdrop.*** His real strength lay, however, in the drama of manners, giving realistic pictures of Russian life among the Russian city classes and the minor nobility. Here he was recognized, from the time of the appearance on the stage of his first pieces, in 1853 and the following years, as without a rival among Russian authors for the theatre. (p. 5)

The tone of ***Poverty Is No Crime,*** written only four years after ***A Family Affair,*** is in sharp contrast with that of its predecessor. In the earlier play Ostróvsky had adopted a satiric tone that proved him a worthy disciple of Gógol, the great founder of Russian realism. Not one lovable character appears in that gloomy picture of merchant life in Moscow; even the old mother repels us by her stupidity more than she attracts us by her kindliness. No ray of light penetrates the "realm of darkness"—to borrow a famous phrase from a Russian critic—conjured up before us by the young dramatist. In ***Poverty Is No Crime*** we see the other side of the medal. Ostróvsky had now been affected by the Slavophile school of writers and thinkers, who found in the traditions of Russian society treasures of kindliness and love that they contrasted with the superficial glitter of Western civilization. Life in Russia is varied as elsewhere, and Ostróvsky could change his tone without doing violence to realistic truth. The tradesmen had not wholly lost the patriarchal charm of their peasant fathers. A poor apprentice is the hero of **Poverty Is No Crime,** and a wealthy manufacturer the villain of the piece. Good-heartedness is the touchstone by which Ostróvsky tries character, and this may be hidden beneath even a drunken and degraded exterior. The scapegrace, Lyubím Tortsóv, has a sound Russian soul, and at the end of the play rouses his hard, grasping brother, who has been infatuated by a passion for aping foreign fashions, to his native Russian worth.

Just as **Poverty Is No Crime** shows the influence of the Slavophile movement, **A Protégée of the Mistress** was inspired by the great liberal movement that bore fruit in the emancipation of the serfs in 1861. Ostróvsky here departed from town to a typical country manor, and produced a work kindred in spirit to Turgénev's *Sportsman's Sketches,* or "Mumu." In a short play, instinct with simple poetry, he shows the suffering brought about by serfdom: the petty tyranny of the landed proprietor, which is the more galling because it is practised with a full conviction of virtue on the part of the tyrant; and the crushed natures of the human cattle under his charge.

> The master grim, the lowly serf that tills his lands;
> With lordly pride the first sends forth commands,
> The second cringes like a slave.
> —*Nekrasov*

Despite the unvarying success of his dramas on the stage, Ostróvsky for a long time derived little financial benefit from them. Discouragement and overwork wrecked his health, and were undoubtedly responsible for the gloomy tone of a series of plays written in the years following 1860, of which **Sin and Sorrow Are Common to All** is a typical example. Here the dramatist sketches a tragic incident arising from the conflict of two social classes, the petty tradesmen and the nobility. From the coarse environment of the first emerge honest, upright natures like Krasnóv; from the superficial, dawdling culture of the second come weak-willed triflers like Babáyev. The sordid plot sweeps on to its inevitable conclusion with true tragic force. (pp. 5-7)

As a dramatist, Ostróvsky is above all else a realist; no more thoroughly natural dramas than his were ever composed. Yet as a master of realistic technique he must not be compared with Ibsen, or even with many less noted men among modern dramatists. His plays have not the neat, concise construction that we prize to-day. Pages of dialogue sometimes serve no purpose except to make a trifle clearer the character of the actors, or perhaps slightly to heighten the impression of commonplace reality. Even in **Sin and Sorrow** and **A Protégée** whole passages merely illustrate the background against which the plot is set rather than help forward the action itself. Many plays, such as **A Family Affair,** end with relatively unimportant pieces of dialogue. Of others we are left to guess even the conclusion of the main action: will Nádya in **A Protégée** submit to her degrading fate, or will she seek refuge in the pond?

Ostróvsky rarely uses the drama to treat of great moral or social problems. He is not a revolutionary thinker or an opponent of existing society; his ideal, like that of his predecessor Gógol, is of honesty, kindliness, generosity, and loyalty in a broad, general way to the traditions of the past. He attacks serfdom not as an isolated leader of a forlorn hope, but as an adherent of a great party of moderate reformers.

Thus Ostróvsky's strength lies in a sedate, rather commonplace realism. One of the most national of authors, he loses much in translation. His style is racy, smacking of the street or the counting-house; he is one of the greatest masters of the Russian vernacular. To translate his Moscow slang into the equivalent dialect of New York would be merely to transfer Broadway associations to the Ilyínka. A translator can only strive to be colloquial and familiar, giving up the effort to render the varying atmosphere of the different plays. And Ostróvsky's characters are as natural as his language. Pig-headed merchants; apprentices, knavish or honest as the case may be; young girls with a touch of poetry in their natures, who sober down into kindly housewives; tyrannical serf-owners and weak-willed sons of noble families: such is the material of which he builds his entertaining, wholesome, mildly thoughtful dramas. Men and women live and love, trade and cheat in Ostróvsky as they do in the world around us. Now and then a murder or a suicide appears in his pages as it does in those of the daily papers, but hardly more frequently. In him we can study the life of Russia as he knew it, crude and coarse and at times cruel, yet full of homely virtue and aspiration. (pp. 7-8)

> *George Rapall Noyes, in an introduction to* Plays *by Alexander Ostrovsky, edited and translated by George Rapall Noyes, Charles Scribner's Sons, 1917, pp. 3-8.*

D. S. Mirsky   (essay date 1927)

[*Mirsky was a Russian prince who fled his country after the Bolshevik Revolution and settled in London. While in England, he wrote two important histories of Russian literature,* Contemporary Russian Literature *(1926) and* A History of Russian Literature *(1927). In 1932, having reconciled himself to the Soviet regime, Mirsky returned to the USSR. He continued to write literary criticism, but his work eventually ran afoul of Soviet censors and he was exiled to Siberia. He disappeared in 1937. In the following excerpt from the revised edition of* A History of Russian Literature, *Mirsky assesses Ostrovsky's contributions to Russian drama.*]

[Ostróvsky] wrote about forty plays in prose besides eight in blank verse. They are of unequal merit, but taken as a whole, doubtless the most remarkable body of dramatic work in Russian. Griboyédov and Gógol had written great and original plays, and each of them is a man of greater genius than Ostróvsky, but it was left to Ostróvsky to create a school of Russian drama, a Russian theater that may be put by the side of the national theaters of the West, if not on equal, at least on comparable terms. The limitations of Ostróvsky's art are obvious. His plays (with few exceptions) are neither tragedies nor comedies, but belong to the middle and bastard kind of drama. The dramatic skeleton in most of them, sacrificed to the exigencies of the slice-of-life method, lacks the firm consistency of classical art. With few exceptions his plays are devoid of poetry, and even where poetry is present, as it is in *The Thunderstorm,* it is a poetry of atmosphere, not of words and texture. Though an admirable master of individualized and typical dialogue, Ostróvsky is not a master of language in the sense Gógol, Leskóv, or (to use an English instance) Synge was. His language is purely representational; he uses it truthfully, but uncreatively. His very raciness of the Russian soil is in a certain sense a limitation, for his plays are always narrowly native and do not have universal significance. Were it not for this limitation, and had he been universal in his nationality, Ostróvsky's place would have been among the greatest. The breadth, the grasp, the variety of Ostróvsky's vision of Russian life are almost infinite. He is the least subjective of Russian writers. His would be a hopeless case for the psychoanalyst. His characters are not in any sense emanations of himself. They are genuine reflections of "the other." He is no psychologist; his characters are not, as Tolstóy's are, inner worlds to which we are introduced by a supreme power of intuition; they are just people as seen by other people. But this superficial realism is not the external, pictorial realism of Gógol and Goncharóv, but a truly dramatic realism, for it gives the characters in their relations to the other characters, which is the simplest and oldest way of narrative and dramatic characterization by speech and action, enriched only by an enormous wealth of social, ethnographic detail. And in spite of this superficiality, they have the individuality and the uniqueness we recognize in our fellow creatures, even without getting inside their skull.

These general remarks on the art of Ostróvsky refer chiefly to his early and most characteristic work, up to about 1861. The subject matter of these plays is taken for the most part from the life of Moscow and provincial merchants and of the lower strata of the official world. The vast and varied picture of the conservative and un-Europeanized life of the Russian merchants was what struck his contemporaries most strongly in the work of Ostróvsky, for the reality underlying literary creation interested them more than the art that transformed it. The critics of the fifties spilled endless ink over the elucidation of Ostróvsky's attitude towards the conservative mainstays of the merchant class. He himself gave disconcertingly abundant food for such discussions and for every kind of interpretation, for his artistic sympathy is distributed in different ways in different plays. Every interpretation, from the most enthusiastic idealization of stolid conservatism and patriarchal despotism to the fierce denunciation of the merchants as an unredeemed kingdom of darkness, could find a peg to hang on in the text of the plays. As for Ostróvsky's own attitude, it was simply unstable, or, to be more exact, the moral and social attitude was a secondary thing to him. His task was to build plays out of the elements of reality as he saw it. An attitude of sympathy or antipathy was to him entirely a matter of dramatic expediency, of pure technique, for, though an "anti-artificial" realist, he felt very keenly the inner laws along which, and not along those of life, he had to construct each play. So his moral judgment over the tyrannical merchant paterfamilias depended on his dramatic function in the particular play. Apart from this it is extraordinarily difficult to extract a social and political *Weltanschauung* out of Ostróvsky.

Technically speaking, the most interesting of all Ostróvsky's plays are the first two, *The Bankrupt* (written

1847-9, published in 1850 under the title *Among Friends One Always Comes to Terms*) and *The Poor Bride* (published 1852, acted 1853). The former was as striking and sensational a beginning for a young author as there is on record in Russian literary history. Gógol in *Marriage* had given an example of a characteristic painting of the merchant milieu. In particular the character of the professional matchmaker practicing among the merchants was already abundantly exploited. In the inclusion of none but unsympathetic characters Ostróvsky also followed the example of Gógol in *Revizór*. But here he went one better and discarded the most time-honored of all traditions of comedy—the poetic justice that punishes vice. The triumph of vice, and precisely of the most unredeemed of all the characters, gives Ostróvsky's play its particular note of bold originality. It was this which incensed even such an old realist as Schépkin, who thought the play cynical and dirty. The realism of Ostróvsky, in spite of the obvious influence of Gógol, is in substance of an opposite nature to Gógol's. It is free from all expressiveness for the sake of expressiveness; it keeps clear of caricature and farce; it is based on a solid, intimate, first-hand knowledge of the life described. The dialogue aims at truthfulness to life, not at verbal richness. The art of using realistic speech without producing the effect of grotesqueness and without obtruding it is a characteristic art of the Russian realists, but it reaches its perfection in Ostróvsky. Finally the untheatrical construction is entirely un-Gogolian, and in the deliberate discarding of all tricks and contrivances at scenic effect Ostróvsky from the outset attains his best. The mainstay of the play is the characters, and the plot is entirely a result of the characters. But the characters are taken in their social aspect. They are not men and women in general, but Moscow merchants and assistants, and cannot be torn away from the social setting.

The Poor Bride is entirely different in tone and atmosphere from *The Bankrupt.* The milieu is not merchants but minor officials. The unpleasantness of it is redeemed by the character of the heroine, a strong girl, in no way inferior to and more actively alive than the heroines of Turgénev. She ends characteristically, after being let down by her romantic, ideal admirer, in submitting to her fate and marrying the successful brute Benevolénsky, who can alone save her mother from imminent ruin. All the characters are masterpieces, and Ostróvsky's skill at building the action entirely on the characters is at its best. But what is especially remarkable is the last act—a bold technical novelty. The play ends on a mass scene, where the crowd discusses the marriage of Benevolénsky and where a wonderfully new note is introduced by the appearance in the crowd of his former mistress. The delicacy and pregnancy of these last scenes, in which the heroes hardly appear, were really a new word in dramatic art. Ostróvsky's power of creating atmospheric poetry is revealed for the first time in this fifth act of *The Poor Bride. In Poverty Is No Crime* Ostróvsky went still further in de-theatricalizing the theater, but with less intrinsic success. The immediate success of the play was great, owing to the original and Slavophil character of the noble drunkard, the ruined merchant Lyubím Tortsóv, who has remained one of the most popular roles in the Russian repertory. But as a play it is much less satisfactory, and the "sliciness" of the technique inclines to mere looseness.

Of the plays written in 1856-61, *The Ward* attains to almost intolerable power in the painting of a character that often reappears in his later work—the selfish, rich, and self-righteous old woman. The three short comedies united by the character of the silly and conceited young clerk Balzamínov (1858-61) are his masterpieces in the comic vein for the characters of Balzamínov and of his mother, fondly doting and yet fully conscious of her son's extreme silliness, and for the saturated painting of their social environment. In another comedy of the same period *Your Drink—My Hangover* (*V chuzhóm pirú pokhmélie*), Ostróvsky concentrated into the character of the merchant Kit Kítych all the essence of the *samodúr*—the willful domestic tyrant who is decided to make everyone do "what my left toe wishes," but who is easily bulliable.

By far the most significant work of this period, and ultimately the masterpiece of Ostróvsky, is *The Thunderstorm.* It is the most famous of his plays and has been most abundantly written about. Dobrolyúbov took it as the text for one of his most effective and influential sermons against the dark forces of conservatism and tradition, and Grigóriev saw in it the highest expression of Ostróvsky's love for the traditional life and character of the undefiled Russian middle classes. In reality it is a purely poetical work, a purely atmospheric creation, a great poem of love and death, of freedom and thralldom. It is intensely local and Russian, and the saturation of the atmosphere with the very essence of Russian *byt* ["mores"] and Russian poetical feeling makes it hardly understandable to a foreigner. For every detail of it is intensified by the background of a whole emotional tradition (expressed perhaps best of all in the lyrical songs of the Russian people), and without this background it loses most of its appeal. *The Thunderstorm* is a rare example of a supreme masterpiece built of exclusively national material.

After 1861 Ostróvsky sought new ways. He devoted himself at one time to historical plays, and in his prose plays he departed from much of his original novelty. He almost abandoned the merchant milieu, which under the influence of the Reforms and of the spread of education was rapidly transforming into a drabber middle class, and he more and more submitted to the traditional method of playmaking, never, however, condescending to use the mere artificial and improbable tricks of the French school. Owing to his example, Russia, unlike most other countries, succeeded in keeping clear from the all-pervading school of Scribe and Sardou. Still there are more intrigue and plot in most of his later than in his early plays, and though the critics as a rule disapproved of them, some later plays of Ostróvsky (*Enough Simplicity in Every Wise Man, The Forest, Wolves and Sheep*) proved even greater favorites with the public than his more characteristic early masterpieces. The first two are distinctly among his best work, and *The Forest* shares with *The Thunderstorm* the honor of being regarded as his masterpiece. Less exclusively original, the comedy is extraordinarily rich in its character drawing. Of all Ostróvsky's plays, it is the one in which the essential nobility of man is most triumphantly asserted. But it also contains the most unsweetened types of cynical and complacent meanness and selfishness in the whole of Russian literature.

Ostróvsky never stood still, but always sought for new ways and methods. In his later plays (*The Dowerless Girl*) he attempted a more psychological method of character drawing. But on the whole his later plays mark a certain drying-up of his creative sources. At the time of his death he dominated the Russian stage by the mass of his work. But the successors he left were minor and uncreative men, who were capable only of writing plays with "grateful parts" for the excellent actors and actresses brought up in the school of Schépkin and of Ostróvsky, but not of carrying on a vital tradition of literary drama. (pp. 234-39)

> *D. S. Mirsky, "The Age of Realism: Journalists, Poets, and Playwrights," in his* A History of Russian Literature Comprising "A History of Russian Literature" and "Contemporary Russian Literature," *edited by Francis J. Whitfield, Alfred A. Knopf, 1949, pp. 205-44.*

Clarence A. Manning   (essay date 1930)

[*In the following excerpt, Manning discusses the depiction of the merchant class in Ostrovsky's plays.*]

We are living in an individualistic age. More and more we are coming to base our philosophy and ethics on the individual, on his joys and sorrows, on his personal accomplishments and failures. We are disregarding his relations with the other members of his own family as negligible factors in his life. It is an age when we are writing and talking of companionate marriage, of liberal divorce, of the theoretical as well as the practical destruction of parental discipline of children; and we feel that we are nearing the solution of those social problems which have worried mankind for thousands of years. Are we really sure that our modern views of love and of freedom, of sentiment and emotion are permanent? Perhaps they too will be swept away before some other system and we will be left ridiculous and benighted hulks on the stream of life.

All this is not an attempt to evaluate modern conditions. Rather it is a plea for sympathy for one who studied a different system, who described a life that is to us merely grotesque and horrible, and who distributed praise and blame with a measure that we can scarce conceive or imagine. Aleksander Nikolayevich Ostrovsky, the greatest of Russian dramatists, and the only talented author of his country who devoted himself exclusively to the drama, seems to-day far removed from real and even possible life. No one can deny that he was a successful playwright and dramatist or that his plays were successful on the stage as well as in the closet. He mastered all the difficulties of the censorship and the opposition of important circles which opposed his exposure of their defects, but nevertheless his point of view seems strange to us and his characters undoubtedly receive a harsher judgment than he ever intended. After all, he lived in a different age. He saw the beginnings of those tendencies which are so vital to us but he saw also the passing of quite a different type of life, and he must have been sorry to see many of its qualities and ideals swept away before the rising tide of progress. (pp. 30-1)

His earliest plays which deal with the merchants of his youth are his most striking and important productions. It is in them that he shows the greatest originality in conception and the keenest observation in character drawing. It is hard to say in many cases whether he approved or disapproved of these old ideals. He dealt with them sympathetically and they are so different from our views that we can hardly understand them. Let us however look at some of them and see what is meant by the phrase, "the Kingdom of Darkness" which was applied to them by many Russian critics.

Perhaps it is in some of the historical plays that Ostrovsky summarizes most clearly this underlying value of Russian life. In the drama *The Pretender Dimitry and Vasily Shuysky,* Dimitry sums up the situation that he finds in these words,

> I do not wonder at such words. You know
> One way and only one to rule—by fear.
> In all and everywhere you rule by fear.
> You all have schooled your wives to show you love
> By many blows and fear; your children too
> From fear dare not to lift their eyes upon you;
> From fear the ploughman ploughs your fertile
> 　fields;
> From fear the soldier marches to the war;
> The general leads him on by fear to battle;
> With fear the envoy guides his daily task;
> From fear you dare not speak in council meeting.
> My father and their sires, as old rulers,
> In Tatar horde, along the mighty Volga,
> Collected fear from the great khan's abode
> And learned from him how best to rule by fear.
> Another means is better and more certain—
> To rule with mercy and with acts of kindness.

Dimitry tries to change this sad state of affairs but it only causes his destruction, for no one of those who have been reared in the old system can understand the new and he falls an easy prey to the machinations of Shuysky. This fear is the outstanding fact of all the historic chronicles of Ostrovsky.

It lies at the root of the autocratic system. It is the mark of Ivan the Terrible in *Vasilisa Melentyevna.* It is the principle of the "Voevoda", the district commander who abuses the people under his charge and drives them to desperation. It is the principle that we find in the dramas of Fonvizin in the eighteenth century. It is perhaps the principle that makes old Bolkonsky in Tolstoy's *War and Peace* refuse to allow his son Prince Andrey to wed Natasha Rostova. It is everywhere, in high and low alike, and above all it is present in the relation of the peasant to his children, his wife, and all his subordinates.

A life of fear seems horrible but there were compensations. With trust and confidence denied, every one was free to do whatever he could unnoticed. As a result we have a lurid picture of life with intrigue, infidelity, scheming, forgery, and every evil abounding but with the absolute maintenance of surface well-being. The master (the father) follows the sixteenth century moral code of the Domostroy and inflicts wounds and blows upon all his subordinates and thereby saves his own soul. Every one lives a life of order and of routine. Every one maintains the commands of the elders, the good old order and the man who sees fit to ignore or disobey this ancestral habit is not merely guilty of imprudence but of sin.

As Ostrovsky shows in his chronicles, this life was characteristic of the Russian court in the days of Ivan the Terrible. It maintained itself well down to the reign of Peter the Great and then it gradually changed. The nobles with a Western education adopted Western ideas and as a result in all too many cases they interpreted these as mere carelessness and thereby wrecked their own financial status. They mortgaged and sold their lands; they neglected their traditional religious and ethical beliefs and finally they saw themselves threatened with extinction. Yet with the years they did acquire a culture and in many cases they were worthy of commendation.

The old order was maintained most strictly by the merchant class of Moscow. Even down into the nineteenth century they did not smoke, because that meant a defiling of the Spirit of God as it came out in the tobacco smoke. They maintained their ancient costume and their old traditions. Ostrovsky knew them well and his plays range over the entire gamut of their lives, now with apparent approval, now with marked disapproval, as befits the subject. Yet even there the corroding or progressive spirit of the modern age was beginning to appear and everywhere we see in his works this conflict of an old and antiquated system of life with a new and often unformed philosophy which can itself lead to as much unhappiness in the hour of its triumph as does the other idea in its moments of defeat.

Again and again in his early dramas Ostrovsky stresses this difference between the merchant on the one hand, and the noble and the educated classes on the other. The one is bound by convention and the teachings of the elders; the other by the possibilities of the situation. Thus in *A Family Picture* the young women would like to undertake a flirtation with a young officer but after all it may be dangerous. A hussar rode his horse straight into the entrance hall of the house of one of their friends. On the other hand the older women see in these nobles and progressive people sinners, people who violate the law of God and man and are not to be mentioned without contempt. The younger women are willing to do anything to attract one of these newer types as husbands. It gives them the possibility of getting out of the house, of meeting people, of lying abed in the morning, and of taking their ease.

The one advantage that these conservative merchant women have is their wealth. We see that clearly in *You Must Sit in Your Own Sleigh.* Here Vikhorev, a retired cavalry officer, is wooing the daughter of a wealthy peasant and quite captivates the imagination of the stupid Avdotya. He confesses frankly that she is no suitable wife for him—"She's not so bad and apparently a very simple girl. How she's in love with me! And I'll get a thousand with her and that's enough. Of course you can't take such a wife up to the capital, but it's all right in the provinces, and you could live in clover." Thus the nobles in their ruined state are as greedy for money as are the merchants who intrigue for the control of fortunes or the officials who seek to have a good income from bribes as in *A Profitable Place.*

The result of these mixed marriages cannot really be fortunate but even more unfortunate are those cases where a woman of education and refinement marries into a peasant or merchant family. Thus in *Sin and Misfortune Can Land on All,* Tatyana marries the shop-keeper Krasnov. Life becomes a living hell for her. Her husband and his relatives watch her, criticize her, and though the husband would like to rise in the cultural scale, he drives her by his rudeness to such despair that she jumps at the chance to have an affair with a former admirer Babayev, and when her husband learns of this, he kills her.

The real basis of this merchant life is the samodur. This is the hard-boiled, limited business man who can brook no obstacles to his will. He realizes perfectly his power, and compared to him Babbitt is a cultured gentleman of the highest rank. Thus in **Poverty Is No Vice,** Gordyey Tortsov is proud of his culture. He has any number of servants and that is his idea of propriety. We can hear him saying haughtily,

> Tell me, isn't everything in order here? Somewhere else, you can find a young fellow serving at table in his shirt-sleeves, or a girl, but I have a functionary in cotton gloves. This functionary, he's a learned man from Moscow; he knows what's proper, where every one is to sit, and what is to be done. And the others! They gather in one room, and sit in a circle, and sing peasant songs. Of course, you have a good time, but I think it's beneath me, it lacks tone. And what they drink, in their ignorance! Liqueurs, cherry bounce. . . . and they haven't a ghost of an idea that there's such a thing as champagne! Oh, if I could only live in Moscow or Petersburg, I'd imitate the latest fashion.

Imitate the latest fashion, even if they didn't understand a word. Many of them love that but the same Tortsov when he fails to marry his daughter to a charlatan, says: "Then to spite him I'll marry my daughter to Mitya". It happens that the poor girl is in love with Mitya but the marriage is arranged only as a whim. Still another one of these characters, in **Intoxication at Another's Feast,** Tit Titich Bruskov declares, "Does any one dare to insult me?" His cowed wife, answers, "No, Tit Titich, no one dares to insult you. You insult everyone else." He proudly replies, "I insult, and I am kind, and I pay money for the privilege. I've paid a lot of money for the privilege in my day".

Thus the samodur interprets his slightest vagary as a law and to his will he sacrifices his children, his family, his friends, his business, everything. He succeeds by sheer brute strength, by the power of money, and by the rule of the ancestral code. He is a terror to everyone, but no one dares to thwart him for an instant.

This is a monstrous type but there is one thing worse, the samodursha, the independent old woman who is the mistress of all she surveys. Can any one be more callous than Ulanbekova in the **Ward**? This heartless woman brings up orphans in luxury and then marries them to peasants. She tells one of them who protests at being married to a drunken rascal,

> My dear, you're not to think of this; you're a girl. You must rely on me, your benefactor. I have reared you and must settle you in life. Besides you must not forget that he's my godson. You should thank me for the honor. And I'll tell you again once for all; I don't like to have people object to my words; I don't like it and that's all. I don't allow any one to do it. Since my youth I've been accustomed to having every word of mine obeyed; it's time for you to know that! It's very strange to me, my dear, that you even dream of contradicting me. I see I've spoiled you.

Not a sign of appreciation of another person's feelings. She even can preach to them this way:

> You have lived here in luxury and wealth, and now

> are marrying a poor man, and you'll be all your life in poverty, and so you must work and do your duty. Forget how you've lived here, because I didn't do it for you; I was only pleasing myself, and you must never think of such a life but always remember your own worthlessness.

The masterpiece of this type is old Kabanova in the **Storm,** the greatest of Ostrovsky's dramas. Here the old woman declares that Katerina cannot love her husband, because otherwise, when he went away, she would have howled for an hour and a half and fallen down on the porch. That was the accepted method as Kabanova understands it, and she abuses Katerina for not doing it. She treats her son as badly as she does his wife. Her daughter has learned the method of acting under this regime. She obeys meekly and slips out the back door to her lover. Katerina is induced to try it but she takes that also too seriously and finally she drowns herself. Her husband who loves her dearly threatens to rebel against the harsh rule of his mother, but she merely sneers, "Wait, until I get you home," and goes off. Here there are signs of revolt but after all these are impotent. We agree to the moral callousness of the old woman but she is the dominating character. Katerina with her charm is really weak. So is the son, and there will be a long way yet to go before they seriously threaten the rule of the old shrew.

It is chiefly in questions of marriage that the fiendish character of the samodur is most clearly shown, for nowhere else is the question of personal taste so much in evidence. The samodur marries his children without consulting their wishes, although often some chance whim comes like a *deus ex machina* to avert a tragic solution. On the other hand the attempts of the young women to rest their marriage on love are little more successful. Take the **Poor Bride.** Here Marya Andreyevna, a poor girl who has no dowry, seeks in vain for a husband. Young Merich she loves ardently but he is merely a Don Juan, flirting lightly with every girl and he easily escapes her awkward attempts to marry him. Finally she submits to her fate and marries old Benevolensky. It is not a marriage of love or of affection. Benevolensky (perhaps we should do him justice and realize that his name means "Well-Wisher") is decidedly limited. He does not read or know music. He is merely a successful business man and he wants an educated wife, in order to appear well in public. Yet after all he is no more impossible than are the young boys who are dallying around Marya. At the marriage a former mistress appears but somehow despite the tears of the wife, there is the assurance that they will get along somehow.

Get along somehow? That is the text of Ostrovsky in one drama after another. Marriages are arranged at the end and carried out in such an indifferent manner that the author almost seems sarcastic. This is especially true in **You Can't Live As You Like.** Here Petr who has married from love, neglects his home and family, and even threatens to kill his wife. She wants to leave him but her father drives her back with the words, "Whom God has joined together, let not man put asunder!" At the end, Petr repents and apologizes and her father says triumphantly, "What did I tell you?" Is it irony or common sense? Critics have argued that it was only a conventional ending, that the wife would be again forgotten, the husband would again misbehave, and the end would be worse than the beginning. Still others have written of it as an illustration of the cruelty of the old system. Why not accept the other solution, that Petr is really reformed? He fears his father's curse; he is a typical member of the old régime. Could he not resolve to act hereafter as he should?

In this as in other plays we can never forget that Ostrovsky is not a conventional preacher. He realized undoubtedly that the old system did have its good sides. Not all his conservative classes are rascals and not all of the educated are intelligent. Take again **Intoxication at Another's Feast.** The schoolteacher and his daughter who spurn the suit of the well-meaning boy are as comical as he is. They lack the wealth and the steadiness, the clear vision and the calm power of the merchant class. There is something lacking in the new system. The folly of an unmitigated denunciation of old Russia had been discussed for nearly two centuries but no one has ever been able to create a working fusion of the two systems of life. That is the teaching of Ostrovsky. Now he is whole-heartedly on the side of the new. Now he realizes the folly of much that is going on and he glorifies the old. The pendulum swings depending upon the plot that he has in hand.

When Ostrovsky returned to modern life after his work on the chronicles, he changed his field of work. The old samodur who was after all a striking figure, a real character, was passing from the scene. Passing were his extreme claims, his frenzied opposition to smoking, his unwarranted belief in himself. The new man is no better, no more honest, no more pure, no more faithful, than the old, but he is different. He has less energy, less power.

The samodur or the samodursha is no longer an impossible but Titanic figure. The newer culprit is petty, indifferent, unscrupulous. In the **Heart Is No Stone,** one of his latest plays, Olga tells how her husband almost on his wedding night embraces harpists in her presence. In general men carry out the first idea that comes into their heads without regard for their wives' feelings. Or again the samodursha in **Wolves and Lambs** degenerates into a quarrelsome, intriguing, dishonest old maid, who schemes and schemes and never triumphs over her misdeeds. She is disagreeable, that's all.

Thus, as we run through the plays of Ostrovsky, we find that they picture the newer life which was replacing that of the stern old patriarchs of the thirties and the forties. As dramatist, he is as expert as ever but there is something missing. His works are now immeasurably nearer to the ordinary comedy of intrigue. The happy ending is not universal but it is often found. There is usually a complicated and amusing plot. Everything is done to make the pieces successful and this goal is often achieved. The works vied and still vie in popularity with the best plays of Russia. They have lived on the stage until now. Nevertheless something has gone out of them. We miss the peculiar flavor of those earlier plays and feel that we are back in the typical continental theatrical atmosphere. There are plays on the stage, as **Talents and Admirers,** which represent the hard and the bright side of the life of a provincial actor. It is good, amusing and dramatic but yet it fails in some way to impress itself upon the reader as the work of thirty years before.

Thus if we will, we may say that the old order changeth, giving place to new. Turgenev caught the great landed estates at the very end of their golden age. His successors were called to tell how the bankrupt nobles endeavored to realize something from their estates and handed the property over to newer and less feeble hands. Ostrovsky likewise paints these nobles more or less in financial difficulties and fits clearly into the same general stream of writing. He shows us also the end of the old merchant class. With all its rascality and its rigidity, with its patriarchal ideas and its unprincipled methods of business, it still was striking. It did appeal to the outside, to the non-Russian, as a curious survival of a vanished era. The new merchant class is no more honest—there is as much use of false papers and of bribery as ever. There is as much failure to consider the rights and feelings of others; there is as much intrigue and contempt, but the picturesque element has gone out of life. We are coming more and more to the drab type of crooked bourgeois, and to face the same problems as the rest of the world.

It is the study of this older and more specialized type of life that is Ostrovsky's field. He has painted as none other this restricted class and he has done it well and fairly. He sees its virtues and its vices; he sees that real values are being lost with the passing of the old type of life but he is keenly aware also of the evils that were inherent in the system. He sees the advantages of the freer atmosphere that the younger people were beginning to breathe but he cannot be blind to some of the obvious mistakes that the new world is perpetuating and introducing. Therefore he stands between the two groups and he lashes now one side, now the other.

It is this impartial point of departure that makes Ostrovsky strange to us to-day. Time has gone on its unrelenting way and we recognize as normal the modern system. We look upon the old now as something monstrous and inhuman. Perhaps the time will come when a new generation will say the same of our modern innovations and in 1950 the conventions of 1920 will seem antiquated. People then will be unable to understand how life exists under present conditions. The certainty of this should make us tolerant of Ostrovsky and make us hesitate to condemn him for seeing the good sides of the old system which was passing in his day. With all his dramas he stands as a guide to one side of Russian life and the student who would understand the origin of present conditions and attitudes cannot pass by these dramas which picture to us as nothing else does the loves and hates, the pride, the bigotry, and the corruption, the virtues and the ideals of the old Russian merchant class, the Kingdom of Darkness. (pp. 32-41)

Clarence A. Manning, "Ostrovsky and the Kingdom of Darkness," in The Sewanee Quarterly, *Vol. XXXVIII, No. 1, January, 1930, pp. 30-41.*

Allardyce Nicoll   (essay date 1949)

[Called "one of the masters of dramatic research," Nicoll is best known as a theater historian whose works have proven invaluable to students and educators. Nicoll's World Drama from Aeschylus to Anouilh *(1949) is considered one of his most important works; theater critic John Gassner has stated that it was "unquestionably the most thorough [study] of its kind in the English language [and] our best reference book on the world's*

dramatic literature." Another of his ambitious theater studies is the six-volume A History of English Drama, 1660-1900 *(1952-59), which has been highly praised for its perceptive commentaries on drama from the Restoration to the close of the nineteenth century. Nicoll was also a popular lecturer on Shakespearean drama and the author of several studies on William Shakespeare's works. In addition, he was the longtime editor of* Shakespeare Survey, *an annual publication of Shakespearean scholarship. In the following excerpt, Nicoll provides an overview of Ostrovsky's career.*]

The work of Alexander Nikolaevich Ostrovski is not well known outside his own country, yet he is unquestionably one of the most important and interesting dramatists of his epoch: without Ostrovski, Chekhov the dramatist might not have been. His first claim to attention is the fact that he was the first Russian author to apply himself exclusively to a professional stage career. Gogol and Griboedov had entered the theatre lightly, airily; Ostrovski made of playwriting his entire life's work. In himself he thus symbolized the Russian theatre's coming of age. This, of course, merely gives him historical significance; intrinsic significance is provided by the quality of his writings. Intensely Slav in sentiment, he seized upon and developed the native realistic style cultivated by his predecessors. Instead of concentrating upon plot, he followed them in exploring character; instead of stressing ideas and problems, he set out to depict the life around him, satirically yet with infinite sympathy. Characteristic of all this school of writing is the peculiar orientation of the poet-creator to the objects of his creation. From one point of view we might be tempted to regard Ostrovski's plays as based on the 'slice-of-life' pattern. Their lack of exact structure and the tendency to prefer a series of loosely related scenes to the logical exposition of a theme would seem to give justification for such a point of view. No less than three of his dramas, instead of being called comedies or dramas, are described as "Scenes" or "Sketches" of Moscow or village life—*Prazdnichnii son—do obieda* (*A Holiday Dream—Before Dinner*), *Vospitannitsa* (*The Ward*) and *Ne vse kotu maslianitsa* (*After the Dinner Comes the Reckoning*). Looking at these, we might indeed be tempted to suppose that Zola's naturalism was here being put into practice. Such a conception, however, would be false: the looseness of structure is apparent merely, and on examination proves itself, like the structure of Chekhov's plays, to be carefully designed. Carefully designed, too, is that quality which so often has puzzled Western critics of this Russian realistic theatre—its seeming uncertainty of mood. Very often we do not know whether to laugh or to cry, whether to praise or to condemn: a character whom we feel to be despicable may suddenly assume admirable virtues; the coarse merchants whom Ostrovski so frequently flays may, in some scenes, be put forward as heroes. The explanation, of course, is that this author, like his companions, is composing his work under the impulse of a peculiar kind of humour: he is satiric, certainly, yet for the things satirized there is in his heart infinite compassion. This is the realm of the so-called *bytovaia komedia*—an almost untranslatable term signifying a play which depicts a way of life— the dramatic expression of the Russian literary movement to which was given the title *Byt*.

With the exception of *Snegurochka* (*The Snow Maiden*) and his unimportant historical dramas, all Ostrovski's plays are realistic, and, with the exception of *Groza* (*The Thunderstorm*), *Grekh da beda na kovo ne zhivet* (*Sin and Sorrow Are Common to All*), and *The Ward,* they are comedies in the sense that they end happily, even though their happiness be bitter. Although among the exceptions stands his best-known play, *The Thunderstorm,* his genius was not well adapted to deal with potentially tragic material. *Sin and Sorrow,* which tells the story of Krasnov, a shopkeeper, married to Tatiana Danilovna, who starts an *affaire* with a young landowner, has little incisiveness of purpose, and the stabbing of the wife by her husband seems to have no inevitability. Infinitely superior is *The Thunderstorm,* yet even it leaves us unsatisfied. Here a similar plot is used. A young wife, Katia, finds herself neglected by her husband and gives way to a handsome lover. In the end the lover abandons her, and, terrified of the husband's wrath, she commits suicide. Death is avoided in *The Ward,* but the atmosphere is no less dark; the last words are spoken by a maidservant who has been a spectator of all the events—"What's fun for the cat is sorrow for the mouse." The ward is Nadia, and basically the entire action which leads towards her betrothal to a man she detests is designed to reveal the evil unconsciously perpetrated by the rich, domineering, self-righteous old dowager, the lady Ulanbekov.

Bespridannitsa (*The Dowerless Girl*) may be taken as transitional between these and the comedies. To a certain extent the plot is tragic in that a girl without a dowry is forced into a loveless marriage, yet the fact that she takes a joy in sacrificing herself, together with the exceedingly vivid manner in which the dramatist deals with the preparations for the wedding, gives the play an atmosphere different from that of *Sin and Sorrow.* Another transitional work is *Bednost ne porok* (*Poverty Is No Crime*), distinguished by the character of Liubim Karpich Tortsov, a sad rogue and a drunkard, albeit lovable, who reveals the pettiness and meanness of his merchant-brother's household and who serves as *deus ex machina* in joining the hands of Liubov and the poor, honest clerk Mitia.

This type of character was a favourite one on the Russian stage, largely because it enabled a contrast to be made with the dull, convention-ridden life of the middle class. Not dissimilar is the Neschastlivtsev of *Les* (*The Forest*), an actor who, though not as successful on the stage as he had hoped, prefers his way of life to that of his bourgeois relations. The rogue, however, is not always presented in such pleasing form as he assumes in the person of Liubim Tortsov. Among Ostrovski's most successful comedies is his very first, *Svoi liudi—sochtemsia* (with an almost untranslatable title: *It's a Family Affair—We'll Settle It Ourselves* is literal, but loses idiomatic significance; perhaps *Birds of a Feather* would best express the theme). In effect, this play is a kind of middle-class Russian *Volpone*. In order to enrich himself a merchant, Bolshov, arranges with a rascally attorney, Rispolozhenski, to fake a bankruptcy: since he has long had loyal service from his clerk, Podkhaliuzin, he decides to pretend to make over all of his property to him. Podkhaliuzin, however, at once sees and seizes his opportunity, holds on to the assets and finds in Olimpiada, Bolshov's daughter, a kindred spirit. The cold-blooded pair marry, and the wretched Bolshov, all his schemes awry, is hoist with his own petard. Typical of the style are the daughter's long opening soliloquy as she reviews in memory the season's dances, and the final words spoken by Podkhaliuzin. The latter has just indulged in his final trick, bilking the dishonest lawyer, who departs muttering enraged curses and accusing his tormentor of many crimes. There-upon the hero turns to the audience. "Don't you believe him," Podkhaliuzin says,

> I mean him who was talking, gentlemen—that's all lies. He's just inventing. Perhaps he only dreamt it. The wife and I, gentlemen, intend to open a little shop: do please favour us with your patronage. If you send your little son to us for an apple, you may be sure he shan't be given a rotten one.

Here the villain-rogue triumphs, although in another kindred work, *Na vsiakovo mudretsa dovolno prostoti* (*Enough Silliness in Every Wise Man,* or, *The Diary of a Scoundrel,* 1868), the trickster is outwitted by forces more honest than his own. A comparison of the two plays shows how difficult it is to pin down Ostrovski to any particular moral code: unlike the French dramatists of the ideological school, he is elusive as life itself.

The comedies mentioned above are thoroughly characteristic of Ostrovski's work as a whole, and perhaps are the best of his writings. In the others the picture of Russian life—sometimes realistically displayed, sometimes coloured with the garish tints of caricature—is expanded along similar lines. *Dokhodnoe mesto* (*A Lucrative Job*) reveals the weakness of the Civil Servants; *Beshenie dengi* (*Rabid Money*) deals with those financial questions which so worried all authors in this age: in one play after another Ostrovski essayed to reveal some fresh aspect of Moscow society. In all he showed himself a master in portraiture—one who perhaps hardly possessed Chekhov's power of universalizing the particular, yet nevertheless a dramatic artist whose worth has not been sufficiently realized outside his own land. (pp. 512-15)

> *Allardyce Nicoll, "From the Medieval to the Materialistic: The Coming of Realism," in his* World Drama: From Aeschylus to Anouilh, *George G. Harrap & Company Ltd., 1949, pp. 485-518.*

Albert Kaspin (essay date 1962)

[*In the following essay, Kaspin discusses Xor'kov and Milašin in* The Poor Bride *as examples of significant character types in Russian literature.*]

Recent Russian criticism and scholarship concerning *The Poor Bride* (*Bednaja nevesta*) has tended, in its concern with the title theme, to follow Dobroljubov's interpretation which appeared over a century ago in his two essays on Ostrovskij [see Further Reading]. Stress is put on reiterating and expanding Dobroljubov's exposition that in the "realm of darkness" there was no way out but marriage to the highest bidder for a poor girl of lower civil-service parentage, even though she was beautiful and intelligent. Following Dobroljubov's comments even further, certain episodic characters (Dunja and Paša) receive special attention. Apparently, however, no importance has been attached to examples of two different types of characters, both of which have interesting antecedants and no less interesting descendants in Russian literature. Certainly worthy of attention in spite of their being minor characters—and especially because they are presented in dramat-

ic form—are Xor'kov, a variant of the superfluous man, and Milašin, who reveals certain traits that relate him to the precursors of the underground man.

The Poor Bride, Ostrovskij's fifth dramatic work, was begun in the summer of 1850 in the wake of the storm aroused by *Svoi ljudi—sočtemsja* which had called Ostrovskij to the unfavorable attention of the authorities and had resulted in his being placed under the surveillance of the Third Section, in his losing his position as a court clerk, and finally in preventing for a time the staging of his plays. Ostrovskij was striving at the time to ease his financial distress by his activities on "the young editorial board" of Pogodin's *Moskvitjanin,* activities that were poorly and infrequently rewarded. It was because he was still troubled by the technical problems connected with writing a full-length drama that work on *The Poor Bride* progressed slowly and that the play underwent revisions even after its appearance in *Moskvitjanin* in February 1852.

For the locale of his play, which takes place in the early 1850's, Ostrovskij remained within the confines of Moscow's *Zamoskvoreč'e* district which he had known so intimately since childhood and of which he was called the "Columbus." This district was noted for its concentration of merchants, but was inhabited also by minor noblemen, civil servants (*činovniki*), and ordinary townspeople (*meščane*). In contrast to *Svoi ljudi—sočtemsja,* in which are satirized the savage mores of the merchant world, this play is concerned with the semi-cultured, lower civil-service milieu. Ostrovskij's turning to this group may have been prompted by a desire to broaden his scope by writing of classes other than the merchant, as well as by a desire to turn away from the merchant world that had been aroused against him by his earlier work. He was again dealing, however, with a world he knew well and of which he was a part. In fact, according to S. M. Maksimov, in his reminiscences of the dramatist, the prototypes for several of the characters in *The Poor Bride* were to be found among Ostrovskij's intimate circle of friends, his acquaintances, and office colleagues. And the heroine's difficult situation had its counterpart in real life.

The Poor Bride was written just before Ostrovskij's temporary change of philosophy was to be reflected in his so-called "Slavophilic" plays which presented a more benign interpretation of Russian merchant life. Even in this play, having the heroine express wishfully at the end the belief that she would attain happiness might be interpreted as an indication of Ostrovskij's changing attitude.

Called a "comedy in five acts," *The Poor Bride* centers around Mar'ja Andreevna Nezabudkina, in whose successful marriage lies the sole hope of her mother, the widow of a minor civil service official, for escape for both of them from impending poverty. Mar'ja sacrifices herself to insure her mother's well-being by accepting Benevolenskij, who, although a scoundrel, is the only one of her four suitors who is financially stable.

One of the unsuccessful suitors is the superfluous man, Mixajlo Ivanovič Xor'kov; another is Ivan Ivanovič Milašin, whose kinship to the underground man will be considered later.

The epithet "superfluous man," first used by Turgenev in a work published in 1850, and given currency by Russian literary critics and historians, came, with variations, to be the term used to describe the educated individual who had become alienated from his milieu and who was unable, because of objective or subjective reasons, to find application for his abilities.

What we know of Xor'kov derives from his appearance in two acts and from what his mother says of him in two others. In addition, we learn from the dramatis personae that he is "a former student," as well as that he is of humble stock, since his mother is described there as "a townswoman" (*meščanka*). Xor'kov's modest antecedants are further underscored by his mother relating to the widow Nezabudkina, with a kind of inverse pride, his comments to her: "It's not important to me, *mamen'ka,* he says, that you are a simple woman and uneducated, while I, he says, am an educated man—I love you and adore you." Again she adds to Nezabudkina: "You know my Miša on his good side; considering his rank, he occupies a high position in society. I, of course, am a woman of low rank, but I don't have any of those low ideas; I am rather far from that circle and am rather refined in my feelings."

These, of course, are the words of a doting mother. Still, by becoming an educated man, Xor'kov had separated himself from the taxpaying class of townspeople (*meščane*) and had become one of the rapidly-increasing group of educated commoners (*raznočincy*). Xor'kov is probably in the civil service, for his mother boasts that he is on the way to become a nobleman, a reference, no doubt, to the fact that university-trained men, by virtue of their education, could by-pass the lowest grades of the civil service ladder and thus be closer to the rank that automatically gave its bearer nobility.

However, Xor'kov probably spends little time at his post, for his mother complains to him of his conduct: "It's strange, Miša: you're an educated man, but, as I look at you, what are you doing? You have no acquaintance at all, you do not work, you loll about the house in a dressing gown with a pipe." The reference to Xor'kov's solitude, sloth and, of course, to the dressing gown recalls the hero of Gončarov's *Oblomov*. Xor'kov is indeed suffering from a *Zamoskvoreč'e* form of what was later identified as Oblomovism: "indolence, deficiency of will, indecision, passivity, procrastination." It was not unusual at that period for a civil service official, especially one in the lower ranks, to visit his office only infrequently. Being enrolled gave the individual social standing, while his salary depended mainly on work actually done. Ostrovskij himself had for a number of years been in the civil service, but had devoted most of his time to literature. Ostrovskij gives another example of this type of work relationship in this play when Milašin says of a rival, the young nobleman Merič, that "he does nothing, he is only listed in the service in order to get the first rank."

In Xor'kov's case it is not only that education has created a chasm that separates him from his original social stratum, but also that that education was of a special kind, one that had an effect on his personality. Xor'kov was a product of Moscow University of the 1840's. This was the period of Professor Granovskij's greatest popularity, of the vogue among Russian students of Hegel and German idealism, of Schiller and romanticism, of intense, endless discussions on philosophy and on esthetic ideals in student cafes, of Belinskij's impassioned articles. Xor'kov was exposed to this heady mixture and became imbued with it, at least in part because his shy, contemplative nature was more conducive to thinking than to doing. When, after such exhilirating experiences, Xor'kov left the refuge of the university and suffered the chilling shock of contact with the brutalities, vulgarities, and stupidities of life about him, he could easily retreat into his shell and try to live in the world of the mind. In addition, the repressive measures following the revolution of 1848 would have dampened any inclinations Xor'kov might have experienced to bring his ideals to life.

In his first speech Xor'kov reveals himself. Having fled from Mar'ja because he became too embarrassed to tell her that he loved her, he sits alone on a bench with bowed head and says:

> I ran away, I became afraid! What a miserable person I am! But what, after all, am I doing? Why am I destroying myself? It has been three years since I graduated, and in these three years I have accomplished absolutely nothing for myself. I feel a cold wave sweeping over me when I recall how I have lived these three years! Indolence, sloth, a grimy bachelor's existence—and no aspirations to get out of this kind of life, no drop of pride! For myself I won't resolve on anything. I know that. My sole salvation is in her, and I don't even dare tell her I love her. No, this must be ended! Can it really be she won't have pity on me? For her I would begin to work, to toil; she alone is capable of binding me to life. O Lord, how I love that girl! How I love her!

For all his weakness of character, Xor'kov is no fool. He has an astute mind and is painfully aware of his deterioration from inactivity and lack of ambition. One suspects it is principally his fear of imminent degeneration that spurs him to dare fall in love with the beautiful Mar'ja: he hopes the power of love will jar him out of his lethargy.

Even more revelatory are his remarks to his mother. Despite his conviction that he can be saved only by Mar'ja's love and that he is superior to his rivals, he defers declaring his love: "Yes, *mamen'ka,* I am educated, I have a kind heart; besides I know that she will be happy with me, that only I am able to appreciate her, that she will perish in that circle, a victim of calculation or ignorance . . . but I am afraid that she will refuse me." And again he says to his mother: "I'll have a talk with her; without fail I will. I must put an end to this somehow . . . But what if she refuses me? Now at least there are hopes, there are dreams, but then what would there be?" Xor'kov holds the uncertainty of the future to be preferable to the certainty of today, for he can see only vileness and unhappiness in the present. He has so little faith in life that he is afraid to risk losing his dream sanctuary.

Xor'kov is quite incapable of meeting a serious challenge. At the first sign of a rebuff he immediately capitulates. When Mar'ja tells him she loves another, Xor'kov sees the collapse of his chance of salvation, of his whole future. He leaves the field to his rivals. He knows that Merič is a philanderer, yet he does not dare warn Mar'ja himself, but gives Milašin some letters to show Mar'ja to prove Merič's perfidy. In his disappointment Xor'kov turns to drink. Later, in a drunken, maudlin state, he makes tearful confession of his love, but it is already too late. Mar'ja has become disillusioned with the handsome poseur Merič and has accepted the proposal of the vulgar Benevolenskij.

Xor'kov understands Mar'ja's predicament and sees through his rivals, but does not take advantage of the situation. He is either too inert or too unselfish. His sincere grief may have aroused pity, but his conduct would hardly have inspired confidence or love in the woe-beset Mar'ja, who herself now needs someone strong for support.

Xor'kov's portrait is the first of several contributions by Ostrovskij to the gallery of superfluous men. The plight of Xor'kov is in some respects even worse than that of Turgenev's unhappy heroes. They, at least, move among people of education and refinement, while Xor'kov has no one with whom he can speak. His university-nurtured *Schöngeistigkeit* ["beautiful spirituality"] puts him out of place in the rough-and-tumble existence of *Zamoskvoreč'e* and acts as a wall between him and the life about him. His learning has estranged him from his environment, an environment he detests and from which he shrinks, but which he lacks the character to struggle against or even to leave. Learning has fostered his natural delicacy and gentleness to the stage where it has enervated him. Rather than act, he prefers to retreat to the beautiful world of his dreams and await events with apprehensive immobility.

A clue to Ostrovskij's concept of Xor'kov is to be found in the latter's surname which apparently derives from *xorëk*, a dialect word meaning "a small island in a river or lake." In his isolation from the stream of life about him, Xor'kov is indeed an island.

In their critical articles Černyševskij and Dobroljubov applied the "superfluous man" label to those members of the gentry who were educated, well meaning, and from whom had been expected to come the leadership that was to guide Russia along the path of social progress, but who, because they had grown up in the post-Decembrist period, had been reared among the mists of German idealism, had become avid and eloquent polemicists, and had dwelt for so long in the realm of ideas that they were incapable of acting effectively, frequently even in personal matters. Černyševskij and Dobroljubov embodied in themselves the idea that leadership was to come from another quarter, from the educated commoners who had been hailed hopefully as being "new men." Ostrovskij's Xor'kov—in his alienation from society because of an education that put him outside the class of his origin and out of contact with life itself, in his frustrating idleness, in his ineptness, in his weakness of character—is an indication that "superfluous men" were to be found not only among the gentry, but had already begun to appear among the educated commoners.

Although Turgenev presented a superfluous man in the character of Rakitin in the play *A Month in the Country*, written in 1850, that work, because of the censors, was published only in 1855. Ostrovskij could therefore have created his Xor'kov quite independently, and, in any case, Xor'kov has traits that make him quite distinct from Turgenev's superfluous men.

In his sensitivity, egocentricity, introspection, lack of will-power, inability to act, and alienation from life, the superfluous man has traits in common with Dostoevskij's diarist of *Notes from the Underground* (1864). However, this underground man has suffered so long from his frustrations that he has come to rationalize his lack of will-power and inability to act as being marks of a superior being. He has become so accustomed to his yoke of moral pain that

he even seeks humiliation, from which he experiences a perverse masochistic satisfaction. Consequently he has a penchant for saying the wrong thing, for placing himself in an awkward position, and for attracting insult. Other manifestations of this unhappy anti-hero who has soured on life are overweening pride, petty spitefulness, and tense neuroticism. An innate feeling of inferiority eggs him on to prove his superiority to himself again and again. He is given to excessive cerebration. His considerable intellectual capacity has been diverted to devising vengeful plans to assert his superiority and to convince himself of the futility and undesirability of pursuing any course other than that of his own inaction. In his fantasies he resorts readily to the idea of committing acts of violence, for with weapon in hand he fancies himself the equal of those individuals whose success is such an irritation to him. He is defeated by the enormity of the chasm that separates the ideal from reality, and from his inability to bridge that gap he retreats into his moral underground of bitter speculation. Finally, he is characterized by a readiness to confess.

Dostoevskij's underground diarist had many precursors. Among these are Puškin's sparsely drawn Evgenij (*Mendnyj vsadnik*) and Germann (*Pikovaja dama*); and, showing increasing self-consciousness, Gogol's Popriščin (*Dnevnik sumasšedšego*) and Akakij Akakievič (*Šinel'*), Turgenev's country squire in *Gamlet Ščigrovskogo uezda* and Čulkaturin (*Dnevnik lišnego čeloveka*), as well as several of Dostoevskij's early heroes. Ostrovskij's Milašin has several features that identify him as a member of this singular fraternity.

The role of Milašin in ***The Poor Bride*** is considerably larger than is that of Xor'kov. He appears in each act, has numerous lines and he serves as a foil for several of the other characters. From an anecdote told by Milašin in the first printed version of the play, but omitted from the final 1859 version, it is clear that he is a civil servant, since he uses the verb *služit'* in a way that includes his own activity. Milašin is in the poor-clerk tradition of Gogol's little men. He is so poor that he admits that he is unable to marry Mar'ja simply because he has no means. This, of course, is quite apart from the fact that Mar'ja does not care at all for him and finds him a bore.

Although he is poor, he is aware of how some officials acquire wealth, but he scorns to follow that path. When he is taunted by Mar'ja's mother that Benevolenskij is a man of means, he exclaims: "Means! And where did he get these means, one should ask? I have a conscience, and because of that no means. It's not difficult to acquire means." For whatever reason Milašin is not a bribe-taker like Benevolenskij.

Having graduated from the *gimnazija,* Milašin had the educational qualifications for entering the service. He is very conscious of his training and proud of it. In trying to prove his superiority over Merič, he asks Mar'ja: "In what way am I worse than a Merič? If I wanted to, I could be a hundred times better than he. The stripling! Didn't study anywhere; learned merely to chatter in French at some boarding school. I at least graduated from the *gimnazija*. How dare he laugh at me?" Characteristic of Milašin, something that is apparent in almost every line he speaks, is his constant preoccupation with himself, the constant comparison he makes of himself with others, and the embittered, argumentative tone, tinged with sarcasm, with which he asserts his superiority over others.

Milašin is aware that he does not cut an attractive figure in society, that he lacks social grace. He is also envious of Merič's success. He tells Mar'ja: "Of course, I'm not as handsome as Merič; I don't go around in high society; I don't speak French. These qualities are highly prized nowadays. Be as stupid as a stump, just know how to make compliments, to chatter . . . That's what is pleasing nowadays. It's terribly annoying."

His pride is hurt that Mar'ja should prefer Merič to him, with all his attributes. It is pride that causes him to answer as he does when he is informed by Merič, who is teasing him, that Mar'ja had told him she did not like Milašin: "It's strange that Mar'ja Andreevna should talk that way. It's even insulting. It's all the same to me, of course: whether she loves me or not, I don't pay any attention. I myself am completely indifferent to her. But why talk? She wants to show by this that I'm running after her. No, I'll leave that to others." His feigning indifference to Mar'ja is obviously his way of saving face before a detested rival. His ego is too great to allow him to admit to another that he could be interested in one who is not interested in him. But this does not deter him from continuing to press his suit with Mar'ja.

Of course, he has an exalted opinion of himself. Even after Mar'ja has made it clear she does not love him, he disregards that unpleasant fact and persists in the illusion of his own attractiveness. When Xor'kov questions whether Mar'ja will believe Milašin, the latter answers:

> MILASIN. She will, without fail she will: she loves me very much.
>
> XOR'KOV. Hardly, Ivan Ivanyč! It seems to me she doesn't love you at all.
>
> MILASIN. Why do you think so? Am I any worse than others? No, excuse me! You don't know me: women like me, too, very much.

Milašin's obtuseness regarding his attractiveness gets him into embarrassing situations. He stubbornly persists in this delusion not only with Xor'kov, but even with Mar'ja herself. His ego will not permit him to admit that Mar'ja could dislike him, and he continues to annoy her.

At least in words Milašin is ready to resort to violence. His answer to Mar'ja, now deserted by Merič, as to how he can help her, is pertinent:

> MILASIN. Do you want me to challenge him to a duel? Do you think I won't challenge him? I certainly will.
>
> MAR'JA ANDREEVNA. What are you thinking of! Why should you do that? By what right?
>
> MILASIN. Yes, actually it is awkward! I just asked, but then, just as you please. Life isn't dear to me . . . I can't bear to see you suffer! Is there absolutely no way in which I can help you?

Caught up in the fervor of the moment, Milašin committed himself before another to a course that would have led him out of fantasy and into action. He was undoubtedly alarmed at the obligation he had offered to assume, and

he backed down with alacrity and relief when Mar'ja would not hear of a duel. Even Milašin realized that he was out of his realm in the field of action.

It is more usual for Milašin to confine his spiteful speculations to himself. In two typical monologues he reveals the quality of his mind, his fantasies, that show his close relationship to the underground man. In the first act, alone at the window, he fumes in exasperation:

> What's this! Merič here again! Well, so he is. That's what I expected. The devil take it, it's annoying. No, I won't permit it. How long I've tried with all my strength to have her like me. I keep on trying again and again . . . and all for nothing; and suddenly someone or other . . . I simply can't stand seeing her flirt with him. If I could just drive him out of here! Marry her? But she won't marry me because I have nothing to live on, and besides, it seems she doesn't like me. Then why do I keep on trying? Just go away, drop it, and pay no attention. But still she ought to be made to feel it. I ought to say to her: "You now have new acquaintances, Mar'ja Andreevna, with whom you are happier than with the old; but you are losing a friend who was devoted to you." She, of course, will argue with me, but I'll say to her: "No," I'll say, "if it's better for you this way, then what is there for me to do here; maybe you're tired of me; farewell," I'll say, " . . . forever." "But why forever, Ivan Ivanyč?" "No," I'll say, "if I say farewell, then it's forever, that's the kind of character I have." I'll take my hat and leave . . . but what will happen then! O, the devil take it! She very likely will even be glad that I'll have gone, and Merič even more so! Then no, I'll stay to spite them; I'll come every day; I'll laugh at Merič right to his face: somehow or other I'll drive him out of here! . . . I'll use any means!

Milašin is the insignificant being, the insulted personality, who always is overlooked and brushed aside. Unable to command attention, he fitfully forces himself on others and, when rebuffed, endlessly analyzes what has occurred to find the flaw in his conduct. He imagines conversations that will stun others by his brilliance and that will unfold his stellar qualities and staunch character. At the wedding reception in the last act, alone, he speaks for the last time at length in the same vein.

Despite his ravings, Milašin is harmless. He is so absurd in his pride, egocentricity, spitefulness, and his efforts to prove his superiority, that he evokes laughter. Although he has the malevolent, splenetic, and humorless characteristics of Dostoevskij's diarist, he differs from the latter in one essential trait: intelligence. Milašin clearly lacks the superior mind of the diarist.

The presentation of a type such as Milašin poses a problem. Gogol', Turgenev, and Dostoevskij usually faced this problem in one of two ways. The first was to have the character make a confession, impulsively blurting his story to some stranger, the author. The other was to have him give free rein to his feelings in letters or in a diary. Neither method is entirely suited for the stage. It would be deadly to have an actor deliver himself of a detailed account of his life and aspirations, and although one or two short letters might be woven into the fabric of a play, more than that would be boring. Ostrovskij tried to solve the problem by giving Milašin numerous lines, by placing him opposite various characters many times, and by the extensive use of monologue. The latter is especially curious because Ostrovskij is noted as a realist and his frequent recourse to the monologue indicates his greater concern for the completeness of his characterization than his interest in the technical smoothness typical of a *pièce bien faite* ["well-made play"].

Xor'kov and Milašin are Ostrovskij's first efforts at presenting the superfluous man and the underground man, types he developed in greater detail in later plays. Xor'kov is of interest because through him Ostrovskij showed that the superfluous man could already be found among the *raznočincy*. Part of Ostrovskij's contribution to these types was that he presented them on the stage. And finally Ostrovskij's method of presenting Milašin partially through monologue constitutes his compromise to a difficult literary problem dictated by the dramatic form in which he wrote. (pp. 312-20)

> Albert Kaspin, "A Superfluous Man and an Underground Man in Ostrovskij's 'The Poor Bride'," in Slavic and East European Journal, Vol. VI, No. 4, Winter, 1962, pp. 312-21.

Marc Slonim (essay date 1964)

[*Slonim was a Russian-born American critic who wrote extensively on Russian literature. In the following excerpt, he discusses the social background of Ostrovsky's works and the reason for their popularity.*]

[The] world of grain dealers, shopkeepers, middlemen, swindlers, shysters, matchmakers, and topers was discovered and introduced into Russian literature by Alexander Ostrovsky. He knew them well, for he was born and lived among them. The son of a poor government clerk, Alexander had spent his childhood in the sedate streets of the 'Across-the-River' quarter, where the clumsily but solidly built houses were surrounded by truck patches and neglected gardens characteristic of their owners. Later on he attended the Law School at the University of Moscow, but did not graduate, and wound up as a clerk in the Court of Equity and the Court of Commerce. In both places he found ample opportunities to study the peculiar Russian breed of merchants and middle-class folk, whose private lives erupted in lawsuits and feuds. At this time his father had resigned from office and had begun practicing as a pettifogger—and from his clients Ostrovsky added to his wealth of observations. In this manner he gathered an enormous amount of material and gained a deep insight into the manners and mentality of a whole class of people that until then, as he claimed, had been 'veiled in the night of ignorance.' In 1856 he undertook a long journey in the Volga region which also enriched his fund of facts, stories, types, and incidents.

As far back as 1847 Ostrovsky had begun to describe the folk 'Across-the-River' in scenes that were later incorporated in his comedy, **It's All in the Family.** The first draft of this play, entitled **The Bankrupt,** had been frequently read aloud in the literary salons of Moscow, at one of which Gogol had heard and liked the piece. Although the play won acclaim, it offended the Moscow merchants and exasperated the authorities. In 1850 Ostrovsky was forced to resign from his position and was put under police surveillance. Until 1861 the censors refused to pass the come-

dy for stage production either in Moscow or St. Petersburg. Between 1850 and 1861, however, Ostrovsky wrote and produced eleven other plays (among them such masterpieces as **Poverty No Disgrace, The Poor Bride, The Thunderstorm**) which assured his success. In the 'sixties he dominated the theater as the creator of a truly national repertoire.

Despite the opposition of influential noblemen, who complained that his plays 'had the fusty smell of the sheepskin coats of peasants and tradesmen,' Ostrovsky won immediate recognition. It was mainly owing to the subject matter and the realism of his plays. He did in the theater what Gogol and Goncharov had accomplished in fiction: instead of the melodramas and lewd farces (mostly translations) that crowded the stage at that time, he offered dramas and comedies whose characters and plots were part of life in Russia, solidly rooted in native soil and genuinely national. The novelty of his subject matter bordered on revelation. The merchants from 'Across-the-River' described by this literary Columbus were not merely illustrative of one class; their psychology and manners belonged to various strata of Russian society.

It was a peculiar world in which crass ignorance was blended with superstition, and the authoritarian pattern of family relation, a rapacious attitude toward property, and mistreatment of the helpless were regarded as perfectly normal. Education hardly crossed the threshold of the stuffy households of Ostrovsky's characters. Some of them, such as the frivolous Lipochka in **It's All in the Family,** were convinced that the highest manifestations of culture consisted of fashionable dress and a parrot-like repetition of two or three phrases in French. His provincial characters did not go even as far as that. In **The Thunderstorm** the merchants of Kalinov, a small town on the Volga and completely cut off from the world, believe any nonsense told them by pilgrims and wandering nuns—that there are dog-headed men living overseas, that the whole world, with the exception of Russia, is divided between two sultans, the Turkish and the Persian, and so on. Dikoi (Wild Man), the tycoon of the town, becomes quite wroth when he hears that thunderstorms are caused by electricity and that lightning can be neutralized by conducting rods. 'What foolishness!' he shouts. 'A thunderstorm is sent us as a visitation, and yet, the Lord forgive me, you want to defend yourself with rods and poles. What are you, a heathen?'

The moral standards had all the rigidity of the Middle Ages. Wives, children, shop clerks, and servants owed absolute obedience to the master. As head of the family and of his business he had unlimited rights and unchallenged authority. The whip hanging on the wall of an 'Across-the-River' bedroom, no mere symbol of masculine authority, was a frequently used instrument of punishment and persuasion. If you beat your wife, ran the proverb, the soup will taste better.

When Bolshov, in **It's All in the Family,** decides to marry off his daughter, he dismisses all the objections of Podkhalyuzin, whom he has chosen as his son-in-law, with: 'Isn't she my daughter? I made her, and I can do whatever I please with her.' The head of the family is convinced that the pattern of divine and social order consists of God in Heaven, the Czar on earth, the father at home, and the master at the shop. And this atmosphere of unlimited authority bred the *samodur,* or petty tyrant. In his comedy, *A Hangover from Other Folks' Wine,* Ostrovsky gives a definition of the *samodur:*

> He's a man who won't listen to anybody or anything; you can split your guts trying to argue with him, but he'll always stick to his point. When he stamps his foot the whole household has to get down on their knees—or may God save us all! He's a wild, wilful man with a heart of stone.

Nor is he only a wilful person (and quite often a blockhead as well); he is given to moods, wants his whims to be taken as law, delights in inspiring fear, and is apt to make most contradictory and absurd decisions. In one of Ostrovsky's comedies the husband keeps thumping the table with his huge fist until his wife is all jittery, whereupon he laughs: 'It's nothing—I merely wanted to be sure and put fear into you. Now, what about some tea?'

The *samodur* enjoys humiliating those under him and usually brags about his money. Dikoi in *The Thunderstorm* boasts of being a Very Important Person, for he has plenty of money: 'You ought to know you're a worm,' he tells Kuligin, a poor inventor. 'I can spare you or crush you, just as I please.' For the sake of money he is ready to cheat and to commit all sorts of base actions, inasmuch as all *samodurs* realize that riches are the basis of authority. Considering property the only sign of achievement or success, they discard any moral or religious scruples when it comes to getting it. Bolshov, in *It's All in the Family,* stages a false bankruptcy to defraud his creditors, but is betrayed by his sneaky accomplice Podkhalyuzin. Korshunov, in *Poverty No Disgrace,* ruins his friend Lyubim, while Lyubim is thrown out into the street by his own brother. Old codgers or whippersnappers—both are equally birds of prey and no pity is shown by either in the ruthless game of acquisition.

The main conflicts in this 'reign of darkness' revolve around money and marriage. Fathers choose mates for their sons and daughters, often with the help of professional matchmakers. The problem of dowry is of primary importance: a poor girl, especially if she is pretty, is doomed to become a victim of lust and depravity, like Larissa, in *Dowerless,* one of Ostrovsky's best plays. In *Poverty No Disgrace* the rich merchant Tortsov suddenly decides that his daughter Lyubov is to marry Korshunov, a shady businessman who has driven his first wife to death by his cruel jealousy. And Lyubov, although she is in love with Mitya, a poor clerk, says to her father: 'I dare not disobey your command.' Everyone is perfectly aware that marrying Korshunov would be her ruin, yet no one voices a protest. Her mother knows of nothing better than to weep, and when Mitya proposes elopement Lyubov answers: 'I must submit to my father's will—such is a maiden's lot, and it must be right, since it has been so ordained from of old.' Fortunately her Uncle Lyubim, an old drunkard, comes in just when the bridal feast is under way, accuses Korshunov of being a swindler and a criminal, and tries to awaken the better feelings of the girl's father.

In *The Thunderstorm* Katerina, married to Tikhon, suffers deeply from the prevalent hypocrisy and sanctimoniousness and from the domineering of her mother-in-law, the ruthless Kabanova. This female *samodur* is a despot who believes only in the observance of church ritual and in traditions: 'What will happen when we old folks die?

How the world will remain in being I don't know!' For her the patriarchal past is the only fount of wisdom and decency. A similar attachment to the past assumes refined forms in such 'nests of gentlefolk' as Berezhkova's, but unfolds in all its crudeness and ugliness in the case of primitive and ignorant people such as Dikoi or Kabanova. Katerina, a sensitive, poetic nature with a profound longing for beauty and freedom, simply cannot comply with the rigid rules of Kabanova. She transgresses the moral code of her environment and, during the absence of her husband, yields to her love for Boris, a somewhat educated young man from Moscow, who is mistreated by his Uncle Dikoi. She pays dearly for her moment of passion and liberty. When Tikhon returns, Katerina cannot pretend and hide what she considers a mortal sin. During a thunderstorm she makes a public confession, and retaliation is swift in coming. Boris is packed off to a place on the Siberian border, without daring to protest. Tikhon, obeying his mother's instructions, suppresses his pity for his unfaithful wife and mistreats her, while Kabanova makes Katerina's life so miserable that finally she throws herself into the Volga.

Katerina, Boris, and the self-taught inventor Kulighin are all above their oppressive environment. 'We have hard ways in our town,' says Kulighin. 'You'll find nothing but coarseness and stark poverty here. Honest labor will never get you more than your daily bread. And whoever has money tries to enslave the poor, so as to get still more.' Boris, the best educated of the three, is too weak and dependent on others. And Kulighin, the *raisonneur* who dreams of solar clocks and lightning conductors, has but a vague hope that education and science will some day cure the ills of his native town.

Despite its tragic end, *The Thunderstorm* showed that there was a 'sunbeam in the realm of darkness,' the title of Dobroliubov's long article on the drama in 1860 [see Further Reading]. Something had gone wrong in the authoritarian system of the Dikois and Kabanovas, those representatives of a new bourgeoisie, whose grasping domination had come to replace the old paternalism of the nobility. They ruled through fear, money, and aggressiveness, but Katerina, Boris, and Kulighin were so many threats to their power.

In addition to being a social drama, *The Thunderstorm* was a drama of tragic love, of a romantic soul whom the stone walls and bars of her domestic prison could not keep from passion. The interplay of realism and symbolic allusions, the drama of action and contrasting characters, the re-creation of a tense atmosphere of love and fate make this play Ostrovsky's best work. It shows the constant inner growth of its author.

In the early 'fifties Ostrovsky associated himself with the group of young Slavophiles connected with *The Muscovite,* a monthly, who acclaimed him as a 'painter of true Russian customs.' As a matter of fact, although Ostrovsky exposed the 'realm of darkness' in several of his first comedies (*It's All in the Family, The Poor Bride*), he also displayed a great deal of sympathy toward the old traditions. This was particularly true in *Know Your Place* (1855), whose heroes, Russakov and Borodkin, might be taken for paragons of the domestic virtues, and in *Poverty No Disgrace,* the very setting of which included the celebration of the Russian Christmas, with its songs, dances, mummers, and old customs. The scapegrace Lyubim Tortsov, who exposes Korshunov, awakens the conscience of his brother, and brings about a happy ending for the two young lovers, was interpreted by the Slavophiles as the embodiment of the 'Russian soul'—expansive, irrational, kind, human even in the slough of drunkenness—while Korshunov, an Anglophile and outwardly a Westernizer, symbolized the corrosive effect of kowtowing to foreigners. Lyubim's speech as he is shown the door: 'Lyubim Tortsov may be a drunkard but he's a better man than you—make way, Lyubim Tortsov is going!' never failed to bring down the house. Tortsov's brother is forever arguing with his wife, who upbraids him for no longer caring for any of 'our Russian ways.' He hires a butler in cotton gloves instead of a youth in a Russian smock or a peasant girl, because he wants to be 'in the swim,' for the same reason that Lipochka, in **It's All in the Family,** wants to learn French. 'Your fashionable falderols,' his wife assures him, 'change from day to day, while our Russian ways have lasted from time immemorial. Folks in the old days were just as smart as we are.'

The class of merchants Ostrovsky depicted was too close to the patriarchal peasantry from which it had sprung to forget the old traditions, some of which went back to the seventeenth century. The men and women of this class reflected the ways of life and characteristics typical of the agricultural population of the Russian steppes—lack of moderation, animal spirits, physical strength, wilfulness combined with Byzantine formalism, a strict code of morals blended with wild impulses. In depicting characters that remained fundamentally Russian even to their eccentricities, Ostrovsky was accomplishing a profoundly national task. This was one of the reasons for his popularity among the Slavophiles. But his association with the *Muscovite* group soon came to an end. He could never be dogmatic and, for the sake of an abstract idea, 'arrange' the facts he had observed. The national traits in his heroes, such as Russakov, Borodkin, or Krasnov, or the idealization of a Lyubim Tortsov could not hide the despotism, ignorance, and other evils of the 'realm of darkness.'

Besides, the political events and the whole social atmosphere of the period contributed to the sharpening of his critical tendency. The disastrous outcome of the Crimean War proved the inefficiency of a regime based on serfdom, a corrupt bureaucracy, and a hierarchy of *samodurs,* great and small. The Slavophiles, boasting of Old Russia's integrity as opposed to the declining West, sounded none too convincing after the victory of decadent Europe over saintly Russia, and Ostrovsky definitely stressed the exposure and criticism in his plays. He became a regular contributor to *The Contemporary* and other reviews of the Westernizers. The liberals, as well as the radicals, saw in him one of their own, even though Ostrovsky never took any political stand and maintained friendly relations with many conservatives.

In 1856 he published **A Profitable Business,** the hero of which, Zhadov, refuses to follow the example of avaricious bureaucrats. An exposé of the latter forms the bulk of the comedy. It was followed, in 1859, by **The Mistress' Pet,** a caustic indictment of rural despotism and, in 1860, by **The Thunderstorm.**

As a writer of increasing reputation who refused to commit himself to any of the existing political or literary groups—except for his allegiance, in a broad sense of the term, to the Realistic movement—Ostrovsky was constantly expanding the range of his plays and turning to new topics that led him far from the world of the merchants. He portrayed the declining nobility in the comedy of **Wild Money,** devoted a series of excellent plays to the life of provincial actors (**The Forest** and **Talents and Suitors** are the best of these), tried his hand at historical dramas, which were the fashion in the late 'seventies, and even wrote a fantastic drama, **The Snow Maiden,** which was to inspire Tchaikovsky and Rimsky-Korsakov.

Not content with his literary activity, this industrious playwright devoted a great deal of his time and energy to the improvement of the situation of actors and writers. The theater in Russia was a State monopoly, and no private theatrical enterprises were allowed in Moscow or St. Petersburg until 1881. Some playwrights offered their plays without any payment in order to have them produced in Moscow and St. Petersburg, since production there amounted to permission to put them on in the provinces. The actors were either treated by the administrators as hirelings of the government, or, in the small towns, considered by the public on a level with mountebanks and prostitutes. Ostrovsky fought for the reform of all legislation dealing with the theater. He also attempted to cultivate in the public a respect for the actor and a higher appreciation of his work. He knew from bitter experience the difficulties of any career connected with the stage: despite his popularity, he made but little money and was always on the verge of poverty. The Administration of the Imperial Theaters, although compelled to produce his plays, disliked these homespun wares which looked so crude next to the graceful French comedies, and put many obstacles in Ostrovsky's way. He succeeded, however, in founding various mutual-aid theatrical associations and, in 1874, he established the Society of Russian Playwrights and Opera Composers for the protection of their rights. This Society functioned all over the country until 1917, and then served as a model for the similar Soviet organization.

In 1886 Ostrovsky was appointed Director of the Moscow Theatrical School and of the repertoire for the Moscow theaters. But this official recognition came too late: the playwright died a few months later.

When his literary heritage is studied in its entirety it reveals, despite the variety of topics, an amazing unity of purpose. Most of his plays pictured the conflict between the wilful and the submissive, the rich and the poor, old age and youth. The warmth and comprehension with which he portrays all the oppressed or ruined victims of the *samodurs* forms the main background of his plays and creates their atmosphere. Ostrovsky's is that famous 'pity' that Europe discovered in Russian Realism, that sympathy for the downtrodden. In Ostrovsky, who avoided lapsing into sentimentality (except for a few 'happy endings,' often tacked on at the insistence of the censors), the pity is enhanced by the pathos of the struggle of the individual for his freedom and dignity. In **The Forest,** Neschastlivtsev (Unlucky), a minor actor, defends his profession before a group of the gentry:

> Mountebanks? *No,* you are the side show performers, we are the noble actors. We love earnestly and, if we dislike somebody, we quarrel and fight, but

when we want to help we do not spare our last cop-
pers. But what about you?

Ostrovsky may appear repetitious and elementary. Several
critics, particularly some early in the twentieth century,
deprecated him as a limited painter of manners, who confined himself to one historical milieu. It is understandable,
they claimed, that he would appeal to his contemporaries,
but only twenty years after his death he had dwindled to
the rank of a regional and outdated playwright. The lack
of interest shown by the West to translations of his work
proved, in their opinion, his limitations: his characters
failed to rise to the universal significance of truly great
works of art, because Ostrovsky used a superficial or
wrong psychology, and lacked any central, unifying idea.

The validity of this criticism was constantly challenged by
facts. Instead of declining, Ostrovsky's popularity in his
country was constantly increasing. During the theatrical
season of 1870 his plays were given daily in four or five
theaters; in 1912 in seven or eight; and in 1940 twenty-
eight Ostrovsky plays were produced daily in the U.S.S.R.
alone. In the previous year the total number of their performances topped 10,000. Tolstoy's prediction of 1886
had come true: Ostrovsky had become a national playwright. No changes in political weather could affect him,
and today, more than 125 years after his birth, he is the
most widely read and most frequently performed playwright of the Soviet Union.

What is the reason for such popularity? It cannot be explained by the scarcity of good Russian plays or by the fact
that in contemporary Russia playwriting is lagging behind
other highly developed theater arts. Ostrovsky has a
steady appeal because he had the knack of portraying Russian characters in a matter-of-fact, realistic way. There is
no mysticism, pathology, or complication in his plays,
even though he presents despots or cranks. His characters
have the Russian exuberance, but not in terms of frenzy
or morbid exaggeration, as in the writings of Dostoevsky.
They are not exceptional, romantic types, but average,
simple men and women, and even their crimes, follies, or
depravities have nothing mysterious or unacceptable
about them. No wonder that for many Europeans and
Americans who seek the 'thrill' of the 'Slave Soul'
Ostrovsky is not spicy enough. In a country of extremes,
struggle, and various forms of political dictatorship, the
conflict between the individual and his environment is always of immediate interest, and this conflict, familial or
social, is Ostrovsky's central theme.

Another reason for his appeal lies in the fact that he is not
only a sound writer but also wholesomely optimistic. According to a prejudice widely prevalent outside of Russia
in Europe and in America, Russian literature is exceedingly morbid. Facts disprove this superficial and faulty conclusion. Pushkin, Goncharov, and Tolstoy, express a vigorous affirmation of human values, a faith in life, and an
acceptance of the universe. Ostrovsky has the same positive spirit, and in that sense he is typically Russian.

The very flavor of Ostrovsky is conveyed to his audience
by his language. He belongs to the auditory type of writer,
for whom the sound of the word, the sonority of a sentence, the intonations of a speech hold first importance.
His dialogue is of the highest stage value because it reproduces living colloquial speech, interspersed with lively re-

marks, amusing slips of the tongue or distortions, with a
generous use of slang, local expressions, and changes of to-
nality. Most of his middle-class protagonists speak an
idiom that is either the Moscow speech of the period or
the unadulterated vernacular of the peasants. Ostrovsky's
language is hardly ever marred by bookish or foreign expressions. It is the country itself, with its steppes, its villages, and provincial towns, that we hear in Ostrovsky's
dramas and comedies and that makes them so difficult to
translate. Even their titles sound odd, since most of them
are nothing but old saws: *Even the Wise Stumble; Sin and
Sorrow Are the Common Lot; It's All in the Family—
We'll Settle It Ourselves; Even a Cat Has Lean Times,*
and so on.

The construction of Ostrovsky's plays is simple. His plots
are logically consistent and avoid surprises, except at the
very end, which is occasionally quite abrupt. The solution
is often presented in the form of a catastrophe, or a change
of mind in one of the main characters. The dramatic intensity, however, never exceeds naturalness. Ostrovsky himself made a distinction between theatrical Realism and
'copying reality.' When the Meiningen theatrical troupe,
famous for its stage Naturalism, came to Russia in 1880,
Ostrovsky, at first enthusiastic, came finally to the conclusion that 'the triumph of the property man and the stage-
hand has nothing to do with Realistic methods.' Like most
Russian Realists, he understood that truth never means
imitation, and that the Realistic approach in art must be
accompanied by interpretation and an organization of material. This conviction directed his artistic creativeness
and is partly responsible for his abiding popularity. It also
accounts for his historical importance. Fonvizin, Griboyedov, and Gogol were great playwrights, but they all left
only a few plays. There was no national repertoire before
Ostrovsky, and many people despaired that there ever
would be one. Ostrovsky proved it was perfectly possible;
he himself has left a legacy of forty-seven original plays—
comedies, dramas, historical chronicles, fantasies, several
plays in collaboration, and translations from Cervantes,
Goldoni, and Shakespeare (*The Taming of the Shrew*)—
thus laying the foundations for an authentically Russian
theater. This fact in itself had a revolutionizing effect.
Moreover, he founded a whole school, which brought
about a revival and a renewal of Russian literature.

All these facts entitle Ostrovsky to a unique place in Russian art: both his admirers and his detractors recognize his
merits as the founder of the modern national theater in
Russia. (pp. 193-202)

> *Marc Slonim, "Critical Realism: Goncharov
> and Ostrovsky," in his* The Epic of Russian
> Literature: From Its Origins through Tolstoy,
> 1950. *Reprint by Oxford University Press,
> 1964, pp. 182-202.*

Norman Henley   (essay date 1970)

*[In the following essay, Henley discusses three types of
characters in Ostrovsky's plays. Henley concludes that
the difficulty in placing each character into a single category demonstrates that Ostrovsky's plays display far
greater psychological complexity than is generally acknowledged.]*

Attention has been given to some of Ostrovskij's specific character types, such as the samodurs (to be discussed) and lovers, but the only inclusive classification made of his characters seems to be that of the exploiters and the exploited (the wolves and the sheep). Since human conflict is central to Ostrovskij's dramaturgy, such a classification has its obvious value. At the same time it is hardly all-inclusive. This article will attempt to categorize Ostrovskij's characters (in his nonhistorical plays) as play-actors, puppets, and rebels.

The play-actors may be subdivided into three groups: the self-seekers, the samodurs, and the histrionically obsessed.

Ostrovskij's first self-seeker is Podzaljuzin in *It's All in the Family (Svoi ljudi—sočtemsja)*. With the exception of his genuine love for Lipočka, Podzaljuzin is almost always playing a role. His role is to orient himself towards that future position in life which may come to him through good fortune and the kind of clever action exemplified by his master and teacher Bol'šov. Early in the play it suits Podzaljuzin's purpose to follow in the footsteps of Molčalin (young subservient official in Griboedov's play *Gore ot uma*), and he says at one point (Act One) to Bol'šov: "But what should I think, sir! That's just as you please. It's our business to be subordinate." But not forever! Before long he has replaced Bol'šov, who is forced to go to prison when Podzaljuzin will not pay Bol'šov's creditors what they are seeking as a settlement for Bol'šov's bankruptcy, although Podzaljuzin's new wealth has actually come to him from Bol'šov. Podzaljuzin is sorry for Bol'šov (who is now his father-in-law) but has no regrets at all for his own actions, since getting to the top justifies the means. Early in Act Two his real attitude is revealed when he interprets conscience in his own way and then says to himself (thinking about Bol'šov), "And why should I be sorry for him? A chance shows itself, well, just don't goof. He acts his own way, but you just chase after your own place."

In *Don't Sit in Another's Sleigh (Ne v svoi sani ne sadis')* Vixarev, another self-seeker, is a young retired cavalry officer from the city who sees a good chance to marry Dunja, daughter of the rich merchant Rusakov, in a provincial town. This will help him to put his finances into order. Vixarev believes in spending money as well as in getting it by the quickest and easiest means. He is so sure that marriage serves an ulterior purpose that near the end he even accuses Dunja, of all people, of wanting to marry him for his social position. However, of special interest for our discussion is the judgment passed on Vixarev by his local rival, the sincere Borodkin, who tells Dunja in Act Two that he himself speaks from the heart, "but with them it's words they've learned, they say one thing and think another."

Indeed, the world of Ostrovskij's self-seekers (and play-actors) is largely a world of words. As Glumov says at the beginning of *To Every Sage His Share of Folly (Na vsjakogo mudreca dovol'no prostoty)*, "How do people make their way? Not always by deeds, most of all by conversation." In Act One of *A Holiday Dream—Before Dinner (Prazdničnyj son—do obeda)*, Bal'zaminov's mother laments the inability of her nitwit son to speak properly and says, "Anyone else who's not good looking'll fool people with words, but that boy of mine doesn't know any clever words at all. Yes, yes! You have to be sorry for him. If he

was only to know some of them clever words, he could gain a lot in our section. We're out of the way, the people don't know much."

Glumov, the main character in *To Every Sage His Share of Folly,* seeks an easy position and profitable marriage by being all things to almost all men, and at first sight he seems to be an archhypocrite. For Glumov himself, however, hypocrisy does not exist. For him his actions are simply a form of deception, which in turn is a form of strategy. With absolute self-confidence he assumes that any end in his interest automatically justifies any means, and there is no reason why conscience (whatever that might be) should interfere with his life. This explains why Glumov feels no repentance at the end when the others, irritated by the public exposure of their various foibles recorded in Glumov's diary, turn on him. Instead he becomes indignant and accuses them, in effect, of making him a martyr. As K. N. Deržavin notes, Glumov knows that he is necessary for the society which bred him. That is the sharp point of Ostrovskij's satire. Glumov is not really an outsider trying to "crash" society but actually is the quintessence of society. The others quickly realize this, and so Glumov leaves them already forgiven; he will be back.

Ostrovskij outdid himself and developed this type of character even more in *Wolves and Sheep (Volki i ovcy)*. In the characters of Glafira and Berkutov he exposes the predatory nature of two brilliant exploiters who take merciless psychological advantage of two morally good characters, the weakwilled Lynjaev and the naive Kupavina. Glafira disarms Lynjaev (whose main aim in life is to stay an easygoing bachelor) by pretending that she is about to enter a convent, and Berkutov pretends that he is not interested in the well-to-do widow Kupavina, which is ironically true since he is really interested in her estate.

In the seldom-discussed but interesting little play *Hangover from Another's Feast (V čužom piru poxmel'e)* Agrafena Platonova tells Ivan Ivanov that Tit Tityč is a "samodur." Since the word is new to Ivanov, Agrafena defines it for him (in Act One) as a man who: "listens to nobody, he's stubborn, he insists on his own way. He'll stamp his foot and say: who am I? All the servants have got to fall at his feet and just lie there, if not there'll be trouble."

The samodur has much of the play-actor in him, but for him play-acting is not a means for reaching the top but rather a way of expressing the fact that he is at the top. It is his way of life. He believes in his role, for he himself is his role, all that he has to do is to project himself onto society just as he is, whether society wants him or not. This is partly why Dobroljubov could rightly claim that Bol'šov has no cause for repentance, on the grounds that Bol'šov has never been accustomed to thinking much about anything. For example, Bol'šov simply cannot imagine that other people might have feelings. For him people are just so many objects in space, good or bad to the degree in which they do or do not get out of his way. He uses the word "conscience" but only to designate an external phenomenon, and at the end he simply feels himself to be unlucky. He never sees any reason to be dissatisfied with himself, and when (in Act Three) his wife complains bitterly that he shows no fatherly feeling for his daughter, he answers: "So there isn't, so what's the harm in that? Must mean that's how God made me."

"Must mean that's how God made me" typifies the self-righteous self-justification of the samodurs. This is why they can engage in absolute self-revelation, condemning themselves in the audience's eyes but not in their own. This type of naive confession, incidentally, is a common device used by Ostrovskij to reveal individual psychological traits, and one should not be tempted, at least with the samodurs, to attribute it to sincerity (in the usual benevolent sense of that word). The frank revelations of self by the samodurs are apt to be declarations of war: this is what I'm like and can afford to be like, so you'd better not cross me.

Although Ostrovskij's samodur may rarely be a benevolent despot (as, for example, the already-mentioned Rusakov), he is usually monstrous, striking examples being Dikoj and Kabanova in *The Thunderstorm (Groza)*. Dikoj is a samodur on the lower level, which is almost physical. He is a loudmouthed ranting bully who reacts instinctively to any sensed threat to his world of power. All the same, as Dobroljubov pointed out, by this time not all is well in the world of samodurism. Resistance is rising against Dikoj's type of samodurism, either brashly (in the person of Kudrjaš) or respectfully (in the person of Kuligin).

Kabanova is a samodur on a higher plane. She is an articulate (if repetitive) apologist for samodurism. For her the world of samodurism, where all is based on respect for tradition and especially respect for the elders with unquestioned authority, is the one and only orthodoxy. Her mission in her remaining years is to combat the heresy of change, a heresy which, as she realizes with her keen mind (a samodur may be narrow-minded but not necessarily stupid), has already made considerable headway. Although everybody is bored by her sermons in defense of samodurism, they pay strict attention (or pretend to), for Kabanova has the courage of her convictions and carries a big stick. Of course, this queen of samodurism can do no wrong, and it should not really surprise anyone that at the end she feels no responsibility whatever for Katerina's suicide.

A third type of play-actor is the histrionically obsessed. Characters of this type resemble or actually are frustrated actors living in the world at large. They are portrayed by Ostrovskij as either ridiculous or noble.

One of Ostrovskij's most engaging characters of the ridiculous type is Merič in *The Poor Bride (Bednaja nevesta)*. To be sure, if one sympathizes completely with Mar'ja (object of his attentions), then Merič may seem at first to be nothing but an unscrupulous adventurer. However, on his own terms, he is a semicomic, semitragic figure. He has been living in a make-believe world of noble posing for so long that he has become a slave to it. He rates himself as the great lover, and, since a great lover needs someone to love and Mar'ja is at hand, why not love her? What distresses him near the end is not the loss of Mar'ja (actually a relief to him) but the possibility that she might think that he had not really loved her. So he even attends her betrothal ceremonies to tell her that he had loved her. But he suddenly realizes what a flat exit this makes, and he changes it to a magnanimous "I love you"!

In the same play is another ridiculous lover addicted to play-acting, though to a much lesser degree than Merič. This is Milašin, a pathetic character. He loves Mar'ja in his strange way, but, already a victim of insecurity, he is terribly frustrated by her failure to reciprocate. This causes him to act and talk in such ridiculous fashion that he worsens his cause and antagonizes her. Nevertheless, knowing that he is unwanted, he persists in posing as a noble lover and on three separate occasions volunteers to sacrifice his life for her.

An early example of a noble character in this genre is Ljubim Torcov in *Poverty's No Vice (Bednost' ne porok)*. Ljubim had visited the theater frequently, and he was so carried away by his love of plays, especially tragedies, that he found it easy to yield to the temptation of dramatizing. As Albert Kaspin says, Ljubim "acts a role and knows he is acting, but this acting has already become a part of him" [see Further Reading entry dated 1962].

Ljubim may be considered a prototype of Nesčastlivcev, a wandering unemployed tragedian in *The Forest (Les)*. Nesčastlivcev is so obsessed by acting that he continually tries to make the life of everyday reality adapt itself to the noble life he has known in roles he has performed in the Shakespearian and Schilleresque tradition. His dramatic world is an ideal world of honor, and he uses that world as a standard, passing judgment on the corrupt world he finds at his aunt's manor. However, during most of the play he does this rather indirectly, in a tone of ironic banter, and it is probably this which tends to disguise the parallel with Griboedov's Čackij (*Gore ot uma*), who also comes out of nowhere and goes off to nowhere after condemning society, but Čackij's condemnations are bitter and specific. At the end Nesčastlivcev gives away all his money to permit Aksjuša to be married, an act which is motivated in part by the kindness of his heart but also certainly by an instinctive impulse to make a noble gesture and to exit on a high note.

The term "puppet," as used here to apply to the second group of Ostrovskij's characters, has nothing to do with the element of animation but serves rather to emphasize the functional nature of this type of character in his plays. The main trait of the puppets is their passiveness. They may be of importance in the play, but they do not aggressively affect the action in crucial moments. Either because of social position or personal weakness (or both) they tend to merge with their environment, which they do not try to change. They drift with developments, coexist with the lot fate has assigned to them.

Probably all of Ostrovskij's minor characters could be considered puppets in one way or another; however, Ostrovskij makes many of these characters quite interesting, especially those on the lower social scale, such as the servants, the matchmakers, and some of the mothers. These are Ostrovskij's folksy characters. Their language and thoughts are down-to-earth, colorful, uninhibited, often original and humorous. The servants in particular may conduct a running common-sense commentary on the insanity and inhumanity witnessed by them. They are usually sorry for the victims of oppression, and they sometimes express their sympathies and disapproval with surprising boldness. Nevertheless, although such expression may affect the audience, it rarely affects the action of the play.

In Ostrovskij's plays (especially his early plays) the male lover is often a weak-charactered puppet. Xor'kov (*The*

Poor Bride), Mitja (*Poverty's No Vice*), Andrej Tityč (*Hangover from Another's Feast*), Leonid (*The Ward/Vospitannica*), and Boris (*The Thunderstorm*) might be considered sincere lovers in comparison with Ostrovskij's play-actor lovers, but otherwise the description is much too flattering. With the possible exception of Mitja, none of them either cares enough or has enough will power to do more than sympathize with his "beloved" at difficult moments. Leonid, for example, who probably could save Nadja's life, at least, when it is obvious that she is contemplating suicide, pretends to sympathize but is actually only trying to save his self-respect and extricate himself from an uncomfortable situation. Boris outdoes even Leonid, being able to tell Katerina that he hopes she will soon be dead and thus out of her suffering! In direct confrontation with Katerina's complete self-sacrifice for Boris, it is almost impossible not to think of Boris as a coward.

Some of Ostrovskij's victimized characters (including the "sheep") are puppets. Certainly Kupavina and Lynjaev in *Wolves and Sheep* are such puppets. It is true that early in the play Lynjaev rouses himself enough to make an effort in the cause of justice, but he abandons the effort completely and immediately when Berkutov comes and takes over the situation.

In *Without a Dowry (Bespridanica)* Larisa, perhaps Ostrovskij's greatest dramatic character after Katerina Kabanova, is, to a large extent, a puppet. Like Katerina, she is endowed with an artistic nature, but, unlike Katerina, she has had an opportunity to develop her talents. In her rather bohemian circle she is a shining light appreciated for her accomplishments by everybody, even by the mercenary Knurov, who is attracted to Larisa for more than her physical beauty. Despite her relatively high level of enlightenment, her blindly naive obedience to her "ardent heart" (to use the title of one of Ostrovskij's plays) betrays her to victimization by Paratov on two separate occasions. At the end she simply does not have the strength to escape through suicide as she wishes to do, but she resigns herself to the thought of becoming Knurov's mistress. Larisa, not a "heroic" heroine, cannot cope with an overwhelmingly difficult situation where nobody gives her real help or sympathy. As Aleksandra Negina, in a similar situation in *Talents and Admirers (Talanty i poklonniki)* says at the end to the lover she is forsaking in favor of financial security: "But you want me to be a heroine. No, how could I possibly fight? What kind of strength do I have!"

The third group of characters, the rebels in Ostrovskij's play, are those who, as victims or witnesses of unjust situations or persons, protest or rebel. As could be expected, Ostrovskij is very sympathetic with such characters, and he often gives them a humanitarian coloring or even halo which, despite a bordering on sentimentality, is often moving.

Ostrovskij's first successful character in this genre was Mar'ja in *The Poor Bride.* Mar'ja has an "ardent heart." Knowing it to be improper she nevertheless takes the initiative in confessing her love for Merič, who does not really reciprocate it. Eventually Mar'ja begins to see the light and complains that Merič does not treat her like a person. Early in the play she sadly and correctly predicts that she will be bargained for like a piece of merchandise

and that she will be taken in marriage for her beauty. In *Without a Dowry* Larisa will complain even more bitterly that nobody loves her for herself, that to others she is only a thing.

Žadov, principal character in *A Profitable Position (Doxodnoe mesto)*, is basically a rebel. Žadov is a reform-minded idealist with dreams and convictions. Although his convictions have an ethereal quality (at one point he calls them his "consolation"), he suffers for them. While he does bring much of his suffering onto himself through naive impracticality, the play makes it only too clear that the fault is much more society's than his. If, however, Ostrovskij made Žadov something of a tragic hero, he had to avoid the danger of making him a saintly bore. He did this, I believe, by giving Žadov an addiction to play-acting *à la* Don Quixote (Žadov himself says at one point that he must give up fighting windmills). It is the ridiculous element in Žadov which helps to make him acceptable to the audience. Moreover, like Griboedov's Čackij, he loves a woman who hardly seems worthy of him. It is his desire to keep his wife which finally makes him yield to the temptation of asking for a "profitable position" with its supplementary income in the form of bribes.

The most striking of Ostrovskij's rebels is Katerina Kabanova (*The Thunderstorm*). Katerina rebels against those who are trying, consciously or not, to dehumanize her; however, her situation is completely hopeless, and her only escape from the "kingdom of darkness" proves to be suicide. Unlike Larisa in *Without a Dowry,* Katerina has some allies: Varvara, Kudrjaš, Kuligin, and even Tixon.

The foregoing is intended to suggest character categories which recur in Ostrovskij's plays, but it would certainly be unwise to attempt to assign all of his characters arbitrarily into one category, for some of his characters may shift from one category to another. This has already been suggested in the case of Žadov, who is mainly a rebel but at times a play-actor. In *Without a Dowry* Larisa is so movingly an innocent victim of callousness that her lamenting protest before her death cannot but make her seem a rebel to the audience at the end, though, as we have indicated, throughout most of the play she has been a puppet. Even such a subjugated puppet as Tixon in *The Thunderstorm* can rise above himself, if only for a moment, to become a rebel, and his anguished denunciation of his mother at the end constitutes the most rebellious lines of the entire play.

One of the most successful combinations of categories is encountered in the character of Nesčastlivcev in *The Forest.* All through the play he play-acts, but at the same time he is fighting (as is Sčastlivcev also) for a recognition of his proper dignity both as actor and human being. At the very end the categories of play-actor and rebel are united in Nesčastlivcev almost simultaneously. As already mentioned, on a sudden impulse he gives away his money (a large sum, especially for him) and then, in true play-actor style, pretends that it is nothing. But shortly after this, when Gurmyžskaja calls the two actors comedians, this is just too much for Nesčastlivcev to take, and he rebelliously blasts out at her (and the audience):

> Comedians? No, we are artists, noble artists, and you are the comedians. If we love, then we love. If we don't love, then we quarrel or fight. If we help

out, then it's with our last earned coin. But you?
You talk your whole life about the welfare of society, about love for humanity. But what have you
done? Whom have you fed? Whom have you entertained? You entertain only yourselves, you amuse
yourselves. You are the comedians, the clowns, not
we . . . Generations of crocodiles! Your tears are
water! Your hearts are a hard sword! Your kisses
are daggers in the breast! . . . Oh, if I could only
vent my rage on this infernal generation of all
bloodthirsty inhabitants of the forests!

The combination of traits inherent in different character
categories reduces the intensity of the characters as types,
giving them an inconsistency, a psychological duality. If
Ostrovskij may lose something by such a diffusion, he also
gains by making the characters in question more humanly
convincing and interesting. Such characters (which are in
the plays not primarily satirical) may not have the universality of a type (such as Molière's Harpagon in *The Miser*
or even Ostrovskij's own Glumov), but all the same they
are convincing in their thoughts, language, and acts as
they struggle for self-recognition and the best possible outcome in tragic situations. This is not peculiarly Russian
but is indeed a form of universality. Therefore, it is high
time that we go beyond D. S. Mirsky's distorted and basically unfair evaluation of Ostrovskij's plays as provincially
Russian and lacking in universal significance [see excerpt
dated 1927]. Now that Russian literary scholarship in
America has come of age, we must stop neglecting
Ostrovskij and start doing justice to a truly great dramatist. (pp. 317-24)

> *Norman Henley, "Ostrovskij's Play-Actors,
> Puppets, and Rebels," in* Slavic and East
> European Journal, *Vol. XIV, No. 3, 1970, pp.
> 317-25.*

Lawrence Hanson   (essay date 1970)

[*In the following excerpt, Hanson discusses the characteristic features of Ostrovsky's dramas and the difficulties they pose for translators and Western audiences.*]

By the time of Ostrovsky's death he had written some fifty
plays as well as a volume of translations from English,
Spanish, French, Italian and Ukranian, and had given the
theatre of his homeland a large and varied repertory of
comedy and drama dealing with national themes and people of almost every class and condition in the country, a
repertory which, theatrically speaking, put Russia on the
map. To this day, at the Ostrovsky Theatre in Moscow,
more than two thirds of his plays are either in the repertory or frequently revived, and many are played regularly
in the theatres of every Russian city.

In short, Ostrovsky was for all practical purposes the
founder of a national drama—greater men had preceded
him but wrote too little to form what could be called a
Russian theatre—and his position in his particular art is
analogous in almost every respect to that of Tchaikovsky
in music. . . . [As] Tchaikovsky, creating a substantial
body of work, established Russian music as a national art
form, unmistakably of its country, so Ostrovsky performed a similar service for the theatre.

But there the parallel ends. Tchaikovsky was famous and
much of his work well known in Western Europe and the
United States some years before he was seriously considered as a master in his own country. Ostrovsky's fame, almost immediate in his own country, has ended there, and
his plays which are staple fare in Moscow, Leningrad, all
the large Russian cities and the travelling companies, are
virtually unknown outside Russia.

It is not that his existence was unknown; as far back as
1868 (just after he had staged his *Even a Clever Man Can
Trip*) one could read in the July number of the *Edinburgh
Review* an anonymous consideration of the dramatist and
his work to date; a detailed and favourable notice. Yet
from that day to this only one or two of his plays have been
staged in this country and a handful translated into English, half of these in the United States.

What are the reasons for this neglect? There are two according to modern critics: the essential Russianness of
many of his plays and the difficulty of translation of all.
This explanation is no doubt valid to a point, but both the
difficulty and the Russianness have been exaggerated.
There are a few plays—possibly one quarter of the
whole—which deal with people and situations so peculiarly Russian that a foreign audience might have trouble in
understanding and appreciating what they saw and heard.
The other three-quarters (more than thirty plays) are either readily comprehensible or readily adaptable to foreign characters and situations.

We are therefore left with difficulty (the word impossibility has been used) of translation as the chief barrier to
knowledge of Ostrovsky outside Russia. But here again
some reservations must be made. In his early merchant
plays Ostrovsky sometimes uses the dialect of the district,
and this is not merely untranslatable but foreign even to
present-day Russians. Perhaps a word should be said
about this. If one imagines, say, the quartiers of Paris
using expressions differing in meaning from one quartier
to another, one will have an impression of Moscow in its
early centuries. The classic example of this curious custom
is perhaps the sixteenth-century ancestor of the famous
composer; he was nicknamed Rakmanin because, in the
district of Moscow in which he lived, that word meant
'generous to a fault' with an emphasis on the fault. In time
this ancestor, being a younger son, adopted the nickname
in place of his rightful surname—a common procedure in
those days; and thus the name Rakhmaninov came into
being. Had the ancestor lived in another district of Moscow he would have been given a different nickname (since
Rakmanin in any other district had a different meaning)
and the Rakmaninov we remember today would not have
been Rakhmaninov.

By the time Ostrovsky was born, this fantastic verbal
melee had almost died out and a standard Russian was
spoken and written in Moscow and indeed (the Ukraine
excepted) everywhere else with no more than the regional
vagaries of pronunciation and occasionally, spelling. The
last stronghold of the medieval custom was of course the
merchant households of Moscow visited by Ostrovsky;
hence his use of words and phrases fit today only for the
scholar to disentangle.

Apart from this formidable obstacle to translation,
Ostrovsky, like all modern playwrights, uses idiomatic
speech frequently, possibly more often than many, but it
is, after all, one of the obvious duties and pleasures of the

Statue of Ostrovsky.

translator to provide the appropriate idioms in his own language. The chief legitimate difficulty with the middle and later Ostrovsky is his penchant for introducing peasant or provincial characters; the resulting dialect is admittedly a stumbling block. But many of his plays do not contain any such characters and many more contain only one or two, and these not carrying the main burden of the play, such as the maidservant in **Talanty i pokloniki** who could easily be dispensed with.

It must be confessed that the translations so far made into English do not support the case put forward here. The few translations in existence either render dialogue literally (often to the point where it makes no sense in English) or provide a translation so free that it retains little of the original economy and pawky humour. The danger, when trying too zealously to accommodate an author to present-day idiom, of merely making him sound vulgar or cheap, is very real. When Ostrovsky is prosaic he should be rendered prosaically, and almost all his idioms, mostly homely, can find their counterpart in an English idiom which is neither smart nor clever but sound. For sound, above all, is what Ostrovsky is.

What is abundantly clear to anyone reading Ostrovsky in the original is that any difficulty in translation has little to do with its merits, and that, when the one does affect the other, it is due to the greatest of his virtues. For his claim to fame is not that he established the Russian drama, great feat though that was; it is that he is one of

the first and best of the social realists on the stage in any country.

This is observable immediately. Like Gogol's *Revizor*, Ostrovsky's **We'll Settle It Amongst Ourselves** does not contain a single estimable character. But unlike Gogol, Ostrovsky does not avoid this difficulty by treating his characters farcically; he asks the theatregoer to accept the fact that such people exist and that they act as they do because they were born with a certain disposition or because circumstances oblige them, being what they are, to act accordingly. Moreover, and even more unlike Gogol, far from ending the play with retribution a mere step away behind the curtain, Ostrovsky's most unlikeable character ends in complete triumph.

This is hard to accept; Nikolai I, fixing a blind eye on the glaring sins of his own court, the secret police and the rest of the corrupt and oppressive regime, was so horrified by this play that in addition to dismissing Ostrovsky from the civil service and ordering strict supervision by the police, insisted that he be summoned to listen to a prepared lecture (given personally by the Minister of Education in Moscow) on the duty of a dramatist to show virtue triumphant, sin punished.

Ostrovsky listened because he had no option, but that was as far as it went. He no doubt observed the stupidity of a monarch who failed to see that the best kind of morality play is one which presents the facts without comment. He no doubt also realised the lack of trust in his own people displayed by the Tsar's instruction. But all this, for Ostrovsky, was beside the point; he declined to learn Nikolai's lesson because he found it diametrically opposed to his conception of a dramatist's duty. He saw his true way clearly; by chance he had been given intimate knowledge of a certain section of human beings in Moscow; he wished to reproduce them and their milieu, with its special problems, on the stage. And (parting company from every other dramatist then writing) he wished them to speak as he had heard them speak, to act as he had seen them act in relation to one another, given a normal set of circumstances, which he had also seen time after time. He was not prepared to follow other dramatists looking for a plot and invent circumstances demanded by the plot. Nor was he, unlike other dramatists, concerned to preach his version of morals or to allow himself to be swayed by any other extra-stage reason which would impede or distort expression of exact truth to life.

This creed he lived up to for the rest of his life, enlarging the range of his plays as the conditions of his life brought him into contact with different kinds of people, and as the social changes in Russia demanded a realistic drama on the stage.

One obvious, though then unheard of result of his aim, was a dialogue which still has the power to appal both romantic and classicist. Like Mussorgsky, he wanted to reproduce on the stage real people using real life speech. In fact, this was impossible; almost all people speak so slovenly that any attempt to copy them would empty a theatre; so he compressed everyday speech into lines speakable by an actor and acceptable to an audience. The impression remains—and it is one of his greatest strengths—that his characters are speaking naturally and inevitably; never does he allow the slightest room for a hint of the unreal.

(And this, in passing, does give a certain amount of difficulty to the translator; in an Ostrovsky play, one cannot find a single example of the smooth cliche of stage dialogue that the experienced translator could render into English in his sleep; all is vividly down to earth. This realism can be surprisingly hard to reproduce in another language.)

The second major result of Ostrovsky's aim to be realistic has also disconcerted many playgoers until they become used to it; this is his abolition of the leading character. In his plays there are no villains, no heroes, no heroines, there are only people into whose minds an audience can enter with ease or difficulty according to the amount of sympathy felt for them. If a member of an audience is prepared to work as well as watch or listen, he will find that every character of an Ostrovsky play has his point of view and that this point of view is, in the eyes of the character, well based. If the member is lazy, he will ally himself with the more obviously sympathetic character and stop there, but he will lose much, above all that prized ability to see the other side of the question.

This abolition of star parts for actors and actresses and focal points for an audience's fervour led straight to Ostrovsky's other great and rare virtue as playwright. One not only looks in vain in his work for hero, heroine, villain, one also looks vainly for the slipshod pasteboard character created merely to convey information, to raise a laugh, to spin out the action. Every one of his characters is drawn in the round and, with very few exceptions, plays an essential part in dialogue and action. And this special virtue of Ostrovsky, which enables his plays to give such solid satisfaction, has been proved over the years in the best of all possible ways, by the reactions of the stage people. If one studies the history of the Russian theatre, one will find that all the great actors and actresses of the two capitals have played most of the roles in the plays; to them—and they have said it—there is no star part in an Ostrovsky play, all the parts are star parts.

The only observable result of the Tsar's lecture and the years of police supervision was that most of his succeeding plays contained at least one character who could be described by a moralist as estimable. But what the playwright conceded with one hand he countered with the other; he allowed his plays to develop and to end as they would if the characters were left to themselves to deal with a certain situation. Thus there could be no question of virtue triumphant because Ostrovsky could not, as an artist, acknowledge such a quality as due for special treatment. What happens in his plays is what must happen if the playwright puts real characters on the stage grappling with a real problem and then steps aside. In some instances nothing conclusive does happen; the audience is shown a group of people working out some situation; if they are the kind of people who would reach a solution, well and good; if not, the play ends without one.

This is social realism in its true form; Ostrovsky was not merely one of the first realistic dramatists, he was a genuine one; he did not, as so many later imitators have done, humbug an audience into thinking that realism consists in an exploitation of outward and unvaryingly unpleasant facets of everyday life. He is concerned solely with the impact of one human being on another; they may be rich or poor, their surroundings pleasant or unpleasant, he never loses sight of this all-important objective.

Not only Nikolai found this new realism (and in those days it was a startling novelty) difficult to accept. In this country, which has seen so much false social realism on the stage, one of the very few Ostrovsky plays to be produced has been deliberately mistitled. *Even a Clever Man Can Trip* became in England *The Diary of a Scoundrel.* A significant change, indeed, for there is no scoundrel in the play. Glumov, regarded with the eye of a moralist, would be found deficient in some directions, but not more so than the people he took in; quite the contrary, as the end of the play carefully indicates. But clearly it was thought that an English audience would insist on a villain, would wish to know in black and white where they were, morally speaking.

But this is to destroy the whole purpose of a dramatist who continued to the end of his life to defy the romantic conventions of the theatre. Far from manipulating his characters, he does not give them so much as a push. The *deus ex machina* is conspicuously absent from his plays; there are no sudden accidents, no unexpected arrivals, no dramatic illnesses or deaths, nothing untoward or unaccountable occurs, nothing that cannot be seen as the inevitable result of one personality impinging on another in a given situation, the situation being one that can be found readily wherever such people live, whether they be merchants, business men, estate owners, peasants, civil servants, actors, or any other of the many strands of society Ostrovsky dealt with before his death. He is always scrupulously just, so much so that it would not be possible to deduce from his plays what kind of man he was, still less to discover his moral standpoint in any one of them.

A contemporary critic, Skabitchevsky, later well known for his book on the folk-novelists, puts the matter simply:

> One scene follows another, all seeming so commonplace, so everyday, yet out of them a drama is imperceptibly coming into being. You could swear that you are not watching a comedy but that life itself is being unrolled before your eyes, as if the author had simply taken away one wall of a room and showed you what was going on in such and such a house. . . . It is impossible to deduce any general principle from his comedies, neither duty against inclination, a collision of passions with a fatal result, antagonism between good and evil, progress or ignorance. In his plays the most varied human relationships are represented; in them, as in life, men stand in different obligatory relationships towards one another, these relationships having their origins in the past, and, having come together, conflicts inevitably arise between these men because of their relationships. As for the outcome of the conflict, this is as a rule unforeseeable and often depends, as so often in real life, on the merest chance, some incident of no importance in itself.

In all the best plays of Ostrovsky—and that means some two-thirds of his output—one sees this social realism carried to a fine art, a very advanced social realism if one considers the state of the theatre in other European countries in the eighteen-fifties—seventies, and it marks the point at which he parts company with his two great predecessors. Gogol and Griboyedov mask their moral purpose very lightly indeed in scathing comedy and farce; they say one thing but quite obviously mean another. Ostrovsky from first line to last means every word his characters choose to say; he does not hide behind farce because he has nothing to hide; he wishes simply to state a known position in society—a position verifiable by any contemporary and, psychologically, by anyone of any age—and to allow it to develop. And this leaves the spectator with the peculiar satisfaction of knowing that he sees and hears the truth, and of realising that the author has paid him the compliment of assuming that he has sufficient judgment to take from a play what it offers him personally. So we are left with the strange proposition that this dramatist who so rigidly eschews the slightest hint of moral preaching may well have, in the long run, a more beneficial effect on his audiences than the most ardent and skilled pamphleteer.

If, despite this collection of virtues, Ostrovsky does not reach the heights of the few great, this is commonly held to be due to his failure to transcend the prosaic in subject and treatment. And if this be true—and the proposition is arguable—it would instance the common happening of a man's strong points or artistic principles proving a stumbling block. Ostrovsky could be a poet—one has only to think of the poetic symbolism of Katerina in **Storm,** of Neschastlivtsev in **The Forest,** of the whole of **Snegurochka**—but the nature of the bulk of his work and aim was opposed to the development of poetry; he wished to show his audience everyday people as they are, and such people are not poets. They may indeed have much that is poetical in their nature if it were ever allowed expression by life as they have to live it, just as they may often have ideas of grandeur (which is also found in plays regarded as great works of art) but usually poetry, like noble thoughts, gives way to the pressure of everyday existence. Ostrovsky knew this, and rather than be false to life, allowed the design of his plays to remain open to the charge of pedestrianism and his dialogue to sound, at first hearing, ordinary. This latter is, of course, a high compliment; the deliberate aim of the dramatist is that the audience shall recognise and so accept the characters put before them, by their realistic speech and action (nothing being more difficult to achieve) and both rule out splendour of conception and treatment obviously poetic.

Finally, Ostrovsky's disregard of the heroic is often seen as fatal to his stature as a great dramatist. The purpose of the theatre was classically intended to hold a mirror to life; this Ostrovsky does *par excellence,* and when the result is grim or depressing, not he but life is to blame. But if life as it is lived rarely touches great heights, it contains plenty of humour, pathos, even inspiration, and for the revelation of these, Ostrovsky, as compassionate as he is clear-sighted, and with a delightfully ironic humour, is one of the best of guides. Certainly, many people wish to look up to a hero, to love a heroine, to detest a villain, and Ostrovsky usually disappoints them. On the other hand, there are many who in the long run prefer truth to the artificial elevation of feelings, and who believe that truth is its own reward. To these, Ostrovsky is great. (pp. xxi-xxix)

> *Lawrence Hanson, in an introduction to* Artistes and Admirers: A Comedy in Four Acts *by Alexander Nikolayevich Ostrovsky, translated by Elisabeth Hanson, Manchester University Press, 1970, pp. vii-xxxvii.*

FURTHER READING

Dobrolyubov, N. A. "Realm of Darkness" and "A Ray of Light in the Realm of Darkness." In his *Selected Philosophical Essays,* translated by J. Fineberg, pp. 218-373, pp. 548-635. Moscow: Foreign Languages Publishing House, 1956.

Two important early essays on Ostrovsky's works. The first is a survey of Ostrovsky's plays up to 1859 in which Dobrolyubov views the playwright's dramatic world as a "realm of darkness," an oppressive environment in which "many of the people become stupefied; they lose the power to think, they lose the will and even the power to feel—all that constitutes intellectual life. . . ." The second essay is a widely discussed analysis of *Groza (The Storm),* focusing primarily on the character of Katerina.

Hoover, Marjorie. *Alexander Ostrovsky.* Boston: Twayne Publishers, 1981, 155 p.

A biographical and critical study of Ostrovsky, including in-depth discussion of his major works.

Kaspin, Albert. "A Re-Examination of Ostrovsky's Character Lyubim Tortsov." In *Studies in Russian and Polish Literature: In Honor of Waclaw Lednicki,* edited by Zbigniew Folejewski, Michael Karpovich, Francis J. Whitfield, and Albert Kaspin, pp. 185-91. The Hague: Mouton, 1962.

Discusses the hero of *Bednost ne porok (Poverty Is No Crime),* noting popular and critical reactions to early performances of the play.

———. "Character and Conflict in Ostrovskij's *Talents and Admirers.*" *Slavic and East European Journal* VIII, No. 1 (Spring 1964): 26-36.

Examines Ostrovsky's dramatic technique in *Talanty i poklonniki,* focusing on those elements that maintain audience interest. Kaspin notes: "In almost every one of his plays, it is out of the multiplicity of cross purposes, out of the conflicting aims and desires of the characters themselves that there arise the tensions that increasingly capture the interest of the spectator."

Lavrin, Janko. "Ostrovsky." In his *A Panorama of Russian Literature,* pp. 147-53. New York: Barnes & Noble, 1973.

Discusses the relationship between Ostrovsky's life and works.

Patrick, George Z. "A. N. Ostrovski: Slavophile or Westerner." In *Slavic Studies,* edited by Alexander Kaun and Ernest J. Simmons, pp. 117-31. Ithaca, N.Y.: Cornell University Press, 1943.

Argues that Ostrovsky was a follower of neither the Slavophiles nor the Westerners, the two major Russian intellectual movements of his time.

Spector, Ivar. "Alexander Nikolayevitch Ostrovsky." In his *The Golden Age of Russian Literature,* pp. 226-42. Caldwell, Idaho: Caxton Printers, 1952.

Includes biographical information, plot summaries, translations of scenes from major works, and a discussion of the role of the merchant class in Ostrovsky's plays.

Wettlin, Margaret. "Alexander Ostrovsky and the Russian Theatre Before Stanislavsky." In *Plays by Alexander*

Ostrovsky, translated by Margaret Wettlin, pp. 7-79. Moscow: Progress Publishers, 1974.

A biographical essay that includes discussion of early productions of Ostrovsky's works and his relationships with important figures in Russian theater.

Zohrab, Irene. "Problems of Translation: The Plays of A. N. Ostrovsky in English." *Melbourne Slavonic Studies* 16 (1982): 43-88.

Analyzes various translations of *Groza* (*The Storm*) and *Les* (*The Forest*), focusing on "the difference between translations which aim to produce dramatic texts for reading purposes, and those which seek to generate theatrical texts for performance."

Friedrich Schelling

1775-1854

(Full name Friedrich Wilhelm Joseph von Schelling) German philosopher.

Schelling was a major figure of the German Idealist and Romantic movements whose philosophical writings encompassed a wide variety of disciplines, including art, religion, and science. While Schelling's ideas have often been considered evasive and his numerous works difficult to reconcile as a unified ideological scheme, he is esteemed as a thinker whose insights were poetic rather than strictly philosophical. Among the important figures who acknowledged a debt to Schelling are the English Romantic poet Samuel Taylor Coleridge, who called Schelling a "great and original genius," and the German Existentialist philosopher Martin Heidegger, who based his *Being and Time* (1927) upon Schelling's question: "Why is there anything at all?"

The son of a Lutheran minister, Schelling was born in Leonberg, a town near Stuttgart. His father taught him Latin, Greek, and Hebrew, and at sixteen he entered the theological seminary at Tübingen. There he lived with Georg Hegel—with whom he would have an ongoing intellectual rivalry—and the poet Friedrich Hölderlin. The three students shared an enthusiasm for the philosophical writings of Baruch Spinoza, Immanuel Kant, and Johann Gottlieb Fichte, and for the political spirit of the French Revolution. Schelling's first published work, *Über die Möglichkeit einer Form der Philosophie überhaupt,* was largely written from the perspective of Fichtean Idealism, which subordinates the natural world as an objective reality to the subjective awareness of the individual ego. In 1798 Schelling joined Fichte as a professor at the University of Jena.

In 1800 Schelling wrote his first important work, *System des transcendentalen Idealismus* (*System of Transcendental Idealism*), which reveals the influence of such Romantic writers as Johann Wolfgang von Goethe and Friedrich von Schiller in its appreciation of such qualities as individualism, antirationalism, and aestheticism. Through his friendship with the philosopher Friedrich Schlegel, Schelling met Caroline Schlegel, the philosopher's wife, and became engaged to her daughter from a previous marriage, Auguste Böhmer. Böhmer died in 1800, and Caroline Schlegel divorced her husband and married Schelling in 1803. After teaching for three years at the University of Würzburg, Schelling accepted a position on the board of the Academy of Sciences in Munich. He produced what many critics consider his most significant work, *Philosophische Untersuchungen über das Wesen der menschlichen Freiheit und die damit zusammenhängende Gegenstände* (*Of Human Freedom*), in 1809. That same year his wife died, and afterward Schelling stopped publishing altogether, though he continued to lecture and write, and he married again in 1812. He continued to serve in various positions in the Academy of Sciences and in the Academy of Arts until 1827, when he became a professor at the Uni-

versity of Munich, and in 1841 he accepted a professorship at the University of Berlin. Schelling died in 1854.

In his earliest work, Schelling had yet to distinguish himself as an original thinker, mainly echoing Fichte's Idealist conception of reality as something primarily dependent on the ego rather than on the natural world of objects existing outside the individual mind. However, critics deem *Philosophische Briefe über Dogmatismus und Kriticismus,* which compares Spinoza and Fichte, and other writings of this period original in their energetic tone and absence of philosophical jargon—aspects of Schelling's style that allied him with the Romantic movement. In 1797 Schelling published a widely read scientific treatise, *Ideen zu einer Philosophie der Natur* (*Ideas for a Philosophy of Nature*), which describes the importance of the natural world in the structure of reality as being equal to that of the ego. During this time, Schelling also published his philosophy of aesthetics in *System of Transcendental Idealism,* and Coleridge adopted and popularized the work's conception of poetry as the reconciliation of contradictory forces. This work, along with the essays in *Vorlesungen über die Methode des academischen Studium* (*On University Studies*) and *Of Human Freedom,* collected in 1803 and 1809 respectively, advance his philosophy of "absolute identity." As Douglas W. Stott has explained: "It is the identity of spirit and nature, subject and object, ideal and real, universal and particular, conscious and unconscious, and particularly the identity of freedom and necessity. . . . This principle of identity or the absolute point of identity of philosophy is also the absolute in and for itself, *one* absolute reality, *one* essence. This *one* absolute, the *one* absolute idea of the identity of the real and the ideal, stands behind Schelling's philosophy during this period." Beginning in 1809 and continuing until the end of his career, Schelling formulated what he termed a "positive" philosophy, defining it as a philosophy based on knowledge of the world unmediated by a system of abstract concepts, in contrast with the rational or "negative" philosophy of Hegel and others. A "positive" philosophy, as Schelling stated, "enters into experience itself and, as it were, grows into cohesion with it." In such works as *Philosophie der Mythologie* and *Philosophie der Offenbarung,* Schelling sought to construct a principle of the divine through an examination of the history of myth and religion, tracing the manner in which concepts of divinity are perceived and transmitted in various cultures and historical periods. Some critics have viewed these writings as precursors of Existentialism because of their questioning of the essence of human consciousness as well as the sense of anxiety that seems to pervade them.

Hegel has been quoted as saying, "Schelling carried on his philosophic education before the public and signaled each fresh stage of his advance with a new treatise," and critics concur that Schelling's career was varied and changeable, as compared with most philosophers of the period who devoted their energies to developing and refining a single system. While some deny that any continuity exists in Schelling's thought, others have found, in the words of James Lindsay, that "the development of Schelling's thought was steadily from an abstract, aesthetic world-view to a living and ethical one."

(See also *Dictionary of Literary Biography,* Vol. 90.)

PRINCIPAL WORKS

Über die Möglichkeit einer Form der Philosophie überhaupt (treatise) 1794
Philosophische Briefe über Dogmatismus und Kriticismus (treatise) 1795
Ideen zu einer Philosophie der Natur (treatise) 1797
  [*Introduction to the Philosophy of Nature,* 1871; also published as *Ideas for a Philosophy of Nature,* 1988]
Von der Weltseele (treatise) 1798
System des transcendentalen Idealismus (treatise) 1800
  [*Introduction to Idealism,* 1871; also published as *System of Transcendental Idealism,* 1978]
Darstellung meines Systems der Philosophie (treatise) 1801
Bruno oder über das göttliche und natürliche Prinzip der Dinge (philosophical dialogue) 1802
  [*Bruno; or, On the Divine and the Natural Principle of Things,* 1984]
Vorlesungen über die Methode des academischen Studium (treatise) 1803
  [*On University Studies,* 1966]
Philosophie und Religion (treatise) 1804

Aphorismen zur Enleitung in die Naturphilosophie (aphorisms) 1806
Das Verhältnis der bildenden Künste zur Natur (treatise) 1807
  [*The Philosophy of Art: An Oration on the Relation between the Plastic Arts and Nature,* 1913-15]
Philosophie der Kunst (treatise) 1809
  [*The Philosophy of Art,* 1980]
Philosophische Untersuchungen über das Wesen der menschlichen Freiheit und die damit zusammenhängende Gegenstände (treatise) 1809
  [*Of Human Freedom,* 1936]
Die Weltalter, Erstes Buch (treatise) 1813
  [*The Ages of the World,* 1942]
*Philosophie der Mythologie (treatise) 1858
*Philosophie der Offenbarung (treatise) 1858
Schellings Werke: Nach der Originalausgabe in neuer Anordnung herausgegeben. 12 vols. (treatises, essays, aphorisms, and philosophical dialogues) 1927-59
The Unconditional in Human Knowledge: Four Early Essays (1794-96) (essays) 1980

*These works were first published in the fourteen-volume *Sämtliche Werke,* 1856-61.

Samuel Taylor Coleridge   (essay date 1817)

[*Coleridge was the intellectual center of the English Romantic movement, and is one of the greatest literary critics in the English language. He was also the first prominent spokesman of German Idealist metaphysics in England and the forerunner of modern psychological criticism, specifically in his conception of the organic nature of literary form—a theory which contends that a work of literature derives and is determined by inspiration rather than by external rules. Though most critics and scholars agree on Coleridge's importance in world literature, they also realize much of his aesthetic philosophy and literary criticism was borrowed, and at times directly translated, from such German thinkers as Schelling, A. W. Schlegel, Immanuel Kant, and Wolfgang von Goethe. According to René Wellek, Coleridge's complete dialectical scheme—his reconciliation of opposites—was derived primarily from German sources. In the following excerpt from his* Biographia Literaria, *Coleridge acknowledges similarities between Schelling's philosophy and his own.*]

In Schelling's **Natur-Philosophie,** and the **System des transcendentalen Idealismus,** I first found a genial coincidence with much that I had toiled out for myself, and a powerful assistance in what I had yet to do. (p. 160)

It would be but a mere act of justice to myself, were I to warn my future readers, that an identity of thought, or even similarity of phrase will not be at all times a certain proof that the passage has been borrowed from Schelling, or that the conceptions were originally learnt from him. In this instance, as in the dramatic lectures of Schlegel to which I have before alluded, from the same motive of self-defence against the charge of plagiarism, many of the most striking resemblances, indeed all the main and fundamental ideas, were born and matured in my mind before I had ever seen a single page of the German Philosopher; and I might indeed affirm with truth, before the more important works of Schelling had been written, or at least made public. Nor is this coincidence at all to be wondered at. We had studied in the same school; been disciplined by the same preparatory philosophy, namely, the writings of Kant; we had both equal obligations to the polar logic and dynamic philosophy of Giordano Bruno; and Schelling has lately, and, as of recent acquisition, avowed that same affectionate reverence for the labors of Behmen, and other mystics, which I had formed at a much earlier period. The coincidence of Schelling's system with certain general ideas of Behmen, he declares to have been *mere* coincidence; while *my* obligations have been more direct. *He* needs give to Behmen only feelings of sympathy; while I owe him a debt of gratitude. God forbid! that I should be suspected of a wish to enter into a rivalry with Schelling for the honors so unequivocally his right, not only as a great and original genius, but as the *founder* of the Philosophy of Nature, and as the most successful *improver* of the Dynamic System which, begun by Bruno, was reintroduced (in a more philosophical form, and freed from all its impurities and visionary accompaniments) by Kant; in whom it was the native and necessary growth of his own system. Kant's followers, however, on whom (for the greater part) their master's *cloak* had fallen without, or with a very scanty portion of, his *spirit,* had adopted his dynamic ideas, only as a more refined species of mechanics. With exception of one or two fundamental ideas, which cannot be with-held from Fichte, to Schelling we owe the completion, and the most important victories, of this revolution in philosophy. To me it will be happiness and honor enough, should I succeed in rendering the system itself intelligible to my countrymen, and in the application of it to the most awful of subjects for the most important of purposes. Whether a work is the offspring of a man's own spirit, and the product of original thinking, will be discovered by those who are its sole legitimate judges, by better tests than the mere reference to dates. For readers in general, let whatever shall be found in this or any future work of mine, that resembles, or coincides with, the doctrines of my German predecessor, though contemporary, be wholly attributed to *him:* provided, that the absence of distinct references to his books, which I could not at all times make with truth as designating citations or thoughts actually *derived* from him; and which, I trust, would, after this general acknowledgment be superfluous; be not charged on me as an ungenerous concealment or intentional plagiarism. I have not indeed (eheu! res angusta domi!) ["Alas! the narrow circumstances at home!"] been hitherto able to procure more than two of his books, viz. the 1st volume of his collected Tracts, and his **System of Transcendental Idealism;** to which, however, I must add a small pamphlet against Fichte, the spirit of which was to *my* feelings painfully incongruous with the principles, and which (with the usual allowance afforded to an antithesis) displayed the love of wisdom rather than the wisdom of love. I regard truth as a divine ventriloquist: I care not from whose mouth the sounds are supposed to proceed, if only the words are audible and intelligible. (pp. 161-64)

Samuel Taylor Coleridge, "Chapter 9," in his
The Collected Works of Samuel Taylor Cole-

ridge: Biographia Literaria; or, Biographical Sketches of My Literary Life and Opinions, *edited by James Engell and W. Jackson Bate, Bollingen Series LXXV, Princeton University Press, 1983, pp. 140-67.*

George Henry Lewes   (essay date 1888)

[*Primarily known for his association with the novelist George Eliot, Lewes was a versatile and prolific man of letters. He wrote philosophical works, scientific studies, literature and drama criticism, biographies, novels, and plays, and served as editor of two prestigious Victorian periodicals, the* Leader *and the* Fortnightly Review. *As an early advocate of positivism, Lewes believed that the scientific principles of observation and verification could be applied to all fields of intellectual inquiry. Guided by this doctrine, which he expounded in his widely read* Biographical History of Philosophy, *Lewes made original and significant contributions to psychology, biology, and philosophy while helping to popularize new discoveries in these fields. In the following essay from that work, Lewes discusses Schelling's views on nature and science.*]

Schelling is often styled the German Plato. In such parallels there is always some truth amidst much error. Schelling's works unquestionably exhibit great power of vivid imagination conjoined with subtle dialectics; if on this ground he is to be styled a Plato, then are there hundreds to share that title with him. His doctrines have little resemblance to those of his supposed prototype. Curiously enough, his head was marvellously like that of Socrates; not so ugly, but still very like it in general character.

Schelling may be regarded as having been the systematizer of a tendency, always manifesting itself, but then in full vigor in Germany—the tendency towards Pantheism. This tendency is not merely the offspring of Mysticism. It may be recognized in the clear Goethe, no less than in the mystical Novalis. In some way or other, Pantheism seems the natural issue of almost every Philosophy of Religion, when rigorously carried out; but Germany, above all European countries, has, both in poetry and speculation, the most constantly reproduced it. Her poets, her artists, her musicians, and her thinkers, have been more or less Pantheists. Schelling's attempt, therefore, to give Pantheism a scientific basis, could not but meet with hearty approbation.

We may here once more notice the similarity, in historical position, of the modern German speculations to those of the Alexandrian Schools. In both, the incapacity of Reason to solve the problems of Philosophy is openly proclaimed; in both, some higher faculty is called in to solve them. Plotinus called this faculty *Ecstasy.* Schelling called it the *Intellectual Intuition.* The Ecstasy was not supposed to be a faculty possessed by all men, and at all times; it was only possessed by the few, and by them but sometimes. The Intellectual Intuition was not supposed to be a faculty common to all men; on the contrary, it was held as the endowment only of a few of the privileged: it was the faculty for philosophizing. Schelling expresses his disdain for those who talk about not comprehending the highest truths of Philosophy. "Really," he exclaims, "one sees not wherefore Philosophy should pay any attention whatever to Incapacity. It is better rather that we should isolate Philosophy from all the ordinary routes, and keep it so separated from ordinary knowledge, that none of these routes should lead to it. Philosophy commences where ordinary knowledge terminates." The highest truths of science cannot be proved, they must be apprehended; for those who cannot apprehend them there is nothing but pity; argument is useless.

After this, were we to call Schelling the German Plotinus, we should perhaps be nearer the truth than in calling him the German Plato. But it was for the sake of no such idle parallel that we compared the fundamental positions of each. Our object was to "point a moral," and to show how the same forms of error reappear in history, and how the labors of so many centuries have not advanced the human mind in this direction one single step.

The first point to be established is the nature of Schelling's improvement upon Fichte: the relation in which the two doctrines stand to each other.

Fichte's Idealism was purely subjective Idealism. The Object had indeed reality, but was solely dependent upon the Subject. Endeavor as we might, we could never separate the Object from the Subject, we could never conceive a possible mode of existence without being forced to identify with it a Subject. Indeed the very conception itself is but an act of the Subject. Admitting that we are forced by the laws of our mental constitution to postulate an unknown something, a Noumenon, as the substance in which all phenomena inhere, what, after all, is this postulate? It is an act of the Mind; it is wholly subjective; the necessity for the postulate is a mental necessity. The Non-Ego therefore is the product of the Ego.

There is subtle reasoning in the above; nay more, it contains a principle which is irrefutable: the principle of the identity of Object and Subject in knowledge. This Schelling adopted. Nevertheless, in spite of such an admission, the nullity of the external world was too violent and repulsive a conclusion to be long maintained; and it was necessary to see if the principle of identity might not be preserved, without forcing such a conclusion.

The existence of the objective world is as firmly believed in as the existence of the subjective: they are, indeed, both given in the same act. We cannot be conscious of our own existence without at the same time inseparably connecting it with some other existence from which we distinguished ourselves. So in like manner we cannot be aware of the existence of any thing out of ourselves without at the same time inseparably connecting with it a consciousness of ourselves. Hence we conclude that both exist; not indeed separately, not independently of each other, but *identified* in some higher power. Fichte said that the Non-Ego was created by the Ego. Schelling said that the two were equally real, and that both were identified in the Absolute.

Knowledge must be knowledge of something. Hence Knowledge implies the correlate of Being. Knowledge without an Object known, is but an empty form. But Knowledge and Being are correlates; they are not separable; they are identified. It is as impossible to conceive an Object known without a Subject knowing, as it is to conceive a Subject knowing without an Object known.

Nature is Spirit visible; Spirit is invisible Nature [Lewes remarks in a footnote: "Our readers will recognize here a favorite saying of Coleridge, many of whose remarks, now become famous, are almost *verbatim* from Schelling and the two Schlegels."]: the absolute Ideal is at the same time the absolute Real.

Hence Philosophy has two primary problems to solve. In the **Transcendental Philosophy** the problem is to construct Nature from Intelligence—the Object from the Subject. In the **Philosophy of Nature** the problem is to construct Intelligence from Nature—the Subject from the Object. And how are we to construct one from the other? Fichte has taught us to do so by the principle of the identity of Subject and Object, whereby the productivity and the product are in constant opposition, yet always one. The productivity (*Tätigkeit*) is the activity in act; it is the force which develops itself into all things. The product is the activity arrested and solidified into a fact; but it is always ready to pass again into activity. And thus the world is but a balancing of contending powers within the sphere of the Absolute.

In what, then, does Schelling differ from Fichte, since both assert that the product (Object) is but the arrested activity of the Ego? In this: the Ego in Fichte's system is a finite Ego—it is the human soul. The Ego in Schelling's system is the Absolute—the Infinite—the All, which Spinoza called Substance; and this Absolute manifests itself in two forms: in the form of the Ego and in the form of the Non-Ego—as Nature and as Mind.

The Ego produces the Non-Ego, but not by its own force, not out of its own nature; it is the universal Nature which works within us and which produces from out of us; it is universal Nature which here in us is conscious of itself. The souls of men are but the innumerable individual eyes with which the Infinite World-Spirit beholds himself.

What is the Ego? It is one and the same with the act which renders it an Object to itself. When I say "myself"—when I form a conception of my Ego, what is that but the Ego making itself an Object? Consciousness therefore may be defined the objectivity of the Ego. Very well; now apply this to the Absolute. He, too, must be conscious of himself, and for that he must realize himself objectively. We can now understand Schelling when he says,

> The blind and unconscious products of Nature are nothing but unsuccessful attempts of Nature to make itself an Object (*sich selbst zu reflectiren*); the so-called dead Nature is but an unripe Intelligence. The acme of its efforts—that is, for Nature completely to objectize itself—is attained through the highest and ultimate degree of reflection in Man— or what we call *Reason*. Here Nature returns into itself, and reveals its identity with that which in us is known as the Object and Subject.

The function of Reason is elsewhere more distinctly described as the total *indifference-point* of the subjective and objective. The Absolute he represents by the symbol of the magnet. Thus, as it is the same principle which divides itself in the magnet into the north and south poles, the centre of which is the indifference-point, so in like manner does the Absolute divide itself into the Real and Ideal, and holds itself in this separation as absolute indifference. And as in the magnet every point is itself a magnet, having a North pole, a South pole, and a point of indifference, so also in the Universe, the individual varieties are but varieties of the eternal One. Man is a microcosm.

Reason is the indifference-point. Whoso rises to it, rises to the *reality* of things (*zum wahren Ansich*), which reality is precisely in the indifference of Object and Subject. The basis of Philosophy is therefore the basis of Reason; its knowledge is a knowledge of things as they *are, i.e.* as they are in Reason.

The spirit of Plotinus revives in these expressions. We have in them the whole key-stone of the Alexandrian School. The Intellectual Intuition by which we are to embrace the Absolute, is, as before remarked, but another form of the Alexandrian Ecstasy. Schelling was well aware that the Absolute, the Infinite as such, could not be known under the conditions of finity, cannot be known in personal consciousness. How, then, can it be known? By some higher faculty which discerns the identity of Object and Subject—which perceives the Absolute as Absolute, where all difference is lost in indifference.

There are three divisions in Schelling's system: the philosophy of Nature, the transcendental philosophy, and the philosophy of the Absolute.

His speculations with respect to Nature have met with considerable applause in Germany. Ingenious they certainly are, but vitiated in Method; incapable of verification. Those who are curious to see what he makes of Nature are referred to his *Zeitschrift für speculative Physik*, and his **Ideen zu einer Philosophie der Natur.** The following examples will serve to indicate the character of his speculations. [Lewes adds in a footnote: "The reader must not complain if he do not understand what follows: intelligibility is not the characteristic of German speculation; and we are here only translating Schelling's words, without undertaking to enlighten their darkness."]

Subject and Object being identical, the absolute Identity is the absolute totality named Universe. There can be no difference except a *quantitative* difference; and this is only conceivable with respect to individual existences. For the absolute Identity is *quantitative indifference* both of Object and Subject, and is only under this form. If we could behold all that is, and behold it in its totality, we should see a perfect quantitative equality. It is only in the scission of the Individual from the Infinite that quantitative difference takes place. This difference of Object and Subject is the ground of all finity; and, on the other hand, quantitative indifference of the two is Infinity.

That which determines any difference is a Power (*Potenz*), and the Absolute is the Identity of all Powers (*aller Potenzen*). All matter is originally liquid; *weight* is the power through which the Attractive and Expansive force, as the immanent ground of the reality of Matter, operates. Weight is the first *Potenz*. The second *Potenz* is Light—an inward intuition of Nature, as weight is the outward intuition. Identity with Light is Transparency. Heat does not pertain to the nature of Light, but is simply a *modus existendi* of Light. Newton's speculations upon Light are treated with disdain, as a system built upon illogical conclusions, a system self-contradictory, and leading to infinite absurdities. Nevertheless this absurd system has led men to many discoveries: it is the basis of a gradually advancing science; while the views of Schelling lead to nothing except disputation. So with his explanation of Electricity: let us suppose it exact, and we must still acknowledge

it to be useless. It admits of no verification; admits of no application. It is utterly sterile.

There are, indeed, general ideas in his *Natur-philosophie*, which not only approach the conceptions of positive science, but have given a powerful stimulus to many scientific intellects. The general law of polarity, for example, which he makes the law of universal nature, is seen illustrated in physics and chemistry; although the presumed relation between heat and oxygen, which he makes the basis of all atomic changes, no chemist will nowadays accept. When, in the second part of this treatise, he theorizes on organic life, the result is similar—namely, some general ideas which seem luminous are enforced by particular ideas certainly false. He maintains that vegetation and life are the products of chemical action: the first consisting in a continual deoxidation, the second in a continual oxidation; as soon as this chemical action ceases, death supervenes, for living beings exist only in the moment of *becoming*. He only expresses the universally accepted idea of life when he makes it depend on the necessant disturbance and re-establishment of an equilibrium, or, as De Blainville defines it, "a continual movement of decomposition and recomposition."

All the functions of Life are but the individualizations of one common principle; and all the series of living beings are but the individualizations of one common Life: this is the *Weltseele,* or *anima mundi.* The same idea had been expressed by Goethe, and has since been presented, under various forms, by Oken and many German naturalists. The idea of a dynamic progression in Nature, is also the fundamental idea in Hegel's philosophy.

Schelling, in his **Jahrbücher der Medicin,** says that Science is only valuable in as far as it is *speculative;* and by speculation he means the contemplation of God as He exists. Reason, inasmuch as it affirms God, cannot affirm any thing else, and annihilates itself at the same time as an *individual* existence, as any thing *out of* God. Thought (*das Denken*) is not my Thought; and Being is not my Being; for every thing belongs to God or the All. There is no such thing as a Reason which *we have;* but only a Reason that *has us.* If nothing exists out of God, then must the knowledge of God be only the infinite knowledge which God has of himself in the eternal Self-affirmation. God is not the highest, but the only One. He is not to be viewed as the summit or the end, but as the centre, as the All in All. Consequently there is no such thing as a being lifted up to the knowledge of God; but the knowledge is *immediate* recognition.

If we divest Schelling's speculations of their dialectical forms, we shall arrive at the following results:

Idealism is one-sided. Beside the Subject there must exist an Object: the two are identical in a third, which is the Absolute. This Absolute is neither Ideal nor Real—neither Mind nor Nature—but both. This Absolute is God. He is the All in All; the eternal source of all existence. He realizes himself under one form, as an objectivity; and under a second form as a subjectivity. He becomes conscious of himself in man: and this man, under the highest form of his existence, manifests Reason, and by this Reason God knows himself. Such are the conclusions to which Schelling's philosophy leads us. And now, we ask, in what does this philosophy differ from Spinozism?

The Absolute, which Schelling assumes as the indifference-point of Subject and Object, is but the πρῶτον αγαθον [first good] and primal Nothing, which forms the first Hypostasis of the Alexandrian Trinity. The Absolute, as the Identity of Subject and Object, being neither and yet both, is but the Substance of Spinoza, whose attributes are Extension and Thought.

With Spinoza also he agreed in giving only a phenomenal reality to the Object and Subject. With Spinoza he agreed in admitting but one existence—the Absolute.

But, although agreeing with Spinoza in his fundamental positions, he differed with him in Method, and in the applications of those positions. In both differences the superiority, as it seems to me, is incontestably due to Spinoza.

Spinoza deduced his system very logically from one fundamental assumption, viz. that whatever was true of ideas was true of objects. This assumption itself was not altogether arbitrary. It was grounded upon the principle of certitude, which Descartes had brought forward as the only principle which was irrefragable. Whatever was found to be distinct and à priori in Consciousness, was irresistibly true. Philosophy was therefore deductive; and Spinoza deduced his system from the principles laid down by Descartes.

Schelling's Method was very different. Aware that human knowledge was necessarily finite, he could not accept Spinoza's Method, because that would have given him only a knowledge of the finite, the conditioned; and such knowledge, it was admitted, led to skepticism. He was forced to assume another faculty of knowing the truth, and this was the Intellectual Intuition. Reason which could know the Absolute, was only possible by transcending Consciousness and sinking into the Absolute. As Knowledge and Being were Identical, to know the Infinite, we must *be* the Infinite, *i.e.* must lose our individuality in the universal.

Consciousness, then, which had for so long formed the basis of all Philosophy, was thrown over by Schelling, as incompetent to solve any of its problems. Consciousness was no ground of certitude. Reason was the organ of Philosophy, and Reason was *impersonal*. The Identity of Being and Knowing took the place of Consciousness, and became the basis of all speculation. (pp. 706-15)

> George Henry Lewes, "Chapter II: Schelling," in his The Biographical History of Philosophy: From Its Origin in Greece Down to the Present Day, *D. Appleton and Company, 1888, pp. 705-15.*

Arthur S. Dewing   (essay date 1910)

[*Dewing was an American philosopher and economist. In the following excerpt, he discusses Schelling's theory of knowledge.*]

Schelling saw clearly the necessity of a Theory of Knowledge as the basis of his philosophical labors. Here, in the problem of how our human consciousness can know the abstract universal of the idealist and the empirical fact of the scientist, Schelling shows himself as a philosophical critic of extended influence and marked significance. (p. 154)

Consistently with the spirit of his own idealism he is interested in the subjective universals which played such an important part in the philosophical speculations of Fichte and his contemporaries. At one time this concept is represented by the Absolute Ego, at another time by the Unconditioned, and again by the Absolute Reason, or simply the Absolute. In whatever form the conception appears, it assumes the role of an all-inclusive universal, conceived presumably by extending the concept of the subjective or consciousness so as to embrace the universe. Schelling wished to strengthen the belief of his readers in the Absolute by weaving the concept into his Theory of Knowledge. Hence the problem: How can our finite processes of knowing realize the existence and the nature of the Absolute? This question becomes one of vital moment to his whole system of idealism.

The relation between the finite consciousness and the absolute consciousness gave Schelling at times considerable difficulty. At one point he almost relinquishes the inquiry altogether, suggesting that it is a matter quite beyond the range of our intelligence; yet almost in the next breath he takes refuge in a kind of Platonic remembrance, suggesting that in a measure we can reproduce in our own consciousness, by a process of "free imitation," some of the essential characteristics of the Absolute consciousness. Beyond this somewhat vague reference Schelling's entire Theory of Knowledge crystallizes about certain types of cognitive process which vary according to the character of the object that each type is especially designed to grasp. It is the problem of the relation of the knower to the known, solved by varying the description of the process of knowing according to the character of the thing known.

If we consider Schelling's work as a whole, it is possible to discover perhaps three of these different forms of the cognitive process. There is one form which Schelling alludes to as Transcendental Knowledge. This process of cognition is of a peculiarly abstract character, so abstract indeed that its object is its own activity. It is described most fully in Schelling's idealistic writing, more particularly in the **System des transcendentalen Idealismus.** A second form of cognition, to which Schelling constantly appeals, is that of the perception of concrete individual objects, things or ideas. This is quite opposite in its description to the previous type. Transcendental Knowledge is so abstract that it can know only itself as its object of knowledge; the intuition of particulars, on the contrary, is directed toward the individual objects of a consciously conceived world. It is, therefore, not at all abstract, but the most individual and "determinate" of all our various states of knowledge. This form of cognition is treated most fully, as would naturally be expected, in those writings of Schelling in which he describes his philosophy of nature. The third form of cognition is in a sense a synthesis of the two previous types. Schelling calls it "Intellectual Intuition." The term is meant to represent a kind of cognitive process which somehow grasps at one bound the richness of all concrete facts. The breadth of its comprehension is universal, while the objects with which it is concerned are concrete and individual. Such attempts to describe an absolute synthesis of opposites are, of course, familiar to students of German Idealism. They meet an analogous conception in the synthesis represented by the third and highest movement of the logical dialectic. Intellectual intuition is mentioned constantly by Schelling from the first essays cast in Fichtean moulds to the advent of the religious philosophy many years later. In a sense it is the capping stone of Schelling's Theory of Knowledge, a kind of ideal state of mind to which he may appeal when he has occasion to describe the cognition of a universal object of any kind.

To understand the trend of Schelling's Theory of Knowledge and the character of its influence on his contemporaries it may be interesting to follow in some detail these three forms of cognition.

Transcendental knowledge (das transcendentale Wissen) is meant by Schelling to represent a state of mind not altogether unfamiliar to students of German idealism. He characterizes it as "knowledge of knowledge"—a kind of cognitive process in which the object of knowledge is somehow lost in the process itself. It represented in Schelling's mind the activity of consciousness struggling to make itself objective, and then to view itself in this position. In this effort it finds the object ever slipping away, a kind of will-o'-the-wisp that eludes the grasp at every turn. Hence arises the evasiveness of the whole activity. Hence, too, one may remark, arises the difficulty which Schelling, or any interpreter of his, will always find in describing transcendental knowledge as something appreciably real and significant.

Beyond this bare description, not altogether free from verbalism, one surmises, Schelling gives us little intimation of the functions and the scope of transcendental knowledge. He tells us that because of the absence of any concrete object, other than merely its own self, transcendental knowledge possesses the highest form of all knowledge—universality—but it is not necessarily the highest "principle of knowledge" nor the "highest principle of being." One may remark in passing that the "highest principle of knowledge" in Schelling's mind was represented by intellectual intuition, the third form of cognitive process to be described presently; and the "highest principle of being" at this period of Schelling's activity was represented by the principle of self-consciousness.

The treatment of transcendental knowledge, from the scattered references throughout the *System des transcendentalen Idealismus,* leads one to believe that the whole subject was far from clear in Schelling's own mind. He saw, evidently, the necessity of reinforcing his own subjective idealism by some precise Theory of Knowledge. Transcendentalism required a state of cognition which does not possess the limitations of our ordinary sense perception. It must have some kind of an 'object,' however, in order to be true knowledge. With these two considerations before him Schelling began his Theory of Knowledge by the verbal concept of a state of cognition so undetermined and undefined as to be in form universal, but yet bearing some resemblance to the finite processes of our ordinary sense perception. Such a state of knowledge seems to involve covertly a contradiction between the unlimited and the limited. But the sweeping, imaginative mind of the young Schelling passed easily over this difficulty, here as elsewhere, by falling back upon the complex staging of a higher synthesis. In view of this he seems to imply that transcendental knowledge has the 'pure form' of universality, yet in the character of viewing itself as object it con-

tains the germ of determined particularity. Thus easily, according to this brilliant transcendentalist, can the infinite and the finite unite in knowledge.

The result of Schelling's treatment of the first of his series of cognitive processes is that he has tried to define what he considers the most abstract and universal form of knowledge. It seems empty, for its only content is itself. It seems futile, for mere knowledge of itself carries us not a bit farther toward a solution of the old problem: "How can we know the world in its reality?" Schelling must have realized this inadequacy; for nowhere except in the *System des transcendentalen Idealismus* does this abstract form of cognition receive more than passing notice. It will be remembered that most of Schelling's time and attention, once he was beyond the immediate influence of Fichte, was devoted to the production of works on the philosophy of nature. Here Schelling shows himself the philosopher of empirical sciences. The problem of knowledge narrows itself to the special problem of the knowledge of objects.

In the effort to supply an adequate background for the empirical facts of science Schelling introduces a new tendency into German idealism. In a sense, he commenced the long series of investigations into the relation between science and philosophy which lead up to the present-day 'nature-philosophy.' Fichte, in the spirit of his own subjectivism, did not attempt to supply a philosophical background for the world of empirical fact, except to state merely that there were conditions under which a subjective process might assume an objective form. Schelling saw that no such verbal solution would meet the concrete richness of science. To his broader vision both nature, in all its multifarious forms, and mind, with its almost infinite possibilities, are phases of one ultimate reality. But Schelling went beyond this new form of Spinozism; he thrust directly into the foreground the old problem of Locke and Leibniz: How can we know of the existence of objective phenomena? In meeting this question fairly Schelling defines his second form of cognition, that of the intuition of individual things.

The intuition of the particular is that which gives us the assurance of the existence of an outside world, and is the first condition of any philosophy of nature. Had Schelling interpreted this presupposition literally, he would have felt no further necessity of dealing with the problem of knowledge in the nature-philosophy. But his mind was so strongly inclined to construct universals at the expense of particulars that he could not rest satisfied with this simple statement. As one essay follows another, he sees more and more in the intuition of particulars an expression of universal spirit, and soon leaves the field of empirical fact to soar into the heights of abstract formalism. Nature is defined as an original, evolving force—a "productivity"—and the individual objects of sense perception as the "mere products (natura naturata)" of this original activity. The particular arises when the "first force of nature" is opposed for a moment of time by its opposite or negating tendency. In the so-called "identity period," after the publication of the *Darstellung meines Systems der Philosophie,* the original simplicity of the problem of sense perception is entirely lost. Schelling reverts first to Spinozism and then to Platonism in his effort to explain how the Absolute may become crystallized from time to time in our simple, ordinary knowledge of particulars. In these efforts there is little of historical significance.

In the *System des transcendentalen Idealismus,* the problem of particular intuition is treated in a very elaborate fashion from the point of view of subjective idealism. Schelling here desires to give an outline of a natural history of self-consciousness in the form of a series of activities. It is, therefore, inevitable that he should meet the problem of particular intuition in an idealistic rather than a naturalistic setting. Schelling, more than either Fichte or Hegel, succeeded in separating the cognitive act of intuition as a fact of knowledge from the metaphysical significance to be attributed to the particular. He asks, to use his own terms, "How the Ego comes to intuit itself as limited?" To explain this he depicts the universal principle of self-consciousness struggling to realize or express itself in concrete situations. It is the plot or spirit of the drama making itself objective and determinate in the successive acts and scenes. The lower strata of these objectifications of self-consciousness correspond to the knowledge of the particular, and are therefore similar in meaning to what was considered as intuition of particulars in the nature-philosophy. Students of Hegel will recall at this point the "sense certainty" and the opening chapters of the *Phenomenologie.* With Schelling this idealistic setting seems to alter the appearance of the problem, as it was stated in connection with the naturalistic writings in the preceding paragraph. In essence, however, the treatment is the same.

The highest level in the series of cognitive processes was called by Schelling Intellectual Intuition (intellectuelle Anschauung). This is to be sharply contrasted with the intuition of particular concrete facts, the description of which connected Schelling most closely with the world of empirical fact. Transcendental intuition represented to him the special form of knowledge which had as its function the knowing of the Absolute in some form. "The transcendental intuition is the organ of all transcendental thinking." The first treatment of this cognitive process occurs in the *Vom Ich als Princip der Philosophie,* at the conclusion of a series of pages in which Schelling has sought to define the Unconditioned Ego in such universal terms that it seemingly cannot be reached by sense perception. In this predicament Schelling must either admit that the Absolute is unknowable, as his critics have contended, or else describe how the ultimate reality of the universe, as the Unconditioned Ego, can be known to human consciousness. Schelling chose the latter course. He brought into the foreground the conception of intellectual intuition, which needs no "object" in the ordinary sense of an object of knowledge. For intellectual intuition the only object is the Absolute Ego—"the Ego is the mere condition for its own intellectual intuition." With this somewhat confusing review, and a casual remark on Kant's attitude toward intellectual intuition, Schelling closes his first observations on the subject. Later on in the same work, when considering the character of the Absolute Ego, Schelling tells us that as the reality of the Ego "is absolutely outside of all time, the form of its intellectual intuition is eternity."

In the *Philosophische Briefe über Dogmatismus und Kriticismus,* Schelling refers to intellectual intuition as an activity of the mind in which the intuited and the intuiting are one, and in the later contributions to the *Fichte-Niethammer Journal* he tells us that the human spirit can abstract from all objectivity and have an intuition of the Absolute. This intuition is intellectual, and through it arises pure self-consciousness.

The tendency to give to intellectual intuition an increasingly important function becomes pronounced in the *System des transcendentalen Idealismus.* In the previous writings Schelling had stated that intellectual intuition could have no object—an assertion which he must have recognized as ridiculous, since the very essence of any cognitive process is to know something. But in these first essays Schelling dreaded above all things to make the Ego any kind of object, fearing to fall into the meshes of the Reinholdian dogmatism, against which he railed in the *Philosophische Briefe.* Now, in the *System des transcendentalen Idealismus,* he conceives of a way of assigning an object to intellectual intuition without detracting from its universal form. This is by asserting that the Absolute of the world-consciousness, as the knower of all processes of knowledge, creates its object by intuiting its own infinite and absolute reality. After 1800 this new interpretation predominates in Schelling's constant effort to explain how we can know the Absolute, and paves the way to a closer connection between intellectual intuition as the form of knowledge and the Absolute as its metaphysical content. Schelling's notes on an essay by Eschenmayer on *Das höchste Princip der Natur-Philosophie* suggests this change. The essay presents a doubt as to how nature as 'pure activity' could be known. The problem is just opposite to Schelling's earlier inquiry as to how the Ego as 'pure subjectivity' could be known. Schelling had already in the *System des transcendentalen Idealismus* met this latter question by asserting that the Absolute Ego, through the act of consciousness, must be both unlimited subjectivity and limited objectivity, in order that it may be known by intellectual intuition. Already before this he had called the limited objectivity, nature. It was, therefore, a comparatively easy step, in answer to Eschenmayer, to bring the two propositions together and assert that the knowledge object of an intellectual intuition was a pure 'subject-object.' It intuited, in an absolute synthesis the pure subject as Ego and the pure object as nature. "What I call nature is nothing more than the pure objective of the intellectual intuition of the pure subject-object." Nature as well as Ego can only be known through intellectual intuition, because by no other means can it be elevated to the position of a correlative with subjectivity. This conception of intellectual intuition has become so firmly fixed that its name is changed to Absolute Reason. With this the Theory of Knowledge becomes merged in the Theory of Reality. Intellectual intuition and its object, the Absolute, become one in the Absolute Reason. In the *Fernere Darstellungen* of the *Neue Zeitschrift,* 1802-3, Schelling returns to the old description of intellectual intuition as the highest principle of knowledge. It "knows the Absolute in and for itself," yet this does not prevent him from devoting the entire section to proving that the intellectual intuition of the Absolute and the Absolute itself are one and the same. This tendency to submerge both knowledge and reality in a form of mysticism becomes more evident in the *Bruno* and the various works immediately following. With this confusion our interest in intellectual intuition ceases.

In summing up Schelling's Theory of Knowledge, it is interesting to note the position of intellectual intuition with respect to the two previous types of cognitive process.

Transcendental knowledge was described as the form of knowing wherein there is no differentiation of object. It could know only itself and was, therefore, empty and sterile. The intuition of particular objects was concerned with limited individuals. It grasped ideas and things. Intellectual intuition now appears as a true synthesis of the two previous types. Students of logical method can see perhaps a resemblance between these three states of cognitive process and the three moments of the dialectic movement of Fichte, Schelling, and Hegel. Schelling himself pointed out no such parallelism, but his mind was so thoroughly saturated with the dialectic method of thought that his thinking fell easily into its moulds. Both transcendental knowledge and the first phase of the logical dialect are alike abstract, vague, and indeterminate. The significance in each case lies in what is to follow. Particular intuition and the antithesis of the dialectic are both concerned with particular, definite objects. Their sphere is the individual. Intellectual intuition, the highest state of knowledge, represents the generality of mere knowing, the most abstract form of the cognitive act, and this same abstractness made concrete through the intuition of an object, the Absolute. Students of Hegel would be inclined to say it represented knowledge made "An-und-fur-sich-sein." Similarly, the synthesis stage of the dialectic represents a logical form embracing both the universality of the thesis and the individuality of the antithesis. Without pressing this analogy too far, however, one cannot help feeling impressed with the importance of Schelling's efforts to bring the absolute idealism of the movement to which he belonged into accord with a Theory of Knowledge. Here lies the importance of his work. In striving to express human knowledge in terms of a cognitive act directed toward certain objects of knowledge, Schelling exerted a marked influence. It was this tendency to demand a solution to the problem of knowledge that is of consequence, rather than the idealistic Theory of Knowledge that took shape beneath his hands. (pp. 157-67)

> *Arthur S. Dewing, "The Significance of Schelling's Theory of Knowledge," in* The Philosophical Review, *Vol. XIX, No. 2, March, 1910, pp. 154-67.*

James Lindsay   (essay date 1910)

[*In the following essay, Lindsay characterizes Schelling's philosophy as influential, but ultimately flawed.*]

In many respects Schelling is a philosopher who cannot be said to have come to his own. Standing between Fichte and Hegel, his characteristic blendings of poetry and science, philosophy and mythology—which made him philosophic center and focus of Romanticism—caused him to be often regarded more as romancer than as seriously constructive philosopher. Unlike Fichte, whose preponderating influence was man, Schelling laid stress upon the world, carrying over into it his wavering subjectivity and his bold phantasy. It was for Schelling an "immediate certainty" that "there exist things outside of us"; and nature formed for him "the sum of all that is purely objective in our knowledge."

Recent idealistic speculation has laid its beginnings so strongly in subjectivity, that it has been needfully reminded by the New Realism of our time of the significance of

aspects like this Schellingian one, wherein the world appears as a datum rather than as a construction. Even if we do not finally rest in Realism, it is necessary to do more justice to objectivity than it has idealistically received. Schelling, for all his hold on objectivity, had an imposing, speculative construction.

The world was to Fichte as self-consciousness erects it; but the self which builds it was to the Romanticists the self of genius—of the constructive artist—and the real world is the world that satisfies such geniuses. Schelling is the most genial of the three speculative thinkers whom we have named, for his ideal of man is just this genial and creative individuality—not, as with Fichte, moral will or character. The Romanticists preferred, to the ethical idealism of Fichte, the less severe mode of interpreting nature, idealistically, in terms of bold statement and striking divination. For Schelling, the greatest problem was the determination of the relationship between nature and mind, between the unconscious and the conscious.

A true metaphysic of nature is a thing of such prime philosophic concern, that it cannot but appear strange that Schelling's philosophy of nature has never received the attention it deserves. To him nature, as unconscious expression of spirit, is visible spirit, and spirit is invisible nature. The absolute intelligence is taken by him as not only giving rise to ideal conceptions, but as creative of the real world. Between such a method as Schelling's of constructing reality from an advancing thought-process, and the intuition on which he insists, there is an inherent contradiction. For him, there was the same Absolute in nature as in mind, their harmony being no mere reflection of thought. If you suppose we transfer our idea to nature, then, holds Schelling, you have not even dreamed what nature is and should be for us. Nature is the counterpart of mind, and produced by it, only that mind may, by its agency, attain to self-consciousness or a pure perception of itself.

"The attempt," according to Schelling, "to account for nature as a production adapted to design, that is, realizing a purpose, destroys the character of nature, and, in fact, the very thing which constitutes it nature. For the peculiarity of nature consists in this, that while its mechanism is blind, it is in that mechanism, nevertheless, adapted to a design. If we destroy that mechanism, we also destroy nature itself." It was indeed this thought of nature's life and action, as constitutive of existent reason, that Hegel expanded into the statement that all that is real or actual is rational. The real thing, to Schelling, is the idea; the idea is the substance—the heart of things; finite existence is a merely derived being, and, loosed from the idea, has no reality. Existence must, in his view, be thought of as substance.

Schelling derives largely from Spinoza, the net result not being Spinozan substance, with matter and mind as inseparable attributes of one being, but an inconceivable background of real being named the Absolute. But Schelling's conception of God is not a simple one, but consists of several, which together sum his inner development. The God-problem occupied him but little at first, God being to him then the world-creating, absolute I, standing in sharpest contrast to the empiric ego of man, which latter exists only through this absolute I. For him the unity of consciousness—in other words, personality—is found only in the finite ego. The infinite ego has no object; neither has it unity of consciousness nor personality. Schelling is still one with Spinoza, but he comes to think differently later. Other stages into which he passed are, periods of interest in the philosophy of nature, and in transcendental idealism.

The mistake of Schelling was to give his idealism an absolute cast, whereby the Idea, as a universal principle of explanation, should be unable to explain the irrational, evil, and contradictory elements of the world. For it can, of course, be urged that, in making Reason all, he fell into an unscientific dogmatism. From consciousness as starting-point of his idealism, he passed to that of the Absolute implied in his philosophy of identity.

Freedom and necessity he sees to be harmonized in God, the absolute synthesis, the identity of the ideal and the real. An infinite process to him is the development of the absolute synthesis. But, again, Schelling's aestheticism finds God really revealed only in art—for him the true religion. The spirit of his teaching may be best gathered from words of his own: "If art is to imitate nature, it has to follow in the wake of the creative power of nature, and not merely slowly to take up architectonically the empty scaffolding of its external forms, and to transfer an equally empty picture of them upon the canvas. It was only for the deep-thinking Grecians, who everywhere felt the trace of the living and working essence, that nature could present many true gods. If we look at things, not with reference to the essence which they contain, but with reference to their empty form, they will not communicate anything to our mind or heart." Art, then, is for Schelling the first revelation of the infinite, in which we are still far from having blended the objectivity of art with the subjectivity of religion.

But Schelling's development presses on to the philosophy of identity; hitherto he has been seeking to overcome Fichtean dualism; he is now centered upon the problem of the Absolute, for solving which man must have intellectual intuition. Such intellectual intuition Schelling believed to be necessary, to save us from narrow subjectivity; and possible, because the Absolute itself dwells in us as essence of our soul. The intuiting self is identical with the intuited or perceived: in the moment of intuition we are not in time, but time—or rather pure, absolute eternity—is in us; with this intellectual intuition, Schelling seeks to know God, the deepest essence of the world, who is also One. This All-One, whom we call God, has knowledge as his form or eternal being: absolute identity is God's essence and form in synchronous fashion.

By the way of philosophical construction, that is, by means of intellectual intuition, Schelling hoped to attain certainty; but it is clear, on scrutinizing it, that this can never become a method of scientific cognition.

God is Reason, in whom all things are comprehended and perfected, so that Reason is already—anticipatory, that is to say, of Hegel—the essence of the world. The Divine unity is, for Schelling, a really existent unity; undifferentiated activity gives way before the abstract monism of a pure unmoved identity; the self-revelation of God is his existence; things then become so many potences, with the absolute identity as their basis; the sum of these potences is the being of the absolute identity—the All, for he is the only real, outside of whom is nothing.

Schelling's philosophy of nature does not provide for any creation of objects, in the ordinary sense of creation. The Schellingian pantheism required the identity of the absolute and the creature to be preserved, so that the absolute must itself enter into the finite, and be immanent in it. The common postulation of an eternal spirit first, then a material world consciously created or produced by it, is by him reversed—matter being to him first and spirit supervening with growing subjectiveness, until pure and perfect ideality is reached, but such spirit, in this late sense, not being Creator of the world. In this way infinite nature came to objectivize itself in its own perfected works. The Absolute is, in all the real products of nature, identical with these, its products—identical with the material world. The real and the ideal are, in the Absolute, identical; the subject and the object, nature and spirit, are identical in the Absolute; and it is through intellectual intuition that we recognize this identity. For Schelling the function of all philosophy is to evolve nature from intelligence or intelligence out of nature. Hegel showed Schelling's system of identity to be but logic, and not concerned with reality.

We are now upon Schelling's pantheistic conception of Deity, in which God and the universe are only two sides or aspects of one and the same thing. God becomes an abstraction, and the world is nothing in particular! But the result was too complete, and led to that study of the rise of the finite out of the infinite, and of the phenomenon of evil, which ended in Schelling's acceptance of theism, of Divine Personality, and of real revelation.

We have seen men of genius and artistic power to be, in Schelling's view, endowed with a faculty of intellectual intuition, which discerns the identity of the One with the All. Such "intellectual intuition" is, for him, "the organ of all transcendental thinking," for this latter aims "to transform into its own object" what is otherwise "no object," so that, in the result, "the producing of the object and the perceiving are absolutely one." The ego itself is such an intuition, such ego being principle of all reality. The sole organ of transcendental philosophizing is, in his view, the "inner sense," whose object is of such a nature that it never can become the object of external intuition. His Absolute is the indifference of real and ideal, of the subjective and the objective. Nature is, to Schelling, really the Absolute, but we have seen how he moved away from conceptual problems to living ones.

In matter, as the simplest form in which the Absolute appears in nature, the real is the predominating element. Its ideal element is pure force within, or rather, the synthesis of two opposite forces, attraction and repulsion. This ideal element or factor gradually overcomes the comparatively inert mass, through light and life, and various dynamic laws come into play. The formative impulse in nature presses on to higher forms in a progressive development. But it is the "eternally unconscious" which is, for him, root of all intelligence, law, and order.

It is, however, one of the fine features of Schelling that the unity of science and the unity of life are focused in him; for, while he attaches himself to the study of the special sciences, he at the same time seeks to construct, or construe out of their essence, their highest principle, namely, the Absolute. Existence is, to Schelling, self-activity, and nature is already self-activity before she arrives at self-consciousness; for nature, to him, is in herself absolute self-movement. Matter is the root of all things—is existence in its first form; but it is still only the unity, or the polar tension of powers or factors which are active in opposite directions. Nature or the universal essence does not stop short without potentiating itself into life. For an actual ground must be an active one, and the stage of pure potence must be overpassed. But the obscurity and indeterminateness of Schelling's treatment make one ask whether, in all the foregoing processes, identity and indifference are preserved?

God is not God of the dead, but of the living, to this richest of the three great speculative thinkers, from whom we set out, in ideas, intuitions, and variety of directions in which he has supplied stimuli. Schelling's thought proceeds in no constant and unvarying direction: his world-view is set to changes of severest type; he thinks such changes are the necessary supplementings of all earlier positions. The World-soul is to him the principle of life. The acceptance of a conscious, actively purposeful Creator raises philosophy in his view. But in a breaking away, a spring (*Sprung*), or falling away from this Creator, does he find the origin of the sense-world, God himself developing through the world, in its historically claimed independence of Him and return to Him.

Teleology in nature was, however, for him only of an unconscious kind. Every organization seemed to him an unconscious purposive product. Schelling's psychology holds nothing to be real save the will, and regards its own psychological function to be to start from the primal will found in nature, and follow the different stages of knowledge up to the active understanding and the practical reason. 'Tis a merit of his to avoid the mistake of Spinoza and others who make of the universe a fact, or a concatenation of facts, while it is really a life. To Schelling, the life of humanity is seen typified or symbolized in nature, wherein spirit has found expression earlier than in man. Schelling, in making man thus an evolution of nature, was reversing the method of Fichte. Schelling's constructive idealism sought to free Fichtean idealism from the arbitrary aspects of the life of finite selves, by providing a theory of the facts of nature, and of the evolution of consciousness, that should be complemental to Fichtean thought. The outer world, then, was a manifestation of spirit, to which outer or natural order the inner world of the ego is inevitably related. These two sciences—mind and nature—Schelling expressly maintains, need and supplement each other, and he declares that a perfect intellectualizing or spiritualizing the laws of nature into laws of thinking or intuition would be "the highest perfecting of the science of nature." For "that theory of nature," he says, "would have attained to perfectness, by virtue of which all nature would resolve itself into intelligence." Man is but nature's last and highest reflection.

The successive stages of phenomenal existence, from nature's lowest forms up to the highest manifestations of life and thought, where sensibility reigns supreme in man, are set forth by means of Schelling's notable—and, it must be said, suggestive—doctrine of potences. All three moments of the Absolute are present, in pursuance of the principles of his theory of identity, in every phenomenon, and all are organic in the end. Man is the sum and content of all the potences. Mechanical and chemical forces are but negative conditions of life: they await vital stimulus that lies exteri-

or to the individual; such is the result of the absolute productivity, which works under the universal law of polarity. "Universal nature," is, for him, common principle of organic and inorganic.

It was here that the defect of Schelling's treatment of the Absolute appeared. Berkeley and Fichte had seen—the former that there is no object without a subject, the latter that, in this sense, the subject makes the object; but Schelling saw that neither can there be a subject without an object—that the objective world equally conditions the existence of the ego. For him, that is to say, the universe has an existence of its own relatively distinct from the thinking subject. This is not to say, however, that the non-ego, in his view, makes the ego—that sense-perception is constitutive of thought, as with Hume, Locke, Condillac.

There is something finely suggestive in the way Schelling asks how the system of nature can be given to us, and does not blindly content himself with the scientific mode of accepting nature as something immediately given. His deeper quest was to know how the system arose for us, and how we are able to perceive it. His dynamic atomism pierced to forces, and was not content with brute facts. But dynamism, endowed with reason or intelligence to a quite fantastical degree, was what formed his philosophy of nature.

But Schelling leaves nature, with her bi-polar laws, standing like an independent entity over against mind, with her bi-polar categories, in unresolved antagonism. This unresolved task was taken up by Hegel, who identified the Absolute with the process itself. Schelling's worlds of mind and matter were supported by the Absolute, who seemed—according to the well-known saying of Hegel—in Schelling's system shot out of a pistol. Schelling, that is to say, does not show why it is there, or what it is, when he ought to have gone on to unify his bi-polar aspects of the world, relating them to an Absolute Being as a primal cause, and deducing their different natures as due to necessary consequences of evolving principles that latently inhered in such originative cause. Schelling's Absolute remains outside of things, if only for the reason that they proceed from Him. His absolute reason was to mean an equilibrium or indifference of subject and object. But if these two coincide in such a blank identity, the absolute unity becomes reduced to empty form or nothingness. Such an Absolute can give no substantial unity, neither can it subserve any purposes of real explanation. His Absolute was to be the center of indifference of the magnet, but the magnet is no magnet at all, for since, by polar logic, subject and object must first be eliminated ere we reach the Absolute as point of indifference, we are reduced to blank nothingness in the process, and never reach a conscious knowledge of the Absolute at all.

It need not be denied that there was something of freedom, and something of elevation, in Schelling's conception of pure and infinite Being as the absolute indifference; but the subject and object, annulled in the process, are never again methodically developed from that indifference. This mode of thinking was characteristic of Schelling's earlier system. This annihilation of consciousness scarcely seems a promising foundation for philosophy; the Absolute is the middle point of the magnet, the center where there ceases to be any difference between the opposing poles of the real and the ideal; the knowledge of the Absolute which he brings us is a recognition of the essential identity and indifference of all things. In its purely pantheistic stage, the main—however variously estimated—service rendered by Schelling's philosophy, was this assertion of the identity of thought and being, this finding of the key to the problem how the ideal world of consciousness and the real world of being should correspond, and come into commerce with each other. Thought and being, the ideal and the real, are to him identical; all activity and movement of the world of appearance are mere *Schein* of the absolute unity.

In Schelling's Absolute there is a dark, irrational ground, which has to be purified, developmentally, ere Personal Being is reached; there is for him something in God which may, no doubt, become God, but is not God. God must have the ground of existence within himself, says Schelling, since nothing exists before or without God; but Schelling does not take this ground to be God, absolutely considered, that is to say, in so far as He exists. But if the world were taken, he says, to be different from God, then would the world have arisen from a ground different from God; but, as nothing can exist outside the Absolute, the solution of the contradiction is to be found, in his view, in the world having its ground in that original ground which is also the ground of the Divine Existence. This ground—or absolute potence—cannot be resolved, but remains as the ground, "the incomprehensible basis of reality."

Naturally, the ascending powers, which are so prominent a feature of his philosophy of nature, are of great consequence in such a system. In that philosophy, as we have seen, the concept of powers and the concept of polarity have fundamental places. His metaphysical idealism draws largely upon analogy; and indeed the philosopher of Romanticism goes so far as to put his own symbolic expositions of nature before the painful searchings of science into the real and reciprocal interconnection of phenomena.

It was his distorted conception of philosophic function—in which Fichte and Hegel in their own ways sinned along with him—that led Schelling to construct nature in his *a priori* fashion, with a fine scorn for the blind and senseless natural science that was everywhere establishing itself since the destruction of philosophy by Bacon and of physics by Boyle and Newton! Having originally claimed nature and spirit to be fundamentally one, Schelling later declared the ground of nature and spirit, the Absolute, to be "the identity of the real and the ideal." The doctrine of identity is thus added to the philosophies of nature and spirit, this philosophy of identity forming indeed their basis. Hence the world-ground is neither nature nor spirit, but the unity of both, rather the indifference of subjective and objective, in which the self-identity of the Absolute is never lost. Such was the goal to which Schelling's thought had traveled from the time when he extolled nature as source of spirit—as, in fact, undeveloped and unconscious intelligence. He had exalted nature to the position of subject, and only from creative nature—*natura naturans*—comes the ego, in this reversion of Fichtean procedure. Nature being to Schelling *a priori,* he thinks we can philosophically construct it anew.

It was his favoring poetical symbolism as a mode of interpretation that made it a more natural result that he should give art the supreme place. But, alike in his teachings and in his want of proper method, Schelling showed himself to be marked by the arbitrariness and lawlessness which were so characteristic of Romanticism.

Schelling does not fail to deal, in his so-called positive philosophy, with the problem of freedom, in relation to good and evil: evil for him arises out of the striving of the individual will against the universal will; man is, for him, free creative activity, and, as such, the essence of the world; his doctrine of freedom, indeed, is marked by insight into the metaphysical essence of the world, but tends to approximate to the irrationalism of Schopenhauer. God at length becomes to Schelling life and personality, not an abstraction; He is becoming and development, not static being; the essence of the world is will, as primary being, though only presaging and unconscious. In the last and highest instance, he insists that there is no existence save willing, which is original existence, self-affirmed and independent of time. Thus the necessities of the ethical life came to influence Schelling's thought more than abstract speculation.

The positive essence of freedom, says Schelling, consists in this, that it is a faculty of good and of evil, so proving the greatest difficulty in philosophy; for he thinks "it is impossible to understand how a faculty for evil can follow from God"; hence "the derivation of human liberty from God cannot be a correct one, but it must, at least in as far as it is a faculty for evil, have a root independent from God." Schelling does not content himself with making freedom the principle of moral action, but regards it as also the principle of consciousness, so making it the common principle of theoretic and of practical philosophy. Nor does he fail to notice an irrational and contingent element in the world, especially in the sphere of organic life. But Schelling is not sufficiently careful to keep the irrationality of individual wills from being, by any possibility, grounded in the last resort in irrationality of the Absolute Will. His philosophy of religion—with its personal God, its freedom, and its individual immortality—is of merely negative value. All birth is, for Schelling, birth out of darkness into light; the process of creation is an inner transmutation of the original principle of darkness into light.

If we desire the dark ground, which is the common root of Deity and the world, to be brought nearer to us, then says Schelling—speaking now as characteristic philosopher of Romanticism—we shall find it to consist of something which is essentially longing—longing to give birth to itself. Man does not at first perceive that he is not really separate from the Absolute, that he is himself an integral part of the Infinite Power, but this identity ever grows in its hold upon him, the infinite spirit acting in him by the different gradations of revelation.

Man has, as we have seen, two principles in him, wherein consists for him the possibility of evil or of good, as he unites himself to the Universal Will or not. But one must recall in this connection that human individuality is a quite insufficient basis for morality, and that it should be realized that moral justification is found for such conceptions as individuality and personality only as they are grounded or set in the universal-human. Schelling came to see that the key to the world's enigma must be found in no categories of nature, but in ethical categories of freedom. What he did not realize was that perfect freedom of the human personality implies that it shall be regarded, as little as possible, as a mere means of divine purpose, and be rather viewed as having end and worth in itself.

Schelling's theism is by no means of a kind that is free from contradictions, when taken as a complete world-view. It does by no means consort well with his pessimistic world-conception. He postulates an immediate, intuitive, and individual knowledge of the Absolute in man, but overlooks that this knowledge is not on all fours with the knowledge which the Absolute itself has. The speculative theism of his later thought was meant to give depth to his originally pure pantheism, while the pure rationalism of his earlier thought was supplemented, later, by a higher empiricism. His later thought made the Divine Personality consist simply in the living unity of the Real and the Ideal—a position not so free from arbitrariness as to be quite easy to justify. The abstract, empty unity, of which his Absolute originally consisted, needed and received from him modification, in respect of the production of the world's multiplicity. In fact, no one presses on more than Schelling from empty speculation to an inquiring comprehension of reality. The irrationalities, discords, oppositions, found in nature and history, are, to Schelling, necessary in order to life. There can be no real unity in his view without such conflict. For only thus does substance first become living, intelligent, willing, active. For the unity of personal being, even in Deity, he must needs postulate an original antithesis in the Absolute. This new mode of conceiving Deity, though interesting and suggestive, does not really carry us far, since the conflict or opposition is entirely within Deity's own nature.

Schelling failed to realize that our individual conscious-

Drawing of Schelling, 1808 or 1809, by Josef Klotz.

ness can perceive only the ready products of the activity of the Absolute, never the precedent producing activity itself. Indeed, it is with the products that our consciousness itself has its rise. Schelling's method has need of an infusion of inductive method, which infers the transcendent in backward fashion from the perceivable. This, however, he came at length to perceive, though the proved insufficiency of the "intellectual intuition." The development of Schelling's thought was steadily from an abstract, aesthetic world-view to a living and ethical one.

In his later philosophy, Schelling begins his ontology with the indeterminate idea of the possibility of becoming (*Seinkönnen*), from which the critical and gradual separation of the ambiguous and indeterminate will educe the true concept of God, which, to Schelling, is that God is the Lord of Being. God was, to him, the Original Possibility of Being; the science of reason shows Him to be the *natura necessaria*—existent in nature or concept, and not merely possible. A still subjectively-thought existence only for Deity; but reason so encloses Him that He is not to be held as essentially so enclosed—in fact, it must postulate Him as actually existing. These ontological suggestions or contentions have been unduly overshadowed by those of Hegel, superior as these latter, even with their exaggerated form, may be. Schelling's theistic conceptions are very unsatisfying, for he holds that God first comes to consciousness in man. In the final stage of Schelling's conceptions of Deity, we find him holding to personality-pantheism, in which all being is God's being, and three personalities are postulated as in Deity. The three potences of his "rational philosophy" are, the negative, the positive, and the harmonization of these two. It was to Schelling—as to Fichte—the task of theoretic philosophy, to give a history of self-consciousness. For him "that which is posited *out of* consciousness is, in its essence, the same as that which is posited *in* consciousness," and so "the knowable must itself bear the impress of the knower." Schelling's philosophy of nature one-sidedly fails to bring out that man's consciousness is not merely consciousness of nature, but is also consciousness of itself, and of its own knowledge. The I, in its self-consciousness, must be held to have other contents than merely that of nature.

It was the principle of his philosophy that brought Schelling to his aesthetic standpoint. He held to two forms of activity in the Absolute: the world of nature sprang out of an infinite, unconscious, necessary activity of the Absolute, while morality was the product of its free, conscious, purposeful activity. The objective world was, for him, only the original, but unconscious poesy of the spirit. The philosophy of Art was the universal organum of philosophy—the keystone of its whole arch—in Schelling's view. To him the idealistic world of art, and the real world objects, are products of one and the same activity.

"But if we are to apprehend it," says Schelling, "as living, the essence must, in its form, not only present itself to us, in general, as active principle, but also as spirit and as science, which realizes itself in its works. Every unity can only be spiritual both in its mode and in its origin, and what else is the aim of every investigation of nature, if it is not to find science in it?" "True, the science by which nature works is not one similar to human science, which is immediately connected with reflection upon itself. No; in the former the idea is not distinct from the act, nor the plan from the execution." Every work of art is, to Schelling, properly the product of genius, purposed yet created, and achieved as by miracle. The work of freedom, it is yet prompted as by nature's necessity, so that conscious and unconscious action here coincide.

The coincidence or meeting together of conscious and unconscious activity yields the real—without consciousness, and—with consciousness—the aesthetic world. Schelling takes man to be that wherein is first found the highest form of beauty: the beauty of the soul is for him the highest signification of nature. He enriched aesthetics at many individual points; his changing aesthetical interests are seen in the three main periods of his philosophic life; the first, in which his art-philosophy is brought into being in his transcendental idealism; the second, in which it appears, broadly developed, in his system of identity; and the third, in which it is marked by theosophic thinness. In the first of these periods Schelling opposed what had been the one-sided moralism of Fichte, who raised Kant's transcendental unity of apperception to the position of a metaphysical essence—the absolutely producing I. Thereby nature, as the product, was left as a mere means or transitional stage, in the confirmation of this I. Schelling, without being conscious of the fact, adopted what had been the view of Leibniz, that all nature is *Ichheit.*

So far from treating aesthetics as mere passage to morality, Schelling made the artistic point of view the controlling one in his whole philosophy of the objective. Nature is extolled by him as an original creative power, and his view ran on into the period of his system of identity, with its equal positing of the subjective and objective elements—will and knowledge. His attempts at knowing and comprehending the unity of the subjective and the objective were various; at one time as the unity of positive productivity and negative conditions, in his philosophy of nature; at another time as abstraction of the objective, in his transcendental idealism; at yet another time as the most original unity, in his system of identity. In the last and most original opposition of active will and passive idea, the world-process tends to appear as a triumph of light or idea over blind and dark will.

If we take so recent a work as Professor Laurie's *Synthetica,* one finds in it not a little that is suggestive of the influence of Schelling. Laurie says "the system of which we form a part is irrational." The irrational element, which figures in Schelling's philosophy, is that which gives it a certain realistic tinge. And yet the system must be taken as idealistic, since in it the universe exists only in thought, thought being but the universal nature in its developmental process, wherein, after all attempts at objectivization, it returns into identity with itself as pure subject. The irrational element is significant, too, of a certain reactionary tendency in Schelling against speculative philosophy, as not without limit, or as marked by inability to reach its final goal. Hence the lingering dualism in Schelling's idealism; his identity doctrine is too abstract and formal; the differences are not really and finally harmonized. Indeed, idealistic as we may admit his system to be, the difficulties as to a coherent world-theory were so great as to work in him an unconscious transition to (an epistemological) transcendental realism. Idealism is the soul of philosophy, he says, realism its body; and it takes these two to make a living whole.

The boldness of Schelling's claim for speculative construction, as able to reach beyond empiric limits, and disclose the inner type of all things, one cannot choose but admire, yet one is, of course, compelled to admit how little nature can be reduced to true unity save by that severe and earnest scientific study of reciprocal and interconnected forces and phenomena which Schelling, in his arbitrariness, undervalued. Yet the fact is not without significance that we have scientists today like Sir Oliver Lodge, Lloyd Morgan and others, who seem disposed to take idealistic interpretations as more ultimate than those yielded by science itself. For any realism must avail but little whose external world is not one revealed in experience.

So, too, his evolutional theory was not realistic enough to face an actual transition of one power into another, instead of each form springing directly out of the infinite productivity itself. Matter was, to Schelling, slumbering spirit, and the evolution he presents to us, in the sphere of reality, is the evolution of the Absolute. But Schelling was idealist enough to hold to the ideality of space and time—space, as such, being nothing real, and time only inner sense becoming, to its own self, object. For Schelling, philosophy's progress is seen first in mythology, and then in revelation.

The evolution of the God-idea in history is traced by him so as to show a passing from pantheism or monotheism to polytheism, and thence to the triune God of revelation. But for him the world's history is just God coming to Himself, and our longing for the actual God is what constitutes religion. With Jacob Boehme, he makes the Absolute the *Urgrund,* the essence prior to all duality, to all ground or existence.

To Schelling's philosophy of nature and transcendental idealism, there has been no nearer approach than Hartmann's philosophy of the unconscious, and Hartmann has sought to bring out the merits of Schelling's metaphysical system. It was a merit, certainly, in Schelling that, to his earlier purely rationalistic philosophy, he added a supplementary positive philosophy, in which freedom and divine will and action are present in more satisfying ways than those which had made the Absolute become personal in man.

Schelling's philosophy shared too largely the weaknesses and limitations of his time to be capable of adoption today, but that does not keep it from being calculated to kindle speculative power anew, to supply weighty thoughts for the healing of the disunion between pantheism and theism, between science and religion, and to point the way to some better world-view of our own making. (pp. 259-75)

James Lindsay, "The Philosophy of Schelling," in The Philosophical Review, *Vol. XIX, No. 3, May, 1910, pp. 259-75.*

Arthur O. Lovejoy   (lecture date 1933)

[*Lovejoy was a German-born American philosopher who founded the field of inquiry known as "the history of ideas."* The Great Chain of Being *(1936), his best known work, examines currents of philosophical history from ancient times through the Romantic movement. In the following excerpt from that work, Lovejoy traces the development of Schelling's theory of theological evolutionism.*]

When the Chain of Being—in other words, the entire created universe—came to be explicitly conceived, no longer as complete once for all and everlastingly the same in the kinds of its components, but as gradually evolving from a less to a greater degree of fullness and excellence, the question inevitably arose whether a God eternally complete and immutable could be supposed to be manifested in such a universe. The question was not always, or at first, answered in the negative; there were numerous eighteenth-century attempts . . . to combine the belief in a Creator who, being always the same and always acting in accordance with the same necessities of absolute reason, could not generate a creation different at one time from what it is at another, with the conviction that the world, being expansive and progressive, *is* essentially different at one time from what it is at another, and that the general order of events in time is not a negligible feature of finite existence, irrelevant to those eternal aspects of things with which metaphysics has to do, but is an aspect of reality of profound significance for philosophy. So long as the two beliefs were held together, the seeming axiom . . . that the antecedent in a casual process cannot contain less than the consequent, or a higher type of being come from a lower . . . could still be precariously maintained. But with the end of that century and the opening decades of the nineteenth these assumptions of the traditional theology and metaphysics began to be reversed. God himself was temporalized—was, indeed, identified with the process by which the whole creation slowly and painfully ascends the scale of possibility; or, if the name is to be reserved for the summit of the scale, God was conceived as the not yet realized final term of the process. Thus for emanationism and creationism came to be substituted what may best be called radical or absolute evolutionism—the typically Romantic evolutionism of which Bergson's *L'évolution créatrice* is in great part a re-editing. The lower precedes the higher, not merely in the history of organic forms and functions, but universally; there is more in the effect than was contained, except as an abstract unrealized potentiality, in the cause.

This development can best be seen in Schelling. In much of his philosophizing between 1800 and 1812, it is true, he has still two Gods and therefore two religions—the religion of a time-transcending and eternally complete Absolute, an "Identity of Identities," the One of Neoplatonism—and the religion of a struggling, temporally limited, gradually self-realizing World-Spirit or Life-Force. The latter is the aspect under which the former manifests itself to us. In its manifestation the principles of plenitude and continuity rule. The temporal order is, as it were, a projection, a spread-out image, of the Absolute Intelligence, and its concrete content consists of the succession of organisms and their states. And any such succession *must,* says Schelling, constitute a progressive graded series, for the following reason:

> Succession itself is gradual, i.e., it cannot in any single moment be given in its entirety. But the farther succession proceeds, the more fully the universe is unfolded. Consequently, the organic world also, in proportion as succession advances, will attain to a fuller extension and represent a greater part of the universe. . . . And on the other hand the farther

we go back in the world of organisms, the smaller becomes the part of the universe which the organism embraces within itself. The plant-world is the most limited of all, since in it a great number of natural processes are lacking altogether.

But the new conception is set forth still more boldly and clearly in the treatise *Ueber das Wesen der menschlichen Freiheit* (1809). Even here vestiges of the Neoplatonic Absolute remain; but Schelling dwells with predilection upon the thesis that God never is, but is only coming to be, through nature and history.

> Has creation a final goal? And if so, why was it not reached at once? Why was the consummation not realized from the beginning? To these questions there is but one answer: Because God is *Life,* and not merely being. All life has a *fate,* and is subject to suffering and to becoming. To this, then, God has of his own free will subjected himself. . . . Being is *sensible* only in becoming. In being as such, it is true, there is no becoming; in the latter, rather, it is itself posited as eternity. But in the actualization (of being) through opposition there is necessarily a becoming. Without the conception of a humanly suffering God—a conception common to all the mysteries and spiritual religions of the past—history remains wholly unintelligible.

Yet the principle of plenitude, with some qualification, and with it the cosmical determinism of Abelard, Bruno, and Spinoza, is once more affirmed by Schelling. It is, says Schelling—still using the phrases of Dionysius and the Schoolmen—because "the act of self-revelation in God is related to his Goodness and Love" that it is necessary. But none the less, or rather, all the more,

> the proposition is absolutely undeniable that from the divine nature everything follows with absolute necessity, that everything which is possible by means of it must also be actual, and what is not actual must also be morally impossible. The error of Spinozism did not at all consist in the assertion of such an inexorable necessity in God, but only in conceiving of this necessity as something lifeless and impersonal.

It recognizes only "a blind and mechanical necessity." But "if God is essentially Love and Goodness, then that which is morally necessary in him follows with a truly metaphysical necessity." Leibniz, on the other hand, was wholly wrong in attributing to God a choice between possible worlds, a sort of "consultation of God with himself" at the conclusion of which he decided upon the actualization of only one among a multitude of possibilities. To assume such a free choice would be to imply "that God has chosen a less perfect world than, when all conditions are taken into account, was possible, and—as some, in fact, assert, since there is no absurdity which does not find some spokesmen—that God could, if he had wished, have created a world better than this one." (This, it will be remembered, had long since been declared by Abelard to be an absurdity.) There thus is not, and never was, a plurality of possible worlds. True, at the beginning of the world-process there was a chaotic condition, constituting the first movement of the Primal Ground (*Grund*), as "a matter still unformed, but capable of receiving all forms"; and there was therefore then "an infinity of possibilities" not yet realized. "But this Primal Ground is not to be assimilated to God; and God, given his perfection, could will only one thing." "There is only one possible world, because there is only one God." But this one possible world cannot contain less than all that was really possible.

The "God" even of this passage, it will be seen, still retains some otherworldly attributes, and the necessity of the production of all possible creatures is still deduced by arguments which are closely akin to the dialectic of emanationism. God is not the *Urgrund,* nor is he the final consummation of the process in which the *Urgrund* gives rise to increasingly various forms and eventually to self-consciousness in man; he remains, here, a perfection prior to the world and yet generative of it as a necessary logical consequence of his essential nature. Yet the generation is a gradual and successive one; and if Schelling meant seriously his emphatic thesis that God is "a life" and therefore "subject to suffering and becoming," he could not consistently hold to this conception of a transcendent Absolute who does not genuinely participate in the world-process in which his self-revelation consists. The two theologies still subsist side by side; but one of them is a survival, the other is an innovating idea which is on the point of destroying the former. (pp. 316-20)

F. H. Jacobi published in 1812 an essay, *Von den göttlichen Dingen und ihrer Offenbarung,* which was chiefly devoted to a vehement and (as Schelling afterwards described it) tearful attack upon this new way of thinking. In the issue which Schelling had raised, Jacobi saw the deepest-reaching antithesis in the entire philosophy of religion. "There can," he wrote,

> be only two principal classes of philosophers: those who regard the more perfect (*Vollkommnere*) as derived from, as gradually developed out of, the less perfect, and those who affirm that the most perfect being was first, and that all things have their source in him; that the first principle of all things was a moral being, an intelligence willing and acting with wisdom—a Creator—God.

Jacobi's reply is rambling and dogmatic; but he takes his stand finally upon what he regards as a self-evident and fundamental axiom of metaphysics: that something cannot "come from nothing" nor the superior be "produced by" the inferior. Such a philosophy as Schelling's, in fact, is, Jacobi asserts, a direct contradiction of a law of formal logic. For, as he observes—the observation is a commonplace of Platonistic theology—the relation of God to the world may, among other things, be conceived as the relation of a logical *prius,* a *Beweisgrund* or reason, to its consequences, the implications deducible from it. But "always and necessarily a *Beweisgrund* must be *above* that which is to be proved by means of it, and must subsume the latter under it; it is from the *Beweisgrund* that truth and certitude are imparted to those things which are demonstrated by means of it; from it they borrow their reality."

To this attack Schelling replied in a piece of controversial writing celebrated for its ferocity and for the damage which it did, at least in the eyes of his contemporaries, to the philosophical reputation of his critic. What is pertinent here is the fact that the attack caused Schelling, not to tone down his theological evolutionism, but to give it more radical and more nearly unqualified expression than before. He might conceivably have met the criticism by pointing out the passages in his previous writings in which the infinity, timelessness, and self-sufficiency of the Abso

lute Identity had been recognized. So far is he from doing this that he now almost unequivocally repudiates such a conception, and quite expressly denies that such an Absolute can be the God of religion. From Jacobi's formulation of the issue, and his estimate of its philosophical significance, Schelling does not dissent; nor does he repudiate his critic's account of the essentials of his doctrine. It is, indeed, Schelling observes, needful to make some distinctions, if the meaning of the doctrine is properly to be understood. Those who held it did not, for example, maintain that the "more perfect sprang from a less perfect being *independent of* and different from itself," but simply that "the more perfect has risen from its own less perfect condition." Nor, accordingly, did they deny that, in a sense, "the all-perfect being—that which has the perfections of all other things in itself—must be *before* all things." But they did deny that it thus pre-existed as perfect *actu* and not merely *potentia.* "To believe that it did," says Schelling,

> is difficult for many reasons, but first of all for the very simple one that, if it were in actual possession of the highest perfection [or completeness], it would have had no reason (*Grund*) for the creation and production of so many other things, through which it—being incapable of attaining a higher degree of perfection—could only fall to a lower one.

Here the central contradiction inherent in the logic of emanationism—but for so many centuries persistently disregarded—was pointed out with the utmost sharpness. The promise and potency, then, of all that evolution should unfold might, if one cared to insist on this, be said to pre-exist from the beginning; but it was a promise unfulfilled and a potency unrealized:

> I posit God [says Schelling] as the first and the last, as the Alpha and the Omega; but as Alpha he is not what he is as Omega, and in so far as he is only the one—God 'in an eminent sense'—he can not be the other God, in the same sense, or, in strictness, be called God. For in that case, let it be expressly said, the unevolved (*unentfaltete*) God, *Deus implicitus,* would already be what, as Omega, the *Deus explicitus* is.

Upon what grounds, in the face of Jacobi's objections, does Schelling justify this evolutionary theology? First of all on the ground that it accords with the actual character of the world of our experience, as that character is disclosed to our everyday observation and to the more comprehensive vision of natural science. On the face of it, the world is, precisely, a system in which the higher habitually develops out of the lower, fuller existence out of emptier. The child grows into a man, the ignorant become learned; "not to mention that nature itself, as all know who have the requisite acquaintance with the subject, has gradually risen from the production of more meagre and inchoate creatures to the production of more perfect and more finely formed ones." A process which is constantly going on before our eyes can hardly be the inconceivability which Jacobi had made it out to be. The new philosophy had simply interpreted the general or 'ultimate' nature of things, and their order in being, in the light of the known nature and sequences of all particular things with which we are acquainted. The "ordinary theism," defended by Jacobi, had, on the contrary, given us "a God who is alien to na ture and a nature that is devoid of God—*ein unnatürlicher Gott und eine gottlose Natur.*"

Again, Schelling observes, the fact of evil, the imperfection of the world, is irreconcilable with the belief that the universe proceeds from a being perfect and intelligent *ab initio.* Those who hold this belief "have no answer when they are asked how, from an intelligence so clear and lucid, a whole so singularly confused (even when brought into *some* order) as the world can have arisen." In every way, then, Schelling finds the picture of reality which accords with the facts is that of a more or less confused and troubled ascent towards fuller and higher life; and the only admissible conception of God is that which is in harmony with this picture. Nor has the contrary view, he declares, the religiously edifying and consoling character to which it pretends. For it "derives the not-good from the Good, and makes God, not the source and potentiality of the good, but the source and potentiality of the not-good." Conceived—as in the theology of absolute becoming it is conceived—as a good in the making, *als ein ins gute Verwandelbares,* evil or imperfection itself is not the hopeless and senseless piece of reality which it must be if conceived as good in the *un*making, as a lapse from a perfection already realized. The God of all the older theology, moreover, had been a God eternally complete, "ready-made once for all," as Schelling puts it. But no conception could be more barren and unprofitable than this; for it is really the conception of "a dead God," not of the God that lives and strives in nature and in man. It is inconceivable, Jacobi had declared, that life should arise out of death, being out of non-being, higher existences out of lower. Is it, then, asked Schelling, easier to conceive that death should arise out of life? "What could move the God who is not a God of the dead but of the living, to produce death. Infinitely more conceivable is it that out of death—which cannot be an absolute death, but only the death which has life concealed within it—life should arise, than that life should pass over into, should lose itself in, death."

Jacobi's error, however—Schelling observes—is a natural consequence of the logical doctrine of the older philosophy from which he never fully emancipated himself; it is, indeed, the crowning example of the pernicious results in metaphysics of the acceptance of the Wolffian theory of knowledge, which based everything upon the logical Principle of Identity, and regarded all certain judgments as "analytical." According to this view, says Schelling—not with entire historical accuracy—"all demonstration is merely a progression in identical propositions, there is no advance from one truth to a different one, but only from the same to the same. The tree of knowledge never comes to bloom or to fruitage; there is nowhere any *development.*" But true philosophy and truly objective science are not a chanting of tautologies. Their object is always a concrete and living thing; and *their* progress and evolution is a progress and evolution of the object itself. "The right method of philosophy is an ascending, not a descending, one"; and its true axiom is precisely opposite to that pseudo-axiom which Jacobi had enunciated:

> Always and necessarily that from which development proceeds (*der Entwicklungsgrund*) is lower than that which is developed; the former raises the latter above itself and subjects itself to it, inasmuch as it serves as the matter, the organ, the condition, for the other's development.

It is—as has too little been noted by historians—in this introduction of a radical evolutionism into metaphysics and theology, and in the attempt to revise even the principles of logic to make them harmonize with an evolutional conception of reality, that the historical significance of Schelling chiefly consists. The question at issue in his controversy with Jacobi is, indeed, as he clearly recognized and emphatically declared, one of the most fundamental and momentous of all philosophical questions, both by its relation to many other theoretical problems, and also by its consequences for the religious consciousness. Schelling's thesis meant not only the discarding of a venerable and almost universally accepted axiom of rational theology and metaphysics, but also the emergence of a new mood and temper of religious feeling. (pp. 321-25)

> *Arthur O. Lovejoy, "The Outcome of the History and Its Moral," in his* The Great Chain of Being: A Study of the History of an Idea, *Cambridge, Mass.: Harvard University Press, 1966, pp. 315-33.*

Emil L. Fackenheim   (essay date 1954)

[*Fackenheim is a German-born Canadian rabbi and philosopher who specializes in modern Jewish philosophy. In the following excerpt, Fackenheim defends Schelling's philosophy as outlined in* Philosophie der Mythologie und Offenbarung.]

When Schelling died a hundred years ago (August 20, 1854), his contemporaries' opinion of him might be summarized as follows. A precocious thinker, Schelling made a great contribution to philosophy around the year 1800, when he was still in his twenties. But he lacked system and thoroughness, and his contribution was soon assimilated and superseded by the system of Hegel. Moreover, he lacked stability. While Hegel spent his whole life working out his system, Schelling changed his standpoint so often as to drive his interpreters to despair. Finally, at least from 1804 on (when Schelling was not yet thirty) these changes were for the worse, for he moved more and more toward mysticism and obscurantism.

This appraisal became conventional opinion, and has remained conventional opinion until this day. In practically any history of philosophy which bothers with Schelling at all one can find this threefold condemnation of his work: that it consists of a number of more or less disconnected systems; that none of these is properly worked out; and that from 1804 on, they get worse and worse. As a result of this opinion, few historians have been interested in Schelling. When in 1944 air raids destroyed the Munich University Library, among the treasures destroyed were thousands of Schelling manuscript pages, mostly written in his later years. It seems that in nearly one hundred years nobody was sufficiently interested in these manuscripts to do anything with them.

But during the last few decades interest in Schelling has revived, at least in Germany and France. This new interest reflects the beginnings of a revision of judgment; indeed, a drastic revision. This is illustrated by the fact that this new interest centers on Schelling's last phase, the phase hitherto most neglected. It is a pity that this revival came too late to make possible the publication of more than a fraction of the manuscripts, before their destruction.

As a result of the new investigations, it has already become clear that the conventional opinion of Schelling is grossly unjust. That opinion is based on the judgment of the contemporaries or near-contemporaries. And these were subject to prejudices which made an adequate understanding of Schelling difficult, if not impossible. Schelling's critics were theologians, positivists and Hegelians. If they were theologians, they looked to Schelling for an apologetic which they did not get, nor were meant to get. If they were positivists, they had even less sympathy with Schelling than they had with Hegel. And if they were Hegelians (as most of them were), they saw the most important criterion of judgment in systematic completeness, the very point in which Schelling was weakest; further, they were bound to regard his development after 1804 as an aberration or an outright betrayal.

To be sure, the conventional opinion is not entirely mistaken. Schelling does lack system and thoroughness; and his consequent tendency to mix the ill-considered, or even the absurd, with the profound confounds the present student as it did the past. But Hegelian prejudices have led to an exaggeration of this vice. Schelling may be weak in execution, but he is strong indeed in programmatic statement. Moreover, the latter strength accounts at least in part for the former weakness. Schelling was able to penetrate with extraordinary swiftness to first principles and ultimate implications. No sooner had he conceived a system than he perceived implications which made it problematic. While others would plod along, working out the details of a system Schelling had outlined, he himself already found it necessary to go beyond it. Thus time and again he faced philosophical crises. If Schelling never worked out any of his systems, this is in part because his systematic tendency was forever at war with his aporematic. But theologians, positivists and Hegelians had this in common: if they were prepared to admit philosophical crises at all, they regarded them as resolved, once and for all.

Because of their blindness to the aporematic element in Schelling's thought, the critics arrived at the opinion that his various systems were more or less disconnected. But this is in fact far from the case. The new system tends to spring from the problems created by the old. Indeed, it is doubtful whether there is any discontinuity in Schelling's development at all. The modern student who fails to perceive a connection does well to suspect that the fault lies, not with Schelling, but with himself.

Because of their prejudices, the critics have been particularly unjust to the philosophy of Schelling's old age. Schelling here made the most radical shift of his entire career. He repudiated absolute idealism, and turned to what can only be called a post-idealistic metaphysics. Absolute idealism now became a mere "negative philosophy," i.e., a mere preface (though a necessary preface) to metaphysics proper, or a "positive philosophy," which did not as yet exist. But Schelling's critics were either hostile to all metaphysics, or else hostile to all but Hegelian metaphysics. Hence they were unable or unwilling to take the program of the positive philosophy seriously. As a result of their prejudices, Schelling's four volume *Philosophie der Mythologie und Offenbarung* is still little known, and less understood.

But the climate of philosophical opinion has changed, and in such a way as to explain the new interest in the philosophy of Schelling's old age. At least one school of contemporary thought can approach that philosophy with sympathy, if not enthusiasm. This is existentialism. Existentialist thought, whatever else it is, is post-idealist, not simply non-idealist or anti-idealist. One might almost say that existentialism is misunderstood to the degree to which this fact is ignored. It is no accident that existentialists tend to see the decisive event for modern metaphysics in the collapse of Hegelianism in the middle of the nineteenth century; and it is a most suggestive fact that practically every existentialist seems to have to struggle with Hegel. This would appear to indicate an agreement that one can neither return to a pre-idealist metaphysics, nor remain with idealism. But this is precisely the conviction which gives rise to Schelling's positive philosophy. (pp. 563-66)

In almost literal anticipation of Heidegger, Schelling asks: "why does anything exist at all? why is there not rather nothing?" The dialectic constructs *a priori* what can be; it knows nothing of existence.

Schelling does not ask: *does* anything exist? The existence of the world is an empirical fact, and the dialectic is object-related from the start: it understands characteristics of the real world. The problem is that dialectic cannot understand the *meaning* of existence; and this means for Schelling that dialectic cannot absorb existence into a system. Dialectic is fragmentary knowledge and must turn to experience for the knowledge of fact.

It might appear, then, that the dialectic constructs *a priori* the nature of the actual world. If so, the positive philosophy would have to answer only a single question: why does this world—which is the only possible world—exist? But this would be to misunderstand Schelling's conception and to reduce it to nonsense. If existence resists dialectical absorption, so does individuality. Reality is not in fact the internal unity which it is in ideal construction. The facts not only appear to, but really do, fall outside each other; and their irrational infinity is as inaccessible to dialectic as the fact of existence itself. Experience encounters, as a brute fact, externality; and along with externality meaninglessness and evil. Thus the second question arises for the new philosophy: why is what exists in discrepancy with what it ideally ought to be? Why is the world "questionable"?

The questions posed by the positive philosophy may well appear non-sensical. How can one ask for the meaning of the meaningless? The meaningless is either ultimately not meaningless, or else it is a brute fact. Schelling emphatically rejects the former alternative: is he, then, not driven toward a simple acceptance of the facts, surrendering the quest for their meaning as itself meaningless? But this would be to ignore the negative achievement of the dialectic. All empirical fact, while indissoluble into dialectic, is yet subject to all-pervasive dialectical qualifications. Dialectic isolates this character of the facts and thus shows them to be in need of explanation. Because of its abstracting from their factuality, dialectic at the same time reveals itself as incapable of the explanation required. Dialectic is thus "negative philosophy," in a double sense. It negates absolute idealism as being a false philosophy, and empiricism as being no philosophy at all.

Internal unity and externality, the *a priori* meaningful and the *a priori* meaningless, are both real characters of the real world; their togetherness in the same world is the problem requiring a solution. This is the situation which gives rise to the positive philosophy.

The questions of the positive philosophy are not nonsensical, but can they be answered? *Qua* dialectically qualified, the facts demand an absolute in terms of which they may be explained; but *qua* facts, they can be explained by no mere idea. The first principle of the positive philosophy cannot be an absolute Idea, but only an absolute Fact. But such a fact is beyond all possible human knowledge. For wherever knowledge grasps fact, it is fact dialectically qualified; and wherever it grasps an Absolute, it is mere idea.

Here the negative philosophy carries out its third and most important negation. It has negated relative fact, as being relative; it has negated absolute Idea, as being mere idea. It now discovers that it cannot think of the Absolute other than as idea, and that it can negate it as such only by negating itself as well. The negative philosophy therefore brings about a radical "crisis of reason" and sets the stage for a radical leap.

"The last aim of rational philosophy," says Schelling, "is to reach God as separate from all relative being." This aim it reaches in one sense, but fails to reach in another. Examples are Aristotle's *actus purus,* or the "necessarily existent" of the scholastics. Rational philosophy here has, in its independence, the principle on which everything depends; but it has it as a mere idea. And this means that the end of rational philosophy, far from being the end of all philosophy, involves a paradox requiring a wholly new point of departure. Rational philosophy is driven to the idea of an absolute Individual who necessarily exists; but this idea, *qua* idea, is universal and non-existent. The form and the content of this idea are in necessary contradiction. In its highest idea reason necessarily points beyond itself; but, equally necessarily, it fails to achieve this beyond. Schelling refers to this pointing-beyond when he says that reason, in its crisis, becomes "ec-static."

Rational philosophy here reaches an unavoidable impasse. From the start, it necessarily abstracts from existence; but what it must *mean* in its last term is the pure Existent beyond all essence. But it cannot attain what it means.

This deadlock can be broken only if it is remembered that rational philosophy, as a whole, is merely the abstract expression of a concrete spiritual condition; it has an existential setting. The idea of God is not only the last concept of reason; it is also the highest expression of a spiritual attitude, viz., philosophical contemplation. In contemplation the philosophizing person seeks to sublate in an Absolute, not just existence in general, but his own personal existence. Contemplation is an attempt at self-surrender and self-oblivion. But just as a mere idea will not absorb any existence, so it will not absorb my own. The logical paradox here turns into a personal paradox which the philosopher lives and suffers. "The self might be satisfied with the purely ideal God, if he could remain in this state of contemplation. But this is impossible. The surrender of action cannot be carried out. Action is inevitable . . . the former despair returns."

Thus for objective philosophical reasons, subjective per-

sonal interest enters. "The last idea of reason . . . has this peculiarity, that the philosophizing subject cannot be indifferent to its existence or non-existence. Here the watchword is: *Tua res agitur.*" The pure Existent is inaccessible to rational detachment because it abstracts from the existence of the thinker.

The finite spirit is in search of the existing God. But in his life he asserts himself and thus has only finite existence; and in his contemplation he has God, but merely in idea. Existence and idea cannot be synthesized in thought. But they can be synthesized in *will.* From the lonely despair brought about by the search for God, a search at once rational and existential, arises the will, not to posit Him—for any such God would again be idea only—but to accept Him, as prior to all thought and experience. Decision is the radical leap from the last idea of the negative to the first principle of the positive philosophy.

This leap is indeed radical and outside all reason. But it is not arbitrary. The predicament from which it arises is the human condition itself, in which rationality itself is rooted. Thus the individual philosopher has the choice only between taking this leap, or remaining within the sphere of the negative philosophy. "The positive philosophy is genuinely free philosophy: the person who does not will it may leave it alone." (pp. 569-74)

Emil L. Fackenheim, "Schelling's Conception of Positive Philosophy," in Review of Metaphysics, *Vol. VII, No. 4, June, 1954, pp. 563-82.*

Ernst Benz   (essay date 1954)

[*Benz was a German philosopher. In the following excerpt from an essay originally published in* Eranos-Jahrbücher *in 1954, he outlines Schelling's approach to mythology.*]

Schelling's approach to mythology takes on a special significance in the light of [the] rediscovery of myth by modern psychology. Consideration of his philosophy of mythology contributes to the modern discussion of the subject something that was previously lacking, namely, the historical factor, an awareness of the relation between the development of mythology and the history of mankind. Modern psychology treats the mythological tradition essentially as a storeroom in which a vast number of mythical archetypes are lined up side by side; according to the psychological or psychopathic state of the individual case, the psychologist picks out this or that archetype as the times or circumstances may require, and employs it as a means of clarifying and overcoming certain psychic tensions and conflicts. The choice of the archetype to be taken from the storeroom is determined largely by the taste and educational level of both physician and patient. But in the storeroom all manner of archetypal variants are jumbled together. Tibetan, Cabalistic, Manichaean, and Christian symbolisms must all pay to psychology their tribute in archetypes and help the psychologist fathom the secret of the psyche beset by the collective unconscious. The mythological tradition of the various nations and religions is, in the words of the New Testament, a "treasure" from which the psychological "house-holder" brings forth "things new and old" as he needs them (Matt. 13:52).

In this situation the utmost importance must be accorded to Schelling's insight that mythology has its history, that the history of mankind and its spiritual and psychic development is the history of myths or, more accurately, of mythmaking, mythogenesis, the mysterious process by which the mythical archetypes grew. Each individual myth has its necessary place within this history. The epoch when a myth made its appearance, when a mythical archetype rose to consciousness, when a god was born and died, is no accident or matter of indifference, for the history of myths, the mythogenic process, is the history of human consciousness. Ultimately, so Schelling believed, this history—and that is what gives it paramount importance—is identical with the history of God himself. The pages of the history of myth are the records of the true theogony.

The mythological traditions of mankind present us with mountains of data that seem to defy all orderly classification. Yet by dint of intense study and an admirable speculative intuition Schelling derived from them a history of myth which to his mind represented the surest index of the history of human consciousness. He believed it to be the history of man's prehistoric development and at the same time of the theogony.

Let us now attempt to enter into Schelling's principal ideas on mythology.

1. In Schelling's view—and to this he attaches the utmost importance—mythology is not theology, but a history of the gods. It presupposes and follows mythogenesis; and theogony, which is a form of mythology, already implies reflection on mythogenesis. In addition to the reigning gods, every mythological system includes some notion of previous gods whom they dethroned. Every polytheistic religion conceives of itself as the outcome of a history, a process of succession: there is always a supreme god who is known to be the successor of another god. After Uranos comes Kronos, after Kronos Zeus. Thus mythology is fundamentally related to history. Myths mark strata in the millennial development of the human spirit; their succession forms a spiritual analogy to biological phylogenesis.

In his very first statement of this relation between myth and history, Schelling invokes the Judaeo-Christian conception of the revelation of God in history: "In so far as revelation sets even the true God in a historical relation to mankind, it seems conceivable that the divine history, given with revelation, had become the substance of polytheism, that its elements had been distorted. A development of mythology from revelation in this sense might have offered a good many noteworthy insights." Here Schelling suggests the possibility that the mythological history of the gods may be a decomposition and distortion of the historical revelation, in which the true God enters into a historical relation with mankind. Thus, at the very beginning of Schelling's study, he attempts to understand the history of mythology on the basis of a Christian history of mankind.

2. How does mythology come into being? What gives rise to "successive polytheism"? When does the history of mythology begin? What brings about the transformation that occurs in the emergence of mythology, of successive polytheism? To these questions Schelling gives the following answer: The origin of mythology cannot be explained "un-

less we presuppose a definite removal of man from his original standpoint." Man was removed from his original standpoint and only then did mythology come into being. This brings us to Schelling's view of the original condition of man, a conception in which he was strongly influenced by the mystical anthropology of Jakob Boehme and above all by Friedrich Christoph Oetinger, the Swabian theosophist. "Man," writes Schelling, "was created at the center of the godhead, and it is essential for him to be at the center, for that alone is his true place. As long as he is there, he sees the things that are in God, not with the usual outward vision bereft of spirit and unity; he sees them, rather, as they gradually coalesced, in man as their head and through him in God." Here Schelling is describing Oetinger's "Adamic insight," or Jakob Boehme's "Central Vision," but he puts a new interpretation on it in line with the idea of development characteristic of his own philosophy: the original man in his initial form sees all things as they are in God, and that means in their inherent order, as they are ultimately epitomized in man as the universal creature and through him are taken up in God. The world in its gradual unfolding is summed up in the consciousness of man, who is its head: man is the medium which communicates the world to God, through which the world is taken back into God. A true communication occurs only where man is wholly at the center of God, where he wholly fulfills his function as the head and integration of Creation. In this state there is no room for mythology, for man is essentially at the center of the godhead; he sees only the one God and all things in Him.

Mythology results from a fundamental change in the relation between man and God: man departs from his essential being in the center of the godhead.

> Once man moves away from the center, the periphery becomes confused for him and the divine unity is distorted, for he himself is no longer divinely above things, but has sunk down to the same level with them. But when, once moved, he strives to assert his central position and the view connected with it, his striving and struggle to hold fast the original unity in a world already shaken and shattered gives rise to the *middle world* which we call a world of the gods and which is, as it were, a *dream of a higher existence,* that man dreams for a while after he has fallen away from it. This world of the gods arises in his mind involuntarily, born of a necessity imposed on him by his original relationship, and endures until his *final awakening,* when, come to self-knowledge, he betakes himself to this extra-divine world, glad to be released from the immediate bond which he is unable to maintain, and all the more eager to replace it with a *mediate* relation which at the same time leaves him free.

Thus the removal of man is a removal from the center of God to the periphery of things. Through it he is reduced to the same level as things; he enters into a world where things are no longer one with God, but dispersed in their particularity, and he himself becomes a thing among things. Banished to the periphery, however, he yearns for the original unity with God and in God and attempts in his alienation to hold the lost unity fast. Alienated from his center, man dreams of his higher lost existence. His dream is mythology.

This sounds like a repetition of the Old Testament doctrine of Adam's fall from grace, and indeed in Jakob Boehme the doctrine of the original man and his loss of Central Vision is developed by allegorical exegesis from the Biblical story of Adam's fall. What distinguishes Schelling from Boehme is that he does not put the accent on man's voluntary transgression. "The world of the gods," he declares, is an "involuntary consequence of a necessity imposed on him by his original relation to God, and the effect of this necessity endures until his awakening." Thus man's original removal from the center of the godhead was itself a necessity, rooted in his own imperfection, in a fundamental deficiency. What was this deficiency?

Schelling replies on the basis of his idea of freedom. In his original immediate relation to God, man was not yet free; he had not yet exercised his freedom; he had to take the step from the center to the periphery in order to transform his immediate, that is to say, unfree relation to God into true love. Mythology is for man the way to freedom and true self-knowledge, to the true knowledge and love of God.

3. Schelling draws a connection between the genesis of mythology and the genesis of peoples, an insight that takes on the utmost importance in the light of modern discoveries concerning prehistoric times. History starts from the unity of mankind, grounded in a unitary principle.

> Such a principle, which left room for no other in the consciousness of man, which admitted of no other beside itself, could only be something infinite; it could only be a God, one God, who completely filled man's consciousness and was common to all mankind, a God who drew man into His own unity as it were, denying him . . . all movement or deviation: only a God of this kind could give permanence to such absolute immobility, to such an absence of development. But just as there was no force better calculated to maintain mankind in a state of unity and perfect rest than the unconditional unity of the God by which it was governed, so, on the other hand, we can conceive of no mightier and more profound upheaval than that which was bound to result when that which hitherto had been unalterably One was itself set in motion, and just this was inevitable once another, or several other, gods appeared in, or emerged from, man's consciousness. This polytheism—however it began . . .—made impossible an enduring unity of the human race. And so polytheism is the ferment of disintegration that was cast among mankind.

Thus the peoples rose not from physical causes but from spiritual movements connected with the first great "removal of mankind." The peoples did not first come into being and then create their myths, but the other way round: it is the mythology of a people that determines its character and history, "or rather, mythology does not determine, but *is* that people's fate (just as a man's character is his fate), its destiny that was allotted to it in the very beginning. Who will deny that the entire history of the Indians, the Greeks, etc., was given them with their theology?"

In the connection between the origins of peoples and of languages Schelling finds confirmation of his view that the peoples emerged from a spiritual movement. The diversification of the one language, which had hitherto been common to all men, meant that the spiritual power which had held mankind in a state of perfect equality was shaken.

This power, which dominated man's consciousness, was the one God. Its breakdown into successive polytheisms was the spiritual cause of the differentiation of the one language into many languages. Once removed from the center of God, the peoples saw things from their various positions on the periphery; seeing them differently, they designated them differently, just as they saw their God in different ways and gave Him different names.

Thus a people is, and develops after the manner of, its mythology. "A people exists as such only after defining itself and making its decision in its mythology." Mythology cannot come into being once a people has defined itself and completed its separation from mankind; nor can mythology arise as long as a people is an invisible part, encompassed in the whole of mankind. No, mythology arises in "the transitional stage, when a people has not yet defined itself but is in the process of separating and closing itself off from mankind."

It is, then, the decision for a particular mythology, a particular God, that creates a people. Not an outside force, but an inner unrest, the feeling that it is no longer all mankind but only a part of it, that it no longer belongs to the absolute One, but has devolved to a particular god or gods—this is the feeling that drives peoples "from land to land, from coast to coast, until each one has found itself alone, separated from all alien peoples, and has found its own appropriate and allotted place."

4. But before we follow the process further, we must cast another glance at the removal of man from the center. Originally, Schelling writes, "mankind was at the center of God, had its being at the center of God," but this state was not a state of perfection, for man was captive; he had not yet exercised his freedom. Mankind was in a state of absolute rest, it had not begun to develop. Though Schelling describes the loss of this condition, the step from the center to the periphery, as a loss of the middle, as an entrance into a dreamlike state, nevertheless, he regards the new state as a step forward, the first step toward true and complete knowledge. Despite appearances to the contrary (and although it is impossible to explain this from our present standpoint), polytheism was truly a transition on the way to a better state, toward the liberation of mankind from a power, in itself beneficent, which, however, repressed its freedom, impeded all development, and so stood in the way of the highest knowledge. Here we see the essential connection between Schelling's philosophy of mythology and his idea of freedom. Removal from the center and dispersion were necessary steps toward freedom; mythology, polytheism, was a necessary path to the liberation of mankind, which is the end of the mythological development.

The process here described has a direct parallel in the theological speculations developed by Schelling in ***The Ages of the World.*** In this work he attempted nothing less than a history of God, an account of His inner movement before He manifested Himself with the creation of the world. Schelling's theology, like his anthropology, is influenced by the speculations of Jakob Boehme and of Oetinger, the Swabian theosophist, who both conceived of a development within God Himself leading from an inner cleavage to the full unfolding of the divine essence. "If primal nature were in harmony with itself, it would remain; there would be an abiding one and never a two, an eternal immobility without progress. As certainly as there is life, there is contradiction in primal nature. . . . Without contradiction there would be no motion, no life, no progress, but eternal immobility, a deathly slumber of all powers." A contradiction lies at the base of the movement toward unity.

In his theory of potency Schelling described this inner movement of God in greater detail.

> There can therefore be no doubt that, if there is to be a succession among the primordial powers of life, only that which encloses and forces back the essence can be the first. What is first in God after the decision, or, since we must assume this decision as having *happened* from all eternity (and hence as still happening), that which is absolutely first in God, in the living God, the eternal beginning of himself in himself, withdraws his essence from without, and retires into himself. . . . But the divine nature does not suffer God to be merely eternal. No, eternal denial of himself; it is likewise his nature to be an essence of all essences, the infinitely self-giving and self-communicating. Thus, while he hides his essence, by virtue of the eternal necessity of his nature, the eternal affirmation of his nature opposes that negation (which is certainly not to be annulled, but remains, although now retreating into the negative). On the other hand, the eternal affirmation thus represses the negating power and precisely thereby develops into an independent being.

But the primal essence as such "remains in a state of perpetual desire, as an incessant seeking, an eternal, never quieted passion to be."

But the first state is not perfection. "To be infinite is by itself no perfection; rather it is the token of the imperfect." So long as the first nature remains nothing but an irresistible urge, so long as "it is not lifted out of this involuntary movement," no freedom is conceivable in it. "It cannot itself avoid this movement; it can only be removed from this movement by something else, and, unquestionably, by something higher," namely, the eternal freedom to be. "God, with respect to his highest self, is not a necessarily real being, but the eternal freedom to be." His development leads from the first nature, which is pure life, pure urge, to eternal freedom. "But in that eternally beginning life there lies the desire to escape from involuntary movement and urgency; and by its mere presence, without any movement (for it is still pure willing itself), as if magically, what is higher awakens the longing for freedom in it. Passionate urge softens into longing, wild desire dissolves into yearning to ally itself, as with its own true or highest self, with the will which wills nothing, with eternal freedom."

Thus there is an intimate connection between God's way to Himself and the way of mankind. The way of man is the way out of the center of God, out of the state of untried freedom, through an existence on the periphery of things, where he tests things in their intrinsic being, and then, endowed with the experience of freedom, back to the center of God. This way of mankind is at the same time the way of a true theogony. In the history of human consciousness, the mysterious history of the gods is enacted, and in the history of the gods there arises the true God, who in the development of human consciousness comes to consciousness of Himself.

The original monotheism of mankind before its entrance into history was no true monotheism, but a henotheism. Its object was not the true One, but a one-sided one, a merely relative monotheism. The elements of the true One, which enters into history only at the end of the mythological development, unfold in successive polytheism; thus mythology is the true genesis of God.

Schelling sums up this idea in a passage that forms the very core of his *Philosophy of Mythology.* This passage provides the key to his interpretations of particular myths, to his view of the history of mythology, and also to his conception of revelation:

> Mythology comes into being through a necessary process (necessary in respect to consciousness), the origin of which loses itself in a suprahistorical realm. Consciousness may resist the process in certain particulars, but cannot impede, much less reverse, it as a whole. . . . Mythological ideas are neither invented nor voluntarily accepted.— Products of a process independent of thought and will, they were unequivocally and undeniably real for the consciousness subjected to them. Peoples and individuals are only *instruments of this process, which they do not perceive as a whole, which they serve without understanding it.* It is not in their power to cast off these ideas, to accept them or not to accept them: for these ideas do not come from outside but are within the mind and men never know how they arise: for they come from the innermost consciousness, on which they imprint themselves with a necessity that permits no doubt as to their truth. . . . Mythology is not allegorical but tautegorical. For it the gods are really existing beings; they are not something else and do not mean something else, but only what they are. . . . The process that creates mythology has its ground and beginning in the first real consciousness of mankind. . . . The succession [of gods within the mythological process] is a movement to which consciousness is actually subjected, a movement *that really takes place.* Even the particulars of the sequence, the fact that this god is followed by that god and not by another, is not arbitrary but necessary, and even when the events and circumstances that make up the history of the gods seem very strange to us, it will always be possible to show from what state of consciousness these representations naturally flowed. . . . Objectively considered, mythology is what it claims to be, true theogony, a history of the gods: but since only those gods who are grounded in God are true gods, the ultimate content of the history of the gods is the Creation, *the real genesis in consciousness of God* to whom the other gods are related only as generative factors.

> Subjectively or genetically, mythology is a theogonic process. It is a *process* that consciousness really effects; in so doing it is compelled to stop at each successive stage which encompasses the preceding stage. Thus it is a movement in the truest sense. It is a real theogonic process, that is, one that is prescribed by an essential relation of the human consciousness to God, a relation grounded in its substance, for in substance the human consciousness is that which naturally (*natura sua*) postulates God. Because the original relationship is a natural

one, consciousness cannot depart from it without inaugurating a process that leads back to it. Thus the human consciousness cannot help manifesting itself as that which produces God, as theogonic.

To the process taking place in the human consciousness there corresponds a real theogonic process, which, according to Schelling, goes back to an objective process in God Himself. And so, speaking of the origin of the peoples, he writes: "When the very same God, who maintained unity as long as He remained undeviatingly identical to Himself, became unlike Himself and variable, it was inevitable that He should disperse the human race just as He had formerly held it together. And just as in His identity He had been the cause of its unity, so in His multiplicity He became the cause of its dispersion."

5. In saying that the mythological process is governed by a necessity of which the peoples and individuals caught up in it are unaware, Schelling is already implying that the whole process of human development is guided by a plan of salvation. Schelling's idea recalls Hegel's "artful device" of reason, which makes use of individuals and peoples in order to carry out its higher plan.

His conception of a necessity inherent in the mythological process leads Schelling to conclude that the process as a whole is both meaningful and beneficial. He expressly rejects the purely negative evaluation of polytheism put forward by the orthodox apologists of the Church. "The usual lamentation about the decline of pure knowledge and its degeneration into polytheism is consequently no more appropriate to the religious standpoint than it is to philosophy or to any true history." Of course polytheism reveals innumerable aberrations, but "false religion as such is never anything more than a dead and hence meaningless vestige of a process which as a whole is grounded in truth." Here again it is clear that he regards the mythological process in the last analysis as part of a general development of mankind toward salvation.

Here we cannot go into the particular degrees and phases of the mythological process as Schelling saw it. It must be remembered that he had only the mythological knowledge of his time to work with. In the past hundred years, research in the history of religions has made great advances. At Schelling's time inquiry, generally speaking, had been limited to the myths of Greek and Roman antiquity. The study of Indian and Egyptian religions was at its beginnings, and only the barest fragments of the religious lore of the ancient Orient had become known. For his time Schelling was amazingly well versed in the religious history of mankind, but since then his knowledge of the mythological material, as well as the interpretation at which he arrived by combining the available data, has long been superseded. Nevertheless, his reflections on the development of mythology are full of profound insights, which, with all our advances in knowledge, retain their significance for anyone who wishes to interpret myths. And such a work as Schelling's treatise **On the Gods of Samothrace** will surely meet with far more understanding today than at the time of its appearance. It is very easy to criticize the details of Schelling's interpretation of ancient myths on the basis of our new knowledge. Criticism of this sort, however, detracts in no way from the value of Schelling's general conception of mythological development as a theogonic process. It would be more accurate to say that a good many

of our students of comparative religion—of varying tendencies—are to blame for their failure to recognize Schelling's insights into the genetic development of myths. For today it is a matter of fundamental necessity that, with our wider knowledge of the history of religions, we resume Schelling's efforts to work out a genetic history of religion which will also be the story of man's earliest development.

Schelling's interpretation of the development of mythology as the pre-history of the human consciousness is still of the utmost relevance to many of the cultural sciences. First of all, there is its bearing on the modern study of mythology and comparative religion. One cannot simply compare everything with everything else. The various myths and religions bear witness to different stages in the development of the human consciousness, to different levels in man's psychic development and knowledge. In the living religions of today we have before us a symbiosis of representations rooted in the most divergent epochs, reflecting the most diverse dimensions of vision and strata of psychic experience. A theogonic conception of the history of religion takes on a particular importance in the light of the discovery that men have inhabited the earth for at least 600,000 years. For aside from the cave paintings of the ice age, the mythical tradition is our only source of information about man's spiritual and religious development during the greater part of this long, obscure period.

A genetic conception should also clarify the psychologist's understanding of the archetype. There is surely a close connection between the development of the individual and that of mankind. Every individual draws on the treasure of images that mankind has assembled over the thousands of years in which it has been viewing the universe, and each one of us is as old as the world. Our primordial ancestors of the Tertiary period are still alive in our darkest depths; the image-creating power of those ancestors who laid the foundations of our cultural heritage is still at work. Our intellectual culture derives from the Greeks and Romans, from Aristotle and the *corpus juris,* but the formation of our deeper strata goes back to the innumerable generations of older ancestors who wrote no books, who achieved their first form of expression in the symbolic art of the cave paintings and in myths. But these myths were recorded in fragments by men of a far later age, who often misunderstood them completely, and only the scientists of a later day learned to interpret them as records of a primordial history of the human soul, as the story of its endeavors to know its essence, origin, and goal.

Schelling's ideas become particularly significant in connection with the relation of Christianity to the non-Christian religions. A new conception of this relation is one of the vital needs of our time. For three reasons: For one thing, the attitude embodied in the old apologetics has become obsolete. Today great demographic movements and the global character of economic and political life have created an entirely new form of coexistence and encounter between the great world religions. Furthermore, the non-Christian religions have embarked on a missionary activity which not only competes with Christianity in what has hitherto been its exclusive preserve but has even made inroads on the secularized society of the Christian mother countries.

The existence of great economic and political blocs demands and indeed necessitates an entirely new form of solidarity among the members of different religions who share the same living conditions. It was possible to condemn a foreign religion totally and fundamentally only so long as Christians had no occasion to become personally acquainted with its adherents; such an attitude became utterly untenable once the Christian was compelled to live with them for better or worse and put his old dogmatic judgments to the test. An experience that was formerly the privilege of a few courageous scholars who investigated foreign religions and, regardless of dogmatic judgments, were not afraid to elucidate their positive religious content is today shared by many. I am speaking not only of educated men who through reading and travel have gained a personal impression of foreign religions but also of numerous members of Christian Churches who live in predominantly non-Christian countries and are obliged to form a community with their neighbors.

A final reason why a purely negative evaluation of non-Christian religions is no longer tenable is that a significant change has set in on the part of the non-Christian religions. Their spiritual leaders have also begun to examine the attitudes and doctrines of their faith with the methods of comparative religion and to criticize the spiritual development of Europe from their own point of view. Such a work as Radhakrishnan's *Eastern Religions and Western Thought,* in which the author critically examines the cultural and religious history of the Christian Occident from the standpoint of the Hindu, with a view to disclosing the points in which a true understanding between Christianity and Hinduism is possible, opens up a new epoch in the relations between the two great religions, an encounter far more appropriate than the old dogmatic monologues to the actual social and cultural structure of our time. In this connection Schelling's ideas take on a new relevance.

With his philosophy of mythology and revelation, Schelling—and herein perhaps lies the greatest significance of this work for our time—laid the foundation for a new view of the relation of Christianity to the non-Christian religions. He was determined not simply to take over or renew the traditional theological opinions and evaluations of this relation. He took a purely scientific point of view toward Christianity as well as other religions and declared expressly: "I intend to consider Christianity just as I have considered mythology; that is to say, I shall try to explain it as far as possible on the basis of its own premises or, in the last analysis, to let it explain itself." He made it very clear that his method has nothing in common with dogmatic theology:

> My aim is not agreement with any dogma of the Church. I have no interest in being what is termed orthodox, and indeed I should experience no difficulty whatsoever in being quite the opposite. To me Christianity is merely a phenomenon that I am trying to explain. As to its meaning, its true significance, we must appraise them according to the authentic documents of Christianity, just as we have sought, for example, to determine the significance of the religion of Dionysos or of some mythological idea through the utterances of the most reliable authors.

Thus Schelling qualifies his view of all religions including Christianity as purely scientific, the reverse of dogmatic.

And he concludes his discussion of Christianity with the remark:

> Moreover, we have merely explained Christianity by itself, just as our explanation of mythology was drawn from mythology itself. Christianity, and the same is true in the last analysis of all significant phenomena, contains the key to our understanding of it: that key is to be sought above all in indications of a divine plan prescribing an order of succession among the highest causes.

This approach carries an all-important consequence. Schelling sharply rejects the view held by many orthodox Protestants in those days—and today further reinforced by "dialectical theology"—to the effect that all non-Christian religions are heathen, hence the diametrical opposite of Christianity, and that all of them, whether primitive or highly developed, are purely and simply the work of demons, so that there can be no question of any continuity between Christianity and other religions. In consequence of this conception, the dialectical school of Protestant theology has taken a hostile attitude toward the scientific study of religions, so breaking off the great tradition of scholarship established by Protestant theologians of the nineteenth and twentieth centuries. And the consequences for the idea and practice of the Christian mission have been equally disastrous.

Schelling points out that the attitude in question is not only historically illogical but fundamentally blasphemous as well:

> If Christianity is nothing other than what it is ordinarily taken for, a mere negation of paganism . . . if Christianity has nothing positive in common with paganism, history falls into two separate halves with no point of contact; the whole continuity of history is broken, Christianity ceases to be the eternal religion it is, which being eternal must also be present in paganism, and becomes something that has been in existence only for a limited time. This is to disparage Christianity.

Schelling held that to tear history apart in this way was to reduce Christianity to an episode and so to blaspheme against God. The history of religions, he stated clearly, is a continuous unity from beginning to end. Even dogmatic theology finds a historical continuity between the Old and the New Testament. But this was not enough for Schelling. Considering the whole history of religions as a theogonic process in which mankind achieves self-awareness, he was bound to draw the entire religious development of the ancient world into the process.

At the very beginning of his *Philosophy of Mythology,* Schelling suggests (as we have seen just above) "that a development of mythology might offer much that is worthy of our attention concerning revelation." By this, as he goes on to say, he means that "the divine history given us in revelation became the substance of polytheism and its elements were distorted into mythological elements." This might sound as though, in comparing it to the Christian revelation, Schelling took a wholly negative view of pagan mythology, judging its contents to be distortions, cast-off shards, *disjecta membra* of revelation. Actually, his whole protracted discussion of the matter argues against a purely negative evaluation of mythology. On the whole, when man enters into a mythological movement and is carried along by it, he is "on the way to the truth; indeed, the mythological movement is itself the way to the truth." (pp. 209-23)

Ernst Benz, "Theogony and the Transformation of Man in Friedrich Wilhelm Joseph Schelling," in Man and Transformation: Papers from the Eranos Yearbooks, *edited by Joseph Campbell, translated by Ralph Manheim, Bollingen Series XXX, Pantheon Books, 1964, pp. 203-49.*

E. D. Hirsch, Jr. (essay date 1960)

[*Hirsch is an American critic and educator best known for his* Cultural Literacy: What Every American Needs to Know *(1987), a controversial indictment of the American educational system. In* Cultural Literacy, *Hirsch states that the average contemporary student is seriously ill-informed about basic historic and literary concepts, and supplies a list of names and terms that he considers indispensable. He expanded the list in* The Dictionary of Cultural Literacy: What Every American Needs to Know *(1988). In conjunction with these publications, Hirsch began the Cultural Literacy Foundation, an organization promoting the teaching of a shared core of knowledge in the nation's schools. In the following excerpt, Hirsch proposes that the works of Schelling and William Wordsworth express a common "pattern of experience" that he designates by the term "Enthusiasm."*]

The pattern of experience shared by Wordsworth and Schelling I call "Enthusiasm." This word, which I have borrowed from [German philosopher Karl] Jaspers, seems preferable, even with its unfortunate connotations, to the word romanticism. I prefer to say Enthusiasm and mean romanticism than to say romanticism and run the risk of raising antipathy and confusion. . . . Besides this, I have no right to claim a larger application for my description before its wider relevance is demonstrated. In any case, Enthusiasm, as I use the term, does not have its modern pejorative connotations but remains much closer to its root meaning: possessed by a god. The term does imply an optimistic and fervid outlook, but this has little in common with the impetuous and impermanent fervor the Germans call *Schwärmerei*. Enthusiasm implies a constant and sober way of confronting reality. There is no jumping from object to object in order to enjoy rapture for its own sake. It is a consistent and disciplined, yet highly affirmative way of experiencing things.

One basic pattern underlies all of Enthusiasm's experience. It might be called the pattern of mutual inclusiveness. To state the matter in purely abstract form, Enthusiasm opposes the notion that A is not Not-A. At one and the same time A is *both* A *and* Not-A. Everything belongs with and implies its other. At first glance, it would seem that Enthusiasm would be much concerned with paradox and, as a matter of fact, many of Enthusiasm's expressions seem highly paradoxical. However, Enthusiasm passes over its necessary paradoxes and focuses attention upon the ultimate reconciliation of things. It does so because it always senses a beyond in reference to which the apparent distinctions between things are overcome. It is the beyond which makes A equal Not-A, not the paradoxical nature

of the entities in themselves. It is the beyond which gives Enthusiasm its bright confidence and high expectancy.

On the surface, this pattern may seem very similar to mysticism with its denial of all distinctions. Sometimes, indeed, Enthusiasm may experience a mystical fusion with the beyond, but this is merely a moment within its experience as a whole. It is a necessary moment, one that sustains Enthusiasm's confidence and expectancy, but in the general course of experience the beyond remains unattained. The subject is always faced with distinctions *to be* overcome, distinctions like that between life and death, the ideal and the real. Yet, at the same time, the task of overcoming distinctions is already implicitly accomplished by the beyond. The *both-and* motif underlies every aspect of experience.

Enthusiasm, then, differs from mysticism in that it preserves a separation from its object. Except for rare mystical moments, the Enthusiast always has a sense of his own selfhood. Yet the distinction between the self and its object has a special character; it is at once separation *and* fusion. Subject and object do not exist in different strata of being but belong to the same essential reality. The subject feels a deep kinship with his object, and the relationship between them can be called a kind of love. There is an awareness of separateness in the relationship and, at the same time, a sense of identity.

Keats described the relationship better, perhaps, than anyone else when he spoke of "fellowship with essence." Subject and object are distinct, yet they have a deep kinship with one another because they both belong to the same essence of things. In Wordsworth and Schelling, this motif is omnipresent. "The external world," said Schelling, "lies open before us in order that we may find again in it the history of our own spirit." And he wrote of the "inner love and kinship which we bear to nature." In like manner, Wordsworth spoke of the "analogy betwixt The mind of man and nature," and he looked

> with feelings of fraternal love
> Upon those unassuming things, that hold
> A silent station in this beauteous world.

Because the subject is not radically different from his object neither has a preferential status. Humanness is thingness and vice versa. Wordsworth once spoke of the "human Soul of universal earth," and felt that

> deeply drinking in the soul of things
> We shall be wise perforce.

The poet always abjured those purely human concerns which eclipse "the impersonated thought." Wordsworth's poetry is at once highly subjective and highly impersonal, and these characteristics are ultimately identical, since they both spring from the sense of kinship between man and thing.

When Schelling proclaimed the *Ichheit* of all things, he was being no more a solipsist than Wordsworth was being when he approved "the impersonated thought." On the contrary, Schelling was denying that reality can be interpreted in purely human terms. With passionate irony, he attacked Fichte's limitation of ego to the I of human consciousness. For Schelling, ego is "simultaneously subjective and objective being." The external world has the same character which the internal world has; that is the very point which the *System of Transcendental Idealism* sets out to demonstrate, and it is the core of the *Identitätsphilosophie*. The philosophy of nature and the philosophy of consciousness are to be brought together, not by asserting, as Kant had done, that reality for us is a product of consciousness but by asserting that mind and the objective world have ultimately the same character. The early works of both Schelling and Hegel passionately attempt to overcome the purely human limitations spelled out in Kant's epistemology. Hegel characterized his whole system as an attempt to demonstrate substance as subject, and this doctrine parallels Wordsworth's notion that humanness is thingness and vice versa.

Despite its confidence in ultimate fusion, Enthusiasm does sense a kind of separation between man and thing, but it always tries to show that the separation is not fundamental and that it can be overcome. The bête noire of Enthusiasm is estrangement; it fights against all "disconnection dead and spiritless" [Wordsworth, "The Ruined Cottage"]; it pits all its energy against any radical separation of things. Kant's *Ding an sich* was insupportable to the early idealists, and they made it the center of philosophical discussion. They flatly rejected all doctrines which held that mind and the physical world belong to different strata of reality. Both Leibnitz and Kant were wrong. Schelling reproached the Kantian by saying that for him the "world and all reality is fundamentally foreign to our spirit." Kant is the devil's advocate; he leaves us "lonely and forsaken amidst the world, surrounded everywhere by spectres."

It was this kind of separation which Wordsworth also strove to overcome. He denied that there was a separate, purely human realm with purely human concerns. For him the countryside was valuable in itself but it was primarily valuable because there the human realm and physical reality truly come together. His poetry focuses on the juxtaposition of man and nature, not on nature alone. There is always a human figure as part of the landscape, although it may simply be the poet himself. Even then it is not simply the scene which the poet describes but also himself as part of the scene. The effect is that of a fellowship between man and nature, between the human and nonhuman. Wordsworth devotes a special section of his poetry to "Poems on the Naming of Places," commemorating, so to speak, the joining of the two realms. It is because the "infant Babe" is no Kantian that he is "bless'd":

No outcast he, bewilder'd and depress'd;
Along his infant veins are interfus'd
The gravitation and the filial bond
Of nature, that connect him with the world.

The child and the world are not fused but interfused. Reciprocity is the fundamental characteristic of the subject-object relationship. Neither the self nor the object loses its self-identity in the relationship, yet the two are joined through a process of "interfusion." The interfusion occurs because both sides have the same essence; subject and object engage in a loving dialectic. Fusion in separation or interfusion is precisely reciprocity, and reciprocity characterizes Wordsworth's own description of subject and object. For him the mind is "fitted" to the external world and

Theme this but little heard of among men—
The external World is fitted to the Mind.

A thing is not "out there," to itself and inaccessible; by the very similarity of its nature to our own, it strikes a responsive chord within us. Yet the object is not simply "in us" exclusively. It is both "out there" and "in us" at one and the same time. By the logic of both-and, Enthusiasm preserves the distinction between mind and thing.

> If consciousness were something absolutely inward and no unmediated contact between it and outward things could be conceived, we would find that we do not at all see things outside of us . . . but that we simply see them in ourselves. If this were so, there could be no possible separation between inner and outer worlds. The outer world would dissolve completely in the inner. And since inner is only distinguishable in contrast to outer, the inner along with the outer world would unavoidably collapse.

Estrangement is conquered not by fusion but by reciprocity.

The reciprocity of subject and object is a true one, for both sides actively participate. Each side gives and receives, so that the process itself is simultaneously one of activity and passivity. For Schelling, the highest moment of being is the union of "utmost passivity with limitless activity," and he speaks of "an activity peaceful as the deepest calm, and a calmness active as the highest activity." This is the very quality which the subject possesses when he engages in a reciprocal relationship with external things. For Wordsworth, that is nature's "glory":

From nature doth emotion come, and moods
Of calmness equally are nature's gift,
This is her glory; these two attributes
Are sister horns that constitute her strength;
This twofold influence is the sun and shower
Of all her bounties, both in origin
And end alike benignant. Hence it is,
That Genius which exists by interchange
Of peace and excitation, finds in her
His best and purest Friend, from her receives
That energy by which he seeks the truth,
Is rouz'd, aspires, grasps, struggles, wishes, craves,
From her that happy stillness of the mind
Which fits him to receive it, when unsought.

The relationship between mind and object is active and reciprocal; even when one side is passive the other is active, so that the union of activity and passivity occurs within an active process, in the same way that fusion occurs within a condition of separation.

When the experience is looked at from the side of the subject, this active reciprocity of subject and object is sensed as fulfillment in striving. The subject actively "aspires, grasps, struggles, wishes, craves," and he also receives "that happy stillness of the mind." But even this happy stillness occurs within a process. Enthusiasm is almost always in movement; it always has a beyond toward which it bends. Schelling said of the mind that "it seeks itself, but even in doing so flees from itself," and Wordsworth said that the soul

         retains an obscure sense
Of possible sublimity, to which,
With growing faculties she doth aspire,
With faculties still growing, feeling still
That whatsoever point they gain, they still
Have something to pursue.

Typically, even in the process of seeking, Enthusiasm senses fulfillment, just as it unites with its object by the process of reciprocity. The patterns are precisely analogous because they are reflections of one another. Unity with the object *is* fulfillment.

Such unity is fulfillment because the object with which Enthusiasm interacts is presented in a special way; it is imbedded, so to speak, in the beyond. Unity with the object is a kind of unity with the beyond, for the reciprocal process itself evokes a sense of "something far more deeply interfused" which dwells in all things, in

> the round ocean, and the living air
> And the blue sky, and in the mind of man.

The beyond is something that subsists within the subject and his object and also beyond them both. Subject and object are unified because of an essence which "rolls through all things." They are akin because they both belong to a greater totality. This totality is apprehended in the object, but it is never fully given in experience; it always reaches beyond, always stretches out toward the "light of setting suns." In the section of "Tintern Abbey" from which these phrases are taken, the word "all" occurs six times in five lines (101-5) and fifteen times between lines 40 and 133. The mind and things are akin because they belong to an infinite totality which unites them.

Because the object is imbedded in an infinite totality, active striving for unity with the object is also striving toward possible sublimity. But the unity is in a sense achieved by the reciprocal process itself. The sense of possible sublimity is also a sense of actual sublimity:

> Our destiny, our nature, and our home
> Is with infinitude, and only there;
> With hope it is, hope that can never die,
> Effort, and expectation, and desire,
> And something evermore about to be.

Infinitude is not only something held before the subject, a beyond never reached; it is also his nature and his home. His hope can never die; what is evermore about to be is also something ever present. Striving never ceases, but in striving itself man fulfills his nature.

For this reason, Enthusiasm is highly affirmative. In the very process of striving it is constantly realizing value. Since the beyond is *both* in experience *and* always just out of reach, everything is presently good and beautiful, even that goodness and beauty which is still to be realized. The character of the subject-object relationship sustains hope and expectation and desire; all oppositions are reconciled in something evermore about to be. The distinctions are not completely overcome in experience; there is always a task, but Enthusiasm strives with the confidence that its task will ultimately be fulfilled, for in experience itself it senses that the task is being fulfilled.

Although Enthusiasm looks before and after and pines for what is not, it does so because of the value in that which is. The beyond is in two places at once, and therefore the entire experience is characterized by the both-and pattern. The striving toward a beyond is at the same time an affirmation of the here and now. The process itself is valuable: "The direct goal of nature in the process I have just described is simply the process itself." "Existence," said Schelling, "is self-affirmation, and self-affirmation is exis-

tence. The one has precisely the same meaning as the other." And Wordsworth's "sentiment of being" was fundamentally

> the deep enthusiastic joy,
> The rapture of the Hallelujah sent
> From all that breathes and is.

Enthusiasm's loving reciprocity with things directly reflects an infinite and loving totality to which subject and object both belong. The beyond reconciles all things in a great self-affirmation, and the subject, along with every aspect of his experience, participates in that affirmation.

> If, therefore, thou hast seen the fullness of existence, as it is for itself, without measure or goal, then thou shouldst also know the inner and holy bond between things and how among themselves, through the unity of the essence to which they belong, they become one.

This I take to be the common structure of experience in Wordsworth and Schelling. (pp. 15-24)

> *E. D. Hirsch, Jr., "The Structure of Experience," in his* Wordsworth and Schelling: A Typological Study of Romanticism, *Yale University Press, 1960, pp. 15-25.*

Frederick Copleston, S. J.   (essay date 1963)

[*Copleston is an English philosopher and Jesuit priest. In the following excerpt, he characterizes the changing nature of Schelling's thought, discusses his place in the history of philosophy, and notes some of the prominent thinkers that he influenced.*]

If we look at Schelling's philosophical pilgrimage as a whole, there is obviously a very great difference between its point of departure and its point of arrival. At the same time there is a certain continuity. For we can see how fresh problems arise for him out of positions already adopted, and how his solutions to these problems demand the adoption of new positions which involve modifications in the old or display them in a new light. Further, there are certain pervasive fundamental problems which serve to confer a certain unity on his philosophizing in spite of all changes.

There can be no reasonable objection to this process of development as such, unless we are prepared to defend as reasonable the thesis that a philosopher should expound a rigid closed system and never change it. Indeed, it is arguable that Schelling did not make sufficient changes. For he showed a tendency to retain ideas already employed even when the adoption of a new idea or set of ideas might well have suggested the advisability of discarding them. This characteristic may not be peculiar to Schelling: it is likely to be found in any philosopher whose thought passed through a variety of distinct phases. But it leads to a certain difficulty in assessing Schelling's precise position at a given moment. For instance, in his later thought he emphasizes the personal nature of God and the freedom of God's creative act. And it is natural to describe the evolution of his thought in its theological aspects as being a movement from pantheism to speculative theism. At the same time his insistence on the divine freedom is accompanied by a retention of the idea of the cosmic Fall and by a persistent inclination to look on the relation between the world and God as analogous to that between consequent and antecedent. Hence, though it seems to me more appropriate to describe his later thought in terms of the ideas which are new rather than in terms of those which are retained for the past, he provides material for those who maintain that even in the last phase of his philosophizing he was a dynamic pantheist rather than a theist. It is, of course, a question partly of emphasis and partly of terminology. But the point is that Schelling himself is largely responsible for the difficulty in finding the precise appropriate descriptive term. However, perhaps one ought not to expect anything else in the case of a philosopher who was so anxious to synthesize apparently conflicting points of view and to show that they were really complementary.

It scarcely needs saying that Schelling was not a systematizer in the sense of one who leaves to posterity a closed and rigid system of the take-it-or-leave-it type. But it does not necessarily follow that he was not a systematic thinker. True, his mind was notably open to stimulus and inspiration from a variety of thinkers whom he found in some respects congenial. For example, Plato, the Neo-Platonists, Giordano Bruno, Jakob Boehme, Spinoza and Leibniz, not to speak of Kant and Fichte, were all used as sources of inspiration. But this openness to the reception of ideas from a variety of sources was not accompanied by any very pronounced ability to weld them all together into one consistent whole. Further, . . . in his later years he showed a strong inclination to take flight into the cloudy realm of theosophy and gnosticism. And it is understandable that a man who drew heavily on the speculations of Jakob Boehme can exercise only a very limited appeal among philosophers. At the same time it is necessary, as Hegel remarks, to make a distinction between Schelling's philosophy and the imitations of it which consist in a farrago of words about the Absolute or in the substitution for sustained thought of vague analogies based on alleged intuitive insights. For though Schelling was not a systematizer in the sense that Hegel was, he none the less thought systematically. That is to say, he made a real and sustained effort to understand his material and to think through the problems which he raised. It was always systematic understanding at which he aimed and which he tried to communicate. Whether he succeeded or not, is another question.

Schelling's later thought has been comparatively neglected by historians. And this is understandable. For one thing . . . Schelling's philosophy of Nature, system of transcendental idealism and theory of the Absolute as pure identity are the important phases of his thought if we choose to regard him primarily as a link between Fichte and Hegel in the development of German idealism. For another thing, his philosophy of mythology and revelation, which in any case belonged to a period when the impetus of metaphysical idealism was already spent, has seemed to many not only to represent a flight beyond anything which can be regarded as rational philosophy but also to be hardly worth considering in view of the actual development of the history of religion in subsequent times.

But though this neglect is understandable, it is also perhaps regrettable. At least it is regrettable if one thinks that there is room for a philosophy of religion as well as for a purely historical and sociological study of religions or a purely psychological study of the religious consciousness.

It is not so much a question of looking to Schelling for solutions to problems as of finding stimulus and inspiration in his thought, points of departure for independent reflection. And possibly this is a characteristic of Schelling's philosophizing as a whole. Its value may be primarily suggestive and stimulative. But it can, of course, exercise this function only for those who have a certain initial sympathy with his mentality and an appreciation of the problems which he raised. In the absence of this sympathy and appreciation there is a natural tendency to write him off as a poet who chose the wrong medium for the expression of his visions of the world. (pp. 142-44)

Schelling's philosophy of Nature exercised some influence on Lorenz Oken (1779-1851). Oken was a professor of medicine at Jena, Munich and Zürich successively; but he was deeply interested in philosophy and published several philosophical works, such as *On the Universe* (*Ueber das Universum*), 1808. In his view the philosophy of Nature is the doctrine of the eternal transformation of God into the world. God is the totality, and the world is the eternal appearance of God. That is to say, the world cannot have had a beginning because it is the expressed divine thought. And for the same reason it can have no end. But there can be and is evolution in the world.

Schelling's judgment of Oken's philosophy was not particularly favourable, though he made use of some of Oken's ideas in his lectures. In his turn Oken refused to follow Schelling into the paths of his later religious philosophy.

The influence of Schelling's philosophy of Nature was also felt by Johann Joseph von Görres (1776-1848), a leading Catholic philosopher of Munich. But Görres is chiefly known as a religious thinker. At first somewhat inclined to the pantheism of Schelling's system of identity, he later expounded a theistic philosophy, as in the four volumes of his *Christian Mysticism* (*Christliche Mystik*, 1836-42), though, like Schelling himself, he was strongly attracted to theosophical speculation. Görres also wrote on art and on political questions. Indeed he took an active part in political life and interested himself in the problem of the relations between Church and State.

Görres's abandonment of the standpoint represented by Schelling's system of identity was not shared by Karl Gustav Carus (1789-1860), a doctor and philosopher who defended pantheism throughout his career. He is of some importance for his work on the soul (*Psyche,* 1846) in which he maintains that the key to the conscious life of the soul is to be found in the sphere of the unconscious.

Turning to Franz von Baader (1765-1841) who, like Görres, was an important member of the circle of Catholic thinkers and writers at Munich, we find a clear case of reciprocal influence. That is to say, though Baader was influenced by Schelling, he in turn influenced the latter. For it was Baader who introduced Schelling to the writings of Boehme and so helped to determine the direction taken by his thought.

It was Baader's conviction that since the time of Francis Bacon and Descartes philosophy had tended to become more and more divorced from religion, whereas true philosophy should have its foundations in faith. And in working out his own philosophy Baader drew on the speculations of thinkers such as Eckhart and Boehme. In God himself we can distinguish higher and lower principles, and though the sensible world is to be regarded as a divine self-manifestation it none the less represents a Fall. Again, just as in God there is the eternal victory of the higher principle over the lower, of light over darkness, so in man there should be a process of spiritualization whereby the world would return to God. It is evident that Baader and Schelling were kindred souls who drank from the same spiritual fountain.

Baader's social and political writings are of some interest. In them he expresses a resolute opposition to the theory of the State as a result of a social compact or contract between individuals. On the contrary, the State is a natural institution in the sense that it is grounded in and proceeds from the nature of man: it is not the product of a convention. At the same time Baader strongly attacks the notion that the State is the ultimate sovereign power. The ultimate sovereign is God alone, and reverence for God and the universal moral law, together with respect for the human person as the image of God, are the only real safeguards against tyranny. If these safeguards are neglected, tyranny and intolerance will result, no matter whether sovereignty is regarded as residing with the monarch or with the people. To the atheistic or secular power-State Baader opposes the ideal of the Christian State. The concentration of power which is characteristic of the secular or the atheistic national State and which leads to injustice at home and to war abroad can be overcome only if religion and morality penetrate the whole of human society.

One can hardly call Karl Christian Friedrich Krause (1781-1832) a disciple of Schelling. For he professed to be the true spiritual successor of Kant, and his relations with Schelling, when at Munich, were far from friendly. However, he was wont to say that the approach to his own philosophy must be by way of Schelling, and some of his ideas were akin to those of Schelling. The body, he maintained, belongs to the realm of Nature, while the spirit or ego belongs to the spiritual sphere, the realm of 'reason'. This idea echoes indeed Kant's distinction between the phenomenal and noumenal spheres. But Krause argued that as Spirit and Nature, though distinct and in one sense opposed, react on one another, we must look for the ground of both in a perfect essence, God or the Absolute. Krause also expounded a 'synthetic' order, proceeding from God or the Absolute to the derived essences, Spirit and Nature, and to finite things. He insisted on the unity of all humanity as the goal of history, and after abandoning his hope of this end being attained through Freemasonry, issued a manifesto proclaiming a League of Humanity (*Menschheitsbund*). In Germany his philosophy was overshadowed by the systems of the three great idealists, but it exercised, perhaps somewhat surprisingly, a wide influence in Spain where 'Krausism' became a fashionable system of thought.

In Russia Schelling appealed to the pan-Slavist group, whereas the westernizers were influenced more by Hegel. For instance, in the early part of the nineteenth century Schelling's philosophy of Nature was expounded at Moscow by M. G. Pavlov (1773-1840), while the later religious thought of Schelling exercised some influence on the famous Russian philosopher Vladimir Soloviev (1853-1900). It would certainly not be accurate to call Soloviev a disciple of Schelling. Apart from the fact that he was influenced by other non-Russian thinkers, he was in any

case an original philosopher and not the 'disciple' of anyone. But in his tendency to theosophical speculation he showed a marked affinity of spirit with Schelling, and certain aspects of his profoundly religious thought are very similar to positions adopted by the German philosopher.

In Great Britain the influence of Schelling has been negligible. Coleridge, the poet, remarks in his *Biographia Literaria* [see excerpt dated 1817] that in Schelling's philosophy of Nature and system of transcendental idealism he found 'a genial coincidence' with much that he had worked out for himself, and he praises Schelling at the expense of Fichte, whom he caricatures. But it can hardly be said that professional philosophers in this country have shown any enthusiasm for Schelling.

In recent times there has been a certain renewal of interest in Schelling's philosophy of religion. For instance, it acted as a stimulus in the development of the thought of the Protestant theologian Paul Tillich [see Further Reading]. And in spite of Kierkegaard's attitude there has been a tendency to see in Schelling's distinction between negative and positive philosophy, in his insistence on freedom and in his emphasis on existence, an anticipation of some themes of existentialism. But though this interpretation has some limited justification, the desire to find anticipations of later ideas in illustrious minds of the past should not blind us to the great differences in atmosphere between the idealist and existentialist movements. In any case Schelling is perhaps most notable for his transformation of the impersonal Absolute of metaphysical idealism into the personal God who reveals himself to the religious consciousness. (pp. 145-48)

> *Frederick Copleston, S.J., "Schelling (3)," in his* A History of Philosophy: Fichte to Nietzsche, *Vol. VII,* Burns and Oates Limited, *1963, pp. 126-48.*

Franz Gabriel Nauen (essay date 1971)

[*In the following excerpt, Nauen traces Schelling's philosophical development from his education at the Tübingen theological seminary through the publication of his* System of Transcendental Idealism.]

At the end of the 18th century, the professors at Tübingen were defending an establishment challenged not only concretely, by the dangers of invasion from France or Austria, but ideologically, by the ideas of the French Revolution and the seemingly seditious teachings of Kant. By and large, the teachers at the *Stift* were able to face this challenge, and channel the discontent of the students into more or less harmless directions. Many of Schelling's classmates at the *Stift* did share both his appreciation of Kant and his sympathy for the French Revolution. But they hoped that Kantianism and traditional Christianity could somehow be reconciled. Following such eminent professors as Bök and Storr, they believed that Kantianism, far from disproving the facts of Christian revelation, had actually overthrown the rationalism of the exponents of natural religion, and had left room once again for orthodox Christian belief.

Schelling's early writings show him gradually breaking with the basic assumptions of the teachers at Tübingen. At first it seemed as if he would try to revolutionize Tübingen from within, while remaining an integrated and highly successful member of his academic community. Indeed, while writing his first German publication, **"On the Oldest Myths"**—published at the age of 18 in his third year at the Stift—Schelling still believed that his critical approach to the prevailing modes of thought could be reconciled with a theological subject of inquiry and with his theological vocation, and was willing to use traditional methods of biblical exegesis and the prevailing philosophical assumptions for his own ends.

At first sight, **"On the Oldest Myths"** appears to be a painfully banal and superficial essay unrelated to Schelling's early philosophical writings. Schelling, like Semmler, Reimarus and Lessing before him, employed the framework of a study of mythology, to ridicule the moral and rational value of many of the most famous stories of the Bible. Schelling, like his predecessors, was attacking through his critical interpretation of Biblical texts, those orthodox Christians who, like his teacher, Gottlieb Storr, in Tübingen, stressed the literal truth of Scripture. But by insisting that these Biblical texts were primitive in nature, he was also implicitly attacking those orthodox Christians who . . . tried to defend the truth of Scripture by giving the Bible a philosophical underpinning and those devotees of the vulgar enlightenment who believed that Scriptural stories were in fact allegorical forms of philosophical truths. Still, at least on the surface, Schelling was concerned in **"On the Oldest Myths"** with showing how oral transmission, pride and the self-interest of priests and princes had perverted the truthful core of many myths.

The reader is appalled by the repetitiveness of the argument and bored by Schelling's perfunctory outrage. For Schelling was not really disturbed either by the superstitious and untruthful element in myth or by the erroneous truths transmitted by them. In fact, he was not even really interested in the myths themselves or in their impact on the mind of a primitive believer. The real object of his patronizing and supercilious pity was not the recipient of myth, but the primitive mythmaker himself.

Unable to abstract, the ancient mythmaker attempted to verbalize his vision of reality by describing the world rather than by explaining it through concepts. The Greek and Hebrew mythmakers tried to explain such universal problems as the role of man in the world, the relation of things and men to their cause and the reason for human misery. But lacking concepts, they were compelled to see man as a thing-among-things in a world without meaning or structure. So inadvertently, the mythmaker explained that which was evident by referring to remote "objective causes" which he was quite unable to comprehend. Without the ability to use concepts, the ancient mythmaker was unable to distinguish between appearance and reality. Even when he used an image such as that of the "breath of life," he meant it literally and most certainly he thought of the soul as a "thing." And man, in the world of myth, thinking of himself as a thing-among-things, understood himself to be not a free agent, but a determined being.

Schelling—we see—was not at all charmed by "natural man" who was totally at the mercy of alien forces which he could not comprehend. Yet by emphasizing not so much the unscientific quality of myth as the unfree consciousness which created it, Schelling was introducing a new perspective for the study of the origins of superstition,

The Tübingen Stift, where Schelling studied with Friedrich Hölderlin and Georg Wilhelm Friedrich Hegel.

unknown to earlier eighteenth century scholars. The chief import of Schelling's new discovery was, however, less its heuristic potential as a device to comprehend remote cultures than the contrast which it implied between the unfree consciousness of primitive man and the spiritual grandeur which the moderns were capable of attaining. Sharply contrasting his own freedom with the abject determinism of the primitive mythmaker, Schelling claimed that man was in the first instance a spirit, and not a being existing in time and space. The key to the knowledge of man did not lie in nature; rather, the key to nature, its "Urbild," lay in the understanding of man. And the vocation of man was not to be a child of nature, but its lawgiver.

Schelling of course did not blame the primitive mythmaker for attempting to comprehend an alien and hostile world with the means at his disposal. He certainly believed, however, that the development of the human mind and its ability to conceptualize now confronted modern man with the challenge of structuring the external world according to laws established by his own reason. Carried to its logical conclusion, this early vision of human freedom had not only purely scientific, but political, social and technological ramifications as well. In **"On the Oldest Myths"** Schelling suggested that modern man through reason did have the potential to win sovereignty over the world of appearance, while ancient man had not. This conclusion became the premise of his first philosophical writings, where, working out the philosophical implications of his own vision of human freedom, Schelling now contested the determinist assumptions no longer of primitive, but of conventional modern thought.

By 1794, his fourth year at the Stift, Schelling, acclaimed by his teachers and his fellow students for his scholarly acumen, abandoned his exegetical ventures—which he considered to be of purely antiquarian interest—and threw himself headlong into the new philosophy inaugurated by Kant and developed by Fichte. Perhaps influenced by his teacher Johann Friedrich Flatt, a newly installed professor of theology at the *Stift,* Schelling from the outset rejected the moderate Kantianism prevalent at Tübingen. Schelling further maintained with Flatt that any attempt to save the tenets of rational theology, challenged by Kant in his *Critique of Pure Reason,* by the "Postulates of Practical Reason," posited in Kant's *Critique* of *Practical Reason,* was insulting both to religion and to the dignity of thought. For reason could not endure a contradiction between knowledge and the will to believe. But instead of following Flatt and returning to orthodoxy, Schelling preferred the intellectual integrity of Fichte's radical Kantianism to the uncertainties of Christian orthodoxy.

But it was not only the uncompromising intellectual honesty of Fichte—so different from the eclecticism which characterized the thinking of his teachers at the *Stift*—which captured young Schelling's fancy. As sober a thinker as Kant had repeatedly asserted that philosophers were now finally capable of solving the age-old problems of philosophy and creating a new metaphysics which would not be subject to future revision. Schelling, enthralled by the speculative verve of Fichte's thought, believed that Fichte was in fact achieving this sublime goal and that he himself could contribute to the rapid acceptance of the new philosophy which would bring the history of metaphysics to a close.

At first sight in fact, Schelling's first philosophical essay *On the Possibility of a Form for Philosophy,* published in 1794, appears to be nothing more than a translation into old fashioned jargon of thoughts better expressed in Fichte's "Concept of a Theory of Science," which had been published a few months earlier. By enthusiastically acclaiming Fichte's philosophy and posing as an amateur preparing the way for a real philosopher, Schelling himself was at least partially responsible for this impression. But despite Schelling's somewhat disingenuous diffidence, and his sincere attempt to integrate his own work into Fichte's philosophical framework, the reader must not overlook the crucial difference between Fichte's essay and Schelling's first major philosophical effort.

Schelling, while paying token homage to the primacy of "practical reason," did not agree with Fichte that moral judgement should be the model for all other modes of thinking. Believing that human freedom was manifest in moral man's unending struggle to subject human passion to the edicts of his will, Fichte felt that this freedom could be extended from the moral sphere to that of human knowledge. The free man was for Fichte not a passive instrument of circumstance or a passive observer of the facts. Rather, the free man was one who was engaged in an endless struggle to make the world about him conform to his own freedom. Schelling, however, believed that human freedom was not so much the struggle for mastery as it was man's total awareness of himself as a free cause of all things. The ego was not simply engaged in an eternal quest for self-realization, but was already the absolute

principle of all knowledge and reality. Fichte's insistence on striving as a chief characteristic of human freedom had led him to accept the "real world," existing institutions, sciences, and arts, as testing grounds for the free man. Schelling, however, starting in his first philosophical essay with the concept of the ego as absolute, soon came to feel that the discovery of human freedom implied a revolutionary reappraisal of all existing social, natural and aesthetic forms.

At first, however, these differences were scarcely perceptible. Schelling considered Fichte his honored teacher and Fichte acknowledged Schelling as a new and brilliant follower. Both Fichte and Schelling believed that they were engaged in different aspects of the same undertaking, and shared philosophical aims. Schelling, in **On the Possibility of a Form for Philosophy,** tried to continue the work which Fichte had begun by showing that not only formal logic, but even the systematic form of philosophy itself, received their ultimate sanction from the unity of the absolute ego.

Fichte, in his essays "Review of Aenesidemus" and "A Concept for a Theory of Science," had derived consciousness, the first principle of theoretical philosophy, from a free, though unconscious act of the ego. By this act, the ego actively opposed to itself the non-ego, and thus supplied the object which consciousness encountered in experience. This act of the ego, however, in turn depended on an even more primary act of the ego through which the ego posited itself. This primal act described in the first principle (or *Grundsatz*) of all philosophy as "Ego-Ego," structured all human thought processes, in science and in morals, and could be derived, according to Fichte, from the entire history of self-consciousness.

Still, in both these essays, Fichte had explicitly presupposed the existence of formal logic as the highest authority on form in philosophy. This lacuna Schelling tried to fill in his essay by deriving the basic logical laws of identity and contradiction from the dynamic self-explication of the absolute ego described in Fichte's *Grundsatz*. The result of this attempted tour de force (which Fichte had carefully circumvented) was that Schelling imposed onto Fichte's argument a completely different estimation of the kind of knowledge man could have of the first principle (*Grundsatz*) of the new science and of the function of this "*Wissenschaftslehre*" in organizing experience. While Fichte believed that he had discovered the abstract principles of human knowledge "through a history of human self-consciousness," Schelling claimed that what Fichte had discovered was the first principle, not only of human knowledge, but of all reality as well.

Both Fichte and Schelling agreed that "consciousness" was capable of conceiving the *Grundsatz,* or first principle, although it could never itself achieve the vision of the Absolute Ego of which this *Grundsatz* was an expression. But this agreement concealed two quite different interpretations of what the word "consciousness" meant. Fichte, following Reinhold, believed that the human mind was capable of conceiving abstractly the transcendent forces which conditioned consciousness. Consciousness itself, however, was restricted to awareness of "things in time and space" of which alone "certain knowledge" was possible. Beyond consciousness, the mind had no real object to focus on and its theoretical insights here were necessarily abstract and partial. Schelling on the other hand, following another intellectual trend begun by Kant, believed that the kind of knowledge concerned with things in time and space, called "consciousness," was necessarily partial and subjective. Man could have "absolute knowledge" of the absolute ego alone and this knowledge, though different in kind, was more rather than less sure than the knowledge man had as consciousness. This "higher" form of knowledge Schelling was soon to call *intellectual intuition.* In **On the Possibility of a Form for Philosophy,** Schelling called this sublime kind of knowledge the "absolute in human knowledge."

For Fichte, only indirect and abstract insight into the absolute source of all knowledge was possible. Through abstraction and reflection it was possible to achieve insight into what this absolute source must be, from what it was not, and so attain a high enough degree of certainty of it to formulate the *Grundsatz.* But human knowledge could never ascend to a vision of the ego in its absolute, original freedom, or to a vision of the ultimate object (*Ding an sich*) posited by the ego. By seeing the *Grundsatz* at work, abstraction could derive the *Grundsatz* itself. This was the highest form of knowledge accessible to man.

Schelling, on the other hand, thought that not only the *Grundsatz* itself, but also its content, was self-evident. Earlier philosophers such as Leibniz and Descartes had tried to base all reality on the self-certainly of the thinking ego. Theoretical philosophy, however, being a science of "consciousness," could never by itself achieve a clear vision of the ego in its freedom. But the knowledge of the ego of itself constituted a higher form of knowledge which while self-evident not only transcended but also unified theoretical and practical knowledge. Though Schelling went to great trouble not to contradict the letter of Fichte's statement, he boldly converted Fichte's epistemological concern into a metaphysical one. The *Grundsatz* did not have to be derived from a history of the human spirit; it was intuited directly as the "absolute in human knowledge." And this fundamental disagreement with Fichte found its expression not only in Schelling's formal, philosophical argument, but also in his completely different estimation of the philosophical status of language.

While Fichte had little faith in words and concepts, and always wrote as if what he was saying barely approximated his thought, Schelling had great faith in the truthfulness of language. Many of his best arguments relied on a careful analysis of the meaning of words, for Schelling believed in the real existence of archetypes. Every form concealed primal form, and indeed Schelling was trying to find the *Urform* for philosophy. By achieving knowledge of this *Urform,* man won direct access to the Absolute.

Fichte preferred to make a much more limited argument for the underlying *Grundsatz* of his *Wissenschaftslehre.* He claimed only that human thought had always worked unconsciously in accordance with its laws, and that from no other *Grundsatz* could all the motions of the mind be derived. The *Grundsatz* could be demonstrated through what Fichte called a "pragmatic history of the human spirit," and in "On a Concept for a Theory of Science," he was far more intent on explaining than on changing human thought. The 'pragmatic history of the human spirit" not only proved that human freedom underlay the speculative ventures of man, but simultaneously acknowl-

edged the relative validity of conventional interpretations of the world. Consequently, Fichte drew very cautious theological inferences from his philosophical position; such tenets of Natural Religion as belief in God, in immortality, and in the infinite perfectibility of man, were not only permissible, but necessary consequences of the encounter of human freedom and an obdurate world. While insisting that man must assert his freedom, Fichte believed that man had no choice but to fill his imagination with such surrogates of freedom in order to comprehend the eternal cleavage between himself as an imperfect being, and the absolute nature of the ego within him.

Fichte was primarily concerned in "On a Concept for a Theory of Science" with "theoretical philosophy" (the exact sciences, "consciousness," and the tenets of Natural Religion) and did not think that he had discovered one absolute principle which could be grasped in contemplation. He claimed only to have established that human freedom—manifest in morality—was behind all meaningful human speculation. Though men, in speaking abstractly for what was right, might be as Kant suggested quite ineffectual in the "world" where nature laid down the rules, man's moral sense stemmed from the basic impulse of his nature to be free. Man must struggle perpetually for a reconciliation between his autonomy and the nature of things. Indeed, this striving to act, this moral sense, was man's assurance of his own free nature and of the unity of his experience in a world in which he often was at the mercy of the facts. Reason for Fichte therefore was primarily "practical." As, however, this battle for freedom never could be won, certain imaginary buttresses of the autonomy of men emerged in consciousness. So the meaningfulness of this struggle was reinforced by the belief in immortality, and the belief in victory, by the belief in God. Still, though science and faith aided men in their struggle, awareness of freedom stemmed solely from striving to be free.

Schelling, on the other hand, ignored completely the caution with which Fichte had induced only the structure rather than the content of human freedom from man's real knowledge of the world. Seeing only that Fichte had shown that all knowledge and all reality in the world could be deduced from a power whose absolute freedom man could share, Schelling ignored Fichte's insistence that real knowledge was possible only as "consciousness" and loudly proclaimed that by intuiting the absolute ego, prior to both human self-consciousness and external reality, man had indeed freed himself from the dominion of objects and of objective truth.

Schelling's dream, expressed in **"On the Oldest Myths,"** that man could escape from the false world of the imagination through reason and achieve legislative power over all reality, now received new meaning. For in **On the Possibility of a Form of Philosophy in General,** man no longer was only the legislator for all laws of science and morals, as he had been already for Kant, but was also the source of "objectivity" in the world. Man was no longer a victim of, but a free source of the facts. Everything that was stemmed from the absolute freedom of his own being. A new universe of knowledge was now possible, as comprehensive as Spinoza's system, but illustrating not human acquiescence, but human freedom.

Schelling in fact intended that his first book, **On the Ego,** published in 1795, be a rebuttal (*ein Gegenstück*) to Spinoza's *Ethics* which would "free men from their slavery to objective truth" and convince them that they themselves were the source of all truth and all reality. If men would only become aware of themselves as totally free beings, capable of asserting the freedom of the absolute ego within them in "intellectual intuition," they would soon realize that their acts could fully express their moral intentions. First the sciences and then mankind itself would be unified, as men, realizing that they shared unrestricted sovereignty over the world, would join together in obeying laws stemming from human autonomy.

Schelling hoped to inaugurate this process by demonstrating that the absolute ego latent within men was the first principle of all truth and the ultimate source of all reality. Schelling here suggested a pantheism as rigorous as that of Spinoza but resting not on "Nature" or "Substance" but on the free ego. From the absolute ego not only the world and knowledge but also morality could be derived. And where Spinoza had held that the wise man saw the necessity of all things, Schelling believed that it was incumbent upon man to make all his acts correspond to his inalienable freedom.

Before 1795, Schelling had believed that awareness of the absolute nature of human freedom implied the struggle for mastery not only over the physical world but over society and politics. While writing *On the Ego,* however, he came to share Spinoza's view that individual moral acts, like other happenings in the world of appearance, were "figments of the imagination." Man, in fact, was sure and free only while thinking himself in intellectual intuition. Indeed, as a being capable of grasping the absolute within himself through intellectual intuition, man should destroy in his mind all the forms which limited and structured the world. From this insight, however, Schelling refused to draw conclusions of moral quiescence.

Man, as a sentient being living in the world (while in thought lifting himself out of the world), should contribute by his acts to the unending task of making the living and visible world correspond to his thought. Not only a "spirit" but also a finite being, partaking of the absolute freedom of the ego, man should exercise his transcendental freedom by trying to make the world about him correspond to the rationality inherent in his mind. Though man could never make the world of appearance *correspond* to his own free nature, he was capable of making his moral acts *reflect* this freedom. Man was not only capable of intuiting the absolute ego within himself in a mystic state; he was also capable of trying to impose his new-won freedom onto matter and society by participating in the attempt to achieve the unattainable goal of making the world outside him correspond to this freedom.

In spite of this dualistic juxtaposition of intellectual intuition and human practice, Schelling tried in *On the Ego* to deduce from the total freedom of the absolute ego some extremely radical moral, ethical and political consequences. In one of his most striking arguments, he suggested that moral action was itself the meaning of history. In fact, the absolute ego created the world so that the ego could achieve tangible victory over the non-ego. Schelling also envisioned an ideal society in which duty and right were identical, freedom achieved, and coercion unnecessary. Still, by stressing that man was capable of becoming

aware of his freedom in intellectual intuition and destroying in his intellect all the bifurcations of the world, Schelling suggested that above human self-expression in the world lay a higher realm of pure awareness. Morality, while pointing the way to true freedom, nevertheless paled beside the mystic heights of intellectual intuition where this freedom was fully revealed. In demonstrating the absolute quality of this freedom, he had denigrated morality itself to the "lower" world of human experience.

The technical arguments in the body of *On the Ego* had the effect of reinforcing this emphasis, and Schelling's original hope that men might achieve both insight and justice in the world was modified by the suggestion that man, while capable of infinite improvement, could never consummate his quest for freedom on the ground of morality alone. Despite man's quest for freedom through history, the final goal of the absolute ego itself remained to destroy "the world as world."

Both Hölderlin and Hegel felt that Schelling was being led astray by his mystical tendencies from their common mission of teaching men to be both spiritually and morally free. Hegel, in a letter to Schelling in 1795, the year *On the Ego* appeared, politely suggested that a philosophy of the ego was all well and good for the philosopher, but that ordinary men must be made aware of their dignity and their rights by an exposé of the repressive ideologies imposed upon them by their masters. Hölderlin, sensing that art might communicate the truth both more easily and more adequately than "intellectual intuition," commented to his friends that Schelling was on the wrong course, and pondered in private on philosophers who abandoned self-consciousness for dangerous mystic delights. Unwilling to part intellectual company with his friends, Schelling was moved by their criticism to try to present his ideas in a form which would be compatible with their mutual goals. In his *Philosophical Letters,* Schelling answered Hölderlin's objections that art rather than speculative insight best reconciled the absolute with human striving, and also attempted to make human moral perfectibility a central characteristic of his vision of human freedom.

Schelling's *Philosophical Letters,* published in the winter of 1795-96, were addressed to an unnamed correspondent who shared not only Schelling's pantheistic world-view, but also his profound contempt for those "vulgar Kantians" who, assuming the fallibility of human reason, held that a determinist world-order and moral freedom had to be reconciled through "moral postulates." This correspondent, however, though agreeing with Schelling that good intentions were futile in a world governed by hostile objective causes, concluded that man had no choice but either to assert his freedom by fighting to the death for his principles or to accept the objective world-order as it was. [The critic remarks in a footnote: "Though the *Philosophical Letters* do not include any letters written by the correspondent, Schelling often answers objections to his views which the correspondent is supposed to be making. It is from these replies that I have drawn my picture of the correspondent."] And the only alternative to the moral quietism of this philosophy of acceptance, claimed Schelling's correspondent, was the stance of the tragic hero. While artists could communicate the unity of existence, either through a lyric reverie or through depicting the heroic though futile freedom of the tragic hero, philosophers, compelled by their trade to acknowledge the eternal cleavage between freedom and necessity, were driven to dogmatism (i.e., determinism) or skepticism. As we shall see, Hölderlin held these views while writing the early versions of *Hyperion,* and thus the unnamed correspondent was almost certainly Hölderlin, with whom Schelling was engaged during the fall of 1795 in long and heated discussions.

Hölderlin, though in Jena an enthusiastic student of Fichte's, was questioning precisely those elements of Fichte's thinking which appealed most to Schelling. He felt that by resting his case on the sublime unity of the absolute ego, Fichte was opening the flood gates to superstition and moral quietism. For without reflection and self-consciousness—which both Fichte and Schelling conceded was absent in intellectual intuition—man lost rational control over the world in which he lived. Schelling was convinced by Hölderlin that it was a mistake to derive moral and political freedom from a doctrine which in itself suggested mystic withdrawal from the world.

In his *Philosophical Letters,* Schelling admitted that intellectual intuition was common to all serious philosophers, be they pantheists, mystics, or voluntarists like himself. In fact, were it not for the problems raised by human experience, there would be no disagreement among philosophers. The difference between the mystic and the free man lay not in their vision of the absolute, but in the role of this vision in structuring experience. For the mystic and the pantheist, the absolute was, or was about to be, realized in the world. For the free man, though it was the goal and purpose of all his act, it remained forever unattainable in the world.

In the *Philosophical Letters,* Schelling was admitting that man and world would never be completely reconciled in history, but he insisted nevertheless that through his own free choice such a reconciliation must be the ultimate goal of the free man. While for the free man awareness of the absolute integrity of his ego and intellectual intuition was the cardinal principle of his speculation, his acts had to express his unending quest to achieve on earth the truth he himself had posited in his total self-assertion. The actions of the free man had to reflect his participation in the human condition; he was committed to the struggle to master objects and relate to his fellow men. To choose to remain in the state of intellectual intuition would be to follow the mystic in rejecting life by denying the reality of human experience. The free man, on the other hand, by making all his acts reflect his attained spiritual freedom could and must act in the world without, however, ever becoming himself a victim of the facts.

Schelling now recognized that his earlier philosophical mysticism was suited only to "gods free from effort and care" and not to men. The philosophy of the free man elaborated in the *Philosophical Letters* was committed to spreading the truth which would make men free—not only in their thoughts but also in their lives. Any other way of reconciling man and nature except through human freedom was illusory and only contributed to human wretchedness. As only consciousness of freedom could make men free, he should expect no help from the external world. Only self-assertion in intellectual intuition and not a vision either of the past or of the future could be a standard for the acts of the free man. Only he who chose to be spiritually free could be morally and politically free.

Schelling held that the current state of the sciences, of political and legal theory, of theology and even of philosophy revealed that this freedom had yet to be achieved. But in the last analysis Schelling did not really believe that the state, society and law could be reformed, for it was the state itself, law itself, which did not correspond to human freedom. The few isolated comments on politics which can be found in Schelling's early writings reveal an extreme form of anarchism which rejects out of hand both law and government. Finding no counterpart to his vision of human freedom in history or in political theory, Schelling insisted that the sense of freedom gained in intellectual intuition was the only sure standard for human decisions.

More moderate in his philosophical position than Schelling, Hölderlin was dissatisfied with the austerity of Schelling's vision. Hölderlin agreed with Schelling that the attempt by the vulgar Kantians to buttress traditional theology by moral arguments and to ignore rational criticism of tradition by stressing the fallibility of human knowledge was itself a misuse of reason. And Schelling accepted in the most general way Hölderlin's alternative to the vulgar Kantians: his emphasis on human struggle. Hölderlin, however, believed that human freedom should be conceived in analogy to the encounter of freedom and destiny in tragedy, which consequently was a perfect medium for communicating the idea of human freedom. While Schelling conceded that a tragic view of the world might be legitimate in art he insisted that it did not stand up to the tribunal of reason. In general, at this stage of his development Schelling distinguished between art and the new philosophy of freedom. Tragedy like any art form was a product of the imagination which presupposed total commitment to an "objective" world on the part of the artist and therefore precluded true freedom. In particular, he insisted that Hölderlin's "tragic vision" could only achieve the semblance of freedom. Hölderlin's conception of human struggle itself implied belief in an objective world order and was incompatible with a philosophy of freedom. If an objective world order was assumed, then any assertion of human freedom was doomed from the outset.

Thus Schelling, the most poetic of the philosophers of German Idealism and personally inclined to move in literary circles, denied poets access to the truth. It must be remembered that the chief aim of German Idealism was to find a form of thinking attuned to ultimate reality. In this quest, the Idealists encountered the romantic poets, also profoundly affected by Kant, who shared with the philosophers an intense hunger for reality and meaning. For example, Schiller and Hölderlin, while intensely conscious of what the philosophers were doing, hoped that art might become a more perfect medium for expressing the truth than abstract speculation burdened by the immense ballast of tradition.

Schelling also differed profoundly from Fichte in his estimation of art. While Fichte tried to harmonize belief and knowledge, aesthetic receptivity and active understanding, Schelling believed that the aesthetic was only a primitive and outdated form of philosophical insight. Fichte felt that art could attain insight into ultimate reality by expressing feelings which could not be grasped by reason; Schelling believed that art was doomed to error from the outset by its commitment to feelings and the imagination. For Schelling the imagination was a spurious form of human activity by which the mind falsely imputed reality to the world of appearance. By committing himself totally to the comprehension of the "object," in effect by acquiescing in it, the poet hoped to win a semblance of freedom. But dedication to the object could not be reconciled with the sovereign autonomy of the ego. The aesthetic experience, while a sublime cousin to dogmatic philosophy, was nevertheless inimical to human freedom. It is apparent to any reader that Fichte was personally indifferent to art, while Schelling had extremely developed aesthetic sensibilities. How then can this extreme iconoclasm of Schelling be explained?

Schelling was engaged in his early writings in a quest for a new, free counterpart to the old passive mystic path. A primary characteristic of his vision of freedom was the denial of reality to the "object." In this undertaking he felt threatened by the poets, whom he saw as engaged in a search for the "object." Man would somehow be reimbursed for the richness he lost in experience by the plenitude of being imparted to his thought by his awareness of freedom. For the absolute ego was so rich in content that it could be the source and end of all human acts and ideas. The aura of unreality which the rejection of the aesthetic implied would be more than offset by a new intense awareness of human vocation. Schelling's vision of human freedom, however, was suitable only for a small intellectual elite. Even if intellectual intuition of the reality of unattainable inner moral and spiritual goals was possible, it, like the old mystic path, was most certainly open only to the few.

Schelling in his *Philosophical Letters* had attempted to reply to the criticism of his friends that his philosophical views had little ethical import and implied a withdrawn elitist attitude towards human affairs. And he did concede to his friends that the free man was committed to experience and must attempt to make the social and natural world around him conform to the dictates of his reason. Nevertheless, he insisted that this venture would never be fully consummated in the real, visible world. Whatever reason there was in human experience received its ultimate sanction solely from the solitary majesty of the sovereign ego knowing itself in intellectual intuition. Like Plato's philosopher, however, the free man must return to the cave. The principle of rationality which governed his own spiritual life was by no means immanent in experience and could be only partially imposed upon it. The ordinary men he encountered could share with the philosopher a sense of freedom by striving through ethical conduct to make the world about them conform to the dictates of their reason. But only the philosopher was fully conscious of his freedom.

Shortly after completing his *Philosophical Letters* Schelling speculated, in writings very much influenced by Hölderlin and certainly not intended for publication, whether there might not be another way besides ethics by which this gulf between the philosopher and his fellow mortals could be bridged. In his **"Fragment for a System,"** (extant only in a copy made by Hegel without title or signature) and his letter of March 21, 1796, to Obereit, an unknown aged scholar who had written him a lengthy letter, Schelling called for a "new mythology" which would con-

vey in aesthetic form for ordinary men the conclusions of the philosophy of freedom. This new mythology—which Schelling contrasted with the popular theology of established religion—would root out the source of popular superstition by destroying the cleavage between the views of ordinary men and those of the philosophical elite.

Influenced by Hölderlin, Schelling seemed to abandon his earlier insistence that the imagination as such belonged not to human freedom but to the "objective world." He suggested in **"A Fragment for a System"** that through a new mythology the creative imagination could be put to the service of reason. In this context the vision of mythology was really nothing more than a device to bridge the gap between the consciousness of philosophical and ordinary man. But in this unpublished and unpublishable text of 1796, Schelling already went beyond this idea to express a thought which was to reappear only in 1801 at the conclusion of his *System of Transcendental Idealism.* Without integrating it into the main course of his argument Schelling prophesied that the day might come when the task of academic philosophy might be completed, and a new philosophy and a new poetry might express the vision of freedom won through speculation. Stressing that the philosopher needed the same aesthetic sensibilities as the poet, Schelling suggested that the highest idea which alone could encompass all the ideas of reason was that of beauty.

Schelling, in response to the criticism of his friends— especially Hölderlin, with whom he conversed at length during the spring of 1796 in Stuttgart—was willing to reconsider both his austere elitism, which he had arrived at in his *Philosophical Letters,* and his rejection of art as an effective means of popularizing his vision of human freedom. Still, it is clear within the context of Schelling's other writings that this extreme tribute paid to art—that the philosopher must have aesthetic sense—was not really an admission that art rather than philosophy should be a model for speculative reasoning. It was rather simply an admission that intellectual intuition could not be arrived at through discursive reasoning but only through a leap analogous in some way to the creativity of the artist. Even in the **"Fragment for a System"** the chief emphasis was not on aesthetic truth but on the dependence of theoretical knowledge on practical reason and of practical reason on a self-determination of the ego. In his published writings immediately subsequent to the **"Fragment for a System,"** Schelling made no mention of art or the idea of beauty. And he adhered strictly to his earlier view that the central notion upon which all knowledge depended was the absolute autonomy of the ego or, according to a new phrase, the "self-determination of the Spirit."

Even in his published writings of the end of the nineties, where Schelling was concerned no longer primarily with epistemology but with the philosophical study of nature, he still insisted that the universe should be conceived of not as an entity separate and distinct from man, but as derived from and analogous to human freedom. It was only in his *System of Transcendental Idealism,* published in 1801, that Schelling publicly asserted that not philosophy but art, as an expression of the fundamental unity of subject and object, was the highest form of human spirituality. But even here he still insisted that though art was the canon from which the principles of philosophical reason should be derived, philosophy still originated in the choice of the philosopher to assert his autonomy.

Schelling in his writings to 1801 attempted to solve consecutively two problems: how to derive all of human experience from human freedom and how to integrate self and world, freedom and nature. In his **"Fragment for a System,"** written at just the moment when, beleaguered by his friends, he was turning from the first question to the second, Schelling tried momentarily to make art the link between these two lines of philosophical inquiry. Reflecting the influence of Hölderlin on his thinking, convincing neither himself nor his reader, Schelling argued that in the course of its own self-discovery the human spirit would eventually discover in the beautiful the means whereby it could find itself in the world, and that it was in art that human freedom and nature reached a state of perfect equipoise.

Within the context of Schelling's philosophical development it should be evident that the poetry alluded to in the **"Fragment for a System"** was really a sort of philosophizing, an expression in universal language of the same decision to assert human autonomy as the more technical ventures in which he himself was engaged. Hölderlin, on the other hand, though he insisted on informing himself of the latest developments in philosophy, believed that the poetic process itself rather than philosophizing was the best description of the process of human self-discovery. Poetry for Hölderlin, far from being a way to express in universal language the conclusions of philosophical speculation, was itself the sublime expression of the commitment of man to experience. As such it was the source and not only the ultimate consequence of valid philosophical reasoning.

It was Hölderlin, not Schelling, who by his own effort tried to create a new poetry which would realize the promise that the beautiful, as the concrete expression of the universal unity of man and experience in intellectual intuition, would integrate self and world and reconcile experience and human freedom. Schelling in his comments on art came close to succumbing to the temptation of making normative philosophical principles out of the irrational prophesies of art without thinking concretely about the way in which art could bridge the gap between philosophical insight and concrete human experience. Hölderlin, on the contrary, believed that the abstract ideas which he had won in philosophical reasoning were not an end in themselves but simply a program for a completely new art form which would record man's valiant attempts to express within real society the basic needs of his own nature.

Hölderlin did not believe that human freedom could achieve mastery over experience simply by asserting itself and then rediscovering itself through protracted philosophical inquiry within the confines of the objective world. Rather, human freedom had to strive to comprehend and structure the world. Art, far from being the final, pure product of the human spirit, incorporating the conclusion of philosophy into its message, was the arena in which the reconciliation between the self and the world, nature and freedom, had to be fought out. Perceived in isolation from the rest of his early thought, the highly abstract characterization of art in the **"Fragment for a System"** seems in perfect accord with Hölderlin's thinking. Still we should not let ourselves be misled to suppose real agreement between Hölderlin and Schelling. Art, for Schelling, was a dimen-

sion of human freedom, which would follow the arduous efforts of human reasoning. For Hölderlin it was the battleground on which the fight for human freedom must be fought. (pp. 28-49)

> *Franz Gabriel Nauen, "Schelling (1792-1796)," in his* Revolution, Idealism and Human Freedom: Schelling, Hölderlin and Hegel and the Crisis of Early German Idealism, *Martinus Nijhoff, 1971, pp. 27-49.*

Thomas F. O'Meara   (essay date 1982)

[O'Meara is an American theologian. In the following excerpt, he describes Schelling's philosophy of religion.]

What does Schelling mean by *religion*? What is the object which his positive system will interpret, this system worked out no longer as an idealist epistemology but as a phenomenology of religion? A tentative answer at this point can give some direction to our voyage along the linear development of what he summed up as historical movement. Spirit's history is theogony, and that process of theogony is threefold. Schelling is always and simultaneously describing three things: (1) the life of God, as God through his active potencies exoterically becomes fully himself; (2) the vital historical line of finite being (other than God but not utterly discrete from him), which has its own realization but which nevertheless bears inwardly the realization of God; (3) the history of human consciousness, both collective and individual, which is bringing to unity nature and spirit in art, in religion, and in their finest expression, philosophy.

"My task is the philosophical explanation of systems of religion and myth." It belongs to philosophy to find the essential content and ultimate purpose of religion. The process which we call religion, myth and philosophy, seems to bridge the gulf between the Absolute and the finite.

Schelling usually wrote of philosophies of "myth and revelation," using less often the phrase "philosophy of religion." The object of his science is the life of the Absolute being realized in the human spirit and world history. If the Absolute becomes fully itself through "tension" and "process," the empirical record of that process is a history which prior to Christ we call myth and after him we name revelation. Revelation expresses with insight and mythology with picture a single process which brings together the ideal and real; the single process is history, religion, theogony.

Religion is the product of divine powers active in consciousness. The place of the process, the tension of the potencies, is consciousness. This consciousness is both the Godhead and the human spirit. The human person as the climax of the universe is placed in the midst of the three powers, open to their influence but ultimately free of each of them. Because of this union of freedom and spirit, the finite consciousness must live amid the influences of the powers, between a discoverable freedom and a false domineering security. Spirit is the subject of the realization of human beings as well as of God.

> The process which begins with the posited tension amid the potencies is a theogonic process—for the potencies effect it and are in themselves theogonic.

But at the same time it is an extradivine process,
not only a process of nature but one which we (initially) call mythology.

This process will include unruliness, error, materialistic
religion.

Schelling's neologism, "tautegory," explains how philosophy will interpret religion and ultimately become revelation. "Mythology is not allegorical but tautegorical—its
gods really exist." Allegory discloses one thing through
something which is different; tautegory discloses the new
through something which is the same. For Schelling
human religion is not the symbolic or cultic representation
of something obscure, whether that be the powers of nature or the heroes of nations. Rather, religion is the life of
knowing and willing expressive of its own progress toward
depth and fullness. This process is the development of
ideal to real, and back again to the fully active ideal-real
of Spirit.

Schelling's system is organic and developmental; it can be
imagined as linear but also as parabolic. Expansion flows
out from the beginning and returns with the spoils of realization: the self-realization of God as an outward motion
and a return. This parabolic model was not foreign to the
earlier philosophy of identity where the Absolute differentiated itself into the real and the ideal in order to become
in a higher synthesis their identity. This pattern (scholars
have recently begun researching its affinity with Plotinus)
was to serve also as the foundation for the later philosophy
of creation and religion.

The dynamism of the human spirit is such that it unfolds
the life of God. In Schelling's later philosophy of religion
the Plotinian motif of fall and re-ascent was retained; what
was new was the relocation of this pattern in the line of
forward movement.

This essay looks first at the process which is both a divine
becoming and a religious history, and, second, at the role
which Christian revelation plays in fulfilling myth, imag-
ing God, and completing religion through idealism.

There is "something before being," a ground of all being
and of the universal system. Schelling's ground is a peaceful, active willing, the source of all that will be. Needful
of nothing, in its ground it wills being. Since willing is forward oriented, the process will be unfolding and eschato-
logical; since it is a process of realization, it will include
both poles of the ideal-real dialectic. It is not a logic but
a phenomenology of will-into-existence. The transcendental structure of Schelling's philosophy remains, but the a
priori categories of the mind have become physical potencies of existence, both ideal and real.

This willing even in its infinite openness contains three
movements: can, must, and ought. These three aspects of
the active essence (*Wesen*) of primal ground can also be
expressed in terms of the subject-object schema: *Seinkönnen* ("potential to being") is the subject; the object is
reines Sein ("pure being"); the subject returned through
objectivity is *reines Sein nun* ("pure being now"). The final
stage—begotten into factual existence—represents the
union of the ideal and the real. In the twelfth lecture of
the ***Philosophy of Revelation*** these powers are called "*Potenzen.*" In Schelling's speculative physics, his writings on
natural philosophy, the potencies had already been pres-

ent not as divine powers but as levels of natural organization. Remaining powers of being, they are now mediators
between the Absolute and the universe, the divine will and
history. They are transcendental horizons of all being. We
might call them vital fields. Schelling employed *Potenz* not
as Aristotelian potentiality but as a striving ready to leap
to fulfillment. Do the *Potenzen* solve the problem which
haunted Schelling's first systems, the distinction between
God and the world? They are not concepts, Schelling repeated, but determinations of the life of the absolute spirit-
as-will, three personalities of the same essence. They are
the deeper meaning of the Christian Trinity. Through the
powers, the God of monotheism becomes worldwide, historical, and so trinitarian.

God is not found in the primal will, or in any one of the
potencies, or in their product. The tension of the powers
is the life of God. The powers are placed outside of the
Godhead yet remain facets of the Godhead's primal being,
will; they are both God and non-God. The world is *part*
of the personal objectification of God. The polarity of freedom and necessity, of subject and object, is the bridge to
the production of the world which is both free and necessary. The first potency delights in real possibility, in the
attraction to beings other than itself. Yet, in this passage
through differentiation, the totality of the divine being is
neither increased nor diminished, for the All has simply
moved from one "form of existence" to another.

The world is not the inner essence of God but an "exoteric
appearance of the deeper theogony." The plurality of the
world rather than being a challenge to the unity of God
is the confirmation of divine vitality. Creation takes place
neither in eternity nor in time, but in a temporal zone
which lies between the chronology of history and the pul-
sation of the burning yet unconsumed primal will. Creation resolves the ideal and the real: the first principle by
its nature has only the desire to maintain itself, and the
second can only go unconditionally beyond the first; a
third power is drawing both to fulfillment, a power which
they recognize as higher and independent.

Once God has led forth innumerable potentialities as realities, the structure is there for finite spirit to be more than
an object, to be a living subject. The divine process continues in the life of the spirit. The external theogony ends not
in the objects of the cosmos but in history made possible
by spirit. The primal will manifests itself in the tension as
process. Schelling's understanding of creation is different
from the view that the world is a logical consequence of
the divine nature (Spinoza) and different from the positing
of God only as the term of his becoming (Hegel). The
world arises through a divine process but one over which
God as *Urgrund* stands, amid but above the potencies
placed in tension.

Does God need the world? "God is God only as Lord, and
he is not Lord without something over which to be Lord.
But God is already, before the world, Lord of the world,
Lord of whether to place the world or not." Although the
divine life is more than detached activity *ad extra,* Schelling no longer would compromise traditional thought by
uncategorically placing a need for creation or incompleteness in God. There is an effort in the later philosophy to
protect the divinity of God. There is an eternal theogony
and a temporal one. In the first, time does not reach to the
heart of God. The linguistic aid to accepting this is the dis-

tinction: esoteric-exoteric, while the systematic key is process. "In the three potencies, which are immanent determinations of absolute spirit in God, and in their ground the category of historical process lies rooted."

Before we pursue the thread of religion further, we must briefly discuss the role for Schelling of the Fall. Searching for an alternative to Plotinian emanation and Aristotelian or Wolffian causality, in 1804 Schelling decided that the world came into an existence apart from God through a leap or a Fall. He admits that such an employment of *Abfall* recalls that "very ancient idea" of original sin. From his first use in 1804 Schelling views the Fall primarily from the perspective of idealist ontology. There is no assertion of moral fault or free choice. In fact, though created by God's freedom in an immediate relationship to God, human persons were not yet free. They had not lived, had not struggled for mastery over self within the potencies. The Fall, then, is not a fall from an original and perfect freedom through a sin, but a creation into concrete existence so that greater freedom can be attained. For the universe the Fall means separateness and limitation. The separation of the second power from the first is *Urzufall,* and from this dissonance the being-process began.

> Man was created at the center of the Godhead and essentially he belongs at that center as his true place. As long as he is there he sees things as they are in God, not with a superficial view empty of spirit and unity . . . but in harmony with man as their head, and through man accepted up into God.

But the Fall brings a change in the relationship between God and humanity.

> Once man moves away from the center, the divine unity is distorted and the periphery becomes confused, for he is no longer divine above things but he has sunk to their level. Since he wants to assert his central position and the insight connected with it (although he now stands in another relationship) he strives to hold onto the original and divine unity in a world destroyed and ripped apart.

The meaning of the Fall, and of the wrath of the father-gods, is the shock of subjectivity, even of an absolute subject, now placed before objective independence. The positing of the world alienates it from God. In the Fall of the world, the Son, the world's potency, also falls. The Father is no longer completely father; the Son will regain serenity in a future, deeper subjectivity. Mirroring the Godhead, creation cannot resolve this tension unless creation becomes spirit, unless the real becomes the ideal.

Schelling's philosophy of religion is an attempt to grasp the full reality of history. For an idealist the important thing about history is consciousness-in-history, the ideal becoming the real and vice versa. History is not primarily the record of political events but the spiritual development of the human race. Thus we partake in the history of myths, in mythmaking. Mythogenesis is the process by which the essential, reflective archetypes in the human consciousness corresponding to theogony come to light. Mythogenesis is the theogonic process as played out during the first epochs in the history of revelation.

The philosophy of mythology is the first part of the philosophy of revelation. Schelling's analysis of the mythical systems of Egypt, India, China, and Greece was not only

an interpretation of the totality of myth but the search for the reproduction of the triadic process in each particular system. Throughout a thousand pages of mythical systems, the word *Bewusstsein* repeated itself: the divine and human consciousness, the idealist realm where history expressed itself in myths.

The history of mythology has four epochs in which the three potencies play out their roles in the transformations and realignments of gods and myths. Every mythological system includes a story of concrete gods. This narrative is a telling of the race's social experience, and so it is myth which forms peoples. Nations emerge not from political pressures but from spiritual movements. "Mythology does not determine but *is* that people's fate (just as a man's character is his fate), its destiny allotted to it from the beginning." Myths, like language and social structure, are a disclosure of the becoming God meeting humanity. The primacy of the ideal over the real is maintained even in the historical phenomenology of religion. Mutual development is grounded on both God and human beings as *Geist.*

Not only does myth mirror theogenesis; the history of myth records psychogenesis. The human spirit finding its way ahead to full freedom is a lesser reflection of God's own development for freedom. The world of gods arises in the human mind spontaneously, born of a necessity imposed by the original relationship. God's way to himself and the path of human history are one: one archetype and one image. "Mythology comes into being through a process which is necessary; its origin is lost in a realm before history. Consciousness may resist the process in certain particulars, but it cannot impede, much less reverse the whole." Theogony is reproduced in the abyss of consciousness and of being. Myth has taken over the role which art and nature played in Schelling's earlier writings. The philosophy of myth is insight into and through the structures of mythogenesis. We recall here the previously mentioned key to Schelling's philosophy of religion: religious forms are not allegory but tautegory. The lives of the gods and goddesses are creations which pictorialize forces active in our minds and wills, and in God's. "Seen objectively mythology is in fact what it claims to be: true theogony, a history of the gods. The ultimate history of the gods is the creation, the real genesis in consciousness, of God."

Although a divine process of revelation lies beneath the history of myth, religion is frequently and inevitably a corruption of spirit. God does not force ideas upon humanity but leads the race through various stages, none of which are fully false, to higher truth. True monotheism can be fashioned only out of the struggles of polytheism. The epochs are transitions to greater insight, greater freedom, gateways to that synthesis which romantic idealism had sought everywhere: in self, nature, art, state, and now finally in religion.

While every religion qualifies as revelation, Christianity marks a higher stage of that process which mythogenesis began. Nevertheless, since mythology is theogony, revelation could hardly be more; and so one asks: What is revelation? It is insight into the real process of God and of history and self; it is a free and true history (more than the myths of Greece or the reason of Kant) which is one with idealism. Neither Schelling's knowledge of theology nor his theological acumen equaled his competent survey of mythology. This was yet another field for him to study, and in the late 1820s when the need for such research made itself felt Schelling was fifty. In his treatment of Christianity he limits his exposition severely. Nevertheless, we know that he was acquainted with some of the theological literature of the time—with D. F. Strauss, with Schleiermacher, whom he considered to be the most intelligent of dogmatic theologians, and with certain of the publications of his Catholic disciples in southern Germany, who since 1802 had viewed him as a counterpart to Hegel.

Schelling treats at length only two specifically Christian doctrines: the Trinity and the Son as Christ. But first let us look at Christianity as a whole. Christianity does not fashion but discloses history; Christian revelation begins at that transitional moment when mythic history begins to return to a God it will find free and complete.

If the epochs of the worldwide history of religion prior to Christ are individually touched by error, still "the process as a whole is truth." Each stage has prepared for the next, and yet the entire process is found in each moment.

> The content of all true religion is eternal and hence cannot be absolutely excluded from any epoch. A religion which is not as old as the world cannot be the true one. Christianity must, therefore, have been in paganism. . . . It is inconceivable that mankind should have remained for thousands of years without links to the principle in which alone there is salvation.

The theophanies of the Old Testament do not seem to be much superior to paganism. Here we might recall that for Schelling the explicit content of any religion is the phenomenal manifestation of the deeper level, the process of theogony and human psychogenesis. Every rite and all doctrinal teachings point to something more profound: so it is not possible to locate revelation or freedom within only one religion.

> If we take paganism, Judaism, and Christianity as the three great forms of all religion, the revelation of the Old Testament is merely the revelation that runs through mythology; Christianity is the revelation which has broken through this husk [paganism], and thereby transcended both paganism and Judaism.

Paganism and Judaism are both prototypes of Christianity. "Christianity was the future of paganism."

If Schelling demeaned Judaism, ranking it amid the religions before Christ, he elevated the oriental religions before and after Christ. His knowledge of the history of Buddhism confirmed for him an organic theory of the universal process of theogonic revelation. A persecution of Buddhism occurred in India at the same time as Christianity appeared further west: this coincidence illustrated the complex but universal presence of the second potency, the Son, in the world. Religious consciousness is, then, collective as well as worldwide.

Creation and history are the places of activity where through individualization lordship is won by the second power. When the Son becomes a power in history, human religion is elevated from the "natural activity" of the potency to its clearer revelation. What in nature is necessary and obscure becomes historical and intuitively clear. In the depth of Christian theology one can intuit that theogo-

ny which positive philosophy describes. Nevertheless, the acceptance of this revelation is not submission to dogmas explained away by reason (as the Enlightenment claims to have done) but insight into the work of God. The shift is also one from the essential to the existential order. Theogony is not only consciousness but, more, relationship to God. Revelation, Schelling says, is the movement from the rational order of nature and myth to the real existence of God active in us.

The history of our planet is the realm of the second potency. Fundamental philosophy sees it as *Sein-müssen*—the objective, existing counterpart to absolute subjectivity; the philosophy of revelation employs the name *Son*. Like the other two *Potenzen* the Son was actively present in every religious and mythical system, but Christianity is the final, explicit stage of his life. Tilliette writes:

> It [*The Philosophy of Revelation*] is a speculative theology, an interpretation of dogmatic statements, but above all it is a philosophy of Christian *religion*. Within this vast philosophy of religion it appears as the second panel of a diptych mythology-Christianity. The relationship of Christianity to paganism is the joint which allows the exposition to expand.

Schelling's lectures on trinitarian theogony led quickly to the generation of the Son and its relation to world and history. While the Father is described at length in terms which are a union of idealism and Böhmeanism, the topic of the Spirit is not well developed either here or at the end of the system. Our conceptualization of the Trinity arises from the encounter of human consciousness with objectivity. Previously theologians had searched for a *vestigium trinitatis* in nature and religion; Augustine had found a trinitarian analogy in the operations of mind and will. This is not what Schelling means. Religion eventually discovers and affirms Trinity in God because the human individual and collective consciousness are a *Gegenbild* of God's becoming.

> Our principles lead us immediately and naturally to a teaching which is the foundational doctrine of Christianity. In *Die Philosophie der Mythologie* I showed that the doctrine of the Trinity in its roots and ground is not specifically Christian . . . but because this is the most primal reality of all there is, Christianity exists.

Our entrance into the life of God is through the Son, for he is potency and Lord of our world. To beget the Son is to begin creation and history. The Son is the realization of God's freedom for being, the breaking of the necessity of not willing. "Before all willing, through the mere necessity of his being God, God, to the extent that he is being-for-itself, places himself in a second form. . . . " The Son is the object of the divine knowledge and will. The time of the Son is a period of exit and return, of risk and realization. Emerging out of freedom this *Potenz* finds that glory is solitude and obedience.

> The *actus* of this self-realization lasts until the time of the complete birth [of the Son]; only at the end is the Son real Son. Since this end is the end of creation, the Son is begotten at the beginning of creation, but is only realized as such at its term.

Schelling's Christianity is Christology. Christ is not the founder of a doctrinal sect. He is the content of Christianity, just as for Christianity history is the content of the universe. As theogony unfolds in the history of human religion, the potency of the Son is present in all religions. But a clearer moment is yet to come. Revelation from the potency active in a "natural" way yields to disclosure. This unveiling is, however, in terms of the Godhead, the apogee, the moment of furthest removal and incipient return.

Creation and history are tragic. Over against the lordship of the subject the solid assertion of objectivity appears not only as distinction but as alienation. So, the second potency's process is lonely and ends not only in Incarnation but upon the Cross. Two Christological themes interest Schelling: the birth of the Son in eternity and time and the terms of that begetting, the *kenosis* of the Incarnation. Schelling's Christology is largely a historical and ontological elaboration of Phil. 2:6-8. What interests Schelling most in this biblical text is the Greek word *morphe*. Does not this show that the Son's pre-existent divinity was a form of God becoming? (*Form* for Schelling pertains to manifestation, mode of being, while *essence* is foundation, ground, and necessity.) Caught up in the epochal movement of the Godhead through the universe, the second potency cannot rest with its first form. *Kenosis* is principally, however, an idealist interpretation of existential Incarnation and secondarily the Crucifixion (more prominent in Paul, Luther, and Hegel). The philosopher singled out from the Crucifixion the Son's obedience. This is the psychological condition of the furthest alienation from the Father. Freedom before, through, and after the Cross: only the one who has the form of God *independent* of God can renounce it and through death arrive at glory *with* God.

It is not surprising that this Pauline passage—the divine person lowering himself into the abyss of historical existence in order to be exalted above all—was appealing. *Kenosis* is historical theogony, a Plotinian *exitus-reditus* extended downward to wounded mortality. The metaphysical tension and the alienation of the powers are set forth in historical terms while the format of ontological polarity is retained. The process of separation to attain a realized freedom continues the differentiation of the ideal realm of the subject. At the same time, the severity of death shows the event of Christ to be the ultimate objectivity. The Cross is historical and so eminently objective. Its blood marks the attainment of a far point in that lonely sphere of the real.

The three *Potenzen* are the three Lords of time. The third potency is spirit. For the idealist, *Geist* is the creative force and the ultimate identity. Spirit, of course, underlies every stage of the developing universe and is the ground of mind and will. Though active from the beginning it must wait for the epoch of the second power, for only after the climactic moment of the Son can the coming of the Spirit, a time of synthesis, occur. Schelling continued to follow the pattern of his early idealist system where subject and object find resolution in a synthesis of both—the ideal-real. Only if God separates beginning from end does he find freedom and possess the infinity of created forms.

How does God resolve human history and personality? History has undergone two important transformations: one from divine indeterminateness to mythogenesis; a second from myth to revelation. We glimpse a third and final one. If Christianity was the future of mythology, is not idealism the future of Christianity? The pattern of the idealist system, of the Fall and its return, remains operative here; the ideal and the real in the human person are to be resolved in Spirit. Schelling's eschatology is protology; it looks backward for ideas. Existence finds climax in consciousness, history in the absolute Spirit. In bringing the Spirit, Christ has brought the possibility of the final era of full freedom. Freedom is the keynote of the time of resolution. The threat of chaos and evil is being subjected to science, to knowing and to fashioning freedom. All other religions must fade except the one of that revelation which is also *Wissenschaft*. Interpreted idealistically the *gnosis* and *charismata* of the Spirit (of which Paul wrote) are a knowledge which now knows no limits, no superstition. No protected corners of darkness escape its light. In the meantime the process continues and slowly penetrates everything prior to the end. "The development after Christ will be subject to the same disturbances, restrictions and counterforces as would affect any natural evolution."

The final stage of the theogonic process, the activity of the third potency in cosmic resolution, is not described at length. The reader must search carefully through the final lectures on revelation for fragments of a completion of the philosophy of religion. What is missing is an idealist ontology of resolution which would correspond to the first part of the positive philosophy, the lectures on the one primal Being leading into the philosophy of religion. Schelling's philosophical imagination seems to have been spent. Distracted by two material segments which excited his curiosity—Satanology and an ecumenical ecclesiology—Schelling deprived his linear process of a worthy conclusion. No doubt recollections about origins are easier than extrapolations of the future. "The past is known: the future believed." (pp. 218-31)

> *Thomas F. O'Meara, " 'Christianity is the Future of Paganism': Schelling's Philosophy of Religion, 1826-1854," in* Meaning, Truth, and God, *edited by Leroy S. Rouner, University of Notre Dame Press, 1982, pp. 216-35.*

Michael G. Vater   (essay date 1984)

[*In the following essay, Vater evaluates Schelling's philosophy of identity as it appears in* Bruno; or, On the Divine and the Natural Principle of Things *(1802).*]

Schelling had the opportunity, which many twentieth century philosophers would account good fortune, to outlive his philosophical positions. In fact he did so several times over, becoming, like Leibniz whom he greatly admired, a philosophers' philosopher, influencing great minds such as Marcel, Heidegger, Tillich, and Habermas, but lacking an audience within the general culture. In 1827 Schelling said of the so-called system of identity, the projected system of which the **Bruno** is but a sketch, "On the one hand, it seems almost impossible that this system is false, but on the other hand, one will sense something in it that prevents one from declaring that it is the ultimate truth. He will recognize that it is true within certain limits, but not unconditionally and absolutely true." Let us turn to the task of evaluating the success of this ambitious piece of metaphysics, while leaving the last word to its sternest critic, Schelling himself.

Recalling that the **Bruno** was penned as a vehicle for discussion between its author and Fichte, let us first address the question whether the dialogue advances any grounds for reconciling their conflicting positions. It is quite plain that it does not, and that the conviction that their differences were irreconcilable hardened in Schelling's mind even as he wrote. The argument makes clear that the only position Schelling and Fichte can share is phenomenalism, the belief that appearances are not what is fundamentally real. Schelling is unequivocal about his belief in the ultimate duality, equiprimordiality, and irreducibility of material and mental phenomena. His claim that the *Science of Knowledge* would reduce the material to the mental dimension is correct. There simply can be no agreement between a subjective idealism that would think away all being or materiality, including nature, and a methodological idealism that wants to preserve the difference of nature and spirit by interpreting them as equally well-founded orders of phenomena. Basic to the two philosophers' longstanding dispute is Schelling's insistence, not only that nature cannot be thought away, but that it is the very foundation for spirit or the realm of consciousness. Fichte had tried to fashion a self-contained philosophy of spirit with but two branches, epistemology and ethics. Schelling's more comprehensive and naturalistic vision of philosophy is well expressed in these remarks on the 'identity-philosophy' made in 1827:

> Thus it follows, from the foregoing determination, that the initial moments of the infinite's positing itself (or since the life of the subject consists in this self-positing, the initial moments of this life) are moments of nature. From this it follows, too, that this philosophy is in nature from its first moves, or that it starts from nature—naturally not in order to remain there, but to later surpass it in ever ascending steps, to emerge from it and become spirit, to elevate itself into an authentically spiritual world. In its beginning, therefore, this philosophy could be called nature-philosophy, but nature-philosophy was only the first part or foundation of the whole [system]. . . . At the start, it was difficult to find a name for this system, since it included the very opposition of all earlier systems within itself, as cancelled. It could in fact be called neither materialism nor spiritualism, neither realism nor idealism. One could have called it 'real-idealism,' inasmuch as within it, idealism itself was based on a realism and developed out of a realism. Only once, in the preface, thus the exoteric part, of my first presentation of this system, did I call it the 'System of Absolute Identity.' I meant that therein was asserted no one-sided real being nor one-sided ideal being, but that only one ultimate subject was to be conceived in that which Fichte called 'the real' and in that which we have become accustomed to call 'the ideal.'

It is plain, then, that no rapprochement with Fichte is possible. The **Bruno** is to be read as the velvet-gloved counterpart of the obviously polemical attacks Hegel unleased in the "Difference" essay and in *Faith and Knowledge*. Perhaps it was with some insight that contemporaries referred to Hegel as Schelling's henchman.

Let us now consider the kind of metaphysics advanced in the **Bruno.** As we have seen, Schelling is quite vocal in his opposition to Kant, and quite daring in his attempt to steer Criticism away from epistemology and back to meta-physics. But the fact remains that Kant had set forth clear arguments that spelled the end of metaphysics, at least as a speculative, if not as a descriptive enterprise. Schelling's metaphysics is highly speculative, however, and the question naturally arises: How could anyone attempt to philosophize in this manner *after Kant?* The answer is very much obscured by Schelling's decision to turn back to the history of philosophy and present himself as Plato risen from the grave—a decision quite consonant with his flashy, arrogant personality. Nonetheless, the answer is simple: Schelling does *Kantian metaphysics.*

When Kant pronounced that "all metaphysicians are therefore solemnly and legally suspended from their occupations," he advanced two general lines of argument: (1) Metaphysics commonly takes categorial concepts meaningful in the context of experience and attempts to apply them beyond the bounds of sense. It errs in that it fails to realize that categorial concepts have no cognitive content; they are but logical functions which interrelate items of experience. Thus talk of substance, causality or a reciprocally determining community of things is meaningless if applied to what is behind or beyond experience. The metaphysician commits the fallacy of misplaced concreteness in his assumption that categories have some positive epistemic content. Hence, to ask after a 'cause of the world' is equivalent to asking whether the rules of chess move one space at a time on the board like pawns or along the diagonal like a bishop. (2) In fixing its sight upon supposed hyper-experiential objects such as the enduring soul, the cosmos as such, and the deity, metaphysics postulates totalities of experience which are not subject to any possible truth-test within experience. Such 'ideas of reason' involve an illegitimate advance from the experience of a finite chain of conditioned entities to a supposed totality of conditions. The ideas of immortal soul and of a personal deity involve the fallacy of reification as well, for 'soul' hypostatizes the empirical stream of consciousness, and 'God' hypostatizes the logical notion of the aggregate of all positive predicates or qualities.

Not only is Schelling keenly aware of Kant's arguments; he is convinced of their truth as well. Careful analysis of the **Bruno**'s argument shows that he indeed follows the limitations on speculation they propose, and that he avoids both sorts of fallacies through his logic of indifference. It is his genius (though some may think it a perverse sort of genius) to have hit upon an *a priori* logical idea which is *nowhere* exhibited in experience, namely indifference or the identity of opposites. Within Schelling's theory, indifference functions both as a connective that links various phenomenal and nonphenomenal domains and as an explanatory device; Schelling need have no recourse to substance-accident or cause-effect relations except when he is talking of the serial interconnection of phenomena within time. As we have seen in detail, indifference explains and unites all the disparate regions of being—mind and matter, soul and body, intuition and concept within consciousness, nature and spirit as the universal orders of appearance, the absolute's form and phenomenal existence, and finally the absolute's form and its identical essence. It is clearly an elegant system, though perhaps a purely formal one, that can establish all these connections with one principle. Thus Schelling is able to avoid causal explanation except in its appropriate context, where one world-state is seen to be determined by another or one intuition determined by its predecessor. He is aware, as well, that questions such as, "Does the absolute cause appearances?" or "What is the cause of separated existence?" are metaphysical in Kant's sense and thus unanswerable, though he clearly shows some uneasiness about not being able to pose and answer the latter question.

Now Kant's first specific objection to metaphysics was that it lifted portions of the logic of experience and employed them out of context. The causal relationship, for instance, is exemplified in any experienced sequence of events where prior members condition or influence subsequent ones; it would therefore be illegitimate to ascribe causality to the unconditional. But indifference or the essential identity of opposites is never clearly and unequivocally exemplified within experience at all. The prime candidate for an experienced instance of indifference would seem to be the correlation between the psychic and somatic aspects of some sensation, but it fails to exhibit indifference the way causally related events exhibit causality. Causality is the only categorical schema available for conceiving the connection of conditioning and conditioned events. The togetherness of psychic and somatic events, however, may be conceived in several ways, for example, (1) either by means of the categories of substance and accident, which leaves open several possible interpretations, namely (a) that both aspects are attributes of a common substance, (b) that the bodily aspect is substantial, while the psychic inheres in it as a quality, and (c) that the psychic aspect is substantial and the somatic accidental, or (2) by means of the logic of indifference. Then too, it is always arguable that psychic and somatic states are simply different. At any rate, if they are indifferently related, this is not *shown* by experience; it is a conclusion attained by pure thought alone, a metaphysical interpretation of the facts that experience furnishes. Schelling cannot, then, be accused of extrapolating a concept which is part of the logic of experience into a pure idea. Indifference may indeed be a pure idea, but since it contradicts the whole logic of experience, the claim can credibly be advanced that it is a genuine idea of reason, not a misplaced concept of reflection. Schelling thus manages to evade the first of Kant's general objections to speculative metaphysics.

Kant's second objection to metaphysics claimed that the ideas of reason are inherently dialectical in that they advance from the experience of conditioned entities such as personal self-consciousness, nature, and the logical ideal of totality to the unconditional posited as a totality of conditions, namely soul, world, and deity. Schelling's metaphysics escapes the fallacies of hypostatizing self-consciousness or the lawlike order of nature by steadfastly maintaining that both orders are strictly phenomenal. There is no nature-in-itself and no enduring or immortal soul. Neither knowing nor being can be attributed to the absolute, nor can either acting according to freedom or acting in conformity with causal mechanism.

But what of the deity, or the absolute, as Schelling calls it? Kant's criticism of conventional philosophical theism claimed that the idea of God illegitimately (1) represented the unconditioned as a totality of conditions, and (2) hypostatized all the positive items that an exhaustive table of contrasting predicates would exhibit. On the first score, the bipolar nature of Schelling's absolute seems to evade the objection, for the absolute is a strictly identical essence

on the one hand, and the totality of all differences held together in the absolute idea on the other. The form-essence distinction, itself the highest instance of indifference and the ontological foundation for all other instances, seems to keep the unconditioned on one side, and the totality of conditions on the other. One cannot deny, however, that Schelling frankly portrays the absolute's form or the absolute idea as a totality of conditions. A Kantian would be justified in asking precisely how we can jump from the conditioned nature of experience to the idea of a totality thereof.

On the second score, Schelling escapes the charge that conventional theism is arbitrary and illogical in describing the deity in terms of positive predicates alone, for Schelling conceives the absolute's form as the totality of all differences, that is, of all contrasting qualities and attributes, positive and negative, held together in an indifferent unity. Theism conceives deity as infinite, perfect, and external to a finite, imperfect world, while Schelling's absolute idea is the indifference of the infinite and the finite, and the coexistence of what we term 'perfect' and 'imperfect' as well. But here again, the Kantian may object that it is precisely the ascent from the fragmentary and successive nature of experience to the idea of a totality that is objectionable.

It is evident, at least, that Schelling carefully considered Kant's objections, even if, in attempting to conform to their letter, he sought to evade their spirit, and that he was consciously working toward the invention of a Kantian-style metaphysics. Consideration of the predominance of speculation on time in the *Bruno,* and of the Kantian manner of that speculation, reinforces this impression. Time is the primitive form of appearance as such. It is what accounts for phenomena being phenomenal, for the durational rather than the eternal form of things' existence, and for the discursive nature of the understanding. Time is made virtually synonymous with individual existence, for the individual separates itself from the eternal community of all things in the absolute precisely by fashioning its own time. And yet time functions as a bridge connecting things' existence in their ideas with separate existence, for it is the expression of the infinite or conceptual dimension, it is responsible for the self-identity, coherence, and cohesion of things, and, in the highest instance, time is itself the stream of consciousness. Now it might be argued that this account of time is fundamentally incoherent, yet the attempt to make external or objective time the framework of finite phenomenal existence and yet make internal time the framework of the discursive synthesis of self-consciousness betokens a vigorous attempt on Schelling's part to bring unity and coherence to the Kantian account of mind.

In all the foregoing discussion of Schelling's attempt to formulate a style of metaphysics immune to Kant's critique, we returned again and again to the concept of indifference. We must now try to measure the validity of this central, enigmatic idea. We have already noted that it formulates a logical connection never exhibited in experience, namely the essential identity of properties that appear to be direct opposites. Only the connected opposites pertain to experience, never their hidden connection. Hence there is a curious invisibility that pertains to every instance of indifference. Within nature, gravity and light are systematizing forces, not things. They never come to appearance; instead, things appear within the systematic framework that they, and space and time as well, provide. Within consciousness, the unity that binds sensation and awareness into the one act of intuition never appears or presents itself as a distinct something, nor does selfhood or the unity of consciousness that connects the moments of thought and intuition. Within the self-conscious organism, body and the stream of consciousness indeed appear, but their indifferent union remains in the background and never presents itself as the substantial element it supposedly is. And the same occurs within the whole scheme of things; the finite and the infinite stand forth in appearance, but never the eternal. Experience exhibits both knowing and being in their distinctness, but never their indifferent or absolute union.

What are we to make of this invisibility of the indifferent? Clearly, it implies the invisibility, and ultimately the ineffability, of the absolute. A metaphysical foundation of appearances that is invisible and ineffable bears both positive and negative philosophical results. Positively, it is true that, if experience never provides a clear instance of an indifferent relation, one is 'safe' from Kantian attacks in characterizing the absolute solely in terms of this nonexperiential form of connection. But on the negative side, the possibility of *arguing* to the absolute is simply cut off, whether by analogical extrapolation from experience or by deductive proof. The absolute must remain a *postulated* otherside of the world of experience, quite beyond the truth-test of experience, and incapable of characterization by any quality or attribute which pertains to experience.

In the last analysis, the only thing that can be said of the absolute is that its nature is indifferent, or unitary and bipolar at the same time. Indifference is a purely logical entity; it involves no quality, mental or physical, for it is only a relation between some set of contrasting qualities.

The question then arises, 'What sort of logical function is indifference?' Is it a connective or a relation, a primitive connective or a derived logical function? It could be interpreted as a relation, but since it essentially involves the connection of opposites, it seems best to view it as complex logical function based on conjunction. As a logical function that simultaneously affirms and denies any and all opposed predicates, it is fundamentally a reversal of the logic of experience. If we denote two contrasting predicates by the functions Fx and Gx, we can represent their indifferent subsistence in the absolute by

$$\sim (Fx \lor Gx) \;\&\; (Fx \;\&\; Gx).$$

Using f(x) and g(x) to represent any and all opposed predicates, the nature of the absolute can be schematically depicted as

$$\sim (f(x) \lor g(x)) \;\&\; (f(x) \;\&\; g(x)),$$

where the left-hand string indicates the absolute's identical essence, the 'neither . . . nor . . . ' of all opposed qualities, and the right-hand side the developed system of differences coexisting in the absolute idea.

Now the fact that we can represent the absolute in simple symbol strings indicates that Schelling's metaphysics of indifference is purely formalistic. And the fact that ordinary logic forces us to read these strings as simple contradictions suggests that the logic of indifference is parasitic upon the logic of experience, just one member of the vast domain of contradictions. Nothing is materially contradictory about $\sim (f(x) \lor g(x))$ as such; negative theology frequently has resort to such expressions. But $(f(x) \;\&\; g(x))$ certainly is a contradiction if g(x) is the denial of f(x), as is the conjunction of the two strings. Now the fact that any and every contradiction applies to the absolute certainly does supply Schelling with a defense against the charge of illicitly borrowing from experience. But that the absolute can only be described in logical terms, and even then only in terms of ordinary logic stood on its head, shows it to be a thin construct indeed.

Here we encounter the chief difficulty with Schelling's identity-philosophy, not that it is a formalism, but that it is an empty formalism, not that it approaches characterizing the *ens realisimum* logically rather than analogically, but that no suitable interpretation can be given to its formulae. Schelling attempts to mediate the opposition of abstract identity and sheer difference, and that of the interrelatedness of phenomena comprehended under scientific laws and their reciprocal exclusion in space and time. He is indeed ingenious in discovering the interrelatedness of things and in suggesting that an ultimate internality grounds all things. He is deficient as a metaphysician, however, in letting the contrast between the internal and the external remain a simple opposition. Schelling simply leaves the sheer identity of the absolute's essence something other than the inclusive difference of the idea; he leaves the absolute the mere unexplained otherside of the phenomenal world, which he correctly views as governed by exclusion and externality. Hegel will ultimately prove himself the more astute thinker by (1) seeing that the ultimate categorial contrast of internality and externality (or selfhood and otherness) must itself be philosophically explained, (2) that explanation of the internal-external relation must ultimately be in terms of one of the relata, and (3) that *thinking,* a rather garden-variety cultural activity, provides the paradigm case of the internal comprehending, or "outflanking," the external.

Though Schelling is ingenious enough to get around Kant's objections, or at least their "fine print," and to point out the path toward a logical metaphysics, he is not sufficiently abstract a thinker to see that his new path leads towards a metaphysics of relations, wherein individuals, either "in idea" or "within appearances," become purely derivative entities. Nor does he possess the foresight to realize that such a project which reduces all entities to complexes of relations and explains all relations through formal, not material, properties, might turn out to be an elegant, though strictly uninterpretable, formal construct.

We reserve the critical last word to Schelling himself, for he eventually became quite aware of the difference between a logical formalism and a philosophy that can claim to capture existence. In his *Lectures on Recent Philosophy,* given in Munich in 1827, Schelling offers a balanced evaluation of his identity-philosophy, though one slightly tinged by the tendency to conflate Hegel's system, characterized by dynamism, with his essentially static early system:

> (1) One cannot reject the system because of its compass or territory, for it encompassed everything knowable, everything that can in any way become an object of knowledge, without excluding

anything. . . . (2) As to its method, it was formulated to exclude any influence by the subjectivity of the philosopher. It was the object of philosophical inquiry itself that supplied the system's content, that successively determined itself according to an immanent principle, a thought progressively specified according to its own inner law. . . . Besides, when one considers how the authority of all natural modes of thought was undermined by Fichte's subjective idealism, how consciousness, dismembered by the earlier absolute opposition of nature and spirit no less than the crass materialism and sensualism, . . . felt itself injured and insulted, then one will understand why this system was initially greeted with a joy that no previous system ever provoked, nor any later one will again provoke. Nor nowadays one does not realize how much one had to *struggle* for what today has become the common good, and in Germany almost an article of faith shared by all high-minded and sensitive men—I mean the conviction that that which *knows* in us is the same as that which *is known*.

Schelling proceeds to discuss the crucial limitation of this philosophy, that it failed to recognize that it was mere thought:

> Now how did it come to pass that this philosophy, in the form in which it first exercised an almost universal attraction, was yet a short time later seen to be limited in its influence, and showed a repelling pole which was little noticed at first? It was not because of the attacks it received from many quarters. . . . It was rather a misunderstanding about itself, a situation wherein the system gave itself out for something (or, as one used to say, let itself be taken for something) that it was not, something that according to its original thought it ought not be. . . . An eternal event is no event. Accordingly, the whole representation of this process [of the absolute subject's development] and this movement was itself illusory. None of it really happened. Everything occurred in mere thought. This philosophy should have realized this; in doing so, it would have set itself beyond all contradiction, but, at the same time, it would have surrendered its claim to objectivity. . . . It should have *recognized* itself to be *pure negative* philosophy. In this way, it would have left a space free for a philosophy beyond itself, for a positive philosophy which considers *existence*, and not given itself out as absolute philosophy, a philosophy which leaves nothing beyond its compass.

(pp. 71-9)

Michael G. Vater, "The Significance of the Philosophy of Identity," in Bruno; or, On the Natural and the Divine Principle of Things, 1802, by F. W. J. Schelling, *edited and translated by Michael G. Vater, State University of New York Press, 1984, pp. 71-9.*

Bernard M. G. Reardon   (essay date 1985)

[*Reardon is an English historian who specializes in the history of philosophy and theology. In the following excerpt, he traces the evolution of Schelling's religious philosophy.*]

[In] embarking on the subject of [the idea of God in the philosophy of Schelling] we must go back to Schelling's first major work, *Vom Ich als Prinzip der Philosophie.* The problem of the existence of a personal deity had occupied him since his student days. In correspondence with Hegel after the latter had left Tübingen he stated his opinion forthrightly. 'We have done', he said, 'with the orthodox conceptions of God. We go farther than the ideal of a personal Being.' As he himself sees it, God is only the absolute 'I': 'Gott ist nichts als das absolute Ich'. Already he had no use for the arguments for divine existence deployed by the theologians. In fact, contemporary apologetic was evasive and dishonest and at odds with any genuine theology. He was especially critical of the moral argument of the Kantians which conceived God as an 'absolute Object' altogether external to the thinking subject. With all a young intellectual's brash confidence he regards himself as Kant's true successor and his own idealism, based on the concept of *das absolute Ich,* as the natural and proper outcome of the critical philosophy. But what did he mean by the phrase?

Schelling's dissatisfaction with the *Critique of Pure Reason* centred on the difficulty, as he saw it, that the various forms under which the mind is there represented as conceiving objects failed to point to a unitary underlying principle. Unless such a principle were to be disclosed, philosophy as essentially the unifying interpretation of experience could make no progress. Happily Fichte, in his *Wissenschaftslehre,* had shown the way forward. The ego is the experiencing subject, over against which is set the non-ego, the world of 'objective' realities present to the experiencing subject's mind. Inasmuch, though, as ego and non-ego stand in reciprocal relation to each other, the one being conditioned by the other, neither can be considered as absolute and so is unable to serve as the wholly unconditioned principle from which philosophy must start. At the same time the absolute principle is to be sought neither in the mere fact of the relativity of subject and object, nor in 'self-consciousness'. Indeed, self-consciousness has to be distinguished from it. What Schelling does therefore is to go beyond subject-object relativities to Fichte's *absolute Ich* or Ego, which not only has absolute causality in itself but is the precondition alike of the ego and the non-ego. The completed system of knowledge, he affirms, has to begin here, with the absolute Ego.

In the light of this principle Schelling faults in turn the theologians of his day, the philosophy of Spinoza and even a post-Kantian like K. L. Reinhold (1758-1823), whose reinterpretation of Kant he otherwise can describe as 'the morning light that precedes the noonday'. The first of these, taking their cue from Kant, introduce God as a moral postulate, but straight away transform him into a moral Being. While, that is, they rejoice in stressing the limitations of the speculative reason they play up the 'thing-in-itself' on moral or 'faith' grounds. Philosophy is thus meanly reduced to the requirements of the pulpit. But to conceive God as an absolute Being, in the way orthodox theology does, is inadmissible.

> Let us posit God as object and assume him to be the real ground of knowledge. Then, as object, he falls within the sphere of our knowledge. But if he is within the sphere of our knowledge he cannot be that whereon the entire sphere itself depends.

God does not, however, exist as an object, he is 'pure, absolute Ego', and to believe in an absolute, infinite object means the annihilation of the believing subject. Objectivity implies the mind's complete grasp of what it knows.

> Inasmuch as the object is a representation in the mind of man, man himself giving the object its form and conditions, man rules it. He has nothing to fear from it; he himself sets its limits. If he abolishes these limits, if the object can no longer be represented in his mind, he finds himself lost.

The error of dogmatism, as Schelling calls this mode of thinking, extends also to Spinoza, admire him as he so much does. Although 'the quiet intuition of rest in the arms of the world' has a profound appeal to many minds—something which the talkative moralism of the theologians lacks—Spinozism spells the end of freedom by identifying subjective causality with objective, since here again the personal ego is annulled. 'Spinoza has set up as the first principle of all philosophy a proposition which could be established only at the end of his system and as the outcome of the most painstaking proof.' He has also made the mistake of absolutizing what is in truth only an intuition of his personal ego, whereas, so Schelling himself maintains, 'everything that exists does so in the ego, outside of which there is nothing'.

Schelling is certain, furthermore, that 'consciousness', the empirical ego, cannot provide an adequate basis for philosophy. The empirical ego is, so to say, only our ordinary, everyday self—a finite experiencing being through whom the true self, the absolute Ego, never achieves total expression. Schelling thus infers that the empirical ego exists through a limitation of the absolute; it is, he would say, an inchoate or fragmentary expression of it, i.e. our ordinary self is in part, but only in part, identifiable with the true self. Hence the causality of the empirical ego is quantitatively but not qualitatively different from that of the absolute. The important difference between the two, however, is that although in everyday experience personality depends on the unity of the consciousness, 'the infinite *Ich* knows no consciousness, no personality.' Yet if we are to speak of God at all it is to the absolute Ego alone that the word can be applied. For the latter is at once the real and the ideal—both that which basically is and that towards which 'reality' is ever moving.

But how is the absolute Ego known? All ordinary knowledge, Schelling replies, derives in the last resort from 'immediate experience'. In the case of the Absolute, on the other hand, that experience is a matter of intellectual perception. Intellectual perception or intuition, but not logical deduction, since logical deduction itself presupposes it. In other words, knowledge of the Absolute is not discursive reflection, it occurs where the perceiving self is one with the perceived self—a moment at which the 'pure absolute eternity is within us'. This intuition of ultimate reality—reminiscent as it is of Schleiermacher's *Gefühl*—is for Schelling, I think, fundamentally religious. He says that Friedrich Heinrich Jacobi, a man of deep spiritual insight, had well described it, but admits nevertheless that it is something extremely difficult to express intelligibly in words, although it has much in common with what in the language of religion is called faith. To have this intuitive knowledge of the original and ideal unity is a state of blessedness; to fall away from it is to decline into sin.

The Absolute, therefore, is to be characterized first and foremost as the ultimately *real*. It is pure Being, as distinct from the specific entities that subsist under the categories of general law, which to it is inapplicable.

> Were there for the Infinite Self mechanism or purpose in nature, for it purpose would be mechanism and mechanism purpose; that is, both would coincide in its absolute Being. Hence even theoretical investigation must consider the teleological as mechanical, the mechanical as teleological, and both as comprised in one principle of Unity.

If God were to exist as object he would be a particular being, even though unique, whereas as absolute he is beyond the categories of being as we know it. The truth of this is brought home to us in a flash of intuitive certainty; we inwardly recognize the Absolute to be 'substantial' in a sense that renders all else accidental. But the absolutely real is also the absolutely *one*. It is not a species nor an individual, but is completely homogeneous, pure self-identity, that wherein being and thought wholly coincide. Finally, it is the ultimate causal principle, of knowledge as of being. 'In the Ego, philosophy through its struggles now gains the highest laurels of its strife; it has found the all-embracing unity.'

But, given the concept of the Absolute, how should the world be thought to have come into existence? Or, as Schelling himself phrases the question, How did the Absolute come out of itself and oppose the world to itself? This is the ancient and residual problem of all metaphysics, that of the one and the many, the transition from the infinite to the finite. The truth is, says Schelling, that as posed it is unanswerable. Thus we have to adopt the opposite procedure, that of starting with the finite but transcending it in a move towards the infinite. For finite and infinite are not juxtaposed as contingent, mutually exclusive entities; the finite is itself an aspect of the infinite. Spinoza understood this in regarding the self as no longer its own (*Eigentum*), but as belonging to an infinite reality. Yet the approach of the finite to the infinite demands never-ceasing effort. If the absolute Ego is theoretically the beginning of the quest, in practice it is its far-distant goal, to be reached only after an arduous journey. But this difficult and toilsome advance is preferable, because more rewarding, than the too-easy assurance offered by the 'moral' God of orthodox theology. As Schelling wrote to Hegel in the letter from which I have already quoted: 'There is no personal God, and our highest strife is to destroy our personality, passing over into the sphere of absolute Being, which however is something not in eternity *possible;* therefore only a drawing-near to the Absolute in action (*praktische*); and therefore—*immortality.*'

To the extent, Schelling concludes, that the infinite Ego is represented schematically as the ultimate goal of the finite ego—and thus external—God can be represented in practice as likewise *external* to the finite ego, but of course only as identical with the infinite Ego. Philosophically, he is saying that God is really to be conceived as the unity anterior to any separation of subjective form and objective content, and that it is only in terms of the absolute Ego that he can rightly be portrayed.

The second stage in the development of Schelling's thought has until fairly recently been the best known and the most influential, the 'philosophy of nature', the first important expression of which was the **Ideen** of 1797.

What we observe in this work is a distinct movement away from Fichte's predominantly subjective, ethical position, and an emphasis now on the non-ego. The world of nature, that is, is felt to be as important as the world of the self. In Fichte's *Wissenschaftslehre* the knowing and willing subject was the focal point of existence, but Schelling has become increasingly disposed to stress the self-existence of the objective world. Nature, however, is not to be understood simply at the level of empirical observation and scientific theory, the truth being that it has a deeper significance of its own which it is the function of speculative or intellectual intuition to penetrate and interpret. Basic to this conception—and astronomy, physics, biology and psychology, although separate sciences, require coordination—is the principle of a dualism of forces in polarity. These opposing forces may be described as, on the one side, positive, active and productive, and on the other as negative, restrictive and limiting. Matter, in truth, *is* force, its properties being repulsion and attraction. In each individual body, so Schelling argues, the forces of attraction and repulsion are in equilibrium, and apart from them nature is not intelligible. But dualism as such being foreign to his mind, Schelling seeks some dynamic, underlying reality, an 'absolute' unity, which the opposition of the forces must itself imply and from which they in fact emanate. But exactly how can the absolute One be conceived of as thus 'going out of' itself? It is a problem, Schelling saw, not easy to solve.

But to go back to the question of these forces—are they really equal? Schelling proceeds to show that they are not, although they are mutually necessary. The former, the 'positive', as we may call it, is of its very nature superior; for it is the positive which determines the fundamental character of reality as conditioned, while the negative simply provides the conditions without which there would be no reality. In other words, the positive is that by which alone the facts of existence can be explained, whereas the negative determines the form of reality through the limitation of those facts. In a sense, therefore, the positive is 'living', the negative 'dead'. Or to put it in another way, the positive can be thought of as a unity, the final condition of all things, whereas it is the function of the negative to break up the unity into multiplicity, imposing the specific conditions which determine what things are. Yet again, the positive may be associated with the organic, the negative with the mechanical. Nature is primarily an organism; though, as Schelling phrases it, the organic does not mean the absence of mechanism, but rather that mechanism obtains where no organism exists.

Thus for Schelling the positive is the ultimate force, the absolute One. It is, he says, 'the age-old idea of a primal "matter", which opens itself out into innumerable phenomena like the many single beams of light broken up in an infinite prism'. A not unfitting designation of this absolute One is *Weltseele,* 'World Soul', a term originating with the ancient Greeks, though here connoting not 'Mind' but physical force, describable variously as 'matter', 'ether', or 'light-ether'. Nor is it to be identified with the actual world-process, since this, as we have noted, involves duality and opposition. It is the 'organic' character of the Absolute, however, that explains life. Dead matter could not produce it. Life and spirit, in other words, are latent in nature, reaching self-consciousness in man. Reality has to be conceived therefore as evolving.

Viewed thus—not as mere 'object', that is, but as 'subject'—nature is essentially dynamic: *natura naturans,* productivity. Being *a priori* it cannot itself be known; we know *of* it only through its products. In a sense indeed product and productivity are mutually opposed, since every product signifies to some extent the limitation, or even the negation, of productive force. Yet this limitation is not purely negative: 'Universal duality, as a principle for explaining nature, is as necessary as the concept of nature itself.' It alone accounts for empirical or 'objective' nature—*natura naturata.* 'Nature as object is that which emerges from an infinite series', though what Schelling is here referring to is nature as a whole, not particular natural objects, inasmuch as 'absolute activity can be represented not by a finite product but only by an infinite one'. Thus empirical nature is never completely achieved or fulfilled; it is always a 'becoming', never, finally, a 'being'. If we ask 'What is the earth?' the answer is that 'its history is woven into that of nature as a whole, and this proceeds upwards from the fossil through inorganic and organic nature to the history of the universe—a single chain'. But the story can never be told in its entirety. 'Our science itself is an infinite task.'

The dialectical method so far adopted by Schelling was still that of Fichte, but applied not, as with the elder thinker, to the active consciousness of the ego but to the process of the non-ego, the external world. In the **System of Transcendental Idealism,** his most schematic work, he offers his own version of the philosophy of consciousness, bringing to the philosophy of nature insights derived from the critical theory of knowledge, to yield 'speculative physics' and 'transcendental philosophy'. The former, dealing with the objective world of nature, shows how intelligent consciousness arises; the latter, beginning with the subject or ego, how it is possible to attain to a knowledge of the 'objective' world of nature. What unifies them is the Absolute as identity of subjectivity and objectivity, so that both inquiries are, as it were, opposite sides of the same coin. But clearly the break with Fichte's thoroughgoing subjectivism is now approaching. The absolute Ego has become Nature. 'The Ego appears subjectively as infinite productivity; objectively, as eternal becoming.'

In tracing the growth of knowledge Schelling distinguishes three stages: from sensation to perception, from perception to reflection, and from reflection to volition. Sensation is simple awareness of the non-ego as limit: self-consciousness passes outward, so to speak, only to encounter the pressure of the non-ego upon it. So for the ego an objective world in *space* comes into being, and therewith immediate consciousness of the self as living and active in *time,* the relation between them being one of *causality.* This perception of the external world gives rise in turn to reflection, while from reflection on the interiority of the self as distinguishable from the not-self comes will, in which the ego takes account of itself as free, active power. Thus we pass from the first and theoretical part of the transcendental philosophy, intended to explain the inner world of the self, to the second and practical part, dealing with the free determination of the self through volition. But the will has to realize itself in terms of moral action—among individuals, in the state and in history. The end of the historical process is for Schelling the gradual realization of freedom under law, a movement towards the perfect state and even, ultimately, 'an Areopagus of peoples, made up of all civilized nations'. But more is wanted, Schelling thinks, than the light of a moral ideal to ensure that the end is attainable. Freedom has to become necessity, and necessity freedom. 'I demand', he says, 'something absolutely objective which, entirely independent of freedom, secures and, as it were, guarantees its highest goal.' Thus within human freedom we must suppose a 'hidden necessity' to be operative, the outcome of which will inevitably be something rational and harmonious. What we have to understand is the fact of an absolute identity between freedom and necessity, although of course it is not present to consciousness. Subjectively, and for inner experience, it is we who act; objectively, however, it is not we but something acting through us. In other words, the whole movement of history must be conceived as a revelation of the unconscious Productivity underlying all things, the Absolute in which real and ideal are one. Thus a perfect moral world-order is the *telos* of the entire historical process, so that we can speak of progress as assured. But because the Absolute is infinite the progressive movement must be unending, never finally complete. Or, to use religious language, God never *is* but gradually and continuously comes to be. His existence therefore cannot be given a logically conclusive demonstration; it can only be divined in the progressive march of history. For this reason God is not an object of *knowledge*—in the strict sense of the word—but only of *faith*, 'the eternal presupposition of action'. True religion is a 'system of Providence'.

The division of the transcendental philosophy into theoretical and practical parts completes an obvious parallelism with Kant's three *Critiques* when a third part introduces a philosophy of art. In neither the theoretical part nor the practical does reason, in Schelling's view, arrive at its highest realization, whereas in art, as he claims with true Romantic fervour, the human ego becomes one with the productive energy of nature. For here at last the self is aware of the cosmic creative power working through its own free acts. What the mind was unconsciously striving after, what the will was consciously seeking without ever fully realizing, art, we are told, actually achieves. Indeed the philosophy of art is 'the true organon of philosophy', and aesthetic idealism the coping-stone of the entire idealist system. 'The work of art reveals to us the identity of the conscious and the unconscious', its fundamental character being 'an unconscious infinite, a synthesis of nature and freedom'. Through his aesthetic sensibility the artist vouchsafes to mankind nothing less than a vision of the ultimate nature of reality, for what 'Providence' is for religion 'Genius' is for art: 'Genius is for aesthetics what the Ego is for philosophy, namely the highest absolute Real, which, while it never becomes objective, is yet the cause of everything that is objective.' Thus it is not ethics but aesthetics which signifies the final stage of the dialectical development of self-consciousness. Necessity and freedom, the unconscious and the conscious, the real and the ideal, nature and spirit are here wrought together in ultimate unity. To understand this is 'infinite satisfaction'. God, it may truly be said, is revealed as Beauty, with the inspired artist as his prophet. The unconscious, impersonal forces present but concealed in man's conscious acts in history have their counterpart in the emotional experience of the artist, in whom something greater than his conscious self flows through him to create what is infinite and eternal.

Title page of Vorlesungen über die Methode des academischen Studium.

By the year 1800 Schelling had completed the earlier phases of his system. In the first he had worked out a doctrine of the 'Object' or Nature, balancing this, in the second, with one of the 'Subject' or Spirit. He also had devised a philosophy of art to explain how in aesthetic experience Nature and Spirit are fused in concrete identity. It remained, however, to elicit and examine the metaphysical implications of that experience and to determine precisely how Nature and Spirit accomplish the union which is thus intuitively discovered. The ***Darstellung meines Systems der Philosophie*** of 1801 marks the beginning of the third phase of the scheme, the 'philosophy of Absolute identity', as Schelling fittingly calls it. The dialogue ***Bruno,*** which appeared in the following year, provided further detail, but it is in the ***Vorlesungen über die Methode des akademischen Studiums,*** published in 1803, that he explores its themes at length. The principle which this new form of the doctrine embodies is that the Absolute is neither Subject nor Object, neither Ego nor Nature, but an original unity which expresses itself in both. This absolute identity of nature and intelligence, of knower and known, is to be found in their common 'neutral' source, reason. 'All philosophy', states Schelling, 'consists in the recollection of the condition in which we were one with nature', and in recognizing the truth that knowledge, as a 'reproduction' of nature, is nature's highest expression. Hence an appropriate name for this philosophy would be 'objective idealism', in contrast to Fichte's 'subjective idealism' in which the ego is all, philosophy now being seen as the systematized knowledge of this 'neutral' absolute.

In setting out his doctrine Schelling draws on Plotinus, Giordano Bruno and Spinoza. He follows Spinoza's geometric method, that is, while Plotinus' *nous* suggests the concept of pure rationality; but Bruno's vitalistic pantheism—along with some hints from Herder and Goethe—supersedes Spinoza's materialistic determinism. The absolute Reason he defines as reason from which the rational intelligence of the individual has been abstracted. It is distinct therefore from any actual process of thinking; as Schelling himself phrases it, it is 'reason in so far as it is thought of as total indifference of the subjective and the objective'. It is equivalent to absolute knowledge, compassing both the 'form' and the 'essence' of the universe. And as the Absolute itself there is nothing outside it. It is the authentic *Ding-an-sich,* the sole 'thing-in-itself'. Accordingly, philosophical understanding is a knowledge of things as they are in themselves.

The problem, however, is to explain the existence of the finite world, the derivation of the many from the One. There can on Schelling's view be nothing 'outside' the Absolute. If the infinite real *contains* all that is then it cannot be the external cause of the universe, and to suppose otherwise has been the cardinal error of almost all philosophies in the past. The absolute Identity cannot 'step outside of itself'; indeed the whole of existence constitutes the absolute Identity. But if the Absolute is pure identity all distinctions must be external to it: as Schelling says, qualitative difference is possible only outside the absolute Totality. To resolve the crux any distinction of subject and object must be deemed illusory except from the point of view of empirical consciousness. The Absolute, that is, produces nothing 'out of' itself; it is not the source of things nor their ground; it is essentially *what they are in themselves.* The usual idea is that nature and spirit proceed from the original unity, so becoming mutually opposed as object and subject. Schelling, however, in his own philosophy of nature, has sought to show that nature, while material and unconscious as 'object', is as 'subject' spiritual and conscious. The transcendental philosophy had similarly demonstrated the same to be true of spirit. Thus everything that is represents the identity of subject and object. Each and every finite entity is the Absolute inasmuch as *in itself,* or at the level of absolute Reason, it is infinite. Ultimate reality is one, qualitatively undifferentiated.

How the empirical consciousness is able to take quite another view, and what status this view has ontologically, Schelling does not inform us, although the obvious fact is that whatever the residual unity which a monism like his may demand, empirical distinctions do remain. Qualitative difference Schelling disallows, as I have just said, but quantitative difference between subject and object he acknowledges, holding that in all things the subjective and the objective are in varying degree mingled. An excess or preponderance of one or the other he calls a 'Potency' or 'Power' (*Potenz*). In nature there is a preponderance of objectivity; in spirit, of subjectivity. The Absolute, however, is the identity of all such Potencies; in other words, were we capable of beholding all things in their totality we

would recognize a perfect equality. On the side of nature the first of these Potencies, Schelling thinks, is weight, with light as the second. The third, organism, is the common product of both. And what we find in the material world is present also in the ideal, where the Potencies are knowledge and action, with reason as the union of the two. In the order of 'values' these latter represent the true, the good and the beautiful respectively. The symmetry is thus complete.

We see, then, that although the Potencies are conceptually differentiated there is no real multiplicity within the One. Such multiplicity as appears is only an aspect of the unity, not something produced by it or generated from it. Empirically there is a process of evolutionary self-expression and self-recognition in the Absolute, but it is not creation *ex nihilo* as Christian theism teaches; it is simply an actualization of what already exists potentially. Nevertheless the Absolute as Subject-Object can exist only in differentiation. Resorting, as Schelling himself frequently does, to religious language, we may say that God has his existence in and through his progressive revelation in human experience, so that man is himself the cause or ground of God's being. But, since the process occurs only *in* the Absolute, and is in fact identifiable with the Absolute, it is no less true to say that God is *self*-caused, arriving at self-knowledge by the actualizing of his inherent potentiality.

In his last years at Jena, Schelling was wont increasingly to speak of the Absolute as divine. He did not indeed simply equate God with the Absolute; rather did he think of him as *natura naturans,* the primal unity of the unconscious World-Self. But this, it is to be noted, is a more static concept than his earlier one, for deity now is less an eternal activity or energizing will than 'rest and inactivity'; activity is to be found in the process of the finite. Hence God is an aspect of the Absolute rather than the whole of it. In himself he is beyond rational comprehension, but he is revealed in human history, in which Schelling distinguishes three successive epochs. The first is that of Nature: the ancient world, with its naturalistic religions, signifies the preponderance of the natural; its finest product was the religion and art of Greece. The epoch of Fate, which follows next, is that of late antiquity, characteristic of which is the mechanical legalism of Rome. But with Christianity the epoch of Providence commences. God became 'objective' for the first time in Christ, although the incarnation is not to be looked on simply as a unique temporal event: it is an eternal act. Christ represents in his own person the sacrifice of the finite in order to make possible the advent of the Spirit as the light of a new world. Thus Christianity's basic dogma is that of the trinity, an admission which should not obscure the fact that Schelling's theological views are nonetheless a good way from orthodoxy. He certainly sets little store by the Bible; replete as it is with legend and superstition, it is an obstacle to reason. A regenerated Christianity will depend on the triumph of speculative knowledge, in which religion will unite with poetry to form truth of a higher order. (pp. 92-102)

The *Philosophische Untersuchungen über das Wesen der menschlichen Freiheit* continues to maintain that God and the world are identical, but only in the sense that antecedent and consequent may be said to be identical. Schelling is seriously concerned, that is, to rebut the charge of pantheism. The visible world, *natura naturata,* is not itself

God, as pantheism in its common meaning supposes. Nor on the other hand does his philosophy imply an acosmism in which finite entities are somehow absorbed and dissolved in the Absolute. His own view is a form of immanentism, holding that all things are contained in God, who is their creative and sustaining principle. Importantly for the personal and moral life, it is an idea that allows room for human freedom. Indeed the paradox is that 'that which is not free is necessarily outside God'. But if God himself is free then the soul of man, which is God's image, is likewise free. 'In the final analysis', Schelling states, 'there is no other existence except Will. Will is original Being—groundlessness, independence of time, self-affirmation are applicable only to Will.' From our standpoint the essence of freedom is in the choice between good and evil, and the fact that we can and do choose between them. But if this is true of the consequent we may presume that it is true also of the antecedent. In which case are we not to deduce that the power of evil, because of his freedom, resides in God himself?

In answering this question guidance comes from human experience and personal introspection. Personality is not simply a 'given', it is an achievement. We emerge, as it were, from darkness into light. There is in our nature an impulsive, urge-driven side, rooted in psychological obscurity, in the subconscious. And it is on this foundation that our personality is built up. But in the process sense contends with spirit, instinct with reason. A man may allow himself to be dominated by sensual desire, or he may submit himself to the control of rationality and the moral law; yet even if he chooses the way of reason his life will not be free of moral conflict and strife. He never succeeds in liberating himself entirely from the pull or the pressures of his darker, subliminal self; the upward path is always hard-going. The power of *choice,* however, is his distinctive quality: 'Man is set on that summit where he has in himself the authority of self-movement towards good or evil. The bond of the principles in him is not necessity but freedom. He stands at the point of decision.' For of course freedom cannot but mean the possibility of evil. Are we, though, to say the same of God? Stimulated by his reading of Boehme, Schelling is prepared to attempt a conceptual analysis of the divine Being himself.

Ultimately, as we have seen, God has to be thought of as sheer unity, the 'absolute indifference', the undifferentiated Ground of all differentiation. As such he is not personal, since personality implies consciousness and self-integration. Yet this original unity, or 'Unground', as Schelling terms it—'a will in which there is no understanding'—divides itself into two equally eternal beginnings. What he intends to affirm by this is, seemingly, that God, being *causa sui,* his own cause, is to be distinguished both as existing and as caused, in such a way that we may conceive of the cause 'as not being itself God'. As Schelling expresses it: 'Since there is nothing before or outside of God he must therefore have the ground of existence in himself', but at the same time there is that 'in God which is not God himself'—i.e. 'that which is the ground of his existence'. But as this is no *temporal* relation of antecedent and consequent the two must be alike eternal. Thus the Absolute, we are to understand, is not simple but complex, distinguishable as simultaneously existence and ground of existence. Yet this original 'grounding' power or 'Will' of God, although inseparable from him, is in itself an irratio-

nality, eluding all understanding. His irrational or unconscious 'volition' can even be described as 'the egoism in God'. But out of it, Schelling maintains, comes a rational Will, loving and self-communicating: 'God himself is begotten in God.'

Thus God's being, from its very complexity, is dynamic and creative. 'The first beginning of creation is the yearning of the One to manifest itself; it is the Will of the Ground.' Nevertheless it is in this creative though irrational 'Will of the Ground' that the principle of evil lies—the divisive and alienating principle which is the opposite of Reason, since Reason *unites.* These two principles coexist in tension in all things. To summarize Schelling's argument in the words of [N. Hartmann]:

> Inasmuch as an original unity obtains between what is embodied in the Ground and what is embodied in the Reason, and inasmuch also as the process of creation is simply an inner transmutation or elevation of the original Dark Principle (*das dunkle Prinzip*) into Light, both being united in every natural existent, if in a limited degree.

In men the Dark Principle subsists as self-will—an appetite and impulse contrary to the universal principle of Reason which thus separates him from God. Yet when this same principle is raised to the Light something higher draws upon him, namely Spirit. In so far as the soul of man is the living identity of both principles it is Spirit, and Spirit is 'in' God. However,

> . . . if the identity of the two principles were as indestructible in the human spirit as it is in God there would be no distinction between God and the human spirit. In other words, God would not manifest himself. Therefore the unity which is indestructible in God must in man be capable of being destroyed. Hence arises the possibility of good and evil.

But although the possibility of evil is grounded in God himself, its realization occurs only in man. The divine personality—if I interpret Schelling aright—is basically a unity, an integrated whole, whereas the human personality is not; its constitutive elements are separable, and in fact are separate, only too obviously. The Dark Principle, the egoistic drive, tends to dominate it, with resulting discord within and disorientation of man's nature. Yet it has to be recognized that without this latent destructive power there would be no order of existence and therefore nothing which could be called good. The potentiality of the one is necessary for the actuality of the other.

Man's freedom, however, does not depend on absoluteness of choice, because it is not completely indeterminate. For his choice is grounded in what he constitutionally is, a rational being—a case, once again, of antecedent and consequent. But there is that also in him, Schelling holds, by which he can direct himself from the universal reason and will of Love and follow the dark, 'natural' and egoistic will of the Ground: 'Man has from eternity attached himself to egoism and self-seeking, and all who are born are born under the influence of the dark principle of evil.' Thus although a man's actions may be predictable he nonetheless is free; for here the determination is an inner one, created by the self's original choice—an act, Schelling thinks, which occurred below the level of consciousness, indeed outside of time and 'in the beginning of creation'. But this inner determination is itself freedom, in that a man's essence is inherently *his own act.* 'Necessity and freedom are mutually immanent, a single reality which appears to be one or the other only when looked at from different sides.' For this Schelling finds an ultimate metaphysical basis, since the Absolute itself embodies that identity of necessity and freedom which is present also in man. It has, I think, to be admitted that Schelling's theory of man's primal, unconscious but determinative choice—the self-positing of the ego—is not easy to understand. For in what can we suppose it to have consisted? The idea presents much the same problem, surely, as does Kant's notion of the origin of the 'radical evil' (*das radicale Böse*) in man. Schelling is evidently concerned to avoid anything suggestive of Calvinistic predestinarianism, while at the same time disallowing the view that man enjoys the liberty of complete indifference. The *tertium quid* he proposes, though, falls a good deal short of clarity.

Of the two conflicting principles in man's nature his own history furnishes the ample record. Without freedom he could have had no history, a condition which provides us with the key to a philosophy of history. From an original state of innocence in unconscious indifference and through increasing struggle and conflict, man's historical Odyssey moves onwards to that final 'Kingdom of God' in which evil, creative though it is, is at last subdued to good. History, that is to say, strives towards unity in a way which reflects the similar drive in nature itself. 'As the plurality of things in nature strives after a unity, and only in such unity reaches completion and the feeling of blessedness, so is the plurality of the world of man.' Schelling's **Weltalter,** had it ever been completed, would have purported to show this; but although he repeatedly announced its forthcoming appearance he never saw the work through to the end.

Yet, as I have just indicated, it is Schelling's contention that, apart from what our viewpoint is identifiable—paradoxically no doubt—as the principle of evil, there would be no finite creation, and thus neither human consciousness nor personality. But also, Schelling points out, no deity either.

> Consciousness begins the moment we become aware of the two principles within us, when we subdivide ourselves, when we set ourselves against ourselves, when with the better part of us we raise ourselves above the lower . . . The same holds true of God . . . The life of God has the closest analogy with the life of man.

Evil, then, it might well be said, is misdirected good, discord mixed with concord, but thereby composing an ultimate harmony. Good, in fact, is the true face of evil in so far as evil has a proper and probably necessary role in the process of the universe. It is in this sense that we can say of evil that it is divinely 'permitted', because God is not simply static Being but Becoming, Life. All life involves process, of which suffering is an inevitable concomitant. In order to become personal God himself entered into process, when he divided the light from the darkness. Being has to express itself in Becoming because it realizes itself only through opposition. Being is achieved *in* Becoming: God 'makes' himself—and suffers in consequence. Yet without the concept of a humanly suffering God, an idea, Schelling believes, common to all the spiritual religions of

antiquity, the course of history would be incomprehensible.

Thus is the divine life realized and manifested in the world-process: cosmogony is theology. The divine consciousness has its beginning in the creation of the world; 'nature' is God's nature, God's 'natural' being. For it is that which is determinate in God: 'The necessity of God is what we designate as the nature of God.' When, however, the 'creative Word' triumphs over the Dark Principle, Spirit emerges, in which the darkness and the light are united, both principles being subordinated to its own self-substantiation as personality. Yet even Spirit is not the cosmic process's highest achievement. The supreme place is reserved for Love, in which the being of God has its final expression and the universe attains the goal of its development. But it is man, we have to recognize, who in Schelling's system stands at the apex of creation. In him 'God first rests; in him is his main end reached'. All else in the natural order is peripheral; man it is who is at the centre of God's being, since he alone, for all his finite existence, is free. Placed, though, as he is between nature and spirit he commands a power that is capable of misuse; and, sadly, he has misused it. But, as the embodiment of the divine, salvation also was in his power. (pp. 106-10)

It is clear that Schelling himself believed that the history of religion is an index of God's self-disclosure, but the problem for him was, while recognizing this, to maintain the Christian religion's uniqueness. His solution of it would appear to be that Christianity manifests in all its fullness the *inner* truth of religion and that it does this not by some implicit logic governing the evolution of the religious consciousness but by God's chosen purpose of free decision. It is this which in Schelling's view constitutes the all-important difference between mythology and revelation, the truth which religion in all its forms seeks to embody being that which is made known, whole and perfect, in Christ. By what means, though, is this distinction and evaluation to be effected? Is Schelling in fact saying that the religious consciousness is 'blind' until philosophy intervenes to interpret it to itself? This certainly was not his intention, nor did he propose to submit revealed religion to criteria of judgment outside itself. Rather did he see his philosophy as articulating a process whereby religion arrives at full *self*-comprehension. A Christian philosophy, that is, will go beyond mere recapitulation of the doctrines and principles of the Christian faith and life by serving as a reasoned elucidation of them. The former are accepted in the first instance on authority, whereas a religious philosophy, as a work of discursive thought, is 'free'. As Schelling himself puts it, 'free religion is only *mediated* through Christianity; it is not immediately *posited* by it'. Basically it is the old scholastic principles of *fides quaerens intellectum,* and there is no suggestion now of an *Aufhebung* of theology by philosophy.

Schelling also has an account to offer of the actual history of Christianity. He distinguishes three main periods, beginning with a 'Petrine', the features of which are law and authority as associated with the Latin peoples and the Roman church. Its theological root is God as the ground of being and identifiable with the First Person of the Christian trinity. The second period he classifies as 'Pauline', although it is not regarded as having properly commenced until the Germanic Protestant Reformation of the sixteenth century. Its keynote is freedom. 'In Paul the principle was at hand through which the church could be freed, not from its unity but from its blind uniformity.' Theologically it relates to the Son. The third period, styled the 'Johannine', is yet to be, but will be recognizable by the convergence of the preceding periods and the reconciliation of authority and freedom in an organically unified Christian community. This will prove to be the age of the Holy Spirit, with the divine love as its energizing power. History then will have reached its goal and God will be all in all.

In Schelling speculative romanticism achieved its most florid expression. To find the One in the All, the infinite in the finite, was with him a passion. Consistently it was the Absolute that lay at the end of his philosophical pilgrimage—beyond the finite consciousness, beyond all empirical inquiry, including the entire range of the special sciences, and, although his thought progressed through a succession of stages, in themselves of sufficient diversity to render it well nigh impossible to speak of his 'system' as though it were a unity, the central conception persisted virtually unaltered. In early life he turned away from Christianity, only to return to it in after years, albeit slowly and tentatively. In the end he arrived at a kind of theism, indeed at a semblance of Christian trinitarianism, but it still was a curiously gnostic or theosophical and quasi-pantheistic religion which for him bore the Christian name, as the young Jakob Burckhardt was one of the first to point out. The reason could have been the presence in his mind of influences, too many and disparate, which he failed properly to assimilate and integrate. Mentally he was highly receptive, but despite his dedication to metaphysics he was without either analytical rigour or the gift for truly architectonic thinking. He could readily systematize, but seemed nonetheless incapable of achieving a firm structure of reasoning. In this he contrasts strikingly with Hegel, who soon learned to know his own mind with commanding certainty. Schelling, for all his precocity and unquestionable fertility in ideas, displayed throughout his life something of the intellectual *flâneur,* the dilettante, even the dabbler. Trained in the sciences, for which he persuaded himself he had an aptitude, his outlook was not scientific; he had over-many interests, with few of them grounded in thorough knowledge. Thus his speculations lost touch with reality, although his conviction of being able to speak on the deepest matters with vision and authority seems never to have been shaken. (pp. 114-16)

> *Bernard M. G. Reardon, "The Idea of God in the Philosophy of Schelling," in his* Religion in the Age of Romanticism: Studies in Early Nineteenth Century Thought, *Cambridge University Press, 1985, pp. 88-116.*

Robert Stern (essay date 1988)

[*In the following excerpt, Stern describes Schelling's conception of nature as a balance of opposing forces.*]

When it first appeared at Easter in 1797, Schelling's *Ideas for a Philosophy of Nature* marked the real beginning of a new phase in his philosophical development. Two years before its publication Schelling had left the Tübingen theological seminary, where he had met and made friends with Hegel and Hölderlin, and had taken up a post as private tutor to an aristocratic family; in 1796 he moved with

the family to Leipzig. There he plunged into a study of medicine, physics and mathematics, and arrived at a picture of nature that emphasized its polarity and dynamism. This new attention to nature led Schelling to break away from the Fichtean themes that had dominated his previous writings. It is true that he retained elements of his previous outlook, and tried to fit his conception of nature into the framework of the Fichtean idealism of his early works; nonetheless, Schelling's discovery of nature represents the start of a fresh phase in his philosophical career. The *Ideas* of 1797 came out of these new reflections on nature, to be followed a year later by *On the World Soul,* the second of Schelling's major works on *Naturphilosophie*. These works at once brought him fame, as well as the support of Goethe, who secured for him a professorship at Jena in 1798.

Six years after its first publication, in 1803, Schelling brought out a second edition of this work, in which he added extensive supplements to the original text. By this time, however, the philosophical background to Schelling's dynamic conception of nature was no longer that of Fichte's dialectic of subject and object, but was now that of his own neo-Platonic philosophy of the absolute. This introduction will begin by explaining Schelling's dynamic conception of nature, and will then examine the effect on this conception of Schelling's change in philosophical outlook between the two editions of the *Ideas.*

In *On the World Soul* Schelling declares that "it is the first principle of a philosophical doctrine of nature to *go in search of polarity and dualism throughout all nature.*" As with Heraclitus, this emphasis on polarity was associated by Schelling with a conception of nature as a balance of opposed forces or tendencies, a balance that when disrupted leads to strife and activity. In particular, Schelling argues in the *Ideas* that matter, which appears to be dead and inert, is in fact nothing more than an equilibrium of these opposed forces, and that it may be "brought to life" when this equilibrium is disturbed and a conflict of forces ensues:

> In the *dead object* everything is *at rest*—there is in it no conflict, but eternal equilibrium. Where physical forces divide, living matter is gradually formed; in this struggle of divided forces the living continues, and for that reason alone we regard it as a visible analogue of the mind.

Schelling, therefore, stands opposed to the Newtonian picture of matter as made up of hard, impenetrable, inert particles that are acted on by forces external to them. He claims that "absolute inertness . . . is a concept without sense or significance," and argues instead that matter is an equilibrium of active forces that stand in polar opposition to one another.

As Schelling acknowledges, this notion of matter is derived in large part from Kant's "construction" of matter in the *Metaphysical Foundations of Natural Science* (1786). There, in the chapter entitled "Dynamics," Kant argues that the apparent solidity and impenetrability of material nature are in fact derived from a repulsive force that must be balanced by an attractive force if matter is not to "disperse itself to infinity." Kant insists that *both* these opposed forces are essential for the construction of matter, and material bodies should be seen as arising from the union of the two:

> That property upon which as a condition even the inner possibility of a thing rests is an essential element of its inner possibility. Therefore, repulsive force belongs just as much to the essence of matter as attractive force; and one cannot be separated from the other in the concept of matter.

In opposition to the "mathematico-mechanical" approach of atoms and the void, therefore, Kant had argued for a "metaphysico-dynamical" conception of matter as made up of a balance of opposed forces.

Kant's "metaphysico-dynamical" conception clearly forms the background to Schelling's account of matter given in the first six chapters of Book II of the *Ideas.* These chapters form the central core of the work. Like Kant, Schelling argues that attractive and repulsive forces are "conditions of the *possibility* of matter": "Matter and bodies, therefore, are themselves nothing but products of opposing forces, or rather, are themselves nothing else but these forces." Like Kant also, Schelling contrasts his understanding of matter with that of the Newtonian atomists, who treat matter as if it were independent of force by allowing "reflection" to separate the latter from the former.

Schelling therefore begins from the presupposition (which, as we shall see, he thinks can only be grounded *philosophically*) that "attractive and repulsive forces constitute the *essence* of matter itself." As a result Schelling claims to be able to dispense with all the efforts of a purely *mechanistic* physics, to explain the gravitational attraction of matter in mechanical terms. In particular, in Chapter 3 of Book II, Schelling sets out to refute the explanation of gravitation offered by the French-Swiss theorist Georges-Louis le Sage, who had postulated an ether of minute particles (*particules ultramondaines*) moving in all directions at high velocity in all parts of space. Le Sage then explained the phenomenon of gravitational attraction by arguing that two ordinary spherical bodies would screen each other from the bombardment of these particles, so that on the side of each body facing the other the impact of particles would be less than that on the other side, and the resulting disequilibrium of force would impel the bodies towards each other. Schelling dismisses this hypothesis, not only on the grounds that it still leaves the motion of the minute particles unexplained, and that the idea of indivisible primary particles is absurd, but also because his (or Kant's) dynamical conception of matter renders le Sage's mechanistic hypothesis redundant.

In the following three chapters of Book II Schelling then goes on to give an explanation of the chemical properties of bodies and chemical processes on the basis of the dynamical account of matter. In the first of these chapters on chemistry he takes up the question of the *qualitative* determination of matter. He argues that although matter in general is constructed from an equilibrium of the "basic forces" (*die Grundkräfte*) of attraction and repulsion, particular qualities of matter in fact derive from an upsetting of this equilibrium, and a predominance of one of these forces over the other; otherwise, Schelling maintains, the forces would simply cancel each other out, in which case neither force would be present in matter to any determinate degree:

> Thus force as such can affect us only insofar as it has a particular degree. But so long as we think of these dynamical forces quite generally—in a wholly indeterminate relationship—neither one of them has a particular degree. We can picture this relationship as an absolute *equilibrium* of these forces, in which the one always cancels out the other, and neither allows the other to grow up to a particular degree. So if *matter* as such is to acquire *qualitative* properties, its forces will have to have a particular degree, i.e., they will have to depart from the generality of the relationship in which the mere understanding thinks of them—or more plainly—they will have to deviate from the equilibrium in which they are originally and necessarily conceived.

From this argument Schelling derives what he calls the "principle of dynamical chemistry": *"All quality of matter rests wholly and solely on the intensity of its basic forces."* The qualities Schelling is referring to here are essentially those of elasticity and mass, where the former is associated with the repulsive force, and the latter with the attractive force. Other properties, such as colour and temperature, are dependent on these primary qualities, especially on the quality of elasticity.

Using this principle of dynamical chemistry, Schelling then goes on to give his account of chemical processes and chemical affinity. As one might expect, he rejects any attempt (e.g., by le Sage or Georges-Louis Leclerc, Comte de Buffon) to offer a Newtonian explanation of chemical affinities in terms of an ether or gravitational attraction (although he grants that these conceptions may have some value as hypotheses, insofar as they help to turn chemistry into a mathematical science). Instead he argues that chemical affinity occurs between bodies with opposite degrees of basic forces (i.e., a high degree of repulsive force and a low degree of attractive force on the one hand, and a low degree of repulsive force and a high degree of attractive force on the other); such bodies, he maintains, will enter into chemical reactions in order to restore their imbalance of basic forces to an equilibrium. Schelling goes on to argue that as a result the way to set a chemical reaction into motion is to upset this equilibrium between the basic forces of two bodies, so that they are forced into combination if a balance of forces is to be restored. The chemical product that results from this combination will be a median of the basic forces of the two opposed bodies. (It has to be said that this conception of the chemical process led Schelling into some strange views: For example, he seems to have held that the paradigm of a chemical reaction is that between a solid and a fluid body, where the former has a high degree of attractive force, and the latter has a high degree of repulsive force. Nonetheless, though the terms and concepts he employs are rather different, Schelling's account is in some respects closer than that of the Newtonians to an account of chemical affinity in terms of opposed electrical charge.)

Now that we have seen how for Schelling matter only enters into chemical interaction when the balance of attractive and repulsive forces within "dead matter" is disturbed, we can look more profitably at Book I of the *Ideas,* where he discusses combustion, light, air, electricity and magnetism.

Schelling's theory of heat and combustion rests on his dynamic conception of matter. On the one hand, he rejects absolutely the caloric theory of heat, which treats heat as an imponderable fluid that enters into chemical combination with the body when it is warmed: Schelling observes that "to postulate a heat-matter as the cause of heat is not to explain the situation, but to pay oneself with words." On the other hand, although he appears to go along with the kinetic theory in accepting that heat is a "mere modification of matter as such," he still rejects any *mechanical* explanation of the expansion of a heated body as being caused by vibrating atoms that push one another apart. In opposition to both these current explanations of heat, Schelling develops a theory more in line with his dynamical explanation of matter, arguing that heat is simply a particular degree of repulsive or expansive force possessed by a heated body, which may be communicated to another body until equilibrium is restored. Nonetheless, although Schelling insists that heat itself does not enter into chemical combination with the heated body, he argues that heat may be the cause of chemical combinations, as occurs, for example, in combustion: In increasing the degree of repulsive force within the body, heating enables it to combine chemically with oxygen, which is "charged" with the opposite attractive force.

In his treatment of light, Schelling is also unwilling to allow the existence of a special "light-stuff" or substance, which can enter into chemical combinations with other forms of matter (although he allows that this view of light may have some value as a scientific *fiction*). Rather, he argues that light is nothing more than "the highest degree known to us of the expansive force"; it differs from heat in that whereas *any* state of matter (gas, liquid or solid) can possess that degree of expansibility or repulsive force felt as heat, only air is capable of that degree of expansive force required in order to be a medium for light.

Air interests Schelling, however, not simply because it is the "medium that conducts to earth the higher forces (light and heat)" but also because the atmosphere displays an equilibrium and interaction of opposed moments. Air is therefore an important instance of the balance of polarity in nature, where the vital air (oxygen) given off by the vegetable kingdom is balanced by the exhalation into the atmosphere of "mephitic gas" (carbon dioxide) by the animal kingdom: "The collectively uniform distribution of substances, which dispenses ever new materials in nicely calculated proportions into the atmospheric cycle, never lets it reach the point where a perfectly pure air would exhaust our vital forces, or a mephitic gas would stifle all seeds of life." Atmospheric air also displays a polar opposition of life-giving oxygen on the one hand, and azotic air (nitrogen) on the other, which in contrast to the former is damaging to all living beings. Schelling rejects absolutely the suggestion of Christoph Girtanner that the elements of atmospheric air are separated into layers, and argues strongly that they must be chemically mixed.

From this account of the duality of air Schelling moves on in the next chapter to a discussion of that polar phenomenon *par excellence*, that favourite of all the Romantics and *Naturphilosophen*, which so excited the popular and scientific imagination throughout the period: electricity. Given that Schelling's philosophy of nature as a whole places such an emphasis on polarity and the basic forces of attraction and repulsion, it is not really surprising that electricity so fascinated him, and his account of it is very much determined by his general dynamic conception of matter as I have analysed it. This conception leads him to reject

Benjamin Franklin's picture of electricity as a subtle elastic fluid, arguing that the postulation of such a fluid is nothing but a "*lazy Philosophy of Nature,* which believes it has explained everything if it postulates the causes of phenomena as basic materials in the bodies, from which they then emerge (*tamquam Deus ex machina*) only when needed to explain some phenomenon in the shortest and most convenient way." Instead Schelling argues that positive electricity is the result of the elasticity of matter, while negative electricity is the result of its cohesion. He then goes on to suggest that this cohesion of matter is caused by oxygen, which he characterizes as a "cohesion-intensifying principle." Schelling brings together both these points in the second-edition supplement to this chapter.

> We can accordingly state the general law of the electrical relation of bodies thus: *That one of the two which enhances its cohesion in opposition to the other will have to appear negatively electric, and that one which diminishes its cohesion, positively electric.* It is evident from this how the electricity of every body is determined, not only by its own quality, but equally by that of the other. As is shown in the foregoing chapter, though very incompletely, the bearing which the electric relationship of bodies has upon that of their oxidizability is intelligible, since this too is determined by cohesion-relationships.

This account of oxygen as causing cohesion in matter, and thereby giving rise to negative electricity, explains Schelling's curious-looking claim in the first edition that "*the basis of negative electrical matter is either oxygen itself or some other basic substance wholly homogeneous with it.*" Given this account of oxygen, Schelling is able to arrive at a dynamical picture of electricity, explaining the negative pole in terms of an increased attractive force caused by oxidation, while at the same time being able to dispense with a unique electrical matter or fluid to account for the presence of this negative electrical charge.

Schelling displays a similar reluctance to allow the existence of imponderable fluids in his discussion of magnetism. While he grants that the one-fluid theory of Franz Aepinus has considerable value as a *hypothesis,* he does not accept that this magnetic fluid is any more than "a (*scientific*) *fiction,* on which to base *experiments* and *observations* (as *regulative*), but not *explanations* and *hypotheses* (as *principle*). For if we speak of a magnetic matter, we have in fact said nothing more by this than what we knew anyway, namely, that there has to be *something* which makes the magnet magnetic." In the case of magnetism, however, Schelling offers little by way of an alternative explanation of the magnetic properties of bodies, although he hints that a chemical explanation may be the most fruitful path to follow.

Now there is no doubt that one major reason for Schelling's hostility towards the postulation of special fluids and matters to account for phenomena like light, heat, electricity and magnetism in Book I of the *Ideas* is his conception of matter as essentially constructed from the polar opposition of dynamical forces, forces that can be used to account for these phenomena, and which need no *further* explanation in terms of matters and fluids. The only explanation that Schelling feels *can* be offered for this polarity of basic forces cannot in fact be given at the level of empirical science at all, but rather must come from outside our possible experience; "we are therefore obliged to ascend to philosophical axioms," to the "higher science" of philosophical explanation. (pp. ix-xvi)

Schelling's philosophical thought, though not without a degree of continuity, is nonetheless notoriously protean, and his outlook changed a good deal between the two editions of the *Ideas.* By 1803 Schelling had worked out his so-called philosophy of identity, most notably in his *Exhibition of My System of Philosophy* (1801) and *Further Exhibitions from the System of Philosophy* (1802), as well as in his dialogue *Bruno; or, Concerning the Divine and Natural Principle of Things* (1802). In these writings Schelling no longer explained the fundamental phenomenon of difference and polarity in the Fichtean way, as the dialectical positing by a one-sided moment of its opposite; rather, Schelling's philosophy now encompassed the absolute, and duality was now understood as the division of a primordial neo-Platonic unity. Thus, whereas in the first edition of the *Ideas* Schelling's deduction of the polarity of nature had been purely dialectical—as the transition of one moment into its opposite or other—in the second edition this polarity is conceived as the unfolding into difference of an original unity. This new conception is neatly summed up in the following passage from Giordano Bruno, which Schelling presents as giving the "creed of true philosophy" towards the end of his eponymous dialogue:

> To penetrate into the deepest secrets of nature, one must not tire of inquiring into the opposed and antagonistic extremes or end points of things. To discover their point of union is not the greatest task, but to do this and then develop elements out of their point of union, this is the genuine and deepest secret of art.

The point of union from which Schelling's identity philosophy begins is the absolute, which is utterly homogeneous and undifferentiated, a Parmenidean One. Now, whereas on a purely dialectical approach this empty absolute would inevitably give rise to its opposite, thereby introducing duality and opposition into the picture, Schelling's identity philosophy is not dialectical in this way; rather, he posits duality as arising *within the absolute itself,* as a "self-division of the undivided absoluteness into subject and object," opposites that must then be brought back to unity, while preserving their difference. This movement gives rise to Schelling's doctrine of three levels or potencies (*die Potenzen*), as a hierarchy of structures that must be repeated by each finite thing or class of things. The first potency is that of relative identity, which involves the transition of unity into difference; the second potency is that of relative difference, which involves the opposite and complementary movement of difference into unity; and both these potencies are encompassed by a third potency of absolute identity, which is the identity of identity and difference. Schelling insists, however, that this third potency, of absolute identity, is in fact primary, and that the other two emerge from it only after the "eternal self-division of the absolute into subject and object," which brings about the introduction of difference into this unity.

In the supplementary Introduction he wrote for the second edition of the *Ideas,* Schelling presents these three levels or potencies using the scholastic terminology of form and essence:

> In this absoluteness and in the eternal act, it [the absolute] is utterly one, and yet, in this unity, again immediately a totality of the three unities, namely, that in which the essence is absolutely shaped into form, that in which the form is absolutely shaped into essence, and that in which both these absolutenesses are again one absoluteness.

Schelling does nothing to explain his use of this terminology here, but a fuller (though by no means unproblematic) account is given by the character called Alexander in the *Bruno.* From this account it is clear that Schelling conceives of a thing's essence as infinite and undifferentiated, whereas its form constitutes the element of limitation and determination; and the absolute, as the form of all forms, unifies this limitation and finiteness with the infinite essence, thereby bringing together both unity and multiplicity in an absolute unity. Moreover, even when in the *Ideas* Schelling uses the different terminology of universal and particular and infinite and finite, the point he is making is basically the same: The absolute is the unity of the twofold movement of unity into difference (or universal into particular, or infinite into finite) and difference into unity (or particular into universal, or finite into infinite).

From this Schelling argues that there must be three levels or potencies in Nature-philosophy. The first potency is the movement of the infinite into the finite, in which the unity of the former gives rise to the spatially differentiated material bodies that make up the world. The second level is made up of the "reverse embodiment of the particular into the universal or essence," in which the universal is given its highest expression in the phenomenon of light. Finally, both these movements are brought together in the primary unity of the third potency, which is represented in the natural world by the organism, as the "perfect mirror-image of the absolute in Nature and for Nature."

In addition, Schelling not only uses this doctrine of potencies to give an account of magnetism (as the transition of identity into difference), electricity (as the transition of difference into unity) and chemistry (as the union of this twofold movement); he also deduces from it the construction of matter that he puts forward in the second edition of the *Ideas.* As in the first edition, he constructs matter from the opposed basic forces of attraction and repulsion; but instead of deducing these forces *dialectically,* as opposites requiring each other in order to come into being, he now simply derives them from the twofold movement of the absolute, as an original unity that produces difference out of unity and unity out of difference.

It should now be clear how in the second edition Schelling's whole philosophy of nature has been rethought against the background of his identity philosophy, in the context of his neo-Platonic meditations on the relation of the one to the many. As a result, nature's polarity is no longer seen as a purely dialectical positing of contraries, but rather as the division of an original unity. "Matter, too, like everything that exists, streams out from the eternal essence, and represents in appearance an effect, albeit indirect and mediate only, of the eternal dichotomizing into subject and object, and of the fashioning of its infinite unity into finitude and multiplicity." With this new philosophy of nature Schelling incorporated the dialectic of contraries into his account of the transition of the one into the many; he thereby succeeded in making the dialectic part of his neo-Platonic conception of reality, an aspect of the dialectic that was only really lost when Hegel managed to break away from Schelling's doctrine of the absolute.

Schelling's *Ideas for a Philosophy of Nature* is a work of considerable historical interest: It offers many insights into the development of Schelling's thought and of post-Kantian German idealism, into the history and philosophy of science of the period, and into the whole intellectual phenomenon of *Naturphilosophie,* which is represented here by one of its most forceful and influential proponents. Moreover, the *Ideas* is of more than merely historical interest. The view of nature, of philosophy and of empirical science that it puts forward is both daring and all-embracing, and as such it should be admired as one of the most startling and original attempts of human speculation to provide us with a total account of the nature of what is. (pp. xx-xxiii)

> *Robert Stern, in an introduction to* Ideas for a Philosophy of Nature as Introduction to the Study of This Science, *1797 by Friedrich Wilhelm Joseph von Schelling, translated by Errol E. Harris and Peter Heath, Cambridge University Press, 1988, pp. ix-xxiii.*

Douglas W. Stott   (essay date 1989)

[*Stott is an American-born German translator who specializes in theological translation. In the following excerpt, Stott explains how Shelling's* Philosophy of Art *is predicated on his understanding of identity and the absolute developed between 1800 and 1804.*]

At the turn of the [eighteenth] century Schelling's . . . philosophical development had progressed into what many subsequently considered to be his most important period, namely, the philosophy of identity. He suggested that the dynamic force (act) at work in the various faculties of the human intellect or spirit was the same (identical) as that which was at work in the production of nature, though viewed merely from a different perspective. At the fundamental level of dynamic force or activity, the *reality* of nature was in fact identical with the *ideality* of the spirit or intellect. In other words, it was not quite correct to assert that the principle of subjectivity itself constituted the first principle of philosophy and of cognition, and that this principle thereby rendered ontologically inferior or subordinate that part of the world that was apparently separate from the human ego. Rather, Schelling pushed the infinite regression of the principle behind self-consciousness back yet a step further. Not the principle of subjectivity as displayed in human self-consciousness—its self-identity—constitutes that first principle, but rather the principle of *identity* itself implied by that configuration. Not the identity of knower and known (and of knower of the identity of knower and known), but rather identity *as such* constituted that first principle. Hence, the absolute manifests itself equally both in the (real) products of nature and in the (ideal) products of the spirit.

Much of Schelling's philosophical activity during this period was directed toward articulating this fundamental vision. The implications of this vision, of course, are considerable, since the two realms into which ordinary understanding separates reality—the subjective and objective—

no longer are really separate, or are separate only from certain perspectives. Ultimately, this identity implies what is now known as the unified field theory in physics, or the systems theory. Schelling asserted that it was the task of the philosophy of nature to investigate the (real) world of nature, and the task of the philosophy of spirit to investigate the (ideal) world of the intellect.

Unfortunately, Schelling was to find that in its rather abstract identity that absolute was particularly recalcitrant when one tried philosophically to derive the palpable world of factical reality from it. How does this absolute actually generate the world around us, and me as an individual human being? How is the transition effected between the abstract quality of absoluteness implied by this understanding of identity *as such,* and the phenomenal world around us?

In the philosophical pieces Schelling wrote during this period—and he wrote a great many—he tried to get at this question from various lines of attack. Most of them, understandably, have Platonic or, more specifically, Neoplatonic overtones. He is never quite satisfied, though, with the interface—or lack of it—between the absolute and the factical world implied by such terms as "emanation" or "outflowing" from the absolute, though he constantly employs these terms. In one philosophical work associated closely with the philosophy of art, the *System der gesammten Philosophie und der Naturphilosophie insbesondere* of 1804, Schelling variously speaks about a thing being a "reflex" or "reflected image" of the All, about "expressions" of ideas, about things "going forth" from the absolute, and especially about things or circumstances "following from" the absolute, and about "results" of the activity within the absolute. Significantly, he did not publish this *System* of 1804, apparently because he was dissatisfied even though it was an accurate exposition of his view of the absolute and its consequences at the time. Neither did Schelling publish these lectures on the philosophy of art, whose composition coincides roughly with that of the *System* of 1804. Although there were several probable reasons for this reluctance, reasons we will discuss shortly, at least one concerned the central problem within the *System* of 1804: the derivation of content from the absolute.

To understand this more clearly, one must comprehend the importance of the concept of the absolute, ground, or first principle in Idealist thinking. It has been said of the work of the twentieth-century theologian Karl Barth that, once one grants him his point of departure in revelation, everything else follows with strict necessity. Schelling ardently wished the same could be said of his own works, and indeed asserted that it could: once this understanding of the absolute has been posited, all else follows with logical necessity; there can be but one philosophy.

Schelling apparently challenged himself in the *System* of 1804 on just this point, and ultimately was not satisfied with his solution. He quickly moved on to rethink his understanding of that absolute first principle grounding the system. The *Philosophy of Art,* however, is yet predicated on this earlier understanding of the absolute.

Having once established the first principle, that of identity, Schelling is concerned with showing scientifically—with strictly systematic methodology—that the world of art as we know it results from the activity characterizing the absolute, and itself constitutes a systematic, self-enclosed whole. In a similar fashion, he believes he has already shown how both the world of nature and the world of the spirit result with equal necessity from that principle, since the dynamic force at work in both is identical (hence, system of identity). What he will actually construct or construe (*construiren, Construktion*) here is the *system of arts necessarily resulting from that principle*. Since it is a system of the individual art forms *as such,* and not one based on a particular selection of works of art (however exemplary one might consider them to be), it necessarily precedes any actual works themselves. It does not precede them temporally, however, as would a system based on principles extracted from actual works, nor is a temporal process involved in its actual generation by the absolute. Rather, it lacks all relationship to time, and precedes actual works of art absolutely, just as the idea of a circle precedes any one, individual circle absolutely. This recalls the problem of the derivation of finite content from an infinite absolute, for if that absolute lacks all relationship to time, how is the temporal world generated from within it?

If, however, we leave this question in abeyance for the sake of proceeding out from that absolute; if, that is, we assume that if finiteness exists at all, some transition must obtain between the absolute and the world of finitude—and not merely a logical transition—we can then analyze what Schelling considers to be a logical sequence proceeding from the absolute ultimately resulting in the real and ideal worlds of nature and the spirit. Everything further, Schelling now asserts, follows with utter necessity. (Schelling argues elsewhere that only from the perspective of finite consciousness itself does this question arise regarding the derivation of content from the absolute, or regarding this transition from infinity to finitude; he does, however, still encounter difficulties deriving finite consciousness.)

Although the principle behind the system—indeed, behind all reality, both real and ideal, behind both the realm of nature and that of the spirit—is absolute identity, that identity is not as purely *one* as it might appear upon first consideration. If one posits identity as such, one has also posited its two possible members, even if they are, as the term implies, themselves identical. If A = A (a common equation that both Fichte and Schelling use), one at least has to consider the unit A from both sides of the equation, and thus recognize difference in identity. This suggests that in some way one is nonetheless dealing with a dualistic first principle. In the works constituting the system of identity, Schelling attributes several terminological pairs to this identity. It is the identity of spirit and nature, subject and object, ideal and real, universal and particular, conscious and unconscious, and particularly the identity of freedom and necessity (the latter pair corresponding to the necessity with which the system of nature operates and the freedom with which, ideally, the human world or world of history should operate). This principle of identity or the absolute point of identity of philosophy is also the absolute in and for itself, *one* absolute reality, *one* essence. This *one* absolute, the *one* absolute idea of the identity of the real and the ideal, stands behind Schelling's philosophy during this period.

In the *System* of 1804, however, and also in the *Philosophy of Art,* Schelling begins referring to this absolute as God. His introduction of the term may be explained per-

haps by the increasing attention he gives the ontological implications of his metaphysical assertions. That is, precisely the problem of the derivation of content from this absolute forced the issue of the ontological status both of the absolute and of that which results from it. The revelatory aspect of art had already played an important role in the *System of Transcendental Idealism,* a role that art arguably never relinquishes during Schelling's long career. In the final sections of that work, he postulates an intuition that discloses or reveals precisely that which the philosopher seeks to establish, namely, the identity of the real and the ideal, the

> *identity of the conscious* and the *unconscious* in the *self,* and *consciousness of this identity.* The product of this intuition [the work of art] will therefore verge on the one side upon the product of nature, and on the other upon the product of freedom, and must unite in itself the characteristics of both.

Only artistic genius, Schelling asserts, is able to effect this union and lend it objective form in a work of art. There inheres, however, an unknown element within this production that makes this union possible in the first place, and which is thus actually the element we intuit in the objective manifestation of the work of art:

> This unknown, however, whereby the objective and the conscious activities are here brought into unexpected harmony, is none other than that absolute [the primordial self] which contains the common ground of the preestablished harmony between the conscious and the unconscious.

The implications for philosophy, and thus for the relationship between art and philosophy, emerge from this expressly revelatory character of art:

> The whole of philosophy starts, and must start, from a principle which, as the absolute principle, is also at the same time the absolutely identical. An absolutely simple and identical cannot be grasped or communicated through description, nor through concepts at all. It can only be intuited. Such an intuition is the organ of all philosophy.—But this intuition, which is an intellectual rather than a sensory one, and has as its object neither the objective nor the subjective, but the absolutely identical, in itself neither subjective nor objective, is itself merely an internal one, which cannot in turn become objective for itself: it can become objective only through the second intuition. This second intuition is the aesthetic.

> The work of art merely reflects to me what is otherwise not reflected by anything, namely that absolutely identical which has already divided itself even in the self. Hence, that which the philosopher allows to be divided even in the primary act of consciousness, and which would otherwise be inaccessible to any intuition, comes, through the miracle of art, to be radiated back from the products thereof.

Hence, in art the philosopher finds revealed objectively that which grounds his entire system, namely, the absolute itself, or absolute identity, and art is granted an expressly revelatory function:

> If aesthetic intuition is merely intellectual intuition become objective, it is self-evident that art is at once the only true and eternal organ and document of

philosophy, which ever and again continues to speak to us of what philosophy cannot depict in external form, namely the unconscious element in acting and producing, and its original identity. Art is paramount to the philosopher, precisely because it opens up to him, as it were, the holy of holies, where burns in eternal and original unity, as if in a single flame, that which in nature and history is rent asunder, and in life and action, no less than in thought, must forever fly apart.

By the time he gave the lectures on the philosophy of art, and by the time he had clarified his understanding of the absolute that we find presented in the *System* of 1804, Schelling had for all practical purposes parted ways with Fichte's one-sidedly subjective understanding of the absolute; the "primordial self" in the passage quoted earlier was itself subsumed under absolute identity, of which it is a mere expression, and the problem of differentiation between the two had become more urgent. This also pressed the issue of the revelatory function of mythology, and likely played a role in Schelling's shifting terminology and introduction of the designation of the absolute as God.

In these lectures, however, Schelling associates several other terminological pairs with the idea of absolute identity as well. The concept of identity itself, and thus the ultimate identity of the various terminological pairs associated with it, constitutes what we may call the basic *organizational* or *relational* principle of the universe, and accordingly also of what Schelling will call the *All*, including the real and ideal worlds (of nature and of the spirit). Since God is now another designation for that absolute, the reader will not go astray if when encountering the term *God* he thinks instead "the ultimate or basic organizational principle of the universe." Indeed, this could apply to the terms *absolute* or *identity* as well. The logical nature of that structure should be noted; it is not an ultimate *being* but rather a relational principle. Additionally, as is consonant with Idealist thinking, it implies the idea of generative *activity*.

In its overall conception, Schelling's system of identity encompasses three distinct "philosophies" that are, however, essentially one: the philosophy of nature, the philosophy of the spirit (transcendental philosophy), and the philosophy of art. The actual object of philosophy *as such,* however, is always the same; it is the *one* essence, the *one* absolute reality, viewed as it manifests itself in nature, in the world of the spirit, and in art. Strictly speaking, one should also speak here of Schelling's philosophy of identity, that is, that philosophy explicating the identity as such of that which is in nature and spirit. The philosophy of art deals with that identity as it manifests itself in the world of art.

A crucial qualification of this one essence, however, is that it is indivisible. Absolute identity as such enters into everything encompassed by the world of nature, spirit, and art. Distinct "things" are then possible only if the entire absolute—the entirety of its quality as absolute identity, including the dual quality of its members—is *posited* under what Schelling calls different *potences*. Although one could also translate the German *Potenz* as *power, exponential,* or *potential,* I have chosen *potence.* The most significant translation of the term from Schelling into English (and, according to the Oxford English Dictionary, the first use of the word in general) occurs in Coleridge's

Biographia Literaria, Chapter 12, in reference to the syntheses of the imagination; Coleridge himself acquires the term from the *System of Transcendental Idealism,* though Schelling employs it elsewhere as well. Coleridge defends his own use of technical terms in philosophy "whenever they tend to preclude confusion of thought, and when they assist the memory by the exclusive singleness of their meaning more than they may, for a short time, bewilder the attention by their strangeness," and thus ventures "to use potence, in order to express a specific degree of a power, in imitation of the Algebraists." I believe the "singleness of meaning" to which Coleridge refers applies in this case, since Schelling's use of the mathematical term in the present philosophical context is not that which one normally expects from the terms *power, exponential,* or *potential,* and the term *potence* may well "assist the memory" and understanding. That is, the central position the term *Potenz* occupies in Schelling's *Philosophy of Art* (as well as in other works) will itself help define the term. (Coleridge mentions the word and then uses it no more in the *Biographia Literaria.*) Schelling himself acquires the word from Giordano Bruno's *De la causa,* though not directly. That is, he did not himself translate it from the Italian, but got it rather—already translated—from an appendix to the second edition of Johann Heinrich Jacobi's *Ueber die Lehre des Spinoza* (1789). Bruno's own term was *potenza,* and likely came from Latin *potentia* as used by Nicholas of Cusa. August Wilhelm Schlegel also uses it in his lecture series entitled *Schöne Literatur und Kunst,* though not in this strictly philosophical context.

This brings us to Schelling's understanding of *duplicity* and *triplicity.* The fundamental principle of organization behind both real and ideal reality is absolute identity. Furthermore, that absolute identity is by nature indivisible, since one cannot speak of the absolute identity of one member of an equation with nothing on the other side. Hence, the principle of organization of any particular thing ("thing" taken here broadly to include products of the worlds of nature and spirit) necessarily manifests a duality or duplicity at its most fundamental level. Whereas in the absolute itself there is no distinction between the two members, in determinate being there must be; what makes it determinate is precisely some *quantitative* qualification that affects its actual being. Although in the *System* of 1804 Schelling goes to great lengths to assure us of the nonreality of such determinate being in the Platonic or Neoplatonic sense, such determinate qualification does obtain in the phenomenal world. That distinguishes it from the absolute.

Concerning actual, finite things, Schelling offers the following proposition in the *System* of 1804:

> *The particularity of finite things through which the real All [first stage of emanation from the absolute] as real, the ideal All as ideal appears, can be based either on a reciprocal preponderance of the one factor over the other or on a balance between the two.*

This, Schelling asserts in the next sentence, concerns merely the method of presentation and thus needs no proof. It is, however, of greater significance than this offhand remark suggests, since the principle of construction is precisely the principle determining the internal organization of all that is, both real and ideal. Instead of a proof he offers an elucidation in which he presents the various possibilities for the *potences*. He also coins a new terminological pair to be applied to the principle of identity, one recalling the origin of that principle in the configuration of knower and known in self-consciousness. The ideal factor (corresponding to the act of knowing) is now called the *affirming* factor, and is active; the real factor (corresponding to the condition of being known) is now called the *affirmed* factor, and is passive. Of self-consciousness one might then say that the affirming element and affirmed element are one. Applied to the particularities within the real and ideal All—that sphere one remove from the absolute from which the actual world of particular things issues—the following principle will obtain:

> *Triplicity of potences is the necessary mode of appearance of the real All as real, as well as of the ideal All as ideal,* for the All can only appear through *finite* things whose differences can be expressed only through three potences, of which the one designates the preponderance of the affirmed condition, the other of the affirming element, and the third the indifference of the two.

That is, a preponderance of the one or other factor results in a condition of *difference;* a balance between the two factors results in a condition of *indifference.* [In a footnote, the critic states: "Schelling's term *Indifferenz* actually implies *nondifference* rather than *indifference* in the sense of apathy or lack of concern. I have retained the cognate *indifference* in keeping with Schelling's own (doubtlessly conscious) use of the foreign term."] The annotation Schelling then adds . . . is significant enough to cite in its entirety:

> *Annotation.* The true *schema* of the immediate issuance from the idea of God would thus be this: God as the prototype is absolute identity in which the real and ideal All is contained. The immediate issuance of the real and ideal All as such is the indifference of the affirming and the affirmed, which for that reason has a double expression: one within the real and the other within the ideal (since absolute identity belongs neither to the one nor to the other). From this indifference there issues in declining order the affirming or the ideal in relative preponderance over the affirmed or real, and the affirmed or real in relative preponderance over the affirming or ideal, both follow or issue in the same way from the indifference within the real and ideal. This same schema can repeat itself into infinity.

The absolute itself transcends these potences, but includes them all. It pours its entire essence into each, such that each contains elements of the other (the entire identity), yet with a preponderance of the one factor over the other. Schelling expresses this mathematically with variations of the following scheme:

$$\frac{\overset{+}{A} = B \qquad\qquad A = \overset{+}{B}}{A = A}$$

These potences, however, though they determine the particular features of things in the real and ideal worlds (of nature and of the spirit or intellect), nonetheless do not determine the thing-in-itself or its essence, but rather only that part belonging to the phenomenal world. Hence, "all differences of *natura naturata* (of the real as well as of the

ideal) are only of a quantitative nature, and are only differences in potence, not in essence."

These principles of duplicity of members and dialectic triplicity of relationships, the first quantitative determinations possible outside absolute identity itself, determine the organization of phenomena both of the world of nature and that of the intellect or spirit. (Phenomena, again, can refer to products of the intellect, since they are included in the finite world.) The principles also thoroughly determine appearances within the world of art, and will be the guiding principles throughout Schelling's presentation.

Let us now return to our point of departure—the three philosophies with one object. In the opening lectures Schelling will say the following:

> There is actually and essentially only *one* essence, *one* absolute reality, and this essence, as absolute, is indivisible such that it cannot change over into other essences by means of division or separation. Since it is indivisible, diversity among things is only possible to the extent that this indivisible whole is posited under various determinations.

This means that the entire absolute*ness* of the absolute will *inform* (*einbilden*) itself into every potence, whether it be a potence of nature, of the spirit, or of art. When Schelling speaks in the following lectures of the *informing* (*Einbildung*) of one factor into another, or of one quality into another, this is what he means. This word recalls the dynamic, generative quality of the absolute, and also suggests that creative, generative, and formative power one associates with the artist. The difference between the various potences depends on the preponderance of the one or other factor of the real or ideal in the potence under consideration, or from the indifference (balance) between the two. Each philosophy—that of nature, of the spirit, or of art—is to be a presentation of this fundamental, primordial identity inherent within the absolute, one manifesting itself as the complete mutual informing of the real and ideal within nature, the spirit, or art. Accordingly, Schelling refers to these three realms as potences as well: the entirety of absoluteness is posited or informed into the potence of nature, of the spirit, and of art, though with varying degrees of preponderance of the one or other factor, or with their indifference. Similarly, within each of these potences we encounter yet another subdivision into triplicity, that is, three more possible potences. In some instances, each of these potences divides itself yet further into three more, and so on ("this entire schema can repeat itself into infinity"). We will consider shortly just how this increasing triplicity manifests itself in the three potences.

In nature, necessity predominates (the factor of the real, of the necessary chain of cause and effect and of physical laws). The dynamic force in nature corresponding to the creative activity within the absolute, or to the conscious activity of the spirit, operates unconsciously in creating that which we call nature. ("Nature is slumbering spirit.") In the spirit itself, freedom is the predominating factor. Human spirit operates consciously and freely in what we call the productions of the spirit (for example, in the activity of philosophy).

One of these products of the spirit is art; yet art presents us with that peculiar set of circumstances mentioned earlier in the discussion of the *System of Transcendental Ideal-*

ism. The conscious spirit in freedom does not operate *alone* within the artist. Otherwise, artistic talent could be taught just as that which we call the rudiments or mechanics of art. We all agree that talent cannot be taught. We sense in every work of genius that some element of necessity is also at work, something analogous to the necessity operating within nature, something that posits its own "laws" with a necessity we ordinarily encounter only in nature. The genius operates quite consciously, but there is always an element not quite under his control, some force acting through him, guiding him in his creation. The ordinary observer senses this as an element of, for lack of a better word, "rightness," even though the order or form imposed on the work of art may well violate what we call natural law. It is in this sense that, as we have seen, the philosophy of art concluded the **System of Transcendental Idealism:** "The work of art reflects to us the identity of the conscious and unconscious activities. . . . Besides what he has put into his work with manifest intention, the artist seems instinctively, as it were, to have depicted therein an infinity, which no finite understanding is capable of developing to the full." That is, the work of art discloses in actuality that identity of the conscious and the unconscious, of spirit and nature, of freedom and necessity, lying behind the philosopher's entire task as the principle of the absolute grounding all knowledge, and the disclosure of which actually constitutes the philosopher's primary goal.

The principles of identity, duplicity, and triplicity will now generate a systematic philosophical structure coordinating both the relationships between the three philosophies among themselves and their internal structures.

Schelling begins with the absolute. The absolute is God; God is both the *idea* and the *being* of absolute, infinite reality. By virtue of the law of absolute identity, *idea* and *being* coincide in God; indeed, God *is* this idea and this being which coincide. Schelling reminds us that an actual circle is clearly not the same as the idea of a circle. The idea of the circle precedes every actual manifestation of a circle, not temporally, but rather absolutely. This is not the case, however, in God. God *is* the identity of being and idea, or *is* absolute identity. God precedes everything—not temporally, since the absolute has no relationship to time whatever, but rather according to the idea.

Formulating this entire complex in terminology analogous to that of human self-consciousness—recalling the terminological pairs of knower-known, active-passive discussed earlier—Schelling also says that God *conceives* (*begreifen*) or *affirms* himself. He conceives himself as an infinitely affirming element (for he is doing the affirming), as infinitely affirmed (for he is affirmed in the passive sense), and as the indifference of the two (for he is both). Strictly speaking, he is neither of the three; it is more accurate to say he is infinite affirm*ation*, the infinite identity of all three. Furthermore, we say that the activity of knowing, conceiving, or affirming is *ideal* (an activity of the intellect or spirit), and that which is known, conceived, or affirmed is *real.* God as knowing, conceiving, or affirming himself is thus an *ideality* encompassing its own reality, and as being known, conceived, or affirmed by himself is a *reality* encompassing its own ideality (the activity of knowing, conceiving, or affirming). In a word, God is a total, absolute identity of ideality and reality, the identity of—to use yet another terminological pair—the universal (ideal) and the particular (real), and is the indifference of the two.

Schelling now deduces his entire series of duplicity and of the ultimate unity or indifference of its members from this essential nature of God as the absolute. God is neither singularly ideal nor singularly real nor singularly the indifference of the two, but is rather all three, or: he is all*ness,* and this suffix *-ness* is as significant as the suffix *-ation* in affirmation, since it is reserved for God alone. In reality—our reality—ideality and reality are always sundered and separate. The concrete circle is never fully congruous with its own idea. The particular or concrete is never fully commensurate with its own universal or its essence.

In a highly significant work of 1802, **Bruno; or, On the Divine and Natural Principle of Things,** Schelling develops an understanding both of the absolute and of the ideas that carries over into his work on the philosophy of art. Particularly in its initial discussions, he works out the philosophical background for the assertion that truth can be equated with beauty and beauty with truth. The fundamental notion is that the more closely a particular, actual thing approximates the perfection of its universal or idea, such that the idea itself (the universal) can be intuited in the particular, the more closely does that particular participate in beauty, which is thus defined as the concurrence of universal and particular intuited in the particular. This is the object of aesthetic intuition. The object of intellectual intuition, on the other hand, is the concurrence of the universal with its particular in the abstract, such concurrence then constituting truth. Hence, beauty (in the concrete) can be equated with truth (in the abstract), and the objects of aesthetic and intellectual intuition are actually the same identity of the universal and the particular, though viewed from opposite directions. This was, as we saw earlier, precisely the point made in the final sections of the **System of Transcendental Idealism.**

Concerning the fundamental separation of the universal and particular in ordinary reality, we find that the idea or universal does appear within that particular—that is the basis for recognition and cognition as such—but never completely; the reality of the particular never completely corresponds to the possibility inherent within its universal. To use Schelling's own words: The positing of the universal of a thing into its concrete is already a limitation (of that universal or idea); hence, the thing—any thing—is never at once and in fact everything it could be essentially or according to its idea or universal. Reality is by definition a privation of ideality. This is not the case, however, in God. Hence, one does not say that God is conscious (ideal); neither is he unconscious (real) or nonconscious, but is rather the absolute unity of the two. He is neither free nor necessary (the opposite of free), but is rather the unity of the two.

This duplicity and the resulting triplicity of relationships, or the triadic structure of the dialectic of the absolute, determines, according to Schelling, the structure of all reality in the larger sense, and does so in a fashion analogous to the inner character of the absolute. Again, the absolute or God is the infinitely affirming, the infinitely affirmed, and the unity of the two, or is the ideal, the real, and the unity of the two. The same is true of reality as such. Proceeding out from the absolute, the next stages are the universe and the All (God is all*ness,* not the All); the universe and the All contain that which is contained in God. For example, the dynamic force in the All conceives itself as infinitely affirming, infinitely affirmed, and as the indifference of the two. There is a real world of nature and an ideal world of the intellect or of spirit; the world—"our" world—constitutes the unity of the two.

The triplicity now continues. Within each of these—the real and ideal worlds—there inheres what Schelling now calls a real series, an ideal series, and the indifference of the two, such that triplicity imprints itself onto our entire reality. We will see that the world of art, as the indifference of the worlds of nature and of the spirit, then constitutes the third element in the triplicity of worlds, recalling yet again the understanding of art presented in the *System of Transcendental Idealism.* As such, the philosophy of art concludes or rounds off the triadic organization of the philosophy of nature, of spirit, and of art.

Following this triplicity further down from the absolute (after the universe and the All), one encounters first the *real* world, reality as the affirmed condition rather than as activity. The infinite affirmed condition of God in the All is the real world, or it is the *informing* (again, Schelling asks that we take this word literally, as active in-form-ing, *Einbildung*) of God's infinite identity into reality. Schelling calls this the real unity, eternal nature, nature in itself (*an sich, natura naturans*). It is not the world of phenomenal nature (*natura naturata*), not nature in its particularity, but rather nature insofar as it is itself a potence of God, namely, insofar as it is God in his infinite affirmed condition.

Here, too, however, we encounter all three unities, and Schelling uses the terms *potence, unity,* and *determination* interchangeably in this sense: that of the affirmed condition, that of the affirming activity, and the indifference of the two, or all three as the infinite affirmation or as the entire essence of God. We recall that God is identity, and each unity accordingly manifests the imprint of the whole, though in a particular potence. These three subpotences, if we may call them such (Schelling does not use this term himself), are actually that which we call the real world of phenomenal nature, and it is the task of the philosophy of nature to investigate this world. The triadic structure disclosing the foci of the philosophy of nature is thus:

1. real potence—affirmed condition—*matter (informing* of the ideal into the real);

2. ideal potence—affirming activity—*light* (ideality resolving all reality); and

3. potence of indifference—*organism.*

It is important to understand these terms relationally, that is, as indicating relational rather than substantive or material features. These potences or unities are the particular results (*Folgen*) of God's affirmation within the *real* All, in the *real* world, within the *real.* Breaking this affirmation itself down further, the real potence within this real world is matter, or, as Schelling calls it, being. This is not matter in and for itself, but rather viewed from the perspective of its phenomenal, corporeal appearance; it is not substance but rather form, *accidens.* Furthermore, matter, as we might expect, is posited with a preponderance of the real, of the affirmed condition. It constitutes the informing of ideality into reality.

The ideal potence, or light, Schelling also calls *activity,* or that ideality that resolves (*auflösen*) all reality within itself. This is essence or the universal. The integration of the two, or the indifference of being and activity, of form and essence, is the organism. The essence of an organism is inseparable from the subsistence of its form.

Although the terminology in Schelling's philosophy of nature may appear somewhat bizarre, it should not unnerve the reader too much. Schelling's concern is to account for the organization both of nature as a whole and of the individual phenomena within nature, and to do so within a unified system, a system from which no part can be extracted without damaging the whole (nature itself, he explains, constitutes an organism), and outside of which no single part can be comprehended. His understanding of matter and light as condition and activity, though based on the limited scientific knowledge of his own age, does betray an impulse to understand and conceive nature as a nonmechanistic system based on a nexus of relations and forces, these relations being inherent within the absolute and manifested within reality as a result of the dynamic, generative aspect of the absolute. In any case, for our present purposes the reader need only follow the triadic structure and the various relationships obtaining within it (duplicity and triplicity).

Let us now move to the ideal world. This constitutes ideality, the activity of affirming. The infinitely affirming activity of God within the All is the ideal world, the informing of his reality into ideality. The act of thinking the concept "tree," for example, constitutes the resolution or informing of reality into ideality. Acting according to an ideal, to take another example, constitutes the elevation or resolution or "taking up" (*aufnehmen*) of reality into ideality. The potences or unities of the ideal world are then:

1. real potence—affirmed condition—*knowledge*—preponderance of the subjective;

2. ideal potence—affirming activity—*action*—preponderance of the objective; and

3. potence of indifference—knowledge and action in indifference nonconscious and conscious in indifference necessity and freedom in indifference—*art.*

Art is the representation (*Darstellung*) of this indifference of the ideal and the real *as* indifference. Art is concerned precisely with this indifference *as indifference,* and constitutes its representation or portrayal, as we can now see, within the *ideal* world of the intellect or spirit. (The representation in the *real world,* or the manifestation within the real world, is the organism.) Art, the work of art, is a product neither of action nor of knowledge alone, neither of freedom nor of necessity alone, neither of conscious nor of unconscious activity alone. As Schelling puts it, "Art is in itself neither mere activity nor mere knowledge, but is rather an activity completely permeated by knowledge, or, in a reverse fashion, knowledge which has completely become activity. That is, it is the indifference of both."

We recall that knowledge is the real potence within the ideal world, the potence of necessity, just as action is the ideal potence within the ideal world, the potence of freedom. In the work of art, as we can now see, both coincide: freedom with necessity, conscious or intentional with nonconscious or unintentional activity. Again, the final section of the *System of Transcendental Idealism* establishes the position of art here.

Schelling also views this complex from the perspective of the ideas themselves, and here, too, we encounter triplicity. The first potence of the real world is matter or being, that of the ideal world knowledge. The idea corresponding to these two potences is that of *truth*. The triadic members are then *being—knowledge—truth*. The second potence of the real world is light or activity, that of the ideal world (free) action; their idea is that of *goodness* or *virtue*. The triadic members are then *activity—free action—virtue*. The third potence of the real world is the organism as indifference, that of the ideal world art as indifference; their idea is *beauty*. The triadic members are thus *organism—art—beauty*.

If we now look more closely at the ideal world (of the intellect or spirit), the world in which art constitutes the third potence, we see that truth manifests itself as necessity, goodness or virtue as freedom, and beauty as the indifference of freedom and necessity, though indifference intuited objectively within the real. Beauty is the informing into unity (*Ineinsbildung*) of the real and the ideal within a reflected image (*Gegenbild*). Art is accordingly an absolute synthesis or mutual interpenetration of freedom and necessity. One can see the analogous position God or the absolute as the absolute unity of freedom and necessity possesses in relation to the work of art, and the enormous metaphysical, revelatory, and symbolic significance Schelling can attribute to the work of art within his system.

At this point we can also see how Schelling understands the German word for imagination (*Einbildungskraft*) in the artist: literally, the power of in-form-ing. It is the power whereby the ideal or universal is in-formed in actual fact into the real or particular; the more fully or completely the artist is able to in-form that ideal or universal into the real or particular, the more beautiful and true will his work of art be. The artist is thus a creator within the reflected image just as God is a creator in the archetype (*Urbild*).

In these lectures, Schelling repeatedly emphasizes that this informing of the ideal into the real is not to be confused with mere correct approximation of nature, what we might call naturalism. In fact, nature or the natural, phenomenal world by definition does *not* constitute a concurrence of the ideal and the real, for no particular object fully renders its own idea or universal, but consists precisely in a privation of that universal. Hence, an approximation of nature in art virtually assures the abrogation of beauty and thus also of truth. A van Gogh sunflower need not approximate the appearance of an actual sunflower, and indeed does not, in order to allow us to intuit the *idea* sunflower; in fact, precisely in its departure from the appearance of an actual sunflower do we sense its closer approximation to that idea that can never be fully rendered in the natural world. In other words, the apparent unnatural particularity of van Gogh's sunflower may well allow us to intuit the idea sunflower or its ideal reality better than any actual sunflower, and thus represents the specific *type* "sunflower" better than any particular natural sunflower could.

The philosophy of nature investigates the real world in its

three potences: matter, light, organism. The philosophy of transcendental Idealism (of spirit) investigates the ideal world in its three potences: truth, action (ethics), art. Art concludes both series, and the *Philosophy of Art* itself accordingly has not merely one series of three potences, but rather two series of three potences each; its *real* series corresponds to the philosophy of nature, its *ideal* series to the philosophy of spirit.

As we saw in the concluding sections of the *System of Transcendental Idealism,* what for philosophy is comprehensible nonobjectively in intellectual intuition (within the ideal) is comprehensible objectively within aesthetic intuition in art as the complete informing into unity of the universal and the particular (within the real). The further constructions of the *Philosophy of Art* thus deal with the particular potences of this informing within art. These particular potences themselves, not only within art, but also within nature and the world of the spirit, represent particular *modes of representation* of the universal within the particular:

> That representation in which the universal means the particular or in which the particular is intuited through the universal is *schematism*.

> That representation, however, in which the particular means the universal or in which the universal is intuited through the particular is *allegory*.

> The synthesis of these two, where neither the universal means the particular nor the particular the universal, but rather where both are absolutely one, is the *symbolic*.

Schelling also calls the third, or symbolic, mode of representation absolute form. In his discussion of mythology, he remarks that as the representation of the forms of the absolute indifference of the universal and the particular within the real as gods, mythology is necessarily symbolic, since the meaning of the gods is simultaneously their being. (Schelling will explain how he considers the symbolic development of mythology to have taken place only within Greek art; the development of modern mythology is still in transition.)

Schelling understands these modes of representation as a progressive series of potences themselves (general categories) in nature, spirit, and art as such. Each particular potence or unity includes all others:

> Nature in the corporeal series: allegorical
> Nature in light: schematic
> Nature in the organism: symbolic
> Spirit in thinking: schematic
> Spirit in action: allegorical
> Spirit in art: symbolic
> Science in arithmetic: allegorical
> Science in geometry: schematic
> Science in philosophy: symbolic

If we now view the world of art as such, we find that the structure of the two series of potences is analogous to that of the real and ideal world. Duplicity and triplicity necessarily recur, and constitute Schelling's *system* of the arts.

Just as in the real world, in nature, ideality is informed into reality, the infinite into the finite, the universal into the particular, so also in the *real* series within art. Hence, the real series in art corresponds to the philosophy of nature. Here, too, we encounter three subpotences analogous to the three potences within the real world.

Schelling calls the real series within art—music, painting, plastic art—the series of the formative arts, since here matter or being itself is elevated into a symbol of the idea; the infinite, the idea is informed into the finite.

The real unity or potence within the real series is music. It may seem somewhat odd that Schelling commences the real series of art in its own real potence with music, seemingly the most unreal or noncorporeal of the arts. We recall, however, that the first potence in the real world, matter, is not matter in and for itself, not substance, but rather form, *accidens,* or the informing of ideality into reality. The same is the case with music in an analogous fashion. Schelling understands music as the first, as it were, the lowest level of the informing of form as such into reality. This is rhythm, represented symbolically by sound. He will also call it the first or lowest level of the informing of unity (here: the unity of regularity) into multiplicity (here: the multiplicity of beats). Naturally, this informing on the first or lowest level is least characterized by the actual substance of the real. In its own turn, music itself encompasses triplicity in the form of three potences, a real and ideal potence, and the indifference: rhythm, modulation or harmony, and melody.

The ideal unity or potence in the real series of art is painting, where the finite or real is taken up into the infinite or ideal, or the particular into the universal. Here, too, we encounter three more subpotences corresponding to the real, ideal, and indifference: drawing, chiaroscuro, and coloring. Within the first potence—drawing—we even encounter three more: perspective, truth, necessity. Its corresponding potence in nature is, not surprisingly, light.

The third potence in the real series of art, that of indifference, is itself the potence in which the real and ideal potences are synthesized: the plastic arts (in nature: the organism). Whereas the first potence is characterized least by actual substance, the third is characterized most by it. Here the real *is* the ideal. In the plastic arts, the real or tangible element *is* the ideal, and vice versa. Here, too, we encounter three more subpotences corresponding to the real, ideal, and indifference: architecture, bas-relief, and sculpture. Carrying the analogy of triplicity even further, Schelling asserts that architecture is the music, bas-relief the painting, and sculpture the indifference of the plastic arts.

This leads us back into the discussion of the various modes of representation. Here, too, Schelling strives to disclose the inherent symmetry: "Music is an allegorizing art, painting schematizes, the plastic arts are symbolic."

The *ideal* series within art—lyric poetry, epic, and drama—corresponds to the ideal world of the spirit or to the philosophy of the spirit. Here language is elevated into a symbol of the idea. In language the particular, finite, or concrete is informed into the universal, infinite, or into the concept, or rather, it is resolved (*aufgelöst*). Accordingly, this is the series of the verbal arts, or poesy. The idea remains relatively ideal.

Here, too, in the ideal series of art, we encounter three subpotences. The real potence in the ideal series of art is lyric poetry, the informing of the infinite into the finite or particular. It corresponds to music as the first potence in the

real series of art, and one can see how Schelling will seek to ground the traditional kinship between music and lyric poetry: both are characterized by particularity, subjectivity, and freedom, and are subordinated to rhythm. This correspondence extends to the mode of representation: "Similarly, in poesy lyric poetry is allegorical."

The ideal potence in the ideal series of art is the epic, the resolution or suspension of the finite or real into the infinite or universal. Necessity predominates here insofar as it is not antithetical to the subject and thus ceases to be necessity as such. As Schelling will point out, necessity is a concept determinable only through antithesis. In his discussion of the various genres included in this potence, he focuses (1) on the displacement of subjectivity (the particular) into the object within the elegy, and of objectivity (the universal) into the poet himself within the idyll, and (2) on the displacement of objectivity (the universal) into the object within the didactic poem, and of subjectivity into the poet himself within the satire. He then focuses on the modern or romantic epic and the novel. The corresponding potence in the real series of art is painting, and the mode of representation follows: "Epic poesy demonstrates the necessary inclination to schematization."

The final potence of the ideal series of art, the synthesis of lyric poetry and the epic, and the concluding genre of the ideal series of art and thus of both series together, is drama, which Schelling deduces as tragedy. Since its corresponding potence in the real series is plastic art as such, the mode of representation is similarly symbolic.

In tragedy there obtains neither a merely subjective conflict between freedom and necessity, as in the lyrical poem, which is characterized by freedom, nor merely pure necessity, as in the epic. Here there must be a real, objective conflict between freedom and necessity, yet such that both as such nonetheless appear in a balance. Since human nature is both subject to necessity and capable of freedom, it constitutes the most appropriate symbol of this equipoise. This condition of balance is achieved when the person who succumbs to necessity nonetheless is victorious over it within his own disposition and elevates himself above it. Schelling deduces drama as tragedy, since the original, absolute manifestation of the conflict between freedom and necessity from which the drama issues is one in which freedom constitutes the subjective, necessity the objective element. Comedy is then merely the intentional reversal of this state of affairs.

Schelling parts company with Aristotle concerning the nature of the misfortune imposed by necessity upon the person. The person does not, as Aristotle suggests, become guilty merely because of an error, but rather through necessity. The tragic person must necessarily transgress; necessity undermines the will itself, and freedom, as Schelling puts it, is attacked on its own turf. The person transgresses by necessity, and without guilt in the ordinary sense, and yet freely accepts the punishment for the transgression. Precisely in this loss of freedom, freedom is affirmed. This constitutes the identity of freedom with necessity, and the art form presenting this objectively and symbolically thus concludes the ideal series of art. (pp. xxx-xlvii)

Douglas W. Stott, in a translator's introduction to The Philosophy of Art: Theory and

History of Literature, Vol. 58 *by Friedrich Wilhelm Joseph Schelling, edited and translated by Douglas W. Stott, University of Minnesota Press, 1989, pp. xxvii-1v.*

FURTHER READING

Benn, A. W. Review of *Werke, Auswahl in Drei Bänden,* by F. W. J. Schelling. *Mind* 33, No. 66 (April 1908): 281-82.
States that "of all Germany's classic thinkers [Schelling] is the most neglected and discredited."

Berlin, James A. "Arnold's Response to Schelling: Agreeing to Disagree." *English Language Notes* XVII, No. 4 (June 1980): 268-73.
Asserts that "even as [Matthew] Arnold denies Schelling's contention that the poet originates the ideas that go into a work of art and, in turn, define an epoch, he echoes Schelling's views on the elements which make for poetic creation—energy, intelligence, and the spirit of the times."

Boas, George. "Voluntarism in the Nineteenth Century." In his *Dominant Themes of Modern Philosophy: A History,* pp. 517-37. New York: The Ronald Press Co., 1957.
Explains the role of inspiration in Schelling's philosophy of art.

Bolman, Frederick de Wolfe, Jr. Introduction to *The Ages of the World,* by F. W. J. Schelling, translated by Frederick de Wolfe Bolman, Jr., pp. 3-79. New York: Columbia University Press, 1942.
Summary of Schelling's career, focusing on the evolution of his ideas on nature and identity.

Bracken, Joseph. "Schelling's Positive Philosophy." *Journal of the History of Philosophy* XV, No. 3 (July 1977): 324-30.
Traces the origins and development of Schelling's "positive philosophy."

Brown, Robert F. *The Later Philosophy of Schelling: Influence of Boehme on the Works of 1809-1815.* Lewisburg, Pa.: Bucknell University Press, 1977, 295 p.
Argues that Jacob Boehme was as a major influence on Schelling's thought.

————. "Schelling and Dorner on Divine Immutability." *Journal of the American Academy of Religion* LIII, No. 2 (June 1985): 237-49.
Cites Schelling as an important source for the writings of Isaac August Dorner, a German Protestant theologian.

Coleman, William. Review of *On University Studies,* by F. W. J. Schelling, translated by Ella S. Morgan. *Isis* 60, No. 4 (Winter 1969): 587-88.
Portrays Schelling as a poetic philosopher who lacked the necessary logical and linguistic skill to form a cogent system.

Di Giovanni, George. "Kant's Metaphysics of Nature and Schelling's *Ideas for a Philosophy of Nature.*" *Journal of the History of Philosophy* XVII, No. 2 (April 1979): 197-215.
Relates Schelling's philosophy of nature to that of Kant.

Engell, James. "Schelling." In his *The Creative Imagination: Enlightenment to Romanticism,* pp. 301-27. Cambridge: Harvard University Press, 1981.
Praises Schelling's conception of the absolute for its inclusion of both reason and the imagination.

Esposito, Joseph L. *Schelling's Idealism and Philosophy of Nature.* Lewisburg, Pa.: Bucknell University Press, 1977, 294 p.
Views Schelling's thought as a crucial link between Fichte's and Hegel's.

Fackenheim, Emil L. "Schelling's Philosophy of Religion." *University of Toronto Quarterly* XXII, No. 1 (October 1952): 1-17.
Explores the tension between faith and reason in Schelling's religious philosophy.

————. "Schelling's Philosophy of the Literary Arts." *The Philosophical Quarterly* 4, No. 17 (October 1954): 310-26.
Evaluates Schelling's approach to literature as it appears in *Philosophy of Art.*

Fichte, J. G. "Fichte's Criticism of Schelling." *The Journal of Speculative Philosophy* XII, No. 1 (January 1878): 160-70.
Translation of an essay written in 1806 by Schelling's friend and colleague. Fichte takes issue with Schelling's "nature philosophy."

Ford, Lewis S. "The Controversy between Schelling and Jacobi." *Journal of the History of Philosophy* III (1965): 75-87.
Chronicles the rivalry between Schelling and Friedrich Heinrich Jacobi.

Heath, Peter. Review of *Bruno; or, On the Natural and Divine Principle of Things,* by F. W. J. Schelling, translated by Michael G. Vater. *The Philosophical Review* XCVI, No. 2 (April 1987): 311-13.
Claims that *Bruno* is "a metaphysic of relations rather than entities, and to that extent it bears only a distant resemblance to the Platonism it professes to revive."

Henderson, J. Scot. "Mr. G. H. Lewes on Schelling and Hegel." *The Contemporary Review* 20 (September 1872): 529-42.
Reproves Lewes [see 1888 excerpt above] for his "imperfect and misleading" treatment of Schelling.

Higonnet, Margaret H. "Madame de Staël and Schelling." *Comparative Literature* 38, No. 2 (Spring 1986): 159-80.
Inquiry into the means by which Madame de Staël learned about Schelling's aesthetic philosophy before introducing it to the French in her *De l'Allemagne.*

Lawrence, Joseph P. "Schelling as Post-Hegelian and as Aristotelian." *International Philosophical Quarterly* XXVI, No. 4 (December 1986): 315-30.
Contends that Schelling "deliberately and successfully thought 'further' than Hegel."

Marx, Werner. *The Philosophy of F. W. J. Schelling.* Bloomington: Indiana University Press, 1984, 96 p.
Focuses on Schelling's conception of history as a product of both freedom and necessity.

Mead, George. "The Romantic Philosophers—Schelling." In his *Movements of Thought in the Nineteenth Century,* edited by George H. Mead, pp. 111-26. Chicago: University of Chicago Press, 1936.

Describes Schelling's theory of the artistic process.

Medicus, Fritz. "The Work of Schelling." *Clio* 13, No. 4 (Summer 1984): 349-68.

Memorial address delivered in 1954 on the centenary of Schelling's death. Medicus emphasizes the prescience of Schelling's writings.

O'Meara, Thomas Franklin, O. P. *Romantic Idealism and Roman Catholicism: Schelling and the Theologians.* Notre Dame: University of Notre Dame Press, 1982, 227 p.

Theological study of Schelling that focuses on "the interplay between faith and culture in the first half of the nineteenth century."

Orsini, G. N. G. "Schelling I—Metaphysics" and "Schelling II—Art and Nature." In his *Coleridge and German Idealism: A Study in the History of Philosophy with Unpublished Materials from Coleridge's Manuscripts,* pp. 192-237. Carbondale, Ill.: Southern Illinois University Press, 1969.

Views Schelling as a major source of Samuel Taylor Coleridge's thought.

Pfeiler, William K. "Coleridge and Schelling's Treatise on Samothracian Deities." *Modern Language Notes* LII, No. 3 (March 1937): 162-65.

Cites Schelling's *The Deities of Samothrace* as an important influence on Samuel Taylor Coleridge's philosophical lectures.

Pratt, Sarah. "The Metaphysical Abyss: One Aspect of the Bond between Tiutchev and Schelling." *Germano-Slavica* IV, No. 2 (Fall 1982): 71-88.

Expands on Andrew Weeks's essay [see below] on Schelling's influence on the Russian poet Fedor Ivanovich Tiutchev.

Reardon, Bernard M. G. "Schelling's Critique of Hegel." *Religious Studies* 20, No. 4 (December 1984): 543-57.

Argues that "Schelling's fundamental objection to Hegelianism . . . is that ultimately it is a panlogism, an absolutization of logic itself."

Singer, Edgar A., Jr. "Thoughts on a Translation of Schelling's *Weltalter:* A Review Article." *The Review of Religion* VIII, No. 1 (November 1943): 39-54.

Review of Frederick de Wolfe Bolman's translation of *Weltalter,* praising Schelling's work as a milestone in post-Kantian philosophy. Singer writes: "The whole drama might be likened to a Divine Comedy, in which the ascent from hell to heaven lay along the dimension of time, instead of along a radius of space. Or it might be caught up in Schelling's own likeness of the *Weltalter* to an epic that tells of an Iliad of estrangement from, followed by an Odyssey of return to, God."

Smid, Stefan. "F. W. J. Schelling's Idea of Ultimate Reality and Meaning." *Ultimate Reality and Meaning* 9, No. 1 (March 1986): 56-69.

Biographical sketch and explication of Schelling's "fundamental hermeneutical principle: human freedom."

Szondi, Peter. "The Notion of the Tragic in Schelling, Hölderlin, and Hegel." In his *On Textual Understanding, and Other Essays,* pp. 43-55. Minneapolis: University of Minnesota Press, 1986.

Contends that Schelling's interpretation of *Oedipus Rex* in his *Philosophical Letters on Dogmatism and Criticism* "marks the beginning of the history of a theory of the Tragic which, unlike previous theories, is not concerned with the effect of the Tragic on the audience, but aims, rather, to understand the phenomenon itself."

Tillich, Paul. *Mysticism and Guilt-Consciousness in Schelling's Philosophical Development.* Translated by Victor Nuovo. Lewisburg, Pa.: Bucknell University Press, 1974, 155 p.

Theological dissertation arguing that Schelling created a metaphysical principle out of the will.

Vater, Michael G. "Schelling's Neoplatonic System-Notion: 'Ineinsbildung' and Temporal Unfolding." In *The Significance of Neoplatonism,* edited by R. Baine Harris, pp. 275-99. Norfolk, Va.: International Society for Neoplatonic Studies, 1976.

Describes the influence of Neoplatonic thought on Schelling's philosophy.

———. Introduction to *System of Transcendental Idealism,* by F. W. J. Schelling, translated by Peter Heath, pp. xi-xxxvi. Charlottesville: University Press of Virginia, 1978.

Explains the function and ramifications of self-consciousness in Schelling's *System.*

Warnock, Mary. "Imagination and Creative Art: Hume, Kant and Schelling." In her *Imagination,* pp. 35-71. Berkeley and Los Angeles: University of California Press, 1976.

Summarizes Schelling's conception of imagination as "the power of seeing things as they are, namely as symbolic, and of creating new symbols (and to a less extent new images) to express the ultimate nature of the world."

Watson, Stephen. "Aesthetics and the Foundation of Interpretation." *The Journal of Aesthetics and Art Criticism* XLV, No. 2 (Winter 1986): 125-38.

Calls *System of Transcendental Idealism* the "masterpiece of [Schelling's] philosophy," viewing the work in terms of Hegel's critique of it.

Weeks, Andrew. "Tiutchev, Schelling and the Question of Influence." *Germano-Slavica* III, No. 5 (Spring 1981): 307-17.

Discusses the influence of Schelling on the Russian Romantic poet Fedor Ivanovich Tiutchev.

Wellek, René. "The Early Romantics in Germany." In his *A History of Modern Criticism: 1750-1950,* pp. 74-82. New Haven: Yale University Press, 1955.

Cites Schelling as an originator of Romantic philosophy.

White, Alan. *Schelling: An Introduction to the System of Freedom.* New Haven: Yale University Press, 1983, 201 p.

Explication of Schelling's philosophy with a discussion of his influences.

Peretz Smolenskin

1842-1885

Russian-born Hebrew novelist and journalist.

Smolenskin is chiefly remembered for his essays and novels delineating the cultural identity of European Jews during the 1870s and 1880s. In these works, many of which were first published in *ha-Shachar,* a Hebrew literary and political magazine that he founded and edited, Smolenskin often criticized the Haskalah, a Jewish intellectual movement that advocated the complete social assimilation of Jews living in Europe. Smolenskin was also an early supporter of the Zionist movement, which sought to establish a Jewish homeland.

Smolenskin was born in Monastyrshchina to impoverished parents. He was accepted into the Jewish academy in Sklov at the age of eleven, becoming the youngest pupil at the school. Smolenskin found the curriculum narrowly focused on Talmudic studies and began studying foreign languages and natural science independently; he was subsequently expelled from the academy for his extracurricular endeavors. He traveled throughout Europe before settling in 1867 in Odessa. There the journal *ha-Melitz* published his essays and reviews, including his scathing review of Meir Halevy Letteris's Hebrew translation of Johann Wolfgang von Goethe's *Faust.* In 1868 Smolenskin moved to Vienna, where he began publishing, editing, and, for the most part, writing his own monthly, *ha-Shachar,* named for a Hebrew word meaning "the dawn."

Originally *ha-Shachar* represented the views of the Haskalah, the members of which, called Maskilim, sought to reform the European Jewry in accordance with principles of reason propounded by such Enlightenment philosophers as Denis Diderot and Voltaire. Moses Mendelssohn, the first and most influential writer of the Haskalah, urged Jews to adopt the customs of non-Jewish Europeans, retaining only the religious observances of Jewish life. Smolenskin grew to disapprove of the movement's aspirations to assimilate, believing that the Haskalah would lead to a disintegration of the moral and spiritual identity of the Jews, and in a series of articles titled *Et la-ta'at* he stressed the identity of Jews as a nation in opposition to the exclusively religious conception of Mendelssohn and the Maskilim. He died of tuberculosis at the age of forty-two.

As part of his vision of a revitalized Jewish life in Europe, Smolenskin advocated the vernacular use of Hebrew, which at the time was primarily the language of religious scholarship. He valued the creation of new Hebrew literature above Hebrew translations of literature from other languages, and refused to publish such translations in *ha-Shachar.* His own novels, among the earliest to be written in Hebrew, enjoyed a widespread readership among European Jews, and critics have observed in Smolenskin's fiction a more tolerant attitude toward the Haskalah than that which is found in his essays. His first novel, *ha-To'eh be-darke ha-hayim,* is based on his youthful wanderings, and, according to critics, generally endorses the principles of the Haskalah. Similarly, *Kevurat hamor* portrays an enemy of the Haskalah as, in the words of Shalom Spiegel, "the essence of all vileness." However, by the time he wrote *Nekam berit,* his last novel, in 1884, Smolenskin had strengthened his anti-Haskalah perspective. In this work, the Russian pogroms of 1881 inspire a renewed faith in Judaism and its traditions. The Russian pogroms and other attacks upon Jews reflected a rise in anti-Semitic sentiment and activity in Europe during the 1880s, and Smolenskin began to champion in his works the efforts of Zionists to establish a Jewish nation outside Europe.

Critical appraisal of Smolenskin has focused on the development of his ideas and his influence on Jewish thought. Although his novels are seen as reflecting his concern for Jewish culture in Europe, his essays and his role as editor of *ha-Shachar* have received greater attention. Spiegel called *Et la-ta'at* "one of the best polemic writings in the Hebrew tongue," praising its passion and eloquence. Furthermore, Smolenskin's Zionist writings are seen as important initial steps in the development of that movement, which culminated in the founding of Israel in 1948. Assessing Smolenskin's contributions, Charles H. Freundlich has written that while his "activity was purely literary and not activist, and while the writing of books alone cannot revive a people, there is little doubt that Smolenskin's name will live on as the writer *par excellence* for the regeneration of the Jewish people in their homeland."

PRINCIPAL WORKS

ha-To'eh be-darke ha-hayim.   3 vols.   (novel)   1868-80
Simhat hanef   (novel)   1872
Kevurat hamor   (novel)   1882-83
Nekam berit   (novel)   1884
*Kol sifre.   6 vols.   (essays and novels)   1901
*Ma'amarim.   4 vols.   (essays)   1925-26
Tseror igrot   (letters)   1959

*Smolenskin's essays *Am olam, She'elat ha-yehudim,* and *Et la-ta'at* are included in these collections.

Nahum Slouschz   (essay date 1909)

[*In the following excerpt, Slouschz summarizes Smolenskin's career and praises his conception of Jewish identity.*]

[Following his studies at a Talmudic academy in Shklow, Perez Smolenskin] cast himself into the whirl of life, became assistant to a cantor at a synagogue, and then teacher of Hebrew and Talmud. The whole gamut of precarious employments open to a scholar of the ghetto he ran up and down again. His restless spirit and the desire to complete his education carried him to Odessa. There he established himself, and there years of work and endeavor were passed. He acquired the modern languages, his mind grew broader, and he gave up religious practices once for all, always remaining attached to Judaism, however.

In 1867 appeared his first literary production, the article against [Meir Halevy] Letteris, who at that time occupied the position of an incontestable authority, in which Smolenskin permits himself to pass severe and independent criticism upon his Hebrew adaptation of Goethe's *Faust.* In the Odessa period falls also the writing of the first few chapters of his great novel, ***Ha-Toeh be-Darke ha-Hayyim (A Wanderer Astray on the Path of Life).*** But his free spirit could not adapt itself to the narrowness and meanness of the literary folk and the editors of periodicals. He determined to leave Russia for the civilized Occident, the promised land in the dreams of the Russian Maskilim, beautified by the presence of Rapoport and Luzzatto. His first destination was Prague, the residence of Rapoport, then Vienna, and later he pushed his way to Paris and London. Everywhere he studied and made notes. A sharp-eyed observer, he sought to probe European affairs as well as Occidental Judaism to their depths. He established relations with Rabbis, scholars, and Jewish notables, and finally he was in a position to appraise at close range the liberty he had heard vaunted so loudly, and the religious reforms wished for so eagerly by the intelligent of his own country. He soon had occasion to see the reverse of the medal, and his disenchantment was complete. Regretfully he came to the conclusion that the modern emancipation movement had brought the Jewish spirit in the Occident to the point at which the Western Jew was turned away from the essence of Judaism. Form had taken the place of substance, ceremonial the place of religious and national sentiment. Heartsick over such disregard of the past, indignant at the indifference displayed by modern Jews toward all he held dear, young Smolenskin resolved to break the silence that was observed in the great capitals of Europe respecting all things Jewish and carry the gospel of the ghetto to the "neo-Gentiles".

The first shaft was delivered in Vienna, where he began the publication of his review *Ha-Shahar (Daybreak).* Almost without means, but fired by the wish to work for the national and moral elevation of his people, the young writer laid down the articles of his faith:

> The purpose of *Ha-Shahar* is to shed the light of knowledge upon the paths of the sons of Jacob, to open the eyes of those who either have not beheld knowledge, or, beholding, have not understood its value, to regenerate the beauty of the Hebrew language, and increase the number of its devotees.
>
> . . . But when the eyes of the blind begin to open slowly, and they shake off the sluggish slumber in which they have been sunk since many years, then there is still another class to be dealt with—those who, having tasted of the fruit of the tree of knowledge, intentionally close their eyes to our language, the only possession left to us that can bring together the hearts of Israel and make one nation of it all over the earth. . . . Let them take warning! If my hand is against the bigots and the hypocrites who hide themselves under the mantle of the truth, . . . it will be equally unsparing of the enlightened hypocrites who seek with honeyed words to alien-

ate the sons of Israel from their ancestral heritage. . . .

War to mediæval obscurantism, war to modern indifference, was the plan of his campaign. *Ha-Shahar* soon became the organ of all in the ghetto who thought, felt, and fought,—the spokesman of the nationalist Maskilim, setting forth their demands as culture bearers and patriots.

At a time when Hebrew literature consisted mainly of translations or works of minor significance, Smolenskin had the boldness to announce that the columns of his periodical would be open to writers of original articles only. The era of the translator and the vapid imitator had come to a close. A new school of original writers stepped upon the boards, and little by little the reading public accustomed itself to give preference to them.

And at a time when disparagement of the national element in Judaism had been carried to the furthest excess, Smolenskin asserted Judaism's right to exist, in such words as these:

> [The wilfully blind] bid us to be like all the other nations, and I repeat after them: Let us be like all the other nations, pursuing and attaining knowledge, leaving off from wickedness and folly, and dwelling as loyal citizens in the lands whither we have been scattered. Yes, let us be like all the other nations, unashamed of the rock whence we have been hewn, like the rest in holding dear our language and the glory of our people. It is not a disgrace for us to believe that our exile will once come to an end, . . . and we need not blush for clinging to the ancient language with which we wandered from people to people, in which our poets sang and our seers prophesied when we lived at ease in our own land, and in which our fathers poured out their hearts when their blood flowed like water in the sight of all. . . . They who thrust us away from the Hebrew language meditate evil against our people and against its glory!

The reputation of *Ha-Shahar* was firmly established by the publication of Smolenskin's great novel ***Ha-Toeh be-Darke ha-Hayyim*** in its columns. In this as in the rest of his works, he is the prophet denouncing the crimes and the depravity of the ghetto, and proclaiming the revival of national dignity.

Smolenskin permitted himself to be thwarted by nothing in the execution of his bold designs, neither by the meagreness of his material resources nor by the animosities which his fearless course did not fail to arouse among literary men.

In 1872, Smolenskin published, at Vienna, his masterpiece ***Am Olam (The Eternal People),*** which became the platform of the movement for national emancipation. Noteworthy from every point of view, this work shows him to have been an original thinker and an inspired poet, a humanist and at the same time a patriot. He is full of love for his people, and his faith in its future knows no limits. He demonstrates convincingly that true nationalism is not incompatible with the final realization of the ideal of the universal brotherhood of men. National devotion is but a higher aspect of devotion to family. In nature we see that, in the measure in which the individuality of a being is distinct, its superiority and its independence are increased.

Differentiation is the law of progress. Why not apply the law to human groups, or nations?

The sum total of the qualities peculiar to the various nations, and the various ways in which they respond to concepts presented to them from without, these constitute the life and the culture of mankind as a whole. While admitting that the historical past of a people is an essential part of its existence, he believes it to be a still more urgent necessity for every people to possess a present ideal, and entertain national hopes for a better future. Judaism cherishes the Messianic ideal, which at bottom is nothing but the hope of its national rebirth. Unfortunately, the modern, unreligious Jew denies the ideal, and the orthodox Jew envelops it in the obscurity of mysticism.

The last chapter of *The Eternal People,* called "The Hope of Israel", is pervaded by magnificent enthusiasm. For the first time in Hebrew, Messianism is detached from its religious element. For the first time, a Hebrew writer asserts that Messianism is the political and moral resurrection of Israel, *the return to the prophetic tradition.*

Why should the Greeks, the Roumanians, desire a national emancipation, and Israel, the people of the Bible, not?. . . . The only obstacle is the fact that the Jews have lost the notion of their national unity and the feeling of their solidarity.

This conviction as to the existence of a Jewish nationality, the national emancipation dreamed by Salvador, Hess, and Luzzatto, considered a heresy by the orthodox and a dangerous theory by the liberals, had at last found its prophet. In Smolenskin's enthusiastic formulation of it, the ideal was carried to the masses in Russia and Galicia, superseding the mystical Messianism they had cherished before.

Smolenskin's combative spirit did not allow him to rest at that. The idea of national regeneration was in collision with the theory, raised to a commanding position by Mendelssohn and his school, that Judaism constitutes a religious confession. In a series of articles (*A Time to Plant, and a Time to Pluck up That Which Is Planted*), he deals with the Mendelssohnian theory.

Proceeding from history and his knowledge of Judaism, he proves that the Jewish religion is not a rigid block of unalterable notions, but rather a body of ethical and philosophical teachings constantly undergoing a process of evolution, and changing its aspect according to the times and the environment. If this doctrine is the quintessence of the national genius of the Jew, it is nevertheless accessible, in theory and in practice, to whosoever desires access. It is not the dogmatic and exclusive privilege of a sacerdotal caste.

This is the rationale of Smolenskin's opposition to the religious dogmatism of Mendelssohn, who had wished to confine Judaism inside of the circle of Rabbinic law without recognizing its essentially evolutionary character. Maimonides himself is not spared by Smolenskin, for it was Maimonides who had set the seal of consecration upon logical dogmatism. The less does he spare the modern school of reformers. Religious reforms, he freely admits, are necessary, but they ought to be spontaneous developments, emanations from the heart of the believers themselves, in response to changes in the times and social relations. They ought not to be the artificial product of a few intellectuals who have long broken away from the masses of the people, sharing neither their suffering nor their hopes. If Luther succeeded, it was because he had faith himself. But the modern Jewish reformers are not believers, therefore their work does not abide. It is only the study of the Hebrew language, of the religion of the Jew, his culture, and his spirit that is capable of replacing the dead letter and soulless regulations by a keen national and religious sentiment in harmony with the exigencies of life. The next century, he predicted, would see a renewed, unified Judaism.

This is a summing up of the ideas which brought him approval and endorsement from all sides, but also, and to a greater degree, opposition and animosity, the latter from the old followers of the German humanist movement. One of them, the poet Gottlober, founded, in 1876, a rival review, *Ha-Boker Or,* in which he pleaded the cause of the school of Mendelssohn. But the new periodical, which continued to appear until 1881, could neither supplant *Ha-Shahar,* nor diminish Smolenskin's ardor. Other obstacles of all sorts, and the difficulties raised by the Russian censor, were equally ineffectual in halting the efforts of the valiant apostle of Jewish nationalism. He was assured the cooperation of all independent literary men, for Smolenskin had never posed as a believer in dogmatic religion or as its defender. On the contrary, he waged constant war with Rabbinism. He was persuaded that an untrammelled propaganda, bold speech issuing from a knowledge of the heart of the masses and their urgent needs, would bring about a natural and peaceable revolution, restoring to the Jewish people its free spirit, its creative genius, and its lofty morality. It mattered little to him that the young had ceased to be orthodox: in case of need, national feeling would suffice to maintain Israel. At this point, it appears, Smolenskin excelled Samuel David Luzzatto and his school as a free-thinker. The Jewish people is to him the eternal people personifying the prophetic idea, realizable in the Jewish land and not in exile. The liberalism displayed by Europe toward the Jews during a part of the nineteenth century is in his opinion but a transient phenomenon, and as early as 1872 he foresaw the recrudescence of anti-Semitism.

This conception of Jewish life was welcomed by the educated as a revelation. The distinction of the editor of *Ha-Shahar* is that he knew how to develop the ideas enunciated by the masters preceding him, how to carry them to completion, and render them accessible to the people at large. He revealed a new formula to them, thanks to which their claims as Jews were no longer in contradiction with the demands of modern times. It was the revenge taken by the people speaking through the mouth of the writer. It was the echo of the cry of the throbbing soul of the ghetto. (pp. 226-36)

Nahum Slouschz, "The National Progressive Movement—Perez Smolenskin," in his The Renascence of Hebrew Literature (1743-1885), *translated by Henrietta Szold, The Jewish Publication Society of America, 1909, pp. 224-36.*

Abraham Solomon Waldstein   (essay date 1916)

[*In the following excerpt, Waldstein describes Smolenskin's opposition to the assimilationist policies of the Haskalah movement and discusses his contribution to the development of Hebrew literature.*]

The biographer of Peretz Ben Moshe Smolenskin, R. Brainin, is obviously right in saying that the Smolenskin whom we know from his novels and essays, is not the one that might have been, had he written under different circumstances. In his works we see only his silhouette, not his real portrait. While his literary personality and great talent were still in the making, his life was cut short, and Hebrew literature was bereft of one of its sincerest, most talented, and most sympathetic writers.

It would perhaps seem strange, at first sight, to speak of a writer of forty-five, who already had behind him some fifteen years of literary activity, as still having been in his literary teens. The talents of Byron and Poe were fully developed before they had reached the years of Smolenskin, and they would probably not have added much to their fame, had they attained to twice their actual age. The literary, at least, the poetic, career of Lamartine was practically ended at forty, though he lived to be well advanced in years. In the case of Smolenskin, however, every page of his writings testifies to the fact that we have before us a man of great literary power, but, at the same time, that this power is artistically unripe, warped, and uncontrolled. And little wonder. Neither were his pre-literary life and training conducive to an adequate preparation for his literary career, nor did the conditions under which he carried on his activity tend fully to bring out his literary powers. Born in poverty and brought up partly under the influence of the Yeshiboth (Talmudic academies), and partly under that of Hasidism,—in an atmosphere, hostile to the spirit of modernism and secular literature, Smolenskin received neither the education nor the literary training necessary for the essayist, novelist, and spiritual leader he later became. And even after he had attained, by sheer richness of talent, greatness of heart, and personal energy, to that ambitious eminence, his work was carried on under the stress of such abject need and forced hurry, that he was not in a position to attend to artistic workmanship. For, Smolenskin was a very busy man, dividing his time between editing and managing a Hebrew monthly—*ha-Shahar*—directing a printing firm, writing essays, novels, and criticisms, and taking a goodly share in general Jewish affairs,—all of which, however, barely yielded him a livelihood.

Smolenskin's literary activity (1869-84) extends over the end of the Haskalah period and the beginning of the revival of the Jewish national spirit, as it expressed itself in the form of the Hibbath Zion movement. (pp. 57-8)

By the end of this period a reaction [to Haskalah had] set in. Even the arch enemies of ultra-orthodox Judaism, such as Lilienblum and Gordon, saw that they had gone too far,—too far from the point of view of Jewish nationalism. For the later phase of the Haskalah movement had been essentially, though not consciously, assimilatory. "Be a Jew in your own house, but a man in society,"—had been the cry. But, as a result, the man was beginning to assert himself at the expense of the Jew, just as the life of the world without was beginning to replace the inner Jewish life, that of the Jewish home, of the synagog, of the Yeshibah. Reality overreached and deceived the devotees of the Haskalah; and therein lies the tragedy of the movement. The Maskilim of the rank and file proved a failure, as Jewish men and women. Even the enlightened Rabbis and teachers, upon whom the leaders had laid so much hope, betrayed them. They formed a class for themselves, haughty and selfish, standing apart from Jewish interests, looking down upon their brethren that still sat in the "benighted" Ghetto, and occupying the function of slaves to the Russian government rather than that of teachers and leaders of their people. This condition naturally could not but wring out a cry of despair from the leaders of the Maskilim, at least from the Hebrew section.

The positive expression of this reaction was the national revival, which began as a comparatively widespread and popular movement, in the early eighties, after the notorious anti-Jewish riots in Russia. This movement, which expressed itself at first in the form of Hibbath-Zion (The Love of Zion), *i.e.,* a return to the land, the language, and the faith of the ancestors, is regarded by some as the product of Jewish repression. Nothing can be more superficial than this opinion. There are no sudden leaps and bounds in nature. Even earthquakes have their history of evolution. The Hibbath-Zion movement, quickened and ripened as it was by the national calamities in the eighties, is undoubtedly to be attributed to the reaction against the Haskalah movement. And if proof be needed for this assertion, we may go to the living fact, Smolenskin, who was the strongest link between the two movements.

In Smolenskin we see the unmistakeable evolution from the Haskalah to the revival movement. He, too, saw in Haskalah a means of uplifting his people, and he, too, made Hasidism a target at which he sped some of his winged and most pointed arrows. The *ha-Shahar*, moreover, was one of the strongholds of the Maskilim, to which the most militant of them contributed their materials. Yet, Smolenskin did not follow the old grooves which they had cut out for him. He was more penetrating and more constructive in his views and ideas. In his consuming love for his people, Smolenskin felt even at the beginning of his career, what the Maskilim were to realize later, that they were over-shooting the mark in their zeal for Haskalah.

Smolenskin developed, in a series of essays published in *ha-Shahar,* an almost systematic theory of the evolution of Jewish history,—a theory that, to a great extent, dominates his works and draws a sharp line of distinction between him and the Maskilim. His view is idealistic, in contradistinction from theirs which was materialistic. Notice, for example, the difference between the materialistic view taken by Gordon in the poem "Zedekiah in the Guard House" and the ideologic view taken by Smolenskin in his essay ***Am Olam,*** as regards the part played by the prophets in Jewish history, and you will see what a contrast there is between the conception of the latter and that of the Maskilim as regards Judaism.

Smolenskin's view of Jewish history is not quite scientific, but it is full of penetration and is instinct with warm feeling for his people. The history of the Jewish people is, according to Smolenskin, indissolubly connected with that of the Torah, not in its theologic sense, but in its moral significance. The Torah was given to the Jews with the purpose of uplifting them spiritually. The external frame that held them together at the beginning of their national existence was, of course, their own country; but what united them as a spiritual body and gave them their characteristic tone was the Torah. It was the spirit of the Torah and its moral greatness that imbued the Jews with national endurance and elasticity even after they had lost their national independence. And Smolenskin lays stress upon the point that the Jews have remained a nation to this day and are not merely a religious sect, as the German-Jewish philosopher, Moses Mendelssohn, asserted. Against this latter theory and its corollary, the so-called Berlin Haskalah, Smolenskin severely inveighed, pointing out its denationalizing tendency and the national havoc which it had wrought among the immediate disciples of Mendelssohn, as well as among later generations. This judgement passed upon Mendelssohn's theory—and, by the way, also upon the man himself,—in one of Smolenskin's most penetrating essays, **"Eth Laasoth,"** naturally met with resentment on the part of the Maskilim, who considered themselves the heritors of the Berlin Haskalah; but it was ultimately adopted in Hebrew literature as a truism.

From this view of Jewish history held by Smolenskin arises his opposition to the extreme reform movement, in the shape which it assumed among the German Jews, and his difference of opinion with the Maskilim as regards the educational endeavors among the Jews. Since the Torah is not merely a religious code but a product of, as well as a stimulus to, the national spirit, and since it continued to develop along national lines all through Jewish history, it follows that it cannot entirely be stripped of its later forms, and be based simply upon a couple of dogmas; for then you strip it of its whole significance, which is really national, and make it a mere theologic abstraction. It is true that Jewish religion needs a pruning, on account of some undesirable shoots which have overgrown it during long ages; but this should by no means be done artificially. Educate the people and the reforms will come by themselves. There is no use in demanding of a blind person that he appreciate the beauties of nature; open his eyes and nature will reveal itself to him in all its grandeur.

Another factor in Jewish nationalism, perhaps more important than religion, was, for Smolenskin, the Hebrew language and literature. If religion is one means of preserving national existence, Hebrew is the only repository for the national attributes and creations. Hence, Hebrew should be cherished as a prime national factor *per se*. And in this respect, again, he differs from the Maskilim, for whom Hebrew was a preferable, but not an essential, channel of Haskalah.

In these two things, then, in the reversion to Jewish religion and in regarding Hebrew as essential to nationalism, Smolenskin was the forerunner of the national revival movement. The third and most important requisite of the revival, the rehabilitation of Palestine, was at first disregarded by Smolenskin, evolving with him only in the course of years.

I have gone to the length of discussing Smolenskin's theory of Jewish history, not only because it is interesting in itself, or in order to point out the difference between him and the Maskilim, but because it is necessary to the understanding of his novels and of the development of Hebrew literature as a whole. Smolenskin came to the latter with a new message,—one that was more positive and constructive than that of the Maskilim. For him, Hebrew as such was of paramount importance. And though encouraging Haskalah and himself marked by many a trait of the Maskil, he freed Hebrew literature, by theory and practice, from the Haskalah tendency, from the tyranny of bias, making it an aim in itself and not merely a means of conveying certain opinions. In this manner, Hebrew literature was given more scope for the purely artistic and literary, and for the freer development of individual character.

Though Smolenskin contributed to the advancement of Hebrew literature by freeing it, in a measure, from the onesidedness of tendency, he could not entirely liberate his own novels from the shackles of the age. As regards appreciation of nature, for example, his novels are as deficient as the other stories of the time. Not a bit of blue sky, fleecy cloud, or green turf do we find in them; they carry us along on their swift currents of events, without giving us time to admire a beautiful scene that we may meet on our way. Nor is the art in his novels flawless. Smolenskin was, it is true, a man of temperament; but his temperament was that of the preacher rather than that of the artist. The plot is not so loose, flimsy, and irrational as, let us say, that of Mapu's *Ayit Zabua*; but there is much even in Smolenskin's novels that is questionable and out of joint. In general, to use a figure of Brunetière, his novels float about in their frames, for Smolenskin makes great use of character and even for the purpose of sermonizing, moralizing, and perorating on anything and everything under the sun. And as it happens with many an author whose vanity gets the better of his artistic taste, Smolenskin prided himself upon his commonplace philosophizing more than upon the really enduring phases of his novels. Thus, in a letter to a friend, he expresses his great satisfaction at the rather banal discussion of the relation of Hamlet to Faust, which, in his eyes, surpasses in importance the whole novel **The Joy of the Wicked,** in which he succeeded in casting up some interesting psychologic problems.

If Smolenskin is diffusive in the plot of his novel, he is, however, capable of dealing with a single situation in a masterly manner. Witness, for example, the scene between the Austrian Jewish detective and the typically Viennese girl (**The Inheritance,** pt. 3, ch. 2). See also the conversation between the "batlanim" (typical Talmudic students) in the synagog, in the introductory chapter of **The Ass's Burial,** and also part of the scene between the emigrants to America (**Pride and Overthrow**),—in all these you will find an abundance of humor and, at the same time, a knowledge of men in the various pursuits of life.

The knowledge of men,—this is another characteristic that distinguishes Smolenskin from the Maskilim. The views and the sympathies of the latter were narrow, bookish; the atmosphere was attenuated, and the sphere of activity limited to one class, the middle class, which was, in its turn, artificially divided into "enlightened" and "unenlightened." In Smolenskin's novels, the range of view is wide, comprehensive. It embraces not only various classes but also various nations. See, for example, **ha-Toeh be-darkey ha-hayyim,** his best known novel, which like *David Copperfield*, though with less coherence of events, is the "truth and fiction" about the life of the author. What a kaleidoscopic view we get here of personages, classes, and peoples! Not only Russian Jewry passes in review before us, in a great many phases and in a variety of classes, but also the Jewries of some other countries, the author reflecting, at the same time, in marginal acute remarks upon other nationalities. It must, however, be owned that Smolenskin was not always just in dealing with other nationalities, his attitude towards them being at times prejudiced by the love he bore his own nation. His view of the Polish revolution may serve as an example of his bias. With a great deal of truth about the inefficiency of the Polish revolutionaries, the bragging and vanity of their leaders and their petty quarrels for office, and, particularly, their thanklessness towards their Jewish allies, he yet treated them with a severity and lack of sympathy tantamount to cruelty.

Smolenskin's novels mark a departure in Hebrew literature in many other important directions. In the first place, he introduced real tragedy into the Hebrew. His predecessors, such as Mapu, kept tragedy in the background. They worked, so to say, deductively. When they introduce us to the scene of action, the great crime—the pivot of the story—has already been committed. The virtuous person, *i.e.,* the Maskil, has been put out of the way, and his family, also composed of the enlightened, is now suffering at the hands of villainy; but we can predict from the very beginning the ultimate triumph of virtue. It is true that Smolenskin's contemporaries, Gordon, for example, who aimed at demonstrating the ill results of bigotry and superstition, have given us tragedies; they were, however, not real, dramatic, but pseudo, tragedies. There was no play of will against will, but of idea against idea. The characters were abstractions, without individuality. Will, character, did not count for much, for the disaster came about by the hard-heartedness of a Rabbi or a predeterminate religious law. Smolenskin, on the contrary, presented tragedy in its really tragic and dramatic elements. Not that he was more pessimistic than the Maskilim. He who entitled one of his novels *The Reward of the Virtuous,* ending it with the exulting words: "Truly, this is the reward of the Righteous!"—can indeed not be accused of pessimism. But, his range of view being more comprehensive than that of the Maskilim, he found in life more tragedy than they. Besides, being a person of great strength of will and character, and of indomitable energy, it was natural for him to endow his heroes with the same qualities. Hence, the really dramatic element in his novels.

The psychologic element, then, plays a great part in Smolenskin's novels; indeed, if it does not always form the axis upon which they revolve, it at least constitutes a component part of them. Even in *ha-Toeh be-darkey ha-hayyim,* primarily a novel of manners, the character of the main hero evolves into tragic individuality; consumed as he is by sexual love for his own sister, whom he, at first, did not know to be any relative of his, and finally killed when hurling himself in passionate despair against a rioting mob in Russia. Similarly, the heroes of his other novels. Note the boldly delineated psychic features of the passionate heroine of *The Inheritance,* Peninah, with all the consciousness of the shame of her sinful parents, and her impetuous humbling of herself before her friends, on account of it. Contrast, at the same time, her character with that of the calm, brilliant Viennese girl, in the same novel; healthy, charming, lively, full of wit, with a loving heart and a pleasant admixture of innocence and common sense. Witness, again, the noble, but fitful and whimsical hero of

the same story, Zerahiah, who brings upon himself, because of his eccentricities, a host of misfortunes and a series of real or imaginary humiliations. Finally, Smolenskin, in at least two of his novels, makes individuality the very pivot of the story. In *The Ass's Burial,* the ultimate ruin and death of the hero are the results of his boastful and vainglorious character; and the motive of *The Joy of the Wicked* hinges upon the fickleness of the hero, who abandons his beautiful wife and child to follow a commonplace girl.

When we speak of the psychologic element of Smolenskin's novels, however, it is to be understood in the relative sense of the word, as compared with other Hebrew novels of the time. Considered by themselves, they leave many a psychologic gap. The characters are at times blurred and indistinct. The distinctive traits of the hero in the *The Ass's Burial,* for example, are not clearly enough delineated to justify the motive of the story. Again, when Smolenskin happens upon a problematic character, he is sometimes at a loss as to the manner of handling it. Take, for example, the heroine of the story related by the "friend of Zarhi," in *Pride and Overthrow.* The author introduces us to a girl of the type of George Eliot's Gwendolen, very beautiful and very whimsical, whose word is law unto her parents and who sets the hearts of all young men aflame. He leaves this enigmatic character, however, so well adapted for deeper psychologic study, entirely undeveloped, and, moreover, gives the story the ridiculous ending of making the heroine elope with a Polish nobleman, who afterwards drives her to commit moral suicide,—an ending that has become almost a hobby with Smolenskin, at least, in some episodes of his novels. And speaking of this heroine, one cannot help thinking of another interesting feature in the novels of Smolenskin, namely, the stress that he lays upon Jewish education as a factor in the development of character, pointing out, in this story and in many others, the moral ills engendered by the lack of such education,—a theory quite in keeping with his national views.

Finally, a word as to the style of Smolenskin. This author is a purist, but not in the same sense as Mapu had been. He never hesitated to make use of a Biblical phrase, whenever it suited his purpose; but he did not abuse this practice, always avoiding the pun and quibble of the Melizah. His style is energetic, exuberant, and full of life; but there is a total absence in it of the imaginative and the figurative, which are essential qualities in the style of fiction.

In short, Smolenskin's novels mark an advance in Hebrew literature. He freed the latter from the tyranny of bias, of tendency and, at the same time, began the emancipation of the individual in fiction, bringing in the personal element and thereby giving character and individuality free scope to develop. By his energy, earnestness, and personal charm, moreover, he gave the Hebrew an impetus which raised it to a height more considerable than that to which it had ever before risen during the last century. His influence was great both upon his contemporaries and upon later writers. In his lifetime he drew about himself a circle of literary friends and he helped to develop many a young talent; and after he was gone, his impress still remained upon Hebrew thought and Hebrew letters. (pp. 58-66)

Abraham Solomon Waldstein, "Peretz Ben Moshe Smolenskin (1839-1884)," in his The Evolution of Modern Hebrew Literature,

1850-1912, *Columbia University Press, 1916,*
pp. 57-66.

Shalom Spiegel   (essay date 1930)

[*Spiegel (1899-1984) was William Prager Professor of
Medieval Hebrew Literature at the Jewish Theological
Seminary of America. In the following excerpt, he considers the impact of Smolenskin's journalism on Jewish
national identity and discusses the strengths and weaknesses of his novels.*]

[Smolenskin's magazine, *Hashachar*,] is usually looked
upon as the dawn of a new phase in Hebrew literature, that
of the national awakening, just as the beginning of the "enlightenment" is usually taken to date from the appearance
of *Hameassef* in Königsberg eighty-five years before. This
is correct, but we must not look for any sudden break with
the earlier trends. For years both Smolenskin and the
magazine stood firmly upon the ideological bases of the
Haskalah, though from the very beginning there peep
forth new ideas of national self-realization, which is only
natural in a "twilight of the gods," during a stage of historic transition.

Smolenskin had the extraordinary faculty, still unsurpassed by Hebrew editors, of discovering and encouraging
contributors, and grouping them around himself. He won
a whole array of talent among both belletristic and scientific writers, so that *Hashachar* became the leading literary
organ, and to this day remains the best source for a knowledge of the spiritual problems and forces of the time.

From the very first, however, Smolenskin himself gave the
tone to the magazine, chiefly by means of his publicistic
articles which, written with contagious enthusiasm and
turbulent persuasiveness, always called out numbers both
of friends and of enemies, passionate approval and passionate condemnation. He had the capacity of the born
journalist to interest the reader; to excite, to compel attention.

In the leading editorial of the first issue of *Hashachar,* defining the policy of the magazine, Smolenskin showed how
little he was edified by occidental emancipated Jewry, to
which the Maskilim of the West looked up with such envy
and reverence. Their undignified aping of everything foreign, even to the forms of religious worship, their indifference to the Hebrew language, which they excluded from
the prayer book itself, their cowardly denial of all messianic hopes, seemed to him high treason to the national sanctities. In white-hot anger he promised to wage war against
such alienating tendencies:

> All peoples set up monuments of stone, build tow-
> ers, pour out their blood like water so that their
> name and their language may not be blotted out.
> They longingly await the day of salvation when
> they will again have their own government, and
> even though that day be remote, they do not cease
> to hope. We, however, have neither monument nor
> land, neither name nor memorials save the one relic
> that has remained to us from the ruins of our sanc-
> tuary, our Hebrew language; yet they regard it with
> shame and contempt. Those who despise the He-
> brew language thereby reject our nation, and have
> neither name nor memorial in the house of Israel;
> they are traitors to their people and their faith.
> They say to us: Let us be like all other nations! And

> I agree with all my heart: Let us indeed be like
> other nations in the pursuit of knowledge, . . . in
> being loyal citizens of the lands of our dispersion;
> but let us, also, like them, be unashamed of the rock
> whence we were hewn. Let us be like them in hon-
> ouring our own language, our own nationhood! It
> is not a shame and a reproach to us to believe that
> there will be an end to our exile, and that the day
> will come when the sceptre will return to the house
> of Israel, just as other nations are not ashamed to
> hope for deliverance from the hands of strangers.

Smolenskin set *Hashachar* a twofold aim where up to that
time Hebrew periodicals had had but one.

> Hitherto the war has been waged only within, but
> now it is carried on both within and without. At a
> time when the eyes of the blind begin little by little
> to open from the sluggish slumber of years, those
> who are already wise of heart deliberately turn their
> eyes away from the language, which is the only
> thing left to us, and which alone can win the hearts
> of all Israel to remain one people.

Smolenskin wants to fight both camps—the obscurantism
that is alien to culture and the assimilation that is alien to
the people, both alike harmful to the furtherance of Judaism that he was fighting for.

On the whole, it can be said of Smolenskin that while in
his publicistic writings he attacked the deserters in the
West, in his novels he was concerned mostly with the fa-
natics of the East. To be sure, this division was neither intended nor without its important exceptions. But it is very
obvious that his belletristic writing is almost throughout
underlain by Maskilic evaluations: opposition to enlightenment is almost always identical with the basest wickedness, is indeed the chief cause thereof. Though Smolenskin
himself seems to have surmounted the Haskalah, he is
more one-sided in his fiction than the earlier Hebrew novelists, who were sometimes able to find a few human traits
in the enemies of enlightenment. An instance in point is
Smolenskin's best-known novel **Hattoëh bedarkhe
hachayim** (*Astray in the Paths of Life*) which ran serially
in *Hashachar* beginning with the first number, went
through several editions, and became one of the most influential books of the epoch. Somlenskin here makes hatred of enlightenment responsible for all the sins which he
heaps upon the characters to the point of caricaturing.

Uniting truth and fiction, the book portrays Smolenskin's
own strayings in life: his youthful struggles at home (first
part); his experiences in the Lithuanian Yeshiba (second
part); and his ramblings among the Chasidim and afterwards in Western Europe (third part). A fourth part,
added to the second edition in 1876, is almost wholly
publicistic, having been written after Smolenskin was so-
bered of all Haskalah delusions.

Despite all its defects, its incoherence and inorganic composition, the innumerable fantastic accidents in the plot,
its naïve psychology and propagandistic aims, **Hattoëh bedarkhe hachayim** won unbelievable influence. It dealt with
no imaginary or bookish problems, but with actual issues,
with the gropings of the youth who were "astray in the
paths of life." What seems to us a literary defect—that it
is a novel with a purpose—was just what Smolenskin's
readers welcomed. They could not understand that literature could be an end in itself, for them it had to be useful,

readily applicable to their own lives. Smolenskin was effective just because he presented contemporary life, not the Biblical or some other remote and romantic past. Moreover, he never merely presented life, but wrote of it as it ought to be; his books were criticisms and incitements to change. While his artistry may have suffered, his enkindling effect upon his readers was due to just that. Still, here and there the artist in him breaks through in many passages that attest his considerable talent for realistic description.

In the latter respect, **Keburath Chamor (The Burial of a Donkey)** is perhaps the best of his novels, being written with much humor and a fresh delight in the telling of a tale. A venturesome wag (Jacob Chaim) plays practical jokes in his ignorant environment, not out of malice, but from sheer exuberance of spirits. However, owing to a spiteful enemy of enlightenment, a local notable named Zebadiah, one misfortune after another befalls him, and finally he is murdered. In revenge and despair his wife Esther has herself baptized. Like the base community leader (Menasse) in **Astray in the Paths of Life,** Zebadiah is caricatured as vice incarnate, the essence of all vileness, Smolenskin still following the naïve psychology of the Haskalah literature that saw in its foes nothing but abomination. However, the frivolous, talkative, good-hearted hero is drawn with sure humor and fidelity to life.

Of Smolenskin's other novels, which to this day have their devoted readers, we shall mention here only the last **Nekam Brith (The Vengeance of the Covenant),** wherein, breaking with the Haskalah ideals forever, he describes the return of Jewish youth to Jewry after the pogroms of 1881. The father is pious and wealthy; the mother an extreme assimilationist; the son, Ben Hagri, though he was taught Hebrew by his father's wish, goes the way of his mother. During his university years he dreams of the time when the last barriers will fall between Jew and Gentile. Even the pogroms, which did not spare his own father's home, could not change his views, since he saw in them only a deplorable accident that ought not to cause loss of faith in the idea itself. Until a terrible personal affront stung him to his inmost soul, and he reverted to his own people. The details of that painful incident are irrelevant. The delineation, the emotional experience, the philosophy to which it gives rise, show no more subtlety than is usual in Smolenskin. But he did grasp the problem itself with a sure intuition. He created herein the first literary prototype which assimilation, particularly in its later stages, produced everywhere and with recurring faithfulness to type. Ben Hagri's way back to his own people is by no means the way of the worst among us. They must taste in their very own persons of the fate that has been ours for centuries; only through personal humiliation can they become aware of the sublime pathos of Jewish martyrdom; but then they respond from their innermost depths. The Talmud rightly says, out of its experience with such Jews, that "in the place where penitents stand, not even great saints may stand."

However, it is not to his novels that Smolenskin owes the honorable place which he holds in Hebrew literature. There is no doubt that in this field he was surpassed by several of his contemporaries whom, for all that, we should hardly care to place on a level with him. It was Smolenskin the publicist, yes, Smolenskin the journalist who, with his

ardor and enthusiasm won even reluctant spirits by storm. Despite his occasional loquacity and his hammer-stroke repetition, an irresistible magnetism radiated from his style, from the vital temperament revealed within it. Furthermore, his earnestness and integrity were sensed between the lines, and won him immediate trust. He may not always have been right in his opinions, the sentiment behind them was always right. His penetrating influence confirms the rightness of Goethe's remark that it is the "personal character of the author that wins him recognition from the public, not the artifices of his talent."

Two lengthy treatises in particular, which are still his most popular works, display Smolenskin in his full stature as an apostle of the national renascence. These are **Am Olam (The Eternal People)** and **Eth lataath (Time to Plant),** both of which ran in serial form in *Hashachar* for several years. It seems preferable to deal with the latter work first, since it is a sort of *pars destruens* for the positive thesis of the former.

Time to Plant is one of the best polemic writings in the Hebrew tongue, an annihilating criticism of Mendelssohn and of the endeavors which, rightly or not, Mendelssohn initiated for Jewish enlightenment. Despite all show of respect, most disparaging criticisms of Mendelssohn the man escape him; yet, on the whole, the idea and the man, the cause and the personality—in so far as so passionate a spirit is capable of this—are kept apart. Smolenskin cannot help showing that Mendelssohn's conciliatory, uncombative temperament is deeply repugnant to him:

> He was a coward by nature and wanted only to be left in peace. He trembled at the sound of a falling leaf, and hated all strife and controversy. Even when surrounded by enemies and opponents, if he could find a place where he might hide silently, he would gladly do so. Such a man cannot be a leader. He did not lead the people, but was pushed onward by them . . . even to a place to which otherwise he would have refused to go.

Centuries after Luther, Mendelssohn rendered the Bible into German, which was no great achievement in itself, nor a service to the Torah. The old Bible translations into Aramaic and Greek were done in times when these were the vernacular tongues of the Jews. But in Mendelssohn's day, "the children of Israel knew Hebrew and not German; they could not understand the source of their faith through a medium still foreign to them." Smolenskin even went so far as to say that Mendelssohn's Bible translation impeded rather than promoted the spread of a knowledge of Judaism, for "when it became known that the children of Mendelssohn and most of his friends and disciples had forsaken the religion of their fathers, how could the pious permit their children to study the Bible and the Hebrew language, seeing that the holy scriptures had become the first step to treason towards Israel?"

But the sharpest shafts of Smolenskin's eloquence are directed against Mendelssohn when he makes him responsible for the notion which since his time has become a creed of the Jewish enlightenment, that we are a religious persuasion and not a people. "I do not say that he was its father, just as I do not say that he was the father of any new idea in Israel. Only his disciples and those who boasted of being his disciples attributed their own thoughts to him, so as to find willing ears; but his passiveness did help to give it much currency."

For Smolenskin the whole future of the Jewish people depended upon a refutation of this theory. For, if we be merely a religious fellowship, we no longer have a common national future, but different destinies for the Jews domiciled in each land of the dispersion. If we be no longer a national unit, Hebrew can at best become the calling of a few scholars; and it would be our duty as, in fact, the Jewish enlightenment has argued since Mendelssohn's time, to lead the Jews to the languages and literatures of their host-nations. But both the hope for national rehabilitation and the most passionate attachment to the Hebrew language could not be extinguished—he felt that he might judge others by himself—in the Jewish soul without destroying that soul itself. Since life refused to give way, he concluded that the theory must be false; and that whoever originated it, whether wittingly or unwittingly, was a false prophet in Jewry. Smolenskin could not but see it as perversity when one, like Mendelssohn, holds the religious commandments and the ritual practices of Judaism obligatory and looks upon those who disregard them as apostates, and yet does not see that it is a far worse betrayal when someone denies its very essence—its most sacred hope, messianism, and the unity of the people. He sees a lack of integrity in the whole conception, which suffers from the same fault as Mendelssohn himself, cowardice.

> To have houses of prayer and choristers and preachers just like the Gentiles, to leave off everything that may not be to their liking, to abandon every opinion that may be unwelcome to them; and since they mistakenly thought the other peoples might take it amiss if we feel ourselves a people, he and they raised their hand to pluck it up by the root.

And in an oft-reiterated, eloquent *quousque tandem,* Smolenskin concludes: how long before we open our eyes and see that it is their cowardice that makes them take a wrong view of things? How long shall we live under the curse of vain fears? "How long until we realize that only the opinions of Mendelssohn and not the spirit of the time is against us?" Opposition to our nationhood comes not from the peoples, but from our wrong estimate of them.

This essay fulfilled a great historic mission. Its occasional personal invective did not impair its purging and educative effect. Its vehemence seemed to say, like Luther, that "he who is in the right may be outspoken." Breathlessly, the Ghetto listened to Smolenskin's refutation. For with Mendelssohn's downfall, the lesser idols lost their hold as a matter of course. Even the half-alienated youth of Russia, whom positivism had robbed of faith in their people, pricked up their ears. "His severe words against Mendelssohn," wrote one of them, "'and his smashing of the god of the Maskilim seemed to me an heroic deed equal to that of Pisarev when he annihilated Pushkin." Jewry too evidently offered potentialities of combat, a chance for great ventures, scope for youthful energies!

One must realize what enormous prestige Mendelssohn enjoyed among the Maskilim in order to understand the whole force of Smolenskin's counterblast. Smolenskin knew that his words would give offense, for

Moses Mendelssohn was to the Maskilim what

Moses the Lawgiver was to the Orthodox, the word of God. To him they looked up, on him they modeled themselves, every syllable that issued from his mouth or did not issue, but was said by others in his name, was considered holy. . . . How many thousands of devout Maskilim are there among us who reject and sneer at the thirteen fundamentals, but who declare: I fervently believe that Moses Mendelssohn was chief of the sages and father of the Maskilim; his law is the unalterable law of truth, his way is without fault or blemish.

Smolenskin considered it his duty to free his generation from submission to the new authority, the infallibility of Mendelssohn. The postulate of freedom to criticize and the quest for truth should apply to one's own party as well.

> The Maskilim applaud and shout with joy when Moses and the prophets and the sages of the Talmud are brought before the bar of judgment; then it is said, let us criticize and examine and test. But let one lay hands upon a *Maskil* who has been set up as a teacher, and they will become just as excited as the Chasidim when their rabbis and saints are attacked. Moreover, there be many among us who will say: You may be right, we are unable to deny the correctness of your words, but such things should only be whispered; why give the obscurantists a chance to raise their heads? Why should the hypocrites say, Behold now, here is a man who is not of our camp, and he too lowers the dignity of their teacher, and admits that he did not serve his people well. All this I knew beforehand, yet did I not hold back, for this is the *time to plant,* and it is our duty to weed out our vineyard.

With these words, Smolenskin overstepped the Maskilic limits of his novels, and paid no heed to the risk of being identified with the orthodox foes of enlightenment. All of Hebrew letters were soon to follow suit.

Smolenskin's affirmation behind the "nay-saying" of **Time to Plant** has been, as said above, formulated in his essay **Am Olam** (**The Eternal People**) and he assumed it as an accepted premise; although, in characteristic manner, and like the born leader that he was, he hammered the definitive principles into the memory of his readers through frequent iteration. Basically, the larger part of **Am Olam** also is polemic and negative and aimed against the religious reforms of Western Jewry—something we need not enter into here. His rejection of reform sprang from his underlying thesis that we are not a religious community, but a people. Israel has not ceased and never will cease to be a people. And just because his religion is not only a profession of faith, but also takes the place of land, government, language, and all those natural institutions which make for national unity, this single, unifying bond must be cherished with the utmost care. Thoughtless changes might impair our unity as a people.

Smolenskin is at pains to show that love for one's own people is not incompatible with universal human ideals, but really fortifies and places these upon their natural basis. For love of one's nation is merely an extension of family feeling and affection; and, just as the former is not conceivable without the latter, so it is not possible to think of a universal brotherhood of mankind without the smaller units of the individual peoples. "If we were suddenly to appear and to proclaim to the multitude: Cast out from your hearts love for all you have loved up to this moment, let not your children and your family be dearer to you than the rest of mankind, would not every man who heard such words ignore and laugh at them?" The aim is identical, only "those who favor love of one's nation set a ladder on the ground whose top reaches the heavens, and go up rung by rung until they reach the top, while those who advocate love of all-humanity wish to leap up to heaven at one bound; therefore those who follow them will necessarily fall and fail. . . ."

I quote these crude formulations in order to obviate any impression that he understood the problem of Jewish (and of general) nationalism in its full implications. He had neither the philosophic nor the poetic finesse of Hess, who in one page could say what Smolenskin's whole essays said, did not say.

Even more. Smolenskin lacked the sheer intellectual energy for overcoming his Haskalah past entirely. His idea of nationhood is still vague and indefinite. We are a people; yet, unlike other peoples, we do not need the outer tokens of nationality (land, government). We are a people of the *spirit*. Such we were even in the days of our national independence, when we still lived in our own land. "We were a people whose life did not depend solely upon a government and a land and laws, one which, when deprived of its land, would lose the foundations of nationality; but since the days of antiquity we have been a people of the spirit, whose Torah was to it as a land and a government and laws. . . ." Israel was born on foreign soil; even before it conquered Canaan it knew itself a people, one people. Hence the idea has never taken root in Israel that it would cease to be a people if, like others, it were to lose its homeland and be dispersed throughout the world. Smolenskin believed that even the results of Bible criticism, which assign a later date to the Torah, to a time when the Jewish people already lived upon its own soil, did not vitiate his theory. For him, not the historic events are important, but the causes which made the children of Israel think their nationhood independent of their land. For centuries the Jews believed the tradition that the Torah was given and the people born before the conquest of the land, a belief to which they cling to this day. Therefore, unlike other peoples, they early learned to think and feel themselves a people of the spirit, whose entity is not destroyed with the loss of their land.

The practical outcome of Smolenskin's conception of spiritual nationhood was that for many years he did not advocate territorial repatriation for the Jews, and even rejected the idea. Though only because it seemed to him impracticable and even dangerous to make a premature attempt whose failure would discredit the idea itself. Nor did he always understand that a Jewish national home could well be reconciled with equality of citizenship for the Jews in the lands of their dispersion—in this respect, also, falling considerably short of Hess. In the few years still granted him after the rise of the *Chibbath Zion,* he threw himself whole-heartedly into the Palestine movement.

However, even in his very first articles in *Hashachar,* and also in *The Eternal People,* his theoretical formulation that a land is not essential for Jewish nationality is opposed by his territorial sentiment, his deep grasp of all the implications of Jewish messianism. When once the satirist M. D. Brandstaetter sent him a parody on the messianic belief, he refused to print it, saying: "I too am one of those who believe in the Messiah and in the day of redemption. And not only do I await the redemption, but I would gladly shed my blood were valiant men to rise among us to save the honor of our people. I shall cling to my faith in the coming of the day of redemption, even though it be far off. . . . " Probably the finest passages in *The Eternal People* are those on the messianic hope, which reveal very clearly the inner conflict where the Maskilic head, which would like to remain sober, yet tries to help the turbulent heart by finding arguments for the seemingly impossible.

> Even though it be pointed out that this hope will never be realized, we ought not to abandon it. For there are many fine ideals which are not realizable, and yet we do not refrain from teaching them to the public and urging youth to hold fast to them. A good thought is good even when it is not translated into action. Just as we do not say to a poor man that he think the less of charitable deeds because it is not within his power to perform them, so we cannot say to a distressed people, Give up your hope of becoming a people with a land and a government of your own because you are unable to give effect to your desire. Even if it be true, as they say, that it is impossible for Israel to return to its land and to restore its state as aforetime. But there is no such thing as impossible. Things which are impossible now may be actualities a few years hence. Had anyone come a hundred years ago to say that the small Greek nation, the remnant of the ancient Greeks, who also are scattered all over the world, would again set up their kingdom, all the people would have laughed at him, saying, What a fool is this prophet! Yet it came to pass because the people willed it with all their hearts. Had Israel wished to find his land, he would long ago have found it. For he could easily have bought it for a price and brought back to it the persecuted Jews from the many lands of their dispersion. Oppression would cease when it became known that they had a land, a land and a government that would take their part in time of need. . . . Then they would be respected like other peoples. . . .

"If Israel willed it" . . . it were no fable. There, once more, is Herzl's teaching, and the concern of those who followed and will for a still undetermined span follow him. To arouse this national will Smolenskin worked with the unparalleled devotion of the apostle who has no fear of the thorny path of propaganda. A grateful people, remembering the sincerity even more than the achievements of his mission, has allotted him a place of honor in the memory of posterity. (pp. 226-41)

> *Shalom Spiegel, "The Homecoming to Zion,"
> in his* Hebrew Reborn, *The Macmillan Company, 1930, pp. 211-42.*

David Polish   (essay date 1943)

[*In the following excerpt, Polish defines Smolenskin's pre-Zionist and Zionist philosophies.*]

Smolenskin's spiritual growth may be divided into two phases. The first was the pre-Zionist phase, which was distinguished by strong negations. The second was the Zionist phase.

. . . . .

The process of negation involved casting off the basic premises of Jewish life in Europe. He was the first Hebrew writer to renounce the most basic premise of all—that Jewish life in the Diaspora is a possibility. He dismissed hope of any future for Diaspora Judaism. His second negation was the dismissal of all contemporary approaches to the Jewish question—Jewish scholarship, *Hasidism, Haskalah.* Finally, Smolenskin rejected the place of European culture in the development of Jewish spiritual and national values.

Smolenskin's despair of the Diaspora is represented in *Hagemul* (1867) and *Nekam berit* (1884). The former is an adaptation of a German work. It tells of a Jewish youth who affirms that there is no room for Judaism in a Poland struggling for her independence, and that with Polish freedom the lot of the Jew will also improve. He devotes himself to the cause of Polish independence, but his Christian associates resent the presence of a Jew in their midst, and betray him to the Russian authorities. In his disillusionment, he sees no hope for Jewry in Poland. He lives to see the attacks on loyal Polish Jews by the erstwhile revolutionists, and he recalls his father's admonition to flee the land. The disillusionment is complete. There is but one escape for Smolenskin—away from Poland. But he does not yet have a destination. (*Nekam berit,* written after the events of 1881, reiterates with heightened bitterness the futility of the *galut* [the Jewish Diaspora], but now the author has found his objective—Palestine.)

Smolenskin repudiated not only the external but the internal forces in Jewish life. This wholesale negation is delineated in *HaToeh.* This is the record of a lost Jewish soul. The leading character personifies the Jew who cannot find a desirable way of life. His personal contacts with many Jews are unpleasant. He constantly encounters corruption and evil in the Jewish communities which he visits. Desperately seeking a happy adjustment, he tries out all sorts of Jewish groups. He finds in the *yeshivot* [religious academies] an excessive devotion to learning which excludes all worldly ambitions. This is repugnant to him. "The love of Torah and the contempt for labor . . . have struck their roots deep" (Book II). He turns from the nationalism of the *yeshivah* to the mysticism of the Hasidim and recoils again. Nor do the Mitnaggedim (opponents of Hasidism) offer greater promise. There follows a brief junket with Haskalah (the "Enlightenment") but the disappointment is inevitable. Haskalah cannot inspire confidence because it stems from enlightenment which the author regards as suspect. France, shrine of liberty and enlightenment, is not free of anti-Semitism (Book IV). Not only is Haskalah disqualified because of this relationship, but its teachings are also untenable. Its "back-to-physical-labor movement" is ridiculed because it emanates from German Jewish merchants and traders, and because Russian Jews, who indulge in hard labor, are no better off than the bourgeoisie (Book IV). The author had hoped that Haskalah would bring happiness and wisdom to his people, but, instead, "I beheld the victims of Haskalah . . . and I cried out, for I have seen evil and trouble . . . " (Book IV).

After each tragic episode which befalls the *"Toeh,"* Smolenskin recalls the utter chaos of Jewish life and the abysmal confusion with which it engulfs him. "I walked among wanderers; wanderers guided me; wanderers persecuted me, aided me, counselled me; and, I like them, was a wanderer in the pathways of life" (Book II). As in *Hagemul,* Smolenskin exposes the emptiness of the ideals in which Jews had put their trust, but he offers no way out, except a warning to others not to err as he did. The story ends with the death of the central figure. He has thus come to the end of a futile Jewish life, but even on the threshold of death he remains bewildered. He is truly the marginal man—divorced from his old way of life, vainly searching for a new.

Kevurat hamor (1874) strikes the same mood, but in this story can be felt the first stirrings of escape from the spiritual trap. In this tale, Smolenskin pits Haskalah against Jewish obscurantism. Like J. L. Gordon, he exposes the bigotry and venality of the communal leaders, their superstition and their relentless hounding of the weak. Because of their authority, they are in a position to dominate the individual and suppress his personal liberty. Smolenskin presents the lone figure of a young *maskil,* a quixotic character, who dares to attempt to overcome his people's debased leadership by laying bare its ignorance and improbity. He cherishes the faith that an objective test of enlightenment versus bigotry will win the day for him. But he is to learn that the people will not follow merely if shown the light. He is to learn that victory is in the hands of those who wield power and authority, those who are organized to impose their collective will. The assassination of the young idealist is a crushing commentary on the futility of his struggle. There is in the story, however, a suggestion of a new approach. It lies in group action. In one scene, the victims of the community's masters meet to plan group resistance against their oppression. This is the first hint that the united efforts of the Jewish people might be an effective check to Jewish dictatorship. This concept is to be developed by Smolenskin in his essays. Its logical result is Zionism.

Smolenskin's third negation involves European culture. This is discussed in *Simhat hanef* (1872). European letters exerted an influence upon Hebrew poetry and prose. Thus European concepts of nationality found access to Hebrew works. Smolenskin was the first Hebrew writer to repudiate this influence. He contended that Jewish nationalism differed from European nationalism, and that to lean upon European standards was to adulterate the Hebraic national expression. He pitted Hebraic against European literary and spiritual values, and sought to prove that the former made for a higher and different kind of nationalism. Much of *Simhat hanef* is a dissertation on this problem. Superficially it is an evaluation of the comparative merits of different literatures. Fundamentally, however, it is an examination of antithetical national values. Smolenskin assigns the defense of European letters to a *maskil* who is also the story's chief scoundrel. The protaganist of Hebrew culture is an opponent of Haskalah and a man of integrity.

Smolenskin attempts to prove that the prototypes of Haskalah literature, among them Goethe and Voltaire, represented everything repugnant to the Jewish national spirit. They are responsible for the resurgence of idolatry in Europe.

Thus, Smolenskin argues, the paganism of Europe's literary giants is incompatible with Jewish values. From this point, he proceeds to indicate that whatever is worthwhile in the works of men like Goethe and Shakespeare is a result of the influence of Hebraic values. Why should modern Hebrew authors follow European currents when their most meritorious elements are Hebraic? Shakespeare's Hamlet and Goethe's Faust are both spiritual heirs of Kohelet and Job. But while Shakespeare and Goethe were of two different nationalities, the authors of both Biblical works were Jewish. Hebrew culture is thus superior on two counts—it is anti-pagan, and it lies at the foundation of what is truly great in European letters. Having established the superiority of Jewish culture, Smolenskin is loathe to equate it with any other. He takes Lessing to task for his parable of the rings. "Had the judges looked carefully they would have seen that the rings were not identical. . . . Come what may, we certainly know which is the original ring. . . . "

Thus was sounded the first note of independence in Hebrew literature. Its only equivalent is to be found in Samuel David Luzzatto's critique of Michal's poetry.

. . . . .

By laying the foundation for Judaism's moral outlook upon authentic Jewish sources, Smolenskin sought to prepare the way for Jewish nationalism. This exposition is a clue to Smolenskin's theory of Jewish nationalism. As developed in his essays, it means basically the fullest modern development by the Jewish people of their spiritual and cultural way of life. It should be noted, however, that even Smolenskin could not effect a tour de force of cultural isolationism. It needs only to be pointed out that **Simhat hanef** shares much in common with Goethe's *Wahlverwandschaften*. Moreover, his essays abound in allusions to European nationalism on which he draws for support and justification of Jewish nationalism.

In his second period, that of political Zionism, Smolenskin arrives at the nationalist solution of the Jewish question through an analysis of two problems. One is the nature and function of reformation in Judaism; the other is the national character of Jewish religion. Both, in effect, are concerned with an analysis of the Jewish spirit. His preoccupation with the former problem is prompted by the need of a rationale for his severely critical attitude toward German Reform and the teachings of Mendelssohn. After assailing them, he establishes his own criteria for reformation in Jewish life. His reasoning, stripped of its ponderous circumlocutions, pursues the following course.

. . . . .

There are two fundamental objections to Reform. One is that it does not have the sanction of the Jewish masses. Secondly, it has failed to unite Israel. Smolenskin's chief argument is that the function of reformation must be to strengthen our national character, but that German Reform has dessicated it. If there are to be any reforms, they must enjoy popular endorsement which would give them authority. The people have the right to repudiate innovators who are in the minority (**Essays,** Vol. I). The reason for thus protecting our religious laws is that our religion is the one uniting factor for all Israel. It should be noted that, to Smolenskin, Jewish religion meant the entirety of Israel's spiritual heritage, not what it meant to his Reform opponents, an arbitrarily defined segment of it. It included the inextricably related ideals of God, Israel, Torah, land, and language. In this particular context, Smolenskin uses the terms religion and nationalism interchangeably. We must, therefore, regard religion not only as a faith, but as

a surrogate for a homeland, language and all other factors which unite other peoples. Just as among free nations, basic changes cannot be made without the consent of the governed, so must our religious heritage be guarded. (pp. 11-14)

The essence of [a Reform] program must be to find a method of uniting the Jewish people.

First of all, there should be national assemblies for the purpose of studying the laws and lightening their burden. Thus new religious practices will be based upon the will of the people and upon the Torah as well. In this way, the whole people will be instructed, and will not have decisions imposed from above.

Second, the unifying process must involve renewing the Jewish hope for redemption. This hope is utterly dependent upon the fostering of the Hebrew language. The enemies of Jewish national hopes try to destroy our language, for without it there is no Torah, and without Torah there is no Jewish people. If we conscientiously desire to make reforms for the purpose of aiding and uniting Israel, we have no other choice but to teach Hebrew to the people.

The third requirement for the unification of Israel is an agency which will undertake this task. Such an agency is the Alliance Israelite Universelle. Without the unifying strength of this group, we are in danger of disintegration as a result of the weakening of our religious observance and of our belief in future redemption.

Thus, religious change by popular approval and in the spirit of Torah; the redemptive urge; the Hebrew language; and the Alliance are the true reforms which must be achieved in Jewish life.

. . . . .

After having established the principle that true reformation must mean the cultivation of nationhood, Smolenskin develops his second thesis. This revolves around the distinctive character of Judaism which embodies religious and national traits in an indivisible entity. His quarrel is with Reform and Haskalah for attempting to split this unity.

Smolenskin begins by attacking the position of Mendelssohn's followers who insisted that we are a religious group only. While Mendelssohn was himself not to blame, his inadequate leadership permitted his followers to corrupt his teachings. Thus, while there can be no objection to necessary reforms, the hypothesis that we have ceased to be a nation is a most dangerous innovation. To Smolenskin, Jewish nationalism and Jewish religion are, in their all-encompassing comprehensiveness, interchangeable.

By creating a dichotomy between the terms, the German Haskalah has furnished anti-Semitism with dangerous weapons and has also weakened our own position. The translation of the Pentateuch alienated an entire generation from the Hebrew language and from Judaism, resulting eventually in wholesale apostasy. Mendelssohn's aping of Germanism not only obstructed the growth of Jewish nationalism but also encouraged the alienation from Hebraic values.

Historically, however, national, and not religious (in the Reform sense), bonds sustained us. This is because our national development has been different from that of other peoples. Our national life has not been dependent upon government, land, or language. What, then, has been the source of our national existence? It has been "the unique spirit of Israel" and our early training. All other nations were born in their own lands. They passed under all sorts of government, but they were conditioned to regard themselves as nations only so long as they occupied their own soil. But Israel, though born in a strange country, nevertheless regarded itself as a nation. For this reason it never developed the notion that, should it be exiled, it would cease to be a national group. In all of our prayers we refer to *Am Yisrael,* not *Dat Yisrael* ["the people of Israel," not "the religion of Israel"]. Just as our nationhood developed without land, so did our government and laws. Among other nations, these factors are relevant only when rooted in a given territory. But Israel had government and laws before it had a land. They were spiritual and hence they could be observed in any place. Israel selected not a temporal but a Divine King. How could such a nation be overthrown?

Thus, with subsequent loss of their state, the Jews did not become an exclusively religious group, for they did not build their unity upon religious foundations. To understand this concept, we must appreciate the distinction between the Jewish and other religions. Among other peoples, religion and nation are separate elements. But in Israel, religion was accepted simultaneously with our national status (*Essays,* Vol. IV).

Our laws are likewise not religious in the accepted sense. They are signs of national unity. They deal with national conduct. This is symbolized by the fact that instead of a specific term for religion, Israel used such terms as *Torah* and *Berit.* The latter signifies an open and contractual acceptance of our religion, not a superimposed cult.

With the exception of Judaism, a religious group is one which differs from others in matters of faith; one whose faith is based upon reward and punishment, and also upon personal salvation. Israel, however, based its faith upon the concept of divine government and not upon a theory of future life. It dealt with the promise of God to take Israel as a people, to redeem them from slavery, and to settle them in their own land. According to this conception, the nations cannot be united until they believe in the One God, until God is enthroned, and until all governments and rulers are removed.

Because our laws and government are spiritual, they must be studied continually. Other peoples must merely *obey* their temporal laws, but we must *study* ours. Study alone reminds us of our unity. We have been made different from all other nations by the Torah, our spiritual way of life, our national abode. Whenever our political fortunes declined, our adherence to Torah intensified. This was due not to the Torah's religious influence, in the sectarian sense, but rather to its capacity for arousing confidence in our ultimate redemption. It was basically a repository of our national consciousness.

In the light of this spiritual definition of Jewish nationalism, our first task must be to renounce the concept that we are a religion and not a nation. "Indeed, we once had a land, but that was not the bond which united us. The land which makes us one is our Torah. . . . "

Refusal to accept the principle of nationhood makes our position in the Diaspora less tenable. Those who attempt to placate our enemies by disclaiming our nationhood imply that those who avow it are disloyal citizens. This plays into the hands of the anti-Semites. The effort to strip ourselves of all national characteristics, including the Hebrew language and the hope for redemption, has earned for us not the approval of the Christian world, but its contempt. Anti-Semitism is not predicated upon Jewish conduct. It will burst forth upon the most "conforming" and the most "emancipated" of Jews. With terrifying accuracy, Smolenskin predicts:

> It is true that for the time being the Jews enjoy security in Germany. They still find shelter in the laws (of the land). Bismark who has been their protector will not suddenly become their enemy. But who knows what another day will bring? Hatred will increase. It will secretly send its shoots and pass from land to land. Who knows what form its fruit will take? Our short-sighted brethren neither see nor believe. . . . They believe that all is well with them, that trouble cannot arise in the nineteenth century. . . . But it is a vain dream. . . . While formerly their enemies were confined to haters of the Jewish religion . . . today they have multiplied until they include . . . (all disgruntled elements). Little by little they will gather around our enemies and at the opportune time, when the government will find need for them, it will abet them in carrying out their designs. Then it will be a time of trouble for Jacob (*Essays,* Vol. III).

Not only must we regard ourselves as a nation, but the outer world also regards us thus. Even if we should secure full equality in the Diaspora, even if religious differences would be eradicated, jealousy of us would still prevail, and we should still be considered a nation (*Essays,* Vol. I).

Recapitulating his concept of Jewish nationalism, Smolenskin writes:

> . . . We are one people and the rules of faith alone are the cornerstone . . . of our national unity. These rules of faith are the belief in One God; the study of Torah in the original—for it is now for us both a land and a language—the hope for a future redemption, which is for us a government. If one adheres to these three principles, then he is for Israel . . . " (*Essays,* Vol. I).

                    . . . . .

Since the repudiation of our nationalism leads to spiritual and political bankruptcy, what are we to do? This question motivates Smolenskin's third proposition, in which he outlines a program of action.

To begin with, he contends that the "Jewish Question" cannot be solved by such efforts as back-to-the-farm movements. We must develop a way of life commensurate with our existing abilities and not with our ancient capacities.

If the nations do not permit us to do this, it is folly to even consider the problem. "Our destinies are not in our own hands but in the hands of others. As long as this condition prevails, there is no hope of saving us in a national way." "We can rescue individuals, but not the group" (*Essays,* Vols. II and III). The only problem which we can solve is the moral problem, namely "How can we renew our covenant as of old, how can we breathe new life into the dry bones?"

Equally ineffective are the efforts of the Alliance Israelite Universelle. Its attempt to help the Jews of Rumania was fruitless. This is due to the lack of universal Jewish acceptance of the proposition that we are a nation. (This statement was written seven years after Smolenskin's earlier endorsement of the Alliance in 1872.) The chief emphasis of the Alliance was upon financial relief. But what Rumanian Jewry wanted was political intervention and spiritual mooring. The Alliance paid lip service to the first and was indifferent to the second. Smolenskin, after visiting Rumania, recognized the need for training Jewish leaders who could guide Rumanian Jewry. The people were enthusiastic, but the Alliance was aloof (*Essays,* Vol. III).

National unity cannot be achieved without first defeating the Berlin Haskalah. This can be done through an increased use of the Hebrew language. By means of a common tongue we can achieve common action. Hebrew alone will not solve our problems but without it the national spirit cannot be revived. Palestine is indispensable for the Jew, but its cause cannot be promulgated except through Hebrew.

From this point on, Smolenskin expatiates on the need for Jewish settlement in Palestine. He advances the theory that Jewish emigration from Europe will lessen anti-Semitism. Further, economic readjustment is possible only in our own homeland. This homeland is Palestine. It is preferable to other territories because it appeals to our national memories, it is capable of cultivation, it is not too distant geographically; Jews settling there will be able to live their own lives; the "Halukkah" Jews of Palestine will be regenerated. The superiority of Palestine over America for settlement purposes is outlined as follows: (a) The migration to America will result in the scattering of the Jewish population. In America a few will prosper while the rest will suffer want and will be without aid. However, in Palestine the needy will be able to turn to the more prosperous settlers who preceded them, for help. (b) We have no guarantee that America's liberal laws will some day not be replaced by restrictive measures. (c) We are in a position to buy land in Palestine from Turkey. (d) We can eventually become a majority and exercise political control within the country. (e) "Upon the idea of Palestine depends the idea of our unity and existence. If (Jewish) groups gather in one place, it will become a center for the learning and regulations of the people, and from there will emanate learning for all the nations." Smolenskin then appeals for a Congress of European Jews to discuss the settlement of Palestine. He presses the urgency of this proposal because "before long persecution will renew its strength . . . and there is no other place where we can hope for sanctuary . . . except Palestine. Oppression has lifted its head . . . because our enemies regret" the equality which they conferred upon us (*Essays,* Vol. IV). Our position in the Middle Ages was better than it is now. Then we were protected by kings and noblemen who enjoyed economic advantage in our well-being. Today, however, our only foothold is business, and it is being torn from under us. If we should lose that, we are doomed in the Diaspora. (pp. 15-19)

> *David Polish, "Peretz Smolenskin's Contribu-*
> *tion to Jewish Thought," in* The Reconstruc-

tionist, *Vol. IX, No. 9, June 11, 1943, pp. 11-19.*

Charles H. Freundlich   (essay date 1965)

[*In the following conclusion to his biography of Smolenskin, Freundlich summarizes Smolenskin's career and assesses his influence on modern Jewish thought.*]

Almost a century has passed since the writings of Smolenskin. In his own day, he was Israel's greatest novelist and this alone would ensure his place in the history of his people. But what of his thought and his philosophy of Judaism? In this area, his work deserves serious attention in understanding the development of modern Israel, the revival of Hebrew and current Jewish Philosophy. Let us summarize his work and view its transition from ideology to reality.

His evaluation of anti-Semitism from the Darwinian perspective led him to advocate the colonization of Palestine. In Palestine, where the Jews would become a majority, there was envisioned a refuge from anti-Semitism. He had little faith in the optimism of the Enlightenment as a solution to the Jewish problem. As long as the Jews were in the Diaspora and were a minority, they would be weak. And as long as they were weak, they would be oppressed. His plea for the restoration of a Jewish state was eloquently expressed in the first issue of his *ha-Shahar* (1868). His only poem, **"Love of the Fatherland,"** underscored his sorrow for the homelessness of the Jewish people.

But he soon withdrew his attention from the external problem of anti-Semitism. Perhaps his stay in Vienna assuaged his feelings about the Czarist oppression of the Jews. Nevertheless, until the pogroms of 1881, he was concerned with the internal "spiritual" problem confronting Judaism. His ***Am olam*** outlined a diagnosis of the Jewish problem and its solution. As he understood it, the crisis in Judaism was caused by the weakening of its national bonds. Enlightenment *a la* Mendelssohn and German Reform Judaism were attacked by him for being the archenemies of Jewish Peoplehood. The bonds of the Jewish people were "spiritual" and consisted of the "Torah", the Hebrew language, and the Messianic Hope. The broadening of the French *Alliance Israelite Universelle* would provide a democratic structure for solving all Jewish problems. Hebrew education, modified reforms, and organized philanthropy were the key areas to be strengthened.

Smolenskin, like Ahad Ha-Am later on, emphasized Hebrew as a literary language, to be used only for spiritual purposes—not to be revived as a spoken genre. Yet his own literary works, his novels, were paving the way for the full revival of Hebrew. More than anyone of his generation, he expressed brilliantly the role of Hebrew, "What shall Hebrew give us? It shall give us dignity to call ourselves Jews!"

While he sensed the need for some reforms in Jewish law, he felt they were of minor significance, and the Jewish people themselves, without Reform Rabbis, conferences or movements, could adapt themselves to the changing times. He thus sided with the traditionalists who were more concerned with *conserving* Judaism than *reforming* it.

After the pogroms of 1881, he modified his nationalist views and advocated full Jewish nationalism including territorialism. He thus laid the foundation for the Zionist platform which was to take form fifteen years later. He anticipated Ahad Ha-Am and viewed the new Israeli community as a "spiritual center" for a Diaspora which would remain for many more years.

His shattering criticism of the *Haskalah* and his denouncement of the theory that the Jews constituted a "religion", were perhaps his greatest contributions to laying the groundwork for modern Zionism. His enthusiasm for the *Alliance* and its potential, anticipated the Zionist organization to be formed twenty five years later.

It is indisputable that Smolenskin's thought was instrumental in building the road to Zion. The odyssey of the homelessness of the Jews draws to a climactic ending. Today, with the realization of the State of Israel, a new chapter has dawned in the history of our people. Multitudes of Jews walk the streets proudly in a free land, speak Hebrew naturally, and carry on a life unhampered by minority status. Is the Zionist dream to be considered fulfilled? Shall history stamp its approval on the Zionist theoreticians from Smolenskin to Herzl, for having solved the Jewish problem?

It is still too early for history to pass final judgment on the Zionist thesis for there still remains much work to be done.

The political aspirations of Zionism *vis-à-vis* the world community has been achieved, with the exception of a rapprochement with the neighboring Arab states. Perhaps this rapprochement will become a reality after the Arab states achieve their own political maturity, expand their educational patterns, liberalize their entire social structure and realize that a progressive Israel, as a neighbor, can be a boon to their own national destiny.

Hebrew, similarly, has been revived as a living genre for daily social intercourse. However, until Israel also produces a literature worthy of the Biblical tradition and comparable in stature to the Hebrew renaissance in the Diaspora of the past century—this revival will still be found wanting.

The relationship of religion and nationhood still needs to be clarified. Smolenskin viewed the "Jewish religion" as an intrinsic part of its nationhood. Yet, the realities of a modern Israel populated by a majority of "secular" Jews who view the militancy of both the Rabbinate and the "religious" political parties as an encroachment on religious freedom, make it appear that a Kulterkamph is in the making. What could be more absurd than the idea of a national revival that revitalized its language and territory but left out the most unique expression of its national life—its law? Until Jewish law becomes revitalized as a modern way of life for *all* its people, "secular" as well as "religious", the full national revival will be incomplete.

The most pressing problem, perhaps, is the working out of a proper dialogue between Israel and the Diaspora. Smolenskin viewed Israel as a "spiritual center" for the Diaspora. To a certain degree, the emergence of Israel has brought about a measure of pride and identity to many of the Diaspora Jews. However, with the emergence of a new Israel identity that has negated the worth of the Diaspora

experience, and the continued dilution of Jewish forms in the west, a parting of ways seems imminent.

For two thousand years, the Jewish people struggled for survival, despite indescribable hardships and inestimable suffering, hoping for the redemption of Israel. Should Israel fail to fulfill the ideals of this Diaspora experience, history would witness the most pitiful waste of human effort.

The Zionist dream did not end the odyssey of the Jew. Rather, it opened a new chapter, and established a vast laboratory, for the rebirth of a people. It is this challenge that Zionism has made possible, rather than the historical accuracy of its ideology, that has made it one of the most successful national movements in modern history.

A world that has been ravaged by the evil and inhumanity from a variety of nationalisms, from Fascism through Nazism, would be well advised to pay heed to Smolenskin's message. Rooted in the high ideals of Israel's prophets, Jewish tradition, and the humanism of the modern age, he underscored the fact that nationalism was a movement of the Spirit. The human spirit was the most vital ingredient in the making of a nation. He thus drew up a blue-print of nationalism worthy of Israel and a universal family of nations. (pp. 261-65)

> *Charles H. Freundlich, in his* Peretz Smolenskin, His Life and Thought: A Study of the Renascence of Jewish Nationalism, *Bloch Publishing Company, 1965, 278 p.*

FURTHER READING

Dubnow, S. M. "The Harbinger of Jewish Nationalism (Perez Smolenskin)." In his *History of the Jews in Russia and Poland: From Earliest Times until the Present Day,* translated by I. Friedlaender, pp. 233-37. Philadelphia: The Jewish Publication Society of America, 1918.

> Views Smolenskin as one who wrote for social rather than artistic reasons.

Greenberg, Louis. "Nationalist Trends." In his *The Jews in Russia,* Vol. I, pp. 130-45. New Haven: Yale University Press, 1944.

> Cites the opinions of Hebrew critics regarding Smolenskin. Greenberg quotes Smolenskin's biographer, Reuben Brainin, who deems Smolenskin "the greatest national philosopher of our latest period, one of the foremost creators of the national literature of our day and the solitary champion of nationalism." Greenberg also quotes J. Klausner's remark: "We have a right to regard both our present day national ideal and the Zionist ideology based upon it as largely the creation of Peter Smolenskin."

Raisin, Jacob S. "Russification, Reformation, and Assimilation." In his *The Haskalah Movement in Russia,* pp. 222-67. Philadelphia: Jewish Publication Society of America, 1913.

Credits Smolenskin with framing the Haskalah of the 1880s, which was "devoted to the development of Hebrew literature and the rejuvenation of the Hebrew people."

Alfred, Lord Tennyson

1809-1892

English poet and dramatist.

Tennyson is considered one of the greatest poets in the English language. He was immensely popular in his lifetime, especially in the years following the publication of his lengthy elegiac poem *In Memoriam.* Epitomizing Tennyson's art and thought, this work was embraced by readers as a justification of their religious faith amid doubt caused by the scientific discoveries and speculations of the time. Queen Victoria declared that she valued it next to the Bible as a work of consolation, thus contributing to Tennyson's stature as the foremost poet of his generation and the poetic voice of Victorian England. While many critics have since found his poetry excessively moralistic, Tennyson is universally acclaimed as a lyricist of unsurpassed skill.

The fourth of twelve children, Tennyson was born in Somersby, Lincolnshire. His father was a rector who maintained his benefice grudgingly as a means of supporting himself and his family. The elder son of a wealthy landowner, he had obtained the rectory when his younger brother was designated as prospective heir to the family's estate. According to biographers, Tennyson's father responded to his virtual disinheritance by indulging in drugs and alcohol, creating an unpleasant domestic atmosphere often made worse by his violent temper. Each of his children suffered to some extent from drug addiction or mental illness, promoting the family's grim speculation on the "black blood" of the Tennysons, whose history of mental and physical debilities, epilepsy prominent among them, had become a distressing part of their family heritage. Biographers speculate that the general melancholy and morbidity expressed in much of Tennyson's verse is rooted in the unhappy environment at Somersby.

Tennyson's first volume of poetry, *Poems by Two Brothers,* included the work of his two elder brothers and was published in 1827. Later that year, Tennyson enrolled at Trinity College, Cambridge, where he won the chancellor's gold medal for his poem "Timbuctoo" in 1829. *Poems, Chiefly Lyrical,* published in 1830, was well received and marked the beginning of Tennyson's literary career; another collection, *Poems,* appeared in 1832 but was less favorably reviewed, many critics praising Tennyson's artistry but objecting to what they considered an absence of intellectual substance. This latter volume was published at the urging of Arthur Hallam, a brilliant Cambridge undergraduate who had become Tennyson's closest friend and was an ardent admirer of his poetry. Hallam's enthusiasm was welcomed by Tennyson, whose personal circumstances had led to a growing despondency: His father died in 1831, leaving Tennyson's family in debt and forcing his early departure from Trinity College; one of Tennyson's brothers suffered a mental breakdown and required institutionalization; and Tennyson himself was morbidly fearful of falling victim to epilepsy or madness. Hallam's untimely death in 1833, which prompted the series of elegies later comprising *In Memoriam,* contributed

greatly to Tennyson's despair. In describing this period, he wrote: "I suffered what seemed to me to shatter all my life so that I desired to die rather than to live."

For nearly a decade after Hallam's death Tennyson published no further poetry. During this period he became engaged to Emily Sellwood, but financial difficulties and Tennyson's persistent anxiety over the condition of his health resulted in their separation. In 1842, yielding to a friend's insistence, Tennyson published his two-volume collection *Poems,* for which reviewers were virtually unanimous in expressing admiration. That same year an unsuccessful financial venture cost Tennyson nearly everything he owned, causing him to succumb to a deep depression that required medical treatment. In 1845 he was granted a government pension in recognition of both his poetic achievement and his apparent need. Contributing to his financial stability, the first edition of his narrative poem *The Princess: A Medley,* published in 1847, sold out within two months. Tennyson resumed his courtship of Sellwood in 1849, and they were married the following year.

The timely success of *In Memoriam,* published in 1850, ensured Tennyson's appointment as poet laureate succeeding William Wordsworth. *Idylls of the King,* considered by Tennyson's contemporaries to be his masterpiece, and *Enoch Arden,* which sold more than forty thousand copies upon publication, increased both his popularity and his wealth, and earned him the designation "the people's poet." Although the dramatic works written later in his career were largely unsuccessful, Tennyson completed several additional collections of poems in the last decade of his life, all of which were well received. In 1883 he accepted a peerage, the first poet to be so honored strictly on the basis of literary achievement. Tennyson died in 1892 and was interred in Westminster Abbey.

Tennyson's first two significant collections, *Poems, Chiefly Lyrical* and *Poems,* were considered by many critics to be of high poetic merit but devoid of meaning or purpose beyond their pure artistry. In a review of the latter collection, philosopher John Stuart Mill urged Tennyson to "cultivate . . . philosophy as well as poetry," expressing a sentiment not uncommon among Tennyson's early reviewers. The collection of *Poems* which appeared in 1842 included radically revised versions of his best poems from the earlier volumes, and addressed such themes as duty, self-discipline, and the complexities of religious faith, offering what critics considered to be a truer representation of human life than that of his early works. Such poems as "The Palace of Art," "St. Simeon Stylites," "The Two Voices," and "The Vision of Sin" reveal an attitude of moral determination that characterizes the collection as a whole, examining the conflict between indulgence and morality while expressing the need for social involvement. If "Recollections of the Arabian Nights," "The Hesperides," and others of Tennyson's earliest poems celebrate, as Jerome Buckley notes, "the flight into an exotic world of pure art," the *Poems* of 1842 demonstrate Tennyson's effort to face and not escape from the world. Nevertheless, Tennyson's attempts to confront important issues and ideas in his works have been regarded as largely unsuccessful. *The Princess,* for example, which examined the education of women in Victorian England, was Tennyson's response to critics who urged him to address the major issues of his day. The focus of the poem, however, shifts from the establishment of women's colleges to a more general consideration of what Tennyson regarded as the unnatural attempt of men and women to assume identical roles in society. Many critics found Tennyson's treatment of the central question, women's education, to be shallow, and thus representative of what they considered the major weakness of his poetry. Summarizing this position, F. L. Lucas has written that Tennyson's detractors condemned him as "intellectually timid, a prophet of comfortable things, a priest without a real faith, a philosopher who could not reason, a political thinker who trimmed over the problems of poverty and turned the Woman's Question into a picnic." Nevertheless, *The Princess* was well received by the British public, to whom its idealism and celebration of domesticity greatly appealed.

Tennyson's next major work, *In Memoriam,* expressed his personal grief over Hallam's death while examining more generally the nature of death and bereavement in relation to contemporary scientific issues, especially those involving evolution and the geologic dating of the earth's history, which brought into question traditional religious beliefs. Largely regarded as an affirmation of faith, *In Memoriam* was especially valued for its reflections on overcoming bereavement. Comprising 132 sections written over the course of nearly two decades, the poem progresses

from despair to joy and concludes with a marriage celebration, symbolically expressing Tennyson's faith in the moral evolution of humanity and reflecting the nineteenth-century ideal of social progress. The success of *In Memoriam* and his subsequent appointment as poet laureate assured Tennyson the opportunity to become the poetic voice of his generation, and in his ceremonial position he composed such poems as "Ode on the Death of the Duke of Wellington" and "The Charge of the Light Brigade," each of which is a celebration of heroism and public duty. *Maud, and Other Poems* was the first collection Tennyson published as laureate, but only his 1832 volume, *Poems,* elicited a more negative response. The title poem is a "monodrama" in which the changing consciousness of the narrator is traced through a series of tragedies that result in his insanity. Confined to an asylum, the protagonist is cured of his madness and asserts his love for humanity by serving his country in the Crimean War. George Eliot and William Gladstone denounced the poem as morbid and obscure, and were among many who disapproved of Tennyson's apparent glorification of war, which he depicted as an ennobling enterprise essential to the cleansing and regeneration of a morally corrupt society. *Maud* has since been reevaluated by critics who find it Tennyson's most stylistically inventive poem, praising its violent rhythms and passionate language. Modern critics largely agree with Christopher Ricks that *Maud* was for Tennyson an "exorcism"; as Ricks explains, "*Maud* was an intense and precarious attempt . . . to encompass the bitter experiences of four decades of a life in which many of the formative influences had also been deformative." Thus madness, suicide, familial conflict, shattered love, death and loss, and untempered mammonism, all central grievings in Tennyson's life, are attacked openly and passionately in *Maud,* with war cultivating the spirit of sacrifice and loyalty which Tennyson felt essential to avert the self-destruction of a selfishly materialistic society.

Tennyson's epic poem *Idylls of the King* followed the controversial *Maud* by examining the rise and fall of idealism in society. "I tried in my *Idylls,*" Tennyson wrote, "to teach men the need of an ideal." F. E. L. Priestley has observed that Tennyson used the "Arthurian cycle as a medium for discussion of problems which [were] both contemporary and perennial," and concludes that the *Idylls* "represent one of Tennyson's most earnest and important efforts to deal with the major problems of his time." Tennyson was concerned with what he considered to be a growing tendency toward hedonism in society and an attendant rejection of spiritual values. *Idylls of the King* expresses his ideal of the British empire as an exemplar of moral and social order: the "Table Round / A glorious company" would "serve as a model for the mighty world." However, when individual acts of betrayal and corruption result from adultery committed by Arthur's wife and Lancelot, the ensuing disorder destroys the Round Table, symbolizing the effects of moral decay which were Tennyson's chief concern for the society of his day.

Tennyson completed a subsequent enlargement of *Idylls of the King* in 1874, and in the decade which followed he focused his efforts on the composition of historical dramas. *Queen Mary,* his first published drama, has been viewed by critics as characteristic of the major flaw of his dramatic works: an unfamiliarity with the limitations of theatrical production. Set changes were frequent and elaborate, and his meticulous adherence to detail lessened the play's dramatic impact. Moreover, Tennyson's verse was cumbersome and ineffective as dramatic dialogue, and *Queen Mary* was withdrawn after twenty-three performances. *Harold*, completed the following year, was less complicated in its dramaturgy than its predecessor, but failed to find a producer during Tennyson's lifetime. While Tennyson completed five more plays, only *The Cup* and *Becket* enjoyed any success on stage, and neither, in Buckley's words, "seriously altered the course of the English theater."

Describing Tennyson's verse as "poised and stationary," Henry James presaged twentieth-century criticism when he stated in 1876 that "a man has always the qualities of his defects, and if Tennyson is . . . a static poet, he at least represents repose and stillness and the fixedness of things, with a splendour that no poet has surpassed." In 1937 Douglas Bush voiced the opinion of many of his contemporaries, writing that Tennyson was "an artist who had consummate powers of expression" but "not very much, except as an emotional poet, to say." Other critics contended that Tennyson's vision of a spiritually elevated world was betrayed by his concessions to a smug and materialistic Victorian ethic. Recent critics, however, have dismissed the generalizations of their predecessors as part of a post–World War I reaction against the Victorian era and its supposed hypocrisy and narrow-mindedness, and Tennyson has once again come to be viewed, not as "the surface flatterer of his time," as T. S. Eliot described him, but as the embodiment of his age, a poet who reflected both the thoughts and feelings of his generation. The skill with which he did so has been the focus of a wealth of modern criticism, and much of the luster of Tennyson's early reputation has been restored, so that a present-day critic may well pose a question similar to that of Henry Van Dyke, who wrote shortly before Tennyson's death: "In the future, when men call the role of poets who have given splendour to the name of England, they will begin with Shakespeare and Milton—and who shall have the third place, if it be not Tennyson?"

(See also *Dictionary of Literary Biography*, Vol. 32.)

PRINCIPAL WORKS

Poems by Two Brothers [with Frederick and Charles Tennyson] (poetry) 1827
"Timbuctoo" (poem) 1829
Poems, Chiefly Lyrical (poetry) 1830
Poems (poetry) 1832
Poems. 2 vols. (poetry) 1842
The Princess: A Medley (poem) 1847
In Memoriam (poem) 1850
"Ode on the Death of the Duke of Wellington" (poem) 1852
Maud, and Other Poems (poetry) 1855
Idylls of the King (poetry) 1859; enlarged edition, 1874
Enoch Arden, Etc. (poetry) 1864
The Holy Grail, and Other Poems (poetry) 1869
Gareth and Lynette, Etc. (poetry) 1872
Queen Mary: A Drama (drama) 1875
Harold: A Drama (drama) 1876
Ballads and Other Poems (poetry) 1880
Becket (drama) 1884

The Cup and The Falcon (drama) 1884
Tiresias, and Other Poems (poetry) 1885
Locksley Hall Sixty Years After, Etc. (poetry) 1886
Demeter, and Other Poems (poetry) 1889
The Death of Oenone, Akbar's Dream, and Other Poems (poetry) 1892
The Foresters, Robin Hood and Maid Marian (drama) 1892

Arthur Henry Hallam (essay date 1831)

[*Hallam was an English poet, essayist, and critic who is chiefly remembered as the subject of Tennyson's elegy* In Memoriam. *In the following excerpt, Hallam offers a favorable assessment of* Poems, Chiefly Lyrical.]

Mr. Tennyson belongs decidedly to the class we [describe] . . . as Poets of Sensation. He sees all the forms of nature with the *"eruditus oculus,"* and his ear has a fairy fineness. There is a strange earnestness in his worship of beauty, which throws a charm over his impassioned song, more easily felt than described, and not to be escaped by those who have once felt it. We think he has more definiteness, and soundness of general conception, than the late Mr. Keats, and is much more free from blemishes of diction, and hasty capriccios of fancy. He has also this advantage over that poet, and his friend Shelley, that he comes before the public, unconnected with any political party, or peculiar system of opinions. Nevertheless, true to the theory we have stated, we believe his participation in their characteristic excellencies is sufficient to secure him a share in their unpopularity. The volume of ***Poems, Chiefly Lyrical,*** does not contain above 154 pages; but it shews us much more of the character of its parent mind, than many books we have known of much larger compass, and more boastful pretensions. The features of original genius are clearly and strongly marked. The author imitates nobody; we recognise the spirit of his age, but not the individual form of this or that writer. His thoughts bear no more resemblance to Byron or Scott, Shelley or Coleridge, than to Homer or Calderon, Ferdusi or Calidas. We [note] . . . five distinctive excellencies of his own manner. First, his luxuriance of imagination, and at the same time his control over it. Secondly, his power of embodying himself in ideal characters, or rather moods of character, with such extreme accuracy of adjustment, that the circumstances of the narration seem to have a natural correspondence with the predominant feeling, and, as it were, to be evolved from it by assimilative force. Thirdly, his vivid, picturesque delineation of objects, and the peculiar skill with which he holds all of them *fused*, to borrow a metaphor from science, in a medium of strong emotion. Fourthly, the variety of his lyrical measures, and exquisite modulation of harmonious words and cadences to the swell and fall of the feelings expressed. Fifthly, the elevated habits of thought, *implied* in these compositions, and imparting a mellow soberness of tone, more impressive, to our minds, than if the author had drawn up a set of opinions in verse, and sought to instruct the understanding, rather than to communicate the love of beauty to the heart. (pp. 620-21)

"Recollections of the Arabian Nights!" What a delightful, endearing title! How we pity those to whom it calls up no reminiscence of early enjoyment, no sentiment of kindliness as towards one who sings a song they have loved, or mentions with affection a departed friend! But let nobody expect a multifarious enumeration of Viziers, Barmecides, Fireworshippers, and Cadis; trees that sing, horses that fly, and Goules that eat rice pudding! Our author knows what he is about: he has, with great judgment, selected our old acquaintance, "the good Haroun Alraschid," as the most prominent object of our childish interest, and with him has called up one of those luxurious garden scenes, the account of which, in plain prose, used to make our mouths water for sherbet, since luckily we were too young to think much about Zobeide! We think this poem will be the favourite among Mr. Tennyson's admirers; perhaps upon the whole it is our own; at least we find ourselves recurring to it oftener than to any other, and every time we read it, we feel the freshness of its beauty increase, and are inclined to exclaim with Madame de Sevigné, *"a force d'être ancien, il m'est nouveau"* ["by force of being ancient, it is new to me"]. (p. 621)

The poems towards the middle of the volume seem to have been written at an earlier period than the rest. They display more unrestrained fancy, and are less evidently proportioned to their ruling ideas, than those which we think of later date. Yet in the **"Ode to Memory"**—the only one which we have the poet's authority for referring to early life—there is a majesty of expression, united to a truth of thought, which almost confounds our preconceived distinctions. The **"Confessions of a Second-Rate, Sensitive Mind,"** are full of deep insight into human nature, and into those particular trials, which are sure to beset men who think and feel for themselves at this epoch of social developement. The title is perhaps ill chosen: not only has it an appearance of quaintness, which has no sufficient reason, but it seems to us incorrect. The mood pourtrayed in this poem, unless the admirable skill of delineation has deceived us, is rather the clouded season of a strong mind, than the habitual condition of one feeble and "second-rate." Ordinary tempers build up fortresses of opinion on one side or another; they will see only what they choose to see; the distant glimpse of such an agony as is here brought out to view, is sufficient to keep them for ever in illusions, voluntarily raised at first, but soon trusted in with full reliance as inseparable parts of self. Perhaps, however, Mr. Tennyson's mode of "rating" is different from ours. He may esteem none worthy of the first order, who has not attained a complete universality of thought, and such trustful reliance on a principle of repose, which lies beyond the war of conflicting opinions, that the grand ideas, *"qui planent sans cesse au dessus de l'humanité"* ["which ever hover above humanity"], cease to affect him with bewildering impulses of hope and fear. We have not space to enter farther into this topic; but we should not despair of convincing Mr. Tennyson, that such a position of intellect would not be the most elevated, nor even the most conducive to perfection of art. The **"How and the Why"** appears to present the reverse of the same picture. It is the same mind still; the sensitive sceptic, whom we have looked upon in his hour of distress, now scoffing at his own state with an earnest mirth that borders on sorrow. It is exquisitely beautiful to see in this, as in the former portrait, how the feeling of art is kept ascendant in our minds over distressful realities, by constant reference to images

of tranquil beauty, whether touched pathetically, as the Ox and the Lamb in the first piece, or with fine humour, as the "great bird" and "little bird" in the second. The **"Sea Fairies"** is another strange title; but those who turn to it with the very natural curiosity of discovering who these new births of mythology may be, will be unpardonable if they do not linger over it with higher feelings. A stretch of lyrical power is here exhibited, which we did not think the English language had possessed. The proud swell of verse, as the harp tones "run up the ridged sea," and the soft and melancholy lapse, as the sounds die along the widening space of waters, are instances of that right imitation which is becoming to art, but which in the hands of the unskilful, or the affecters of easy popularity, is often converted into a degrading mimicry, detrimental to the best interests of the imagination. A considerable portion of this book is taken up with a very singular, and very beautiful class of poems, on which the author has evidently bestowed much thought and elaboration. We allude to the female characters, every trait of which presumes an uncommon degree of observation and reflection. Mr. Tennyson's way of proceeding seems to be this. He collects the most striking phenomena of individual minds, until he arrives at some leading fact, which allows him to lay down an axiom, or law, and then, working on the law thus attained, he clearly discerns the tendency of what new particulars his invention suggests, and is enabled to impress an individual freshness and unity on ideal combinations. These expressions of character are brief and coherent: nothing extraneous to the dominant fact is admitted, nothing illustrative of it, and, as it were, growing out of it, is rejected. They are like summaries of mighty dramas. We do not say this method admits of such large luxuriance of power, as that of our real dramatists; but we contend that it is a new species of poetry, a graft of the lyric on the dramatic, and Mr. Tennyson deserves the laurel of an inventor, an enlarger of our modes of knowledge and power. (pp. 626-27)

One word more, before we have done, and it shall be a word of praise. The language of this book, with one or two rare exceptions, is thorough and sterling English. A little more respect, perhaps, was due to the *"jus et norma loquendi"* ["proper and normal language"], but we are inclined to consider as venial a fault arising from generous enthusiasm for the principles of sound analogy, and for that Saxon element, which constitutes the intrinsic freedom and nervousness of our native tongue. We see no signs in what Mr. Tennyson has written of the Quixotic spirit which has led some persons to desire the reduction of English to a single form, by excluding nearly the whole of Latin and Roman derivatives. Ours is necessarily a compound language; as such alone it can flourish and increase; nor will the author . . . be likely to barter for a barren appearance of symmetrical structure that fertility of expression, and variety of harmony, which "the speech, that Shakspeare spoke," derived from the sources of southern phraseology. (p. 628)

Arthur Henry Hallam, "On Some of the Characteristics of Modern Poetry, and on the Lyrical Poems of Alfred Tennyson," in The Englishman's Magazine, Vol. 1, August, 1831, pp. 616-28.

John Wilson Croker   (essay date 1833)

[*Croker made extensive contributions to the* Quarterly Review, *the most prominent conservative periodical of the early nineteenth century. While Croker was a noteworthy critic of literature and historical writings, he had a greater role in guiding the political direction of the* Quarterly Review. *Croker, who was First Secretary of the Admiralty and a friend to Tory leaders in the English government, so effectively channeled the government's views into the* Review *that, from 1830 to 1850, the journal was considered the voice of the old Tory party. In the following excerpt, Croker presents a sarcastic review of Tennyson's second collection,* Poems.]

[*Poems*] is, as some of his marginal notes intimate, Mr. Tennyson's second appearance. By some strange chance we have never seen his first publication, which, if it at all resembles its younger brother, must be by this time so popular that any notice of it on our part would seem idle and presumptuous; but we gladly seize this opportunity of repairing an unintentional neglect, and of introducing to the admiration of our more sequestered readers a new prodigy of genius—another and a brighter star of that galaxy or *milky way* of poetry of which the lamented Keats was the harbinger. . . . (p. 81)

[It] is very agreeable to us, as well as to our readers, that our present task will be little more than the selection, for their delight, of a few specimens of Mr. Tennyson's singular genius, and the venturing to point out, now and then, the peculiar brilliancy of some of the gems that irradiate his poetical crown.

A prefatory sonnet opens to the reader the aspirations of the young author, in which, after the manner of sundry poets, ancient and modern, he expresses his own peculiar character, by wishing himself to be something that he is not. The amorous Catullus aspired to be a sparrow; the tuneful and convivial Anacreon . . . wished to be a lyre and a great drinking cup; a crowd of more modern sentimentalists have desired to approach their mistresses as flowers, tunicks, sandals, birds, breezes, and butterflies;—all poor conceits of narrow-minded poetasters! Mr. Tennyson (though he, too, would, as far as his true-love is concerned, not unwillingly be 'an earring,' 'a girdle,' and 'a necklace,') in the more serious and solemn exordium of his works ambitions a bolder metamorphosis—he wishes to be—*a river!*

"SONNET"

Mine be the strength of spirit fierce and free,
Like some broad river rushing down *alone*—

rivers that travel in company are too common for his taste—

With the self-same impulse wherewith he was thrown—

a beautiful and harmonious line—

From his loud fount upon the echoing lea:—
Which, with *increasing* might, doth *forward flee*—

Every word of this line is valuable—the natural progress of human ambition is here strongly characterized—two lines ago he would have been satisfied with the *self-same* impulse—but now he must have *increasing* might; and indeed he would require all his might to accomplish his ob-

ject of *fleeing forward,* that is, going backwards and forwards at the same time. Perhaps he uses the word *flee* for *flow;* which latter he could not well employ in *this* place, it being, as we shall see, essentially necessary to rhyme to *Mexico* towards the end of the sonnet—as an equivalent to *flow* he has, therefore, with great taste and ingenuity, hit on the combination of *forward flee*—

—doth forward flee
By town, and tower, and hill, and cape, and isle,
And in the middle of the green *salt* sea
Keeps his blue waters fresh for many a mile.

A noble wish, beautifully expressed, that he may not be confounded with the deluge of ordinary poets, but, amidst their discoloured and briny ocean, still preserve his own bright tints and sweet savor. He may be at ease on this point—he never can be mistaken for any one else. We have but too late become acquainted with him, yet we assure ourselves that if a thousand anonymous specimens were presented to us, we should unerringly distinguish his by the total absence of any particle of *salt*. But again, his thoughts take another turn, and he reverts to the insatiability of human ambition:—we have seen him just now content to be a river, but as he *flees forward,* his desires expand into sublimity, and he wishes to become the great Gulf-stream of the Atlantic.

Mine be the power which ever to its sway
Will win *the wise at once*—

We, for once, are wise, and he has won *us*—

Will win the wise at once; and by degrees
May into uncongenial spirits flow,
Even as the great gulphstream of Flor*ida*
Floats far away into the Northern seas
The lavish growths of southern Mex*ico!*

And so concludes the sonnet.

The next piece is a kind of testamentary paper, addressed 'To —,' a friend, we presume, containing his wishes as to what his friend should do for him when he (the poet) shall be dead—not, as we shall see, that he quite thinks that such a poet can die outright.

Shake hands, my friend, across the brink
Of that deep grave to which I go.
Shake hands once more; I cannot sink
So far—far down, but I shall know
Thy voice, and answer from below!

Horace said 'non omnis moriar,' meaning that his fame should survive—Mr. Tennyson is still more vivacious, 'non *omnino* moriar,'—'I will not die at all; my body shall be as immortal as my verse, and however *low I may go,* I warrant you I shall keep all my wits about me,—therefore'

When, in the darkness over me,
The four-handed mole shall scrape,
Plant thou no dusky cypress tree,
Nor wreath thy cap with doleful crape,
But pledge me in the flowing grape.

Observe how all ages become present to the mind of a great poet; and admire how naturally he combines the funeral cypress of classical antiquity with the crape hatband of the modern undertaker.

He proceeds:—

And when the sappy field and wood
  Grow green beneath the *showery gray,*
And rugged barks begin to bud,
  And through damp holts, newflushed with May,
  Ring sudden *laughters* of the jay!

Laughter, the philosophers tell us, is the peculiar attribute of man—but as Shakspeare found 'tongues in trees and sermons in stones,' this true poet endows all nature not merely with human sensibilities but with human functions—the jay *laughs,* and we find, indeed, a little further on, that the woodpecker *laughs* also; but to mark the distinction between their merriment and that of men, both jays and woodpeckers laugh upon melancholy occasions. We are glad, moreover, to observe, that Mr. Tennyson is prepared for, and therefore will not be disturbed by, human laughter, if any silly reader should catch the infection from the woodpeckers and jays.

Then let wise Nature work her will,
  And on my clay her darnels grow,
Come only when the days are still,
  And at my head-stone whisper low,
  And tell me—

Now, what would an ordinary bard wish to be told under such circumstances?—why, perhaps, how his sweetheart was, or his child, or his family, or how the Reform Bill worked, or whether the last edition of the poems had been sold—*papæ!* our genuine poet's first wish is

And tell me—*if the woodbines blow!*

When, indeed, he shall have been thus satisfied as to the *woodbines,* (of the blowing of which in their due season he may, we think, feel pretty secure,) he turns a passing thought to his friend—and another to his mother—

If *thou* art blest, my *mother's* smile
Undimmed—

but such inquiries, short as they are, seem too commonplace, and he immediately glides back into his curiosity as to the state of the weather and the forwardness of the spring—

If thou art blessed—my mother's smile
Undimmed—*if bees are on the wing?*

No, we believe the whole circle of poetry does not furnish such another instance of enthusiasm for the sights and sounds of the vernal season!—The sorrows of a bereaved mother rank *after* the blossoms of the *woodbine,* and just before the hummings of the *bee;* and this is *all* that he has any curiosity about; for he proceeds—

Then cease, my friend, a little while
That I may—

'send my love to my mother,' or 'give you some hints about bees, which I have picked up from Aristæus, in the Elysian Fields,' or 'tell you how I am situated as to my own personal comforts in the world below'?—oh no—

That I may—hear the *throstle sing*
  His bridal song—the boast of spring.
Sweet as the noise, in parchèd plains,
  Of bubbling wells that fret the stones,
  (*If any sense in me remains*)
Thy words will be—thy cheerful tones
As welcome to—my *crumbling bones!*

'If any sense in me remains!'—This doubt is inconsistent with the opening stanza of the piece, and, in fact, too modest; we take upon ourselves to re-assure Mr. Tennyson, that, even after he shall be dead and buried, as much *'sense'* will still remain as he has now the good fortune to possess.

We have quoted these two first poems in *extenso,* to obviate any suspicion of our having made a partial or delusive selection. We cannot afford space—we wish we could—for an equally minute examination of the rest of the volume, but we shall make a few extracts to show—what we solemnly affirm—that every page teems with beauties hardly less surprising.

'The Lady of Shalott' is a poem in four parts, the story of which we decline to maim by such an analysis as we could give, but it opens thus—

On either side the river lie
Long fields of barley and of rye,
That clothe the world and *meet the sky*—
And *through* the field the road runs *by.*

The Lady of Shalott was, it seems, a spinster who had, under some unnamed penalty, a certain web to weave.

Underneath the bearded barley,
The reaper, reaping late and early,
Hears her ever chanting cheerly,
Like an angel singing clearly. . . . . .
No time has she to sport or play,
A charmèd web she weaves alway;
A curse is on her if she stay
Her weaving either night or day. . . . . .
She knows not—

Poor lady, nor we either—

She knows not what that curse may be,
Therefore she weaveth steadily;
Therefore no other care has she,
    The Lady of Shalott.

A knight, however, happens to ride past her window, coming

    —from Camelot;
From the bank, and *from* the *river,*
He flashed *into* the crystal *mirror*—
"Tirra lirra, tirra *lirra,*" (*lirrar?*)
    Sang Sir Launcelot.

The lady stepped to the window to look at the stranger, and forgot for an instant her web:—the curse fell on her, and she died; why, how, and wherefore, the following stanzas will clearly and pathetically explain:—

A long drawn carol, mournful, holy,
She chanted loudly, chanted lowly,
Till her eyes were darkened *wholly,*
And her smooth face *sharpened slowly,*
    Turned to towered Camelot.

For ere she reached upon the tide
The first house on the water side,
Singing in her song she died,
    The Lady of Shalott!

Knight and burgher, lord and dame,
To the plankèd wharfage came;
Below *the stern* they read her name,
    The Lady of Shalott.

We pass by two—what shall we call them?—tales, or odes, or sketches, entitled **'Mariana in the South'** and **'Eleänore,'** of which we fear we could make no intelligible extract, so curiously are they run together into one dreamy tissue—to a little novel in rhyme, called **'The Miller's Daughter.'** Miller's daughters, poor things, have been so generally betrayed by their sweethearts, that it is refreshing to find that Mr. Tennyson has united himself to *his* miller's daughter in lawful wedlock, and the poem is a history of his courtship and wedding. He begins with a sketch of his own birth, parentage, and personal appearance—

> My father's mansion, mounted high,
>   Looked down upon the village-spire;
> I was a long and listless boy,
>   And son and heir unto the Squire.

But the son and heir of Squire Tennyson often descended from the 'mansion mounted high;' and

> I met in all the close green ways,
>   While walking with my line and rod,

A metonymy for 'rod and line'—

> The wealthy miller's mealy face,
>   Like the *moon in an ivytod.*
> He looked so jolly and so good—
>   While fishing in the mill-dam water,
> I laughed to see him as he stood,
>   And dreamt not of the miller's daughter.

He, however, soon saw, and, need we add, loved the miller's daughter, whose countenance, we presume, bore no great resemblance either to the 'mealy face' of the miller, or 'the moon in an ivy-tod;' and we think our readers will be delighted at the way in which the impassioned husband relates to his wife how his fancy mingled enthusiasm for rural sights and sounds, with a prospect of the less romantic scene of her father's occupation.

> How dear to me in youth, my love,
>   Was everything about the mill;
> The black, the silent pool above,
>   The pool beneath that ne'er stood still;
> The meal-sacks on the whitened floor,
>   The dark round of the dripping wheel,
> *The very air about the door,*
>   *Made misty with the floating meal!*

The accumulation of tender images in the following lines appears not less wonderful:—

> Remember you that pleasant day
>   When, after roving in the woods,
> ('Twas April then) I came and lay
>   Beneath those *gummy* chestnut-buds?
> A water-rat from off the bank
>   Plunged in the stream. With idle care,
> Downlooking through the sedges rank,
>   I saw your troubled image there.
> If you remember, you had set,
>   Upon the narrow casement-edge,
> A *long green box* of mignonette,
>   And you were leaning on the ledge.

The poet's truth to Nature in his 'gummy' chestnut-buds, and to Art in the 'long green box' of mignonette—and that masterly touch of likening the first intrusion of love into the virgin bosom of the Miller's daughter to the plunging of a water-rat into the mill-dam—these are beauties which, we do not fear to say, equal anything even in Keats.

We pass by several songs, sonnets, and small pieces, all of singular merit, to arrive at a class, we may call them, of three poems derived from mythological sources—Œnone, the Hesperides, and the Lotos-eaters. But though the subjects are derived from classical antiquity, Mr. Tennyson treats them with so much originality that he makes them exclusively his own. Œnone, deserted by

> Beautiful Paris, evilhearted Paris,

sings a kind of dying soliloquy addressed to Mount Ida, in a formula which is *sixteen* times repeated in this short poem.

> Dear mother Ida, hearken ere I die.

She tells her 'dear mother Ida,' that when evilhearted Paris was about to judge between the three goddesses, he hid her (Œnone) behind a rock, whence she had a full view of the *naked* beauties of the rivals, which broke her heart.

> *Dear mother Ida, hearken ere I die:—*
> It was the deep mid noon: one silvery cloud
> Had *lost his way* among the pined hills:
> They came—*all three* the Olympian goddesses.
> Naked they came—
>
> . . . . .
>
> How beautiful they were! too beautiful
> To look upon; but Paris was to me
> *More lovelier* than all the world beside.
> *O mother Ida, hearken ere I die.*

In the place where we have indicated a pause, follows a description, long, rich, and luscious—Of the three naked goddesses? Fye for shame—no—of the 'lily flower violet-eyed,' and the 'singing pine,' and the 'overwandering ivy and vine,' and 'festoons,' and 'gnarlèd boughs,' and 'tree tops,' and 'berries,' and 'flowers,' and all the *inanimate* beauties of the scene. It would be unjust to the *ingenuus pudor* of the author not to observe the art with which he has veiled this ticklish interview behind such luxuriant trellis-work, and it is obvious that it is for our special sakes he has entered into these local details, because if there was one thing which 'mother Ida' knew better than another, it must have been her own bushes and brakes. We then have in detail the tempting speeches of, first—

> The imperial Olympian,
> With archèd eyebrow smiling sovranly,
> Full-eyèd Here;

secondly of Pallas—

> Her clear and barèd limbs
> O'er-thwarted with the brazen-headed spear,

and thirdly—

> Idalian Aphrodite ocean-born,
> Fresh as the foam, new-bathed in Paphian *wells*—

for one dip, or even three dips in one well, would not have been enough on such an occasion—and her succinct and prevailing promise of—

> The fairest and most loving *wife* in Greece;—

upon evil-hearted Paris's catching at which prize, the tender and chaste Œnone exclaims her indignation, that she herself should not be considered fair enough, since only yesterday her charms had struck awe into—

> A wild and wanton pard,
> Eyed like the evening star, with playful tail—

and proceeds in this anti-Martineau rapture—

> *Most* loving is *she?*
> Ah me! my mountain shepherd, that my arms
> Were wound about thee, and my hot lips prest
> Close—close to thine in that quick-falling dew
> Of *fruitful* kisses. . . . . . .
> Dear mother Ida! hearken ere I die!

After such reiterated assurances that she was about to die on the spot, it appears that Œnone thought better of it, and the poem concludes with her taking the wiser course of going to town to consult her swain's sister, Cassandra—whose advice, we presume, prevailed upon her to live, as we can, from other sources, assure our readers she did to a good old age.

In the **'Hesperides'** our author, with great judgment, rejects the common fable, which attributes to Hercules the slaying of the dragon and the plunder of the golden fruit. Nay, he supposes them to have existed to a comparatively recent period—namely, the voyage of Hanno, on the coarse canvas of whose log-book Mr. Tennyson has judiciously embroidered the Hesperian romance. The poem opens with a geographical description of the neighbourhood, which must be very clear and satisfactory to the English reader; indeed, it leaves far behind in accuracy of topography and melody of rhythm the heroics of Dionysius *Periegetes.*

> The north wind fall'n, in the new-starrèd night.

Here we must pause to observe a new species of *metabolé* with which Mr. Tennyson has enriched our language. He suppresses the E in *fallen,* where it is usually written and where it must be pronounced, and transfers it to the word *new-starrèd,* where it would not be pronounced if he did not take due care to superfix a *grave* accent. This use of the grave accent is, as our readers may have already perceived, so habitual with Mr. Tennyson, and is so obvious an improvement, that we really wonder how the language has hitherto done without it. We are tempted to suggest, that if analogy to the accented languages is to be thought of, it is rather the acute ( ) than the grave ( ) which should be employed on such occasions; but we speak with profound diffidence; and as Mr. Tennyson is the inventor of the system, we shall bow with respect to whatever his final determination may be.

> The north wind fall'n, in the new-starrèd night
> Zidonian Hanno, voyaging beyond
> The hoary promontory of Soloë,
> Past Thymiaterion in calmèd bays.

We must here note specially the musical flow of this last line, which is the more creditable to Mr. Tennyson, because it was before the tuneless names of this very neighbourhood that the learned continuator of Dionysius retreated in despair, . . . but Mr. Tennyson is bolder and happier—

> Past Thymiaterion in calmèd bays,
> Between the southern and the western Horn,
> Heard neither—

We pause for a moment to consider what a sea-captain might have expected to hear, by night, in the Atlantic ocean—he heard

> —neither the warbling of the *nightingale*
> Nor melody o' the Libyan lotusflute,

but he did hear the three daughters of Hesper singing the following song:—

> The golden apple, the golden apple, the hallowèd fruit,
> Guard it well, guard it warily,
> Singing airily,
> Standing about the charmèd root,
> Round about all is mute—

mute, though they sung so loud as to be heard some leagues out at sea—

> —all is mute
> As the snow-field on mountain peaks,
> As the sand-field at the mountain foot.
> Crocodiles in briny creeks
> Sleep, and stir not: all is mute.

How admirably do these lines describe the peculiarities of this charmèd neighbourhood—fields of snow, so talkative when they happen to lie at the foot of the mountain, are quite out of breath when they get to the top, and the sand, so noisy on the summit of a hill, is dumb at its foot. The very crocodiles, too, are *mute*—not dumb but *mute.* The 'red-combèd dragon curl'd' is next introduced—

> Look to him, father, lest he wink, and the golden apple be
>   stolen away,
> For his ancient heart is drunk with overwatchings night
>   and day,
> Sing away, sing aloud evermore, in the wind, without stop.

The north wind, it appears, had by this time awaked again—

> Lest his scalèd eyelid drop,
> For he is older than the world—

older than the *hills,* besides not rhyming to 'curl'd,' would hardly have been a sufficiently venerable phrase for this most harmonious of lyrics. It proceeds—

> If ye sing not, if ye make false measure,
> We shall lose eternal pleasure,
> Worth eternal want of rest.
> Laugh not loudly: watch the treasure
> Of the wisdom of the west.
> In *a corner* wisdom whispers. Five and three
> (*Let it not be preached abroad*) make an awful mystery.

This recipe for keeping a secret, by singing it so loud as to be heard for miles, is almost the only point, in all Mr. Tennyson's poems, in which we can trace the remotest approach to anything like what other men have written, but it certainly does remind us of the 'chorus of conspirators' in the Rovers.

Hanno, however, who understood no language but Punic—(the Hesperides sang, we presume, either in Greek or in English)—appears to have kept on his way without taking any notice of the song, for the poem concludes,—

> The apple of gold hangs over the sea,
> Five links, a golden chain, are we,
> Hesper, the Dragon, and sisters three;
> Daughters three,

Bound about
All round about
The gnarlèd bole of the charmèd tree,
The golden apple, the golden apple, the hallowèd fruit.
Guard it well, guard it warily,
Watch it warily,
Singing airily,
Standing about the charmèd root.

We hardly think that, if Hanno had translated it into Punic, the song would have been more intelligible.

The **'Lotuseaters'**—a kind of classical opium-eaters—are Ulysses and his crew. They land on the 'charmèd island,' and eat of the 'charmèd root,' and then they sing—

Long enough the winedark wave our weary bark did
    carry.
This is lovelier and sweeter,
Men of Ithaca, this is meeter,
In the hollow rosy vale to tarry,
Like a dreamy Lotuseater—a delicious Lotuseater!
We will eat the Lotus, sweet
As the yellow honeycomb;
In the valley some, and some
On the ancient heights divine,
And no more roam,
On the loud hoar foam,
To the melancholy home,
At the limits of the brine,
The little isle of Ithaca, beneath the day's decline.

Our readers will, we think, agree that this is admirably characteristic, and that the singers of this song must have made pretty free with the intoxicating fruit. How they got home you must read in Homer:—Mr. Tennyson—himself, we presume, a dreamy lotus-eater, a delicious lotus-eater—leaves them in full song.

Next comes another class of poems,—Visions. The first is the **'Palace of Art,'** or a fine house, in which the poet *dreams* that he sees a very fine collection of well-known pictures. An ordinary versifier would, no doubt, have followed the old routine, and dully described himself as walking into the Louvre, or Buckingham Palace, and there seeing certain masterpieces of painting:—a true poet dreams it. We have not room to hang many of these *chefs-d'œuvre,* but for a few we must find space.—'The Madonna'—

The maid mother by a crucifix,
    In yellow pastures sunny warm,
Beneath branch work of costly sardonyx
    Sat smiling—*babe in arm.*

The use of this latter, apparently, colloquial phrase is a deep stroke of art. The form of expression is always used to express an habitual and characteristic action. A knight is described *'lance in rest'*—a dragoon, *'sword in hand'*—so, as the idea of the Virgin is inseparably connected with her child, Mr. Tennyson reverently describes her conventional position—*'babe in arm.'*

His gallery of illustrious portraits is thus admirably arranged:—The Madonna—Ganymede—St. Cecilia—Europa—Deep-haired Milton—Shakspeare—Grim Dante—Michael Angelo—Luther—Lord Bacon—Cervantes—Calderon—King David—'the Halicarnassëan' (*quære,* which of them?)—Alfred, (not Alfred Tennyson, though no doubt in any other man's gallery *he* would have had a place) and finally—

Isaïah, with fierce Ezekiel,
    Swarth Moses by the Coptic sea,
Plato, *Petrarca,* Livy, and Raphaël,
    And eastern Confutzee!

We can hardly suspect the very original mind of Mr. Tennyson to have harboured any recollections of that celebrated Doric idyll, 'The groves of Blarney,' but certainly there is a strong likeness between Mr. Tennyson's list of pictures and the Blarney collection of statues—

Statues growing that noble place in,
    All heathen goddesses most rare,
Homer, Plutarch, and Nebuchadnezzar,
    All standing naked in the open air!

In this poem we first observed a stroke of art (repeated afterwards) which we think very ingenious. No one who has ever written verse but must have felt the pain of erasing some happy line, some striking stanza, which, however excellent in itself, did not exactly suit the place for which it was destined. How curiously does an author mould and remould the plastic verse in order to fit in the favourite thought; and when he finds that he cannot introduce it, as Corporal Trim says, *any how,* with what reluctance does he at last reject the intractable, but still cherished offspring of his brain! Mr. Tennyson manages this delicate matter in a new and better way; he says, with great candour and simplicity, 'If this poem were not already too long, *I should have added* the following stanzas,' and *then he adds them*—or, 'the following lines are manifestly superfluous, as a part of the text, but they may be allowed to stand as a separate poem,' *which they do;*—or, 'I intended to have added something on statuary, but I found it very difficult;'—(he had, moreover, as we have seen, been anticipated in this line by the Blarney poet)—'but I had finished the statues of *Elijah* and *Olympias*—judge whether I have succeeded,'—and then we have these two statues. This is certainly the most ingenious device that has ever come under our observation, for reconciling the rigour of criticism with the indulgence of parental partiality. It is economical too, and to the reader profitable, as by these means

We lose no drop of the immortal man.

The other vision is **'A Dream of Fair Women,'** in which the heroines of all ages—some, indeed, that belong to the times of 'heathen goddesses most rare'—pass before his view. We have not time to notice them all, but the second, whom we take to be Iphigenia, touches the heart with a stroke of nature more powerful than even the veil that the Grecian painter threw over the head of her father.

            —dimly I could descry
The stern blackbearded kings with wolfish eyes,
    Watching to see me die.
The tall masts quivered as they lay afloat;
    The temples, and the people, and the shore;
One drew a sharp knife through my tender throat—
    Slowly,—and *nothing more!*

What touching simplicity—what pathetic resignation—he cut my throat—*'nothing more!'* One might indeed ask, 'what *more*' she would have?

But we must hasten on; and to tranquillize the reader's mind after the last affecting scene, shall notice the only two pieces of a lighter strain which the volume affords. The first is elegant and playful; it is a description of the author's study, which he affectionately calls his **'Darling Room.'**

> O darling room, my heart's delight;
> Dear room, the apple of my sight;
> With thy two couches, soft and white,
> There is no room so exqui*site;*
> No little room so warm and bright,
> Wherein to read, wherein to write.

We entreat our readers to note how, even in this little trifle, the singular taste and genius of Mr. Tennyson break forth. In such a dear *little* room a narrow-minded scribbler would have been content with *one* sofa, and that one he would probably have covered with black mohair, or red cloth, or a good striped chintz; how infinitely more characteristic is white dimity!—'tis as it were a type of the purity of the poet's mind. He proceeds—

> For I the Nonnenwerth have seen,
> And Oberwinter's vineyards green,
> Musical Lurlei; and between
> The hills to Bingen I have been,
> Bingen in Darmstadt, where the *Rhene*
> Curves towards Mentz, a woody scene.
> Yet never did there meet my sight,
> In any town, to left or right,
> A little room so exqui*site,*
> With *two* such couches soft and white;
> Not any room so warm and bright,
> Wherein to read, wherein to write.

A common poet would have said that he had been in London or in Paris—in the loveliest villa on the banks of the Thames, or the most gorgeous chateau on the Loire—that he had reclined in Madame de Staël's boudoir, and mused in Mr. Roger's comfortable study; but the *darling room* of the poet of nature (which we must suppose to be endued with sensibility, or he would not have addressed it) would not be flattered with such common-place comparisons;— no, no, but it is something to have it said that there is no such room in the ruins of the Drachenfels, in the vineyard of Oberwinter, or even in the rapids of the *Rhene,* under the Lurleyberg. We have ourselves visited all these celebrated spots, and can testify, in corroboration of Mr. Tennyson, that we did not see in any of them anything like *this little room so exquis*ITE. (pp. 82-95)

> *John Wilson Croker, in an originally unsigned essay titled "Poems by Alfred Tennyson," in* The Quarterly Review, *Vol. 49, No. XCVII, April, 1833, pp. 81-96.*

John Stuart Mill   (essay date 1835)

[*An English essayist and critic, Mill is regarded as one of the greatest philosophers and political economists of the nineteenth century. At an early age, Mill was recognized as a leading advocate of the utilitarian philosophy of Jeremy Bentham, and he was a principal contributor to the* Westminster Review, *an English periodical founded by Bentham that later merged with the* London Review. *During the 1830s, after reading the works of William Wordsworth, Samuel Taylor Coleridge, and Auguste Comte, Mill gradually diverged from Bentham's utilitarianism and acknowledged the importance of intuition and feelings, attempting to reconcile them with his rational philosophy. As part owner of the* Lon-*don and* Westminster Review *from 1835-40, Mill was instrumental in modifying the periodical's utilitarian stance. He is considered a key figure in the transition from the rationalism of the Enlightenment to the renewed emphasis on mysticism and the emotions of the Romantic era. In the following excerpt, Mill reviews Tennyson's first two volumes of poetry, finding many of the poems in these collections lacking in meaning and urging Tennyson to cultivate a philosophy which would add depth to his poetry.*]

There are in the character of every true poet, two elements, for one of which he is indebted to nature, for the other to cultivation. What he derives from nature, is fine senses: a nervous organization, not only adapted to make his outward impressions vivid and distinct (in which, however, practice does even more than nature), but so constituted, as to be, more easily than common organizations, thrown, either by physical or moral causes, into *states* of enjoyment or suffering, especially of enjoyment: states of a certain duration; often lasting long after the removal of the cause which produced them; and not local, nor consciously physical, but, in so far as organic, pervading the entire nervous system. This peculiar kind of nervous susceptibility seems to be the distinctive character of the poetic temperament. It constitutes the capacity for poetry; and not only produces, as has been shown from the known laws of the human mind, a predisposition to the poetic associations, but supplies the very materials out of which many of them are formed. What the poet will afterwards construct out of these materials, or whether he will construct anything of value to any one but himself, depends upon the direction given, either by accident or design, to his habitual associations. Here, therefore, begins the province of culture; and, from this point upwards, we may lay it down as a principle, that the achievements of any poet in his art will be in proportion to the growth and perfection of his thinking faculty.

Every great poet, every poet who has extensively or permanently influenced mankind, has been a great thinker;— has had a philosophy, though perhaps he did not call it by that name;—has had his mind full of thoughts, derived not merely from passive sensibility, but from trains of reflection, from observation, analysis, and generalization; however remote the sphere of his observation and meditation may have lain from the studies of the schools. Where the poetic temperament exists in its greatest degree, while the systematic culture of the intellect has been neglected, we may expect to find, what we do find in the best poems of Shelley—vivid representations of states of passive and dreamy emotion, fitted to give extreme pleasure to persons of similar organization to the poet, but not likely to be sympathized in, because not understood, by any other persons; and scarcely conducting at all to the noblest end of poetry as an intellectual pursuit, that of acting upon the desires and characters of mankind through their emotions, to raise them towards the perfection of their nature. This, like every other adaptation of means to ends, is the work of cultivated reason; and the poet's success in it will be in proportion to the intrinsic value of his thoughts, and to the command which he has acquired over the materials of his imagination, for placing those thoughts in a strong light before the intellect, and impressing them on the feelings. (pp. 418-19)

[Tennyson] possesses, in an eminent degree, the natural endowment of a poet—the poetic temperament. And it appears clearly, not only from a comparison of the [*Poems, Chiefly Lyrical* and *Poems*], but of different poems in the same volume, that, with him, the other element of poetic excellence—intellectual culture—is advancing both steadily and rapidly; that he is not destined, like so many others, to be remembered for what he might have done, rather than for what he did; that he will not remain a poet of mere temperament, but is ripening into a true artist. Mr. Tennyson may not be conscious of the wide difference in maturity of intellect, which is apparent in his various poems. Though he now writes from greater fulness and clearness of thought, it by no means follows that he has learnt to detect the absence of those qualities in some of his earlier effusions. Indeed, he himself, in one of the most beautiful poems of his first volume (though, as a work of art, very imperfect), the '**Ode to Memory**,' confesses a parental predilection for the 'first-born' of his genius. But to us it is evident, not only that his second volume differs from his first as early manhood from youth, but that the various poems in the first volume belong to different, and even distant stages of intellectual development;—distant, not perhaps in years—for a mind like Mr. Tennyson's advances rapidly—but corresponding to very different states of the intellectual powers, both in respect of their strength and of their proportions.

From the very first, like all writers of his natural gifts, he luxuriates in sensuous imagery; his nominal subject sometimes lies buried in a heap of it. From the first, too, we see his intellect, with every successive degree of strength, struggling upwards to shape this sensuous imagery to a spiritual meaning; to bring the materials which sense supplies, and fancy summons up, under the command of a central and controlling thought or feeling. We [may see] . . . , by the poem of '**Mariana**,' with what success he . . . [has occasionally done] this, even in the period which answers to his first volume; but that volume contains various instances in which he has attempted the same thing, and failed. Such, for example, are, in our opinion, the opening poem, '**Claribel**,' and the verses headed '**Elegiacs**.' In both, there is what is commonly called imagination—namely, fancy: the imagery and the melody actually haunt us; but there is no harmonizing principle in either;—no appropriateness to the spiritual elements of the scene. If the one poem had been called 'A Solitary Place in a Wood,' and the other, 'An Evening Landscape,' they would not have lost, but gained. In another poem, in the same volume, called '**A Dirge**,' and intended for a person who, when alive, had suffered from calumny—a subject which a poet of maturer powers would have made so much of, Mr. Tennyson merely glances at the topics of thought and emotion which his subject suggested, and expatiates in the mere scenery about the grave.

Some of the smaller poems have a fault which in any but a very juvenile production would be the worst fault of all: they are altogether without meaning: none at least can be discerned in them by persons otherwise competent judges of poetry; if the author had any meaning, he has not been able to express it. Such, for instance, are the two songs on the Owl; such, also, are the verses headed '**The How and the Why**,' in the first volume, and the lines on To-day and Yesterday, in the second. If in the former of these productions Mr. Tennyson aimed at shadowing forth the vague

aspirations to a knowledge beyond the reach of man—the yearnings for a solution of all questions, soluble or insoluble, which concern our nature and destiny—the impatience under the insufficiency of the human faculties to penetrate the secret of our being here, and being what we are—which are natural in a certain state of the human mind; if this was what he sought to typify, he has only proved that he knows not the feeling—that he has neither experienced it, nor realized it in imagination. The questions which a Faust calls upon earth and heaven, and all powers supernal and infernal, to resolve for him, are not the ridiculous ones which Mr. Tennyson asks himself in these verses.

But enough of faults which the poet has almost entirely thrown off merely by the natural expansion of his intellect. We have alluded to them chiefly to show how rapidly progressive that intellect has been. There are traces, we think, of a continuance of the same progression, throughout the second as well as the first volume.

In the art of painting a picture to the inward eye, the improvement is not so conspicuous as in other qualities; so high a degree of excellence having been already attained in the first volume. . . . [We] may refer, in that volume, to . . . '**Recollections of the Arabian Nights**,' '**The Dying Swan**,' '**The Kraken**,' and '**The Sleeping Beauty**.' The beautiful poems (songs they are called, but are not) '**In the Glooming Light**,' and '**A Spirit Haunts the Year's Last Hours**,' are (like the '**Mariana**') not mere pictures, but states of emotion, embodied in sensuous imagery. From these, however, to the command over the materials of outward sense for the purpose of bodying forth states of feeling, evinced by some of the poems in the second volume, especially '**The Lady of Shalott**' and '**The Lotos-Eaters**,' there is a considerable distance; and Mr. Tennyson seems, as he proceeded, to have raised his aims still higher—to have aspired to render his poems not only vivid representations of spiritual states, but symbolical of spiritual truths. His longest poem, '**The Palace of Art**,' is an attempt of this sort. As such, we do not think it wholly successful, though rich in beauties of detail; but we deem it of the most favourable augury for Mr. Tennyson's future achievements, since it proves a continually increasing endeavour towards the highest excellence, and a constantly rising standard of it.

We predict, that, as Mr. Tennyson advances in general spiritual culture, these higher aims will become more and more predominant in his writings; that he will strive more and more diligently, and, even without striving, will be more and more impelled by the natural tendencies of an expanding character, towards what has been described as the highest object of poetry—'to incorporate the everlasting reason of man in forms visible to his sense, and suitable to it.' For the fulfilment of this exalted purpose, what we have already seen of him authorizes us to foretell with confidence, that powers of execution will not fail him; it rests with himself to see that his powers of thought may keep pace with them. To render his poetic endowment the means of giving impressiveness to important truths, he must, by continual study and meditation, strengthen his intellect for the discrimination of such truths; he must see that his theory of life and the world be no chimera of the brain, but the well-grounded result of solid and mature thinking;—he must cultivate, and with no half devotion, philosophy as well as poetry.

It may not be superfluous to add, that he should guard himself against an error, to which the philosophical speculations of poets are peculiarly liable—that of embracing as truth, not the conclusions which are recommended by the strongest evidence, but those which have the most poetical appearance;—not those which arise from the deductions of impartial reason, but those which are most captivating to an imagination, biassed perhaps by education and conventional associations. That whatever philosophy he adopts will leave ample materials for poetry, he may be well assured. Whatever is comprehensive, whatever is commanding, whatever is on a great scale, is poetical. Let our philosophical system be what it may, human feelings exist: human nature, with all its enjoyments and sufferings, its strugglings, its victories and defeats, still remain to us; and these are the materials of all poetry. Whoever, in the greatest concerns of human life, pursues truth with unbiassed feelings, and an intellect adequate to discern it, will not find that the resources of poetry are lost to him because he has learnt to use, and not abuse them. They are as open to him as they are to the sentimental weakling, who has no test of the true but the ornamental. And when he once has them under his command, he can wield them for purposes, and with a power, of which neither the dilettante nor the visionary have the slightest conception.

We will not conclude without reminding Mr. Tennyson, that if he wishes his poems to live, he has still much to do in order to perfect himself in the merely mechanical parts of his craft. In a prose-writer, great beauties bespeak forgiveness for innumerable negligences; but poems, especially short poems, attain permanent fame only by the most finished perfection in the details. In some of the most beautiful of Mr. Tennyson's productions there are awkwardnesses and feeblenesses of expression, occasionally even absurdities, to be corrected; and which generally might be corrected without impairing a single beauty. His powers of versification are not yet of the highest order. In one great secret of his art, the adaptation of the music of his verse to the character of his subject, he is far from being a master: he often seems to take his metres almost at random. But this is little to set in the balance against so much excellence; and needed not have been mentioned, except to indicate to Mr. Tennyson the points on which some of his warmest admirers see most room and most necessity for further effort on his part, if he would secure to himself the high place in our poetic literature for which so many of the qualifications are already his own. (pp. 419-24)

John Stuart Mill, "Tennyson's Poems," in The London Review, *Vol. I, No. 2, July, 1835, pp. 402-24.*

Edgar Allan Poe   (essay date 1844)

[*One of the foremost American authors of the nineteenth century, Poe is widely regarded as the architect of the modern short story and the principal forerunner of aestheticism in America. His self-declared intention, both as a critic and as a literary theorist, was the articulation and promotion of strictly artistic ideals in a milieu he viewed as overly concerned with the utilitarian value of* literature. *Specifically, Poe's theory of literary creation is noted for two central points: (1) a work must create a unity of effect on the reader to be counted successful; (2) the production of this single effect should not be left to the hazards of accident or inspiration but should to the minutest detail of style and subject matter be the result of rational deliberation on the part of the author. Along with these theoretical concepts, Poe's most conspicuous contribution to literary criticism was his analytical approach, which focused on the specifics of style and construction. In the following excerpt, he praises the evocative quality of Tennyson's poetry.*]

I am not sure that Tennyson is not the greatest of poets. The uncertainty attending the public conception of the term "poet" alone prevents me from demonstrating that he *is*. Other bards produce effects which are, now and then, otherwise produced than by what we call poems; but Tennyson an effect which only a poem does. His alone are idiosyncratic poems. By the enjoyment or non-enjoyment of the **"Morte d'Arthur,"** or of the **"Œnone,"** I would test any one's ideal sense.

There are passages in his works which rivet a conviction I had long entertained, that the *indefinite* is an element in the true πoιησιơ. Why do some persons fatigue themselves in attempts to unravel such phantasy-pieces as the **"Lady of Shalott?"** As well unweave the *"ventum textilem."* If the author did not deliberately propose to himself a suggestive indefinitiveness of meaning, with the view of bringing about a definitiveness of vague and therefore of spiritual *effect*—this, at least, arose from the silent analytical promptings of that poetic genius which, in its supreme development, embodies all orders of intellectual capacity.

I *know* that indefinitiveness is an element of the true music—I mean of the true musical expression. Give to it any undue decision—imbue it with any very determinate tone—and you deprive it, at once, of its ethereal, its ideal, its intrinsic and essential character. You dispel its luxury of dream. You dissolve the atmosphere of the mystic upon which it floats. You exhaust it of its breath of faery. It now becomes a tangible and easy appreciable idea—a thing of the earth, earthy. It has not, indeed, lost its power to please, but all which I consider the distinctiveness of that power. And to the uncultivated talent, or to the unimaginative apprehension, this deprivation of its most delicate grace will be, not unfrequently, a recommendation. A determinateness of expression is sought—and often by composers who should know better—is sought as a beauty rather than rejected as a blemish. Thus we have, even from high authorities, attempts at absolute *imitation* in music. Who can forget the sillinesses of the "Battle of Prague?" What man of taste but must laugh at the interminable drums, trumpets, blunderbusses, and thunder? *"Vocal music,"* says L'Abbate Gravina, who would have said the same thing of instrumental, "ought to imitate the natural language of the human feelings and passions, rather than the warblings of Canary birds, which our singers, now-a-days, affect so vastly to mimic with their quaverings and boasted cadences." This is true only so far as the "rather" is concerned. If any music must imitate anything, it were assuredly better to limit the imitation as Gravina suggests.

Tennyson's shorter pieces abound in minute rhythmical lapses sufficient to assure me that—in common with all poets living or dead—he has neglected to make precise investigation of the principles of metre; but, on the other hand, so perfect is his rhythmical instinct in general, that, like the present Viscount Canterbury, he seems *to see with his ear.* (pp. 1331-32)

Edgar Allan Poe, "Marginalia," in his Essays and Reviews, *edited by G. R. Thompson, The Library of America, 1984, pp. 1331-62.*

George Eliot   (essay date 1855)

[*An English novelist, essayist, poet, editor, short story writer, and translator, Eliot was one of the greatest English novelists of the nineteenth century. Her work, including the novels* The Mill on the Floss *(1860) and* Middlemarch: A Study of Provincial Life *(1871-72), is informed by penetrating psychological analysis and profound insight into human character. Played against the backdrop of English rural life, Eliot's novels explore moral and philosophical issues and employ a realistic approach to character and plot development. In the following excerpt, Eliot, while expressing a high appraisal of Tennyson's overall poetic achievement, attacks* Maud *for its "morbid" tone and apparent advocation of warfare.*]

If we were asked who among contemporary authors is likely to live in the next century, the name that would first and most unhesitatingly rise to our lips is that of Alfred Tennyson. He, at least, while belonging emphatically to his own age, while giving a voice to the struggles and the far-reaching thoughts of this nineteenth century, has those supreme artistic qualities which must make him a poet for all ages. As long as the English language is spoken, the word music of Tennyson must charm the ear; and when English has become a dead language, his wonderful concentration of thought into luminous speech, the exquisite pictures in which he has blended all the hues of reflection, feeling, and fancy, will cause him to be read as we read Homer, Pindar, and Horace. Thought and feeling, like carbon, will always be finding new forms for themselves, but once condense them into the diamonds of poetry, and the form, as well as the element, will be lasting. This is the sublime privilege of the artist—to be present with future generations, not merely through the indirect results of his work, but through his immediate creations; and of all artists the one whose works are least in peril from the changing conditions of humanity, is the highest order of poet. . . . (p. 596)

Such a poet, by the suffrage of all competent judges among his countrymen, is Tennyson. His **"Ulysses"** is a pure little ingot of the same gold that runs through the ore of the Odyssey. It has the "large utterance" of the early epic, with that rich fruit of moral experience which it has required thousands of years to ripen. The **"Morte d'Arthur"** breathes the intensest spirit of chivalry in the pure and serene air of unselfish piety; and it falls on the ear with the rich, soothing melody of a *Dona nobis* swelling through the aisles of a cathedral. **"Locksley Hall"** has become, like Milton's minor poems, so familiar that we dare not quote it; it is the object of a sort of family affection which we all cherish, but think it is not good taste to mention. Then there are his idyls, such as the **"Gardener's Daughter,"**—works which in their kind have no rival, either in the past

or present. But the time would fail us to tell of all we owe to Tennyson, for, with two or three exceptions, every poem in his two volumes is a favourite. The ***Princess,*** too, with all that criticism has to say against it, has passages of inspiration and lyrical gems imbedded in it, which make it a fresh claim on our gratitude. But, last and greatest, came **In Memoriam,** which to us enshrines the highest tendency of this age, as the Apollo Belvedere expressed the presence of a free and vigorous human spirit amidst a decaying civilization. Whatever was the immediate prompting of **In Memoriam,** whatever the form under which the author represented his aim to himself, the deepest significance of the poem is the sanctification of human love as a religion. If, then, the voice that sang all these undying strains had remained for ever after mute, we should have had no reason to reproach Tennyson with gifts inadequately used; we should rather have rejoiced in the thought that one who has sown for his fellow-men so much—

> generous seed,
> Fruitful of further thought and deed,

should at length be finding rest for his wings in a soft nest of home affections, and be living idyls, instead of writing them.

We could not prevail on ourselves to say what we think of *Maud,* without thus expressing our love and admiration of Tennyson. For that optical law by which an insignificant object, if near, excludes very great and glorious things that lie in the distance, has its moral parallel in the judgments of the public: men's speech is too apt to be exclusively determined by the unsuccessful deed or book of today, the successful doings and writings of past years being for the moment lost sight of. And even seen in the light of the most reverential criticism, the effect of *Maud* cannot be favourable to Tennyson's fame. Here and there only it contains a few lines in which he does not fall below himself. With these slight exceptions, he is everywhere saying, if not something that would be better left unsaid, something that he had already said better; and the finest sentiments that animate his other poems are entirely absent. We have in *Maud* scarcely more than a residuum of Alfred Tennyson; the wide-sweeping intellect, the mild philosophy, the healthy pathos, the wondrous melody, have almost all vanished, and left little more than a narrow scorn which piques itself on its scorn of narrowness, and a passion which clothes itself in exaggerated conceits. While to his other poems we turn incessantly with new distress that we cannot carry them all in our memory, of *Maud* we must say, if we say the truth, that excepting only a few passages, we wish to forget it as we should wish to forget a bad opera. And this not only because it wants the charms of mind and music which belong to his other poetry, but because its tone is throughout morbid; it opens to us the self-revelations of a morbid mind, and what it presents as the cure for this mental disease is itself only a morbid conception of human relations.

But we will abstain from general remarks, and make the reader acquainted with the plan and texture of the poem. It opens, like the gates of Pandemonium, "with horrible discord and jarring sound,"—with harsh and rugged hexameters, in which the hero, who is throughout the speaker, tells us something of his history and his views of society. It is impossible to suppose that, with so great a master of rhythm as Tennyson, this harshness and ruggedness are otherwise than intentional; so we must conclude that it is a device of his art thus to set our teeth on edge with his verses when he means to rouse our disgust by his descriptions; and that, writing of disagreeable things, he has made it a rule to write disagreeably. These hexameters, weak in logic and grating in sound, are undeniably strong in expression, and eat themselves with phosphoric eagerness into our memory, in spite of our will. The hero opens his story by telling us how "long since" his father was found dead in "the dreadful hollow behind the little wood," supposed to have committed suicide in despair at the ruin entailed on him by the failure of a great speculation; and he paints with terrible force that crisis in his boyhood:—

> I remember the time, for the roots of my hair were stirr'd
> By a shuffled step, by a dead weight trail'd, by a whisper'd fright,
> And my pulses closed their gates with a shock on my heart as I heard
> The shrill-edged shriek of a mother divide the shuddering night.

An old neighbour "dropt off gorged" from that same speculation, and is now lord of the broad estate and the hall. These family sorrows and mortifications the hero regards as a direct result of the anti-social tendencies of Peace, which he proceeds to expose to us in all its hideousness; looking to war as the immediate curative for unwholesome lodging of the poor, adulteration of provisions, child-murder, and wife-beating—an effect which is as yet by no means visible in our police reports. It seems indeed that, in the opinion of our hero, nothing short of an invasion of our own coasts is the consummation devoutly to be wished:—

> For I trust if an enemy's fleet came yonder round by the hill,
> And the rushing battle-bolt sang from the three-decker out of the foam,
> That the smoothfaced snubnosed rogue would leap from his counter and till,
> And strike, if he could, were it but with his cheating yard-wand, home.

From his deadly hatred of retail traders and susceptibility as to the adulteration of provisions, we were inclined to imagine that this modern Conrad, with a "devil in his sneer," but not a "laughing devil," had in his reduced circumstances taken a London lodging and endured much peculation in the shape of weekly bills, and much indigestion arising from unwholesome bread and beer. But no: we presently learn that he resides in a lone house not far from the Hall, and can still afford to keep "a man and a maid." And now, he says, the family is coming home to the Hall; the old blood-sucker, with his son and a daughter, Maud, whom he remembers as a little girl, "with her sweet purse-mouth, when my father dangled the grapes." He is determined not to fall in love with her, and the glance he gets of her as she passes in her carriage, assures him that he is in no danger from her "cold and clear-cut face,"—

> Faultily faultless, icily regular, splendidly null,
> Dead perfection, no more.

However, he does not escape from this first glance without the "least little touch of the spleen," which the reader foresees is the germinal spot that is to develop itself into love. The first lines of any beauty in the poem are those in which he describes the "cold and clear-cut face," breaking his sleep, and haunting him "star-sweet on a gloom profound," till he gets up and walks away the wintry night in his own dark garden. Then Maud seems to look haughtily on him as she returns his bow, and he makes fierce resolves to flee from the cruel madness of love, and more especially from the love of Maud, who is "all unmeet for a wife;" but presently he hears her voice, which has a more irresistible magic even than her face. By-and-bye she looks more benignantly on him, but his suspicious heart dares not sun itself in her smile, lest her brother—

> That jewell'd mass of millinery,
> That oil'd and curl'd Assyrian Bull,

may have prompted her to this benignity as a mode of canvassing for a vote at the coming election. A fresh circumstance is now added in the form of a new-made lord, apparently a suitor of Maud's—

> a captain, a padded shape,
> A bought commission, a waxen face,
> A rabbit mouth that is ever agape.

Very indignant is our hero with this lord's grandfather, for having made his fortune by a coal-mine, though the consideration that the said grandfather is now in "a blacker pit," is somewhat soothing to his chafed feelings. In the denunciations we have here of new-made fortunes, new titles, new houses, and new suits of clothes, it is evidently Mr. Tennyson's aversion, and not merely his hero's morbid mood, that speaks; and we must say, that this immense expenditure of gall on trivial social phases, seems to us intrinsically petty and snobbish. The gall presently overflows, as gall is apt to do, without any visible sequence of association, on Mr. Bright, who is denounced as—

> This broad-brimm'd hawker of holy things,
> Whose ear is stuft with his cotton, and rings
> Even in dreams to the chink of his pence.

In a second edition of **Maud,** we hope these lines will no longer appear on Tennyson's page: we hope he will by that time have recovered the spirit in which he once wrote how the "wise of heart"

> Would love the gleams of good that broke
> From either side, nor veil his eyes.

On the next page, he gives us an agreeable change of key in a little lyric, which will remind the German reader of Thekla's song. Here is the second stanza:—

> Let the sweet heavens endure,
>   Not close and darken above me,
> Before I am quite, quite sure
>   That there is one to love me;
> Then let come what come may
>   To a life that has been so sad,
> I shall have had my day.

At length, after many alternations of feeling and metre, our hero becomes assured that he is Maud's accepted lover, and atones for rather a silly outburst, in which he requests the sky to

> Blush from West to East,
>   Blush from East to West,
> Till the West is East,
>   Blush it thro' the West,

by some very fine lines, of which we can only afford to quote the concluding ones:—

> Is that enchanted moan only the swell
> Of the long waves that roll in yonder bay?
> And hark the clock within, the silver knell
> Of twelve sweet hours that past in bridal white,
> And died to live, long as my pulses play;
> But now by this my love has closed her sight
> And given false death her hand, and stol'n away
> To dreamful wastes where footless fancies dwell
> Among the fragments of the golden day.
> May nothing there her maiden grace affright!
> Dear heart, I feel with thee the drowsy spell.
> My bride to be, my evermore delight,
> My own heart's heart and ownest own, farewell.
> It is but for a little space I go:
> And ye meanwhile far over moor and fell
> Beat to the noiseless music of the night!
> Has our whole earth gone nearer to the glow
> Of your soft splendours that you look so bright?
> *I* have climb'd nearer out of lonely Hell.
> Beat, happy stars, timing with things below,
> Beat with my heart more blest than heart can tell,
> Blest, but for some dark undercurrent woe
> That seems to draw—but it shall not be so:
> Let all be well, be well.

We are now approaching the crisis of the story. A grand dinner and a dance are to be held at the Hall, and the hero, not being invited, waits in the garden till the festivities are over, that Maud may then come out and show herself to him in all the glory of her ball-dress. Here occurs the invocation, which has been deservedly admired and quoted by every critic:—

> Come into the garden, Maud,
>   For the black bat, night, has flown,—
> Come into the garden, Maud,
>   I am here at the gate alone;
> And the woodbine spices are wafted abroad,
>   And the musk of the roses blown.
>
> For a breeze of morning moves,
>   And the planet of Love is on high,
> Beginning to faint in the light that she loves
>   On a bed of daffodil sky,—
> To faint in the light of the sun she loves,
>   To faint in his light, and to die.

Very exquisite is that descriptive bit, in the second stanza, where the music of the verse seems to faint and die like the star. Still the whole poem, which is too long for us to quote, is very inferior, as a poem of the Fancy, to the **"Talking Oak."** We do not, for a moment, believe in the sensibility of the roses and lilies in Maud's garden, as we believe in the thrills felt to his "inmost ring" by the **"Old Oak of Summer Chace."** This invocation is the topmost note of the lover's joy. The interview in the garden is disturbed by the **"Assyrian Bull,"** and the "padded shape." A duel follows, in which the brother is killed. And now we find the hero an exile on the Breton coast, where, from delivering some stanzas of Natural Theology *à propos* of a shell, he proceeds to retrace the sad memories of his love, until he becomes mad. We have then a Bedlam soliloquy, in which he fancies himself dead, and mingles with the images of Maud, her father, and her brother, his early-fixed idea—the police reports. From this madness he is recovered by the news that the Allies have declared war against Russia; whereupon he bursts into a pæan, that

the long, long canker of Peace is over and done.

It is possible, no doubt, to allegorize all this into a variety of edifying meanings; but it remains true, that the ground-notes of the poem are nothing more than hatred of peace and the Peace Society, hatred of commerce and coal-mines, hatred of young gentlemen with flourishing whiskers and padded coats, adoration of a clear-cut face, and faith in War as the unique social regenerator. Such are the sentiments, and such is the philosophy embodied in *Maud;* at least, for plain people not given to allegorizing; and it, perhaps, speaks well for Tennyson's genius, that it has refused to aid him much on themes so little worthy of his greatest self. Of the smaller poems, which, with the well-known **"Ode,"** make up the volume, **"The Brook"** is rather a pretty idyl, and **"The Daisy"** a graceful, unaffected recollection of Italy; but no one of them is remarkable enough to be ranked with the author's best poems of the same class. (pp. 596-601)

> *George Eliot, in an originally unsigned essay titled "Belles Lettres," in* The Westminster and Foreign Quarterly Review, *Vol. LXIV, No. CXXVI, October, 1855, pp. 596-615.*

Walter Bagehot   (essay date 1859)

[*Bagehot is regarded as one of the most versatile and influential authors of mid-Victorian England. In addition to literary criticism, he wrote several pioneering works in the fields of politics, sociology, and economics. As editor of the London* Economist, *he was instrumental in shaping the financial policy of his generation. Despite their diverse subject matter, Bagehot's works are unified by his emphasis on factual information and his interest in the personalities of literary figures, politicians, and economists. His works are also noted for their humorous tone, reflecting Bagehot's belief that "the knack in style is to write like a human being." Many modern commentators contend that it is partially because of the "readable" quality of his prose that Bagehot's writings, which were primarily composed as journalistic pieces, are still enjoyed today. In the following excerpt, Bagehot compares Tennyson's verse with that of John Keats, Percy Bysshe Shelley, William Wordsworth, and Samuel Taylor Coleridge.*]

Where is Mr. Tennyson to be placed in the rank of our poets? We know that he has genius; but is that genius great or small, when compared with others like it?

It is most natural to compare him with Keats and Shelley. The kind of readers he addresses is, as we observed, the same: a sort of intellectual sentiment pervades his works as well as theirs: the superficial resemblances of the works of all the three are many. But, on the other hand, Mr. Tennyson is deficient in the most marked peculiarity which Shelley and Keats have in common. Both of these poets are singularly gifted with a sustained faculty of lyrical expression. They seem hurried into song; and, what is more, kept there when they have been hurried there. Shelley's "Skylark" is the most familiar example of this. A rather young musician was once asked, what was Jenny Lind's charm in singing. "Oh," he replied, "she went up so high, and staid up high so long." There is something of this sustainment at a great height in all Shelley's lyrics. His strains are profuse. He is ever soaring; and whilst soaring, ever singing. Keats, it is true, did not ascend to so extreme an elevation. He did not belong to the upper air. He had no abstract labour, no haunting speculations, no attenuated thoughts. He was the poet of the obvious beauty of the world. His genius was of the earth—of the autumn earth—rich and mellow; and it was lavish. He did not carry his art high or deep; he neither enlightens our eyes much, nor expands our ears much; but pleases our fancies with a prolonged strain of simple rich melody. He does not pause, or stay, or hesitate. His genius is continuous; the flow of it is as obvious at the best moments as the excellence, and at inferior moments is more so. Mr. Tennyson, on the other hand, has no tendencies of this kind. He broods. . . . There are undoubtedly several beautiful songs in his writings,—several in which the sentiment cleaves to the words, and cannot even in our memories be divorced from them. But their beauty is not continuous. A few lines fasten upon us with an imperious and ever-mastering charm; but the whole composition, as a whole, has not much value. The run of it, as far as it has a run, expresses nothing. The genius of Mr. Tennyson is delineative; it muses and meditates; it describes moods, feelings, and objects of imagination; but it does not rush on to pour out passion, or express overwhelming emotion.

In the special lyrical impulse, therefore, we think it indisputable that Mr. Tennyson is inferior both to Keats and to Shelley. To Shelley he is moreover evidently inferior in general intensity of mind. This intense power of conception is, indeed, the most striking of all Shelley's peculiarities. There is something nervously exciting about his way

Arthur Henry Hallam

of writing, even on simple subjects. He takes them up so vividly into his brain that they seem to make it quiver, and that of a sensitive reader at times quivers in sympathy. The subjects are no doubt often abstract; too abstract, perhaps, occasionally for art. But that only makes the result more singular. That an excitable mind should be stimulated by the strong interest of the facts of the world, by the phenomena of life, by the expectation of death, is what we should expect. It is intelligible to our understanding, and in obvious accordance with our experience. But that this extreme excitement should be caused in the poet's mind very often, and in the reader's mind sometimes, by the abstractions of singular tenuity, is what few would expect. So, however, it is. The mind of Shelley seems always to work in a kind of pure rare ether, clearer, sharper, more eager than the ordinary air. The reader feels that he is on a kind of mountainous elevation, and perhaps he feels vivified by it: at times almost all persons do so, but at times also they are chilled at its cold, and half-frightened at the lifelessness and singularity. It is characteristic of Shelley that he was obliged to abandon one of his favourite speculations, "dizzy from thrilling horror." Of all this abstract intensity Mr. Tennyson has not a particle. He is never very eager about any thing, and he is certainly not over-anxious about phantoms and abstractions. In some respects this deficiency may not have injured his writings: it has rather contributed to his popularity. The English mind, which, like its great philosophers, likes to work upon "stuff," is more pleased with genial chivalric pictures than with chiselled phantoms and intense lyrics. Still, a critic who appreciates Shelley at all, will probably feel that he has a degree of inner power, of telling mental efficiency, which Mr. Tennyson does not equal. Horrible as the *Cenci* must ever be, it shows an eager and firmer grasp of mind—a greater tension of the imagination—than the **Idylls.**

Over Keats, however, Mr. Tennyson may perhaps claim a general superiority. We are, indeed, making a comparison which is scarcely fair; Keats died when he was still very young. His genius was immature; and his education, except the superficial musing education he gave himself, was very imperfect. Mr. Tennyson has lived till his genius is fully ripe, and he has gathered in the fruits of his century. No one can read his poems without feeling this: some of his readers have probably felt it painfully. Twenty years ago, when there was an idea in the high places of criticism that he was a silly and affected writer, many ignorant persons thought they were showing their knowledge in laughing at a language which nevertheless was both most emphatic and most accurate. The amount of thought which is held in solution,—if we may be pardoned so scientific a metaphor,—in Mr. Tennyson's poetry, is very great. If you come to his poems a hundred times, it is very probable that you will even to the end find there some new allusion, some recondite trace of high-bred thought, which you had not seen before. His reflections are often not new; he would not advance for himself perhaps, his just admirers, we are sure, would not claim for him, the fame of an absolutely original thinker. But he indicates the possession of a kind of faculty which in an age of intellect and cultivation is just as important, possibly is even more important, than the power of first-hand discovery. He is a first-rate *realiser;* and realisation is a test of truth. Out of the infinite thoughts, discoveries, and speculations which are scattered, more or less perfectly, through society, certain minds have a knack of taking up and making their own that which is true, and healthy, and valuable; and they reject the rest. It is often not by a very strict analysis or explicit logical statement that such minds arrive at their conclusions. They are continually thinking the subjects in question over: they have the details of them in their minds: they have a floating picture of endless particulars about them in their imaginations. In consequence, by musing over a true doctrine, they see that it is true: it fits their picture, adapts itself to it, forms at once a framework for it. On the contrary, they find that a false tenet does not suit the facts which they have in their minds: they muse over it, find out its unsuitability, and think no more of it. The belief of these remarkably sane and remarkably meditative persons about the facts to which they devote their own understandings is one of the best criteria of truth in this world. It is the discriminating winnow of civilisation, which receives the real corn of the true discoverer, and leaves the vexing chaff of the more pompous science to be forgotten and pass away. This kind of meditative tact and slow selective judgment Mr. Tennyson possesses in a very great measure; and there is nothing of which Keats was so entirely destitute. It does not, perhaps, occur to you while reading him that he is deficient in it. It belongs to an order of merit completely out of his way. It is the reflective gift of a mature man: Keats's best gifts are those of an impulsive, original, and refined boy. But if we compare—as in some degree we cannot help doing—the indications of general mind which are scattered through the three writers, we shall think, perhaps, that in these Mr. Tennyson excels Keats, even remembering the latter's early death, and, in consequence, giving him all fair credit for the possibilities of subsequent development; just as we found before that the intellectual balance seemed, when similarly adjusted, to incline against Mr. Tennyson, and in favour of Shelley.

Some one has said that Tennyson was a drawing-room Wordsworth. There is no deep felicity or instruction in the phrase, but it has some superficial appropriateness. Wordsworth's works have no claim to be in the drawing-room: they have the hill-side and the library, and those places are enough for them. Wordsworth, as we know, dealt with two subjects, and with two subjects only,—the simple elemental passions, "the pangs by which the generations are prepared," and in which they live and breathe and move; and secondly, the spiritual conception of nature, which implies that the universe is, in its beauties and its changes, but the expression of an inherent and animating spirit. Neither of these subjects suits the drawing-room. The simple passions are there carefully covered over; nature is out-of-doors. Mr. Tennyson, however, has given some accounts of the more refined and secondary passions in Wordsworth's intense manner; and if he does not give the exact sketches of external nature, or preach any gospel concerning it, he gives us a mental reflex of it, and a Lotus-eater's view of what it ought to be, and what it is rather a shame on the whole that it is not, which are not inadmissible in a luxurious drawing-room. A little of the spirit of Wordsworth, thus modified, may be traced in Mr. Tennyson; and perhaps this is the only marked trace of a recent writer that can be found in his writings. If we were to be asked as before, whether Mr. Wordsworth or Mr. Tennyson were the superior in general imaginative power, we think we should say that the latter was the superior, but that Wordsworth had achieved a greater task than he has as yet achieved, with inferior powers. The

mind of Wordsworth was singularly narrow; his range peculiarly limited; the object he proposed to himself unusually distinct. He has given to us a complete embodiment of the two classes of subjects which he has treated of: perhaps it would be impossible to imagine one of them—the peculiar aspect of outward nature which we mentioned—to be better delineated; certainly as yet, we apprehend, it is not delineated nearly so well any where else. Although we should be inclined to believe that Mr. Tennyson's works indicate greater powers, we do not think that they evince so much concentrated efficiency, that they leave any single result upon the mind which is at once so high and so definite.

If we were asked, as we shall be asked, why we think Mr. Tennyson to have greater powers than Wordsworth, we would venture to allege two reasons. In the first place, Mr. Tennyson has a power of making fun. No one can claim that, of all powers, for Wordsworth, it is certain: no human being more entirely destitute of humour is perhaps discoverable any where in literature, or possibly even in society. Not a tinge of it seems ever to have influenced him. He had, through life, the narrow sincerity of the special missionary; but he had not, what is all but incompatible with it, the restraining tact of the man of the world, which teaches that all things and all gospels are only now and then in season; that it is absurd always to be teaching a single doctrine; that it is not wise to fatigue oneself by trying to interest others in that which it is perfectly certain they will not be interested in. The world of "cakes and ale," indisputably, is not that of Wordsworth. There are quite sufficient indications that Mr. Tennyson appreciates it. Secondly, it may be said that, far more completely than Wordsworth, and far more completely than any other recent poet, Mr. Tennyson has conceived in his mind, and has delineated in his works, a general picture of human life. He certainly does not give us the whole of it, there is a considerable portion which he scarcely touches; but an acute eye can observe that he sees more than he says; and even judging exclusively and rigidly from what is said, the amount of life which Mr. Tennyson has delineated, even in these *Idylls* only, far surpasses in extent and range that which Wordsworth has described. Wordsworth's range is so narrow, and the extent of life and thought which these *Idylls* go over, slight as is their seeming structure, is so great, that perhaps no one will question this conclusion. Some may, however, deny its sufficiency; they may suggest that it does not prove our conclusion. In Shelley's case, it may be said that we allowed a certain defined intensity to have a higher imaginative value than a more diffused fertility and a less concentrated art; why is not Wordsworth entitled to share the benefit of this doctrine also? The plea is very specious, but we are not inclined to think that it is sound. Shelley has shown in a single direction, or in a few directions, an immense general power of imagination and mind. We may not pause to prove this: it is in the nature of allusive criticism to be dogmatic; we must appeal to the memory of our readers. On the other hand, we think, by a certain doggedness of nature, by high resolution, and even, in a certain sense, by an extreme limitation of mind, Wordsworth, with far less of imagination, was able in special directions to execute most admirable works. But the power displayed is, in a great degree, that of character rather than of imagination. He put all his mind into a single task, and he did it. Wordsworth's best works are the saved-up excellencies of a rather barren nature; those of Shelley are the rapid productions of a very fertile one. When we are speaking of mere intellectual and imaginative power, we run, therefore, no risk of contradiction in ranking Mr. Tennyson at a higher place than Wordsworth, notwithstanding that we have adjudged him to be inferior in the same quality to Shelley.

Perhaps we can, after this discussion, fix, at least approximately and incompletely, Mr. Tennyson's position in the hierarchy of our poets. We think that the poets of this century of whom we have been speaking,—and Coleridge may be added to the number,—may be, in a certain sense, classed together as the intellectualised poets. We do not, of course, mean that there ever was a great poet who was destitute of great intellect, or who did not show that intellect distinctly in his poems. But the poets of whom we speak show that intellect in a further and special sense. We are all conscious of the difference between talking to an educated man and to an uneducated. The difference by no means is, that the educated man talks better; that he either says better things, or says them in a more vigorous way. Possibly uneducated persons, as a rule, talk more expressively, and send whatever meaning they have farther into the hearer's mind; perhaps their meaning on the subjects which they have in common with educated men, is not very much inferior. Still there is a subtle charm about the conversation of the educated which that of other persons has not. That charm consists in the constant presence and constant trace of a cultivated intellect. The words are used with a certain distinct precision; a distinguishing tact of intellect is indicated by that which is said; a discriminating felicity is shown in the mode in which it is said. The charm of cultivated expression is like the charm of a cultivated manner; it is easy and yet cautious, natural and yet improved, ready and yet restrained. The fascination of a cultivated intellect in literature is the same. It is more easy to describe its absence, perhaps, than its presence. The style of Shakespeare, for example, wants entirely this peculiar charm. He had the manifold experience, the cheerful practicality, the easy felicity of the uneducated man; but he had not the measured abundance, the self-restraining fertility, which the very highest writer may be conceived to have. There is no subtle discretion in his words: there is the nice tact of native instinct; there is not the less necessary, but yet attractive, precision of an earnest and anxious education. Perhaps it will be admitted that the writers we have mentioned—Shelley, Coleridge, Keats, Wordsworth, and Tennyson—may all be called, as far as our own literature is concerned, in a peculiar sense the intellectualised poets. Milton indeed would, in positive knowledge, be superior to any of them, and to many of them put together, but he is an exceptional poet in English literature, to be classed apart, and seldom to be spoken of in contrast or comparison with any other; and even he, from a want of natural subtlety of mind, does not perhaps show us, in the midst of his amazing knowledge, the most acute and discriminating intellectuality. But if we except Milton, these poets may almost certainly be classed apart: and if they are to be so, we have indicated the place which Mr. Tennyson holds in this class in relation to all of them save Coleridge. . . . [Coleridge] will long be a problem to the critics, and a puzzle to the psychologists. But, so far as the general powers of mind shown in his poems are concerned,—and this is the only aspect of his genius which we are at present considering,—we need have no hesitation in saying that they are much inferior to those shown

in the poems of our greatest contemporary poet. Their great excellence is, in truth, almost confined to their singular power in the expression of one single idea. Both "Christabel" and the "Ancient Mariner" are substantially developments of the same conception; they delineate almost exclusively the power which the supernatural has, when it is thrust among the detail of the natural. This idea is worked out with astonishing completeness; but it is left to stand alone. There are no characters, no picture of life at large, no extraordinary thoughts, to be found in these poems; their metre and their strangeness are their charm. After what has been said, we need not prove at large that such an exclusive concentration upon such an idea proves that these poems are inferior, or rather indicate inferior imaginative genius to that of Tennyson. The range of the art is infinitely less; and the peculiar idea, which is naturally impressive, and in comparison with others easy to develop, hardly affords scope for the clear exhibition of a very creative genius, even if there were not other circumstances which would lead us to doubt whether Coleridge, rich and various as were his mental gifts, was possessed of that one. On the whole, we may pause in the tedium of our comparative dissertation. We may conclude, that in the series of our intellectualised poets Mr. Tennyson is to be ranked as inferior in the general power of the poetic imagination to Shelley, and to Shelley only. . . . (pp. 387-94)

Walter Bagehot, in an originally unsigned essay titled "Tennyson's Idylls," in The National Review, *London, Vol. IX, No. XVIII, October, 1859, pp. 368-94.*

Henry James (essay date 1875)

[*As a novelist James is valued for his psychological acuity and complex sense of artistic form. Throughout his career, he also wrote literary criticism in which he developed his artistic ideals and applied them to the works of others. James admired the self-consciously formalistic approach of contemporary French writers, particularly Gustave Flaubert, whose style contrasted with the loose, less formulated standards of English novelists. On the other hand, he favored the moral concerns of English writing over the often amoral and cynical vision which characterized much of French literature in the second half of the nineteenth century. His literary aim was to combine the qualities of each country's literature that most appealed to his temperament. In the following excerpt from a review of Tennyson's drama* Queen Mary *that originally appeared in* The Galaxy, *James characterizes Tennyson's poetry as "static" rather than dramatic.*]

A new poem by Mr. Tennyson is certain to be largely criticised, and if the new poem is a drama, the performance must be a great event for criticism as well as for poetry. Great surprise, great hopes, and great fears had been called into being by the announcement that the author of so many finely musical lyrics and finished, chiselled specimens of narrative verse, had tempted fortune in the perilous field of the drama.

Few poets seemed less dramatic than Tennyson, even in his most dramatic attempts—in *Maud,* in *Enoch Arden,* or in certain of the *Idylls of the King.* He had never used the dramatic form, even by snatches; and though no critic was qualified to affirm that he had no slumbering ambition in that direction, it seemed likely that a poet who had apparently passed the meridian of his power had nothing absolutely new to show us. On the other hand, if he had for years been keeping a gift in reserve, and suffering it to ripen and mellow in some deep corner of his genius, while shallower tendencies waxed and waned above it, it was not unjust to expect that the consummate fruit would prove magnificent.

On the whole, we think that doubt was uppermost in the minds of those persons who to a lively appreciation of the author of *Maud* added a vivid conception of the exigencies of the drama. But at last *Queen Mary* appeared, and conjecture was able to merge itself in knowledge. There was a momentary interval, during which we all read, among the cable telegrams in the newspapers, that the London *Times* affirmed the new drama to contain more "true fire" than anything since Shakespeare had laid down the pen. This gave an edge to our impatience; for "fire," true or false, was not what the Laureate's admirers had hitherto claimed for him. In a day or two, however, most people had the work in their hands.

Every one, it seems to us, has been justified—those who hoped (that is, expected), those who feared, and those who were mainly surprised. *Queen Mary* is both better and less good than was to have been supposed, and both in its merits and its defects it is extremely singular. It is the least Tennysonian of all the author's productions; and we may say that he has not so much refuted as evaded the charge that he is not a dramatic poet. To produce his drama he has had to cease to be himself. Even if *Queen Mary,* as a drama, had many more than its actual faults, this fact alone—this extraordinary defeasance by the poet of his familiar identity—would make it a remarkable work.

We know of few similar phenomena in the history of literature—few such examples of rupture with a consecrated past. Poets in their prime have groped and experimented, tried this and that, and finally made a great success in a very different vein from that in which they had found their early successes. But the writers in prose or in verse are few who, after a lifetime spent in elaborating and perfecting a certain definite and extremely characteristic manner, have at Mr. Tennyson's age suddenly dismissed it from use and stood forth clad from head to foot in a disguise without a flaw. We are sure that the other great English poet—the author of *The Ring and the Book,*— would be quite incapable of any such feat. The more's the pity, as many of his readers will say!

Queen Mary is upward of three hundred pages long; and yet in all these three hundred pages there is hardly a trace of the Tennyson we know. Of course the reader is on the watch for reminders of the writer he has greatly loved; and of course, vivid signs being absent, he finds a certain eloquence in the slightest intimations. When he reads that

> —that same tide
> Which, coming with our coming, seemed to smile
> And sparkle like our fortune as thou saidest,
> Ran sunless down and moaned against the piers,

he seems for a moment to detect the peculiar note and rhythm of *Enoch Arden* or *The Princess.* Just preceding

these, indeed, is a line which seems Tennysonian because it is in a poem by Tennyson:

> Last night I climbed into the gate-house, Brett,
> And scared the gray old porter and his wife.

In such touches as these the Tennysonian note is faintly struck; but if the poem were unsigned, they would not do much toward pointing out the author. On the other hand, the fine passages in *Queen Mary* are conspicuously deficient in those peculiar cadences—that exquisite perfume of diction—which every young poet of the day has had his hour of imitating. We may give as an example Pole's striking denial of the charge that the Church of Rome has ever known trepidation:

> What, my Lord!
> The Church on Petra's rock? Never! I have seen
> A pine in Italy that cast its shadow
> Athwart a cataract; firm stood the pine—
> The cataract shook the shadow. To my mind
> The cataract typed the headlong plunge and fall
> Of heresy to the pit: the pine was Rome.
> You see, my Lords,
> It was the shadow of the Church that trembled.

This reads like Tennyson doing his best not to be Tennyson, and very fairly succeeding. Well as he succeeds, however, and admirably skilful and clever as is his attempt throughout to play tricks with his old habits of language, and prove that he was not the slave but the master of the classic Tennysonian rhythm, I think that few readers can fail to ask themselves whether the new gift is of equal value with the old. The question will perhaps set them to fingering over the nearest volume of the poet at hand, to refresh their memory of his ancient magic. It has rendered the present writer this service, and he feels as if it were a considerable one. Every great poet has something that he does supremely well, and when you come upon Tennyson at his best you feel that you are dealing with poetry at its highest. One of the best passages in *Queen Mary*—the only one, it seems to me, very sensibly warmed by the "fire" commemorated by the London *Times*—is the passionate monologue of Mary when she feels what she supposes to be the intimations of maternity:

> He hath awaked, he hath awaked!
> He stirs within the darkness!
> Oh Philip, husband! how thy love to mine
> Will cling more close, and those bleak manners thaw,
> That make me shamed and tongue-tied in my love.
> The second Prince of Peace—
> The great unborn defender of the Faith,
> Who will avenge me of mine enemies—
> He comes, and my star rises.
> The stormy Wyatts and Northumberlands
> And proud ambitions of Elizabeth,
> And all her fiercest partisans, are pale
> Before my star!
> His sceptre shall go forth from Ind to Ind!
> His sword shall hew the heretic peoples down!
> His faith shall clothe the world that will be his,
> Like universal air and sunshine! Open,
> Ye everlasting gates! The King is here!—
> My star, my son!

That is very fine, and its broken verses and uneven movement have great felicity and suggestiveness. But their magic is as nothing, surely, to the magic of such a passage as this:

Yet hold me not for ever in thine East;
How can my nature longer mix with thine?
Coldly thy rosy shadows bathe me, cold
Are all thy lights, and cold my wrinkled feet
Upon thy glimmering thresholds, where the stream
Floats up from those dim fields about the homes
Of happy men that have the power to die,
And grassy barrows of the happier dead.
Release me and restore me to the ground;
Thou seëst all things, thou wilt see my grave;
Thou wilt renew thy beauty morn by morn;
I, earth in earth, forget these empty courts,
And thee returning on thy silver wheels.

In these beautiful lines from **"Tithonus"** there is a purity of tone, an inspiration, a something sublime and exquisite, which is easily within the compass of Mr. Tennyson's usual manner at its highest, but which is not easily achieved by any really dramatic verse. It is poised and stationary, like a bird whose wings have borne him high, but the beauty of whose movement is less in great ethereal sweeps and circles than in the way he hangs motionless in the blue air, with only a vague tremor of his pinions. Even if the idea with Tennyson were more largely dramatic than it usually is, the immobility, as we must call it, of his phrase would always defeat the dramatic intention. When he wishes to represent movement, the phrase always seems to me to pause and slowly pivot upon itself, or at most to move backward. I do not know whether the reader recognizes the peculiarity to which I allude; one has only to open Tennyson almost at random to find an example of it:

For once when Arthur, walking all alone,
Vext at a rumour rife about the Queen,
Had met her, Vivien being greeted fair,
Would fain have wrought upon his cloudy mood
With reverent eyes mock-loyal, shaken voice,
And fluttered adoration.

That perhaps is a subtle illustration; the allusion to Teolin's dog in **"Aylmer's Field"** is a franker one:

—his old Newfoundlands, when they ran
To lose him at the stables; for he rose,
Two-footed, at the limit of his chain,
Roaring to make a third.

What these pictures present is not the action itself, but the poet's complex perception of it; it seems hardly more vivid and genuine than the sustained posturings of brilliant *tableaux vivants.* With the poets who are natural chroniclers of movement, the words fall into their places as with some throw of the dice, which fortune should always favour. With Scott and Byron they leap into the verse *à pieds joints,* and shake it with their coming; with Tennyson they arrive slowly and settle cautiously into their attitudes, after having well scanned the locality. In consequence they are generally exquisite, and make exquisite combinations; but the result is intellectual poetry and not passionate—poetry which, if the term is not too pedantic, one may qualify as static poetry. Any scene of violence represented by Tennyson is always singularly limited and compressed; it is reduced to a few elements—refined to a single statuesque episode. There are, for example, several descriptions of tournaments and combats in the **Idylls of the King.** They are all most beautiful, but they are all curiously delicate. One gets no sense of the din and shock of battle; one seems to be looking at a bas relief of two contesting

knights in chiselled silver, on a priceless piece of plate. They belong to the same family as that charming description, in Hawthorne's *Marble Faun,* of the sylvan dance of Donatello and Miriam in the Borghese gardens. Hawthorne talks of the freedom and frankness of their mirth and revelry; what we seem to see is a solemn frieze in stone along the base of a monument. These are the natural fruits of geniuses who are of the brooding rather than the impulsive order. I do not mean to say that here and there Tennyson does not give us a couplet in which motion seems reflected without being made to tarry. I open **Enoch Arden** at hazard, and I read of Enoch's ship that

—at first indeed
Thro' many a fair sea-circle, day by day,
Scarce rocking, her full-busted figure-head
Stared o'er the ripple feathering from her bows.

I turn the page and read of

The myriad shriek of wheeling ocean fowl,
The league-long roller thundering on the reef,
The moving whisper of huge trees that branched
And blossomed in the zenith;

of

The sunrise broken into scarlet shafts
Among the palms and ferns and precipices;
The blaze upon the waters to the east;
The blaze upon his island overhead;
The blaze upon the waters to the west;
Then the great stars that globed themselves in Heaven,
The hollower-bellowing Ocean, and again
The scarlet shafts of sunrise.

These lines represent movement on the grand natural scale—taking place in that measured, majestic fashion which, at any given moment, seems identical with permanence. One is almost ashamed to quote Tennyson; one can hardly lay one's hand on a passage that does not form part of the common stock of reference and recitation. Passages of the more impulsive and spontaneous kind will of course chiefly be found in his lyrics and rhymed verses (though rhyme would at first seem but another check upon his freedom); and passages of the kind to which I have been calling attention, chiefly in his narrative poems, in the **Idylls** generally, and especially in the later ones, while the words strike one as having been pondered and collated with an almost miserly care.

But a man has always the qualities of his defects, and if Tennyson is what I have called a static poet, he at least represents repose and stillness and the fixedness of things, with a splendour that no poet has surpassed. We all of this generation have lived in such intimacy with him, and made him so much part of our regular intellectual meat and drink, that it requires a certain effort to hold him off at the proper distance for scanning him. We need to cease mechanically murmuring his lines, so that we may hear them speak for themselves.

Few persons who have grown up within the last forty years but have passed through the regular Tennysonian phase; happy few who have paid it a merely passive tribute, and not been moved to commit their emotions to philosophic verse, in the metre of **In Memoriam**! The phase has lasted longer with some persons than with others; but it will not be denied that with the generation at large it has visibly declined. The young persons of twenty now read Tennyson (though, as we imagine, with a fervour less intense than that which prevailed twenty years ago); but the young persons of thirty read Browning and Dante Rossetti, and Omar Kheyam—and are also sometimes heard to complain that poetry is dead and that there is nothing nowadays to read.

We have heard Tennyson called "dainty" so often, we have seen so many allusions to the "Tennysonian trick," we have been so struck, in a certain way, with M. Taine's remarkable portrait of the poet, in contrast to that of Alfred de Musset, that every one who has anything of a notion of keeping abreast of what is called the "culture of the time" is rather shy of making an explicit, or even a serious profession of admiration for his earlier idol. It has long been the fashion to praise Byron, if one praises him at all, with an apologetic smile; and Tennyson has been, I think, in a measure, tacitly classed with the author of *Childe Harold* as a poet whom one thinks most of while one's taste is immature.

This is natural enough, I suppose, and the taste of the day must travel to its opportunity's end. But I do not believe that Byron has passed, by any means, and I do not think that Tennyson has been proved to be a secondary or a tertiary poet. If he is not in the front rank, it is hard to see what it is that constitutes exquisite quality. There are poets of a larger compass; he has not the passion of Shelley nor the transcendent meditation of Wordsworth; but his inspiration, in its own current, is surely as pure as theirs. He depicts the assured beauties of life, the things that civilisation has gained and permeated, and he does it with an ineffable delicacy of imagination. Only once, as it seems to me (at the close of *Maud*), has he struck the note of irrepressible emotion, and appeared to say the thing that must be said at the moment, at any cost. For the rest, his verse is the verse of leisure, of luxury, of contemplation, of a faculty that circumstances have helped to become fastidious; but this leaves it a wide province—a province that it fills with a sovereign splendour.

When a poet is such an artist as Tennyson, such an unfaltering, consummate master, it is no shame to surrender one's self to his spell. Reading him over here and there, as I have been doing, I have received an extraordinary impression of talent—talent ripened and refined, and passed, with a hundred incantations, through the crucible of taste. The reader is in thoroughly good company, and if the language is to a certain extent that of a coterie, the coterie can offer convincing evidence of its right to be exclusive. Its own tone is exquisite; listen to it, and you will desire nothing more. (pp. 165-77)

> *Henry James, "Tennyson's Drama," in his* Views and Reviews, *1908. Reprint by Books for Libraries Press, 1968, pp. 165-204.*

Henry W. Longfellow   (poem date 1877)

[*Longfellow was an American poet, novelist, essayist, and translator, whose poetry is characterized by gentle simplicity and a melancholy reminiscent of the German Romantics. He is credited with having been instrumental in introducing European culture to his American readers, and in popularizing American folk themes abroad. In the following poem, entitled "Wapentake"*

and dedicated "to Alfred Tennyson," Longfellow expresses his admiration for Tennyson's verse.]

> POET! I come to touch thy lance with mine;
>   Not as a knight, who on the listed field
>   Of tourney touched his adversary's shield
> In token of defiance, but in sign
> Of homage to the mastery, which is thine
>   In English song; nor will I keep concealed,
>   And voiceless as a rivulet frost-congealed,
>   My admiration for thy verse divine.
> Not of the howling dervishes of song,
>   Who craze the brain with their delirious dance,
>   Art thou, O sweet historian of the heart!
> Therefore to thee the laurel-leaves belong,
>   To thee our love and our allegiance,
> For thy allegiance to the poet's art.

> *Henry W. Longfellow, "Wapentake," in* The Atlantic Monthly, *Vol. XL, No. CCXLII, December, 1877, p. 731.*

Walt Whitman   (essay date 1887)

[*Considered one of America's greatest poets, Whitman was a literary innovator whose poetry decisively influenced the development of modern free verse. His masterpiece, the poetry collection* Leaves of Grass *(1855), focused on themes of death, immortality, and democracy, and was controversial during the author's lifetime for its frank treatment of sexuality and lack of such conventional poetic devices as rhyme, regular meter, and uniform length of line and stanza. Whitman actively promoted an image of himself as the definitive poet of American democracy and the common people. In the following essay, Whitman reviews Tennyson's poetry from an American perspective.*]

Beautiful as the song was, the original **'Locksley Hall'** of half a century ago was essentially morbid, heart-broken, finding fault with everything, especially the fact of money's being made (as it ever must be, and perhaps should be) the paramount matter in worldly affairs.

> Every door is barr'd with gold, and opens but to golden keys.

First, a father, having fallen in battle, his child (the singer)

> Was left a trampled orphan, and a selfish uncle's ward.

Of course love ensues. The woman in the chant or monologue proves a false one; and as far as appears the ideal of woman, in the poet's reflections, is a false one, at any rate for America. Woman is *not* 'the lesser man.' (The heart is not the brain.) The best of the piece of fifty years since is its concluding line:

> For the mighty wind arises roaring seaward and I go.

Then for this current 1886-7, a just-out sequel, which (as an apparently authentic summary says) 'reviews the life of mankind during the past sixty years, and comes to the conclusion that its boasted progress is of doubtful credit to the world in general and to England in particular. A cynical vein of denunciation of democratic opinions and aspirations runs throughout the poem, in marked contrast with the spirit of the poet's youth.' Among the most striking lines of this sequel are the following:

Envy wears the mask of love, and, laughing sober fact to
   scorn,
Cries to weakest as to strongest, 'Ye are equals, equal-
   born.'
Equal-born! Oh yes, if yonder hill be level with the flat.
Charm us, orator, till the lion look no larger than the cat;
Till the cat, through that mirage of overheated language,
   loom
Larger than the lion Demos—end in working its own
   doom.

      . . . . .

Tumble nature heel over head, and, yelling with the yelling street,
Set the feet above the brain and swear the brain is in the
   feet.
Bring the old Dark Ages back, without the faith, without
   the hope
Beneath the State, the Church, the throne, and roll their
   ruins down the slope.

I should say that all this is a legitimate consequence of the tone and convictions of the earlier standards and points of view. Then some reflections, down to the hard-pan of this sort of thing.

The course of progressive politics (democracy) is so certain and resistless, not only in America but in Europe, that we can well afford the warning calls, threats, checks, neutralizings, in imaginative literature, or any department, of such deep-sounding and high-soaring voices as Carlyle's and Tennyson's. Nay, the blindness, excesses, of the prevalent tendency—the dangers of the urgent trends of our times—in my opinion, need such voices almost more than any. I should, too, call it a signal instance of democratic humanity's luck that it has such enemies to contend with—so candid, so fervid, so heroic. But why do I say enemy? Upon the whole is not Tennyson—and was not Carlyle (like an honest and stern physician)—the true friend of our age?

Let me assume to pass verdict, or perhaps momentary judgment, for the United States on this poet—a removed and distant position giving some advantages over a nigh one. What is Tennyson's service to his race, times, and especially to America? First, I should say, his personal character. He is not to be mentioned as a rugged, evolutionary, aboriginal force—but (and a great lesson is in it) he has been consistent throughout with the native, personal, healthy, patriotic spinal element and promptings of himself. His moral line is local and conventional, but it is vital and genuine. He reflects the upper-crust of his time, its pale cast of thought—even its *ennui.* Then the simile of my friend John Burroughs is entirely true, 'his glove is a glove of silk, but the hand is a hand of iron.' He shows how one can be a royal laureate, quite elegant and 'aristocratic,' and a little queer and affected, and at the same time perfectly manly and natural. As to his non-democracy, it fits him well, and I like him the better for it. I guess we all like to have (I am sure I do) some one who presents those sides of a thought, or possibility, different from our own—different, and yet with a sort of home-likeness—a tartness and contradiction offsetting the theory as we view it, and construed from tastes and proclivities not at all our own.

To me, Tennyson shows more than any poet I know (perhaps has been a warning to me) how much there is in finest verbalism. There is such a latent charm in mere words, cunning collocations, and in the voice ringing them,

which he has caught and brought out, beyond all others—as in the line,

And hollow, hollow, hollow, all delight,

in 'The Passing of Arthur,' and evidenced in 'The Lady of Shalott,' 'The Deserted House,' and many other pieces. Among the best (I often linger over them again and again) are 'Lucretius,' 'The Lotos Eaters,' and 'The Northern Farmer.' His mannerism is great, but it is a noble and welcome mannerism. His very best work, to me, is contained in the books of *The Idylls of the King,* all of them, and all that has grown out of them. Though indeed we could spare nothing of Tennyson, however small or however peculiar—not 'Break, Break,' nor 'Flower in the Crannied Wall' nor the old, eterally-told passion of 'Edward Gray:'

Love may come and love may go,
   And fly like a bird from tree to tree
But I will love no more, no more
   Till Ellen Adair come back to me.

Yes, Alfred Tennyson's is a superb character, and will help give illustriousness, through the long roll of time, to our Nineteenth Century. In its bunch of orbic names, shining like a constellation of stars, his will be one of the brightest. His very faults, doubts, swervings, doublings upon himself, have been typical of our age. We are like the voyagers of a ship, casting off for new seas, distant shores. We would still dwell in the old suffocating and dead haunts, remembering and magnifying their pleasant experiences only, and more than once impelled to jump ashore before it is too late, and stay where our fathers stayed, and live as they lived.

May-be I am non-literary and non-decorous (let me at least be human, and pay part of my debt) in this word about Tennyson. I want him to realize that here is a great and ardent Nation that absorbs his songs, and has a respect and affection for him personally, as almost for no other foreigner. I want this word to go to the old man at Farringford as conveying no more than the simple truth; and that truth (a little Christmas gift) no slight one either. I have written impromptu, and shall let it all go at that. The readers of more than fifty millions of people in the New World not only owe to him some of their most agreeable and harmless and healthy hours, but he has entered into the formative influences of character here, not only in the Atlantic cities, but inland and far West, out in Missouri, in Kansas, and away in Oregon, in farmer's house and miner's cabin.

Best thanks, anyhow, to Alfred Tennyson—thanks and appreciation in America's name. (pp. 1-2)

> *Walt Whitman, "A Word about Tennyson," in*
> The Critic, *New York, Vol. 10, January 1,*
> *1887, pp. 1-2.*

George Saintsbury   (essay date 1895)

[*Saintsbury has been called the most influential English literary historian and critic of the late nineteenth and early twentieth centuries. Saintsbury adhered to two distinct sets of critical standards: one for the novel and the other for poetry and drama. As a critic of novels, he maintained that "the novel has nothing to do with any beliefs, with any convictions, with any thoughts in the strict sense, except as mere garnishings. Its substance must always be life not thought, conduct not belief, the passions not the intellect, manners and morals not creeds and theories . . . The novel is . . . mainly and firstly a criticism of life." As a critic of poetry and drama, Saintsbury was a radical formalist who frequently asserted that subject is of little importance, and that "the so-called 'formal' part is of the essence." In the following excerpt, he praises the descriptive and rhythmic elements of Tennyson's verse.]*

[We] have quite recently found some persons saying that "Tennyson is as great as Shakespeare," and other people going into fits of wrath, or smiling surprise with calm disdain, at the saying. If what the former mean to say and what the latter deny is that Tennyson has a supreme and peculiar poetic charm, then I am with the former and against the latter. He has: and from the very fact of his having it he will not necessarily be appreciated at once, and may miss appreciation altogether with some people.

The recent publication anew of the earliest *Poems by Two Brothers* has been especially useful in enabling us to study this charm. In these poems it is absolutely nowhere: there is not from beginning to end in any verse, whether attributed to Alfred, Frederick, or Charles, one suggestion even of the witchery that we Tennysonians associate with the work of the first-named. It appears dimly and distantly—so dimly and distantly that one has to doubt whether we recognise it by anything but a "fallacy of looking back"—in **"Timbuctoo,"** in **"The Lovers' Tale"** quite distinctly, but uncertainly; and with much alloy in the pieces which the author later labelled as "Juvenilia."

It is true that these "Juvenilia" have been a good deal retouched, and that much of the really juvenile work on which the critics were by no means unjustly severe has been left out. But the charm is there. Take the very first stanza of **"Claribel."** You may pick holes in the conceit which makes a verb "I low-lie, thou low-liest, she low-lieth," and you may do other things of the same kind if you like. But who ever wrote like that before? Who struck that key earlier? Who produced anything like the slow, dreamy music of the variations in it? Spenser and Keats were the only two masters of anything in the remotest degree similar in English before. And yet it is perfectly independent of Spenser, perfectly independent of Keats. It is Tennyson, the first rustle of the "thick-leaved, ambrosial" murmuring which was to raise round English lovers of poetry a very Broceliande of poetical enchantment for sixty years to come during the poet's life, and after his death for as long as books can speak and readers hear. (pp. 28-30)

I believe that, in so far as the secret of a poet can be discovered and isolated, the secret of Tennyson lies in that slow and dreamy music . . . and I am nearly sure that my own admiration of him dates from the time when I first became aware of it. "Claribel," of course, is by no means a very effective example; though the fact of its standing in the very forefront of the whole work is excessively interesting. The same music continued to sound—with infinite variety of detail, but with no breach of general character—from **"Claribel"** itself to **"Crossing the Bar."** At no time was Tennyson a perfect master of the quick and lively measures; and in comparison he very seldom affected them. He cannot pick up and return the ball of song as Praed—another great master of metre if not quite of music, who

preceded him by seven years at Trinity—did, still less as Praed partly taught Mr. Swinburne to do. There is nothing in Tennyson of the hurrying yet never scurrying metre of "At a Month's End," or the Dedication to Sir Richard Burton. His difficulty in this respect has not improved **"The Charge of the Light Brigade,"** and it is noticeable that it impresses a somewhat grave and leisurely character even on his anapæsts,—as for instance in the **"Voyage of Maeldune."** If you want quick music you must go elsewhere, or be content to find the poet not at his best in it.

But in the other mode of linked and long-drawn out sweetness he has hardly any single master and no superior:

> At midnight the moon cometh
> And looketh down alone.

There again the despised **"Claribel"** gives us the cue. And how soon and how miraculously it was taken up, sustained, developed, varied, everybody who knows Tennyson knows. **"Mariana"** is the very incarnation, the very embodiment in verse of spell-bound stagnation, that is yet in the rendering beautiful. The **"Recollections of the Arabian Nights"** move something sprightlier, but the **"Ode to Memory,"** by far the greatest of the "Juvenilia," relapses into the visionary gliding. Even in **"The Sea Fairies"** and **"The Dying Swan,"** the occasional dactyls and anapæsts rather slide than skip; and the same is the case with the best lines in **"Oriana"** and (naturally enough) with the whole course of the **"Dirge."** All the ideal girl-portraits except **"Lilian"** (the least worthy of them) have this golden languor, which is so distinctly the note of the earlier poems that it is astonishing any one should ever have missed it. Yet, as I have said, I believe I missed it myself for some time, and certainly, judging from their criticisms, contemporaries of the poet much cleverer than I never seem to have heard it at all.

When the great collection came it must have been hard still to miss it; yet how little the English public even yet was attuned is shown by the fact that both then and since one of the most popular things has been *The May Queen,* which, if anything of Tennyson's could be so, I should myself be disposed to call trumpery. **"The Lady of Shalott"** is very far from trumpery, and perhaps the poet's very happiest thing not in a languid measure; but even **"The Lady of Shalott"** does not count among the poems that established Tennyson's title to the first rank among English poets. **"The Lotos-Eaters," "The Palace of Art," "A Dream of Fair Women," "Œnone," "Ulysses,"** (though perhaps it will be said that I ought not to include blank verse pieces,) all have the trailing garments of the night, not the rush and skip of dawn; and though there are some exceptions among the rightly famous lyrics, such as **"Sir Galahad"** and the admirable piece of cynicism in **"The Vision of Sin,"** they are exceptions. Even **"Locksley Hall"** canters rather than gallops, and the famous verses in **"The Brook"** are but a *tour de force.*

But it would be impossible here to go through the whole of the poet's work. He can do many things; but he always (at least to my taste) does his best in lyric to slow music. And I doubt whether any one will again produce this peculiar effect as he has produced it. It must be evident, too, how much this faculty of slow and stately verse adds to the effect of *In Memoriam.* If the peculiar metre of that poem is treated (as I have known it treated by imitators) in a light and jaunty fashion—to quick time, so to speak—the effect is very terrible. But Tennyson has another secret than this for blank verse. This is the secret of the paragraph, which he alone of all English poets shares with Milton in perfection. There is little doubt that he learnt it from Milton, but the effect is quite different, though the means resorted to are necessarily much the same in both cases, and include in both a very careful and deliberate disposition of the full stop which breaks and varies the cadence of the line; the adoption when it is thought necessary of trisyllabic instead of dissyllabic feet; and the arrangement of a whole block of verses so that they lead up to a climax of sense and sound in the final line. Almost the whole secret can be found in one of the earliest and perhaps the finest of his blank verse exercises, the **"Morte d'Arthur,"** but examples were never wanting up to his very last book.

These two gifts, that of an infinitely varied slow music and dreamy motion in lyric and that of concerted blank verse, with his almost unequalled faculty of observation and phrasing as regards description of nature, were, I think, the things in Tennyson which first founded Tennyson-worship in my case. And these, I am sure, are what have kept it alive in my case, though I have added to them an increasing appreciation of his wonderful skill in adjusting vowel values. His subjects matter little: I do not know that subject ever does matter much in poetry, though it is all important in prose. But if I have been right in my selection of his chief gifts, it will follow almost as the night the day that the vague, the antique, and to some extent the passionate, must suit him better than the modern, the precise, the meditative. Not that Tennyson is by any means as some misguided ones hold, a shallow poet; the exquisite perfection of his phrase and his horror of jargon have deceived some even of the elect on that point, just as there have been those who think that Plato is shallow because he is nowhere unintelligible, and that Berkeley cannot be a great philosopher because he is a great man of letters. But art, romance, distant history (for history of a certain age simply becomes romance), certainly suit him better than science, modern life, or argument. Vast efforts have been spent on developing schemes of modernised Christianity out of *In Memoriam;* but the religious element in that poem is as consistent with an antiquated orthodoxy as with anything new and undogmatic; and the attraction of the poem is in its human affection, in its revelation of the House of Mourning, and above all in those unmatched landscapes and sketches of which the poet is everywhere prodigal.

It is perhaps (if I may refine still further on the corrections of impressions which years of study have left) in the combination of the faculty of poetical music with that of poetical picture drawing that the special virtue of Tennyson lies. There have been poets, though not many, who could manage sound with equal skill; and there have been those, though not many, who could bring with a few modulated words a visual picture before the mind's eye and almost the eye of the body itself with equal sureness and success. But there have hardly been any, outside the very greatest Three or Four, who could do both these things at the same time in so consummate a fashion. The very musical poets are too apt to let the sharp and crisp definition of their picture be washed away in floods of sound; the very pictorial poets to neglect the musical accompaniment. Tennyson

never commits either fault. The wonderful successions of cartoons in the **"Palace"** and the **"Dream"** exhibit this in his very earliest stage. If any one has ever in this combination of music, draughtsmanship, and colour equalled him who wrote,

> One seemed all dark and red, a tract of sand,
> And some one pacing there alone,
> Who paced for ever in a glimmering land,
> Lit with a low large moon,

I do not know him. The first stanza of **"The Lotos-Eaters"** has the same power of filling eye and ear at once, so that it is almost impossible to decide whether you hear the symphony or see the picture most clearly. And at the very other extreme of the poet's poetical life, in those famous lines which united all competent suffrages (though one egregious person I remember called them "homely" and divers wiseacres puzzled over the identity of the "pilot" and the propriety of his relation of place toward the "bar"), this master faculty again appeared.

> With such a tide as moving seems asleep,
> Too full for sound or foam,

are words which make the very picture, the very foamless swirl, the very soundless volume of sound, which they describe.

No! In the impressions given by such a poet as this, when they have been once duly and fairly received, there can be no correction, except a better and better appreciation of him as time goes on. The people who have liked what was not best, or have not liked what was best, may grow weary of well admiring. Those who look rather at the absence of faults than at the presence of beauties may point to incongruities and mediocrities, to attempts in styles for which the poet had little aptitude, to occasional relapses from the grand manner to the small mannerism, and so forth. But those whose ears and eyes (if not, alas! their lips) Apollo has touched, will never make any mistake about him. They may as in other—as in all—cases be more or fewer as time goes on: there may be seasons when the general eye grows blind and the general ear deaf to his music and his vision. But that will not matter at all. So long as the unknown laws which govern the presentation of beauty in sight and sound last, beauty will be discovered here just as we ourselves after two thousand years find it in the ancient tongues which we cannot even pronounce with any certainty that we are nearer to the original than Mr. Hamerton's little French boy was when he tried to vocalise that very stanza of **"Claribel"**, to which I have referred above. (pp. 31-40)

George Saintsbury, "Tennyson" and "Tennyson (Concluded)," in his Corrected Impressions: Essays on Victorian Writers, *Dodd, Mead and Company, 1895, pp. 21-30, 31-40.*

G. K. Chesterton   (essay date 1903)

[*Regarded as one of England's premier men of letters during the first half of the twentieth century, Chesterton is best known today as a colorful bon vivant, a witty essayist, and creator of the Father Brown mysteries and the fantasy* The Man Who Was Thursday *(1908). Much of Chesterton's work reveals his childlike joie de vivre and reflects his pronounced Anglican and, later, Roman Catholic beliefs. His essays are characterized by their humor, frequent use of paradox, and chatty, rambling style. In the following excerpt, he defends Tennyson's poetry against charges that it is "commonplace."]*

The attempts which have been made to discredit the poetical position of Tennyson are in the main dictated by an entire misunderstanding of the nature of poetry. When critics like Matthew Arnold [See Jump, *Tennyson: The Critical Heritage,* in Further Reading], for example, suggest that his poetry is deficient in elaborate thought, they only prove, as Matthew Arnold proved, that they themselves could never be great poets. It is no valid accusation against a poet that the sentiment he expresses is commonplace. Poetry is always commonplace; it is vulgar in the noblest sense of that noble word. Unless a man can make the same kind of ringing appeal to absolute and admitted sentiments that is made by a popular orator, he has lost touch with emotional literature. Unless he is to some extent a demagogue, he cannot be a poet. A man who expresses in poetry new and strange and undiscovered emotions is not a poet; he is a brain specialist. Tennyson can never be discredited before any serious tribunal of criticism because the sentiments and thoughts to which he dedicates himself are those sentiments and thoughts which occur to anyone. These are the peculiar province of poetry; poetry, like religion, is always a democratic thing, even if it pretends the contrary. The faults of Tennyson, so far as they existed, were not half so much in the common character of his sentiments as in the arrogant perfection of his workmanship. He was not by any means so wrong in his faults as he was in his perfections.

Men are very much too ready to speak of men's work being ordinary, when we consider that, properly considered, every man is extraordinary. The average man is a tribal fable, like the Man-Wolf or the Wise Man of the Stoics. In every man's heart there is a revolution; how much more in every poet's? The supreme business of criticism is to discover that part of a man's work which is his and to ignore that part which belongs to others. Why should any critic of poetry spend time and attention on that part of a man's work which is unpoetical? Why should any man be interested in aspects which are uninteresting? The business of a critic is to discover the importance of men and not their crimes. It is true that the Greek word critic carries with it the meaning of a judge, and up to this point of history judges have had to do with the valuation of men's sins, and not with the valuation of their virtues.

Tennyson's work, disencumbered of all that uninteresting accretion which he had inherited or copied, resolves itself, like that of any other man of genius, into those things which he really inaugurated. Underneath all his exterior of polished and polite rectitude there was in him a genuine fire of novelty; only that, like all the able men of his period, he disguised revolution under the name of evolution. He is only a very shallow critic who cannot see an eternal rebel in the heart of the Conservative.

Tennyson had certain absolutely personal ideas, as much his own as the ideas of Browning or Meredith, though they were fewer in number. One of these, for example, was the fact that he was the first of all poets (and perhaps the last) to attempt to treat poetically that vast and monstrous vision of fact which science had recently revealed to mankind. Scientific discoveries seem commonly fables as fantastic in the ears of poets as poems in the ears of men of science. The poet is always a Ptolemaist; for him the sun still rises and the earth stands still. Tennyson really worked the essence of modern science into his poetical constitution, so that its appalling birds and frightful flowers were really part of his literary imagery. To him blind and brutal monsters, the products of the wild babyhood of the Universe, were as the daisies and the nightingales were to Keats; he absolutely realised the great literary paradox mentioned in the Book of Job: "He saw Behemoth, and he played with him as with a bird."

Instances of this would not be difficult to find. But the tests of poetry are those instances in which this outrageous scientific phraseology becomes natural and unconscious. Tennyson wrote one of his own exquisite lyrics describing the exultation of a lover on the evening before his bridal day. This would be an occasion, if ever there was one, for falling back on those ancient and assured falsehoods of the doomed heaven and the flat earth in which generations of poets have made us feel at home. We can imagine the poet in such a lyric saluting the setting sun and prophesying the sun's resurrection. There is something extraordinarily typical of Tennyson's scientific faith in the fact that this, one of the most sentimental and elemental of his poems, opens with the two lines:

> Move eastward, happy earth, and leave
> Yon orange sunset waning slow.

Rivers had often been commanded to flow by poets, and flowers to blossom in their season, and both were doubtless grateful for the permission. But the terrestrial globe of science has only twice, so far as we know, been encouraged in poetry to continue its course, one instance being that of this poem, and the other the incomparable "Address to the Terrestrial Globe" in the "Bab Ballads."

There was, again, another poetic element entirely peculiar to Tennyson, which his critics have, in many cases, ridiculously confused with a fault. This was the fact that Tennyson stood alone among modern poets in the attempt to give a poetic character to the conception of Liberal Conservatism, of splendid compromise. The carping critics who have abused Tennyson for this do not see that it was far more daring and original for a poet to defend conventionality than to defend a cart-load of revolutions. His really sound and essential conception of Liberty,

> Turning to scorn with lips divine
> The falsehood of extremes,

is as good a definition of Liberalism as has been uttered in poetry in the Liberal century. Moderation is *not* a compromise; moderation is a passion; the passion of great judges. That Tennyson felt that lyrical enthusiasm could be devoted to established customs, to indefensible and ineradicable national constitutions, to the dignity of time and the empire of unutterable common sense, all this did not make him a tamer poet, but an infinitely more original one. Any poetaster can describe a thunderstorm; it requires a poet to describe the ancient and quiet sky.

I cannot, indeed, fall in with Mr. Morton Luce in his somewhat frigid and patrician theory of poetry. "Dialect," he says, "mostly falls below the dignity of art." I cannot feel myself that art has any dignity higher than the indwelling and divine dignity of human nature. Great poets like Burns were far more undignified when they clothed their thoughts in what Mr. Morton Luce calls "the seemly raiment of cultured speech" than when they clothed them in the headlong and flexible patois in which they thought and prayed and quarrelled and made love. If Tennyson failed (which I do not admit) in such poems as **"The Northern Farmer,"** it was not because he used too much of the spirit of the dialect, but because he used too little.

Tennyson belonged undoubtedly to a period from which we are divided; the period in which men had queer ideas of the antagonism of science and religion; the period in which the Missing Link was really missing. But his hold upon the old realities of existence never wavered; he was the apostle of the sanctity of laws, of the sanctity of customs; above all, like every poet, he was the apostle of the sanctity of words. (pp. 250-57)

G. K. Chesterton, "Tennyson," in his Varied Types, *Dodd, Mead and Company,* 1903, pp. 249-57.

A. C. Bradley   (essay date 1910)

[*Bradley was an English educator and critic noted especially for his contributions to Shakespearean scholarship. Though English poetry was his primary focus, Bradley also wrote on philosophical subjects and religion. In the following excerpt, Bradley discusses Tennyson's consideration of immortality in* In Memoriam.]

An understanding of [*In Memoriam*] may be furthered, and the necessity for detailed explanations of particular passages may be avoided, if we . . . raise the questions: How does Tennyson habitually think of the soul and its future, and on what does his faith appear to be based?

Here certain cautions must be borne in mind. In the first place we must distinguish between that which is all-important and that which is of secondary interest. For example, it is evident that to Tennyson the fact of immortality was both certain and essential; but his ideas as to the precise nature of the future life or lives stand on another level. It is useful to review these ideas, because they show us the world in which his imagination was accustomed to move; but they were not to him matters either of certainty or of great practical import. And, in the second place, we have to remember that Tennyson neither was nor professed to be a philosopher, and we must not expect from him either the exactness of language or the form of consecutive reasoning which are required in philosophy. In one section of **In Memoriam** (XLVIII.) he disclaims the intention of dealing fully or even seriously with the problems on which he has touched. Up to the time when he finished the poem he does not appear to have made any study of philosophers; and though a few of his later poems bear marks of some reading of this kind, and even employ terms too technical for poetry, in general the language remains that of imagination, and the form of argumentation or strict statement is never adopted. The reader, therefore, must not expect system or definition; he must not press hardly on single phrases or sentences, but must use them in order to feel his way into the poet's mind.

If we try to picture the soul's history, as Tennyson habitually imagines it, our first question must be: When did this history begin? Sometimes, we find, he imagines a previous existence, or more than one, in which the soul was either embodied or else 'floated free'; and certain strange longings and dim visions which haunt its earthly life are regarded as faint recollections of a previous state (so, *e.g.,* in **'The Two Voices,' 'The Ancient Sage,' 'Far, Far Away'**). But much more often, and in **In Memoriam** probably always, the earthly life is thought of as the first life of the soul, which is then figured as coming from the 'deep' of a larger spiritual being, or as detaching itself, or being detached, from the 'general soul.' This process is coincident with, or the spiritual complement of, certain changes in matter which issue in the body of the soul; and later, through experience gained by means of this body, the soul develops into self-consciousness or personality (XLV.). That which is deepest and most real in it is sometimes spoken of as will or free-will, to Tennyson the 'main-miracle, apparently an act of self-limitation by the Infinite, and yet a revelation by Himself of Himself.'

The life on earth need not be considered here. At death the union of soul and body is dissolved. The idea that thereupon the soul passes at once to a final state of bliss or woe, is on the whole foreign to the poet's mind, and is repudiated (in 'The Ring'). So is the idea that at the end of the earthly life the soul at once remerges into the general soul so as to lose its individuality (XLVII.). And again the idea that at death the soul falls into a long sleep from which it will awake unchanged, though entertained as a possibility in XLIII., is evidently not habitual with the poet. He habitually imagines the soul as entering on a second individual life immediately after death. The new life is almost always, if not always, thought of as implying a new embodiment; and sometimes, perhaps generally, this embodiment is supposed to take place on some other world or 'star.' The soul's second life, if it lived well on earth, is regarded as free from many of the limitations and defects of the first. Though occasionally described as though it were an existence of merely contemplative happiness, it is generally imagined as a life of activity in which the soul takes part in some common work and so advances on the path of progress. Usually, though not always, the poet thinks of the soul as remembering its past and its earthly companions; occasionally he imagines it as being, at least for a time, peculiarly 'near' to the beloved on earth and perhaps even able to 'touch' them without the intervention of sense; as a rule, and in **In Memoriam** habitually, he thinks of a reunion and recognition, in the next life, of souls dear to one another in this.

The second life is supposed to be succeeded by death, on which follows a third embodied life; and this process is repeated again and again for ages, the soul in each embodiment reaching a higher stage of being, and approaching more and more nearly to God. The union with God in which this progress would presumably terminate, the poet naturally does not attempt to imagine; but it is noticeable that, if we may judge from XLVII. and the phrases quoted in *Memoir,* the idea of an *ultimate* 'absorption into the divine' was not, like the idea of an immediate absorption, repugnant to him; and perhaps with this we may connect the fact that in the trance-experience which he several times described, 'the loss of personality (if so it were)' seemed to him 'no extinction but the only true life' (*Memoir*). Of the future of souls which grew worse with time in their earthly state he does not write, but, as his later poems show, he could not entertain the belief that any soul would in the end be excluded from a God of love. The 'larger hope' of LV., and perhaps the

> one far-off divine event
> To which the whole creation moves [Epilogue],

are phrases which refer to the final reconciliation or union of all souls with their divine source.

How many of the ideas just summarised were to the poet matters of belief and of essential importance we do not know; and therefore, in turning to the question of the basis of his belief in immortality, we must dismiss the greater part of them, and must understand by 'immortality' simply the conscious and indefinitely prolonged life of the soul beyond death. For this was to him undoubtedly a matter of fixed belief, and of an importance so great that life without the belief in it seemed to him to have neither sense nor value. We must remember also that immortality was to his mind a fact of the same order as the existence of a God of love, so that what is said of the grounds of his faith in the one may often be taken to apply also to the grounds of his faith in the other; and where the two ideas are not regarded as thus coordinate, the belief in immortality is considered as a consequence of belief in God, so that the basis of the latter is indirectly also the foundation of the former.

In the first place, then, it is clear that God and immortality are to the poet matters not of knowledge or proof, but of faith. Concerning them

> We have but faith: we cannot know;
> For knowledge is of things we see.

We embrace them 'by faith, and faith alone,'

> Believing where we cannot prove. (Cf. CXXXI.)

This position is maintained throughout Tennyson's poetry, and is set forth most fully and maturely in the following lines from **'The Ancient Sage:'**

> Thou canst not prove the Nameless, O my son,
> Nor canst thou prove the world thou movest in,
> Thou canst not prove that thou art body alone,
> Nor canst thou prove that thou art spirit alone,
> Nor canst thou prove that thou art both in one:
> Thou canst not prove thou art immortal, no
> Nor yet that thou art mortal—nay my son,
> Thou canst not prove that I, who speak with thee,
> Am not thyself in converse with thyself,
> For nothing worthy proving can be proven,
> Nor yet disproven: wherefore thou be wise,
> Cleave ever to the sunnier side of doubt,
> And cling to Faith beyond the forms of Faith!

The ideas of God and immortality, in the next place, are not for the poet the result of reasoning upon the phenomena of external Nature. He appears to have held consistently throughout his life, that if we did not bring them with us to the examination of Nature, but simply used our reason upon it without taking into account the evidence derived from our own nature, we should not believe either in God or in immortality. As an undergraduate he voted No on the question raised in the Apostles' Society, Is an intelligible First Cause deducible from the phenomena of the universe? He would say, on looking through the microscope, 'Strange that these wonders should draw some men to God and repel others. No more reason in one than

in the other'(*Memoir*). And so the poet in *In Memoriam* declares:

> I found Him not in world or sun,
> Or eagle's wing, or insect's eye. (CXXIV.)

Nay, in his dark hour, it even seems to him that the message of Nature is a terrible one; that, 'red in tooth and claw with ravine,' she 'shrieks against his creed'; that the world is a process of ceaseless change, in which individual existences arise to pass without return; that its forces show no token that they value life more than death, good more than evil, or the soul more than a grain of sand. And though these are but 'evil dreams' born of his distress, and Nature appears to him far otherwise when he views it, as he habitually does, in the light of ideas derived from another source, he is still constant to the position that Nature, regarded by itself, would not convince him of immortality or God.

So far all is clear. And the positive question, Whence then, according to the poet, is the faith in these ideas derived? admits of an easy answer in general terms. 'Such ideas,' he says, 'we get from ourselves, from what is highest within us.' But when we proceed to ask, What is this 'highest within us'? we find difficulties, and it is certainly not safe to found an answer, as is often done, upon three or four lines in a single section of *In Memoriam.* Our best plan will rather be to collect and place in order some crucial passages from various poems, and then to elicit a result from them.

In **'The Two Voices'** one voice pleads that the senses tell us 'the dead are dead.' The poet answers:

> Who forged that other influence,
> That heat of inward evidence,
> By which [man] doubts against the sense?
>
> He owns the fatal gift of eyes,
> That read his spirit blindly wise,
> Not simple as a thing that dies.
>
> Here sits he shaping wings to fly:
> His heart forebodes a mystery:
> He names the name Eternity.
>
> That type of Perfect in his mind
> In Nature can he nowhere find.
> He sows himself on every wind.

This does not mean that he imposes his own fancies on the universe; rather, these inward evidences are regarded as the witness of the power which reaches 'through Nature moulding men,' and 'revealing' itself 'in every human soul.' (*Memoir*).

They are often said to come through feeling, or are called feeling. God, to the Ancient Sage, is

> That which knows
> And is not known, but felt thro' what we feel
> Within ourselves is highest.

And, in particular, as love is the highest we feel, we must believe that God is Love. So in *In Memoriam* (CXXIV.) the 'evil dreams' which Nature lends are opposed by feeling or the heart:

> A warmth within the breast would melt
> The freezing reason's colder part,
> And like a man in wrath the heart

Stood up and answered 'I have felt';

and, in his distress, the poet cries to what he 'feels is Lord of all.' In *In Memoriam,* again, it is chiefly (though not solely) the presence of love within himself that makes the poet declare that, without immortality, life would be valueless, and man a monster, because combining the contradictory attributes of love and mortality: and in **'Vastness'** the similar passionate assertions that nothing in the world could matter if man were doomed to perish, are suddenly broken off with the words:

> Peace, let it be! for I loved him, and love him for ever: the
> dead are not dead but alive.

Finally, in **'The Two Voices'** the poet appeals to mysterious intimations:

> Heaven opens inward, chasms yawn,
> Vast images in glimmering dawn,
> Half shown, are broken and withdrawn.
>
>   . . . . .
>
> Moreover, something is or seems,
> That touches me with mystic gleams,
> Like glimpses of forgotten dreams.

So in the **'Holy Grail'** and the **'Ancient Sage'** reference is made to the inward evidence of exceptional moments when everything material becomes unreal or visionary, yet there is in the soul 'no shade of doubt, But utter clearness,' and man

>   feels he cannot die,
> And knows himself no vision to himself,
> Nor the high God a vision.
>
>   ['Holy Grail']

And so, in *In Memoriam,* not only is this trancelike experience one in which the soul comes 'on that which is,' and for a moment seems to understand the riddle of the world (XCV.), but the cry of distress to what is felt as Lord of all is immediately followed by the vision of the reality behind appearances:

> And what I am beheld again
>   What is, and no man understands. (CXXIV.)

If now we consider these various passages, what answer do they give to our question concerning the basis of the poet's faith? They show at once that it does not suffice to take the stanza ending 'I have felt,' and to reply: Tennyson thinks that the emotions or 'heart' cannot be satisfied without a belief in God and immortality, and that is the sole ground of his belief. For this account of the matter, even if it were satisfactory for one passage, evidently does not apply to others. The 'highest within us' seems to be generally accompanied by emotion, but not always, or even generally, to be an emotion. Often it is love, but it is obviously not so in the lines quoted from **'The Two Voices,'** nor apparently in those from the **'Holy Grail'** and the **'Ancient Sage'**; and love, to which the appeal is made in *In Memoriam,* XXXIV., XXXV., is coupled with other high activities and achievements in LVI., and is not referred to at all in the lines from XCV. or the last lines of CXXIV. The 'highest within us' means many things, and its meaning could be further extended if we went beyond our list of passages.

Nor is the use made of this consciousness of a higher al-

ways the same. It seems to be of two distinct kinds. Sometimes the poet, looking at that which he feels to be highest in himself, finds it to point beyond earthly experience; and on this characteristic of it he founds what is, in effect, an *argument* in favour of immortality or the divine origin of the soul. So it is with the shaping of wings that yet can never fly on earth; or the presence of the ideas of eternity and perfection which cannot be derived from mere nature nor realised here; or the mysterious intimations of **'The Two Voices.'** So it is also with love, which appears to the poet to imply in its very nature the immortality both of itself and of its object. To him the existence of these tokens of immortality in man, if it were coupled with the fact of mortality, would make man an inexplicable 'monster,' and deprive both his life and the history of the earth of all their meaning. This then is one way in which his consciousness of the best within him yields a basis for the poet's faith; and when he replies to the freezing reason 'I have felt,' the feeling he appeals to is not the desire to be immortal, nor yet a feeling that he is immortal, but the feeling of love, which he points to as a fact inconsistent with the theory of the world put forward in his dark mood by his reason.

But there is another way. When King Arthur says that there are moments when he *feels* he cannot die; when God is said to be *felt* through what we feel within ourselves is highest; when the poet speaks of that which he *feels* is Lord of all, there is a more direct appeal to something called feeling. Here the poet does not point to something within him which seems to imply immortality or God, and from which therefore these may be inferred; the feelings of which he speaks are, or give, an immediate assurance of God or of immortality. It would probably be vain to attempt to define these 'feelings' more exactly, or to ask whether the poet's meaning was simply that at certain moments, recognised by him as his highest, he was unable to doubt the existence of God and immortality, or whether he meant that at these moments he appeared to himself to have a direct and positive apprehension of the soul as immortal, and of God as Love. What is clear is that, on the one hand, these feelings are not merely what we generally call emotions, since a certainty of God and immortality is conveyed in them; and that, on the other hand, the assurance they convey is direct or immediate, not dependent on reasoning or 'proof.' Such phrases, in the descriptions of the trance-like state, as *'came on* that which is,' *'beheld* what is,' *'knows* himself no vision,' are evidently meant to indicate this same immediate certainty.

It is on the second of these two kinds of 'inward evidence' that the poet seems to lay most stress. And the reason of this doubtless is that the first kind obviously involves a process of reasoning, and that to him this process is not accompanied by the conviction of certainty. It falls short of 'proof.' Thus in **'The Two Voices'** the presence in the soul of certain ideas, activities, and feelings, was taken to point to the divine origin and the immortality of that soul, but it did not give the 'assurance' for which the poet longed, and which came later when, at the sound of a mysterious inner voice which whispered hope,

> From out [his] sullen heart a power
> Broke, like the rainbow from the shower,
>
> To feel, altho' no tongue can prove,
> That every cloud, that spreads above
> And veileth love, itself is love.

In the same way it seems clear to him that a being who can love as he loves, and who yet is doomed to perish, is a 'monster,' a 'dream,' a 'discord'; but this does not give him *assurance* that the soul is not such a monstrosity. On the other hand the 'feelings' of which he speaks in the passages quoted, like the experience of the trance-like state, involve for him no process of inference, do not pretend to 'prove,' and do carry with them the 'assurance' he requires.

Indeed, the language used of these feelings and experiences is of such a kind that one is tempted to ask why, after all, the poet should declare that

> We have but faith: we cannot know;
> For knowledge is of things we see:

since the immediate certainty claimed for these feelings would appear to be, or to justify, something more than faith or a believing of what we cannot prove. Perhaps he distrusted what he could not suppose to be the common possession of mankind. Or perhaps his answer would be found in Wordsworth's lines which tell us that it is

> the most difficult of tasks to *keep*
> Heights which the soul is competent to gain.

She gains them, he might say, in exceptional moments; and the experience of these moments, when she is conscious of being at her best, becomes the light of her life. But they come rarely, and they pass quickly away, or, it may be, are 'stricken thro' with doubt' (xcv.). The soul sinks back and loses its contact with reality, and in the long intervals between these visits must rely on memory and hope, living in the assurance, not of vision or feeling, but of faith in what it once saw and felt. This faith is not an adherence to something which reason declares false, but it is an adherence to something which reason cannot prove to be true; for that which can be 'known' or proved is always a limited and subordinate truth, while the 'systems and creeds' which strive to render intelligible to the soul the experience of her highest moments, lack on the one hand the 'assurance' of those moments themselves, and on the other hand the certainty of the lower truths which can be proven and are not 'worthy proving.' (pp. 49-66)

> *A. C. Bradley, in his* A Commentary on Tennyson's "In Memoriam", *revised edition, 1910. Reprint by Archon Books, 1966, 251 p.*

Alfred Noyes   (essay date 1924)

[*Noyes was an English poet and prose writer temperamentally and stylistically wed to the poetry of an earlier age, particularly that of William Wordsworth and Alfred, Lord Tennyson. Although a prolific writer popular with the reading public, Noyes was never recognized as an important poet by most critics. In the following excerpt, he examines the function of rhythm and meter in Tennyson's poetry.*]

[Rhythm] and metre, so far from making the poet's expression of his thought unnatural, are his chief means (*when he has mastered his instrument*) of bringing his thought into harmony, consciously or unconsciously, with the rhythms of Nature herself. This is one reason why a thought expressed in verse by a master has often a preci-

sion and a universality that makes it immortal. . . . (p. 152)

There is nothing mechanical in that vowel-music which, at its simplest, may appear to be hardly more than the careful balancing of the long ō, ōr, and ōō sounds, one against another, as in innumerable lines of Milton:

> *Sonōrous* metal *blōwing* martial sounds;

or:

> High on a *throne* of royal state that far
> Outshone the wealth of *Ormus* or of Ind,
> Or where the *gorgeous* East with richest hand
> Showers on her kings barbaric pearl and *gold,*
> Satan *exalted* sat;

or, in Tennyson:

> *Mournful Œnone* wandering *forlorn;*

or:

> The *moan* of doves in *immemorial* elms.

In itself this may seem a trivial matter; but it is only one of innumerable and more subtle harmonies of tone that the poet evolves *when he is the master of his instrument,* and evolves quite naturally, because his mastery enables him to forget his instrument, and to express himself through it, just as in the evolution of articulate language itself from sounds that imitated the sounds of Nature an instrument was gradually perfected through which men might express their highest thoughts and deepest emotions. The development of

> Sweet articulate words
> Sweetly divided apart

into an instrument of thought is unconsciously, and again in its simplest form, represented in Tennyson's own song by the Lakes of Killarney. Beginning with the echoes of a bugle among the hills, it gradually rises into a music that has a spiritual significance:

> O hark, O hear, how thin and clear,
>   And thinner, clearer, farther going,
> O, sweet and far, from cliff and scar
>   The horns of elf-land, faintly blowing.
> Blow, bugle, let us hear the purple glens replying;
> Blow, bugle; answer, echoes; dying, dying, dying.
>
> O, Love, they die in yon rich sky;
>   They faint on hill and field and river.
> Our echoes roll from soul to soul
>   And grow for ever and for ever.
> Blow, bugle, blow; set the wild echoes flying;
> And answer, echoes, answer; dying, dying, dying.

The connection between the development of thought and the development of language has been emphasized by many of the evolutionary philosophers. It is worth our while to examine here some sentences in which the materialist, Haeckel, unconsciously conceded to the poets a power of thought above his own:

> In the wider sense language is common to all the higher gregarious animals. It is effected either by touch or by signs, or by sounds having a definite meaning—the song of the bird, the bark of the dog, the chirp of the cricket, are all specimens of animal speech. Only in man, however, has that articulate

speech developed which has enabled his reason to attain such high achievements.

There are certain consequences of that unusually true statement of the eminent materialist; and they have a very direct bearing upon literary values, and upon such poetry as that of Homer, Vergil, Milton, and Tennyson. The bearing is obvious enough upon such direct pieces of onomatopœia as

Myriads of rivulets hurrying through the lawns,
The moan of doves in immemorial elms,
And murmuring of innumerable bees.

Here is language fulfilling one of its primary functions, but on an instrument exquisitely perfected: the soft quick syllables that are crowded into the first of these lines giving the very sound and movement of the brooks; the deep slow vowel-sounds on ō and ōr in the second line, with the repetition of the alliterative m, giving the calm music of the dove-haunted woodland; and the murmuring vowels of the last line giving, to any reader who wishes to make it so, the exact sound of the thing it depicts. It is language used as Vergil used it:

Formosam resonare doces Amaryllida sylvas,

but with more subtlety and more variety than the hexameter allowed.

Again, in the great line from **"Boädicea,"** in that marvellous unrhymed metre of Tennyson's own invention, the onomatopœia is perfect: he describes an army that

Roared as when the roaring breakers boom and blanch on
the precipices.

The reduplication of the roar, the boom of the breaking wave, the sharper sound in the word *blanch* as it whitens after the heavy shock, and the swift hissing retreat in the word "precipices"—it is a perfect imitation in articulate language of the thing it depicts; and, again, it is the method of Vergil:

Panditur interea domus omnipotentis Olympi,

where the very doors of the gods are heard to open. Or again where, in the **"Morte d'Arthur,"** Sir Bedivere, in armour, climbs down through the rocks to the lake:

Dry clashed his harness in the icy caves
And barren chasms, and all to left and right
The bare black cliff clanged round him . . .

The whole passage rings like steel on stone.

The points on which I am dwelling here are, of course, elementary in the technique of poetry, though they are not so elementary as those which are so frequently dwelt upon by writers who have only recently discovered that it is possible to break the regular beat of an iambic pentameter, and have therefore come to the erroneous conclusion that firmness of line and precision of handling are evidence of inferior workmanship, or that a merely vague wavering or fluttering of the syllables, inexpressive of anything but the minor poet's vacuity, is evidence of a super-subtle art. It is only the firmness of the normal line, the backbone of the work, that makes the departure from it significant.

But this is only the beginning of the matter. It is quite demonstrable that, above and beyond all this, the possession of a great and subtle instrument of language connotes in certain poets—and Tennyson is among them—a power to deal with certain profound ideas as no man could possibly deal with them without that instrument. Inability to express certain fine shades of thought, inability to reach certain heights of expression, even for the most eminent men of science, remains nothing less than inability. And this is one of the explanations of the perpetual conflict between certain kinds of materialistic science in the nineteenth century and certain kinds of religion. The failure, on both sides, was in their inability to express the fullness of their own thought; and it was just here that Tennyson, in some degree, through the exquisite perfection of his instrument, came near to reconciling them. When Tennyson speaks of a soul descending

from the distance of the abyss
Of tenfold-complicated change,

he is expressing perfectly an idea which, in that form, is full of significance to every man of science; but has never been expressed in science or philosophy so precisely or completely. This again is demonstrable; and, if any reader doubts it, he has only to produce an equally terse arrangement of words to express the same idea. The possession of this instrument of language connoted in Tennyson the intellectual power that developed it and was in turn developed by it. It became an intellectual and spiritual instrument; and through it he was able to express gradations of thought which, as he developed them, reacted upon his powers of thought; so that, one step leading to another, he was able to attain to heights of vision beyond the range of the philosopher whose exposition of this very development I quoted above. The music which in Tennyson's early poems gave us that marvellous unstopped tone of the fen wind blowing over the reeds, begins with *In Memoriam* to soar into loftier regions.

It is interesting to make a direct comparison of the two methods.

Haeckel, employing his own not very precise instrument, writes as follows:

Our monistic view, that the great cosmic law applies throughout the whole universe, is of the highest moment. It not only involves, on its positive side, the essential unity of the cosmos, but it marks the highest intellectual progress, in that it definitely rules out the three central dogmas of metaphysics—God, freedom and immortality. We assign mechanical causes to phenomena everywhere. To the solution of the world-riddle the nineteenth century has contributed more than all its predecessors. *In a certain sense, indeed, it has found the solution.*

The last sentence is stupendous in its crudity; and the whole paragraph, under analysis, resolves itself into a pitiable exhibition of human weakness. Compare with this clumsy picture of the "universe" the exquisite precision of Tennyson gazing

Where all the starry heavens of space
Are sharpened to a needle's end;

compare with the bland cocksureness of Haeckel the deep inner voice of that passage from *In Memoriam:*

And what I am beheld again
What is, and no man understands;

And out of darkness came the hands
That reach through Nature, moulding men.

Or (to put it on its very simplest ground), with the mud-
dled denials of a materialist who, while declaring that we
know nothing but the report of our own senses, is yet
ready to affirm that these can tell us the whole truth, compare that cry of the great poet to the "living will," and the
higher "monism" of the last great lucid stanza of *In Memoriam:*

> One God, one Law, one Element,
> And one far-off divine event
> To which the whole creation moves.

Whatever else may be said about this conception, it was
one that, demonstrably, Haeckel was unable to formulate,
because he had not the intellectual instrument. The reverence that characterized all the work of Tennyson when he
confronted those fundamental problems proceeded from
clearness of vision, not from haziness or limitation. He
was quite demonstrably able to realize infinitely more of
the vastness and mystery of the universe than the materialistic philosopher could realize. He wished to accept all the
facts and then find their reconciliation, if possible. In one
stanza, for instance, he sets two great arguments one
against the other:

> Who trusted God was Love indeed,
> And Love creation's final law,
> Though Nature, red in tooth and claw
> With rapine, shrieked against the creed.

No phrase has been used more often as a text by the modern pessimists than that "red in tooth and claw" of the
third line. A whole group of writers has specialized in that
particular aspect of things which Tennyson summed up
and expressed in one line of a complicated and highly organized poem. Lord Morley, for instance, used it as a criticism of the faith of Wordsworth; forgetting, apparently,
the faith of the man who originated the phrase. Tennyson,
in giving that clean-cut phrase to the world, demonstrated
by its very vigour that he was more alive to that aspect of
Nature than those who have been forced to borrow the
phrase from him. But he was able to consider a hundred
other aspects also:

> Earth, these solid stars, this weight of body and limb,
> Are they not sign and symbol of thy division from Him?
>
> Speak to Him, thou; for He hears, and spirit with spirit
> can meet.
> Closer is He than breathing, and nearer than hands or feet.

This many-sidedness of Tennyson's work has never been
fully recognized. His early Arthurian poems practically
founded the Pre-Raphaelite school in England. There was
a **"Lady of Shalott"** school; a Lancelot school; and a
school that specialized in a form of beauty that Tennyson
drew, in one golden line, revealing the "warm white apple
of her throat." But in Tennyson the sacred mount of Camelot rose into heights of symbolism. The mighty hall that
Merlin built was built to the golden numbers of modern
philosophy; with its four great zones of sculpture:

> And in the lowest beasts are slaying men,
> And in the second men are slaying beasts,
> And in the third are warriors, perfect men,
> And in the fourth are men with growing wings.

In *Maud,* again, he was the leader of the "spasmodic
school"; but behind the emotional love-story, and the political interpretation that has been thrust upon it, there are
depths of thought unsounded yet by modern criticism. In
form it was unique in our literature—a long dramatic
poem, consisting entirely of lyrics joined together in such
a way that each lyric represents a scene in the action.
Moreover, the metres of these lyrics were quite new in English poetry. Many of them depend for their effect on a development of the device which was noticed above in **"The
Dying Swan,"** the holding over of the rhyme from the line
in which it was expected, for a fuller effect in a subsequent
line. But here the method was occasionally elaborated into
long swiftly moving stanzas:

> We are puppets, Man in his pride, and Beauty fair in her
> flower;
> Do we move ourselves, or are moved by an unseen hand
> at a game
> That pushes us off from the board, and others ever suc-
> ceed?
> Ah, yet we cannot be kind to each other here for an hour;
> We whisper, and hint, and chuckle, and grin at a brother's
> shame;
> However we brave it out, we men are a little breed.

It is a curious fact that many of the modern critics of the
"derivative" poetry of Tennyson have never yet discovered that he was among the greatest of metrical inventors,
and have never yet realized that the originality of many
later poets often consists in reproducing the most conventional measures in a degraded form. It ought to be the aim
of the poet, in his technique, to develop the instrument
which he has inherited. In his heritage he is derivative, he
is bound to be derivative; but in his use of his heritage he
ought to be creative; and it is only the right kind of derivative poet who can ever be creative or, in the truest sense
of the word, original. His thought should naturally lead
him into new developments of rhythm and metre and
music. This is the true line of rebellion against the constraints of the past; but it involves patience and labour. In
recent years the ground has shifted under our feet, and
modern critics are now calling the hunt for the easier way,
"rebellion." The rebellion that achieves anything is difficult, and as long as art. It involves solid work, with hand
and brain; and neither "genius" nor youth can evade it,
if they desire to reach their goal. It is just here that a revival of attention to the work of Tennyson might be salutary
to a generation in a hurry.

The opening satire in *Maud* upon his own age, as fierce as
anything in Juvenal, is another example of the fact that I
tried to emphasize at the beginning of this essay—the
plain fact that Tennyson was the exact opposite of the
complacent accepter of things as they were in the Victorian period:

> Sooner or later I too may passively take the print
> Of the golden age—why not? I have neither hope nor
> trust;
> May make my heart as a mill-stone, set my face as a flint,
> Cheat and be cheated, and die: who knows? We are ashes
> and dust.

These quatrains, with their regular, alternate rhymes, establish the normal measure, which he then proceeds to
elaborate into some of the most exquisite of his metrical
fugues, if that word may be borrowed from music to suggest the effect of the deferred rhyme. . . . There are few

passages in Tennyson, or in any other poet, so masterly as those in which he begins to depart from his established measure, defer the rhyme, and surprise the ear, taking wider and wider curves in the stanza before coming to the full close of music and meaning in the final line.

Music and meaning, I say, for they are inseparable here. Whenever he varies the instance of the rhyme he does it for a purpose, to secure a definite effect, as he did in **"The Dying Swan";** but here the purpose is larger and more significant. In the following passage, for instance, which gives the lover's vision in the dark, the first four lines are again a regular quatrain, rhyming alternately; but, after that, he sweeps off into a magnificent fugue of verse which is fully closed only in the fourteenth line:

> Cold and clear-cut face, why come you so cruelly meek,
> Breaking a slumber in which all spleenful folly was drowned,
> Pale with the golden beam of an eyelash dead on the cheek,
> Passionless, pale, cold face, star-sweet on a gloom profound;
> Woman-like, taking revenge too deep for a transient wrong
> Done but in thought to your beauty, and ever as pale as before
> Growing and fading and growing upon me without a sound,
> Luminous, gem-like, ghost-like, death-like, half the night long
> Growing and fading and growing, till I could bear it no more;
> But arose, and all by myself in my own dark garden-ground,
> Listening now to the tide in its broad-flung ship-wrecking roar,
> Now to the scream of a maddened beach dragged down by the wave,
> Walked in a wintry wind by a ghastly glimmer, and found
> The shining daffodil dead, and Orion low in his grave.

If it be read aloud, with a slight dwelling upon the rhyme-sounds, the exquisite structure of the whole becomes apparent even to those who have no inward ear for verse; but it is almost impossible that work of this kind should be fully appreciated in the English-speaking world to-day. It is only too clear that this poetry requires more of its readers than all but a few can give; and a very few experiments suffice to show that the readers who can follow this music in their minds, or can even follow it metrically, are far fewer than men of letters suspect. This is an additional reason for withstanding the foolish depreciation of our Vergil, and, I may add, it is one of my motives for endeavouring to make these technical details clearer. A world that is rapidly losing its power to take in anything but picture-writing need have little fear that appreciation of "one good custom" in literature will corrupt it, or cramp its own endeavours.

A little later, in *Maud,* after the lovers' meeting at night, there comes a passage of incomparable beauty where again the rhyme arrangement has what I have called the fugue effect. It is an impression of the summer night, as the lover lingers on in the great dark garden, listening to the sound of the sea and watching the mightier movement of the starry heavens. For precision and power in conveying the thousand and one intangible things that make up such an impression—the silence, the peaceful sounds, and the inner depths of passion—this music is unmatched anywhere. It is the supreme "nocturne" of English poetry. Here, if there be any truth in the theories of impressionism, is an impression in poetry more exquisite than any that was ever painted. We need no further truth than the sheer beauty of that summer's night; but here, for once, dreams are caught in a net of twilight, and made to surrender their secret in flawless music, intricate, wild, and precise as the rhythms of the universe, whose divine wildness is folded in a divine law:

> Is that enchanted moan only the swell
> Of the long waves that roll in yonder bay?
> And hark, the clock within, the silver knell
> Of twelve sweet hours that past in bridal white,
> And died to live, long as my pulses play;
> And now by this my love has closed her sight
> And given false death her hand and stolen away
> To dreamful wastes where footless fancies dwell
> Among the fragments of the golden day.

The last ten words give the most precise and beautiful description of the nature and origin of dreams that is to be found in poetry.

After the tragedy, when the lover, outlawed for ever by his blood-guilt, is wandering alone on the Breton coast, there is an almost miraculous touch, so slight, so quiet that its tremendous dramatic significance may easily be missed by those who do not realize that they are here in the presence of a master, whose every syllable demands the closest attention. It is one of the passages which justify the declaration of Jowett about this poem: "No poem since Shakespeare seems to show equal power of the same kind, or equal knowledge of human nature"; and the equally emphatic statement of Ruskin that "no admiration can be too extravagant." In quoting these statements I do not wish to use them as a mere "argument from authority"; but it is ridiculous that any generation should leap to the opposite opinion without proper consideration and without taking the trouble to read the work in question. In one flagrant instance a well-known writer actually denied in public that one of the greatest lines in this poem was to be found in the works of Tennyson. If this were not arrogance gone mad, I certainly do not know what to call it; and I know of no better remedy than a little authority.

The passage, which I have selected as an example of Tennyson's Shakespearean power of depicting human nature and the tremendous forces that attack the soul and are dominated by the soul, is that in which he gives the lover's curious brooding over a minute shell at his feet on the seashore. It can be compared only with the musing of Hamlet over apparently trivial matters; but here there is something added, a suggestion that the besieged mind of the blood-guilty outlawed man is groping, groping for a sign, some little nucleus of evidence that there is a meaning, a guiding hand, a steersman of the universe. It has often been treated as if it were only a pretty interpolation, a lyric, complete in itself; and, in fact, it seems to stand quite aloof from the great tempestuous movement of the preceding and subsequent scenes of the poem. But, in itself, it contains the explanation of this; and it is by that very aloofness that, with almost uncanny power, it suggests the beginnings of the outcast's madness and the question whether the delicate cells of the brain will withstand the shock. It was the device of a supreme master, an incomparable master, to suggest this by a sudden contrast of extreme stillness, and by a passage that in itself is so exquisitely logical and sane:

> See what a lovely shell,
> Small and pure as a pearl,
> Lying close to my foot,
> Frail, but a work divine,
> Made so fairily well
> With delicate spire and whorl,
> How exquisitely minute,
> A miracle of design. . . .
>
> Slight, to be crushed with a tap
> Of my finger-nail on the sand,
> Small, but a work divine,
> Frail, but of force to withstand,
> Year upon year, the shock
> Of cataract seas. . . .

And so the music gradually swells up again, through subtle gradations, now of prayer that his lost love may be comforted, now of hope that the slain man may still be living, and now of intense longing:

> O, that 'twere possible
>   After long grief and pain
> To find the arms of my true love
>   Round me once again!

The frail mind ceases to withstand the terrible forces that are attacking it; its cosmos breaks up into the chaos of madness; and he imagines himself to be dead and buried alive, and unable to sleep. The movement of the lines (which is again a "fugue effect") in those passages of madness, is more fitly to be compared with the first part of Goethe's *Faust* than with *Hamlet;* but in their exact representation of the movement of the troubled mind they are beyond anything that Goethe ever wrote:

> Dead, long dead,
> Long dead!
> And my heart is a handful of dust,
> And the wheels go over my head,
> And my bones are shaken with pain,
> For into a shallow grave they are thrust,
> Only a yard beneath the street,
> And the hoofs of the horses beat, beat,
> The hoofs of the horses beat,
> Beat into my scalp and my brain,
> With never an end to the stream of passing feet,
> Driving, hurrying, marrying, burying,
> Clamour and rumble, and ringing and clatter,
> And here beneath it is all as bad,
> For I thought the dead had peace, but it is not so;
> To have no peace in the grave, is that not sad?
> But up and down and to and fro
> Ever about me the dead men go;
> And then to hear a dead man chatter
> Is enough to drive one mad.

Then, in the final scenes, depicting the gradual return to sanity, the music once again broadens and deepens into a vaster movement, in which the individual finds himself at one with the universal. It is possible, for any one who wishes to do so, to narrow the significance of that last section of a great poem and turn it into a merely local militaristic manifesto. But those who wish it must have forgotten their Shakespeare; and they must be entirely ignorant of the mind of Tennyson as expressed not only here, but in scores of passages throughout his work, on one of the great hopes of the world. That hope will not be furthered

by foolish assaults upon those who have seriously endeavoured to grapple with one of the greatest problems in the evolution of the race, and envisaged it clearly, from a hundred points of view, as in itself it really is.

This breadth of vision is, in fact, the glory of Tennyson. It is as absurd to seize one detail in his presentation of the universe, and attempt to limit him to that, as it would be to describe him as the pessimistic exponent of a Nature "red in tooth and claw." It is equally foolish to concentrate attention on his weaker poems. These things exist in every poet; and, on the whole, in proportion to the magnificent body of his work, they are rarer in Tennyson than in any other English poet. His technical skill; his landscape work; his development from the mere artist into one of those great sage poets, looking out over the whole field of human affairs from a central position; his power of keeping always "an equal mind"; and, in the life of his own heart and intellect, as in all that concerned the State of Man and the City of God, his faith in law as the only guide through what is merely a chaos in many lesser poets;—all these things place him with the greatest on the roll of the world's literature. (pp. 152-67)

> *Alfred Noyes, "Tennyson and Some Recent Critics," in his* Some Aspects of Modern Poetry, *Hodder and Stoughton, 1924, pp. 133-76.*

Harold Nicolson   (essay date 1925)

[*Nicolson was an English diplomat, politician, author, and critic who wrote prolifically on literature, history, and politics. In the following excerpt, he analyzes the strengths and weaknesses of Tennyson's poetry.*]

Were an anthology of Tennyson's poetry to be compiled for the purpose of including only such poems as can appeal directly to the literary taste of to-day, the result might well be both curious and illuminating. Such a volume would, in the first place, be far more bulky than might be imagined. And, in the second place, it would be found, I think, that in any honest and intelligent process of rejection and selection a great many of the more famous and popular poems would be discarded—it would be found, that is, that in the end the Victorian Tennyson, the didactic and the narrative Tennyson, had disappeared, and that someone quite different had emerged in his place. Were I myself to make such a selection, I should from the first be tempted to reject the **Idylls of the King**, the **Idylls of the Hearth,** or at any rate **Enoch Arden,** "**Dora**" and "**Sea Dreams,**" the "Keepsake" verses, most of the ballads and dramatic pieces, and some of the later theological compositions. I should also, I think, reject both the "**Locksley Halls.**" On the other hand, I should include all the "Classical" poems, with the exception of "**Lucretius**" and "**The Death of Oenone**"; I should include nearly all the early Romantic poems, together with the "**Kraken**" and the "**Ode to Memory**"; I should give "**The Vision of Sin**" and "**The Palace of Art**" in their entirety; I should include "**The Northern Farmer,**" while rejecting the other dialect poems; I should give the lyrics from **The Princess** while omitting the main narrative; I should include the whole of "**The Two Voices**" and **Maud** and nearly the whole of **In Memoriam;** I should give "**Boädicea**" and the other experiments in quantity; and finally, I should retain practically all the occasional poems, the dedications, epitaphs and such pieces as **"The Daisy"** and **"Will Waterproof's Lyrical Monologue."**

Such a selection would doubtless be arbitrary and personal. I do not think, however, that, as regards the two general categories of the selected and the rejected, there would to-day be much dispute. For these categories do actually represent a basic divergence of taste between the nineteenth and the twentieth century; they represent, that is, the divergence between absolute or if you prefer it, "pure," poetry and applied poetry. For whereas the Victorians cared mainly for applied poetry, for poetry as a vehicle, either of instruction or diversion, for poetry either as a sermon or a novel; we, caring less for the object or even the form of a poem, insist that it shall possess an "absolute" quality, that it shall be an end unto itself. And it is because of this conviction of "poetry for poetry's sake," that we are particularly apt to resent the intrusion of any extraneous purpose. Now, the great mass of Tennyson's poetry is . . . "applied" poetry; nor, even as such, is it of a very high quality. His didactic poetry suffers from a lack of intellect and education, his dramatic poetry is marred by the fact that, unlike Browning, he was not a creative analyst of character. But if we can isolate this great mass of his "applied," of his didactic and narrative, poetry, there remains a very important residue of "absolute" poetry, and it is because of the value, of the very remarkable value, of this "absolute" poetry that he will survive.

For should anyone doubt the real importance of this distinction between the "absolute" and the "applied" poetry of Tennyson, let him cast a glance at the many incidental or occasional poems which figure in the collected works. Although these poems constitute applied poetry to the ex-

tent that they are written for the avowed purpose of conveying some compliment or message, yet the object of the poem is in effect subsidiary to the subject. The occasional verses of Tennyson stand, that is, midway between his subjective and his objective poetry. For whereas in the latter we are continually disconcerted by the suspicion that the thing could be done far better either in the form of a novel with a purpose or in a volume of philosophical or religious essays, in the former, in his lyrical poetry, we are convinced that verse alone offers the accordant form of expression. In the intermediary category of his occasional verses we may feel, of course, that he could as well have put it all into a letter, yet we must admit that his choice of the forms of verse has raised the communication to a far higher and more memorable level. And the fact that we are so pleasurably surprised by the quality of Tennyson's occasional verse shows, I think, that the moment he can rid himself of the obsession of his "message" and his mission, from that moment he begins to write very good poetry indeed. And if so slight a thing as incidental and often perfunctory versification can cause us pleasure, how far more penetrating should be the effect of those subjective emotions which forced him, almost against his will, to give them lyrical expression! (pp. 272-74)

Tennyson's occasional verses are, as I have said, of considerable interest, not only because of their intrinsic quality, but also because they are generally exempt from the intention of striking some particular attitude or conveying some particular moral. They are taken, so to speak, in his stride, and they show, better than his didactic poems or his cautionary tales, how wide, and indeed lavish, was his range of interest. They show him, moreover, in a pleasant light as a quite human, quite urbane, almost genial man of culture. They are an invaluable antidote to the Victorian fog which obscures so many of his poems. Even the odes which he would write from time to time in his official capacity as Poet Laureate are better than those of his predecessors, infinitely better than those of his immediate successor and imitator in that office. They produce the same pleasurable feeling of satisfaction at the achievement of something intricate and deliberate, as is conveyed by a polished copy of Latin verses; and, of course, the Wellington ode is in a class by itself. But apart from the official poems, there is a great mass of incidental verse, dedications, epitaphs and the like, which, whether they be incised with the stately condensation of some Roman inscription, or composed with the flowing lucidity of some of the lighter odes of Horace, carry with them a very welcome and a very mellow savour of the humanities.

Take this, for instance, from the lines to F. D. Maurice:—

Three stanzas of The Princess, *written by Tennyson for presentation to a friend.*

> You'll have no scandal while you dine,
> But honest talk and wholesome wine,
>   And only hear the magpie gossip
> Garrulous under a roof of pine:
>
> For groves of pine on either hand,
> To break the blast of winter, stand;
>   And further on, the hoary Channel
> Tumbles a billow on chalk and sand;
>
> Where, if below the milky steep
> Some ship of battle slowly creep,
>   And on thro' zones of light and shadow
> Glimmer away to the lonely deep,

We might discuss the Northern sin
Which made a selfish war begin;
   Dispute the claims, arrange the chances;
Emperor, Ottoman, which shall win.

Even better, perhaps, are the lines to FitzGerald, in which, after recalling his visit to Woodbridge in 1876, and the pigeons and the vegetarianism of it all, Tennyson sends his friend **"Tiresias"**:—

         which you will take
My Fitz, and welcome, as I know,
   Less for its own than for the sake
Of one recalling gracious times,
   When, in our younger London days,
You found some merit in my rhymes,
   And I more pleasure in your praise.

One is pleased by the urbanity of this, by the supple Horatian felicity with which the last line closes the movement; and, indeed, there is a real place in poetry for the urbane. (pp. 274-76)

Equally intermediate in character is Tennyson's treatment of Nature. For although much of his Nature poetry is, it must be owned, written with the old desire to instruct, with the wish, even, to display his powers of observation, or his peculiar felicity in condensing such observation into accurate and concentrated expression, yet one has but to read through any of the longer poems to be pleasantly stimulated at recurrent intervals by some chance simile or illustration of Nature such as opens a sudden rift of blue in the heavy clouds which hang so often upon his poetry. It is not that Tennyson's Nature poetry is as a rule more subjective or more "absolute" than his other themes—it is that, in approaching the eternal and illimitable inspiration of Nature, the emotional ecstasy depends perhaps more upon the temperament of the reader than upon the imaginative impulse of the poet himself. For if the reader is at all sensitive to the inspiration of Nature, it will require but the slightest stimulus of "recognition," some incidental allusion vivid or merely accurate, in order to inflame his own imaginative recollection, and to afford him that startled realisation of the identity of the personal with the eternal which is, in effect, the essence of the highest poetic appreciation. As a theme, Nature herself contains all the necessary elements for such appreciation: she combines, in a perpetual surprise, the minute and the infinite, the precise and the unknowable, the momentary and the eternal. One has but to feel assured that the poet is himself sensitive to these sublime contrasts for his Nature poetry to be affected almost automatically, and by processes which, if applied to other themes, might well fail to produce any nervous vibration. And with Tennyson at least you have such an assurance. One of the few subjective poems which he wrote on this theme figures fittingly upon the base of his most appropriate statue, that rugged masterpiece of Watts which stands in shambling untidiness under the Lincolnshire sky and in the shadow of the three cathedral towers which grace and dominate the wide, sad county of his birth:—

Flower in the crannied wall,
I pluck you out of the crannies,
I hold you here, root and all, in my hand,
Little flower—but *if* I could understand
What you are, root and all, and all in all,
I should know what God and man is.

It is not, however, merely this sense of the spirituality of Nature which gives to Tennyson's treatment of the subject so peculiar an interest. It is also that his observation of Nature is curiously concentrated and detailed. This concentration arises, not only from his unwillingness to record facts which he had not actually experienced, or to describe phenomena which he had not actually examined, but also from the more practical cause of his extreme short sight. The result is that the Nature poetry of Tennyson so often deals, on the one hand, with the tiny and incidental phenomena of the foreground, and, on the other, with the vast and illimitable movements in the background: there is no middle distance. And, as a result, the essential contrast of Nature—the contrast between the microscopic and the illimitable, between the speedwell and the stars—is continually, even if only indirectly, emphasised. And the emotional reality of this contrast gives to Tennyson's Nature poetry, whether he be speaking of the minute or of the infinite, a very peculiar significance.

It is important, in discussing Tennyson's powers of observation, to keep in mind this emotional reality, since there are moments when his habits of accuracy, his method of storing and "working up later" some observed phenomena—the rippled shadow on a cow's neck when drinking, the foam flakes scudding along the beach at Mablethorpe, the flat leaves of water-lilies tugging at their stems in a gust of wind, the little tufts of thrift upon some Cornish headland—might savour otherwise of the perfunctory, or even of the prosaic. And it must be admitted that at times Tennyson's habits of accuracy, his predilection for the scientific, his sudden relapses into botany, his interest in pond life, are apt to throw the shadow of "Madam How and Lady Why" over some of his most stimulating references to Nature. It is unfortunate, for instance, on reading in Section X of *In Memoriam* lines as good as:—

Than if with thee the roaring wells
   Should gulf him fathom-deep in brine;
   And hands so often clasp'd in mine
Should toss with tangle and with shells,

to turn to the note and find the following:—

   Section X, verse v, *tangle,* or "oar-weed" (*Laminaria digitata*).

But then the notes to the Eversley Edition should in any case be read only by the healthy-minded.

If we are resolved, therefore, to steel ourselves against these relapses into the accurate, and to bear in mind Tennyson's essentially emotional attitude towards Nature, his powers of observation and portrayal will then become for us of great value and interest. For how often, and with what economy of language, does he set before us such penetrating touches as the soft smell of the earth after rain, as the colours of the autumn woods reeling behind the smoke of burning weeds, as the crumpled leaf of a poppy when first liberated from its sheath, as the rustle of the poplar leaves like the patter of rain, as the breeze of early dawn stirring the flowers of a garden, or as the sound in every mood of falling waters? It may be said, of course, that his pictures of Nature savour too much of the Rectory garden, of the soft, steaming monochrome of the Isle of Wight, of the trim complacency of Surrey; that they recall a little too vividly the water-colours of Mrs. Allingham.

There are moments when this is true enough, such as the description of the cottage-gardens in **"Aylmer's Field"**:—

> Her art, her hand, her counsel all had wrought
> About them: here was one that, summer-blanch'd,
> Was parcel-bearded with the traveller's-joy
> In autumn, parcel ivy-clad; and here
> The warm-blue breathings of a hidden hearth
> Broke from a bower of vine and honeysuckle:
> One look'd all rosetree, and another wore
> A close-set robe of jasmine sown with stars:
> This had a rosy sea of gillyflowers
> About it; this. . . .
> A lily-avenue climbing to the doors;
> One, almost to the martin-haunted eaves
> A summer burial deep in hollyhocks.

All this perhaps is too sweet to be wholly true. But in the main the Nature poetry of Tennyson, restricted as it is to his actual range of observation, is a faithful and stimulating picture of English country scents and sounds and habits. (pp. 277-80)

If Tennyson's appreciation of the more tender processes of Nature has, perhaps, too domestic a flavour, his sense of the infinities of sea and sky is on a larger, and indeed a sterner, scale. Ever since his schoolboy days, the sense of water, the sound of water, had meant a great deal to him, and his earlier poems abound with impressions of the great North Sea rollers booming along the flat beach at Mablethorpe. The Isle of Wight, when it came, furnished him with other scenes and echoes, and with the scream of the shingle sucked back by the retreating wave. His visits to Cornwall gave him one simile, at least, of arresting truth and beauty:—

> So dark a forethought roll'd about his brain
> As on a dull day in an Ocean cave
> The blind wave feeling round his long sea-hall
> In silence.

His voyage to Norway in 1858 remains in one of his few deep-sea similes:—

> as a wild wave in the wide North Sea
> Green-glimmering toward the summit, bears, with all
> Its stormy crests that smoke against the skies
> Down on a bark, and overbears the bark . . .

And finally it was the slow movement of Lymington harbour-mouth which inspired what is perhaps the finest of all his references to the sea:—

> But such a tide as moving seems asleep,
>   Too full for sound and foam,
> When that which drew from out the boundless deep
>   Turns again home.

Of his sense of the infinity of space I have already spoken, but some further mention must here be made of the many striking passages in which he speaks of the stars. His knowledge of astronomy was slightly above that of the ordinary amateur, and we hear of him in the 'sixties going down frequently to Fairfax road to look through Lockyer's six-inch equatorial. And after dinner, sometimes, at Farringford, he would take them all on to the roof and point out Venus. "Can you imagine," he would say, as he said later in the second **"Locksley Hall,"** "roaring London and raving Paris *there* in that point of peaceful light?" "While I said *there*," he would add, "the earth has whirled twenty miles." Scattered throughout his poems there are

many passages which show how deep was the feeling which possessed him for the majesty and the distance of the stars. As early as the first **"Locksley Hall"** we hear of "great Orion sloping slowly to the West," or we find him watching the Pleiades:—

> rising thro' the mellow shade,
> Glitter like a swarm of fire-flies tangled in a silver braid.

And later, when his renown had grown to wider proportions, he would gaze at the Nebula in the sword of Orion and be filled with dismay at the insignificance of human fame:—

> A single misty star
> Which is the second in a line of stars
> That seem a sword beneath a belt of three,
> I never gazed upon it but I dreamt
> Of some vast charm concluded in that star
> To make fame nothing.

If, therefore, we can find in the felicitous humanism of Tennyson's incidental verses a relief from the heavy shallowness of his didactic and narrative poetry; if we can discover in his loving and precise observation of Nature an interest which is quite detached from the usual conception of him as devoted only to the applied purposes of poetry; we can also, I think, look to his technical proficiency as a master of the English language to provide a genuine stirring of purely literary enjoyment.

I have not the aptitude, nor indeed the space, to discuss in detail the technical aspects of Tennyson's prosody and language. Much has been written on the subject. . . . It may be said, perhaps, that he never fully justified the prosodic promise of his early poems, which, tentative as they were, yet showed a metrical originality such as causes us to wonder at the contemporary strictures of Coleridge and the later criticisms of Swinburne. The extraordinary dexterity with which, by the shifting of the stress, by the interchange of vowel sounds, and by the use, and sometimes the abuse, of alliteration, he was able to vary the inherent monotony of *In Memoriam;* the mastery which he abundantly displayed in the trochaic measure—a measure so naturally adapted to the English language; the success of his experiments in quantity, of such pieces as the Phalaecian hendecasyllables, or **"The Battle of Brunanburh,"** make one regret that he was not more often, as in **"The Daisy,"** tempted to adopt original verse forms, and that he confined himself predominantly to blank verse, in which, proficient as he indubitably was, he did not possess the skill of Browning or the mellow movement even of Matthew Arnold. One has only to read the panting, spasmodic interjections of *Maud,* or the frenzied sweep of **"Boädicea,"** the rattling galliambics of which, so unlike the effeminacy of the **"Attis,"** have all the fire of Borodine's *Igor,* to realise what a remarkable talent Tennyson possessed for accommodating the movement of his verse to its subject, for marking the gradations of his theme by the subtlest changes of key or intonation.

His skill in this important and intricate branch of his art is conveniently illustrated by his famous lines to Catullus. He had, in the summer of 1880, been travelling in the Dolomites with his son, Hallam Tennyson. They had gone down to Garda and had rowed out one evening to the peninsula of Sirmio. As they rowed across the lake the poignant movement of the old Catullan choriambics, fused with the elegiacs to his brother, mingled in the poet's consciousness with the rhythmic beating of the oar:—

> Paene insularum, Sirmio, insularumque.

and he produced the following famous stanza:—

> Row us out from Desenzano, to your Sirmione row!
> So they row'd, and there we landed—"O venusta Sirmio"—
> There to me thro' all the groves of olive in the summer glow,
> There beneath the Roman ruin where the purple flowers grow,
> Came the "Ave atque Vale" of the Poet's hopeless woe,
> Tenderest of the Roman poets, nineteen hundred years ago,
> "Frater Ave atque Vale"—as we wandered to and fro
> Gazing at the Lydian laughter of the Garda Lake below
> Sweet Catullus' all-but-island, olive-silvery Sirmio!

The subtlety with which these lines are constructed, instinctive and subconscious as they probably were, merits some analysis. For, of the two currents of emotion which gave birth to the poem, the first is the actual beauty of the moment—the flat lake, the encircling mountains and the Italian boatmen, singing, doubtless, to their oars—and the second is the plangent recollection of Catullus—of how, so many years ago, he had looked upon this little jutting strip of olives as his own, how he had come so gaily back to it from Bithynia, and how he had lost the brother whom he loved. There are therefore two musical *motifs* in the poem—the *motif* of the rowers, represented by the vowel "o," and the *motif* of Catullus, represented by the broad Roman "a." The music is set to eight rhythmic beats, as is general in all such water songs from the Volga to the Elbe, and in the first line, as well as in the first two beats of the second, the rowing motif predominates. With the broader vowel of "landed," however, it ceases to obtrude—becomes indeed an undertone to what follows and passes in recurrent echoes among the hills. The transition between the "o" motif and the "a" motif is marked by the intermediately broad vowel of "there," which word is repeated and echoed predominantly in the two lines that follow. In the fifth line, the "a" *motif* is definitely introduced by the "Ave atque Vale," which is repeated in the opening of the seventh line, and echoed in the lesser tones of "wandered," "at," "Lydian," "laughter," "Garda" in the verse that follows. And the poem ends with the sighing rustle of the concluding line, in which the two dominant *motifs* are fused in a crowd of gentler vowels. (pp. 282-86)

This very dexterous manipulation of vowel sounds can be illustrated from other poems of Tennyson, and might be said, indeed, to constitute his most original contribution to the harmonics of the English language. We have the authority of Sir C. Stanford that "it was his perfection of vowel balance which made his poetry so difficult to set to music," and he was himself fully aware of his talent in this direction, and would at times exploit it somewhat unduly. He would take infinite trouble to exclude the harsher gutturals and sibilants from his verse, and he had a prejudice against the vowels "i" and "ē." He even went so far on one occasion as to inform Rawnsley that "the finest line he had ever written" was:—

> The mellow ouzel fluted in the elm.

It must be admitted, indeed, that Tennyson was apt to ex-

aggerate the importance of harmonics, and to rely a little too often and too lavishly upon the mere devices of verse—upon onomatopœia, epanaphora and alliteration. (pp. 286-87)

[Tennyson's use of the onomatopœic device] was a talent which was inherent in him, and as early as **"Mariana"** we find:—

> The sparrow's chirrup on the roof,
>   The slow clock ticking, and the sound
> Which to the wooing wind aloof
>   The poplar made. . . .

In later years the thing became a habit, and of almost irritating frequency. For while one can well admire the "moan of doves in immemorial elms," the "murmuring of innumerable bees," and the "long wash of Australasian seas," one cannot wholly welcome such expressions as "oilily bubbled up the mere," or such a simile as:—

> like an iron-clanging anvil banged
> With hammers.

Nor can the device be wholly legitimate when applied to visual and not to aural impressions, as in the following:—

> And I rode on and found a mighty hill
> And on the top a city wall'd: the spires
> Prick'd with incredible pinnacles into heaven.

But at its best the use which Tennyson makes of onomatopœia is effective enough, and one cannot but respect the skill with which the introduction of the four leading labials in the last two lines of the following passage marks the transition from the preceding gutturals:—

> Dry clashed his harness in the icy caves
> And barren chasms, and all to left and right
> The bare black cliff clang'd round him as he based
> His feet on juts of slipping crag that rang
> Sharp-smitten with the dint of armed heels—
> And on a sudden, lo! the level lake
> And the long glories of the winter moon.

Coupled with Tennyson's use of onomatopœia must be mentioned his employment of the devices of epanaphora, or repetition, and alliteration. The former he could use, at times, with great effect, as when:—

> The rain of heaven and their own bitter tears,
> Tears, and the careless rain of heaven mixt
> Upon their faces;

or even when:—

> The lizard, with his shadow on the stone
> Rests like a shadow;

but in his narrative poems, and with the purpose of giving an impression of speed and continuity to his blank verse, he is apt to employ the device with too much frequency, and we find, for instance, in a passage of *The Princess,* fourteen out of seventeen consecutive lines beginning with the same word "and."

His abuse of the trick of alliteration has been severely commented on. He derived it, doubtless, as he derived his onomatopœia, from too appreciative a study of the *Æneid.* But at times, and in combination with onomatopœia, he can use it with almost miraculous effect, as in the inter-

change of the letters "d," "s" and "h" in the famous Wye
passage of *In Memoriam:*—

> The Danube to the Severn gave
>   The darken'd heart that beat no more;
>   They laid him by the pleasant shore,
> And in the hearing of the wave.
>
> There twice a day the Severn fills;
>   The salt sea-water passes by,
>   And hushes half the babbling Wye,
> And makes a silence in the hills.
>
> The Wye is hush'd nor moved along,
>   And hush'd my deepest grief of all,
>   When fill'd with tears that cannot fall,
> I brim with sorrow drowning song.

I have dealt hitherto with the more technical aspects of
Tennyson's style, its general beauties being sufficiently obvious and familiar. The development of his style was, in
truth, as has been said, a progression "from the luxuriant
to the heroic." The early affectations, the lispings of
"Claribel," the abundance of epithets, the abuse of double
or archaic words disappeared with his increasing power of
selection and condensation. This power of condensation,
which was indeed remarkable, led him at times into irritating tricks of periphrasis and elaboration. The sea becomes
"the ocean mirrors rounded large," a poacher appears as
"the nightly wirer of the innocent hare," and "the foaming
grape of Eastern France" is, I suppose, to be interpreted
as champagne. Such tricks are harmless enough, and have
their precedent in even greater poetry, but there are occasions when Tennyson's use of periphrasis is illegitimate,
in that it deliberately produces a false sense of beauty. The
lines, for instance:—

> Or where the kneeling hamlet drains
> The chalice of the grapes of God,

do not, as one vaguely hopes, refer to some village in the
Alban hills, but to early service at Clevedon parish
church; and the simplicity essential to his meaning is
marred by the elaboration of the language in which that
meaning is conveyed. Nor am I one of those who relish the
verbal contortions in which the game-pie of **"Audley
Court"** is so intricately involved; for food, apart from
drink, is a subject for epic poetry alone.

Such elaboration is not, however, the dominant characteristic of Tennyson's maturer style, and indeed, one can observe in his later poems a determined endeavour to prefer
the direct to the elaborate, and even the Anglo-Saxon to
the Latin word. Nor does he indulge over-much in the device, so popular with English poets from Milton to Fleck-
er, of enlivening the grey colours of our native speech by
the introduction of resonant and flamboyant foreign
names. He is at his best, and he knows that he is at his best,
in the flow of direct and simple narrative, as in the nine
initial lines with which the scenery of the sea-village is
sketched as the introduction to *Enoch Arden.* And indeed
the impression which emerges from any unbiassed reading
of Tennyson is not that of his many tricks and affectations,
but of a very outright simplicity, continuity and stateliness; more definitely, perhaps, of a remarkable gift of condensation, of a condensation which could produce such
lines as the following:—

> And one, the reapers at their sultry toil.

> In front they bound the sheaves. Behind
> Were realms of upland, prodigal in oil,
>   And hoary to the wind,

and of a directness which could evolve:—

> Not wholly in the busy world, nor quite
> Beyond it, blooms the garden that I love.
> News from the humming city comes to it
> In sound of funeral or of marriage bells;
> And, sitting muffled in dark leaves, you hear
> The windy clanging of the Minster clock;
> Although between it and the garden lies
> A league of grass, wash'd by a slow broad stream,
> That, stirred with languid pulses of the oar,
> Waves all its lazy lilies, and creeps on,
> Barge-laden, to three arches of a bridge,
> Crown'd with the Minster towers.
>
>   The fields between
> Are dewy-fresh, browsed by deep-udder'd kine,
> And all about the large lime-feathers blow,
> The lime a summer home of murmurous wings. . . .

(pp. 288-92)

In its technical and narrow sense lyrical poetry implies a
form of words written to be sung to the lyre or other accompaniment; in its applied and extended meaning it is interpreted as the poetry of personal experience or emotion.
The latter interpretation is the more comprehensive and
important. The former, however, is not without its interest
and its instances. For the songs of Tennyson, written separately as interludes to break the flow of narrative, are
among the best in the English language, and in them we
find, as rarely in his other poems, the absolute vatic ecstasy; the "purest" poetry, perhaps, which he ever composed.
For in his songs, and predominantly in the songs incorporated in *The Princess,* his poetic energy was concentrated
wholly on the magic of words. He sang, for once, "but as
the linnets sing"; he sang, for once, "without a conscience
and an aim." The result comes to one with a shock of delight. For they vibrate, these songs of Tennyson, with
something vague and poignant, with:—

> I knew not what of wild and sweet,
> Like that strange song I heard Apollo sing
> While Ilion like a mist rose into towers.

And they vibrate with more than this—they vibrate, at
last, with that "divine excess," with that glimpse of the Di-
onysiac, that unmistakable sense of impulsive continuity
falling haphazard upon the right, the only word; they vibrate with that conviction of the inevitable and the inimitable, with that conviction of the inspired, which only the
greatest lyric poets can achieve in the moments when they
feel the force and beauty of their own genius:—

> For Love is of the valley, come thou down
> And find him; by the happy threshold, he,
> Or hand in hand with Plenty in the maize,
> Or red with spirted purple of the vats,
> Or fox-like in the vine; nor cares to walk
> With Death and Morning or the silver horns,

or again:—

> Now sleeps the crimson petal, now the white;
> Nor waves the cypress in the palace walk;
> Nor winks the gold fin in the porphyry font:
> The fire-fly wakens: waken thou with me.
>
> Now droops the milk-white peacock like a ghost,

And like a ghost she glimmers on to me.

Now lies the earth all Danäe to the stars,
And all thy heart lies open unto me.

Now slides the silent meteor on, and leaves
A shining furrow, as thy thoughts in me.

Now folds the lily all her sweetness up,
And slips into the bosom of the lake:
So fold thyself, my dearest, thou, and slip
Into my bosom and be lost in me.

This poem is clearly beyond criticism and even elucidation. The sheer melody of the verse, unaided as it is by the agency of rhyme, is by itself remarkable. The poem can stand, I think, second only to the odes of Keats, to which, in the quality of its inspiration, it bears a resemblance, faint but unmistakable. And unconscious, also. For although the critic may find in the skill with which the word "up" is placed at the end of the last stanza an echo of the even greater skill which induced Keats to construct the Ruth stanza of the "Nightingale" upon the corner-stone of "hath," yet with Tennyson it is evident and welcome that this song at least came all unconsciously, and with such elaboration only as is given to something born already essentially completed from the soul.

Nor are his other songs, although they seldom reel to the same drunken sense of beauty, much inferior in quality. The first verse, at least, of **"Ask Me No More,"** with the sad echo of the hollow-toned vowels in which he so delighted, and with the skilful shifting of the stress in the fourth line, is haunting enough:—

Ask me no more: the moon may draw the sea;
The cloud may stoop from heaven and take the shape,
With fold to fold, of mountain or of cape;
But O too fond, when have I answer'd thee?

Ask me no more.

Nor can I see how the two following verses, familiar as they are, can fail to be classed in the first rank of lyrical poetry:—

Ah, sad and strange as in dark summer dawns
The earliest pipe of half-awaken'd birds
To dying ears, when unto dying eyes
The casement slowly grows a glimmering square;
So sad, so strange, the days that are no more.

Dear as remember'd kisses after death,
And sweet as those by hopeless fancy feigned
On lips that are for others; deep as love,
Deep as first love, and wild with all regret;
O Death in Life, the days that are no more.

And with what relief from the panting spasms of *Maud* do we slide into:—

There has fallen a splendid tear
From the passion flower at the gate.
She is coming, my dove, my dear;
She is coming, my life, my fate;
The red rose cries, "She is near, she is near,"
And the white rose weeps, "She is late."
The larkspur listens, "I hear, I hear,"
And the lily whispers, "I wait."

Few indeed are the occasions when Tennyson rises to his own poetic level, when the tremulous intensity of his emotion wells up suddenly within him and passes into that plangent wistfulness to which his lyre was so perfectly attuned. "A little flash" will come to him at moments, "a mystic hint," and, suddenly, he will write songs such as these, or let fall a verse such as:—

Between the loud streams and the trembling stars,

or conceive **"Ulysses,"** and the inspired line:—

And see the great Achilles whom we knew,

or strike upon the infinite beauty of the conclusion to **"Tithonus":**—

Thou seest all things, thou wilt see my grave:
Thou wilt renew thy beauty morn by morn;
I earth in earth forget these empty courts,
And thee returning on thy silver wheels.

It is with an almost melancholy satisfaction that one cites these scattered instances of poetic ecstasy, regretting, as one cannot but regret, how few they are, how seldom they occur, how rarely—how very rarely—the wide and continuous middle level of his poetry is relieved even by the swallow-flights of song. One feels that, like the youthful horseman of the **"Vision of Sin":**—

He rode a horse with wings, that would have flown,
But that his heavy rider kept him down.

This may be so. But even if we are of those who resent the fact that Tennyson was so emphatically not "of the howling dervishes of song," we must admit, I think, that his "middle level" is in itself a remarkable achievement of stately continuity and craftsmanship. (pp. 293-96)

And then there is *In Memoriam.* Not that artificially constructed synthesis which appeared in 1850, with its prologue and its epilogue, with its three arbitrary divisions of Despair, Regret and Hope, ticked off symmetrically by the successive Christmas Odes; not the theological treatise on the conflict between faith and doubt, religion and dogma, belief and science; but the original Μηνισ; those plangent elegies which were scribbled in the old account-book, scribbled in odd unhappy moments during the seven years from 1833 to 1840; those lonely, wistful, frightened elegies. (pp. 296-97)

For the most durable impression of *In Memoriam* is that of a poem which renders, with an infinitely subtle melody, the "muffled motions" of a human soul overwhelmed by some immense personal disaster, of a soul crushed suddenly by irreparable grief. There is the first numbed insensibility to what has happened—his mind dwells only on the physical aspect, the dumb thought that "he is gone," the instinctive fusion of Arthur Hallam with the ship sailing slowly with his coffin from Trieste; the relief at feeling that he is at last in England; the incredible fact that one so vivid and so intimate should suddenly have become speechless and unreveal'd—the cry "Where wert thou, brother, those four days?" And, on the heels of this, the identification of his own blind sorrow with the dumb movements of Nature:—

But Summer on the steaming floods,
And Spring that swells in narrow brooks,
And Autumn, with a noise of rooks,
That gather in the waning woods,

And every pulse of wind and wave
Recalls, in change of light or gloom,

> My old affection of the tomb,
> And my prime passion in the grave.

In section after section we have the sensitive response of his bruised and languid nerves to the moods of Nature. Whether it be that first sad October:—

> Calm is the morn without a sound,
>   Calm as to suit a calmer grief,
>   And only thro' the faded leaf
> The chestnut pattering to the ground:
>
> Calm and deep peace on this high wold,
>   And on these dews that drench the furze,
>   And all the silvery gossamers
> That twinkle into green and gold:
>
> Calm and still light on yon great plain
>   That sweeps with all its autumn bowers,
>   And crowded farms and lessening towers,
> To mingle with the bounding main:
>
> Calm and deep peace in this wide air,
>   These leaves that redden to the fall;
>   And in my heart, if calm at all,
> If any calm, a calm despair,

or the wilder month that followed:—

> To-night the winds begin to rise
>   And roar from yonder dropping day;
>   The last red leaf is whirl'd away,
> The rooks are blown about the skies;
>
> The forest crack'd, the waters curl'd,
>   The cattle huddled on the lea;
>   And wildly dash'd on tower and tree
> The sunbeam strikes along the world:
>
> And but for fancies, which aver
>   That all thy motions gently pass
>   Athwart a plane of molten glass,
> I scarce could brook the strain and stir
>
> That makes the barren branches loud;
>   And but for fear it is not so,
>   The wild unrest that lives in woe
> Would dote and pore on yonder cloud
>
> That rises upward always higher,
>   And onward drags a labouring breast,
>   And topples round the dreary west,
> A looming bastion fringed with fire.

With this despair mingles the galling sense of waste, of resentment almost, that he who bore "the weight of all the hopes of half the world," that so radiant a promise, should have been quenched as if gratuitously. Such thoughts flit sombrely, with sad, incessant wings pulsating in the dim recesses of the poet's grief, and

>   circle moaning in the air
> Is this the end? Is this the end?

They kill within him the interest of life itself, the joy even of the coming spring, the love of home; they "make a desert in the mind"; the "purple from the distance dies"; the "bases of his life" are drowned in tears. And through this veil of tears looms gradually the great problem of immortality, the agonised faith in ultimate reunion, the struggling hope, the torturing doubt, the dread of Nature's vicious cruelty:—

> I falter where I firmly trod,
>   And falling with my weight of cares
>   Upon the great world's altar stairs
> That slope thro' darkness up to God
>
> I stretch lame hands of faith, and grope,
>   And gather dust and chaff, and call
>   To what I feel is Lord of all,
> And faintly trust the larger hope.

In the pauses of such bitter spasms he dwells with almost morbid insistence on the past: he forces himself to recall the features and the accents of his friend, he visualises little vivid incidents in that dawn-golden time, he traces lovingly the course of those four years of friendship, the "tracts that pleased us well," the "path by which we twain did go"; and in an agony he cries:—

> How changed from when it ran
>   Thro' lands where not a leaf was dumb;
>   But all the lavish hills would hum
> The murmur of a happy Pan.

And thus gradually, through bitter reactions and long pauses of uncertainty, he works out his conviction of love and immortality. But the interest of *In Memoriam,* to me at least, centres not in the triumphant notes of its conclusions, but in the moods of terror and despair through which the ultimate conviction is attained.

Again and again this terror would seize and rack him, leaving him with quivering pulses sobbing as:—

> An infant crying in the night,
> An infant crying for the light
> And with no language but a cry.

There are moments, such as the first anniversary of Hallam's death, when the wan hopelessness of it all descends upon him as a cloud:—

> Risest thou thus, dim dawn, again,
>   And howlest, issuing out of night,
>   With blasts that blow the poplar white,
> And lash with storm the streaming pane?
>
> Day, when my crown'd estate begun
>   To pine in that reverse of doom,
>   Which sicken'd every living bloom,
> And blurr'd the splendour of the sun;
>
> Who usherest in the dolorous hour
>   With thy quick tears that make the rose
>   Pull sideways, and the daisy close
> Her crimson fringes to the shower; . . .
>
> Lift as thou may'st thy burthen'd brows
>   Thro' clouds that drench the morning star,
>   And whirl the ungarner'd sheaf afar,
> And sow the sky with flying boughs,
>
> And up thy vault with roaring sound
>   Climb thy thick noon, disastrous day;
>   Touch thy dull goal of joyless gray,
> And hide thy shame beneath the ground.

And there are moments, "in the dead unhappy night, and when the rain is on the roof," when he is in the dark and alone, when he lies there with the moon upon his bed, and the sense of night around him—moments when his nerves ache with fear and loneliness; moments when he sees:—

> A gulf that ever shuts and gapes,
> A hand that points, and palled shapes
> In shadowy thoroughfares of thought;

And crowds that stream from yawning doors,
 And shoals of pucker'd faces drive;
 Dark bulks that tumble half alive,
And lazy lengths on boundless shores.

It was at moments such as this, when "the blood creeps and the nerves prick," that he would yearn with passionate intensity for Hallam, that he would lie there crushed by his own fear and loneliness, and that he would cry out in agony:—

Speak to me from the stormy sky!
 The wind is loud in holt and hill,
 It is not kind to be so still,
Speak to me, dearest, lest I die.

This haunting wail of fear and loneliness piercing at moments through the undertones of *In Memoriam,* echoes a note which runs through all the poetry of Tennyson, and which, when once apprehended, beats with pitiful persistence on the heart. It proceeds from that grey region between the conscious and the unconscious; from that dim glimmering land where mingle the "Voices of the Dark" and the "Voices of the Day"; from the uncertain shadow-edges of consciousness in which stir the evanescent memories of childhood or the flitting shapelessness of half-forgotten dreams. It is a cry that mingles with the mystery of wide spaces, of sullen sunsets or of sodden dawns; the cry of a child lost at night time; the cry of some stricken creature in the dark; "the low moan of an unknown sea":—

The first gray streak of earliest summer-dawn
The last long stripe of waning crimson gloom,
As if the late and early were but one—
A height, a broken grange, a grove, a flower
Had murmurs "Lost and gone and gone":
A breath, a whisper—Some divine farewell—
Desolate sweetness—far and far away.

And thus, in that "ever-moaning battle in the mist" which was the spiritual life of Tennyson, there were sudden penetrating moments when he would obtain:—

A glimpse of that dark world where I was born;

when, once again, the "old mysterious glimmer" would steal into his soul, and when, in a sombre flash of vision, he would see his life:—

all dark and red—a tract of sand,
 And someone pacing there alone,
Who paced for ever in a glimmering land,
 Lit with a low large moon.

To the vibration of so sad a cadence I should wish to leave him, trusting that the ultimate impression, thus attuned, will prove more poignant and more durable than any hollow reverence for what was once admired. The age of Tennyson is past; the ideals which he voiced so earnestly have fallen from esteem. The day may come, perhaps, when the conventions of that century will once again inspire the thoughtful or animate the weak. But, for the moment, it is not through these that any interest can be evoked. And thus, if we consider it reasonable and right that Tennyson should also stand among the poets, let us, for the present, forget the delicate Laureate of a cautious age; the shallow thought, the vacant compromise; the honeyed idyll, the complacent ode; let us forget the dulled monochrome of

his middle years, forget the magnolia and the roses, the indolent Augusts of his island-home; forget the laurels and the rhododendrons.

Let us recall only the low booming of the North Sea upon the dunes; the grey clouds lowering above the wold; the moan of the night wind on the fen; the far glimmer of marsh-pools through the reeds; the cold, the half-light, and the gloom. (pp. 297-303)

> *Harold Nicolson, in his* Tennyson: Aspects of His Life, Character and Poetry, *Houghton Mifflin Company, 1925, 308 p.*

T. S. Eliot (essay date 1936)

[*Perhaps the most influential poet and critic to write in the English Language during the first half of the twentieth century, Eliot is closely identified with many of the qualities denoted by the term Modernism: experimentation, formal complexity, artistic and intellectual eclecticism, and a classicist's view of the artist working at an emotional distance from his or her creation. He introduced a number of terms and concepts that strongly affected critical thought in his lifetime, among them the idea that poets must be conscious of the living tradition of literature in order for their work to have artistic and spiritual validity. In general, Eliot upheld values of traditionalism and discipline, and in 1928 he annexed Christian theology to his overall conservative worldview. Of his criticism, he stated: "It is a by-product of my private poetry-workshop: or a prolongation of the thinking that went into the formation of my verse." In the following excerpt, Eliot praises Tennyson's artistry, but asserts that his poetry suffers from suppressed emotion and a lack of dramatic depth.*]

Tennyson is a great poet, for reasons that are perfectly clear. He has three qualities which are seldom found together except in the greatest poets: abundance, variety, and complete competence. We therefore cannot appreciate his work unless we read a good deal of it. We may not admire his aims: but whatever he sets out to do, he succeeds in doing, with a mastery which gives us the sense of confidence that is one of the major pleasures of poetry. His variety of metrical accomplishment is astonishing. Without making the mistake of trying to write Latin verse in English, he knew everything about Latin versification that an English poet could use; and he said of himself that he thought he knew the quantity of the sounds of every English word except perhaps *scissors.* He had the finest ear of any English poet since Milton. He was the master of Swinburne; and the versification of Swinburne, himself a classical scholar, is often crude and sometimes cheap, in comparison with Tennyson's. Tennyson extended very widely the range of active metrical forms in English: in *Maud* alone the variety is prodigious. (pp. 175-76)

In some of Tennyson's early verse the influence of Keats is visible—in songs and in blank verse; and less successfully, there is the influence of Wordsworth, as in **'Dora.'** But . . . in the two Mariana poems, **'The Sea-Fairies,'** **'The Lotos-Eaters,' 'The Lady of Shalott'** and elsewhere, there is something wholly new.

All day within the dreamy house,
 The doors upon their hinges creak'd;

> The blue fly sung in the pane; the mouse
> Behind the mouldering wainscot shriek'd,
>   Or from the crevice peer'd about.

The blue fly sung in the pane (the line would be ruined if you substituted *sang* for *sung*) is enough to tell us that something important has happened.

The reading of long poems is not nowadays much practised: in the age of Tennyson it appears to have been easier. For a good many long poems were not only written but widely circulated; and the level was high: even the second-rate long poems of that time, like "The Light of Asia," are better worth reading than most long modern novels. But Tennyson's long poems are not long poems in quite the same sense as those of his contemporaries. They are very different in kind from *Sordello* or *The Ring and the Book*, to name the greatest by the greatest of his contemporary poets. *Maud* and *In Memoriam* are each a series of poems, given form by the greatest lyrical resourcefulness that a poet has ever shown. The *Idylls of the King* have merits and defects similar to those of *The Princess*. An *idyll* is a 'short poem descriptive of some picturesque scene or incident'; in choosing the name Tennyson perhaps showed an appreciation of his limitations. For his poems are always descriptive, and always picturesque; they are never really narrative. The *Idylls of the King* are no different in kind from some of his early poems; the **'Morte d'Arthur'** is in fact an early poem. *The Princess* is still an idyll, but an idyll that is too long. Tennyson's versification in this poem is as masterly as elsewhere: it is a poem which we must read, but which we excuse ourselves from reading twice. And it is worth while recognizing the reason why we return again and again, and are always stirred by the lyrics which intersperse it, and which are among the greatest of all poetry of their kind, and yet avoid the poem itself. It is not, as we may think while reading, the outmoded attitude towards the relations of the sexes, the exasperating views on the subjects of matrimony, celibacy and female education, that make us recoil from *The Princess*. We can swallow the most antipathetic doctrines if we are given an exciting narrative. But for narrative Tennyson had no gift at all. For a static poem, and a moving poem, on the same subject, you have only to compare his **'Ulysses'** with the condensed and intensely exciting narrative of that hero in the XXVIth Canto of Dante's *Inferno*. Dante is telling a story. Tennyson is only stating an elegiac mood. The very greatest poets set before you real men talking, carry you on in real events moving. Tennyson could not tell a story at all. It is not that in *The Princess* he tries to tell a story and failed: it is rather than an idyll protracted to such length becomes unreadable. So *The Princess* is a dull poem; one of the poems of which we may say, that they are beautiful but dull.

But in *Maud* and in *In Memoriam*, Tennyson is doing what every conscious artist does, turning his limitations to good purpose. . . . *Maud* consists of a few very beautiful lyrics, such as **'O Let the Solid Ground,' 'Birds in the High Hall-Garden,'** and **'Go Not, Happy Day,'** around which the semblance of a dramatic situation has been constructed with the greatest metrical virtuosity. The whole situation is unreal; the ravings of the lover on the edge of insanity sound false, and fail, as do the bellicose bellowings, to make one's flesh creep with sincerity. It would be foolish to suggest that Tennyson ought to have gone through some experience similar to that described: for a poet with dramatic gifts, a situation quite remote from his personal experience may release the strongest emotion. And I do not believe for a moment that Tennyson was a man of mild feelings or weak passions. There is no evidence in his poetry that he knew the experience of violent passion for a woman; but there is plenty of evidence of emotional intensity and violence—but of emotion so deeply suppressed, even from himself, as to tend rather towards the blackest melancholia than towards dramatic action. And it is emotion which, so far as my reading of the poems can discover, attained no ultimate clear purgation. I should reproach Tennyson not for mildness, or tepidity, but rather for lack of serenity.

> Of love that never found his earthly close,
>   What sequel?

The fury of *Maud* is shrill rather than deep, though one feels in every passage what exquisite adaptation of metre to the mood Tennyson is attempting to express. I think that the effect of feeble violence, which the poem as a whole produces, is the result of a fundamental error of form. A poet can express his feelings as fully through a dramatic, as through a lyrical form; but *Maud* is neither one thing nor the other: just as *The Princess* is more than an idyll, and less than a narrative. In *Maud*, Tennyson neither identifies himself with the lover, nor identifies the lover with himself: consequently, the real feelings of Tennyson, profound and tumultuous as they are, never arrive at expression.

It is, in my opinion, in *In Memoriam*, that Tennyson finds full expression. Its technical merit alone is enough to ensure its perpetuity. While Tennyson's technical competence is everywhere masterly and satisfying, *In Memoriam* is the less unapproachable of all his poems. Here are one hundred and thirty-two passages, each of several quatrains in the same form, and never monotony or repetition. And the poem has to be comprehended as a whole. We may not memorize a few passages, we cannot find a 'fair sample'; we have to comprehend the whole of a poem which is essentially the length that it is. We may choose to remember:

> Dark house, by which once more I stand
>   Here in the long unlovely street,
>   Doors, where my heart was used to beat
> So quickly, waiting for a hand,
>
> A hand that can be clasp'd no more—
>   Behold me, for I cannot sleep,
>   And like a guilty thing I creep
> At earliest morning to the door.
>
> He is not here; but far away
>   The noise of life begins again,
>   And ghastly thro' the drizzling rain
> On the bald street breaks the blank day.

This is great poetry, economical of words, a universal emotion in what could only be an English town: and it gives me the shudder that I fail to get from anything in *Maud*. But such a passage, by itself, is not *In Memoriam*: *In Memoriam* is the whole poem. It is unique: it is a long poem made by putting together lyrics, which have only the unity and continuity of a diary, the concentrated diary of a man confessing himself. It is a diary of which we have to read every word.

Apparently Tennyson's contemporaries, once they had accepted *In Memoriam,* regarded it as a message of hope and reassurance to their rather fading Christian faith. It happens now and then that a poet by some strange accident expresses the mood of his generation, at the same time that he is expressing a mood of his own which is quite remote from that of his generation. This is not a question of insincerity: there is an amalgam of yielding and opposition below the level of consciousness. Tennyson himself, on the conscious level of the man who talks to reporters and poses for photographers, to judge from remarks made in conversation and recorded in his son's *Memoir,* consistently asserted a convinced, if somewhat sketchy, Christian belief. And he was a friend of Frederick Denison Maurice—nothing seems odder about that age than the respect which its eminent people felt for each other. Nevertheless, I get a very different impression from *In Memoriam* from that which Tennyson's contemporaries seem to have got. It is of a very much more interesting and tragic Tennyson. His biographers have not failed to remark that he had a good deal of the temperament of the mystic—certainly not at all the mind of the theologian. He was desperately anxious to hold the faith of the believer, without being very clear about what he wanted to believe: he was capable of illumination which he was incapable of understanding. The 'Strong Son of God, immortal Love', with an invocation of whom the poem opens, has only a hazy connexion with the Logos, or the Incarnate God. Tennyson is distressed by the idea of a mechanical universe; he is naturally, in lamenting his friend, teased by the hope of immortality and reunion beyond death. Yet the renewal craved for seems at best but a continuance, or a substitute for the joys of friendship upon earth. His desire for immortality never is quite the desire for Eternal Life; his concern is for the loss of man rather than for the gain of God.

> shall he,
> Man, her last work, who seem'd so fair,
>   Such splendid purpose in his eyes,
>   Who roll'd the psalm to wintry skies,
> Who built him fanes of fruitless prayer,
>
> Who trusted God was love indeed,
>   And love Creation's final law—
>   Though Nature, red in tooth and claw
> With ravine shriek'd against his creed—
>
> Who loved, who suffer'd countless ills.
>   Who battled for the True, the Just,
>   Be blown about the desert dust,
> Or seal'd within the iron hills?

That strange abstraction, 'Nature', becomes a real god or goddess, perhaps more real, at moments, to Tennyson than God (**'Are God and Nature Then at Strife?'**). The hope of immortality is confused (typically of the period) with the hope of the gradual and steady improvement of this world. Much has been said of Tennyson's interest in contemporary science, and of the impression of Darwin. *In Memoriam,* in any case, antedates *The Origin of Species* by several years, and the belief in social progress by democracy antedates it by many more; and I suspect that the faith of Tennyson's age in human progress would have been quite as strong even had the discoveries of Darwin been postponed by fifty years. And after all, there is no logical connexion: the belief in progress being current already, the discoveries of Darwin were harnessed to it:

> No longer half-akin to brute,
>   For all we thought, and loved and did
>   And hoped, and suffer'd, is but seed
> Of what in them is flower and fruit;
>
> Whereof the man, that with me trod
>   This planet, was a noble type
>   Appearing ere the times were ripe,
> That friend of mine who lives in God,
>
> That God, which ever lives and loves,
>   One God, one law, one element,
>   And one far-off divine event,
> To which the whole creation moves.

These lines show an interesting compromise between the religious attitude and, what is quite a different thing, the belief in human perfectibility; but the contrast was not so apparent to Tennyson's contemporaries. They may have been taken in by it, but I don't think that Tennyson himself was, quite: his feelings were more honest than his mind. There is evidence elsewhere—even in an early poem, **'Locksley Hall,'** for example—that Tennyson by no means regarded with complacency all the changes that were going on about him in the progress of industrialism and the rise of the mercantile and manufacturing and banking classes; and he may have contemplated the future of England, as his years drew out, with increasing gloom. Temperamentally, he was opposed to the doctrine that he was moved to accept and to praise.

Tennyson's feelings, I have said, were honest; but they were usually a good way below the surface. *In Memoriam* can, I think, justly be called a religious poem, but for another reason than that which made it seem religious to his contemporaries. It is not religious because of the quality of its faith, but because of the quality of its doubt. Its faith is a poor thing, but its doubt is a very intense experience. *In Memoriam* is a poem of despair, but of despair of a religious kind. And to qualify its despair with the adjective 'religious' is to elevate it above most of its derivatives. For "The City of Dreadful Night," and the "Shropshire Lad," and the poems of Thomas Hardy, are small work in comparison with *In Memoriam:* it is greater than they and comprehends them.

In ending we must go back to the beginning and remember that *In Memoriam* would not be a great poem, or Tennyson a great poet, without the technical accomplishment. Tennyson is the great master of metric as well as of melancholia; I do not think any poet in English has ever had a finer ear for vowel sound, as well as a subtler feeling for some moods of anguish:

> Dear as remember'd kisses after death,
> And sweet as those by hopeless fancy feign'd
> On lips that are for others; deep as love,
> Deep as first love, and wild with all regret.

And this technical gift of Tennyson's is no slight thing. Tennyson lived in a time which was already acutely time-conscious: a great many things seemed to be happening, railways were being built, discoveries were being made, the face of the world was changing. That was a time busy in keeping up to date. It had, for the most part, no hold on permanent things, on permanent truths about man and god and life and death. The surface of Tennyson stirred about with his time; and he had nothing to which to hold fast except his unique and unerring feeling for the sounds of words. But in this he had something that no one else had. Tennyson's surface, his technical accomplishment, is intimate with his depths: what we most quickly see about Tennyson is that which moves between the surface and the depths, that which is of slight importance. By looking innocently at the surface we are most likely to come to the depths, to the abyss of sorrow. Tennyson is not only a minor Virgil, he is also with Virgil as Dante saw him, a Virgil among the Shades, the saddest of all English poets, among the Great in Limbo, the most instinctive rebel against the society in which he was the most perfect conformist.

Tennyson seems to have reached the end of his spiritual development with *In Memoriam;* there followed no reconciliation, no resolution.

> And now no sacred staff shall break in blossom,
>   No choral salutation lure to light
>   A spirit sick with perfume and sweet night,

or rather with twilight, for Tennyson faced neither the darkness nor the light, in his later years. The genius, the technical power, persisted to the end, but the spirit had surrendered. A gloomier end than that of Baudelaire: Tennyson had no *singulier avertissement.* And having turned aside from the journey through the dark night, to become the surface flatterer of his own time, he has been rewarded with the despite of an age that succeeds his own in shallowness. (pp. 178-90)

> *T. S. Eliot, "In Memoriam," in his* Essays Ancient & Modern, *Faber & Faber Limited, 1936, pp. 175-90.*

W. H. Auden   (essay date 1944)

[*Often considered the poetic successor of W. B. Yeats and T. S. Eliot, Auden is also highly regarded for his literary criticism. As a member of a generation of British writers strongly influenced by the ideas of Karl Marx and Sigmund Freud, Auden considered social and psychological commentary important functions of literary criticism. As a committed follower of Christianity, he considered it necessary to view art in the context of moral and theological absolutes. Thus, he regarded art as a "secondary world" which should serve a definite purpose within the "primary world" of human history. This purpose is the creation of aesthetic beauty and moral order, qualities that exist only in imperfect form in the primary world but are intrinsic to the secondary world of art. While he has been criticized for significant inconsistencies in his thought throughout his career, Auden is generally regarded as a fair and perceptive critic. In the following excerpt, from his introduction to a 1944 edition of Tennyson's poetry, he asserts that Tennyson, though a gifted lyricist, composed vacuous poetry of simple emotion, having "no talent" for dramatic or epic form.*]

[Tennyson] had the finest ear, perhaps, of any English poet; he was also undoubtedly the stupidest; there was little about melancholia that he didn't know; there was little else that he did. (p. 222)

A poet may write bad poetry in three ways. He may be bored or in a hurry and write work which is technically slipshod or carelessly expressed. From this fault, of which Shakespeare is not infrequently guilty, Tennyson is quite free. Secondly, by overlooking verbal and visual associations he may be unintentionally funny at a serious moment; e.g., in describing the martyrdom of St. Stephen, Tennyson writes:

> But looking upward, full of grace,
> He pray'd, and from a happy place
> God's glory smote him on the face.

And in his dedicatory poem to Lord Dufferin, on whose yacht his own son had died:

> But ere he left your fatal shore,
>   And lay on that funereal boat,
>   Dying, "Unspeakable" he wrote
> "Their kindness," and he wrote no more;

Thirdly, he may suffer from a corruption of his own consciousness and produce work, the badness of which strikes the reader as intentional; i.e., in the case of carelessness or accidental bathos, one feels it would only have to be pointed out to the poet for the latter to recognize it instantly, but in the case of this kind of badness, one feels certain that the poet is very pleased with it. The faults, for instance, of the following extracts, could not be cured by literary criticism alone; they involve Tennyson's personality.

> Love for the maiden, crown'd with marriage, no regrets
>   for aught that has been,
> Household happiness, gracious children, debtless competence, golden mean;
>
> For think not, tho' thou would'st not love thy lord,
> Thy lord has wholly lost his love for thee.
> I am not made of so slight elements.
> Yet must I leave thee, woman, to thy shame. . . .
> I did not come to curse thee, Guinevere,
> I, whose vast pity almost makes me die . . .
> Lo, I forgive thee, as Eternal God
> Forgives: do thou for thine own soul the rest.
>
> Kiss in the bower,
>   Tit on the tree!
> Bird mustn't tell,
>   Whoop! he can see.

For poetry which is bad in this essential sense, there are different specific causes in each case, but they may all, perhaps, be included in one basic error; trash is the inevitable result whenever a person tries to do for himself or for others by the writing of poetry what can only be done in some other way, by action, or study, or prayer. That is why so many adolescents write poetry. Those who have no poetic gift quickly give it up, but those who have talent, and hence discover that *something* can be achieved by artistic creation, namely a consciousness of what one really feels, remain subject to the temptation to think that everything can be achieved in this way; the elimination, for example, of unpleasant or disgraceful feelings, particularly if they are talented enough to acquire a professional status and rich enough to need no other occupation. This temptation was, in Tennyson's case, particularly acute. In the first place, his genius was lyrical, and the lyric poet is perpetually confronted with the problem of what to do with his time between the few hours when he is visited by his muse. If Tennyson, like others before and after him, occupied himself from his fiftieth to his seventieth year with epic and dramatic forms for which he had no talent whatsoever, it would be unjust to attribute this wholly or even mainly to a conceited ambition to rival Milton and Shakespeare; one, by no means the least important factor, was certainly the laudable wish not to be as idle in the second half of his life as he had been in the first. As we know from the lives of other lyric poets, the alternative to writing long, unreadable poems is apt to be the less innocent and not necessarily more fruitful pastime of debauchery.

And in the second place, the feelings which his gift revealed to Tennyson were almost entirely those of lonely terror and desire for death. From the **"Song"** written when he was still an undergraduate

> The air is damp, and hush'd, and close,
> As a sick man's room when he taketh repose
>   An hour before death;
> My very heart faints and my whole soul grieves
> At the moist rich smell of the rotting leaves,
>   And the breath
>   Of the fading edges of box beneath.
> And the year's last rose.

to **"Demeter"** written when he was nearly eighty.

> . . . . and see no more,
> The Stone, the Wheel, the dimly-glimmering lawns,
> Of that Elysium, all the hateful fires
> Of torment, and the shadowy warrior glide
> Along the silent field of Asphodel.

The note successfully struck is consistently that of numb elegiac sadness. Nietzsche's description of Wagner applies in a lesser degree to Tennyson too.

> Nobody can approach him in the colours of late Autumn, in the indescribably touching joy of a last, a very last, and all too short gladness; he knows of a chord which expresses those secret and weird midnight hours of the soul when cause and effect seem to have fallen asunder and at every moment something may spring out of nonentity. . . . He knows that weary shuffling along of the soul which is no longer able either to spring or to fly, nay which is no longer able to walk . . . his spirit prefers to squat peacefully in the corners of broken-down houses: concealed in this way, and hidden even from himself, he paints his really great masterpieces, all of which are very short, often only one bar in length—there only does he become quite good, great and perfect, perhaps there alone. . . .

When one begins to make a selection from Tennyson's work, one is startled by the similarity of the symbolic situations his best poems present. One can almost construct an archetypal pattern and say that the Tennysonian subject must contain one or more of the following elements:

1. An act of desertion, whether by marriage or by death; e.g., **"Mariana and Oenone"** (desertion of a man by a woman), *In Memoriam* (desertion of a man by a man), **"Rizpah"** (desertion of a mother by a son), **"Demeter"** (desertion of a mother by a daughter), **"Despair"** (desertion by God).

2. An insensitive, cruel other; e.g., **"Oenone"** (Aphrodite), **"Locksley Hall"** (husband), *Maud* (brother), **"Rizpah"** (The Law).

3. An accidental crime committed by the hero; e.g., **"Oriana,"** *Maud,* **"Tiresias."**

4. A thief; e.g., *Maud* (grandfather), **"Despair"** (son).

5. A contrast of landscape. The barren landscape of loneliness and passion (rocks and sea) versus the fertile landscape of coziness and calm (village and river plain).

In no other English poet of comparable rank does the bulk of his work seem so clearly to be inspired by some single and probably very early experience.

Tennyson's own description of himself as

> An infant crying in the night;
> An infant crying for the light.
> And with no language but a cry

is extraordinarily acute. If Wordsworth is the great English poet of Nature, then Tennyson is the great English poet of the Nursery . . . , i.e., his poems deal with human emotions in their most primitive states, uncomplicated by conscious sexuality or intellectual rationalization. (No other poetry is easier, and less illuminating, to psychoanalyze.)

Two admissions of Tennyson's, that the first poetry which excited him was his own, and that at the age of five he used to walk about saying "Alfred, Alfred" are significant, as are his lines on science.

> Let Science prove we are, and then
> What matters Science unto men.

Two questions: Who am I? Why do I exist? and the panic fear of their remaining unanswered—doubt is much too intellectual and tame a term for such a vertigo of anxiety—seem to have obsessed him all his life. (pp. 224-28)

> *W. H. Auden, "Tennyson," in his* Forewords and Afterwords, *edited by Edward Mendelson, Random House, 1973, pp. 221-32.*

Cleanth Brooks   (essay date 1947)

[Brooks is the most prominent of the New Critics, an influential movement in American criticism which also included Allen Tate, John Crowe Ransom, and Robert Penn Warren, and which paralleled a critical movement in England led by I. A. Richards, T. S. Eliot, and William Empson. Although the various New Critics did not subscribe to a single set of principles, all believed that a work of literature had to be examined as an object in itself through a process of close analysis of symbol, image, and metaphor. For the New Critics, a literary work was not a manifestation of ethics, sociology, or psychology, and could not be evaluated in the general terms of any nonliterary discipline. For Brooks, metaphor was the primary element of literary art, and the effect of that metaphor of primary importance. Brooks's most characteristic essays are detailed studies of metaphoric structure, particularly in poetry. According to René Wellek, "Brooks analyzes poems as structures of opposites, tensions, paradoxes, and ironies with unparalleled skill." For Brooks, irony is the most important of these elements and, as Wellek notes, "indicates the recognition of incongruities, the ambiguity, the reconciliation of opposites which Brooks finds in all good, that is, complex poetry." Brooks's criticism strongly influenced critical writing and the teaching of literature in the United

States during the 1940s and 50s. In the following excerpt, he examines the effects of paradox and ambiguity in Tennyson's "Tears, Idle Tears."]

Tennyson is perhaps the last English poet one would think of associating with the subtleties of paradox and ambiguity. He is not the thoughtless poet, to be sure: he grapples—particularly in his later period—with the "big" questions which were up for his day; and he struggles manfully with them. But the struggle, as Tennyson conducted it, was usually kept out of the grammar and symbolism of the poetry itself. Like his own protagonist in **In Memoriam,** Tennyson "fought his doubts"—he does not typically build them into the structure of the poetry itself as enriching ambiguities.

Yet substantially true as this generalization is, Tennyson was not always successful in avoiding the ambiguous and the paradoxical; and indeed, in some of his poems his failure to avoid them becomes a saving grace. The lyric **"Tears, Idle Tears"** is a very good instance. It is a poem which, from a strictly logical point of view, Tennyson may be thought to have blundered into. But, whether he blundered into it or not, the poem gains from the fact that it finds its unity in a principle of organization higher than that which seems to be operative in many of Tennyson's more "thoughtful" poems.

Any account of the poem may very well begin with a consideration of the nature of the tears. Are they *idle* tears? Or are they not rather the most meaningful of tears? Does not the very fact that they are "idle" (that is, tears occasioned by no immediate grief) become in itself a guarantee of the fact that they spring from a deeper, more universal cause?

It would seem so, and that the poet is thus beginning his poem with a paradox. For the third line of the poem indicates that there is no doubt in the speaker's mind about the origin of the tears in some divine despair. They "rise in the heart"—for all that they have been first announced as "idle."

But the question of whether Tennyson is guilty of (or to be complimented upon) a use of paradox may well wait upon further discussion. At this point in our commentary, it is enough to observe that Tennyson has chosen to open his poem with some dramatic boldness—if not with the bold step of equating "idle" with "from the depth of some divine despair," then at least with a bold and violent reversal of the speaker's first characterization of his tears.

The tears "rise in the heart" as the speaker looks upon a scene of beauty and tranquillity. Does looking on the "happy Autumn-fields" bring to mind the days that are no more? The poet does not say so. The tears rise to the eyes in looking on the "happy Autumn-fields" *and* thinking of the days that are no more. The poet himself does not stand responsible for any closer linkage between these actions, though, as a matter of fact, most of us will want to make a closer linkage here. For, if we change "happy Autumn-fields," say, to "happy April-fields," the two terms tend to draw apart. The fact that the fields are autumn-fields which, though happy, point back to something which is over—which is finished—*does* connect them with the past and therefore properly suggests to the observer thoughts about that past.

To sum up: The first stanza has a unity, but it is not a unity which finds its sanctions in the ordinary logic of language. Its sanctions are to be found in the dramatic context, and, to my mind, there alone. Indeed, the stanza suggests the play of the speaker's mind as the tears unexpectedly start, tears for which there is no apparent occasion, and as he searches for an explanation of them. He calls them "idle," but, even as he says "I know not what they mean," he realizes that they must spring from the depths of his being—is willing, with his very next words, to associate them with "some divine despair." Moreover, the real occasion of the tears, though the speaker himself comes to realize it only as he approaches the end of the stanza, is the thought about the past. It is psychologically and dramatically right, therefore, that the real occasion should be stated explicitly only with the last line of the stanza.

This first stanza, then, recapitulates the surprise and bewilderment in the speaker's own mind, and sets the problem which the succeeding stanzas are to analyze. The dramatic effect may be described as follows: the stanza seems, not a meditated observation, but a speech begun impulsively—a statement which the speaker has begun before he knows how he will end it.

In the second stanza we are not surprised to have the poet characterize the days that are no more as "sad," but there is some shock in hearing him apply to them the adjective "fresh." Again, the speaker does not pause to explain: the word "fresh" actually begins the stanza. Yet the adjective justifies itself.

The past is fresh as with a dawn freshness—as fresh as the first beam glittering on the sail of an incoming ship. The ship is evidently expected; it brings friends, friends "up from the underworld." On the surface, the comparison is innocent: the "underworld" is merely the antipodes, the world which lies below the horizon—an underworld in the sense displayed in old-fashioned geographies with their sketches illustrating the effects of the curvature of the earth. The sails, which catch the light and glitter, will necessarily be the part first seen of any ship which is coming "up" over the curve of the earth.

But the word "underworld" will necessarily suggest the underworld of Greek mythology, the realm of the shades, the abode of the dead. The attempt to characterize the freshness of the days that are no more has, thus, developed, almost imperceptibly, into a further characterization of the days themselves as belonging, not to our daylight world, but to an "underworld." This suggestion is, of course, strengthened in the lines that follow in which the ship metaphor is reversed so as to give us a picture of sadness: evening, the last glint of sunset light on the sail of a ship

> That sinks with all we love below the verge . . .

The conjunction of the qualities of sadness and freshness is reinforced by the fact that the same basic symbol—the light on the sails of a ship hull down—has been employed to suggest both qualities. With the third stanza, the process is carried one stage further: the two qualities (with the variant of "strange" for "fresh") are explicitly linked together:

> Ah, sad and strange as in dark summer dawns . . .

And here the poet is not content to suggest the qualities of sadness and strangeness by means of two different, even if closely related, figures. In this third stanza the special kind of sadness and strangeness is suggested by one and the same figure.

It is a figure developed in some detail. It, too, involves a dawn scene, though ironically so, for the beginning of the new day is to be the beginning of the long night for the dying man. The dying eyes, the poem suggests, have been for some time awake—long enough to have had time to watch the

> . . . casement slowly [grow] a glimmering square. . . .

The dying man, soon to sleep the lasting sleep, is more fully awake than the "half-awaken'd birds" whose earliest pipings come to his dying ears. We know why these pipings are sad; but why are they *strange?* Because to the person hearing a bird's song for the last time, it will seem that he has never before really heard one. The familiar sound will take on a quality of unreality—of strangeness.

If this poem were merely a gently melancholy reverie on the sweet sadness of the past, Stanzas II and III would have no place in the poem. But the poem is no such reverie: the images from the past rise up with a strange clarity and sharpness that shock the speaker. Their sharpness and freshness account for the sudden tears and for the psychological problem with which the speaker wrestles in the poem. If the past would only remain melancholy but dimmed, sad but worn and familiar, we should have no problem and no poem. At least, we should not have *this* poem; we should certainly not have the intensity of the last stanza.

That intensity, if justified, must grow out of a sense of the apparent nearness and intimate presence of what is irrevocably beyond reach: the days that are no more must be more than the conventional "dear, dead days beyond recall." They must be beyond recall, yet alive—tantalizingly vivid and near. It is only thus that we can feel the speaker justified in calling them

> Dear as remember'd kisses after death,
> And sweet as those by hopeless fancy feign'd
> On lips that are for others. . . .

It is only thus that we can accept the culminating paradox of

> O Death in Life, the days that are no more.

We have already observed, in the third stanza, how the speaker compares the strangeness and sadness of the past to the sadness of the birds' piping as it sounds to dying ears. There is a rather brilliant ironic contrast involved in the comparison. The speaker, a living man, in attempting to indicate how sad and strange to him are the days of the past, says that they are as sad and strange as is the natural activity of the awakening world to the man who is dying: the dead past seems to the living man as unfamiliar and fresh in its sadness as the living present seems to the dying man. There is more here, however, than a mere, ironic reversal of roles; in each case there is the sense of being irrevocably barred out from the known world.

This ironic contrast, too, accounts for the sense of desperation which runs through the concluding lines of the poem. The kisses feigned by "hopeless fancy" are made the more precious because of the very hopelessness; but memory takes on the quality of fancy. It is equally hopeless—the kisses can as little be renewed as those "feign'd / On lips that are for others" can be obtained. The realized past has become as fabulous as the unrealizable future. The days that are no more are as dear as the one, as sweet as the other, the speaker says; and it does not matter whether we compare them to the one or to the other or to both: it comes to the same thing.

But the days that are no more are not merely "dear" and "sweet"; they are "deep" and "wild." Something has happened to the grammar here. How can the *days* be "deep as love" or "wild with all regret"? And what is the status of the exclamation "O Death in Life"? Is it merely a tortured cry like "O God! the days that are no more"? Or is it a loose appositive: "the days that are no more are a kind of death in life"?

The questions are not asked in a censorious spirit, as if there were no justification for Tennyson's license here. But it is important to see how much license the poem requires, and the terms on which the reader decides to accord it justification. What one finds on closer examination is not muddlement but richness. But it is a richness achieved through principles of organization which many an admirer of the poet has difficulty in allowing to the "obscure" modern poet.

For example, how can the days of the past be *deep?* Here, of course, the problem is not very difficult. The past is buried within one: the days that are no more constitute the deepest level of one's being, and the tears that arise from thinking on them may be said to come from the "depth of some divine despair." But how can the days be "wild with all regret"? The extension demanded here is more ambitious. In matter of fact, it is the speaker, the man, who is made wild with regret by thinking on the days.

One can, of course, justify the adjective as a transferred epithet on the model of Vergil's *maestum timorem;* and perhaps this was Tennyson's own conscious justification (if, indeed, the need to justify it ever occurred to him). But one can make a better case than a mere appeal to the authority of an established literary convention. There is a sense in which the man and the remembered days are one and the same. A man is the sum of his memories. The adjective which applies to the man made wild with regret can apply to those memories which make him wild with regret. For, does the man charge the memories with his own passion, or is it the memories that give the emotion to him? If we pursue the matter far enough, we come to a point where the distinction lapses. Perhaps I should say, more accurately, adopting the metaphor of the poem itself, we *descend* to a depth where the distinction lapses. The days that are no more are *deep* and *wild,* buried but not dead—below the surface and unthought of, yet at the deepest core of being, secretly alive.

The past *should* be tame, fettered, brought to heel; it is not. It is capable of breaking forth and coming to the surface. The word "wild" is bold, therefore, but justified. It reasserts the line of development which has been maintained throughout the earlier stanzas: "fresh," "strange," and now "wild"—all adjectives which suggest passionate, irrational life. The word "wild," thus, not only pulls into focus the earlier paradoxes, but is the final stage in the preparation for the culminating paradox, "O Death in Life."

The last stanza evokes an intense emotional response from the reader. The claim could hardly be made good by the stanza taken in isolation. The stanza leans heavily upon the foregoing stanzas, and the final paradox draws heavily upon the great metaphors in Stanzas II and III. This is as it should be. The justification for emphasizing the fact here is this: the poem, for all its illusion of impassioned speech—with the looseness and *apparent* confusion of unpremeditated speech—is very tightly organized. It represents an organic structure; and the intensity of the total effect is a reflection of the total structure.

The reader, I take it, will hardly be disposed to quarrel with the general statement of the theme of the poem as it is given in the foregoing account; and he will probably find himself in accord with this general estimate of the poem's value. But the reader may well feel that the amount of attention given to the structure of the poem is irrelevant, if not positively bad. In particular, he may find the emphasis on paradox, ambiguity, and ironic contrast displeasing. He has not been taught to expect these in Tennyson, and he has had the general impression that the presence of these qualities represents the intrusion of alien, "unpoetic" matter.

I have no wish to intellectualize the poem—to make conscious and artful what was actually spontaneous and simple. Nevertheless, the qualities of ironic contrast and paradox *do* exist in the poem; and they *do* have a relation to the poem's dramatic power.

Those who still feel that "simple eloquence" is enough might compare **"Tears, Idle Tears"** with another of Tennyson's poems which has somewhat the same subject matter and hints of the same imagery, the lyric **"Break, Break, Break."**

> Break, break, break,
>   On thy cold grey stones, O sea!
> And I would that my tongue could utter
>   The thoughts that arise in me.
>
> O, well for the fisherman's boy,
>   That he shouts with his sister at play!
> O well for the sailor lad,
>   That he sings in his boat on the bay!
>
> And the stately ships go on
>   To their haven under the hill;
> But O for the touch of a vanished hand,
>   And the sound of a voice that is still!
>
> Break, break, break,
>   At the foot of thy crags, O sea!
> But the tender grace of a day that is dead
>   Will never come back to me.

It is an easier poem than **"Tears,"** and, in one sense, a less confusing poem. But it is also a much thinner poem, and unless we yield comfortably and easily to the strain of gentle melancholy, actually a coarser and a more confused poem. For example, the ships are said to be "stately," but this observation is idle and finally irrelevant. What relation has their stateliness to the experience of grief? (Perhaps one may argue that the term suggests that they go on to fulfill their missions, unperturbed and with no regard for the speaker's mood. But this interpretation is

forced, and even under forcing, the yield of relevance is small.)

Again, consider the status of the past as it appears in this poem: the hand is vanished, the voice is still. It is true, as the poem itself indicates, that there is a sense in which the hand has not vanished and the voice is yet heard; otherwise we should not have the poem at all. But the poet makes no effort to connect this activity, still alive in memory, with its former "actual" life. He is content to keep close to the conventional prose account of such matters. Memory in this poem does not become a kind of life: it is just "memory"—whatever that is—and, in reading the poem, we are not forced beyond the bounds of our conventional thinking on the subject.

In the same way, the elements of the line, "the tender grace of a day that is dead," remain frozen at the conventional prose level. The day is "dead"; the "tender grace" of it will never "come back" to him. We are not encouraged to take the poignance of his present memory of it as a ghost from the tomb. The poet does not recognize that his experience represents such an ironical resurrection; nor does he allow the metaphors buried in "dead" and "come back" to suffer a resurrection into vigorous poetic life. With such phenomena the poet is not concerned.

Of course, the poet *need* not be concerned with them; I should agree that we have no right to demand that this poem should explore the nature of memory as **"Tears, Idle Tears"** explores it. At moments, men are unaccountably saddened by scenes which are in themselves placid and even happy. The poet is certainly entitled, if he chooses, to let it go at that. Yet, it should be observed that in avoiding the psychological exploration of the experience, the poet risks losing dramatic force.

Mere psychological analysis is, of course, not enough to insure dramatic force; and such analysis, moreover, carries its own risks: the poem may become unnatural and coldly rhetorical. But when the poet is able, as in **"Tears, Idle Tears,"** to analyze his experience, and in the full light of the disparity and even apparent contradiction of the various elements, bring them into a new unity, he secures not only richness and depth but dramatic power as well. Our conventional accounts of poetry which oppose emotion to intellect, "lyric simplicity" to "thoughtful meditation," have done no service to the cause of poetry. The opposition is not only merely superficial: it falsifies the real relationships. For the lyric quality, if it be genuine, is not the result of some transparent and "simple" redaction of a theme or a situation which is somehow poetic in itself; it is, rather, the result of an imaginative grasp of diverse materials—but an imaginative grasp so sure that it may show itself to the reader as unstudied and unpredictable without for a moment relaxing its hold on the intricate and complex stuff which it carries. (pp. 167-77)

> *Cleanth Brooks, "The Motivation of Tennyson's Weeper," in his* The Well Wrought Urn: Studies in the Structure of Poetry, *1947. Reprint by Harcourt Brace Jovanovich, Inc., 1956?, pp. 166-77.*

F. E. L. Priestley   (essay date 1949)

[*Priestley is a Canadian educator and critic. In the fol-*

lowing excerpt, he examines Idylls of the King *as an allegorical expression of Tennyson's philosophy.*]

One of the most persistent heresies in Tennyson criticism is the belief that the *Idylls* are literature of escape. Ever since Carlyle, with his usual vigour and not unusual critical myopia, greeted the first group with remarks about "finely elaborated execution," "inward perfection of vacancy," and "the lollipops were so superlative," the myth has persisted that the poems are mere tapestry-work, "skilfully wrought of high imaginings, faery spells, fantastic legends, and mediaeval splendours . . . suffused with the Tennysonian glamour of golden mist, . . . like a chronicle illuminated by saintly hands . . . "; "a refuge from life"; "a mediaeval arras" behind which Tennyson fled from "the horrors of the Industrial Revolution."

The *Idylls* are so far from being escape that they represent one of Tennyson's most earnest and important efforts to deal with major problems of his time. Their proper significance can only be grasped by a careful reading, not of separate idylls, but of the complete group in its final form. The misunderstandings by critics have, I think, arisen largely from the reading of detached idylls, a habit encouraged by Tennyson's mode of composition and publication.

The real deficiency of the *Idylls* grows out of their piecemeal composition; quite clearly Tennyson's intention, and with it his treatment, passed through three stages, introducing inconsistencies which only complete revision and a larger measure of rewriting of the earlier idylls could have removed. Tennyson began in the eighteen-thirties with **"Morte d'Arthur,"** which is conscientiously epic in style, and follows Malory very closely. But even at this stage he was not content merely to "remodel models," and recognized that only the finding of a modern significance in the Arthurian material would redeem his poem "from the charge of nothingness." It seems evident, however, that he could see at this time no satisfactory way of continuing the epic treatment, and his next step was to abandon the "epyllion" for the "idyll." The titles, *Enid and Nimuë: The True and the False,* of 1857, and "The True and the False: Four Idylls of the King," in the proof-sheets of 1859, suggest a development of intention. The title of 1859 gives primacy to the exemplary and didactic function of the stories, with Enid and Elaine as types of fidelity, Nimuë (Vivien) and Guinevere as types of the false and unchaste. The moral message is, however, very general, and the treatment is for the most part rather like that of the **"English Idylls"**; **"Nimuë"** in particular offers a convincing portrayal of ordinary human psychology. Critics who approach these poems as typical of the *Idylls* may perhaps be forgiven for believing that the poet is concerned chiefly with a translation of the Arthurian material into a poetical variety of realistic fiction. But the style retains reminiscences of the epic, and **"Enid"** and **"Nimuë"** often suggest symbolic overtones, especially in Earl Doorm. Tennyson's final intention appears ten years later, with the provision of the main framework of symbolic allegory in **"The Coming of Arthur," "The Holy Grail,"** and **"The Passing of Arthur." "Pelleas and Ettarre"** and the later poems complete the pattern, but however unified the total structure has been made thematically, the treatment remains heterogeneous. **"Lancelot and Elaine"** belongs quite clearly to a different *genre* from **"The Holy Grail"**—

to the *genre* of **Enoch Arden** or **"Aylmer's Field,"** not to that of **"The Vision of Sin."**

Nevertheless, the twelve poems do in fact form a pattern, and this pattern is best appreciated by interpreting the whole in terms of Tennyson's last intention, and recognizing that it is not his primary purpose to re-vivify Malory's story in a dramatic narrative, but to use the Arthurian cycle as a medium for the discussion of problems which are both contemporary and perennial. The *Idylls* are primarily allegorical, or (as Tennyson preferred to put it) parabolic. It is important to remember that the allegory is not simple. Tennyson himself, after reading reviews of the 1869 volume, complained: "They have taken my hobby, and ridden it too hard, and have explained some things too allegorically, although there is an allegorical or perhaps rather a parabolic drift in the poem. . . . I hate to be tied down to say, '*This* means *that*,' because the thought within the image is much more than any one interpretation." (pp. 35-6)

Tennyson himself tells us something. His earliest note identifies Arthur with religious faith, and the Round Table with liberal institutions. Much later, in conversation with Knowles, he said, "By Arthur I always meant the soul, and by the Round Table the passions and capacities of a man." Arthur's relationship to his knights is likened by Guinevere to that of the "conscience of a saint" to his "warring senses." And again, Tennyson is quoted in the *Memoir* as saying, "The whole is the dream of a man coming into practical life and ruined by one sin. Birth is a mystery and death is a mystery, and in the midst lies the tableland of life, and its struggles and performances. It is not the history of one man or of one generation but of a whole cycle of generations." According to his son, Tennyson "felt strongly that only under the inspiration of ideals, and with his 'sword bathed in heaven,' can a man combat the cynical indifference, the intellectual selfishness, the sloth of will, the utilitarian materialism of a transition age. . . . If Epic unity is looked for in the *Idylls,* we find it . . . in the unending war of humanity in all ages—the worldwide war of sense and soul, typified in individuals. . . . "

Arthur is, then, in the most general sense, soul or spirit in action. It is significant that he is constantly associated with the bringing of order out of chaos, harmony out of discord. His city is ever being built to music, "therefore never built at all, And therefore built for ever." The life of man, the life of society—each depends upon a principle of order, upon the recognition of a set of spiritual values to which all is harmonized. Arthur as soul is a symbol of these spiritual values, ideals, aspirations, and is consequently for Tennyson identified with the religious faith which must animate man, society, and nation. The Round Table is the symbol of the order, individual or social, which the values create. It is "an image of the mighty world," the cosmos created by spirit. The tragic collapse of Arthur's work in the *Idylls* is an allegory of the collapse of society, of nation, and of individual, which must follow the rejection of spiritual values.

But Tennyson is not so naïve as to think that the problem of retaining spiritual values is a simple one. From the first, we are faced with the most fundamental doubt of all: that of the validity of the values. What are the origins of our ideals? Some give to Arthur a naturalistic origin, saying that he is the son of Uther by Gorlois' wife; but Uther and

Ygerve were both dark in hair and eyes, and "this king is fair Beyond the race of Britons and of men." Nevertheless many, among them Modred, deny the supernatural origin of Arthur, "some there be that hold the King a shadow, and the city real." Those who accept Arthur accept him in one of two ways. Bellicent, by knowing Arthur, has felt the power and attraction of his personality, and intuitively has known his kingship. (Arthur has comforted her in her sorrow; "being a child with me," as she grew greater he grew with her, was stern at times, and sad at times, "but sweet again, and then I loved him well.") Gareth, on the other hand, accepts Arthur as proved by his works: to his mother's objection that Arthur is "not wholly proven king" he replies,

> "Not proven, who swept the dust of ruin'd Rome
> From off the threshold of the realm, and crush'd
> The idolaters, and made the people free?
> Who should be king save him who makes us free?"

But the difficulty remains: the authenticity of Arthur's kingship is not established so that all *must* accept him. And even over those who acknowledge him king his power is not complete nor permanent. At the institution of the Order of the Round Table, a momentary likeness of the king flashes over the faces of the knights as they have the brief clear vision of Arthur's divine authority, but soon some are thinking of Arthur as merely human, others are recognizing his authority while they defy it, others are starting to complain that his system of vows is too strict for human nature to observe. Bound up in this fundamental problem of Arthur's authority is the whole set of fundamental problems of moral philosophy: the origin of our moral ideals, the sanctions attached to them, the nature of obligation, and so on.

Further problems are brought out by Arthur's marriage to Guinevere. Soul must act through Body; Thought must wed Fact; the Spirit must mix himself with Life; the Idea must be actualized:

> " . . . for saving I be join'd
> To her that is the fairest under heaven,
> I seem as nothing in the mighty world,
> And cannot will my will nor work my work
> Wholly, nor make myself in mine own realm
> Victor and lord. But were I join'd with her,
> Then might we live together as one life,
> And reigning with one will in everything,
> Have power on this dark land to lighten it,
> And power on this dead world to make it live."

It is only through alliance with the temporal that the eternal can work in the temporal, and since for Tennyson the prime function of an ideal is to work in the temporal, the alliance is necessary. It nevertheless brings the inevitable danger of separation and of conflict.

From the start, then, the stability of Arthur's realm, of the reign of spirit, is threatened in two ways; its collapse occurs when the challenge to Arthur's authority becomes more widespread and open, and the rebellion of the flesh within the realm becomes more violent. The defection of Guinevere is by no means the sole, or perhaps the chief, cause of the failure of Arthur's plans. It is, to be sure, important, since it tends constantly to reinforce other influences operating towards the catastrophe. But the activities of Vivien, her capture of Merlin, the revolt against the vows typified by Tristram, the effects of the Grail quest, and the stealthy work of Modred are all profoundly significant.

Vivien and Tristram are both associated with the court of Mark, a court of active and irreconcilable evil. When Mark tries to bribe his way into the Order, he has his gift burned by Arthur and his petition indignantly rejected: "More like are we to reave him of his crown Than make him knight because men call him king." Mark, inasmuch as men *do* call him king, stands for a set of values accepted by many but absolutely opposed to the Christian values Arthur stands for. Mark's values are defined by Vivien and Tristram. Vivien's whole being is dedicated to one purpose, the destruction of the Order; she has no fleshly motive for her wickedness, nor does she need any; her motive is essentially the hate felt by evil for the good.

> "As love, if love be perfect, casts out fear,
> So hate, if hate be perfect, casts out fear.
> My father died in battle against the King,
> My mother on his corpse in open field;
> . . . born from death was I
> Among the dead and sown upon the wind. . . . "

Her song, "The fire of heaven is not the flame of hell," echoes Lucretian themes of materialist naturalism, and at once recalls the similar songs in **"The Vision of Sin"** and **"The Ancient Sage."** Her values are thoroughly hedonist. "I better prize the living dog than the dead lion." "What shame in love, So love be true." Her weapons are slander and seduction. But it is to be noted that she succeeds only where some weakness already exists for her to exploit. She vanquishes Merlin only because he is already prey to "a great melancholy," a sense of "doom that poised itself to fall," a premonition of

> World-war of dying flesh against the life,
> Death in all life and lying in all love,
> The meanest having power upon the highest,
> And the high purpose broken by the worm.

He is overcome finally by weariness and Vivien's feigned repentance.

Merlin's surrender seems to signify more than the mere defeat of Reason by Passion, although this is undoubtedly in part what is meant. But Merlin, we are told, knew the range of all arts, was the king's chief builder, "was also Bard, and knew the starry heavens." His charm, the secret of his power and the preserver of his authority and indeed of his function, came to him from a seer to whom "the wall That sunders ghosts and shadow-casting men Became a crystal." If Merlin represents Reason, then, it is quite clearly not Reason in its empirical or even discursive sense; he is endowed with what Tennyson would call Wisdom, rather than Knowledge; like the poet, he threads "the secretest walks of fame," and sees "thro' life and death, thro' good and ill." It is Vivien's complaint that he does not belong wholly to her; it is her boast finally that she has made Merlin's glory hers. The authority belonging properly to the intuitive reason, which is not bound to sensation and phenomena, but can penetrate to ideal reality, has been usurped by the senses. Reason has been reduced to "empirical verification," and "closed in the four walls of a hollow tower, From which was no escape for evermore." The overthrow of Merlin means the rejection of that faculty which perceives the ideal, the faculty of the poet and seer.

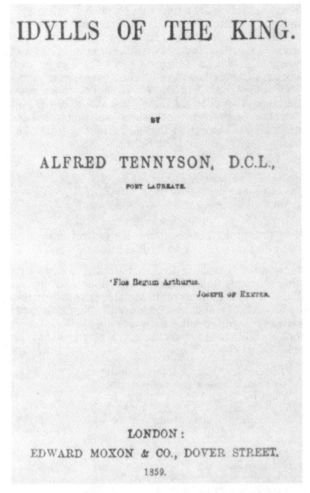

Title page for the first volume of Tennyson's Idylls of the King.

With his removal, the task of Vivien becomes much simpler, for Merlin has been the chief support of Arthur's system, the chief witness of Arthur's kingship. After he is gone, the reality of the ideal, the validity of Arthur's kingship, is judged by other standards. Even Guinevere can question the value of the Round Table; she resorts to the false but comforting doctrine of the fallen: "He is all fault who hath no fault at all," and glibly attributes to Arthur her own defection: "A moral child without the craft to rule, Else had he not lost me." The cause Vivien represents has won: Guinevere values imperfection and evil (since they are natural) above perfection and good; she admires craft more than virtue; and she judges worth by success in craft. These are the ethics of materialism, naturalism, utilitarianism. Once the higher ethical system is undermined, all codes go. The last virtues to be discarded are the merely barbarian "sporting" virtues; Gawain breaks an oath readily, even when sworn by the honour of the Table Round, but it still stirs him to see three attacking one. Yet even these, when become a mere code of sportsmanship not based upon any deeper ideal, are abandoned, and the last tournament is simply a struggle for prizes. The change in attitude is symbolized by the absence of Arthur as president, and by the victory of Tristram, who now replaces Vivien as a symbol of "Mark's way."

In him the naturalist philosophy of the court of Mark has become more conscious and rationalized. He repeats the doctrines of hedonism, but his motivation is different from Vivien's. He is a sceptic. Vivien has always recognized the value of what she is attacking; she knows that Arthur is right, and that her own life is wrong and evil. But Tristram is prepared to defend by argument his own rejection of the vows: "The vow that binds too strictly snaps itself— . . . ay, being snapt—We run more counter to the soul thereof Than had we never sworn." He questions the foundation of Arthur's authority, of the authority of spiritual values, by an appeal to the "natural":

> "The vows!
> O, ay—the wholesome madness of an hour—
> They served their use, their time; for every knight . . .
> Did mightier deeds than elsewise he had done,
> And so the realm was made. But then their vows . . .
> Began to gall the knighthood, asking when
> Had Arthur right to bind them to himself?
> Dropt down from heaven? Wash'd up from out the deep?
> They fail'd to trace him thro' the flesh and blood
> Of our old kings. Whence then? a doubtful lord
> To bind them by inviolable vows,
> Which flesh and blood perforce would violate. . . . "

The only validity Tristram grants at any time to the vows is a pragmatic one: they served their use. He challenges their permanent validity by a naturalistic argument— Arthur cannot be traced "thro' the flesh and blood Of our old kings," i.e. the spiritual values Arthur represents are not derived from the ruling elements of our physical nature. The morality Tristram seeks is one founded in those elements; he is the type of those who talk about making morality "conform to the facts of human nature." What he would advocate is an attitude which accepts the good and evil of human nature indifferently, which recognizes the naturalness of man's frailties, and which, making "naturalness" the norm, gives free play to the passions. It is worth noting that Guinevere's sin occupies a subordinate place in Tristram's argument; he attributes the downfall of the Round Table primarily to the impossible strictness of the vows.

Guinevere had at one point also drawn comfort in her error from the belief (or hope) that goodness was impossible for ordinary human nature; she had spoken scornfully of Arthur,

> "Rapt in this fancy of his Table Round,
> And swearing men to vows impossible,
> To make them like himself."

Even the faithful fool Dagonet is moved to cry out bitterly that Arthur is the king of fools, who

> Conceits himself as God that he can make
> Figs out of thistles, silk from bristles, milk
> From burning spurge, honey from hornet-combs,
> And men from beasts.

All of these characters give strong expression to the naturalistic argument and challenge the authority of religion and of systems of ethics from the point of view of evolutionary naturalism.

But the problem is wider; it involves the whole difficulty of the relationship of the ethical ideal to the humanly possible. And Tennyson undertakes a solution. In the first place, he argues that the vows are brought into disrepute, and indeed are made almost impossible to follow, if they are exaggerated into an excessive asceticism. Mark and Vivien recognize their first opportunity when they hear that a few of the younger knights have renounced marriage,

> So passionate for an utter purity
> Beyond the limit of their bond are these,
> For Arthur bound them not to singleness.

Sir Pellam shows another aspect of asceticism which has its dangers: he holds that heavenly things must not be defiled with earthly uses; his heir is Garlon, the poisonous vessel of scorn and slander. Some of the meaning of the Grail poem is to the same general effect; ideals are for application to life, to human nature. If they involve a turning of the back upon life, they are barren at best, destructive at worst. The strict vow is for the exceptional, for Galahads or perhaps even Percivales. But, asks Arthur,

> "What are ye? Galahads?—no, nor Percivales
> . . . but men
> With strength and will to right the wrong'd, of power
> To lay the sudden heads of violence flat. . . .
> Your places being vacant at my side,
> This chance of noble deeds will come and go,
> Unchallenged. . . . "

There is a special significance, perhaps, in the fact that the chance of noble deeds was not being seized *before* the Grail vision. Percivale's decision to pursue the Grail arose out of dissatisfaction with the condition of the court,

> "vainglories, rivalries,
> And earthly heats that spring and sparkle out
> Among us in the jousts, while women watch
> Who wins, who falls, and waste the spiritual strength
> Within us, better offer'd up to heav'n."

The society is already pervaded with a sense of spiritual frustration; the ideal of service is already lost; the old order is already vastly changed. And the turning to the Grail quest marks for most of the knights a withdrawal from the everyday problems involved in Arthur's original purpose, to "have power on this dead world to make it live," to inform the real with the ideal. For those who find the revelation, it is well, but few find it.

The Grail poem undoubtedly expresses, as most critics recognize, Tennyson's rejection of the ascetic way of life, at least as a normal vocation. But I think there is more in it. "One has seen," says Arthur, "and all the blind will see." And when the knights return, each has seen according to his sight.

> "And out of those to whom the vision came
> My greatest hardly will believe he saw.
> Another hath beheld it afar off,
> And, leaving human wrongs to right themselves,
> Cares but to pass into the silent life."

Quite clearly, the true purposes of ordinary life are not served at all by the Grail quest. Galahad, in his success, is as much "lost to life and use" as Merlin; he has passed out on to the great Sea, beyond the limits of human life; he has been willing to lose himself to save himself. But the others, while wishing to stay in life, are seeking an easy way to spiritual certitude in the shift and clash of moral values. Without having any deep inward conviction, they insist on seeing the unseen. Arthur is content to let the vi-

sions come, and many a time they come. Not directly and deliberately seeking the vision, he sees more than most of the Grail adventurers. The restless quest for religious certainty, for most an inevitably fruitless quest, brings a paralysis of the will, as Tennyson had known as he wrote **"Supposed Confessions,"** and **"The Two Voices,"** and as Carlyle and Arnold had known. If man's proper task is undertaken, that of establishing the kingdom of the highest ideal on earth, then the "visions" will come as a deep and passionate conviction that all pertaining to the flesh is vision, and "God and the Spiritual the only real and true," and then will come to man the

> moments when he feels he cannot die,
> And knows himself no vision to himself,
> Nor the high God a vision, nor that One
> Who rose again.

(These lines, said Tennyson, are the central lines of the **Idylls**.) The proper way to faith is through works.

It is thoroughly consistent that those who seek to *know* Arthur's origins find no certainty. Arthur's royalty and holiness, and the holiness of the vows, are not to be empirically proved, "Thou canst not prove the Nameless"; they are either recognized immediately, or not at all. Guinevere is for long blind to them; at the end it is as if a veil has been lifted:

> "Thou art the highest and most human too,
> Not Lancelot, nor another. Is there none
> Will tell the King I love him tho' so late?
> Now—ere he goes to the great battle? None!
> Myself must tell him in that purer life. . . .
>
>   Ah my God,
> What might I not have made of thy fair world,
> Had I but loved thy highest creature here?
> It was my duty to have loved the highest;
> It surely was my profit had I known;
> It would have been my pleasure had I seen."

The whole problem appears in that "had I known," "had I seen." What had prevented her from knowing, and seeing?

> "False voluptuous pride, that took
> Full easily all impressions from below,
> Would not look up, or half-despised the height
> To which I would not or I could not climb."

The defect of recognition proceeds from a defect of will.

In Guinevere's repentant insight we are also given Tennyson's second answer to the naturalistic argument. The vows present the paradox: The highest is the most human too. A morality which merely conforms to our nature is based upon less than the highest possibility of our nature; we are most human when we transcend our ordinary selves. The ideal must not, like the ascetic ideal, be so remote that it seems obviously unattainable; nor must it, like the naturalistic ideal, be so close that it seems obviously attained. But it is the essence of ethics to be not descriptive, but normative; not to tell us how we behave, but how we ought to behave. The ethics of naturalism confuse the prescriptive end of ethics with the descriptive end of science.

The causes of Arthur's failure, then, are many. All round are the powers of the wasteland, powers of violence, hate, and lust. How far these and the powers of the North represent an active diabolic spirit of evil, and how far primitive atavistic forces within the individual soul and within society, does not matter—nor, I think, would Tennyson have felt it necessary to decide. Assisting them are the false philosophies represented by Mark, Vivien, and Tristram. These operate at two levels: as rationalizations in the individual, and as popular modes of thought in society. Both society and individual are secure against these powers of disintegration as long as there is a clear recognition of the spiritual values which give coherence to society and individual. This clear recognition is threatened in three ways: by doubts of the foundation and validity of the ideals; by a separation of the ideals from the actual, either in an exaggerated asceticism or in a withdrawal; and by the ignoring of the primary importance of action, and the abandonment of ethical problems in the quest for religious certainty.

The failure of Arthur's work presents the basic problem of the moral order. And here, in the last of the poems, whether deliberately or forced by the earlier pattern established in **"Morte d'Arthur,"** Tennyson changes the relationship of the king to the theme. He is no longer so much a symbol of Soul, or of the Ideal, as of defeated mankind asking a question. The poems have hitherto displayed how evil triumphs, how "bright things come to confusion"; now Arthur asks the deeper question why.

> "I found Him in the shining of the stars,
> I mark'd Him in the flowering of His fields,
> But in His ways with men I find Him not."

God's hand is visible in the physical order, but not in the moral; the history of the stars and of the flowers shows a pattern, but not the history of man. The problem of evil is an urgent one for Arthur. His whole work has been based upon belief in an ultimate moral order, in a system wherein good must finally prevail—and yet, as he looks back upon the history of his Round Table, he sees the Cosmos which he created out of Chaos succeeded merely by a new Chaos. And with the final doubt of the moral order, Arthur doubts himself: "I know not what I am, Nor whence I am, nor whether I be king." But as he prepares for death by the surrender of Excalibur, symbol of his kingship, the "arm, clothed in white samite, mystic, wonderful," which catches the flung sword, by its very appearance and action proclaims again the reality of his kingship, and by its repetition of the beginning affirms the pattern. What the pattern is, Arthur cannot see; but that his life began with a solemn arming and ends with a solemn disarming suggests the completion of a cycle, a cycle whose meaning may not be clear to Arthur, but is clear to those who armed him.

With the reassurance thus established, Arthur is able to affirm a faith in the order of the historical process. The flux of events is not a blind flux; the growth and decay of institutions, of societies, is not a mere mechanical sequence of phenomena. Nor does the fact of change carry implications of moral relativity. Every new order is a mode of actualization of the ideal: "God fulfils himself in many ways, Lest one good custom should corrupt the world." The ultimate truth is the paradox of the permanence of the ideal which underlies the transitory shifting phenomena. The history of Arthur "is not the history of one man or of one generation but of a whole cycle of generations." The war of Sense and Soul is an "unending war

of humanity in all ages." The Ideal which Arthur symbolizes has found embodiment in many forms, in many ages, in many places; it has fought its battles and has, in each form, yielded place to new. It passes but never dies. As Bedivere watches the speck of Arthur's barge, it vanishes "into light, And the new sun rose bringing the new year."

Tennyson is asserting through the *Idylls* the primacy of the Unseen, the ultimate reality of the Spiritual, which is manifested in a constant succession of phenomena, and gives permanent meaning to them. The phenomena are not merely shadows or illusions; they are "real" in that they are the temporal actualization of the ideal. Man's task is not to pierce through the evil of appearances and brush it aside; it is to recognize the relationship of appearance to an ideal reality which he cannot fully know, and to work in the realm of phenomena towards more complete actualization of the ideal in so far as he knows it. And Tennyson believes that the activity of working itself brings fuller knowledge. His idealism, in short, serves to guarantee the religious and ethical values (both for the individual and for society), while not permitting a retreat into contemplative passivity; the temporal aspects of individual and social problems are the aspects under which we are bound to see, and bound to attack them. The Creed of Creeds must be worked out by human hands; the watchword is "Do Well." The task is not to be fulfilled by a denial of human nature and of human problems; asceticism is a retreat. Nor is it to be fulfilled by the search for personal intellectual certainty of the Unseen; this again is a retreat from the real duty.

Man's proper task is that of securing order and harmony in all phases of human activity: in the individual, the harmony of senses, passions, reason, ordered by conscience; in society, harmony of individuals and of social groups in their relations to each other, ordered again by conscience operating as a sense of justice, loyalty, duty or responsibility, and love. The threats to order come from within and without. Within there are crimes of sense: lust, pride, anger, gluttony; and crimes of malice: slander, wilful breach of trust, envy of the lost good, and so on. Without there are active powers of malevolence and brutality, symbolized traditionally in the poem by the powers in the North. These have success only against those already weakened internally.

When the real nature of the *Idylls* is properly understood, it is possible to appreciate their quality, which is essentially that of dramatic allegory. The twelve poems fall naturally into three groups of four, corresponding closely to the three acts of modern drama. The first act opens with the highly symbolic **"Coming of Arthur,"** and closes with **"Geraint and Enid."** Each of the four poems it includes has what can be considered a happy ending, and the general theme of all is the establishing of order and the victory of good over evil. Arthur is characterized by sharp clarity of vision; Gareth shows similar sureness and fixity of purpose. Gareth knows from the first his end in life, and recognizes easily Arthur's kingship. He finds freedom in service, and resolutely overcomes the Star Knights and the Knight of the Castle Perilous. He and Enid provide exemplars of the ideals of Arthur. Geraint and Lynette, in their perverse obstinacy and reluctant recognition of values represent internal obstacles to be overcome, rather than external forces threatening the good. But we are kept aware, during the triumphs, of the threats to Arthur's reign. The knights are few, and include slothful officers, mean-spirited knights like Sir Kay. Outside the court lie the wasteland and the dark powers of the North, violent and brutal, denying Arthur's kingship and doubting his origin. And already there is suggestion of falseness at the very heart of the realm; it is a rumour about Guinevere that leads Geraint to mistrust Enid. All these elements moderate the pattern of success and prepare for the second act.

This opens powerfully with the grim **"Balin and Balan,"** and ends with the climax of **"The Holy Grail."** The forces of disruption move suddenly into sharp focus: the illicit love of Lancelot and Guinevere, formerly an uncertain and shadowy rumour, becomes a hard certainty; evil emerges, conscious, deliberate, and triumphant, in Vivien and Garlon. The fierce and tragic opening is modulated through the **"Merlin and Vivien"** to the pathetic involvement of the innocent Elaine, and finally to the complex pattern of splendid holiness, shameful sin, glorious achievement, and foolish futility of **"The Holy Grail."** Arthur, who in the first act is shown presiding at the Hall of Justice, is left at the end of the second "gazing at a barren board, And a lean Order—scarce return'd a tithe."

The last act opens with the bitterly ironic **"Pelleas and Ettarre."** Pelleas is reminiscent of Gareth, particularly in his youthful eagerness and zeal, but he has none of Gareth's clarity, and his conception of knighthood is not, like Gareth's, one of religious service; it is wholly secular. His is the ideal of the courtly lover, seeking fame for a lady. He is abashed by the fleshly beauty of the harlot Ettarre, "as tho' it were the beauty of her soul." Ettarre is no Lynette or Enid; she values experienced worldliness, not young enthusiasm. And when Pelleas, betrayed by Ettarre and Gawain, goes half mad with disillusionment, it is significant that he turns against Arthur and the vows. **"The Last Tournament"** completes the theme of corruption by presenting the form which the spirit has left. The irony becomes deeper and all-pervading, in the title of the tournament, the prize offered, and the winner. Victory goes merely to the most experienced, who is also the most open repudiator of all that Arthur stands for. The defence of Arthur is given to Dagonet, the fool, the sad and lonely remnant of the king's following. All that remains is for the form to collapse. The last two idylls present the *dénouement,* and in the repentance of Guinevere a final statement, now tragic, of the worth of what has decayed. The choric comment by Arthur in the last poem sets the whole action in cosmic perspective, with a levelling off of emotion, and an affirmation of faith in order. The total dramatic effect seems to me to have considerable power.

That Tennyson sees a particular relevance for his own time in what he is saying is clear enough. The *Idylls* present in allegory the philosophy which pervades the whole of Tennyson's poetry, the philosophy which he felt it necessary to assert throughout his poetic lifetime. Penetrating all his poetry is the strong faith in the eternal world of spirit, expressed particularly in **"The Higher Pantheism,"** **"De Profundis," "The Ancient Sage,"** at the end of **"Locksley Hall Sixty Years After"** and in **"Merlin and the Gleam."** The assertion of the validity and necessity of idealism is reinforced by continual warnings of the dangers of materialism: **"The Vision of Sin,"** *Maud,* **"Aylmer's Field," "Despair,"** and **"Lucretius"** are the chief ve-

hicles for these warnings. Like most sensitive thinkers of his day, Tennyson was deeply concerned with the growing materialism, with the new hedonism, with the utilitarian ethic with its relativism and naturalism, with the attack on the religious foundation of the Christian ethic not merely by the higher critics but particularly by those who were applying evolutionary principles to show the "natural" origin of moral ideas. He was concerned with the apparent decay of ethical principles in commercial, political, and social life, and with the growing tendency to defend all sensual gratification as "natural." He saw that religious leaders were not always effective in combatting these tendencies, since they were on the defensive, and were busy trying to "demonstrate," to "prove" Christianity. The expenditure of effort against Huxley over the Gadarene swine is significant and symptomatic. The laity could hardly be blamed for thinking that Christian doctrine ought to be susceptible of the same kind of verification as scientific fact; they either wearied and perplexed themselves in the search for certainty, or sank into agnosticism. Tennyson is asserting in the *Idylls* that Christianity is not so much a set of facts to be argued about as a system of principles to be lived by; that the proof of these principles is to be established not by external empirical evidence, but by the power with which they unify and give stability and meaning to the life of man and of societies. He wants to make the reader understand how these principles become neglected, and what must happen to individuals and societies who neglect them. He is voicing a warning to his own age and nation, and to all ages and nations. He is consistently opposing a revival of the Lucretian philosophy, with its materialism, its naturalism, and its secularism. To him it is the philosophy of pessimism and despair, of defeat and social destruction.

Against the Lucretian spirit Tennyson upholds the Vergilian. The two have been well characterized by the late Professor C. N. Cochrane:

> The one holds up an ideal of repose and refined sensual enjoyment; the other, one of restless effort and activity. Lucretius urges the recognition that men are limited as the dust; that the pursuit of their aspirations is as vain and futile as are the impulses of religion, pride, ambition which ceaselessly urge them on. The purpose of Vergil is to vindicate those obscure forces within the self by which mankind is impelled to material achievement and inhibited from destroying the work of his own hands. . . . The one . . . accepts the intellectual assurance of futility, the other . . . , like all enlightened men, is beset by the problem of finding a reasonable ground for his faith.

The last line of Tennyson's **"Lucretius"** presents acutely the implications of the Lucretian philosophy: "Thy duty? What is duty?" The man or society who can find no answer must perish. (pp. 36-49)

F. E. L. Priestley, "Tennyson's 'Idylls'," in University of Toronto Quarterly, *Vol. XIX, No. 1, October, 1949, pp. 35-49.*

E. D. H. Johnson   (essay date 1958)

[*In the following excerpt, Johnson examines* In Memoriam *as a reflection of Tennyson's artistic development.*]

The tendency to regard **In Memoriam** exclusively as spiritual autobiography has obscured the importance of this work as a record of Tennyson's artistic development during the formative years between 1833 and 1850. Yet among the components of the ordeal through which the poet passed in his journey to faith was the search for an aesthetic creed answerable alike to his creative needs and to the literary demands of the age. Of the lyrics making up **In Memoriam,** approximately one quarter relates to this concern; and when taken together, they constitute an index to Victorian poetic theory and practice as suggestive in its way as the testimony of *The Prelude* with reference to the poetry of the Romantic generation.

In tracing the stages through which Tennyson came to an awareness of his mission as a poet, there is no need to get involved in the perplexing problem of dating the sections of **In Memoriam.** A. C. Bradley's *Commentary* has demonstrated the organic unity of the elegy in its published form. With three Christmas seasons as chronological points of division, it falls into four parts, the dominant mood progressing from an initial reaction of despair over Hallam's death (1-27), through a period of philosophic doubt (28-77), to nascent hope (78-103), and finally, to a confident assertion of faith (104-131). This [essay] will undertake to show, first, that Bradley's schematization lends itself equally well to a formal analysis of the evolution of the Tennysonian poetic, and secondly, that the processes of philosophic and aesthetic growth exhibited in the poem are so interrelated in their successive phases as ultimately to be inseparable.

Shattered by grief during the early months of his bereavement, Tennyson found in poetry an anodyne bringing temporary release from obsessive introspection:

> But, for the unquiet heart and brain,
> A use in measured language lies;
> The sad mechanic exercise,
> Like dull narcotics, numbing pain. (5)

At this time he makes of art a private ceremony, a votive offering to the friend on whose sympathetic encouragement he had been accustomed to rely (8). Vacillating between "calm despair" and "wild unrest," he senses the want of emotional perspective necessary to sustained and disciplined creativity. So crippled seems the shaping power of the imagination that the poet is even provoked to surmise whether the shock of sorrow has not alienated "all knowledge of myself":

> And made me that delirious man
> Whose fancy fuses old and new,
> And flashes into false and true,
> And mingles all without a plan? (16)

Yet this very impulse toward self-scrutiny had begun to knit "the firmer mind" which Tennyson attributes in the eighteenth lyric to the purgative effect of suffering. The important grouping which follows (19-21) shows the poet at a provisional resting-place affording respite to assess the essentially lyric quality of his response to the experience which he is undergoing. His poetic faculties, incapable of dealing with the full impact of this experience, are commensurate only with the "lighter moods . . . , / That out of words a comfort win." Nevertheless, as though perfec-

tion of manner might serve to compensate for superficiality of content, the elaborately wrought metaphors of the nineteenth and twentieth poems point in their deliberate artifice to a notable increase in artistic detachment. Despite the fact that he continues to describe his method of compensation as "breaking into song by fits" (23), Tennyson must by now have begun to entertain thoughts of future publication; for the twenty-first lyric introduces a new element of anxiety over the poet's responsibility to his audience. The slighting comments of a chorus of imaginary interlocutors anticipate the kind of criticism which may be expected to greet a work so subjective in mode. The first speaker condemns the unabashed display of feeling as a eulogy of weakness, while to the second it seems that the poet's inclination "to make parade of pain" originates from an egoistic motive. The third speaker, in drawing attention to the encroachments of democracy on established institutions and to the challenge to received opinions made by science, asks more weightily: "Is this an hour / For private sorrow's barren song?" To which objections Tennyson, unable as yet to surmount his sense of personal deprivation, can only reply by again pleading that he writes solely in order to give vent to emotions that spontaneously well up: "I do but sing because I must, / And pipe but as the linnets sing."

The passing of the first Christmastide left Tennyson in a more stable frame of mind and disposed, in consequence, to try to come to intellectual terms with the fact of Hallam's death. As the second part of **In Memoriam** shows, however, the search for a meaning in the experience, at least in its initial stages, had no other effect than to involve the mind in the heart's distress. The lyrics relating to poetic theory in this part of the elegy occur in clusters, as follows: 36-38, 48-49 (with which 52 belongs), 57-59, and 75-77. It is significant that each of these groups follows on a section of philosophic inquiry in which speculations precipitated by the irresolvable problems of death and change culminate in a paroxysm of doubt. Whereas the poet had previously looked to art to provide a release from emotional despair, he now discovers its further efficacy in allaying the tormenting "dialogue of the mind with itself."

Tennyson's increasing uneasiness over the limited scope of his work is implied in the derogatory reference of the thirty-fourth lyric to "some wild poet, when he works / Without a conscience or an aim." Yet, what message can be derived from the bleakly materialistic findings of modern historical and scientific knowledge hopeful enough to set beside the homely truths embodied in Christ's parables? In an age of unfaith art perforce abdicates its ethical function in favor of the kinds of teaching that issue in action, "In loveliness of perfect deeds, / More strong than all poetic thought" (36). Guiltily aware of the shaky foundations of his own belief in the Christian revelation, the poet cries: "I am not worthy ev'n to speak / Of thy prevailing mysteries" (37). By so much as daring to trespass on such matters he stands convinced of having "loiter'd in the master's field, / And darken'd sanctities with song." In dismay at the presumption of this first venture beyond the confines of immediate sensation, he falls back on the consolation offered by his "earthly Muse" with her

> little art
> To lull with song an aching heart,
> And render human love his dues . . .

For all the continuing modesty of his pretensions, Tennyson could take additional gratification from the sense that each poem of *In Memoriam* had the truth of fidelity to the mood which had inspired it. Thus, in the sequence preceding the forty-eighth poem, the author's inconclusive brooding, this time over the related enigmas of individual identity and personal immortality, again results in a disavowal of any higher significance for his lyrics than as "Short swallow-flights of song, that dip / Their wings in tears, and skim away." In this very diffidence, however, he recognizes subservience to "a wholesome law," not unlike the Keatsian Negative Capability. And, if his songs leave unplumbed the deeps of human experience, it can at least be asserted in their defense that by giving voice to whatever fancy is uppermost at the moment they register the full range of the poet's sensibility: "From art, from nature, from the schools, / Let random influences glance" (49).

The note of pessimism sounded in the thirty-fifth lyric recurs in the famous fifty-fourth, -fifth, and -sixth poems, formidably reinforced by Tennyson's reading in evolutionary doctrine. Before the blank futility of the view of life here revealed he recoils in horror, conscious of the indignity to Hallam's memory in further pursuing so wild a train of thought (57). At the same time, by forcing him out of purely subjective involvement in his grief, this crisis of doubt leaves in its wake newly won reliance on the capacity of the mind under trial not just to endure, but to grow in dignity. "Wherefore grieve / Thy brethren with a fruitless tear?" the spirit of poetry inquires: "Abide a little longer here, / And thou shalt take a nobler leave" (58). In a still more confident mood the ensuing lyric, which first appeared in the fourth edition of *In Memoriam* (1851), testifies to Tennyson's satisfaction in the discovery that he has gained the power to sublimate private feelings, and as a result to display his sorrow

> With so much hope for years to come,
>   That, howsoe'er I know thee, some
>   Could hardly tell what name were thine.

Furthermore, just as he has experienced the humanizing effect of suffering (66), so the poet is brought to realize that his constant endeavor to give artistic expression to his ordeal has been a cathartic exercise:

> And in that solace can I sing,
>   Till out of painful phases wrought
>   There flutters up a happy thought,
> Self-balanced on a lightsome wing . . . (65)

His philosophic misgivings momentarily dormant, Tennyson undertakes in the lyrics immediately preceding the seventy-fifth to memorialize Hallam's brilliant promise and the loss to the age resulting from his untimely death. This subject is deemed too taxing for "verse that brings myself relief"; but there has occurred a significant shift in the reasons which the poet gives for his reluctance to tackle themes of high seriousness. The burden of the blame is now laid on the unpoetic temper of the time, rather than on the writer's own lack of endowment: "I care not in these fading days / To raise a cry that lasts not long." And although, admittedly, no work of art can withstand the erosion of time (76), Tennyson, like Arnold, feels that the hope for modern poetry is nullified from the outset by a hostile *Zeitgeist*. Counteracting this pessimism, however, is the creative self-fulfillment which he increasingly derives from the writing of his elegy; and the tone on which the second part ends is anything but apologetic in the earlier manner:

> My darken'd ways
> Shall ring with music all the same;
> To breathe my loss is more than fame,
> To utter love more sweet than praise. (77)

The attitude of stoic resignation with which Tennyson greets the second Christmas season is prelude to the recovery of hope in the third part of the poem. Concurrently, art ceases to be valued so much as a distraction from the central conflict in which the writer's deeper thoughts and emotions are involved. The process of spiritual regeneration thus has its aesthetic analogue in the closer identification of artistic considerations with the main themes of the elegy. For example, the coming of spring in the eighty-third lyric is made an image not only for the healing principle of growth, but also for the reawakening of the creative impulse which, too long sorrow-bound, now "longs to burst a frozen bud / And flood a fresher throat with song."

That Tennyson remained distrustful of the promptings of the poetic imagination is evident from the long retrospective eighty-fifth lyric in which he considers whether his pretended communion with Hallam's spirit is not willful self-deception: "so shall grief with symbols play / And pining life be fancy-fed." Yet, there is no disposition to discount the importance of artistic endeavor as a means of assimilating experience:

> Likewise the imaginative woe,
>   That loved to handle spiritual strife,
>   Diffused the shock thro' all my life,
> But in the present broke the blow.

As if poetry were, indeed, the spontaneous voice of hope reborn, Tennyson is more and more inclined to trust its directive power. Significant in this respect is his changing response to nature. In the first part of *In Memoriam* the phenomenal world had been invoked more often than not to mirror and hence to intensify subjective moods. In the second part the natural order had been questioned in more impersonal terms in a vain attempt to establish some sanction for human values. The eighty-eighth lyric, however, takes the form of a transcendental paean in praise of the beauty and vitality inherent in nature:

> And I—my harp would prelude woe—
>   I cannot all command the strings;
>   The glory of the sum of things
> Will flash along the chords and go.

The series of poems beginning with ninety is climaxed by the mystical revelation of the ninety-fifth, in which Tennyson fleetingly achieves union in the spirit with Hallam. Although his friend's own search for faith is ostensibly the subject of the following lyric, the moral that "There lives more faith in honest doubt, / Believe me, than in half the creeds" is unmistakably derived from the writer's own experience. And by the same token, it is his own poetic progress that Tennyson has in mind when he equates the struggle for intellectual certitude with artistic growth:

> one indeed I knew
> In many a subtle question versed,
> Who touch'd a jarring lyre at first,
> But ever strove to make it true:

Perplext in faith, but pure in deeds,
    At last he beat his music out.

The departure from Somersby, now first announced, is symbolic in more senses than one; and the allegorical one hundred and third poem fittingly brings the third part of *In Memoriam* to a conclusion with Tennyson's resolve to rededicate his poetry to more ambitious goals. The interpretation of this lyric offers no special difficulties, but its theme becomes more meaningful if viewed in relation to the stages through which the poet had passed in attaining the conception of his role here set forth. The opening four stanzas rehearse the elements of the first part of the elegy when Tennyson had devoted his art ritualistically to the private image of Hallam enshrined in his heart. The summons from the sea, here as in **"Ulysses"** and elsewhere a metaphor for the life of active commitment in pursuit of transmundane goals, suggests through the device of the river journey the severe struggle with doubt in the second part of the poem, a struggle now looked back on as integral to the attainment of artistic as well as spiritual maturity. The quest is consummated in the final stanzas where the poet is reunited with Hallam—but a Hallam transubstantiated into the type of ideal humanity to the service of which the writer will henceforth exert his talents.

The third Christmas, observed in a new abode, ushers in the great New Year's hymn (106) with its exultant proclamation of progress toward the earthly paradise. His vision cleared and his purpose steadied by the perception of a goal which will enlist the altruistic devotion enjoined on him by Hallam's example, Tennyson is now ready to don the bardic mantle: "Ring out, ring out my mournful rhymes, / But ring the fuller minstrel in." No longer will he embrace isolation out of a refusal to connect the life of the imagination with the general life:

I will not shut me from my kind,
    And, lest I stiffen into stone,
    I will not eat my heart alone,
Nor feed with sighs a passing wind . . . (108)

No longer will he make the mistake of seeking the meaning of his experience in the cloudlands of subjective consciousness amidst the delusions of "vacant yearning": "What find I in the highest place, / But mine own phantom chanting hymns?" For in the wisdom sprung from associating his loss with the common lot, he can now perceive that all along "a *human* face" had shone on him from the "depths of death" within a landscape of sorrow overarched by "*human* skies" (italics added).

As the group of lyrics extending from one hundred and twenty to one hundred and twenty-five makes clear, the assumption of the Carlylean role of poetic sage paradoxically provided Tennyson with an argument in final vindication of the subjective mode of his elegy. Like the confessional writings of his great contemporaries, Carlyle's *Sartor Resartus,* Mill's *Autobiography,* and Newman's *Apologia,* the message of *In Memoriam* was addressed to the age; but the persuasiveness of the message in each of these works resided precisely in the essentially private nature of the experiential evidence which backed it up. The Victorian autobiographers thought of themselves as representative figures within the context of their times; and however intimate the circumstances from their lives selected for narration, they admitted nothing in which the particular could not be subsumed under the guise of the typical.

Thus, when Tennyson declares, "I trust I have not wasted breath" (120), it is in the hope that the record of his own victory over doubt will guide others, similarly beset, along the road to faith.

The mood of affirmation which characterizes the concluding poems of *In Memoriam* is expressive not only of the poet's acceptance of love as the pervasive cosmological principle, but also of renewed delight in creative activity as an aspect of this faith. The boon conferred by willed belief has been

To feel once more, in placid awe,
    The strong imagination roll
    A sphere of stars about my soul,
In all her motion one with law. (122)

And so Tennyson can invoke Hallam's genius to sustain poetic utterance which, no longer shadowed by grief will joyfully sing once more its author's responsiveness to the beauty of the world:

be with me now,
    And enter in at breast and brow,
    Till all my blood, a fuller wave,

Be quicken'd with a livelier breath,
    And like an inconsiderate boy,
    As in the former flash of joy,
I slip the thoughts of life and death;

And all the breeze of Fancy blows,
    And every dew-drop paints a bow,
    The wizard lightnings deeply glow,
And every thought breaks out a rose.

In the end, then, Tennyson turns back to the life of the imagination, rediscovering in its resources confirmation of the intuitions which formed the basis of his religious faith: "But in my spirit will I dwell, / And dream my dream, and hold it true" (123). The one hundred and twenty-fifth lyric develops in more straightforward terms the quest motif embodied in the allegory of the one hundred and third. In casting a backward glance over the stages of his spiritual pilgrimage, the poet explicitly identifies with each a distinguishing aesthetic manifestation:

Whatever I have said or sung,
    Some bitter notes my harp would give,
    Yea, tho' there often seem'd to live
A contradiction on the tongue,

Yet Hope had never lost her youth,
    She did but look through dimmer eyes;
    Or Love but play'd with gracious lies,
Because he felt so fix'd in truth;

And if the song were full of care,
    He breathed the spirit of the song;
    And if the words were sweet and strong
He set his royal signet there;

Abiding with me till I sail
    To seek thee on the mystic deeps,
    And this electric force, that keeps
A thousand pulses dancing, fail.

And when, three poems later, he seeks a figure to encompass the organic totality of his experience, it is the process of artistic creation that comes to mind:

I see in part
    That all, as in some piece of art,
Is toil coöperant to an end.

Tennyson's emergence from his long night of sorrow over Hallam's death into the light of living faith is dramatized through the bold device of appending an epithalamion as epilogue to the elegy. He here takes final leave of the threnodic vein in which his suffering had found voice, "No longer caring to embalm / In dying songs a dead regret." The poetry born of subjective striving with private emotion no longer suffices the artist to whom the passing years have brought knowledge of the transcendent power of love:

> For I myself with these have grown
> To something greater than before;
>
> Which makes appear the songs I made
>   As echoes out of weaker times,
>   As half but idle brawling rhymes,
> The sport of random sun and shade.

The Prologue to *In Memoriam,* dated 1849, seven years later than the Epilogue, was clearly conceived as a setpiece to introduce the elegy; and this fact explains the deprecatory tone of its final stanza. The rather formal and perfunctory ring of these lines simply reemphasizes the poet's intention, foreshadowed in the Epilogue, to devote himself henceforth to more public themes:

> Forgive these wild and wandering cries,
>   Confusions of a wasted youth;
>   Forgive them where they fail in truth,
> And in thy wisdom make me wise.

In the opening lyric of *In Memoriam* Tennyson had adumbrated the view of evolutionary progress which controls his method in the elegy and furnishes the key to the poem's structure: "men may rise on stepping-stones / Of their dead selves to higher things." These "stepping-stones," as psychologically distinguished by the author, ascend through three orders of consciousness: the emotional, identified with man's sensory being; the intellectual, identified with the human mind; and the intuitive, identified with the realm of spirit. Following Bradley's quadripartite arrangement, the consecutive stages of growth recorded in the poem may be roughly diagrammed as follows:

Part One: Despair (ungoverned sense)
Part Two: Doubt (mind governing sense, i.e. despair)
Part Three: Hope (spirit governing mind, i.e. doubt)
Part Four: Faith (spirit harmonizing sense and mind)

If now a corresponding diagram is constructed to illustrate the stages of aesthetic growth in the elegy, it will appear that the demands which Tennyson made on his art in each of the four parts were directly responsive to the psychological needs of the phase through which he was passing:

Part One: Poetry as release from emotion
Part Two: Poetry as escape from thought
Part Three: Poetry as self-realization
Part Four: Poetry as mission

In Memoriam, as a poem of spiritual quest, represents the Way of the Soul. It is not less surely a poem of aesthetic quest, which sets forth the Way of the Poet. Tennyson came to the writing of his elegy fresh from such compositions as **"The Lady of Shalott," "Oenone," "The Palace**

of Art," and **"The Lotos-Eaters."** With its publication he was to attain the laureateship and to go on to the planning of **Maud** and the early **Idylls of the King.** Bridging, as it does, the earlier and later work, *In Memoriam* is quite as much a testament to artistic as to philosophic growth. (pp. 139-48)

E. D. H. Johnson, " 'In Memoriam': The Way of the Poet," in Victorian Studies, *Vol. 2, No. 1, December, 1958, pp. 139-48.*

John D. Rosenberg   (essay date 1959)

[*An American educator and critic, Rosenberg is the author of the highly regarded study* The Darkening Glass: A Portrait of Ruskin's Genius *(1961). In the following excerpt, Rosenberg examines Tennyson's treatment of the implications of evolutionary science for Christian faith in* In Memoriam.]

In Memoriam was composed over a seventeen-year period, from 1833, when Arthur Hallam died, to 1849, the year before Tennyson published the elegy dedicated to his friend. The poem was widely read as an orthodox testament of Victorian faith, and as such it has been reread and misread in our own century. Yet the opening lines (among the last to be composed), in which the tone of affirmation is struck after years of the doubter's agony, betray an astonishing uncertainty. The Prologue is clogged with qualifications working antiphonally against the statement of faith, which is most vigorously offered in the first line but then retracted, celebrated, denied, and asserted through not only the Prologue but the entire poem. Admittedly only a poet with a great ear is capable of such counterpoint, but the mindless poet would be equally incapable of handling the subtler modulations of Tennyson's theme. The ear itself is here an intellectual instrument used not to rouse our admiration for a variation in vowel but to initiate the reader to the contrasting tones and rhythms by which Tennyson is later to reveal his agonized or exultant soul.

Thus, although the first line of the Prologue invokes the "Strong Son of God, immortal Love," the poet admits that "We have but faith: we cannot know" (l. 21): he can only *"trust"* (l. 39) that Hallam lives eternally with the Strong Son of God. This final admission is extraordinary, for it climaxes seventeen years of obsessive meditation on the death and after-life of the poet's friend. It epitomizes the energetic conflict between doubt and the will to believe which makes **In Memoriam** the most dramatic as well as the most religious of English elegies. This is the point of T. S. Eliot's important comment on the poem [see excerpt dated 1936]: "It is not religious because of the quality of its faith, but because of the quality of its doubt."

In the early sections of **In Memoriam,** when the sudden pain of loss is at its keenest, images of darkness and death are forced upon us. The Strong Son of God, embraced by faith in the Prologue, gives way to Tennyson's clasping of Death in the raven blackness and *danse macabre* of Section I. Death's predominance is further symbolized in Section II by the old yew tree, whose roots grasp at the headstones of the dead and whose branches are without bloom. Sorrow, Priestess of Death in Section III, tells the poet that the sun is dying and that nature herself is a lifeless phantom. With Section VI we come upon a series of domestic idylls, "little pictures" of Victorian life which are, unhappily, interspersed throughout the poem. Each of the idylls depicts a miniature of humanity suffering under the weight of mortality. The last, with its overtones of romantic love, prepares us for the great seventh section:

> Dark house, by which once more I stand
>   Here in the long unlovely street,
>   Doors, where my heart was used to beat
> So quickly, waiting for a hand,
>
> A hand that can be clasp'd no more
>   Behold me, for I cannot sleep,
>   And like a guilty thing I creep
> At earliest morning to the door.
>
> He is not here; but far away
>   The noise of life begins again,
>   And ghastly thro' the drizzling rain
> On the bald street breaks the blank day.

In making this pained visitation, the poet has become a nocturnal creature ("I cannot sleep"), the darkness shrouding him "like a guilty thing" and severing him from the normal waking world. With the self-evident opening of the third stanza—"He is not here"—Tennyson is forced to recognize anew his first shocked astonishment at Hallam's death. That shock is heightened by a probable allusion to the Gospels, in all of which, save that of St. John, the angel announces before the empty sepulcher, "He is not here" but has risen in immortal glory. Yet Tennyson, standing before the darkened, empty house—itself an image of the tomb—is nowhere more conscious of Hallam's *mortality,* a consciousness painfully intensified by the contrast between the dead friend and the risen God.

We feel ourselves closer to Hallam's death in the opening sections of **In Memoriam** than at any other point. That event clouds all of nature and grates against the harmony of life itself. Before the dark house, as the "blank day" breaks, Tennyson hears the waking sounds of the city as a *"noise of life,"* a distant cacophony from which, in the hostility of his isolation, he is utterly apart. The dawn, symbol of rebirth, is without light—merely a lesser darkness looming through the rain. The poem has reached a point analogous to the heavy close of the eighth stanza of Wordsworth's Immortality Ode:

> Full soon thy Soul shall have her earthly freight,
> And custom lie upon thee with a weight,
> Heavy as frost, and deep almost as life!

The note must change or Tennyson will lapse into inaudibility, chilled into silence by those tears of Section III which grief "hath shaken into frost."

The poem now moves to a series of lyrics (Sections IX through XVII) about the "fair ship" which bears the "lost Arthur's loved remains" home to England. Hallam, who died on land, dies once more as Tennyson pictures him engulfed "fathom-deep in brine," the "hands so often clasp'd" in his, now tossing "with tangle and with shells" (X, ll. 17-19). The clasping of hands is weighted, as it was in Section VII, with the sense of impossibility; it has yet to become Tennyson's symbol of reunion in the shared immortal life. Still, there has been a change. The tears once shaken to frost have thawed, as the poet tells us in Section XIII that his eyes now "have leisure for their tears."

On the first joyless Christmas after Hallam's death (XXX) Tennyson prays that "The light that shone when Hope was born"—the hope of immortal life—be lit again. Without that hope he is convinced that "earth is darkness at the core" (XXXIV), a vast dark house from which the human race is doomed never to arise. He asserts the immortality of the soul not as a religious dogma but as a personal necessity. The argument recalls Arnold's claim in the preface to *God and the Bible* that one of the two evident facts about Christianity is "that men cannot do without it." **In Memoriam** is Tennyson's assertion that *he* could not do without its promise of personal immortality. "The cardinal point of Christianity," his son quotes him as saying, "is the Life after Death."

Tennyson's obsession with that life makes much of **In Memoriam** inaccessible to the modern reader. Our own obsessions have become secularized and we are at a loss to follow a poet who through some thirty-seven stanzas (XL-XLVII) pursues such questions as, Do the dead remain inactive until some general awakening (XLIII), or do they at once begin a new life, forgetting us entirely (XLIV)? It would seem that the problem of a poet's beliefs embarrasses us in direct proportion as they approach us in time. We know all about the ghost in *Hamlet,* scrupulously suspending our disbelief in him so that we may believe in the exigencies of Hamlet's dilemma. But the "ghost" of **In Memoriam** eludes us completely. Because he eludes us, we conclude in our secret hearts that Tennyson, if not the stupidest, is certainly the most naïve of poets. Yet to overlook Tennyson's passionate quest for Hallam's "ghost" is to fail to see that **In Memoriam** is one of the great love poems in English.

For Hallam when alive was very nearly the center of Tennyson's life, and Hallam dead was the focal point of his life during the poem's composition. Despite its overlay of conventional pastoral elegy, **In Memoriam** is deeply, in places almost obnoxiously, personal. Herein lies its uniqueness and distressing modernity among the major English elegies. Edward King is irrelevant to *Lycidas;* Keats is only the occasion for *Adonais;* but Arthur Hallam—above all Tennyson's love for Hallam—is the overriding subject of **In Memoriam.** Indeed, Tennyson's unending speculation on immortality is rooted in his inexhaustible impulse to visualize and to *touch* Hallam. Hence the ubiquitous image of the hand.

After the victorious affirmation concluding the immortality group—"And I shall know him when we meet" (XLVII)—Tennyson plunges into the panic despair of Section L:

> Be near me when my light is low,
>   When the blood creeps, and the nerves prick
>   And tingle; and the heart is sick,
> And all the wheels of being slow. . . .

The regressive movement culminates in Sections LIV-LVI. The poet compares himself to

> An infant crying in the night;
>   An infant crying for the light,
> And with no language but a cry. (LIV, ll. 18-20)

The primitive fear of "Be near me . . . " here becomes a plea for release from the animal terror of extinction. Without assurance of that release, Nature herself is a hostile goddess, a shrieking Fury "red in tooth and claw" (LVI, l. 15). "I bring to life, I bring to death" (LVI, l. 6), she cries, usurping the work of the Prologue's Strong Son of God who "madest Life" and "madest Death" (ll. 6-7). Shall man, Nature's final creation, who "trusted God was love indeed,"

> Who loved, who suffer'd countless ills,
>   Who battled for the True, the Just,
>   Be blown about the desert dust,
> Or seal'd within the iron hills? (LVI, ll. 17-20)

We are at the opposite pole from the confident assertion of Section XLVII—"And I shall know him when we meet." Hallam's death, first felt by Tennyson alone, has here been generalized to include the whole of living nature in one arid, iron negation.

Nature retains her hostility in the great lyric marking the first anniversary of Hallam's death (LXXII), a day which rises howling, blasts the poplar and the rose, and is "mark'd as with some hideous crime"—the slaying of Hallam. Only with the second Christmas after his death is there a clear release from the paralyzing preoccupation with loss. "O last regret," Tennyson exclaims, "regret can die!" (LXXVIII). He can now grace his theme with paradox, marking that detachment from the past necessary for the full growth of his faith in Hallam's immortality.

Death, the dark-handed criminal of the anniversary poem, becomes "holy Death" in LXXX, sanctified by contact with Hallam. In LXXXIV Tennyson feels "The low beginnings of content." In LXXXVII, lingering outside Hallam's former rooms at Cambridge, he is for the first time capable of recollection in tranquility (st. 6-10), a tranquility which becomes absolute in LXXXIX as he recalls his friend's idyllic visits to the Tennyson home at Somersby. But after these calm retrospects Tennyson's desire for the sight and touch of Hallam returns with increased intensity. In XCIII he cries to Hallam, "Descend, and touch, and enter," a desire gratified in XCV, one of the four or five climactic lyrics of *In Memoriam.*

It opens in the calm of evening with the poet and his family together on the lawn. The trees lay their "dark arms" about the fields, and as night falls the family departs, symbolizing the larger society from which Tennyson's grief has isolated him. He reads Hallam's letters written during the period of friendship (the "glad year" of l. 22) and finds that the dead leaves still retain their life. Then the dead man himself becomes a living spirit which "touches" Tennyson's own, their souls now intertwined as were once their hands:

> So word by word, and line by line,
>   The dead man touch'd me from the past,
>   And all at once it seem'd at last
> The living soul was flash'd on mine,
>
> And mine in this was wound, and whirl'd
>   About empyreal heights of thought . . .

The two souls "come on that which is" and feel "the deep pulsations of the world." But Tennyson's "trance" is at length "stricken thro' with doubt" (l. 44), and the blinding flash of his vision fades into the less revealing light of the visible world:

> And suck'd from out the distant gloom
>   A breeze began to tremble o'er

The large leaves of the sycamore,
And fluctuate all the still perfume,

And gathering freshlier overhead,
  Rock'd the full-foliaged elms, and swung
  The heavy-folded rose, and flung
The lilies to and fro, and said,

"The dawn, the dawn," and died away;
  And East and West, without a breath,
  Mixt their dim lights, like life and death,
To broaden into boundless day.

The breeze speaks only four words, which Tennyson translates into a parable interpreting much of *In Memoriam.* Light and dark, day and night—*"like life and death"*—are dual aspects of that single reality to which the poet aspires, the eternal life-after-death in which Hallam will not appear in a moment's flash but abide with Tennyson in the lasting light of "boundless day."

Section XCV reveals the symbolic structure of *In Memoriam* with unusual clarity. That structure at times parallels and at times is independent of the poem's formal division into seasons. Within this section Tennyson achieves the transition from images of darkness and death to light and the promise of reunion with Hallam. The parallel movement in the formal organization of the poem is marked by Section CVI ("Ring out, wild bells, to the wild sky"), which celebrates the third Christmas after Hallam's death. Although it contains irrelevancies and its manner is forced, the dramatic success of this set-piece is unquestionable. The *tone* is right, for the wild ringing of the bells to the wild sky counterbalances the earlier hysteria of grief and the high-pitched shrieking of nature red in tooth and claw. Tennyson now rings out his "mournful rhymes" and rings in "the Christ that is to be" (l. 32). When in quieter voice, he simply tells us that his regret has blossomed into an April violet (CXV, l. 19).

Yet *In Memoriam* demands a more articulate response to the angry questions of Sections LV and LVI than the mere ringing of bells. How can we be certain that God and Nature are not at strife, that immortal Love does in fact govern all creation? Tennyson never attains absolute assurance; instead he attempts something perhaps braver and certainly more difficult—the synthesis of a nightmare with a vision of felicity. For that synthesis he draws on two great myths, the myth of Progress and the Christian vision of the Kingdom of Heaven on Earth. With these he slays the dragon of doubt first shocked into formidable being with Hallam's death in 1833 and later grown to monstrous proportions with Tennyson's reading of Lyell's *Principles of Geology* in 1837. From geological evidence Lyell argued that "species cannot be immortal, but must perish one after the other, like the individuals which compose them." Thus man, the creation of immortal Love in the Prologue, appears in Sections LV and LVI neither to share his maker's immortality nor to inhabit an earth guided by any conceivable laws of love: "A thousand types are gone," Nature cries, "I care for nothing, all shall go" (LVI, ll. 3-4).

This, then, is the nightmare. Whence the vision of felicity, of faith rather than extinction? Tennyson points to the answer in Section CXVIII, in which man, "Who throve and branch'd from clime to clime," becomes at last "The herald of a higher race" (ll. 13-14). Geology had revealed life as an "idle ore" (l. 20), a desert dust sealed within the iron hills of an earth darkened to the core. But evolution speaks to us of the living forms which may perpetuate the dead.

With increased confidence Tennyson asserts in Section CXXIV that if doubt had ever shaken faith, his heart had stood firm and answered "I have felt." He had once been like "a child in doubt and fear . . . a child that cries" (ll. 17, 19), a conscious echo of the infant of Section LIV, "An infant crying in the night . . . And with no language but a cry." He had then extended lame hands of faith to God but gathered only dust and chaff (LV, ll. 17-18). Now, as when Hallam's soul had flashed on his in Section XCV, he again beholds "What is,"

> And out of darkness came the hands
> That reach thro' nature, moulding men.

Yet these hands, which Tennyson has sought throughout the poem, are not Hallam's but those of the immortal Love of the Prologue which "madest Life" and "madest man" and here shape and animate mankind.

The metamorphosis of Hallam's hands into those of the divinity would be more startling, were it not that in the latter part of **In Memoriam** Tennyson annihilates the distinction between the human and the divine. And with that annihilation Tennyson achieves the synthesis earlier alluded to, drawing at once on the assumptions of nineteenth-century science and orthodox Christianity. The evolutionary argument of Section CXVIII (man thriving from clime to clime) answered adequately to Tennyson's fears of racial extinction in Sections LV and LVI. Yet it failed to guarantee the personal immortality of Hallam. God, reaching hands through nature, might be Love indeed; but for Tennyson it was a feeble love which could not preside over the placing of his own immortal hand in Hallam's. Evolution offered no such union; Christianity did. Thus in the closing lyrics Tennyson joins the promise of the one—Progress—to the promise of the other—Immortality. Evolution's proffered "higher race" becomes interchangeable with Christianity's promised Kingdom of Heaven on Earth. Hallam himself is a citizen of both realms, of the heavenly city which is to be manifested on earth and of the earthly city which is to evolve into the divine.

It is not surprising, then, that as the poem draws to its close we find Tennyson simultaneously employing the language of religion and of Victorian science. Section CXXVII is especially pertinent, for it contains linguistic strata of Geology and the Apocalypse. Mountains tremble, sheets of ice topple from their peaks

> And molten up, and roar in flood;
> The fortress crashes from on high,
> The brute earth lightens to the sky,
> And the great Aeon sinks in blood.

Earlier (XXXV) Tennyson had described, with geological accuracy, streams which slowly "Draw down Aeonian hills, and sow / The dust of continents to be." Now he deliberately abandons Lyell's hypothesis that the present configuration of the earth is the product of wholly natural forces such as erosion. He reverts to the discredited concept of cataclysmic upheavals and in place of "continents to be" we read of the great Aeon sinking in blood, "compass'd by the *fires of hell*" (l. 17). The language, no longer

scientific, recalls that of the destruction of the Great Babylon, of "fire come down from heaven . . . and thunders, and lightnings; and . . . a great earthquake, such as was not since men were upon the earth."

Hallam, witness to this incandescent holocaust, "*smil-[eth]*, knowing all is well" (l. 20). The line is very nearly incredible. The smile is diabolic or divine, expressing either pyromaniacal joy or sublime content in the knowledge that the flaming of the earth is prelude to a finer order and a higher race. From the vantage point of the gods Hallam now sees what Tennyson (at the conclusion of CXXVIII) sees only in part:

> That all, as in some piece of art,
> Is toil coöperant to an end.

The cataclysm is subsumed in the cosmic work of art.

Throughout the later poems Hallam has been progressively depersonalized, assuming many of the attributes of the Prologue's Strong Son of God. As human he anticipates evolutionary progress; as divine he fulfills the Gospel's promise of everlasting life. Thus the paradoxical address to Hallam in Section CXXIX: he is "Known and unknown, *human, divine*." Uncertain of Hallam's identity in Section CXXX—"What art thou then? I cannot guess"—he can nonetheless assert, "I shall not lose thee tho' I die." With the promise of that final possession Tennyson concludes the poem proper:

> O living will that shalt endure
>   When all that seems shall suffer shock,
>   Rise in the spiritual rock,
> Flow thro' our deeds and make them pure. . . .
>
>   Until we close with all we loved,
>   And all we flow from, soul in soul.

Tennyson himself glossed "living will" as "Free will in man." Yet in the Prologue he writes "Our wills are ours, to make them thine." This transfer of will enables us to accept the cataclysm of CXXVII as that which only "seems [to] suffer shock," a flaming instant of destruction in the eternity of rebirth, just as the loss of Hallam was a long moment's darkness preceding boundless day. The progression from death to life is again implicit in the reference to the "spiritual rock" from which Moses struck water in the desert and which Paul called the rock that "was Christ"—the same rock from which man partakes of the baptismal waters of rebirth and on which Tennyson bases his faith that we shall "*close* with all we loved . . . soul in soul." The image, appropriately, is of an embrace; the clasping of hands has led to the union of souls.

Had Tennyson concluded **In Memoriam** without appending the Epilogue, he would have spared us the longest and most damaging of the poem's domestic idylls. There is much bad verse in another great long poem of the nineteenth century, *The Prelude*. But Wordsworth's ineptitudes are rarely offensive; they are merely unfortunate lapses into prose. Tennyson never deviates into prose but occasionally postures himself into verse. That posture in much of the closing epithalamium is mannered and false, although it is true that the marriage Tennyson celebrates has its symbolic relation to the whole poem: "It begins," he said, "with a funeral and ends with a marriage—begins with death and ends in promise of a new life—a sort of Divine Comedy, cheerful at the close."

Precisely as "cheerful" is grossly inadequate to the tone of the *Paradiso,* so it is disastrously inadequate to the conclusion of **In Memoriam.** Wrapped in the spell of wedding cheer, Tennyson can refer to the preceding lyrics as "echoes" of a weaker past, as "half but idle brawling rhymes" (ll. 22-23). He here rejects the larger grief and the larger joy of **In Memoriam** in favor of the lesser pleasantries of Celia Tennyson's marriage, on a bright Victorian forenoon, to Edmund Lushington. A greater poet, or one less responsive to the demands of his contemporaries, would have embraced both experiences, felt no compulsion to disparage the earlier part of the poem in order to exalt the "cheer" of its conclusion.

Fortunately, however, Tennyson is the master of many styles. Nowhere are they called upon to accomplish more than in the closing verses of the Epilogue. The wedded pair depart; the feast draws to an end and the poet retires in darkness, withdrawing into that isolation from the family group which preceded the flashing of Hallam's soul on his in Section XCV. From the language of polite conversation he moves to that of resolution and prophecy. The twenty-seventh stanza clearly marks the transition:

> Again the feast, the speech, the glee,
>   The shade of passing thought, the wealth
>   Of words and wit, the double health,
> The crowning cup, the three-times-three,
>
> And last the dance;—till I retire.
>   Dumb is that tower which spake so loud,
>   And high in heaven the streaming cloud,
> And on the downs a rising fire:
>
> And rise, O moon, from yonder down,
>   Till over down and over dale
>   All night the shining vapor sail
> And pass the silent-lighted town,
>
> The white-faced halls, the glancing rills,
>   And catch at every mountain head. . . .

I have begun to quote a sentence—one of the longest in English poetry—which extends through ten stanzas and thirty-nine lines. Yet it is a compact unity which gathers into its imagery and statement the longer statement of the entire poem. It transports us from the lesser "noise of life" in society to the enfolding quiet of nature. We move from microcosm to macrocosm, the moonlight serving Tennyson's lyric and symbolic intention precisely as the snow, falling faintly through the universe upon all the living and the nonliving, serves Joyce's intention at the close of "The Dead."

The moonlight, playing on mountain and star, touches the "bridal doors" behind which "A soul shall . . . strike his being into bounds,"

> And, moved thro' life of lower phase,
>   Results in man, be born and think,
>   And act and love, a closer link
> Betwixt us and the crowning race
>
> Of those that, eye to eye, shall look
>   On knowledge; under whose command
>   Is Earth and Earth's, and in their hand
> Is Nature like an open book.

The foetus, recapitulating the "lower phases" of evolution, will develop, as had Hallam, into a closer link with the crowning race of perfected mankind, whose advent had

been "heralded" in Section CXVIII. That race will look on knowledge not as "A beam in darkness" (Prologue, 1. 24) but "eye to eye," just as Hallam in the penultimate stanza "lives in God," seeing Him not through a glass darkly but "face to face":

> Whereof the man that with me trod
>   This planet was a noble type
>   Appearing ere the times were ripe,
> That friend of mine who lives in God,
>
> That God, which ever lives and loves,
>   One God, one law, one element,
>   And one far-off divine event,
> To which the whole creation moves.

Hallam is at once the noble type of evolution's crowning race and forerunner of "the Christ that is to be." The Strong Son of God of the Prologue again emerges, long after Nature's discordant shriek, as *immortal Love*—the God which "ever lives and loves." His creation, one element, resolves under one law the antitheses of life and death, darkness and light, destruction and rebirth.

With the "one far-off divine event" we confront Tennyson's final effort at uniting evolutionary science and Christian faith. For that event holds out the promise both of the Kingdom of Heaven, when all shall "live in God," and the Kingdom of Earth, when all shall have evolved into gods. The nineteenth century's conviction of man's perfectibility and Christianity's conviction of man's redemption become interchangeable. The synthesis is not without its inconsistencies, perhaps its absurdities; but it is the more remarkable in that the hundred years which followed the publication of **In Memoriam** have produced no like attempt more daring, persuasive, or eloquent. (pp. 228-40)

John D. Rosenberg, "The Two Kingdoms of 'In Memoriam'," in The Journal of English and Germanic Philology, *Vol. LVIII, No. 1, January, 1959, pp. 228-40.*

Jerome Hamilton Buckley   (essay date 1961)

[*Buckley is an American educator and critic who has written extensively on Victorian literature. In the following excerpt, he surveys Tennyson's dramas.*]

Published in 1875, **Queen Mary** was developed not as a single dramatic structure but as a sprawling panorama, a pageant unfolded with a cinematic abundance and little regard for the limitations of the theater. The twenty-three separate scenes demanded frequent and often elaborate change of sets. The "Dramatis Personae" included forty-four characters drawn from all ranks of society and listed in addition a small army of nameless supernumeraries, "Lords and other Attendants, Members of the Privy Council, Members of Parliament, Two Gentlemen, Aldermen, Citizens, Peasants, Ushers, Messengers, Guards, Pages, Gospellers, Marshalmen, etc." Though the text and cast were severely cut for the production at the Lyceum in April 1876, in which Henry Irving appeared as King Philip, no editing could impose a real coherence upon the work. James's criticism of the printed play [see excerpt dated 1908] could have been applied with almost equal force to the acted version: **Queen Mary** in either form was but "a dramatized chronicle, . . . taking its material in pieces, as history hands them over, and working each one up into an independent scene—usually with great ability." The playwright, James complained, "has embroidered cunningly the groundwork offered him by Mr. Froude, but he has contributed no new material."

Tennyson indeed hewed so closely to the line of fact that he was not content to accept Froude's brilliant but biased interpretation as a full or adequate account of the sixteenth-century struggle. He carefully examined many primary and secondary sources, from Foxe's *Book of Martyrs* and the correspondence of Archbishop Parker down to the latest social and ecclesiastical histories of the period. Though his own loyalties were essentially Protestant, he tried to be scrupulously fair to the claims of Catholicism, for which his new friend W. G. Ward had given him some real respect, and he strove in particular to do justice to the Queen herself, whom he felt Froude had misrepresented. If his scholarly caution, his reluctance to simplify by omission, needlessly complicated the action of his play, it nonetheless gave him a sharp sense of the instability, conflict, and confusion of Marian England. Whatever his inexperience and naïveté as dramatist, he succeeded admirably in suggesting the temper of an age. . . . (pp. 200-01)

Apart from its faithfulness as an historical record, which mitigates its power as a play, the strength of **Queen Mary** lies in its able characterizations. Each of the principal figures—except Philip of Spain, who in his ruthless self-sufficiency approaches caricature—emerges as a subtly rounded personality. Cranmer, in particular, is drawn in all the complexity of divided motives as politician and martyr, a man of courage, remorse, humility, and proud conviction. Cardinal Pole, driven to follow the courses of least resistance, is a convincing blend of sensitivity, fearfulness, and cruelty born of disappointment. And the princess Elizabeth, who hovers in the background as a symbol of ultimate social renewal, effectively combines sympathetic understanding with an imperious reserve willing to bide its time. But most impressive of all is the Queen herself, a real woman of tragic depth, far removed from the monster she had been in Victor Hugo's *Marie Tudor*. In the beginning Mary has the capacity to rise above the wrongs she has suffered, to forgive her enemies, even to practice a measure of tolerance so long as she may retain her religious faith. In the end she is destroyed by her unreasoning passion, her obsessive love for the loveless Philip. At first her desire is simply a yearning that troubles her private dreams; "It breaks my heart," says an attendant lady, "to hear her moan at night / As tho' the nightmare never left her bed." But ultimately her frustrations determine the violence she inflicts upon her whole realm. Abandoned by the Spaniard, she loses all purpose in living and with it all true title to sovereignty. As Lord Howard explains,

> Her life, since Philip left her, and she lost
> Her fierce desire of bearing him a child,
> Hath, like a brief and bitter winter's day,
> Gone narrowing down and darkening to a close.

Here the mood recalls that of the thwarted Guinevere or, more distantly, of the abandoned Oenone. Indeed, if Tennyson had paid less heed to the political background and given the character of his protagonist more centrality, he might have found for **Queen Mary** what the play most seriously lacks, a subject, such a theme as animates many

of his more vital poems: the betrayal of the social conscience by a passionate self-interest.

Harold, published a year later, shows a considerable advance in structure. Each of its scenes—the number is reduced to eleven—develops a situation which contributes directly to the action of the play as a whole; and the key scene especially, in which Harold swears under duress to support the claim of William to the English throne, attains by skillful timing a high dramatic tension. Perhaps because he had fewer records to draw upon, Tennyson introduces many fewer characters than in **Queen Mary** and much less subsidiary historical detail. He focuses the interest of the drama where it should be, on the conduct of his hero. Unfortunately, however, Harold with all his strength, courage, and (except for the one false oath) truthfulness is too uncomplicated a person to command our sustained attention, and few of the others with whom he has to contend are drawn with enough color to assume a genuine life. The women who appear as rivals for Harold's love seem particularly factitious: Edith is a frail creature of sweet and ultimately maudlin sentiment, and Aldwyth is but a villainous schemer from popular melodrama. Far inferior in characterization to **Queen Mary,** this second chronicle could not expect even the brief *succès d'estime* in the theater which greeted the first. It awaited production on a public stage for over fifty years.

On a visit to Battle Abbey in 1876, Tennyson wrote a prefatory sonnet for **Harold** celebrating the field of Senlac "Where might made right eight hundred years ago." In effect the sonnet defines the theme of the play: the defeat of right by might, which may finally establish a new right but which first must demand the sacrifice of old values. Tennyson's ethical sympathies lie entirely with Harold, whose practical goodness resembles the intuitive religion of King Arthur and oddly prefigures the Victorian Broad-Church rejection of a rigid dogmatism:

> O God! I cannot help it, but at times
> They seem to me too narrow, all the faiths
> Of this grown world of ours, whose baby eye
> Saw them sufficient.

Harold instinctively resents the piety which drives Edward the Confessor, as it drove the seekers of the Holy Grail, to an ascetic withdrawal from social responsibility. Edward, who according to the "heretical" Archbishop Stigand has "A conscience for his own soul, not his realm," speaks with all the self-righteous unction of Tennyson's St. Simeon Stylites:

> I have lived a life of utter purity:
> I have builded the great church of Holy Peter:
> I have wrought miracles—to God the glory—
> And miracles will in my name be wrought
> Hereafter.—I have fought the fight and go—
> I see the flashing of the gates of pearl—
> And it is well with me, tho' some of you
> Have scorn'd me—ay—but after I am gone
> Woe, woe to England!

The woe in large part is of Edward's own making; for his indifference and indecision have irreparably weakened the English cause, and his approval—half envious and half fearful—of the disciplined Norman church has encouraged William to seek in the same assured and quite un-English orthodoxy spiritual sanction for his own quite secular designs. At the last Harold—without time enough to rally the England that Edward in his self-absorption has rebuked and neglected—must perish, resisting in vain an alien faith and a new order of despotic power.

The tension between might and right persists in **Becket,** which Tennyson had already begun before the publication of **Harold.** But now the wrong is mixed. Neither Becket himself nor Henry II, his antagonist, is blameless; both are betrayed by the external magnitude of office and the unconfessed falsity within, the personal desire for absolute dominion. Far from being a mere villain or even a ruthless self-seeker like the Conqueror, Henry is a genial and on the whole benevolent leader, eager for peace (on his own terms), filled with understanding of his subjects, often impulsive and hot-tempered, but relatively reasonable until pushed to the end of his patience by Becket's opposition to his authority and driven to sigh in exasperation, "Will no man free me from this pestilent priest?" Becket, on the other hand, is depicted as restless, ambitious, self-confident, able to inspire malice in his rivals and great affection in the common people, ready to give his all with intensity to his work whether as Chancellor at odds with the church or as Archbishop in conflict with the state. His sin, of which he never reaches full awareness, is pride of spirit, an arrogance commingling with his saintly strength of conviction. From the beginning of his tenure as primate he knows that he will resist rather than appease the king, who has hopefully elevated him:

> I served King Henry well as Chancellor;
> I am his no more, and I must serve the Church.
> This Canterbury is only less than Rome,
> And all my doubts I fling from me like dust,
> Winnow and scatter all scruples to the wind,
> And all the puissance of the warrior,
> And all the wisdom of the Chancellor,
> And all the heap'd experiences of life,
> I cast upon the side of Canterbury.

Before long he has exercised the power of anathema so freely that the ironic Walter Map, who serves briefly as Tennyson's chorus character, may warn him, "My lord, you have put so many of the King's household out of communion, that they begin to smile at it." Finally, as the death hour approaches, John of Salisbury, his most faithful confidant, must beg him to recognize the possible self-interest that may conceal itself in sanctified attitudes:

> And may there not be something
> Of this world's leaven in thee too, when crying
> On Holy Church to thunder out her rights
> And thine own wrong so pitilessly? Ah, Thomas,
> The lightnings that we think are only Heaven's
> Flash sometimes out of earth against the heavens. . . .
> Thou hast waged God's war against the King; and yet
> We are self-uncertain creatures, and we may,
> Yea, even when we know not, mix our spites
> And private hates with our defence of Heaven.

But Becket, committed wholly to the idea of self-sacrifice, declares himself as the agent of God's will quite "prepared to die" and refuses even to hear his friend's pointed reminder that "We are sinners all, / The best of all not all-prepared to die." Thus with magnificent consistency and fortitude, but without ever achieving complete self-confrontation, he faces the doom he has anticipated since he first considered the gravity of his new position: "I may come to martyrdom. / I am martyr in myself already."

As the murderers leave the fallen Becket, a "storm bursts" over the cathedral and "flashes of lightning" illumine the stage. Lest he be accused of forcing an effect, Tennyson explains in a footnote that the elements actually did so behave at the time of the assassination. Yet no appeal to fact can guarantee that a play will enjoy an independent life of its own. Once again Tennyson is embarrassed by the raw materials of history and too cautious to take imaginative liberties. J. R. Green, the medievalist whom he consulted about matters of historical detail, was grateful for the vivid portrayal of Henry and his court. But the succession of accurate tableaux does not achieve dramatic movement. Like **Queen Mary, Becket** is a loose chronicle with several striking characters and some ably framed separate scenes but no real coherence of total action. The subplot, which involves Henry's love for Rosamund de Clifford and the jealousy of his wife Eleanor, is intended to provide relief from the often rather arid debate between church and crown, but it succeeds only in proving a melodramatic distraction. Eleanor of Aquitaine is reduced to an enraged tigress. Rosamund, who appeared with some romantic grace in **"A Dream of Fair Women,"** is scarcely more credible than the sentimental Edith of **Harold.** And the encounter between the two, where Eleanor points a dagger at Rosamund's bosom and Becket steals up from behind just in time to wrench the weapon from her hand, may have had some parallel in fact but assuredly has no place in a serious work of art.

Rebuffed in his efforts to bring **Becket** to the stage, Tennyson published the play in 1884 with an apologetic dedication declaring that it was "not intended in its present form to meet the exigencies of our modern theatre." But he never abandoned hope that, properly edited, it might one day be produced; and in the last year of his life his confidence seemed after all well placed, for Irving after many delays finally agreed to reshape the piece as a personal vehicle. On February 6, 1893—exactly four months after Tennyson's death—**Becket** began its highly successful run of one hundred and twelve nights at the Lyceum with Irving as the Archbishop and Ellen Terry as Rosamund. Thereafter Irving repeatedly revived the role both in London and on tour, convinced, as he said, that "the play made me. It changed my whole view of life." Few later actors have shared Irving's enthusiasm, and **Becket** has more and more been relegated to the low dusty shelves where it awaits the very few readers of arm-chair literary drama. Since 1935, when it has been appraised at all, it has suffered by comparison with *Murder in the Cathedral,* to which it bears little resemblance. Less varied and precise in characterization than **Becket,** Eliot's play gains from its narrowed concentration on theme and its deft use of the anonymous interpretive Chorus of Women. Less dependent on fact, it attains far greater freedom of language, a poetry uninhibited by the standards of a documentary realism and at the same time closer than Tennyson's blank verse to the rhythms of real human speech. Whereas Eliot has attempted to create a new form suited to his own idiom, Tennyson sought to adapt his gifts of style and imagination to the demands of an outmoded convention, to the "exigencies" of a theatre that had not existed since the early seventeenth century. The difference in approach helps define Tennyson's major limitation as dramatist. (pp. 201-08)

Four new plays followed the composition of **Becket**. . . . (p. 208)

The slightest of the four is **The Falcon,** a one-act sentimental comedy, derived from Boccaccio's tale of the Count Federigo who, having squandered all his wealth but his falcon, does not hesitate to sacrifice even the cherished bird when he must extend the hospitality of his table to the Lady Giovanna. Tennyson thought his own version of the anecdote "stately and tender," and the play in fact enjoyed a limited success as part of a double bill at the St. James' Theatre in the winter of 1879-80. But, apart from its gentle irony, the piece has little dramatic substance. Though the exposition is adroit, the characters are flat and the happy denouement too easy and too rapid to be convincing. The dialogue in prose achieves some fluency and humor, but the verse spoken by the Count and the Lady is stilted in its old-world formality. Nowhere do we find the mark of Tennyson's peculiar strength, the power (as in the **Idylls,** for instance) to suffuse an old story with a freshly felt emotion.

Finished in 1881 but first produced in 1892 by Augustin Daly in New York, **The Foresters—Robin Hood and Maid Marian** proved more popular than its author had any right to expect. Particularly attractive to the American audience in a mood of genial Anglophilia was the lyric which opened the second act, "There is no land like England," the "National Song" (suppressed after publication in 1830), written, as Tennyson told Daly, "when I was nineteen." The bulk of the play might well have been the product of even earlier years, for the sentiment and derring-do are incredibly juvenile. The scene, for instance, in which Robin meets the disguised Marian, swears his love to her, and kneels as she shows him her sword, belongs only in the Neverneverland of Peter Pan. Robin's men dash to the rescue, and Much speaks:

> Our Robin beaten, pleading for his life!
> Seize on the knight! wrench his sword from him!
> >   (*They all rush on Marian*)
> ROBIN (*springing up and waving his hand*)
> >   Back!
> Back all of you! this is Maid Marian
> Flying from John—disguised.
> >   MEN
> Maid Marian? she?
>
> >   SCARLET
> Captain, we saw thee cowering to a knight
> And thought thou wert bewitch'd.
>
> >   MARIAN
> >   You dared to dream
> That our great Earl, the bravest English heart
> Since Hereward the Wake, would cower to any
> Of mortal build. Weak natures that impute
> Themselves to their unlikes, and their own want
> Of manhood to their leader!

The less "romantic" stretches of **The Foresters** are scarcely more adult. The good bad men of Sherwood, paragons all of virtue in revolt against tyranny, retain throughout a storybook naïveté; and their attempts at humor, largely in the form of shameless punning, read like boyish imitations of the bantering of Shakespeare's clowns. Tennyson was able to persuade himself that his subject matter had a certain historical gravity, for he claimed to have sketched in the play "the state of the people in another

great transition period of the making of England, when the barons sided with the people and eventually won for them the Magna Charta." Such sober implications, however, are seldom apparent in the text; despite frequent hits at the villainy of Prince John, the manner of the whole is incompatible with cogent political commentary. Certainly no shadow of significance touches the Fairy Scene which Tennyson introduced at Irving's suggestion and in the stage copy transferred to the end of the third act—as his note tells us—"for the sake of modern dramatic effect." Sir Arthur Sullivan, who set all the songs to music, may have been largely responsible for making these facetious fairy rhymes the most warmly applauded lines of the play. If so, we can only wish that Gilbert had helped Tennyson furnish Sullivan a more rollicking libretto. For **The Foresters** is really a comic operetta which has failed to recognize its inherent burlesque.

Tennyson's two "tragedies," **The Cup** and **The Promise of May,** both of which were written and produced in the early eighties, at least give some scope to his more serious conviction. Suggested by W. E. H. Lecky's account of a story in Plutarch, **The Cup** concerns the revenge of a Galatian priestess, Camma, who, having seen her husband slain by the covetous Synorix, feigns love for the latter and so induces him to share with her a poisoned chalice. Lest he err in detail, Tennyson consulted the archaeologist Sir Charles Newton of the British Museum about the worship of Artemis in Galatia; but he felt freer than in the chronicle plays to mold his characters to his own purpose, and he strove to make Synorix a prototype, like his Tristram, of the sensualist who, denying the claims of a moral idealism, seeks fulfillment in selfish passion. But again he found the dramatic medium a distinct handicap. "The worst of writing for the stage," he complained, "is, you must keep some actor always in your mind." He had written **The Cup** expressly for Irving, and he could do little afterwards to change Irving's false interpretation of Synorix as "a villain, not an epicurean." Once in production, **The Cup** was Irving's own project. Irving devised the elaborate décor, the massive sculptured pillars, the antique lyres, and the sacred flames burning musky perfumes. He enlisted Ellen Terry for the role of Camma, and he helped select the hundred beautiful girls who served as vestal virgins, her attendants in the temple. The opening night, which attracted "a most distinguished audience—one of the richest in literature, art, science, and politics that has ever been seen at the Lyceum," seemed an aesthetic event of the first magnitude. We may guess the quality of the performance from a newspaper review which appeared the next morning:

> Not only do the grapes grow before us, and the myrtles blossom, the snow mountains change from silver-white at day to roseate hues at dawn; not only are the pagan ceremonies enacted before us with a reality and fidelity that almost baffle description, but in the midst of this scenic allurement glide the classical draperies and sea-green robes of Miss Ellen Terry, who is the exact representation of the period she enacts, while following her we find the eager glances of the fate-haunted Mr. Irving.

The two acts so heavily mounted must have seemed almost static in effect, but few in the audience left the theatre dissatisfied, for *The Corsican Brothers* by Dion Boucicault, which completed the Lyceum bill, supplied all the movement anyone could have asked. The materials from which Tennyson at another time might have made an effective classical idyl had been shaped by Irving into a lavish spectacle, and *The Cup* accordingly began its long successful run.

The Promise of May, on the other hand, fared ill from the beginning. Gladstone, who attended the opening at the Globe, thought it a good play but "above the comprehension of the vast mass of the people present." On the third or fourth night the Marquess of Queensberry, who felt that he saw its drift only too plainly, rose from his seat to denounce the piece as an "abominable caricature" of free thought and a gross insult to the British Secular Union, of which he was president. The ensuing commotion in the back rows was quelled just in time to avert a riot, but not soon enough to save the play's reputation. To no avail did Herman Vezin, the actor who filled the role of Edgar the tendentious rationalist, defend the tragedy in a letter to the press as a serious drama of ideas. "So also, in time," he concluded, "will plays presenting social and moral problems crowd out dramatic trivialities which amuse for an hour and are then forgotten. Mr. Tennyson . . . has inserted the thin edge of the wedge . . . in this, the boldest experiment in the modern drama." But, though the prediction was sound, the defense was not a happy one. The playwright was not Bernard Shaw; and the play, with its old-fashioned awkward plotting, stock sentiment, and melodramatic gesture, did not bring new life to the English theatre.

Nevertheless, though hastily written and poorly edited for the stage, *The Promise of May* as the only one of the seven dramas with a contemporary setting does deal in ideas which Tennyson considered of immediate relevance to his own age. The story, to be sure, is contrived and improbable: Edgar, the city intellectual, seduces and abandons a naive country girl named Eva, then returns in disguise five years later and professes love for her sister Dora until the disgraced Eva reappears to expose, yet forgive with her dying breath, his perfidy. But Tennyson was far more interested in the motivations of Edgar than in the details of the action. Despite Queensberry's objection, Edgar is not a caricature of the honest "secularist," though his use or misuse of the secularist creed is plainly intended to suggest the necessity of a higher faith. He is not perhaps a "freethinker" at all, but rather a sensualist who, having followed the courses of self-indulgence to the point of satiation, seeks to rationalize his conduct by the logic of various disturbing new philosophies. Toying with the proposition that man is but "an automatic series of sensations," he denies any possible responsibility for moral decision, yet claims for himself the right to cultivate pleasurable sensation and to ignore the painful experience of others. Like the hero of *Maud* before the coming of love, he argues from the analogy of nature that amoral self-development is the one law of an evolutionary world. When eager to free himself from the "entanglement" with Eva, he declares marriage "but an old tradition" and professes to find comfort in the belief that the immanent revolution, "the storm . . . hard at hand," will sweep away all established institutions. He looks to the day of liberation:

> And when the man,
> The child of evolution, flings aside
> His swaddling-bands the morals of the tribe,
> He, following his own instincts as his God,

> Will enter on the larger golden age,
> No pleasure then taboo'd; for when the tide
> Of full democracy has overwhelm'd
> This Old World, from that flood will rise the New.

But later when he begins to feel the power of a remorse which his hedonism cannot explain, he grows skeptical of his own too easy nonconformities. Perhaps because, as he admits ironically, he has now inherited his uncle's wealth, he denounces his erstwhile positions as "a Socialist, / A Communist, a Nihilist—what you will"; all these are now but

> Utopian idiotcies.
> They did not last three Junes. Such rampant weeds
> Strangle each other, die, and make the soil
> For Caesars, Cromwells, and Napoleons
> To root their power in.

But whatever their coloring, radical or reactionary, Edgar's speculations touch on many issues of real moment to Tennyson throughout his creative life, and Edgar himself is also, by endowment at least, an artist—"Born, happily, with some sense of art, to live / By brush and pencil." His intellectual crime lies not so much in the error of his opinions as in his proud aesthetic detachment from any consistent point of view. As the epigraph to the play labels him, he is "A surface man of theories, true to none." Like the Soul in **"The Palace of Art,"** he aspires to a godlike autonomy, an independence of all social and ethical ties; and, like the Soul's, his pride must be ultimately destroyed. Yet, since he appeals to modern knowledge to redeem him from traditional reverence, his sin is more than aesthetic; he is to the poet a symbol of the selfseeker who in a world of shifting values finally cannot believe even in the self. Because it says all this much too didactically and not just because it offended the "freethinkers," *The Promise of May* fails utterly as drama. Tennyson, however, concerned almost exclusively with his theme, refused to see the disastrous limitations of the play. He had tried, he said, to give the public "one leaf out of the great book of truth and nature"; and the public had rejected his effort. Bitterly disappointed, he wrote no more for the stage.

None of the plays seriously altered the course of the English theater. **Becket,** the most successful on the boards and perhaps the strongest of the seven, did little more than remind Irving and his fellow actors that there was still a place and even an audience for poetic drama. And *The Promise of May,* in most respects the weakest, demonstrated only that a playwright with ideas could stimulate controversy. But apart from their slight influence and despite their many defects, all remain a testimony to the remarkable, even if misdirected, energy that carried the aging poet into his last decade. Tennyson brought enthusiasm and resourcefulness to his dramatic experiment, and he gained from it both personal stimulus and new perspective on his work. Returning to his poetry, he found himself better able to objectify and so to release his emotion. More and more now he conceived of even the lyric as a dramatic utterance from a given situation. The dominant form of all his volumes from 1880 to the end is accordingly the monologue—the musing, the laughter, or the lament of an imagined character not to be directly identified with the author. "Under the mask of his Dramatis Persona" he could express at will the most intimate or the most alien feeling and yet maintain such detachment as would give the sentiment an independent life of its own. His experience as dramatist shows ultimately to best advantage in the vitality and abundance of his last poems. (pp. 208-15)

Jerome Hamilton Buckley, in his Tennyson: The Growth of a Poet, *Cambridge, Mass.: Harvard University Press, 1961, 298 pp.*

Valerie Pitt (essay date 1962)

[*Pitt is an English educator and critic. In the following excerpt, she evaluates the strengths and weaknesses of Tennyson's poetry.*]

Tennyson cannot be regarded as anything but a major poet. But greatness in poetry has its varieties and its degrees, and when we come to consider Tennyson's work something seems lacking in it, some element of vitality, or significance which we find and respond to in the works of other poets who are commonly called great. The reader of Tennyson, however much he admires or enjoys him, is left with a sense of a potentiality which remains in much, though not all, of his work, only half fulfilled. It is time now to consider this incompleteness in Tennyson's achievement. (p. 247)

[The diction of Tennyson's] early poetry, with its insistent subordination of the rational sense to the total mood of the poem, and its sensitiveness to sound and movement was the instrument of a particular sensibility. Tennyson was not a follower, but himself as much a revolutionary as Wordsworth. He had to create, like him, a new poetic method for a new need, and like his, his diction was modified over sixty years of a varied experience.

The revolutionary nature of his poetry, of which he was not himself conscious, laid Tennyson open to certain dangers. There was nothing in the poetry of the period against which he could measure his achievement. When he was a young man, struggling for recognition, the critics saw the hope of the future in the tedious Shakespearean verse of Sir Henry Taylor; they admired Barry Cornwall, Miss Procter, Miss Elizabeth Barrett, and a whole tribe of album verse-makers less talented than these. There was no norm of judgment. The reviewers were not entirely unjust when they stigmatised Tennyson's first work as of 'the Cockney School'; for what they meant was that the young poet showed signs of a lush provincialism, a tendency to private whimsy, and the cultivation both of an eccentric sensibility and an eccentric use of language. And they were right: these faults reappear in various forms in a great deal of Tennyson's work; in the early poetry they appear as extravagance in feeling and diction. But the fault is not entirely Tennyson's. What the reviewers did not realise was that the tradition on which they based their own judgments, the Augustan tradition of the mean based on reason, was no longer available to younger poets. Sensibility had changed, the language was changing, the very forms of reason were no longer those which would be recognised by the poets of the great era. The new poet had to create his own discipline: to make and maintain his own tradition.

It is in the making of that tradition that some of the historical interest of Tennyson's work lies. Over nearly sixty years of a writing life he remains an experimentalist. He continually invents or modifies styles and techniques: not

for the sake of technical achievement, though it is a factor in Tennyson's art that he enjoyed the actual manipulation of words and metres, but principally to articulate new ways of thinking and feeling, to turn a private intuition into a public philosophy. There is a central Tennysonian manner: in the blank verse of the *Idylls* Tennyson created a characteristic mode, a mode which influenced and dominated the style of minor poets both in his own generation and the next. But the central Tennysonian manner was not his only manner; the monumental marble of the *Idylls of the King* encloses only a part of his work, and even this is not entirely marmoreal. Much of the rest of his work is exploratory: the tone of his voice differs from period to period. Until *In Memoriam* the better part of his writing was lush and descriptive, consciously and deliberately poetic as in "The Gardener's Daughter"; it relied for its effects on sensuous associations, and is, within limits, the expression of a highly developed literary sensibility. The style of *In Memoriam* is nothing like so lush: it is poetry of a different kind from that of "The Palace of Art" or *The Lady of Shalott.* There is no enamel-work in it, it is reflective and argumentative, where it uses symbols it uses them in the context of analogical argument, and its choice of metaphor and analogy is more likely to lie in the range of the *gemütlich* than in that of the fantastic. There is another shift of style in the *Maud* volume, and still another in [his later poems]. . . . These variations in manner, none of which necessarily precludes, or is uninfluenced by the others, were usually provoked by a variation in subject matter or, more importantly, in Tennyson's apprehension of it. The style of the first period, with its sensuous intensity and dream symbolism, reflected . . . the mode in which the young Tennyson realised the world. This dream style, the drift and lull of sounds would be inappropriate both to the theme of *Maud* and to Tennyson's imagination of it. The combination of lyric and dramatic monologue, the easing of rhythms from formal song patterns to an almost conversational movement within those formal patterns gives *Maud* an aliveness, a reality which chimes with Tennyson's awareness of the individual in relationship with other men, but it does not smother his vivid expression of the private, exclusive consciousness of the estranged mind.

This continued creation and recreation of medium, the adaptation of style to vision, provides the background for a judgment of Tennyson's work. It forces us to regard him as a professional poet, that is, a poet who was interested in the techniques of poetry as well as in its content; professional in the sense in which Milton and Pope were professionals. And a judgment on technique is a valid judgment on his work. Auden's dictum [see excerpt dated 1944] that Tennyson had the finest ear of any English poet does not, I think, imply that there is something shameful about having a good ear, much less that Tennyson's metrical skill is mere virtuosity. It is one of Tennyson's achievements that he extended the range and the possibilities of English metrical systems, and poets can still learn a lot from his handling of sound and movement. But this does not mean that his technique was impeccable. On the contrary, the variety of his methods made it more likely that he would misjudge the needs of his subject, and the want of practice in a particular form led him into ineptitudes just as it led Wordsworth into the clumsiness of the early Lyrical Ballads. Wordsworth was clumsy, Tennyson over-musical or monotonous, and both show the faults of an unpractised hand. On the other hand the freedom of continued experiment imparts that flexibility and variety to his writing which Mr Eliot insists on as his peculiar merit [see excerpt dated 1936]. It is these qualities which make the easy, the generalised judgment dangerous. Not all Tennyson's early, moody poetry is good, not all his later moral poetry is bad. The poetry of mood can fall into its characteristic excess, into cloying richness, or stifling but unconvincing atmospherics:

> But sometimes in the falling day
>   An image seem'd to pass the door,
> To look into her eyes and say,
>   'But thou shalt be alone no more.'
> And flaming downward over all
>   From heat to heat the day decreased,
> And slowly rounded to the east
>   The one black shadow from the wall.

It can degenerate into melodramatic trickery:

> I rose up in the silent night:
> I made my dagger sharp and bright.
>   The wind is raving in turret and tree.
> As half-asleep his breath he drew,
> Three times I stabb'd him thro' and thro'.
>   O the Earl was fair to see!

His moral poetry cannot be dismissed on the ground that it is not *his genre;* still less on the facile assumption that all morality is ruinous to art. There may indeed be no place in the visual arts or in music for instruction, but there is a legitimate genre of instructive verse, to which belong, for instance, the *Essay on Man,* the *Ode to Duty,* and Ulysses' speech on Order in *Troilus and Cressida.* The judgment of Tennyson turns, given the present assumptions about his art, on whether he does or does not succeed in this genre.

It was of course in moral poetry that his difficulties were most acute, and his handling of his technical problems least secure. For, by a paradox, instructional poetry rarely instructs; it articulates the poet's convictions, or his moral intuitions, within the framework of accepted and often traditional doctrines. The poet can utilise familiar systems, they are a common ground between him and his reader. But no such traditional system of morality was available to Tennyson: he was not able to realise his own moral and spiritual intuitions in terms of the religious and ethical doctrines familiar in his own time. Where he had a common ground with his generation and shared a common knowledge with them, Tennyson's instructional verse was confident and clear, as we see, for instance, in the lectures and the arguments about women's rights in **The Princess:**

> This world was once a fluid haze of light,
> Till toward the centre set the starry tides,
> And eddied into suns, that wheeling cast
> The planets: then the monster, then the man;
> Tattoo'd or woaded, winter-clad in skins,
> Raw from the prime, and crushing down his mate;
> As yet we find in barbarous isles, and here
> Among the lowest. . . .
>   . . . . .
>
> Here might they learn whatever men were taught:
> Let them not fear: some said their heads were less:
> Some men's were small; not they the least of men;
> For often fineness compensated size;
> Besides the brain was like the hand, and grew

> With using; thence the man's, if more was more;
> He took advantage of his strength to be
> First in the field: some ages had been lost;
> But woman ripen'd earlier, and her life
> Was longer; and albeit their glorious names
> Were fewer, scatter'd stars, yet since in truth
> The highest is the measure of the man,
> And not the Kaffir, Hottentot, Malay,
> Nor those horn-handed breakers of the glebe,
> But Homer, Plato, Verulam; even so
> With woman: and in arts of government
> Elizabeth and others; arts of war
> The peasant Joan and others; arts of grace
> Sappho and others vied with any man.

Psyche's argument is supported by some of Tennyson's constant themes, an account according to the so-called 'nebular hypothesis' of the origin and development of the world, the idea of progress, and the firm conviction that 'the highest is the measure of the man'. He had already expressed these in the ringing tones of **"Locksley Hall":**

> But I count the gray barbarian lower than the Christian
>   child.
>
> I, to herd with narrow foreheads, vacant of our glorious
>   gains,
> Like a beast with lower pleasures, like a beast with lower
>   pains!
>
> Mated with a squalid savage—what to me were sun or
>   clime?
> I the heir of all the ages, in the foremost files of time—
>
> I that rather held it better men should perish one by one,
> Than that earth should stand at gaze like Joshua's moon
>   in Ajalon!
>
> Not in vain the distance beacons. Forward, forward let us
>   range,
> Let the great world spin forever down the ringing grooves
>   of change.
>
> Thro' the shadow of the globe we sweep into the younger
>   day:
> Better fifty years of Europe than a cycle of Cathay.

These views can be regarded as in some sense moral, for they are certainly concerned with the place of man (and woman) in society, and in the physical universe. They are not, of course, non-controversial: the nebular hypothesis, for instance, was one of the earliest causes of the standing controversy between religion and science. But the idea of progress, of the world evolving from a cloud of light, and the brain of man growing by use through the ages was familiar to the reading public of the forties, so that it was not unreasonable to present the less familiar topic of female equality and female rights in these terms. The poetry is not perhaps great, but it is firm and pleasing. Where Tennyson's moral attitude is in line with that of his contemporaries, he displays the same quiet virtues:

> We might discuss the Northern sin
> Which made a selfish war begin;
>   Dispute the claims, arrange the chances;
> Emperor, Ottoman, which shall win:
>
> Or whether war's avenging rod
> Shall lash all Europe into blood;
>   Till you should turn to dearer matters,
> Dear to the man that is dear to God;
>
> How best to help the slender store,

> How mend the dwellings, of the poor;
>   How gain in life, as life advances,
>   Valour and charity more and more.

There is no need in such passages to enter into an elaborate explanation, or defence of valour and charity, though it does sometimes seem as if criticism of this kind of poetry arises from the dislike of the virtues which the Victorians took for granted.

Tennyson's major fault in exhortatory poetry is one of technique; he is inclined to over-ornamentation. Instructional verse, perhaps from the familiarity of the subject, or the need to persuade, perhaps simply from the fact that it belongs to the Augustan tradition, retains the convention of periphrasis. There is a legitimate use of this device, but Tennyson often misuses it, and elaborates his sentiments beyond their capacity.

> Pray for my soul. More things are wrought by prayer
> Than this world dreams of.

So far so good: even if the sentiment is unacceptable the expression is terse and plain; even the slightly conscious word 'wrought' is better for its purpose than its synonyms, done, made, created, worked. But the passage goes on:

> Wherefore, let thy voice
> Rise like a fountain for me night and day.
> For what are men better than sheep or goats
> That nourish a blind life within the brain,
> If, knowing God, they lift not hands of prayer
> Both for themselves and those who call them friend?
> For so the whole round earth is every way
> Bound by gold chains about the feet of God.

Something, certainly, is added to Arthur's statement by this, and there is a vividness in the presentation of animal sentience, the 'blind life within the brain', with its contrast between blindness and life, frustration and power, which quickens our awareness of the consciousness of man. But most of the passage is nothing but an elaboration of the first statement, a rococo superstructure on the original theme. The decorative gold-leaf of Tennyson's expression is thickest in the final image:

> The whole round earth is every way
> Bound by gold chains about the feet of God.

The whole passage evokes the visual memory, not of Victoriana but of elaborate seventeenth-century title pages, and the emblematic designs for masques. There is nothing of course essentially wrong with this kind of decorated art. The **"Morte d'Arthur"** was written in a consciously archaic and artificial style, and Arthur's speech represents a certain kind of rhetorical achievement. The elaboration, the vivid image serve to make the passage memorable, and to be remembered is one of the virtues of instructional verse. But sooner or later someone is sure to ask whether the gold chain really adds anything to our sense of the value and the necessity of prayer, whether it does not direct our attention away from the sentiment to the decoration. This stylised image breaks away from the main structure, and appears like the carved bits of baroque altars lying about antique shops and ateliers, a curio, an *objet d'art,* rather than a functional part of the argument. This tendency of Tennyson's art (he lends himself very much to the aphoristic quotation) does not matter so much in his earlier work. Later it was to be dangerous to him.

Successful didactic poetry is normally concerned with a subject matter which is both familiar to the audience and easily reducible to intellectual formulae. It is easy to translate sentiments about moral behaviour into poetry, into a certain kind of poetry: the achievement is rather rhetorical than poetic. The more difficult task is to translate direct moral experience into common terms. Oddly enough it is when Tennyson is concerned with his own experience, or with convictions realised through experience, that he is least secure in his handling of his material. Here we must distinguish; the record of his search for the moral meaning of great experience in **In Memoriam** presented difficulties in expression which are quite different from those which arose in his expression of the settled philosophy of **"The Ancient Sage."** In **In Memoriam** Tennyson's discovery of moral and spiritual purpose is communicated to the reader as a shared experience, and in the long run perhaps this is the best way to express moral conviction. But Tennyson's own anger in **"Locksley Hall Sixty Years After,"** his personal spirituality in **"The Ancient Sage"** are recognised by the reader, not felt or shared. This failure to communicate has, like Tennyson's other failures, a technical cause. Technique must be understood here as something more than the mere manipulation of language and metre. The inarticulateness of Tennyson's later poetry arises from his want of a certain kind of intellectual skill, his inability to understand his own experience, to formulate it to himself before expressing it to others. One of the troubles lay in what is perhaps his major virtue as a poet; his intelligence was of an intuitive and synthesising kind, it was not analytical. Even supposing that it had been, the condition of the language in the Victorian period did not favour the composition of the precise intellectual poetry which both the subject and the purpose of **"The Ancient Sage"** and the other poems of this group demand. Swinburne made devastating fun of the verbal confusion of **"The Higher Pantheism"**:

> One, who is not, we see; but one, whom we see not, is;
> Surely, this is not that; but that is assuredly this.
>
> What, and wherefore, and whence: for under is over and
>   under;
> If thunder could be without lightning, lightning could be
>   without thunder.
>
> Doubt is faith in the main, but faith, on the whole, is
>   doubt;
> We cannot believe by proof; but could we believe without?

The parody makes a legitimate point. Swinburne did not however, realise that in **"The Higher Pantheism"** Tennyson was attempting an exactness of meaning of which the curious imprecision of Victorian writing had robbed the language. His subject stems from an experience of the real which is, or was believed to be, transsensuous, and which indeed appears inconsistent with the evidence of the senses. He did not try to describe what he felt although that would be comparatively easy. In **In Memoriam,** in passages of the **Idylls of the King,** and even in **"The Ancient Sage"** he had already achieved an adequate and revealing expression of the subjective aspects of religious experience, of what it feels like to enter into states of trance or exultation. In **"The Higher Pantheism"** and elsewhere he wished to objectify that experience, to present it as part of an interpretation of reality, an interpretation which the experience is believed to validate, and which carried certain consequences in the field of ethics. But it was precisely in matters of this kind that there was no common ground between Tennyson and his age. The Victorians were susceptible to 'uplift' and, beneath a sober front, highly imaginative; they responded to weirdness and to the preternatural with a kind of delicious spiritual titillation, shown in their fondness for the ghost story and the pseudo-mediaeval. But, perhaps because of this, they were deeply suspicious of the mystical. The kind of thing Tennyson described was beyond their normal experience, and, until the end of the century, not within the range of their normal theological and philosophical vocabulary. A comfortable middle-class and nationalist Protestantism, a spikily rational scientific scepticism—neither of these could in the least accommodate the absorption of personality into 'his great World-self and all in all'. Tennyson seems to have been well aware of this. **"The Higher Pantheism"** and **"The Ancient Sage"** have the form of an argument, or a lesson; they are attempts to explain and define. As so often in such cases the explanation proceeds by negatives:

> And when thou sendest thy free soul thro' heaven,
> Nor understandest bound nor boundlessness,
> Thou seest the Nameless of the hundred names.

In these negatives Tennyson attempted to emphasise the transsensuous quality of religious experience and the non-material nature of the Nameless. Normal experience does not touch on these realms of being and therefore normal experience cannot comprehend or give warrant for them:

> Thou canst not prove the Nameless, O my son,

At the same time Tennyson wished to emphasise that the normal experience of the visible world is the channel through which we come to know the Nameless, and it is this position, perfectly familiar to older traditions, but not to the Victorians, which led him into tedious paradox.

All this may be philosophically sound, but for Tennyson it is poetically disastrous. For in the negative paradox of these poems he attempts to move from the imaginative and sensuous world into that of the conceptual, and he has not the equipment for it. There was no technical vocabulary for his doctrine: he had to invent it—as he does, for instance, in **"De Profundis." "De Profundis"** . . . is an intolerably bad poem, but not because there is anything wrong with the sentiment; it is, after all, a strange thing to reflect that an hour, a week, a month ago, this particular infant was not. The evil is that Tennyson has confused the mysterious but undoubtedly material arrival of his elder son with the mysteriousness of immaterial being and brooded on it so long that both spiritual reality and actual birth have disappeared into a mist of mysteriousness:

> Out of the deep, my child, out of the deep,
> From that great deep, before our world begins,
> Whereon the Spirit of God moves as he will—
> Out of the deep, my child, out of the deep,
> From that true world within the world we see,
> Whereof our world is but the bounding shore—
> Out of the deep, Spirit, out of the deep,
> With this ninth moon, that sends the hidden sun
> Down yon dark sea, thou comest, darling boy.

It is very difficult, in this wilderness of seas, and shores, and moons, to hang on to the plain fact that Hallam Tennyson, like anyone else, was born of a woman's womb. But the fault in the passage is not only that Tennyson has, as

it were, floated away from a physical reality, it is that he is out of touch with any reality. 'The great deep' in the *Idylls of the King* is indeed symbolic, but as a symbol its vividness is derived in part from its existence in a non-symbolic context. The deep here is the sea beyond Lyonnesse of the Arthurian tales, the real sea dashing against the Cornish rocks, and against the bleak Lincolnshire coast of Tennyson's boyhood. The mysteriousness which it symbolises is also felt in experience. But in **"De Profundis"** the word 'deep' suggests none of this, it has no lien on a concrete palpable world: what is more, it is not conceptual in significance, not the verbal sign for one of a class of deeps. It is simply a counter or label for an important element in Tennyson's system. He has named something or other 'the deep' and he repeats the word over and over again like an enchanter's spell in which it is vital that the words should be emptied of common meaning. It is as if he expected us to realise the significance of what he is saying by making a ritual of a word. Then, to make matters worse, he elaborates on the word *deep* in a way which adds something to his meaning, but which does not help us to apprehend anything about the deep which would justify its use as a symbol:

> Out of the deep, my child, out of the deep,
> From that true world within the world we see,
> Whereof our world is but the bounding shore.

Any attention to a real 'deep', lake, or sea, or deep hole in the earth, makes nonsense of this sentence. The word has in fact been stretched and stretched beyond its original content like the rubber of a balloon blown up almost to bursting point.

Aldworth, Tennyson's home near Haslemere in Surrey.

This inflation of language is the characteristic fault of Tennyson's later poetry. He acquired a whole vocabulary, a set of counters which for him stand for complex realities, but which for the reader have no value at all, words and phrases like *deep, Nameless, noble, forms of faith, Highest in the Highest,* and it seems as if he thought the mere repetition of them would communicate his meaning. This habit of style is the end product of the mannerism we have already discussed: the use of the striking periphrasis, image, or aphorism, which is detachable from the main body of the work, and which seems a kind of stucco decoration on experience. To some extent periphrasis helps to convey Tennyson's meaning:

> That which knows
> And is not known, but felt through what we feel
> Within ourselves is highest.

This is at least a means of defining an object of knowledge by its effects on us. Even 'the Nameless of the hundred Names' has some value in suggesting identity. But there comes a point in these poems when the reader is aware that Tennyson is concerned more with the striking phrases than with clarity: he has forgotten that language has a function. What shall we understand by this, for instance?

> the pain
> Of this divisible-indivisible world
> Among the numerable-innumerable
> Sun, sun and sun, thro' finite-infinite space
> In finite-infinite Time—

The irony of this is that it has clearly begun as an attempt to translate into poetry some of the difficult awareness of the depths of space, but the striking paradox is too obviously enjoyed by the poet, he cannot resist repeating the effect. The need to explain and define, combined with the enjoyment of elaboration, has developed into a garrulousness which defeats both enjoyment and understanding.

What is so odd about Tennyson's adoption of this oracular but unenlightening manner is that he was capable of a kind of writing in which the images used both have a power over the imagination and yet are the means of carrying forward an argument. . . . He was experimenting with a half-analogical, half-impressionistic imagery as early as "Isabel," and some of the finest passages of *In Memoriam* are the expressions both of mood and of reflection:

> Now dance the lights on lawn and lea,
>   The flocks are whiter down the vale,
>   The milkier every milky sail
> On winding stream or distant sea;
>
> Where now the seamew pipes, or dives
>   In yonder greening gleam, and fly
>   The happy birds, that change their sky
> To build and brood; that live their lives
>
> From land to land; and in my breast
>   Spring wakens too; and my regret
>   Becomes an April violet,
> And buds and blossoms like the rest.

Every detail of this passage belongs to the description of Spring and helps to create the mood of the season, but equally every detail helps to point the analogy between the state of the season and the new view of his experience in Tennyson's mind—the wider, brighter horizons, the birds that change their sky as he himself returns from the exile of continual grief, the rebirth of the April violet which is like the rebirth of hope in his mind. How far he could develop this analogical method of writing can be seen in **"The Voice and the Peak."** In this poem the reader's attention is directed not so much to the qualities of a particular scene as to the familiar feelings of awe, to the sense of something beyond the world of sense, but glimpsed through it and in it, which for the Victorian was roused by mountain peaks, stars, and falling water:

> The voice and the Peak
>   Far over summit and lawn,
> The lone glow and long roar
>   Green-rushing from the rosy thrones of dawn!
>
> All night have I heard the voice
>   Rave over the rocky bar,
> But thou wert silent in heaven,
>   Above thee glided the star.

Tennyson is not so much concerned with the mountain as with a total experience, the mountain in the physical world, the sense of awe in the watcher. He strives to draw the two realities together by isolating and emphasising those elements of mountain scenery which lend themselves to associations of awe:

> Thou wert silent in heaven,
>   Above thee glided the star.

And by the use of a certain dissonance in vowel sounds, a dissonance which is not unpleasant in itself, he suggests the hollow noise of wind and falling water at a distance, sounds which excite a sense of the alien:

> The lone glow and long roar
>
> Rave over the rocky bar

As the poem develops it is clear that the Peak comes to stand for the total experience of reality, and finally the Peak and its voice for symbols of the relation between the permanent and the transient. Or to speak more accurately, Tennyson attempts to present his awareness of these relationships through the analogy of a known relationship, that of the Peak and the waterfall. The Peak, that is, stands for a conception in Tennyson's mind, and his argument is worked out by reference to it. But this concept is based on an interpretation of experience in which the mountain itself played a part. This lien on physical reality has a salutary effect on the poetry. The careful statement of emotional associations with which it opens establishes the Peak as a reality to which the imagination responds: it is not, like the deep of **"De Profundis,"** a magician's meaningless word. There is here a real sense of the 'finite-infinite', there is the Peak that 'standest high above all', from which the waters flow down with a thousand voices like the voices of time, the Peak which seems to be the very image of eternity: and there is the geological peak, which is no more permanent than anything else. Tennyson does not need to be explicit and impressively paradoxical about this relationship. The imagery establishes it for him:

> The deep has power on the height,
>   And the height has power on the deep;
> They are raised for ever and ever,
>   And sink again to sleep.
>
> Not raised for ever and ever,
>   But when their cycle is o'er,

The valley, the voice, the peak, the star
  Pass, and are found no more.

It is man's awareness of these physical things which gives them their mysterious power and their symbolic value:

The Peak is high and flush'd
  At his highest with sunrise fire;
The Peak is high, and the stars are high,
  And the thought of a man is higher.

In returning to the finite character of his symbol Tennyson completes his statement about the relationship between the permanent and the transient. Only the mind of man can comprehend and transcend the enormous division between infinity and the finite. His theme is much the same as it was in **"De Profundis,"** but it is a good deal more lucid when apprehended through the image of the mountain than in the earlier poem's conflict of abstractions. (pp. 253-67)

[The success of **"The Voice and the Peak"** illustrates first] . . . Tennyson is able, for once, to use images from the common stock, images which were neither exclusively Victorian, like the subject pictures in **In Memoriam,** nor so intolerably hackneyed as to be emptied of meaning. Victorian sensibility had been trained to respond to mountains, to regard them as the proper objects of awe. If the age had read nothing else, it had read *Childe Harold* and Mrs Radcliffe; the more cultured of its members, at this late period, had also read Rousseau, Wordsworth, Coleridge and Shelley. Everyone made his private visits to the Alps, and stayed, like Walpole, Byron, Ruskin, and the whole family of the Dorrits, at the hospice of St Bernard. The educated Victorian was also familiar with, even if he disliked, the idea of a never-ceasing change in the universe:

Not raised for ever and ever,
  But when their cycle is o'er,
The valley, the voice, the peak, the star
  Pass, and are found no more.

Tennyson was lucky. His own sensibility was not normally responsive to mountains, but to flat wastes and seas, so that when his imagination was seized by the mountain he could write of it with freshness and confidence, yet, because of the familiarity of the image, he had no need to enter into tedious explanations, or to spend his energies on the recreation of private emotion.

But the vision of reality in **"The Voice and the Peak"** is Tennysonian rather than Victorian. Tennyson's awareness of the natural world as a fleeting dream, or as the symbol of the infinity from which it arises is equally alien to the sturdy Protestantism, and the sturdier materialism of his age. The coincidence of his insights with common symbols was accidental, and on the whole the Victorian public misunderstood him. This does not mean of course that Tennyson himself never had a belief in common with any of his fellows. The schizophrenia of Victorian culture was not a simple matter of the artist contracting out of the common life; the common life itself is riddled with contradictions. . . . The fact is that the Victorian mind was furnished not with common beliefs but with odds and ends, the left-overs and experiments of incongruous systems. Its archetypal figure is the character in *Alice* who could believe several impossible things before breakfast, but most Victorians could do more, they could confuse to-gether mutually exclusive philosophies and religions. (pp. 267-68)

We need not then attempt to explain or justify Tennyson's failures in terms of too close an alignment with a stodgy public, or again as the result of a fastidious withdrawal from the real problems of his age. The disintegration of a culture under the pressure both of intellectual and social change affected both Tennyson and his readers, and it robbed both of standards of judgment by which to measure their achievement. And yet the measure of Tennyson's importance is increased by the difficulties of his background. He did not succumb to temptation as Arnold and Swinburne, in their different ways, succumbed. Against the shift and instability of the period he built a central poetic tradition which served his successors as a support. Dr Leavis quite rightly shows that Yeats emancipated himself from the Tennysonian convention, but the fact remains that the convention was there for Yeats to use and develop until he was mature enough to discard it. It is after all only small poets who allow themselves to be imprisoned by the style and the sensibility of their predecessors, and Yeats was not a small poet. But even the great need support when they begin: the Tennysonian tradition supported not only Yeats but Eliot, whose poetry with its exploitation of associations, its cadences like a tired voice falling to silence, its movement from significant complexes of images to paradoxical balances of words and verbal definitions, is more Tennysonian than perhaps Eliot himself realises. It is the measure of a poet that he expands the possibilities of the language. That Tennyson did so while creating and maintaining a poetic tradition which the first mass audience in the world could accept, and in which it found comfort, was in itself a considerable achievement. That he did so in a cultural situation unpropitious to literature, suggests an unusual greatness. (pp. 269-70)

Valerie Pitt, in her Tennyson Laureate, *1962. Reprint by University of Toronto Press, 1969, 292 p.*

K. W. Gransden   (essay date 1964)

[*Gransden is an English educator, poet, and critic. In the following excerpt, he discusses the importance of the "Epilogue" to* In Memoriam.]

[If] **In Memoriam** is read as Tennyson intended it to be, the poems of grief and despair at the beginning of the cycle cannot be extracted from the sequence and given special emphasis as though they were representative of the whole poem. The Victorians did not make this mistake, but some modern critics have tended to see in the poem a reflection of our modern static mental condition, even though this means ignoring, or at best belittling, the considerable intellectual and spiritual hard work done in the later poems of the cycle. The cynic of today may smile at the thought that Queen Victoria found in **In Memoriam,** next to the Bible, her best comfort after Albert's death; yet it is hard to see how, if the Queen had read the poem as, say, Mr. T. S. Eliot seems to have read it [see excerpt dated 1936], she could have found much comfort in it. The slick answer here is, of course, that the Victorians found what *they* wanted and we find what *we* want; that we are more impressed by the documentation of despair than by the documentation of hope; and that, anyway, what Tennyson thought he had achieved may not correspond to what he did achieve. But Tennyson was a highly conscious and self-conscious artist, and a man of the highest intelligence and sensibility. Seventeen years after Hallam's death, he would not have taken the trouble to arrange the poem as he did, and to work out the concluding arguments of the sequence, if he had wanted to leave the poem as a poem of despair (even if it was, in Mr. Eliot's words, despair of a religious kind).

The early poems of the sequence, like VII (**'Dark House by Which Once More I Stand'**) linger in the reader's mind because they speak to our condition, they can be fitted into the tradition of urban *angoisse* established by Baudelaire, Verlaine and Rimbaud; Tennyson's London is the London, it seems, of *The Waste Land,* 'flaring like a dreary dawn'. For the modern reader, using the two-column collected edition of Tennyson, *In Memoriam* is stuffed like a collection of miscellanea into the middle of a cabin trunk, with the result that the sequence seems a mere collection of lyrics, inviting us to pick and choose. In the poem as originally published, in an octavo volume of over two hundred pages, each poem starting on a fresh page, it is somehow much easier to trace a development (as in Meredith's sequence *Modern Love*). Moreover, it must not be forgotten that the great English elegies, *Lycidas* or *Adonais,* always move from personal grief towards the acceptance of some kind of immortality (whether orthodox Christian or pantheistic) which triumphs over grief. Consequently, to give the earlier grief-dominated poems too much emphasis is to place too much strain on a part of the whole, to alter the poem's structure, to reduce its stature, to ignore Tennyson's own intentions and the tradition in which he is writing.

That the poem moves away from despair is particularly (some critics would say over-) emphasised in the epilogue, which celebrates the marriage of Tennyson's sister Cecilia with Edmund Lushington. This marriage took place in 1842, eight years before the publication of *In Memoriam,* so that it cannot be seen as a last-minute addition, tagged on in order to provide a happier happy ending. Indeed, it is clear from the poem's opening stanzas that the epilogue was composed as an epithalamium on and for the occasion itself, so that its incorporation into *In Memoriam* as the poet's last word must have been deliberate.

In the epilogue Tennyson looks back on his own grief, already at the time of writing eight years away and by the time of publication seventeen. He contrasts his old mood with his present one, which he describes, rather loftily, as

> No longer caring to embalm
> In dying songs a dead regret,
> But like a statue solid-set,
> And moulded in colossal calm.

This is reasonable if one takes Tennyson to mean (what the closing poems of the sequence have already announced) that he has exorcised his grief, subsumed it in a new understanding and acceptance: all passion spent. But the image seems to do rather more than this: the words 'embalm', 'dead' and 'statue' suggest that all feeling has gone, that the poet is no longer capable of feeling and does not wish to be. 'Colossal' is of course directly suggested by 'statue' (the Colossus of Rhodes) but in its ordinary

modern sense the adjective nevertheless makes a heavy claim, as if of some larger-than-life stability. After the humility, the self-effacement, the subordination of the self to Hallam's memory, made in the poem, the epilogue seems to show Tennyson as self-aggrandising, boasting about the impressiveness of his new state. He does, it is true, also say that though regret is dead, love is more, but to this he adds that in the last few years

> I myself with these have grown
> To something greater than before.

In the poem itself it was Hallam, and Tennyson's love, that grew vaster and finally became all-pervasive. Now Tennyson appears to be making this claim for himself. Consequently, critics have tended to dismiss the epilogue (even Bradley said the style of its writing was mannered) and have used it to support their argument that the more hopeful note of the later poems is a false one.

I think Tennyson took the marriage as an omen, the symbol of a new start. He may have felt in its finality a residue of discomfort and disloyalty to Hallam for which he had to compensate by citing his own changed attitude. But the attitude has been completely prepared for: it is the self-control achieved at the end of the cycle. The forward-looking tone of the epithalamium is prepared for as early as LXXXV, in which Tennyson admits that he is beginning to be more interested in the future than in the past and feels the need to apologise to Hallam for appearing to desert him, the work of autotherapy and commemoration being already almost complete. The two statements that he counts it 'crime to mourn for any overmuch' and that he cannot forget 'the mighty hopes that make us men' are a warning that the point of no return between past and future is about to be reached.

Tennyson does not expect others to learn wisdom from his experiences if he cannot learn any himself; the epilogue is evidence that he had learnt something, and that what he has learnt is not only self-control but *self-confidence*. In the hour of despair man feels small in his helplessness, and when things go well with him again he seems to fill out, to assert himself again, to take up room on earth proudly instead of trying to creep into a corner and disappear. Moreover, self-control means, not that one has ceased to feel but that one does not *appear* to feel. One is no longer vulnerable. (Tennyson does not say that he *is* a statue but that he is *like* one.) The calm of the epilogue recalls the calm despair of XI: but that calm was as uncontrollable as a calm before a storm, ready at any moment to give way to another onrush of wild unrest. In contrast, the new calm is impervious to external influence (nature's moods are as irrelevant now as they seemed relevant then). So the lines may be taken quite literally: regret *is* dead; we recall

> . . . and my regret
> Becomes an April violet . . .

The violet goes, but we remain: no longer the slaves of our feelings or of our mortality. And the statue is a work of art, and it is through a work of art that Tennyson has achieved his new strength and insight.

But the most important part of the epilogue is the last six stanzas, for they state, more firmly than anything in the preceding poem, Tennyson's faith in the moral evolution of man. Here he re-affirms his belief that a race will one day be born which shall 'look on knowledge'. Of this race Hallam is called a 'noble type, appearing ere the times were ripe'. The idea here is one of correspondence, a familiar one in Christian art: Hallam is to the race to be what an Old Testament figure was to a New Testament one: a prophetic emblem. (But throughout his work Tennyson uses 'type' both in its old theological sense and in its nineteenth-century scientific sense, of a group of organisms having a common pattern. If a perfect specimen of any group can be found, this will serve as a model, exemplar or ideal. The whole article on 'type' in the N.E.D. should be read.) Tennyson thus reinforces as a belief amounting to a prediction what in CXVIII had been a hope, a prayer: 'let the ape and tiger die'. The marriage by turning the poet's mind towards the future gives him new encouragement to believe that man will improve and be 'no longer half akin to brute'. The children of the marriage will be one step nearer the generation which will justify the whole troublesome human experiment: they will be

> a closer link
> Betwixt us and the crowning race

Tennyson is careful not to say when this will be, and CXXVII, one of the few political poems in the sequence, shows that he felt further troubles and upheavals would have to be endured but that the enlightened dead could look beyond these revolutions and smile, knowing what was to follow.

Thus *In Memoriam* ends with the assertion of a regenerative principle as do the last plays of Shakespeare: but a regenerative principle for which we may have to wait patiently through many generations. Meanwhile, man's development on earth is, as we have seen in previous evolutionary poems in the sequence, paralleled by the instant development of the good man in heaven. So Hallam both foreshadows the crowning race and catches up with it in heaven; the dead and the unborn share an insight for which the living seek in vain. And the 'one far-off divine event to which the whole creation moves' is the arrival of the regenerative principle itself, when the long heartbreaking process will be complete. A late poem called **'The Making of Man'** makes this clear (again the tiger and the ape represent stages left behind in the process of spiritual evolution):

> Where is one that, born of woman, altogether can escape
> From the lower world within him, moods of tiger or of ape?
>> Man as yet is being made, and ere the crowning Age of ages,
> Shall not aeon after aeon pass and touch him into shape?
>
> All about him shadow still, but, while the races flower and fade,
> Prophet-eyes may catch a glory slowly gaining on the shade,
>> Till the people all are one and all their voices blend in choric
> Hallelujah to the Maker 'It is finish'd. Man is made.'

We should remember that the idea of a better race was current in the nineteenth century. Mill wrote that Bentham 'lived in a generation of the leanest and barrenest men whom England had yet produced, and he was an old man when a better race came in with the present century'. In the *Idylls* Arthur's knights are called 'the fair beginners of a nobler time'; and Wordsworth in *The Excursion*

prayed that his life should 'express the image of a better time' and asked why the vision of Paradise should be

> A history only of departed things
> Or a mere fiction of what never was.

Thus I do not feel with Mr. Eliot that the faith of *In Memoriam* is a poor thing but that it follows a great tradition of faith in what Wordsworth called 'sovereign man'; nor do I feel that the poems of Hardy and Housman . . . or Thomson's *City of Dreadful Night* with its bleak, mannered pessimisms are characteristic derivatives. What all these writers lack, and what Tennyson and Wordsworth possessed and show in all their work, is piety. This does not preclude feelings of despondency and despair: but it does involve a faith in the existence of something larger, both in human capacity and in the universe as man reads it: and this the late romantic pessimists—egotists whose egotism remained their goal instead of being their philosophic springboard—conspicuously lacked. If I had to single out a poem which obviously derives from *In Memoriam,* I should pick J. A. Symonds's 'A Vista':

> These things shall be! A loftier race
> Than e'er the world hath known, shall rise
> With flame of freedom in their souls
> And light of knowledge in their eyes.

The concept of the golden age is one of the oldest in European poetry, but for Tennyson it is the ultimate goal, never yet attained, an improvement on, not a repetition of, prelapsarian perfection.

What Tennyson claims in *In Memoriam* is that he has won a significant spiritual victory not only over personal despair—

> not in vain,
> Like Paul with beasts, I fought with Death

—but over the false general pessimism engendered by scientific materialism, the dead end of up-to-dateness:

> I think we are not wholly brain,
> Magnetic mockeries . . .
>
> Not only cunning casts in clay:
> Let Science prove we are, and then
> What matters Science unto men,
> At least to me? I would not stay.

And this argument came to be accepted by Victorian scientists. In his book on *Darwinism,* which appeared in 1889 and which ends with a quotation from *In Memoriam,* A. R. Wallace, arguing that the process of natural selection cannot account for man's spiritual qualities, wrote:

> We who accept the existence of a spiritual world can look upon the universe as a grand consistent whole adapted in all its parts to the development of spiritual beings capable of indefinite life and perfectibility. To us the whole purpose, the only *raison d'être* of the world—with all its complexities of physical structure, with its grand geological progress, the slow evolution of the vegetable and animal kingdoms, and the ultimate appearance of man— was the development of the human spirit in association with the human body.

Thus the vision with which *In Memoriam* ends may be read as a new metaphor for man's innate capacity for moral greatness, a capacity to which all the major poets of the eighteenth and early nineteenth centuries had borne witness. Tennyson thus stands almost at the end of a tradition: 'And the great Aeon sinks in blood'. The value of *In Memoriam* lies in the fact that in it not only Tennyson's spiritual survival but man's is at stake. He moves on from despair with a Bunyanesque steadfastness which we ought to admire in him as he admired it in Hallam:

> He faced the spectres of the mind
> And laid them.

Three years before, in *The Princess,* Tennyson had published some lines which closely correspond to the end of *In Memoriam,* lines celebrating marriage as the symbol of hope not only for the two concerned but for the human race:

> And so these twain, upon the skirts of Time,
> Sit side by side, full-summ'd in all their powers,
> Dispensing harvest, sowing the To-be,
> Self-reverent each and reverencing each;
> Distinct in individualities,
> But like each other ev'n as those who love.
> Then comes the statelier Eden back to men:
> Then reign the world's great bridals, chaste and calm:
> Then springs the crowning race of human kind.
> May such things be!

To this the practical princess says 'I fear they will not': the poet-prince replies 'Dear, but let us type them now'. Hallam 'typed' (i.e. both prefigured and perfectly exemplified) what man can become: a married couple can do more, they can take a practical step towards the crowning race. One recalls, reading these lines, Adam and Eve, the slow climb back to Paradise: yet not the old Paradise of innocence, but a new and better Paradise to which accumulated experience and moral wisdom contribute. Meanwhile, the individual can only do his best within existing limitations:

> O we will walk this world,
> Yok'd in all exercise of noble end,
> And so thro' those dark gates across the wild
> That no man knows.

The journey may be long, but man must go on, keeping the vision in his mind; he dies, and all his generation die, but his successors take up the pursuit.

> And we, the poor earth's dying race, and yet
> No phantoms, watching from a phantom shore
> Await the last and largest sense to make
> The phantom walls of this illusion fade,
> And show us that the world is wholly fair,

These lines from **'The Ancient Sage'** are perhaps the finest summing up of the Tennysonian vision. Phantom is a favourite word of Tennyson's, and 'phantom shore' also occurs in the poem to Virgil. But man is no phantom, because human vision, and only human vision, can see beyond the phenomenal world. The crowning race will be endowed with the 'last and largest sense' which will allow it to see reality, not through a glass darkly, but clearly. The 'dream of good' from which man now keeps waking because of the limitations of his own mental darkness, is an inkling of that perfection 'behind the veil'.

Man's capacity to understand his limitations, to grasp his predicament, and to place it in a larger context of human development, began to decline during the last decades of the nineteenth century. The visionary power and the steadfastness began to fade. One sees this clearly in Arnold, prophet of modern *angst.* Lines like

> Still the same ocean round us raves
> But we stand still and watch the waves

express the static nature of modern impotence, and emphasise by contrast the way in which, in *In Memoriam,* the human spirit is still asserting itself against time and space, doubt and despair. It is a historical document from a time when the odds against man were heavy but not overwhelming. The artist still had 'a conscience and an aim', wanting to teach because his readers wanted to learn. Though enmeshed in a new complex of scientific data Tennyson could still, without either ignoring or being ignorant of these data, speculate on man's spiritual nature with something of the old traditional grandeur. Our own age is overwhelmed with data which seem beyond assimilation and impossible to ignore. Tennyson is, if we like, the last great poet to link those soon to be notorious two cultures which now threaten to diminish the stature of man. (pp. 60-8)

> *K. W. Gransden, in his* Tennyson: In Memoriam, *Edward Arnold (Publishers) Ltd., 1964, 72 p.*

John D. Jump   (essay date 1974)

[*In the following excerpt, Jump provides a biographical background to Tennyson's works and surveys his major poetry.*]

Dr George Clayton Tennyson, the Rector of Somersby in Lincolnshire, had entered holy orders against his inclination; he found his income insufficient to maintain his large family in what he considered decency; and he bitterly resented the preferment of his younger brother as their wealthy father's heir. Resentment unhinged his mind. He wrecked his health by taking to drink, and drinking tended to make him ungovernably violent. After years of misery, his wife had to insist upon a separation.

Alfred, born in 1809, the third of their children to survive infancy, grew up under the shadow of the family feud and in the gloomy presence of this learned and cultivated but unhappy and demented man. He evidently regarded his father with pity and fear, with anger and love, and at times with plain hostility. Trinity College, Cambridge, where he was admitted late in 1827, must have seemed to offer a haven from domestic storms. But Alfred was bored and lonely there until he met Arthur Henry Hallam in the spring of 1829. The two young men quickly became firm friends. Each could give the other support by his sympathetic understanding of the moods of despondency to which both were subject. They joined the 'Apostles', an informal debating society which included many of the ablest undergraduates among its members; and before the end of the year Hallam fell in love with Tennyson's sister Emily.

Hallam found satisfaction, and greatly assisted his friend, by acting as Tennyson's literary agent. He worked hard to get *Poems, Chiefly Lyrical* (1830) a favourable reception, and but for him Tennyson would not have brought out his second volume, *Poems,* as early as 1832. He praised Tennyson 'as promising fair to be the greatest poet of our generation, perhaps of our century'. Then, in the autumn of 1833, he died suddenly while touring in Austria with his father. Tennyson and his sister lost in Hallam a man whom both loved deeply and who fully returned the love of both. Tennyson's whole life seemed shattered; for a time he wished to die.

Not that Hallam's death was solely responsible for this wish. The circumstances of Tennyson's early life, and possibly hereditary factors, had predisposed him to melancholia. Poems written before as well as after the autumn of 1833 express the desperate loneliness he was always prone to feel and the craving for oblivion to which it constantly led. Shortly before Hallam's death J. W. Croker had produced a brutally sarcastic review of *Poems* (1832; dated 1833), writing with the avowed intention of making another Keats of his victim. Hurt, despondent, and bereaved, Tennyson lapsed into the 'ten years' silence' which preceded the launching of his next collection, *Poems* (1842).

Early in this period, in 1834, he fell in love with Rosa Baring of Harrington Hall, near Somersby. Her wealth made her unattainable, and he soon came to see her as a rather commonplace young woman. But he was always to remember vividly the intensity of his brief, thwarted passion. In 1836 he fell in love with Emily Sellwood, a Lincolnshire solicitor's daughter, who was to become his wife after an engagement greatly prolonged and even interrupted by his lack of funds, by her family's anxiety about the mental health of the Tennysons generally, and by her own misgivings regarding his religious faith.

Poems (1842) comprised two volumes: the first contained selected poems, often much revised, from the earlier collections, the second a slightly greater amount of new verse. Both the public and the reviewers responded favourably. But, whereas Tennyson had written much during the greater part of the 'ten years' silence', he wrote little during the years immediately before and after the publication of *Poems* (1842), that broke it. Acute financial problems and the apparent loss of Emily were aggravating his recurrent fierce melancholia. Late in 1843 his friend Edward FitzGerald—subsequently to become famous for *The Rubáiyát of Omar Khayyám*—found him more hopeless than he had ever seen him; and in the following year Tennyson was receiving medical treatment. He continued to be a source of anxiety to his friends until after the publication of *The Princess* (1847).

From about that time, however, things took a turn for the better. Tennyson's financial position improved. A reading of *In Memoriam* in manuscript dispelled Emily's anxiety about his religious faith, and they married in the summer of 1850. Emily was to be a devoted and tireless wife, and their friends soon noted with pleasure the change in Alfred's health and spirits. For some years his reputation as a poet had been growing steadily, and towards the end of 1850 he succeeded William Wordsworth as Poet Laureate. (pp. vii-viii)

One after another [Tennyson's] books augmented his reputation. Admittedly, many reviewers complained that *Maud* (1855) was obscure and morbid. But the reading public did not lose interest, and the first four *Idylls of the King* (1859) and *Enoch Arden* (1864) raised his popularity to such a pitch that a writer in a weekly paper could think

it likely that the age would become known as the age of Tennyson. (p. ix)

Even as brief a biographical summary as this can leave no one in doubt regarding certain sources of the melancholy which finds expression in one after another of Tennyson's poems. His deep love for his home must have made the distresses and frustrations of life at Somersby almost unbearable. They find an indirect outlet in his writing. He evokes an oppressive sense of decay in the 'Song' beginning 'A spirit haunts the year's last hours'; he uses a beautifully particularized setting to compel his reader to share the loneliness and dejection of the abandoned woman in **'Mariana'**; and in **'The Two Voices'** he confronts the case for escaping the weariness, the fever, and the fret of life by suicide.

The voice which tempts the speaker to this conclusion seems to come from within himself. It is a 'still small voice', which does not so much originate lines of argument as develop disconcertingly those which the speaker himself advances in trying to resist despair. It punctures his human pride by pointing out that there must be many creatures superior to man in a universe that is boundless; it undercuts his faith in progress by asking what is the significance of progress along a scale that is infinite; it derides his wish to leave an honourable name; and it seeks to allay the dread of something after death by persuading him that the dead are at peace. But the speaker needs to believe that death does not end all. Despite the voice's insistence upon the fact of pain, he wants 'More life, and fuller'; and he is strengthened in this desire by the sight of a happily united family walking to church. When the sceptical voice dies away, the second voice of the poem's title cheers the speaker by hinting at a 'hidden hope' of a divine love.

As this necessarily selective outline will have suggested, the argument of **'The Two Voices'** follows the vagaries of feeling rather than the routine of logic. The poem's rhyming triplets, which almost ask for a dubitative pause after each third line, serve well to record a process of anxious and tentative brooding. Admittedly, **'The Two Voices'** does not achieve the assured success of **'Mariana'** or the **'Song'**. It is awkward in some places, flat in others; and many twentieth-century readers have found its churchgoing family too good to be true. Nevertheless, it does honestly face the issues it raises, and it is frequently moving and memorable.

Since a draft of it existed three months before Tennyson learned of Hallam's death, the bereavement cannot have prompted the poem. Work on it continued for some time, however, so we may assume that grief at Hallam's death entered into **'The Two Voices'** as finally published. Tennyson himself declared that **'Ulysses'** was what he wrote under the immediate sense of the loss, with the feeling 'that all had gone by, but that still life must be fought out to the end'. The speaker in this dramatic monologue has resolved to embark upon a new, perilous, and possibly final voyage. Yet his mood is elegiac; a tone as of mournful acquiescence casts doubt on the strenuousness of his resolution. As a result, we imagine him less as striving, seeking, finding, and refusing to yield than as standing, in the words of a Victorian reviewer, 'for ever a listless and melancholy figure on the shore'. The ambiguity of the portrait springs from Tennyson's utter honesty. Life had indeed to be fought out to the end, but by one whom grief had immobilized and in whom early experience had implanted a longing for oblivion. **'Ulysses'** is one of the most complex and poignant of his shorter pieces.

The work that most readily brings Hallam to mind is *In Memoriam.* Critics have sometimes exaggerated the degree of unity that resulted when Tennyson arranged almost a gross of short lyrics to form this long philosophical poem. Admittedly it opens with the first crushing onset of grief, and it closes with the marriage of a sister of the poet. 'It was meant to be a kind of *Divina Commedia,* ending with happiness', stated Tennyson. Its three Christmas passages, implying a fictional span of almost exactly three years between the opening and the close, can be read as marking clear stages in the mourner's emotional and spiritual recovery: the first Christmas Eve falls 'sadly' (xxx), the second 'calmly' (lxxviii), and the third 'strangely' (cv). Lyrics marking other anniversaries serve this purpose, too. But when all has been said we must let Tennyson remind us that the lyrics 'were written at many different places, and as the phases of our intercourse came to my memory and suggested them. I did not write them with any view of weaving them into a whole, or for publication, until I found that I had written so many.'

This did not prevent him from distinguishing nine natural groups of lyrics in *In Memoriam* as finally shaped. A list of the nine, with some indication of their leading subjects or themes, will take us about as far as it seems reasonable to go in trying to see the poem as a strictly organized whole:

1 Grief at the news of Hallam's death overwhelms the mourner (i-viii).

2 In imagination, he follows the ship that is bringing home his friend's body for burial (ix-xx).

3 He recalls the four years of friendship he and the dead man had known (xxi-xxvii).

4 The pain of loss would be insupportable but for the hope of survival after death (xxviii-xlix).

5 Needing to believe in personal immortality and in the enduring value of human endeavour, the mourner longs for his friend to approach and sustain him (l-lviii).

6 His reliance upon Hallam's spirit continues despite the extent of their separation (lix-lxxi).

7 Though his grief is growing calmer, his dependence persists, and he still begs his friend's spirit to come to him. From about this point, springtime imagery tends to displace autumn and winter imagery. A fleeting mystical experience, recorded in xcv, forms the climax and turning-point of the poem (lxxii-xcviii).

8 The mourner's departure from the childhood home which Hallam had visited signalizes a fresh start (xcix-ciii).

9 The New Year hymn, cvi, further emphasizing this, leads to a series of affectionate and admiring recollections of his friend and to confident assertions of faith in the divine love (civ-cxxxi). This faith is the theme also of the prologue, which Tennyson wrote late but used to introduce the entire poem. A lyric on his sister's wedding forms the epilogue.

The need to believe in survival after death and in the enduring value of human endeavour had prevailed by the end of **'The Two Voices.'** In the fifth group of lyrics composing *In Memoriam,* Tennyson reaffirms it in face of the appalling fact that not only individuals like Hallam but whole species of living creatures have been ruthlessly and arbitrarily swept away in the long course of time. The reaffirmation is cruelly difficult. What rôle can mind or spirit have had in the process traced by the geologists? Does not this process invite explanation in purely material or physical terms? Only 'faintly', in defiance of the evidence, can Tennyson 'trust the larger hope'. This, at all events, is as far as he can go in the first half of *In Memoriam.*

In the final group of lyrics he achieves a more confident assertion of faith. He rejects materialism as cripplingly reductive. Men cannot be satisfactorily explained as 'wholly brain' or mere 'cunning casts in clay'. Moreover, the evolutionary process moves towards the fulfilment of a providential plan; it is bringing into being 'a higher race', which was anticipated in Hallam. This providential plan implies a loving God. Experience of the kind recorded in xcv enables the poet to affirm his belief in the divine love. Simply and firmly, he can declare, 'I have felt.'

So the poem as a whole traces the gradual alleviation of the pain of bereavement and the eventual confirmation of an intuitive faith in the 'Strong Son of God, immortal Love'. But while we are actually reading it we pay less heed to these processes than to the particular phases of thought and feeling captured in the separate lyrics. Tennyson's stanza-form lends itself exactly to this presentation of a series of intellectual and emotional states, each one of which in turn appears to be almost immutable. The four lines composing the *In Memoriam* stanza are all iambic tetrameters. The second and third derive firmness and emphasis from their couplet rhyming. While the first and fourth, thanks to the rhymes which link them, seem to wrap around the couplet, their separation from each other weakens the conclusiveness of the fourth. The stanza turns on itself, encloses itself, pauses in earnest reflection, yet seems always to hint at resumption.

Tennyson's contemporaries had found much to admire in the short pieces published by 1842. Yet some even of the friendliest of them were not completely satisfied. They looked for something more strenuous and sustained. They wanted him to write a long poem, to handle an important contemporary subject, to show a deeper human sympathy, and to preach sound doctrine. Tennyson had responded with *The Princess* (1847), a fanciful contribution to the current discussion of women's education. Ironically, the poetic romance which forms the main part of this work has kept its appeal less well than have the exquisite and moving lyrics which are supposedly incidental to it. But with *In Memoriam* Tennyson solved his problem by shaping a long prophetic poem, as demanded by his critics, from the short personal lyrics that came more naturally to him.

Maud (1855) is another long poem made up of short lyrics. These purport to be the dramatic utterances of a young man whose distresses broadly resemble those of Tennyson himself: his father, wronged, resentful, and finally unbalanced, appears to have committed suicide; his mother has been lonely and unhappy; the wealth and social standing of Maud's family constitute as great a barrier to his union with her as those of Rosa Baring's family did to her union with Tennyson; bitter experience had made Tennyson quite as angrily aware of financial malpractices as his hero was to be; and when his hero expresses the grief of bereavement and the longing for reunion with a dead lover in the lyric beginning 'O that 'twere possible' (II.iv) he is elaborating lines that Tennyson had written immediately after Hallam's death. Was the happily married and successful Poet Laureate perhaps trying to come to terms through a fictional plot with the pains and grievances of his own earlier life?

He called the poem 'a little *Hamlet*'. Like the prince, its hero has been deprived of his inheritance by the man whom he holds responsible for his father's death. He sees this man as representative of a whole Mammon-worshipping age. Denouncing it in the manner of Thomas Carlyle or Charles Kingsley, he resolves to bury himself in himself (I.i).

He then sets eyes on this man's daughter, Maud, for the first time since childhood. He tries to dismiss her from his mind as 'Faultily faultless, icily regular, splendidly null' (I.ii). But he cannot forget her looks—though he thinks her proud—and he is captivated by her voice when she sings 'A passionate ballad gallant and gay, / A martial song like a trumpet's call' (I.v). Delighted when Maud shows him friendship, he nevertheless suspects 'some coquettish deceit' (I.vi).

Maud's brother, a selfish and arrogant young dandy with a genuine affection for his sister, is the principal obstacle to their developing relationship. Although their fathers have pledged long ago that the hero and Maud shall become man and wife, the brother wishes to marry her to the effete grandson of a wealthy, ruthless mine-owner.

But Maud and the hero draw together in love. Her acceptance of him is marked by the grave and beautiful lyric, 'I have led her home' (I.xviii). In this, a steady, assured, and customary iambic rhythm prevails for the first time at any length in a poem mainly characterized by hectic and throbbing anapaestic, or mixed anapaestic and iambic, patterns. The hero swears 'to bury / All this dead body of hate' (I.xix). The famous lyric in which he waits eagerly, impatiently, feverishly for her to leave the dance at the Hall, her home, and join him in the garden marks the climax of the poem (I.xxii).

The hero's fortunes now resemble Romeo's more closely than Hamlet's. Just as Romeo fights with Juliet's kinsman Tybalt and is banished, so the hero fights with Maud's brother and goes into exile. There are extenuating circumstances: the brother acts in defiance of the fathers' pledge and of the lovers' mutual affection; he calls the hero a liar and strikes him in the presence of his 'grinning' rival (II.i); and he receives his wound in a formal duel, after which he admits, 'The fault was mine' (II.i). Maud's death follows quickly on this calamity.

The hero retains two clear images of her. One shows her as she appeared when he was a happy accepted lover; the other shows her as she appeared when she uttered her 'passionate cry' (II.i) of grief at the bloodshed. This second image becomes the 'phantom' that haunts him in his exile and madness, a symbol of his guilt. His madness is powerfully rendered in a lyric, II.v, which incorporates disordered reminiscences of all that has gone before.

Part III associates his recovery of his reason, and the final disappearance of the 'phantom', with his ceasing to bury himself in himself and instead devoting himself to a great cause. 'It is better to fight for the good than to rail at the ill' (III.vi).

This is on the whole the hero's version of what happens in *Maud*. Does the poem present any alternative version? A play allows different characters to take different views of what is going on—Lear's differs from Cordelia's, and hers from Goneril's and Regan's—but *Maud* is not a play. All the lyrics come from the hero's mouth. In such dramatic monologues as 'My Last Duchess', 'Andrea del Sarto', and 'The Bishop Orders his Tomb', Browning allows his characters to give their own accounts of things, but at the same time, by permitting a little over-insistence, for example, or by briefly releasing passions which the characters strive to repress, he implies alternative accounts which the reader may share with him. In this sense, Tennyson's lyrics are hardly dramatic at all. If we were to learn that the poem had not been written by Tennyson but by a young man who had himself loved Maud, shot and perhaps killed her brother, and enlisted in the army, we should find this only too easy to believe.

Does this matter? May we not read the poem as a series of lyrics expressing the changing moods of an isolated, unhappy, angry, neurotic young man; who is lifted out of his misery when he finds his love returned but is plunged into even deeper misery when circumstances lead him to wreck that love; and who emerges from his consequent madness only when he finds a great and noble cause which he can serve?

That 'great and noble cause' troubles many readers. They cannot view the Crimean War in that light. With the wisdom of hindsight, they can see that it was unnecessary; and they know that it was going to be mismanaged. But we can hardly blame the hero, or Tennyson, for not knowing all this at the time. What matters in the poem is that the hero is devoting himself to what he believes to be a struggle against falsehood and tyranny.

It is plausible enough, psychologically speaking, that he should be able to overcome his personal grief and guilt by achieving solidarity with others in such a movement. Moreover, he believes that the war will do for the nation something comparable with what he expects military service will do for himself. In the opening lyric and later he has castigated contemporary selfishness and greed. He has denounced the evils permitted or even encouraged by Victorian capitalism, and he has protested against the materialism of the age. He now trusts that the challenge of war will elicit in Englishmen a stronger sense of solidarity with, and of responsibility towards, one another and so lead them to eliminate these evils. Much of his criticism of the aggressive individualism of his time is justified; and both then and later men have urgently needed a strong sense of collective purpose. However, war seems an intolerably ruthless, destructive, and wasteful way of supplying this want, and one that can hardly supply it permanently.

Yet we scrutinize the poem in vain for any recognition by Tennyson that this is so. He is apparently content that the war should be fought to cure his hero's neurosis and to raise standards of behaviour in commerce and industry. In short, he seems to have surrendered his poem to his hero. Understandably, there were contemporaries who criticized Tennyson for identifying with his hero's bellicosity while sitting safely at home in the Isle of Wight.

Tennyson seems to identify not merely with his hero's bellicosity but with all his hero's changing and often passionate moods. As a result, *Maud* is not only a poem about a somewhat feverish hero; it is a somewhat feverish poem about such a hero. It is a skilfully planned series of personal lyrics written in an assumed character. This character is not dramatically projected. We are left to judge for ourselves the reliability of his testimony; we receive little or no guidance from the poem itself.

But his changing and often passionate moods are rendered with a marvellous intimacy and persuasiveness. *Maud* may hardly deserve the subtitle, *A Monodrama*. It is, however, a compelling, moving, exciting, lyrical sequence.

Tennyson cast several of his finest shorter poems in the form of dramatic monologues. In most of them, as in *Maud,* there is little point in trying to distinguish between what the character says and what the poem says. This is evidently the case with 'Ulysses'; and in 'Tithonus', also commenced shortly after Hallam's death, Tennyson places in a suitable speaker's mouth his own recognition that there are terms on which even immortality would become a curse and would produce a longing for extinction. 'Ulysses' and 'Tithonus' are two of the subtlest, richest, and most truly personal of his poems.

But they hardly aspire to be 'dramatic' in the sense in which 'St. Simeon Stylites' may be so described. In this, the speaker has sought salvation by mortifying the flesh. For thirty years he has confined himself to the top of a high pillar; he has grown emaciated, deformed, diseased; but he has, he hopes, acquired a degree of sanctity sufficient to qualify him to be a miraculous healer on earth and one of the blessed hereafter. Tennyson allows him to grow over-insistent in his pleading. Argumentatively, he asks Christ who, if not he, may be saved: 'Who may be made a saint, if I fail here?' He boasts that 'no one, even among the saints, / May match his pains with mine'. Though he thanks God for 'His bounty' in making him an 'example to mankind, / Which few can reach to', his words inadvertently disclose his arrogant assumption that he has by his own effort 'reached' the state to which he is ostensibly thanking God for raising him.

By such touches, Tennyson makes his poem convey meanings which Simeon does not intend. As we read, we see Simeon both through his own eyes and through those of an independent observer. His monologue is dramatic in the sense in which one hesitates to apply the term to *Maud* or 'Ulysses' or 'Tithonus'. To say this is not to decry these three works and others like them; it is merely to define the kind of success characteristic of these more subjective monologues.

The grotesque traits in the portrait of Simeon may serve to remind us that Tennyson's writings exhibit a considerable variety both in content and in form. His melancholia and his efforts to dispel the fears it aroused, dominate most of the poems reviewed so far. *Maud* is not alone in bringing home to us how acute was his awareness of the subrational forces, both in the individual and in the world generally, that make for madness, violence, and destruction, and how earnestly he strove to understand and to

manage these forces within his own life. The complement of this painful awareness is a craving for stability, security, and peace of mind. This can be expressed mawkishly, as in the evocation of 'settled bliss' at the end of 'The Miller's Daughter'. But it can equally be communicated with serene finality by the compellingly suggestive detail of a landscape, as when he speaks of the knolls 'where, couch'd at ease, / The white kine glimmer'd, and the trees / Laid their dark arms about the field' (*In Memoriam,* xcv) or of 'The pillar'd dusk of sounding sycamores' ('Audley Court').

His poetic renderings of natural phenomena are rarely less than brilliant. Patient and sensitive observation is served in them by his supreme skill in the handling of words, by what Walt Whitman called his 'finest verbalism'. During his later years, readers noted the conjunction of such verbalism with a gentle sadness and tenderness and spoke of him as the English Virgil. During his earlier years, its manifestation in such poems as 'Mariana', the 'Song' ('A spirit haunts the year's last hours'), 'The Lady of Shalott', and 'The Lotos-Eaters' led them to regard him as the successor to John Keats. His language in these is rich, deliberate, incantatory. 'The Lady of Shalott' shows how readily it can give access to that mediaeval dream-world which attracted so many nineteenth-century writers and painters.

Though Tennyson mediaevalizes in several early lyrical poems, his most distinguished achievement in that direction is an epic fragment, 'Morte d'Arthur'. In this, a poet who longed for settled ways comes to terms, through an Arthur who is dying, or passing to Avilion, with the irresistible and often violent processes of change. The fragment is haunting, poignant, and compelling.

Tennyson knew that many critics were currently demanding poems about contemporary life. So in self-defence he enclosed his fragment in what amounted to an apology, 'The Epic'. Gradually conquering his timidity, he returned to the Arthurian material in middle age and eventually produced what many Victorians thought his masterpiece, *Idylls of the King.* Like *In Memoriam* and *Maud,* this is a long work built up from relatively short, separate items. Four of these appeared in 1859: 'Enid', 'Vivien', 'Elaine', and 'Guinevere'. Readers understandably saw them simply as four cabinet pictures related to the Arthurian legends. As picture followed picture during the next quarter-century, however, it became clear that there was what Tennyson called 'an allegorical or perhaps rather a parabolic drift' designed to unite them into a single whole. Thanks to this, the complete set of twelve *Idylls* offers an elaborate treatment of the struggle in human life between soul and sense.

The first of the *Idylls* as finally arranged, 'The Coming of Arthur', opens the cycle with appropriate hints and ambiguities. 'Merlin and Vivien' and 'The Holy Grail' are among the most successful of those that follow. The finest of all is the last, 'The Passing of Arthur', which incorporates 'Morte d'Arthur' almost without alteration.

At the opposite extreme from the *Idylls,* with their collective aspiration to something like epic status, stand the songs and short lyrics in *The Princess.* These are among Tennyson's most delicate and evocative creations; here if anywhere, art aspires towards the condition of music. In particular, 'Tears, Idle Tears', 'Now Sleeps the Crimson

Petal', and 'Come Down, O Maid' call both for high praise and for a confession that critical analysis cannot go very far towards explaining their charm. Equally fine achievements occur elsewhere. Many examples could be taken from *In Memoriam* and *Maud.* But two independent lyrics will suffice to complete this review: 'Break, Break, Break' expresses with poignant indirectness the poet's desolation at Hallam's death; and 'Crossing the Bar' sums up with simple dignity the outcome of a lifetime's brooding on faith and doubt.

Many of his shorter poems are neither songs nor song-like lyrics. 'To E. FitzGerald' is an urbane and cordial Horatian ode; 'Northern Farmer—Old Style' and 'Northern Farmer—New Style' are humorous and racy dialect poems; the satirical impulse which contributes to them leads in 'A Character' to a cool scrutiny of the victim's polished self-esteem; a similar satirical impulse enables the hero of *Maud* sharply to characterize his lover's overbearing brother (I.xiii); the vigorous rhetoric of 'The Charge of the Light Brigade', a poem on which Tennyson did not particularly pride himself, would shame most other Poets Laureate; and 'Vastness' shows him late in his career resorting again to the denunciatory, prophetic tones already heard in 'Locksley Hall' and in several sections of *Maud.*

But 'Vastness' within itself exemplifies the variety of Tennyson's work. After a thirty-five-line Jeremiad, he breaks off, pauses, and quietly concludes, 'Peace, let it be! for I loved him, and love him for ever: the dead are not dead but alive.' Here, as in 'In the Valley of Cauteretz', the elderly poet can for the moment think of nothing but the greatly loved friend who died when they were both young and who has been present to him ever since. (pp. ix-xix)

> *John D. Jump, in an introduction to* Alfred Tennyson: In Memoriam, Maud and Other Poems, *edited by John D. Jump, J. M. Dent & Sons Limited, 1974, pp. vii-xx.*

Herbert F. Tucker, Jr.   (essay date 1983)

[*In the following excerpt, Tucker examines what he considers a deterministic view of life expressed in Tennyson's poetry.*]

The account that Tennyson gives of the way he wrote *Maud* in 1854-55, at the middle of his career, suggests something important about everything he wrote. Here is Aubrey de Vere's report:

> Its origin and composition were, as he described them, singular. He had accidentally lighted upon a poem of his own which begins, "O that 'twere possible," and which had long before been published in a selected volume got up by Lord Northampton for the aid of a sick clergyman. It had struck him, in consequence, I think, of a suggestion made by Sir John Simeon, that, to render the poem fully intelligible, a preceding one was necessary. He wrote it; the second poem too required a predecessor: and thus the whole poem was written, as it were, *backwards.*

The backward genesis of an intricate work of over a thousand lines is indeed "singular," as de Vere says. The most singular thing, however, may be that the composition of *Maud* was not a freakish episode but a quite typical in-

stance of Tennyson's approach to his art. His longest work, *Idylls of the King* (1885), an epic matured during the course of forty years and more, proceeds from King Arthur's mysterious birth, through the rise and decline of Camelot, to Arthur's mysterious death. But it was the last idyll, "The Passing of Arthur," that came first, published in 1842 as the "Morte d'Arthur" and written nine years before that. While the parallel is not exact, we can say with some justice that in keying his epic to its foregone conclusion Tennyson wrote *Idylls of the King* backward, as he had written *Maud.* Likewise, he composed the elegies that make up *In Memoriam* (1850) over the better part of two decades; and as Christopher Ricks has observed, the resolutions of the poem, the easiest and most easeful lyrics, were those that came to Tennyson first. His leisurely expansion of a handful of elegies into a poem of major proportions was largely a backing and filling maneuver—"if there were a blank space I would put in a poem"—that supplied preparatory complications as afterthoughts to the emotional stabilities they precede in the text we read today. Perhaps to provide an emblem of this compositional process, Tennyson prefaced the finished poem with a prologue dated 1849, a retrospective introduction that forecasts and summarizes the plot of the elegies that follow. The idea of a prefatory last word, an origin that serves a work as its goal, must be nearly as old as literate culture. Yet *In Memoriam* so pervasively implies that "all, as in some piece of art, / Is toil coöperant to an end" (128.23-24) that the final vision of "One far-off divine event / To which the whole creation moves" (Epilogue 143-44) seems to describe the creatively ordained evolution of the poem, as well as the evolving universe the poem has come to celebrate.

Even when, to the best of our knowledge, the process of composition was straightforward, Tennyson delighted to enclose his poems in frames that give the illusion of retrospective return. Sometimes, as in *The Princess* (1847) or "Aylmer's Field" (1864), a scene of narration opens and closes a poem whose narrated events recede into the mythic or historical past. Sometimes, as in "Oenone," "The Hesperides," and "The Lotos-Eaters" (1832) or "Lucretius" (1868), a past-tense narrative preface embeds and distances the present urgency of lyric voice. Sometimes Tennyson more subtly introduces dramatic speeches like those of the title figures of "Ulysses" (1842), "Tithonus" (1860), and "Tiresias" (1885), who speak without mediation in the present yet fill the present with their longing to get back to an earlier state. More subtly still, even in such comparatively rare instances of naked lyric address as "Break, Break, Break" (1842), "The Eagle" (1851), "Flower in the Crannied Wall" (1869), and "Crossing the Bar" (1889), Tennyson's theme and imagery gravitate toward some inevitable ground in the power of God, the drift of nature, or the obsessions of human nature. And for Tennyson, through an inextricable compounding of temperament and biographical accident, human nature itself usually involves a fixation on the past, on the days that are no more.

Whether we inspect the circumstances of textual composition, then, or the emotional texture of the verse, we find in Tennyson a poetry of aftermath. What drew him repeatedly to imagine terminal or retrospective lyric situations, and also fostered his retrograde procedure in the composition of longer poems, was a fascination with inevitability.

Although his was a century remarkable for its faith in progress and hope for the future—currents of the zeitgeist by which Tennyson could scarcely remain untouched—his genius gave its real allegiance to an older and darker wisdom that discerns in the present the determining hand of the past. This allegiance may explain why in the private realm his poems yield well to a psychoanalysis of desire, why his public poems disclose a fatalist or teleological view of history, and why imitation and allusion form so large a part of his work. Tennyson prized the past as the temporal locus of a power more important to him than the past itself: the power of what cannot be changed. His poetry is a coming to terms with the inevitable, and to approach it as such is to appreciate the relation between the notes of helplessness and authority that produce its distinctive tone. The following remarks on Tennyson's handling of character, action, and atmosphere should illuminate the connections between his undeniable limitations and his great strengths; they should also prepare us to see how the shaggy mystic and the precise formalist in him can have consorted together so well.

Writing at the first crest of Tennyson's immense popularity, Matthew Arnold described as definitively modern those situations "in which there is everything to be endured, nothing to be done." We might read into Arnold's criticism of his own *Empedocles on Etna* a sidelong glance at the works of his modern, all too modern contemporary. There is something of an ethical vacuum in Tennyson's poetry. Tennyson is simply not very interested in investigating and assessing the interplay of motive and action, and those who seek primarily these things in poetry will not read him for long with much pleasure. Of course we find no shortage of moral exhortation or argument in his public set pieces or in the Horatian mode he developed in the early 1830s, years before gaining the laureateship. But to set forth rules for conduct is not to imagine the ethical crisis, the awareness of other minds, and the resultant dramatic pressure of choice that have provided central themes for English poets of character from Chaucer onward. The interest of an absorbing poem like **"The Two Voices"** (1842) scarcely inheres in the drama of the modern psychomachia, though that is where Tennyson probably expected his readers to find it. The heavy reliance on generalizing epigram and illustrative emblem, the virtual absence of context, the ultimate passivity of the earnest yet bemused speaker before the injunctions of the voices he hears—all conspire against the credible formation of character in a poem that seeks, after all, to render a character-forming crisis of faith. The "monodramatic" form of *Maud,* in contrast, makes a virtue of Tennyson's defects by dwelling on isolated moods and letting their serial juxtaposition do the work of dramatic development.

The obvious comparison with his contemporary Browning shows that, while Tennyson could create character and sustain its moods, he could not dramatize it beyond a relatively narrow range of internal and external action—a range of action that is most compelling, in fact, when it addresses those conditions or psychological mechanisms that thwart change. Conservative in most respects, Tennyson was nowhere more conservative than in a psychology that embraced the determination of character, either by the blood or by the unalterable early past. His speakers are notable for their lack of pluck: they exhibit determination rarely and suffer it often. Typically they come into voice after the fact, once some determining deed has been committed and the irrevocable consequences of that deed are making themselves felt. They bring to their postfactual situations a belated commentary, and it is the burden of Tennyson's unsurpassed rhetoric to persuade us of the validity of situations for which belated commentary is all that can be offered.

A conviction of inevitability as profound as Tennyson's spells the death of a certain kind of ethical curiosity. His speakers are responsive but not responsible, at least inasmuch as responsibility implies the capacity for present or future action; and Tennyson makes them most convincing when he cleaves to his psychological conservatism and does not force them (the way he forces, say, Princess Ida) to transform themselves. As Tennyson's characters are seldom responsible, so they are seldom guilty. Though we may understandably convict Mariana or Ulysses of serious crimes against themselves and against virtually anybody else who may impinge on their consciousness, we should also observe that Mariana and Ulysses do not experience guilt directly or practice the conscious arts of self-justification. Instead they baffle their guilt, projecting it into a landscape from which it may return with alien, ominous authority. When for characters like Guinevere and Launcelot in the *Idylls* guilt is a given of the tale—that is, when for Tennyson as author the inevitable takes the authoritative shape of antique legend—the behavior of the characters is more revealing still. Guinevere and Launcelot, much like their poet, treat guilt as a given, and this acceptance of an uncontested guilt is the equivalent, in character, of Tennyson's odd narrative elision of the moments of their fall and redemption.

Sometimes the drama of self-justification becomes explicit, but then it also becomes unacceptably schematic. Tennyson knew as much when he created, in **"St. Simeon Stylites"** (1842), a character who substitutes a dogma of sin and atonement for any real grappling with a conviction of guilt; this monologue may provide the best character sketch anywhere in Tennyson, and, significantly, its subject is a characteristic evasion of guilt. (One can only wish that the poet's awareness of such tendencies toward ethical abstractness had stayed with him, and stayed his hand, when he lent his support to King Arthur's formal and vacuous apologia in the eleventh of the idylls.) Finally, the guilt-ridden second part of *Maud* may serve as an exception that not only proves the rule but also suggests why Tennyson clung to it elsewhere. Here for once a character confronts guilt without stay or prop, and madness is the result. Character itself dissolves into a welter of constituencies that can be brought to order only, it seems, through repeated submission to the inevitable, or as the last words of the poem have it, "the purpose of God, and the doom assigned" (3.59). Tennyson's career, I want to argue, makes sense as a series of just such submissions to an inevitable doom. *Maud* has been convincingly read as a poem à clef expressing obliquely the frustrations of Tennyson's earlier love life and of his familial and social position, but we might also approach it allegorically as a work rich with "autobiographical" significance for the poet as well as for the man.

When there is everything to be endured and nothing to be done, endurance will be a leading virtue, the index of a speaker's strength will be the deepening stasis of a mood, and action itself will take the strictly subordinate place it takes in Tennyson's poetry. Critics who contend that Tennyson really couldn't tell a proper story have to contend first with the enormous success of **Enoch Arden** (1864), **Idylls of the King,** and other narratives among an audience whose authentic taste for moving narration Tennyson manifestly knew how to meet. Still, anyone who reads widely in Tennyson's collected works will know what such critics mean. There is something about the stories he tells best, in their climactic emphasis on inhibition or in their diffuse sense of breakdown, that scandalizes the assumptions behind our critical metaphors of narrative "development" and "progression." Something opposes the thrust of narrative and deflects the poetry in an allegorical direction that has made readers since Walter Bagehot suspect that, whatever a Tennyson poem is ostensibly about, its real subject lies elsewhere. When undertaking an actual story, Tennyson consistently opts for descriptive over narrative effects, and even then he gives atmospheric or local description priority over physical description of characters or analysis of their minds. (In similar fashion, on the smallest scale, he gives adjectival and adverbial modifiers syntactic priority over main subjects and predicates.) For longer works, he goes out of his way to devise narrative structures that deemphasize plot and intensify lyric mood: **In Memoriam** and **Maud** are collections of lyrics in which narrative continuity is only implied; the fragmentation of the Arthurian legend into discrete vignettes, *idylls* of the king, may be Tennyson's most striking departure from his sources; even **The Princess** presents itself as an improvised medley, a multimedia event for mixed voices.

The case against Tennyson's narrative ability can rest more firmly on his disinclination than on his incompetence: he could convey action with thrift and force when he wanted to, but he did not often want to. We might say, recalling his determinist notions about character, that Tennyson's imagination was reluctant to believe in the efficacy of human action. Thus, when his characters conceive and attempt to execute plots, their plots are always frustrated: the frustration may be comic, as when the broken purposes of Princess Ida and her suitor lead to a higher harmony, or it may be tragic, as when the governing vision of Camelot decays. But in either case some external power, in the guise of providence or inertia, balks independent initiative. Such instances of independence are rare: far more often in Tennyson action begins as reaction, where the proximate stimulus matters less than some distant final cause, the call of the occult, the holy, the other. The Kraken stirs only when stirred by the distant fire of apocalypse; from the first the Lady of Shalott suffers under a curse that any course of action seems doomed to fulfill; the poet himself anticipates **"Crossing the Bar"** only in response to "one clear call" from beyond.

This last poem suggests the relevance to Tennyson's other proclivities of his lifelong fondness for the quest. As a plot motif the quest permits plenty of action, but action in which the actors are subordinated to some authority outside themselves. Consider the mingled vigor and acquiescence of Tennyson's questers: on their travels the Magus in **"The Devil and the Lady"** (written before 1825), Galahad, Percivale, and company in **"The Holy Grail"** (1869), and the thinly veiled figure of the poet in **"Merlin and the Gleam"** (1889) meet with the most marvelous things, but by the standards of romance they *do* remarkably little.

They experience wonders without confronting them; Tennysonian experience, it appears, is not a mode of self-expression but a pressure exerted on the self from without. Even Odysseus, that archetypal Western adventurer, becomes in Tennyson's Ulysses a figure for whom "all experience" is somewhere out there, "an arch wherethrough / Gleams that untravelled world whose margin fades / Forever and forever when I move" (19-21). Tennyson's questers "move," like Ulysses, through space and time in order that they may be moved inwardly. "When he wishes to represent movement," Henry James observed of Tennyson, "the phrase always seems to me to pause and slowly pivot upon itself, or at most to move backward" [see excerpt dated 1875]. His figures do not actively adopt perspectives, they find themselves in contexts; and the backward movement of his phrases and plots, insisting on the belatedness of context, acknowledges the inevitable power he enshrined in the past.

Tennyson put so little stock in action, and in the capacity of human character to conceive a plot and bring it to fulfillment, because his interest lay instead in *passion,* a term whose etymological connection to *passivity* his poetry consistently reinforces. It is this connection, I think, that explains his uncanny knack for making a landscape describe both an environmental and a mental state. This gift has been hailed retrospectively as a presymbolist technique; although Tennyson's important influence in this regard deserves further charting, I want to suggest that his sense of landscape is both more literal and less merely technical than such a categorization implies. If for Tennyson experience is the pressure of event, and usually of scene, upon the self, his renditions of inner and outer weather will coincide. In fact they never do quite coincide in Tennyson, as I shall suggest more fully in a moment, and it was left for later generations to alloy perception and passion in the extreme simplification of the pure poetic image. But Tennyson helped cast the crucible of imagism: the atrophy of character and action is sufficiently advanced in his poetry to let us say that his prime achievement consists in rendering the still, scenic imagery of an unalterable mood—and in composing the superb verbal music that, for him more than for any of his contemporaries, is no mere medium of rendition. Tennyson's acoustic tact, like that of Keats, reminds us both that emotion is feeling and that poetry is body language, although his great departure from Keats lies precisely in his paradoxical use of body language as a means for transcending bodily life and anything like ordinary emotion.

Tennyson's presentations of character and action, however principled they may be, remain relatively slender accomplishments. But to the reader who is willing to tolerate a certain ethical and practical poverty, Tennyson offers the twin compensations of his richest gifts: the sustained evocation of emotional atmosphere and the atmospheric and physical acoustics of one of the most fulfilling voices in English tradition. These gifts are profoundly allied, and we might approach the basis of their alliance by positing a typical Tennysonian setting and pursuing a few of its implications. His scenes are more literally "set" than those of most writers: vivid, immediate details stand out like jewels against a shadowy background. The vacancy of the middle distance probably owes something to the poet's myopia, but his visual complaints and lifelong fear of blindness confirm the suggestions of several readers that for Tennyson detail served the ends of defense: his lovingly precise visualization of what was at hand arose in response to an awareness of a threat from beyond, a sentence of doom that was nearing its period. The face of his poetry is set to westward, to "a land / In which it seemèd always afternoon" (**"The Lotos-Eaters"** 3-4)—and the longer after noon, the more evocative the tension between foreground and encroaching depth. Indeed, the time of day most in keeping with Tennyson's poetry of aftermath is dusk—a scene bathed in the half-light after sunset, not before dawn—a time of day that purchases its comprehensive overview at the sacrifice of any will to alter what past events have rendered inevitable. When dawn does rise, more often than not it rises on an emphatically terminal situation: the deathbed figure in **"Tears, Idle Tears"** from *The Princess,* the hopeless speaker of the seventh lyric from *In Memoriam,* and especially Tithonus greet the dawn with the poignant sense of discrepancy that engenders in Tennyson not irony but its cousin melancholy. Tennysonian dusk is a liminal hour, and its threshold has a clear sensory and psychic direction, away from sight into sound and feeling, away from character into passion, away from conscious will into mystic passivity. The field of vision at this hour features what is precious in evanescence: a fugitive gleam, a glimmering ghost, a shape or reflection that pales into oceanic gloom—each, perhaps, like the glint of the discarded sword Excalibur, the wraith of an abandoned intention.

The most memorable and characteristic moments in Tennyson's poetry occur as sight is swallowed up in darkness and the visual is overwhelmed by an ascending power of sound that moans round with many voices, voices that themselves merge—as in the long view Tennyson's precariously achieved personae merge—into the roar or pulse of an inevitable, unutterable power. The haunt of this power Tennyson calls "the deep," a locality he approaches when the light of sense goes out and yields to auditory and kinesthetic evidences of a music that is both heard and felt, though hardly understood. When he wants an objective correlative to the power of the great deep, he habitually imagines the sea, which is less often briny or wine dark than oral in its attributes: vocal, devouring, or both. Thus, to take a famous instance, in the magnificent verse paragraph that closes **"Ulysses"** the "dark broad seas" first "gloom" afar, in the privation of sight (45), then acquire the blind, increasingly intimate power of voice and—finally, primally—of thirst, as they surround and ingest Tennyson's hungry-hearted speaker: "the deep / Moans round with many voices"; "It may be that the gulfs will wash us down" (55-56, 62). Yet even so persuasively embodied a sea is ultimately a figure for an inner tide of feeling that sweeps back beyond individual emotions to an epiphany of the inevitable, "that which is" (*In Memoriam* 95.39), with a rhythm, at once cardiac and astral, to which the whole creation moves.

Tennyson was never comfortable about fixing this inevitable power to form or linking its manifestations to any inherited or devised intellectual system. Had he been able to do so more consistently he might have written the kind of poetry his Victorian public hoped they were reading when they pored over *In Memoriam.* But his intuitions of the music of the deep remained too sensuously concrete for that—Hallam was right to class his friend among the poets of sensation—and Tennyson remains an essentially

modern, which is to say an essentially romantic, religious poet. A primary task of literary criticism, for better or worse, is to conceptualize the sensuous workings of imagination; Tennyson makes this task unusually difficult by keeping his intuitions of inevitable power as conceptually and even mythically vague as they are physically urgent. We may do his imagination the least violence by respecting the temporality implied by his habitually musical representation of power. **"The Mystic"** of 1830 "hath heard / Time flowing in the middle of the night, / And all things creeping to a day of doom" (38-40). The resolutely unmystical speaker of **"Locksley Hall"** (1842) has likewise felt "the deep heart of existence beat forever like a boy's" (140)—though by now a more canny Tennyson uses a speaker's repudiation of this rhythmic sympathy to define one stage of an admittedly helter-skelter development. The same speaker can be recognized a decade later in *Maud,* and at one of the imaginative peaks of the poem he returns to the mystic measure of simultaneous intimacy and enormous distance: "Beat, happy stars, timing with things below" (1.679). The posthumously published **"Akbar's Dream"** (1892), where "the living pulse of Alla beats / Through all His world" and where the sun is conclusively hymned as a cosmic metronome, "the flame that measures Time" (39-40, 201), follows the oriental detour of Tennyson's final phase back to the same pulse that had fed the ear of the young mystic of **"Timbuctoo"** (1829), in rapt attention to "the lordly music flowing from / The illimitable years" (214-15).

In these musical intuitions, as in the "deep pulsations" of the "Aeonian music" from *In Memoriam* that measures out "The steps of Time—the shocks of Chance— / The blows of Death" (95.41-43), Tennyson hears not a person or a principle but what he calls "Eternal process" (82.5), not timeless sublimity but the sublime measure in and of time itself. His vision of transcendence is an audition of transience, and an audition made to measure: even when Tennyson registers the eternal process as linear or flowing, he takes care to break the flow into rhythmic units—from pulses to aeons—that creep or beat with a fundamentally musical organization. At the same time, he is equally careful to keep the eternal process from sounding much more concrete than this elemental rhythm suggests. An exception proving this rule of tact occurs in **"Tithonus,"** possibly Tennyson's greatest poem but in many respects a special case; Tithonus displays an extraordinary lust for the concrete by giving the weird music he hears an anthropomorphic source and shaping it as song: "That wild song I heard Apollo sing / While Ilion like a mist rose into towers" (62-63). The otherwise comparable music to which Merlin ascribes the building of Camelot is, more typically, free of origin and contour: "the city is built / To music, therefore never built at all, / And therefore built for ever" (**"Gareth and Lynette"** 272-74). What perennially recurs at points of imaginative climax for Tennyson is itself a sense of eternal recurrence, a perception of rhythm that, by all contemporary accounts, dominated the poet's obsessive recitals of his own works for captive visitors and friends and that should inform our discussion of the effects of formal repetition in his verse. His metrical mastery, his circling syntax, and his manipulation of stanzaic forms do different jobs, of course, in different poems. But one way of seeing Tennyson whole is to grasp these repetitive devices as modes of approach to, or recession from, musical intuitions of an inevitable "burden"—something he felt as a pressure and expressed in the half-mimetic, half-protective mediations of song.

In order to understand how Tennyson took up the burden of eternal process as both a weight and a shield, we should consider how its rhythmic movement bears an ambiguous relation to human mortality and thus to human time generally. On the one hand—the hand of Keats is discernible here—the process means death to the individual self, and in two ways. Its measure enforces the march of a life from youth through age to the grave; and those who, en route, would listen to the music they are obeying can do so only by dying to the life of normal consciousness and into "weird seizures" like those that punctuate *The Princess* or into the kind of trance known by Arthur in **"The Holy Grail,"** by the Ancient Sage (1885), and throughout his life by Tennyson himself (possibly in the less visionary, more pathological form of mild epilepsy). On the other hand—arguably the hand of Shelley—this figurative death or self-annihilation discloses intimations of immortality: Tennyson never represents the process as other than eternal, and in yielding to its vibration he enjoys a state that can know no death.

Recognitions of the power, the process, the deep music of doom came to Tennyson early and seem never to have deserted him for long. Since these recognitions demanded nothing less than the extinction of what he regarded as human personality, they came to prompt in him an ambivalence almost as deep as the power itself. This ambivalence manifests itself variously in his reliance on binary devices for the structuring of individual poems and in his corresponding habit of balancing complementary poems within the volumes he published. It is more generally manifest in the melancholy that typifies the Tennysonian spirit. The elegiac tone and gesture of farewell that are hallmarks of his poetry have been derided in our century as the signs of an indulgent sentimentality, but we can better understand his melancholy if we recognize that it proceeds from his honesty. What Tennyson regrets is the self's passing away, an imaginative necessity imposed by a power whose authority he would not shirk yet could not accept without a murmur. That murmur, the self's lament for the self, in counterpoint to the rhythmic groundswell of doom, generates Tennyson's poetic theme: his subject and his music. Passionately melancholic and authoritatively passive, his speakers remain the victims of circumstance, and in a double sense: they regard themselves as heirs of a past they cannot control, and at the same time they invest the present scene of aftermath with an enveloping power that dissolves the will. Coming to terms with the inevitable, they lament what they know too well to resist it.

The close link between the atmospheric inevitability of Tennyson's poetic world and the formal inevitability of his poetic style is apparent in his talent for ending even otherwise undistinguished poems with an authority that makes it extraordinarily hard to imagine how they might have ended in any other way. Influential poets and readers of English poetry during the first half of our century denigrated Tennyson in the mistaken, if valiant, belief that they might avoid his influence. But even these detractors conceded his remarkable verbal gift. Tennyson is the most finished, the most inevitable of poets, at least of poets in romantic tradition, and the inevitability that marks his style also characterizes the attitude that lies behind the

style. One reason Tennyson's poems dependably create in us the impression that they *had* to conclude as they did is that Tennyson seems often to have been subject to that impression about events in the world as well as in poems.

Finding imagined or actual events inevitable is a far cry from being in command of them, but it can offer a semblance of command, one that Tennyson sees reflected in the command of poetic form. The comprehensive elaboration of his art seems to have given him a hold on himself and on his world; it also gave him a large measure of his hold on contemporary readers. Apropos of Tennyson's versification, W. H. Auden offered this speculation on "the relation between the strictness and musicality of a poet's form and his own anxiety": "the more conscious he is of an inner disorder and dread, the more value he will place on tidiness in the work as a *defence,* as if he hoped that through his control of the means of expressing his emotions, the emotions themselves, which he cannot master directly, might be brought to order" [see excerpt dated 1944]. Composition as a means to composure: Auden half sneers at the idea ("tidiness in the work"), but twentieth-century readers taught by T. S. Eliot that poetry in general may be an escape from emotion and that Tennyson's poetry in particular is great for the emotions of doubt and dread it never did quite escape should be prepared to find in Tennyson's post-factual strategies and in the impeccability of his style the marks of a disturbingly modern sensibility. As Tennyson once declared to his son, with a characteristic blending of sage generality and modest confession: "The artist is known by his self-limitation" [see Tennyson, Hallam, Lord, *Tennyson: A Memoir,* in Further Reading]. Tennyson resorted to self-limitation as a means of self-definition, a way of making himself known not only to himself but to others, in part because he wrote in and of a century that witnessed the disintegration of traditional limits and goals. Well aware that the great world around him was spinning down the ringing grooves of change but fearfully ignorant of its destination, Tennyson defended against his ignorance by imagining terminal situations in accomplished verse. Yet in leaping to the ends of things his imagination was too honest not to import into its defensive stronghold much of the melancholy helplessness that characterized the present it could only partially escape.

A poet's grammar is an aspect of imaginative form, and we could describe in grammatical terms the Tennysonian discrepancy between that which is and that which might have been as a tension between indicative and subjunctive moods. An attempt to write the generative grammar of Tennyson's imagination could indeed begin with his success in animating the latent ambiguity of those past-tense forms that do double duty in English as subjunctives. Consider, for example, the lyric seed out of which he bred *Maud:*

> O that 'twere possible
> After long grief and pain
> To find the arms of my true love
> Round me once again!

(2.141-44)

"O that 'twere possible": the verb denotes a situation contrary to fact. But through an emotionally trustworthy if philologically shaky homonymy that is part of the traditional wisdom of our language, the verb also invites us to conceive this hypothetical situation as part of a story set in the past and to live through the story, in imagination, to the end. As we know, that is what Tennyson did when he backed into the plot of **Maud:** in providing the antecedent action necessary "to render the poem fully intelligible," he added to the yearning "that 'twere possible" his speaker's awareness that, once upon a time, the consummation of true love *was* possible. The postfactual and the contrafactual implications of Tennyson's verb mix the inevitabilities of memory and desire. Remorse enriches yearning to produce the emotional complex, deep as first love and wild with all regret, that is the condition for Tennyson's idle tears; and the **Maud** lyric ends with the speaker's longing "to weep, and weep, and weep / My whole soul out to thee" (2.237-38).

A fuller consideration of Tennyson's historical position would return us, I think, to the central dilemma outlined above: his poetry is caught between the desires of the self and the demands of a power whose recognition exacts, in one way or another, the dissolution of the self. To the latter imperative he owes his utter authority of manner, to the former the submerged lyric drive whose strength we must largely infer from his pervasive melancholy, which is a symptomatic response to the incompatibility of the two imperatives he faced. It is impossible to say whether Tennyson's authority or his melancholy had the greater appeal for contemporary readers, especially since after his earliest poetry the two are rarely found apart. But an important clue to his popularity is probably that, writing

Tennyson in 1888.

during a crisis of authority, he was able simultaneously to gratify conflicting needs. The seal of certitude allayed publicly a cultural malaise that the note of melancholy was secretly feeding all the while.

Tennyson was no hypocrite; a sense of scruple, if anything, produced his peculiarly undogmatic certitude and his vagueness about the object of his grief. Yet these very characteristics arguably made his dilemmas and resolutions more available for public adoption. It did not strike Aubrey de Vere as strange that a lament of erotic frustration like "O that 'twere possible" should occupy a place first in a volume got up "for the aid of a sick clergyman" and later in a long poem containing some of the bitterest social invective Tennyson ever published. Presumably something in the poem's theme of loss, and in the peculiar kind of "aid" it offered through the expression of loss, struck a common chord that resounded through the multiple discontents of the age. Nowadays our analysis of Victorian malaise would include among its interlocking causes industrialization and the consequent alienation of workers from traditional modes of labor, rapid restratification of English social classes, correlative shifts in the political power base, the crumbling of religious orthodoxy, and much more. Tennyson's special fitness for the role of Victoria's laureate was that he could consistently and inventively let a reading public touched by any or all of these causes imagine that the situation was awful and that it was also, somehow, at last, all right. He spoke for a modern malaise, and he spoke to it. His readers responded—as they can still respond—to the expression of an inconsolable loss beyond words, a content irreducible to form, and at the same time to a polished style offering a genuine consolation of its own, a reassuring meassage independent of thematic content.

Auden's comment about the relation of formal to emotional control draws on the plausible assumption that what sounds right to a poet succeeds because it also feels right. Like the more rhetorical pronouncements we meet in Arnold's literary criticism, Tennyson's obiter dicta on the stylistic properties of other poets often disclose his sympathy or antipathy to what those poets say as much as to the way in which they say it. He seems to have been moved especially by turns of phrase that emphasize the sense of inevitable aftermath we find in his own writing; and on more than one revealing occasion, he gives other writers' suggestive phrases yet more emphatic twists in the direction of a Tennysonian doom. William Allingham, a minor Victorian poet whose lionizing of Tennyson appears throughout the ingenuous diary he left behind, twice records the laureate's admiration for the following two lines from Keats's "Ode to a Nightingale":

> Charm'd magic casements, opening on the foam
> Of perilous seas, in faery lands forlorn.
>
> (27 July 1884)

The words are quoted accurately (by Tennyson, we may presume, as well as by Allingham), but Keats's syntax has been truncated to make the lines appear more Tennysonian than Keatsian. Keats wrote that in hearing the voice of the nightingale he heard the same song that had filled the ears of emperor, clown, and the biblical Ruth: "The same that oft-times hath / Charm'd magic casements. . . ." Tennyson lops off the subject and the auxiliary verb of Keats's clause and effectively transforms

"Charm'd" into a past passive participle that links up with "forlorn" to frame the active participle "opening." As Tennyson remembers them, Keats's lines suggest a magic that performs itself without the benefit of magician, the work of an agency even more mysterious than the one the "Ode" had addressed. Tennyson's memory, like much of his best poetry, avoids confrontation with the cause and relishes its effects instead.

Of course, the surest evidence of poets' verbal susceptibilities occurs in their own works, and we might look further at the way two of Tennyson's best-known poems grew from the germ of a phrase transplanted from its context into his imagination. Hallam Tennyson writes, "My father's poems were generally based on some single phrase like 'Someone had blundered': and were rolled about, so to speak, in his head, before he wrote them down." Hallam's specific example comes from **"The Charge of the Light Brigade,"** which the poet wrote after reading the phrase "some hideous blunder" in the *Times* for 13 November 1854; "and this," writes his son, "was the origin of the metre of his poem" (1:268, 381) Bearing in mind the effect on Tennyson of Keats's "Charm'd magic casements," we should suspect that the germinal phrase from the *Times* supplied him with more than meter. Our suspicion is confirmed when we see how this unusually action-packed poem never does get back to the precipitating blunder, which remains the deed of an unspecified agent ensconced in the pluperfect: "Someone had blundered" (12). The Light Brigade are a heroic company for Tennyson in that they are doomed—accursed rather than charmed, but at all events "framed," performing the will of a power they cannot question. In describing the Light Brigade as "hurried to their doom by some inextricable error" and the British soldier as "not paralyzed by feeling that he is the victim of some hideous blunder," the *Times* had evidently given Tennyson an idea as well as a sound. That he remembered his debt as a metrical one betokens the indivisibility of idea from sound in the poet's mind; the compression of passivity into valor, together with the alliterative hum of doom ("victim of some hideous blunder"), presented him with what he so often needed in order to compose: an emotionally congenial subject and a tonic refrain to which he might build his battering stanzas.

Occasionally, then, Tennyson might recall phrasing like Keats's verbatim but in such a way as to revise its sense; at other times he might find a rough-hewn phrase like "some hideous blunder" and roll it about in his head until he had smoothed its wording into consonance with his own internal measure. An early lyric that furnishes an extreme instance of this latter process is **"Mariana."** The poem begins with an epigraph attributed—appropriately enough for my argument—to Shakespeare's *Measure for Measure: "Mariana in the moated grange."* Strictly speaking, Tennyson's attribution is incorrect, since the closest wording in Shakespeare is the speech of Duke Vincentio: "I will presently to St. Luke's; there at the moated grange resides this dejected Mariana" (3.1.256-58). That "moated grange" is what drew Tennyson to Mariana: like the phrases we have already discussed, it is a past passive construction, and Tennyson based on it one of his most perfect distillations of formidably defended victimage and fixation on the past. In turn the power of this evocation seems to have colored Tennyson's verbal memory. He plucked Mariana and her grange from the Duke's declara-

tive sentence, isolated her in a fragment, condensed Shakespeare's phrasing, and substituted "in" for "at." This revision immures Mariana yet further in a murmur of *m*'s and *n*'s that seems to proceed from her own name and implies the self-enclosure, the tyranny of Mariana over herself, that is the un-Shakespearean subject of Tennyson's altogether original poem.

In his civilized, often urbane authority, his unremitting estimate of the sacrifices that self-conscious life in civilization exacts, and his painstaking elaboration of a verse that gives expression to both, Tennyson is the most Vergilian of English poets. A principal difference between Augustus' imperial laureate and Victoria's is that, where Vergil faced Homer as his major precursor, Tennyson faced the English romantics. Hence Tennyson's best work gives priority to the problems of the imperial self, rather than to those of political and cultural empire, and replaces Vergil's rationalized Olympian pantheon with a mythology of the divided psyche, under the regime of an irresistible power he spoke by but could not name. As a Victorian romantic, Tennyson tends toward lyric and idyllic forms instead of toward the didactic and epic forms refined by Vergil; but across nearly two millennia the congruence of these poets' sensibilities is striking, particularly in their attitudes toward form itself.

Tennyson's late tribute **"To Virgil"** (1882) records the salute of one kindred spirit to another, in shared sympathy with the vision of the tears in things, Vergil's *lacrimae rerum:* "Thou that seëst Universal Nature moved by Universal Mind; / Thou majestic in thy sadness at the doubtful doom of human kind" (11-12). Yet Tennyson reserves his highest praise for Vergil the "lord of language," who captured "All the charm of all the Muses often flowering in a lonely word" (3, 6). Not a *single* word, a *lonely* word: it is as if the *lacrimae rerum* were also *lacrimae verborum,* as if the magical "charm" and the pathetic "charm" of poetic language were one and the same. For Tennyson, Vergil expresses not the pathos of a sublime isolation but the sublimity of a pathos that words can approximate and poetic rhythm can convey. Across vast space and time, the sympathetic vibration of an "ocean-roll of rhythm" joins the poet of a perished empire with the spokesman of "the Northern Island sundered once from all the human race" (16, 18)—sundered once but since redeemed into community with the European culture sown by Vergil that had led in England to the development of the accentual-syllabic prosody Tennyson was among the last great poets to cultivate. There is an abyss in things, replenished first by tears and then by the patient art of the poet as human communicant. Vergil's majesty, like Tennyson's, inheres in the measure of his "sadness," and not vice versa: tears well up from the depth of a despair that is divine, and the poet's definitively human touch makes language of a cry, shapes an idyll from idle tears. Thus it is as a touchstone of the human, as the formalist artist who respects the ends of things and "is known by his self-limitation," that Tennyson salutes Vergil in the last words of the poem: "Wielder of the stateliest measure ever moulded by the lips of man" (20).

His focus on Vergil's "measure," as on the "metre" he heard in a newspaper article, shows us once more how poetic rhythm served Tennyson as a way of capturing and transmitting the deep music of the doubtful doom of humankind—again, "Aeonian music measuring out / The steps of Time—the shocks of Chance—/ The blows of Death." The point of this capture, the "use in measured language" (*In Memoriam* 5.6), was for Tennyson mimetic and expressive at once. He intended his rhythms to imitate the pulse of inevitability that he felt within the core of human experience and that he intuited beyond its further reaches and to express the deep if somewhat narrow range of moods that arise in acknowledging, and submitting to, the inevitable. Tennyson hoped to achieve by incantation—"The charm of all the Muses"—what could not be achieved, he was sure, by the reasoning mind. His aim was not to master the inevitable but to take its measure in the music of doom, to render it not intelligible but perceptible and communicable as the ground of a fate we should otherwise share without quite knowing it. (pp. 8-18)

> *Herbert F. Tucker, Jr., "Tennyson and the Measure of Doom," in* PMLA, *Vol. 98, No. 1, January, 1983, pp. 8-20.*

Ann C. Colley   (essay date 1983)

[*Colley is an American educator and critic. In the following excerpt, she examines Tennyson's use of madness as a metaphor for social disorder in* Idylls of the King.]

Many of Tennyson's contemporaries were convinced that they were living in a country and in an age literally madder than all others. In the popular mind England and insanity were all too frequent companions. The physician Alfred Beaumont Maddock was one of many to register alarm. In 1854 he wrote that "in no other country, compared with England, do we find such numerous and formidable examples of this extensive scourge." Later Tennyson's Dr. Matthew Allen also remarked on the nation's poor health. Alluding to the common belief, he wrote: "It need scarcely be mentioned, that the present constitution of society is not in a healthy state. . . . Discord and disseverment prevail to an extent which seem to threaten its decomposition and destruction." For all of these believers the metaphor of madness touched a sensitive spot and must have seemed as much a reality as a poetic device.

Of all the poems demonstrating Tennyson's sensitivity to his contemporaries' sense of England's unhealthy state, none illustrates it more thoroughly and indeed more anxiously than the *Idylls of the King.* Here Tennyson resurrects the legendary Camelot to expose simultaneously the forces threatening contemporary England's moral fiber and the excesses enslaving the minds of the nation's inhabitants. (p. 87)

Because Tennyson shared in the public's fear that England and its subjects had lost control and had become slaves to their passions, it is not surprising that when he wrote the *Idylls* he made use of madness in his characters, and its infectious spread through the kingdom, as a metaphor for the breakdown of order and as the fatal genesis of that collapse. Madness is to be expected in a poem that anxiously explores the ruin of the nation's morality and, thus, its sanity. It is also not surprising that in the *Idylls* he uses madness as he does in his other poetry to mirror despair, disorder, inordinate passion, and civil chaos. Indeed the metaphor of madness is most appropriate, for not only is there precedent for it in Tennyson's poetry and in the trea-

tises concerning the nation's "insanity," but also in the public's familiarity with the metaphor. For them as well as for Tennyson madness was familiar as a metaphor of disorder and as a real threat. Madness is a most appropriate gauge of the fall of Camelot.

Because madness plays such a vital role in Tennyson's vision of the fall, and because it allows him to link his fears to his sense of the nation's distress, it emerges as a binding, central force in the *Idylls.* As a result, the *Idylls* is Tennyson's most extensive inquiry into madness as a reality and madness as a metaphor. With such a concentrated use of the metaphor, contrary to what many might expect, the *Idylls* exceeds even *Maud* in its exploration of madness. The madness in the poem as it appeared in its final, published form (1883) should be considered at length.

Significantly, when the *Idylls* opens, madness belongs to the past. For the moment, it is conquered, and all is held in balance. Soon, however, as the realm begins to deteriorate, all kinds of madness appear and infect the inhabitants of Camelot. The insanity extends far beyond that usually associated with Lancelot, Balin, and Pelleas. In the end it seems even to reach King Arthur. He leaves Camelot in "confusion."

The first idyll, **"The Coming of Arthur,"** opens with multiple and conflicting accounts of the king's birth, the variety of which immediately suggests that the king is born with a multiple inheritance: he is born of anger, passion, bitterness, sweetness, nobility, and love. With this inheritance, he emerges as a person who contains within him the bestial and the noble passions. He is at once baseborn and sublime or "more than man." Initially as king he unites and controls these warring elements so that he and his kingdom are balanced. He and "his knighthood for a space / Were all one will" (ll. 514-15). They draw in "the petty princedoms" so that all function harmoniously. Moreover, because he can balance these passions, he is able to transform the "great tracts of wilderness / Wherein the beast was ever more and more, / But men less and less" (11. 10-12) into an orderly society. No longer do the wolves roam his land and devour children; no longer do the children fall victim to the beastly and excessive passions of their forebears. To complete the harmony, Arthur marries, an act that is necessary in the minds of Tennyson and his contemporaries who, despite certain fears for those with a predisposition to madness, maintain that few are whole without marriage and without uniting the masculine and feminine elements of their character. The marriage as a representation of this wholeness, however, cannot last long in the *Idylls,* for already the seething passions are surfacing and tyrannizing the kingdom and the citizens. Even in this first idyllic section there are hints of the evil lurking below and the madness waiting to break out, for Gawain bursts into song and wildly dashes about while Modred eavesdrops hoping to find a means of overthrowing the king (ll. 319-24).

In the second idyll, **"Gareth and Lynette,"** order continues to dominate, but the challenge posed to that order or sanity by the bestial passions becomes slightly more visible. As yet, though, neither the individual inhabitants of Camelot nor Camelot itself is overwhelmed and maddened by the baser instincts as Lucretius was. The mood throughout the idyll is idealistic. It is replete with allusions to a fairy-tale world where wishes come true and with proclamations or evidence of Gareth's faith in King Arthur's court. Gareth's innocence within such a world allows him to overcome potentially treacherous moments. Later, however, Tennyson will tip Gareth's innocence upside down and place his faith within the context of a fallen world that does not even have the benefit of the virtues and illusions belonging to the fairy tale.

This second idyll opens with affectionate banter between Gareth and his mother and with his telling the story of the goose and the golden eggs. Through the telling of the story, Gareth disarms his mother's objections to his leaving home for Camelot. In leaving, Gareth turns his back on a life of idleness (his weak father's life), always so dangerous in Tennyson's mind, and goes forward. When Gareth comes to the gates of Camelot his companions are frightened. Armed with his innocence and idealistic faith, Gareth is not bothered by the shadowy, illusory movements that meet him as he enters Camelot, or by the riddle of the king's birth that has no answer (ll. 184-231). He enters "with all good cheer." Believing in Arthur's order of the Knights of the Round Table, he willingly takes the difficult vows "Of utter hardihood, utter gentleness, / And, loving, utter faithfulness in love, / And uttermost obedience to the King" (ll. 542-44). By believing in and becoming a vassal to Arthur's order, he is able to combat the excessively proud and nasty prodding of Lynette, to overcome the four destructive knights, to survive his journey through the maddening mire, to save the baron, and, in the end, with Lancelot's help, to save the "blooming boy" from a death in life. He controls pride, despair, savagery, doubt, peril, lawlessness, insanity, the passions, and the temptations met in the various stages of life. His victories over the "wronger of the Realm" are the conquests of Arthur's ideal soul. They mirror the king's judicious hold over the realm which Gareth has witnessed in Arthur's court. Gareth's victories are analogous to Arthur's victories over himself, for even he must control his base inheritance (he is "baseborn") which periodically threatens to unseat him. For example, when the widow of Arthur's enemy requests his aid, the king's tense reply reflects his inner turmoil. Control, however, wins:

> "We sit King, to help the wronged
> Through all our realm. The woman loves her lord.
> Peace to thee, woman, with thy loves and hates!
> The kings of old had doomed thee to the flames,
> Aurelius Emrys would have scourged thee dead,
> And Uther slit thy tongue: but get thee hence—
> Lest that rough humour of the kings of old
> Return upon me!"
>
> [ll. 363-70]

This power, though, is possible only in an innocent, fairyland setting. As Tennyson knew only too well, the shadows and riddles of one's inheritance always threatened to disrupt even the best situations.

Beginning in the next idyll, **"The Marriage of Geraint,"** the ideal state begins to totter. The wise Merlin's warning that Gareth is passing into a city where "the King / Will bind thee by such vows, as is a shame / A man should not be bound by, yet that which / No man can keep" (**"Gareth and Lynette,"** ll. 265-67) contains truth. These vows are the ideal, and, in reality, they are impossible. People are normally more vulnerable than Gareth was. As people and a nation progress in life, from their morning to their evening, they are going to meet with conflict; they fall into

battle with the mire of despair, lust, pride, anger, and anarchy; and many are going to become victims of these vices. It will not always be possible to rescue the child from death or madness; to save the innocent or nobler self from the darker, deadlier self. It will not always be possible to fall and laugh as Gareth has done:

> And Gareth crying pricked against the cry;
> But when they closed—in a moment—at one touch
> Of that skilled spear, the wonder of the world—
> Went sliding down so easily, and fell,
> That when he found the grass within his hands
> He laughed.
>
> [**"Gareth and Lynette,"** ll. 1191-95]

In the future idylls madness will become a more immediate and ominous threat. It will not be dismissed as quickly as it is in this second idyll, where madness is a word used lightly and where it is as illusory as the knight who is the Star of Evening. Gareth's fight with that "madman" is long, but Gareth wins. In the future such struggles with madness will be harder. Once a person is touched by its lawlessness, rarely will he regain order. Balin will return to the court and be reprieved, but his sanity is only to be temporary. The nation too will not recover from its infliction. From **"The Marriage of Geraint"** on, Tennyson describes how many lose these battles, how many tumble and become lost in the mire of their tyrannizing passions. Neither the people nor the nation can break their habits and release their saner selves.

The long, hot summer, the season for madness and the heat of excessive passion, begins in the next two idylls, **"The Marriage of Geraint"** and **"Geraint and Enid,"** when Lancelot's and Guinevere's sexual passion for one another has begun to gain control. No longer can their affair be kept secret. Rumors spread, and with those rumors corruption extends from the two lovers to many in Arthur's court. Their effect on the court is very much tied to Tennyson's discomfort with and distrust of sexual passion. No passion is as contaminating as theirs; it too easily destroys the mind's and the nation's delicate balance, too frequently rouses the monster madness from its sleep. Because Lancelot and Guinevere have not repressed their lust, they and others will weaken and become more vulnerable to other excesses. Geraint is the first to be sullied and victimized by their affair. Before learning of their "guilty love" (ll. 24-28) Geraint has exhibited "exceeding manfulness / And pure nobility of temperament" (ll. 211-12), but afterward he fears he is effeminate, dashes madly into the wilderness, and distorts what he hears. He has lost control of the delicate relation between his masculine and feminine qualities, which, of course, the ideal King Arthur exhibits. Now the knowledge of Guinevere's and Lancelot's passion transforms Geraint's moments of splenetic behavior (as when he shouted at the armorer and "flashed into sudden spleen") into a prolonged, mad fury; it transforms his effeminate tendencies (his wearing of the long purple scarf with the gold apple dangling from it) into impotency; and it turns his scrupulous attention to his wife's deportment and clothing into a dangerous obsession, and, finally, into a sexual fantasy. Because of Guinevere's sin, the fear envelopes him "lest his gentle wife, / Through that great tenderness for Guinevere" (ll. 29-30) become as tainted as she. Like the mad lovers in case studies and those belonging to the literary convention, Geraint's mind is seized by one mastering thought, causing him to distort all that goes on around him. To give a sense of just how deeply Geraint is trapped by his unhealthy obsession, Tennyson repeats phrases and locks them into an obsessive pattern. For example, when Geraint madly refuses to leave Enid's side, Tennyson uses the trapped syntax to speak of the consequences. Geraint grows

> Forgetful of his promise to the king,
> Forgetful of the falcon and the hunt,
> Forgetful of the tilt and tournament,
> Forgetful of his glory and his name,
> Forgetful of his princedom and its cares.
>
> [ll. 48-54]

The consequences of Geraint's monomania are almost fatal. His excessive anger, pride, jealousy, and fear fight to rule him. Under their domain, losing his grip on reality, Geraint mistakes his wife's motives, deceives King Arthur, talks to himself, and babbles to others. He is an example of those who "Do forge a life-long trouble for [themselves], / By taking true for false, or false for true" (**"Geraint and Enid,"** ll. 3-4). Geraint's excesses lead him to those "Gray swamps and pools, waste places of the hern, / And wildernesses, perilous paths" (ll. 31-32)— wild places that complement the chaos, danger, and barrenness of his sick mind. Like any truly sick person he vacillates between wrath and despair, between irrationality and rationality. In the more rational moments, Geraint and Enid come to a smoother landscape, a meadow cared for by mowers. But even there Geraint displays excessive behavior—an indication of his continuing unbalanced state. Without realizing it he ravenously consumes all the mowers' food; and then, when he understands what he has done, he overpays them "fifty fold." Later he pays the host with "five horses and their armours," a payment that the amazed host admits is equal to five times the cost of a room at his inn.

Geraint's appetite and payments are as out of proportion as his judgment. His monomania affects not only his "appetite" but also his sense of the world around him. He rides "as if he heard not"; he hears only half, as when waking from his sleep to catch the last few words of his wife's speech. Sometimes he neither hears nor sees. Enid must do that for him. She says: "I hear the violent threats you do not hear, / I see the danger which you cannot see" (**"Geraint and Enid,"** ll. 420-21). In the end, lawlessness nearly overwhelms Geraint. His excesses lead him to the Earl of Doorm's wasteland. Here the "wild Limours" attacks "all in a passion uttering a dry shriek." Although Geraint stuns this mad lover, he receives a terrible wound. He totters. Losing his balance, he falls from his horse. The struggle with Limours, though, is a turning point for Geraint. He begins to find a way out of his living death, to release himself from the lawless lord's estate—a realm resembling an asylum. Among its inhabitants are a man-at-arms "half whistling and half singing a coarse song" and another "flying from the wrath of Doorm / Before an ever-fancied arrow" (ll. 522-32).

It is logical that Limours unbalances Geraint, for Limours's excessive passion for Enid mirrors Geraint's and, furthermore, comments on Guinevere and Lancelot's affair. His fate mirrors what Geraint's might have been if Enid had not kept her husband in touch with reality. Limours has become "wild" because he is completely subjected to his own sensations. There is no one to help him

hear or see, he says, except "Enid, the pilot star of my lone life, / Enid, my early and my only love, / Enid, the loss of whom hath turned me wild—" (ll. 306-8). Geraint survives only because he is cared for by Enid, a person who shields her head from the sinful sun and the fires of madness, who shuns "the wild ways of the lawless tribe." Governed by moderation, she refuses to eat and participate in Geraint's lawless appetite, and can therefore protect him. Eventually with Enid's help Geraint's manliness and balance return. The earl slaps Enid, and her cries for help awaken and arouse Geraint's masculinity. He takes his sword, an emblem of Arthur's order, and "with a sweep of it / Shore through the swarthy neck" of the Earl of Doorm. The taking of the sword is an act by which Geraint simultaneously regains his sanity and his masculinity.

With harmony restored, Geraint and Enid can now mount the same horse and ride together back to King Arthur's court, where the king's reigning order promises to nurse Geraint back to health. In the court an image of restored inner harmony awaits them. Edyrn, who had believed himself "well-nigh mad," is now, in Arthur's words, "One of the noblest, our most Valorous, / Sanest and most obedient" knights (ll. 909-10). Unfortunately, though, the court is no longer a perfect place. The restored harmony is not secure. Experience has broken the innocence, and Enid realizes that governed passion may soon erupt to tyrannize once more. When she meets Edyrn and remembers his former, destructive self, she cannot help shrinking "a little." As Tennyson adds: "In a hollow land, / From which old fires have broken, men may fear / Fresh fire and ruin" (ll. 820-22)—an autobiographical statement from Tennyson, who periodically had seen madness break out and threaten to consume him and his family; and, moreover, a poignant statement for his contemporaries, who had feared that the horrors of the French Revolution and the chaos of brutal democracy might break out on English soil and upset the nation's delicate balance.

Enid fears more than Edyrn. She also lives in horror of the "bandits scattered in the field." Although Geraint seems to be whole again, and although the Earl of Doorm is dead, the earl's lawless followers, like the rumors of Guinevere and Lancelot's affair, are very much alive, although scattered. Geraint too is suspicious. He can "never take again / That comfort from" Enid's and Guinevere's "converse which he took / Before the Queen's fair name was breathed upon" (ll. 948-50). Shadows also hover over the king's justice. There is still a belief that man and nation can "repent," but now that belief is qualified. Significantly, Arthur is not blind to the difficulties:

> The world will not believe a man repents:
> And this wise world of ours is mainly right.
> Full seldom doth a man repent, or use
> Both grace and will to pick the vicious quitch
> Of blood and custom wholly out of him,
> And make all clean, and plant himself afresh.
>
> [ll. 899-904]

All these fears, suspicions, shadows, and qualifications seem to be Tennyson's attempt to show how easy it is to doubt. Like Arthur, Tennyson worries about that doubt. He wants people to hold on to their idealism and beliefs, for without them the Limours and the lawless bandits of Doorm will turn civilization into a wild place. Doubting brings people closer to their madness. It causes people to neglect the task of weeding out their evil passions. Like Yniol, Enid's father, they stand idly by allowing their kingdoms to topple over from disuse; they stand there in old and rusty arms, tyrannized like Edyrn, who if only given the chance to live under Arthur's order can be made sane again.

The hot summer and the fevers of madness continue to blast through **"Balin and Balan."** They bring with them a confusion more perilous than that in the previous idylls. People's doubts, wrath, pride, and lust are more lethal than ever. Moreover, what Enid and Tennyson had feared comes true. The old fires break out afresh and consume. Only for a while does Balin find inner harmony, but all too soon the anger and "outer fiends," which his brother Balan had begged him to control, rage. He cannot recover his sanity as Edyrn and Geraint had. In "middle May," the season of madness, Balin fights "hard with himself" to repress his moods but cannot. He vows, "I will be gentle," but fails. He kills his brother and falls into despair, crying "My violences, my violences!"

Throughout this idyll Balin's struggle to control his violence is his quest. He desperately wants to heed his brother's warning, so he accepts Arthur's invitation to "walk with me, and move / To music with thine Order and the King" (ll. 72-74), and he tries to "learn what Arthur meant by courtesy, / Manhood, and knighthood" (ll. 155-56). Neither the invitation nor the lesson is strong enough to destroy the disorder threatening Balin's stability. Already the king's order is slipping away. Balin ends up going on a journey that takes him the very opposite of where he wishes to go. Ironically, instead of keeping him within Arthur's promised order, Balin's quest leads him away from Camelot into the chaotic wilderness filled with hallucinations—a sure sign of insanity. His flight from court horrifyingly echoes the maddened figure in the previous idyll, who stumbled through the lawless woods "flying from the wrath of Doorm / Before an ever-fancied arrow" (**"Geraint and Enid,"** ll. 530-31). Balin's madness is similar:

> He felt the hollow-beaten mosses thud
> And tremble, and then the shadow of a spear,
> Shot from behind him, ran along the ground.
> Sideways he started from the path, and saw,
> With pointed lance as if to pierce, a shape,
> A light of armour by him flash, and pass
> And vanish in the woods; and followed this,
> But all so blind in rage that unawares
> He burst his lance against a forest bough,
> Dishorsed himself, and rose again.
>
> [ll. 316-25]

Eventually he falls under the power of King Pellam, the enemy of order, who will not pay tribute to Arthur's court. Balin can no longer bridle his passion, so his horse does not carry him back to Camelot as Gareth and Enid's had. Instead it crushes him. When Balin falls from his horse there is no laughter. That was possible only in Geraint's fairy-tale world. Death replaces not only laughter, but also marriage and the future promise concluding the previous idylls. Balin and Balan die tyrannized by madness. As Balin admits, "My madness all thy life has been thy doom, / Thy curse, and darkened all thy day; and now / The night has come" (ll. 608-10).

Once more Guinevere's and Lancelot's lust has tipped the balance, for Balin lost control after the shock of overhearing the queen and her lover's amorous conversation in the garden. The shock of his discovery unleashes his madness. He gives in to its fury, blaming his inheritance from an angry father, and turns his back on Arthur's court.

The queen's guilty passion, however, is not the only root of Balin's madness. Despair and unwillingness to have complete faith in Arthur's order also unbalance him. Both conspire to destroy his trust. Balin fears: "Too high this mount of Camelot for me: / These high-set courtesies are not for me" (ll. 221-22). Like his anger, his doubts distort his judgment. He chooses to follow not only shadows, as Geraint did, but also shadows of shadows. Believing that to become one of Arthur's knights is "beyond *my* reach," he mistakenly and single-mindedly champions Guinevere as an image of purity and order: " 'No shadow' said Sir Balin 'O my Queen, / But light to me! no shadow, O my King, / But golden earnest of a gentler life!' " (ll. 202-4). His delusion and his single-mindedness bring their own madness, creating more confusion. Despite Sir Garlon's scorn of Guinevere's purity, Balin insists she is the "fairest, best and purest." Later, despite Vivien's blatant distortion of Guinevere and Lancelot's garden conversation, Balin believes her account is the truth. Vivien's "truth" is yet another blow to his chaotic mind. Once more the shock excites his madness. Emitting a "weird yell, / Unearthlier than all shriek of bird or beast" (ll. 535-36), Balin goes wild. His brother believes the shriek to be that of the "wood-devil I came to quell." In a moment of utter chaos the brothers do not recognize each other and attack. Indeed Balin has momentarily turned into a wood-devil: "his evil spirit upon him leapt, / He ground his teeth together, sprang with a yell, / Tore from the branch, and cast on earth, the shield" (ll. 529-31). But his death is not the death of the demon in the woods. The real demons are left to scatter like the lawless lords, "to dwell among the woods" and bring destruction and madness closer to the center of Arthur's order. Vivien with her "truth" is the real wood-devil, not Balin. From this moment on, the survivors are the destroyers.

In the next idyll, **"Merlin and Vivien,"** Balin's disorderly world creeps closer to Camelot, for despair, passion, and madness attack Merlin, the very architect of the order. Like a cancer, the warring passions are multiplying and gradually overtaking the individual's healthy soul and that of the nation. In this idyll Vivien is a demon driven by her lust and pride. She pursues Merlin into the woods, where she wears down his resistance to her sensuous touch and entangles him in his own lust and weaknesses. She leaves him trapped within the walls of a hollow tower, locked within the cells of madness, useless, and tyrannized by his passion. Merlin has allowed "the meanest" to have power "upon the highest." In the end, Merlin is "lost to life and use and name and fame." His end is prophetic of Guinevere's. She too will be locked within the convent's hollow walls, useless and barren.

Merlin's fall comes because he is first melancholy's victim.

> Then fell on Merlin a great melancholy;
> He walked with dreams and darkness, and he found
> A doom that ever poised itself to fall,
> An ever-moaning battle in the mist,
> World-war of dying flesh against the life,

Death in all life and lying in all love,
The meanest having power upon the highest,
And the high purpose broken by the worm.

[ll. 187-94]

In this warped state he is most vulnerable. He has little power to resist Vivien's wiles. He despairs too easily; therefore he gives in too easily. His fall is a pessimistic image of what Tennyson considers is happening to his country, and it is also a reminder that the wisest and the cleverest are as vulnerable as their inferiors. As Tennyson once commented, "Some loyal souls are wrought to madness against the world. Others, and some among the highest intellects become the slaves of the evil which is at first half disdained."

As the heat of summer continues, so madness continues to gauge the passions' assault on the ideal order. In **"Lancelot and Elaine,"** madness comes to and from those whose minds are as trapped as Merlin's. They too are held in hollow towers, tyrannized by their lust. The story in this idyll centers on Elaine, who, like her family, lives apart from Arthur's realm and is therefore unsullied by its moral erosion. Corruption comes, however. This time it is neither Guinevere nor Vivien whose sensuous touch destroys; it is Lancelot's which brings death and confusion.

Before Lancelot's arrival in her father's kingdom of Astolat, Elaine is an innocent "lily maid." After he comes, however, and she catches a glimpse of his guilty love, Elaine's innocence disappears. Lancelot's "mellow voice" arouses her and unbalances her mind. Immediately her infatuation distorts her perception and sets her off on a destructive quest to gain Lancelot's love. She begins by misinterpreting his courteous ways, mistakenly thinking "all was nature, all perchance, for her." Then, in a manner reminiscent of Tennyson's tyrannized and maddened lovers, she dwells "all night long" on Lancelot's face. Sudden flashes of wild desire govern her, and she impetuously offers her red sleeve, a symbol of her passion, as a favor to Lancelot to carry with him to the tournament he has left Camelot to attend. Foolishly Lancelot accepts and gives her his shield. So wrapped up is he in his passion for Guinevere that he is not sensitive to Elaine's. After he leaves for the tournament, Elaine climbs to her tower, takes the shield, and "there kept it, and so lived in fantasy." She is now like all those before her whose passion has possessed them and trapped them in a hollow, barren world. Nothing now exists for her but her passion and her false idea of Lancelot's intentions. After the tournament, when she is nursing the wounded Lancelot, she immoderately exclaims: "I have gone mad. I love you: Let me die." Lancelot will not and, worse, cannot give his love, for he is bound by his passion for the queen. Therefore, denied his presence and his love, Elaine once more retreats to that mad tower and mixes "Her fancies with the sallow-rifted glooms / Of evening, and the moanings of the wind" (ll. 995-96). Now, so lost is she in her delusion, that she cannot recognize truth. Her self-deception echoes Balin's, for she does not believe the rumors her father tells her about Lancelot's affair.

Sweet father, all too faint and sick am I
For anger: these are slanders: never yet
Was noble man but made ignoble talk.
He makes no friend who never made a foe.
But now it is my glory to have loved
One peerless, without stain.

[ll. 1079-84]

In the end, like a hysteric, she wills her death. As she dies, so separated is she from her true and saner self that her father barely recognizes her: "So dwelt the father on her face, and thought / 'Is this Elaine?' " [ll. 1023-24].

Elaine's loss of self parallels Lancelot's. Because he cannot break the hold of his lust, he too loses his way and himself. Angry with himself, yet still drawn by his desire for Guinevere, he decides to attend the king's tournament rather than remain in Camelot pretending to the king to be suffering from an unhealed wound (ll. 88-159). His journey to the jousts, like his warring mind, is not straightforward. It is impetuous and chaotic.

Then got Sir Lancelot suddenly to horse,
Wroth at himself. Not willing to be known,
He left the barren-beaten thoroughfare,
Chose the green path that showed the rarer foot,
And there among the solitary downs,
Full oft lost in fancy, lost his way.

[ll. 158-63]

Lancelot is as lost in his fancy as Elaine is in hers.

Throughout the rest of the idyll Lancelot progressively loses his grasp on his sanity. Periodically the anxieties stemming from his divided loyalty to Guinevere and to Arthur, his battle between his sense and his conscience, spur the madness seething within him. At times he appears very much like Balin, for he becomes another demon of the woods: "His mood was often like a fiend, and rose / And drove him into wastes and solitudes / For agony, who was yet a living soul" (ll. 250-52). Lancelot's disguise at the tournament is yet another manifestation of this loss of self. By pretending to be a "stranger knight," he is acting out, maybe even acknowledging, this loss; furthermore, he is courting death. After the tournament he lies almost fatally wounded. Like his madness, his existence is a living death. The disguise and the wound at once echo and reverse Gareth's harmless, innocent, and advantageous charade as the kitchen knave. In that early idyll, before corruption had spread, Gareth's noble nature showed through the disguise. The charade did not bury his true self. Indeed it permitted Gareth to find himself. Now, however, in a disorderly and maddening climate, deception is evil. It is a means by which Lancelot strays further from his nobler nature. In fact, that nobler nature is so weakened that people at the tournament do not, at first, see through his disguise. After the tournament Lancelot has so little moral strength that he is unable to rescue Elaine, to help her "from herself." Moreover, he has little drive to save himself. While he is recovering from his wound he resolves to give up Guinevere. But, as the narrator knows too well, after Lancelot's physical health returns, his passion will also revive to war with and tyrannize his conscience once more.

Yet the great knight in his mid-sickness made
Full many a holy vow and pure resolve.
These, as but born of sickness, could not live:
For when the blood ran lustier in him again,
Full often the bright image of one face,
Making a treacherous quiet in his heart,
Dispersed his resolution like a cloud.

[ll. 873-79]

Elaine's and Lancelot's lust and their resulting loss of self find their parallels among other figures in this idyll. Gawain and Guinevere are two examples. Gawain comes to Astolat on a quest to find Lancelot and give him the tournament prize, but being more enthralled with Elaine and lost in his desire for her, he forgets his mission. Elaine asks him:

> O loyal nephew of our noble King
> Why ask you not to see the shield he left,
> Whence you might learn his name? Why slight your King,
> And lose the quest he sent you on, and prove
> No surer than our falcon yesterday,
> Who lost the hern we slipt her at, and went
> To all the winds?
>
> [ll. 648-54]

Gawain's lust crowds out any remaining loyalty to the king's order. Guinevere's passion distorts her judgment and turns her into "the wild Queen." She cannot recognize the truth, that Arthur is human, that he has "a touch of earth." Her jealousy when she learns of Elaine is completely out of proportion, and she acts rashly, throwing the tournament's prize into the water.

In all cases this madness is barren, a living death. The king's description of Lancelot at the end of the idyll as "a lonely" person and "heirless" is also true for Elaine, Guinevere, and Gawain. All are lost to their passion and consequently themselves. Arthur, whose personal order is ideally balanced and whose will controls his passion, knows better than those whose lives become a living death, and he realizes that freedom can come only with control, with limits. As Arthur tells Lancelot, "Free love, so bound, were freest." Excess binds rather than liberates. It locks people into hollow towers.

As in **"Lancelot and Elaine,"** much of the emphasis in the first half of the *Idylls* is on the destructive excesses of pride, anger, despair, jealousy, and desire, and on their challenge to the individual's as well as to the nation's sanity. Throughout this half, those excesses have spread and have come close to overwhelming Camelot. They have surfaced as madness, an emblem of the order's unbalance, but for the most part that madness has remained outside the kingdom's gates. Given Tennyson's and his contemporaries' concern for England's sanity and their fear of immoderation, however, it is inevitable that this chaos enters those gates. In the idyll **"The Holy Grail,"** the madness that had once been held outside the realm in exile—like Balin—is now within. Arthur's absence in this idyll signals the entrance of disorder, and perhaps more significantly the people's growing disbelief in his order.

In **"The Holy Grail"** Tennyson concentrates on the distortion and insanity found in the quest for the spiritual and nonmaterial, a quest that held Tennyson's close attention. This idyll reflects his anxiety concerning England's religious crisis. Like England, Camelot is an unbalanced state suffering from a loss of faith. Tennyson watches nervously as its subjects, damaged by doubt, worn down by the excesses of the previous idylls, and lacking the benefit of any clear vision, attempt to fill the existing void with a meaning and a faith which, in his mind, take people further and further away from religious faith. These attempts send them on quests that increasingly distort their understanding and allow them to fall deeper into their personal quagmires. As Tennyson said to his son Hallam: "Faith declines, religion turns from practical goodness and holiness to superstition. . . . These seek relief in selfish spiritual excitement."

Tennyson's concern for false religious visions was topical as well as personal. In the nineteenth century not only were there numerous investigations into the physical and emotional sources of apparitions, but there was also a clinical interest in religious enthusiasm and hysteria. With few exceptions physicians easily linked these apparitions or "delusions" with insanity. In 1824, for instance, Alexander Morison talked about an insanity that comes from "excessive devotion, and contrition or remorse of conscience," and he identified doubt in religious doctrines "previously professed" as one source of madness. Four years later George Man Burrows recognized, as most Victorians did, the danger of "exuberance of zeal on any subject," and he, like many others, found religious enthusiasm the most dangerous exuberance of all. He writes: "excess of religious enthusiasm, unless tempered by an habitual command over the affective passions, usually and readily degenerates into fanaticism." To this distrust was added the fear of mass hysteria. Sensitive to the contagious nature of passion, people were all too aware that religious experiences can be no more than a form of hysteria. Mesmerism also undermined the validity of religious enthusiasm, for it had popularly demonstrated the power of suggestion and the power of one individual over another.

Tennyson has these concerns very much in mind throughout **"The Holy Grail."** He parades one false vision after another. Time and time again he illustrates how the defining qualities of character and people's expectations and excesses trap and deceive them. He also demonstrates how dangerous such religious delusions are; how they can, as the physicians claimed, quickly arouse hysteria or insanity, spread from person to person, and tyrannize not only minds but nations. (pp. 93-107)

Throughout the *Idylls* King Arthur has seldom spoken—even though his presence has always been felt. In **"Guinevere,"** however, Tennyson does give Arthur his chance. For 165 lines the king lectures the queen, reminding her of his humanity, his love for her, the need for moderation, and, of course, her sins. The lecture is a curious mixture of compassion and severity, and a powerful one. Many readers, especially twentieth-century readers, have experienced difficulties with the king's speech. Many have been annoyed by its self-righteous tone. They find his words too high-minded. They are annoyed with his moralistic posture because they claim that he has no right to be so critical. They claim that he is not "blameless." These readers want to blame "the blameless King" for Camelot's fall. Certainly the many references scattered throughout the *Idylls* to the impossibility of the king's vows encourage such thoughts. However, the blame does not lie with him or with his naïveté. It rests with the individuals, the citizens of Camelot, and not with the king. As Tennyson once said, "Take away the sense of individual responsibility and men sink into pessimism and madness." Such is the problem in the *Idylls.* The fall belongs to those individuals who are unwilling to believe in or to follow the king's vows. Camelot would have survived had people not only continued to believe in the ideal, but had they also, through moderation, maintained a harmonious balance.

Tennyson's contemporaries would have had little difficulty with the king's lecture. They would have found him "blameless," for they too believed in moderation, and they too were involved in the battles of the *Idylls.* They knew that to keep order they must fight their bestial forces; that they must not lose sight of order and must exercise their wills. For a public that felt threatened by the passions and constantly searched for new ways in which to govern themselves and their nation, the effects of madness in Tennyson's *Idylls* were all too familiar. For these reasons the public would have also been most sensitive to Tennyson's praise of Prince Albert in the dedication preceding the *Idylls.* Tennyson lauds the prince for many qualities:

> And indeed He seems to me
> Scarce other than my king's ideal knight,
> "Who reverenced his conscience as his king;
> Whose glory was, redressing human wrong;
> Who spake no slander, no, nor listened to it;
> Who loved one only and who clave to her—"
> Her—over all whose realms to their last isle,
> Commingled with the gloom of imminent war,
> The shadow of His loss drew like eclipse,
> Darkening the world. We have lost him: he is gone:
> We know him now: all narrow jealousies
> Are silent; and we see him as he moved,
> How modest, kindly, all-accomplished, wise,
> With what sublime repression of himself,
> And in what limits, and how tenderly;
> Not swaying to this faction or to that;
> Not making his high place the lawless perch
> Of winged ambitions, nor a vantage-ground
> For pleasure; but through all this tract of years
> Wearing the white flower of a blameless life,
> Before a thousand peering littlenesses,
> In that fierce light which beats upon a throne,
> And blackens every blot.
>
> [ll. 5-27]

The praise mirrors Arthur's speech to Guinevere and suggests an equation between Arthur and Prince Albert. Both "loved one only" and, more important, both exercised moderation—both were "blameless."

Buried among the praise is the curious phrase "sublime repression"—a phrase that has puzzled many. However, in the light of the public's fears and the *Idylls*'s concerns, the phrase is not so puzzling, but is clearly appropriate. To survive personally and to survive as a healthy nation, people must repress their doubts and their excesses. And in Tennyson's mind, given the necessity and the difficulty of this task, this repression is indeed "sublime." Tennyson suggests that his audience follow Albert's and Arthur's example: the audience must themselves exercise "sublime repression." They must be more aware of how the bestial forces constantly bombard and erode the will, upsetting the delicate balance, sending them and their nation headlong into madness. The *Idylls* is indeed an example not only of the sublime nature of repression, but of its necessity. The fall of Camelot is the fall of "sublime repression." (pp. 114-16)

> *Ann C. Colley, in her* Tennyson and Madness, *The University of Georgia Press, 1983, 176 p.*

F. B. Pinion　(essay date 1984)

[*Pinion is an English educator and critic who has written extensively on nineteenth-century literature. In the fol-* lowing *excerpt, he examines patriotic and political subjects and themes in Tennyson's poetry.*]

Tennyson grew up in a period when, as a result of the horrors produced by the French Revolution, and by the long struggle against Napoleonic imperialism, anti-Gallic sentiments in England were almost endemic. Nevertheless the jingoism of 'English Warsong' and 'National Song' against 'the ancient enemy', even though they appeared in 1830, and however rousing their choric metres, is as astonishing as the triteness of their clichés: hearts of oak, Merry England, the only land of the free. The sonnet **'Buonaparte'** (1832) boasts of the lessons 'the island queen who sways the floods and lands From Ind to Ind' taught the French. Revolutionary and imperialist alarms from France brought Tennyson more than once to boiling-point. He damns the 'blind hysterics of the Celt' and the 'red foolfury of the Seine' in *In Memoriam* (cix, cxxvii) and, in **'Beautiful City'** (1889), observes how often Paris, 'the crater of European confusion', with its 'passionate shriek for the rights of an equal humanity', had proved its revolution to be only evolution 'Rolled again back on itself in the tides of a civic insanity'.

The admiration which Tennyson could not help voicing late in life at the end of *Harold* for heroism in defence of England appears early in **'Hail Briton!'**, where he contrasts the 'haughtier aims' of the Saxons who 'gave their bodies to the death' with contemporary politicians who aim at nothing higher than popular applause. A nobler testimony to the influence of such patriots on their countrymen appear in **'Tiresias'**:

> No sound is breathed so potent to coerce,
> And to conciliate, as their names who dare
> For that sweet mother land which gave them birth
> Nobly to do, nobly to die.

Though elated by the passing of the electoral Reform Bill in 1832, Tennyson reveals a rooted distrust of demagogues during this period. In **'Woe to the Double-Tongued'** he optimistically forecasts the doom of these 'Lords of the hustings, whose mob-rhetoric rends The ears of Truth', these 'blind leaders of the blind' who wish to foment riots and 'civil blood'. **'Hail Briton!'** betrays the fear that 'the neighbourhood of . . . unstable Celtic blood' will rouse passion and destroy judgment. Traditional law and order are threatened by loud-mouthed ranters against all forms of power, each (unlike freedom-fighters of the past) less interested in the general good than in becoming 'the light ephemeris That flutters in the popular breath'. Extreme political parties leave 'The middle road of sober thought', and the bonds of fellowship are snapped; wisdom lags behind knowledge, and temporary expedients are preferred to 'seasonable changes'. The fable of 'The Goose' suggests that a revolution will destroy what is of most value.

For Tennyson this is freedom of speech. If it were lost, he declares in **'You Ask Me, Why, Though Ill at Ease'**, he would leave Britain, however great and wealthy it might be, for a warmer clime; he stays because it is a land 'Where Freedom slowly broadens down From precedent to precedent', and where 'diffusive thought' is given time to work. The subject is continued in **'Love Thou Thy Land'**, which begins with emphasis first on reverence for traditional values, then on the need for knowledge. Progress will not come if people give priority to personal gain; it needs to be based on discussion and experience; it comes from growth or gradation, not from conservative or innovatory extremism. He believes that, even if the clash between old and new continues to create civil strife, the wise will learn from error, and the future will benefit. **'Of Old Sat Freedom on the Heights'** expresses the wish that her age-old wisdom will retain its perennial youth and save England from extremes. More despondently **'I Loving Freedom for Herself'** declares that 'change by just degrees With reason and with law' may bring unprecedented progress, but offers cold comfort in the thought that, if the worst should happen, Confusion and War like Order and Peace are ministers of Truth. We learn from our mistakes; there is a divinity that shapes our ends, rough-hew them how we will. Beyond the altruistic dream of love that will 'leaven all the mass, Till every soul be free', the poem **'Freedom'** (Tennyson's first political utterance as a peer') is contrived entirely from old ideas, and even from some of his early verse. Hallam Tennyson comments, 'It carried on the feeling of his old political poems, the same feeling which Bacon had expressed, that "Men in their innovations should follow the example of time itself, which indeed innovateth greatly, but quietly, and by degrees scarce to be perceived." '

A French invasion scare after Louis Napoleon's *coup d'état* roused Tennyson in January 1852 to write a number of verses, all but one of which were published anonymously or pseudonymously in the press. **'Rifle Clubs!!!'**, directed principally against Napoleon the slaughterer, is notable for its condemnation of peace born of sloth or avarice. **'Britons, Guard Your Own'** stresses friendship for the French people, but works on anti-Catholic feeling against their dictator, who has won the support of Rome. **'For the Penny-Wise'** emphasizes the folly of British military unpreparedness, as 'The Penny-Wise', with its reference to 'Four hundred thousand slaves in arms' in France, had done. Two poems signed 'Merlin' in *The Examiner* continue the campaign. **'The Third of February, 1852'** takes the House of Lords to task for appearing to condone the *coup d'état:* England is the one voice in Europe, and must speak out against 'this French God, the child of Hell' synonymous with war; descendants of barons who spoke in manly strain at Runnymede may 'dodge and palter with a public crime' but, despite the bawling of Manchester Liberal peacemongers, the tyrant will not be spared one hard word, and England's honour will be maintained. The second, **'Hands All Round!'**, is in popular form, its choric appeal for freedom against tyranny being climaxed with 'the great name of England'. It states that 'the best cosmopolite' is the true patriot, and the true Conservative is he who 'lops the mouldered branch away'; it admits that 'Too much we make our Ledgers, Gods'; toasts the wiser French, and America, 'Gigantic daughter of the West', urging her not to stand by while the mother country resists tyrant powers unaided. Another poem, appearing a week later, praises the manly style of these two poems, and trusts that the freedom of the press will not be abused; anonymity assists it in the furtherance of public ends, and **'Taliessin'** urges it not to 'work with faction's tools To charm a lower sphere of fulminating fools'. He then turns to cankers of the state, attacking mammonism ('hogs' in 'commercial mire' that discount higher values), the worship of Respectability, with church observances to atone for weekly worldliness (as in Samuel Butler's Musical Banks), and the feebleness of a Church more interested in forms than in truth. After lamenting the revival of Ro-

manism (free subjects plunging their doubts among Carlylean 'old rags and bones') and the reduction, by young intellectual students of the universe, of the One in all to 'An essence less concentred than a man', he asserts the need for 'a manlike God', Godlike men, and readiness for war. Early 1852, in short, saw a critical ferment in Tennyson which broke out later in *Maud.* Another French invasion scare in 1859 led to the publication of **'Riflemen Form!'** (adapted from a poem written in January 1852) and to the writing of **'Jack Tar'**, in which the nation's dependence on the common sailor, rather than on quarrelling party politicians, is underlined.

The greater harmonies of **'Ode on the Death of the Duke of Wellington'** befit the burial of a national hero. Tennyson was not commissioned as Poet Laureate to compose it, but felt that it was expected of him. Most of it was written with changing forms of appropriate music in mind: solemn at first in processional pageant, then lighter in thanksgiving through which the tolling bell is heard. Variation continues, from the sound of the sorrowing anthem within St Paul's, and the booming of the cannon, to the happier note of the warrior's victories, which make him worthy to be laid by the side of Nelson; the solemn tone returns with serious hopes for national protection, followed by thoughts of duty and honour as the heroic leader is slowly borne to glorious burial. More peaceful notes, with reflections on the distress caused by his loss, countered by the hope that his soul will have nobler work to do, preface the lowering of the coffin, where lengthened lines consort with the accompaniment of the Dead March and emotional stress, after which the ode concludes calmly, with a glance at the Duke's renown, then at his committal to Christ and God. The ending may not have satisfied its author, but the whole work is to be commended for avoidance of conformity to those traditional artificialities that tend to ossify most English odes written for grand occasions. There are many admirable details of phraseology in this carefully executed poem; it reveals qualities which Tennyson expected in great statesmen; and his hint at the 'slothful overtrust' of politicians could not have been lost in its juxtaposition with reflections on the greatness of one who 'never sold the truth to serve the hour, Nor paltered with Eternal God for power'. Possibly first composed with Wellington in mind, **'Will'** contrasts the strong and the weak in images derived from the Scriptural parable of the wise man who built his house on a rock and the foolish man who built his house on the sand. The first of Tennyson's images resembles Wordsworth's on fortitude in 'Elegiac Stanzas suggested by a Picture of Peele Castle'; the second is idiosyncratic and unforgettably evocative:

> as one whose footsteps halt,
> Toiling in immeasurable sand,
> And o'er a weary sultry land,
> Far beneath a blazing vault,
> Sown in a wrinkle of the monstrous hill,
> The city sparkles like a grain of salt.

The Crimean War inspired the ending of *Maud* and **'The Charge of the Light Brigade'**, which was written in a few minutes after Tennyson had read an account in *The Times* of a gallant but a suicidal action at Balaclava. A phrase, which he remembered as 'someone had blundered', recalled the movement of Chatterton's 'Song to Aella', and he adopted this metre for a similar subject. Tennyson's verses were much appreciated by soldiers in hospital at

Scutari, and proved so popular that he was induced many years later by A. W. Kinglake, historian of the war, who sent him a memorandum on the subject, to commemorate an even greater action in **'The Charge of the Heavy Brigade at Balaclava'**. Its exciting rhythms are varied in accordance with the changing movements of an astonishingly bold uphill cavalry charge which proved successful against tremendous odds. Recollections of strictures against *Maud,* and a discussion with Laura Tennant on the *Pembroke Castle,* made the poet realize that he could wrongly be branded a militarist. In **'Epilogue'**, which is based on this conversation, he states his views on war and war poetry very plainly: he looked forward to the end of war, and to the time when imperialism for commercial ends would cease; 'who loves War for War's own sake Is fool, or crazed, or worse'. Nevertheless he believed that heroic patriotism should be praised, even if it were for a country in the wrong; in justification of his own verse he wrote, 'The song that nerves a nation's heart, Is in itself a deed.'

The theme of **'Ode Sung at the Opening of the International Exhibition'** turns significantly to hopes for world peace and prosperity; (three lines were added to the first draft when Prince Albert died in December 1861, the whole being set to music by Sterndale Bennett for four thousand singers):

> O ye, the wise who think, the wise who reign,
> From growing commerce loose her latest chain,
> And let the fair white-winged peacemaker fly
> To happy havens under all the sky,
> And mix the seasons and the golden hours;
> Till each man find his own in all men's good,
> And all men work in noble brotherhood,
> Breaking their mailed fleets and armed towers,
> And ruling by obeying Nature's powers,
> And gathering all the fruits of earth and crowned with all
>   her flowers.

British imperialism persisted, and so did Tennyson's admiration of gallantry. In 1879, more than twenty years after the event, having learned many details from survivors and official records, he wrote **'The Defence of Lucknow'**, a dramatic account of long resistance by a 'handful' of English during the Indian Mutiny. In 1885 he wrote **'The Fleet'**, which was published in *The Times* as a warning against neglect of naval defences. Pride in 'old England' which Nelson 'left so great' assumes an imperial dimension: it is lord of every sea and, its small army being scattered, the fleet is her all-in-all. Should those who have the ordering of it bring about England's disgrace, 'the wild mob's million feet' will kick them from office, 'But then too late, too late'. More equable and neat are two short poems on the wisdom of avoiding political extremes at home: **'Compromise'** urges the way of caution when the steersman is confronted with 'two channels, moving to one end', one straight to the cataract, the other a detour; **'Politics'**, addressed to Gladstone, ends with 'while the hills remain, Up hill "Too-slow" will need the whip, Down hill "Too-quick", the chain'.

'The Queen of the Isles', written on Queen Victoria's accession to the throne in 1837, purveys not only some stock Tennysonian responses but the poet's reinforcement of Victorian attitudes on Britain's role in international affairs. A lengthy toast is proposed in vigorous, facile, regular rhythm, wishing her, among other things, a lengthy

reign, hearts of oak in council who are no slaves of party, supremacy on the seas to ensure prosperity and balance of power, and readiness to respond with cannon roar like the judgment of God against despots and fools. **'To the Queen'**, the Poet Laureate's dedication of a new edition of *Poems* in 1851, is very different, typical of many epistolary poems he wrote in directness, sincerity, and seemingly conversational ease. His wish is that she may reign long, that 'children of our children' may say she 'wrought her people lasting good', her land had peace, and her statesmen knew when to increase freedom by passing decrees which maintained the throne 'Broad-based upon her people's will, And compassed by the inviolate sea'. The 'Dedication' to *Idylls of the King,* written soon after Prince Albert's death, pays respect to qualities in the Prince Consort that approached the Arthurian ideal. Unswayed by factions, using his high position neither as 'the lawless perch Of winged ambitions' nor as 'a vantage-ground For pleasure', laborious for the people of England 'and her poor', a promoter of international trade, and genuinely interested in science and art, he was 'a Prince indeed'. **'To the Queen'**, composed at the end of 1872 as an epilogue-dedication of the enlarged *Idylls of the King,* proudly rejects the suggestion of a London journal that Canada, too costly an imperial burden, should be relinquished:

> Is this the tone of empire? here the faith
> That made us rulers? this, indeed, her voice
> And meaning, whom the roar of Hougoumont
> Left mightiest of all peoples under heaven?
> What shock has fooled her since, that she should speak
> So feebly?

Some detect 'signs of storm', but Tennyson sees those loyal to the Queen 'loyal to their own far sons, who love Our ocean-empire with her boundless homes For ever-broadening England, and her throne In our vast Orient'.

In the early 1830s Tennyson had believed there was no land as great as Britain, and the world would not forget who 'taught the peoples right'. Preservation of the Empire is the central thought in **'Hands All Round'**, which he adapted from the 1852 version for the Queen's 1882 birthday. The same thought runs through 'Opening of the Indian and Colonial Exhibition by the Queen' (1886), and brings his ode 'On the Jubilee of Queen Victoria' to a climax, after an appeal to the affluent to improve the lot of the lowly and destitute. According to C. V. Stanford, who set this to music, the final lines were added at the Queen's suggestion: 'Are there thunders moaning in the distance? Are there spectres moving in the darkness?' the poet asks, trusting that her people will be led by 'the Hand of Light'. Neither the Queen nor the Poet Laureate could have had an inkling of the worldwide disasters that would accrue in the next sixty years as a result of imperial aggression and colonial rivalries.

Tennyson knew that the present was fatal daughter to the past at home, but he was not disposed to 'play Tiresias to the times' openly. In 1870 he thought England 'the most beastly self-satisfied nation in the world'. At a time of agitation for a further extension of the franchise in 1884, reassurance came with the thought that commonsense had usually 'carried the day without great upheavals', and would continue to be England's salvation provided 'our statesmen be not idiotic'. The viciousness of society, with the poor starving in great cities, convinced him in 1887 that 'a mighty wave of evil' was passing over the world, the outcome of which he would not live to see. Suppression of his fears led to a violent poetic eruption, but only through a mask, in 'Locksley Hall Sixty Years After', where he despondently asks whether 'the Federation of the world' which he predicted in 'Locksley Hall' will ever be attained:

> Earth at last a warless world, a single race, a single
>   tongue—
> I have seen her far away—for is not Earth as yet so
>   young?—
>
> Every tiger madness muzzled, every serpent passion
>   killed,
> Every grim ravine a garden, every blazing desert tilled,
>
> Robed in universal harvest up to either pole she smiles,
> Universal ocean softly washing all her warless Isles.

From depression Tennyson swings to euphoria in his Jubilee ode, where he notes 'prosperous auguries' for the Queen and Empress of India. Although the two were inextricably linked, he remained far more assured about the rightness of British imperialism than he did about the state of England and western Europe. There he saw the working of evil forces which would inevitably result, sooner than later, in some kind of 'Armageddon'.

Apart from references to the growing anxieties of his later years, Tennyson's most damning indictments and home-truths reflect fitful alarms rather than undying convictions. On the question of full democracy he was as conservative as Wordsworth in his later years, believing with Goethe that 'The worst thing in the world is ignorance in motion'; he wished demagogues would remember that 'Liberty forgetful of others is licence, and nothing better than treason.' Unlike Wordsworth, whose beliefs were reinforced through years of agonizing over contemporary struggles for political freedom and independence, Tennyson was never roused to great poetic heights by passionately held political principles which made him unwaveringly single-minded in the condemnation of his country's glaring defects. (pp. 153-61)

> *F. B. Pinion, in his* A Tennyson Companion:
> Life and Works, *The Macmillan Press Ltd.,
> 1984, 267 p.*

Herbert Foltinek   (essay date 1985)

[*In the following excerpt, Foltinek examines "The Charge of the Light Brigade," focusing on Tennyson's treatment of societal constraints which impart a measure of inevitability to human existence.*]

Tennyson's 'Charge of the Light Brigade', one of the most familiar poems in the language, has fared badly in English studies of a more recent date. Barred from most anthologies it usually receives scant notice as a deplorable chauvinistic aberration which even the most sympathetic interpretation could not hope to ameliorate. Lord Tennyson himself, it is often pointed out, seems to have felt somewhat embarrassed about the composition on reflection. At one time he even thought of discarding it from the canon altogether. And yet he had taken considerable pride in the poem when it first appeared and is said to have been fond of reciting it in his old age. While this wavering attitude

admits of various explanations, it might well indicate that the 'Charge' cannot be all that easily dismissed as a collection of sabre-rattling sentiments. There is no denying that the apparent simplicity and rhetorical direction of the rousing ballad tend to favour such ready-made responses, yet these can hardly be reconciled with its highly elliptical texture from which further and even contradictory meanings may be deduced. The following . . . will elaborate this line of argument through a structural analysis that relates the poem to the historical context in which it originated, at the same time exploiting the vantage point of the twentieth-century reader, who is better equipped to assess the codes of war poetry than a Victorian literary audience. (p. 27)

Critics who dismiss the 'Charge' as a piece of chauvinism often seem quite oblivious of the genesis of the work. There is no doubt that the news of the engagement in which British forces had conducted themselves with exemplary courage must have affected the author deeply. As Poet Laureate he might even have felt called upon to compose a tribute to the Queen's troops who had fought so bravely for a good cause. But this is the point where Tennyson's motivation becomes problematical. The operation had after all not ended in victory and the newspaper reports dwelt on the sheer lunacy of the instruction that had triggered off the carnage. Why should he then have chosen to commemorate a debacle which cast serious doubt on the competence of the British command, instead of celebrating a victorious operation? The often alleged inclination of the English to glory in defeat will hardly serve as a satisfactory explanation in this case. Conversely, it seems most probable that the author was initially moved to protest at the bungle, which in fact receives emphatic attention in the ballad. This view is fully supported by the circumstances of the composition. In the standard *Memoir* of 1897 Hallam Tennyson claims that the 'Charge' was spontaneously written on 2 December 1854, "in a few minutes", after his father had been struck by the words "some one had blundered" in an article in *The Times* of November 13, where the "disaster" was treated at some length. There is probably no way of explaining how it came about that a newspaper more than two weeks old, referring to an event that had happened three weeks before the report should have excited the poet to such an extent. By that time Tennyson must have been sufficiently informed about the virtual loss of the Light Cavalry Brigade and could hardly have been impressed by yet another write-up of the affair unless it contained additional information or offered a new aspect that might put the incident in a different light. The first news had already reached England by the end of October. In the following weeks the British press had duly reported the debacle, commenting pointedly on the misleading order. We may then conclude that the inspiration for the poem came entirely from the emotive word "blunder", which must have made a great impact on Tennyson, so that he chose to employ it in a prominent position.

In fact, Hallam Tennyson was not quite accurate when he recorded the composition of the 'Charge' years later. For one thing, the poet was not only indebted to an article in *The Times* of November 13, but also to an additional report in the following number, which may have reached him at the same time. More to the point, the article of November 13, to which Hallam Tennyson explicitly refers, actually used a slightly different phrase in discussing the event. It spoke in fact of "some hideous blunder" committed by the commanders, which Tennyson with or without thinking must have rephrased into the more colloquial and more dynamic "some one had blundered". In this way the key phrase of the poem came into existence. When Hallam Tennyson described its genesis he traced the sentence wrongly to *The Times,* but it had been of Tennyson's own making. One can see why the words should have imprinted themselves so emphatically on his mind. Apart from their ominous import, they already contain the brisk dactylictrochaic metre of the poem, which, as in many other cases, seems to have been rhythmically conceived by its author. At this point already Tennyson may have phonetically associated the word "blundered" with "hundred", thus attaining the first rhyme link of the composition.

Commentators have been at pains to point out that not "six hundred" but 673 cavalry were involved in the operation, as if excessive poetic licence had made the poet guilty of a false statement that required correction. Yet the two accounts in the newspaper had been quite inconsistent in this respect, as Tennyson himself indicated when he submitted the manuscript for publication. The first article had in fact mentioned seven hundred combatants, whereas the report in the following issue of *The Times* (14 November 1854), which the poet seems to have perused together with the first contribution, erroneously reduced the figure to 607. In addition, a nineteenth-century reader would have recalled the frequent appearance of the figure six hundred among the round numbers of the Old Testament. A few contemporary critics also complained about the impurity of the rhyme which connects the blunt "blundered" with the portentous "six hundred". The harshness may, however, have been intentional. The rough rhyme is indeed repeated in the following stanzas where "hundred" is linked with "wondered", "sundered" and "thundered", gaining additional emphasis in the process.

"Blundered", "wondered", "thundered"—we might go further and assume that the word had struck Tennyson so forcefully because it expressed the essence of the incident: hundreds of lives lost as the result of a flagrant mistake committed by somebody high up whose authority would never be called in doubt. Actually, the "hideous blunder" was made up of a series of failures, misunderstandings, and plain follies. But this is not how the common man judges the origin of a spoilt undertaking. An error of such magnitude will always be traced back to some anonymous offender, a privileged person no doubt, but one totally unqualified for the job. At the same time even a bungled order remains an imperative, as the soldier well knows, since the business of war requires absolute discipline, even against the individual's better knowledge. Thus an error may give rise to brave actions, though it will always remain a blunder which even the staunch self-sacrifice of the soldier could not ennoble into an act of fate. The role of fate, as Tennyson may have seen it, concerned only the suffering men, who rode to their doom in full awareness of the folly of the instruction. But could they really have known the scope of the mistake when the signal was given?

This raises the issue of the location of the conflict, which seems to have been quite ordinary and certainly lacking in sublime effects. Not a weird region circled by the "moaning sea" nor a picturesque gorge, but a wide stretch of undulating ground formed the setting of the encounter. Doubtless, Tennyson's imagination could have turned the scene into a doom-laden landscape, but he chose to reduce it to the bare outlines and the stylised lay-out that his account required. In the **'Charge'** Tennyson entirely forgoes his inclination for evocative scene-painting. The actuality of scattered military postings across a hilly and broken country is transformed into the framing of a ritual. The flat sloping basin along which the cavalry advanced becomes a narrow corridor that might have been specifically constructed for the ordeal. Biblical images and traditional emblems evoke the obsessive dread of a confined passage surrounded by danger. The first article in *The Times* already employs the phrase "Valley of Death", which may have stimulated Tennyson's retentive and imaginative faculties. This is, then, a descent into infernal regions, the Pilgrim's Progress through the dark valley of the shadow of death past the mouth of hell. Though the military goal is still upheld, the mission proceeds as a veritable endurance test, a purgatory where only extreme fortitude can ensure survival. Passing through fire, braving death, the men are set to fulfil their task as if everything depended on their conduct. Only a schematised setting would have suited this allegorical rendering. What Tennyson wishes to convey is the essence of the action as he conceived it, not the incident itself, as it really happened. Hence the actual details of the environment had to be discarded.

For the same reason no individualisation of the riders is attempted. The six hundred know their predicament and move and suffer in one body. In the actual engagement the subsidiary units fared differently under their officers, some of whom proved excellent commanders. The retreat in particular seems to have comprised a variety of skirmishes and daring maoeuvres. Many of the men limped home on their own having lost their horses, others carried injured comrades to safety. Not so in the ballad, where the survivors return as they have advanced, as a collective, apparently even democratically constituted group. While no distinction is made between the officers and other ranks, the entire body of men are raised to a higher station as the "noble six hundred".

At the same time, the poem could not entirely omit the role of the commanders, as military actions are never collectively determined. The textual history of the composition is very revealing in this respect. The original printed version ascribes the imperative "Forward, the Light Brigade!" to Nolan, the unfortunate staff officer whose impetuosity seems to have largely contributed to the catastrophe—

> 'Take the guns,' Nolan said:
> Into the valley of Death
> Rode the six hundred. (1854. 11-14)

The 1855 reading in ***Maud, and Other Poems,*** which Tennyson soon discarded, cites one "captain" only, whereas the final text opts for an anonymous "he":

> Half a league, half a league,
> Half a league onward,
> All in the valley of Death
> Rode the six hundred.
> 'Forward, the Light Brigade!
> Charge for the guns!' he said:
> Into the valley of Death
> Rode the six hundred. (1-8)

A comparison of the extant variants as listed by Edward Shannon and Christopher Ricks supports the view that the author was deeply concerned about the ill-fated operation and was indeed searching for its cause. Doubtless he would have known that a mere captain could never have ordered the advance of a whole brigade. In fact Captain Nolan, who was killed in the fight, had only delivered the cryptic brief to Lord Lucan, adding that the troops should be set in motion forthwith. The decision to advance thus became Lucan's responsibility. The immediate order came, of course, from General Cardigan, who headed the charge so daringly and so obtusely. It seems as if the original wording sought to ascertain the false impulse of the action, tracing the initiative to a personage who was widely regarded as the scapegoat and whose name could be safely included. The 1855, altogether less outspoken version contained in *Maud, and Other Poems,* substitutes the entirely non-committal "captain", apparently still seeking to fix the blame of the debacle on a particular officer. But then the poet's attitude must have changed, possibly under the impact of the publicity which the poem had received in the meantime among the troops themselves. The later, less restrictive reading raises the issue to another level altogether. In its final form the poem is no longer trying to probe the circumstances of the mistake. What matters is solely the relationship between the men and the actuating authority, which is determined by mute obedience on their part.

It may have seemed unusual to Tennyson's contemporaries that a verse composition written in praise of the famous engagement should have omitted the name of Cardigan, who was shortly to receive a hero's welcome upon his return to England. To be sure, later readers of the final version might have associated the mysterious "he" of line 6 with him, as the ineffable speaker in **'The Lotos-Eaters'** is commonly identified as Ulysses—"'Courage!' he said, and pointed toward the land". It is improbable, however, that such an understanding would have significantly modified the reception of the text. The ambiguity of the words contributes to the overall effect of the poem, which would be marred to some degree if a clear-cut attribution helped to decide the issue. The speaker of the ominous words is after all quite unimportant. Whoever tells the cavalry to advance is merely acting out an instrumental part soon to be relinquished. For he too shares their predicament, responding obediently to what he conceives to be a gross error. In the "Valley of Death" all the participants sink or rise to the same level. The aspect of leadership that figures so large in traditional tales of military exploits becomes irrelevant once the brigade has been set in motion. We are now in a position to consider the crucial lines of the poem within their specific context:

> 'Forward, the Light Brigade!'
> Was there a man dismayed?
> Not though the soldier knew
> 　Some one had blundered:
> Their's not to make reply,
> Their's not to reason why,
> Their's but to do and die:
> Into the valley of Death
> Rode the six hundred. (9-17)

At first sight the second line of the second stanza might seem difficult if not impossible to accept. As a rhetorical question it may, however, hold more truth than the present-day reader can be expected to allow. After all, the soldiers of the Light Cavalry Brigade had been anxiously waiting for the signal to advance throughout the entire morning. In such a state every change of the current situation seems most welcome indeed. The excitement caused by the order, when it finally came, would have suspended the natural reaction of fear at least temporarily. As already noted, it seems unlikely that all and sundry could have immediately realised the lunacy of the operation. This is, however, a probability which Tennyson is not prepared to admit. Characteristically, he is emphatically speaking in the collective once more. "The soldier" who knew it all, represents a large body of troops, including high-ranking officers, who are thus reduced to the notions of the common man. For the common man may be expected to grasp the desperate situation intuitively and to foresee its outcome. A bungle has occurred for which he will have to pay, as is always the case. Unflinchingly he sets about his task:

> 　　　neither pride
> Nor hope rekindling at the end descried,
> So much as gladness that some end might be.

In this connection the function of the speaker in the **'Charge'** will have to be established. Tennyson obviously intended the verse to serve as a popular account in the tradition of the ballad. The metrical form and irregular stanzaic arrangement follow a somewhat different pattern; the brisk presentation, frequent use of repetition and simple diction, however, clearly point in this direction. The narrator or mediator is therefore best understood as a messenger who has weighty tidings to impart. Hence the abrupt delivery, hence the elliptical and yet heavily redundant style. In communicating the incident the speaker is acting out the part of the agents involved or alternatively commenting on past actions. The latter standpoint determines the final stanza: the ballad ends with a word of praise for the "six hundred" men who were killed or survived the charge. In the second stanza, however, the attitude expressed is that of the riders themselves. All of them, officers and privates, are aware that every command, even a blatantly erroneous one, is to be carried out, that orders are never to be debated, that men in action, whatever their place in the military or social hierarchy, cannot afford to reflect on the intelligence behind a line of conduct that is mapped out for them. "Obedience is the bond of rule."

"Their's not to reason why." Undoubtedly these lines speak primarily of military regulations, of the blind obedience of men in uniform throughout the ages, but the words have still wider implication. As mentioned above, Tennyson liked to declaim the poem and recordings of his delivery are extant. It is striking that he should have emphasised the word "knew" in reciting the lines under discussion, thus stressing the contradiction implied. For how could the truly obedient subordinate ever have surmised the event of a blunder if the most elementary mental process was expressly prohibited for him? Or is forbidden knowledge the cause of death, as suggested in the Biblical parable? It is unlikely that Tennyson was unaware of the subtle irony which his words convey. In fact, the inconsistency of the argument expresses the psychological dilemma of the situation quite adequately: we know only too well what we dare not think about.

In an earlier assessment of the **'Charge'**, Christopher Ricks has argued that the poem is indirectly concerned with the idea of suicide, which pervades Tennyson's early poetry, but can also be discovered in his later works. In armed combat self-extinction loses the stigma that traditionally attaches to it in Western society and is esteemed an honourable line of behaviour instead. There is little doubt that military actions have sometimes been prompted by an urge for annihilation. Seen from this angle, the enthusiastic self-sacrifice of soldiers, which was often observed in World War I, loses its heroic note but gains a profoundly human significance which would have appealed to Tennyson. It is important to note in this connection that his description deviates at one point from the steadfast regularity that otherwise characterises the advance. In the last stanza lavish praise is bestowed on the "wild charge" of the Light Brigade as if the poet had for once yielded to a secret conviction that the ride had a suicidal aspect—

> When can their glory fade?
> O the wild charge they made!
> All the world wondered.
> Honour the charge they made!
> Honour the Light Brigade,
> Noble six hundred! (50-55)

But the ballad is not merely an expression of suicidal determination. "Their's but to do and die." Inevitably the contemporary reader will be reminded of kamikaze missions, of guerilla assaults, and terrorist raids whose purpose is to inflict destruction on others through self-immolation. Would the Victorian Laureate have shuddered at the ferocities of a barbaric age that was still to come? The hero of **Maud,** a monodrama written shortly after the **'Charge'**, certainly approves of violent, self-destructive actions when they are inspired by genuine conviction:

> It is better to fight for the good than to rail at the ill;
> I have felt with my native land, I am one with my kind,
> I embrace the purpose of God, and the doom assigned.

The various analogies to which the text relates would suggest that the 'Charge' comprises a still wider potential of meaning. Though the eventual clash between the British horsemen and their opponents undoubtedly forms the climax of the narrative discourse, the main theme of the poem is struck by a note of stoic endurance in the face of better knowledge:

> Not though the soldier knew
>   Some one had blundered:

Even the suicide-motif arises from the argument advanced in the second stanza where the moment of awareness is expressly articulated. "Their's but to do and die": the steady progress of the collective body of troopers who pass lemming-like to their doom will raise associations that are more closely related to contemporary everyday life than to military engagement. The common man has become painfully aware of the infinite variety of administrative mishaps that devolve upon him in the shape of coercive patterns imposed from above. Legal restrictions, bureaucratic regulations, rigid codes of professional conduct, technocratic directions—the individual's existence is weighed down by constraints that we often know to be erroneous and yet are forced to comply with, since the

rhythms of contemporary life depend on our enactment of predetermined roles. Moreover, the predicament requires distinctly more than sheeplike obedience. Fortitude and active dedication are called for if the rigorous discipline of the modern state is to be maintained. Advancing or retreating with the steady measure of a pendulum, men may at all times be forced into situations that could terminate in personal annihilation. It appears to be a peculiar feature of our seemingly unheroic age that self-destruction is silently condoned whenever unpremeditated complications occur. The phraseology which modern man applies to such cases amply indicates that the traditional ritualistic aspect has not entirely vanished. A high incidence of mortality is termed a "slaughter" or registered as the "death-toll", innovative projects are often held to involve considerable "sacrifice of life", and individual suffering may assume "tragic" dimensions when personal extinction has become inevitable. Modern society is still prepared to acknowledge the importance of unflinching loyalty on the part of the individual. Yet no purgatorial purification or spiritual reward, not even the certainty of lasting public esteem could still be attained through acts of selfless devotion, and this is precisely the point where the **'Charge of the Light Brigade'** falls short of illustrating the human condition in our time. Tennyson ended his poem on a note of praise promising everlasting glory for the victims of an administrative mess. He might have been profoundly perplexed to hear about a reading that revealed a subversive sub-text behind his patriotic war-song. And yet, as Robert Browning would have put it, "who can say?" (pp. 30-6)

Herbert Foltinek, "'Their's Not to Reason Why': Alfred Lord Tennyson on the Human Condition," in A Yearbook of Studies in English Language and Literature, *Vol. 80, 1985-86, pp. 27-38.*

FURTHER READING

Archer, William. "Mr. Alfred Tennyson." In his *English Dramatists of To-Day,* pp. 334-51. London: Sampson Low, Marston, Searle, & Rivington, 1882.

> Analysis of Tennyson's first four dramas. Archer concludes that "Tennyson's forte evidently lies not in the construction of dramas but in the dramatic interpretation of history."

Beach, Joseph Warren. "Tennyson." In his *The Concept of Nature in Nineteenth-Century English Poetry,* pp. 406-34. New York: Russell & Russell, 1966.

> Examines Tennyson's view of nature, science, and evolution, finding him to be a "dualist" who associates nature with the objective world and God and immortality with the subjective. According to Beach, Tennyson regards nature as a "distressful necessity" by which "man's spirit is eclipsed and divided from God."

Beetz, Kirk H. *Tennyson: A Bibliography, 1827-1982.* Metuchen, N. J.: The Scarecrow Press, 1984, 528 p.

> Most comprehensive guide to secondary sources.

Bloom, Harold. "Tennyson, Hallam, and Romantic Tradition." In his *The Ringers in the Tower: Studies in Romantic Tradition,* pp. 145-54. Chicago: The University of Chicago Press, 1971.

Examines Tennyson's poetic vision and place in the Romantic tradition.

———. "Tennyson: In the Shadow of Keats." In his *Poetry and Repression: Revisionism from Blake to Stevens,* pp. 143-74. New Haven: Yale University Press, 1976.

Examines Tennyson's "revisionist genius for internalizing Keats."

———. *Man and His Myths: Tennyson's "Idylls of the King" in Critical Context.* N. Y.: New York University Press, 1984, 360 p.

Critical explication of *Idylls of the King,* along with a survey of the critical issues involving the poem.

———, ed. *Modern Critical Views: Alfred Lord Tennyson.* New York: Chelsea House Publishers, 1985, 199 p.

Selection of representative twentieth-century criticism, including essays by G. M. Young, Christopher Ricks, John Rosenberg, and Robert Bernard Martin.

Buckley, Jerome Hamilton. *Tennyson: The Growth of a Poet.* Cambridge: Harvard University Press, 1961, 298 p.

Important critical biography.

———. "The Persistence of Tennyson." In *The Victorian Experience: The Poets,* edited by Richard A. Levine, pp. 1-22. Athens: Ohio University Press, 1982.

Relates Buckley's personal experience in studying Tennyson amid changing critical perspectives, and discusses Tennyson's "artistry . . . as a conscious and unconscious reflection of the culture that produced it."

Bush, Douglas. "Tennyson." In his *Mythology and the Romantic Tradition in English Poetry,* pp. 197-228. New York: W. W. Norton & Company, 1963.

Examines Tennyson's use of mythology and classical themes. Bush asserts that "classical themes generally banished from [Tennyson's] mind what was timid, parochial, sentimental, inadequately philosophical, and evoked his special gifts and his most authentic emotions, his rich and wistful sense of the past, his love of nature, and his power of style."

Chesterton, G. K. "Tennyson." In his *The Uses of Diversity: A Book of Essays,* pp. 18-23. London: Methuen & Co. Ltd., 1927.

Defends Tennyson's artistic skill against the "coldness towards him" which has resulted from "his weakness . . . [in] being fashionable."

Eggers, J. Philip. *King Arthur's Laureate: A Study of Tennyson's "Idylls of the King,"* New York: New York University Press, 1971, 274 p.

Examines *Idylls of the King* in its social and historical context.

Elsdale, Henry. *Studies in the Idylls: An Essay on Mr. Tennyson's "Idylls of the King,"* London: Henry S. King and Co., 1878, 197 p.

Early study of the first ten books of *Idylls of the King.* Elsdale examines the unity of the work, concluding that it "constitute[s] essentially one long study of [human] failure."

Empson, Sir William. "Empson on Tennyson." *The Tennyson Research Bulletin* 4, No. 3 (November 1984): 107-09.

Remarks on Tennyson taken from Empson's part in a BBC program entitled *Tennyson: Eighty Years On.*

Ford, George H. " 'A Great Poetical Boa-Constrictor,' Alfred Tennyson: An Educated Victorian Mind." In *Victorian Literature and Society,* edited by James R. Kincaid and Albert J. Kuhn, pp. 146-67. Columbus: Ohio State University Press, 1984.

Concludes that Tennyson possessed the inquisitive intellect representative of an educated mind in the Victorian era.

Fulweiler, Howard W. "The Argument of 'The Ancient Sage': Tennyson and the Christian Intellectual Tradition." *Victorian Poetry* 21, No. 3 (Autumn 1983): 203-16.

Argues that Tennyson's religious faith was rooted in "the Christian philosophical tradition," opposing the prevalent view that it was strictly intuitive.

Genung, John F. *Tennyson's "In Memoriam": Its Purpose and Its Structure.* Boston: Houghton, Mifflin and Company, 1899, 199 p.

Focuses on the influence of Victorian thought on *In Memoriam.*

Gilbert, Elliot L. "The Female King: Tennyson's Arthurian Apocalypse." *PMLA* 98, No. 5 (October 1983): 863-78.

Examines Tennyson's treatment of sexual role-reversal and the assertion of female authority in *Idylls of the King.*

[Gladstone, William Ewart]. Review of *Idylls of the King,* by Alfred Lord Tennyson. *The Quarterly Review* 106, No. 212 (October 1859): 454-85.

Includes a brief discussion of each of Tennyson's earlier works, beginning with *Poems* (1842). Gladstone asserts that *Idylls of the King* gives Tennyson "a new rank and standing" by its "dramatic power."

Gosse, Edmund. "A First Sight of Tennyson." In his *Portraits and Sketches,* pp. 127-34. New York: Charles Scribner's Sons, 1912.

Gosse's reflections on first meeting Tennyson, conveying a sense of the esteem in which Tennyson was held during his lifetime.

Gray, J. M. *Thro' the Vision of the Night: A Study of Source, Evolution and Structure in Tennyson's "Idylls of the King".* Montreal: McGill-Queen's University Press, 1980, 179 p.

Explication of *Idylls of the King* that purposes to demonstrate structural coherence and the integrity of Tennyson's poetic vision.

Grigson, Geoffrey. "Alfred Tennyson." In his *Poets in Their Pride,* pp. 124-35. London: Phoenix House Ltd., 1962.

Biographical background to Tennyson's development as a poet.

Gwynn, Stephen. *Tennyson: A Critical Study.* London: Blackie & Son, 1899, 234 p.

Analysis of Tennyson's major works that includes a biographical sketch and chapters considering Tennyson's treatment of love, religion, politics, and nature.

Hair, Donald S. *Domestic and Heroic in Tennyson's Poetry.* Toronto: University of Toronto Press, 1981, 251 p.

Examines Tennyson's use of domestic themes and images in his works, describing his treatment of the family as a model of social order and a source of heroic character and action.

Hinchcliffe, Peter. "Elegy and Epithalamium in 'In Memoriam.'" *University of Toronto Quarterly* 52, No. 3 (Spring 1983): 241-62.
Argues for the structural and thematic coherence of *In Memoriam.*

Hughes, Linda K. *The Manyfaced Glass: Tennyson's Dramatic Monologues.* Athens: Ohio University Press, 1987, 311 p.
Study of the importance and diversity of Tennyson's use of the dramatic monologue, a structure in which "almost a fifth of his poems, and some of his finest" are written.

[Hunt, Leigh]. Review of *Poems, Chiefly Lyrical,* by Alfred Tennyson. *The Tatler,* nos. 149, 151 (24 February, 1831; 26 February 1831): 593-94, 601-02.
Positive early review. Hunt concludes with the assertion that Tennyson "has the universal and loving eye of a true poet, and must not condescend to pretend otherwise."

Johnson, E. D. H. "Tennyson." In his *The Alien Vision of Victorian Poetry,* pp. 3-70. Princeton: Princeton University Press, 1952.
Argues that Tennyson's artistic vision was "sublimated" rather than suppressed by his concessions to the literary fashions of his day.

Jones, Richard. *The Growth of the Idylls of the King.* Philadelphia: J. B. Lippincott Company, 1895, 161 p.
Includes a discussion of sources for *Idylls of the King* and presents Tennyson's manuscript revisions as part of a consideration of the poem's purpose.

Joseph, Gerhard. "Tennyson's Three Women: The Thought within the Image." *Victorian Poetry* 19, No. 1 (Spring 1981): 1-18.
Examines the significance of the three-queen consort in *Idylls of the King.*

———. "Tennyson's Stupidity." *University of Hartford Studies in Literature* 15, No. 2 (1983): 55-62.
Discusses "the mystery of human sorrow" as a persistent theme in Tennyson's poetry.

Jump, John D., ed. *Tennyson: The Critical Heritage.* London: Routledge & Kegan Paul Limited, 1967, 464 p.
Presents thirty-five critical essays and reviews of Tennyson's works by his contemporaries.

Kingsley, Charles. "Tennyson." *Fraser's Magazine* XLII, No. 249. (September 1850): 245-55.
Favorable review of *In Memoriam.*

Lang, Andrew. *Alfred Tennyson.* 1901. Reprint. New York: AMS Press, 1970, 233 p.
Biographical and critical study.

Langbaum, Robert. "The Dynamic Unity of *In Memoriam.*" In his *The Modern Spirit: Essays on the Continuity of Nineteenth- and Twentieth-Century Literature,* pp. 51-75. New York: Oxford University Press, 1970.
Argues that "the backtrackings, the changes of mood, style, and levels of intensity, even the apparent contradictions" evident in *In Memoriam* "are all signs of the genuineness of the experience and coherent aspects of a single developing consciousness," and thus proof of the poem's "dynamic unity."

Larkin, Philip. "The Most Victorian Laureate." In his *Required Writing: Miscellaneous Pieces 1955-1982,* pp. 182-87. New York: Farrar, Straus, & Giroux, 1982.
Occasioned by the release of Christopher Ricks's annotated edition of Tennyson's works, Larkin reviews Tennyson's poetry, asserting that "to open the complete works of Tennyson is to enter the Victorian age itself."

Lucas, Frank Laurence. *Tennyson.* London: Longmans, Green & Co., 1957, 40 p.
Critical biography focusing on Tennyson's poetic skill and praising his evocation of "that natural beauty of the much-loved earth."

MacCallum, M. A. *Tennyson's "Idylls of the King" and Arthurian Story From the XVIth Century.* Glasgow: James Maclehose and Sons, 1894, 435 p.
Discusses the literary history of the Arthurian legend and examines Tennyson's allegorical treatment of this legend in *Idylls of the King.*

McKay, Kenneth. *Many Glancing Colours: An Essay in Reading Tennyson, 1809-1850.* Toronto: University of Toronto Press, 1988, 287 p.
Detailed analysis of Tennyson's early works.

McSweeney, Kerry. *Tennyson and Swinburne as Romantic Naturalists.* Toronto: University of Toronto Press, 1981, 222 p.
Examines what the critic regards as the suppression in Tennyson's poetry of "a sense of man's life as part of nature."

Martin, Robert Bernard. *Tennyson: The Unquiet Heart.* Oxford: Clarendon Press, 1980, 643 p.
Most comprehensive biography of Tennyson's life and career.

Meynell, Alice. "Tennyson." *The Dublin Review* 146, No. 292 (January 1910): 62-71.
Positive overview of Tennyson's verse occasioned by the centenary of his birth.

O'Donnell, Angela G. "Tennyson's 'English Idyls': Studies in Poetic Decorum." *Studies in Philology* LXXXV, No. 1 (Winter 1988): 125-44.
Establishes eight poems as the canon of Tennyson's "English Idyls," examining the significance of each poem's inclusion in this group and the importance of its designation.

Page, Norman, ed. *Tennyson: Interviews and Recollections.* Totowa, N. J.: Barnes & Noble Books, 1983, 202 p.
Reminiscences of Tennyson, including contributions by Queen Victoria, Thomas Carlyle, Edward FitzGerald, and C. L. Dodgson.

Pallen, Condé Benoist. *The Meaning of "The Idylls of the King": An Essay in Interpretation,* 1904. Reprint. New York: Haskell House, 1965, 115 p.
Analysis of the major themes and characters of *Idylls of the King.*

Palmer, D. J., ed. *Tennyson.* London: G. Bell & Sons Ltd., 1973, 279 p.
Nine essays on various aspects of Tennyson's life and

works by prominent Tennyson critics, including Lionel Madden, John D. Jump, and John Killham.

Peltason, Timothy. "Tennyson, Nature, and Romantic Nature Poetry." *Philological Quarterly* 63, No. 1 (Winter 1984): 75-93.
> Examines Tennyson's depiction of nature and its relationship to that of the English Romantic poets.

———. "Tennyson's Philosophy: Some Lyric Examples." In *Philosophical Approaches to Literature,* edited by William E. Cain, pp. 51-72. London: Associated University Presses, 1984.
> Discusses the underlying philosophy of Tennyson's poetry.

Reed, John R. *Perception and Design in Tennyson's "Idylls of the King."* Athens: Ohio University Press, 1969, 270 p.
> Examines Christian tradition and moral design in *Idylls of the King.*

Ricks, Christopher. *Tennyson.* New York: The Macmillan Company, 1972, 349 p.
> Critical biography in which Ricks seeks to accomplish "three things: to create a sense of what Tennyson in his private life underwent and became; to make an independent exploration of his poetry, seeking to comprehend its special distinction and to establish distinctions; and to suggest some of the relationships between the life and the work."

Rosenberg, John D. *The Fall of Camelot: A Study of Tennyson's "Idylls of the King,"* Cambridge: The Belknap Press of Harvard University Press, 1973, 182 p.
> Analysis of *Idylls of the King* as "the subtlest anatomy of the failure of ideality in our literature."

Ryals, Clyde de L. *From the Great Deep: Essays on "Idylls of the King,"* Athens: Ohio University Press, 1967, 204 p.
> Examines *Idylls of the King* as a philosophical poem and a forum for "much of Tennyson's most mature thought."

Shaw, W. David. *Tennyson's Style.* Ithaca: Cornell University Press, 1976, 347 p.
> Study of Tennyson's poetic technique in his major works.

Shires, Linda M. " 'Maud,' Masculinity and Poetic Identity." *Criticism* XXIX, No. 3 (Summer 1987): 269-90.
> Examines Tennyson's reaction to the increased authority of women in nineteenth-century society.

Sinfield, Alan. *The Language of Tennyson's "In Memoriam,"* Oxford: Basil Blackwell, 1971, 223 p.

Analysis of the diction, syntax, imagery, sound, and rhythm of *In Memoriam.* Sinfield's work has become a standard reference on Tennyson's artistry.

Stevenson, Lionel. "Alfred Tennyson." In his *Darwin Among the Poets,* pp. 55-116. Chicago: University of Chicago Press, 1932.
> Discusses Tennyson's treatment of evolutionary theory.

Tennyson, Charles. *Alfred Tennyson.* New York: The Macmillan Company, 1949, 579 p.
> Biography by Tennyson's grandson.

———. *Six Tennyson Essays.* London: Cassell & Co. Ltd, 1954, 197 p.
> Includes essays on Tennyson's humor, politics, religion and artistry.

Tennyson, Hallam, Lord. *Alfred Lord Tennyson: A Memoir.* London: Macmillan and Co., 1897, 516 p.
> Memoir by Tennyson's son that includes correspondence to and from Tennyson, as well as his own reflections on his works.

———. *Tennyson and His Friends.* London: Macmillan & Co., 1911, 503 p.
> Contains recollections of Tennyson by many who knew him, as well as Tennyson's own correspondence with various friends and acquaintances.

Tennyson, Hallam, ed. *Studies in Tennyson.* Totowa, N. J.: Barnes & Noble Books, 1981, 229 p.
> Collections of essays resulting from a series of lectures which commemorated the centenary of the birth of Tennyson's grandson and biographer, Charles.

Van Dyke, Henry. *The Poetry of Tennyson.* London: Elkin Mathews and John Lane, 1889, 378 p.
> Appreciation of Tennyson's works that focuses on the personal and spiritual aspects of his poems.

Watts-Dunton, Theodore. "Alfred, Lord Tennyson." In his *Old Familiar Faces,* pp. 120-76. New York: E. P. Dutton and Company, 1916.
> Reflections on Tennyson's personal life and character.

Weygandt, Cornelius. "Tennyson, the Victorian Oracle." In his *The Time of Tennyson: English Victorian Poetry as it Affected America,* pp. 99-120. 1936. Reprint. Port Washington, N. Y.: Kennikat Press, Inc., 1968.
> Surveys Tennyson's major works, highlighting their reception and influence in America.

Frances Trollope

1780-1863

(Born Frances Milton) English travel writer and novelist.

Trollope is best known as the author of *Domestic Manners of the Americans,* an indictment of early nineteenth-century American principles, tastes, and manners. Her first literary work, *Domestic Manners* propelled Trollope to fame and remains one of the most renowned books about American life of the period. While Trollope was also a prolific travel writer and novelist, she is valued almost exclusively for her observations regarding American behavior.

Trollope was the second of three children born to a clergyman's family in a village near Bristol. Raised and educated by her father, Reverend William Milton, after her mother's early death, she acquired a facility with languages and a talent for writing that for years were expressed only in her lively correspondence. Until the early 1800s the family maintained a household in Bristol as well as in rural Heckfield; when Reverend Milton remarried and settled permanently in Heckfield, his children established a residence in London. There Frances met a young barrister, Thomas Anthony Trollope, and in 1809 they married. By 1818 the Trollopes had six children and were deeply in debt. They borrowed money freely, and after several years of increasing financial hardship, Trollope traveled to the United States with three of her children in 1827, planning to participate in an experimental utopian community in Tennessee, while her husband maintained their farm in England. Disillusioned by the squalor of the surroundings, however, she moved almost immediately to Cincinnati. There she collaborated with entrepreneur Joseph Dorfeuille on several museum exhibits, including a cleverly faked supernatural manifestation, the "Invisible Girl," whose voice resounded in a seemingly empty room, and a waxwork depiction of hell, featuring the skeletons of executed criminals and electrified wires providing a foretaste of eternal torment. The moderate financial success of these ventures encouraged Trollope to pursue a more ambitious endeavour: the "Trollope Bazaar," a combined market and cultural center offering luxury goods and such events as art exhibits and concerts. Trollope was unable to meet the costs of building the fantastic structure intended to house the enterprise, and merchandise shipped from England by her husband to stock the bazaar was seized to cover her debts, leaving her bankrupt.

Although at age fifty-two she had never written for publication, Trollope began *Domestic Manners of the Americans* in a final effort to profit from her sojourn abroad. Loans from friends enabled her to travel more widely in the United States, and she returned to England in 1831 with the manuscript nearly completed. Published in 1832, the book was enormously popular in England, where many readers were predisposed to think the worst of Americans, and a *succès de scandale* in the United States, where people were outraged to find themselves portrayed so negatively. However, the income from the sale of *Domestic Manners* and from two novels—*The Refugee in*

America and *The Abbess: A Romance*—was not sufficient to satisfy creditors, and the Trollopes fled to Belgium in 1834 to keep Thomas Trollope from debtors' prison. Trollope continued to write prolifically, producing a novel or a travel book nearly every year thereafter until 1856. As she attained financial success and public renown, she was able to live well, financially assist her children, and travel extensively. Her son Anthony, who later became one of the most famous novelists in England, began writing and publishing fiction with his mother's assistance in 1844; she saw the appearance of several novels in his acclaimed Barsetshire series before her death in 1863.

Domestic Manners combines straightforward descriptions of cities and landscapes with an assessment of American social habits, many of which Trollope considered uncouth. She deemed the Americans' lack of formal etiquette the direct result of their egalitarian form of government, and portions of her book argue strenuously for preserving the monarchy in England, lest that country too fall prey to bad manners. In *Domestic Manners* and in five succeeding travel volumes—*Belgium and Western Germany in 1833, Paris and the Parisians in 1835, Vienna and the Austrians, A Visit to Italy,* and *Travels and Travellers: A Series of Sketches*—Trollope measured each culture against En-

303

gland, her acknowledged ideal: a monarchy in which a rigid class hierarchy affords social stability by preventing the lower classes from assuming equality with the upper. While her place descriptions are considered unremarkable and her attempts at political analysis unsophisticated, Trollope is commended for her manners analysis and for her commentary in *Domestic Manners* on three issues: the vanquishing of native Americans, the limited opportunities afforded women, and the iniquity of slavery.

Of Trollope's more than thirty novels, many are unexceptional melodramatic romances that adhere to the conventions and display the defects of much popular fiction of the period, including sensational plots and one-dimensional characters. A number of Trollope's novels, however, undertake such serious themes as the slavery system in the United States and child labor and factory conditions in England. Trollope also attracted attention with her creation and development of strong, individualistic women characters in her fiction. In *The Widow Barnaby, The Widow Married: A Sequel to the Widow Barnaby,* and *The Barnabys in America; or, Adventures of the Widow Wedded,* the audacious Martha Barnaby pursues matrimony and wealth, remaining undaunted by misfortune. While the figure of the manipulative, middle-aged husband-hunter was not new to fiction, such a character had never been central to a series of novels or portrayed in such a way that appealed widely to readers and critics. In other novels, including *Charles Chesterfield; or, The Adventures of a Youth of Genius, The Blue Belles of England, Jessie Phillips: A Tale of the Present Day,* and *The Attractive Man,* such stock figures as the fortune-hunter, the fallen woman, and the pseudo-intellectual are presented with acuity and often with pointed satire. In her works Trollope frequently allowed these characters to prosper, or at least avoid the death or dishonor usually accorded them in nineteenth-century literature.

Largely unread today, Trollope's novels have been studied by modern critics interested in her portrayal of strong and unconventional women characters, and *Domestic Manners* retains historical interest for its lively account of an English traveler's response to America.

(See also *Dictionary of Literary Biography,* Vol. 21.)

PRINCIPAL WORKS

Domestic Manners of the Americans. 2 vols. (travel essays) 1832
The Refugee in America (novel) 1832
The Abbess: A Romance (novel) 1833
The Mother's Manual; or, Illustrations of Matrimonial Economy: An Essay in Verse (poetry) 1833
Belgium and Western Germany in 1833. 2 vols. (travel essays) 1834
Tremordyn Cliff (novel) 1835
The Life and Adventures of Jonathan Jefferson Whitlaw; or, Scenes on the Mississippi (novel) 1836; also published as *Lynch Law,* 1857
Paris and the Parisians in 1835. 2 vols. (travel essays) 1836
The Vicar of Wrexhill (novel) 1837
Vienna and the Austrians, with Some Account of a Journey through Swabia, Bavaria, the Tyrol, and the Salzbourg. 2 vols. (travel essays) 1838

The Life and Adventures of Michael Armstrong, the Factory Boy (novel) 1839
The Widow Barnaby (novel) 1839
The Widow Married: A Sequel to the Widow Barnaby (novel) 1840
Charles Chesterfield; or, The Adventures of a Youth of Genius (novel) 1841
The Blue Belles of England (novel) 1842
A Visit to Italy. 2 vols. (travel essays) 1842
The Barnabys in America; or, Adventures of the Widow Wedded (novel) 1843
Jessie Phillips: A Tale of the Present Day (novel) 1843
Young Love (novel) 1844
The Attractive Man (novel) 1846
Travels and Travellers: A Series of Sketches (travel essays) 1846
Father Eustace: A Tale of the Jesuits (novel) 1847
The Three Cousins (novel) 1847
Town and Country (novel) 1848; also published as *Days of the Regency,* 1857
The Young Countess; or, Love and Jealousy (novel) 1848
The Lottery of Marriage (novel) 1849
The Old World and the New (novel) 1849
Petticoat Government (novel) 1850
Mrs. Mathews; or, Family Mysteries (novel) 1851
Second Love; or, Beauty and Intellect (novel) 1851
The Young Heiress (novel) 1853
The Life and Adventures of a Clever Woman (novel) 1854
Gertrude; or, Family Pride (novel) 1855
Fashionable Life; or, Paris and London (novel) 1856

American Quarterly Review (essay date 1832)

[*In the following excerpt, an American reviewer of* Domestic Manners of the Americans *comments on the limited range of Trollope's travels in the United States and questions the scope of her judgment, powers of observation, and standards of comparison.*]

It is not our purpose to review [*Domestic Manners of the Americans*] with any desire to expose or correct a single misrepresentation. We have no wish, and, certainly, see no particular necessity, to set Mrs. Trollope right in any of her misstatements. Her mistakes are numerous; but rather, we are disposed to think, the fault of her education—which appears to have been somewhat French and flippant, and by no means calculated for a comprehensive survey of her kind or kin—and not the result of any inclination on the part of the lady. She is particularly careful, indeed, at frequent intervals of her book, to induce us to attribute her errors—though she does not believe that she has made any—to the simple and single defect of vision, mental or physical; and is assiduously urgent, in discarding from her speech—in the hearing of her auditors, at least—all of those prejudices and preferences, either of birth or education, which she appears to be conscious have sometimes the effect of giving colour to all objects of human speculation, whether abroad or at home. With these reservations, clearly made, and as clearly recognised and understood, we will venture to look into the volume, which, if it has not, to employ the language of the writer in reference to the reception among us of Basil Hall's book on the same subject, been productive of a "moral earthquake," has, nevertheless, to the infinite amusement of the well-informed in our country, occasioned some annoyance to many of that thin-skinned gentry, the journalists. If it be the subject of any gratification, as doubtless it will, to know that she has fully succeeded in stirring up the bile of certain among them, Mrs. Trollope may felicitate herself thereupon, with all the pride and triumph of an Englishwoman. It is, indeed, the chief objection to the reprint before us, that it has been thought proper, by the American publishers, to preface it with an exordium, conceived in a peevish and fretful spirit, and altogether written in a puerile taste. The irony is not always perceptible, and is calculated immediately to provoke the sneer and sarcasm, which it would seem to have been the devout desire of the writer to avert.

The travels of Mrs. Trollope have been neither very various nor very wide. Indeed she has merely skirted a small frontier of our country, in its least cultivated and settled regions; and, if we except a few weeks passed in some few of the eastern and middle regions, can scarcely be said to have been in it at all. She entered the Mississippi at New Orleans—made a pause of some seventy hours in that city—sympathized with a little negro, who, though a slave, appeared to be most unreasonably contented and happy—became acquainted with a milliner, and, through her, with a venerable gentleman of the New-Harmony faith, who dealt freely in maxims, "wise saws and modern instances;" and thus prepared and provided with this amount and specimen of New Orleans society, took her departure. To a lady of her tact and talent, this glimpse of three days was enough, undoubtedly, to enable her to know all that was to be known, and to speak confidently and freely upon the characters, manners, and conditions of the place; and, accordingly, with the aid of a steam-boat journeyer, who happily fell in with her on her departure from New Orleans, she details to us something of those distinctions which make the various classes of its society. She speaks with sovereign contempt of the creole aristocracy, who, it seems, have the audacity to give "grand dinners and dine together," and commiserates the fate of the "beautiful and amiable quadroons," who are not admitted to a glimpse of this ultra elysium; but, on the contrary, are silly enough to be satisfied, and even pleased, with their own—such as it is. There is not quite a chapter devoted to this city—the narrative, in most cases, being lamentably diversified with speculative digression, and passing cursorily, with the lady's mood, into the consideration of various other topics. (pp. 109-11)

Mrs. Trollope, from New Orleans, proceeds to Memphis, on board a steam boat, which, though large and convenient, has, it appears, separate cabins for the ladies and gentlemen—an arrangement which the English lady does not seem altogether to approve. It has too much formality about it, and although, were the cabins in common, some one of either sex might be incommoded, yet this evil, in the plenitude of her refinement, she considers more than counterbalanced by the starched and stiffened air of the popular manners, consequent to this arrangement. The gentlemen, too, it appears, insist somewhat tenaciously upon the exclusive possession of their division; and the tone in which this feature of the local custom is dwelt

upon by the writer, would lead us to the unavoidable inference, that Mrs. Trollope had become on board a perfect Mrs. Pry—had peeped and peered in all sections—

Look'd in the baths and God knows where beside;

and, most probably, exposed herself to some few hints of the aforesaid exclusiveness. She appears evidently to have been a very inquisitive body, and her book is much swollen by a petty and peevish complaining of repelling coldness here, and uncourteous indifference there, in cases where, without undergoing the usual, and, in America, the necessary forms of introduction, she has instituted a rigorous inquiry into concerns and customs, commonly held private and domestic. It is on this occasion, and on board this boat, that she first remarks, with a degree of severity, in strict proportion with its justice, upon the too current, if not fashionable, and vile habit of chewing tobacco, and voiding its offensive juices all around; utterly indifferent to situation and to decency. On this subject, she well merits a hearing; and if her rebuke have any effect in diminishing the number of those cursed and cursing with this noxious indulgence, we shall gladly forgive her all the other offences of her volume. Her sarcasms on this subject run all through the book, and are properly conceived and well written. We quote a single paragraph at the conclusion of the second chapter.

> I hardly know any annoyance so deeply repugnant to English feelings as the incessant, remorseless spitting of Americans. I feel that I owe my readers an apology for the repeated use of this, and several other odious words; but I cannot avoid them, without suffering the fidelity of description to escape me. It is possible that in this phrase "Americans," I may be too general. The United States form a continent of almost distinct nations, and I must now and always, be understood to speak only of that portion of them which I have seen. In conversing with Americans, I have constantly found that if I alluded to any thing which they thought I considered as uncouth, they would assure me it was local and not national; the accidental peculiarity of a very small part, and by no means a specimen of the whole.

It would appear from this, that Mrs. Trollope had suffered some occasional misgivings, and been warned, that she was not exactly among the American people, though in America—that portion of the people, at least, from which the nation is to derive its character, and by which, alone, it would be legitimately represented. It is to be regretted however, that she so frequently overlooks and forgets the reservation, here made, and holds up as the make and model of a great people—great, even in achievement, not less than in number—the drunken boatman of a frontier river, or the ditcher of some interior canal, who, in many, if not most cases, is a faithful transcript from her own exclusively temperate and sedate regions of Wapping and the Strand.

We shall not pursue, step by step, the route taken by Mrs. Trollope. Her course is easily indicated, and the merest glance at the map, will satisfy any one, even unacquainted with the geography of the United States, how very small is the portion of that country, comparatively speaking, which she has seen. It will be found that the greater part of the three years which she spent within its limits, was employed in journeyings into and about a region, which, until within the last twenty-five years, had little or no sign of civilization—was partly in possession, and under the control of, the Aborigines; and to which, the citizens of the United States are, to this moment, almost as much strangers as Mrs. Trollope herself. Much of it has been settled by the destitute myriads of foreigners who are ingrate and foolish enough annually to fly from the fashion, the fertility and feeling of their own European dwellings— preferring plenty and ease and independence on the Ohio and Mississippi, though coupled with rudeness of speech and uncouth manners. Many of its leading features are foreign, and we have been more than once amused with the complaint of the lady, uttered in reproof of some custom decidedly European in its origin, and perhaps a transfer directly from her own country. (pp. 112-13)

From Memphis, our traveller proceeds to Cincinnati, touching at various points of location, on or about the Ohio and Mississippi rivers. On this route she gives us some woeful accounts of the miserable condition of those who inhabit it—many particulars of her narrative most certainly having their foundation in truth. The only mistake which she can be said to have made, is in so hastily seizing upon the fortunes of some single individual or family—some exile, doubtless for good and sufficient reason, and making that the standard and specimen of the American people. As well might the American traveller, with like temper and truth, from the stews of London produce and set up the model, and draw the character of that nation, in which Mrs. Trollope never appears to have heard of boxing and bruising and beer drinking—of mobs and individual ruffians—of a penal code more sanguinary than that of Draco; and in a population of a million and a half, the existence of a class, as the London statistical writers allege, five thousand in number, who would cut one's throat for a shilling. She has never heard of squalid misery—of outrageous crime—of brutal licentiousness—of ill manners, in this utopian and blessed region. It is no wonder therefore that she should be startled in the wildernesses of the new world, with exhibitions of boorishness and brutality among the men, and of a silly air of mock modesty among the women. She endeavours to make a pathetic picture of a Mississippi wood cutter—a creature met with but seldom, and not recognised, and scarcely known as representing any distinct class in the country. The text is illustrated by a rude plate, representing the log dwelling and its wretched inmates. The description, taken only as that of a singular and isolated case, is doubtless correct in all leading particulars. In any estimate of the resources of the nation, it is surely unnecessary to say, that such a class forms no subject of consideration.

At Cincinnati, Mrs. Trollope spent nearly two, out of the three years passed in our country. In all this period she never saw a beggar; and this fact, which, of itself, speaks volumes for the nation of which it is recorded, not only fails to elicit from this very impartial narrator, the applause for our policy and people, which, by any unjaundiced spirit would most certainly have been expressed, but actually furnishes her with an occasion to sneer at our deficiencies in other respects—in the arts, the sciences, learning, literature and amusements—which deficiencies, with a strange philosophy, she avers to arise from this distaste to beggary—a feeling in turn, solely attributable to the *"auri sacra fames"* ["cursed hunger for gold"]—the vile and besetting sin, in this lady's estimation of American-

ism. Their industry becomes a reproach, and an argument against them; and that very condition of things, so far as individual prosperity is affected, for which the British democracy is now struggling, is ascribed to this same democracy, as far less grateful and necessary than the absolute poverty and destitution, crime and misery, which in their own, and, in every country, must be the certain result of the many labouring and living only for the ease, the refinements and the luxuries of the few. This, indeed, is the true and only comparison which should be made—the condition and character, the present and future prospects of the British labouring classes, and the American people at large—who are, all of them, workingmen in a greater or less degree. (pp. 115-16)

We must now finish with Mrs. Trollope's book. Our object has been, rather to let our own people see a little of what has been said about them, whether well or ill-founded, just or unjust, and not to offer any vain qualifications of the one, or defences or denials of the other. In the performance of this duty, however, we have not hesitated to remark, here and there, cursorily and without study, upon various particulars, more with a feeling of nationality, or, we should say, Americanism, than from a sense of any necessity, or the influence of any great desire, to correct Mrs. Trollope, or to console our readers for the poor opinions entertained of them by that wise and venerable lady. Her notices are evidently written in a mood rather unfavourable to the consideration of the peculiarities of any people whomsoever. She regards all things with a querulous and unquiet spirit, and a jaundiced and wandering eye. Her chief topics of complaint, in the review of Americans and American customs, other than those of which we have spoken, and the truth of which, in a spirit of equity rather than of law, (for it would be difficult, under the general issue, for the lady to prove much of her narration,) we have freely admitted, are apt among all reasonable and not ill-tempered people, to provoke a smile. They are mostly evils of the tea-table and the toilet—subjects, we grant, of infinite importance among the young and budding of her sex, but, we should think, not exactly such as should very greatly provoke the anger, or occasion the severe censure of an ancient and intelligent personage of Mrs. Trollope's dimensions. Few of our defects are material ones—none, according to her account, irremediable—yet, they are sufficient, it would seem, to subject their proprietors to the seven-fold curse—the "doom of sores"—*"a capite ad calcem."* She admits the country to be "fair to the eye, and most richly teeming with the gifts of plenty"—she has "never seen a beggar" within its limits—she beholds all prosperous who desire to be so—many wise, intelligent, agreeable—mostly virtuous—all willing to please—and yet, what with the lack of the arts in every mud-hovel in every wilderness, (a growth, by the way, entirely of the closet and hot-house,) the deficiency of *mannerists* from London or Paris—the absence of snug coterie and literary lady, in all quarters in which it may please our traveller to place her abode—she has seen nothing to "soften the distate which the aggregate of her recollections has left upon her mind."

It is impossible for us to say what were Mrs. Trollope's anticipations when she came to our country. What did she expect to see—what could have been her ideas of a young people, whose history has only been peculiar, and calculated to provoke attention, from the extreme severity and hardship of their early fortunes? It is more than probable, that knowing little or nothing of the history of the United States, she looked for every thing—not merely the things to which in her own land she had been familiar, but those for which her fancy had sighed; and *omne ignotum pro magnifico* ["everything unknown is taken as grand"]—she looked for the *spolia opima* ["rich spoils"] of the two worlds of fiction and reality—the one for herself, and the other, in Cincinnati, for her son; and, from all accounts, found neither; besides, as she says, "spending a great deal of money." On the subject of her anticipations, however, she keeps us woefully in the dark—her standards of contrast and comparison are, indeed, for ever before our eyes. She compares the miserable township on the Ohio and Mississippi—its streets scarcely marked out, and the trees certainly not yet removed from them, with London and Paris, &c.; and puts in opposition, the manners and customs of a poor and scattered peasantry on our frontier—not to the working classes—the peasants and manufacturers of her own country at large, in England, Scotland, and Ireland, but with what the lady has been accustomed, herself, to encounter in the exclusive circles of her metropolitan world. If, in her seclusion at Cincinnati, she suffers a tedious evening, she exclaims, "ah! how different in London!" and this standard is forever present to her imagination. (pp. 129-31)

"Mrs. Trollope and the Americans," in American Quarterly Review, *Vol. XII, No. XXIII, September, 1832, pp. 109-33.*

The Quarterly Review   (essay date 1834)

[*In the following excerpt, the reviewer commends the straightforward descriptions in* Belgium and Western Germany in 1833 *while noting numerous typographical errors in the volume.*]

Mrs. Trollope is, we think, extremely well adapted to the task of planning and executing a 'pleasure tour,' (as the Germans call it,) and giving a correct and spirited report of her seeings and hearings, for the benefit of us home *voyageurs autour de nos chambres* ['armchair travelers']. With the tact and quick observation of a woman, and much of the unpretending good sense of an Englishwoman, she unites great activity, bodily as well as mental, sound views on most topics, political and religious, a lively style, good feeling and good spirits, and much unprejudiced fairness in her judgments on men and manners. If she has but 'little learning,' her good sense prevents its being 'a dangerous thing;' and every reader of any taste must like her and her work all the better for the absence of all pretension to more than she possesses. We verily believe she started to write a tour in Germany, with scarcely any other apparatus than a common guide-book, and a passport duly *viséd*—without having got up, *more solito,* Madame de Staël's *Allemagne,* or dipped into Frederic of Prussia's Correspondence, or marked quotations (like Sir A. B. Faulkner) in the first chapter of *Tacitus de Moribus Germanorum.* Then, although she follows Lord Bacon's advice, and 'diets in such places where there is good company,' she neither engages, nor prates about, Italian couriers, and *britschkas* and *extra post* horses; she can breathe in a *lohn kutsch,* and make her observations very shrewdly and like a lady in the *eilwagen* and the *wasser diligenz;* and

she rationally prefers the lively *table d'hôte* to expensive and uninforming repasts in her bed-room. The result is, she has produced [**Belgium and Western Germany in 1833**], two very agreeable and companionable volumes upon Belgium and Rhenish Germany, full of animated description and natural observation, free from conventional rhapsodies and second-hand criticism,—never dogmatizing, and seldom theorizing. . . . Though she spends some days at the Universities of Bonn and Heidelberg, she is not drawn into sublime disquisitions about Kant's philosophy, or *transcendental* raptures upon Goethe and Schlegel. She describes the castles on the Rhine without swelling her volumes with every legend appurtenant to them from Schreiber or Gottschalk; and she clearly states what she sees in the vaults of the supposed secret tribunal at Baden, without extracting an elaborate history from Sir Francis Palgrave, or bewildering herself in the controversy as to its constitution and fall; nor does she reproduce, from a thumbed copy of *Childe Harold,* Byron's noble but hackneyed descriptions of the river and the castles 'where ruin greenly dwells;' nay, her chapters are headed by plain prose tables of contents, instead of useless and sentimental mottoes—in the reciprocation of which we observe a considerable traffic among the poetasters and 'standard novelists' of this age of puffing.

Let us not be supposed for a moment to undervalue the travels of persons of real science, and of historical and antiquarian knowledge. We know hardly any works more delightful than Saussure's *Travels* in the Alps and Humboldt's in South America, for their union of scientific observation with glowing and animated description; and the details which we have of the northern countries from Clarke (enriched by Heber's notes), of Italy from Eustace and Forsyth, and of India from Heber, acquire a tenfold value from the real familiarity of those authors with the history and antiquities of the countries they visit. But what we dislike, and what Mrs. Trollope's work is far superior to, is the book of travels, so common in these days, compiled from guide-books, gazetteers, and topographical dictionaries, instead of the actual use of the tourist's ears and eyes—with centos of inapt quotations—profound displays of title-page learning—shallow lectures on general politics—crude generalizations from scanty particulars—in short, all that indicates misplaced industry at home, with little note-taking and careless observation on the spot.

But though her readers will readily forgive Mrs. Trollope for not being a profound antiquary, or even a German scholar, and will doubtless applaud with us her contempt for the too common affectation of learning and languages, we really wish she had possessed herself of some good dictionary of proper names, or had at least copied them correctly from the guide-books and road-posts which fell in her way. It is really distressing to find, in her generally accurate volumes, our old acquaintances the German towns and villages, rivers, and mountains, so metamorphosed in name as to be hardly recognizable. The town of *Bruchsal* is turned into *Bronchsal,* the *Murg* river into the *Moury,* the *Bergstrasse* into *Bergstross* (it is not the beautiful chain of hills which is called Bergstrasse, but the *chaussée* at their feet—the *mountain-road*): *Braubach* is *Branbach, Rheinfels* is *Rhinefels* or *Rhinfels, Marbourg* is *Marberg,* and *Starkenburg* is *Storkenberg:* the termination *burg*—fortress or town, and *berg*—mountain, being generally confounded. The *Fulda* river is written the *Foulde,* the *Sie-ben-gebirge* are turned into *Sieben-geberg,* the town of *Deutz* into *Deuty; Rolundseck* is divided into *Roland Seck* (i. e. *dry Roland,* instead of *Roland's nook*); *Nonnenwerth* is turned into *Nonnenworth;* Bethmann the banker is curtailed of his final *n*—the Marquis of Sommariva of his second *m*—and *Danekker* the sculptor is transformed to *Dennecker.* We point out these *errata,* which will be more offensive to her foreign readers than to many of her English ones, in order that Mrs. Trollope may correct them in a future edition. From various circumstances, we have little doubt that this one has not had the advantage of being carried through the press under her own inspection.

Having thus summed up her typographical demerits, we have pleasure in saying that we think her style considerably strengthened and improved since her Tour in America. Her observations are also more sober and just than was always the case in that amusing volume; and if her present work does not excite so many 'broad grins' as the former, it is in part owing to the difference of subject, but also because it has less of extravaganza and caricature. (pp. 203-06)

A review of "Belgium and Western Germany in 1833," in The Quarterly Review, *Vol. LII, No. CIII, August, 1834, pp. 203-33.*

Fraser's Magazine for Town and Country (essay date 1838)

[In the following excerpt, Trollope is criticized for her attacks on Evangelicalism in The Vicar of Wrexhill.*]*

If against the inroads of the evangelical party the orthodox church has need of a defender, it hardly would wish, we should think, to be assisted *tali auxilio.* Mrs. Trollope has not exactly the genius which is best calculated to support the Church of England, or to argue upon so grave a subject as that on which she has thought proper to write.

With a keen eye, a very sharp tongue, a firm belief, doubtless, in the high-church doctrines, and a decent reputation from the authorship of half-a-dozen novels, or other light works, Mrs. Trollope determined on no less an undertaking than to be the champion of oppressed Orthodoxy. These are feeble arms for one who would engage in such a contest; but our fair Mrs. Trollope trusted entirely in her own skill, and the weapon with which she proposed to combat a strong party is no more nor less than this novel of **The Vicar of Wrexhill.** It is a great pity that the heroine ever set forth on such a foolish errand; she has only harmed herself and her cause (as a bad advocate always will), and had much better have remained at home, pudding-making or stocking-mending, than have meddled with matters which she understands so ill.

In the first place (we speak it with due respect for the sex), she is guilty of a fault which is somewhat too common among them; and having very little, except prejudice, on which to found an opinion, she makes up for want of argument by a wonderful fluency of abuse. A woman's religion is chiefly that of the heart, and not of the head. She goes through, for the most part, no tedious processes of reasoning, no dreadful stages of doubt, no changes of faith: she loves God as she loves her husband—by a kind of instinctive devotion. Faith is a passion with her, and not a calcu-

lation; so that, in the faculty of believing, though they far exceed the other sex, in the power of convincing they fall far short of them.

Oh! we repeat once more, that ladies would make puddings and mend stockings! that they would not meddle with religion (what is styled religion, we mean), except to pray to God, to live quietly among their families, and move lovingly among their neighbours! Mrs. Trollope, for instance, who sees so keenly the follies of the other party—how much vanity there is in Bible Meetings—how much sin even at Missionary Societies—how much cant and hypocrisy there is among those who desecrate the awful name of God, by mixing it with their mean private interests and petty projects—Mrs. Trollope cannot see that there is any hypocrisy or bigotry on her part. She, who designates the rival party as false, and wicked, and vain—tracing all their actions to the basest motives, declaring their worship of God to be only one general hypocrisy, their conduct at home one fearful scene of crime, is blind to the faults on her own side. Always bitter against the Pharisees, she does as the Pharisees do. It is vanity, very likely, which leads these people to use God's name so often, and to devote all to perdition who do not coincide in their peculiar notions. Is Mrs. Trollope less vain than they when she declares, and merely *declares,* her own to be the real creed, and stigmatises its rival so fiercely? Is Mrs. Trollope serving God, in making abusive and licentious pictures of those who serve Him in a different way? (pp. 79-80)

Mrs. Trollope may make a licentious book, of which the heroes and heroines are all of the evangelical party; and it may be true, that there are scoundrels belonging to that party as to every other: but her shameful error has been in fixing upon the evangelical *class* as an object of satire, making them necessarily licentious and hypocritical, and charging upon every one of them the vices which belong to only a very few of all sects. Another writer, because the Rev. Mr. Hackman murdered a young lady, or the Rev. Dr. Dodd forged a bill of exchange, might, with fully as much justice, declare all clergymen to be murderers, and the whole body of the Church of England to be a set of forgers. (p. 80)

There can be little doubt as to the cleverness of this novel, but, coming from a woman's pen, it is most odiously and disgustingly indecent. As a party attack, it is an entire failure; and as a representation of a very large portion of English Christians, a shameful and wicked slander. (p. 85)

"Trollope's 'Vicar of Wrexhill'," in Fraser's *Magazine for Town and Country, Vol. XVII, No. XCVII, January, 1838, pp. 79-85.*

Tait's Edinburgh Magazine (essay date 1839)

[In the following excerpt, the critic commends Trollope's skill in making the title character of The Widow Barnaby *the book's most attractive figure despite this character's divergence from traditionally appealing qualities of the literary heroine.]*

Let us hope it may be something else than the mere corruption of human nature which makes us always relish the works of this shrewd and lively authoress best, when, as the Yankee bookseller phrased it, she "Trollopizes a bit."

She is nothing if not satirical, or little more than the herd of ordinary fictionists; while, in her own peculiar walk of design, she approaches an H. B.

The Widow Barnaby's portraiture is no doubt exaggerated into extravagant caricature, despite which, we fear, there is strong, true, and staring resemblance. The Widow's coarse rouge, laid on as with a trowel, and her prodigality of false ringlets, do not more outrage nature than many traits of her character; yet the real woman is there: not that nature is ever chargeable with producing so thoroughly selfish, heartless, and audacious a piece of feminity, though a certain concurrence of circumstances does, in a vitiated society, tend to form female characters in many points strongly resembling that of Mrs Barnaby, with her low ambition, her paltry pride, her impudent and palpable dissimulation, her intense, mean selfishness, her brazen audacity, her cunning and quick wit, and her falsehoods, gross as the mother that bore them. The adventures of so odious a personage must be cleverly and skilfully managed to prevent fatigue and disgust in the reader, in spite of the constant efflux of the amusing or the broadly ludicrous. Without contrast and relief, it might not be easy to proceed far with the Widow Barnaby, as the key to her mean and vile character is obtained at once, instructively and divertingly as she is afterwards developed in many a well-imagined incident. The relief is found in the sentimental involvements and adventures of the widow's niece, Agnes Willoughby, a heroine of the shy, timid, and fascinating Evelina cast, with the beauty of an angel, the voice of a seraph, a fund of latent enthusiasm under the meekest, simplest guise, and the power of fascinating every creature that comes within the sphere of her varied attractions, save only the hard and brazen Barnaby. That matchless widow is, however, the true heroine of the piece, and we have neither eyes nor ears save for her. (p. 157)

> *"Mrs. Trollope's 'Widow Barnaby'," in* Tait's Edinburgh Magazine, *Vol. LXIII, No. VI, March, 1839, pp. 157-67.*

Tait's Edinburgh Magazine (essay date 1841)

[*In the following excerpt, the critic commends Trollope's satiric depiction of London literary society in* Charles Chesterfield; or, The Adventures of a Youth of Genius.]

[*Charles Chesterfield; or, The Adventures of a Youth of Genius*] is an exceedingly clever, but on the whole, a rather disagreeable book. We must not, however, complain that the probe of the surgeon is sharp to the touch, or the healing medicine of the physician bitter to the taste, if the state of the patient demand their application. Chesterfield unfolds or points to a condition of society, as respects literature in the capital, which may well fill simple provincials with surprise and dismay. There may be a good deal of exaggeration, and some very glaring caricature; but if one-tenth of these representations are from the life, then is literary young England to the full as profligate as *La jeune france* is sometimes described. The story is simple as regards the leading interest—the fortunes of the *Genius,* who, by the way, is an inconceivable ninny; but there is a good deal of play at cross-purposes beneath; with a lover who seems to embody the author's conception of a true English gentleman, and with a heroine, who is a beautiful

delineation of refined womanhood, whether as the high-minded daughter of a profligate fashionable father, or as the mistress of a fastidious lover. But the principal actors are the *coterie* people, and the patrons of literature, art, and Lions. For some of the sketches of these *readings* and literary *soirées,* Mrs. Trollope must have, we presume, drawn a good deal on her imagination, and no doubt some little upon her Parisian experiences. Her most rampant literary lion is Mr. Marchmont, the editor of the *Regenerator,* the "leading periodical of Europe." For impudence, ignorance, assumption, and knowledge of the weak sides of fair patronesses of a certain age, he is not amiss; but the principal literary lady, Mrs. Sherbourne, far surpasses him both in artist-like delicacy of handling, and, we sadly fear, in general truth of resemblance. Yet as there cannot be three Mrs. Sherbournes in all London—perhaps not two, was it worth while to degrade a whole class for the purpose of cleverly satirizing an individual? Any thing more despicable it is impossible to conceive, in the way of authorship, than this lady; the poor poet, who goes from house to house boring people to purchase his rhyming wares, by a kind of, what is called in Scotland, "gentle begging," being an honourable and delicate person in comparison with the Mrs. Sherbournes. Here is the original, very skilfully painted we make no doubt, and very odious when finished:—

> Those who are familiar, personally, with the authorial world of London, must know, or have known, more than one person in many points exceedingly like Mrs. Sherbourne. She was, beyond all doubt, past her first youth, but she was in the fullest meridian of her second. A period, it may be observed, infinitely more thought of and cared for by the fair possessor, than the first, which in most cases is pretty much permitted to take care of itself, without any very active attempts to improve upon nature. Not so with the period which we venture to denominate the second; and it may be, that the consciousness felt by beauties in their second stage of bloom, of their charms being in a great degree the result of their own ingenious industry, may be one reason for the increased value they set upon them. At any rate, Mrs. Sherbourne did very dearly value all the beauty she had left, and certainly watched over it with quite as much care as any mother could do over her child. . . .
>
> Such was the person of Mrs. Sherbourne. To describe her mind as accurately would be more difficult. She certainly was not without talent—far from it; but it was of a flimsy, loose, and unstable quality. No one was more ready to pronounce an opinion, yet there was probably no subject under Heaven, except her own beauty, and that of all the young men of her acquaintance, on which she really had one.
>
> (p. 722)

The degrading artifices, the coquetries, the cajolery of this personage, her mental prostitution,—for we can find no softer term,—are well depicted, though terribly exaggerated—the patch of coarse rouge being needed to give effect to the heroine of the book as of the stage—but yet with a general colouring of truth. Her best scene is that in which she cleverly outwits the great lion—the editor of the *Regenerator* himself. (p. 723)

But Marchmont, besides being a lion and a gallant, is also

a keen man of business; getting all the articles for the *Regenerator* from simpletons like young Chesterfield, the Genius, without payment, and managing to drive the best bargains possible with the Mrs. Sherbournes. The mixture of the slashing critic, the enthusiastic poet, and the *Lintot,* is exceedingly amusing. (pp. 723-24)

From the lectures with which the oracle of the *Regenerator* indoctrinates his pupil and protegé Chesterfield, the entire secrets of modern successful authorship may be learned. All literature is now comprehended in two grand divisions, the *transcendental* and the *burlesque.* So said Mr. Marchmont; and Chesterfield, who placed all his glory in being allowed to appear in the pages of the *Regenerator,* modestly requested for a specimen of excellence in each of these styles. The *Transcendental* he obtains in form of a desperate tale, entitled *Desperation,* in the Ainsworth and Dickens style, which contains a copious admixture of the *burlesque,* the one style heightening the effect of the other. The secret of the burlesque is very successfully shown by a pretty, light, and graceful prologue, which Chesterfield has written *gratis* for Mrs. Sherbourne's play, being turned into it, by the simple process of changing all the *v's* into *w's,* and *vice versa,* and by sinking the aspirates, and supplying superfluous *h's.* Marchmont says—

> "Your prologue, in the state you gave it to me, could have produced no possible effect, except setting the good people to sleep before their time, which would not have been fair, you know, to Mrs. Sherbourne. But if distinctly delivered as I have left it, having merely transposed every *v* and *w* throughout the four stanzas, and managed the aspirates according to the laws of modern wit, the effect, as you will see, will be electrical. Nobody can stand it. The young, the old, the grave, the gay, all yield together to the mysterious *spell* (forgive the pun) produced by this mode of writing. Yet it is a very simple operation. But it may perhaps be necessary for you repeatedly to note the fact, before you can be able to conceive it."

Chesterfield could not be made all at once to comprehend the mighty *spell,* which produces such effects. At a subsequent interview he says—

> "Shall I confess to you, that even now I do not well understand the reason of your altering the spelling of my lines. Why does every body enjoy it so much!"

> "Is it possible that you do not yourself taste the exquisite burlesque!" demanded Marchmont, looking at him with genuine astonishment.

> "I perceive that the words so pronounced sound very strangely, but they might be made to sound more strangely still, if more letters were changed," observed Charles.

> "Egad, that's very true, boy, and I don't know but we might make some use of it—but it must be in a totally different manner. This, you see, is genuine London lingo. The manner, you know, in which the very lowest of the people talk in the streets."

> "Is it indeed!" said Charles.

> "To be sure it is. Didn't you know that!" returned Mr. Marchmont, in a tone of considerable contempt.

> "I had no idea of it, sir. You know I have never been in London before, and as yet I have walked very little in the streets. It seems to me, then," added the young man, musingly, "that this species of composition is intended wholly for London!"

> "Nonsense! That's utter nonsense, Chesterfield. The whole world must learn the cockney tongue, if they do not know it already. I tell you once for all, that cockney slang, and cockney pronunciation is the very essence, the very marrow, the very life and soul of English wit at the present day; and if you don't understand it, you must learn to understand it; and if you don't like it, you must learn to like it; and if you refuse to make use of it, you may just shut up shop and run away."

> "I will learn it, I will like it, and I will make use of it," exclaimed Charles, eagerly.

We have the authority of the *Quarterly Review* for saying that the greatest admirers of this sort of *lingo,* and of the heroes and heroines that use it, are ladies of rank and fashion, who soar above the vulgar trammels and strait-lacing of middle-life society. This should satisfy Mrs. Trollope, who is a great stickler for social order, of the propriety and legitimacy of cockney slang and of the style of the slang-whangers.

The reader will have a better idea of the tone of this production from these extracts than from anything we can say. The satire is free and unsparing, and far, we fear, from being wholly uncalled for, whether as respects editors, critics, publishers, or authors. Yet is the novel anything but fair as a general picture of those classes; and, from its very structure and object, an acrid production. (p. 727)

> *A review of "Charles Chesterfield; or, The Adventures of a Youth of Genius," in* Tait's Edinburgh Magazine, *n.s. Vol. VIII, No. XCV, November, 1841, pp. 722-27.*

Henry T. Tuckerman   (essay date 1864)

[*In the following excerpt, Tuckerman notes some reasons for the outcry against* Domestic Manners of the Americans *in the United States.*]

[*Domestic Manners of the Americans* by Mrs. Trollope] . . . is superior to the average of a like scope, in narrative interest. It is written in a lively, confident style, and, before the subjects treated had become so familiar and hackneyed, must have proved quite entertaining. The name of the writer, however, was, for a long period, and still is, to a certain extent, more identified with the unsparing social critics of the country than any other in the long catalogue of modern British travellers in America. Until recently, the sight of a human foot protruding over the gallery of a Western theatre was hailed with the instant and vociferous challenge, apparently undisputed as authoritative, of "Trollope!" whereupon the obnoxious member was withdrawn from sight; and the inference to a stranger's mind became inevitable, that this best-abused writer on America was a beneficent, practical reformer.

The truth is, that Mrs. Trollope's powers of observation are remarkable. What she sees, she describes with vivacity, and often with accurate skill. No one can read her Travels in Austria [*Vienna and the Austrians*] without acknowledging the vigor and brightness of her mind. Personal disappointment in a pecuniary enterprise vexed her judgment; and, like so many of her nation, she thoroughly disliked the political institutions of the United States, was on the lookout for social anomalies and personal defects, and persistent, like her "unreasoning sex," in attributing all that was offensive or undesirable in her experience to the prejudice she cherished. Moreover, her experience itself was limited and local. She entered the country more than thirty years ago, at New Orleans, and passed most of the time, during her sojourn, amid the new and thriving but crude and confident Western communities, where neither manners nor culture, economy nor character had attained any well-organized or harmonious development. The self-love of these independent but sometimes rough pioneers of civilization, was wounded by the severe comments of a stranger who had shared their hospitality, when she expatiated on their reckless use of tobacco, their too free speech and angular attitudes; but, especially, when all their shortcomings were declared the natural result of republican institutions. Hence the outcry her book occasioned, and the factitious importance attached thereto. Not a single fault is found recorded by her, which our own writers, and every candid citizen, have not often admitted and complained of. The fast eating, boastful talk, transient female beauty, inadequate domestic service, abuse of calomel as a remedy, copious and careless expectoration, free and easy manners, superficial culture, and many other traits, more or less true now as then, here or there, are or have been normal subjects of animadversion. It was not because Mrs. Trollope did not write much truth about the country and the people, that, among classes of the latter, her name was a reproach; but because she reasoned so perversely, and did not take the pains to ascertain the whole truth, and to recognize the compensatory facts of American life. But this objection should have been reconciled by her candor. She frankly declares that her chief object is "to encourage her countrymen to hold fast by the Constitution that insures all the blessings which flow from established habits and solid principles;" and elsewhere remarks that the dogma, "that all men are born free and equal has done, is doing, and will do much harm to this fair country." Her sympathies overflow toward an English actor, author, and teacher she encounters, and she feels a pang at André's grave; but she looks with the eye of criticism only on the rude masses who are turning the wilderness into cities, refusing to see any prosperity or progress in the scope and impulse of democratic principles. "Some of the native political economists," she writes, "assert that this rapid conversion of a bearbrake into a prosperous city is the result of free political institutions. Not being very deep in such matters, a more obvious cause suggested itself to me, in the unceasing goad which necessity applies to industry in this country, and in the absence of all resources for the idle." Without discussing the abstract merits of her theory, it is obvious that a preconceived antipathy to the institutions of a country unfits even a sensible and frank writer for social criticism thereon; and, in this instance, the writer seems to have known comparatively few of the more enlightened men, and to have enjoyed the intimacy of a still smaller number of the higher class of American women; so that, with the local and social data she chiefly relied on, her conclusions are only unjust inasmuch as they are too general. She describes well what strikes her as new and curious; but her first impressions, always so influential, were forlorn. The flat shores at the mouth of the Mississippi in winter, the muddy current, pelicans, snags, and bulrushes, were to her a desolate change from the bright blue ocean; but the flowers and fruits of Louisiana, the woods and the rivers, as they opened to her view, brought speedy consolation; which, indeed, was modified by disagreeable cookery, bad roads, illness, thunder storms, and unpleasant manners and customs—the depressing influence of which, however, did not prevent her expatiating with zest and skill upon the camp meetings, snakes, insects, elections, house moving, queer phrases, dress, bugs, lingo, parsons, politicians, figures, faces, and opinions which came within her observation.

With more perspicacity and less prejudice, she would have acknowledged the temporary character of many of the facts of the hour, emphasized by her pen as permanent. The superficial reading she notes, for instance, was but the eager thirst for knowledge that has since expanded into so wide a habit of culture that the statistics of the book trade in the United States have become one of the intellectual marvels of the age. Her investigation as to the talent, sources of discipline, and development, were extremely incurious and slight; hence, what she says of our statesmen and men of letters is too meagre for comment. The only American author she appears to have known well was Flint; and her warm appreciation of his writings and conversation, indicates what a better knowledge of our scholars and eminent professional men would have elicited from so shrewd an observer. The redeeming feature of her book is the love of nature it exhibits. American scenery often reconciles her to the bad food and worse manners; the waterfalls, rivers, and forests are themes of perpetual admiration. "So powerful," she writes of a passage down one of the majestic streams of the West, "was the effect of this sweet scenery, that we ceased to grumble at our dinners and suppers." Strange to say, she was delighted with the city of Washington, extols the Capitol, and recognizes the peculiar merits of Philadelphia. In fact, when she writes of what she sees, apart from prejudice, there are true woman's wit and sense in her descriptions; but she does not discriminate, or patiently inquire. Her book is one of impressions—some very just, and others casual. She was provoked at being often told, in reply to some remark, "That is because you know so little of America;" and yet the observation is one continually suggested by her too hasty conclusions. With all its defects, however, few of the class of books to which it belongs are better worth reading now than this once famous record of Mrs. Trollope. It has a certain freshness and boldness about it that explain its original popularity. Its tone, also, in no small degree explains its unpopularity; for the writer, quoting a remark of Basil Hall's, to the effect that the great difference between Americans and English is the want of loyalty, declares it, in her opinion, is the want of refinement. And it is upon this that she harps continually in her strictures, while the reader is offended by the identical deficiency in herself; and herein we find the secret of the popular protest the book elicited on this side of the water; for those who felt they needed to be lectured on manners, repudiated such a female writer as authoritative, and regarded her assumption of the office as more than gratuitous. (pp. 225-29)

Henry T. Tuckerman, "British Travellers and Writers—Continued," in his America and Her

Commentators, *Charles Scribner, 1864, pp. 193-251.*

Donald Smalley   (essay date 1949)

[*Smalley is an American educator and critic who has written extensively on Victorian literature. In the following excerpt, he discusses public and critical reaction to* Domestic Manners of the Americans *and surveys Trollope's principal novels with American settings.*]

Frances Trollope's **Domestic Manners of the Americans** reached the public on March 19, 1832. It could not have come out at a better time. Agitation for the reform of Parliament along more democratic lines was at its highest pitch. The Tories snatched at her disparaging tale of life in a democracy as potent propaganda. The powerful Tory *Quarterly Review* praised Mrs. Trollope as "an English *lady* of sense and acuteness" and rejoiced that her book on America appeared at a moment "when so much trash and falsehood pass current respecting that 'terrestrial paradise of the west.'" Friends of the Reform Bill damned Mrs. Trollope's two volumes as loudly as the Tories praised them. The Whig *Edinburgh Review* called her an irresponsible caricaturist who drew her sketches not with pen and Indian ink but with vitriol and a blacking brush. Her book, it said, was nothing but four-and-thirty chapters of American scandal.

But Britons of both parties read her book and relished it for the racy genre pictures of American life with which its pages abound. Before the end of the year, **Domestic Manners** had run through four editions, "Yankeeisms" were a conversational fad, and Mrs. Trollope was a literary lion, well launched at the age of fifty-two upon her remarkable career as a writer of novels and travel books. In the next quarter-century she was to publish no less than one hundred and thirteen volumes.

In the United States an outraged citizenry read **Domestic Manners** as they had read no travel book before it. Lieutenant E. T. Coke, a British subaltern who was at New York when Mrs. Trollope's book first appeared there, found the commotion that it created "truly inconceivable."

> The Tariff and Bank Bill were alike forgotten, and the tug of war was hard, whether the **Domestic Manners,** or the cholera, which burst upon them simultaneously, should be the more engrossing topic of conversation. At every corner of the street, at the door of every petty retailer of information for the people, a large placard met the eye with, "For sale here, with plates, **Domestic Manners of the Americans,** by Mrs. Trollope." At every table d'hote, on board of every steam-boat, in every stage-coach, and in all societies, the first question was, "Have you read Mrs. Trollope?" And one half of the people would be seen with a red or blue half-bound volume in their hand, which you might vouch for being the odious work; and the more it was abused the more rapidly did the printers issue new editions.

Newspapers in every section of the country made a pastime of reviling Mrs. Trollope, though they also quoted long sections from her book. Even the polished quarterlies denounced her "coarse exaggeration" and "bitter carica-

ture"; a Western editor indexed his review under "Lies of an English lady." American journalists soberly repeated, and probably believed, that "libeling the United States" had netted her "the immense profit of between one hundred and thirty and one hundred and forty thousand dollars."

Frances Trollope was soon one of the best-known of British authors throughout America, and the worst-hated. She was lampooned in prose and poetry and on the stage; she was travestied in cartoons. She became a folk character. A frontiersman named his "hound with a number of whelps" after her. A circus band played "Mrs. Trollope's March" to the roar of a lion. "A Trollope! a Trollope!" became the accustomed cry from the pits of theaters when gentlemen failed to sit properly in the boxes. A German traveler reported viewing a wax figure of Mrs. Trollope in New York. "She appeared in the form of a goblin and the public is given the pleasure to see her in this form for the price of admission." In Maine an English tourist encountered a traveling menagerie which advertised "'an exact likeness' of the celebrated Mrs. Trollope":

> . . . this exact likeness turned out to be the figure of a fat red-faced *trollop,* smoking a short pipe, and dressed in dirty flannel and worsted, and a ragged slouched hat.
>
> "This," said the showman, "is the purty Mrs. Trollope, who was sent over to the United States by the British lords, to write libels against the free-born Americans." The figure excited a good deal of attention, and was abused in no measured terms.

More than one responsible person in England and America feared that behind such smoke there might lurk the sparks of an international "incident." An American writer, Timothy Flint, half-seriously plotted the course by which Mrs. Trollope's book could lead to open war.

> We first fight the wordy war of tongue and pen. The emergency comes, and evil passions, and concentrated and long-gathered bitternesses concur with reasons of state, and the passions of a dominant party, to engender a war, and we redden the ocean and the land with human blood, that is spilled because Mrs. Trollope had no letters of recommendation, and was a short dumpling and ill-dressed figure—a war of a frock and a petticoat.

No blood was spilled, but the war of words, kept in motion by the works of other critical British travelers, went on for years and was a serious factor in Anglo-American relations.

To a modern reader, the amount of resentment that Mrs. Trollope raised is apt to seem out of all proportion to the modest pretensions of her book. She carefully disavows at the start any claim to furnish "complete information" about America. Her subject, she insists, is simply "the daily aspect of ordinary life," and she proposes to limit herself to recording her own observations during her three years and six months in the United States. Few travelers, as a matter of fact, have written so intimately of their day-to-day experiences and their thoughts and feelings in a strange land. **Domestic Manners** is essentially the story of Frances Trollope. It neither promises nor affords a rounded view of American society. Because she came to the United States as a threadbare business woman, her tale

American caricature of Trollope from 1833.

has a good deal more to do with petty tradesmen and their wives, with trips to market and revival meetings, with cheap travel and cheap boarding-houses, than it has to do with American drawing-rooms. Because her own experiences were not happy, she paints an unflattering picture of life in the New World. And because she wrote of her own adventures and denied any intention of doing more than that, she felt free to criticize everything and everybody in the offhand manner that is a privilege of the personal raconteur. It was this airy irresponsibility of Frances Trollope's that, more than anything else, infuriated American reviewers. She could speak lightly of her "gossipy pages," but thousands on two continents read them. She modestly disclaimed any right to sit upon the judge's bench, and then proceeded, in effect, to pronounce opinion upon all America from a tradesman's front parlor and a stagecoach seat.

There is no good reason, however, to believe the charges of her American reviewers that she willfully distorted her account of what she saw. She was ambitious for detail and for accuracy. She early developed the habit of jotting down particulars and pursued it often at strange times and in strange places. She did not let her sense of propriety keep her from chatting with the wife of a publican or peering beneath the flap of a camp-meeting tent. She describes

the mores of the back country with a downright frankness that shocked her bluestocking friends. In the preface to her ***Belgium and Western Germany in 1833*** she wrote an oblique reply to the charges of her critics.

> My little volumes on America have been much read. Many have said that this was owing to their being written with strong party feeling: but I—who am in the secret—know that such was not the case. The cause of their success, therefore, must be sought elsewhere; and I attribute it solely to that intuitive power of discerning what is written with truth, which is possessed, often unconsciously, by every reader. Be he pleased, or displeased by the pictures brought before him, he feels that the images portrayed are real; and this will interest, even if it vex him.
>
> I have an inveterate habit of suffering all I see to make a deep impression on my memory; and the result of this is a sort of mosaic, by no means very grand in outline or skilful in drawing; but each morsel of colour has the reality of truth—in which there is ever some value.

While the storm of criticism against her was at its fiercest, Americans could concede that she had struck truth on many, or perhaps most, points. Washington Irving, who toured the West a few months after *Domestic Manners* was published, took the book along with him and read it "not without acquiescence." With the passage of time, even Cincinnati, which was her principal subject and had by all odds greatest cause to complain of the sharpness of her pencil, came to see her in a fairer light. "Her book," says Charles Anderson, looking back upon events that he had witnessed as a young man, "was too just a picture of our people to make her anything in their opinion than the very opposite of what she was." "That her book aroused the hot indignation of Cincinnatians was altogether proper," Charles Frederick Goss writes in his history of the city (1912), "but that she gave a pretty true account of affairs here is also true." Her scenes of American life, it is now generally agreed, are as honest as they are sharp-cut and graphic. Of course they are limited in perspective. They represent America in the age of Jackson as it was seen and felt by an especially English Englishwoman who had strong personal reasons for viewing the New World with disenchanted eyes. (pp. viii-xii)

Any second book "by Mrs. Trollope, the author of *Domestic Manners of the Americans*," was assured of an audience. *The Refugee in America* was praised and condemned and held in the public notice by partisan reviewers who judged it by what they had thought of *Domestic Manners.* In large part *The Refugee* is simply run-of-the-mine fiction of its time. Mrs. Trollope was satisfied with no one less than a young earl for her hero, and the Countess of Darcy, his mother, figures prominently in the action. Subscribers to the rental libraries had their expected ration of aristocracy. The plot is made up of deep intrigue, disguise, and pursuit, culminating in a trial at Westminster Hall. There Lord Darcy is cleared of a charge of murder by the last-minute appearance of the girl he loves, with incontrovertible proof of his innocence. The girl is an American, an unspoiled, adaptable maiden who easily sees the merits of imitating English speech and English manners. It is in the American scenes that the novel comes to life, and these contain much clever writing. There is hardly a detail of American life, to be sure, that is not twice-told material for the reader of *Domestic Manners;* but to the average devotee of the three-volume novel *The Refugee*'s American settings must have been new and satisfying. Perhaps the most notable fact about this first novel is that in it Mrs. Trollope adopted the practice that she was to follow with rare exceptions throughout her career, one that provided her a reliable market for a quarter-century: she gauged her audience and gave them what they wanted. Critics might abuse her novel as they had abused *Domestic Manners;* so long as her books sold, she did not care greatly. She had no high opinion of herself as a producer of literature; she wrote not for posterity but for money to supply the needs of her family. (p. lxiv)

For *The Life and Adventures of Jonathan Jefferson Whitlaw; or, Scenes on the Mississippi,* Mrs. Trollope put aside the lighter tone that she had used to satirize the United States and its inhabitants in *Domestic Manners* and *The Refugee in America.* Her present plan was to make a deadly serious attack upon Negro slavery, and she chose as her vehicle a tale heavy with melodrama and dominated by an appalling villain. Son of a river squatter, Jonathan Jefferson Whitlaw rises to wealth and power by cunning and total lack of scruples. He is opposed in his designs by Juno, an aged Negress who exerts power over whites and blacks alike by preying upon their superstitious natures. Ultimately Juno proves the nemesis of Whitlaw; he dies under the daggers of four slaves whom she has set upon him and is buried beneath the floor of her hut. But before his evil career is ended, Whitlaw has driven Juno's half-white granddaughter, reared as an English heiress, to escape his threats by suicide; he has also contrived the death of the hero. This enlightened young Kentuckian, who has blocked Whitlaw's plans by championing the Negroes, dies at the hands of a lynching party. Altogether *Jonathan Jefferson Whitlaw* is a grim tale, full of persecution and violence. It suffers from improbabilities of plotting, but it possesses memorable scenes and characters and is easily one of Mrs. Trollope's strongest performances. (pp. lxvii-lxviii)

In 1843, a year after the appearance of Charles Dickens's *American Notes,* Frances Trollope published *The Barnabys in America,* her third novel dealing with life in the United States. The simple, somewhat foolish Widow Barnaby was a favorite character whom Mrs. Trollope had already carried through two novels [*The Widow Barnaby* and *The Widow Married: A Sequel to the Widow Barnaby*]. *The Barnabys in America* is a broad-humored, leisurely, and practically plotless satire upon American customs and American prejudices. In the course of the Barnabys' travels about America the widow's Irish husband changes parts as often as a low comedian on a rural circuit and thus allows his creator to poke fun at a number of American types, including the swaggering, bragging tobacco-chewer and the hypocritical revivalist minister. The widow herself decides to write a book about America, but unlike the author of *Domestic Manners* she shows great adaptability and few scruples; she fits readily into the environment of the moment. She is lionized in the South because she praises slavery and in the North because she condemns it. She is eager for advice about her book and receives large amounts of that commodity. Her advisers differ sharply in their ideas upon the proper handling of particular subjects, but as to the general point of view she should adopt all are agreed. "All I want," one American woman informs her, "is that you should portray us out to the world for just what we really are, and that is the finest nation upon the surface of God's whole earth, and as far ahead in civilization of Europe in general, and England in particular, as the summer is before winter in heat."

Perhaps Mrs. Trollope meant originally to turn a part of the laughter toward herself; the Widow Barnaby takes notes and asks questions even as she herself had done a dozen years earlier. But the widow is far more often Mrs. Trollope's foil than her likeness. The single sheet of "Justice Done at Last" which the widow reads to an admiring American audience is a wildly fulsome eulogy on "the free-born, the free-bred, the immortal, and ten hundred thousand times more glorious country," to which all others put together cannot in any respect hold a candle. One member of the audience exclaims: "Admirable!" An American dignitary who is of the party objects to the word. "Admirable? It is *first-rate,* ma'am." There was no doubt in the minds of readers which way the satire pointed, but it was too broad in tone and too familiar in theme to hurt or surprise anyone.

Six years later Mrs. Trollope published her fourth and last novel of American life. She was now within one year of threescore and ten, and she may have felt that it was time to make her peace with the Americans. At least, **The Old World and the New** deals more kindly with the United States than any of her earlier books. The Stormonts come to the New World because they cannot see their way to remaining solvent in England. After inspecting a wild forest tract in New York, they move on to Ohio, where they purchase fifteen hundred acres of land, most of which is already cleared. Their farm is only ten miles from Cincinnati. The Stormonts are much better pleased with this city than Mrs. Trollope had been; they admire its "busy prosperity" and its "magnificent position." Fortunately, they have enough capital to establish themselves without hardship. "Nothing is so difficult as to get along in the United States without ready money," Mrs. Trollope observes. "Nothing is so easy with it."

The Stormonts prosper in the New World even from the start. Before long they decide to build a more spacious residence. . . . Within six weeks after the English family had moved into their new house, they had become acquainted with "all the most distinguished families among the aristocracy of Cincinnati."

English families in Mrs. Trollope's earlier novels had been glad to shake the dust of the United States from their shoes, but the Stormonts, even when they could return to the Old World in comfort, prefer to stay in Ohio and see their children grow into full-fledged Americans. After all, Mrs. Trollope reflects, twenty years and the advent of the transatlantic steamship have greatly lessened differences between England and America:

> It is an obvious and a very agreeable fact, that the social intercourse between the old country and the new, has been rapidly increased, and is still rapidly increasing, in consequence of the great comparative facility with which an excursion across the Atlantic may now be made; and the natural and inevitable effect of this has been the formation of many warm and cordial friendships between individuals who were born of the same race, but with this formidable barrier dividing them.

Now that easy communication between the two countries has been effected, Americans are steadily improving through the benefits of travel. In time they may even learn how to speak English. (pp. lxxi-lxxiii)

> *Donald Smalley, in an introduction to* Domestic Manners of the Americans *by Frances Trollope, edited by Donald Smalley, Alfred A. Knopf, 1949, pp. vii-lxxvi.*

Joseph Wood Krutch (essay date 1954)

[*Krutch is one of America's most respected literary and drama critics. Noteworthy among his works are* The American Drama since 1918 *(1939), in which he analyzed the most important dramas of the 1920s and 1930s, and* "Modernism" in Modern Drama *(1953), in which he stressed the need for twentieth-century playwrights to infuse their works with traditional humanistic values. A conservative and idealistic thinker, he was a consistent proponent of human dignity and the preeminence of literary art. His literary criticism is characterized by such concerns; in* The Modern Temper *(1929)*

he argued that because scientific thought has denied human worth, tragedy has become obsolete, and in The Measure of Man *(1954) he attacked modern culture for depriving humanity of the sense of individual responsibility necessary for making important decisions in an increasingly complex age. In the following excerpt, Krutch summarizes strengths and weaknesses of* Domestic Manners of the Americans.]

Daughter of an impractical clergyman and married to a highly unsuccessful lawyer, Mrs. Trollope . . . found herself responsible for a numerous and expensive family. What she really wanted to do was to preside over a salon full of "interesting people," but she took time out to launch a series of hair-brained schemes for achieving solvency. She began by leasing two farms to be managed by the incompetent husband, who then promptly retired to his study to compile an Ecclesiastical Encyclopedia. When she was already past forty she fell under the spell of an eloquent female Owenite and set out with some of the children to join a colony near Memphis, Tennessee, which proposed to educate whites and Negroes together as a lesson in equality. Finding there only a dismal huddle of shacks, she soon shook its mud from her feet and proceeded to Cincinnati, where after a series of unpleasant encounters with pigs and people she sank what remained of the family money in an Atheneum-Bazaar where the barbarous Cincinnatians were to be exposed to culture after the promise of desirable merchandise for sale had lured them in.

When both the English and the American establishment collapsed completely and simultaneously, she had her great idea. She had never written anything for publication, but why not a book on **Domestic Manners of the Americans**? She had seen too much of them. Making a hasty circuit of some Eastern cities, chiefly in order to be able to say that she had been there, she dashed off a book full of exuberant descriptions of pigs in the street, spitting in the dining-room, and invincible ignorance.

From one point of view almost everything was wrong with the book. Mrs. Trollope was a thoroughly incompetent observer who saw everything in terms of the irritation or the pleasure of the moment, and as her famous son Anthony was to say many years later, "her politics were always an affair of the heart, as indeed were all of her convictions." She also managed to convey the impression that the manners of a frontier town were approximately the same as those of the Eastern seaboard, and she thus paved the way for the long-enduring European conviction that redskins were scalping pedestrians on Fifth Avenue well down into the nineteenth century.

In other respects the book was exactly right. Mrs. Trollope was sometimes witty and always vivacious. She was curiously shrewd as well as curiously gullible, and she laid the colors on thick. In England Tories bought the book to confirm their opinion that "leveling" didn't work; Liberals to denounce it as a libel on the promise and the achievement of democracy. In America everybody bought it for the same reasons—whatever they may be—which still lead Americans to buy any reasonably readable book which ridicules them vigorously. The other thing that was right was simply this: Cincinnati was probably almost as bad as she described it. She would have exaggerated if exaggeration had been possible, but it probably wasn't.

Sometimes one suspects her of inventing; sometimes she sounds as though her leg had been pulled by citizens who realized that they could never make her believe them civilized and so might as well play the role of really extraordinary barbarians. But too many other visitors to frontier America—some before and some after her time—have reported much the same situation to make it possible to dismiss all the testimony.

Given her vivacity, she might under happier circumstances have produced a real classic of humor—something, say, like Mark Twain, who saw much the same world a generation later, or like the too little known chapter about the Pike County pig herders in Clarence King's *Mountaineering in the Sierras.* But because she was unhappy, desperate, and in the angry mood of a romanticist faced with grim reality, she wrote only a best-seller which pulled the family out of the pit and assured the moderate success of the novels and travel books she wrote later. Of course she never realized that at least half the joke was on her. When she excoriated the inhabitants of Cincinnati for their failure to support a phrenological institute she was not on very secure ground, but when she became one of the first to describe the American addiction to spitting copiously, incessantly, and inaccurately she probably knew what she was talking about. Who knows how much international understanding would have been facilitated if the citizens of our young republic had not been so enthusiastically addicted to "chawing"?

Fortunately the manners of Americans have changed a good deal since Mrs. Trollope's time. Unfortunately those of English visitors have not always changed as much. (p. 366)

> *Joseph Wood Krutch, "She Didn't Like 'Chawing'," in* The Nation, *New York, Vol. 178, No. 17, April 24, 1954, pp. 365-66.*

Roger P. Wallins   (essay date 1977)

[*In the following essay discussing* The Life and Adventures of Michael Armstrong, the Factory Boy, *Wallins assesses Trollope's success in reconciling her desire to expose the evils of the factory system with her aspiration to produce an artistically accomplished, marketable novel.*]

The nineteenth-century social novel generally establishes a limited area in which to identify and perhaps offer solutions to a particular problem, often some aspects of the living and working conditions of factory workers, miners or, less frequently, agricultural laborers. It seems to have begun with *Oliver Twist,* Charles Dickens' first attempt to treat at length such serious social problems as the adverse effects of the New Poor Law and the existence of criminal training-schools in the slums of large cities. Dickens' novel has survived because he was able to incorporate his social criticism into a work that has not only topicality but also artistic merit. It is this latter quality, by which a novelist transcends the issues to be discussed in his work, that ultimately determines a novel's durability. And it is this quality which poses the primary dilemma for a social novelist: how to propagandize without sacrificing the artistic integrity of the work.

Frances Trollope and Charlotte Tonna, who published so-cial novels almost simultaneously in 1839-40, are significant for their commentaries on factory life despite critical recognition of their works' artistic deficiencies. Mrs. Tonna is important to us as a "social historian" because, in *Helen Fleetwood,* she is the first social novelist to use recorded testimony from Royal Commission and Parliamentary Committee reports (the "blue books") as dialogue in her fiction. Although recent critics claim little artistic merit for her novel [the critic cites Ivanka Kovacevic and S. Barbara Kanner, "Blue Book into Novel: The Forgotten Industrial Fiction of Charlotte Elizabeth Tonna, *Nineteenth Century Fiction* 25, 1970], they do compare it favorably with Mrs. Trollope's *Michael Armstrong,* that "much inferior and farfetched extravaganza" significant nonetheless for reflecting the author's detailed observation during her visit to Manchester factories. In preferring *Helen Fleetwood,* these critics seem to be ignoring a major difference in the motivation behind the two novels. And while "motivation" is in itself not a justifiable criterion for critically judging a work of art, it often helps to explain why a given work takes the form or the approach it does. Mrs. Tonna's purpose was "unashamedly propagandistic": although she viewed "fabrication" distastefully, she wished to inform readers of *The Christian Lady's Magazine,* in which her novel was originally published, about the evils exposed by the blue books. Mrs. Trollope also intended to "draw the attention of her countrymen to the fearful evils inherent in the Factory system," as she states in her Preface. But she had another major purpose which influenced her choice of subject in the first place: she wanted to sell novels, and she recognized that agitation for factory reform was seizing the popular mind. In other words, she wanted her story to have a social purpose and to appeal to a wider audience than Mrs. Tonna apparently chose to address.

In this purpose she was faced with the dilemma of the social novelist. Critics of *Michael Armstrong* too readily dismiss the work as an inartistic failure, and overlook the slight but very real success Mrs. Trollope achieves in resolving this dilemma. An examination of the artistic difficulties Mrs. Trollope encounters in this novel, and of her methods and success in solving them, will help to deemphasize critical concern about the "social" aspects of the work and will increase emphasis on the "novel" as art. Where her desire to "tell a good story" conflicts with her social purpose, we must ask if she does violence to the one in order to do justice to the other.

Michael Armstrong has two plot strands. In the main one, the sadistic Sir Matthew Dowling owns many factories in the Lancashire manufacturing town of Ashleigh, in one of which young Michael and his lame brother Edward are employed. Pressured by a noblewoman, Mary Brotherton, into taking Michael out of the factory and into his own home, Sir Matthew responds by plotting to place his despised charge in the more brutal and more isolated Deep Valley Mill, owned by Elgood Sharpton. Workers in this mill supposedly are "apprenticed," but actually are legally bound slaves until the age of twenty-one. With no parents and no authorities near enough to check on conditions, the young workers often sicken and die before their apprenticeship is to terminate. Michael manages not only to survive but to escape from Deep Valley, and the rest of the novel describes his ultimately successful quest to be reunited with his brother. In such a summary, this plot strand is easy enough to understand; it develops in conjunction with the minor strand, Mary Brotherton's attempts to learn about factory conditions.

But we must ask whether Mrs. Trollope fails to integrate the two plot strands that she creates to convey her social message. Does she fail artistically in other areas? For example, does she find it necessary to emphasize social ideas by entering her pages in her own voice or by including lengthy dialogue which distracts attention from the major events of the plot? And does her social thesis preclude attempts to create developed characters?

Certainly, the characters in *Michael Armstrong* are types, rather than realistically complex individuals. Michael is the innocent young factory child whose destruction is planned by the consummate villain, Sir Matthew Dowling. Sir Matthew is evil throughout, and gleefully plots new ways by which to rob his young workers of their humanity; but Mrs. Trollope provides no motivation for such an attitude, and this is certainly a failing in characterization. For Sir Matthew is hardly believable either as a factory owner or—which he also is—as a family man with children of his own. His character may, in fact, weaken Frances Trollope's claim that her picture of factory life is true. He owns many mills, is the wealthiest man in the vicinity, and forces his employees to work long hours. Yet, according to both the compilers of the blue books and such apologists for the manufacturers as Charles Babbage and Andrew Ure, large manufacturers in particular were most careful to protect the well-being of the workers. The smaller employers, those who owned few mills, had to squeeze work out of their men in order to realize what they considered a decent profit. In giving Sir Matthew the wealth and position of a large master but the antisocial drives of a small one, Mrs. Trollope has created an atypical owner. Indeed, his characterization led one contemporary reviewer to charge that *Michael Armstrong* is "an exaggerated statement of the vices of a class, and a mischievous attempt to excite the worst and bitterest feelings against men who are, like other men, creatures of circumstances, in which their lot has been cast. . . ."

On the other hand, and despite this exaggeration in her portrait, Mrs. Trollope's characters fit her purposes in *Michael Armstrong,* for they enable her not only to expose factory working conditions but to comment on them. The reader recognizes, for example, that whatever Sir Matthew approves of, Mrs. Trollope opposes. So it is with her attack on the ineffectiveness of factory legislation, an attack the periodicals began as early as 1833. Sir Matthew boasts that "old Sir Robert Peel's bill was to all intents and purposes a dead letter within two years after it was passed," a statement which would merely show the law's ineffectiveness and the need for stronger legislation. However, Dowling adds that it was an "absurd bill for the protection of infant paupers," and that "it was the easiest thing in the world to keep the creatures so ignorant about the bill, after the first talk was over, that they might have been made to believe any thing and submit to any thing. . . . They must either do what the masters would have them, or STARVE." Such an attitude provides clear delineation of his character while simultaneously reinforcing Mrs. Trollope's general concern for factory children.

In creating such a character as Sir Matthew Dowling, Mrs. Trollope was appealing to a known Victorian taste for melodrama. The melodramatic element in *Michael Armstrong* is in fact one major reason that the novel has sunk into oblivion. For Sir Matthew's evilness is devoid of any redeeming qualities; he engenders in the reader no sympathetic understanding and no desire to understand. Similarly, Michael's purity and innocence are cloying in their own way: born good, raised good, he survives all the machinations of Sir Matthew and remains the good-natured, kind, and innocent youth who finally—melodramatically, of course—achieves personal happiness. But Michael's character also enabled Mrs. Trollope to convey social criticism because he had the Victorian audience's complete sympathy, evoked partly by his good nature and partly by the evil that Sir Matthew does to him. Thus the Victorian reader was agitated by the factory conditions in which such good young boys had to work, and by the poverty in which they were forced to live. When Michael is temporarily rescued from Sir Matthew's clutches, he tells his rescuer, "I should very much like never to go to work at the factory any more." He thus expresses the desire held by every factory child in the book, and helps enforce the author's social message.

Mrs. Trollope thus achieves some artistic success with her characterizations. She is less fortunate in the narrative techniques she employs to convey social information to her readers. Too often she intrudes into the story in her own voice in order to comment directly on events and on the living and working conditions of the young factory workers. Her intrusions are occasionally so long that her readers can lose sight of the major plot action. At times, too, her comments are not immediately relevant to their context. Of the several major examples of such intrusions, one can serve to indicate the magnitude of her artistic difficulty. Praising her young hero's moral character late in the novel, Mrs. Trollope addresses the reader at length about the deleterious effects of factory work. She concludes her two-page digression by emphasizing the hopelessness of such workers' lives: "The factory operative alone, of all to whom God has given the power of thought, is denied the delicious privilege of hope. It is this which degrades their nature." But such a comment is irrelevant to her hero, she immediately admits, and thus confesses to a major narrative digression for her social purposes alone.

Occasionally, though too rarely to compensate for her more lengthy and less relevant ones, her intrusions are more organic. Perhaps her finest use of the technique is her early description of the inside of Dowling's mill: "All this [noise and impure air] is terrible. But what the eye brings home to the heart of those, who look around upon the horrid earthly hell, is enough to make it all forgotten; for who can think of villanous (*sic*) smells, or heed the suffering of the ear-racking sounds, while they look upon hundreds of helpless children, divested of every trace of health, of joyousness, and even of youth?" This picture of suffering children, sufficiently tied to the immediate scene to be relevant to the story, emphasizes her basic social theme and is guaranteed to gain the reader's sympathy.

Mrs. Trollope often conveys necessary information by reporting discussions between characters, but such a narrative technique creates a major artistic problem: the tedium inherent in pages of dialogue asserting the author's viewpoint on a social issue. When Mary Brotherton, a member of the upper class interested in the welfare of factory workers becomes a close friend of Mr. Bell, a local champion of factory workers, Mrs. Trollope fails to integrate their long discussions effectively into the rest of her story. The climax of her attack on the factory system occurs in chapter xix, which is almost entirely devoted to a discussion between the proselytizing Bell and his protege. It is the culmination of earlier discussions between Miss Brotherton and other characters, but far surpasses them in scope of material discussed, in length of passages, and in dullness. Wanting to get this propaganda into the story, Mrs. Trollope has chosen the method of explicit discussion, Mr. Bell answering Miss Brotherton's questions. She has set her story aside, and let the social concern override it.

Nonetheless, in a few other places in *Michael Armstrong,* Mrs. Trollope varies the discussion technique sufficiently to overcome these artistic difficulties and to reinforce her views indirectly. Mary Brotherton, for example, initially seeks answers to her questions about factory working conditions from some poorly informed people who echo arguments proposed by Andrew Ure and other apologists for the manufacturers: that factories provide employment for many people who otherwise would be unable to work. One of her aquaintances tells her that factory work, "such a blessing as it is to the poor," should not be considered unhealthy, for "There's numbers of [medical men] that declare it's quite impossible to tell in any way satisfactory that it can do 'em any harm at all." This idea is taken from the 1832 Sadler Committee Report, which passes no moral judgments about doctors who, when asked if injury would result from a child's standing for twenty-three hours in a hot and dusty room, replied, "I have no fact to direct me to any conclusion." But some of the periodical writers who reviewed this report did disapprove of such answers, and maintained that harsh working conditions obviously would harm children. One was Anthony Ashley Cooper, Lord Ashley, writing for the *Quarterly Review* in 1836. Ashley had unsuccessfully sponsored a Ten Hours Bill in 1833, and in *Michael Armstrong* Mrs. Trollope was supporting his most recent bill before Parliament. She clearly reflects Lord Ashley's point of view in her many scenes of factory children in physical distress. Thus she adds a complexity to the "discussion technique" means of conveying information to the reader: by exposing false points of view, she makes her own more immediately acceptable to her readers.

In particular, she shows by example that current working conditions harm children. Edward Armstrong, Michael's brother, lame when Mary Brotherton removed him from Dowling's mill, grows strong and healthy under her care. This event is part of the plot-action of the story which, tying together characterization and narrative technique, should provide the most telling examples of the author's artistic success or failure in combining social concern with an "interesting story." In *Michael Armstrong,* we have noted, Mrs. Trollope attempts to develop two plot strands: the adventures of young Michael first with Sir Matthew and then at Deep Valley; and the desire of the upper-class Mary Brotherton to learn about factory conditions and, as a result, to help both Michael and his brother Edward. Clearly the two strands are thematically related, but Mrs. Trollope's intense social message finally prevents her from unifying them.

For almost the entire first half of the novel, Mrs. Trollope does effect a good balance between her story of Michael's difficulties with Matthew Dowling and her story of Mary Brotherton's awakening to the realities of the harsh life of the factory worker. Dowling unwillingly takes Michael out of the factory and into his home, where he plots to place the youth in Deep Valley Mill; Mary Brotherton observes Michael's unhappiness with his position and with Sir Matthew, and determines to learn more about the conditions in which factory operatives—from whose labor her own father became wealthy—work and live. The emphasis is clearly on young Michael, the Mary Brotherton plot being subordinate to the title character's.

Nearly halfway through the novel, however, Mrs. Trollope begins to shift her emphasis. Michael is apprenticed to Elgood Sharpton at Deep Valley; after much false information, Mary Brotherton learns the truth about the evils of factory life and, missing Michael, instead takes his brother Edward out of the factory to be nursed back to health. But Miss Brotherton is still concerned about Michael and, for most of the rest of the novel, searches for him.

The shift occurs at this point, for Mary becomes interested in factory reform in general through Mr. Bell. Mrs. Trollope uses their acquaintance for the long question-and-answer session in chapter xix that we have examined. The second half of the novel becomes increasingly episodic as Mrs. Trollope alternates rapidly between Michael's adventures and Mary's learning. Since the sections concerning Mary Brotherton's desire to learn about factory life have little action in the first place, the increased attention paid to her decreases the emphasis on the real "story" of the novel, Michael's, and is for social-issue purposes only. Further weakening the novel's structure in the last quarter of the book, Mrs. Trollope compresses time greatly: Michael escapes from Deep Valley where he has worked for three years (ch. xxv); his brother Edward, under Mary's care, has recovered (ch. xxvi); Michael is rescued from a suicide attempt by a farmer who gives him work until, at age eighteen, Michael visits Ashleigh where he attends a meeting for factory reform and hears Mary Brotherton and Edward (ch. xxvii). Mrs. Trollope then slows the pace from the hectic passage of seven years in three chapters as she winds up the melodrama: by chapter xxx Matthew Dowling is going insane; he dies in the next chapter; and Mrs. Trollope uses her final two chapters to tie loose ends together and to ensure that Michael will live happily ever after. It is an absurdly quick conclusion to the two plot strands which diverge widely in the second half of the book.

Mrs. Trollope seems to have recognized her difficulties, although she is unable to avoid them. In Mary Brotherton's reference to Michael as "a hero of romance," Mrs. Trollope acknowledges the episodic and romantic nature of the second half of the novel. It is her way of admitting that her characters do not develop, do not change: Michael is always the pure and innocent hero, Sir Matthew the evil manufacturer. It is her means of explaining away—if not excusing—her own authorial intrusions and certainly the long question-and-answer discussions between characters. It is her acceptance too of her digressive, episodic plot, especially in the second half of the novel.

Nonetheless, we must recognize her early successful integration of her two plot strands and, just as importantly, the variation of the discussion technique which she introduces in Mary Brotherton's quest for knowledge. By Mary's insistent questioning, and more especially by the inadequate answers she receives early in the novel, we see her in the process of developing ideas about factory work and workers. As she questions the stereotyped generalizations she receives, we become as involved in the process of learning as she is. It is artistically unfortunate, to be sure, that Mrs. Trollope found it necessary to abandon this method of development in favor of the more typical—and more tedious—propagandizing, through Mr. Bell's responses in chapter xix. But it is to her credit that, at least for a time, Frances Trollope saw, recognized, and attempted to resolve the artistic difficulties inherent in the subgenre she chose. (pp. 5-14)

> Roger P. Wallins, "Mrs. Trollope's Artistic Dilemma in 'Michael Armstrong'," in *Ariel: A Review of International English Literature, Vol. 8, No. 1, January, 1977, pp. 5-15.*

Helen Heineman (essay date 1979)

[*Heineman is an American educator and critic who has written extensively on Victorian literature and women's studies, and is among the foremost Trollope scholars. In the following excerpt from her* Mrs. Trollope: The Triumphant Feminine in the Nineteenth Century, *she examines Trollope's portrayal of Martha Barnaby, the audacious widow who figures prominently in three novels.*]

After four novels peopled by lifeless aristocrats [*The Refugee in America, The Abbess: A Romance, Tremordyn Cliff, A Romance of Vienna*], and two serious exposés of "repulsive" subjects [*The Life and Adventures of Jonathan Jefferson Whitlaw; or, Scenes on the Mississippi, The Vicar of Wrexhill*], in December 1838, Mrs. Trollope entered the popular field of the literature of roguery with *The Widow Barnaby.* William Makepeace Thackeray, another writer sensitive to popular tastes, had begun his career with this kind of fiction, even while complaining a year after the appearance of the first widow book that "the public will hear of nothing but rogues . . . and the only way in which poor authors, who must live, can act honestly by the public and themselves, is to paint such thieves as they are."

But in the early Victorian period, coaching, sporting, gambling, cheating, hunting, adventuring, and living by one's wits had been the material of male writers about male characters, who used their sketches to reinforce a masculine sense of unlimited freedom and dominance. Dickens used the form, as did Borrow, Hook, Marryat, Mayhew, and Thackeray. The few women picaras were always minor characters, in most cases low types and gypsies, the best of whom usually repented at the end. Contemporary standards did not permit a woman at the center of a tale of roguery. It would be an undignified spectacle for a female to rove the world in search of her fortunes and fair game. With the widow Barnaby, Mrs. Trollope created the feminine picaresque, a lady ready to pack her trunks of a moment's notice, one who enjoyed herself immensely while exploring and exploiting life's possibilities for a middle-aged woman.

In this, Mrs. Trollope diverged from the stereotyped heroines of the day, these "suffering angels," in Thackeray's telling phrase, "pale, pious, pulmonary, crossed in love, of course," and added a new dimension to the treatment of women in fiction. Far from being wilting or spiritual, the widow Barnaby was, in one reviewer's words, "showy, strong-willed, supple-tongued, audacious, garrulous, affected, tawdry, lynx-eyed, indomitable in her scheming, and colossal in her selfishness—*Was für eine Frau* ['such a woman'] is the widow Barnaby."

Mrs. Trollope's successful portrayal of this new kind of heroine greatly impressed her generation. Even Thackeray once confessed: "I do not care to read ladies' novels, except those of Mesdames Gore and Trollope." Some ten years after the widow's appearance, he brought out his own great version in the wily Becky Sharp. The similarities between the widow Barnaby and Becky are striking. Both are completely passionless; their hearts are really never engaged, even by the men they relentlessly pursue. When they chance to be occasionally discarded, they simply seek fresh conquests unperturbed. Neither has a conscience, and both are dedicated, from the outset, to getting on in the world as they find it. Both tap their admirers for presents, and both learn quickly and well how to lead the gullible to ruin by means of their husbands' card-playing prowess. Neither places much faith in gambling as a permanent living, but they indulge their husbands, even while plotting themselves to secure something far more grandiose and permanent. Creatures of total mendacity, absolute cheats and liars, they are remarkably appealing heroines. The widow, like Becky, leaves a comfortable home in search of greater things. Neither is forced by absolute necessity. They are not low-born prostitutes and criminals like Moll Flanders. Mrs. Trollope's widow is a woman of the middle class with a little money, who is driven by ambition and aspiration to search for more. She could easily have stayed in Silverton and lived a genteel and respectable life. Becky could have stayed with the Crawleys, but both want something more. They refuse to settle for that "lamentable insignificance" which Mrs. Trollope had found so regrettable in American women. And while Thackeray ultimately put the fascinating Becky in her place and punished her, Mrs. Trollope dispatched her widow on to ever greater triumphs, as her creator revelled in the fanciful exploration of aspiration in a woman, middle-aged, coarse, and vulgar though she was.

Mrs. Trollope found the faults, foibles, vulgarities, and vagaries of her widow both amusing and deeply congenial to her writing talents. Her earlier fiction had drawn praise for its satiric portrayals of minor low-life characters, whom reviewers had found more in her line than noble heroes and heroines. Martha Barnaby was gossipy, vain, complacent, pretentious, and vulgar, a social-climber of epic proportions, and a compendium of all the worst middle-class vices. But in addition, Mrs. Trollope clearly gave this favorite character not only a large dose of her own ebullient personality but also some obviously autobiographical touches. The widow was always able to pick herself up after losses, dropping unsuccessful ventures without undue regrets and moving on to the next scheme. A woman whose horizons seemed endlessly expanding, she cheerfully endured a whole host of transplantings and radiated, in spite of her faults, a special brand of *joie de vivre.* In the greatest of her swindles, the widow even decided to pose as an authoress with plans to make money by writing a best-selling travel book on the United States!

Mrs. Trollope enjoyed her heroine so much that she brought her back in two sequels, which allowed ample opportunity to develop situations well suited to her talents. (pp. 157-59)

Mrs. Trollope had originally conceived of Martha Barnaby as the stereotyped husband-hunting widow. Gradually, over the course of three novels (*The Widow Barnaby,* 1838; *The Widow Married: A Sequel to the Widow Barnaby,* 1840; and *The Barnabys in America; or, Adventures of the Widow Wedded,* 1843), she evolved a more fully developed and complex character. In the first book, Martha Compton eagerly attaches herself to the best prospects currently quartering in the vicinity. As the years pass (along with the regiments and her matrimonial prospects) Martha, failing to catch a young husband, settles for the older (if admirable) Mr. Barnaby, the apothecary, who soon conveniently dies, leaving her as sole executor and sole legatee in possession of a tidy £400 a year. The remaining action concerns her humorous attempts to land a rich and fashionable husband. Advancing toward middle age, she rouges her cheeks, affects dark false curls, and concocts elegant draperies to conceal an increasingly ample figure, thus completing the conventional aspects of the stock character.

Elements of Mrs. Trollope's original plot were openly derivative, a tribute to the great success of Dicken's *Pickwick Papers,* itself an important variant of the literature of roguery. While Mrs. Trollope was writing her novel, she discussed *Pickwick,* the broad humor of which did not overwhelm her, even while she was notably impressed by its sales:

> I doubt . . . if I have so much fun in me as heretofore, for I do not laugh at "Boz" half so perseveringly as most others do, and as I will not put this obtusity down to my want of capacity, I must attribute it to my age. You, my dear friend, who are . . . some half score of years or more my junior, can judge of these popular pleasantries more fairly, and I really wish you would tell me, if you go on number after number sharing the ecstasy that causes thirty thousand of the *Pickwick Papers* to be sold monthly.

While the Pickwickian vein is not evident in the first volume (which she had completed by August), the last two, in plot and style, bear evidence of hopes to capitalize on the current mania. Thus, in the second volume, Mrs. Barnaby sets her sights on the fashionable (if aging and fat) Lord Muckleberry. The resulting contretemps clearly owed its conception to the Bardell-Pickwick affair, and in the ensuing lawsuit, complete with letters now dubbed the "Barnaby Papers," Sergeant Buzfuz is cited by name.

If the character and plot had emerged from old recipes, they soon became uniquely her own. In the return of the character as *The Widow Married,* Mrs. Trollope expanded the husband-hunting heroine to suggest that the conventional female stances, the "cult of true womanhood" that she had scorned in *Domestic Manners,* masked vicious realities in the contemporary marriage market. Although Mrs. Barnaby was not above using pretenses of delicacy and helplessness to win a husband ("Alas! . . . there is so much weakness in the heart of a woman. . . .

We are all impulse, all soul, all sentiment"), Mrs. Trollope assures the reader that her heroine made "very sure of the Major's rent-roll before she bestowed herself and her fortune upon him; for notwithstanding her flirting propensities, the tender passion had ever been secondary in her heart to a passion for wealth and finery." Similarly, the tender girl who faints at the thought of meeting a man clearly does so only for effect. By emphasizing the insincerity of the expected polite female behavior, Mrs. Trollope makes the widow's exploitation of it not only endurable but laudable. She at least is honest with herself, if not with others.

With exquisite irony, Mrs. Trollope demolishes the myth that contemporary marriages were built on love. In one of the book's minor episodes, a man discreetly inquires of his future sister-in-law:

> Alas! before I can throw myself at her feet, the odious trammels of the world force from me another inquiry, hardly less necessary, such unhappily is the formation of society, than the first. Before I offer my hand in marriage to your sister . . . it is absolutely necessary that I should ascertain from you whether our united incomes would amount to such a sum as I should deem sufficient for ensuring the happiness of the woman I so fondly adore.

When the sister reveals that she alone has all the money, the gentleman instantly switches gears:

> How can I make known—how, by any language used by man, can I hope to explain the vehement revulsion of feeling which has taken place in my very heart of hearts since first I entered this fatal room.

Without missing a step, he now proposes marriage to "the angelic woman" before him:

> Oh! Louisa! he added, throwing himself on his knees before her, determined, as it seemed, to stake all on this bold *throw,* "Oh! Louisa! it is yourself: Speak to me, adored Louisa! Tell me my fate in one soul-stirring word—will you be my wife?"

This broadly farcical scene could stand as a paradigm of the book. Things are seldom what they seem, especially when the rhetoric is most fulsome and heart-stirring. In a society built upon such hypocrisies, the Barnabys of this world are bound to succeed.

The independent Mrs. Barnaby, never accepting male domination, and "a vast deal too clever to believe a single word of all [her husband] said," must have come as a refreshing breeze to those women who felt cramped by the inhibiting manners and rhetoric of the time. Her lesson was one easily mastered. While paying lip-service to the conventions, women must always safeguard their rights and financial independence. With each of her husbands, Mrs. Barnaby won the battle to keep her money to herself; significantly, the Trollopes had worked out a similar arrangement.

At the end of *The Widow Married,* when her third husband, Major Allen, is caught cheating at cards, Mrs. Barnaby leads the family in flight from England and prosecution. As they depart for a sojourn in the United States, the reader feels as sure that they will land on their feet across the Atlantic as that Mrs. Trollope will bring them back again. And indeed, three years later, the widow returned in all her full-blown glory a third time, in what was to prove the best of the widow books, if not the most successful of all Mrs. Trollope's thirty-four novels: *The Barnabys in America.*

The widow's new appearance represents Mrs. Trollope's most ingenious combination of her American experience and the character of the widow Barnaby. It was right and proper to send her favorite female character on "an expedition . . . to a land which all the world knows I cherish in my memory with peculiar delight." What followed was a farcical vision of what, in Mrs. Trollope's most mischievous dreams, might indeed (and perhaps should) have happened to a traveler in America. The family lands in New Orleans, certain that Mrs. Barnaby's cleverness and the major's skill at cards will bring success in the new world. In the subsequent adventures, Mrs. Barnaby increasingly resembles Mrs. Trollope—well-built, highly colored, a matriarchal type, with a flair for the dramatic, who has had to leave the old world for financial reasons. Mrs. Barnaby's instant acceptance in polite American society surely burlesques Timothy Flint's published explanation for "the circumstances which caused [Mrs. Trollope] so uncourteous a reception at Cincinnati." [In "Travellers in America, etc." in *Knickerbocker, or New York Monthly Magazine* 2, 1833, he] had singled out:

> The habit of the ladies there of estimating people according to their show and dress. Had she come with numerous letters, and been an elegant figure dressed in the most approved fashion, there is no doubt, that she would have made her way in every circle.

Twelve years later, past all bitterness and enjoying her many successes, Mrs. Trollope presented Mrs. Barnaby, gradually unfolding to the delight of the New Orleans ladies eight hampers full of velvets, satins, and lace (all unpaid for). With this elegant wardrobe, Mrs. Barnaby is launched in the best circles and thereafter proceeds swiftly to swindle everyone. Mrs. Trollope's honest and innovative business venture had been a miserable failure; Mrs. Barnaby's frauds are a huge success.

Mrs. Trollope's prejudices are, as always, quite clear. The clash of English and American values is again resolved when an Englishman marries and carries back to London the only decent American girl in the book so that she can share "his heart, his hand, a noble settlement, and the alliance of an ancient English race, whose motto might very honestly have been—*Sans peur, et sans reproche*" ["without fear and without reproach"]. There are the usual number of American types, from the "patriot lady" to the "evangelical saints," from slave-owners and Quakers to New York speculators. Mrs. Barnaby and family swindle them all, and masquerading as an itinerant preacher, the major is even able to fool the deadly serious female members of the United States Needle Steeple Congregation.

All of these adventures gradually emerge as a vicarious revenge, or as Mrs. Barnaby describes one ruse:

> As a jest played off to avenge, as it were, the numberless tricks which we hear of as practised against our countrymen it is more than justifiable; and in that light, my dearest major, it commands my warmest and most patriotic admiration.

At long last the sharpies have been outdone by the English, a feat that Mrs. Trollope herself was unfortunately unable to accomplish in real life. *The Barnabys in America* documents all of Mrs. Trollope's prejudices about America and satirizes all her grudges. She makes fun of everyone—the gullible Americans, the vulgarians of the old world, and even the middle-aged English lady, who several years ago crossed the Atlantic and wrote a book about the Americans.

The central swindle is Mrs. Barnaby's ingenious plan to write a book on America and thus procure access to the best society. In her proposed work, she assures the Americans, she will counteract all the perfidious lies published previously by other English travelers. Ever since the publication of [Captain Basil] Hall's volumes and *Domestic Manners*, Americans had railed against the lies of superficial English tourists. In Mrs. Trollope's satiric novel, a true "patriot lady," beseeches Mrs. Barnaby to write "an out and out good book of travels upon the United States," declaring that

> there has never yet been a single volume written upon the United States, that was not crammed with the most abominable lies from beginning to end, and . . . any body who would come forward to contradict all these wicked and most scandalous falsehoods, would be rewarded in the very noblest manner possible: first, by a great quantity of money; and next, by the admiration and respect of all the people in the country.

This lady expects only one thing from Mrs. Barnaby:

> All I want in return is that you should portrait us out to the world for just what we really are, and that is the finest nation upon the surface of God's whole earth, and as far ahead in civilization of Europe in general, and England in particular, as the summer is before winter in heat.

Musing upon the project, Mrs. Barnaby considers the book she might write about America if she wanted to tell the truth, for the inhabitants were "curious enough, to be sure," and the work would "amuse the folks at home to know, if one did but dare to tell it." But she quickly rejects this notion, since the endeavor is primarily a question of dollars:

> It would be just as easy for me to write all truth as all lies, about this queer place, and all these monstrous odd people but wouldn't I be a fool if I did any such thing?—and is it one bit more trouble I should like to know, writing them all in one sense instead of the other?

Mrs. Barnaby's project is Mrs. Trollope's answer to those who claimed she had told outrageous lies about the Americans in order to make money.

At a big evening party in her honor, Mrs. Barnaby endures the first public test of her talents, as she reads sections from her work, entitled "Justice Done at Last, or The Travels of Mrs. Major Allen Barnaby through the United States of America." One paragraph of exaggerated and meaningless praise is particularly welcomed:

> Nobody properly qualified to write upon this wonderful country could behold a single town, a single street, a single house, a single individual of it, for just one single half-hour, without feeling all over to

his very heart convinced, that not all the countries of the old world put together are worthy to compare, in any one respect, from the greatest to the very least, with the free-born, the free-bred, the immortal, the ten hundred thousand times more glorious country, generally called that of the "Stars and the Stripes!" The country of the Stars and the Stripes is, in fact, and beyond all reach of contradiction, the finest country in the whole world, and the simple truth is, that nobody who really knows any thing about it, can ever think of calling it any thing else. It is just the biggest and the best, and that is saying everything in two words.

To cries of "admirable, admirable," Mrs. Barnaby bows gracefully, smelling of lavender water, coyly pushes back her curls, and carefully smoothes down the pages while the credulous Americans nod with pleasure. The novel's pattern is a mirror image of **Domestic Manners,** refracted into pure parody. Here, says Mrs. Trollope, is what the Americans wanted in an author; here, too, is what they deserved. Suddenly, while the audience is still ruminating on the fulsome praise of the talk, Mrs. Barnaby intrudes five "harmless" questions, which for a moment dispel the giddy and superficial mood and give a glimpse of the critical author of **Domestic Manners** and **Jonathan Jefferson Whitlaw.** She would appreciate it, she tells her listeners, if they would answer these queries:

> 1. In what manner does the republican form of government appear to affect the social habits of the people?
>
> 2. How far does the absence of a national form of worship produce the results anticipated from it?
>
> 3. At what degree of elevation may the education of the ladies of the union be considered to stand, when compared to that received by the females of other countries?
>
> 4. In what manner was slavery originally instituted?
>
> 5. And what are its real effects, both on the black and on the white population?

The questions, however, do not disturb the Americans, and Mrs. Barnaby continues her progress. Pandering to southern prejudices, she claims to include praise of slavery as the highest institution known to man. All goes well until the major wins too heavily at cards and the family must move to Philadelphia, where Mrs. Barnaby again poses as a famous authoress, traveling incognito. This time, for her audience of abolitionist Quakers, she proposes a book that will help wipe out the menace of slavery from the face of the earth. The task of appearing demure and principled requires a complete and troublesome metamorphosis in dress only:

> From her morning gown she abstracted every bow, together with a deep trimming of very broad imitation black lace from the cape of it, which left this addition to her grave-coloured silk dress of such very moderate dimensions as entirely to change its general effect, and to give to her appearance a snug sort of succinct tidiness, such as it had probably never exhibited before.
>
> The cap she selected for the occasion was one which owed almost all its Barnabian grace to a very magnificent wreath of crimson roses, which ran

twiningly and caressingly round the front of it, and these being removed by the simple operation of withdrawing a few pins, left as decent a cap as any one could wish to see.

> Of her half-dozen luxuriously-curling "fronts," she chose the least copious and the least curling, and having bedewed it with water from a sponge, induced its flowing meshes to repose themselves upon her forehead with a trim tranquility that might have befitted a Magdalen.

With a talent for impersonation rivaled only by her creator, Mrs. Barnaby manages to leave Philadelphia five hundred dollars richer. The Quakers, who have naively hoped to use the Englishwoman for their own purposes, are both poorer and wiser.

After successfully duping the Quakers, the family again departs; this pattern is repeated a third and fourth time, after which, richer by some ten thousand dollars, they return to England, well satisfied with themselves and with America. As the book rolls to its hilarious conclusion, the reader realizes that Mrs. Barnaby is actually Mrs. Trollope in disguise. This transformation had already begun in **The Widow Married,** when Mrs. Trollope had her heroine reflect upon her progress from adversity to pleasure and profit in a triumphant monologue:

> I do sometimes think . . . that great abilities, thorough real cleverness I mean, is a better fortune for a girl . . . than almost any money in the world. . . . I don't mind telling you that my father and mother . . . had no more right to expect that I should ever be in such a place as this, ordering court-dresses for myself and my daughter, than you have to be Queen of England. Oh! dear!—how well I remember going shopping in our little town, where my father was the rector. . . . I have managed from that time to this to get on monstrous well.

In the last book, Mrs. Barnaby several times soliloquizes on this important theme, marveling over her great success:

> I do wonder sometimes where I got all my cleverness from. There isn't many, though I say it, that shouldn't—but that's only when nobody hears me—there isn't many that could go on as I have done, from the very first almost, that I remember any thing, always getting on, and on, and on. There's a pretty tolerable difference, thank Heaven! between what I am now with judges and members, and I don't know who all, smirking and speechifying to me, and what I was when my name was Martha Compton, without two decent gowns perhaps, to my back, and not knowing where on earth to get another when they were gone!

Mrs. Barnaby and Mrs. Trollope certainly were women who succeeded on their own efforts. Moreover, both shared a keen interest in life. As Mrs. Trollope noted fondly of her heroine:

> To do her justice, [she] seldom felt any thing to be tedious; she could always find, or make opportunities for displaying both her mind and body to advantage; and who that does this can ever find any portion of existence fatiguing?

Besieged by her admirers, she heartily enjoys her success: "I wonder what would happen if I were to take into my head to make myself a queen? I wonder whether anybody, or anything, would be found able to stop me?" Falling into a deep sleep, "she became . . . the subject of her own high imaginings." In a brief dream dialogue with her husband, Martha Barnaby has a vision of her own womanly greatness:

> It is not *you* who have written all these books; and if, as you all justly enough say, a title must and will be given, as in the case of Sir Walter and Sir Edward, it cannot be given to *you.* No, Donny, no. It must and will be given to ME. Yes, yes; hush, hush, hush. I know it, I know it. I know perfectly well, Major Allen, without your telling me, that no ladies ever are made baronets. I know I can't be Sir Martha, foolish man, quite as well as you do, and I know a little better, perhaps that *you* will never be Sir anything. . . . Why should I not be called Lady Martha?

Since she cannot be Sir Martha, her husband must become Mr. Barnaby! In the end, the major, in a burst of honest admiration, changes his name to Barnaby "as a still farther compliment" to the cleverness of "his ever-admired wife." Clearly conceding her preeminence, the major salutes her "with all the fervour of young affection. . . . I can never hope to equal you in anything." In one way or another, the superiority of women had been Mrs. Trollope's theme since *Domestic Manners.* Surely, Martha Barnaby is her apotheosis of the new woman. (pp. 159-67)

> *Helen Heineman, in her* Mrs. Trollope: The Triumphant Feminine in the Nineteenth Century, *Ohio University Press, 1979, 316 p.*

Janet Giltrow   (essay date 1981)

[*Giltrow is a Canadian educator and critic. In the following excerpt from an essay contrasting* Domestic Manners of the Americans *with Susanna Moodie's* Roughing It in the Bush *(1852) and* Life in the Clearings *(1852), she theorizes that Trollope's dissatisfaction with her social and economic situation affected the tone and content of her book.*]

Travel narrative comes about as a result of the writer's separation from his cultural habitat and his term abroad in a place where he is an alien and a stranger. On his return home, the narrator addresses the community of which he is a member on the subject of places and societies foreign to him and his audience, comparing what he found abroad with what he had known at home. His narration is the verbal signal of his reincorporation into his native mileu; it repairs the breach which occurs when one group member is estranged from his community, and the publication of details of the writer's whereabouts during his absence compensates for the alienation he has experienced.

Collections of letters-home are the mode of travel commentary which most clearly demonstrate the social function of the genre. Letters reserve the absentee's place at home, simulating the face-to-face connections that have been temporarily ruptured. As they reconstruct the writer's alien experience, they reintroduce him into the familiar world he left behind. Many travel books are cast in the form of a series of letters to actual or fictive recipients. Other travel books are logs or journals composed with minute regularity for the benefit of home readers. In travel narrative where these structures are not explicit—where the chapter or the sketch rather than the letter or the day is the organizational unit of prose—exposition nevertheless performs the same rhetorical purpose of accounting for the writer's absence.

While the traveler is abroad, his accustomed social relationships are interrupted. To replenish this void, he may resort to letter-writing, to journalizing, or, ambitiously, to narration. Written language then stands in for every other form of social relatedness. Cut off from this supportive network of connections he is used to at home, the traveler is on his own—except for this connecting verbal strand. Often, the foreign community will not recognize his social status: his cultural assets are discounted, his idiom misunderstood, his identity mistaken. To counteract feelings of anonymity and alienation, the travel narrator can reassure himself of his continued membership in the community he left behind by becoming very pronounced indeed in his expression of native cultural attitudes and habits. Away from home, we perhaps most emphatically declare our national provenance and identity.

The travel narrator is alone, detached from the scenes he describes and unassimilated by the foreign community. At their most extreme, the conditions of travel lead to social disorientation, anomie, feelings of being *dépaysé* ["out of one's element"]. But the traveler's isolation has a counterpoise in the affinity he feels with the culture he addresses—an affinity amounting sometimes to homesickness. Even at the most remote quarters of the earth, home exerts an irresistible attraction and travel narrative advances toward a denouement of homecoming. Having embarked, some travelers and travel writers never get home again. Nevertheless, the idea of getting home continues to structure and inspire narrative. In its circularity—its obedience to the round-trip-travel narrative differs from literature posed on a quest theme, for its goal is its point of departure. When the one-way journey of permanent emigration is the actual experience of the writer, but round-trip travel remains his ideal of a due course, his consequent art is often poignant with disappointment and unresolvable alienation.

Frances Trollope's *Domestic Manners of the Americans* is clearly a travel book: it begins with the writer's embarkation from England; it includes large, discursive, informational units comparing life in the New World to life in the Old; it concludes with the writer's departure from the foreign scene. Susanna Moodie's *Roughing It in the Bush* also begins with her departure from home; it includes substantial information on Canadian life, organized for the benefit of European readers. In contrast to Trollope, however, Moodie never made the return trip: her book ends with the family's move from the bush to Belleville, which was a more congenial site but still no asylum on this cheerless continent. (pp. 131-33)

[*Domestic Manners of the Americans*] was published in London in 1832, the year of the Moodies' departure. Moodie may have known the book, for it had an extremely successful publication, but that possibility has less to do with the similarities between *Domestic Manners* and *Roughing It* than coincidences in the authors' social and economic situations. The Moodies came to Canada to avoid the ignominy of a moderate but, to them, intolerable poverty; they expected to enhance magically their meager assets.

When Trollope sailed in 1827 she left behind a horrendous tangle of debts and financial disappointments which she hoped to sort out in short order by investing a small capital on the American frontier. Both families were nearly obliterated financially by the North American economic structure.

Both Moodie and Trollope were, in a sense, exceptionally bad travelers: every detail of their existence reminded them that they were abroad and not at home. But if their disgruntlement made them bad travelers, it made them very good travel writers, giving them a profound sense of relocation, of having been radically transported and set down elsewhere. On a superficial level, the occasion of **Domestic Manners** can be compared to that of *Roughing It in the Bush* and *Life in the Clearings*. Both writers saw something of the wilderness: Trollope spent a few weeks on the Tennessee frontier; Moodie lived six years in the Canadian bush. Both women knew town life, too: Trollope passed two years in Cincinnati, and by the early 1850s, when *Roughing It* and *Life in the Clearings* were published, Moodie had been more than ten years at Belleville. The pleasure tour described in *Life in the Clearings* corresponds to the more extensive tourism which concluded Trollope's sojourn in the United States. But the most profitable basis for comparing **Domestic Manners** to *Roughing It* and its sequel lies in the fact of each writer's cultural alienation from the site of her economic project.

For brilliant recklessness, the Trollopes' scheme for financial recovery far surpasses the Moodies' drab attempts at homesteading. Donald Smalley's introduction to the 1949 edition of **Domestic Manners** provides a background to which Trollope herself never directly refers: the enterprise which occupied her during her two years at Cincinnati was the construction of an enormous, arabesque emporium known as "The Bazaar," to house all the social and cultural business Trollope believed the city lacked and desired. Imported "fancy goods" were to be displayed for sale; an "Exchange" would be a setting for coffee-house conviviality; a ballroom, theater and gallery would host important events. The edifice was architecturally eclectic, supplying at once *all* the design deficiencies of a frontier town. Strangest of all, the building actually was constructed, the "fancy goods" arrived, and a few evenings of dramatic recitations did occur. Unfortunately, the people of Cincinnati did not appreciate the opportunity offered them, and ignored this facsimile of European culture—as far as this was possible, given the dimensions and singularity of the thing. Irony lies in the fact that Trollope, creator of this prominent public fantasy, isolates bad taste and "want of refinement" as distinguishing characteristics of Americans.

Frances Trollope left England in 1827; three years and nine months later she was back. Just less than half of **Domestic Manners** deals with her arrival in America and her residence in Cincinnati. The remainder of the book follows her to Baltimore, Washington, Philadelphia, New York, Niagara and through the terrains which intervene. During this second phase she industriously collected material for the travel book that represented her only hope of recouping some of the devastating losses incurred by the unfortunate voyage. The greatest part of her memoirs refers to the social landscape, but she looked at nature, too.

The Trollope Bazaar.

For both Trollope and Moodie, nature and wilderness are separate quantities. Although neither can establish any firm esthetic connection with wilderness and neither comes near [Catharine Parr] Traill's ability to discover structure in organic forms, both women were schooled in nature description. They responded fluently and easily to sites like Niagara, for Niagara was a familiar text, existing within a received verbal tradition. It demanded only marginal innovation to renew it, and nothing like the profound revisions of esthetic and rhetorical convention required by the infinite vacuity of unpeopled forests and plains.

But Trollope was not absolutely silent about wilderness. Faced with elemental nature at the mouth of the Mississippi, she declares the scene uninteresting: "Only one object rears itself above the eddying waters; this is the mast of a vessel long since wrecked in attempting to cross the bar, and it still stands, a dismal witness of the destruction that has been, and boding prophet of that which is to come." This introduction to the continent has at least its forlorn relic with which to construe a meaning; when Trollope truly penetrates to the wilderness, an undelineated blankness and unutterable meaninglessness confront her. This is certainly all she finds at Nashoba, an experimental settlement in Tennessee founded on libertarian principles and intended for the education of emancipated slaves. Even the highly civilized *raison d'être* of Nashoba cannot make up for the negative environment in which it exists, and for its lack of familiar, humane objects: "Desolation was the only feeling—the only word that presented itself . . . " when Trollope arrived. Unnerved by this indescribable emptiness, she decamps after ten days and flees Nashoba.

She is better pleased by the views along the Ohio, as she makes her way to Cincinnati, but even those are regrettably limited in esthetic reference: "were there occasionally a ruined abbey, or feudal castle, to mix the romance of real life with that of nature, the Ohio would be perfect." Trollope's sentiments are typical: many other travelers in America, Washington Irving and Henry James among them, lament the esthetic incompleteness of even the most exquisite scenery when it is unassimilated by an historical tradition.

As early as Frances Brooke's *History of Emily Montague* (1769) European travelers were critical of the North American's lack of interest in celebrated scenery. At Niagara Trollope describes the American tourist as ignorantly nonchalant "before the god of nature," as indifferent and irreverent as Moodie's fellow guest. At Cincinnati the Trollopes were unique among the populace for the pleasure they took in nature: "A row upon the Ohio was another of our favourite amusements; but in this I believe, we were also very singular, for often, when enjoying it, we were shouted at, by the young free-borns on the banks, as if we had been so many monsters." However, in spite of regular picnics and excursions, Trollope cannot love her location: "On first arriving, I thought the many tree-covered hills around very beautiful, but long before my departure, I felt so weary of the confined view that Salisbury Plain would have been an agreeable variety."

Cincinnati may be an interesting place to visit, but it is no place to live, Trollope observes: "The more unlike a country through which we travel is to all we have left, the more we are likely to be amused; everything in Cincinnati had this newness, and I should have thought it a place delightful to visit, but to tarry there was not to feel at home." Trollope is arrested and impatient in an inhospitable environment. And however distasteful the scenery becomes, it is a minor problem compared with the difficulties of living in a society hostile to her own values and ambitions. Throughout her residence at Cincinnati Trollope remains in a state of nervous irritation over every feature of frontier society. Her hypersensitivity distinguishes her from the community around her, isolating her as a person habituated to the refinements of civilization. Where every delicate pleasure and subtle amenity are missing, the individual accustomed to them is at a loss: "where the whole machine of the human frame is in full activity, where every sense brings home to consciousness its touch of pleasure or pain, then every object that meets the sense is important as a vehicle of happiness or misery. But let no frame so tempered visit the United States, or if they do, let it be with no longer pausing than will store the memory with images, which, by the force of the contrast, shall sweeten the future."

Trollope pauses much longer than the brief interval she recommends. Rather than enjoy the traveler's pleasure in notable differences and the opportunity for discursive comparison-making, she has to live through the profundity of the abysmal contrast.

Like Susanna Moodie, Frances Trollope is intensely concerned with social insubordination and class order in a society which does not acknowledge her claims to station and status. Like Moodie, she finds the behavior of her servants a sign of the corruption of traditional social values. Until she finds a deferential English servant-girl, she is abused and exploited by "free-born" servants who come and go as they please and boldly declare their own terms.

Moodie puts up with being called "woman"; Trollope endures worse, for she is referred to as "old woman." She is forced into social relations with those she regards as her inferiors, and even invited to the home of a greengrocer. These humiliations do not go unaccounted. In her writing, to redress the offense, Trollope adopts a tone of amused disdain remarkably like Moodie's. She goes to the grocer's house, but only to observe and "report" and flesh out the irony of her social predicament. Like Moodie at Belleville, she is an aloof spectator, a social sightseer. Trollope describes her "amusement": "Had I not become heartily tired of my prolonged residence in a place I cordially disliked, and which moreover I began to fear would not be attended with the favourable results we had anticipated, I should have found an almost inexhaustible source of amusement in the notions and opinions of the people I conversed with; and as it was, I often did enjoy this in a considerable degree." Again, comedy and social satire serve the hapless alien stationed in a foreign habitat.

This foreign place is not merely incompatible with the social assumptions of the European visitor; it openly announces its hatred and contempt for her: "We received, as I have mentioned, much personal kindness; but this by no means interferred with the national feeling of, I believe, unconquerable dislike, which evidently lives at the bottom of every truly American heart against the English. This shows itself in a thousand little ways, even in the midst of the most kind and friendly intercourse, but often in a manner more comic than offensive." Trollope says she was neither disappointed nor injured by this popular loathing for her kind. Once she finds that she cannot be loved in America, that she will be only misunderstood and reviled, she becomes stoical, feeling the same "amusement" Moodie felt at insults to her art and dignity:

> One lady asked me very gravely, if we had left home in order to get rid of the vermin with which the English of all ranks were afflicted? "I have heard from unquestionable authority," she added, "that it is quite impossible to walk through the streets of London without having the head filled." I laughed a little, but spoke not a word.

Like Moodie, who spoke out when she found an audience but kept quiet at Cobourg, Trollope dispenses her opinions generously at home but hoards them here, for she finds it impossible to communicate with citizens of the Republic: "I have conversed in London and in Paris with foreigners of many nations, and often through the misty medium of an idiom imperfectly understood, but I remember no instance in which I found the same difficulty in conveying my sentiments, my impressions, and my opinions to those around me, as I did in America." One need hardly wonder at the length and fluency of her memoirs when one learns that she was virtually incommunicado for almost four years—all those sensations and opinions stopped-up, pressing to flood forth and inundate a receptive audience.

Upon one occasion, however, Trollope does find a sympathetic interlocutor. At Philadelphia, in a grassy square, she spies an interesting-looking woman playing with a child: "There was something in her manner of looking at me, and exchanging a smile when her young charge performed some extraordinary feat of activity on the grass, that persuaded me she was not an American. I do not remember who spoke first, but we were presently in a full flow of conversation." This young woman is a homesick European, a German who is disdainful of Americans. " 'They do not love music,' " she complains. " 'Oh no! and they never amuse themselves—no; and their hearts are not warm, at least they seem not so to a stranger. . . . But I will not stay long, I think, for I should not live'." Trollope admires the German, with her languishing spirit and her negative analysis of American manners.

Trollope despises the artificiality of those manners. When some ceremony or social procedure comes to her attention, she finds it silly or pretentious. But when the matrix of social conventions is missing, she deplores its absence, for she finds the idea of social and economic independence "unnatural." Mournfully, she describes the existence of a backwoods family, and then offers her interpretation of the meaning of such a life: "These people were indeed independent . . . but yet it seemed to me that there was something awful and almost unnatural in their loneliness. No village bell ever summoned them to prayer, where they might meet the friendly greeting of their fellow-men. When they die, no spot sacred by ancient reverence will receive their bones. . . ." Trollope turns to the idea of lonely death as the best way of registering her emotional response.

After four years of "attentive observation" Trollope can unconditionally assert that in America "the moral sense is on every point blunter than with us." A society so lacking in moral equipment is a society incapable of comprehending Trollope's values and certainly incapable of endorsing her art. The popular uproar in America which followed news of the London publication of **Domestic Manners** could only have confirmed her opinions on the impossibility of communication between the European traveler and Americans.

Had Trollope's North American journey not included a two-year residence in the West, she might have kept an objective interest in novelty—for, as she says, the more novel the scene the more valuable it is to the traveler. But as it was, comparisons and contrasts were of no mere academic, instructive interest; they were personal crises to be endured. For every social and cultural asset—class, capital, sensibility—to be discounted and for the traveler to be left bankrupt and socially demoralized required some quick action to recuperate the loss. Like Moodie, Trollope saw that the best way to recover a personal investment was to make a literary inquiry into the very foreignness of the manners so alien to her own interests. Trollope, rather than waste her experiences in regret and dismay, husbanded them to retail in a better market. One of her few happy social experiences in America was her half-hour of intense conversation with the homesick German. **Domestic Manners** expands the measure of that moment, telling the whole story and getting home again.

Susanna Moodie did not get home again. Her only way of retraversing her route lay in dispatching an appeal to her distant audience. She asks for commiseration. Frances Trollope, on the other hand, was sure that her course would restore her eventually to her home; her appeal to her audience satisfies her need to redress the offenses she suffered at the hands of a society which demeaned her. She expresses her outrage through denunciation.

Frances Trollope is only an interesting footnote to American literary history. Samuel Clemens refers to her appreciatively in *Life on the Mississippi* [see Further Reading], but he is less an inspiration to him than a source of historical background for his documentation of his own journey. She belongs in the British tradition, voicing esthetic, political and social attitudes which were familiar and attractive to her English audience. (pp. 137-42)

With their passage across the Atlantic, Moodie and Trollope felt themselves vanishing anonymously into a social and cultural void. Travel was at best disorienting; at worst, it was an existential threat. For both women, the idea of death expressed the loss they felt and the danger they faced. In Trollope's book, it is the backwoods settler who is destined for a remote grave, and the homesick German who will die for lack of sympathy; she herself is finally secure in the round-trip itinerary which will restore her to England. (p. 143)

> Janet Giltrow, " 'Painful Experience in a Distant Land': Mrs. Moodie in Canada and Mrs. Trollope in America," in Mosaic: A Journal for the Interdisciplinary Study of Literature, Vol. XIV, No. 2, Spring, 1981, pp. 131-44.

Helen Heineman (essay date 1984)

[*In the following excerpt from her biographical and critical study of Trollope, Heineman examines the development of strong, unconventional female characters in Trollope's fiction between 1841 and 1856.*]

The success of her Widow Barnaby books inspired Trollope to create more females with initiative. Also, in 1843, she had completed the last of her fiction of social reform, a genre which increased her own sense of influence and in which she had used women as the primary agents of enlightenment. That same year she left England to take up residence in Italy. This physical distancing enabled her to explore the position of women from a new vantage point. Over the next ten years she functioned as a skillful professional writer. Seldom a year passed without one or two new romances from her pen. The books were all written with enthusiasm and gusto; her success as a writer was due to her ability to describe reality in a light, satiric fashion. In general, however, the books did not differ from the rather conventional love stories then on the market. She too told of young heroines seeking and accomplishing marriage. New, however, was her introduction of a variety of subplots populated by intelligent and self-willed girls, who simply did not fit into the accepted mold. While the widow Barnaby had conquered through her enterprise and loquacity, these characters added sexuality to obtain power over men. In these peripheral creations Trollope continued to develop a more congenial female character, whom she cast in a supporting, but crucial role, as villainess, siren, unhappy wife, and, most important of all, fortune hunter.

The first two books in which such characters appear are works overlapping from the previous period, and in general their subject matter is more literary than feminist.

Taken together, *Charles Chesterfield; or, The Adventures of a Youth of Genius* and *The Blue Belles of England* satirized the London literary scene. In a most unusual circumstance, both appeared simultaneously in monthly parts, between July 1840 and December 1841, in two different magazines, the *New Monthly* and the *Metropolitan Magazine.* Thus Trollope continued to exploit the monthly serialization and to attack the literary conventions of her day; all the prevailing fads and especially the hypocrisy of the so-called "Moderns" became the subject of her ridicule.

The plot of *Charles Chesterfield* follows the fortunes of a young son of a substantial farmer, who unexpectedly inherits a legacy from a considerate godmother and departs for London hoping to become a brilliant literary success. "It was the world, it was London, for which he panted. Fame, renown, applause . . . such as he had heard tell of . . . as having been achieved by an individual called Sir Walter Scott, and by another named Lord Byron." In town, he is introduced by a swindling patron to a literary coterie, including the famous critic Marchmont, who attaches himself to the naive Chesterfield, circulating him among celebrities and instructing him on the techniques of modern literature. Soon Charles becomes somewhat entangled with a Mrs. Sherbourne, a literary lady. In the third volume, disenchanted with these parasites, Charles begins to see his new friends for what they are, as Mrs. Sherbourne threatens to sue him for breach of promise, and his poetic work is rejected by an honest publisher. Finally Charles returns to the country, marries his old sweetheart, and becomes an honest clergyman, thus rejecting the lure of London's "heartless puppetshow" and fame.

In this book Trollope focuses primarily on the critic Marchmont, whose characterization enables her to attack the inflated ideas of literary genius then in fashion. Marchmont affects long hair and an "uncovered throat" à la Byron and Shelley and drinks freely for inspiration, for, as he says, "even the mighty steam engine itself wants oil." Always presumably too distracted to hear what is being said to him, he is admired by some who gush: "Does it not remind you of the stories we have heard of Sir Isaac Newton? Beyond all question his power of withdrawing the soul from outward objects is one of the most precious privileges which nature accords to genius." Introducing Chesterfield to Marchmont, the artistic Mrs. Gibson calls out: "Descend! Come down! 'Tis time."

Trollope also uses the character of Marchmont to expose the nonsense of the modern notion of "originality." Marchmont finds the only obstacle to Charles's successes is his extensive formal education. As he explains of his own background: "My grammar is mankind, my friend; my dictionary is in the clouds. The winds are my syntax, and rushing cataracts my prosody!" Tradition is unimportant. "This pitiable reverence for antiquity is now happily passing from the earth for ever." But the quality of Marchmont's talent becomes clear in the very first stanza of his poem "On a star seen at midnight."

> Bright candle in an everlasting stick!
> How soothingly thy trembling rays descend
> Upon a heart from o'erwrought feeling sick,
> Whose leaping pulses towards madness tend!

Trollope's view of artistic inspiration had little to do with either "leaping pulses" or madness. Her position was later adopted by her novel-writing son Anthony: *"Labor omnia vincit improbus"* ["never-ending work conquers all"]. She had but scorn for Marchmont's inflated ideas of artistic genius.

Marchmont's first assignment for Charles is to review a new book, *The Philosophy of Suicide.* When the protégé protests that the topic is itself a contradiction in terms, Marchmont uses the occasion to enunciate his philosophy of literary criticism. "Don't ever take the same side of a question as all the old fogies." Emphasize incongruity—concentrate on form ("the sparkling style"), not content. "You need not trouble yourself to say clever things." Instead, "make people stare a little . . . by saying something startling and wild." Along the way, "avoid all words and phrases which tend to give a precise and clearly-defined idea to the mind." Marchmont, it turns out, is also the influential editor and reviewer of a literary magazine, the *Regenerator,* a substantial portion of which "is devoted to the passing sentence on the literary productions of the day." Influenced mainly by the name, reputation, or political principles of the authors and not the quality of their books, Marchmont takes pleasure in anonymously demolishing literary products with his "cut-and-thrust maneuvering from behind a golden screen."

Worse, he bluntly confesses to Chesterfield that most reviewers do not actually read the books they describe, and giving Charles his list of notes for his own forthcoming articles, he demonstrates how easy critical comment can be. One simply takes the title, uses one's prejudices, and starts:

> 1. *Thoughts on a Future State of Existence.*
> Execrable. Bigotry. Intolerance. 19th Century. Stumbling-block in the progress of thought. To be done savagely, but jocosely.
>
> 2. *The Tyranny of Passions: or Absolution by Right Divine.*
> Admirable, Courage of truth. Strength of Argument. Irresistible reasoning. First-rate talent. Commanding intellect. To be done in a high transcendental tone of enthusiasm.

Charles wonders if "this omnipotent business of reviewing" can really be "all humbug" and chance. No, says Marchmont, all depends on knowing the author or his principles. Conservatives are always attacked, while avant-garde writers, like the author of *The Convict Footman,* are praised to the skies, with the kind of literary "hype" still familiar one hundred and forty years later. "We hail these volumes as the advent of a new era in the history of man." Having so long been flayed by the reviewers, Trollope enjoyed counterattacking with her completely odious creation, Marchmont.

More significant in terms of the development of her future themes was the appearance of more strong women characters, predictably cast in subsidiary plots. In her lineup she included two artistic ladies, the first the fraudulent Mrs. Gibson, "in every sense of the phrase, a woman *à prétention.*" Mrs. Gibson is hostess to all the bright lights of the day and receives "nearly the whole host of living authors (she has 47 upon her list)." Her second distinction is her massive work illustrating *Paradise Lost.* In her sacred back parlour she collects and colors etchings, pasting them beneath the relevant sections of Milton's great epic. To depict the rebellion of the angels, for example, Mrs. Gibson uses a plate showing the breaking up of the school at Dotheboy's Hall from *Nicholas Nickleby,* an idea with which "everybody is delighted." At the novel's end this literary hack work is "superbly bound in 43 volumes" and becomes one of Mrs. Gibson's "lions."

To contrast with this female dilettante Trollope created Mrs. Sherbourne, another fanciful version of herself, a woman who lived entirely from the proceeds of her writing of popular works of fiction. "No circulating library from the Orkneys to the Land's End, dared to confess that they had not got Mrs. Sherbourne's last work; and *The Condemned One—The Entranced One—The Corrupted One—The Infernal One—The Empyrean One*—and *The Disgusting One,* and all in succession, conveyed her intensity into every village of the empire, and brought in return wherewithal to 'live and love, to dress and dream' (which in one of *Occasional Poems* she had declared ought to be the whole of woman's existence), very much to her satisfaction." But Trollope had a more serious purpose for her character than just self-portraiture. She wanted to comment on the problems of literary women in a field managed predominantly by men. Aware of a limited talent and large needs, Mrs. Sherbourne, like so many other female writers, was forced to use personal charms to advance her career.

> Her professional existence depended upon her welcoming without reserve all those who could assist her in her pursuits, either by criticism or patronage. . . . Her existence glided on through a series of small literary labours, cheered by a series, equally unbroken, of small literary flirtations, each helping forward the other by a reciprocity of influence, by no means unskillfully managed.

In *Charles Chesterfield* her main efforts at flirting and flattery are expended on Marchmont. As Trollope notes: "Whenever she wished to produce an effect . . . she understood perfectly well how to make common cause between her books and her beauty, without ever permitting the one to outshine the other." Moreover, all she does must be done without "the slightest approach to indiscretion." Yet clearly, her beauty and her literary talent were both essential to her success:

> Mrs. Sherbourne would as soon have thought of putting her impassioned language, her original views on all subjects, her boasted knowledge of Italian, or any other of her manifold accomplishments upon the shelf, as her beauty. Her prose and poetry, her hands and feet, her wit and her white shoulders, her philosophy and her long ringlets, her large eyes and her little Italian vocabulary, were one and all part and parcel of herself, and one and all part and parcel of "that by which she lived."

Mrs. Sherbourne uses Marchmont to get good reviews for her new play, *The Matchless Minstrel.* Never forgetting her concentration on "the *wherewithal* by which all that she most loved and liked was to be obtained," she puts out of her mind Marchmont's distasteful ugliness and disagreeable personality, remembering only that he is "one of the omnipotent WE, and member of the secret tribunal, in whose frown there was death, and whose smile brought food, lodging, hackney-coaches, and satin gowns." So she

smiled at him and put on the necessary pretense of delicate weakness. Later, she contracts to sell him her memoirs, but again not without the prerequisite pretenses:

> Oh Mr. Marchmont! You little guess what it is for one so utterly unfit to breast the storms as I am, to offer my second soul, as I may call it, for sale! To carry my sorrows and my joys to market! To ask, to urge—even such a noble mind as yours, to give me gold for turning traitor to my own precious thoughts, and laying bare my heart of hearts to all men!

Marchmont accepts the memoirs, but reminds Mrs. Sherbourne of the secret of literary success. Someone must be found to "sing out that such a work is too improper to read"; then it will have enormous sales. Surely Trollope referred obliquely here to the unwritten good turn the critics had done in their many attacks upon the "coarseness and vulgarity" of her own novels.

The Blue Belles of England, which appeared simultaneously, is another clever satire on the fashionable London literary world. The book begins as Constance Ridley comes of age and into £30,000. Even as Charles Chesterfield had wanted to win literary renown, Constance's ambition is to make personal acquaintance with those who "had acquired honourable fame" in the arts. Through her friends the Hartleys, she contrives to get "introduced to the London world," a favor for which she must help pay expenses. As is so often the case with Trollope's heroines, Constance has a foolish brother, Sir James. "Everything belonging to, or emanating from, the mind of the brother was little, trifling, and dwarfish. Even his faults were on a small scale."

One of the Hartley girls, Margaretta, decides to lure Sir James into marriage. She does not love him. Indeed, since a crush at age sixteen, she tells her mother, "I have never been the victim of any tender passion whatever." Sir James, vain and rich, is fair game to her. He, for his part, thinks himself safe. As he tells Constance, "I'll defy all the women in London, old or young, to catch me." Margaretta is the first in what was to be a long series of aggressive but curiously attractive fortune hunters. She exploits opportunity and male vanity to win a rich husband in a "steadfastly purposed and patient" campaign. She tells her mother: "There is not a girl in London, let her advantages be what they may, who could compete with me in this charming chase. . . . He comes to me as constantly, and as naturally, for my little compliments to himself . . . as Cloe [the horse] does to the footman to be fed; and you will see, Mamma, that before long he will find out that he cannot do without them." In fact, she finds Sir James "such an uncommon fool, and so utterly devoid of everything like the spirit and feeling of a man," that she considers her activities "very dull work, [and] very difficult too."

But this side of her nature is carefully hidden as, simpering, she plays the part of the timid maiden. "She made her appearance, raised her timid eyes, averted her blushing cheek, gave her trembling hand, and performed every other part of the routine expected and required with the most irreproachable propriety of demeanour." Her subsequent marriage is one long exercise of tyranny over Sir James. Without power, she candidly concludes, there was nothing to "sustain her under what she felt to be a most prodigious bore." The phenomenon, the author assures the reader, "is by no means uncommon," and modestly adds: "Never, perhaps, had there been a finer example seen of a strutting, vain, and silly coxcomb, subjugated to the tyranny of an artful and ingenious wife," who just happened to be more violent, headstrong, imperious, and unreasonable than himself.

Contemporary reviewers noticed that the best parts of Trollope's novels now often had to do with these determined women and their machinations. The *Spectator* wrote of *The Blue Belles:*

> Mrs. Hartley and her husband-hunting daughter Margaretta, and the bragging baronet Sir James Ridley, whom that designing lady trepans into marriage, are the best-drawn characters in the novel. In the anatomizing of baser natures, Mrs. Trollope is skillful and diverting, though the amusement is of a disagreeable kind.

Properly reflecting Frances Trollope's own creative instincts, the reviewer admitted, "when the fate of the heroine alone engages the attention, the interest . . . flags."

Constance, the conventional heroine, is dazzled by the fashionable literary world, whose main hostess, Lady Dart, insists "it has been the favorite object of my existence . . . to collect round me all that nature had let slip through her fingers upon us of divine." Many of the names of those present are thinly veiled versions of celebrities from the real literary world, like Mr. Lodhart (the critic Lockhart). The center of attention is the poet Mortimer, who is surrounded by "the Blue Belles of England," admiring coteries of women who follow in the wake of successful authors. As one of the Miss Hartleys explains:

> One hundred and twenty . . . sent their albums . . . beseeching that [Mortimer] would write a few original lines in his own delicious vein of poesy therein. Seventy modestly entreated that he would only vouchsafe to inscribe his name at full length on a scrap of paper . . . One hundred and three requested . . . a small lock of his hair; and fifty-two sent him poetry of their own composing.

Many of the book's ladies have literary aspirations. Lady Dart keeps a notebook (her "museum of ideas"), and Lady Georgiana Grayton is "a prodigious verse-writer." Everywhere, women are striving to advance themselves through a variety of means, either literary or marital. Most innovative as a female character is one of Mortimer's special friends, the unique Mrs. Gardiner-Stewart. Like some of the book's other women, even while married to a pleasant and polite nonentity, who appears at parties and does not interfere with his wife's diversions, she too is searching for power and control over men. A "very sweet woman," she surrounds herself with beautiful things—plate, linen, perfumes, and keeps "that vulgar article called daylight" out of her rooms with silk curtains and venetian blinds. Her house is a "palace of dainty devices." The drawing room is scented by "a delicate incense from Arabian gums" and lit by tapers and decorated with flowers and "hangings of lemon-coloured satin, gilt ornaments, and a multitude of mirrors." She "hated standing," and settles herself prevailingly upon her sofa in "an attitude exceedingly recumbent." As the narrator suggests, "no one living could exhibit symptoms of being *ennuyée* more conspicuously than Mrs. Gardiner-Stewart." This lethargic pose masked an inner determination and toughness as, with "closed eye-

lids" and an "air of perfect and very soft and beautiful repose," she listens to the whispered compliments of admirers and controls the fates of many of the gentlemen who haplessly swarm around her alluring presence. She is one of the earliest portrayals of the siren figure, later so masterfully developed by Anthony Trollope in *Barchester Towers* with his Signora Neroni.

In the second volume Constance accepts the marriage proposal of Mortimer, the poet. Soon, however, she sees him "as he really was, artificial, vain, little-minded, and insincere." A Mr. Fitzosborne has, instead, "so many of the higher qualities which were wanting in her affianced husband." To extricate herself from this difficult position without harming others is her task in the third volume. After an appropriate number of delays and misunderstandings, Constance and Fitzosborne are united. In the end Constance has come to see what Frances Trollope set out for her readers, the fickle shallowness of the London literary scene, both the lionized artist and the coteries of hangers-on.

With the writing of **Charles Chesterfield** and **The Blue Belles** Trollope embarked upon a succession of works treating the men, women, and manners of the age. Her perception of the ludicrous and the power of satire remained undiminished, making these works vigorous and popular, as she turned ever more intensely to analysis and criticism of her own society.

The main interest of **Young Love** is not its conventional romantic plot, from which the author herself turns pointedly aside: "And this, gentle reader, is all the love-making between my hero and heroine with which I can favour you." Instead, Trollope introduces Amelia Thorwald, surely one of her most unscrupulous fortune hunters. Reviewers found her "rather too much of a heartless profligate." Her maneuvers, her mock marriage, her lies, the episodes she inhabits "have something revolting about them," wrote one critic. Yet once again, the real vitality of the book lies in the machinations of a fortune hunter.

Amelia goes quickly to work in the usual surroundings of country society, selecting for herself the man who possesses the most economic and social power, Alfred Dermont, "the first young man in the company, . . . the richest, and the handsomest," the one with "the greatest power of making her conspicuous by his attentions." As in the usual situations created by Trollope, Amelia has no romantic feelings for the prey, "a horrible bore" she calls him to a female confidante: "Whether my poor shattered spirits will bear the wear and tear of his young love . . . from noon till dewy eve . . . I cannot tell." The lack of emotional involvement is a constant with this character type. The new ingredient in Amelia is precisely her hope to marry someone she truly likes. She prefers another man, the older and more sophisticated Lord William, and gambles all on one more try at him, even while keeping the naive Alfred on a string, "a dangerous game" as her female mentor warns.

In this book Trollope uses the device of letters to get inside the real Amelia, about whom, in company, there is nothing "natural or involuntary." As the narrator pointedly notes: "Nothing can assist the development of character so effectually as the perusal of confidential epistles." Amelia's letters are directed to an older woman who has also suffered in life, going from teaching to a "very advantageous marriage," to destitution and misery, to lady's maid, and in her final transformation, to clothes merchant. Amelia writes her sympathetic friend in confidence, "opening an aching and overfull heart" about the "insipid and wearisome boy" she will have to marry if she can "hope for nothing better."

In the end Amelia abandons the sure catch to marry her choice, whom she wins by acting a scene of dramatic pathos, telling him she is being compelled to marry Alfred against her will. Later, Lord William proves to be a cad, deceiving and abandoning Amelia. But she is indomitable to the last, admitting to having been taken in, while claiming that "it is a sort of thing that no woman, let her be ever so clever, need be ashamed of." Amelia and Lord William are divorced, and she disappears, the "latter scenes of her career" shrouded in darkness. Trollope will not punish Amelia for her valiant attempt to win both security and a man she can at least find interesting. (pp. 100-10)

By the time Trollope published **The Three Cousins** [in 1847], reviewers were commenting on the pattern discernible in her female characters. *John Bull* noted: "Mrs. Trollope has written a great deal, and hence she sometimes copies herself; that is, we have essentially the same characters, acting from analogous motives, but externally diversified by differences of situation. . . . Her own sex she seems to have studied with profound attention, and *no living writer so keenly satirises the heartless woman of the world,* or so admirably exposes all the elaborate devices by which artificial manners are made to represent natural impulses." After five years of describing such characters, the fortune hunter had become Trollope's recognized special domain.

This story concerns three cousins, ladies aged 52, 34, and 18. The eldest is Mrs. Morrison, the wife of the Bishop of Solway, who takes an interest in her young cousin, the penniless Laura Lexington. Mrs. Morrison is a "New Woman" of 1847. "Every idea that was new had wonderful attraction for her. The new idiom of Carlyle, the new colouring of Turner, the new preaching of Newman . . . etcetera, etcetera, all excited an enthusiastic degree of interest in her mind." An elderly relative, Sir Joseph Lexington, with an illegitimate son Frederick, takes a liking to young Laura. The plot revolves around the question of how Sir Joseph will dispose of his money. He invites Laura to his estate, gives her gifts, and outfits her with new clothes. The third cousin, Mrs. Cobhurst, a widow of 34, is the husband- and fortune-hunting villainess, who attaches herself to the Lexingtons, hoping to catch Sir Joseph for herself.

Mrs. Cobhurst is a fading beauty. The reader meets her as she undresses before a mirror, removing false tresses and artificial flowers, washing her face of its cosmetics and quickly extinguishing her candle, "not wishing to look at herself in the glass afterwards." She tries to look like eighteen and perseveres with the "murderous work" of flirting for a living. Once again, the lady has little interest in the man she seeks to trap. "She was very far from being such an extremely silly body as really to care three straws about 'the bright vision' himself. She had gone through too many flirtations in the course of her long military experiences . . . for one affair more or less, . . . to touch her tranquillity." She is a woman on the make, a lone widow without protection or assistance of any kind, but with "a brain which, if bestowed upon a warlike monarch, might have made him the pest of his age." Instead, Mrs. Cobhurst is only "a restless schemer in a little way." Such, Trollope insists, is the fate of women in the marriage market.

The less interested young cousin Laura meanwhile falls in love with Frederick. These potenially convenient arrangements are interrupted by the machinations of Laura's father and, of course, Mrs. Cobhurst. When Sir Joseph dies, a will found in an old desk reveals that Frederick is really legitimate, upon which all the cousins and couples sort themselves out, some happily, others more resignedly. The book's postscript belongs to Mrs. Cobhurst. Failing to trap Sir Joseph, she has merely moved on to the next opportunity and "has been flirting a good deal for some weeks past with a rising young barrister, . . . endeavouring to make good her dream for a great niece's share of the unbequeathed portion of the late Sir Joseph's personal property." Though she has failed to get her man, Mrs. Cobhurst is indomitable to the last. As her creator characterizes her, "She had great resources in an intellect, that was never for an instant at a loss for expedients, in perseverance that was never wearied, in courage that was never daunted, and in principles that had never stood in her way upon any occasion since she reached the mature age of 21." (pp. 113-15)

[**The Young Countess; or, Love and Jealousy** and **Town and Country**] are devoted in different ways to accounts of unhappy marriages. Both feature enterprising women who rise above the conditions of their unfortunate unions. The young countess of the title is widowed and finds the death of her old and boring husband a release. Nevertheless, she wishes to observe the proprieties, and spends a year of mourning at a ruined old castle which, to beguile the time, she decides to restore, even re-creating its old dungeon in faithful detail. Lonely, she invites the penniless orphan Caroline de Marfeld to stay with her. Soon the Countess decides to make her protégée a permanent resident of the castle and sets up a fund for her. Anticipating a theme she would soon develop more fully, Trollope thus has her heroine seek out a friend of her own sex. She pointedly explains the countess's need in a long aside to the reader. Her heroine, she writes, needs "a dear, faithful, intimate friend, of her own sex, before whom all ceremony might be banished, every thought revealed, and with whom every project might be discussed before it was brought forward to meet the light of day."

When the castle is complete, the countess invites a party of guests, one of whom is Alfred de Hermanstadt, with whom she falls passionately (and jealously) in love. When she suspects he loves Caroline, she locks him up in her newly built dungeon. In time the countess regrets her actions, endows an abbey of nuns, and makes Alfred her heir on condition that he marry Caroline. Fourteen years later, the reader learns that the countess has become the abbess and, in the last scene of the novel, she is reconciled with the others as she visits the dungeon in which she had imprisioned Alfred. Despite the highly colored melodrama of this somewhat ridiculous plot, the novel nevertheless features a heroine who finally finds both power and peace on her own, the real world offering no other simple possibilities.

Town and Country, in its narrative technique, also looks ahead to the novels of Trollope's last period. The book features a narrator with a heavily female voice, speaking on behalf of women in oppressive marriages and, more important, uses letters and extracts from journals in order to get inside the thinking of the women, especially the heroine. Harriet's mother opens her heart in letters to "the earliest friend of her youth, from whom her marriage had separated her." Harriet herself keeps a journal, "an extract or two" from which "will throw more light upon the subject than any narrative."

Harriet undertakes a May-December union with a man thirty years her senior, not unlike Dorothea's marriage to Casaubon in George Eliot's *Middlemarch* some thirty years later. Mr. Cuthbert appeals to Harriet as a source of knowledge and power. She is proud that he has found her "neither too young, too ignorant, nor too silly for him to converse with." Attracted to him because he treats her as an equal and favors her with intelligent conversation, she marries him, to her subsequent regret. But her thirst for enlarged experience and broader horizons is analogous to that of the unscrupulous fortune hunters of this period. Not until Trollope's late novels would she give her readers heroines who found power within themselves and not in the men they successfully or unsuccessfully hunted, or accepted to their ultimate distress. (pp. 117-19)

In the last period of her writing career (1850-1856) Trollope scrapped all subterfuge and allowed her strong, free-spirited women to function as heroines of the main plot. They appear as happy, self-sufficient, often older women who get along beautifully on their own. Their most frequent sources of distress are the demands of unreasonable fathers or the oppressions of weak and worthless husbands. As they achieve their variety of victories, they defiantly disregard the social and economic imperatives to marry, around which so many middle-class Victorian ladies shaped their lives.

Appropriately enough, the series begins with a story of female self-rule in *Petticoat Government.* A wealthy ward in Chancery is sent to the charge of her two maiden aunts, who struggle for the exclusive right to guard the profitable heiress. A compromise is reached, and the girl spends six months with each aunt. But these female communities abound in suspicion and squabbling. The spinster aunts (who secretly wish to be married) are only interested in their niece for her money. Finally the young heroine marries her cousin, son of another long-lost aunt, and the three form their own community far away from England.

The plot is predictable, and while there is talk throughout about women living satisfactorily without marriage, the arrangements the reader sees are all failures. Nevertheless, this novel ushers in a series of major heroines who realize their true identities aside from marriage and, in some cases, primarily in the company of other women. In these late books the mixed female character, who appeared as comical or deviant before, now achieves her apotheosis as the clever woman whose essential self is unengaged by relationships with men.

Second Love is a novel whose plot abounds not in love, but in unhappy marriages. Some characters wed for the wrong reasons, both emotional and financial, and others are shown struggling to cope with unhappy unions, like Mrs. Selcroft, whose situation is the one Frances Trollope most often depicted in these late novels. "The sworn-to-be-obedient wife of a man who often required the practice of such a faculty in his helpmate," Mrs. Selcroft kept the knowledge of her husband's inferiority hidden in her bosom, as the narrator pointedly comments, "poor lady, as carefully concealed in her heart, as an incendiary keeps his dark lantern in his bosom." Her daughter Lucy is franker and more independent, "exceedingly clever, and not only very capable of taking care of herself, but moreover of a disposition which might make it difficult for any one else to take care of her effectually." She is an intellectual girl, unwilling "to delude herself into the belief that she could love [her father] as sincerely as she honoured her mother." Not surprisingly, her father finds her more difficult to manage than her mother.

Throughout the novel, the narrator (clearly speaking in Trollope's voice) pities the mother for her unshakable belief in wifely submission and praises Lucy for resisting her father's tyrannical and unjust commands. Her plucky skirmishes with her father bring out a pointed moral: men who "have the happiness of possessing a good and affectionate daughter, will do well to content themselves with the blessing, while they carefully avoid the dangerous attempt of endeavouring to convert her into a hood-winked slave. It is just possible that occasionally such a plan may answer with a wife, but with a daughter, unless she happen to be an idiot, NEVER." Trollope's words and the logic of her plot undermined the Victorian idea that women must blindly obey the men in their lives. At this novel's conclusion those who resist throughout are suitably rewarded with the demise or departure of offending husbands or fathers.

Mrs. Mathews begins as the fifty-year-old Mary King looks back on her life and considers the ideas and passions she has outgrown. First, she no longer believes that women's best years are those of their youth. She writes: "I am quite conscious . . . of being in the very highest prime and vigour of existence. When I was younger, I was less so." More important, she has dispensed with the need for romantic love and marriage. Tough and independent, she exults in her maturity and the free spirit of her singleness, even as her elderly father worries about what will become of his daughter after his death. Strongly convinced "that men only were capable of taking care of the money concerns of a family," he pressures his daughter to marry his old friend, Mr. Mathews. Protective and patriarchal, he wonders what will she do about signing the rent receipts, ordering the wine, and repairing the drains of the home pastures. Even more important, "And oh Mary! Mary! Who will sit at the side of the fire with you through the long winter evenings?" Surely, he reasons, a woman needs a man for companionship above all.

Complying with his wishes, the clear-headed Mary weds, but not without strong feelings of oppression: "She did not like the idea of belonging to any man." She negotiates a marriage settlement that will preserve much of her wonted independence, insisting on a separate allowance, the right to dispose of her own property, and the privacy of a section of the house for her own use. Despite these provisions, she soon finds all her worst apprehensions about marriage correct. After her father's death, Mr. Mathews shows his true colors, becomes belligerent and masterful, and in general throws Mary's happy and orderly life into turmoil. Finally, after a series of singular complications, Mrs. Mathews prevails and regains her independence. After making a will in her favor, Mr. Mathews accommodatingly dies. This easy resolution to all the heroine's difficulties should not obscure the lesson of this remarkable novel. In marriage Mary must struggle to obtain her rightful position and belongings. In the single life lay a power women had as yet not discovered.

In *Mrs. Mathews* Trollope succeeded in making a totally unromantic heroine the focus of a popular novel. A sturdy, sensible, resourceful woman, Mary King Mathews is a plain heroine who, unlike Charlotte Brontë's Jane Eyre and Lucy Snowe, finds no dashing, erotic Rochester or fascinating Paul Emanuel. Mrs. Mathews must cope with a marriage to a selfish, grasping old bachelor whom she does not love. The focus in this unusual novel is the struggle between the sexes—not a romantic one like the clashes described by the Brontë's, but a life-and-death competition between rivals for property and the rights of inheritance, which ends not in reconciliation or compromise, but with the destruction of the male and the triumphal coming into her own of the single female. (pp. 123-26)

The mother of the heroine of [*Gertrude; or, Family Pride*] is another lady who must cope with an unsuccessful marriage. Having recognized that "her husband was a pompous fool, incapable of acting from rational motives; incapable of forming a rational opinion; and pretty nearly incapable of uttering a rational word," she resolves, with "steady, quiet perseverance," to make the best of life with "one of the dullest men that ever lived as a husband and companion." Perhaps, she reasons with practical wisdom, far worse would have been to have married "a man who, with less of dullness, had a greater propensity to interfere with the opinions of his wife and who might have interfered more fatally still with the occupation of her time." Eventually she discovers the great truth that Trollope's women always come to: "her only resource against something very like despair must be sought in herself." Like Mrs. Mathews, she furnishes her own apartments according to her own taste and makes constant additions to her fine old library. She also bears a daughter who provides her with the happiness she has not found in marriage. Her only fear is "that the intellect of her child might resemble that of its father." When she dies, a close female friend becomes young Gertrude's companion. For women, motherhood and friendship are life's only unalloyed pleasures. With this novel Trollope's interest in depicting the female community has begun.

Trollope's last heroine, Clara Holmwood [in *Fashionable Life; or, Paris and London*] is another woman on her own. Taught by a schoolmaster, not a governess, her education, "a very strange one," had "led her considerably beyond the limits usually fixed, as the *ne plus ultra* of female education." Impervious to social pressures that she join the smart set, she will accept as a close friend only a penniless old maiden aunt. In a plot similar to that of *Mrs. Mathews,* Clara's dying father worries about his daughter's future and is anxious that she find a suitable husband before he dies. Without her knowledge or consent, he appoints the odious sycophant Dr. Brixbourg as her guardian. Mr. Holmwood, "like all other discreet men of business . . . was not, nor ever had been, in the habit of

talking to the ladies of his family concerning his financial affairs, either private or commercial." When he dies in Clara's nineteenth year, he leaves her £100,000, but she must live the remaining two years of her minority with the Brixbourg family. Like many of her creator's heroines, she resolves to endure this trial patiently, but not without first making formal arrangements about her rights. Aunt Sarah must stay with her, along with her schoolmaster, for she resolves to continue her studies in Latin, French, and English. Her only regret is that she has never studied the law, an omission that has left her unsure about Dr. Brixbourg's rights to compel her to obey his wishes. Before long a young man falls in love with Clara, not with her beauty but, as the author notes, with "the tone and quality of her mind." Henry Hamilton, however, is too noble to pursue a girl of large fortune and sails for Australia to forget the one he loves. His departure leaves Clara free to face the question so many of Trollope's heroines encountered. What will she do with herself? How shall she shape the unknown future that lies before her?

Characteristically, her first thought is not of marriage but a profession. "Had I been persuaded into believing that I possessed a talent for painting, or for sculpture, or for music, or for astronomy, I might have amused my life, by fancying that I was making progress towards something desirable, but never having been conscious of possessing any talent at all, my existence must, of necessity, be a very shapeless one." Yet, "conscious of an elastic spring within her which, if one scheme of existence failed, would give her energy to try another," she turns, like her creator before her, to the next resource—traveling!

Indeed, she sets out cheerfully, perhaps too happily for the conventional heroine who has just lost her lover. The author needs to explain such feelings to readers who expected that the girl would languish: "That this state of mind was in her case reasonable, can scarcely be denied." Yet, not "every young girl as abruptly disappointed in the hopes of an apparently well-placed attachment, as she had been, could, or should, be expected to bear it so well." The generalization that follows is intended for Trollope's female readers: "There is probably no very reasonable hope of mending the matter; but as society is now constituted, the happiness of English women seems to depend too much upon the *accident* of being married, or not married."

Clara certainly does not let her happiness depend on Henry Hamilton. Coming of age, she leaves the home of her odious guardian and goes to Paris, where she once again negotiates suitable living arrangements, without reference to marriage. When she meets Lady Amelia Wharton, who is poor but has good social connections, Clara decides to set up housekeeping with her friend and, of course, Aunt Sarah. Her proposal is quite businesslike: "What say you to our entering into partnership together for a month or two?"

Pooling their resources efficiently, the women arrange to keep house together for the ensuing winter at least. Lady Amelia is quite contented with these arrangements and tells her seventeen-year-old daughter, Annie, who will also be a member of the group, "our present mode of life certainly appears likely to be very agreeable, and we should be sadly silly to destroy our enjoyment of it, by perpetually dwelling on its possible termination."

The women get along without struggle or suspicions of one another, and their establishment is soon "as celebrated for . . . hospitality as for . . . elegance." Indeed, "in all that passed between Lady Amelia Wharton and Clara Holmwood concerning their partnership establishment, it would be difficult for the most captious fault-finder to name any point upon which either of them could have been found wanting, either in genuine liberality of feeling, or in the unobtrusive and graceful expression of it."

The women enjoy one another's company, even while "each was so essentially different from the others." Aunt Sarah is "gentle, quiet, peaceful." Annie Wharton, a "high born, graceful little beauty, contrived to animate and embellish the existence of the insignificant old maid." Trollope's picture is one of shared happiness and considerable "freedom from social slavery." Lady Amelia, for her part, is not at all anxious to see her daughter married off. "Marriages, they say," she explains, "are made in heaven; and though I am not sure that this is part of my faith, I am greatly inclined to think that the less busy we make ourselves about it on earth, the better. It will come when it will come." The statement has a tone of resignation. The reader knows nothing of Lady Amelia's own marriage besides her lonely and penniless state. Her reluctance to hurry her daughter into uncertainties is understandable, but surely at odds with fictional depictions of Victorian mothers.

Soon the author is calling the ladies "partners in the firm of Wharton and Holmwood," a business venture whose goal is not financial gain but rather the "very considerably increased enjoyment of each, and all, of the fair ladies of whom the family was composed." The arrangement, unlike marriage, was one in which one might amuse oneself or withdraw at will. As Trollope pointedly notes: "Perhaps of all the goods the gods can give, the most precious is freedom of will and action." In describing the living arrangements to her old schoolmaster, Clara praises above all "the sister-like terms" under which the women live together.

In the second volume Annie Wharton does become attached to a young man, Victor Dormont. So that they can marry, Clara settles some money on her. At once the women plan to take the young couple into their circle. "Why should they not live with us here?" Upon the agreement of all the women, they give up their third drawing room to the couple. As Clara observes; "You and your daughter, and I and my aunt, though not particularly likely from our very different portions in life to think and feel alike, have formed, since we have been together, a very happy family; and I much doubt if, in any matters of domestic arrangement, we should be likely to differ." Thus, "none of those tearful separations occurred which will often cause a parting bride to sigh, even at the moment when the dearest wish of her heart is fulfilled."

When Victor's financial speculations fail, he conveniently commits suicide. Fortunately, Annie has had a baby and thus, "the strongest feeling of her nature, *maternal love*" will save her. Since he had also secretly involved Clara's money in his schemes, she must return to England penniless, where a returned Henry Hamilton, who has inherited £400 a year, can now marry her. Eventually she gets her fortune back, and everyone lives happily ever after. All this action, however, takes place in the last four chapters

of volume 3 and is clearly not the part of the novel upon which Trollope lavished her closest attention. The bulk of her story was a paean of praise for the pleasure and power of sisterhood.

With this novel, her thirty-fourth since she had begun a writing life at fifty-three, Trollope ended her career, giving artistic expression to a vision of female independence and sisterhood that stands out prominently in the world of Victorian patriarchy. (pp. 129-33)

Helen Heineman, in her Frances Trollope, *Twayne Publishers, 1984, 163 p.*

FURTHER READING

Review of *Domestic Manners of the Americans,* by Frances Trollope. *The Athenaeum,* No. 230 (24 March 1832): 187-88.
  Commends Trollope's powers of observation and description but suggests that she drew incorrect conclusions from her experiences in the United States.

Review of *Domestic Manners of the Americans,* by Frances Trollope. *The Athenaeum,* No. 231 (31 March 1832): 204-06.
  Focuses on Trollope's commentary on religious practices in the United States, concluding that "We have seldom met with so much talent united to such sad prejudice."

Baker, Ernest A. "The Predecessors of Dickens." In his *The History of the English Novel: The Age of Dickens and Thackeray,* pp. 203-36. London: H. F. & G. Witherby Ltd., 1936.
  Briefly notes the sensational reception of *Domestic Manners of the Americans* and commends the humor and satire of *The Vicar of Wrexhill, The Widow Barnaby, The Widow Married,* and *The Barnabys in America.*

Bethke, Frederick John. "Writings about Mrs. Frances Milton Trollope, 1832-1972." In his *Three Victorian Travel Writers: An Annotated Bibliography of Criticism on Mrs. Frances Milton Trollope, Samuel Butler, and Robert Louis Stevenson,* pp. 3-55. Boston: G. K. Hall & Co., 1977.
  Annotated bibliography of criticism on Trollope's travel books.

Chaloner, W. H. "Mrs. Trollope and the Early Factory System." *Victorian Studies* IV, No. 2 (December 1960): 159-66.
  Assesses Trollope's depiction of factory conditions in *The Life and Adventures of Michael Armstrong, the Factory Boy* and describes her methods of researching the novel.

Dickens, Charles. Letter to Frances Trollope. In his *The Letters of Charles Dickens, Vol. I: 1833 to 1856,* edited by Mamie Dickens and Georgina Hogarth, p. 94. New York: Charles Scribner's Sons, 1879.
  Letter of 16 December 1842 in which Dickens credits *Domestic Manners of the Americans* with the reform of "many social features of American society." He writes: "I am convinced that there is no writer who has so well and accurately (I need not add so entertainingly) described it, in many of its aspects, as you have done."

Review of *A Visit to Italy,* by Frances Trollope. *The Dublin Review* XIV, No. xxvii (February 1843): 255-68.

> Negative review of Trollope's Italian travel book focusing on her misrepresentations and misinterpretations of Roman Catholicism.

Heineman, Helen. "Frances Trollope in the New World: *Domestic Manners of the Americans.*" *American Quarterly* XXI, No. 3 (Fall 1969): 544-59.

> Textual and stylistic analysis of *Domestic Manners,* assessing its popular appeal and enduring notoriety.

——. " 'Starving in That Land of Plenty': New Backgrounds to Frances Trollope's *Domestic Manners of the Americans.*" *American Quarterly* XXIV, No. 5 (December 1972): 643-60.

> Corrects longstanding misrepresentations of Trollope's reasons for traveling to the United States in 1827 using information drawn from recently discovered letters.

——. "Frances Trollope's *Jessie Phillips:* Sexual Politics and the New Poor Law." *International Journal of Women's Studies* 1, No. 1 (January-February 1978): 96-106.

> Considers ways that Trollope's novel illustrates the inequities of the bastardy clause in the New Poor Law of 1834.

——. "Frances Trollope." In her *Restless Angels: The Friendship of Six Victorian Women,* pp. 183-213. Athens: Ohio University Press, 1983.

> Account of the circumstances surrounding Trollope's 1827-31 sojourn in the United States. Heineman includes discussion of Trollope's return to England and her rigorous work habits.

Johnston, Johanna. *The Life, Manners, and Travels of Fanny Trollope: A Biography.* New York: Hawthorne Books, 1978, 242 p.

> Anecdotal, noncritical biography based largely on earlier biographical accounts.

Kestner, Joseph. "Men in Female Condition of England Novels." In *Men by Women,* edited by Janet Todd, pp. 77-99. New York: Holmes & Meier Publishers, 1981.

> Includes discussion of characterization in Trollope's novel *The Life and Adventures of Michael Armstrong, the Factory Boy* in an analysis of male characters in industrial fiction written by women between 1830 and 1850.

Lancaster, Clay. "The Egyptian Hall and Mrs. Trollope's Bazaar." *Magazine of Art* 43, No. 3 (March 1950): 94-9, 112.

> Account of Trollope's unsuccessful business ventures in Cincinnati in 1828, describing the design and construction of the building intended to house her proposed marketplace and cultural center.

McCourt, Edward A. "Mrs. Trollope among the Savages." *The Dalhousie Review* XXVIII, No. 2 (July 1948): 124-32.

> Assesses the circumstances that led Trollope to write *Domestic Manners of the Americans* and notes some salient qualities of the work, concluding that "*Domestic Manners of the Americans* is an extremely shrewd, if prejudiced, summary of national characteristics and aspirations."

Mitchell, Sally. "Lost Women: Feminist Implications of the Fallen in Works by Forgotten Women Writers of the 1840's."

The University of Michigan Papers in Women's Studies 1, No. 2 (June 1974): 110-24.

> Includes discussion of *Jessie Phillips: A Tale of the Present Day* in an examination of ways that women novelists of the period treated the theme of the seduced woman and unwed mother.

Review of *Vienna and the Austrians, with Some Account of a Journey through Swabia, Bavaria, the Tyrol, and the Salzbourg,* by Frances Trollope. *The Quarterly Review* LXV, No. cxxix (December 1839): 263-72.

> Comments on Trollope's growing fame as a travel writer and assesses the acuity of her observations of Austrian nobility and high society.

Sadleir, Michael. Introduction to *Domestic Manners of the Americans,* by Frances Trollope, pp. xi-xxvi. New York: Dodd, Mead & Co., 1927.

> Recounts the circumstances of the volume's composition and its reception on publication. Sadleir includes commentary on several of Trollope's social purpose novels.

——. "Anthony's Mother." In his *Trollope: A Commentary,* pp. 37-116. Rev. ed. New York: Farrar, Straus & Co., 1947.

> Admiring account of Trollope's life and personality that dismisses her literary career as unimportant artistically and significant primarily because it afforded her the means to support her family.

Sagmaster, Joseph. "Fist Across the Sea." *The Kenyon Review* XII, No. 2 (Spring 1950): 365-68.

> Proposes a relationship between Trollope's financial failure in the United States and the acerbity of *Domestic Manners of the Americans.*

"Frances Trollope: Her Books." *The Saturday Review* (London) 80, No. 2095 (21 December 1895): 841-42.

> Questions the artistic merit of Trollope's many published volumes but commends her courage and industry.

"Mrs. Trollope's Visit to Italy." *The Spectator* 15, No. 746 (15 October 1842): 997-98.

> Favorable review of *A Visit to Italy.*

Stebbins, Lucy Poate, and Stebbins, Richard Poate. *The Trollopes: The Chronicle of a Writing Family.* New York: Columbia University Press, 1945, 394 p.

> Account of the lives and literary careers of Frances Trollope and several of her children, focusing on Anthony Trollope.

Review of *The Attractive Man,* by Frances Trollope. *Tait's Edinburgh Magazine* XII, No. cxliv (December 1845): 784-805.

> Favorable review commending in particular the vivid characterizations in the novel.

Trollope, Anthony. "My Mother." In his *An Autobiography,* pp. 18-30. New York: Harper & Brothers, 1883.

> Reminiscences about his mother's character, life, and literary career.

Trollope, Frances Eleanor. *Frances Trollope: Her Life and Literary Work from George III to Victoria.* 2 vols. London: Bentley & Son, 1895.

> Authorized biography by a daughter-in-law of Trollope who had access to unpublished letters and family papers.

Trollope, Joanna. Introduction to *Domestic Manners of the Americans,* by Frances Trollope, pp. v-ix. London: Century Publishing, 1984.

> Biographical sketch noting the sensational reception of *Domestic Manners of the Americans.*

Trollope, Thomas Adolphus. *What I Remember.* 2 vols. New York: Harper & Brothers, 1888.

> Autobiography by Trollope's eldest son commended for its accuracy.

Twain, Mark. *Life on the Mississippi,* pp. 132ff. Toronto: Bantam Books, 1981.

> Authorized edition of Twain's 1896 volume, containing scattered references to "poor candid Mrs. Trollope" and the angry American reception of *Domestic Manners of the Americans.*

Review of *Belgium and Western Germany,* by Frances Trollope. *The Westminster Review* XXII, No. xliv (1 April 1835): 514-18.

> Disparages Trollope's travel book about Belgium and Germany, contending that her "pretensions to refinement, and penchant towards aristocracy, betray a vulgar taste endeavouring to be fine."

Wilson, Rufus Rockwell. "Foreign Authors in America, Part II." *The Bookman* (New York) XII, No. 6 (February 1901): 589-97.

> Notes the "storm of protests" that greeted the publication of *Domestic Manners of the Americans* in the United States. Wilson attributes to Trollope "a sincere desire to be truthful and moderate" and suggests that personal difficulties she encountered in the United States influenced the negative tone of her volume. He concludes that "perhaps what most piqued her subjects at the time was consciousness of the truth behind her strictures, and the wit and humour with which she pointed them."

John Trumbull

1750-1831

American poet and essayist.

Trumbull was a noted satirist and prominent member of the Connecticut Wits, a loosely organized group of writers whose works celebrated the literary and political independence of America and promoted the cause of Federalism. His best known works are *The Progress of Dulness,* a satirical poem on the ineffectual educational practices of his time, and *M'Fingal,* a mock epic poem that ridicules the position of British loyalists during the American Revolution. The latter work enjoyed enormous popularity during the Revolutionary period, and critics note its significance both as a skillfully wrought work of literature and as an impassioned argument in favor of American independence.

Born in Westbury (now Watertown), Connecticut, Trumbull was the son of Reverend John Trumbull, a Congregationalist minister and classical scholar. A precocious child, the younger Trumbull learned to read when he was two years old, wrote his first poem at the age of four, and began learning Greek and Latin when he was five. He passed the Yale College entrance exam when he was seven years old, but, because of his youth and poor health, continued to study at home for another six years. At Yale Trumbull studied theology, ancient languages, mathematics, and literature, earning his bachelor's degree in 1767. Continuing as a graduate student at Yale, he collaborated with Timothy Dwight, a fellow student and member of the Connecticut Wits, on two series of periodical essays, "The Meddler" and "The Correspondent." He also became an active proponent of educational reform; in 1770, believing that the liberal arts had been neglected at Yale, Trumbull defended the study of literature in his master's oration, which was published as *An Essay on the Uses and Advantages of the Fine Arts.* He later satirized what he saw as the mediocrity of the educational practices of the time in *The Progress of Dulness,* published anonymously in three parts between 1772 and 1773.

While working as a tutor at Yale, Trumbull began to study law, and after being admitted to the bar in 1773, he moved to Boston to further his studies in the law office of John Adams. However, he continued his avocational interest in literature, and in 1775 several leaders in the movement for independence asked him to write a satire ridiculing the British loyalists. Shortly after a proclamation declaring martial law was issued by General Thomas Gage, governor of Massachusetts and commander of the British forces in the colonies, Trumbull wrote a verse parody of the proclamation, mocking the British soldiers and encouraging Gage to go back to England. Later in 1775, Trumbull incorporated approximately fifty lines of this parody into *M'Fingal: A Modern Epic Poem. Canto First, or The Town Meeting. M'Fingal* was a popular success among American revolutionaries, and George Washington, James Madison, and Thomas Jefferson all owned copies. In 1782 Trumbull published a revised and expanded edition, entitled *M'Fingal: A Modern Epic Poem in Four Cantos,* divid-

ing the initial canto into two and adding a third and fourth. During the 1780s Trumbull collaborated with others among the Connecticut Wits on *The Anarchiad,* a satiric poem written in support of a strong federal government. He devoted the following three decades to his legal career, serving in a variety of legislative and judicial positions in Connecticut. Considering the writing of political satire inconsistent with his responsibilities as a judge, Trumbull wrote little during these years and waited until he had retired to issue a collected edition of his works. Trumbull died at his daughter's house in Detroit in 1831.

In his first important satire, *The Progress of Dulness,* Trumbull critiqued "those general errors, that hinder the advantages of education, and the growth of piety." *The Progress of Dulness, Part First; or, The Rare Adventures of Tom Brainless* follows the educational development of Tom Brainless, a lazy young man who pursues a career in the ministry because he dislikes hard work. After sleeping his way through four years of college, Brainless teaches school for a year and is later certified to preach by a group of clergy who declare that, although he can barely read or write, "he's orthodox, and that's enough." In response to people who called the author an "open reviler of the Clergy," Trumbull dedicated the preface of the second part of

The Progress of Dulness to "the Envious and Malicious Reader" and suggested that his critics "might each of them have sate for the picture of Tom Brainless." The second and third parts of *The Progress* portray the similarly poor educations of Dick Hairbrain, a country fop, and Harriet Simper, a coquette, and the subsequent effect these have on their development. Although less renowned than *M'Fingal, The Progress of Dulness* has been praised for its wit and its insightful exposure of educational mediocrity.

The 1776 edition of *M'Fingal* takes the form of a debate between Honorius, a prominent member of the Whigs, who favored limiting the power of the monarchy, and Squire M'Fingal, a Scottish Tory loyal to Britain. Honorius accuses the British of seeking excessive power over the colonies. M'Fingal speaks in defense of Great Britain. M'Fingal's "defense," however, ironically reveals the truth of Honorius's charges. The third and fourth cantos added in 1782 continue the debate between Honorius and M'Fingal. A fight breaks out when the Whigs grow tired of listening to the Tory squire; M'Fingal is subsequently tarred and feathered. The poem ends when a clandestine meeting in M'Fingal's cellar is disrupted by the Whigs, and M'Fingal sneaks out, deserting his fellow Tories. Trumbull later claimed in a letter that his initial purpose in writing *M'Fingal* was, "with as much impartiality as possible, [to] satirize the follies and extravagancies of my countrymen, as well as of their enemies." Recent scholars, however, have discovered two previously unpublished letters written in 1775 which show that the 1776 edition of *M'Fingal* was primarily intended to ridicule the Tories. The revised edition of 1782 is more generally thought to display the "impartiality" of which Trumbull wrote, reflecting his disapproval of the conduct of his countrymen during the chaotic years immediately following the Revolution. Critics frequently note similarities between *M'Fingal* and Samuel Butler's widely renowned satire on English Puritans, *Hudibras* (1663-78), particularly in Trumbull's use of epigrammatic octosyllabic couplets, also known as Hudibrastic verse.

Eighteenth- and nineteenth-century criticism of Trumbull's work is almost exclusively devoted to *M'Fingal*, focusing on its role as political propaganda and debating its merits as literature. More recent evaluations have renewed interest in *The Progress of Dulness* and the "Meddler" and "Correspondent" essays. However, Trumbull's reputation as one of the most talented satirists in early American literature rests primarily on *M'Fingal*.

(See also *Dictionary of Literary Biography,* Vol. 31.)

PRINCIPAL WORKS

An Essay on the Uses and Advantages of the Fine Arts (essay) 1770
The Progress of Dulness, Part First; or, The Rare Adventures of Tom Brainless (poetry) 1772
The Progress of Dulness, Part Second; or, An Essay on the Life and Character of Dick Hairbrain of Finical Memory (poetry) 1773
The Progress of Dulness, Part Third, and Last: Sometimes Called The Progress of Coquetry; or, The Adventures of Miss Harriet Simper (poetry) 1773
M'Fingal: A Modern Epic Poem. Canto First, or The Town Meeting (poetry) 1776; also published as

M'Fingal: A Modern Epic Poem in Four Cantos [revised and enlarged edition], 1782
The Poetical Works of John Trumbull, LL.D. (poetry, letters, and essay) 1820
The Anarchiad: A New England Poem [with David Humphreys, Lemuel Hopkins, and Joel Barlow] (poetry) 1861
The Satiric Poems of John Trumbull (poetry) 1962
The Meddler (1769-70) and the Correspondent (1770-73) (essays) 1985

John Trumbull (essay date 1773)

[*In the following preface to the second part of* The Progress of Dulness, *Trumbull offers a satirical response to critics of the first part.*]

It is become an universal custom for every Author, before he gives himself up to the fury of the Critics, to make his dying speech in a Preface; in which, according to the usual style of criminals, he confesses his faults, tells the temptations that led him to the crime of scribbling, gives good advice to the rest of his fraternity, and throws himself upon the mercy of the Court. These speeches are commonly addressed to a sort of imaginary being, called the *kind, courteous, candid* and sometimes, *benevolent Reader.* Not that I would deny the existence of such a being, as an Epicurean once did of the soul, because he could not find an account of it, in the complete zoology of animals. The first part of this Poem met with very kind reception from many of this class: nor am I concerned least the second should receive any ill usage from them. Authors have much more to fear from readers of a different stamp; and though we are usually loth to speak out so plainly, the truth is, we should not make such long prologues to the Candid, were we assured of our safety from the attacks of the Malicious. For my own part, being an enemy to ceremony and circumlocution, and having moreover some outstanding accounts to settle, I shall directly address myself to this last kind of Critic; assuring him however, upon my word of honour, that I was not moved to do him this homage, as the Indians are to worship the devil, out of any fear of his power to do mischief; since I have already experienced that his malice has its proper antidote in his impotence.

To the envious and malicious reader:

May it please your Worship, or your Reverence; or your Ill-nature, by what title soever dignified and distinguished:

As you have expressed great resentment against the first part of this Poem and its Author, you might perchance think yourself slighted, if I should let the second come abroad without paying you my proper acknowledgements. I own myself much your debtor; and am only sorry that the number of your brotherhood is so inconsiderable, that the world may perhaps think this dedication almost entirely needless. Had a greater number shown themselves affected, I should have had more grounds to hope that the Poem might be useful. Satire is a medicine very salutary in its effects, but quite unpleasant in its operation; nor do I know a more evident symptom that the potion has taken its proper effect, than the groans and distortions of the Patient.

I had the pleasure, my Illnatured Reader, on the first publication of my poem, to hear the remarks made upon it by a cluster of your fraternity, who might each of them have sate for the picture of *Tom Brainless*. And as you may have frequent occasion to talk against it yourself, and yet be at some loss what to alledge in its reproach, I will do you the favor to acquaint you with the result of their criticisms; in order to save you the trouble of so much thinking, and assist you a little in the style and expression of your resentments.

It was determined by the meeting, *nem. con.* that the whole piece was low, paltry stuff, and both scurrilous in the sentiments and dirty in the style; that it was evident, the Author knew nothing of language, or versification, and was incapable of writing with any degree of elegance; that he was an open reviler of the Clergy, and an enemy to truth and learning; that his apparent design was to ridicule religion, disgrace morality, sneer at the present methods of education, and in short, write a satire upon *Yale-College* and the ten commandments; that he treated the subject in the most partial and prejudiced manner, and must certainly be either a Separatist, or a Sandemanian. Though the truth of the assertions in the poem could not so conveniently be denied, yet much was said against the intention of the Author; and it was affirmed that if indeed the world in one or two points was not quite so good, as they could wish it, yet things in the present state could never be altered for the better, and it was folly, or madness alone could propose it.

Now to give you as much light as possible into this matter, I would assure you, the Author had very little hopes that the world would, in his day, arrive at the point of perfection, from which it is at present he knows not how many leagues distant; and his expectations are not very sanguine, that these pictures of the modern defective manners will do much service. He is fully sensible, that the moral World is as difficult to be moved out of its course, as the natural; that there is in it as much power of resistance or *vis inertiae,* as the Philosophers term it; and that the projectors are equally at a loss for engines and foothold. He is as much satisfied that the present year hath borne a sufficient number of fools to keep up the breed, as that there has been a tolerable crop produced every season, for these forty years past. But he thought, though perhaps the picture might not reclaim many, there could be no harm in trying his hand at the draught: In which, if the good people, who sate for the painting, have the ill hap to find themselves drawn with a wide mouth, a long nose, or a blear eye, he begs of them to get a little acquainted with their own faces, and see whether these be not their real defects of nature, before they begin to rail at the Painter, for the badness of their resemblance.

I am fully sensible, my Illnatured Reader, that you have good reasons in your own breast, to account for your resentment against my first essay, and direct you in the manner of your remarks. You ought in gratitude to defend that carelessness in the examination of Candidates for preaching, to which it is not at all impossible, but you may yourself be indebted for your reverence and your band. Justly may you despise the study of those finer Arts and Sciences, of which, in a smooth journey through life, you never once

knew the want, or perceived the advantages: justly should you undervalue them in comparison with that ancient Learning, which from experience you rightly term *Solid,* as your own wits were never able to penetrate it. With good reason also do you affirm the satire to be levelled at the Clergy in general, since that assertion is the best method of preventing the public from dragging to view those particular men, at whom it is, and ought to be, pointed; though you might discern, with any other eye than that of wilful prejudice, that the Author hath the highest veneration for the ministerial robe, or he would never thus trouble himself about the spots that defile it. As for those, *however dignified in station,* who rail at the **Progress of Dulness,** to gain favour with a particular party, or order of men, he thinks them unworthy the notice of an answer. He would hint only to such as hope to screen themselves in the croud, and draw on him the resentment of those he esteems, by affirming the satire to be general, that he would thank them, if they would so far throw off the mask, that by acquiring a right to their names, he may have an opportunity hereafter to render it more particular. He especially recommends this hint to two Persons, the haughtiest Dullard, and the most impertinent Coxcomb of this age; from whom he has already received numberless favours, and who by their future good conduct may stand a chance, at some fortunate period, to figure at the head of a Dedication to the first and second parts of the **Progress of Dulness.**

And now, my Evil Reader, with regard to the Poem before you, which is properly a counterpart to the other, I design pretty much to let it speak for itself. Perhaps, since I have now endeavoured to ridicule and explode both extremes, this second part may assist you a little to judge what are the sentiments I would wish to enforce: but in plain truth, I have very little hopes of you. Nevertheless before I leave you, I will tell you one secret, and give you a few words of advice. The secret, which I am sure you would never have been able to discover, is this; In conformity to the delicacy of your taste, I have raised the style of this part, about two degrees by the scale, higher than the other. The advice is, that it will be no unwise proceedure in you to hint that the spirit of the piece is not well supported, nor this part half so good as the first: and an observation, or two, upon the Author's impudence, seasonably introduced, might not be wholly without effect. But as to the old trite way of calling men, Heretics, Deists and Arminians, it hath been lately so much hackneyed and worn out by some Reverend Gentlemen, that I cannot promise it would do you any manner of service.

I cannot conclude without declaring to the world in this public manner, that whoever shall take on himself this character, by criticizing on these Poems in the method above specified, shall have my free licence and permission to appropriate to himself the whole of this dedication, and be distinguished for the future by the title of my Envious and Malicious Reader: and I do assure him that this preface was written purposely for him; not designing however to exclude from a proper share every one, who shall join with him in those sentiments, from this first day of January, new style, A.D. 1773, henceforth, and as long as the world shall endure, be the same term longer or shorter. (pp. 47-52)

John Trumbull, in a preface to "The Progress

of Dullness," in The Satiric Poems of John Trumbull, *edited by Edwin T. Bowden, University of Texas Press, 1962, pp. 47-52.*

John Trumbull   (letter date 1775)

[*In the following excerpt from a letter to John Adams, Trumbull explains his purpose in writing* M'Fingal.]

To Expose a number of the principal Villains of the day, to ridicule the high blustering menaces & great expectations of the Tory party, & to burlesque the achievements of our ministerial Heroes, civil, ecclesiastical & military, was my whole plan. This could be done with more spirit in dialogue than plain narration, & by a mixture of Irony & Sarcasm under various Characters & different Styles, than in an unvaried harangue in the Author's own person. Nor is it a small beauty in any production of this kind, to paint the manners of the age. For these purposes, the Description of a Townmeeting & its Harangues, appeared the best Vehicle of the Satire. Had there been any one grand Villain, whose Character & History would have answered exactly, I should have made use of him & his real name, as freely as I have the names of others. But I could think of no *One,* & therefore substituted a fictitious Character, of a Scotch Tory Expectant, which I hope is not drawn so illy, but that the world might find hundreds perhaps to whom it might be properly applied. The other Speaker has properly speaking no Character drawn, & no actions ascribed to him. He is any one whose Sentiments are agreeable to his Speeches.

The Picture of the Townmeeting is drawn from the life, & with as proper lights, shades & Colouring as I could give it, & is I fancy no bad likeness.

> *John Trumbull, in a letter to John Adams on November 14, 1775, in* John Trumbull *by Victor E. Gimmestad, Twayne Publishers, Inc., 1974, p. 88.*

John Adams   (letter date 1785)

[*The second president of the United States, Adams was a political writer who helped to draft the Declaration of Independence. In the following excerpt from a letter to Trumbull, Adams offers praise for* M'Fingal, *but encourages the poet to focus his talents on more worthy subjects.*]

If I speak freely of [*M'Fingal*], I can truly say, that altho' it is not equal to itself throughout (and where is the Poem that is so?) yet there are many Parts of it equal to any thing, in that kind of Poetry, that ever was written.

Give me leave, however, to repeat, what I believe I have formerly said to you, in some Letter or Conversation—at least I have long thought of it, and said it to others—that altho' your Talent in this way is equal to that of any one, you have veins of Poetry of superior kinds. I wish you to think of a subject which may employ you for many years, and afford full scope for the pathetic and sublime, of which several specimens have shown you master in the highest degree. Upon this plan I should hope to live to see our young America in Possession of an Heroick Poem, equal to those the most esteemed in any Country.

John Adams, in a letter to John Trumbull on April 28, 1785 in The Historical Magazine, *Vol. IV, No. 7, July, 1860, p. 195.*

John Trumbull   (letter date 1785)

[*In the following excerpt from a letter to the Marquis de Chastellux, Trumbull offers a revised explanation of the circumstances surrounding the composition of* M'Fingal *and his design for the poem.*]

[*M'Fingal*] was written merely with a political view, at the instigation of some leading members of the first Congress, who urged me to compose a satirical poem on the events of the campaign in the year 1775. My design was to give, in a poetical manner, a general account of the American contest, with a particular description of the characters and manners of the times, interspersed with anecdotes, which no history would probably record or display: and with as much impartiality as possible, satirize the follies and extravagancies of my countrymen, as well as of their enemies. I determined to describe every subject in the manner it struck my own imagination, and without confining myself to a perpetual effort at wit, drollery and humour, indulge every variety of manner, as my subject varied, and insert all the ridicule, satire, sense, sprightliness and elevation, of which I was master. In a word, I hoped to write a burlesque poem, which your Boileau would not have condemned, with those of Scarron and Dassouci, "aux plaisans du Pont-neuf."

To throw this design into a regular poetical form, I introduced M'Fingal, a fictitious hero, who is the general representative of the party, whom we styled Tories, in New-England. The scenes in which he is engaged, the townmeeting, the mobs, the liberty-pole, the secret cabal in the cellar, the operation of tarring and feathering, &c. were acted in almost every town. His exertions in favor of Great-Britain are regularly completed by his flight to Boston, to which event every incident in the poem tends: in the course of which, all the transactions of the war, previous to the period of his flight, are naturally introduced in narration. The subsequent events are shown in the customary and ancient poetical way in a vision; in which I availed myself of the claims of the Scotch Highlanders, to the gift of prophecy by second-sight, as a novel kind of machinery, peculiarly appropriate to the subject, and exactly suited to a Poem, which from its nature must in every part be a parody of the serious Epic. In the style, I have preferred the high burlesque to the low (which is the style of *Hudibras*) not only as more agreeable to my own taste, but as it readily admits a transition to the grave, elevated or sublime: a transition which is often made with the greatest ease and gracefulness, in the satirical poems of Pope and Despreaux. (pp. 231-33)

> *John Trumbull, in a letter to the Marquis de Chastellux on May 20, 1785, in his* The Poetical Works of John Trumbull, LL.D., *Samuel G. Goodrich, 1820, pp. 230-33. Reprinted by Scholarly Press, 1968.*

The Monthly Review, London   (essay date 1793)

[*In the following excerpt, the critic praises* M'Fingal *as a successful imitation of Samuel Butler's* Hudibras *(1662-80) but objects to Trumbull's "slovenly rhymes."*]

Turn and turn about, says one old proverb; every dog has his day, says another: British royalists have for more than a century enjoyed a poet laureat in Butler; and the American republicans are now supported by no mean satirist, in the person of the writer of [*M'Fingal*], who possesses a genius which may claim respectable affinity with that which produced the celebrated *Hudibras.*

We are informed that the author of this burlesque epic poem is John Trumbull, Esq. an eminent Counsellor in the state of Connecticut, a near relation of the late Governor Trumbull of that state, and of Mr. Trumbull the painter; and that he is known in his own country for many other works of genius, and of utility, both in prose and verse.

M'Fingal is a successful imitation of *Hudibras;* and the adventures that are celebrated in it are more consistent; probably because, as we are informed, the character of the principal hero was not drawn for any particular person, but stands as representative of the tory faction in general. The author's language is not usually so careless as that which we find in Butler's work; and this attention may be thought to impose some restraint on the freedom of his humour; yet, misled, probably, by that general applause which covers the slovenly rhymes that are often to be found in his model, he tags the ends of some of his lines with words in which the coarsest ear must disown any correspondence of sound:—but humourous poets should always bear in mind Butler's rule, though, like many other preceptors, he paid but little attention to it himself; and, if one line contains the sense, they should give us, at least, a rhyme in the other. (pp. 34-5)

Chronology fixes the time of this ludicrous tale in the year 1775, at the opening of the American war; and the poem, we understand, was first published in Connecticut, in 1782, toward its conclusion. . . . [There] can be little doubt of its having contributed to the good humour of the Americans, after the success of their cause; and in England, the liberal mind will not deny it a place on the same shelf with our *Hudibras;* a distinction which it well merits in every point of view: except with regard to the horrid rhymes, which are still worse than those that debase the witty performance of Butler.

These master-pieces of rival doggrel have struck a fair balance between royalists and republicans, between high churchmen and puritans; and the comparison may serve to soften the rancour of honest men, of all opinions, toward each other. Such recriminations shew more clearly than the most laboured arguments, that the love of power, under whatever disguise, is the same passion, and pursues its object by similar practices. (p. 45)

A review of "M'Fingal: A Modern Epic Poem, in Four Cantos," in The Monthly Review, *London, Vol. X, January, 1793, pp. 34-45.*

William Cullen Bryant   (essay date 1818)

[*Bryant was the first American poet to receive substantial international acclaim. His poetic treatment of the themes of nature and mutability identifies him as one of the earliest figures in the Romantic movement in*

American literature. In the following excerpt, Bryant compares M'Fingal *with* The Progress of Dulness, *preferring the latter.*]

M'Fingal, the most popular of the writings of [John Trumbull], first appeared in the year 1782. This pleasant satire on the adherents of Britain in those times, may be pronounced a tolerably successful imitation of the great work of Butler—though, like every other imitation of that author, it wants that varied and inexhaustible fertility of allusion, which made all subjects of thought—the lightest and most abstruse parts of learning—every thing in the physical and moral world—in art or nature, the playthings of his wit. The work of Trumbull cannot be much praised for the purity of its diction. Yet perhaps great scrupulousness in this particular was not consistent with the plan of the author, and, to give the scenes of his poem their full effect, it might have been thought necessary to adopt the familiar dialect of the country and the times. We think his *Progress of Dulness* a more pleasing poem, as more finished, and more perfect in its kind, and though written in the same manner, more free from the constraint and servility of imitation. The graver poems of Trumbull contain some vigorous and animated declamation. (p. 201)

William Cullen Bryant, "Essay on American Poetry," in The North American Review, *Vol. VII, No. 2, July, 1818, pp. 198-211.*

Samuel Kettell   (essay date 1829)

[*An American author and editor, Kettell is chiefly remembered for his* Specimens of American Poetry, with Critical and Biographical Notices, *compiled in answer to the question "Who reads an American book?" In the following excerpt from that work, Kettell discusses the influence of* M'Fingal *during the American Revolution.*]

Although Trumbull's fame as a poet has rested mainly upon *M'Fingal,* yet the modern reader would probably assign as high a rank to his earliest piece, *The Progress of Dulness.* This is a satire in Hudibrastic verse upon the errors and absurdities which were then prevalent in the literature and manners of the author's neighborhood. The pedantry and ignorance of the members of the learned professions, the preposterous customs on the subject of education, the coxcombry and conceit of fashionable life, are handled with a felicitous power of sarcasm. Had he produced no other work than this, it would have sufficed to bring him into distinguished notice. But it has attracted little regard compared to the more popular and national work, *M'Fingal.*

M'Fingal has had a greater celebrity than any other American poem, owing partly to its intrinsic merit, but more, doubtless, to the time and circumstances which gave it birth. It was written, at the request of some members of the American Congress, in 1775, with a view to aid the struggle for independence, which had then just begun. The period had arrived when England and America were to be separated. Reflecting men saw the necessity of this, long before it was visible to the common people. A redress of grievances had been the end of their views; the thought of independence was forbidden by their reverence for their king, their love of England, and their respect for its power.

It was a task no less difficult than necessary for the crisis, that the American people should be roused to active and bloody resistance; that the breasts which had been accustomed to glow with loyalty should burn with indignation; that the filial feeling should give place to resentment; and that the language of prayer and petition should be laid aside for the accents of hostility.

In this critical moment the keen sighted politicians of the day did not overlook the influence, which the still lingering respect toward England, and the deep sense of her power, must exert over the colonists. They understood the advantage which would be gained, if this respect and dread of power could be made to give place to scorn and contempt. They foresaw that if the Americans could despise the English, they would more boldly face them in battle; that if they could once laugh at them by their firesides, and in the camp, at night, they would beat them in the field on the morrow.

The wit of Trumbull was in this extremity a better reinforcement than regiments. He had been an attentive spectator of the events which had preceded, and which opened the war; he had watched with a satirical eye, the errors and follies of England and her officers; and felt with indignation the wrongs which had been inflicted on his country. He had already drawn more than one keen shaft from his quiver, and found, with unerring aim, the vital part of his country's enemies. But there was now a requisition for help on all who could give it; and while others, at the earliest call of a suffering country, drained their purses and their veins in her behalf, Trumbull could not refuse the contribution of such timely aid as he had to bestow.

It was at this moment, and to serve this emergency, that *M'Fingal* was written. Its direct object was to pour contempt upon the British and their Tory friends, and consequently to inspire the lovers of liberty with confidence, and give point and efficacy to their indignation. It is probable that the author, now but twentyfive years of age, appearing on the stage when everything was turned to politics, educated in a country where the taste for the luxuries of literature was either not formed, or was absorbed in more stirring excitements, and when literary competition did not yet exert much influence in stimulating to effort, had little in view, in composing *M'Fingal,* beyond the immediate political effect. His purpose was, to influence immediately and strongly the common people. The style and subject of his work were therefore prescribed to him by the occasion which he was to serve; the one must be coarse and familiar, adapted to the plain apprehension of common minds; the other must be the British and the Tory party. He was not at liberty to choose, even if his taste had inclined him, to the higher and more inspired language of the muse; nor might he seize upon some great event, over which distance had thrown its mist, and to which time had lent its enchantment. He must be popular, at the risk of being short lived; he must serve his country, and take the chance of being remembered as a patriot, and forgotten as a poet.

In truth, we suspect if *M'Fingal* had not lived beyond the war, and, after having answered it immediate design, had passed with other productions of the day into oblivion; that the author had not been disappointed. Such must have been the fate of a work written in the heat of party excitement, and possessing in its very constitution the ele-

ments of decay, if, indeed, the breathing of genius may not have endowed it with immortality.

M'Fingal is a burlesque poem, directed against the enemies of American liberty, and holding up to particular scorn and contempt, the tories and the British officers, naval, military, and civil, in America. It is a mercile satire throughout: whatever it touches, it transforms; kings, ministers, lords, bishops, generals, judges, admirals, all take their turn, and become in the light or associations in which they are exhibited, alternately the objects of our merriment, hatred, or scorn. So wedded is the author to his vein of satire, that even M'Fingal, the friend of England, and the champion of the tories, is made the undisguised scoffer of both them and their cause.

The story of *M'Fingal* is this: the hero, a Scotchman, and justice of the peace in a town near Boston, and who had two gifts by virtue of his birth, "rebellion and the second sight," goes to a town meeting, where he and one Honorius, make speeches at each other through two whole cantos. At the end of the second canto, the town meeting breaks up tumultuously; and the people gather round a liberty pole erected by the mob. Here M'Fingal makes a virulent speech of near two hundred lines, at the end of which he is pursued, and brought back to the liberty pole, where the constable is swung aloft, and M'Fingal tarred and feathered. M'Fingal is set at liberty; he goes home, and at night makes a speech to some of his tory friends in his cellar, extending through the rest of the poem, leaving only room to tell that the mob broke off his address in the middle by assaulting the house, and that M'Fingal escaped to Boston. These are all the incidents, and this the whole story of a poem of four cantos, and consisting of some thousands of lines.

The work is written after the manner of *Hudibras,* sometimes affecting the carelessness of its versification and the drollery of its rhymes, and occasionally verging into the more artificial and dignified manner of Pope. It often condescends to deal in the coarse language and revolting images of its prototype, and even surpasses it, we think, in free allusions to scripture. In its general manner, it is characterized by less of levity than *Hudibras,* and more of vivacity than the *Dunciad.* It frequently and happily imitates them both, sometimes in the quaint humor of Butler, exhibiting new and striking analogies between images altogether remote and dissimilar; and sometimes in the unrelenting manner of Pope, holding up the objects of its satire to hatred and abhorrence. If it seldom or never rivals the more exquisite passages of either, we are almost ready to admit that it is because they are inimitable.

The gifts of the author seem to lie in a keen perception of the ridiculous, and a ready talent for seizing upon the true point of humor. The excellencies of the poem therefore are found in the address with which a satirical light is made to play upon the objects of the writer's fancy, and that power of ridicule, which like an uneven glass, throws everything that is seen through it, into absurd and ridiculous positions. The principal defects of the work, considered without relation to the objects for which it was written, are a want of creative imagination; a barrenness of incident and consequent deficiency of interest in the story; a cast of extravagance and a tone of bitterness in the sentiments, which, however natural for the time and fitting to the occasion, must ever after be beyond the sympathy of the reader.

There is another weighty deduction to be made from the merit of the work. Burlesque poetry is but an inferior species of composition, and the masters of it can claim but a second place in the temple of the muses. We may admit with Johnson that *Hudibras* has made Butler immortal, but we wish with Dryden, that he had written a different work. We feel it to be in some sense a prostitution of poetry, to busy it with the faults and follies of men. The free and chosen haunts of the muse are in the lofty mountains, along the margin of the silver rivulet, through silent valleys, in solitary woods, on the sea-shore, in the blue sky, on the sailing cloud. Here she communes with nature, and discourses of loveliness and beauty. It is not willingly, but by compulsion, that she leaves these scenes for the crowded haunts of men, to deal with vice and deformity. The change is almost fatal to her charms. In the narrow streets of the city we hardly recognize the enchantress. Her white wing becomes soiled and drooping; her brow furrowed with indignation; her lip curled in scorn; a quiver of poisoned arrows is at her back; a whip of scorpions in her hand. The silver music of her voice is gone; her inspired language is exchanged for the vulgar speech of men; her fancy is filled with images of deformity! Who that has been her companion in the lone mountain, by the wild waterfall, and in the trackless wood; when weary, has reposed on beds of wild roses, when thirsty, has kissed the lip of a virgin fountain, that ever before has flowed untouched in its secret bower—who, that has lived and communed with her thus, would wish to see her degraded to the business of a satirist and scourge?

Yet in contemplating *M'Fingal,* if we cannot admire the poet, we must acknowledge the debt we owe the patriot. It is in the light of history and not by the tests of literary criticism, that we would estimate the value of the work. Let it be tried by the stern question, why was it written, and what has it done? the answer is a proud one.—It was dictated by patriotism, and served efficiently the cause it was designed to promote. While most satires have originated in personal malice, or feelings nearly allied to it, this was written in an hour of national trial, to serve the cause of justice and humanity. The *Dunciad* was designed to blast the enemies of Alexander Pope; *M'Fingal* to confound the enemies of liberty. The higher motives which gave birth to the last, cannot indeed elevate it to the literary rank of the other; yet while critics deny to *M'Fingal* a place among the English classics, the name of Trumbull is honorably registered in the annals of American Independence. (pp. 178-83)

Samuel Kettell, "John Trumbull," in his Specimens of American Poetry, *Vol. I, S. G. Goodrich and Co., 1829, pp. 175-98.*

Frederick Sheldon   (essay date 1865)

[*In the following excerpt, Sheldon notes the popularity of* M'Fingal *but suggests that the work lacks any permanent value.*]

[John] Trumbull's *chef d'œuvre* is *M'Fingal,* begun before the war and finished soon after the peace. The poem covers the whole Revolutionary period, from the Boston tea-

party to the final humiliation of Great Britain: Lord North and General Gage, Hutchinson, Judge Oliver, and Treasurer Gray; Doctors Sam. Peters and Seabury; passive obedience and divine right; no taxation without representation; Rivington the printer, Massachusettensis, and Samuel Adams; Yankee Doodle; who began the war? town-meetings, liberty-poles, mobs, tarring, feathering, and smoking Tories; Tryon, Galloway, Burgoyne, Prescott, Guy Carleton; paper-money, regulation, and tender; in short, all the men and topics which preserve our polyphilosophohistorical societies from lethargic extinction. *M'Fingal* hit the taste of the times; it was very successful. But although thirty editions were sold in shops or hawked about by peddlers, there was no copyright law in the land, and Trumbull took more praise than solid pudding by his poetry. It was reprinted in England, and found its way to France. The Marquis de Chastellux, an author himself, took an especial interest in American literature. He wrote to congratulate Trumbull upon his excellent poem, and took the opportunity to lay down "the conditions prescribed for burlesque poetry." "These, Sir, you have happily seized and perfectly complied with. . . . . I believe that you have rifled every flower which that kind of poetry could offer. . . . Nor do I hesitate to assure you that I prefer it to every work of the kind,—even to *Hudibras.*" Notwithstanding the opinion of the pompous Marquis, nobody reads *M'Fingal.* Time has blotted out most of the four cantos. There are left a few lines, often quoted by gentlemen of the press, and invariably ascribed to *Hudibras:*—

> For any man with half an eye
> What stands before him can espy;
> But optics sharp it needs, I ween,
> To see what is not to be seen.
>
> But as some muskets so contrive it
> As oft to miss the mark they drive at,
> And though well aimed at duck or plover,
> Bear wide and kick their owners over.
>
> No man e'er felt the halter draw
> With good opinion of the law.

The last two verses have passed into immortality as a proverb. Perhaps a few other grains of corn might be picked out of these hundred and seventy pages of chaff. (p. 192)

Frederick Sheldon, "The Pleiades of Connecticut," in The Atlantic Monthly, *Vol. XV, No. LXXXVIII, February, 1865, pp. 187-201.*

Moses Coit Tyler   (essay date 1898)

[*An American teacher, minister, and literary historian, Tyler was one of the first critics to adopt a scholarly approach to the study of American literature. His* History of American Literature during the Colonial Time: 1607-1765 *(1878) and* The Literary History of the American Revolution: 1763-1783 *are examples of his methodical research, authoritative style, and keen insight. In the following excerpt from the latter work, Tyler argues against the traditional view of* M'Fingal *as an imitation of* Hudibras, *claiming that the distinctive features of* M'Fingal *can more easily be attributed to the influence of Charles Churchill.*]

The traditional and, indeed, the stereotyped criticism upon *M'Fingal,* that it is an imitation of *Hudibras,* is undoubtedly the judgment most naturally formed at the first glance, and from indications apparent on the surface of the two poems. Thus, *M'Fingal* certainly follows *Hudibras* in its general literary type—that of the burlesque epic; and yet even here one needs to observe the distinction that, while Butler chose the low burlesque, which does not admit of grave or elevated passages, his follower adopted the high burlesque, and availed himself of the privilege it confers, by transitions that are serious and dignified. Then, too, the verse of *M'Fingal* is obviously the verse which since Butler's time has been called Hudibrastic, that is, the rhymed iambic tetrameters of the earlier English poets, depraved to the droll uses of burlesque by the Butlerian peculiarities, to wit, the clipping of words, the suppression of syllables, colloquial jargon, a certain rapid, ridiculous jig-like movement, and the jingle of unexpected, fantastic, and often imperfect rhymes. Furthermore, in many places Trumbull has so perfectly caught the manner of Butler, that he easily passes for him in quotation. This is especially the case with some of those shrewd aphorismal couplets which abound in *M'Fingal* as they do in *Hudibras,* and which, as taken from the former, are sometimes attributed to the latter.

Beyond these aspects of resemblance, it is doubtful whether the relation of *M'Fingal* to *Hudibras* be not rather one of contrast than of imitation. The hero of the one poem is a pedantic Puritan radical of the time of Oliver Cromwell; the hero of the other is a garrulous and preposterous high-church Scottish-American conservative of the time of George the Third. Each poem is an attempt to exhibit, chiefly through the speeches and the ludicrous and lugubrious adventures of its hero, the questions at issue in a period of revolutionary convulsion; but the earlier poem is a satire on the ideas and methods of the party of progress, while the later one is a satire on the ideas and methods of the party of conservatism. Moreover, in plot, in arrangement, in incident, there is in *M'Fingal* scarcely a trait that can be accounted as a reproduction of *Hudibras.* Finally, in the essential qualities of Hudibrastic wit,—in oddity of comparison, in extravagance of fancy, and in the amusing effects produced by a sudden and grotesque assemblage of remote historical and literary allusions,—there is in *M'Fingal* little apparent effort to follow its prototype.

The truth is, that a much closer intellectual kinship existed between Trumbull and Charles Churchill, than between Trumbull and Samuel Butler; and so far as Trumbull's originality in satire was moulded and tinged by the manner of any other satirist, it was not so much by the author of *Hudibras,* as it was by his own powerful contemporary, the author of the "Prophecy of Famine," and of "The Ghost." Churchill was Trumbull's true model. It is to Churchill's influence that we are to attribute peculiarities in *M'Fingal* far more fundamental and decisive than any which can be traced to the influence of any other writer. Indeed, what should perhaps be regarded as the most serious fault in *M'Fingal,*—the alien and unreal note imparted to this New England mock-epic by the prominence of the Scottish element in the satire,—can be accounted for in this way, and in this way only. Of such a poem the hero at least should have been not only a native but a typical New Englander, and thus the main force of the satire

should have been made to fall, as the author undoubtedly meant that it should fall, upon that powerful class of New England conservatives who then stood forth against the politics of the Revolution. By taking for this Yankee epic a title which, owing to peculiar literary associations, was then intensely Scottish, and by concentrating the reader's derision upon its Scottish hero, and upon Malcolm, his Scottish confederate, a certain local genuineness is lost to the poem; the true direction of the satire is turned aside; and a pair of Scottish Loyalists are dragged in and thrust forward as the real objects of all this satiric venom which really belonged to Loyalists of the pure American type, like Hutchinson, and Leonard, and Oliver. By a glance at the nearly contemporary satires of Churchill, particularly at the two that are mentioned above,—in which the leading note is an angry and contemptuous vituperation of the Scottish element then so prominent in English politics and in English society,—it will be made clear that it was from Churchill that Trumbull derived a trait which, though entirely pertinent and very effective in an English satire of that time, had much less fitness in an American satire, and therefore gave to it a rather pointless and weakening feature.

It would be a mistake, however, to infer that the influence of Churchill upon Trumbull is to be discovered only in Trumbull's faults. This is very far from being the case. For example, the verse of *M'Fingal* seems to have a flow and a freedom characteristic of Churchill: this verse is indeed Hudibrastic, but in the main it is the Hudibrastic verse, not of *Hudibras,* but of "The Ghost." Moreover, in the sprightliness and energy of *M'Fingal,* in the robustness of its thought, in its glow of expression, and in the special quality of its wit, which, for the most part, is direct and spontaneous rather than artificial and subtle, one is apt to recognize the sturdy and invigorating tone of the later English satirist.

We should be doing injustice, also, to the variety and the breadth of Trumbull's literary training, if, in dealing with the composition of *M'Fingal* as revealing the influence of its author's literary masters, we should discover only the influence of Churchill and of Butler. Trumbull was, according to the best opportunity of his place and time, a catholic student of letters; and in all his work as a satirist, particularly in this work, one finds in many quiet and indirect ways, the evidence of his manifold contact with all the masters of his art.

As regards the literary relationships of this poem, one notable peculiarity is its delicate and effective use of parody as a means of humorous effect: itself a burlesque epic, it carries the privilege of burlesque into every detail of style. Through Trumbull's memory, which was of the miraculous sort, there seemed to be ever floating strains and melodies borne to him from the myriad-voiced choir of English song; and continually, as he told of his droll hero, and of his hero's adventures, snatches of English classic verse became entangled in his lines, and were detained by him there, and were comically transformed into travesty. Thus, through the opening lines of *M'Fingal* one hears amusing echoes of the opening lines of *Hudibras;* and as from this beginning of the first canto, one reads on and on to the end of the last canto, the ear is continually caught, and the fancy is titillated, by playful reverberations from the ballad of "Chevy Chase," from *Paradise Lost,* from the poetry of Dryden, of Swift, of Pope, of Prior, of Macpherson, of Gray.

After all that may be said of the uses which Trumbull made of his literary masters, it remains true that his poem of *M'Fingal* is a work of essential originality. The form is an old one; but into that old form Trumbull put the new life of his own soul, and of his own time. He did not invent the burlesque epic; but he did invent his own treatment, under the form of a burlesque epic, of the social and political dispute involved in the American Revolution. In the construction of his poem, he has shown not only originality, but high artistic skill. The plot has a unity, a symmetry, a consistency which one looks for in vain in such masterpieces as *Hudibras* and *The Dunciad;* the story, though a slight one, is sufficient for the comically didactic purpose for which it is framed; in the management of this story the author avoids those bewildering digressions and those excesses of loquacity in which Butler so often loses himself and the company of his readers; finally, the story advances, by a natural and life-like progress, through a variety of ridiculous circumstances, to a conclusion wherein the ludicrous quality of the satire reaches a fitting and powerful culmination.

No literary production was ever a more genuine embodiment of the spirit and life of a people, in the midst of a stirring and world-famous conflict, than is *M'Fingal* an embodiment of the spirit and life of the American people, in the midst of that stupendous conflict which formed our great epoch of national deliverance. Here we find presented to us, with the vividness of a contemporary experience, the very issues which then divided friends and families and neighborhoods, as they did entire colonies, and at last the empire itself; the very persons and passions of the opposing parties; the very spirit and accent and method of political controversy at that time; and at last, those riotous frolics and that hilarious lawlessness with which the Revolutionary patriots were fond of demonstrating their disapproval of the politics of their antagonists. No one can now fully understand and enjoy *M'Fingal* who is not, in a rather special sense, a student of the American Revolution; but he who is so, will find in it an authentic, a marvelously accurate, a most diverting rehearsal of the logic, the anger, and the humor of an epoch in our national experience which can never cease to have for us either a profound importance or an absorbing charm.

Satire is, of course, one of the less noble forms of literary expression; and in satire uttering itself through burlesque, there is special danger of the presence of qualities which are positively ignoble. Yet never was satire employed in a better cause, or for loftier objects, or in a more disinterested spirit. Often has satire been but the ally of partisan selfishness and malice, or of the meanness of personal spite. To add derision to defeat, to overwhelm with scoffs and with pitiless ridicule a great party which was already overwhelmed with disaster, to fling mocks and jibes at men who, never lacking ability or courage, were then crushed and powerless, and able to move neither tongue nor hand in reply—that was the object of the author of *Hudibras.* To appease the stings of literary vanity, to avenge himself on his rivals, to make the world ring with his wrath at a group of paltry and obscure personal enemies—that was the object of the author of *The Dunciad.* Now the author of *M'Fingal* wrote his satire under no personal or petty motive. His poem was a terrific assault on men who, in his opinion, were the public enemies of his country; and he did not delay that assault until they were unable to strike back. *M'Fingal* belongs, indeed, to a type of literature never truly lovely or truly beautiful,—a type of literature hard, bitter, vengeful, often undignified; but the hardness of *M'Fingal,* its bitterness, its vengeful force are directed against persons believed by its author to be the foes—the fashionable and the powerful foes—of human liberty; if at times it surrenders its own dignity, it does so on behalf of the greater dignity of human nature.

That *M'Fingal* is, in its own sphere, a masterpiece, that it has within itself a sort of power never attaching to a mere imitation, is shown by the vast and prolonged impression it has made upon the American people. Immediately upon its first publication it perfectly seized and held the attention of the public. It was everywhere read. "Its popularity was unexampled." It became "the property of newsmongers, hawkers, peddlers, and petty chapmen." Probably as many as forty editions of it have been issued in this country and in England. It was one of the forces which drove forward that enormous movement of human thought and passion which we describe as the American Revolution; and in each of the great agitations of American thought and passion which have occurred since that time, occasioned by the French Revolution, by the war of 1812, and by the war which extinguished American slavery, this scorching satire against social reaction, this jeering burlesque on political obstructiveness, has been reëdited, has been republished, has been sent forth again and again into the world, to renew its mirthful and scornful activity in the ever-renewing battle for human progress. (pp. 443-50)

> *Moses Coit Tyler, "The Satirical Masterpiece of John Trumbull: 1775," in his* The Literary History of the American Revolution, 1763-1783, *Vol. I, 1763-1776, second edition, G. P. Putnam's Sons, 1898, pp. 426-50.*

Annie Russell Marble   (essay date 1907)

[*In the following excerpt, Marble discusses Trumbull's works, focusing on* M'Fingal. *Marble notes that although* M'Fingal *has several defects as a work of literature, it was effective as a piece of political propaganda.*]

The question has been asked . . . whether satire was a natural or an accidental form of literary expression on the part of Trumbull. He once asserted that his native taste was imaginative rather than satirical, and that the latter trend came from the political conditions which confronted and stirred him. Evidence from his literary efforts of varied types, and also from reading some of his keen, satiric pleas and letters, seems to indicate that satire was a legitimate expression of his witty, penetrating mind. Doubtless it was fostered both by the political conflict, and also by his devotion to the English essayists of satirical form. Before the patriotic impulse had awakened within him, he had chosen to write in burlesque and satire. Unlike [American poet Philip Morin] Freneau, he showed no proof of a poetic temperament, before or after the stress of war and national federation. His work that has lived in memory has been that of the satirist and scholar. His only attempts at verse of lyrical kind were labored and stilted.

Among his burlesques, *The Progress of Dulness* will take rank as inventive and forceful. This was conceived when the leaders of progressive methods in education, among whom was Trumbull, were trying to overthrow prejudices and false standards at Yale. The satire was in octosyllabic meter, in three parts, published at intervals of a few months. The first issue told of the career of Tom Brainless, a dull lad who had been sent to college to fritter time away upon titled, uninspiring texts. He succeeded in "hood-winking" professors, so that he was passed through college and entered the school of theology. With the same spiritless, droning routine, he became a minister. In his pulpit he is thus portrayed:

> In awkward tones, nor said nor sung,
> Slow rumbling o'er the faltering tongue,
> Two hours his drawling speech holds on,
> And names it preaching when 'tis done.

The type of the teacher unworthy the name was also satirized:

> Then throned aloft in elbow chair,
> With solemn face and awful air,
> He tries, with ease and unconcern,
> To teach what ne'er himself could learn;
> Gives law and punishment alone,
> Judge, jury, bailiff all in one;
> Holds all good learning must depend
> Upon his rod's extremest end,
> Whose great electric virtue's such
> Each genius brightens at the touch;
> With threats and blows, incitements pressing,
> Drives on his lads to learn each lesson,
> Thinks flogging cures all moral ills
> And breaks their heads to break their wills.

Beside this dull master of the rod is the teacher who was long known as "the book-worm," thus portrayed with justice as well as wit:

> Read ancient authors o'er in vain,
> Nor taste one beauty they contain,
> And plodding on in one dull tone,
> Gain ancient tongues and lose their own.

The first part of this burlesque was reprinted, in a corrected edition, the year after its appearance. In a preface note, Trumbull explained its purport thus:

> The subject is the state of the times in regard to literature and religion. The author was prompted to write by a hope that it might be of use to point out, in a clear, concise, and striking manner, those general errors, that hinder the advantages of education, and the growth of piety. The subject is inexhaustible; nor is my design yet completed.

As proof of the last sentence, he published this same year, 1773, the second part of the burlesque. Here the character ridiculed was Dick Hairbrain, antitype of the first dull collegian, but equally familiar then and today. His foppish airs, his feather brain, his swagger and swearing, his skeptical opinions exploited after a hasty reading of Hume and Voltaire—such qualities were delineated with keen, biting sarcasm. The style in this part was more earnest than in the earlier issue. There were lines of moral teaching, mingled with the portrayal of the rakish student:

> More oaths than words Dick learned to speak,
> And studied knavery more than Greek.

The career of this young man abroad, his excesses and failures to win respect or success, are told with vividness, until

> In lonely age he sinks forlorn,
> Of all, and even himself, the scorn.

To complete the trilogy of characters, misguided and educated according to wrong standards, Trumbull introduced in the third part Miss Harriet Simper, a vain coquette. In a preface the author affirmed "that the foibles we discover in the fair sex arise principally from the neglect of their education, and the mistaken notions they imbibe in their early youth." The same thought was thus expressed in ironical verse:

> And why should girls be learn'd or wise?
> Books only serve to spoil their eyes.
> The studious eye but faintly twinkles,
> And reading paves the way to wrinkles.

To give a touch of romantic unity, Trumbull depicted his coquette in various flirtations; she is scorned by Dick Hairbrain and marries Tom Brainless, to escape the "stigma of being an old maid."

This burlesque was popular as a production of wit, and it exerted no little influence as a rebuke to the conditions of the time which fostered such drones, fops, and coquettes. The pages contain some pictures of society and epigrams which are relevant today, as:

> Follies be multiplied with quickness,
> And whims keep up the family likeness.

> Good sense, like fruit, is rais'd by toil,
> But follies sprout in every soil.

(pp. 119-24)

[In November 1773 Trumbull went to Boston] to the law office of John Adams. This year gave new impulse to his interests and literary activities. He had taken a mild part in urging freedom of expression in America and had praised the tendency toward resistance. Now he came into personal contact with statesmen who had already shown their radical opposition to the Stamp Act and other measures of injustice. Soon after he reached Boston, the affair of the tea-ships took place, and the military discipline directed against Boston increased the political ferment. All these steps, tending toward independence and war, must have impressed a young man so keen and zealous for reform as Trumbull was. His legal chief, John Adams, was recognized as one of the leaders among the patriots and was sent to Philadelphia to attend the Continental Congress of 1774 while Trumbull was in his office.

The influence of these agitations, and the political principles involved, may be read in the literary work of Trumbull during this year and the following. His first writing in verse, **"The Destruction of Babylon"** was probably only the completion of an earlier effort. With the exception of a few lines, which might be applied to the situation in Boston and the incipient thought of freedom, the poem showed no distinct marks of its author's environment. At about the same time he wrote certain light fables in verse, as **"The Owl and the Sparrow"** and **"To a Young Lady Who Requested the Author to Draw Her Character."** These are merely occasional verses, with bits of covert sarcasm.

Quite a new spirit permeates **"An Elegy on the Times,"** which was first printed at Boston, September, 1774. The author said that it was written soon after the Boston Port Bill. It had a tone of sadness as well as of courage, as if Trumbull still hoped that the worst might be averted, but, if necessary, he would defend his country's rights with his pen. A few stanzas show the deepening zeal of this awakened patriot:

> In vain we hope from ministerial pride
> A hand to save us or a heart to bless:
> 'Tis strength, our own, must stem the rushing tide,
> 'Tis our own virtue must command success.

> . . . . .

> Then, tell us, NORTH, for thou art sure to know,
> For have not kings and fortunes made thee great;
> Or lurks not wisdom in th' ennobled brow,
> And dwells no prescience in the robes of state?

> And tell how rapt by freedom's sacred flame
> And fost'ring influence of propitious skies,
> This western world, the last recess of fame,
> Sees in her wilds a new-born empire rise,—

> A new-born empire whose ascendant hour
> Defies its foes, assembled to destroy,
> And like Alcides, with its infant power
> Shall crush those serpents, who its rest annoy.

These stanzas seem faulty judged by poetical canons, but they were superior to the majority of verses of these years. Philip Freneau's best satires began to appear within a few months, but Trumbull preceded in literary evidence of patriotism, combined with keen wit. By his contemporaries he was called "the finest satirical lance of the age," and was urged to write yet other poems for the cause of freedom. He had come into friendly relations with James Otis, John Hancock, John Adams, and Thomas Cushing. The influence of these patriots doubtless incited Trumbull to the burlesque stanzas which were afterward expanded into his masterpiece of satire, *M'Fingal.* To the Marquis de Chastelleux, after *M'Fingal* had become known in Europe as well as in America, Trumbull wrote that "it was written merely with a political view, at the instigation of some of the leading members of the first Congress who urged me to compose a satirical poem upon the events of the campaign of 1775." (pp. 125-28)

The first canto of *M'Fingal,* published in Philadelphia, was soon circulated through the newspapers and reprinted in several editions. It was viewed with dismay by the British leaders, for it was too popular to be counteracted by any Tory satire. The second canto came within the year 1776, but the third part was deferred until 1782.

M'Fingal, the Loyalist, is a well-conceived and sustained character. His introduction was preceded by a few lines of general ridicule:

> When Yankees, skill'd in martial rule,
> First put the British troops to school;
> Instructed them in warlike trade,
> And new manoevres of parade,
> The true war-dance of Yankee reels,
> And *manual exercise* of heels;
> Made them give up, like saints complete,
> The arm of flesh, and trust the feet.
> And work like Christians undissembling,
> Salvation out by fear and trembling;

> Taught Percy fashionable races
> And modern modes of Chevy-Chases;
> From Boston, in his best array,
> Great Squire M'Fingal took his way,
> And grac'd with ensigns of renown,
> Steer'd homeward to his native town.

> . . . . .

> His fathers flourished in the Highlands
> Of Scotia's fog-benighted islands;
> Whence gained our Squire two gifts by right,
> Rebellion and the Second-sight.

In contrast with M'Fingal was the character of Honorius, the staunch Whig, generally considered a portrait of John Adams. In the scene of the town-meeting, which has its forenoon and afternoon sessions respectively in Cantos I and II, Honorius speaks boldly regarding the arrogance and injustice of England and her decline in power. Gage had explained to various colonial officers, among them Governor Trumbull of Connecticut, that he sent his troops to Concord merely "to prevent a civil war." This statement was used with caustic effect in the speech of Honorius, in Canto II:

> There, when the war he chose to wage,
> Shone the benevolence of Gage;
> Sent troops to that ill-omen'd place,
> On errands mere of special grace;
> And all the work he chose them for,
> Was to *prevent a civil war.*
> For which kind purpose he projected
> The truly certain way t' effect it,
> To seize your powder, shot and arms,
> And all your means of doing harms;
> As prudent folks take knives away,
> Lest children cut themselves at play.
> And yet, when this was all his scheme,
> The war you still will charge on him;
> And tho' he oft has sworn and said it,
> Stick close to facts and give no credit.

In a fractious temper, M'Fingal tries to respond, taunting the Whigs with both cowardice and foolishness. Interrupted by sharp questions and sarcasms from Honorius, he pleads in vain the cause of British justice. At last, recognizing that he is losing ground, he passes into a trance of second-sight, and depicts his vision of the grand rewards assured to the Tories who will stand by their king in the conflict. In the great day of British victory—

> Whigs subdued, in slavish awe,
> Our wood shall hew, our water draw,
> And bless that mildness, when past hope,
> Which sav'd their necks from noose of rope.

By this speech of M'Fingal, Honorius has gained a point— exposure of the greed and disloyalty of the Tories—and he breaks forth into an eloquent plea for patriotism. M'Fingal and his friends find their only resource in stirring up a riot by hisses; and thus ends the town-meeting.

When this satire, of fifteen hundred lines, was reprinted in Hartford, London, Boston, and elsewhere, it attracted universal attention. In England there was much speculation as to its authorship. It was accredited to Butler and other wits. Some affirmed that it was the work of a British officer who had been superseded in command, and who chose this method of venting his wrath. In the **"Memoir"** to his *Poetical Works,* Trumbull referred to the various surmises regarding the authorship of *M'Fingal,* and said that there were ascribed to him

> Jests he ne'er uttered, deeds he ne'er atchiev'd,
> Rhymes he ne'er wrote, and lives (thank heaven) he
> never lived.

The fact that Trumbull was the author of this satire was known, however, long before the third canto was written. This came in response to a popular demand. There he depicted his Scottish orator as seized by a mob and tried by a hastily convened court at the foot of a Liberty Pole; he was convicted of Toryism, and condemned to a coat of tar and feathers. The illustration of this scene in later editions was rude, but vigorous. In the last canto the once vainglorious leader of the Loyalists had assembled his anxious, dwindling followers to cheer them with another vision. Meanwhile, the entrance of the Whig forces scattered the company, and the frightened M'Fingal escaped to Boston.

The last portion of the satire was weak, in contrast with the earlier, spirited cantos, although there were two passages of clever construction. The first was the famous scene of the tar-and-feather process, once so popular as a means of punishment. This description by Trumbull was long a favorite "piece" for recital by schoolboy orators:

> So from the high-raised urn the torrents
> Spread down his sides their various currents:
> His flowing wig, as next the brim,
> First met and drank the sable stream;
> Adown his visage stern and grave
> Roll'd and adhered the viscid wave;
> With arms depending as he stood,
> Each cuff capacious holds the flood:
> From nose and chin's remotest end
> The tarry icicles descend;
> Till, all o'erspread, with colors gay,
> He glitter'd to the Western ray
> Like sleet-bound trees in wintry skies,
> Or Lapland idol carved in ice.
> And now the feather-bag display'd
> Is waved in triumph o'er his head,
> And clouds him o'er with feathers missive
> And, down upon the tar adhesive:
> Not Maia's son, with wings for ears,
> Such plumage round his visage wears;
> Not Milton's six-wing'd angel gathers
> Such superfluity of feathers.

There is more wit and ease in the second familiar portion, where M'Fingal makes his recantation, to escape from the taunts of the patriots:

> I here renounce the Pope, the Turks,
> The King, the Devil and all their works;
> And will, set me but once again at ease,
> Turn Whig or Christian, what you please.

This satire, as a whole, may be censured for many offenses against literary taste and many examples of strained meter. It must be regarded, however, not as a finished poem, like Butler's *Hudibras* or Churchill's "The Ghost," although it resembles these in form. It was a hastily written weapon of warfare. Its purpose was utilitarian and its effect upon the contending parties cannot be overstated. It represented progressive patriotism against reactionary fears. Few writings of that day reached such a wide circulation. It was reprinted in piratical editions until, we are told, it brought about, in 1783, the passage of an "Act for the Encouragement of Literature and Genius," by the

General Assembly of Connecticut, which secured to authors their copyrights within the state.

While we recognize the specific aim of this burlesque and its immediate service to patriotism, we still find, within its lines, atmosphere and silhouettes of characters of the past which are well worth remembrance, apart from its purpose. Not alone external pictures of the times are here, but also a clear presentation of the mental processes of Whig and Tory, in the period which preceded secession. If the humor is broad and the words often uncouth, such were the traits of the classes which were represented—the sturdy, uneducated farmers, the rude soldiers, the blacksmiths, storekeepers, and other characters of early village life in America. (pp. 129-35)

> Annie Russell Marble, "John Trumbull: Satirist and Scholar," in her Heralds of American Literature, *The University of Chicago Press, 1907, pp. 107-45.*

Clare I. Cogan   (essay date 1922)

[*In the following excerpt, Cogan provides an overview of Trumbull's major works.*]

[John] Trumbull, through personal effort rather than through collegiate encouragement, was steeped in the tradition of [Addison, Steele, Swift, Pope, Prior, Gay, and Johnson]. During his brief span of productivity, he tried his hand, at times with not mean success, at their every type. He experimented—especially in the heroic couplet— now in translation from the classics, now in Biblical paraphrase. He touched upon the subject-matter of Milton and of Gray in odes and elegies that suggest the eighteenth-century beginnings of the Romantic Movement in Great Britain. He presented various forms of social satire, now in the heroic couplet and the philosophic tone of Pope, now in the lighter tone and octosyllabics of Gay's *Fables,* now (as in *The Progress of Dulness*) in a form that verges on the Hudibrastic. And finally, in heroic couplet, in elegiac quatrain, and in ode, but chiefly in the octosyllabics of Butler and of Churchill, Trumbull turned to patriotic themes, and became (notably in *M'Fingal*) the political satirist of the American Revolution. (pp. 80-1)

Of the subjectivism which, never dead, ran quietly beneath the blatant individualism of the eighteenth century, we find traces in the minor writers of the Augustan period. The lyric genius is always romantic, the spirit of quest, the wonder of the individual. The renaissance of this spirit has its beginning on the one side in renewed interest in things Mediaeval, and on the other in Milton's *Il Penseroso.* From the "Goddess sage and holy" to the place of sepulchre is a far cry. Under the stern classic regime, one's feelings had been kept decently repressed; but the new movement allowed of expansiveness, and its followers in search of emotion went to the brink of the grave. Not the eternal *whither,* but the physical aspects of dissolution, gave a theme sung from Blair and Young to our own Bryant. With this revival, a new interest in the elegiac form arose; and it is in this garb that Gray, the high-priest of the Grave-yard School, presents his melancholy lay. The "Elegy" is a more refined type than many of the other contributions of the time. The gentle philosophic spirit, the tone of tenderness, just saved from sentimentalism by the sincerity of the author, the delicate phrasing, the master-handling of a classic form, place it very close to poetry of the highest rank. This work was undoubtedly the influencing factor in Trumbull's **"Elegy on the Death of Mr. Buckingham St. John."** The subject, of course, precluded treating of the humble objects of Gray's masterpiece; the device of having the disembodied St. John relate his own end, is too forced to compare with the tale "some hoary-headed Swain may say." The opening verses show, however, in form, in melody, in personal element, and in melancholic strain, the strongest influences of the "Elegy in the Country Churchyard." Trumbull's consideration of the shortness of life's day,

> The approaching hour shall see the sun no
> more
> Wheel his long course . . .

reminds one strongly of Bryant's later lines:

> Yet a few days, and thee
> The all-beholding sun shall see no more
> In all his course.

A composite of eighteenth century expression in America, to be true to its model, must hold a web of romance.

"On the Vanity of Youthful Expectations" is delightfully young. Two things nearly save young John from being a prig—mudpies and this poem. To normal adolescence, the world is all wrong: from adoring Mother to the veriest stranger extends a conspiracy to cheat one-and-twenty out of his man's estate. Every youth is an incipient Shelley, rebellious and longing for the golden days. With the first love affair ended, the victim appears a sadly wise and disillusioned man.

> Come, Sadness, come, mild sister of Despair, . . .
> How vain the wish, that grasps at things below.

This spirit is not melancholy but melodramatic; and Trumbull is enjoying his misery. As an expression of fleeting emotion in elegiac form, it is of the romantic school, bound round with neo-classic phrases and capitalized personification, as "waves that roar," "when night sits gloomy," "vain Hope," and "gaudy Flattery." The exceptions to the rule were in danger of becoming fixed romantic signposts, as the sporting sheep, rural joys, and ghosts at even-tide! The title reminds one of *The Vanity of Human Wishes;* but Trumbull sobs with Goldsmith rather than philosophizes with Johnson.

For an example of the dominance of the imagination over fact and form, one looks to the **"Ode to Sleep."** Here Trumbull manages an unusual expression of emotion, an outward sign of inner grace, an externalization obtained by metaphor, hyperbole, and sense of aspiration. It is a call back, now to *L'Allegro,* again to *Il Penseroso,* and has an outlook far beyond the geographic boundaries of land and water, and the neo-classic limits of measure and manner:

> Give the astonished soul to rove,
> *Where never sunbeam stretch'd its wide domain. . . .*
> In fields of *uncreated spring,*
> A loft where realms of endless glory rise,
> And *rapture paints* in gold the *landscape of the skies.*

For the purposes of art, the **"Ode"** had better end with the graceful conceit,

> I clasp the fair, . . .
> Press to my heart the dear deceit, and think the
> transport true.

The neo-classical formula for a poet was genius plus training. Trumbull had too little genius and too much training: the over-conventionalized spirit that helped him toward success in satire, made the **"Ode to Sleep"** fall just short of a romantic success.

Saint Beuve's remark that nothing resembles a hollow so much as a swelling, Babbitt uses to illustrate the difference between romanticism and neo-classicism. They are antipodals, the hole conveying an idea of contrast, not negation. The ideals of each are as positive poles, differing not in degree but in kind. Nineteenth century romanticism is not a repudiation of the classic movement at its best; it is a wedding of the lustiness of the Elizabethan period with the elegance of the Augustan—nuptials which Trumbull at least foretells.

"Characters," "a fragment of a Moral Essay in the manner of Pope," is founded upon the premise that

> There's some peculiar in each leaf and grain.

Some now unknown local celebrities measured by this rule are exposed to ridicule; but, even at the time of their belated presentation, the point of the sarcasm must have been lost. The work is interesting merely as an early American specimen of philosophic satire. The characters bear stock neo-classic names, and exhibit stock neo-classic vices. The apostrophe to riches is in kindred spirit to Pope's

> If wealth alone then make and keep us blest,
> Still, still be getting; never, never rest.

Curio's gifts of gold, "trophied arches," "gilded spires," "flowery banks," "lucent waves," "robes of pomp and power," are quite stereotyped; and the intimation that nature's defects are supplied by the art of a stranger parallels Epistle IV, of the *Moral Essays.* Trumbull need not have pointed out the influence of Pope on this work. It bears the unmistakable ear-marks, in its philosophizing content, in its heroic couplet measure, in its striving for antithetical expression and parallel construction, in its word-hoard drawn from the eighteenth century vocabulary, in its characters with the same mark of trade, and in its occasional catalogue method. We have many such lines as

> Gold, houses, chattels, lands, whate'er thy name,

or

> Wit, learning, wisdom, every worth in one,

as against Pope's

> Gold, silver, ivory, vases sculptured high,
> Paint, marble, gems, and robes of Persian dye,

or

> Wit, spirit, faculties, but make it worse.

At times, Trumbull achieves expressions which, quoted apart from the context, would be credited to the Master,

> Fear'd by the brave, and flatter'd by the wise.

And either cease to be, or to be poor.

By learning, taught to doubt and disbelieve,

By reasoning, others and himself deceive.

The philosophic spirit is typical of the youthful Trumbull; and, for a just estimate, consideration must be given his intense moral earnestness. This approach can be better made through the ["Meddler" and "Correspondent"] Essays, where, following the Addisonian tradition of urbanity but with sincerity of purpose and with the didacticism of a preacher, he assails such vanities as incensed the "Spectator," and later, adding a local color, flays impostors religious, educational, medical, literary, and political that infested the North. Trumbull gave to American literature its once distinguishing mark—moral earnestness—and turned the eyes of provincials inward seeking new possibilities.

If the **"Ode to Sleep"** is the high water mark of Trumbull's romantic spirit, his lighter poems may be considered as the flow-tide of his poetic neo-classicism. First places in this society-verse are usually given to Matthew Prior and John Gay. It is quite natural that Trumbull should take the latter as his model, for both Trumbull and Gay are distinctly imitative in thought as well as in form, and lack originality as well as singularity. Certainly, initiative is not one of Trumbull's qualities; his resolute conservatism—what is good enough for Old England is good enough for the New—had found expression in the **"Future Glory of America."** Americans must

> . . . ope heaven's glories to th' astonish'd eye,
> And bid their lays with lofty Milton vie:
> Or wake from nature's themes the moral song,
> And shine with Pope, with Thompson [*sic*] and
>   with Young.

In this spirit of imitation, the lighter verses are cast. Diplomacy is never a characteristic of a satirist; but Trumbull evinces a carelessness verging on foolhardiness when he attempts to give **"Advice to Ladies of a Certain Age."** Prior stuck to "noble, lovely, *little* Peggy," or "dear five year old"; Pope's beshorn virgin is young; but Trumbull dares to address "thou remnant left of ancient time." Youth rushes in where elders fear to tread! Here we get the first use in our author of the octosyllabic verse as practiced by Gay and his followers, a verse-form which we shall find quickly taking on Hudibrastic characteristics. This short tetrameter line seems especially suited to the English humorous genius. It is preëminently a meter for nimbleness of mind, sharpness of wit, and lightness of heart. In this manner, Trumbull defends the Fair from the attacks of the gossips, and warns the latter to repent. Occasionally the rhyme is a bit forced; there is no subtlety in the arraignment, little geniality in the spirit, and no disguise of the didactic purpose; but there are a directness of manner and a confinement of thought to the two lines, that reminds one of Swift. The trenchant phrasing of **M'Fingal** is at least once foreshadowed:

> Thieves heed the arguments of gibbets,
> And for a villain's quick conversion,
> A pillory can outpreach a parson.

With greater success, Trumbull takes up after the fashion of Gay a fable of love, **"The Owl and the Sparrow."** His easy assimilation of classic lore, and his adaptation of it to frivolous use, makes for a lighter touch than is always attained by Gay and his school. We have here in full use the Hudibrastic tricks, of elision, as *met'physician, neighb'ring,* of forced masculine rhyme, *thrush—bush, grove—love,* of feminine rhymes in which two monosyllables are made to correspond to a dissyllable, *pen it— senate.*

> Each stock and stone could prate and gabble,
> Worse than ten labourers of Babel,

gives an exact rhyme of Butler,

> Which made some think, when he did gabble,
> Th' had heard three labourers of Babel;

and Trumbull repeats it in **M'Fingal,**

> Or like the variegated gabble,
> That crazed the carpenters of Babel.

The use here of still another rhyme is of interest:

> Each Bullfrog croak'd in loud bombastic,
> Each Monkey chatter'd Hudibrastic.

The argument that Trumbull is writing with Butler in mind is strengthened when we find in his unpublished **"Epithalamium,"** a work following the progression of Spenser's wedding song, written in bad taste and worse verse, these lines,

> Thou my muse
> Who never didst thine aid refuse,
> Whether I sung in high *bombastic*
> Or sunk to simple *Hudibrastic.*

The fable turns on Pope's line,

> Every woman is at heart a rake.

Of the same genus but different species is the fable **"To a Young Lady, Who Requested the Writer to Draw Her Character."** This is conventional flattery in which grandiloquence is substituted for sincerity and humor.

John Trumbull, English Colonial, seems to have reacted simultaneously against the wordy militancy of the religious leaders and the prevailing system of education in New England. As his opinions on the religious condition found expression in his Essays, so his educational views were first recorded in the "Meddler" papers III, IV, and IX, and later expanded in the **Progress of Dulness.** Leaving aside for the present Trumbull's political contributions, we find that, of his thirty-five hundred odd verses, about fifty per cent. belong to the **Progress.** The name is conformable to the eighteenth century creed—indeed the *Dunciad* evolved from just such a title. But Trumbull's work, in its vigor, spirit, intelligibility, and wit, reminds one more specifically of the moral paintings of Hogarth than of the finish and beauty of line of Pope. This work, written in the midst of his many occupations, bears on the formal side the same mark as his other compositions, that is, an attitude toward life of the British light essayist, deepened by a moral earnestness, and caught up in the tetrameter of Butler. There is, however, another element found only in some of the "Correspondent" papers—the conscious background of New England town and college.

In a letter to Silas Deane dated January 8th, 1772, Trumbull makes mention of his **Progress of Dulness,** the general scheme of which he had already sketched. The vast opportunities for satire on methods of education and the proceedings of the clergy, the author appreciates but is hesitant to stress, not wishing "to make a new set of enemies." Deane, apparently having no such scruples, would advise a broadening and deepening of the work, to which Trumbull replies "perhaps I may." The force of the satire on both points makes one feel that Deane triumphed. The brief, prefacing Part I, explains in detail motive and plan, and leaves no vital message for Tom Brainless to deliver. As an indictment of actual conditions in school and church, the work shows study of the situation, clear thinking, and hardheaded judgment. Tom's progression to college is much the same as that of the wealthy country child of "Meddler" IX.

> The young lad . . . if he is an only child, or has tender parents, . . . is discovered to be a remarkable genius, and as soon put to school. The parents, [are] confirmed in this notion by the schoolmaster, who is often a dunce and generally a parasite.

Addison's fairy touch Trumbull does not understand; his is the hit-and-hit-again system. The careers of his lads and lass he follows from early beginning to age, leaving nothing to the imagination. Tom, without undue exertion, reaches college, suffers acutely from prevalent college maladies of headache and eye-strain, dozes through four years, and comes forth with a sheep-skin.

In this instance, however, the story is not the thing. Trumbull is at his best when, using it as a spring board, he jumps to such questions as the place of the classics in college education, the proper method of their presentation, and the relative importance of the sciences. Again, in the earnestness of the reformer, he interrupts the story to make direct comment; and in these passages one catches an echo of Pope, emphasized occasionally by such a borrowing as

> Thy space a point, thy life a day,

Which undoubtedly is a rephrasing to fit another metre of

> His time a moment, and a point his space.

(pp. 83-92)

En route to the ministry, Tom is, for forty pounds a year, sidetracked into teaching. At the expiration of the term, he resigns, much to the joy of the children, and the sorrow of the parents who must

> . . . Seek again, their school to keep,
> One just as good, *and just as cheap.*

Even Trumbull does not feel a necessity for explaining! But on with Tom to the ministry he goes, with only a plaintive

> Perhaps with genius we'd dispense;
> But sure we look at least for sense.

This is not mere social satire; the verse is but the froth of sane and serious thinking. The doctrine is not of destruction, but of conservation; and, for its propagation, Trumbull becomes as great a controversialist as his enemies in the opposing camps.

The beau and the belle of Addisonian ancestry are treated in much the same way in Parts II and III. Convivial Dick Hairbrain finds an extramural college life suited to his spe-

cial faculties; and, as the lad is bent, the man inclines, until, too old for further joys, he repents; the judgment is Trumbull's, not mine. Miss Simper is of the class of women who so look, that they need not be heard. Trumbull, trained under a mother of education and ability, rebels at this status, and advocates education as a panacea. After Harriet, a cure is required. The fair lady of many flirtations, she falls victim to the wiles of Dick; but that gentleman, devoted to life, liberty, and pursuit of his own happiness, steps aside; and Harriet is forced to bestow her hand on the Reverend Tom.

The Progress of Dulness is satire, purely intellectual, with no trace of tenderness or emotion, and with nothing of the divine understanding that can forgive men for their very childishness. It lacks the geniality of Addison, the brotherhood of Steele. One is minded more of the harshness of Swift, without his personal rancour, the keenness of Butler, without the peculiarities that mark his style, the vision of Dryden, without the dignity of his matter and manner. It is not good poetry as poetry: no single verse challenges attention for beauty of form or of conception. But the thought carries the lines, and the strong common sense, lightened by humor tinged with irony, gives frequently a terseness of expression that makes for quotability.

Trumbull always hitched his wagon to a literary star with the result that he challenges comparison with the greatest of eighteenth century writers. This fact exposes his weaknesses; but it is nevertheless a not unworthy compliment to the aspirations of the American youth, or to his accomplishments that bear the indubitable mark of his ambition.

The early struggles attending the nation's birth found but little echo in Trumbull's poetry; and, were it not for his outburst at the very moment of America's need, one would feel that the passing events but little stirred him. The **"Future Glory of America"** (1770) predicts her greatness in Arts. The heroic couplets **"Addressed to Messrs. Dwight and Barlow, on the Projected Publication of Their Poems in London"** (1775) are interesting in light of the feud, largely American, over "native" literature. But of impending war there is no word.

The **"Elegy on the Times"** (1774) and the **"Genius of America"** (1777-78) show an aroused Trumbull: in the first, colonial, provincial if you will, but with a devotion to liberty which in the second becomes a fixed determination to protect and save her. The moral of the **"Elegy"** is of the Pollyanna type. Probable chastisement of England does not enter into the prophecy. America, the good child, will be freed; and John Bull, the proverbial bad boy, will be punished by—possibly poetic justice. The sixty-eight stanzas of the poem are mostly given over to stock eighteenth century phrases, "hostile beaks," "pointed thunders," "bloody standards," mixed occasionally with "sympathetic tears." But let us remember that, in all this, there is only a hint of rebellion; and, when we consider that it is in celebration of the "Tea Party," and written by a law student in the office of John Adams, the **"Elegy"** is very mild indeed.

The **"Genius of America: An Ode,"** consists of sixteen stanzas, the last three of which were written to commemorate "the expulsion of the British forces from the continent to Staten and New-York Islands, after the battle of Monmouth." The poem may be an attempt at patriotic expression. "Proud Albion" is accused for her unjust assaults; the glories of Washington, Warren, Putnam, and Greene, are related; the effects of war are dissected; but there is not one soul-stirring call to arms, not a word that the eager young defenders might cherish in their hearts, not a gleam of comfort for those who are bereaved.

Trumbull, despite his own estimate, was not temperamentally a poet; he was by nature a reformer, and perhaps the law gave outlet to this corrective tendency. His reactions against local conditions would never have perpetuated his name. His meed of fame after a century and a half is due entirely to his literary warfare in favor of America independent.

The first really incendiary article which can be definitely ascribed to Trumbull, is his burlesque of the broadside issued by General Gage, June 12, 1775. Notes in warfare are not particularly impressive, and this one in parody was published in two sections in the *Connecticut Journal and Hartford Weekly Intelligencer,* for August 7th and 14th. To us the burlesque carries an appeal stronger than its undeniable cleverness, and that is its temerity. In the doubtful state of the colonies, it required no small courage thus to stimulate a nation's morale. Gage and Trumbull's accounts of the Lexington affair are typical examples of their respective "Proclamations":

> A number of armed persons, to the amount of many thousands, assembled on the 19th of April last, and from behind walls and lurking holes, attacked a detachment of the King's troops, who not suspecting so consummate an act of phrenzy, unprepared for vengeance, and willing to decline it, made use of their arms only in their own defence. Since that period the rebels, deriving confidence from impunity, have added insult to outrage; have repeatedly fired upon the king's ships and subjects, with cannon and small-arms; Have possessed the roads, and other communications by which the Town of Boston was supplied with provisions; with a perposterous parade of military arrangement, they affect to hold the army besieged.

Of which Trumbull says:

> And now to tell the things that past
> The nineteenth day of April last,
> Of your armed rebels, twenty dozen,
> Whom our fears multiplied to thousands, . . .
> Attack'd our peaceful troops, I sent,
> For plunder, not for slaughter meant;
> Who little mischief then had done,
> But killed twelve men at Lexington;
> Who show'd their love to peace and virtue,
> And prov'd they'd no intent to hurt you.
> For did not every reg'lar run,
> As soon as e'er you fir'd a gun; . . .
> Convey'd themselves with speed away,
> Full twenty miles in half a day . . .
> And since assuming airs so tall,
> Because we did not kill you all,
> Have dar'd with jibes and jeers confounded,
> Insult the brave, whose backs you wounded; . . .
> Fire on us at your will, and shut
> The town as tho' ye'd starve us out,
> And with parade preposterous hedg'd,
> Affect to hold us here besieg'd,
> (Tho' we, who still command the seas,
> Can run away whene'er we please.)

J. Hammond Trumbull was the first to point out that, of the two hundred and sixteen lines of this burlesque, fifty were later incorporated in the *M'Fingal.*

The invigorating effect of the **"Proclamation"** perhaps was the reason that Trumbull, when America's fortune was at low ebb, was called upon for another contribution. His response, *M'Fingal,* is a brave piece in face of trouble and disaster. At the time, it was welcomed here and abroad as a clever imitation of Butler; and, in later years, a probable influence by Churchill has been alleged. Both contentions are true; and still neither fact is strong enough to account for *M'Fingal*'s popularity. Not the art of the poem, but its tone of uncompromising devotion to freedom, its picture, its caricature if you will, of the troublous period of our nation's youth, explain its republication especially at times of great national consciousness. The twenty odd editions of the poem before 1800 are accounted for by the Revolution and its aftermath; the editions ascribed by the *Cambridge History of American Literature* to Baltimore, 1812, Augusta, 1813, and Hallowell, 1813, synchronize with the beginning of America's "second war for independence," as the edition of Hudson, 1816, and the inclusion of *M'Fingal* in the complete *Poetical Works* of Trumbull, 1820, follow that war's conclusion; and the Lossing editions of 1860 and 1864 consciously or unconsciously voice the patriotism of the period of the Civil War. (pp. 92-7)

The first edition of *M'Fingal,* consisting of one canto, and printed in Philadelphia where the second Continental Congress was then in session, bears the date 1775. It was, however, really issued early in 1776—almost at the same moment as Paine's *Common Sense.* The same year saw it reprinted in London. These two editions, each consisting of 1480 lines, differ in but one particular: in the English edition, the names of Bute and Mansfield are represented by initials. In the completed version, 1782, the original poem with but slight changes—and these in way of additions—becomes the first two cantos, while the new material forms the third and fourth. The first two cantos describe a town meeting—evidently not very far from Boston—in which the opposing arguments of Whig and Tory are presented by Honorius the rebel and Squire M'Fingal the loyalist. Such is the presentation, however, that not only the speeches of Honorius—Give us liberty or give us death!—but also the argument of M'Fingal—Whatever is is right!—tend to strengthen the case against the rule of Britain. Trumbull has here a subtle advantage in being able to write the addresses of both sides! In the third canto, argument gives place to action: the mob presents M'Fingal with a coat of tar and feathers and carts him through the town. In the fourth canto, M'Fingal, humbled and converted, makes to his own followers a final speech in which, from the vantage-point of Trumbull in 1782, he "foresees" unerringly the outcome of the war.

The influence of Churchill upon Trumbull's epic, appears both in its verse-form and in its subject-matter. In making the hero a Scotchman gifted with second sight—when so many perfectly good New England loyalists were at hand—this influence has been unfortunate. M'Fingal's nationality tends to obscure the fact that, after all, the struggle was primarily a civil strife. As for the verse-form of the poem, it is the octosyllabic couplet of Churchill's "The Ghost," but with more of the peculiarities that are associated with Butler's *Hudibras.* Churchill and Trumbull were both intellectually superior to Butler. The former assailed bitterly men of prominence, of success; Trumbull leveled his attack at the enemy when his own cause seemed almost hopeless; Butler, however, made game of a lost cause. Churchill makes some attempt at characterization; but Trumbull's characters like Butler's are merely pegs upon which to hang his ideas, about which to cluster his epigrammatic sentences, his pointed apothegms, his unexpected allusions (the fruit of his wide reading), his quaint turns of expression, and his unusual and fanciful rhymes. The vulgarity of both of his predecessors Trumbull escapes. The usual accompaniments of Hudibrastic verse, as to rhymes and elisions, we have in full measure—good, bad, and indifferent; but Trumbull rarely resorts to the use of Latin terms, of words in an unusual sense, or to unusual words. His erudition allows of the most foreign and unexpected comparisons and allusions. Milton, Virgil, Blackstone, Homer, Waller, Cervantes, Aristophanes, and a score of others flit across the pages; but bookishness is counterbalanced by the popular journalistic touch, and so the danger of too great subtlety is averted.

Like all satirists, Trumbull is partisan; the cause of England is painted black; the actions of her armed men are such as we have been taught belong only to the Teutons; their leaders are stupid or worse; and above and beyond all, that bugbear of bigots, the power of Rome, is second-sighted by Trumbull as by his lineal descendants in this generation. Aloft and alone, the emblem of purity, stands America, triumphant.

With *M'Fingal* ends Trumbull's literary career. With the exception of contributions to *The Anarchiad,* which are indistinguishable from those of his collaborators, Trumbull forsakes the Muse and worships at the shrine of Justice. Unlike his principal contemporary among American poets, Trumbull escaped the ultra-radical influences of the French Revolution and thereby escaped also the epithet which Washington flung at that contemporary: "that *rascal* Freneau." Unlike Freneau, although he lived to see the war of 1812, he did not sing its naval victories. But Trumbull, whatever be his limitations as a poet, is worthy of a rereading if only for his success in his three major works: the romantic beauty of portions of his **"Ode to Sleep,"** his earnest demand, in *The Progress of Dulness,* for educational reform, and, in *M'Fingal,* his illustration of the fact that, in the America of the Revolution, it was possible to be at the same time an effective political satirist and a gentleman. (pp. 97-9)

> *Clare I. Cogan, "John Trumbull: Satirist," in*
> The Colonnade: 1919-1922, *Vol. XIV, 1922,*
> *pp. 79-99.*

Alexander Cowie   (essay date 1931)

[*In the following excerpt, Cowie examines* M'Fingal, *arguing that Trumbull's aim in writing the poem was more literary and less revolutionary than has generally been acknowledged.*]

The tendency of our literary historians to assign individual writers to groups or schools for purposes of general criticism and interpretation has its uses, particularly where minor writers are concerned; but occasionally such a prac-

tice leads to serious misinterpretation of a writer who, although he resembles the group in many respects, is fundamentally different in temperament or literary methods. It has been customary to refer to John Trumbull as if he were a flaming revolutionist of the same stripe as Paine or Freneau and to credit him with an all-absorbing love of country which impelled him to write his greatest poem, *M'Fingal.* With the exception of V. L. Parrington, who does not go deeply into the matter, historians and critics have generally followed one another in making unfounded comments touching Trumbull's revolutionary caliber. M. C. Tyler, for example, speaks of the "fierce note" which one finds in Trumbull's poetry after 1774 and of the poet's "strain of passionate sympathy with the direction and tone of . . . Revolutionary politics." Carl Holliday confidently asserts that Trumbull composed *M'Fingal* "not through an itching for fame, but through genuine love of country." In *The Cambridge History of American Literature* Will Howe writes of the "anger" with which Trumbull composed his epic.

Inasmuch as Trumbull sided with the Colonies against the Crown, it is perhaps natural to assume hastily that his motives in writing the poem were purely patriotic and that he wrote it spontaneously in a mood of fierce indignation. Yet a closer examination of *M'Fingal* leads to the belief that although Trumbull by no means harbored Loyalist opinion as definitely as Crèvecoeur, he was far from a bigoted Whig even at the outbreak of the Revolution. In Cantos I and II (written 1775) he satirizes not only the Tory point of view but the town-meeting as a whole. He raises laughter at the Colonists for their indecision in the face of varying "winds of doctrine," and he rebukes them for their boisterous conduct. The Squire acidly ridicules the Whigs' mode of conducting an argument, and in a trenchant speech he charges them with ingratitude. Moreover, their patriotism, he finds, is not unmixed with self-interest. These and other passages in the first two cantos indicate that Trumbull did not write in the uncompromisingly partisan spirit which characterized, for example, Freneau. It is in the third canto, however—which, although not published until 1782, was fully planned and partly written in 1775—that Trumbull loosed his keenest shafts of satire at the Whigs. In this part of the poem the unlettered proponents of democracy are mocked in thorough fashion:

> . . . For Liberty, in your own by-sense,
> Is but for crimes a patent license,

to

> Dispute and pray and fight and groan
> For public good, and mean your own;
>
> . . . . .
>
> And when by clamours and confusions,
> Your freedom's grown a public nuisance,
> Cry "Liberty," with powerful yearning,
> As he does "Fire!" whose house is burning;
> Though he already has much more
> Than he can find occasion for.
> While every clown that tills the plains,
> Though bankrupt in estate and brains,
> By this new light transform'd to traitor,
> Forsakes his plough to turn dictator,
> Starts an haranguing chief of Whigs,
> And drags you by the ear, like pigs.
> All bluster, arm'd with factious licence,

New-born at once to politicians.
Each leather-apron'd dunce, grown wise,
Presents his forward face t'advise,
And tatter'd legislators meet,
From every workshop through the street.
His goose the tailor finds new use in,
To patch and turn the Constitution;
The blacksmith comes with sledge and grate
To iron-bind the wheels of state;
The quack forbears his patients' souse,
To purge the Council and the House;
The tinker quits his moulds and doxies,
To cast assembly-men and proxies.
From dunghills deep of blackest hue,
Your dirt-bred patriots spring to view,
To wealth and power and honors rise,
Like new-wing'd maggots changed to flies . . .

First and last throughout *M'Fingal,* Trumbull introduced a number of condemnations of raucous democracy which were so aptly phrased that for many years after the Revolution they were torn from their contexts and used by the Federalists as texts for diatribes against those radical moves which threatened the stability of the government. Most of the vituperation of the Whigs in the poem issues, to be sure, from the mouth of the Tory Squire; and the arguments against the Whigs are of course far outweighed by the ridicule of the Loyalists. Yet it is obvious that Trumbull wrote many of the Squire's speeches *con amore;* and the fairness, not to say generosity, with which Trumbull states the case against the rebels moves one to inquire how far it is reasonable to characterize the poet as a revolutionist, a blind partisan of "liberty." A brief review of some of the aspects of his life before he wrote *M'Fingal* may be illuminating.

The son of a conservative clergyman, Trumbull seems to have been from his earliest days a person of irreproachable conduct and respect for law and order. As a sophomore in college, he testified against a fellow-student charged with stealing "fowls." When in 1766 Yale College underwent a revolution which resulted in the forced resignation of President Clap, Trumbull does not appear to have been a leader in the movement. His earliest poems were formal, correct imitations of classical poets and slightly indecent lampoons with a strong literary flavor. After he was graduated from college this future revolutionist, one learns, went home to play in the sand. He carried on his first venture in the satirical essay with the moral support of Timothy Dwight. In 1772 he began the composition of *The Progress of Dulness* but was tempted to give it over lest he "make a new set of Enemies." With the encouragement of Silas Deane he pushed the work to a conclusion. The first part contained a spirited attack upon the methods of education in American colleges, particularly Yale College; but after a stormy reception had been accorded that work, Trumbull proceeded to make the second and third parts far more conventional in their satire, less offensive to particular people and institutions. In 1774, after two years of academic retirement as a Yale tutor, he went to Boston to perfect his legal training in the office of John Adams. Here he was in a position to study intimately the preparations of his countrymen for opposing Great Britain by force. His first poem intended for national circulation, **"An Elegy on the Times"** (1774), called forth by the Boston Port Bill, did indeed attack the British ministry, but it bore a message of prudence that seemed untimely to those in whose eyes the Port Bill was a gross act of tyranny. The

Boston Tea-Party, there is reason to believe, appeared to Trumbull an unjustifiable act of violence. Among the most eloquent stanzas in the Elegy is that in which the poet counsels watchful waiting:

> But oh my friends, the arm of blood restrain,
> (No rage intemp'rate aids the public weal;)
> Nor basely blend, too daring but in vain,
> Th' assassin's madness with the patriot's zeal.
>
> Ours be the manly firmness of the sage . . .

Now, for a twenty-four-year-old youth to recommend "the manly firmness of the sage" in preference to fighting does not argue the presence of much rebel blood in his veins. Indeed this poem was so mild in its tenor that when a year later his New Haven publishers brought out a reprint of it, they felt obliged to apologize for its note of caution. Again, in 1774, on the very eve of the Revolution, Trumbull wrote to John Adams, apropos of the political situation in Massachusetts, that he hoped "no violent measures" would be taken "till the sense of the whole continent" was known. These may have been words of wisdom, but they were not the words of a headlong revolutionist.

The truth is that Trumbull hated mobs and disorder, and he feared violence. When, in August 1774, John Adams, Trumbull's preceptor, left Boston to attend the First Continental Congress, Trumbull, instead of remaining in Boston at the focus of Revolutionary activity, withdrew to New Haven. He took no active part in the Revolution. In 1777, when New Haven was exposed to invasion and, forsooth, business fell off, he retired to the relative security of his native hamlet, Westbury. Revolutionists should be made of sterner stuff!

It appears, then, that although in the period preceding the Revolution Trumbull was definitely aligned with the Whigs, he was by no means a restless rebel agitator. What was his attitude after the commencement of hostilities? He was slow to enter the lists,—slower than Freneau, who was two years his junior. Indeed, instead of volunteering at once as a rebel propagandist, Trumbull had virtually to be conscripted as a penman of the Revolution. In the spring of 1775 Silas Deane suggested that Trumbull write a satire on General Gage, who had succeeded in rendering himself absurd with his proclamations and his generally indiscreet conduct. Trumbull toyed with the idea for a time and then dropped it until late in the summer, when he finally produced a two-hundred line poem, the only revolutionary verse he wrote during the first six months of the war. In the fall of 1775 Trumbull began the composition of *M'Fingal.* Silas Deane's remark had stuck in his mind, and other members of the Continental Congress had joined in a request that Trumbull write a comic poem on the campaigns of 1775. The poet diffidently complied. After he had completed what now stand as Cantos I and II of *M'Fingal,* he wrote a letter to his literary adviser to learn his judgment of the work. This letter has remained practically unknown; and no one, so far as can be ascertained, has related it properly to the subject of Trumbull's zeal as a revolutionary writer. It will be observed how casually the poet speaks of his revolutionary purpose. The letter reads in part:

> Give me leave, Sir, to introduce to your acquaintance one Squire McFingal, a Gentleman, who has

been a Month or six weeks under my care, & who seems desirous of seeing a little of the world. I can say little more in his commendation than that I believe he is perfectly harmless; for indeed I am, upon longer acquaintance, got pretty much out of conceit of him myself, & if you like him no better I shall not wonder if you order him into close Custody. Without a metaphor, you remember, Sir, last spring you recommended to me to attempt a burlesque on General Gage's victories. I wrote you an answer, rather declining it, for reasons I then gave you; & you dropped the matter. It ran, however, in my mind, & I had so much regard for your commands, that I attempted a little sketch or two, but without being able to please myself, & so threw aside the thought for that time. But lately on shewing what I had sketched to one or two friends here, they advised me to throw the whole into some consistent form & go on with it. This (as I had nothing else either of business or amusement) I complied with, & it has produced the thing I here send you. I know it is too long, & too tedious & too—in short, too badly written & has too little wit in it. But I am heartily tired of it, & if it has no merit now, I shall never give it any. Many would call it inelegant & incorrect, but as my notions of the degree of elegance and correctness proper for this style are not just like the Ideas of your merely grammatical Critics, I would not wish it altered in that respect. My Plan you will see comprehends yours, & takes in a larger field,—& one main view I had, was to record a few of the most inveterate enemies of our Country, whom I should wish to see otherwise gibbeted up than in my verse. If you approve of the piece on the whole, do what you please with it. If any particular part do not answer, strike it out, & preserve the connection in any way you chuse. I am sensible many couplets may be omitted without affecting the sense. If it should appear broad [*sic*], more notes would perhaps be wanting. I leave it all to your better judgment. If you shew it to any Gentlemen with you, unless Mr. J. Adams, I must beg you not to tell the author's name. Do not let the Copy go out of your hands. If you suppress it, I beg you to return it to me. I have no other, except the first rough draft. I have been doubting this fortnight, for it is so long since it was finished, whether to send it to you, or consign it to oblivion. On the whole I have determined to send it. And so fourthly & lastly, I have to enquire of you, your opinion of the piece, & what you design to do with it: which I beg the favour of you by a line, to inform me. . . .

This letter reveals four significant facts. First, Trumbull did not himself originate the idea of his writing a satire on the Tories. Second, far from rushing rashly into print upon the outbreak of the Revolution, he dallied with the idea of writing the poem until he had sufficient leisure. Third, he wished to exercise extreme caution to preserve his anonymity. Fourth, he was not so much excited over the opportunity of serving his country as he was concerned to produce a literary work which would be a credit to him.

The foregoing is not meant as a general denial of the effectiveness of *M'Fingal* as a poem written in the Whig interest. Trumbull expended his genius for ridicule generously in lashing the British and American Tories; once engaged in the business of writing satire, he was not the man to leave a task half done. *M'Fingal* remains probably the most distinguished patriotic poem on the subject of the

Revolution written by an American. Although not to be compared in point of political effectiveness with Paine's *Common Sense,* which appeared at the same time as *M'Fingal,* Trumbull's poem was doubtless a serviceable weapon against the Crown. Yet it should be understood that *M'Fingal* was not the work of a reckless radical or a blind revolutionist. It is obvious not only from the letter quoted above but from a perusal of the poem that its author was less concerned for the fate of his country than for the fate of his poem. Rich in classical allusions, verbal subtleties, and echoes of other poets from Homer to Churchill, *M'Fingal,* written in the cause of revolution, smells less of battle than of the lamp. Trumbull was by nature a poet of the library. If the times required his presence in the market-place, why, he submitted with as good grace as possible, but he still bore the mien of a scholar.

For a full understanding of the apparent diffidence with which Trumbull undertook the composition of *M'Fingal,* one additional fact is needed. It had been stipulated by his friends that the poem should be a burlesque. Now, despite Trumbull's great talent for burlesque and satire, he was evidently loath to stake his reputation as a poet on comic or satiric verse. He was aware that even in 1775 Puritan America frowned upon a poet who wasted his substance in comic writing. Moreover, he was himself of the opinion that "humorous writings are usually temporary in their

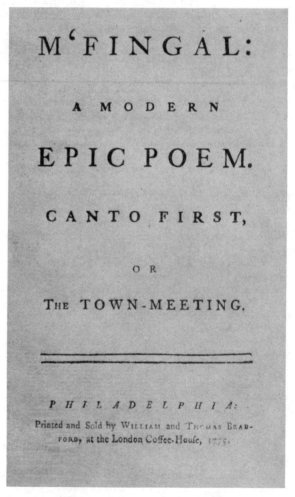

Title page of the first edition of M'Fingal.

Subjects; times change, the ridicule is lost, & the Writer forgotten." Hence from early youth, although he easily threw off brilliant comic poems from time to time, he nursed the delusion that he was destined to excel as a writer of elegiac or of epic poetry, and he sedulously practiced in a serious vein. Even as late as 1785 John Adams wrote in a letter to Trumbull that although *M'Fingal* was all right in its way as a *jeu d'esprit,* Trumbull's great poem remained to be written, namely, a serious heroic work. Trumbull never gratified the wish of Adams, but he well knew that in eighteenth-century America there was a strong demand for "sublime" and "pathetic" poetry,—a demand that was ultimately silenced by Dwight's *Conquest of Canaän* and Barlow's *Columbiad.*

In the light of the material presented in this paper it appears to be a mistake to assume that because Trumbull was a "poet of the Revolution," he was therefore a revolutionist *par excellence.* Seen in its proper perspective, *M'Fingal,* although called forth by a political crisis, is first of all a finished literary production. In view of the poet's proneness to deliberation, it is a little excessive to refer to his "strain of passionate sympathy" with the Revolution. Trumbull's letter to Silas Deane, quoted above, is sufficient refutation of the assertion that he composed *M'Fingal* "not through an itching for fame, but through genuine love of country." Nor did Trumbull probably write with "anger"; some malice there appears to have been in his nature, but his writing seldom if ever shows anger or high indignation.

John Trumbull was an urbane gentleman of sufficient income and aristocratic tastes. His principal powers were not imaginative or emotional, but intellectual. By temperament something of a recluse and a scholar, he loved the quiet of his study. By profe— a lawyer, he deplored all violent interruptions of the established order of things. In his early youth he made spirited, if conventional, attacks upon incompetence and ins   y in education, religion, and medicine. As the years passed, he grew increasingly conservative; after the war he became, like most of the Hartford Wits, a staunch Federalist. At the time of the outbreak of the Revolution his opinions were those of a moderate liberal; consequently when he found himself thrown among the Whigs, he espoused their cause with what warmth his nature possessed: if he was no revolutionist, he was at least a patriot. But more than a patriot he was an ambitious man of letters. He conceived of himself as destined to shine in a rôle for which he was not fitted by nature, that of the elegiac or the epic writer; and he was reluctant to base his claim to fame as a poet upon satire, which was of the devil, or upon humor, which was ephemeral. His friends, however, and circumstance induced him to write the only poem for which posterity could ever thank a man with his gifts, the comic satire, *M'Fingal.* (pp. 287-95)

Alexander Cowie, "John Trumbull as Revolutionist," in American Literature, *Vol. 3, No. 3, November, 1931, pp. 287-95.*

Alexander Cowie   (essay date 1938)

[*In the following essay, Cowie examines Trumbull's critical writings on poetry in order to illuminate his poetic theory.*]

When John Trumbull deserted letters for the law, American literature lost not only a poet but a critic. How great was the loss of the poet is not here the consideration: his achievement for better or worse is well known to scholars. Less is known of the critic. Incidental comments are available in a few of Trumbull's published letters, but the bulk of his critical writing exists only in manuscript form among the Tyler papers at Cornell University. Though most of the items in this collection were written in the 1770's and 1780's, a few date from a later period, so that there are comments, sometimes amounting to no more than memoranda, on a variety of writers from Homer to Byron.

Too much must not be expected of Trumbull's critical utterances in a period when the most ardent devotées scarcely considered a literary career even possible in America. There is little likelihood that he considered publishing these, both because there was slight demand or market for American criticism and because the essays, though occasionally rich in detail and polished in phrase, are as wholes unfinished. Nevertheless they contain materials of real importance to the student of early American criticism. To give some idea of the range and quality of Trumbull's critical writing, discussion will be centered chiefly about a few topics: his conception of a critic; his general outlook on poetry; his use of epic and mock epic forms; his preferences in prosody; his conception of poetic diction; his attitude toward neo-classicism and Pope; and his reaction to romanticism. These items may not altogether coalesce, but they will perhaps serve to introduce an early American writer of moderate-conservative temperament who, despite certain limitations and a few very evident blunders, was a discerning critic with a fairly well-defined set of principles.

Nowhere did Trumbull set down a complete formula for the characteristics of the ideal critic—perhaps because Pope had already done so. It is evident that he had little use for the average journalistic critic, whose judgments, especially if he were a British reviewer appraising an American book, were likely to be determined by national prejudices:

> And see, where yon proud Isle her shore extends
> The cloud of Critics on your Muse descends!
>
> . . . . .
>
> Such men to charm, could Homer's muse avail,
> Who read to cavil, and who write to rail;
> When ardent genius pours the bold sublime,
> Carp at the style or nibble at the rhyme;
> Misstate your thought, misconstrue your design,
> And cite, as samples, every feebler line?
> To praise your muse be your admirer's care;
> Her faults alone the critics make their share.

Among less biased critics, mostly unnamed, he finds the principal fault to be ignorance. In judgment of the classics particularly, modern critics go astray because of their habit of "borrowing mistaken & unjust remarks from each other" for the reason that "they have either not read the Authors they criticise, or are incapable of making proper observations & distinctions." This point he presses home by commenting on certain critics who settle upon Cicero as "the most vainglorious of all antient Writers," whereas if the critics had been "equally versed in the writings of the other Antients, they might have discovered that this vainglorious manner of speaking one's own praises was not peculiar to Cicero, & was rather Characteristic of the antient Ages, than of the Temper of that great Orator."

Less conventionally, he exposes an error of Lord Kames in the latter's comment on Lines 51-58 of Pope's "Eloisa and Abelard," which discuss the value of letters to "some banish'd lover" or "captive maid." Anent this passage Lord Kames had said, "These thoughts . . . are very pretty; they suit Pope extremely, but not Eloisa." "It happens unfortunately for the Critic," observes Trumbull, "that these are the very sentiments of Eloisa, versified, & that no passage in the whole Poem is more closely copied from her original letters"—which he quotes. "Critics," says Trumbull, "should be careful not to betray their ignorance & should avoid their dogmatical assertions till they have a thorough knowledge of the Subject." From making such errors as these, whether in the ancient or in the modern field, Trumbull was protected by his exceptionally wide knowledge of the theory and practice of literature.

Trumbull's theory of poetry must be inferred largely from his critical remarks upon various writers. He was essentially no more creative as a critic than as a poet: chiefly he selected, shaped, and modified such critical tradition as was handed down through the ages. His standards were, of course, preponderantly intellectual, rather than emotional. With Wordsworth's later definition of poetry as the spontaneous overflow of powerful feelings he could have had no sympathy. For him, as a true neo-classicist, the essential thing was not the *generation* of powerful emotion, or even of original thought, but the adequate expression of it. For expression, there were available norms and standards. For thought, there was the generalized experience of the race. He was wary of individuality. There is no question that he accepted Johnson's dictum that "the business of a poet is to examine, not the individual, but the species; to remark general properties and large appearances." He seems to have been in full accord with Johnson's further remark that the poet should "exhibit in his portraits of nature such prominent and striking features as *recall the original to every mind.*" Such an admonition was no encouragement to the poet to venture into new syntheses; it was no spur to the essentially creative mind. The poet was not to establish, but to discover and to record. The new was suspect. With this general attitude Trumbull was in agreement. He himself said that there are two kinds of originality, "originality of thought & Originality of manner," but he wanted too much of neither. The past provided not only all needed precedents for great poetry but also the rules and canons necessary for producing or criticizing poetry. The critical law, deriving ultimately from Aristotle, Horace, Quintilian, and Longinus and expounded by Boileau, Dryden, and Pope, was already complete; Trumbull looked for no additional revelation, no new prophets. Among modern commentators he probably preferred Pope. In most respects he placed Pope above Dryden as a poet:

> Pope in his manner of writing is an inimitable Original. . . . By manner of writing I mean method, style, expression, versification &c. As to his versification I do not regard the objection, that it is formed upon Dryden's. I do not call him an Imitator, who improves an Art to a perfection of which his Master had no Idea.

At all events Trumbull was essentially at home in the eighteenth-century critical and poetical environment symbolized by the sway of Pope, and such adverse comments on it as he made indicate that he wished not the establishment of a new order but a sane revision of the old.

On the theory of that form of composition which he evidently regarded as the highest manifestation of the poetic genius, namely, epic poetry, Trumbull has left very little direct comment. Doubtless he subscribed to the terms laid down in Aristotle's *Poetics,* and there was an end on't. His familiarity with the great epic poems is clear not only from allusions to them in his own works but also from his list of their authors in the order of excellence. First place in the list is occupied jointly by Homer and Milton. Thereafter appear in order Virgil, Tasso, Camoens, Ariosto, Ossian, Spenser, Dwight, Lucan, Ercilla, Statius, Cowley, Claudian, Voltaire, and Silius Italicus. There is no detailed discussion of the writers. The impudence of ranking Dwight immediately below Spenser may be laid partly to near-sighted loyalty: Trumbull and Dwight were fellow-students and fellow-tutors at Yale. Apparently Trumbull did not question the status of *The Faerie Queene* as an epic but rather objected to Spenser's poetry on other grounds. The chief value of *The Faerie Queene,* he thought, lay in its "fanciful descriptions of Scenes that have no foundation in Nature or Possibility." Its allegory he did not prize: "Spenser's Fairy Queen considered merely as an Allegory is a poor, threadbare performance & inferior to Bunyan. . . . He who reads it merely with a View to the Allegory loses all its beauty." Of the other writers listed, Milton receives the most frequent mention in Trumbull's miscellaneous writing. On the basis of other comments it may be inferred that he valued Milton for two principal virtues, his powers of description and his superior organizaton. In *M'Fingal* he cites Milton twelve times as a source for a phrase or an image. Eleven of the references are to *Paradise Lost* and only one to *Paradise Regained.* Of the latter Trumbull had a comparatively low opinion. In 1772 he wrote to Silas Deane:

> I have been lately reading over again Milton's *Paradise Regained.* I entirely am of your opinion that it never did any honour to his genius; but I cannot think quite so meanly of it, as you seem to. The sentiments, though seldom very striking, are just, & some of the descriptions, particularly that of the banquet Satan raises in the second book, the scene of viewing all the kingdoms of the world, in the third, & that of a stormy night, followed by a fair morning towards the end of the fourth, are animated with a considerable portion of Milton's Spirit. On the whole I think it would have done Honor to a Genius of the second rank. We are disgusted with it, because it is beneath what we expect from Milton.

In sum, it is clear that of the four great English poets Trumbull by far preferred Milton. Chaucer he ignored; Shakespeare he referred to only a few times, albeit in terms of homage; Spenser he occasionally cited, seldom borrowed from, and once parodied. Milton he imitated. He honored Milton as the author of the finest epic in our language; and the epic, he appeared to believe, was the highest form of poetry.

Nevertheless Trumbull of course honored the epic more in the breach than in the observance of its basic rules of decorum. And hence arose a problem—a problem peculiarly American. While Dwight was employing a vast Scriptural metaphor to celebrate Washington's service to his country, and Barlow was borrowing the prophetic eye of Columbus to pierce future history, Trumbull was dissipating his poetical energies upon such comparatively small fry as General Gage, Lord North, and Gentlemanly Johnny Burgoyne. His wide learning was diverted to antic uses. In the race for poetical fame, therefore, he seemed destined to lose to both Barlow and Dwight, who with tortoiselike determination plodded through leagues of heroic couplets over a period of from ten to fifteen years. The hare, in the meantime, having frolicked through half his stint (Cantos I and II of *M'Fingal*), lay down and dozed through the Revolution. But the fable must now be reversed, for the hare awoke betimes, finished his journey (Cantos III and IV were published in 1782), and, as posterity at least can see, essentially won the race. Dwight and Barlow duly crossed the line, in 1785 and 1787 respectively, and they were at once granted high praise; but with the passage of time, their performances have suffered serious devaluation.

Yet Trumbull had to fight for the prestige of *M'Fingal:* America apparently preferred the serious epic. Along with the praise that greeted the appearance of the poem, there was also adverse criticism which rankled in Trumbull's mind. In conservative courts of opinion such a satire or burlesque savored slightly of the irreligious. From this objection there were three possible appeals. The first was classical precedent. Had not Homer used burlesque in the twenty-first book of the *Iliad?* Had not Cratinus parodied the epic? Had not Aristophanes parodied Euripides? It is true that Aristotle's *Poetics* says little of comedy (the comic commentary having been lost), yet comedy, though recognized only later than tragedy, was of honorable estate in the Athenian theatre at the time of Aristophanes.

A second appeal might have been to neo-classical practice and opinion. In England, Trumbull's "problem" would not have existed, for there the serious epic had passed its heyday, and lighter forms were being preferred. Dryden had long since written *MacFlecknoe* and Pope *The Rape of the Lock* and *The Dunciad,* leaving his own serious epic, *Brutus,* uncompleted—for reasons which Austin Warren has plausibly conjectured, namely, the poet's "instinctive feeling that the age of the epic had passed and the age of other and more sophisticated forms had arrived; the sense that his own powers were better suited to satire and its derivatives, the mock-heroic and the burlesque." And to this feeling Lord Kames had given the weight of his approval, in part, at least, in 1762:

> A burlesque poem, such as the Lutrin or the Dispensary, may . . . though they assume the air of history, give entertainment chiefly by their pleasant and ludicrous pictures . . . it is not the aim of such a poem, to raise our sympathy: and for that reason a strict imitation of nature is not required. [In a] poem professedly ludicrous . . . the more extravagant the better.

With such opinions as these Trumbull marched comfortably.

When, however, he came to plead for his own burlesque epic, *M'Fingal,* Trumbull used mainly a different appeal more suitable to puritan America (which talked about the classics more than it read them), namely, the Scriptural. In 1783, in an article on copyright, Trumbull complained of the damaging effect on sales of an adverse moral opinion:

> If [the poet] attempt humour and ridicule, he is at once dreaded and hated as a satirist, and every witty passage in his writings shall be wrested and distorted to found a charge of irreligion and profligacy . . .

The problem was brought home to him specifically with reference to a couplet in the fourth canto of *M'Fingal,* which, says Trumbull, "the sour censures of Hypocrisy have fixed upon as prophane, & a proof of the Author's contempt of the Sacred Writings—"

> As Baal his prophets left confounded,
> And Bawling Vot'ries gash'd & wounded.

In order to confute such petty criticism Trumbull had recourse to Scripture itself:

> The beauties of fine writing contained in the Bible have been so often considered in every other view, that it is unnecessary for any one to remark on them, more particularly, than to join with Critics of the best taste, in observing that the Eloquence & Poetry of the Inspired Writers are almost infinitely superior to the Sublimity of the greatest human Genius.—But it may with equal truth be remarked, that altho' the subjects of the sacred Writings, being of the serious kind, do not afford frequent occasions for Humour, Irony or Satire, yet in a variety of instances that style is introduced, & many Passages may be mentioned which have never been excelled by the most witty satirist of antient or modern Ages.

Whereupon Trumbull refers to various passages in Scripture which he regards as satirical, including the fable of Jotham, Elijah's sarcasm on Baal's prophets, portions of the *Book of Job*—most of which he describes as "sarcastic & contemptuous, several of them highly humourous." The very passage in *M'Fingal* cited against him above, he maintains, is no more deeply satirical than passages on the worship of idols in *Isaiah,* Chapter 44. The popularity of *M'Fingal* in its own time, despite such strictures as these, proves that the public was not wholly "grave," but the problem was a real one; and Trumbull was doubtless vexed by well-meant comments to the relative disparagement of *M'Fingal,* as when John Adams wrote to him in 1785 that although *M'Fingal* was very well in its way, yet Trumbull should exert himself to exhibit his gifts for "Poetry of superior kinds," meaning the serious epic. Nor did the feeling against satire and humor wholly recede for a generation to come.

Not only did Trumbull champion the cause of satire and humor, but he attempted to establish its final legitimacy by making suggestions for its improvement. It is one of Trumbull's distinctions that he took the technique of humorous writing seriously. He employed the term *burlesque* somewhat loosely, using it interchangeably with *parody.* He divided it, however, into two distinguishable types, the high burlesque and the low, terms which in modern parlance would be comparable to mock heroic and travesty, the mock heroic treating a little subject in heroic fashion and the travesty debasing a large subject by treating it meanly. *Hudibras* Trumbull regarded as low burlesque and *M'Fingal* as high burlesque. He preferred the high, he said, because it "readily admits a transition to the grave, elevated or sublime." Apparently he was not apprenhensive lest (in Pope's words) "Farce and Epic get a jumbled race," for in *M'Fingal* the debate between Honorius, who seriously expounds his views, and M'Fingal, who trips on his own arguments, is one of the less fortunate features of the poem. Nowhere did Trumbull wholly justify his apparent inconsistency in this respect.

He did, however, insist upon the importance of organization, and as E. A. Richards has pointed out, "*M'Fingal* can easily stand all ordinary tests of conception, design, ingenuity, and vigor." Believing that the bane of most humorous writing is casualness and inconsequentiality, Trumbull asserted that "this kind of poetry [*i.e.*, burlesque] . . . demands a regular plan and design." He professed to having been "disappointed in reading almost every poem of the sort, by its irregularity and deficiency in this view." The author of the *Lutrin*

> gets rid of his story in a very singular way, by desiring his patron to finish it. Garth . . . ends his Dispensary by sending his hero to the Elysian fields to consult the goddess Hygeia, who gravely advises him to go home and apply by petition to the Secretary of State. The fourth book of Pope's Dunciad has scarcely any connection with the former parts, either in manner or design. Indeed all these poems seem to have been intended merely as vehicles for ridicule and satire; and when those topics are exhausted, the work of course is at an end.

A well-articulated design, then, Trumbull believed indispensable as a framework for wit and drollery.

Nor did he confine his interest in plan to humorous writing: it is significant that his first award to serious epic writers went to two poets who excelled in design, Homer and Milton. Moreover, his disapproval of sundry other writers was often based upon their lack of plan. Young's satires he condemned as a "meer tissue of Epigrams," and the same poet's *Night Thoughts,* though he thought well of them in some ways, he labelled as "the most extraordinary mass of thoughts, good, bad & indifferent, that ever were thrown together on Paper." But he insisted upon organization particularly for the epic and for its impish alter ego, the burlesque epic.

For other poems he had other criteria as well. And first there was the test of versification. "Scarcely any subject has been less attended to than English Prosody," wrote Trumbull in 1785. He himself was an interested and discerning student of prosody, perhaps one of the earliest in the history of American criticism to give the matter much attention. His first important comments on the subject appeared as a section in Noah Webster's *Grammatical Institute of the English Language.* After first discussing the difference between accent and emphasis, Trumbull proceeds to an analysis of the "heroic measure," which, he tries to prove, "admits of a greater variety of feet, than the heroic measure of any language with which [he is] acquainted." Recognizing the long debate among grammarians on the question of the essential nature of English prosody, he offers his opinion that English verse is based on a system of accent and emphasis rather than of variation of long and short vowels. An elaborate classification of metrical feet follows the discussion; and the whole section, some thir-

teen pages in the *Institute,* is concluded by pertinent directions for reading verse. In general, Trumbull's conception of versification is that which one would expect of a conservative eighteenth-century writer. Though he, as a comic writer, used the octosyllabic couplet, frequently with Hudibrastic rhymes, in his more famous poems, it is clear that he favored in general the decasyllabic couplet which he also used, for modern English poetry.

Trumbull was well aware of the extent to which blank verse was growing in favor, but he did not approve. His admiration for Milton's *Paradise Lost* on other grounds, we now realize, must have been intense in view of his dislike of its meter. His objections to blank verse and his suggestions for its improvement he outlined in a memorandum to James Hillhouse in 1814, shortly after the latter had employed the form in a comparatively long poem, "The Judgment":

> Too near resemblance to Prose is the natural defect of blank verse. . . . To avoid this fault some confined their versification to single lines, & their minute & monotonous melody returned as regularly as the click of a chronometer. Others to throw it out of prose adopted a style of inflated pomp and loaded their lines with sounding & unmeaning Epithets; of this fault Thomson has given too many examples in his Seasons. . . . Milton affected Archaisms & Greek or latin forms of expression. . . . Cowper's Task in the choice of words & the arrangement of sentences is generally no more than plain prose, many pages if printed as such would scarcely be suspected of being intended as verse. . . . But the most general fault of blank verse is diffusion and prolixity. Single thoughts are drawn out like threads in a glasswork to immense length. . . . The style in blank verse ought to be as much condensed as that of Pope. Every elliptical form of expression, every omission of the relative or connective, that does not lead to harshness or obscurity tends to give strength as well as conciseness. Laboured transitions, & the introduction of minute & unnecessary circumstances . . . ordinary arrangement of the parts of a sentence & even the peculiar melody of prosaic numbers ought to be avoided. . . . No unnecessary word or epithet should ever be introduced merely to fill out the line. . . . This is easily avoided, for blank verse not only admits the period to end in any part of the line, but claims the frequent & forcible caesural pauses as one of its peculiar ornaments. The free use of polysyllables . . . often adds a graceful variety, & renders the lines more flowing & harmonious.

Regarding the use of elliptical expressions here referred to, Trumbull had already spoken his mind emphatically on the subject, in terms that explain his relative coolness toward Spenser. In defending one of Dwight's poems (presumably an early draft of *The Conquest of Canaan*) to Silas Deane he remarked:

> As to abbreviations in the versification, I do not think it possible to write in english rhyme-verse without. It is impossible to avoid them without running into the drawling Style of old Spenser. The fault is in the Language—not in the Poet.

By the same token, although he probably failed to appreciate some of the finer qualities of Milton's verse, he could take satisfaction in the precision of phrase and condensation of thought which, despite its length, characterizes

Milton's writing in *Paradise Lost.* Moreover, Milton availed himself of those means of varying his blank verse to which Trumbull alluded in his letter to Hillhouse. In all these comments, as well as in other criticism, it is evident that Trumbull placed the highest value upon condensed thought and sententious expression and favored those metrical practices which fostered such qualities. Never did he use the Spenserian stanza, and it is clear that, like Pope, he thought the Alexandrine "needless." He had no natural inclination to "linked sweetness long drawn out," whether in Milton, Spenser, or any other poet.

In his criticism of description and diction in poetry, he again proved himself essentially a middle-of-the-roader. "No Poet ever gained immortality," he remarked, "unless he excelled in description or *passion,*" for "the reader must see the object." As a youngster he drew up a list of rules for description, governing such matters as point of view, selection, arrangement, and dominant tone. Like his century, he valued decorum, deprecated gaudiness, believed that formality was compatible with a decent simplicity, and required of the poet a certain chastity of diction. Anyone who has read the concluding verses of his own **"Essay on the Fine Arts"** (1770) may well question his right to criticize other writers on the score of stilted, stereotyped, or extravagant diction; yet practice is one thing and precept another. In the prose preamble to this very same work, Trumbull indicated his awareness of the devitalizing effect of imitation and inbreeding. Long before the romantic movement brought about some correction of the abuses Trumbull had in mind, he here called attention to a decline in eighteenth-century English poetry by reason of what he termed a

> luxurious effeminacy, which hath caused a decay of genius, and introduced a false taste in writing. Their Men of learning are infected with pedantry. They are great admirers of antiquity and followers in the path of servile imitation. They sacrifice ease and elegance to the affectation of classic correctness, fetter the fancy with the rules of method, and damp all the ardour of aspiring invention.

Trumbull was one of the earliest critics in America to attack "poetic diction" as inimical to true poetry. He expressed himself on this and related points on more than one occasion. As early as 1778, he noted that since the time of Thomson

> most of the English Poets have been meer imitators—& have debased the Style of Poetry. Swelling Epithets, & a laboured attention to pompous versification & a perpetual aim at description, give the modern English verse a great resemblance to the Style of Claudian in the decline of Latin Poetry. I wish I had not too much followed that manner myself in some of my more laboured productions.

In such criticism and confessions one finds the probable reason why Trumbull professed that he would "not give a fig to be the Author of all the Poems of Whitehead, Jennings & half a Hundred Writers in Dodsley's Collection." The quality he seems most to have missed in these and other writers of the time was what he called the "antient Simplicity of writing." Hence his admiration of Gray's "Elegy" (which he preferred to the odes) and of Goldsmith. Of the latter he said:

> But the most original writer in this long lost Style

of simplicity is Goldsmith. . . . He has a peculiar talent of introducing little circumstances, which all other poets would have passed over as too low for poetry, in such a manner as to heighten the beauty of his descriptions, & place the object described in a more natural & agreeable view. His Deserted Village is a masterpiece; his Ballad in the Vicar of Wakefield & some other little pieces have the same kind of merit.

In a second comment, earlier in date but more specific in character, he cites the same evil, namely, overwrought diction and imagery, in the poetry of his countryman, Timothy Dwight, whose *Conquest of Canaan* he read and criticized in progress. In 1770 he alluded jocularly to Dwight as "a late Poet [who] has filled his work with so much thunder and lightning, that upon reading it, I could not but compare his head to vulcan's shop, in which an hundred Cyclops were perpetually employed in forging thunderbolts." A little later, when, presumably, the whole poem was available, Trumbull picked up the same theme, and from criticizing Dwight specifically passed to a general criticism of poets afflicted with severe cases of poetic diction, with definite examples of the clichés to which he objected:

> Many poets, especially modern ones, . . . imagine the sublimity of stile to consist in its entire deviation from common & natural expression. . . . They form a poetical vocabulary, which needs a glossary to explain it—A sword becomes *the steely vengence,* a rivulet, the *streamy rain,* a stone, a *craggy ruin* &c. They involve everything in metaphor. . . . A hero must do nothing like other people . . . when he exclaims—*his voice in thunder driven, starts all the host & rends the clouds of heaven.* . . . The frequency of metaphor renders the stile always forced, generally obscure, often absurd or liable to double meanings. A thousand examples of this last observation occur in this poem.

> A second fault in the stile of this poem is *prolixity.* Four or five lines are often used to express an idea, which Pope would have explained more clearly in one. . . .

> [In description, this] author seems rather to aim at dazzling the mind by a number of sublime images. If the subject does not afford them, he calls in the aid of metaphor & comparison. When he is about to paint any object, he seems to range all nature to cull out a few sublime circumstances, & groups them together in a kind of *glowing patchwork.* This leads astray the mind from the object, or renders the descriptions often pompously obscure.

Nursing such ideas as these, Trumbull might have been expected to welcome the first stirrings of romanticism in his time, which promised, among other things, some correction of false standards of diction and imagery. His fellow critic, Joseph Dennie, as early as 1801, hailed Wordsworth as a poet who "has forsaken . . . extravagance . . . and has recalled erring readers from sounds to things, from fancy to the heart." But Trumbull did not welcome the new movement. His advancing age of course militated against any complete revision of his poetic faith. He recognized that the domination of Pope must pass. Yet in their eagerness to "throw off the shackles" the new writers, he felt, had gone beyond liberty into license. They trampled on almost every principle Trumbull cherished. He valued organization: the new writers often jumbled their images together "without object, connection or design." He admired careful versification: they indulged in a metrical "confusion . . . founded on principles entirely discordant." He believed in restraint: they substituted the "rant of a maniac" for imaginative writing, the "horrid & the unnatural" for the "sublime." These purveyors of false raptures and shudders found their admirers among the unjudicial, with whom "excentricity passes for genius."

Trumbull's animadversions proved that satiric blood still ran strong in his veins. Looking back over the first harvest of romantic poetry and other contemporary items, he remarked with more asperity than discrimination:

> Every Novelty now caught the public attention. The lullaby of *Wordsworth's* lyrical ballads. *Crabbe's Borough. Thalaba. Kehama.*

Nor had he much more respect for the Scotch and German tributaries:

> The public devoured with great voracity the productions of Schiller & Kotzbue, with Bürger's Lenora carried off by a ghost & all the tremendous horrors of German sublimity—They welcomed numeros emigrations of elves & brownies & warlocks, & water-kings, fresh from the highlands of Scotland—ready to cast the glamour over the eyes of the reader.

It is a fair guess that the beauty of "Tintern Abbey," with its flowing blank verse and its subtle study of the spirit, was almost entirely lost upon him; it is easy also to infer his entire disapproval of such poems as "Simon Lee" and "The Leech Gatherer." Although he had praised Goldsmith for his "little circumstances, which all other poets would have passed over as too low for poetry," he did not wish to wallow in the commonplace with Wordsworth. At all events, he incongruously classed Wordsworth with Crabbe and others of a school of writers whom he condemns as having

> sought originality by attempting to dignify by verse objects the most vulgar and disgusting. Instead of endeavoring, like their predecessors, to soar to the summit, they employ themselves in digging for gold & diamonds in the caverns & vaults of Parnassus, or bathing in the muddy bottom of the streams of Helicon.

Of Coleridge he speaks briefly in a paragraph headed "Wildness of imagination." Coleridge's colleagues in sin he does not specify, but to Trumbull they all wrote "as though a poetical Bedlam was about to be erected on the summit of Parnassus, and they were striving to show themselves qualified for professorships in that academy." It is possible that among these lawless potential professors he would include Byron, whom he presently dismisses with the brief comment, "Byron does not excel in description—in passion & feeling only—but of the *worst* sort."

One more poet passes under peevish review during this twilight of Trumbull's criticism. In Thomas Moore he acknowledged a certain elegance, but he could not be expected to take kindly to the "poet of Voluptuousness." He had read Moore, even going to the trouble of copying out in his own hand a number of passages from *Lalla Rookh;* but he expresses in brilliant phrase his scorn for Moore's tawdry evasions of reality, likening him to

a Boy-sorcerer chacing rainbows of his own creation. His poetic fire is mostly phosphoric—full of glare & glimmer & glitter but cold as Spenser's enchanted Beauty, formed out of a snowball. It is the frostwork of Helicon. "It smiled, shone, and it was cold." He delights in gaudy image, & exclaims with his own Peri. Oh am I not happy! I am, I am.

In the eagerness with which Trumbull seizes upon the line "Oh am I not happy! I am, I am,"—a line which is a virtual appeal for parody—he had doubtless forgotten that he once complained of critics who quoted "every feebler line." He did, however, come close to putting his finger upon Moore's descriptive method when he added: "Moore seldom describes the object—he at once tells us what it was like and spends all his genius in painting the simile." Here was an unpleasant element of romanticism which John Trumbull found foreign to his principles: rendering experience indirectly, whether through showy figures or through the mood of the writer. He demanded first of all a clear picture of the object—not a muddy or misty reflection of it in the disordered brain of a neurotic poet. Even Wordsworth's sober self-analysis he did not approve. Trumbull was interested in man, not men; he did not value the subjective approach to experience which marked the habit of many romantic poets. This was the principal reason why, though a little prone to be critical of neo-classical poetry, he could not respond more readily to a movement which found inspiration as much in a rill by a cottage as in the springs of Helicon, and which was ready to scrap ancient precepts of writing for the impulse from a vernal wood. (pp. 773-93)

> *Alexander Cowie, "John Trumbull as a Critic of Poetry," in* The New England Quarterly, *Vol. XI, No. 4, December, 1938, pp. 773-93.*

Edwin T. Bowden   (essay date 1962)

[*In the following excerpt from his preface to* The Satiric Poems of John Trumbull, *Bowden discusses* The Progress of Dulness *and* M'Fingal, *commenting that, although Trumbull's works seem archaic, "the eighteenth century still has a great deal to say to the twentieth."*]

Historically [John Trumbull] cannot be called a "two poem man," yet that is the impression he offers the modern reader. It is hardly fair, however, to attack Trumbull for not being a more consistent or a more prolific or a more dedicated poet than he was. Even if his was only a minor talent when compared to that of the great poets of the world, it is an interesting and an entertaining and a competent talent that did offer two fine long satiric poems that can still hold the amused attention of the reader in the second century after their publication. Perhaps by the very definition of the term that is not so minor after all.

The Progress of Dulness, 1773, has from its first publication attracted less attention than ***M'Fingal,*** although it is in many ways the more readable of the two today. For the period during and after the Revolution it did not have the nationalistic or historical immediacy to hold the same attraction, and the next age to some extent simply accepted the reputation given the poems by the earlier. At first glance too ***The Progress of Dulness*** seems more dated than ***M'Fingal:*** the poem of the Revolution is about past events, of course, but events so clearly past that they cause no confusion and offer a certain historical interest. *The Progress of Dulness* is in many respects about the same problems and the same crotchets of human nature that exist today, but it uses a tradition and a vocabulary that belong to the past and presents characters drawn from the literary conventions of the eighteenth century that may seem quaintly archaic. The reader today is liable to a certain confusion, a little like that engendered by eating lunch in an olde tea shoppe beside the superhighway. But after the first glance, the poem begins to speak directly to the modern reader as he recognizes in Trumbull's Tom, Dick and Harriet the friends or relatives or classmates he knows for himself. Even if we no longer call our gay young men "fops" or our silly girls "coquettes," we recognize in the eighteenth century types—for all their ruffles and tuckers—the human being that is still with us. And if the details of our formal education and our college curriculum have changed since Trumbull's day, we still recognize the college's reluctance to leave the old and the tried, and we can still laugh, if somewhat painfully, at youth's aptness at learning nothing at all, old or new. Of course it is a cliché that human nature does not change, but it is one that explains why the poem can still provide an amusing hour.

Part One, the adventures of Tom Brainless, is probably the best section of the poem. The youthful Trumbull knew the college and the students he was talking about, and his satire is apt and fitting. The student who arrives with glowing letters of recommendation, only to prove a lazy dunce, is hardly unknown today. The college curriculum, whose staid conservatism so bothered the young Trumbull, has changed in its content if not in its character, but that does not lessen Trumbull's wit at its expense. And any teacher today will smile at the conclusion of Tom's school teaching experience:

> The year is done; he takes his leave;
> The children smile; the parents grieve;
> And seek again, their school to keep,
> One just as good, and just as cheap.

Turning Tom into a dunce in the clergy, "As thieves of old, t' avoid the halter, / Took refuge in the holy altar," does not perhaps strike us as quite so funny—as apparently it did not a number of Trumbull's contemporaries—but it was not intended to. A satirist without some edge to his wit is hardly a satirist at all. And so Part One goes, sometimes an attack on the dullard that Tom represents, and sometimes an attack on the foibles of the institutions that shelter him. With the abandon of a young satirist, Trumbull strikes out at whatever seems to need correction or chastisement, and thoroughly enjoys himself while doing it.

Parts Two and Three, the careers of Dick Hairbrain, the country fop and man about town, and of Harriet Simper, the silly young coquette, do not quite come up to the same standard. Perhaps Trumbull had been frightened at the abuse he apparently received from those who read personal references into Part One or who thought it simply an attack on the college or the clergy. Or perhaps in reaching out beyond his own experience toward the stock figures of English satire he exceeded his maturity or his observation. Whatever the reason, the satire of the last two parts is milder and the immediacy is less. But they still have amusement to offer and an occasional sting that may be felt yet. In one respect both parts are a direct continuation

of Part One and carry on something of its effectiveness, for both are equally concerned with the problems and the failures of education. Education, in fact, may be called the central theme of the poem as a whole: Tom is the satiric example of the dullard in school; Dick, the wastrel and the careless; Harriet, the silly and the misguided. And the system through which they are put is little better: the college of Tom and Dick offers no intellectual immediacy or excitement, devoting itself to the learned and the stuffy, and Harriet's schooling shows the failure of the popular view of education for women:

> And why should girls be learn'd or wise?
> Books only serve to spoil their eyes.
> The studious eye but faintly twinkles,
> And reading paves the way to wrinkles.

In an America today so exercised over the shortcomings of its education, the poem seems particularly alive. Parts Two and Three have their other pleasures too, of course, for we can still enjoy the glance at the young man and the pretty miss out to charm the world and make it their private dish. If they do not emerge as very believable characters, or if their progress reminds us of the many other "progresses" of the century—even the much harsher ones of a Hogarth—it doesn't make much difference, for the effect of the satire remains, and the many surface details of scene and clothing, gossip and manners are there to charm and amuse us.

Something of Trumbull's satiric intentions—as well as the popular effect of his satire—appears in the biting prefaces to the three parts. Trumbull dropped the preface to the second part in the 1820 edition, and subsequent editions have not generally reprinted even those to the first and third parts. It is too bad, for some of the human interest of the poem is in them. In the preface to Part One Trumbull carefully points out his intention to attack the errors of the colleges and also the laxity of the clergy in its failure to exclude the ignorant and irreligious, all in hopes that he can contribute to improvement. But the preface to Part Two shows that the public had failed to understand what he was doing. Almost inevitably, Part One had been read by some as simply an attack on the college and the clergy; and Trumbull roars back in counterattack against "the Envious and Malicious Reader." Most later commentators seem to take his words at their face value and to see Trumbull as an embittered man striking back at his enemies. Of course there is some bitterness, but it is difficult to read the preface with all that solemnity and seriousness; the last paragraph alone—offering the preface to anyone who wants to deserve it—would seem enough to indicate that Trumbull is enjoying himself too and means the preface in its own way to be as comic as the poem itself, comedy founded on satire. Whatever the exact intention, the preface does have a bite that is still effective—apparently too strong a bite for the older and more staid John Trumbull when he came back to it. Yet there must have been something to his sensitivity to criticism, for the preface to Part Three is much more restrained and very careful to point out exactly what he is doing in the poem to follow: he is not attacking womanhood itself but the neglect of women's education that leads to the foibles that men find. One wonders whether the women accepted such careful distinctions. Trumbull, in fact, keeps protesting his virtuous intentions so explicitly that the modern reader would like to protest himself. But even in enforced mildness,

Trumbull is not entirely tamed and manages—perhaps in a forgetful moment—to get in a word about being "ignorantly or wilfully misunderstood." John Trumbull may have had his feelings, but there is no question that he was human.

By the time of the publication of *M'Fingal,* he had become more judicious. Or perhaps he is equally personal and immediate but has simply chosen the popular position so that he has the protection of the impersonality of political warfare and nationalistic sentiment. All right thinking citizens had to agree with him, and his attacks no longer seemed private spite or radical opinion but the patriotic and spirited efforts of a good American. After the first canto appeared in 1776, friends even urged him to continue it as a patriotic duty and a valuable contribution to the national spirit in the war. The completed version of 1782 appeared in time to catch the new American nationalism in its first full growth, and the poem continued to hold patriotic approval for the next century. It is no surprise to find the poem, despite its length, Trumbull's most popular work from the time of its first publication to the present. Even before its final version in the collected works of 1820, it went through twenty-three editions, not counting a number of pirated editions. An illustrated edition of 1795, apparently one of the reprints published with Trumbull's express consent, points to the sort of popular reading that it was receiving. And as an indication of its acceptance among professional men of letters, an edition of 1799 now in the Humanities Research Center of the University of Texas may be pointed out. On the back of the title page Joseph Dennie (1768-1812), the popular essayist, editor, man-about-letters of the day, has written: "John Trumbull Esq. is the author of this poem. which in copious wit, is second only to the cantos of Butler & in vigor, dignity & greatness is superior even to the 'surpassing worth of Sr. Hudibras.' When the Politics of McFingall are forgotten, when the name of whig becomes obsolete, & Anglo Americans & Englishmen wonder at antient animosity, this poem will be read, respected & admired by every lover of the Jocund muse." Trumbull at last had found public approval of his satire, at the expense perhaps of something of his own interest and private concerns.

M'Fingal takes the proper stand certainly and lambastes the Tories and the English with the necessary vigor. When the Scotch Tory M'Fingal speaks for his party he succeeds only in making a fool of himself and in bringing laughter down on the Tory position—and laughter, as Trumbull had discovered, was a powerful and frightening weapon. On closer reading, however, particularly at a safe distance from the high feelings of the day, the weapon is not aimed entirely at the Tories. Often M'Fingal's attacks on the patriotic Whigs have a sting that M'Fingal's own ludicrousness cannot soothe or lessen. In the third canto, for instance, lines 41-108 have enough validity to make them difficult to dismiss even for the staunch patriot. A few of the lines will demonstrate the tone:

> For Liberty in your own by-sense
> Is but for crimes a patent licence;
> To break of law th' Egyptian yoke,
> And throw the world in common stock,
> Reduce all grievances and ills
> To Magna Charta of your wills,
> Establish cheats and frauds and nonsense,
> Fram'd by the model of your conscience.

Trumbull was a moderate, and a lawyer too, and could not bring himself to accept the violent fanaticism of the day that took from even an enemy his traditional and legal rights and denied the whole concept of deliberation and due means. Liberty poles, tar and feathers, and lynchings, even when on the right political side, were hardly what Trumbull was supporting, and even while he jeers at the Tories he takes care to glance acidly at the super patriots who would take the law into their own hands. He has other reservations about the patriots too—particularly when they are as dull and as long-winded as the Tories—but the careful reader will discover them for himself. It is enough to say that even in a time of high emotion Trumbull retained the objective, even disinterested, eye of the true satirist, and hit out at what he believed needed chastisement. The occasion and the subject of his comic satire had changed but the satire itself had not. Unlike his earlier work, however, *M'Fingal* provoked no public indignation; the explanation is probably simply that we enjoy seeing the other fellow attacked, and in the pleasure are likely not to recognize ourselves, at least for the moment.

Trumbull seems never to have been a flaming patriot anyway; his nature, his education, even his family inheritance were all against it. At best perhaps he should be called a literary patriot, for his interests in large part even in *M'Fingal* are literary interests. The poem itself suggests its familiar literary background, and if there were any doubt, Trumbull's letter to the Marquis de Chastellux discussing the poem, later printed in the 1820 edition, would point out his deliberately "literary" intention. The rough verse with its comic hudibrastic rhymes echoes Butler, of course, and often points to Trumbull's familiarity with the verse of Charles Churchill and Swift and Pope and other satiric poets of the century. In particular the poem illustrates Trumbull's familiarity with the conventions of the mock heroic, or "high burlesque" as he calls it in his letter to the marquis, the humorous parody of the conventions of the heroic epic of the sort most familiar today in such greater works of the time as Dryden's *MacFlecknoe* or Pope's *Rape of the Lock.* Canto Three in particular illustrates the technique when M'Fingal's single combat and heroic defeat are described as they might have been by one of the great epic poets in a moment of drunken comedy. To avoid any possible failure to recognize the parody, Trumbull in a note to line 262 even points out the similarity to Homer, Virgil and Milton, and later in the verse itself makes his point after a mock epic simile:

> The deadly spade discharg'd a blow
> Tremendous on his rear below:
> His bent knee fail'd, and void of strength,
> Stretch'd on the ground his manly length;
> Like antient oak o'erturn'd he lay,
> Or tow'rs to tempests fall'n a prey,
> And more things else—but all men know 'em,
> If slightly vers'd in Epic Poem.

The poem is full too of "low" burlesque literary allusions, either particular or general; not only heroic verse but the other all but sacred—and even the sacred—classics are given their share of comic use, sometimes in apparent parody of the scholarly tendency of the day to make all points by classical or Biblical reference, sometimes in the simple fun of burlesque, sometimes just because Trumbull could assume that his readers would see the comic point buried in the reference. To read the poem with full enjoyment, one ought now to be as steeped in the traditions of literature as Trumbull himself was.

And yet it is not necessary for the reader to recognize all of the literary references or even to know a great deal about the literary traditions in order to enjoy the poem. The problem is similar to that posed by the many references to historical details of the revolutionary period: if they are recognized, fine; if not, the greater part of the enjoyment of the poem still remains. And after all, for those who want to go into the details, the notes are always there at the end of this edition. The general political situation must be understood, of course, and the general literary aim of the poem, but beyond that no special knowledge is necessary. For the true pleasure of the poem for most modern readers is not, or at least not entirely, in its historical interest but in its general display of wit and humor for a satiric end. If it were not for the satiric wit, in fact, the poem would be a little disappointing. It is not great poetry and does not pretend to be; Trumbull too often lets his comic purpose override even his poetic sensitivities. As comic verse it does occasionally rise to fine passages of real poetic wit such as the characterization of "Gentleman Johnny":

> Behold that martial Macaroni,
> Compound of Phoebus and Bellona,
> With warlike sword and singsong lay,
> Equipp'd alike for feast or fray,
> Where equal wit and valour join;
> This, this is he, the famed Burgoyne.

But the passages are not generally long sustained, and the reader must too often content himself in long sections with a few memorable couplets:

> True to their King, with firm devotion,
> For conscience sake and hop'd promotion.

It seems fair to say too that the poem is too long; Trumbull might better have left the debates in the town meeting of the first and second cantos condensed into one canto, as it was in the original printing, and might have foreshortened even more the detailed panorama of the war offered by M'Fingal's second sight in the fourth canto. Then too, the characterization is weak; M'Fingal is seldom more than a disembodied comic voice, and his Whig opponent of the first two cantos, Honorius, is so clearly and so dully a trumpet for the proper sentiments that it is difficult even to remember his name. Only those real, historical persons attacked—Gage, Howe, Loring, Hutchinson, and the like—have a life of their own, and that is the life of caricature.

If one is willing to read simply for the amusement that the poem has to offer, however, he will not be disappointed. For Trumbull's satiric wit is there in profusion, even if the occasion and the structure of the poem, even the character of the speakers, exist only to offer an opportunity for the wit. The best advice would seem to be to relax and enjoy it, just as it would be enjoyable today to read a wit with a fine sense of the ludicrous commenting on our own wars and politics, our great rumbling national actions and our petty local tempests, our national saints and our devils, our friends and our enemies. The American revolution now seems far back in time, but Trumbull with his timeless sense of the comic makes us see that people then were not so much different from people now, and that human

wit can live even when the occasion that called it forth has long since disappeared. In this sense of living on past its own time and occasion *M'Fingal* is like *The Progress of Dulness.* Both poems amuse by reminding us in a witty fashion of the foibles and the foolishness of the human being, and both astonish us a little—in a provincial pride that would have delighted John Trumbull—that even the eighteenth century still has a great deal to say to the twentieth. (pp. 11-20)

> *Edwin T. Bowden, in a preface to* The Satiric Poems of John Trumbull *edited by Edwin T. Bowden, University of Texas Press, 1962, pp. 7-23.*

Victor E. Gimmestad   (essay date 1974)

[*In the following excerpt, Gimmestad analyzes* M'Fingal, *tracing the influence of Trumbull's readings on the work and examining its reception in revolutionary circles.*]

M'Fingal, the principal work for which we know Trumbull, has had a distinctive role in American culture and history. It had its origin in some of its author's patriotic verse and in the urging of some members of the Continental Congress who perceived the necessity to raise colonial morale by ridiculing the British. The first canto was written and printed in the last months of 1775 and was published early in 1776. In 1782, the author expanded the poem to four cantos by dividing the first one of 1776 into two with some modifications and by adding a third and fourth.

The first two cantos of the completed satire dealt with a town meeting in which M'Fingal and Honorius debate contemporary issues, the former supporting the Tory side and the latter the Whig. The third involved a liberty pole, a mock-heroic individual combat, and a tarring and feathering. The fourth presented a vision of the events of the Revolutionary War, including the surrender of Cornwallis. Intended as mock epic, it was written in Hudibrastic verse which moved more like that of Swift and Churchill than that by Butler. It satirized the opponents of the colonial Whigs mainly through a Scotch Tory who derived his name from James Macpherson's Ossianic *Fingal: An Ancient Epic Poem* (1762). Trumbull's *M'Fingal* contained many allusions not only to the epics by Homer, Virgil, and Milton but also to the Bible. *M'Fingal* had an impact during the war which is difficult to assess but which was probably strongest on the educated classes because of its literary nature. The fact that the completed poem was pirated in 1782 helped bring about copyright laws in Connecticut, but editions were printed in other places without the knowledge or consent of the author. The poem made him famous, and, ironically, gave him the name M'Fingal in the popular mind. Begun in a dark hour in American history, *M'Fingal* became associated with patriotism in times of crisis; and it has entered into our national heritage as an important legacy. (pp. 77-8)

When he began writing *M'Fingal,* Trumbull aimed at the high burlesque rather than the low. There are several evidences of this fact. First, when he wrote to Silas Deane on May 27, 1775, he suggested that the style of *The Dunciad* might be better than that of *Hudibras.* Second, he said to

De Chastellux in 1785 that he had aimed at the high burlesque. And last, there is Joel Barlow's preface to the London edition of 1792 in which the point is made. Because Barlow lived for a time in Trumbull's house in Hartford during the 1780's, he must have become familiar with his host's ideas about his recently completed poem and could speak with authority.

Though Trumbull was aiming for the high burlesque, *M'Fingal* resembles *Hudibras* in several ways. Like the great English mock epic, it attacks persons; it includes a knight and a squire; it contains the "mixture of Irony & Sarcasm" which Trumbull admired in Butler; and it uses the octosyllabic couplet, unusual rhymes, and double rhymes. Nearly one-sixth of the couplets have double rhymes, used for humorous effect. They sometimes rival Butler's for cleverness: "dozy"—"idiocy," "submission"—"addition," "atrabilious"—"peccadilloes," and "Erie, or"—"Superior."

In addition, there are over twenty examples of resemblances or borrowings mentioned by J. Hammond Trumbull in his annotated copy of Nathaniel Patten's 1782 edition. In the resemblances, no direct indebtedness is claimed; but passages from *Hudibras* usually are cited. In seven instances, there is an assertion of demonstrable influence: on the gift of prophecy, on guns which miss the mark, on the justification for lying, on Caligula, on the characterization of the Commonwealth, on the owl paraded around Rome, and on an upside-down empire. In the last of these, *M'Fingal* reads, "Whose crupper had o'ertopp'd his head. / You've push'd and turn'd the whole world up- / Side down, and got yourselves at top." The comparable passage in *Hudibras* is, "Which now had almost got the upper- / Hand of his head, for want of crupper." One passage in the 1782 edition was so close to *Hudibras* that the author altered it in 1820. Canto I, lines 63-64 read, "Nor only saw he all that was / But much that never came to pass." In *Hudibras,* similar lines are "He could foretel whats'ever was, / By consequence to come to pass." For the 1820 edition Trumbull altered his lines to read, "Nor only saw he all that could be, / But much that never was, nor would be."

Conversant with other English authors of the seventeenth and eighteenth centuries, Trumbull may have been influenced by a number of them. From Prior could come "a kind of easy elegant humour & natural description." Trumbull himself said he sought to imitate Churchill and Swift in his Hudibrastic poems; and he seems principally indebted to Churchill, particularly for the verse patterns and movement of "The Ghost." In a passage describing qualities he himself strove for, Trumbull wrote: "Churchill aims at sprightliness & vivacity of imagination. His thoughts flow rapidly, & the expression is bold and glowing. The style often bears a nearer resemblance to the Horatian Odes, than to the Poetry from which it takes its name. Indeed this Style is capable of most of the Beauties of the higher kinds of Poetry." And from Swift probably stemmed the use of humor in description, of combining a conversational style with irony, both of which he credited that British author with having introduced into English poetry.

In addition to the references to historical volumes in the poem, there are numerous allusions to the Bible and to various literary works. Those to the Bible run over forty in number, almost all being from the Old Testament. There are several allusions or references to mock epics, but there are many more to epics, principally—in that order of frequency—to those by Milton, Homer, and Virgil. There are many to ancient authors and to Classical mythology, but there are fewer to more recent works and authors, and these are to ballads. References are to the British Samuel Johnson, Bunyan, Shakespeare, Swift, Thomas Tickell, Edmund Waller, Gray, Prior, General Burgoyne, and Sir Walter Scott; and to the Americans Jonathan Sewall and Cotton Mather. These many allusions give a decidedly literary cast to *M'Fingal.*

The use of a Scotch Tory as M'Fingal has puzzled many readers. Trumbull never explained his choice, but he may well have had three ideas in mind. First, he found the "machinery" of the second sight, reputedly possessed by the Highlanders, advantageous because it would enable him to use the device of prophecy found in some epics. Second, the Scottish members of Parliament supported the ministry in repressive measures against the colonies, and only two voted to repeal the Stamp Act. And, third, however rebellious the Scots may have been at home, they generally were Tories in the colonies, particularly in the Carolinas. As Lossing has pointed out [in his notes to the 1860 edition of *M'Fingal*], Jefferson referred in the original draft of the Declaration of Independence to " 'Scotch and foreign mercenaries.' "

An estimate of the effectiveness of *M'Fingal* as propaganda necessarily is only approximate. The inevitable comparison with Thomas Paine's *Common Sense* and *The Crisis* shows Trumbull's work at a disadvantage, for it was less partisan, it contained many literary allusions which were meaningless to those with little schooling, and poetry was a form less popular than the essay. It seems likely that the influence of *M'Fingal* was felt most among the educated. In this group it could have affected the choice of those who were wavering between the opposing camps, and it gave both assurance and a weapon to the literate patriots. For them, it probably had a value not foreseen by anyone when the request or "order" was sent to Trumbull—that value consisted in its possessing literary stature sufficient to remind readers of Butler's mock epic. Being of such quality, *M'Fingal* helped rid the patriots of their feeling of cultural inferiority, a mighty service not only in 1776 but also in 1782, when the problems of independence loomed closer. Desperately needing something to bolster morale, the patriots welcomed an author who was favorably compared with eminent English writers.

As the records tell us, the satire was esteemed by the revolutionaries in both its 1776 and 1782 editions. On February 21, 1776, Abigail Adams wrote to her husband that "If Mack Fingal [*sic*] is published be so good as to send it." On July 25 of the same year Enoch Hale, brother of Nathan Hale, recorded his purchase of *M'Fingal* for a shilling. In 1782, although General Cornwallis had surrendered and the war was nearly over, copies of the recently published complete *M'Fingal* were favorably received for their combination of patriotic and literary merit. Both Jeremiah Wadsworth and Humphreys wrote about it to General Nathanael Greene, who did not receive his copy until December. He knew Trumbull personally and spoke of the high regard in which he and others held the poet. On September 29, 1782, he wrote to Trumbull that "Many people of this Country wish to get you to become a settler here. Governor Mathews desird [*sic*] me to write you on the subject. Men of taste and genius are much courted and encouraged by the principal Inhabitants." Other leaders also welcomed the patriotic poem. Aaron Burr wrote to Jeremiah Wadsworth, "I am really obliged to you for Mc Fingal. I have read it more than once with great pleasure." Madison wrote about the stir it made in Philadelphia and sent copies to Edmund Randolph, Governor Benjamin Harrison, and Edmund Pendleton. Humphreys carried a copy from the author to Thomas Jefferson. John Jay was acquainted with it and referred to it. Washington owned a copy, which later was in the Huth Library in England but is now back in America in the Chapin Library at Williams College.

Any satisfaction which Trumbull may have derived from the popularity of *M'Fingal* was lessened by the fact that satire often was thought inferior or immoral. Even John Adams later urged his former law student to use his "veins of Poetry of Superior kinds," that is, the epic. Trumbull wisely declined any attempt at a form to which he did not feel equal, despite his ambition to write in the "sublime" or "pathetic" style. But what irritated Trumbull was the carping criticism that satire was sinful. In January 1783 he recorded some of his thoughts in an unpublished essay called **"On Satirical Productions."** Since the most important detractors presumably were clergymen, he met them on their own ground and cited the fable of Jotham, Elijah's speech to Baal's prophets, the Book of Job, and many other examples to buttress his point that the Bible has "many Passages . . . which have never been excelled by the most witty Satirist of antient or modern ages." Adding a few remarks at the end of the essay, he mentioned examples of irony in Scripture also. Though he hoped he could silence his critics, he recognized that arguing with those "who are determined not to be convinced" was futile.

Trumbull opens the first canto with mockery of British might as displayed at Lexington and Concord. Then he describes Squire M'Fingal, the representative of the Tories and the possessor of second-sight, making his way to his home town. In a jocular reference to the reputed gift of prophecy, the author writes:

> For any man with half an eye
> What stands before him can espy;
> But optics sharp it needs, I ween,
> To see what is not to be seen.

These frequently quoted couplets are often mistakenly attributed to *Hudibras*.

Though endowed with prophetic powers, M'Fingal is not always helpful to his cause and its adherents. As the author tells it:

> But as some muskets so contrive it,
> As oft to miss the mark they drive at,
> And though well aim'd at duck or plover,
> Bear wide, and kick their owners over:
> So fared our 'Squire, whose reas'ning toil
> Would often on himself recoil,
> And so much injured more his side,
> The stronger arguments he applied;
> As old war-elephants, dismay'd,
> Trod down the troops they came to aid,
> And hurt their own side more in battle,
> Than less and ordinary cattle.

Because M'Fingal arrives late at the town meeting, the Whig leader Honorius begins speaking first. He utilizes the popular idea that political states, like people, have their various ages; and he charges that Great Britain is now grown old and has lost her senses, even claiming in the Declaratory Act to be all-powerful. In his effort to reassure his countrymen by his ridicule of England, Trumbull draws a satiric comparison:

> "As madmen, straw who long have slept on,
> Style themselves Jupiter and Neptune:
> So Britain in her airs so flighty,
> Now took a whim to be Almighty;
> Urg'd on to desperate heights of frenzy,
> Affirm'd her own Omnipotency."

In his accusations, Honorius insists that Britain has been deaf to pleas and has sent Gage, a prime liar, to Boston. Though that officer bungles his falsehoods, he is a threat:

> "Yet fools are often dangerous enemies;
> As meanest reptiles are most venomous:
> Nor e'er could Gage, by craft or prowess,
> Have done a whit more mischief to us;
> Since he began th' unnat'ral war,
> The work his masters sent him for."

Having castigated Gage, Honorius condemns the "Tory expectants," the "dastard race" of those clergymen, lawyers, merchants, and judges

> " . . . who long have sold
> Their souls and consciences for gold;
> Who wish to stab their country's vitals,
> Could they enjoy surviving titles."

When M'Fingal gives a signal, his adherents, who follow him "like files of geese," make an uproar. M'Fingal then begins his first speech, which is full of unintended irony. Charging that the Whigs are too stupid to understand logic, he defends the Anglicans:

> "Have not our High-church Clergy made it
> Appear from Scriptures, which ye credit,
> That right divine from heaven was lent
> To kings, that is, the Parliament,
> Their subjects to oppress and teaze,
> And serve the devil when they please?"

He continues, naming clergy:

> "Have ye not heard from Parson Walter
> Much dire presage of many a halter?
> What warnings had ye of your duty,
> From our old rev'rend Sam. Auchmuty;
> From priests of all degrees and metres,
> T' our fag-end man, poor Parson Peters?"

M'Fingal advises the colonials to bear silently the plague of modern kings sent by God, and he extols the reasoning powers of "scribblers" on the Tory side, such as Massachusettensis.

In a passage appealing to religious sentiment, Honorius challenges the Tory:

> " 'Twas then belike," Honorius cried,
> "When you the public fast defied,
> Refused to heaven to raise a prayer,
> Because you'd no connections there."

Replying, M'Fingal asks whether heaven had sent Judge Peter Oliver, an "ignoramus"; Sewall, a "wit of water-gruel"; and Nat. Ray Thomas, the "Marshfield blunderer"; Thomas Hutchinson; or Treasurer Harrison Gray. Then Honorius reminds the Tories how Hutchinson has lied—a fact that does not disturb M'Fingal, who defends all brother Ananiases:

> Quoth he, "For lies and promise-breaking,
> Ye need not be in such a taking:
> For lying is, we know and teach,
> The highest privilege of speech;
> The universal Magna Charta,
> To which all human race is party."

After excusing lies further, M'Fingal calls for a dinner recess.

The first canto, which establishes the poem as a mock epic, is distinguished from the third and fourth cantos by the greater intensity of its opposition to the British and the Tories. The poem tells of inglorious military expeditions, lists opposition heroes, and includes a debate, which is carried on at a town meeting. To ridicule the opposition, Trumbull employs scorn and occasionally invective, as when he calls Parson Samuel Peters a "fag-end man." Indicative also of the author's seriousness are the many references to the Bible and the few to the *Iliad,* the *Odyssey,* the *Aeneid, Paradise Lost,* and *Fingal.* Sometimes he makes a sharp satiric stroke by echoing a biblical passage, as he does with Acts 17:28 when he writes "In them, who made you Tories, seeing / You lived and moved and had your being." In the first Canto also is the one satirical reference to the metaphysical divines with whom he had been battling for over five years. Contributing to the humor in a lighter way are over one hundred fifty double rhymes, a greater number than in any of the other cantos. The first canto, as well as the second one, reflects strongly the patriotic involvement of Trumbull in Boston and New Haven.

Canto II opens with mock-heroic lines about the sun which are reminiscent of the **"Epithalamion"** and then goes to the dinner:

> (Nor shall we, like old Homer, care
> To versify their bill of fare)
> Each active party, feasted well,
> Throng'd in, like sheep, at sound of bell;
> With equal spirit took their places,
> And meeting oped with three *Oh Yesses.*

M'Fingal rises and calls the Whigs ungrateful. In another unknowingly ironical speech, he cites the colonials' supposed debt to Charles I, Archbishop Laud, soldiers, governors, judges, and clergymen. In addition, he maintains the British " 'brought all felons in the nation / To help you on in population.' " He derides patriotism and insists " 'That self is still, in either faction, / The only principle of action' "; and he questions doing anything for posterity. M'Fingal then calls the Whigs cowards, reminds them of British military might, and, incongruously, mentions that the British used Indians against the colonials as well as instigated slave revolts.

Honorius answers the challenge on British military strength by citing Gage's proclamation. M'Fingal makes the ridiculous answer that Providence chooses its own instruments:

> "To pay a tax, at Peter's wish,
> His chief cashier was once a fish;
> An ass, in Balaam's sad disaster,

> Turn'd orator and saved his master;
> A goose, placed sentry on his station,
> Preserved old Rome from desolation;
> An English bishop's cur of late
> Disclosed rebellions 'gainst the state;
> So frogs croak'd Pharaoh to repentance,
> And lice delay'd the fatal sentence:
> And heaven can ruin you at pleasure,
> By Gage, as soon as by a Caesar."

With unwitting irony M'Fingal cites Colonel Nesbit's tarring and feathering of a farmer, Colonel Alexander Leslie's ineffective trip to Salem, Gage's statement that he tried to avert civil war, the battle of Lexington, the actions of Abijah White, and the British soldiers who mistook "whizzing beetles" for whizzing bullets. With second sight M'Fingal foresees gallows for Whigs; the sack of cities; the arrival of the British navy and its thieving of provisions; the bombast of Gage, Admiral Samuel Graves, and Captain James Wallace; the coming of prodigies; and "new setts / Of home-made Earls in Massachusetts."

Honorius responds with a stirring call for liberty: " 'Tis Freedom calls! the raptured sound / The Apalachian hills rebound.' " Scornfully, Honorius addresses the fainthearted:

> "And ye, whose souls of dastard mould
> Start at the bravery of the bold;
> To love your country who pretend,
> Yet want all spirit to defend."

Such persons Honorius advises to go home and hide behind the aprons of their "more heroic wives." Tumult breaks out, and "Plumed Victory" sits on the pulpit-canopy ready to join the winning side. But suddenly a shout comes from outside, and the meeting breaks up. Like a knight and his squire, M'Fingal and the constable sally outdoors.

Written originally as part of Canto I, the second canto resembles the first in most respects and differs in only a few. It includes such mock-epic conventions as a meal, Plumed Victory, a knight and squire, omens, speeches, and innocuous battles. It makes its points with irony and invective. It contains many allusions to the Bible and several to epics, particularly to the *Iliad.* Proportionately, it contains fewer double rhymes than the first canto. It differs in including a pun (on Lord North's name) and in referring to two mock epics—the *Batrachomuomachia* and *Hudibras.* And in Canto II there are verses Washington may have thought particularly apt, for in his copy of the Hudson and Goodwin edition there are penciled double lines which he likely made beside "What has posterity done for us, / That we, least they their rights should lose, / Should trust our necks to gripe of noose?"

The third canto differs considerably from the first two. Trumbull followed the earlier recommendation of Silas Deane to use different styles in each part, and he also heeded the advice of those friends such as Humphreys who urged him to complete the poem as literature by filling the canto with literary allusions and echoes. Furthermore, although he had outlined parts of Canto III by the first part of October 1775, he could scarcely have written them as they now stand. For example, the speech of M'Fingal at the liberty pole, around which a noisy crowd has gathered, was startlingly different from his earlier bumbling and ridiculous harangues. With the Revolution almost over, the poet endorsed the views of the American upper classes toward the lower ones by evincing little sympathy for the social revolution taking place along with the political one. M'Fingal's speech condemning the mob lacks the irony of those in the first two cantos; and we recognize the difference between the philosophy of "life, liberty, and pursuit of happiness" in the Declaration of Independence and that of "life, liberty, and property" incorporated in the colonial charters and in the Constitution.

M'Fingal, in fact, at first sounds as straightforward as Honorius when he addresses the patriots as "dupes to every factious rogue / And tavern-prating demagogue" and when he charges that, for them, liberty "Is but for crimes a patent license." He accuses them of hypocritical selfishness when he says they "Dispute and pray and fight and groan / For public good, and mean [their] own." And Honorius actually voices the author's own sentiments when he observes,

> "And when by clamours and confusions,
> Your freedom's grown a public nuisance,
> Cry 'Liberty,' with powerful yearning,
> As he does 'Fire!' whose house is burning;
> Though he already has much more
> Than he can find occasion for."

Continuing, M'Fingal scornfully derides the weakness of Congress and the election of tradesmen as legislators. Gradually he works into his old habit of unintentional irony, but not before the author has condemned weak central government and paper money. Returning to his former style, M'Fingal alludes to North, the Earl of Bute, and Governor Tryon and to the mobs in New York which have done work cheered by the patriots.

But the Whigs grow tired of M'Fingal's harangue, and a fight breaks out. The description of the ensuing battle parodies the epic accounts, among them that between the Lapithae and Centaurs in the twelfth book of Ovid's *Metamorphoses*. M'Fingal cries " 'King George' " three times, draws his sword, and enters the melee. A powerful Whig with a spade bests him in combat with "a blow / Tremendous on his rear below." When the supporting Tories have vanished, and M'Fingal and the constable are caught, the constable is hoisted to the top of the liberty pole, where he, like Socrates in *The Clouds,* thinks more clearly, and renounces Toryism. M'Fingal, however, stands "heroic as a mule," and argues that punishment will merely "provoke" offenders, as "No man e'er felt the halter draw, / With good opinion of the law." A bench of justice is established, and M'Fingal and his aid are quickly sentenced to tarring and feathering, with a subsequent ride through town. As in a description in Claudian, tar streams down from M'Fingal's head. After the feathering, he outdoes several rival literary figures:

> Not Maia's son, with wings for ears,
> Such plumage round his visage wears;
> Nor Milton's six-wing'd angel gathers
> Such superfluity of feathers.
> Now all complete appears our 'Squire,
> Like Gorgon or Chimaera dire;
> Nor more could boast on Plato's plan
> To rank among the race of man,
> Or prove his claim to human nature,
> As a two-legg'd unfeather'd creature.

After the ride through town, the two men are brought

back to the pole and stuck to it. M'Fingal then speaks and reveals that his prophetic sight predicts a Whig victory. He concludes by directing the constable to call a Tory meeting.

Distinguishing the third canto are the liberty pole, which, like the town meeting, was a New England institution; the fewer biblical references; the increased number of literary allusions; the seven references to Milton; the smaller number of double rhymes; and the one triple rhyme in the poem—"trouble ye"—"jubilee." It continues the mock-epic conventions, of course, one of which is a ridiculous individual combat. All in all, the canto has a decidedly more literary cast than the first two.

The fourth canto opens with an appropriate mock-heroic description:

> Now Night came down, and rose full soon
> That patroness of rogues, the Moon;
> Beneath whose kind protecting ray,
> Wolves, brute and human, prowl for prey.
> The honest world all snored in chorus,
> While owls and ghosts and thieves and Tories,
> Whom erst the mid-day sun had awed,
> Crept from their lurking holes abroad.

The "Tory pandemonium" meets in the cellar of M'Fingal, in which he addresses the assemblage from a turnip bin. With his second sight he perceives John Malcolm, Governor Tryon's aid, who does most of the prophesying. Referring to actual events of the war, more than in the third, the author, through Malcolm's words, cites patriot victories and pays graceful compliments to Washington and to General Greene, his correspondent and friend. The defeats of Burgoyne and Cornwallis are announced along with the ultimate patriot victory. The vision ends when the constable announces that the Whigs are coming, and M'Fingal makes "good his rear" with an ignominious exit and leaves for Boston. This craven action fittingly concludes the poem.

The fourth canto has the deepest literary hue of all the cantos. The longest of the four divisions, it has nearly twice as many literary allusions, many being to Classical mythology, to Virgil, and to Milton. It has fewer double rhymes than either of the first two cantos. It is so impartial that it and number three must have been in Trumbull's mind when he wrote to De Chastellux that he had tried to point out the faults of both sides in the Revolution. (pp. 88-100)

> *Victor E. Gimmestad, in his* John Trumbull,
> *Twayne Publishers, Inc., 1974, 183 p.*

Bruce Granger   (essay date 1976)

[*In the following excerpt, Granger discusses Trumbull's "Meddler" and "Correspondent" essays.*]

The widespread success of Richard Steele and Joseph Addison's serial publications, "The Tatler," "The Spectator," and "The Guardian," at their appearance between 1709 and 1714 established a new genre overnight. Throughout the eighteenth century the journalistic and objective style of essay established in those publications remained the most nearly representative type of prose written on both sides of the Atlantic. From its inception the periodical essay was moral in purpose and social in point of view. The matter ranged through manners and morality, philosophical reflection, character, criticism, and humor. In the half century separating the first American essay serial, Benjamin Franklin's "Dogood" papers (1722), from John Trumbull's efforts in this genre, no fewer than seven important serials appeared in the press; so that when Trumbull ventured into prose in 1769 at age nineteen, he had an established tradition within which to work.

So heavily classical and theological was Trumbull's formal education that only by pushing beyond its limits in defiance of authority did he win through to becoming a poet and, what is here important, an essayist. Late in life he remembered that "The Spectator and Watts' Lyric Poems were the only works of merit in the belles-lettres" in his father's library, and that when he attended Yale College in the 1760s "English poetry and the belles-lettres were called folly, nonsense and an idle waste of time." Among the literary exercises he engaged in to stimulate an interest in belles-lettres while a graduate student and a tutor at Yale were two essay serials, "The Meddler" and "The Correspondent." At a time when most American writers were participating in the Revolutionary debate, Trumbull "showed little disposition to employ public events as topics for his writing." Where politics was concerned, he could say with Addison's Spectator, "I never espoused any Party with Violence, and am resolved to observe an exact Neutrality between the Whigs and Tories, unless I shall be forced to declare myself by the Hostilities of either Side." If Trumbull avoided political controversy, he did not hesitate to engage in theological and philosophical disputation. As the first part of *The Progress of Dulness* (*The Rare Adventures of Tom Brainless*) led church and school authority in Connecticut to condemn him as "an open reviler of the Clergy, and an enemy to truth and learning," so his attacks in "The Correspondent" on metaphysical writers and incompetent or hypocritical clergymen "very much enraged some Persons of eminence."

The Meddler, "not influenced by fame" but by "a desire to make trial of his genius," at once explains that his series "will consist of essays, chiefly of the moral, critical and poetical kinds, upon miscellaneous and mostly unconnected subjects; . . . I shall carefully avoid all strokes of party spirit and personal satire, with every thing that may have the least tendency to immorality." And indeed, except for the eighth number on hypocrisy in religion, he does avoid partisanship, unlike the Correspondent, whose essays followed shortly.

In the first number "The Meddler," following the plan of "The Spectator" and other English serials, introduces the club. A few friends, notably Mr. Thomas Freeman and John Manly, Esq., will "meet every week at the dwelling-house of the author" to assist "in compiling and correcting my writings." Freeman, a country gentleman modelled on Sir Roger de Coverly, "is a great humourist, has an odd and peculiar way of thinking, and a ready discernment of every thing ridiculous, in writings, actions or conversation: but at the same time is a great admirer of every thing that is just and beautiful. He is a friend to sincerity and plain dealing, and consequently an enemy to all kinds of affectation and hypocrisy, which he never fails to lash with satyrical indignation." Manly is very like him, though not

in disposition. "Folly, ignorance and affectation, which move the mirth of *Mr. Freeman,* are regarded, by Mr. Manly, with an eye of pity and contempt only." Another member of the club is Jack Dapperwit, descended from "The Spectator's" Tom Dapperwit. "His favourite author is Tristram Shandy, whose manner he endeavours to imitate in conversation, but so unluckily, that with very little portion of his humour, he attains only to a rambling incoherence of style and [confusion] of sentiment, which however among such company as he esteems polite, passes him off for a person of the greatest strength of wit and genius." Finally there is the Clergyman, "a person of great genius and merit, reverenced by all his acquaintance, and heartily welcomed by us, whenever he visits our society." But the Meddler's club is in effect stillborn; its members appear only once again, to argue about Freeman's recipe for making a popular preacher.

At the end of his first number the Meddler expresses the hope that he can contribute his assistance "towards instructing the unlearned, diverting and improving the learned, rectifying the taste and manners of the times, and cultivating the fine arts in this land." His essays fulfill this promise to instruct and entertain by ranging through the conventional subjects, notably manners. Several times we glimpse the coquette and the fop, who will emerge fully developed in *The Progress of Dulness.* The following mock-advertisement announcing the sale of Isabella Sprightly's estate is a foreshadowing of Harriet Simper:

> *Imprimis,* all the Tools and utensils, necessary for the trade of a Cocquet; viz. several bundles of darts and arrows, which are well-pointed, and capable of doing great execution, a considerable quantity of patches, paint, brushes and cosmetics, for plaistering, painting and white washing the face, and several dozens of *Cupids,* with all their appurtenancies, very proper to be stationed on a *ruby lip,* a *diamond eye,* or a *roseate cheek.*
>
> *Item.* As she proposes by certain ceremonies to transform one of her humble servants into an husband, and keep him for her own use, she offers for sale, Floris, Daphinis, Cynthis, Cleanthies, and several others whom she won, by a constant attendance on business, during the space of four years. She can prove her indisputable right to them, by certain deeds of gift, bills of sale and attestations, commonly called love letters, under their own hands. They will be sold very cheap, for they are all either broken-hearted, or broken-winded, or in a dying condition; nay, some of them have been dead this half year, as they declare and testify in the above mentioned.
>
> N. B. Their hearts will be SOLD separate.

Similarly, the Meddler's account of how boys are trained up to foppery prefigures Dick Hairbrain. The country lad, after proper preparation, is sent off to college. His first acquaintance there, "who, ten to one is a rake, a coxcomb, or a gamester . . . makes a tool of him to execute his own purposes," whereupon he wastes his time and loses his ambition. The city lad, when he is fifteen or sixteen, "commences beau; is caressed by the Ladies, envied by all his brother-beaus and despised by all persons of sense and judgment[;] he spends his time in fashionable amusements, in gaming, in parties of pleasure, in 'squiring the Ladies to balls, plays and other places of resort, until in a few years, he becomes antiquated and is elbowed out by younger gallants, . . . a most miserable creature, destitute and unworthy of notice and regard."

One of the Meddler's contributors, the Schemer, contends that we Moderns "exceed the Antients in all the polite arts and sciences; . . . dress, dancing, compliments, curses, drinking, swearing, gaming, poetry, fighting and dying, and, in a word, every qualification that belongs to a *gentleman* and a *man of honour,* in the modern acceptation of the words." His satirical explanation is heavy-handed: "All the elegance and beauty of dress have undoubtedly been added in modern ages. The antients have nothing to boast of, either in variety of fashions, or superfluity of decorations: they dressed for advantage and not for ornament. Necessity was their instructor, and plainness their model. . . . The art of cursing and swearing is almost wholly of modern invention. *Aristophanes, Plautus, Terence, Horace,* and a few more, who might perhaps have been gentlemen, had they lived in these days, do indeed make a few slight attempts in the practice; but they have not an oath, or a curse fit for the mouth of a modern gentleman." In "every polite and populous town" in America let there be erected two universities, "one for the education of gentlemen, and the other for the education of taylors. . . . In the college for the education of gentlemen, beside the usual officers, let there be a dancing-master, a fencing-master, a gaming-master, and above all, a professor of swearing: this post will require, a gentleman of superior abilities and uncommon application, and may probably fall to some experienced seaman."

The Meddler, complying with a request for his views on good and bad breeding, presents a set of characters more vividly drawn than the members of his club. In contrast to Eusebius, who "places politeness, in such behaviour to others, as he would desire them to shew towards him," are three examples of how not to behave. The first is the fop Abaxus:

> As soon as he rises in the morning, which is about eleven, he is attended by his valet, who spends about two hours in adjusting the back parts of his dress; . . . Then his barber passes about an hour in regulating his hair; after which he sometimes spares time enough to hurry down his breakfast; which being finished, he devotes about two hours of his time, to the contriving of fashions for the good of mankind, and [then] commits his important discoveries to paper, . . . When his hours of study, which he looks upon as the most advantageous and profitable part of his life, are over, he appears at the play house, or at any other assembly, where he may have an opportunity of shewing his accomplishments, either of dancing or dress.

Licentio bullies his inferiors and is insolent to his superiors: "Yesterday, as soon as he was dressed, he rang the bell for his servant; after he had given him his orders, observing something in his gait or dress, which offended his good breeding[,] he followed him to his chamberdoor, and being very well gifted in the art of kicking, with one stroke, laid him at the bottom of the stairs. Soon after he proceeded to a coffeehouse, where the waiter happening to spill some coffee upon a gentleman's coat, he stepped up to him, and brandishing his cane in the genteelest manner, very politely knocked him down; then throwing him a guinea, marched off in triumph." Pephasio is awkwardly attentive

to the fair sex: "When he first enters a company of ladies, he makes a most extraordinary bow; for beginning at the right hand person, he stares each one in the face, till he arrives at the left hand one, then bowing his head very low, turns it over his left shoulder. . . . One of the ladies dropping her fan, Pephasio in haste to pick it up, happened to step upon one corner of her apron: for which, with an appearance of much sorrow and confusion, he asked (if I am not mistaken) some thousand and odd pardons."

As literary critic Trumbull was strongly influenced by Lord Kames's *Elements of Criticism* (1762), which he read at Yale. "Upon a sense common to the species," writes Kames, "is erected a standard of taste, which without hesitation is apply'd to the taste of every individual. . . . We have the same standard for ascertaining in all the fine arts, what is beautiful or ugly, high or low, proper or improper, proportioned or disproportioned." The criticism present in "The Meddler," and later in "The Correspondent," conforms to Kames's insistence on aesthetic uniformitarianism. Echoing the judgment of Addison, who sought to establish "a Taste of polite Writing" by distinguishing between true and false wit, Trumbull's Meddler writes, "True Wit depends upon genius and nature, the false upon labour or affectation; true Wit is always accompanied with good-nature, politeness and a fine taste, the false with the grossest offences against modesty, good-manners or good-sense." Among the kinds of false wit that prevail in writing, and especially in conversation, are "the art of talking unintelligibly," ridicule and raillery, and *double-entendre.* This last, "though mostly peculiar to the male sex, would not have so universally prevailed among them, had it not met with the approbation and encouragement of the female; since it is well known that their taste and opinion is the standard of politeness."

Elsewhere the Meddler praises the literary excellences of the Bible, maintaining that the finest passages in "heathen poets" like Milton, Homer, Shakespeare, Ossian, Virgil, and Pope do not compare with "the first chapter of Genesis, the books of Job, Psalms, Isaiah, Ezekiel, Daniel, Joel, Nahum, the last chapter of Habackkuk, the book of Revelations, the description of our Saviour's passion, with numberless other places too many to be enumerated." "The perfect harmony and agreement that reigns throughout every part of the scriptures is a great and powerful proof of their divine inspiration; for all human compositions on the subject of morality, where they have not been directed by the Bible, are full of gross inconsistencies and absurdities."

Among the dishes the Meddler prepares for his readers in the final number are several consisting of literary criticism. He describes "a late Poet" (Timothy Dwight) who "has filled his work with so much thunder and lightning, that upon reading it, I could not but compare his head to Vulcan's shop, in which an hundred Cyclops were perpetually employed in forging thunderbolts." To critics who, like Addison, blame Milton "for mingling allegory with reality, and introducing sin and death, as actors," in *Paradise Lost,* the Meddler replies, "I leave it to the reader to judge whether, Sin and death only excepted, any other fictitious persons could properly be made the porters of hellgate." And viewing *Clarissa* as a conduct book, he advises, "If any Lady is desirous to know how to avoid the delusive snares of man, let her attend to the story and imitate the character of Clarissa; and if any man is desirous of learning how to deceive innocence, and betray unguarded female virtue, and in a word to become an incarnate devil, let him attend to the observations and imitate the character of Lovelace."

On one occasion, Trumbull, sounding more like Swift than Addison, engages in humor for its own sake. The Meddler is handed a manuscript by "some learned Writer" consisting of miscellaneous essays. The first satirizes "those trifling projectors who trouble the world with pompous essays, upon subjects of no importance," like the study of words, points, and signs.

> We see many persons staring at a sentence or paragraph, not because they find any thing in it worth notice, but because it is ushered by a pointing hand and has the rear brought up by a sign of admiration. Hence we may judge what great advantages would accrue from introducing signs, to express every passion; . . . How many modern Comedies, although raked together with great labour of imagination, have been read over without a single smile, and for this reason only, that the authors of them were ignorant of any method or sign, by which to discover whereabouts the wit and humour lay? and how many Tragedies have failed of moving the reader, only for want of a few signs of crying inserted in proper places?

The next essay "ridicules and exposes those vain pretenders to science, who endeavour to explain and account for the mysterious works of nature, by the finespun imaginations of their own brain." One such pretender maintains that the tongue and fingers are the only channels "by which our ideas are let out of the brain; . . . If these channels are any way obstructed, they presently begin to swell, foam and ferment and press prodigiously against the skull; till with pushing by each other, fighting for place, crouding, squeezing, and mixing with the brain, they breed such uproar and sedition in the head, that the patient cannot chuse but to fall into fits of raving and delirium, which after some continuance terminate in settled and downright madness." "Some persons have nevertheless been remedied by trepanning, which is cutting open the head, as when a cask is likely to burst, we ease it by boring a vent. . . . I have bought all the instruments and apparatus necessary for this part of Surgery, and am determined to send my servant with a gimlet, to perform the necessary operation upon every mad Author, Poet, Lover and Enthusiast of my acquaintance."

When the Meddler took leave of his readers at the end of the tenth number, "only desiring them to call in, and accept of another collation, next week," there was no hint that Trumbull was breaking off the series. A month later, on February 23, 1770, he initiated a new serial, "The Correspondent."

Assuming "the character of an universal Correspondent, to receive letters from all the world, to return suitable answers, and to patronize such writings, as nobody else would take any notice of," Trumbull's Correspondent promises to "vindicate [the World's] character from all . . . undeserved aspersions" and encourage "merit and virtue." With an eye to the theological and philosophical disputation in which he will soon be engaged, he announces that he will at times "attempt to employ the style of humour and irony; since it is allowed by the greatest men of all ages, that ridicule is the best method of disgracing known falshood."

Trumbull discontinued "The Correspondent" after only eight numbers, explaining later, "My leaving New Haven & engaging in an employment that left me no leisure for such amusements, made me soon drop the design." He did not resume the series until February 12, 1773, by which time he had returned to Yale as tutor. Remembering how the first numbers so enraged "some Persons of eminence" that "they called the Author, all the *rogues, rascals, knaves* and *scoundrels,* that could be invented," the Correspondent now wishes "to avoid the character of a Party-satirist. . . . my desire is to furnish, if I can, an entertaining series of miscellaneous essays." In spite of this profession he persists in making "satirical observations on the reigning follies and vices of the times" until finally his enemies threaten that "he is to be assaulted in private, caned, kicked and cudgelled; he is to have his nose cut off, his eyes knocked out, and his head beaten to a mummy; besides which, he is to be hanged, tarred and feathered, with several other punishments of so grievous a nature, that being employed at present in business more important, and engaged in amusements more agreeable, he declares that he hath neither leisure, nor inclination to undergo half of them." In a word, the Correspondent is a more contentious and less genial character than the Meddler.

While the Correspondent ranges through the conventional subject matter of the periodical essay, he instructs the reader more and diverts him less than the Meddler had done. In the area of manners there are essays on the government of families, flattery, the art of begging, and dunces. On the subject of dunces, three of whom Trumbull was just then portraying in *The Progress of Dulness,* the Correspondent wishes to vindicate the Egyptian god Theuth, inventor of the useful arts and sciences, who, finding that many of his countrymen are dunces, invents for them such pernicious arts as gaming, swearing, and debauchery. Theuth, ordering "all rogues, fools, simpletons, scoundrels and vagabonds in the kingdom" to convene "before his temple at the city of *Thebes*" on April 1, 1694, proceeds

> to lay down rules about ruffles, hairdresses and periwigs; shews them how to handle a cane, a fan, and a snuff box; unfolds to them the whole art of swearing and prophaneness, and gives them a compleat academy of compliments. He then produces a pack of cards, and a box of dice, and spends a long time, in explaining to them, the different kinds of gaming, and shewing them, how to calculate the chances of wagers. He directs them to the institution of clubs and lodges, and teaches them how to give out toasts, and drink bumpers. He gives some laudable hints about the erecting of brothels and concludes his instructions with a long explanation of the Freethinker's Creed.

Assuring them that "Sense, and Wisdom shall be out of fashion, and Honesty and Conscience shall be turned out of doors: And Coxcombs shall pass for Wits and Genius's, till the end of Dunces shall come," he commands the assembled company: "Retire then to your tents, ye Simpletons, game, dress, drink, revel, and carouse. Let your hearts be warmed with thankfulness, and your tongues sound forth the praise of *Theuth.* Let this day be remembered by your posterity as the period of gladness, and the first of *April,* as the anniversary of Fools." Fearful for his own country's future, the Correspondent warns: "*America* seems designed by Providence for the last stage of Arts and Sciences; for their final seat when they have bid adieu to the other parts of the world. Great part of their train have already arrived. *Sense* and *Genius* came over with the first European Settlers; *Fancy* and *Invention* have begun to appear; But *Humour* and *Satire* having scarcely landed, the cultivation of the soil seems almost at a stand; *Folly* and *Dulness* have made great progress, and in many places there is danger least the Tares should overrun the Wheat."

When the second part of **The Progress of Dulness (The Life and Character of Dick Hairbrain)** appeared, one of the Correspondent's friends, probably David Humphreys, asked, "Do you expect the world to mend? / Let me advise you better friend." The Correspondent (Trumbull himself) replies:

'Tis true the world will ne'er be good!
Nor is't our int'rest that it should:
For what should sat'rists live upon,
If all the fools and knaves were gone?

. . . . .

T'our praise be't spoken, now for twenty year,
Rogues, cheats & fools were never plentier;

. . . .

Were there no fools beneath the skies,
What were the trick of being wise?

. . . . .

While fools and knaves are nine in ten,
We'll pass for wits and honest men.

These lines reinforce the judgment made in the second part of **The Progress of Dulness,** wherein Trumbull expresses satisfaction "that the present year hath borne a sufficient number of fools to keep up the breed" and says of fops like Dick Hairbrain,

As fire electric draws together
Each hair and straw and dust and feather,
The travell'd Dunce collects betimes
The levities of other climes;
And when long toil has giv'n success,
Returns his native land to bless,
A Patriot-fop, that struts by rules,
And Knight of all the shire of fools.

Morality, not noticeably present as a subject in "The Meddler," is often the concern of the Correspondent, who discourses on greed, knavery as a vocation, lying and defamation, pride, Negro slavery, and medical quacks. These last two subjects are of particular interest in that they reveal Trumbull adapting his material to an American audience. "We have a natural, moral, and divine right of enslaving the Africans," asserts the Correspondent. "Is not the enslaving of these people the most charitable act in the world? With no other end in view than to bring those poor creatures to christian ground, and within hearing of the gospel, we spare no expence of time or money, we send many thousand miles across the dangerous seas, and think all our toil and pains well rewarded. . . . And are they not bound by all the ties of gratitude, to devout [*sic*] their whole lives to our service, as the only reward that can be

adequate to our superabundant charity!" At the end the Correspondent takes a universal view of the subject: "I would just observe that there are many other nations in the world, whom we have equal right to enslave, and who stand in as much need of Christianity, as these poor Africans. Not to mention the Chinese, the Tartars, or the Laplanders, with many others, who would scarcely pay the trouble of christianizing. I would observe that the Turks and the Papists, are very numerous in the world, and that it would go a great way towards the millennium, if we should transform them to Christians." While Trumbull's Congregationalism helps explain the slur on Roman Catholics, it is difficult to reconcile this frontal attack on Negro slavery with his known conservatism and moderation. It is unfortunate but a sign of youth that his irony lacks the subtlety of, say, Franklin's letter to the Philadelphia press, "On the Slave Trade."

Medical quacks, like metaphysical writers and incompetent or hypocritical clergymen, engross the Correspondent's attention. In all countries, he declares, Death "hath a set of retainers to his business, whom the learned distinguish by the name of Quacks and Mountebanks."

These Creatures know as little of physic, as of conjuration, are as poorly acquainted with the machinery of the human body, as of the air-pump, & are so far from understanding the operations of their potions, that they are entirely ignorant of the plainest principles of philosophy. Their stock and materials for setting up trade are, an old family-book of receipts, which they apply at a venture, as chance may be propitious; a portmanteau, stuffed with herbs and roots, to which they have given some fantastical name, and in which they pretend to have discovered some unaccountable virtues; and an extraordinary gift of impudence, to extol the miracles of their medical applications, deride the practice of regular Physicians, and vent hard words of terrible sound, of which neither they, nor their gaping admirers know any meaning.

As for their education, "after devoting four years to the business of Idleness, they live perhaps six months with some one, who has had the same liberal advantages, and then sally forth into the world to help diseases kill mankind. . . . I am well satisfied, that if there were but one hundredth part so many diseases in the world, as Quacks have infallible cures, this life would be little preferable to that, which we may charitably conclude they will one time experience." Among the instances of quackery "that have fallen under my observation, in the practice of some among the most noted Physicians in this colony," consider the following case:

A Woman, three or four months advanced in a state of pregnancy, being troubled with some peculiar disorders, applied to a Physician, who had for a great number of years been celebrated in all parts of the country, for extraordinary skill in such cases. The old Doctor, when he arrived, found her in a very languid state; but bade her be of good courage, for he had cured hundreds in the same condition, and was acquainted with an infallible remedy, in these disorders. . . . He ordered a distilled liquor to be prepared from the *uterus, foetus & secundines* of a pregnant ewe; arguing that those parts, which had served such excellent purposes in a brute animal, would undoubtedly, by help of their experience perform the same good offices in the human body. I cannot omit, that the butcher, who was employed to procure the necessary ingredients, being something of an humourist, very wisely recommended to the Doctor, on the strength of his reasoning, to have the brains also saved out to be distilled for himself, and taken as a nostrum to promote medical knowledge.

The Correspondent is convinced that "these matters can never be properly regulated, but by the interposition of the Legislative Authority of the Colony. Affairs of far less importance have been thought worthy their notice, and been the subject of a multiplicity of debates. A Lawyer shall not be allowed to practice in any court of judicature, till he have undergone a strict examination, and taken a solemn oath of faithfulness in his business and fidelity to his clients. . . . Very wise regulations are also established among the Clergy, and very just laws enacted to restrain an unbounded licence of Preaching." Surely, then, "some public examination of young Practitioners, some regular licence might be insisted on." Law, divinity, and physic were associated one with the other in the mind of the eighteenth century, as the Correspondent's last remarks suggest. It is revealing that Trumbull the essayist, who would be studying law within six months, never attacks that profession as he often does the other two.

The Correspondent reflects philosophically on the blessings of folly, love of esteem, public spirit, and what dying does for a man's reputation. "Dying is certainly the most expeditious way of gaining a reputation; it makes almost as great a change in a man's character, as his estate; it will transform a Scoundrel into a Gentleman, a notorious Cheat into a Man of Piety, and the most insignificant Scribbler into a great Genius." Consider the cobbler Samuel Snip:

> . . . such was his increase of piety, that it may justly be affirmed, not a day passed, in which he did not as well amend the temper of his soul, as the shoes of his customers. . . . So great was the fame of his honesty and integrity, that he was often appealed to in disputes between his neighbours, & made arbitrator of several considerable wagers at the tavern & ale-house. . . . He sustained many honorable offices in this town. In the forty-sixth year of his age, he was solemnly set apart to the ecclesiastical office of a Sexton, which he exercised with much care and fidelity to his dying day. He kept the church in the utmost neatness, dug graves with great alacrity, and rang the bells with peculiar harmony and modulation. . . . He was for many years one of the School-committee for a certain district in the town; in which office, in conjunction with two Blacksmiths and a Barber, he was always particularly frugal of the public money, and engaged the cheapest schoolmaster that offered himself for sale.

"And at last, full of days and full of honours, when, with *Caesar,* he had lived long enough both for nature and glory, to the unspeakable loss of his bereaved friends and his weeping country, this Glory of Sextons, this Flower of School-committees, this Ornament of Corporals, and Phoenix of Cobblers was snatched away by relentless Death, in the 81st year of his age."

The Correspondent hopes that he draws his characters to life, but cautions "all those who find their own characters drawn, to take as little notice of it as possible, and remember that although the arrow be shot at random, among the flock, yet the bird that flutters is certainly known to be wounded." His gallery includes Xantippus the slanderer, Dogmaticus the fool, the dunces Castalio and Garrulas, and the hypocrites Sombrio and Malicio. On weekdays Sombrio leaves the door open so that he may be seen at morning prayers, for he "is sensible that he shall never procure the reputation of performing secret duty, unless mankind find it out; and how shall they find it out, unless they catch him in the very act?" "On Sunday he takes his broad-brimmed hat and black wig, which is never profaned with powder, and, without any levity in his walk, proceeds to church. Being there comfortably built up in the faith by a nap, he returns home, thinking the people all the way spy in him nothing less than little Saint or Angel in embryo."

The fact that the Correspondent chooses to instruct his readers more and divert them less than the Meddler explains why none of his essays are purely humorous and why only two focus on literary criticism. Aware that his satirical method has won him numerous enemies, he defends the use of personal satire under special circumstances. "The first is the case of personal injury. He, who endeavours to ruin my character, gives me an equal right over his own; and common sense will always justify the man, who exposes unprovoked slander, or revenges himself on a malicious aggressor." The second case "is when a man stands forth as the champion of injured innocence, against the assaults of open malevolence, or the ambush of secret slander." Finally, "when a Man's vices, by their nature and tendency, become hurtful to the public, every member of the society is injured by his conduct, and hath as just a right to expose his character, or designs, so far as they influence the morals of mankind, as he would have to remove a public nuisance." But "if it be in our power," adds the Correspondent, "let us expose the vice without naming the person, or dragging forth the character to public view." For the most part eighteenth-century practice observed these injunctions on the use of satire. Trumbull's own writings, both prose and poetry, always do.

In view of the epistolary nature of the periodical essay it is not surprising that the Correspondent should offer his thoughts on letter writing. "I shall at present remark on the serious, the complimentary, and the whimsical letter writer, the lady, the lover, and the satirist; and endeavour to point out in each which is ridiculous." Serious letter writers "are extremely apt to be well with help from above, to remain yours in the Lord, and to send salutations for compliments." The complimentary letter writer begins in a lofty manner, "Incomparable friend, I received your inimitable letter, and am eternally obliged to your condescending goodness, that you would demean your dignity to write to one, whose weak abilities are so far beneath the task of returning an equivalent answer." "The whimsical letter writer hates pedantry and affectation; he has heard that an easy, natural style is the chief beauty of letters; and thinks a sprightliness of imagination the only mark of genius. To avoid stiffness in style, he never finishes a period; to avoid method, he loses all connection; and to be witty, he strains at things so uncommon, that he deviates into the downright flightiness of nonsense." "The high bombast of love letters hath been so often exposed, that it may save a satirist the trouble; but the cringing submission of their usual style deserves equal notice." Here is how such a letter would run:

> Madam, upon the strictest examination finding myself absolutely good for nothing, I have thought proper to offer myself to you: hoping that you will esteem me so highly, as to be willing to spend the rest of your life with me. As I have fallen entirely out of favor with myself, I doubt not of obtaining favor of you; and I think you cannot but be extremely obliged to me for the offer of an heart and hand, which I set not the least value on, and assure you are entirely unworthy of your notice. If you will be so kind as to accept of me on this representation, it will save me the trouble of dying for love, which I design otherwise to set about immediately; being resolved to get rid of myself, as soon as possible, either by marriage or hanging, both of which, it is said, go by destiny.

Trumbull, who planned to move to Boston in the fall of 1773, has the Correspondent announce in July, "As the Copartnership between the Correspondent and the Public will soon be dissolved, all persons, that have any accounts to settle . . . are desired to send them in as soon as possible." One contributor, chagrined at hearing this news, praises the Correspondent for "the Plainness, the Freedom, the Honesty, and Integrity of your Dealings; your prudent Choice of Commodities; the Importance of your Fund; and the Regularity, and Justness of your Accounts." Soon word comes that "on Monday last, agreeably to his own predictions, departed this life the noted Correspondent, who for some time past hath existed in the public papers." Of his life all that is known for certain is "that he died in the tenth year of his age." Opinions differ as to the cause: one physician "affirms that he died of the Catarrh, or dripping of the brains"; another, "that he died of the *Caput mortuum.*" "He was embalmed by his friends, and the last offices will be performed to him, as soon as they have complied with the injunctions of his will, which he hath ordered his executor to publish in the next paper." In his last will and testament, which brings the series to an end, the Correspondent bequeaths to the public all his "literary productions, which were composed for their own use and entertainment," adding, "I return my sincere thanks for the general kindness I have received from the Public, and desire only that the same goodness may still be extended towards my memory, that my writings may be read with candour, as they were composed without malevolence, and that a judgment of my character or designs may not be formed from the accounts of those men, who find it their interest and make it their business, by the most improbable falshoods to oppose, misrepresent and defame me."

Trumbull's prophecy in 1770, "This Land her Steele and Addison shall view," was never fulfilled, even though the periodical essay continued popular into the first years of the nineteenth century. Although Timothy Dwight dubbed Joseph Dennie "the Addison of the United States," it was a title the author of the "Lay Preacher" essays did not earn the right to wear. Certainly Trumbull was not the American Addison, nor did he claim to be. The Meddler and the Correspondent are thin disguises assumed by a young man who was unable, or perhaps unwilling, to put dramatic distance between himself and his readers. Of the conventions associated with the periodical essay—including dream vision, moral dialogue, beast

fable, genealogy and adventures, transformation, foreign visitor, and oriental tale—Trumbull availed himself of only a few: for instance, fictitious letter, aptronym, and mock-advertisement. Like Franklin, who initiated the tradition in America, and Irving, who presided over its demise, Trumbull began his career as a serial essayist. Whereas Franklin and Irving developed into wide ranging prose writers, Trumbull found poetry his proper element. Nevertheless, it is worth remembering that he served an apprenticeship as essayist and that these apprentice works not only illuminate the meaning of poems like *The Progress of Dulness* but left the serial essay tradition in America permanently enriched. (pp. 273-86)

> Bruce Granger, "John Trumbull: Essayist," in Early American Literature, *Vol. X, No. 3, Winter, 1975-76, pp. 273-88.*

Robert D. Arner   (essay date 1977)

[In the following excerpt, Arner examines Trumbull's poetic technique.]

Trumbull's two major poems, *The Progress of Dulness* and *M'Fingal,* were both initially published in partial versions. The first grew out of Trumbull's essay series, "The Correspondent," and his efforts to revise the curriculum at Yale during his first year as tutor, when he and Dwight sought to introduce modern literature into the program of study. The first part of *Progress,* featuring the adventures of a ministerial student named Tom Brainless, was published in 1772, and parts two and three, the *Life and Character of Dick Hairbrain* and *The Progress of Coquetry; or, The Adventures of Miss Harriet Simper,* appeared in January and September of the next year. Perhaps, as some have thought, Trumbull was actually acquainted with the fop and the coquette upon whom he modeled these last two characters, but nevertheless they do not have the authority of portraits drawn from life. They seem rather like those early eighteenth-century American portraits, where stylized costume, gesture, and pose carry the message of status and type at the expense of individualized character study.

Foppery and coquetry, if they ever existed in New England as they are represented in the poem (only Dick Hairbrain's rusticity carries conviction on this count), have long since passed out of fashion as primary concerns for satire. Not so the abuses, misuses, and illusions of a college education which Trumbull treats in Canto I, easily the best part of the poem. Modern Trumbullians who complain about the present quality of college graduates or of Ph.D.'s who could not read their own diploma if it were written in Latin may take either comfort or despair from Tom Brainless, whose

> wit and learning now may
> Be proved by token of diploma,
> Of that diploma, which with speed
> He learns to construe and to read. . . .

What Trumbull is against, of course, is not the learning of Latin, but the rote memorization of a dead language that, imperfectly acquired at best, is of no practical advantage even to the future minister except to make him proud in the possession of a parchment. Education in New England, apparently, had not changed much between Tom

Brainless's school days and Benjamin Franklin's "Dogood No. IV" (1722), but American schools would eventually walk down a much straighter and narrower path of practicality than either Trumbull or Franklin (see also Franklin's "Proposals Relating to the Education of Youth in Pensilvania" of 1749) dreamed of, perhaps to its present dead end.

In the first section of **Progress,** Trumbull frequently manages an ironic compression more reminiscent of the closed couplets of Alexander Pope than of Butler's galloping overruns: "And hear no prayers, and fear no fine," for instance, deliberately confuses even as it separates over a medical caesura the worlds of the spirit and the flesh, at the same time implying through its ironic echo of the Psalmist's "fear no evil," its alliterative stress, and the end positioning of "fine" that this world is more worrisome to the would-be minister than the next; "Sermons to study, and to steal" again employs alliteration to align two very different verbs with a single noun in order to enforce the flat contradiction between the act of stealing and the content of most sermons. To demonstrate the debasement of true learning, what better way than to show classical Latin at the service of sloth and triviality, this time through rhymes which are reticently metaphoric:

> With sleepy eyes and count'nance heavy,
> With much excuse of *non paravi,*
> Much absence, *Tardes* and *egresses,*
> The college-evil on his seizes. . . .

> What silly rules in pomp appear!
> What mighty nothings stun the ear!
> *Athroismos, Mesoteleuton,*
> *Symploce* and *Paregmenon!*
> Thus, in such sounds high rumbling, run
> The names of jingle and of pun. . . .

> The scholar dress that once array'd him,
> The charm, *Admitto te ad gradum.* . . .

Shortly after the publication of **Progress,** Trumbull's growing involvement in the revolutionary cause turned his attention to matters more pressing than the quality of higher education, and, while in Boston studying law with John Adams, he wrote his **"Elegy on the Times"** (1774), a serious attack on the Boston Port Bill which opens with an echo of Goldsmith's *Deserted Village* (1770) and, therefore, an implicit reminder that Britain has been guilty of similar inhumanities in the past. On August 7 and 14, 1775, there followed a burlesque poem, **"By Thomas Gage . . . A Proclamation,"** and later that year, at the request of some members of the Continental Congress, the first version of **M'Fingal.** In a letter to the Marquis de Chastellux dated May 20, 1785, Trumbull acknowledged the congressional urgings and added that his original intention had been "to satirize the follies and extravagances of my countrymen, as well as of their enemies." Since we know that he had outlined the third canto and composed parts of the forth as early as 1775, there is no strong reason to doubt this *post facto* statement, as some have done, and accuse the poet of compromising an originally democratic work by adding criticism of the "patriotic" rabble in the finished version of 1782. It is, indeed, in part this balanced view which lifts **M'Fingal** far above the level of other diatribes that passed for political satire in the early years of the Republic.

Squire M'Fingal at the liberty pole.

In the first and second cantos of **M'Fingal,** the Tory M'Fingal and the Whig Honorius debate at length the causes that impell to separation. The forum for their debate is the town meeting, backbone of New England democracy, but when the session ends in a shouting match between the two factions, with every blockhead wishing to have his say, Trumbull has already laid the foundation for his criticism of unrestrained liberty. What the Whigs cannot demonstrate by force of logic, they prove by force of arms in Canto 3, in which M'Fingal leads an assault upon a Liberty Pole outside the meeting house. The attack is repulsed, the laborer's spade besting the aristocrat's sword, and M'Fingal is seized, tarred and feathered, paraded through the town on a cart, and eventually returned to the steps of the meeting house. There, his backside glued to the pole and his optics made gloomy by the flowing pitch, he foresees an ultimate Whig victory. In Canto 4, he calls a convocation of Tories in his cellar and elaborates upon his gloomy vision as it was revealed to him in a dream by another high-ranking Tory, one Malcolm, who was almost lynched by a patriotic mob. The meeting is interrupted by Whig rabble, however, from whom M'Fingal flees toward Boston as the poem closes.

As in **Progress,** in this satire Trumbull occasionally calls upon compression and the suggestiveness of syntax to make his ironic equations: "Till all this formidable league rose / Of Indians, British troops, and Negroes. . . . " For the most part, however, he enjoys his greatest degree of success in this poem with historical and literary allusions. Again the example of Pope, and especially of *The Dunciad,* lurks under the Butlerian surface. There is, for instance, some of Pope's metaphorical interplay between the abstract and the concrete in Trumbull's naming—Honorius and Justic Quorum balanced against Abijah White, Malcolm, and a host of other Tories—but it is the real names that work most effectively. In general, Trumbull's rhymes and catalogues of names, often functioning simultaneously as mock heroic devices, work to implicate the Tories and the British in the creation of a world of improbability and poetic dissonance, to draw them into the unusual, the freakish, and away from the order represented by the traditionally strong masculine rhymes of the heroic couplet. The names may also operate in more specific contexts; "consign'd" pairs with "Burgoyned" and "follies" with "Cornwallis" in tightly compressed statements of what were, for Americans at the time, the essential qualities of these two British generals. So, too, the underlying theme of Tory self-interest is well served by an individualized roll call of M'Fingal's heroes as he expects to see them in their future glory:

> Behold! the world shall stare at new setts
> Of home-made Earls in Massachusetts;
> Admire, array'd in ducal tassels,
> Your Ol'vers, Hutchinsons and Vasalls;
> See join'd in ministerial work
> His Grace of Albany, and York.
> What lordships from each carved estate,
> On our New-York Assembly wait!
> What titled Jauncys, Gales and Billops;
> Lord Brush, Lord Wilkins and Lord Philips!
> Aloft a Cardinal's hat is spread
> O'er punster Cooper's reverend head.
> In Vardell, that poetic zealot,
> I view a lawn-bedizen'd Prelate;
> While mitres fall, as 'tis their duty,
> On heads of Chandler and Auchmuty!

Interlayered among these catalogues are numerous literary allusions, most to the Old Testament but some, significantly in context, to the book of Revelation. Persistently if not systematically, the story of Israel's delivery from Egyptian bondage unfolds behind the day's events at the meeting house and elsewhere, reminding us of Trumbull's strong New England heritage and establishing the frame of values within which the satire operates. "Will this vile Pole, devote to freedom," demands M'Fingal scornfully,

> Save like the Jewish pole in Edom;
> Or like the brazen snake of Moses,
> Cure your crackt skulls and batter'd noses?

Here and in the lines immediately following them in the third canto, Trumbull seems to be at least partly on M'Fingal's side, decrying the patriot's concept of liberty as "But for crimes a patent license, / To break of law th' Egyptian yoke, / And throw the world in common stock." At other moments, however, the Scotsman stands alone, blasphemously elevating Lord North to the divinity of Christ and proclaiming a Second Coming with material rewards for the faithful:

> I see the day, that lots your [the Whigs'] share
> In utter darkness and despair;

> The day of joy, when North, our Lord,
> His faithful fav'rites shall reward.
> No Tory then shall set before him
> Small wish of 'Squire or Justice Quorum;
> But to his unmistaken eyes
> See lordships, posts and pensions rise.

The final cantos of *M'Fingal* and undetermined contributions to *The Anarchiad* in 1786 all but mark the end of Trumbull's poetic career. A combination of ill health and increasing judicial responsibilities kept him from an occupation which was at best, perhaps, chiefly a response to his country's needs. A few "Newscarrier's Addresses," another brief essay serial ("The American"), and, it is thought, a substantial body of anonymous political prose which may well never be definitely attributed to him just about tally his productivity after the adoption of the Constitution. Though he achieved considerable proficiency as a political satirist, Trumbull often remarked that he wielded the satirist's pen only reluctantly, because the age demanded it. On the evidence of his **"Newscarrier's Address"** for New Year's, 1824, we may easily believe this, for even the highly partisan politics of the constitutional crisis, bitter as they often became, do not appear to have scarred him permanently. An aging man, he could look back on that time of domestic turmoil and good-naturedly reflect:

> Democracy and Federalism
> That caus'd such uproar once, and schism,
> Have stoutly fought their quarrel out,
> Till nought was left to fight about.

(pp. 236-40)

Robert D. Arner, "The Connecticut Wits," in American Literature 1764-1789: The Revolutionary Years, *edited by Everett Emerson, The University of Wisconsin Press, 1977, pp. 233-52.*

Robert A. Ferguson   (essay date 1984)

[*In the following excerpt, Ferguson discusses the influence of Trumbull's legal training on his works and literary career.*]

John Trumbull's talent made him the most celebrated American poet of the eighteenth century, and his critical expertise brought vital leadership to the country's first school of poetry, the Connecticut Wits. But these achievements have always seemed minor when placed against a precocity that promised so much more. By the age of four Trumbull had read the Bible through and was writing verse. At seven, in 1757, he gained admission to Yale College, and, by nine, with Milton and Thomson as guides, he had versified half of the Psalms. He was a leading intellectual at Yale as a young tutor in the early 1770s and a recognized poet before he was twenty-five. All of this activity flowed from a strong, particular, and continuing sense of purpose. From the beginning Trumbull sought "to build a name" in literature, and it was no idle boast when he later wrote John Adams of his determination "to be the most learned Man in America." And yet his best poems, *The Progress of Dulness* (1772-1773) and *M'Fingal* (1775-1782), hardly convey such talent, energy, and ambition. Trumbull was the first to acknowledge his own failure. He excluded everything done in later life, almost forty years, from his *Poetical Works,* when they appeared in 1820.

What happened to the brilliant young writer compared by contemporaries to Swift and Butler? Were American audiences simply unreceptive to the uses and meaning of poetry—particularly satiric poetry? Did Trumbull ossify within a rigid neoclassical tradition? Was this son, grandson, and great-grandson of somber Connecticut clergymen unable to appreciate his own genius for humorous verse? These are the questions biographers have asked in exploring a lost talent, but their answers fail to account for the poet's situation. Trumbull had the intellectual support of community leaders, and his best efforts received popular acclaim. Although committed to neoclassical tenets, he championed the formal study of modern literature on its own terms. Certainly no one in the early republic had a clearer notion of the value and meaning of humor. Satire was "a medicine very salutary in its effects," and Trumbull clearly enjoyed "the groans and distortions of the Patient" who received his "potion." He also understood his central role as a pioneer in American humor. "I have the honour," he once observed, "of being the first, who dared by Satire to oppose the party of controversial Scribblers, & set this part of America an example of the use of Ridicule & Humour, to combat the whims of dogmatical Enthusiasts."

Successful, eager, and perceptive, Trumbull nonetheless stood in the way of his own talent, and his legal career helps to explain why. In effect, the lawyer's goals came to contain those of the poet through the affinities of law and letters in early republican culture. These affinities, the presence of a legal mind within the poetry, are clearest in Trumbull's best works. *The Progress of Dulness* dramatizes the eighteenth-century American intellectual's vocational movement away from the ministry and toward law. *M'Fingal* epitomizes the lawyer's peculiar ambivalence regarding Revolutionary politics. Both poems project the tensions and aspirations that undermined Trumbull's creativity. Examined closely, they illuminate the problems that led toward later silence.

Sixteen hundred lines of jingling tetrameter couplets, *The Progress of Dulness* satirizes three different character types: Tom Brainless, a drudge of a divine, who "deals forth the dulness of the day" from a country pulpit; Dick Hairbrain, who moves from yokel to fop on the strength of his father's wealth; and Harriet Simper, who rises and falls as the traditional coquette in "gaudy whims of vain parade." Of the three sections, only part one, *The Rare Adventures of Tom Brainless,* has the bite of true satire. Here Trumbull attacks the loose educational standards of Yale College and the errors of a Connecticut clergy enmeshed in doctrinal wrangling and mediocrity. These were bold targets for an American writer in 1772, particularly for a youth of twenty-two whose father then presided as a leading minister of the region and a trustee of Yale. Trumbull, a true son of New England, meant only to "point out . . . those general errors, that hinder the advantages of education and the growth of piety." Even so, he soon found himself branded "an enemy to truth and learning" by certain "Reverend Gentlemen." Ministers were quick to find "an open reviler of the Clergy" whose "apparent design was to ridicule religion, disgrace morality, sneer at the present methods of education, and, in short, write a satire upon Yale-College and the ten commandments."

The strength of such resentment reveals *The Progress of Dulness* for what it is: the first popular work to document the diminished status of the clergy in Revolutionary America. As one historian has put it, "In 1740 America's leading intellectuals were clergymen and thought about theology; in 1790 they were statesmen and thought about politics." Tom Brainless' inept ministry is the fanciful projection of this change; it "does little good, and little harm," in part because it is so irrelevant. Trumbull's characterization traces a descent across the generations. The parson who instructs Tom has forgotten the ancient languages that his pupil can never learn. "From heaven at first your order came," the poet reminds all brothers of the cloth, but smaller minds have long since reduced truth and conviction to a narrow search for orthodoxy. The ministers who gather for Tom's ordination sermon know that Brainless is incompetent both in name and in fact. They admit him anyway:

> What though his learning be so slight,
> He scarcely knows to spell or write;
> What though his skull be cudgel-proof!
> He's orthodox, and that's enough.

Later in *The Progress of Dulness* Trumbull describes the empty social posturing of a modern church service: "To church the female squadron move, / All arm'd with weapons used in love." The explicit contrast is to the sincerity and vigor of New England's first Community of Saints:

> Each man equipp'd on Sunday morn,
> With psalm-book, shot and powder-horn;
> And look'd in form, as all must grant,
> Like th' ancient, true church militant.

In a telling juxtaposition, the poet's generation of churchmen struggle against themselves in vain theological debate. No shot and powder-horn here! They are scribbling dogmatists who "fight with quills, like porcupines."

Not least in Trumbull's portrait of declension is his pervasive humor. That the poet presumes to satirize "where dreaded satire may not dare" gives final proof of the minister's lost hegemony in American culture. Nor is Trumbull slow to trace the implications of a dwindling vitality in religious thought. About to enter the law office of John Adams in Boston, he deliberately stings the clergy with the new choice of young men on the rise:

> [When] fools assume your sacred place,
> It threats your order with disgrace;
> Bids genius from your seats withdraw,
> And seek the pert, loquacious law.

The shift in professional preferences that began in the generation of John Adams was in full swing when the poet wrote these lines. A decade later, Trumbull's contemporary and sometime collaborator, Noah Webster, summarized the result: "Never was such a rage for the study of the law. From one end of the continent to the other, the students of this science are multiplying without number."

Significantly, Tom Brainless "starves on sixty pounds a year" in his country parish. Ministers on fixed incomes were swamped by the inflationary spirals of the Revolutionary and post-Revolutionary periods, while lawyers rode the crest upon the only profession that was both lucrative and secure. Did Trumbull's hopes for wealth and place as a lawyer squelch his penchant for satire? It has been argued that "there was no circle in America into which he [Trumbull] could escape for approval and praise after an onslaught upon the dullards. He had to live among his victims—and eventually expect them to be his legal clients and political supporters." No wonder the poet of 1772 worried about making "a new set of Enemies." He consciously diluted his satire in the last two parts of *The Progress of Dulness,* giving special credence to a couplet in the closing section: "So priests drive poets to the lurch / By fulminations of the church." And yet the same poet was quite willing to challenge and cudgel his "malicious attackers," any one of whom might "have sate for the picture of Tom Brainless." Greater issues than careerism and financial security tempered Trumbull's humor— issues concerned with the intrinsic connection of law and politics and with the intellectual ascendancy of the lawyer in Revolutionary America.

A closer look at *The Progress of Dulness* suggests a troubled and troubling vision of America. The collective cognomen "Tom, Dick, and Harriet" reaches for generic significance, and Trumbull uses his caricatures to excoriate two related evils in American society: impiety and a growing materialism. These ills are the ones deplored by most eighteenth-century American intellectuals in their calls for a return to virtue through education, public service, and a right sense of religion. In fact, the second part of *The Progress of Dulness* ends with just such a call. But Trumbull's happy man who applies "the will of heaven" and "studious pain" to achieve "heart-felt peace of mind" and the praise of his community is a strangely disembodied figment with no part to play in the society of Brainless, Hairbrain, and Simper. There is no clear path to virtue in *The Progress of Dulness.* For while folly is punished in Trumbull's poem, the fates of his characters raise more questions than they answer.

In part one, laziness and ignorance reward the Reverend Tom Brainless with the obscurity that he manifestly deserves. However, Trumbull saves his sharpest barbs for Brainless' opponents, the New Light Divines who try to rejuvenate the clergy and reconstitute religious fervor in the second half of the eighteenth century. *The Progress of Dulness* may praise the true church militant, but it seeks no modern equivalent. Like Adams and Jefferson before him, Trumbull has absorbed the rational-legal temperament of Lord Kames. He wants nothing to do with dogmatism, enthusiasm, and revivalism as mechanisms of social improvement. Conventionally in favor of piety, he distrusts the wellsprings of emotion that supply religious conviction.

The poet hopes instead that "bright philosophy" and "ethics" will combine with common sense to "teach the laws divine."

> Oh! might I live to see that day,
> When sense shall point to youths their way;
> Through every maze of science guide;
> O'er education's laws preside;
> The good retain, with just discerning
> Explode the quackeries of learning.

The secular humanism in this passage encourages a cool head, not a warm heart. Trumbull's sensationalist stress— "When sense shall point to youths their way"—also leaves

plenty of room for the materialism of a Dick Hairbrain or a Harriet Simper. Implicitly, the poet places rationalism and worldly prudence on a par with religious conviction, but since virtue still rests upon piety, the overall result is a kind of moral confusion. Trumbull's solutions compound his problems and reflect uncomfortable transitions in New England life.

The punishments of Dick and Harriet in parts two and three of *The Progress of Dulness* are even more problematic. Fop and coxcomb, Dick fails not because of his moral deficiencies but because of poor fiscal management. In a crass world of Hairbrains, wealth keeps Dick's "name / Rank'd in the foremost lists of fame" and excuses every form of bad behavior. Only bankruptcy can expose and condemn. As Trumbull admits, "The coxcomb's course were gay and clever, / Would health and money last for ever." Harriet Simper's difficulties can be summarized in similar terms: given the opportunity, she fails to marry well. Her coquetry attracts "deserving lovers" along with the usual "powder'd swarm" of dandies. Alas, Harriet does not know when to stop or, more important, whom to choose. The absence of true virtue has less to do with missing her goal in life—a good match—than lack of discernment. Harriet's flaw, like Dick's, is a failure to apply common sense and prudence in worldly matters. Although Trumbull would wish it otherwise, his characters are punished not because they play games with life but because they don't play life's game well enough.

America has become a place in which simple "country manners" give way to the "vain parade" of the "pop'lous city." In *The Progress of Dulness* primitive virtues have been lost, but meaningful culture remains a distant prospect. "The half-genteel are least polite," warns the poet. As if to foreshorten this disastrous middle stage in cultural development, Trumbull hustles Dick and Harriet into premature old age, each within a few lines. Unfortunately, the immediate future promises nothing better. In a final thrust Trumbull marries off the vulgar Simper to the ignorant Brainless. Little can be expected from this version of an American union.

Such negativism left the poet of 1773 with a problem. *The Progress of Dulness* undercut an intrinsic optimism in early republican literature and contradicted the poet's own resolutions. Trumbull had written his poem "for the universal Benefit of Mankind" and "to promote the interests of learning and morality." There was bombast in the use of these abstractions but also intense inner conviction. The value of poetry lay in public service. If the story of Tom, Dick, and Harriet failed to "conduce to the service of mankind," then Trumbull "had spent much time in the studies of the Muses in vain."

The subordination of creativity to service put a high premium on the social vision of the writer, and this impulse, in turn, prompted the strongest possible presentation of country during the political turmoil of the 1770s. What *The Progress of Dulness* lacked was an articulate plan for the future of America. One consequence was that its design was "by many . . . ignorantly or wilfully misunderstood." Trumbull would try to rectify his mistake by including just such a vision in his next major effort, *M'Fingal,* but even then he hesitated—not from a fear of failure but over the uncertain impact of success. The stipulation that a literary work serve given social ends placed a heavy responsibility upon the writer who decided to publish. To those who encouraged the plan of *M'Fingal* in 1775, Trumbull at first opposed "grounds of Diffidence." "But suppose such a piece to succeed," he asked, "What would be its Effect?"

Trumbull feared the discrepancy between creative aims and public reactions, and in *M'Fingal* there was cause for worry. The poet's hopes for his mock-epic of the Revolution were complicated—far more complicated than his first readers realized. On one level, he lampooned the loyalist opposition through the rancorous persona of M'Fingal, a Scottish Tory who condemns the Revolution in a New England town meeting and is tarred and feathered for his pains. Here was the patriotic bluster that early republicans reveled in. Beneath the surface, however, Trumbull sought "impartiality" and wrote to "satirize the follies and extravagancies of my countrymen, as well as of their enemies." This more balanced view served other purposes than humor and chauvinism. By looking at both sides, the poet wanted to curb the radical impulses in Revolutionary politics and impose a conservative theory of order.

Like most Whig lawyers of the day and particularly like his mentor and lifelong leader John Adams, Trumbull was for the Revolution but against revolution. Mob excess represented at least as grave a danger to liberty as British tyranny. The democratic tendencies in Revolutionary politics had to be resisted because only a balance of aristocratic and popular components could hope to produce a responsible government. In this Trumbull followed the Polybian view of mixed government set forth by the Whig lawyers of England after the Glorious Revolution and followed closely by Adams and other American leaders in their own Revolutionary debates. There was, of course, much disagreement over the proper arrangement of aristocratic and popular components—Trumbull and generations of Federalists after him wanted "a *speaking* aristocracy *in the face of a silent* democracy"—but everyone agreed that only an impartial rule of laws could safeguard a proper mixture of influences and controls. Accordingly, what Trumbull criticized most in the revolutionary zealots of *M'Fingal* was their loss of respect for law. Too much rebellion undermined the legal foundations of constitutional government.

M'Fingal begins with a communal debate between Honorius, leader of the Whigs, and M'Fingal, who speaks for the Tories, at a town meeting. Even though these exchanges fill two of the poem's four cantos, Trumbull's narrative soon reaches the "Uproar and Rage and wild Misrule" that his character M'Fingal has foreseen as the logical outcome of revolution. Meaningful debate quickly becomes impossible. By cantos three and four, as open rebellion succeeds, the "vengeance of resentful Whigs" gives way to "the Mob, beflipp'd at taverns." The last Tories must meet alone at night and in secret. In the concluding lines of Trumbull's mock-epic, they flee in terror as their hiding place is invaded by "the rage of mob." Every form of authority and restraint is swept away in *M'Fingal.* The town constable is tarred and feathered. The chairman of the town meeting, Trumbull's clearest symbol of moderation, literally disappears as he tries "the peace to keep." "Like Sol half seen behind a cloud," he brings the meeting to order, but as tempers flare he moves "out of view, / Be-

neath the desk." Predictably, no one waits for this invisible moderator to gavel the meeting to a close. Even Honorius loses control. The speaker of the moment when an unidentified shout from outside the hall abruptly terminates debate, Honorius is not heard from again. Whig direction passes from the implicitly aristocratic orator to an unnamed brawler. This final leader in *M'Fingal* is "the stoutest wrestler on the green," and he fights with a worker's spade.

Trumbull explains exactly what has happened. Because the town is "torn by feuds of faction," it is subject to mercurial shifts that shake the body politic:

> So did this town with ardent zeal
> Weave cobwebs for the public weal,
> Which when completed, or before,
> A second vote in pieces tore.

These unsettled circumstances gradually destroy the natural order in the state, displacing a necessary aristocratic leadership and turning society on its head.

> For in this ferment of the stream
> The dregs have work'd up to the brim,
> And by the rule of topsy-turvies,
> The scum stands foaming on the surface.
> You've caused your pyramid t' ascend
> And set it on the little end.

Unleashed, the populace "make the bar and bench and steeple / submit t' our Sovereign Lord, The People." The inevitable result is "Anarchy from chaos." Once law becomes a momentary expression of popular opinion instead of an objective base for mutual restraint, mobs "cry justice down, as out of fashion" and "reduce all grievances and ills / To Magna Charta of your wills." In the pivotal scene of *M'Fingal,* just such a mob arbitrarily tries, sentences, and punishes M'Fingal in what Trumbull calls "an imitation of legal forms . . . universally practiced by the mobs in New-England" during the Revolution. The poet-lawyer calls this imitation of legal forms "a curious trait of national character," and his own constant wordplay upon legal terminology in *M'Fingal* draws attention to a larger problem.

For while *M'Fingal* celebrates the victory of patriotism over tyranny, it also points to a crying need for civic balance and respect for law—virtues lost in the Revolution. In this sense, Trumbull's Scottish Tory summarizes common American fears. By rejecting the British constitution ("That constitution form'd by sages, / The wonder of all modern ages"), the new states are turning away from the old, safe balances, risking "wild confusion" in "new-cast legislative engines." New balances must have seemed tenuous indeed in 1782, the year in which *M'Fingal* appeared, and there is much to puzzle over in the poet's brief glimpse of the future:

> This Rebel Empire, proud and vaunting,
> From anarchy shall change her crasis,
> And fix her pow'r on firmer basis;
> To glory, wealth and fame ascend,
> Her commerce wake, her realms extend.

The only certainty in this vision of empire is present chaos. After the calls to virtue in *The Progress of Dulness,* what is one to make of a future order built so entirely upon commercial prosperity? Post-Revolutionary theorists feared that America lacked the aristocratic components for a properly balanced, mixed form of constitutional government, and Trumbull seems to supply that deficiency here by predicting a new aristocracy of wealth and place. But could an Honorius lead such an empire? Would he want to? And if he could and did, what was to prevent an emerging nation of materialistic Hairbrains?

Trumbull and many others turned for answers to a conservative and legalistic republicanism. "The friends of order, justice, and regular authority," they were certain that a proper respect for law would supply leadership and insure virtue. Here was the crux of the matter for conservative republican intellectuals and the literature they wrote. They meant to create a controlling rule of law in a nation of laws, a goal that became an obsession when legal authority was challenged in the 1780s. The poet's last important work, *The Anarchiad* in 1786 and 1787, is a tale of woe precisely because the rule of law has been threatened by a general weakness in the Confederation of States and by the particular turmoil of Shays's Rebellion in Massachusetts. In *The Anarchiad* Trumbull and his collaborators, the other Connecticut Wits, still believe that virtuous leaders can "bid laws again exalt the imperial scale, / And public justice o'er her foes prevail," but in 1786 Shays's "mob-compelling name" has overwhelmed "the new-born state," and "Law sinks before [the] uncreating word" of Chaos. Everyone's worst fears have been confirmed: "Lo, THE COURT FALLS; th' affrighted judges run, / Clerks, Lawyers, Sheriffs, every mother's son."

The poet did not write for publication again. Shays, of course, fell quickly and a stronger constitution soon replaced the weak Articles of Confederation, but the events of the next decade, the democratizing course of the Revolution, left Trumbull and his friends fighting the same ideological battles over and over again. The factional splits between Federalist and Republican, the Whiskey Rebellion of 1794, the conflicts over the Alien and Sedition Acts of 1798, and, above all, the Republican victory of 1800 elicited the same cries of dismay previously heard in *The Anarchiad.* At some point in this period, Trumbull concluded that satiric writings no longer "checked and intimidated the leaders of disorganization and infidel philosophy" as they once had done. A growing threat to law and order from radical democracy required action instead of poetry.

Trumbull served first in 1789 as state's attorney for Hartford County and then as town representative to the legislature. Appointed a judge for the superior court of Connecticut in 1801, he killed whatever was left of the poet. "The character of a partizan and political writer," he explained, "was inconsistent with the station of a judge and destructive of the confidence of suitors in the impartiality of judiciary decisions." Jeffersonian attacks upon a Federalist judiciary in 1801 may have hastened this movement toward a defensive and exclusive professionalism, but the lawyer's decision necessarily grew from the writer's original aims. The poet of *M'Fingal* and the judge of the superior court were anxious defenders of the same precarious republicanism. Behind the transition was the same legal mind of the period, acting the role of ideological guardian. (pp. 100-11)

> *Robert A. Ferguson, "The Post-Revolutionary*
> *Writers: Trumbull, Tyler, and Brackenridge,"*
> *in his* Law and Letters in American Culture,

Cambridge, Mass.: Harvard University Press, 1984, pp. 96-128.

Peter M. Briggs (essay date 1985)

[*In the following excerpt, Briggs discusses Trumbull's difficulties in creating a uniquely American version of the English tradition of satirical humor.*]

There was laughter on these shores, of course, before there were scribes to record it, and for this reason any study of early American humor is likely to begin with notions easier to suppose than to demonstrate. Europeans met Indians in solemn conclave, and then each party went home with their own people to mock the dress, burlesque the manners, and parrot the mispronunciations of the other. Between decks of the Mayflower children whispered together, making foolish faces and mimicking the solemnity of their parents. Near New Amsterdam English travelers mocked Dutchmen, and the Dutch in their turn ridiculed the English. In the South children had to be taught not to snicker at the great man's funny-sounding name, General Oglethorpe. Everywhere older settlers tested the gullibility of newcomers by telling tall tales; new arrivals laughed uncertainly and looked forward to the day when they would possess the humorous self-assurance of older settlers. And, as with every great venture, things went wrong—it was rainy and muddy, or snowy and cold, or hot and dusty; mosquitoes were everywhere, or chiggers, or flies; crops failed or were eaten by pests; guns misfired and wagons broke; food spoiled and neighbors gossiped; children died, wives complained, and men got drunk—and people laughed ruefully at all these things because there was little else to be done.

In a sense, then, there is no identifiable beginning to a native tradition of American humor. By the same token we should recognize that nearly all of the early American humor that we do possess now is belated humor, humor that had to wait until people had the time, detachment, and inclination to write it down, along with the expectation of an audience to share it. Recording humor in a literary form changes its nature, of course: gone are the immediacy, spontaneity, and all the theatrical effects of personal delivery; in their place come the formal conventions of literary humor—the careful control of perspective and tone and pace, the building and shaping of audience expectations, the artful contrivance of economy, irony, and wit, the licensed improprieties of the professed humorist, and so on. To formalize humor in literature, then, is naturally a conservative gesture in a double sense: it preserves materials by setting them apart from the world of ephemera; and it performs this act of preservation by accomodating new materials to older cultural forms and conventions. (There are many more new jests in the world than there are new ways of telling them.) The higher one aspires as a humorist—for example, if one would be a formal verse satirist rather than a mere jokester—the more one is likely to be inspired yet circumscribed, challenged yet embarrassed by what has already been done well by one's predecessors in the humorous tradition.

Hence, there is another kind of belatedness in humor, a self-conscious awareness of one's debt to honored predecessors for the basic tools of one's trade, an indebtedness that may extend from fundamental conventions to bits of felicitous phrasing that the later humorist is anxious to revive or unwilling to forego. New literary opportunities and old literary obligations are often simultaneous and coincident; and, just as Dante was conducted by the shade of Virgil, so the latterday humorist is likely to find his work prompted and shaped and haunted by the spectres of Juvenal and Horace, Rabelais and Cervantes, Swift and Pope. Significantly, the shade of Virgil finally left Dante in Purgatory.

My subject, then, is the simultaneous newness and oldness of early American satirical humor, and the rich possibilities and subtle difficulties of accommodating the new with the old that American humorists encountered as they sought the right combination of "European-ness" and "American-ness," local color and general significance, personal idiosyncrasy and a representative voice. My principal examples are drawn from the works of John Trumbull, a Yale graduate (class of 1767) and a member of that loosely connected circle of poets—Timothy Dwight, Joel Barlow, David Humphreys, Lemuel Hopkins—generally known as the Connecticut Wits. Trumbull was not the first American literary humorist (George Alsop, Ebenezer Cook, Benjamin Franklin, William Byrd II, Dr. Alexander Hamilton, and others came earlier), but he was one of the most accomplished, and he also aspired higher than most, which meant that he confronted more directly the problem of combining the new and the old in an attempt to establish America as an appropriate setting for traditional kinds of literary humor. By now several generations of critics have concluded that Trumbull was basically a secondary figure in the development of American poetry and satire, a precocious poet whose early works suggested a literary promise that was never fulfilled in mature works, and there is no need here to challenge this assessment. Yet Trumbull is an enjoyable poet just as he stands, and there is useful instruction even in the works of secondary poets. Trumbull's struggles to domesticate his muse provide a clear instance of some of the general difficulties of cultural transmission and the particular difficulties and ambivalences of realizing America and American-ness in a literary form.

Seen from a sufficient philosophical distance, the rise of learning and the arts in America seemed natural, even inevitable. The translation of the fruits of older cultures westward to be renewed in younger and flourishing cultures was a well-established literary convention, and, insofar as one subscribed to this convention, the matter of carrying English culture to her colonies in North America seemed a simple and straightforward one, as direct and predictable as the westward movement of the sun. In a poem originally titled "America, or the Muse's Refuge: A Prophecy" (written 1726, published 1752) George Berkeley celebrated the future glory of America and particularly her fugitive muse:

> There shall be sung another golden age,
> The rise of Empire and of Arts,
> The Good and Great inspiring epic Rage
> The wisest Heads and noblest Hearts.

Berkeley concluded his prophecy with the most famous lines he ever wrote: "Westward the Course of Empire takes its Way. . . . Time's noblest Offspring is the last." He sought to support his hopeful vision with constructive action, projecting the establishment of a colonial college

in Bermuda, and, when that project failed for want of funding, sending books to Harvard and both books and monies to Yale. (John Trumbull would later hold a Berkeley scholarship as a graduate student at Yale.) Others in England shared Berkeley's hope for an American golden age, even after the Bermuda project failed. As late as 1774, almost on the eve of the Revolution, Horace Walpole could write of America's prospects with undimmed enthusiasm:

> The next Augustan age will dawn on the other side of the Atlantic. There will, perhaps, be a Thucydides at Boston, a Xenophon at New York, and, in time, a Virgil at Mexico, and a Newton at Peru. At last, some curious traveller from Lima will visit England and give a description of the ruins of St. Paul's.

Not surprisingly, matters looked somewhat different, if one stood on the opposite shores of the Atlantic. American colonists would gladly have embraced a native Thucydides or a village Virgil, but none raised his voice, and the resistless wave of European culture moving westward seemed more likely to overwhelm than to encourage the early signs of a distinctively American culture. By the middle of the eighteenth century American colonials were dependable importers of English culture—poetry, plays, and novels, of course, but also music, prints, paintings, theological works, instructional books, and so on. They had the money to pay for such cultural imports, but seemingly little prospect for repaying English culture in kind. The most they could hope was that their evident provincialism would not last forever, that at some indefinite future time, America might beget artists who would prove that colonial culture represented—not exactly something new, but a legitimate *extension* of English culture. For the present, however, there was little to be done beyond learning a graceful acceptance of provincial status. (pp. 13-16)

In his *Recherches philosophiques sur les Américains,* published in 1768, Cornelius DePauw, a French natural scientist, lent an unhelpful hand to American cultural confidence when he wondered rather pointedly whether America really possessed all the promise that others attributed to it. He argued on quasi-scientific grounds that America's climate was naturally unwholesome and perverse: American conditions caused European plants and domestic animals to become stunted and unhealthy, while noxious native plants and wild animals thrived; America was naturally a land of small crops and large weeds, stunted livestock and large mosquitoes. The possible analogy between blighted American nature and dwarfish American culture was obvious to contemporary observers, and although it is doubtful that DePauw's arguments ever persuaded a single American *not* to write a poem, play, or whatever, still the currency of such ideas suggests the deep ambivalence that many American colonials, still taking many of their cues from European attitudes, must have felt toward their own cultural endeavors.

Viewed against this doubt-filled background, the early career of John Trumbull seems oddly smooth and straightforward, unimpeded by his colonial status and circumstances. . . . In 1769, when he was still only nineteen, Trumbull collaborated with Timothy Dwight (who was seventeen) to launch a series of mildly satirical familiar essays, "The Meddler" papers, modeled loosely on Addison and Steele's *Spectator* papers, which appeared in *The Boston Chronicle.* In 1772-73, while he was serving as a tutor at Yale, Trumbull showed his independent-mindedness and self-confidence by publishing the first of the two poems for which he is remembered. *The Progress of Dulness,* which satirized among other things contemporary educational attitudes at Yale. Here was a writer unwilling to be circumscribed by the austere pieties of provincial life.

The three parts of *The Progress of Dulness* describe satirically the careers of three representative colonial types. In Part I Trumbull presents Tom Brainless, a farm boy who grows up to become first a dull and empty-headed scholar, then a tyrannical schoolmaster, and at last a provincial preacher who urges his dozing congregation toward salvation with the help of bold dogmatism and secret plagiarism. Part II presents Dick Hairbrain, son of a colonial farmer turned squire, who uses his opportunity to attend college to launch a career as a wit, fop, and debauché. In the final part Trumbull describes Miss Harriet Simper, a pretty girl who, through the efforts of her mother and other relatives, grows up to become a colonial coquette, doomed after countless fashionable flirtations and a frustrated love affair with Dick Hairbrain to settle down to a dull marriage with Tom Brainless. *The Progress of Dulness* is usually described as a satire of contemporary educational attitudes and practices (which it certainly is), but it also implies a broader indictment of colonial society as ill-educated, pretentious, short-sighted, complacent, and shallow. The satire itself is a well-managed one: witty, controlled, and multifaceted, quite an accomplished performance for a satirist of twenty-three.

My interest here, however, is not so much in *The Progress of Dulness* as a promising individual performance, but rather in its satirical genealogy, its evident indebtedness to some of the prevailing traditions of English satire. In fact, Trumbull's poem can be read as a composite of elements borrowed from the English satirists whom he most admired. The syntax, tone, and basic narrative structure of the poem are derived from Swift's various "Progress" poems—"The Progress of Love," "The Progress of Beauty," "The Progress of Poetry"—all of which explore a general theme by tracing the particular misadventures of a burlesque anti-hero or heroine. Trumbull's rough meter is Butlerian or Swiftian, as is also his tendency to include long lists of unlovely satiric particulars. Trumbull's informality of address and his affection for asides to the reader may be Swiftian, or they may derive from Charles Churchill, whose works were much admired in America by 1770. The poet's main theme, the prevalence of Dulness in the colonies, is clearly traceable to Pope's *Dunciad,* but in the various parts of his poem Trumbull borrows from other poems of Pope as diverse as *The Rape of the Lock, An Essay on Man,* and the *Epistle on the Characters of Women.* Modern scholars have also noted echoes from Waller, Dryden, Etherege, Prior, Gay, and others. Indeed, no small part of the art of Trumbull's poem is his easy and unobtrusive conflation of materials from such heterogeneous resources into a form that has its own energy and coherence.

Still, many of Trumbull's borrowings are too obvious to be hidden. Clearly they represent implicit tributes to earlier satirists, but they also serve the poet as an economical

way of orienting his own satire and of making it more resonant and generally significant. For example, he portrays Tom Brainless as a preacher struggling to put together a credible sermon—

> Round him much manuscript is spread,
> Extracts from living works, and dead,
> Themes, sermons, plans of controversy,
> That hack and mangle without mercy,
> And whence, to glad the reader's eyes,
> The future dialogue shall rise.

—a passage that clearly recalls Pope's energetic description of Colley Cibber struggling to rise through desperation and plagiarism into creativity:

> Round him much Embryo, much Abortion lay,
> Much future Ode, and abdicated Play;
> Nonsense precipitate, like running lead,
> That slip'd thro' Cracks and Zig-zags of the Head;
>
> . . . . .
>
> Next' o'er his Books his eyes began to roll,
> In pleasing memory of all he stole, . . .

In effect, Tom Brainless's lack of comprehension, wit, and substance is tied by allusion to a much longer tradition of dull, stolen hackwork, and Grub Street reaches across the ocean to embrace an American divine.

More generally speaking, Trumbull's entire presentation of Tom Brainless stands as an extended allusion to *The Dunciad:* Tom's rise through education to dull, dogmatic mediocrity recapitulates in miniature many of the abuses of learning satirized by Pope—the self-pleased wanderings of muddle-headed dullards whose notions of learning dissociate it from any ideas of natural order or human usefulness. Yet there is no *conspiracy* against civilization in *The Progress of Dulness:* Tom Brainless is a cultivated fool, but not a threat to any larger notion of civilization. To be sure, Trumbull was not an Alexander Pope, and his poem lacks the intensity, the seriousness, and the scope of Pope's poem; the story of Tom Brainless is not an American *Dunciad.* Yet it should be pointed out that a part of the relative lack of significance of Tom's story has little to do with Trumbull's abilities or aspirations. The American colonies in 1772 simply did not possess an intellectual, social, and political establishment that was or even, I dare say, could have been imagined to be comparable to Britain's—no capital, no court, no Parliament, no Prime Minister, no Oxford or Cambridge, not even a Grub Street or Smithfield or Drury Lane. The presence of such a backdrop of all-encompassing, integrated, and sinister cultural power is an important grounding to the satire in *The Dunciad:* Pope was writing about a society—really, a civilization—that could at least be conceived to operate, and to degenerate, as an integrated whole. Since America was not similarly centralized and integrated, Trumbull was forced by simple circumstance to employ metaphors of cultural decline in more restricted and less resonant ways. To put the matter plainly, Pope himself could not have written an American *Dunciad* at the time. More of this hereafter.

If the story of Tom Brainless springs principally from *The Dunciad,* the stories of Dick Hairbrain and Miss Harriet Simper derive from *The Rape of the Lock.* Both Dick and Harriet are foolish young things, trying out their self-centered pretensions and vanities upon the colonial social scene: Dick learns of up-to-date skepticism and stylish vices, while Harriet toys with foppish lovers and dotes upon the latest London fashions. Pope's Belinda, inevitably, provides the appropriate model and point of reference for comparable vanities and follies in Dick and Harriet, and Trumbull repeatedly recalls small details from Belinda's world in order to dramatize theirs. (pp. 16-20)

To appreciate the full (though intermittent) artfulness of Trumbull's poem, however, it is necessary to dwell, not on passages where he latched onto one particular model and sought to "translate" it to American circumstances, but on those passages where he deftly combined different resources to highlight his own subject. Consider, for example, his portrayal of Dick Hairbrain, returned from a European grand tour with all his affectations intact:

> As fire electric draws together
> Each hair and straw and dust and feather,
> The travell'd Dunce collects betimes
> The levities of other climes;
> And when long toil has giv'n success,
> Returns his native land to bless,
> A Patriot-fop, that struts by rules,
> A Knight of all the shire of fools.

The burlesque simile is characteristically Swiftian or Butlerian, but it may also recall Pope's depiction of the "needy Poet" in *The Dunciad* as a "vile straw that's blown about the streets, . . . now loose, now fast, And carry'd off in some Dog's tail at last." Certainly Trumbull's whole portrait of Dick Hairbrain as grand tourist glances at Pope's depiction of "young Aeneas," " . . . saunter[ing] Europe round, And gather[ing] ev'ry Vice on Christian ground." Finally Trumbull's description of young Dick as "Knight of all the shire of fools" echoes Dryden's description of Sir Fopling Flutter, another grand tourist, in his epilogue to Etherege's *Man of Mode:*

> True Fops help Natures work, and go to school,
> To file and finish god-a'mighty's fool.
> Yet none Sir *Fopling* him, or him can call;
> He's Knight o' th' Shire, and represents ye all.

In other words, Trumbull has marshalled a whole tradition of fops and fools who stand just behind his presentation of Dick and serve to amplify its meaning.

More generally speaking, Trumbull can be seen thinking through his satiric situation, his characters, his themes, his strategies, in terms of the achievements of his English predecessors in satire. This is good neoclassical practice, of course, and much the same thing that Pope or Churchill had done before him; satirists strengthen their works by the implicit insistence that such works do not stand alone, that they are parts of an honorable tradition. At the same time, however, this continual recollection of English predecessors suggests cumulatively a reluctance or an inability on Trumbull's part to imagine a distinctively American kind of satire, a new set of satiric norms and metaphors to go with a new setting for satire. (What exactly does "knight of the shire" mean in a land with no knights and in one where the term 'shire' was rapidly falling into disuse?) Obviously it was neither possible nor even desireable for Trumbull to invent a wholly new complement of satiric devices to reestablish satire on a new continent—new satire would inevitably continue to reflect its ancestors, even if those ancestors were an ocean away—and the poet was, after all, writing for an audience that had grown up on En-

glish kinds of satire. Nonetheless, it does not seem as if Trumbull's notions of satire have in any significant way been expanded or augmented by removal to America, and in some ways they clearly have been diminished by distance. In fact, there is little in *The Progress of Dulness* that is distinctively American: the satirist's heroes and heroine are definitely provincial, borrowing their thoughts and tastes from a world they conceive as more sophisticated than theirs, but for the most part they could be inhabitants of *any* province—a Cornish coquette, a Scottish preacher, an Irish fop. Their American-ness is subsumed in general provincialness. More significantly, it is clear that Trumbull's ideas of wit and satire are still basically London-centered; Connecticut and its local peculiarities are impediments to be overlooked, not resources for a new, strongly rooted American satire. In short, Trumbull wrote a rather good satire, but he was failing in important ways to "imagine" the literary potential of an American setting.

Trumbull dealt more directly with American materials in his more mature satire *M'Fingal,* published in parts in 1776 and 1782. Basically this poem tells the story of an American Tory, Squire M'Fingal, who seeks to discredit or subvert the efforts of American patriots to assert political independence from Britain: M'Fingal, defeated first in argument, then in a drunken brawl among enflamed partisans, finally becomes the victim of revolutionary zeal as he is tarred and feathered by vengeful patriots. Trumbull's mock-heroic poem is ostensibly an imitation of Butler's *Hudibras,* but Trumbull himself admitted that he had more often followed Swift and Churchill as models than Butler. A modern reader might be most struck by the number of Miltonic parodies that are sprinkled throughout the poem. Again, Trumbull was clearly thinking through his satiric situation in terms of the achievements of honored predecessors.

Still, *M'Fingal* does deal directly with subject matters and settings that are contemporary and distinctively American. M'Fingal attends a real town meeting, real troops march on a real Boston Common, and the various arguments in the poem between patriots and loyalists are based upon recent political events within the colonies. Yet even here there is a paradox. Consider as an instance M'Fingal's first glimpse of the Liberty pole in the town square which he and his Tory companions subsequently seek to pull down:

> When sudden met his angry eye,
> A pole, ascending thro' the sky,
> Which num'rous throngs of Whiggish race
> Were raising in the market-place;
> Not higher school-boys kites aspire,
> Or royal mast or country spire,
> Like spears at Brobdignagian tilting,
> Or Satan's walking-staff in Milton;
> And on its top the flag unfurl'd
> Waved triumph o'er the prostrate world,
> Inscribed with inconsistent types
> Of liberty and thirteen stripes.

Obviously the subject matter is local, particular, and American, but what is more interesting is Trumbull's method of imagining the Liberty pole—high as a royal mast, a Brobdignagian spear, Satan's walking-staff. It could be argued that Trumbull is writing from M'Fingal's point of view and that these English-derived metaphors are really artful reflections of the hero's Tory outlook. Yet it seems more likely, here as elsewhere, that Trumbull is revealing in himself a certain Toryism of the imagination, showing an ongoing figurative and imaginative indebtedness to English culture even as he and his fellow patriots celebrated political independence from England.

One further instance of this phenomenon in *M'Fingal* should confirm the point. Toward the end of the satire, M'Fingal, like many of his epic predecessors, is granted a vision of the future. Unwillingly, he sees the rout of his fellow Tories, the triumphs of the patriots, and the eventual rise of a new and independent nation. His vision concludes with a prophecy of America's future greatness:

> To glory, wealth and fame ascend.
> Her commerce rise, her realms extend;
> Where now the panther guards his den,
> Her desart forests swarm with men.
> Her cities, tow'rs and columns rise,
> And dazzling temples meet the skies;
> Her pines descending to the main,
> In triumph spread the watry plain.
> Ride inland lakes with fav'ring gales,
> And croud her ports with whit'ning sails;
> Till to the skirts of western day,
> The peopled regions own her sway.

It is tempting to read Trumbull's apotheosis of America as an anticipation of Americans' nineteenth-century assertion of their "manifest destiny"—and perhaps it is—but it should also be pointed out that Trumbull's vision is a fairly close imitation of Pope's celebration of *English* destiny at the end of *Windsor Forest.* Aiming to describe an American future, Trumbull is once again swept unwillingly back into an English past.

To a significant extent, then, the newly independent Americans were forced to laugh at their British brethren with borrowed laughter, at least in their fledgling literature, and to assert their independence with cultural forms derived from the very people against whom they rebelled. (Recall that "Yankee Doodle," which American revolutionaries enthusiastically adopted as a kind of unofficial national anthem, had earlier been a marching tune used by British soldiers. And, when George Washington arrived at New York to be inaugurated as first president of the new republic, he was greeted by a mixed chorus singing a patriotic ode written by an American, one Samuel Low; the tune for the ode was a borrowed one, however—the music of "God Save the King.") John Trumbull and his fellow Wits, like many other Americans of the revolutionary generation, were saddled with all the implicit contradictions that accompanied a successful political revolution that was not, and not even *intended* to be, a cultural revolution. The business of establishing political independence from Britain was a relatively easy matter compared with the more subtle, ambivalent, and tortuous task of establishing some sort of imaginative independence.

It is an unpleasing and ultimately unprofitable task simply to dwell upon the derivative qualities of Trumbull's satiric verse or to trace similar signs of poetic belatedness in the works of the other Connecticut Wits. Let us just assume the conclusions toward which such musings might lead: that the Connecticut Wits were not as talented, polished, or persistent as their greatest predecessors in English satire; that the Wits were overvalued in their own time, large-

ly for patriotic reasons; and that the Wits have been faintly praised by modern critics, partly because of earlier overpraising, but more because the Wits had little lasting impact upon the development of English or American satire. (Of course, the Wits were imitating satiric models that were already somewhat out of date, even at the time they wrote, and their efforts coincided with the relative decline in popularity of satire and other neoclassical kinds of "wit" in England.) Still, Trumbull and his fellow Wits are often enjoyable in themselves, and they are critically interesting insofar as their relative lack of success reveals something both about the nature of satire and about the processes of cultural transmission.

What, then, might be learned from their example?

First, something about the inevitable tension between theory and practice in satire. In theory the Wits should have been more successful than they were: the rise of satire in American newspapers before and during the Revolution suggests an audience eager for and responsive to satire, and the Wits could claim for themselves not only personal energy and precocious ability, but, thanks to the Revolution, great issues and occasions for satire as well. Moreover, satire *should* do well in unsettled times—recall that most participants in the Revolution and its aftermath learned to fear American anarchy as much as English oppression—simply because satire is well suited to the needs of writers (and readers) who know what they are against, though not necessarily what they are for. Unfortunately, however, theory cuts the other way as well. Revolutionists generally believe (or pretend to believe) in new beginnings for individuals and for societies; satirists, mindful of the persistence of human vices and follies, seldom if ever trust notions of new beginnings. The Wits were at least partially caught, then, between their revolutionary patriotism and the skepticism inherent in their chosen vocation. Trumbull's Tories are a loutish bunch, but too often his patriotic Whigs are little better.

Second, the example of the Connecticut Wits suggests something about the imaginative condition of the American colonies. That the American Revolution was a political revolution far more than it was a cultural one is obvious, but some of the consequences of this notion are worth emphasizing. To put the issue bluntly, colonialism implies a state of mind and a state of imagination as well as a political situation, and the state of mind may be far harder to transcend than political constraints. At least initially, the colonial writer is beholden to the mother country and its culture for all the components of his craft—his conventions, his metaphors, the themes and settings that are considered appropriate for art, his very language and its artistic potentialities. A contemporary English satirist whom Trumbull read put the matter succinctly: "No man lives long enough to get rid of his nursery." The Connecticut Wits knew America well, and yet they had a difficult time *imagining* it for literary purposes; to a surprising extent, the territory was theirs, but their imaginations were not. Or to put that matter more forcefully, it is most surprising the extent to which their cultivated imaginations, well stocked with a close knowledge of the best English models, stood between them and those native conditions they might have "realized" in lasting literature. In an oftquoted letter to his wife Abigail, John Adams explained the necessity of his participation in the Revolution by looking ahead to the longer prospects of his family:

> —I must study Politicks and War that my sons may have liberty to study Mathematicks and Philosophy. . . . Geography, natural History, Naval Architecture, navigation, Commerce and Agriculture, in order to give their Children a right to study Painting, Poetry, Musick, Architecture, Statuary, Tapestry and Porcelaine.

Note that the artistic pursuits are all in the third generation: implicitly Adams knew what others were reluctant to recognize, that a true imaginative revolution might well be the work of generations.

Third, the example of Trumbull and his fellow Wits suggests some lessons about satire, and particularly the portability of satire. In his Preface to *A Tale of a Tub,* Jonathan Swift's hack narrator announces with considerable confidence that

> . . . nothing is so very tender as a *Modern* Piece of Wit, and, . . . apt to suffer so much in the Carriage. Some things are extreamly witty *to day,* or *fasting,* or *in this place,* or *at eight a clock,* or *over a Bottle,* or *spoke by Mr.* What d'y'call'm, or *in a Summer's Morning:* Any of which, by the smallest Transposal or Misapplication, is utterly annihilate. Thus, *wit* has its Walks and Purlieus, out of which it may not stray the breadth of a Hair, upon peril of being lost.

To be sure, Swift's Hack is not exactly an authority on this or any other matter, and clearly Swift is making fun of the notion that all wit is merely local and transitory. Still, the Hack may have a point, though for reasons of which he cannot quite conceive. Consider the case of John Trumbull. Although Trumbull was not as fine a poet as Pope, still he could write down a fool or knave in a manner nearly as devastating as Pope's—and yet his fools and knaves do not seem to *matter* as Pope's did. Why not? The fact is that satire depends for its force, richness, and resonance upon an imaginative context as well as a circumstantial one, and that imaginative context was far thinner in America than in London. Consider the simple matter of geography: the business of carrying the Smithfield muses to the ear of kings was really quite different from carrying a rumor of impending dullness from New Haven to Hartford (formerly Suckiaug), with stops at Middletown and Wethersfield. Pope was writing satire within a frame of reference that was not only well established but also celebrated—Grub Street and St. Paul's, Smithfield and St. Stephen's—and that well-known geography implies an important dimension of the meaning of his satire. Trumbull had no such substructure to rely upon. Moreover, Pope could build upon an imaginative landscape that accompanied the geographical one, and Trumbull could not. A new Belinda floating on the Housatonic or the Quinnipiac simply could not mean what that former Belinda floating on the Thames had meant. The Thames implied an open-ended set of imaginative associations—mythical Trojans, Romans, Britons; Elizabeth I meeting Leicester, battles and treasons and trysts; poetry by Spenser, Drayton, Milton, Dryden, and a hundred others. The accumulation of these associations forms the basis of Belinda's significance, both real and imaginary. The Housatonic, on the other hand, simply implied an unknown river with a rather exotic name, and nothing that a new Belinda could say or do

would much alter its imaginative associations. What is true of Pope's geography in *The Rape of the Lock* or *The Dunciad* is also true in other realms of reference: lords and lapdogs, sylphs and sycophants, mayors and madams—all find their true significance in relation to one another and in relation to a whole, elaborately encoded vision of English "civilization." Clearly Pope enriched and focused existing associations by raising them to satiric intensity, and therein lies much of the greatness of his works, but he was not forced—as Trumbull often was—to postulate those underlying designs and relationships before embellishing them. My general point is a simple one: great satire is most often characterized by economy, intensity, and resonance, and these virtues are not wholly within the individual satirist's power. The satirist must have the talent and the wit to make the most of what he is given in the way of imaginative context, but if he is given little, there is little that he can make of it, whatever his talents. In short, transporting satire may remove it from those contexts, real and imaginary, which did not create but rather *permitted* its most fundamental virtues.

This notion of the imaginative context of satire has another implication worth considering. A Popean kind of satire makes appeal most often for its positive values to historical ideals, not abstract ones, and most of history, both literary and civic, was an ocean away, as far as Americans were concerned. This oceanic remove from history does not necessarily eliminate the possibility of historical resonance in satire or elsewhere, but it makes any such resonance a much more distant one. (The very fact that the American experiment could be considered alternatively as a fulfillment of past history or as an escape from it implies the underlying tentativeness of all contemporary statements of its historical relationships.) Moreover, an Alexander Pope was able to write satire upon the basis of some notion, real or imagined, of historical and moral order, social coherence, metaphysical balance *betrayed:* satire was a sad record and consequence of the falling away from a coherent and integrated order, civilized in its parts, beautiful and sanctified as a whole. Americans in 1776 or 1789 were much more in the position of discovering and asserting that their culture *had* a true center, a coherence, an order, a teleology—and to such labors a satirist need not apply. By nature conservative and skeptical, satire is best suited to charting known territories and traditional values, not to imagining new ones.

John Trumbull and his fellow Wits seem to mark the stretching-thin of an older English tradition of satiric humor more clearly than they signal a new beginning for American satire. Still, their example was not without influence: a significant number of later writers—Washington Irving and Oliver Wendell Holmes, Sr., provide ready instances—continued to seek to embrace and assert the cosmopolitan ease and urbanity that they admired in their greatest British predecessors. Yet the true beginnings of a more distinctively American kind of literary satire lie elsewhere—and that "elsewhere" is, of course, another story, the story of an oral and quasi-oral satiric humor that grew out of promotional literature and tall tales, and the literary impersonation of rustic earthiness and crackerbarrel wisdom and humor. This alternative tradition of humor and satire had fewer literary pretensions—in fact, it often seemed to pride itself on its lack of "refinement"—and therefore was less haunted by European literary precedents. This new humor was a boisterous child, energetic, brash, familiar and plain-spoken, irreverent, insistently uninhibited—and, as we all know, that energetic native child eventually grew up to become Mark Twain. Of course, Twain possessed more historical distance from European origins than the Wits had, and he was not one to be daunted by British predecessors or circumscribed by European precedents. Yet it *is* worth recalling how many times over the course of his career Twain brought European characters, social institutions, codes of expression and behavior, particularly English ones, into his own works, seemingly just to make fun of them. To be sure, Twain was jauntily American, and he played the role to the hilt. Yet he seems also to have felt the need for a wise caution, running up to twist the lion's tail one more time, just to make sure that the lion was *still* dead. (pp. 21-9)

> *Peter M. Briggs, "English Satire and Connecticut Wit," in* American Quarterly, *Vol. 37, No. 1, Spring, 1985, pp. 13-29.*

FURTHER READING

Cowie, Alexander. *John Trumbull: Connecticut Wit.* Chapel Hill: University of North Carolina Press, 1936, 230 p.

A biographical study of the relationship between Trumbull's life and works that includes chapters on *The Progress of Dulness* and *M'Fingal.*

———. "John Trumbull Glances at Fiction." *American Literature* 12, No. 1 (March 1940): 69-73.

A previously unpublished critical essay by Trumbull preceded by Cowie's commentary. Cowie notes that "[Trumbull's] criticism of the novel . . . betrays some lack of perspective; but it is an interesting and indicative example of early American criticism of fiction."

Gimmestad, Victor E. "John Trumbull's 'Epithalamion'." *The Yale University Library Gazette* 48, No. 3 (January 1974): 178-82.

Discusses the publication history of Trumbull's poem "Epithalamion" and notes several biographical and historical facts that may affect interpretation of the poem.

———. "Joel Barlow's Editing of John Trumbull's *M'Fingal.*" *American Literature* XLVII, No. 1 (March 1975): 97-102.

Provides evidence that Barlow edited the 1792 edition of *M'Fingal* and discusses Trumbull's objections to Barlow's alterations of the poem.

———. "John Trumbull's Original 'Epithalamion'." *Early American Literature* X, No. 2 (Fall 1975): 158-66.

Textual analysis of several published and unpublished versions of the "Epithalamion." Gimmestad presents what he considers Trumbull's original version of the poem.

Granger, Bruce Ingham. "Hudibras in the American Revolution." *American Literature* XXVII, No. 4 (January 1956): 499-508.

Examines the Hudibrastic tradition in early American literature. Granger faults the fourth canto of *M'Fingal* for "tediousness" but praises Trumbull's narrative and artistic control, citing *M'Fingal* as one of the poems that "left the tradition permanently enriched."

Grey, Lennox. "John Adams and John Trumbull in the 'Boston Cycle'." *The New England Quarterly* IV (July 1931): 509-14.

Argues against a common view that the character Honorius in *M'Fingal* was intended as a portrayal of John Adams.

Howard, Leon. *The Connecticut Wits.* Chicago: University of Chicago Press, 1943, 453 p.

A highly regarded literary and biographical study of the works and lives of John Trumbull, Timothy Dwight, David Humphreys, and Joel Barlow.

Mize, George E. "Trumbull's Use of the Epic Formula in *The Progress of Dulness* and *M'Fingal.*" *Connecticut Review* 4, No. 2 (April 1971): 86-90.

A brief discussion of epic conventions in Trumbull's major works.

Parrington, Vernon Louis. Introduction to *The Connecticut Wits,* edited by Vernon Louis Parrington, pp. ix-xlviii. New York: Harcourt, Brace and Co., 1926.

An essay on the historical, philosophical, religious, and literary background of the Connecticut Wits. Parrington discusses *M'Fingal,* commenting that "[Trumbull's] refined tastes ill fitted him for the turmoil of revolution."

Schulz, Max F. "John Trumbull and Satirical Criticism of Literature." *Modern Language Notes* LXXIII, No. 2 (February 1958): 85-90.

A presentation of Trumbull's critical views based on an examination of several unpublished manuscripts.

Trumbull, J. Hammond. "The Origin of *M'Fingal.*" *The Historical Magazine* III second series, No. 1 (January 1868): 1-10.

A comparison of General Gage's proclamation with Trumbull's parody of it. The critic, Trumbull's son, also notes that approximately fifty lines from this parody were incorporated in the 1775 edition of *M'Fingal.*

Van Dover, J. K. "The Design of Anarchy: *The Anarchiad,* 1786-1787." *Early American Literature* 24, No. 3 (1989): 37-47.

Discusses *The Anarchiad* as the literary response of the Connecticut Wits to the turbulent political climate in the years preceding the Constitutional Convention. Van Dover observes that although the work had little influence, it "did articulate the responses of a group of literate, concerned, and often witty young men to the crises of their time."

Noah Webster

1758-1843

American lexicographer, educator, essayist, editor, journalist, and historian.

Webster is best remembered for his *American Dictionary of the English Language,* which, along with his popular textbooks on spelling and grammar, first standardized and documented a distinctly American form of the English language. Webster was also a notable political figure of postrevolutionary America, writing numerous essays in support of American independence from England and advocating a strong federal government. While Webster also wrote on such diverse subjects as economics, literature, and epidemiology, he is distinguished primarily as a lexicographer and educator who greatly furthered American cultural unity after the Revolution.

Webster was born in 1758 in West Hartford, Connecticut. In 1774 he enrolled in Yale College, and after postponing his studies briefly to serve in the Revolutionary Army, he graduated with a bachelor's degree in 1778. Webster subsequently began to study law while supporting himself teaching primary school in Connecticut. He was admitted to the bar in Hartford in 1781, but did not practice immediately, working instead as a schoolteacher in Goshen, New York. At this time Webster reacted against what he perceived as the Anglocentrism of textbooks used in the United States and began writing his *Grammatical Institute, of the English Language,* a three-volume series comprising a spelling book, a grammar text, and a guide to reading and speaking. The *Grammatical Institute* established reforms in language based on American usage that were widely accepted throughout the United States, and the first part, known as the "Blue-Backed Speller," became one of Webster's most popular and financially rewarding works.

During the 1780s and 1790s Webster devoted himself to politics and journalism. His treatise *Sketches of American Policy* appeared in 1785, supporting centralized government of the states and emphasizing national sovereignty in both politics and culture. Webster distributed the pamphlet during a series of tours through the United States in the mid-1780s, which he undertook to publicize his textbooks and lobby for legal rights for authors. The latter effort by Webster is credited with influencing the enactment of copyright laws by most of the thirteen states during the late 1780s and the first federal copyright statute, which was passed in 1790. Webster founded and edited the *American Magazine,* a general-interest periodical based in New York City, in 1787, writing a number of essays in defense of the proposed U.S. Constitution. After the magazine went out of business in 1788, he married and moved back to Hartford to practice law. However, at the request of several prominent politicians, including Alexander Hamilton and John Jay, Webster returned to New York in 1793 to edit the pro-Federalist newspaper the *American Minerva,* and in 1794 he became the editor of the *Herald,* publishing articles in both periodicals on political, educational, and economic issues.

In 1798 Webster moved to New Haven, Connecticut, distancing himself from politics to better pursue his other intellectual interests. Webster's first dictionary, *A Compendious Dictionary of the English Language,* was published in 1806, and is noted for its inclusion of numerous Americanisms. He devoted the following two decades to the compilation and research of the more extensive *American Dictionary of the English Language,* while also writing books of grammar, biography, and history. By 1825 Webster had completed the *American Dictionary,* which contained approximately 70,000 words, substantially more than previous dictionaries of the English language. When the work was published three years later, it provoked varied responses from the American public. Many readers resisted what they considered radical divergences from standard British spelling and pronunciation, and during Webster's lifetime the book was not a financial success. Following the publication of the *American Dictionary,* he worked on an adaptation of the Bible, which appeared in 1833, modified to include current American diction and to replace words that Webster felt were coarse or impious with more euphemistic terms. He died of pleurisy in 1843.

Criticism of Webster's work generally addresses the linguistic innovations of *An American Dictionary of the En-*

glish Language or surveys his writings on both language and politics to evaluate his contribution to American cultural nationalism. Scholars praise Webster's *American Dictionary* for revising the spelling and pronunciation of numerous English words based on American usage. For example, Webster replaced the British noun endings "-our" and "-re" with the American "-or" and "-er," instituting reforms that have since been thoroughly incorporated into the language. The dictionary is also lauded for presenting lucid definitions, for frequently quoting American writers as authorities on word usage, and for including numerous technical terms from the arts and sciences. Webster's etymologies in the *American Dictionary,* however, have been frequently criticized for relying too heavily on biblical theories of the origins of language and underutilizing European innovations in philology developed during the first half of the nineteenth century. Commentators also debate the extent to which Webster was dependent on Samuel Johnson's *Dictionary of the English Language,* which first appeared in 1755 and was considered a seminal lexicographic work. In general critics agree that Webster relied upon Johnson's work to a greater degree than he acknowledged. Among Webster's other writings, his textbooks and political essays have received the most attention. Typically these writings are acclaimed for an insightful combination of cultural and political nationalism. Some commentators, however, observe problematic contradictions between the revolutionary democratic views espoused by Webster during his early career and his emphasis on elite central authority, religious dogma, and rigid social order during his later years.

Following Webster's death the publication rights to his *American Dictionary* were acquired by George and Charles Merriam, who issued numerous editions of the work, and by the mid-1860s the abridged version of the dictionary had become the standard lexicographic authority for most educational institutions in the nation. Today Merriam-Webster Incorporated continues to publish the work under the Webster name in significantly revised and updated versions, and it has earned international recognition as a principal authority on the English language. Although Webster's other writings are not as well known, his political essays are considered important expressions of his cultural objectives, and Webster's textbooks are acknowledged as instrumental to the development of early American education, earning him the nickname "Schoolmaster to America."

(See also *Dictionary of Literary Biography,* Vols. 1, 37, 42, 43, and 73.)

*PRINCIPAL WORKS

†*A Grammatical Institute, of the English Language, Comprising, an Easy, Concise, and Systematic Method of Education, Designed for the Use of English Schools in America.* 3 vols. (textbooks) 1783-85
Sketches of American Policy . . . (essay) 1785
An Examination into the Leading Principles of the Federal Constitution Proposed by the Late Convention Held at Philadelphia, with Answers to the Principal Objections That Have Been Raised Against the System, by a Citizen of America (essay) 1787
Attention! or, New Thoughts on a Serious Subject: Being an

Enquiry into the Excise Laws of Connecticut; Addressed to the Freemen of the State (essay) 1789
Dissertations on the English Language; with Notes, Historical and Critical (essays) 1789
The New England Primer, Amended and Improved . . . [editor] (textbook) 1789
A Collection of Essays and Fugitiv Writings on Moral, Historical, Political, and Literary Subjects. . . (essays) 1790
John Winthrop, A Journal of the Transactions and Occurrences in the Settlement of Massachusetts and Other New-England Colonies, from the Year 1630 to 1644 [editor] (history) 1790
The Little Reader's Assistant . . . (textbook) 1790
The Prompter; or A Commentary on Common Sayings and Subjects, Which Are Full of Common Sense, the Best Sense in the World . . . (essays) 1791
Effects of Slavery on Morals and Industry (essay) 1793
The Revolution in France, Considered in Respect to Its Progress and Effects (essay) 1794
A Brief History of Epidemic and Pestilential Diseases; with the Principal Phenomena of the Physical World, Which Precede and Accompany Them, and Observations Deduced from the Facts Stated. . . . 2 vols. (history) 1799
Ten Letters to Dr. Joseph Priestly, in Answer to His Letters to the Inhabitants of Northumberland (letters) 1800
Miscellaneous Papers on Political and Commercial Subjects . . . (essays) 1802
Elements of Useful Knowledge. . . . 4 vols. (essays) 1802-12
A Compendious Dictionary of the English Language (dictionary) 1806
A Dictionary of the English Language; Compiled for the Use of Common Schools in the United States (dictionary) 1807
A Philosophical and Practical Grammar of the English Language (essays) 1807
Letters to a Young Gentleman Commencing His Education: To Which Is Subjoined a Brief History of the United States (letters and history) 1823
An American Dictionary of the English Language. . . . 2 vols. (dictionary) 1828; also published as *A Dictionary of the English Language: Abridged from "The American Dictionary", for the Use of Primary Schools and the Counting House* [abridged edition], 1830
Biography for the Use of Schools (biography) 1830
An Improved Grammar of the English Language (textbook) 1831
History of the United States, to Which is Prefixed a Brief Historical Account of Our [English] Ancestors, from the Dispersion at Babel, to Their Migration to America, and of the Conquest of South America, by the Spaniards (history) 1832
The Holy Bible, Containing the Old and New Testaments, in the Common Version [adaptation] (religious texts) 1833
Value of the Bible, and Excellence of the Christian Religion: For the Use of Families and Schools (textbook) 1834
Instructive and Entertaining Lessons for Youth; with Rules for Reading with Propriety, Illustrated by Examples: Designed for Use in Schools and Families (textbook) 1835

The Teacher: A Supplement to "The Elementary Spelling Book" (textbook) 1836

Mistakes and Corrections . . . (essay) 1837

A Manual of Useful Studies: For the Instruction of Young Persons of Both Sexes, in Families and Schools (textbook) 1839

A Collection of Papers on Political, Literary, and Moral Subjects (essays) 1843

The Letters of Noah Webster (letters) 1953

On Being American: Selected Writings, 1783-1828 (essays) 1967

*Webster's textbooks and dictionaries have been frequently revised and abridged. Only significant early editions are included.

†The first volume of this series was also published in revised editions as *The American Spelling Book: Containing an Easy Standard of Pronunciation* in 1787 and *The Elementary Spelling Book; Being an Improvement on "The American Spelling Book"* in 1829. The third volume was also published in a revised edition as *An American Selection of Lessons in Reading and Speaking* in 1787.

Noah Webster   (essay date 1828)

[*What follows is Webster's preface to the original publication of* An American Dictionary of the English Language.]

In the year 1783, just at the close of the revolution, I published an elementary book [part one of *A Grammatical Institute, of the English Language*] for facilitating the acquisition of our vernacular tongue, and for correcting a vicious pronunciation, which prevailed extensively among the common people of this country. Soon after the publication of that work, I believe in the following year, that learned and respectable scholar, the Rev. Dr. Goodrich of Durham, one of the trustees of Yale College, suggested to me, the propriety and expediency of my compiling a dictionary, which should complete a system for the instruction of the citizens of this country in the language. At that time, I could not indulge the thought, much less the hope, of undertaking such a work; as I was neither qualified by research, nor had I the means of support, during the execution of the work, had I been disposed to undertake it. For many years therefore, though I considered such a work as very desirable, yet it appeared to me impracticable; as I was under the necessity of devoting my time to other occupations for obtaining subsistence.

About twenty seven years ago, I began to think of attempting the compilation of a Dictionary. I was induced to this undertaking, not more by the suggestion of friends, than by my own experience of the want of such a work, while reading modern books of science. In this pursuit, I found almost insuperable difficulties, from the want of a dictionary, for explaining many new words, which recent discoveries in the physical sciences had introduced into use. To remedy this defect in part, I published my *Compendious Dictionary* in 1806; and soon after made preparations for undertaking a larger work.

My original design did not extend to an investigation of the origin and progress of our language; much less of other languages. I limited my views to the correcting of certain errors in the best English Dictionaries, and to the supplying of words in which they are deficient. But after writing through two letters of the alphabet, I determined to change my plan. I found myself embarrassed, at every step, for want of a knowledge of the origin of words, which Johnson, Bailey, Junius, Skinner and some other authors do not afford the means of obtaining. Then laying aside my manuscripts, and all books treating of language, except lexicons and dictionaries, I endeavored, by a diligent comparison of words, having the same or cognate radical letters, in about twenty languages, to obtain a more correct knowledge of the primary sense of original words, of the affinities between the English and many other languages, and thus to enable myself to trace words to their source.

I had not pursued this course more than three or four years, before I discovered that I had to unlearn a great deal that I had spent years in learning, and that it was necessary for me to go back to the first rudiments of a branch of erudition, which I had before cultivated, as I had supposed, with success.

I spent ten years in this comparison of radical words, and in forming a synopsis of the principal words in twenty languages, arranged in classes, under their primary elements or letters. The result has been to open what are to me new views of language, and to unfold what appear to be the genuine principles on which these languages are constructed.

After completing this synopsis, I proceeded to correct what I had written of the Dictionary, and to complete the remaining part of the work. But before I had finished it, I determined on a voyage to Europe, with the view of obtaining some books and some assistance which I wanted; of learning the real state of the pronunciation of our language in England, as well as the general state of philology in that country; and of attempting to bring about some agreement or coincidence of opinions, in regard to unsettled points in pronunciation and grammatical construction. In some of these objects I failed; in others, my designs were answered.

It is not only important, but, in a degree necessary, that the people of this country, should have an *American Dictionary* of the English Language; for, although the body of the language is the same as in England, and it is desirable to perpetuate that sameness, yet some differences must exist. Language is the expression of ideas; and if the people of one country cannot preserve an identity of ideas, they cannot retain an identity of language. Now an identity of ideas depends materially upon a sameness of things or objects with which the people of the two countries are conversant. But in no two portions of the earth, remote from each other, can such identity be found. Even physical objects must be different. But the principal differences between the people of this country and of all others, arise from different forms of government, different laws, institutions and customs. Thus the practice of hawking and hunting, the institution of heraldry, and the feudal system of England originated terms which formed, and some of which now form, a necessary part of the language of that country; but, in the United States, many of these terms are no part of our present language,—and they cannot be, for the things which they express do not exist in this country. They can be known to us only as obsolete or as foreign words. On the other hand, the institutions in this country which are new and peculiar, give rise to new terms or to new applications of old terms, unknown to the people of England; which cannot be explained by them and which will not be inserted in their dictionaries, unless copied from ours. Thus the terms, *land-office; land-warrant; location of land; consocation* of churches; *regent* of a university; *intendant* of a city; *plantation, selectmen, senate, congress, court, assembly, escheat,* &c. are either words not belonging to the language of England, or they are applied to things in this country which do not exist in that. No person in this country will be satisfied with the English definitions of the words *congress, senate* and *assembly, court,* &c. for although these are words used in England, yet they are applied in this country to express ideas which they do not express in that country. With out present constitutions of government, *escheat* can never have its feudal sense in the United States.

But this is not all. In many cases, the nature of our governments, and of our civil institutions, requires an appropriate language in the definition of words, even when the words express the same thing, as in England. Thus the English Dictionaries inform us that a *Justice* is one deputed by the *King* to do right by way of judgment—he is a *Lord* by his office—Justices of the peace are appointed by the *King's commission*—language which is inaccurate in respect to this officer in the United States. So *constitutionally* is defined by Todd or Chalmers, *legally,* but in this country the distinction between *constitution* and *law* requires a different definition. In the United States, a *plantation* is a very different thing from what it is in England. The word *marshal,* in this country, has one important application unknown in England or in Europe.

A great number of words in our language require to be defined in a phraseology accommodated to the condition and institutions of the people in these states, and the people of England must look to an American Dictionary for a correct understanding of such terms.

The necessity therefore of a Dictionary suited to the people of the United States is obvious; and I should suppose that this fact being admitted, there could be no difference of opinion as to the *time,* when such a work ought to be substituted for English Dictionaries.

There are many other considerations of a public nature, which serve to justify this attempt to furnish an American Work which shall be a guide to the youth of the United States. Most of these are too obvious to require illustration.

One consideration however which is dictated by my own feelings, but which I trust will meet with approbation in correspondent feelings in my fellow citizens, ought not to be passed in silence. It is this. "The chief glory of a nation," says Dr. Johnson, "arises from its authors." With this opinion deeply impressed on my mind, I have the same ambition which actuated that great man when he expressed a wish to give celebrity to Bacon, to Hooker, to Milton and to Boyle.

I do not indeed expect to add celebrity to the names of *Franklin, Washington, Adams, Jay, Madison, Marshall, Ramsay, Dwight, Smith, Trumbull, Hamilton, Belknap, Ames, Mason, Kent, Hare, Silliman, Cleaveland, Walsh, Irving,* and many other Americans distinguished by their writings or by their science; but it is with pride and satisfaction, that I can place them, as authorities, on the same page with those of *Boyle, Hooker, Milton, Dryden, Addison, Ray, Milner, Cowper, Davy, Thomson* and *Jameson.*

A life devoted to reading and to an investigation of the origin and principles of our vernacular language, and especially a particular examination of the best English writers, with a view to a comparison of their style and phraseology, with those of the best American writers, and with our colloquial usage, enables me to affirm with confidence, that the genuine English idiom is as well preserved by the unmixed English of this country, as it is by the best *English* writers. Examples to prove this fact will be found in the Introduction to this work. It is true, that many of our writers have neglected to cultivate taste, and the embellishments of style; but even these have written the language in its genuine *idiom.* In this respect, Franklin and Washington, whose language is their hereditary mother tongue, unsophisticated by modern grammar, present as pure models of genuine English, as Addison or Swift. But I may go farther, and affirm, with truth, that our country has produced some of the best models of composition. The style of President Smith; of the authors of the *Federalist;* of Mr. Ames; of Dr. Mason; of Mr. Harper; of Chancellor Kent; (the prose) of Mr. Barlow; of the legal decisions of the Supreme Court of the United States; of the reports of legal decisions in some of the particular states; and many other writings; in purity, in elegance and in technical precision, is equaled only by that of the best British authors, and surpassed by that of no English compositions of a similar kind.

The United States commenced their existence under circumstances wholly novel and unexampled in the history of nations. They commenced with civilization, with learning, with science, with constitutions of free government, and with that best gift of God to man, the christian religion. Their population is now equal to that of England; in arts and sciences, our citizens are very little behind the most enlightened people on earth; in some respects, they have no superiors; and our language, within two centuries, will be spoken by more people in this country, than any other language on earth, except the Chinese, in Asia, and even that may not be an exception.

It has been my aim in this work, now offered to my fellow citizens, to ascertain the true principles of the language, in its orthography and structure; to purify it from some palpable errors, and reduce the number of its anomalies, thus giving it more regularity and consistency in its forms, both of words and sentences; and in this manner, to furnish a standard of our vernacular tongue, which we shall not be ashamed to bequeath to *three hundred millions of people,* who are destined to occupy, and I hope, to adorn the vast territory within our jurisdiction.

If the language can be improved in regularity, so as to be more easily acquired by our own citizens, and by foreigners, and thus be rendered a more useful instrument for the propagation of science, arts, civilization and christianity; if it can be rescued from the mischievous influence of sciolists and that dabbling spirit of innovation which is perpetually disturbing its settled usages and filling it with anomalies; if, in short, our vernacular language can be redeemed from corruptions, and our philology and literature from degradation; it would be a source of great satisfaction to me to be one among the instruments of promoting these valuable objects. If this object cannot be effected, and my wishes and hopes are to be frustrated, my labor will be lost, and this work must sink into oblivion.

This Dictionary, like all others of the kind, must be left, in some degree, imperfect; for what individual is competent to trace to their source, and define in all their various applications, popular, scientific and technical, *sixty* or *seventy thousand* words! It satisfies my mind that I have done all that my health, my talents and my pecuniary means would enable me to accomplish. I present it to my fellow citizens, not with frigid indifference, but with my ardent wishes for their improvement and their happiness; and for the continued increase of the wealth, the learning, the moral and religious elevation of character, and the glory of my country.

To that great and benevolent Being, who, during the preparation of this work, has sustained a feeble constitution, amidst obstacles and toils, disappointments, infirmities and depression; who has twice borne me and my manuscripts in safety across the Atlantic, and given me strength and resolution to bring the work to a close, I would present the tribute of my most grateful acknowledgments. And if the talent which he entrusted to my care, has not been put to the most profitable use in his service, I hope it has not been "kept laid up in a napkin," and that any misapplication of it may be graciously forgiven.

> *Noah Webster, in a preface to his* An American Dictionary of the English Language, Vol. 1, *1828. Reprint by Johnson Reprint Corporation, 1970.*

Basil Hall (essay date 1829)

[*In the following excerpt from his 1829 collection of narratives based on his travels in North America between 1827 and 1828, Hall recalls a visit with Webster in New Haven during which they discussed Webster's inclusion of Americanisms in* An American Dictionary of the English Language.]

In the evening I had the pleasure of being introduced to Mr. Noah Webster, of New Haven, a gentleman who has been occupied during the last forty years of his life in preparing a dictionary of the English language, which, I find, has since been published. He includes in it all the technical expressions connected with the arts and sciences, thus giving, he hopes, as complete a picture as possible of the English language, as it stands at this moment, on both sides of the Atlantic.

We had a pleasant discussion on the use of what are called Americanisms, during which he gave me some new views on this subject. He contended that his countrymen had not only a right to adopt new words, but were obliged to modify the language to suit the novelty of the circumstances, geographical and political, in which they were placed. He fully agreed with me, however, in saying that where there was an equally expressive English word, cut and dry, it ought to be used in preference to a new one. 'Nevertheless,' said he, 'it is quite impossible to stop the progress of language—it is like the course of the Mississippi, the motion of which, at times, is scarcely perceptible; yet even then it possesses a momentum quite irresistible. It is the same with the language we are speaking of. Words and ex-

pressions will be forced into use, in spite of all the exertions of all the writers in the world.'

'Yes,' I observed; 'but surely such innovations are to be deprecated?'

'I don't know that,' he replied. 'If a word becomes universally current in America, where English is spoken, why should it not take its station in the language?'

'Because,' I said, 'there are words enough already; and it only confuses matters and hurts the cause of letters to introduce such words.'

'But,' said he, reasonably enough, 'in England such things happen currently, and, in process of time, your new words find their way across the Atlantic, and are incorporated in the spoken language here.' 'In like manner,' he added, 'many of our words, heretofore not used in England, have gradually crept in there, and are now an acknowledged part of the language. The interchange, in short, is inevitable; and, whether desirable or not, cannot be stopped or even essentially modified.'

I asked him what he meant to do in this matter in his dictionary.

'I mean,' he said, 'to give every word at present in general use, and hope thereby to contribute in some degree to fix the language at its present station. This cannot be done completely; but it may be possible to do a great deal.'

I begged to know what he proposed to do with those words which were generally pronounced differently in the two countries. 'In that case,' said he, 'I would adopt that which was most consonant to the principles of the English language, as denoted by the analogy of similar words, without regarding which side of the water that analogy favoured. For example, you in England universally say *chivalry*—we as generally say *shivalry*; but I should certainly give it according to the first way, as more consistent with the principles of the language. On the other hand, your way of pronouncing the word deaf is *def*—ours, as if it were written *deef*; and as this is the correct mode, from which you have departed, I shall adhere to the American way.'

I was at first surprised when Mr. Webster assured me there were not fifty words in all which were used in America and not in England, but I have certainly not been able to collect nearly that number. He told me too, what I did not quite agree to at the time but which subsequent inquiry has confirmed as far as it has gone, that, with very few exceptions, all these apparent novelties are merely old English words, brought over to America by the early settlers, being current at home when they set out on their pilgrimage, and here they have remained in good use ever since. (pp. 118-19)

> *Basil Hall, "A Naval Officer Sees All Sections, 1827-8," in* America through British Eyes, *edited by Allan Nevins, revised edition, Oxford University Press, 1948, pp. 103-19.*

Horace E. Scudder (essay date 1881)

[*A noted American author of short stories for children during the late nineteenth century, Scudder was the editor of the* Riverside Magazine for Young People *and founder of the Riverside Literature series, which provided editions of literary works for schools. Also known as a critic and biographer, he was the editor of the* Atlantic Monthly *during the 1890s and author of such acclaimed studies of American writers as* James Russell Lowell: A Biography *(1901) and* American Men of Letters: Noah Webster, *the first comprehensive book on Webster's life and career. In the following excerpt from the latter work, Scudder relates Webster's textbooks and dictionaries to the concepts of individualism and nationalism in the United States after the Revolution.*]

Noah Webster's name abides, connected with the great work which he initiated, and the monument will keep his name imperishable. It never can be an uninteresting study to the people how the man, whose name is a household word, wrought and achieved. . . . There was nothing concealed in his nature. His vanity made him open, and his strong self-reliance gave him a boldness of expression which makes it possible for any student to measure his aims.

The chief discovery yet to be made of Webster, if any is possible, lies in the direction of history. I do not suppose that if the entire correspondence of Webster with his contemporaries could be produced, we should find him any more potent as a public man . . . ; but a more thorough comprehension of the forces at work in the organization of national life may yet enable us to see with greater distinctness the degree of Webster's power and function. The last result of historical study is the determination of national genius, and for that time and the slow evolution of national character are requisite. I am sure that the dignity of Webster's position in our history is more intelligible to-day than it was in his own time. I am confident that the twentieth century will give him a juster meed than we are giving him to-day.

It was at once his fortune and his misfortune to pass his life contemporaneously with the birth and adolescence of a great nation, and to feel the passion of the hour. There is unquestionably a parochial sort of nationality which it is easy to satirize. No one could well set it out in stronger light than Webster himself in [the preface to his **Dictionary;** see excerpt dated 1828]. . . . He is judiciously silent concerning the American poets of his time, being careful, even,—most unkindest cut!—not to commit himself to the support of Joel Barlow's heroic verse; but he produces a list of American prosaists, whom he places back to back with their English fellows. He has a proper sense of the importance of language to a nation, and appears to be perplexed by the implied question: If Englishmen and Americans speak the same language, how in the world are we to tell them apart and keep them apart? Then again, since there has been a revolution resulting in governmental independence, what stands in the way of a complete independence, so that the spick and span new nation may go to the language tailors and be dressed in a new suit of parts of speech? "Let us seize the present moment," he cries, "and establish a national language as well as a national government." Never was there such a chance, he thinks, for clearing away the rubbish which has accumulated for generations in our clumsy, inelegant language. Hand him the Bible which people have foolishly regarded as a great conservator of the English tongue, and he will give you a new edition "purified from the numerous errors." Knock

off the useless appendages to words which serve only to muffle simple sounds. Innocent iconoclast, with his schoolmaster ferrule!

It is worth our while to make serious answer to these serious propositions, since the true aspect of native literature may thus be disclosed. The Revolution, which so filled Webster's eyes, was unquestionably a great historic event by reason of its connection with the formal institution of a new nation; but the roots of our national life were not then planted. They run back to the first settlements and the first charters and agreements; nor is the genesis of the nation to be found there; sharp as are the beginnings of our history on this continent, no student could content himself with a conception of our national life which took into account only the events and conditions determined by the people and the soil of America. Even in actual relations between America and Europe there never has been a time when the Atlantic has not had an ebbing as well as a flowing tide, and the instinct which now sends us to the Old World on passionate pilgrimages is a constituent part of our national life, and not an unfilial sentiment. In the minds of Webster and many others, England was an unnatural parent, and the spirit of anger, together with an elation at success in the severing of governmental ties, made them impatient of even a spiritual connection. But the Revolution was an outward, visible sign of an organic growth which it accelerated, but did not produce; and the patriotic outcries of the generation were incoherent expressions of a profounder life which had been growing, scarcely heeded, until wakened by this event. The centripetal force of nationality was at work, and it is possible now, even from our near station, to discover the conjunction of outward circumstance and inward consciousness which marks nationality as an established fact. It was a weak conception of nationality which was bounded by Webster's definition; but his belief in his country and his energetic action were, in reality, constantly overpassing that conception. In spite of the disposition to regard a written constitution as the bottom fact, there was the real, substantial, organic nation, and that saved the paper nation from erasure,—a fate which easily overtakes South American republics. A nation which could immediately be placed in the world's museum, duly ticketed and catalogued, with its distinct manners, dress, language, and literature,—this was a conception which resulted logically from theories which held the nation itself to be the creation of popular will or historic accident; but a nation slowly struggling against untoward outward circumstance and inward dissension, collecting by degrees its constituent members, forming and reforming, plunging with rude strength down dangerous ways, but nevertheless growing into integral unity,—this has been the historical result of the living forces which were immanent in the country when the nation was formally instituted.

Now there never has been a time from Webster's day to this when Americans have not believed and asserted that nationality consisted mainly in independence, and waxed impatient not merely of foreign control and influence, but even of hereditary influence: the temper which calls for American characteristics in art and literature is often scarcely less hostile to the past of American history than to the present of European civilization. It is a restless, uneasy spirit, goaded by self-consciousness. It finds in nature an aid and abettor; it grows angry at the disproportionate place which the Cephissus, the Arno, the Seine, the Rhine, and the Thames hold on the map of the world's passion. We are all acquainted with the typical American who added to his name in the hotel book on the shores of Lake Como, "What pygmy puddles these are to the inland seas of tremendous and eternal America!" But these are coarser, more palpable signs of that uneasy consciousness which frets at a continued dependence on European culture.

There is no doubt that Webster was right when he set himself the task of Americanizing the English language by a recourse to *The Spelling Book.* He succeeded very largely in determining the form of words; but he did more than this, while he failed in the ambitious and preposterous task which he set himself. He did more; by his shrewdness and his ready perception of the popular need he made elementary education possible at once, and furnished the American people with a key which moved easily in the lock; he failed where he sought the most, because language is not a toy or a patent machine, which can be broken, thrown aside at will, and replaced with a better tool, ready-made from the lexicographer's shop. He had no conception of the enormous weight of the English language and literature, when he undertook to shovel it out of the path of American civilization. The stars in their courses fought against him. It is so still. We cannot dispense with European culture, because we refuse to separate ourselves from the mighty past, which has settled there in forms of human life unrepresented among us. We cannot step out of the world's current, though it looks sluggish beside our rushing stream, because there is a spiritual demand in us which cries louder than the thin voice of a self-conscious national life. This demand is profoundly at one with the deeper, holier sense of national being which does not strut upon the world's stage. The humility of a great nation is in its reverence for its own past, and, since that is incomplete, in its admiration for whatever is noble and worthy in other nations. It is out of this reverence and humility and this self-respect that great works in literature and art grow, and not out of the overweening sensitiveness which makes one's nationality but a petty jealousy of other people.

It is possible for us thus to discriminate between a nationality which is a mere posture and that which is a plain expression of positive organic life. When we measure the force of the latter we are compelled to a finer analysis, and its illustrations are to be sought in subtler manifestations. Webster well exemplifies, by the very rudeness of his mind, phases of Americanism which may be traced in more delicate lines elsewhere. There can be no doubt that self-reliance, which was both the cause and the effect of local self-government long practiced, has been a powerful factor in American life; that an indifference to the past has often been only the obverse of an elastic hope, a consciousness of destiny; that a fearlessness and a spirit of adventure have been invited by the large promises held out by nature; that an expansiveness of mind, and an alertness and facility in intellectual device, have been encouraged by the flexile condition of American society. All things have seemed possible to the ardent American, and each has secretly said to himself:—

> I . . . had resolved to be
> The maker of my destiny.

These elements of character have entered into literature,

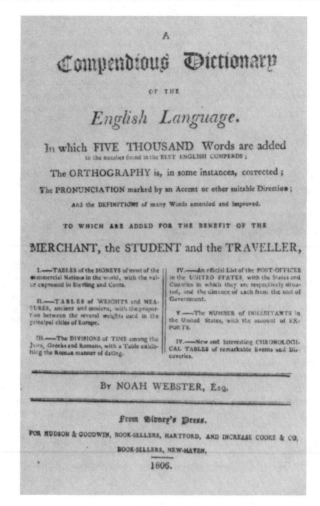

Title page of Webster's first dictionary.

the exponent of character; and Webster, with his self-reliance, his indifference to the past, his consciousness of destiny, his courage and resolution and quick fitting into his country's work, stands easily as the first aggressive American in our literature. In him we see roughly marked what future critics will discern of men more readily assigned a place in universal literature. The Americanism of Hawthorne, for example, differs from that of Webster in quality rather than in essence. They were both content with America and New England. Hawthorne, with his shrug at old buildings and his wish that all over two hundred years of age should be burnt down, was repeating Webster's contempt of the musty halls of collegiate Cambridge; and Hawthorne, Yankeeizing the Greek myths, and finding all Rome but the background for his Puritan maiden, was asserting that new discovery of Europe by America which has ever since been going on, and was illustrated by Webster's excursions in language to bring back English variations from American usage.

The ease with which Webster walked about the Jericho of English lexicography, blowing his trumpet of destruction, was an American ease, born of a sense that America was a continent and not a province. He transferred the capital of literature from London to Boston, or New York, or Hartford,—he was indifferent so long as it was in the United States. He thought Washington as good an authority on spelling as Dr. Johnson, and much better than King George. He took the Bible as a book to be used, not as a piece of antiquity to be sheltered in a museum, and with an American practicality set about making it more serviceable in his own way. He foresaw the vast crowds of American children; he knew that the integrity of the country was conditioned on the intelligibility of their votes, and he turned his back on England less with indifference to her than with an absorption in his own country. He made a Speller which has sown votes and muskets; he made alone a Dictionary, which has grown, under the impulse he gave it, into a national encyclopædia, possessing an irresistible momentum. Indeed, is not the very existence of that book in its current form a witness to the same Americanism which Webster displayed, only now in a firmer, finer, and more complex form?

In the high walks of scholarship, where nationality would seem to be effaced, we have had very recently a capital illustration of the inevitable tendency of national traits to seek expression. The Appendix to the *Revised Version of the New Testament* contains the variations proposed by the American company from the text as otherwise determined. There were in the English company men of radical temperament and of conservative; there were in the American company like distinctions; nevertheless the final separation between the two companies is largely on this line, and one can easily see how much sympathy, Webster, for example, would have expressed with the position which the American company took, a position not of dissent but of independent assertion.

The separation between England and America which was so effectual in Webster's conception, and thus determined much of his thought, was really incipient and not complete. The two countries are more widely separate to-day than they were then, while the outward signs of separation are in many ways less conspicuous. The forces of national life have been diverging, and the resultant in character and literature is more sure and ineffaceable.

It should be observed that the individualism which characterizes American life was more marked in the first years of the republic than it is now. After we have reasoned away all we will of a revolutionary cataclysmal element in the separation of the United States from the British Empire, there still remains a sharp determination of individual life, historically evident, and very influential in the formation of national character. In the earliest years the centripetal force for union was barely superior to the centrifugal force for state independence; but the political thought which justified state sovereignty had its logical issue in an isolated individuality. Common sense and prudence, to be sure, are always defeating logic; but the logical conception helps us to understand tendencies, and it is not difficult to see that the word independence, which was on every one's lips at the close of the last century, was not the sign of a political thought only, but expressed the habit of mind with which persons everywhere regarded life in its varied relations. The breaking up of old political connections not only unsettled the social fabric, it affected necessarily all the relations which the person held to society; and it was only as a profounder political unity disclosed itself in the nation that each man put forth more confidently his hand to his fellow. The historian of the Union will not fail to

observe how with the growth of that Union there began to spring up societies and corporations of every kind, the interdependence of the States extending itself to the interdependence of all interests involved in the State, and the whole fabric of society feeling its web and woof grow firmer and denser.

The career of Webster illustrates this truth. He worked alone, and his solitariness was not wholly due to his idiosyncrasies. It was in part the penalty paid by a student of the time. The resolution and self-reliance of an American were his, and so was the individuality. That such enterprises are not now conducted single-handed is owing not to a lack of courage but to the greater complexity of life, the more constant sense of interdependence, the existence of greater solidarity in intellectual pursuits. Webster was unable to believe that a company of scholars could ever be formed who should carry forward a revision of the Bible, and therefore he made the attempt himself. Individual criticism has been abundant ever since, but no one, however learned or popular, has ever been able to impress his work upon the community. The most carefully organized body of scholars submits the results of its ten years' conference to the votes of the world. The history of Webster's ***Dictionary*** is parallel with the growth of national life out of individualism. (pp. 279-94)

> *Horace E. Scudder, in his* American Men of Letters: Noah Webster, *edited by Charles Dudley Warner, Houghton, Mifflin and Company, 1881, 302 p.*

Harry R. Warfel   (essay date 1934)

[*An American critic and educator, Warfel wrote textbooks on English grammar and composition as well as studies of American literature. He was particularly interested in the development of American nationalism and American intellectual thought, focusing in the works of his later career on the interrelationship between language and literary structure. In addition to his major biography,* Noah Webster: Schoolmaster to America *(1936), Warfel edited several volumes of Webster's essays and letters. In the following essay, he favorably evaluates Webster's adaptation of the Bible.*]

When, at the age of seventy, Noah Webster completed his great ***American Dictionary of the English Language*** (1828), he might well have considered his labors done. But his orderly plan for the improvement of American education included another and crowning work. By his [***Grammatical Institute, of the English Language***], comprising a spelling-book, a grammar, and a reading-book, he had supplied the correct standard in language for our schools, given a religious tone to all our text-books, and had fostered patriotic pride. His ***Dictionary*** became the undisputed arbiter of spelling and definition. The great popular text-book, the Bible, needed amendment in language, he believed, so that it might conform to the American idiom, not forgetting American morality. Five years he engaged in this enterprise, and published the first American revised edition of the Holy Bible in December, 1833.

Webster looked upon this revision as the most important enterprise of his life; yet his work is almost forgotten. At the time of its publication no minister of the gospel or teacher of theology hazarded a commendation of it. Many condemned the temerity of one man for attempting to improve the King James Version, the work of many and reverend scholars. In their eager hostility, these critics forgot that Wycliffe, Coverdale, Tyndale, and Luther had all worked alone. It was forgotten, too, that the King James Bible was a revision, not a new translation. Webster sought for his own time and country precisely the same correctness and purity at which his predecessors had aimed.

He approached the Bible with reverence, for a pious probity, akin to John Woolman's, guided his steps from youth to old age. The moral and religious precepts scattered through his text-books were not seeds craftily sown to increase his sales: they sprang from a mind convinced of the truths of Calvinism as interpreted to New England. "The longer I live," he wrote his daughter Harriet,

> the stronger is my faith in the truth of the scriptures, and in the truth of that creed in which I have been educated. I am perfectly well satisfied that what is denominated "moderate Calvinism" is the genuine religion preached by Christ and his apostles, and that there is no other genuine religion. I rest all my hope on the doctrines of that system, and commit myself cheerfully to that savior who preached them.

Unlike some recent translators, Webster was unwilling to alter, without cause, the beautiful simplicity of the version of 1611. He wished only to correct those faults which impaired its beauty, obscured its sense, or offended feelings of decency. This care for propriety of speech, in addition to accuracy of language, lays his work open, nowadays, to a kind of censure he could hardly have expected. "Whenever words," he wrote, "are understood in a sense different from that which they had when introduced, and different from that of the original languages, they do not present to the reader the *Word of God*." To attain the correct Word, he diligently compared the version of 1611 with the Hebrew and Greek originals, altering only those passages in which changes seemed imperative. He showed far more restraint than the authors of the revised version which was prepared some fifty years later.

Webster early recognized that language was a living form, in which old words took on new meanings. Thus, he substituted "hinder" for the Elizabethan "let," "button" for "tache," "advanced" for "stricken in years," "boiled" for "sodden," "interest" for "usury," "insane" for "mad," and so forth. He made these changes because a version of Scripture designed for popular use should consist, he believed, of words used in their common sense. Obsolete words had no place in the text, for they did not convey to untrained readers the true significance of the original.

Vulgar words and expressions were the more offensive, he thought, because they appeared in a setting which seemed to give sanction to their daily use. Euphemistic expressions were substituted in all such cases. He exchanged "O that" for "Would God" or "Would to God," because the original passages did not contain the name of the Supreme Being, and because the insertion of them in the version of 1611 had given countenance to their introduction into discourse and public speech, with a levity that is incompatible with a due veneration for the name of God. "God forbid," likewise, was changed, following MacKnight, to "By

no means." One can not be certain that he reasoned correctly, though he wrote: "Language which cannot be uttered in company without a violation of decorum or the rules of good breeding, exposes the scriptures to the scoffs of unbelievers, impairs their authority, and multiplies or confirms the enemies of our holy religion." [A footnote added to the text states that "this expression of opinion would be puzzling to any one who failed to remember how often and completely intellectual leaders of an age will talk, and even write, some of its cant. Noah Webster lived at the beginning of that time when people took up with the notion of connecting mealy mouths with good morals. It is not astonishing, therefore, that he should have thought he believed that the coarseness of the Bible had ever cost 'our holy religion' so much as a single convert or communicant. Although Webster may have had Thomas Paine in mind, the 'scoffs of unbelievers' have not always been directed at the indecorous language of Scripture. The story of Jonah and the whale, for instance, is the favorite approach for persons who would impair the 'authority' of Holy Writ."]

Many grammatical changes were incorporated, particularly in the use of the articles, in the agreement of subject and verb, and in the pronouns. "Who" was substituted for "which," when the reference was to persons; "its" for "his," when the reference was to plants and things without life; and "my" and "thy" replaced the adjectives "mine" and "thine." These changes were designed to avoid the pitfalls into which children, trained to say "Our Father which," fell when they recited in public school. The personality of the Deity seemed to have been removed by the older usage. However small this point may seem to be, the psychological factor demanding the change is tremendous, as any school-teacher knows.

Although Webster's aim was to preserve the sense of the version of 1611 by expressing it more clearly, he did not hesitate to correct errors. Thus, "Ye blind guides, which strain at a gnat, and swallow a camel" became "strain out a gnat." In this emendation Webster for the first time in English rendered Jesus's saying as He said it, and corrected the figure of speech. "For I know nothing by myself" (1 Corinthians IV, 8) was correctly altered to "For I know nothing against myself." Some geographical names were corrected, such as Ethiopia (Genesis II, 13) and the Red Sea (Deuteronomy I, 1,) which became Cush and Suph, respectively. Most of Webster's improvements were adopted by the authors of the revised version, and it is probable that Webster's work, though slow to gain a footing, helped to make the success of the later work possible.

Webster knew that he laid himself open to charges of arrogance and improper aims, but his life-long passion for accuracy in philological details led him to risk opprobrium. When, in 1821, he proposed this revision to Dr. Moses Stuart, a professor at Andover, the faculty agreed that "the feelings (not to say the prejudices) of the public would not probably admit change." During the completion of his *Dictionary* he laid aside his plan for a corrected Bible. Freed at seventy for other labors, he set about the work with consistent, if conservative courage.

His revision of the Bible was Noah Webster's crowning achievement. Not only did it bring to completion his labors in philology, but it rounded out his cherished plan for giving the United States a body of literature from which correct language could be derived. His school-books were designed for the instruction of the young; his dictionaries regulated, so far as books can, the spellings and meanings of words; the Bible gave Americans Scripture for daily reading correctly translated into their own language. Webster's innovation was not so great as Wycliffe's or Luther's, and yet in his own mind he believed that his Bible would play as large a part as theirs in reforming the common speech. Toward this end he pleaded that his version be made the American standard, even as his **Dictionary** was the standard for orthography. The longer the time that variations existed, the further people would be drawn from the great source of moral wisdom. Disagreements over a faulty text would weaken faith. He foresaw our plight today, when a multiplicity of versions destroys the unifying idiom of the version of 1611. The only sound reason for alteration was a change in meaning.

The Revolution had fired Webster with patriotic ardor. He designed his books to enhance our reputation and unity as a nation.

> The language of the Bible [he wrote] has no inconsiderable influence in forming and preserving our national language. On this account, the language of the common version ought to be correct in grammatical construction, and in the use of appropriate words. This is the more important, as men who are accustomed to read the Bible with veneration, are apt to contract a predilection for its phraseology, and thus to become attached to phrases which are quaint or obsolete. This may be a real misfortune; for the use of words and phrases, when they have ceased to be a part of the living language, and appear odd or singular, impairs the purity of the language, and is apt to create a disrelish for it in those who have not, by long practice, contracted a like predilection. It may require some effort to subdue this predilection; but it may be done, and for the sake of the rising generation, it is desirable.

Webster was the first to write an American school-book, a history of commerce, and a history of epidemical fevers; the first, also, to compile an American dictionary, and revise Scripture. Although he is probably known least for this last important labor, his real achievement lies in the revised version. (pp. 578-82)

> *Harry R. Warfel, "The Centenary of Noah Webster's Bible," in* The New England Quarterly, *Vol. 7, September, 1934, pp. 578-82.*

H. L. Mencken (essay date 1948)

[*From the era of World War I until the early years of the Great Depression, Mencken was one of the most influential figures in American letters. His strongly individualistic, irreverent viewpoint and writing style helped establish the iconoclastic spirit of the Jazz Age and significantly shaped American literature of the time. As a social and literary critic, Mencken excoriated numerous facets of American life that he perceived as humbug, and his literary criticism encouraged American authors to shun the Anglophilic, moralistic bent of nineteenth-century literature and to practice realism. Mencken is also noted for his acclaimed study* The American Language: An Inquiry into the Development of English in the United States, *which was first published in 1919 and*

is recognized as an important early examination of the formation of American English. The following excerpt is from the second supplement to that work, last revised by Mencken in 1948. Here, he outlines the influence of part one of A Grammatical Institute, of the English Language *and Webster's major dictionaries on English spelling in the United States after the Revolution. The italicized passage indicates Mencken's condensed treatment of material from previous editions.*]

The influence of Webster's Spelling Book was really stupendous. It took the place in the American schools of Dilworth's [*textbook*], *the favorite of the Revolution generation, and maintained its authority for nearly a century.* Dilworth's book, the official title of which was *A New Guide to the English Tongue,* was published in London in 1740. Seven years later Benjamin Franklin reprinted it in Philadelphia, and thereafter it was constantly on the press in America until the Webster Speller, first published in 1783, began to overhaul it. Webster himself had been nourished upon it in youth, and was sufficiently convinced of its merits to imitate it, even to the extent of lifting whole passages. Dilworth's reading lessons, for example, began with a series of pious dithyrambs in monosyllables, more or less reminiscent of the Old Testament, and Webster's began with a palpable paraphrase of them. Thus:

Dilworth

No man may put off the law of God,
The way of God is no ill way.
My joy is in God all the day.
A bad man is a foe to God.

To God do I cry all the day.
Who is God, but our God?
All men go out of the way of thy law.
In God do I put my joy, O let me not sin.

Pay to God his due.
Go not in the way of bad men.
No man can see God.
Our God is the God of all men.

Who can say he has no sin?
The way of man is ill, but not the way of God.
My son, go not in the way of bad men.
No man can do as God can do.

Webster

No man may put off the law of God.
My joy is in his law all the day.
O may I not go in the way of sin!
Let me not go in the way of ill men.

A bad man is a foe to the law.
It is his joy to do ill.
All men go out of the way.
Who can say he has no sin?

The way of man is ill.
My son, do as you are bid.
But if you are bid, do no ill.
See not my sin, and let me not go to the pit.

Rest in the Lord, and mind his word.
My son, hold fast in the law that is good.
You must not tell a lie, nor do hurt.
We must let no man hurt us.

Dilworth shut down after six stanzas of this dismal doggerel, but Noah went on to ten, and then followed with five more printed frankly as prose. The latter began in the tone of the dithyrambs, but quickly proceeded to more worldly matters, thus:

> A good child will not lie, swear, nor steal. He will be good at home, and ask to read his book; when he gets up he will wash his hands and face clean; he will comb his hair, and make haste to school; he will not play by the way, as bad boys do.

Webster also borrowed the general arrangement of Dilworth, with lists of progressively more difficult words alternating with reading lessons, and not a few of his lists— e.g., *big, dig, fig, gig, jig, pig, wig*—he took over bodily. He also levied upon Daniel Fenning's *Universal Spelling Book*, first published in 1756, though he testified late in life that he had not studied from it in his boyhood. It was, he said, "in the country, but was not used in my neighborhood." But we have his own testimony that he sweated through Dilworth in the Hartford primary-school, along with the New England Primer, a Psalter and the Bible. "No geography," he said in his old age, "was studied before the publication of Dr. Morse's small books on that subject, about the year 1786 or 1787. No history was read, as far as my knowledge extends, for there was no abridged history of the United States." [In a footnote, the critic observes that "Dr. Jedidiah Morse's first geography was actually published in 1784."] The Catechism at the end of the Primer, as Warfel points out [see Further Reading entry dated 1936], greatly influenced American pedagogical method until the Revolutionary era, and Webster showed that influence by casting some of his hortations in the form of questions and answers, e.g., "Henry, tell me the number of days in a year," "Charles, how is the year divided?" and "John, what are the seasons?" He was sufficiently homiletic, God knows, but now and then something almost akin to poetry crept into his lessons:

> Emily, look at the flowers in the garden. What a charming sight. How the tulips adorn the borders of the alleys, dressing them with gayety. Soon the sweet pinks will deck the bed, and the fragrant roses perfume the air. Take care of the sweet williams, the jonquils and the artemisia. See the honeysuckle, how it winds about the column, and climbs along the margin of the windows. Now it is in bloom: how fragrant the air is around it; how sweet the perfume after a gentle shower or amidst the soft dews of the evening. Such are the charms of youth when robed in innocence; such is the bloom of life when decked with modesty and a sweet temper.

Webster's Spelling-Book, even in its heyday, was by no means without rivals. It not only had to buck the entrenched Dilworth; it was also beset by innumerable imitations. There was no national copyright until 1790, and the States did not offer any protection to authors until 1782, when Webster himself began besieging their Legislatures. In his preface to his revised edition of 1803, he complained bitterly that his imitators "all constructed their works on a similar plan," borrowing his lists of words (as he had borrowed some of Dilworth's), or altering them "by additions, mutilations and subdivisions, numerous and perplexing." But he had a stout heart and was a relentless salesman, and he could boast in the same preface that the

sales of the Spelling-Book to date had reached 3,000,000. He went on:

> Its reputation has been gradually extended and established, until it has become the principal elementary book in the United States. In a great part of the northern States it is the only book of the kind used; it is much used in the middle and southern States, and its annual sales indicate a large and increasing demand.

How many copies were sold before it was at last displaced by more "scientific" texts is unknown, for it was republished, sometimes with the author's license and sometimes as piracy, by dozens of enterprising Barabbases in all parts of the country. Mrs. Roswell Skeel, Jr., Noah's great-granddaughter, tells me that she has heard estimates running to 400,000,000, but believes that 100,000,000 would be "very much nearer an accurate guess." It seems to have made its way in the South more slowly than in the North, probably because schools were much fewer there, but once it was established it became almost immovable. During the Civil War discreetly revised editions were brought out at Macon, Raleigh and Atlanta, and Warfel reported in 1936 that it was still to be found in an occasional southern school. From 1930 to 1942 the American Book Company, the present publisher, averaged a sale of 4000 a year. Within recent years peddlers hawking the book from door to door have been in operation in Texas.

Even more influential than the old blue-back speller was Webster's series of dictionaries, and especially the ***American Dictionary*** of 1828. He began work on them in 1800, and six years later brought out a preliminary draft under the title of ***A Compendious Dictionary of the English Language.*** In 1807 he followed with ***A Dictionary of the English Language; Compiled for the Use of Common Schools in the United States.*** Both sold fairly well, but they were belabored with ferocity by Webster's numerous enemies, and he spent a large part of his time during the next half dozen years in defending himself against their attack. Meanwhile, he continued to amass materials for the larger dictionary that he had in mind, and in 1824 went to Europe to consult the philologians and libraries of England and France. The former apparently paid him little attention, but he seems to have found what he wanted in the libraries and in January, 1825, he finished his manuscript at Cambridge. He had a publisher in waiting, to wit, Sherman Converse of New York, but when the time came to make a contract with the printer, Hezekiah Howe of New Haven, it turned out that Converse was short of the needed money, so Webster himself had to borrow enough to cover Howe's bill. The first edition, in two volumes quarto, was of 2500 copies, selling at $20 a set. It went off quickly enough, but there was no profit in it, and in 1829 Webster employed Joseph E. Worcester (1784-1865) to prepare an abridgement in one volume. This abridgement sold very well, but Worcester followed it soon afterward with a dictionary of his own [*A Comprehensive Pronouncing and Explanatory Dictionary of the English Language*], and for years thereafter this dictionary and Webster's fought for favor.

Worcester's had one advantage: it was free from the attempts at reform in spelling and pronunciation that Webster had undertaken, and was thus preferred by the more conservative pedagogues of the time. But Webster's, though its etymologies were often fanciful and most of its innovations in spelling had to be dropped after his death, gradually made its way with the plain people, and by 1840 it was generally accepted as the American authority *par excellence.* In 1840, when he was past eighty and close to death, old Noah mortgaged his home in Hartford to bring out a second edition. When he died in 1843 George and Charles Merriam, of Springfield, Mass., bought the rights to the dictionary from his quarreling heirs, and employed one of his sons-in-law, Chauncey A. Goodrich, to prepare a new edition. This appeared in 1847, in one volume selling at $6. Warfel says that it "took immediate hold" and that "the presence of a Webster dictionary in almost every literate household dates from this year."

During the century since then Webster has had to meet some very stiff competition—from the *Century Dictionary* after 1891, from the *Standard* after 1895, and from the *Concise Oxford* after 1911—, but it still holds its own, and four Americans out of five, when they think of a dictionary, think of it. The Merriams, who were smart business men, employed competent philologians to supervise the revisions which stretched from 1859 to 1934, and those revisions gradually made the position of the work unassailable. Today it is accepted as authority by all American courts, is in almost universal use in the schools and colleges, is the official spelling guide of the Government Printing Office, and has the same standing in the overwhelming majority of American newspaper, magazine and book publishing offices. How many copies of it have been printed and circulated to date cannot be ascertained, for as the copyrights on the successive editions expired many other publishers entered into competition with the Merriams, and scores of different editions are still in circulation. That the total sales of all these editions—some of them for the vest-pocket and selling for as little as ten cents—have equalled the sales of the Webster Speller is certainly possible, if not exactly probable. Thus Webster lives in American literary history as the author of the two champion best-sellers of all time. Nor has his singular success been confined to his native land. Said the *Literary Supplement* of the London *Times* on May 29, 1943:

> All the English-speaking nations can join this week in commemorating the centenary of the death on May 28, 1843, of that patriarchal dictionary-maker, Noah Webster. His actual dictionary, it is true, may now be out of date, just as Johnson's is; but it lives on eponymously—"a Webster" having become almost a synonym for a dictionary—and spiritually in the American language itself, which, though English, is no longer that of England or of colonial New England, but of a great and independent nation. Webster, in fact, was in his own sphere as much a founder of his nation as Washington, and consciously so; for he had the vision to perceive that his country, which ceased to be a colony when he was a young man, must henceforward grow its own culture, look no more to London and Europe for its sanctions, and speak and write no longer as a provincial. In his own way Webster was as the Pericles of his country, who presented it with an enduring temple in which to enshrine its words; or as its Augustus, who found its spelling to be of roughcast and left it of polished marble.

(pp. 271-76)

H. L. Mencken, "American Spelling," in his

The American Language: An Inquiry into the Development of English in the United States, *1936. Reprint by Alfred A. Knopf, 1962, pp. 271-331.*

Joseph W. Reed, Jr.   (essay date 1962)

[*Reed is an American painter and literary critic who has written extensively on nineteenth-century literature. In the following essay, he assesses the extent to which Webster relied on the 1799 edition of Samuel Johnson's* Dictionary of the English Language *in compiling* An American Dictionary of the English Language.]

Borrowing—even plagiarism—is no sin to lexicographers. They may borrow from a single source or from a shelffull of sources. Genealogies have been traced for most important dictionaries, but simple notation of debt to this or that forebear does not provide enough detail for us to assess originality. Examination of individual changes, additions, and omissions is necessary if the lexicographer is to be accorded more originality than a scissors-and-paste editor. Unfortunately, the student's eagerness for detail pales to the bulk of collation necessary to distinguish original work from borrowings. The project is put aside for the coming dawn of enlightenment when the machines really do all we are told they can: when copy text is established on a roll of magnetic tape, when collation is taken over by the tireless eyes of the automated page scanner.

It has long been recognized that Noah Webster frequently consulted the 1799 London edition of Samuel Johnson's *Dictionary of the English Language* when he was drafting **An American Dictionary of the English Language** (1828). Johnsonians make much of this in anniversary exhibitions; Webster aficionados minimize the connection, pointing to Webster's advances, in etymology and in the number of words covered, and to his more scientific method. Data for assessment of Webster's specific debt to Johnson have been lacking.

Chiefly to satisfy curiosity I undertook a limited collation of only the entries that appear under the letter *L.* This was a sample of convenient size and had the added virtue of its position in the book: Webster had by this time settled down to a regular *modus operandi.* [In a footnote, Reed states, 'After drafting his dictionary through *B* he "found the *want of research"* and "spent ten years in making a Synopsis of twenty languages." Following this interruption, he apparently drafted straight through the alphabet (letter to Samuel Latham Mitchell, Dec. 12, 1823, in **Letters,** ed. Harry R. Warfel [1953]).'] Conclusions drawn from such a sample must be fragmentary: Johnson was only one of Webster's sources; *L* is only one letter (2,024 words and 4,505 meanings out of approximately 70,000 words and perhaps 150,000 meanings given in the 1828 **Dictionary**). The arbitrary nature of point-for-point collation naturally blurs some dependencies (such as order of definitions); it offers no insight at all into such matters as etymology, which Webster was treating in terms of an apparently wholly new theory. The conclusions are just, then, only where the two texts are close enough for meaningful comparison, and only insofar as the *L*'s are representative of the total work. Thoroughly reliable conclusions await the time when we are replaced by the kindly and peripatetic Univac.

Before starting on the 1828 ***Dictionary,*** Webster regarded Johnson and his lexicography with a jaundiced eye. He was foreign authority: 'The question . . . is whether an *American citizen shall be permitted to correct and improve English books* or whether we are bound down to receive whatever the English give us.' He was fallible, 'often betrayed into errors by his natural indolence which led him to write often without investigation, or he must have been pressed by disease and poverty to send his papers to the press in an unfinished state.' He was 'injudicious . . . to select Shakespeare as one of his principal authorities.' In a bill of particulars drawn up in 1807 (to answer objections of a critic of his 1806 [***Compendious Dictionary of the English Language***]), Webster repeated these assertions and added to them charges that Johnson had inserted 'a *multitude of words*' that did not belong in the language, and 'vulgar and cant words'; that he exhibited '*want of discrimination*' in distinguishing different senses of a given word and in defining words which were nearly synonymous. Johnson's etymology was 'inaccurate' and his examples were irrelevant or were 'taken from authors who did not write the language with purity' (such as Sir Thomas Browne) [***A Letter to Dr. David Ramsay, of Charleston, (S.C.) Respecting the Errors in Johnson's Dictionary, and Other Lexicons*** (New Haven, 1807)].

Webster's determination to rectify Johnson's errors and shortcomings was but one of the many aims he set for the 1828 ***American Dictionary.*** He began work on it in 1805 and completed it in January, 1825. Once he had finished basic research, most of his compilation was done in a workroom, where he had set up

> a large circular table . . . about two feet wide, built in the form of a hollow circle. Dictionaries and grammars of all obtainable languages were laid in successive order upon its surface. Webster would take the word under investigation, and standing at the right end of the lexicographer's table, look it up in the first dictionary which lay at that end. He made a note, examined a grammar, considered some kindred word, and then passed to the next dictionary of some other tongue. He took each word through the twenty or thirty dictionaries, making notes of his discoveries and passing around his table many times in the course of a day's labor of minute and careful study.

The 1799 Johnson was among the books on the table.

The striking similarity of many of the definitions is immediately apparent. I have recorded this similarity in three degrees: transfer, revision, and influence.

Webster copied 333 of Johnson's definitions word for word (Johnson himself not infrequently borrowed his phrasing from Nathaniel Bailey). Of these, Johnson is cited as source for the definition in only sixteen instances. Webster made very slight alterations (no more than three words changed, transposed, omitted, or added) in 987 definitions. These I noted as revisions. The narrowest interpretation of this category (in eighty-six instances) involved only one word:

Lace, n.3

> *J.* A plaited string with which women fasten their clothes.

W. A plaited string with which females fasten their clothes.

Webster used *female* for Johnson's *woman* almost universally. The altered word makes no substantive change in definition, but must be considered a revision. Slightly more substantive revisions follow:

Lousy, adj. 1

> *J.* Swarming with lice; overrun with lice.

> *W.* Swarming with lice, infested with lice.

Lacerable, adj.

> *J.* Such as may be torn.

> *W.* That may be torn.

Of 987 revisions, Webster credits Johnson with the definition of eighteen.

I recorded 161 influenced definitions, a category difficult to delimit. Webster clearly used Johnson's definition as a starting point for such meanings, but added or qualified to such an extent that they cannot be considered revisions. Still, he retained words or phrases with a distinctly Johnsonian ring, such as:

Lake, n.2

> *J.* A middle colour, between ultramarine and vermilion, yet it is rather sweet than harsh. It is made of cochineal.

> *W.* A middle color between ultramarine and vermilion, made of cochineal.

Webster unquestionably wrote the definition with his Johnson at his elbow, but omitted so much that an exact degree of debt is difficult to establish.

Of all 4,505 definitions written by Webster (including new definitions and all definitions of new words), 1,481, or about one third, were culled from Johnson or show unmistakable signs of Johnson's influence. Since about 30 percent of Webster's words had not been treated by Johnson at all, the extent of verbal similarity is remarkable.

Webster had committed himself to a cleansing of the 'Augean stable' of Johnson's authorities, but when the cleansing took place it seems to have been more a matter of quantity than quality. Where Johnson gave three and occasionally four authorities or examples of usage for one definition, Webster seldom included more than one. Webster's frequent practice, when he felt that his definition indicated clearly enough the use of the word, was to give only the author's name, thus ignoring, or not even realizing, the historical value of such quotations. [In a footnote, Reed observes, 'This may, of course, represent nothing more than a survival of Webster's original intention to give his readers more for their money: *"One half* of the whole bulk of Johnson's Dictionary is composed of quotations equally useless. *One half* of all the money that has been paid for the book, and which, in fifty years, must have been a very great amount, has been taken from the purchasers for what is entirely useless".']

Collation reveals that Webster borrowed 872 authors' names or quotations from Johnson's exemplification. Since the total number of examples employed by Webster was only 1,320 in the sample examined, about 66 percent were culled from Johnson. Apparently, Webster's dislike for Sir Thomas Browne had subsided between 1807 and 1828 (or he simply found it easier to use examples already assembled); for citations from Browne and many other sixteenth- and seventeenth-century writers pepper the pages, cited by name or quotation. Neither is Shakespeare slighted, for all his 'low scenes and vulgar characters.'

Webster's principle for selecting exemplifications, however, was not purely lexicographic. In his copy of Johnson's 1799 *Dictionary,* Webster placed a large black mark beside one of Johnson's authorities for *lame,* v.t. Johnson quotes Swift: 'If you happen to let a child fall, and *lame* it, never confess.' Webster seems to have objected not to the propriety of the usage but to the poor moral example set by the quotation. He includes *lame,* v.t. in his **American Dictionary** of 1828, but cites only Dryden's name for authority.

Similarity in phrasing of definition and in authorities cited indicates that Webster not only had Johnson's *Dictionary* near at hand on his 'circular table,' but that he must have consulted Johnson first and last, changing Johnson's wording only to amplify or extend, or when he found just cause to doubt his accuracy or his taste.

I found that only twenty of Johnson's words or phrases and twenty-seven of his meanings were completely omitted by Webster. There is little reason to criticize Webster's discretion in these omissions, but in the light of his criticism of Johnson's 'words that do not belong in the language,' it seems remarkable that he found so little to excise.

For 120 of Johnson's words or phrases, Webster inserted in italics his opinion on their prevalence or propriety. Apparently, Webster felt that the English language would be better without these words, but he did not have the heart to exclude them from his 'complete' dictionary. Webster omitted similar cautionary comments which Johnson had inserted beside ten words, thus welcoming back into the canon of proper diction words which Johnson had considered improper or obsolete.

In the Introduction to the **American Dictionary** (1828) Webster noted as one of the 'principal faults' in Johnson's *Dictionary* 'the omission of the participles or most of them.' Johnson included only some participles of irregular verbs. Webster added 112 participles and comparative and superlative adjectives not treated by Johnson. Webster not only listed participles as separate words but, as a rule, defined them in full.

Webster criticized Johnson for his 'defective . . . work . . . in words of the sciences.' In this instance, at least, his criticism withstood the glaring light of his own investigations, for the inclusion of 253 technical words not considered by Johnson represents perhaps the most significant single characteristic of the **American Dictionary,** involving what may be considered a new concept of lexicography. Technical vocabularies of law, medicine, religion, industry, transportation, seamanship, architecture, ancient history, agriculture, heraldry, and all the natural sciences found their way into Webster.

Webster's dependence on the phrasing of technical sources seems to have been at least as faithful as his dependence on Johnson. I have traced only one of these: *The Mariner's*

Dictionary (cited by Webster as *Mar. Dict.*). In the *L*'s there are thirty-four new technical terms and twenty new technical meanings from the vocabulary of seamanship, most of which can be traced to *The Mariner's Dictionary; or, American Seaman's Vocabulary of Technical Terms, and Sea Phrases* . . . [1805; this was an American pirated edition of J. J. Moore, *The British Mariner's Vocabulary; or, Universal Dictionary of Technical Terms and Sea Phrases* . . . (1801)]. The few omitted were for the most part specialized senses of other words having a more significant general meaning (e.g., *labor*). Quite a few of Webster's definitions (e.g., *leech-line*) are direct transfers from this source, and many more depend heavily on its phrasing as, for example:

Mar. Dict.

Lateen sail, a triangular sail, frequently used by xebecks, polacres, settees, and other vessels navigated in the Mediterranean Sea.

Lateen yard, a long yard, used to extend the preceding sail upon it, is slung about one-quarter from the lower end, which is brought down as [*sic*] the tack, while the upper end is raised in the air, in an angle of about 45 degrees.

Webster

Lateen, adj. A *lateen* sail is a triangular sail, extended by a *lateen* yard, which is slung about one quarter the distance from the lower end, which is brought down at the tack, while the other end is elevated at an angle of about 45 degrees; used in xebecs, polacres and setees, in the Mediterranean. *Mar. Dict.*

Webster could not resist revising the orthography of the names of the exotic vessels, but there seems to be no other significant difference.

The advance of technology from 1755 to 1828 alone does not explain Webster's improvement in technical lexicography. Perhaps Johnson would have been somewhat loath to admit that such words were a legitimate part of the English language. Certainly (except for certain fields such as medicine), Johnson did not feel that technical vocabularies of the sciences were the lexicographer's province. Webster not only made these vocabularies accessible to the layman, but by doing so brought lexicography to a turning point. By introducing matter previously limited to technical and professional books, and encyclopedias, Webster did more than perhaps any other lexicographer to initiate the encyclopedic dictionary. Whether or not this new scope served the best interests of lexicography is a question.

In addition to participles and words drawn from technical vocabularies, Webster included 428 words not considered by Johnson. The description 'new' may be applied to these only with qualification. Most of the terms which were 'new' with Webster were very old words; many were already obsolete or used only in archaic or poetic diction by the beginning of the nineteenth century.

Webster explained this in the Preface:

The catalogue of *obsolete* words in Johnson has been considerably augmented by Mason and Todd. I have, though somewhat reluctantly, inserted nearly the whole catalogue, which, I presume, amounts to seven or eight, and perhaps ten thousand words. Most of these may be useful to the antiquary; but to the great mass of readers, they are useless.

In introducing these obsolete words, apparently from Mason and Todd, Webster made no distinction between truly obsolete words and archaic forms of current words. Sometimes he inserted a note in italics (e.g., *Obs., little used, not now used*), but for the most part they are included without comment. Thus, *lab* (*'obs.'*), *labile* (*'not used'*), and *ladkin* (*'little used'*) are annotated, but *lachrymable, laic, launder,* n., *laundress,* v.i., *lazarlike,* and *leapingly* are not commented upon. *Langure* (obs. form of *languor,* v.), *lee* (obs. form of *lie,* v.i.), *lere* (*learn*), and *leve* (*believe*) are designated as obsolete words, but not as early forms of surviving words.

Most of these 'new' words which are still in active use were also current in Johnson's time, and must have been overlooked by him in compiling his *Dictionary.* The *OED* cites Johnson's speech (as recorded by Boswell) as authority for *laxly* and *literate,* and one of his letters for *luminousness.* His close friends—Boswell, Goldsmith, Garrick, and Mrs. Piozzi—are authorities for several others (*lagoon, landed, landslip, letter-press, liqueur,* and *low-bred*); either these were oversights or Johnson ruled them out on grounds of taste.

There were few genuine Americanisms. Webster, as he advanced in his studies of language, became more and more reluctant to call any word an Americanism. He sometimes noted *United States* or *New England* for authority, but in the 1828 Preface [reprinted above] he did not care to venture an opinion as to the extent of American coinage:

> As to Americanisms, so called, I have not been able to find many words, in respectable use, which can be so denominated. These, I have admitted and, noted as peculiar to this country. I have fully ascertained that most of the new words charged to the coinage of this country, were first used in England.

Even with the advanced etymology and lexicography at our disposal today, it is difficult to determine genuine American coinages which have not been used previously in England or in one of the English dialects. Americanisms in the *L*'s with a clearly established pedigree are *land-office, letter-case, lister, livestock, loan-office, loan-officer, locate,* v.t., and *lull,* v.i. Of somewhat more dubious heritage are *lengthy, limsy,* adj., *loan,* v.t., and *lonesomeness.* A few words which had been obsolete in English for some time are listed by Webster with a new meaning; evidently they are dialectal survivals which had undergone a gradual change in American usage, or (much less likely) words picked up from reading and made current by use. Of these, *lope,* n. has perhaps the clearest history.

Webster introduced 281 new meanings for words appearing in Johnson; 100 of these might be considered technical meanings analogous to the new technical vocabulary. Technological redefinition is perhaps best exemplified in the definitions for *lithography,* n.:

> *J.* The art or practice of engraving upon stones.

> *W.* The art of engraving, or of tracing letters, figures or other designs on stone, and of transferring them to paper by impression; an art recently in-

vented by Mr. Sennefelder of Munich in Bavaria. *Journ. of Science.*

Johnson was thinking of gravestones; Webster, of the graphic process later made famous by Toulouse-Lautrec.

Two or more of Johnson's numbered definitions are often compressed by Webster into a single unit, or one of Johnson's definitions may be broken into two parts. A kind of fragmentation popular with Webster is the separate citation of theological meaning or scriptural connotation. For example, *light,* n., carries thirteen meanings (n.15 through n.26 and *light of the countenance*) dependent upon Biblical interpretation. The meanings listed under these headings are either not valid in any other context (e.g., 'joy,' 'Christ,' 'saving knowledge,' 'prosperity; happiness,' 'support,' 'Gospel,' 'gifts and graces of Christians,' 'a true Christian,' 'a good king'), or else they have already been expressed in an earlier nontheological definition (e.g., 'understanding'). In all, there are forty-six such theological fragmentations in the sample examined.

A few changes in meaning resulted from Webster's eager equivocation to avoid naughty words:

> *lecher,* n.

> *J.* A whoremaster.

> *W.* A man given to lewdness; one addicted, in an exorbitant degree, to the indulgence of animal appetite, and an illicit commerce with females.

Some conventional meanings were Americanized by Webster; the ***American Dictionary*** should, after all, be a clarion call to democracy:

> *lady,* n.1

> *J.* A woman of high rank; the title of *lady* properly belongs to the wives of knights, of all degrees above them, and to the daughters of earls, and all of higher ranks.

> *W.* A woman of distinction. Originally, the title of lady was given to the daughters of earls and others in high rank, but by custom, the title belongs to any woman of genteel education.

Few of the new meanings, however, are of distinctly American etymology; *levee,* n.3 ('A bank or causey, particularly along a river') and *liberal,* adj.7 ('free; not literal or strict; as a *liberal* construction of law') seem clearly American. Doubtful American meanings are so numerous that I list none here.

Webster took the majority of his illustrations and authorities from Johnson. For the 448 new illustrations inserted in the *L*'s, he had stated [in the Preface] a distinct purpose: to draw attention to 'American authorities' and scientists ('Franklin, Washington, Adams, Jay, Madison, Marshall, Ramsay, Dwight, Smith, Trumbull, Hamilton, Belknap, Ames, Mason, Kent, Hare, Silliman, Cleaveland, Walsh, Irving'). In spite of this intention, more than half of the illustrations he added to Johnson (at least in the *L*'s) came from the Bible and an encyclopedia. Johnson had quoted liberally from the Bible, but apparently not nearly often enough to please Webster. The encyclopedia fulfilled another of Webster's desires: precision of statement in definition and illustrative quotations which amplified definitions with scientific facts, leaving little opportunity for misinterpretation. Historical authority of Addison and Sidney must give way to technical authority of the herald of the new age: the encyclopedia.

Webster and Johnson had basically divergent attitudes toward lexicography and toward their role as lexicographers. The difference is manifested in the simplest definitions:

lion, n.

J. The fiercest and most magnanimous of four-footed beasts.

W. A quadruped of the genus Felis, very strong, fierce and rapacious. The largest lions are eight or nine feet in length. The male has a thick head, beset with long bushy hair of a yellowish color. The lion is a native of Africa and the warm climates of Asia. His aspect is noble, his gait stately, and his roar tremendous.

Johnson observes the characteristics of the animal and places it in the humanistic hierarchy of beasts, arranged by attribution of human qualities. He is primarily interested in the figurative lion: his definition is literary. With no more than Johnson's definition as a guide, no one could spot a lion in a roomful of beasts. Webster describes the animal in scientific terms and places it in a zoological hierarchy. The description is reminiscent, though, of the definition of a 'horse' given in Mr. Gradgrind's utilitarian school in Dickens's *Hard Times.* These are the facts on the lion: they enable the reader to identify one if he happens to run across it. Johnson's definition is literary and humanistic; Webster's, scientific and encyclopedic.

Perhaps the key to their differences is found in their definitions of *lexicographer:*

J. A writer of dictionaries; a harmless drudge, that busies himself in tracing the original, and detailing the signification of words.

W. The author of a lexicon or dictionary.

The characterization is inverted. Johnson depicts his role ironically and humbly but, in a sense, better describes Webster the lexicographer than he describes himself. Webster uses the word *author,* implying a man of literature with a literary approach; Johnson was more properly the 'author of a lexicon.'

The value of Webster's work was recognized more and more as the years passed and Johnson's slipped into partial oblivion. Each man created a monument to himself in a single work. In the time-honored manner of the lexicographer, Webster used what Johnson had compiled, in spite of his previous aversion to Johnson's 'want of discrimination' and his 'vulgar words and offensive ribaldry.' What Webster compiled required at first committees and later whole offices to revise. Webster so much widened the scope of lexicography that he assured himself of a kind of immortality. Lexicography was no longer a one-man job: one man could never 'improve' his work as he had 'improved' Johnson's. Undeniably, he had added 'by his own toil, to the acquisitions of his ancestors.' (pp. 95-105)

Joseph W. Reed, Jr., "Noah Webster's Debt to Samuel Johnson," in American Speech, *Vol. XXXVII, No. 2, May, 1962, pp. 95-105.*

Homer D. Babbidge, Jr. (essay date 1967)

[*Babbidge was a distinguished American educator and university administrator who specialized in American studies. In the following excerpt, he surveys Webster's career and examines his contribution to American political and cultural nationalism.*]

The altogether human habit that leads us to identify a man by a single personal trait or physical attribute—to remember a Benedict Arnold for his treachery alone—has for more than a century categorized one of America's most illustrious and many-faceted historical figures as "the man who made the dictionary." The great *An American Dictionary of the English Language* stands today as a monument to Noah Webster, but the full dimensions of his career have been obscured in its shadow.

Such a truncated reputation does Webster a grave injustice, for in terms of vision, ability, dedication, and versatility, he deserves a place among that extraordinary group of men known to us today as founders of the American nation. Webster was a prominent author, editor, and publicist long before he began work on his famous dictionary; indeed, had it not been for that astonishing accomplishment, he might be better known to us today as a striking representative of early American nationalistic thought. A brief list of claims made in his behalf by those who have looked beyond the curtain of his lexicographic success suggests the dimensions of his career. He has been called "Schoolmaster to America," "the Man Who Taught the Masses How To Read and Write," "the Father of American Copyright Law," "the First Historian of Epidemic Disease," and "the Colossus of the Federalists." He was a founder of the Connecticut Academy of Arts and Sciences, Amherst College, and what was perhaps the first philological society in America. He held a variety of public offices—from judge to legislator—in both Connecticut and Massachusetts, and worked, throughout the eighty-five years of his life, as a schoolteacher, magazine and newspaper editor and publisher, lawyer, lecturer, farmer, author, and essayist. In breadth of interest and accomplishment, Webster had few superiors in the glittering Age of American Enlightenment. Though a certain humorless rigidity of character and manner—his detractors called him "the Monarch"—denied Webster the role in national politics he might otherwise have enjoyed, he made vital contributions to the emergence of the American nation, both politically and culturally. But these prior accomplishments disappeared from the public consciousness, like so many sandpiper tracks from the ocean shore, under the wave of fame that followed on the publication, in 1828, of *An American Dictionary of the English Language.* So dramatic was this culminating event in his career that its earlier acts and scenes have been forgotten. (pp. 3-4)

In a sense, Noah Webster's career had two distinct acts. The first—and most appealing, from hindsight—was his career as a militant advocate of American union and cultural and political independence. For fifteen years, from 1782 to 1797, Webster toiled with enthusiasm and dedication to instill in the hearts and minds of his fellow citizens some of his own passionate love of liberty and to persuade them of the great truth of his life, that liberty could be preserved only through the strength that comes of unity. Webster's career as a "cultural nationalist" entitles him to unchallenged eminence in American life, for his broadly

4 Any individual of a family descending in a collateral line; any descendant from a common parent or stock.

5. Branches of a bridle. Two pieces of iron bent iron which bear the bit, the cross chains & the curb. Encyc

6 In gothic architecture, the branches of ogives are the arches of gothic vaults, traversing from one angle to another diagonally, & forming a cross between the other arches, which make the sides of the square, of which the arches are diagonals. Harris

7. A warrant a commission given to a pilot. Laws of Massachusetts

8 A chandelier — — .. — –: — — Ash

Branch v.i. To shoot or spread in branches; to ramify; as a plant; a as horns.

2. To divide into separate parts, or subdivisions; as a mountain; a stream; or a moral subject; to ramify.

3 To speak diffusively; to make many distinctions or divisions in a discourse;

4 To have horns shooting out Milton

Branch v.t. To divide as into branches; to make subordinate divisions. Bacon

2 To adorn with needle work, representing branches, or flowers, or twigs. Spenser

Branch'ed pp. Divided or spread into branches; separated into subordinate parts; adorned with branches; furnished with branches.

Branch'er n. One that shoots forth branches;

2 A young hawk when he begins to leave the nest, & take to the branches.

Branch'ery n. The ramifications or ramified vessels dispersed through the pulpy part of fruit. Encyc. Ash.

Branch'iness n. Fulness of branches. — Johnson

Branch'ing ppr. Shooting in branches; dividing into several subordinate parts.

Branch'ing a. Loaded with branches coming out without order. Martyn.

Manuscript page from Webster's An American Dictionary of the English Language.

conceived ideal of union and its cultural dimensions surpasses that of his more famous contemporaries.

The second act of Webster's career only partly negated the first. In it, he emerges not so much as an individual proponent of national unity, but as a classic symbol of the lost cause of American Federalism. Disillusioned by what he considered the demoralization of American politics, Webster turned, with the century, from political activism to moral criticism, his shining vision of the new America tarnished. With increasing piety and diminishing humanness, Webster moved away from the affairs of men to the pursuits of the mind and the spirit. He became, in his later years, the very model of the irascible, crotchety conservative, looking with equal disdain upon the folly of his youth and its reflection in nineteenth-century democratic practice.

Bred of stolid Connecticut Puritan stock, nurtured in the stern Calvinism of the eighteenth century, and educated at the orthodox little college at New Haven, the Webster of provincial, propertied, and pious loyalties seems a perfectly natural product of his environment. That he should have played an important role in organizing the Hartford Convention of 1814—because the federal government did not adequately reflect the *"northern* or *commercial* interest"—seems more natural than his statement, in 1785, that "the interest of individuals must always give place to the interest of the whole community."

Webster's early devotion to revolutionary ideals can be attributed to exposure during his youth to the contagious spirit of political independence then abroad in New England and, more particularly, to the especially potent form of the virus that affected Yale College while he was there. His intense devotion to these ideals indicates the extraordinary grip this radical spirit had on the mind of Yale's wartime generation.

Professor David Potter discusses the role of Yale College as a seedbed not only of independence but also of union among the American colonies [in "Nathan Hale and the Ideal of American Union," *Connecticut Antiquarian,* (June, 1954)]. He quite properly cites the farewell address of Timothy Dwight as a high-water mark in the tide of sentiment that caused the class of 1769 to appear at graduation "wholly dressed in the manufactures of our own country." To Dwight, a young tutor at the college during Webster's undergraduate career, must go considerable credit for Webster's infection with these advanced ideals.

Webster derived from his career at Yale an exciting concept of American nationality and destiny—the concept of a nation that John Trumbull of the class of 1768 described as "the first in letters as the first in arms." The cultural baptism he received in the atmosphere there during the Revolutionary War, including an undergraduate glimpse of the great George Washington and an uncomfortable, but perfectly safe, march to join in the Battle of Saratoga, confirmed Webster as a patriot in the broadest sense of his own definition. Before he had reached his majority, Webster saw the visions of liberty and union as two sides of the same political and cultural coin.

Once out of Yale, however, Webster had some difficulty finding the right medium for the expression of his sentiments. He tried his hand at schoolteaching, taking time out when he could afford it to study law. By the time his first book appeared in 1783, he had been admitted to the Connecticut bar and had satisfied himself that schoolmastering was not a sufficient outlet for his growing ambitions. In his famous *The American Spelling Book* (Part I of *A Grammatical Institute, of the English Language*), Webster sought to "promote the honour and prosperity" of America by establishing American independence in this rudimentary branch of literature. Encouraged by public response, he ventured to take a more prominent place in public affairs. Returning to his native Hartford, he peppered the Connecticut *Courant* with anonymous letters on a variety of political and economic subjects and, in 1785, published his *Sketches of American Policy.* This slender volume, revealing Webster's considerable debt to Rousseau and other contemporary democratic writers, contained a plea for strong national government, which Madison was later to acknowledge as an "early" expression of the sentiment that culminated in the Constitution of 1787. Believing that no one else had yet formulated such clear views on the need for a strong central government, Webster gave them wide play during an extensive lecture tour through the colonies in 1785-86. As a result of this tour—on which Webster promoted both the adoption of copyright laws and the sale of his book—his views on language matured. Taken together, the preface to Webster's *A Grammatical Institute, of the English Language,* his *Sketches of American Policy,* and his *Dissertations on the English Language* (not published until 1789) represent a comprehensive statement of the cultural nationalism that Webster was determined to promulgate.

Webster's nationalism had two essential characteristics, remarkable not so much for their novelty as for their directness and simplicity. First, it embodied the familiar conviction that only in union was there sufficient strength to ensure liberty. In that sense, Webster shared the characteristic of all the great leaders of American independence, "the whole-heartedness with which they embraced the ideal of Union as well as the ideal of Freedom." Of the local, colonial liberty that existed under the Articles of Confederation, Webster cried in 1787, "From such liberty, O Lord, deliver us!" He saw in the inability of the national government to enforce its policies "a ridiculous farce, a burlesque on government, and a reproach to America," because it permitted individual states to negate common policy and gave America no effectual protection against alien intrusion.

The second feature of Webster's nationalism was inextricably bound up with his devotion to political union. He believed that a sense of nationality was vital to the preservation of unity, just as union was essential to liberty. Of political affairs he observed, "We ought to generalize our ideas and our measures. We ought not to consider ourselves as inhabitants of a particular state only, but as *Americans,* as the common subjects of a great empire." Nor was this concept of nationality limited to his adage that selfishness is "self-ruin, and that *provincial interest* is inseperable from *national interest."* Webster saw Americanism as something intimately tied up with everyday matters of dress, speech, manners, and education; he argued that a true spirit of nationality could develop only from a sense of distinctiveness in the personal, daily life of the people. Cultural independence was the mortar for the stones of political union, just as union was the foundation of liberty.

Conspicuous by its absence from Webster's thinking was that spirit of egalitarian democracy and humanitarianism that had characterized the nationalism of contemporary French thinkers and that subsequently became a vital part of American national purpose. As radical as his views were in the context of his background, Webster, even in his earliest political essays, cautioned against the kind of direct democracy that had prevailed in early Greece, where an "illiterate and credulous" people "under no restraint" had provided "capricious and irregular" government. He advocated, instead, a representative democracy held in check by a strong constitution vigorously enforced. He saw property ownership as the real source of power in society and felt that the general distribution of property in America assured that civil power would remain with the people. He saw as the great task facing America the creation of a constitution, a set of laws, and a system of education that would constructively harness the popular will and provide effective protection for the rights of person and property. Believing that "the privileges of freemen are interwoven into the very feelings and habits of the Americans," he concerned himself politically with the ways and means of institutionalizing liberty. In this respect he was more an objective political scientist than a militant advocate of democratic institutions, more a protector than a promoter of democracy.

Qualifications on Webster's debt to the egalitarians are apparent also in his efforts against slavery. Though offended by the "injustice" of slavery and active in founding one of the nation's first abolitionist societies, the Connecticut Society for the Promotion of Freedom and the Relief of Persons unlawfully holden in Bondage, Webster in his *Effects of Slavery on Morals and Industry* (1793) concerns himself with the harmful economic and social effects of slavery, rather than with its offenses against mankind. His gradualist approach to emancipation and his preoccupation with the dollars-and-cents value of freeing the slaves suggest that Webster was not a passionate humanitarian. No matter what spirit later generations might choose to infuse into their institutions, Webster's objective was to secure for them the freedom to make that choice. Such freedom, he believed, could be obtained only through the development of union, both political and cultural.

Webster devoted his prodigiously active career from 1783 to 1800 to the task of developing a spirit of American nationality. On the political front, he served as a publicist for the new Constitution (1787–88). In 1793, he founded the daily *American Minerva* (later renamed the *Commercial Advertiser*) in New York and worked assiduously as its editor until 1798, to promote the policies—notably neutrality—of Washington's administration. Although considered a spokesman for such leading Federalists as Jay and Hamilton (both of whom had encouraged the establishment of the newspaper), Webster felt that his tireless efforts were nonpartisan and constructive and that his single enemy was "disunion," the only "really formidable" threat to America. In these journalistic efforts he did much to promote the figure of Washington as a symbol of Americanism, as well as to defend the policies of his administration. Webster composed pamphlets stressing the economic advantages and cultural importance of political union; he wrote one of the first comprehensive histories of the Revolutionary War, gave wide circulation to the addresses of Revolutionary thinkers, and otherwise helped

to build a nucleus of American folklore on which he and others could begin to elaborate a sense of American being.

Webster paid particular attention to the more intimate aspects of national character. Worthy of the fame it brought him was his development of the concept of an American language—a modified usage by means of which Americans would be distinguishable from their English forebears. Throughout his long and varied career, from the "Blue-Backed Speller" [Part I of *A Grammatical Institute, of the English Language*] to the great Dictionary, this was the dominant chord in the nationalistic score of Webster's life. Long after political disillusionment had robbed him of his enthusiasm for democracy and for the government that fostered it, the aged Webster could devote himself to the cause of a national language with the full measure of his patriotism. In this work Webster was an effective publicist. He pointed a schoolmasterly finger of shame at his fellow citizens for their dependence on European and English standards in speech, as well as manners and dress. Incessantly, he appealed to their self-respect, accusing them of lack of character in failing to make their own independent way through life. He capitalized on a lingering hostility toward the British in order to accomplish his ends and at times took advantage of American ignorance of Europe to caricature and attack its manners and morals. His ability to marshal economic, social, political, and moral arguments in a way that appealed to a wide range of Americans was impressive. He could accentuate the positive by extolling the future glory of America, and he could frighten Americans by describing the untold evils in store for American youth in the dens of European debauchery. He sold abolition on economic grounds and made opposition to simplified spelling smack of treason. He could be moralistic, even sanctimonious, or he could be bitter and vituperative. All things were fair for Webster in his private war to create an American spirit, for he divined that without the spirit, the union was lost; and without the union, liberty was lost.

Always, however, the dominant note in Webster's writing was an appeal to that germ of nationalistic sentiment that lingered from the Revolution, when a pressing common cause had excited a sense of national identity among the thirteen colonies. For example, in appealing for the adoption of an American system of education, Webster stated, "But every child in America should be acquainted with his own country. He should read books that furnish him with ideas that will be useful to him in life and practice. As soon as he opens his lips . . . he should lisp the praises of liberty and of those illustrious heroes and statesmen who have wrought a revolution in his favor."

Thus did Webster attempt to tease the Revolutionary spirit of Americans out into broader fields and to diffuse it through the customs and institutions of the new country. Throughout his life he directed special attention to American education, partly because the youth of America had not been exposed firsthand to the glorious spirit of '76 and partly because he believed that "the only practicable method to reform mankind is to begin with children." He agreed with Montesquieu that educational practice should be related to the political principles of a nation, and he argued forcefully for an indigenous American system of education. One of the first American educators to recognize the unique function of education in a republican form of government, Webster endeavored in his extensive series of schoolbooks to acquaint young Americans with the political history of their country in general and its political institutions in particular. His **"Federal Catechism,"** included in *An American Selection of Lessons in Reading and Speaking,* suggests the religiosity of Webster's devotion to this objective, and his later opinion that Americans were as advanced as Europeans in their study and knowledge of politics undoubtedly served to justify the importance he attached to such study.

That Webster had an economic interest in the extension of patriotic sentiment, insofar as it prompted the sale of books that were based on this kind of appeal, cannot be disregarded. He worked hard to win endorsement for his schoolbooks and to promote their sale, just as he labored for a body of copyright law that would ensure an income from these sales. But Webster's career is studded with too many economically unprofitable acts of patriotism to justify a belief that he promoted nationalism merely to sell his books. While Webster did create a demand for his own books, he performed the same service for many other authors whose profits exceeded the meager royalties that he realized on most of his works. Moreover, his interest in Americanism outlasted his concern for royalties. Long after the Revolutionary spirit had waned, he reissued *An American Selection of Lessons in Reading and Speaking* "to instruct our youth in what belongs to this country." What is perhaps more impressive, the doughty schoolmaster dared to do what few authors in his limited circumstances would: He withdrew one of his books from the market "on the ground of . . . imperfections," an act described by a biographer as "a precious example of integrity" [see Warfel entry dated 1936 in Further Reading].

Webster's varied activities in the promotion of American nationalism attracted the abuse and ridicule so characteristic of the period. Republican partisans considered him a virtual monarchist, and the reactionary William Cobbett called him a "toad in the service of sans-culottism." Though this criticism may be taken as evidence of Webster's effectiveness, his sensitivity to it was partly responsible for his temporary retirement from public life, in 1789, when he wrote President Washington, "I wish now to attend solely to my profession and to be unknown in any other sphere of life." It was a factor, too, in Webster's final retirement from the role of publicist, in 1798, when he announced his intention to "pursue, with little interruption, my taste for science." His withdrawal to New Haven in 1798, an act of great significance in Webster's life, was a symbolic retirement to the sidelines of national affairs and marked the beginning of the career that made him famous. His political comments thereafter, though frequent and militant, served only to emphasize his failure to follow in the flood of democratic sentiment that was sweeping America.

Disenchanted by the sober study of the French Revolution he had made for the *American Minerva* and alarmed by the similarity between the mushrooming democratic clubs and the despised Jacobins, Webster showed signs of losing faith in the government he had helped to create. Never an egalitarian, and always a staunch advocate of property as the basis of franchise, Webster now saw control of what was to have been the glorious new America falling into the hands of the ignorant, emotional rabble. He saw in equal

suffrage a "monstrous inversion of the natural order of society" and in the ability of people without property to tax those who had accumulated it a "species of oppression that will ultimately produce a revolution." A ringing Federalist victory in the Connecticut elections of 1798 was momentarily reassuring, but he cautioned a Fourth of July audience that year to proceed with care, observing that *"Experience* is a safe pilot, but *experiment* is a dangerous ocean, full of rocks and shoals."

In this new role, Webster became a virtual prototype of the disillusioned Federalist. He still believed in liberty—individual and collective—and in the union that made it possible. "Man is too feeble to protect himself," he said in 1802, "and unless he can protect himself, he is not free." What alarmed him was the susceptibility of the people, who, he believed, were putting into office a group of self-seeking, corrupt, and immoral men. Webster's essential confidence in the people had been based on the "substantial yeomanry" that he saw about him in Connecticut—these being moderately well educated and, in large part, property-owning. Immigration, population increases, and a more complex economy could only detract from that confidence, which had never been unlimited. On the eve of a period that posterity would one day call the zenith of democracy and the nadir of education, Webster saw the people re-enacting the tragedy of early Greece, where a similar populace had been "generally at the command of some noisy demagogue." He attacked Jefferson and "partisans" on both sides for exciting the passions of the people and urged that the people be given an opportunity to contemplate the "pernicious effects" of "hasty councils," for he remained essentially confident that "it is morally impossible that the body of a people can be enemies to public happiness."

He longed for a government "where *constitution* and *law* and *wisdom* have the control," instead of the popular democracy of Jefferson and his followers. So strong was his belief in representative constitutional government that the first evidence of partisan popular rule—especially the spoils system—left him stunned and horrified. At first, Webster clung to the view that courageous, enlightened leadership could remedy the situation; thus, he charged the Federalist leaders with attempting "to resist the force of current popular opinion instead of falling into the current with a view to direct it." But he, too, eventually pulled himself up onto the bank when it became apparent that he could do nothing but be drowned in that current. In the pious quietude of his old age, Webster would one day yearn for a community to which he could remove himself "to be freed from our democracy." "We deserve all our public evils," he said. "We are a degenerate and wicked people. That a kind Providence may watch over . . . all of us is [my] prayer."

Disillusioned as he was by what the American people chose to make of their freedom despite his warnings, Webster did not surrender his desire to promote a sense of Americanism among them. He observed in 1800 that "nothing like a well-defined national character" existed outside New England [*Ten Letters to Dr. Joseph Priestly* (1800)], and he sought new outlets for the expression of his patriotic values and new means for their dissemination throughout the United States. He found these in what he called "literary pursuits," which "afford the highest satisfaction without the vexations, disappointments, and endless perturbations" that he had encountered in the arena of public affairs.

After his withdrawal from public affairs, Webster took two steps that fixed the course of his life thereafter: He gave himself to the church and he devoted his talents almost exclusively to the elevation of American science and letters. Webster may have felt that his contributions here would ultimately have beneficial political effects on the people, but he also believed that there was intrinsic value in the two labors of his later life—the extension of religious morality and the elevation and general diffusion of learning. Of Timothy Dwight's line, "Be freedom, and science, and virtue, thy fame," Webster was, despite his conservatism, able to salvage two-thirds. His formal commitment to virtue took place in the winter of 1807-8, when he publicly espoused the "moderate Calvinist" Church, though he recalled that a reading of Samuel Johnson's *Rambler* had led him in his youth to "a firm resolution to pursue a course of virtue through life, and to perform all moral and social duties with scrupulous exactness." The transformation that took place in 1808 was a repudiation of his earlier "mistake" of "attending to the duties which man owes to man," while neglecting those he owed "to our Creator and Redeemer." That this new view of virtue was to intrude at times upon his personal and literary life was immediately evident, for on October 13, 1808, he wrote his classmate and friend Joel Barlow explaining why he could not, as he had intended, write a public review of the latter's *Columbiad:* "Of the poem as a poem I can conscientiously say all, perhaps, which you can expect or desire, but I cannot in a review omit to pass a severe censure on the atheistical principles it contains."

Webster was to express his thanks for divine favor frequently thereafter, for his new-found religious faith was an indispensable support to him in the greatest labor of his life. At the same time, however, his religious orientation led him increasingly to a moral view of political affairs that made it difficult for him to recall the realities of the political world. The one word that Webster actually created—to describe the effects of the French Revolution—was defined in his great dictionary as follows:

> Demoralize—To corrupt or undermine the morals of; to destroy or lessen the effect of moral principles on; to render corrupt in morals.

So convinced was Webster of the essential morality of his own position that he fell into the error of assuming the absence of morality in the views of those who opposed him. Over and over again he was to bemoan the demoralization of American government. Webster devoted considerable energy during the remaining thirty-five years of his life to the promotion of religious morality, in and out of politics. His revision of the Bible in 1833 and his central role in the founding of Amherst College in 1820 "for the education of pious young men for the gospel ministry" attest to the force of his conviction and are in contrast to its less constructive applications in the area of politics.

Webster's abundant energies, stimulated by a renewed sense of moral responsibility but frustrated in the channels of political life, poured with steady force into the riverbed of his literary course. It seems doubtful that Webster could have completed the 1828 dictionary had not his sen-

timents ruled out continued extensive participation in political affairs and allowed him to concentrate all his energy, ambition, and public spirit on the single goal of promoting the intellectual dignity of America.

Webster's first major undertaking after his withdrawal from New York, the preparation of *A Brief History of Epidemic and Pestilential Diseases,* was one of the most impressive scientific labors to emerge from the young nation and convincingly demonstrated that Webster was determined to make a mark for American science. Though since proven wrong in its speculations on the causes of epidemic diseases, the work is a bench mark of careful historical research, and the labor that produced it was excellent preparation for the mammoth work Webster was to undertake next.

According to his own accounts, Webster's formal venture into lexicography began at the turn of the century. The germ of the idea having been planted some years before, Webster had begun to make marginal notes of errors, new usages, and unfamiliar words in his extensive reading during his active editorial career, in subconscious preparation for his first formal effort at defining words. The motivation for the work, however, had been with him from his youth, when in the course of his early lectures he began to develop his views on **"Reasons Why the English Should Not Be Our Standard, Either in Language or Manners."** His earliest literary research led him to find fault with the work of Robert Lowth and Samuel Johnson, two great standards of the day, and he began at once to plant his explosive nationalist spirit in whatever faults he could find. Webster delighted in detonating his charges in print and conducted a systematic campaign to crack the walls of English convention even before he began the constructive effort of his great dictionary. His extensive research during the first quarter of the nineteenth century only added to his enthusiasm, and by 1816, when challenged by John Pickering for his lack of respect for English literary authority, Webster gave free run to his sentiments. His philological and etymological studies had, he told Pickering, led him to "withdraw much of . . . [his] confidence" in the great English writers and had made him "look with astonishment upon the errors and false principles which they have propagated." He leveled criticism at Johnson over and over again, as he had in an open letter to Judge Dawes on July 25, 1809, in which he stated that "the definitions which constitute the whole value of *Johnson's* Dictionary are deficient in precision beyond anything I could have imagined."

Webster knew well that such criticism rang hollow without a better dictionary to replace the one he challenged. Faultfinding had come easily to one whose entire career had been devoted to breaking the "charm of veneration" of foreign authorities. Providing the constructive alternative was a backbreaking labor, but its successful completion properly earned for its executor the eternal regard of his country. A quarter-century of persistent work, "beating the track of the alphabet with sluggish resolution" (as Johnson saw the lexicographer's task), years of study in dozens of languages, the construction of an extensive theory of etymology, an extended trip to Europe, and the writing *by hand* of more than seventy thousand entries—these were the chief, though far from sole, occupations of Webster between the ages of forty-two and seventy. When, with trembling hand, Webster completed the last entry in his manuscript, he had forged the most impressive link in that "band of national union" that had been the single object of his career. He had given America its own independent standard of language—one that was good enough to become, in a few short years, the standard of the English-speaking world. Thus did Webster, by diverting his nationalist spirit into the remote channel of literary scholarship, make his greatest single contribution to the elusive object of his life. He had fulfilled, in part, his prediction of an earlier year that "We shall realize a new species of independence—an independence flattering to generous minds, and more productive of wealth than all the laws of power or the little arts of national policy" [*An American Selection of Lessons in Reading and Speaking*].

His devotion to Washingtonian policies, his abhorrence of political parties, his attachment to property and commerce, his tendency to equate New England values and interests with those of the nation, and his ultimate political disillusionment made Noah Webster a brilliant personification of "Steady Habit" Federalism. But when political disenchantment came and he found the times intolerant of his antique views, Webster defied the prototype. He largely resisted the tendency of the old-line Federalists to abandon their original confidence in the destiny of America; instead, he funneled his energies into constructive literary channels.

The thread of patriotism in the varied pattern of Webster's life thus sustained itself in political disillusion. From that day in 1782, when, with "the American army . . . lying on the bank of the Hudson" and with "no certain prospect of peace," he undertook his first book "to promote the honour and prosperity of . . . America," to the climactic achievement of his great dictionary in 1828, which he presented to the public with wishes "for the glory of my country," Webster's life was dedicated to the ideals of American liberty and union. For this, despite his ultimately unpopular political views, posterity must rank Noah Webster as one of America's most devoted patriots.

The genius of Webster's contribution to America's self-image was his recognition that union is built not of laws and policies or of economic and political advantage alone, but of all of these welded together by the spirit and symbols of national self-consciousness. His life was a combination of breadth of conception and interest, as reflected in his extraordinary range of writings, and a marked singleness of purpose. Politics was only one important expression of the varied media through which he tried to promote that single object—the creation of a free and unified America. His writings on history, geography, science, and simplified spelling, though less important, were similar links in the chain of unity he tried to forge during his lifetime. And the two great monuments of his career—the "Blue-Backed Speller" and *An American Dictionary of the English Language*—though they stand as the most important evidence of Webster's work, are nonetheless only parts of that same unity. (pp. 4-15)

Homer D. Babbidge, Jr., in an introduction to On Being American: Selected Writings, 1783-1828 *by Noah Webster, edited by Homer D. Babbidge, Jr., Frederick A. Praeger, Publishers, 1967, pp. 3-15.*

Richard M. Rollins   (essay date 1976)

[*Rollins is an American historian who specializes in U.S. history and American thought and language. In the following excerpt, he argues that* An American Dictionary of the English Language *significantly reflects the undemocratic authoritarianism that characterized Webster's thought during his late career.*]

"I finished writing my dictionary in January, 1825," Noah Webster once recalled. It was a solemn moment:

> When I had come to the last word, I was seized with a trembling which made it somewhat difficult to hold my pen steady for writing. The cause seems to have been the thought that I might not then live to finish the work, or the thought that I was so near the end of my labors. But I summoned the strength to finish the last word, and then walking about the room a few minutes I recovered.

So ended twenty-five years of constant, daily labor. The finished product was, by all standards, a monumental achievement. With 70,000 entries, all written out by his own hand, it was a massive work, the last major dictionary ever compiled by a single individual. It has become, in the form of its successors, an integral part of American culture. As early as the mid-nineteenth century the name Webster had become synonymous with a dictionary.

Virtually everyone believes that the *American Dictionary of the English Language* was a nationalistic tract. So pervasive is this belief that many historians . . . discuss the work in the context of rising nationalism without really stating that the work was thus motivated. They write as if Webster's nationalism was common knowledge and that there could be no other explanation for his work. . . . Even Lawrence J. Friedman [see Further Reading], who correctly notes Webster's alienation, portrays the dictionary as a patriotic work. Those who have concentrated on Webster or the dictionary itself have been even more adamant in their conclusions. Homer D. Babbidge [see excerpt above] represents the attitude and methodology most commentators employ. He consistently confuses Webster's nationalistic statements of the 1780s with his later work, as if nothing occurred between 1783 and 1841.

Nationalism is too simple an explanation. When the work is considered within the context of Noah Webster's life, it becomes apparent that it was stimulated by much more than patriotism. That was undoubtedly an important factor in his early conceptions, but the *American Dictionary* was the product of a lifetime. It reflected the events and inheritances of that human life and contained all the biases, concerns, and ideals of a specific individual. Indeed, it was an extension of his whole personality, and one must read it carefully to understand the tale it tells. Webster's main motivation for writing and publishing it was not to celebrate American life or to expand independence. Instead, he sought to counteract social disruption and reestablish the deferential world order that he believed was disintegrating.

Over the course of his eighty-four years, Noah Webster changed from an optimistic revolutionary in the 1780s, convinced that man could perfect himself and that America was the site of a future utopia, to a pessimistic critic of man and society. His buoyant nationalism dissolved under the pressures of the events of the 1780s and 1790s. The question that commanded his attention during the last fifty years of his life was the conflict between freedom and order. As with many others who perceived themselves as America's moral stewards after 1800, his answer to that problem was that all Americans should submit their hearts and minds to an authoritarian God and mold themselves in the image of Quiet Christians. Good citizens were not disruptive; they were obedient to the wishes of a social leadership consisting of pious, elderly property owners. Webster's definitions of words, both in his private correspondence and in the dictionary itself, as well as his method of etymology, reflect this view. If Americans would only see the world through the eyes and mind of Noah Webster as set forth in his dictionary, Christian peace and tranquility would reign. Webster's main motivation was social control, and his dictionary was a means of achieving it.

The change in Webster began in the 1780s. Dissent in Connecticut, Shays' Rebellion in Massachusetts, chaotic election procedures in the South, and economic instability convinced him that an authority capable of enforcing order was necessary, that the Articles of Confederation must be replaced. In 1787, the Pennsylvania delegation to the Constitutional Convention asked him to write a defense of the new government. Webster happily complied, expressing his view of the new system as a balance between revolutionary ideals and social stability [in *An Examination into the Leading Principles of the Federal Constitution . . .*].

The development of Webster's interest in language coincided with an emerging emphasis on order. Throughout his life he exhibited a dualistic attitude toward language. It was a subject worthy of study by all Americans for its own sake, but also a means to a greater end. In 1789 he published the first significant American essay on linguistics, *Dissertations on the English Language. . . .* His concept of language as a tool of social change had emerged. Webster believed that cultural as well as political independence was necessary for the new nation to survive. Like Schlegel, Grimm, Horne Tooke, and other Europeans, Webster believed that a connection between language and the nation existed. "A *national language* is a bond of *national union*," he said, and it should "be employed to render the people of this country national. . . ."

Yet Webster's anxiety increased in response to the events of the 1790s. The growth of the democratic societies, mob violence, the activities of Genêt and his supporters, and especially the political battles and public vituperation dismayed him. The terror in France was a turning point. Shocked by the widespread use of the guillotine, Webster became convinced that man was innately depraved and that the expansion of human freedom and self-reliance brought only anarchy, chaos, murder, and brutality. Events in France seemed a portent of America's future, and thus he opposed efforts at progressive social change. The great experiment had produced only a people characterized by corruption, vice, deceit, and debauchery.

On July Fourth of 1798 Webster gave an oration in New Haven in which he summarized the events of the previous twenty years and predicted the nation's future. It amounted to little more than a call for imposition of authority and a means of enforcing its wishes. Utopia had become a frightening den of iniquity; agitation and dissent must cease, a source of cohesion must be found. "Let us never forget that the cornerstone of all republican government is," he said, "that the will of every citizen is controlled by the laws of supreme will of the state."

His criticism of the developing nation after 1798 was profound. The concept of equality seemed fallacious, and democracy threatened civilization itself. Only fatherly figures of authority could be trusted to govern. People would be freer and happier "if all were deprived of the right of suffrage until they were forty-five years of age, and if no man was eligible to an important office until he was fifty. . . ." All power should be vested in "our old men, who have lost their ambitions chiefly and have learnt wisdom by experience."

Conversion to evangelical Protestantism in 1808 provided Webster with more detailed explanations of all his fears. With men like John Jay, Stephen Van Rensselaer, Timothy Dwight, John Cotton Smith, and Elias Boudinot, Webster believed that religion provided the only viable basis for civilization. They saw themselves as "their brother's keepers," and were determined to oversee America's return to tranquility through their own moral stewardship. They formed large organizations, including the American Bible Society, the American Tract Society, and the American Sunday School Union in order to spread their doctrines of Quiet Christian deference and to enhance public acquiescence. In everything he wrote after 1808, from ordinary school books to evangelical tracts and including his own version of the Holy Bible, Webster proclaimed that fearful worship of God was the first step to civil order, that government should be run by the elderly, pious, and wealthy. He summed up his conception of the influence of religion on behavior and society:

> Real religion implies a habitual sense of divine presence, and a fear of offending the Supreme Being, subdues and controls all the turbulent passions; and nothing is seen in the Christian, but meekness, forbearance, and kindness, accompanied by a serenity of mind and a desire to please, as uniform as they are cheering to families and friends.
>
> [*Letter from Noah Webster, Esq., of New Haven, Connecticut, to a Friend in Explanation and Defense of the Distinguishing Doctrines of the Gospel* (1809)]

Americans should not agitate for social change but must instead be obedient followers of the law as laid down by the moral stewards. All would be chaos without total obedience to God:

> . . . we are cast on the ocean of life, without chart, or compass, or rudder—nay, we are ignorant of our own port—we know not where we are bound—we have not a ray of light to guide us in the tempestuous sea—not a hope to cheer us amidst the distresses of this world, or tranquillize the soul in its passage into the next—and all beyond the present state, is annihilation or despair!
>
> ["Letter to a Young Gentleman Commencing His Education," *A Collection of Papers on Political, Literary, and Moral Subjects* (1843)]

In this frame of mind, far from one of exuberant nationalism, Webster wrote his dictionary.

It is natural to draw direct links between Webster's early

nationalism and his *American Dictionary.* And of course Webster encouraged this in the title and in his preface to his most famous work [see essay dated 1828]. He noted that the chief glory of a nation arose from its authors and stated that American writers were equal to Englishmen. He even named those on this side of the Atlantic whom he considered comparable to the best of Europe. Franklin, Washington, Adams, Jay, Madison, Marshall, Dwight, Trumbull, and Irving were his more well-known favorites. Nonetheless, the nationalist context is insufficient to explain the book. Perhaps as an indication of what was to come, Webster did not mention the internationally famous American who symbolized all that he loathed, Thomas Jefferson. Thomas Paine and other earlier American celebrators of democracy and freedom were also neglected. As George Krapp, the most respected twentieth-century student of the development of the English language has noted, merely naming Franklin, Washington, and others as authorities "is quite a different matter from the narrow patriotic zeal which was rampant in the years immediately following the Revolution" [see Further Reading].

In addition, Webster himself indicated that his views had changed. "It is not only important, but, in a degree necessary," he said in the opening pages, "that the people of this country, should have an *American Dictionary* of the English language. . . . " He did not advocate the development of a new language, or even a new dialect. Instead, he perceived himself to be writing merely an "American" dictionary of the English language, which is different from creating a whole new language. And he further explained his position, noting that the body of the language was basically the same as that of England. He added a revealing statement: "It is desirable to perpetuate that sameness."

Thus the end product of Webster's toils was anything but a new "American tongue." He included only about fifty Americanisms, a fact which prompted H. L. Mencken to label Webster an incompetent observer of his own country [*The American Language: An Inquiry into the Development of English in the United States* (1923)]. The lexicographer's nationalism had in fact reached a low point in 1814, when he helped draft the first circular calling for the Hartford Convention. In that year he also denounced the Constitution as naive and wildly democratic, ridiculed the concept of universal white male suffrage, and called for division of the union into three separate countries [in *An Oration, Pronounced before the Knox and Warren Branches of the Washington Benevolent Society, at Amherst* . . . (1814)].

The *American Dictionary* was perfectly acceptable in England. The first edition of 2,500 copies was quickly followed by an English edition of 3,000, and one major student of lexicography had noted that Webster's crowning achievement was quite suitable for use in America and England. Indeed, his dictionary was received more warmly across the Atlantic than in the United States. Warfel stated that "soon Webster became the standard in England . . . " [see Further Reading entry dated 1936]. When his publisher went bankrupt, copies of the English edition were sold without change in America.

Yet another incident suggests that his dictionary was not a nationalistic tract. When the second American edition was published in 1841, he sent a copy to Queen Victoria. Significantly, he told the person carrying it to her that

"our common language is one of the ties that binds the two nations together; I hope the works I have executed will manifest to the British nation that the Americans are not willing to suffer it to degenerate on this side of the Atlantic." Half a century earlier he had despised England and all that it stood for. Now he told the Queen that he hoped his dictionary might furnish evidence that the "genuine descendants of English ancestors born on the west of the Atlantic, have not forgotten either the land or the language of their fathers."

Webster made his intentions in the dictionary explicit. The values expressed within the work were his. "In many cases, I have given brief sentences of my own," he declared, "and often presenting some important maxim or sentiment in religion, morality, law or civil policy. . . . "

While Webster's work in etymology exhibited the influence of his social and political values, he sincerely believed that it was new, scholarly, and in fact the most important part of his work. As Laird correctly notes [see Further Reading], of all the causes he supported over his long life, and they were legion, "none was dearer to him than was the pursuit of etymologies, and in nothing so much as in his vast synopsis of 'language affinities' . . . did he repose his hopes for the gratitude and admiration of society." As early as 1806 Webster had vowed [in his preface to *A Compendious Dictionary of the English Language*] to "make one effort to dissolve the chains of illusions" surrounding the development of language. A year later he had begun to compile the dictionary by concentrating merely on definitions and correcting errors in orthography. This had led him "gradually and almost insensibly" to investigate the origin of the English language. He had been surprised to learn that the path of development of all European languages was an unexplored subject. All other etymologists had "wandered into the field of conjecture, venturing to substitute opinions for evidence. . . . " By 1809 he had concluded that language had begun in Asia and migrated outward. At about this time, Webster stopped working on definitions and orthography and spent ten years compiling his synopsis of the affinities of languages, on which his etymology in his dictionary was based. Four years before his death he still believed that his work was superior to any others and that any other etymology, including those by "the German scholars, the most accurate philologists in Europe, appears to be wholly deficient."

Yet, according to modern etymologists, it was Webster who was in error, not the Europeans. In fact, his etymology has been judged a failure. George Krapp has come close to explaining Webster's errors. "In short," he said, "it was really spiritual, not phonological truth in which Webster was primarily interested." He seems to have thought "that the truth of a word, that is the primitive and original radical value of the word, was equivalent to the truth of the idea."

Webster's etymology was a literal extrapolation of Scriptural truth, the only concrete truth, as far as he was concerned, into another field. Since 1808 he had believed that the Bible was factually correct, and that it must be accepted as such. Without it, there was no basis for civilization itself. Thus his rejection of European etymologists is no mystery. Their scientific attempts to unravel the development of language led away from the story of the Tower of Babel. They were challenging the validity of the Bible, the only rock upon which peace and tranquillity could be secured.

In 1806, as he began his etymological studies, Webster commented specifically on this subject. He believed that etymology illuminated not just the origins of words but the development of human history as well. The etymology of the languages of Europe "will throw no inconsiderable light on the origin and history of the several nations who people it, and confirm in no small degree, the scriptures account of the dispersion of men."

In the final analysis, Webster had no choice but to write Christian etymology, regardless of the methodology and insights of other authors. The only ultimate truth was contained in the Scriptures, and it dictated the mere truth of words. Beside Christ, Schlegel and Grimm were insignificant. They challenged the validity of Christianity, and if the authority of the Scriptures was demolished, there was simply no hope for mankind. Without literal belief in Biblical truth, he said in 1823, "we are cast on the ocean of life, without chart, or compass, or rudder." Only "annihilation and despair" could result if the Scriptures were found invalid in any area. Given this vision, Webster was incapable of seeing the development of language in any framework of explanation other than that set forth in the Bible.

Webster introduced his etymology with a literal belief in the origin of language according to Genesis. Vocal sounds, he noted, were used to communicate between Adam and Eve. "Hence we may infer that language was bestowed on Adam, in the same manner as all his other faculties and knowledge, by supernatural power; or in other words was of divine origin. . . ." "It is therefore probable that *language* as well as the faculty of speech, was the immediate gift of God." Webster then traced the Biblical story of the development of man, which was the basis for all the deviations of the words in the two volumes. As Joseph Friend notes [see Further Reading], no amount of hard work, not even the labor of a quarter of a century, could overcome the limitations imposed by this Scriptural literalism. He accepted without question the story of the Tower of Babel and the confusion of tongues. Before that time all mankind had spoken a common language, which Webster called "Chaldee," and which modern etymologists agree was a fantasy. When those in Babel were dispersed, they divided into three groups, each led by a son of Noah: Shem, Ham, and Japheth. The last had eventually migrated to Northern Europe, and thus all the languages of that area were labeled "Japhetic." This development, believed Webster, could be traced through the existence of certain words that reappeared in several languages, as well as through the existence of words with similar construction and meaning in various languages.

One example of Webster's etymology will illustrate both his change in viewpoint over time and his authoritarian cast of mind. In 1789 he had remarked that the word "God" had come from the concept "good," and that His nature was the explanation of that derivation [*Dissertations on the English Language* . . .]. In 1826 he specifically rejected that idea. Instead, he noted that "Supreme Being" was taken from "supremacy or power." Thus "God" was "equivalent to lord or ruler, from some root signifying to press or exert force."

In attempting to understand the *American Dictionary* and the man who wrote it, we must recall that Webster's view of language was dualistic. It was, of course, to be studied for its own sake, but it was also something much more. Language, he believed, influenced opinion and behavior. If people had a clear understanding of "equality," they would act in certain ways. Language could be used as a means to a greater end. It could be altered and manipulated, and in so doing, one could affect millions of people. Although he never explicitly said so, Webster assumed this from the very beginning of his work. It is implicit in his early attempts—later repudiated—to forge an "American tongue" as a way of encouraging independence from a vile and corrupt England, and to further his utopian dreams. Even in 1788 he could conceptualize the use of language in purifying society. In that year he called for studies which would "show how far truth and accuracy of thinking are concerned in a clear understanding of *words*." Language should be studied "if it can be proved that *mere use of words* has led nations into error, and still continues the delusion. . . ." As early at 1790 he was engaged in manipulation of language as a means of influencing opinion and behavior. He had just completed another book, he told a friend. "I have introduced into it some definitions, relative to the slave trade," he said, "calculated to impress upon young minds the detestableness of the trade."

Webster's disillusionment with man and society was accompanied by the conclusion that the definition of words played a role in American development. "There is one remarkable circumstance in our own history which seems to have escaped observation," he noted in 1838, "which is, the mischievous effect of the indefinite application of terms." A year later he wrote an essay in which he summed up his entire life's work in linguistics, philology, etymology, and lexicography. "It is obvious to my mind, that popular errors proceeding from a misunderstanding of words," he said, "are among the efficient causes of our political disorders. . . ."

The thought process which led to etymological error also led to certain definitions. His correspondence and publications offer the opportunity to observe the way in which definitions were formed. Indeed, examples of the influence of social events and opinions abound, including the formulation of definitions which appeared almost intact decades later in his dictionaries. They reveal that his strong social and political values and his longing for public submission to authority dictated what he believed should be the correct understanding of important words.

He wrote that an incorrect understanding of the word "pension" had been partially responsible for social discord in the 1780s. Congress had granted a pension to officers who had served in the Continental Army. Many had protested, and a convention held in Middletown, Connecticut, had called for its repeal. This unrest had distressed Webster. It had been "a remarkable, but unfortunate instance of the use of the word, in a sense so indefinite that the people at large made no distinction between *pensions* granted as a provision for old officers, and *pensions* granted for the purpose of bribery for favor and support." Obviously Webster thought that the half-pay for officers was the first type of pension, while to the convention it was the second kind. In his dictionary he was careful to say that it meant "to grant an annual allowance from the public treasury to a person for past services. . . . " No example of the misunderstanding of words, he noted, was as important as that surrounding the phrase "union of church and state." He understood the aversion of many Americans to the unification of ecclesiastical and civil authority because of the European experience. Along with many others, Webster had spoken in favor of their separation in the 1780s. But times had changed, and by 1838 his conception of that relationship had also changed. Now the union of the two meant that "all laws must have *religion for their basis.*" In this sense, there was a strong need for a "union of civil and ecclesiastical powers; in support of the laws and institutions." This union was the seedbed of Quiet Christians and the heart of his concept of social relations.

"Jacobinism," "democrat," and "republican" were prominent words that Webster's biases led him to define in significant ways. The first, he said in 1799, was not merely the philosophy of a French political faction. It was instead "an opposition to established government and institutions, and an attempt to overthrow them, by private accusations or by violent or illegal means." "Democrat" was "synonymous with the word *Jacobian* in France. . . . " Democratic organizations arose from the attempt to "control our government by private associations." By 1800 the word signified "a person who attempts undue opposition to our influence over government by means of private clubs, secret intrigues, or by public popular meetings which are extraneous to the Constitution." "Republicans," on the other hand, were "friends of our Representative Governments, who believe that no influence whatever should be exercised in a state which is directly authorized by and developed by legislation." Similar definitions appeared in his dictionary.

A key word, the definition of which he felt could influence action, was "free." Most Americans were convinced that all men were free to act according to their own wills. The idea that this abstract condition was natural and was a basic part of American life was widely upheld, or so thought Noah Webster. To him it was absurd, and in fact "contributed to the popular licentiousness, which often disturbs the public peace, and even threatens extensive evils in this country." A misunderstanding of "free" threatened the permanency of government, because it led people to feel that somehow individuals were "*above* the constitutional authorities." It was also simply incorrect. Instead, all individuals, from the time of their birth, were subject to the demands of their parents, of God, and of the government of the country in which they lived. There would be fewer problems in society, said Noah Webster, if Americans understood that "*No person is born free,* in the general acception of the word *free.*"

"Equality" and "equal" were also crucial terms. "Nothing can be more obvious than that by the appointment of the creator, in the constitution of man and of human society," he wrote a few months before his death, "the conditions of men must be different and *unequal.*" The common American assumption that all men must be equal in conditions in which they lived was false. The Declaration of Independence was wrong when it began by affirming as a self-evident truth that "all men are born *equal.*" That was the work of the infamous idealist, Thomas Jefferson, and as a universal proposition had to be rejected. In their intellectual and physical powers men were born "*unequal,*"

and hence inequality was a basic part of human life. Webster said that most of the men of the earlier generation had maintained that each person was born with an "equal natural right to liberty and protection . . . ," something far different than total equality, an idea that led to agitation over the right of suffrage. The founders had believed in equality of opportunity, with which Webster had no argument. "But *equality of condition* is a very different thing and dependent on circumstances over which government and laws have no control."

Most importantly, when people expected equality of condition, it led inevitably to opposition to authority, chaos, and ultimately anarchy. Misunderstanding of the words *"free* and *equal"* influenced "the more ignorant and turbulent part of the community" to become "emboldened" and to "take the law into their own hands, or to trample both constitution and law under their feet." The very concept of equality of condition could culminate in disaster:

> . . . It is not for the interest and safety of society that all men should be equal. Perfect equality, if such a state could be supposed practicable, would render due subordination impossible, and dissolve society. All men in a community are equally entitled to protection, and the secure enjoyment of their rights. . . . Superiority in natural and acquired endowments, and in authority derived from the laws, is essential to the existence of social order, and of personal safety.

In his dictionary Webster listed nineteen definitions of the words "equal" and "equality." His faith in equality among men is conspicuous only by its absence.

Webster's emphasis on Quiet Christian behavior appears throughout the definitions in the ***American Dictionary*** itself. The reader is reminded of his divinely-directed role in life and the values by which he should live. The fear of God, absolute and rigid controller of all things, the depravity of man, and the character traits of meekness, humility, passivity, and wholehearted submission to proper authority are celebrated in the definitions of hundreds and perhaps thousands of words. This was done in two ways: either through definitions outlining deferential conduct, or through quotes illustrating the meaning of the word. He defined "author," for instance, as "One who produces, creates, or brings into being. . . . " Webster could have stopped there, with an objective statement, as other lexicographers did. Instead he added "as, God is the *author* of the Universe," thus reminding the reader of His fearful power.

Webster interjected his obsession with authority into the most intimate of human relationships. The verb form of "love" was "a sense to be pleased with," to which he added a significant set of examples of its usage, again designed to instruct the Quiet Christian:

> The Christian *loves* his Bible. In short, we *love* whatever gives us pleasure and delight, whether animal or intellectual; and if our hearts are right, we *love* God above all things, as the sum of all excellence and all the attributes which can communicate happiness to intelligent beings. In other words, the Christian *loves* God with the love of complacency in his attributes, the love of benevolence towards the interests of his kingdom, and the love of gratitude for favors received.

The noun form of "love" was also used in a similar way. Webster gives another example of the use of religion in forming deferential, Quiet Christian personalities and demeanor:

> The *love* of God is the first duty of man, and this springs from just views of his attributes or excellencies of character, which afford the highest delight to the sanctified heart. Esteem and reverence constitute ingredients in this affection, and a fear of offending him is the inseparable effect.

The dictionary also evidenced Webster's disgust with politicians and politics. He defined them as men "of artifice or deep contrivance" rather than people engaged in government or management of affairs. The adjective form of "politician" meant "cunning; using artifice." His own longing for a return to some former time before the rise of democratic politics was indicated in his definition of "polity." He quoted Ezra Stiles, who said, "were the whole Christian world to revert back to the original model, how far more simple, uniform and beautiful would the church appear, and how far more agreeable to the ecclesiastical *polity* instituted by the holy apostles."

The Quiet Christian image appears throughout the dictionary. "Laws" were "the *laws* which enjoin the duties of

A
Grammatical Institute,
OF THE
ENGLISH LANGUAGE,
COMPRISING,

An easy, concise, and systematic Method of

EDUCATION,

Designed for the Use of *English* Schools
In *AMERICA*.

IN THREE PARTS.

PART I.

CONTAINING,

A new and accurate Standard of Pronunciation.

By NOAH WEBSTER, A. M.

Usus est Norma Loquendi.   CICERO.

HARTFORD:
PRINTED BY HUDSON & GOODWIN,
FOR THE AUTHOR.

Title page of the first edition of Webster's renowned spelling book.

piety and morality, and prescribed by God and found in the Scriptures." Under "submission" Webster again insists that the Quiet Christian should be full of "resignation," meaning "entire and cheerful *submission* to the will of God [which] is a Christian duty of prime excellence." The only individual who could be "esteemed really and permanently happy" is the one "who enjoys a peace of mind in the favor of God," not unlike the mental tranquillity he had found in 1808. Defining "improve," he commands that "it is the duty . . . of a good man to *improve* in grace and piety." He tells us that "the distribution of the Scriptures may be the *instrument* of a vastly extensive reformation in morals and religion." Webster's view of the family appears in his definition of "marriage" as "instituted by God himself, for the sexes, for promoting domestic felicity and for securing the maintenance and education of children." The helplessness of a man is accented when he tells us under "meritorious" that "we rely for salvation on the *meritorious* obedience and suffering of Christ."

The dictionary is saturated with commands to be quiescent. Only a few examples will suffice as a general indication of the flavor of the work. "Good breeding forbids us to use *offensive* words." "A man is *profane* when he takes the name of God in vain, or treats sacred things with abuse and irreverence." "*Perfect rectitude* belongs only to the Supreme Being. The more nearly the *rectitude* of men approaches to the standard of divine law, the more exalted and dignified is their character. Want of *rectitude* is not only sinful, but debasing." "Freedom" is defined in one sense as "violation of the rules of decorum," while Webster warns us to "beware of what are called innocent *freedoms.*" Webster's denial of freedom and advocacy of submission to authority is consistent. "Freedom" in another sense is defined as "license."

"Duty" is a key concept, and in defining it Webster commands us to obey virtually any authority:

> That which a person owes to another; that which a person is bound, by any natural, moral or legal obligation, to pay, do or perform. Obedience to princes, magistrates and the laws is the *duty* of every citizen and subject; obedience, respect and kindness to parents are the *duties* of children; fidelity to friends is a *duty;* reverence, obedience and prayer to God are indisputable *duties;* the government and religious instruction of children are *duties* of parents which they cannot neglect without guilt.

"Submission" was synonymous with "obedience," and "*submission* of children to their parents is an indispensible duty." "Government" meant "control; restraint." In this definition he added that "Children are often ruined by a neglect of *government* in parents." Under "inferior" Webster commands us to "Pay due respect to those who are superior in station, and due civility to those who are *inferior.*"

"Liberty" is one of the most revealing terms in the *American Dictionary.* His first definition was simply "freedom from restraint. . . ." To this, however, he added some interesting distinctions. Most important were the two types of liberty that John Winthrop had spoken of in 1645. "*Natural liberty*" meant the "power of acting as one thinks fit, without any restraint or control, except from the laws of nature." Like Winthrop, he emphasized that this condition was impractical and was always "abridged by the establishment of government." He was not speaking of the Lockean notion of a government as a compact between men, but of the need for restraint on human liberty. *"Civil liberty,"* on the other hand, was the liberty "of men in a state of society" in which natural liberty was "abridged and restrained" not to enhance cooperation or distribution of goods, but for "the safety and interest of the society, state or nation." Civil liberty he stated was "secured by established laws, which restrain every man from injuring or controlling others." He was undoubtedly thinking of the turmoil since the 1780s when he noted that "the restraints of law are essential to *civil liberty*."

Perhaps the most revealing definition in the entire two-volume work was that of "education." This one small paragraph in many ways summed up much of Webster's life. Education had always been of interest to him, not only for its own value, but as a means of social change of one sort or another. In the early 1780s it had been an instrument of increasing both cultural independence from England and reform as well, and these two motivations were behind his first attempt to Americanize the schools systematically. After 1808 Webster had seen schools as institutions for producing Quiet Christians, as a means of insuring tranquility by teaching a specific form of conduct [*A Plea for a Miserable World . . .* (1820)]. Through them discipline could be instilled and the unruly passions of men checked and limited. His definition of education did not stress the increase of learning, of understanding or comprehending the world. Value-laden words emphasizing this side of education appear only twice: "enlighten the understanding," and "arts and science." The second occurrence is almost thrown in as if an afterthought. But terms espousing authoritarian control appear nine times in the space of three sentences: "formation of manners," "discipline," "correct the temper," "from the manners and habits of youth," "fit them for usefulness in their future stations," "manners," "religious *education*," "immense responsibility," "duties." And this is not counting the use of "instruction," a term he chose instead of "learning" or other, less authority-laden terms. Finally, notice that an education in manners, arts and science is merely "important." A religious education, with all its overtones of the Quiet Christian, is "indispensible."

One last definition demonstrates the interrelationship between religion, politics, behavior, and language that existed in Webster's mind. Under "reason," he quotes an author who said "God brings good out of evil, and therefore it were but *reason* we should trust God to govern his own world." Implicit is the notion that man should follow God's laws, not his own reason. Thus reason was used to advocate its opposite.

Every phase of the *American Dictionary* affirms the author's concern with authority and social control; exuberant nationalism is absent. The same obsession appears in the dedication of the work. One might expect a man who labored for twenty-five years on a single book to acknowledge the role played by those who influenced him. Modern scholars usually mention the work of those who came before them or others in the field. But, of course, Webster could not do that. If Webster had been a strong nationalist, as most historians have said, one might expect long paeans to American freedom, or celebrations of the heroes of the Revolution. But the *American Dictionary* was a product of Webster's evolving ideas about America. The work exhibited the values and beliefs of the evangelical movement of the early nineteenth century whose major emphasis was limiting human actions, not of the nationalistic fervor of the late eighteenth century. In his dedication Webster said:

> To the great and benevolent Being, who during the preparation of this work, has sustained a feeble constitution, amidst obstacles and toils, disappointments, infirmities and depression; who has twice borne me and my manuscripts in safety across the Atlantic, and given me strength and resolution to bring the work to a close, I would present the tribute of my most grateful acknowledgments

(pp. 415-30)

Richard M. Rollins, "Words as Social Control: Noah Webster and the Creation of the 'American Dictionary'," in American Quarterly, *Vol. XXVIII, No. 4, Fall, 1976, pp. 415-30.*

Bruce Southard   (essay date 1979)

[*In the following essay, Southard discusses Webster's writings on grammar.*]

While most people in America know that the name *Webster* is inextricably bound with the word *dictionary,* fewer know that the first name which accompanies the dictionary's Webster is *Noah,* and not *Daniel.* Still fewer know that Noah Webster was one of the leading proponents of a strong Federal constitution, that he provided one of the first American studies on epidemiology, or that he wrote a treatise on the decomposition of white lead paint. Unfortunately, Webster has also been forgotten for one of his most important roles, that of America's first great student of language. Indeed, if one examines recent histories of language study, he will not even find Webster's name. Were Webster's observations on language as far-fetched as his theories on the spread of pestilential diseases, his absence from historical accounts of linguistics would be understandable. What is true, however, is that Noah Webster, almost 200 years ago, was making observations about language that are being discovered anew today. Moreover, he early focused on an issue that is still a matter of great controversy—the question of what "correct" English is. Had Webster's comments been heeded, generations of American students and teachers would have been spared frustrating years of misguided instruction.

That Webster's ideas about language have been ignored is undoubtedly due not only to the man himself and to the times during which he formulated his theories, but also to inconsistencies which appear in his works. Cantankerous and unpleasant as an old man, Webster was self-righteous and dogmatic as America's first young grammarian. "After all my reading and observation for the course of ten years," he wrote in the preface to his *Dissertations on the English Language,* "I have been able to unlearn a considerable part of what I learnt in early life; and at thirty years of age can, with confidence, affirm that our modern grammars have done much more hurt than good." The grammars of which Webster wrote were those of Robert Lowth and his followers. Lowth, a leading proponent of the idea that there is a right and a wrong way to use language, was undoubtedly brought to his position because of his familiarity with Latin, a dead language that seemed to have grammatical rules fixed for all time. Believing that Latin represented the highest form of language, a form of which English was but a corrupt example, Lowth developed a series of rules based upon Latin grammar books and designed to show not only what was correct in English, but also what was incorrect. "The authors [of grammar books]," Webster continued in his preface to *Dissertations,* "have labored to prove what is obviously absurd, viz. that our language is not made right; and in pursuance of this idea, have tried to make it over again, and persuade the English to speak by Latin rules, or by arbitrary rules of their own. Hence they have rejected many phrases of pure English, and substituted those which are neither English nor sense."

In place of arbitrary or Latinate rules, Webster took the position reached by American structural linguists in the 1930s—the grammarian must look to the language itself for the rules to be followed. In his *Philosophical and Practical Grammar of the English Language,* Webster pointed out that language is of two kinds, spoken and written, and that one must look to the spoken language for the general patterns that can be formulated as grammatical rules: "The grammar of a particular language is a system of *general principles* derived from natural distinctions of words, and of *particular rules* deduced from the customary forms of speech in the nation using that language." Perhaps the clearest indication of what Webster meant is to be found in a letter written in January 1798, [*A Letter to the Governors, Instructors, and Trustees of the Universities, and Other Seminaries of Learning, in the United States, on the Errors of English Grammars*]. In the letter, Webster noted that the school children of this country were being taught that English is formed by a series of rules existing independently of the language, and he wished to "make a few observations to refute this egregious error." He argued that the grammarian does not create the rules of a language; rather, he finds the already existing grammatical structure and strives to codify it. Using the presence or absence of the plural marker *s* as an example, Webster explained that the grammarian observes the uniformity of termination of singular and plural nouns, and adopts that regularity as a "rule." The grammarian, then, searches out and reduces to order the structural patterns of the language. "Thus," wrote Webster, "in every instance *grammar is built solely* on the *structure of language.* That which is not found in the *practice of speaking a language* can have *no place* in a grammar of that language; it must be the *arbitrary dictum* of the compiler and of *no authority.* [¶] I have thought it necessary to say this much on a mistake which appears to be material. Grammars are made to show the student what a language *is,* not how it *ought to be.*"

Thus was the battle joined between the traditional grammarians and those who might well be called the "Websterian" grammarians, a battle that was to flourish in the first half of the twentieth century as American structuralism came to the fore, and a battle that continues today. On the one hand are those who say, "Don't split an infinitive" or "Two negatives in a sentence are equivalent to an affirmative," a rule first formulated by Robert Lowth himself. On the other hand are those who say, "Look to the language itself for any rules."

But what type of language should one examine? Some argue even now that, if one looks to actual usage for the rules of language, he must consult the best users of language—the learned, the best writers, or the members of the highest social class. Webster anticipated such a position and rejected it: "An attempt to fix a standard on any particular class of people is highly absurd: As a friend of mine once observed, it is like fixing a light house on a floating island. It is an attempt to *fix* that which is in itself variable" (*Dissertations*). If the language standard cannot be fixed on a particular class of people, then how shall it be fixed? For Webster, "the answer is extremely easy; *the rules of the language itself,* and the *general practice of the nation,* constitute propriety in speaking. If we examine the structure of any language, we shall find a certain principle of analogy running through the whole." Such statements were radical in the late 1700s; clearly, some traditional grammarians and most laymen would find them radical today. Moreover, early in his career Webster crowed about the superiority of the American yeomanry, an attitude not likely to win admirers among the British-educated grammarians then preparing textbooks. Webster was attacked by other grammarians, and his basic principles were ignored.

Another factor undoubtedly contributing to Webster's lack of influence on the study of grammar was an inconsistency in his own works, for his theoretical pronouncements often contradicted his pedagogical materials. For instance, in [part two of] his *Grammatical Institute, of the English Language,* Webster wrote that "two negatives destroy each other and amount to an affirmative." Twenty-three years later, however, in his *Philosophical and Practical Grammar,* he inveighed against that rule. Some of Webster's inconsistency can be attributed to his growth as a language scholar, as evinced by his changing view of Robert Lowth. In 1784, Webster praised Lowth by quoting Dr. Ash's characterization of him as "the greatest man, perhaps, that ever wrote on the subject [of grammar]" (*Institute*). And, despite Webster's occasional disagreements with Lowth's analyses, the *Grammatical Institute* of 1784 is clearly influenced by Lowth's *Short Introduction to English Grammar.* Only three years later, however, when Webster brought out the first revised edition of part two of the *Grammatical Institute,* the encomium to Lowth was deleted and Webster acknowledged that, in respect to some points, he had changed his opinion. In the preface to the revised edition, Webster observed that, "when a Lowth, an Ash, and a Priestley differ from each other in opinion, the curious inquirer has no resource, but to look for satisfaction in the state of the language itself."

While Webster was formulating his own theories about language, however, he was faced with the practical consideration of writing books that would outsell those of his competitors. From his thirtieth birthday, when he vowed to "leave writing and do more lucrative business," to his eightieth year, when he had to mortgage his home in order to publish the second edition of his *American Dictionary of the English Language,* Webster was concerned with amassing enough wealth to finance his scholarly activities, as well as to provide for his large family. Though he was an indefatigable promoter, Webster had to have a product conservative enough to appeal to the masses. Thus, his *Grammatical Institute,* a work designed for the general public which went through two editions and at least twenty printings, was far more influential than the more scholarly *Philosophical and Practical Grammar,* which had only one printing.

Webster's political writings show a similar inconsistency. From 1782 to 1797 he devoted himself to the cause of national unity, though he never fully embraced the concept of egalitarian democracy then attracting French intellectuals. As his essay *Revolution in France* shows, by 1794 Webster was "appalled" at the events taking place in France and at the "idle theories of upstart philosophers." Nevertheless, he remained a devoted Federalist who believed in constitution and law as the safeguards of freedom, and not in the popular democracy practiced by the American yeomanry whom he once had so glowingly praised, but whom he had come to view as ignorant, gullible people putting into office corrupt and immoral men. By 1798 Webster essentially withdrew from public political affairs by moving from New York to New Haven, where he devoted himself to scholarship.

When Franklin Edgerton in his examination of nineteenth-century American linguists ["Notes on Early American Work in Linguistics," *Proceedings of the American Philosophical Society* (1944)] dismisses Webster as "a great but paradoxical figure," he identifies the contradictory nature of Webster's work but fails to emphasize what is edifying and original. Edgerton praises John Pickering and Peter Stephen Du Ponceau as the greatest American linguists in the first half of the nineteenth century; and, ignoring Webster's *Dissertations* and *Philosophical and Practical Grammar,* he asserts that Pickering's [*A Vocabulary, or Collection of Words and Phrases Which Have Been Supposed to Be Peculiar to the United States of America* (1816)] is "perhaps the earliest serious attempt at a scientific study of American English." The selection of such a work as the earliest scientific study of American English reveals the attitude of many American language scholars during the nineteenth century and the first half of the twentieth, for Pickering displays a debilitating Anglophilia.

Pickering's opening sentence shows him to be no admirer of American English: "The preservation of the *English language* in its purity throughout the United States is an object deserving the attention of every American, who is a friend to the literature and science of his country." He asserts that the American language is losing its purity by creating new words, adding new meanings to old words, and retaining words which are obsolete in England. Such changes, he notes with horror, might lead to a language "that is to be called at some future day the American tongue!" Some hundred years later, H. L. Mencken finally realized Pickering's forebodings with the title of his *American Language.* To prevent such a change in language, Pickering urged "that our scholars should lose no time in endeavoring to restore it to its purity, and to prevent future corruption." Invoking such authorities as Benjamin Franklin and the British-educated John Witherspoon, and ignoring Webster, whose grammars he studied as a child, Pickering suggested that "every unauthorized word and phrase" should have a "discountenancing mark" set upon it. The primary purpose of his *Vocabulary,* obviously, was not to give a scientific account of Americanisms, but rather to list those words which were not "authorized" and which needed to be expunged from American English. But

what, one might ask, is the authority that determines the acceptability of an English word? Pickering was quite clear: "well educated *Englishmen,*" especially "the best authors" would determine which words constitute pure English.

Everything that Pickering wrote was directly opposed to Webster's statements on language. In December 1816 Webster published a letter to Pickering intended "to correct what I apprehend to be erroneous opinions." Noting "the unfriendly dispositions manifested towards me by men of high standing in the republic of letters . . . and the virulence with which every effort to detect errors in long received opinions has hitherto been assailed—a virulence by no means compatible with a candid desire of improvement and probably not warranted by the low estimate which even my opposers have formed of my talents, labors, and public services," Webster proceeded to a scathing appraisal of Pickering's work. Examining Pickering's contention that Americans were creating new words, Webster asserted that Pickering improperly used the term "new words," in that most words are derived in one fashion or another from already existing forms. Be that as it may, "new words will be formed and used, if found necessary or convenient, without a license from Englishmen." In like manner, Webster demonstrated that language, of necessity, compels its users to expand the number of meanings a word may possess. He focused on the "profound ignorance of the principles on which language is formed" displayed by those who object to the conversion of such nouns as *test* or *advocate* to verb forms *to test* and *to advocate,* forms upon which Pickering placed his "discountenancing mark." "The common people," wrote Webster, "without any reasoning on the subject or any guide but habit or convenience, pursue a correct principle in conformity with analogy when they say, they *yard* their cattle, *spade* their gardens, and *bridge* the rivers." As for local and obsolete expressions, Webster stated "that words of local use exist in all languages and countries; and it is impossible to prevent it." In short, language does not conform to the wishes of any outside authority.

In concluding his examination of Pickering's work, Webster articulated three principles that continue to be ignored even today:

> *First.* The man who undertakes to censure others for the use of certain words and to decide what is or is not correct in language seems to arrogate to himself a dictatorial authority, the legitimacy of which will always be denied. . . .
>
> *Secondly.* Very few men are competent to decide upon what is national practice and still fewer upon what is radically correct in language. . . .
>
> *Thirdly.* But the most weighty objection against any attempts to fix a limit to the use of words and phrases is its utter impracticability. There is and there can be no tribunal of competent jurisdiction for this purpose. Nor is it necessary or useful that there should be. Analogy, custom, and habit form a better rule to guide men in the use of words than any tribunal of men voluntarily or arbitrarily instituted.

Although Webster's critique of Pickering's *Vocabulary* appeared almost thirty years after his first writings on language, even the early writings consistently made a number of theoretical, if not pedagogical, observations about language that have recently come to be accepted by linguists, if not by the general public. One example is his analysis of the verb system. Robert Lowth had written that "there are three kinds of verbs; Active, Passive, and Neuter Verbs." Moreover, according to Lowth, time is expressed by present, past, or future tenses. These ideas are echoed by Webster's fellow countryman, Lindley Murray, whose English grammars provided the major competition for Webster's own works. Murray's statement concerning the types of verbs is identical to Lowth's, but he expands the notion of tense "to consist of six variations, viz. the Present, the Preterimperfect, the Preterperfect, the Preterpluperfect, and the first and second futures."

Webster's examination of the verb system led to quite different conclusions: "The only [classification of verbs] in English which seems to be correct and sufficiently comprehensive, is, into *transitive* and *intransitive*" (**Grammar**). Presaging Noam Chomsky's transformational grammar, which in its formative stages had the "Passive Transformation" as a keystone, Webster described the passive as follows: "In this form of the verb, the agent and object change places. In the transitive form the agent precedes the verb and the object follows; as 'John has convinced Moses.' In the Passive form the order is changed, and the agent follows the verb preceded by a preposition; as 'Moses is convinced by John.'"

As for tense, Webster wrote that "the English verb has but two variations of ending to express time; the present as *love, write;* and the past, as *loved, wrote*" (**Dissertations**). Webster pointed out that English has no way of inflecting the verb to indicate future time, and that to pretend *shall* and *will* are instances of the future tense is to misrepresent the English language. "In strictness of speech therefore, we have no future tense of the verb in English." Webster did, however, present a scheme for representing time which more closely corresponds to the actual system of English. The verb, in company with a series of auxiliaries, is capable of showing at least six different times, each verbal time capable of being expressed as definite or indefinite. These six times are present, past, perfect, prior-past ("He had received the news before the messenger arrived"), future, and prior-future ("They will have performed their task, by the appointed hour") (**Grammar**).

Webster's differences with the traditional grammarians extend to areas other than the verb. Eschewing the nominative, accusative, genitive, and dative case system of which the traditionalists wrote, Webster simply noted that "in English . . . names have two cases only, the *nominative,* or simple name, and the *possessive*" (**Grammar**). He denied the existence of the eight parts of speech, contending that there were two major classes, one containing nouns and verbs, and the second containing five species of words of secondary use. Once more demonstrating his independence from the traditional grammarians, Webster chose to rename these species of words (as some 150 years later Charles Fries did in his *Structure of English*). Webster's two major classes of words thus yield seven parts of speech: names, verbs, substitutes, attributes, modifiers, prepositions, and connectives. These classes are similar to, but not identical with, the traditional grammarian's nouns, verbs, pronouns, adjectives, adverbs, prepositions, and conjunctions.

In defining the sentence, Webster was to take what is even now a fairly modern position. A sentence for Webster was not "a complete thought," but a group of words "in due order" forming a complete proposition. The proposition he defined as "in philosophical language," consisting of a subject and a predicate connected by an affirmation, in some instances the affirmation being included in the verb. Illustrating his point with the sentences "God is omnipotent" and "The sun shines," Webster identified "God" as the subject, "omnipotent" as the thing affirmed, and "is" as that which forms the affirmation. "Shines" contains both the predicate and its affirmation.

In his views on subject-verb agreement, on negation, and on mood in English, Webster took a common-sense position that schoolma'ams have been trying to eradicate since the mid 1700s. For example, he noted that, although *you* was originally plural in number, national usage demands it be marked for both the singular and the plural. The overt marker of singularity, according to Webster, is the inflectional ending of the verb, for "to assign the substitute to its verb, is to invert the order of things. The verb must follow its nominative—if that denotes unity, so does the verb." Webster then listed fourteen literary citations of "you was" or "was you," adding that "these writers did not commit mistakes in the use of the verb after *you*—they wrote the language as established by national usage."

Discussing occurrences of multiple negation in a sentence, Webster noted that it is

> nearly impossible, in my opinion, ever to change a usage which enters into the language of every cottage, every hour and almost every moment. . . . "He did not owe nothing," in the vulgar language, and "He owed nothing" in the style of the learned, mean precisely the same thing. It makes no difference that men of letters denounce vulgar language as incorrect . . . and rash indeed is the innovator who attempts to change an idiom which has the stamp of authority of thousands of years.

Webster was realist enough to note, however, that despite the advantages of a uniform national language, he did not expect either the learned or the common man to change this particular speech practice. And, in discussing mood, he noted that grammarians have, without effect, tried to inject a subjunctive into English, which neither has nor requires it. "People in practice," he pointed out, "pay no regard to it" (**Dissertations**). Despite Webster's observations on such matters, grammarians still try to enforce artificial rules that the common users of language continue to reject. *The American Heritage Dictionary,* for instance, labels the double negative an illiteracy to be avoided; and the authors of a recent grammar book discuss the subjunctive in English, though observing that it "appears most often in formal writing and in the speech of educated people."

In a "last effort" to bring his views on grammar to the public, Webster appended an abridged version of his **Philosophical and Practical Grammar** to his 1828 dictionary. His "advertisement" to this abridgement lamented,

> It needs the club of Hercules, wielded by the arm of a giant, to destroy the hydra of educational prejudice. The club and the arm I pretend not to possess, and my efforts may be fruitless; but it will ever be a satisfaction to reflect that I have discharged a duty demanded by a deep sense of the importance

of *truth.* It is not possible for me to think with indifference, that half a million of youth in our schools are daily toiling to learn that which is not true. It has been justly observed that *ignorance* is preferable to error.

Clearly, Webster did not have the club and arm needed to bring truth to the study of America's national language. Indeed, America still needs a clear definition of what her national language is, a definition that relies upon the language itself and not upon arbitrary dictums of self-appointed experts. Faced with a continuing lack of support, linguistic geographers in this country are still struggling to provide a scientific account of regional language variation, a project begun over forty years ago. In the meantime, popularized accounts of American English, designed to heighten linguistic insecurity by making people believe that there is a "strict" way of speaking, make the best-seller lists.

In concluding his letter to John Pickering, Webster wrote:

> I am not ignorant, Sir, of the narrowness of the sphere which I now occupy. Secluded in great measure from the world, with small means and no adventitious aids from men of science, with little patronage to extend my influence and powerful enmities to circumscribe it, what can my efforts avail in attempting to counteract a current of opinion? Yet I am not accustomed to despondence. I have contributed in a small degree to the instruction of at least four millions of the rising generation; and it is not unreasonable to expect that a few seeds of improvement planted by my hand may germinate and grow and ripen into valuable fruit when my remains shall be mingled with the dust.

As we now know, the currents of opinion ran so strongly against Webster's writings that few of his seeds grew. The period of rapprochement between the United States and England following the War of 1812 helped insure that British English and British grammars would continue to serve as an ideal, if not a model, for American speech. The excesses of the French Revolution helped destroy the intellectual attractiveness of the egalitarianism first espoused by Webster and, coupled with a developing social stratification of speech in the United States, made people less willing to adopt the language of the "yeomanry." Nevertheless, Noah Webster did identify many qualities of what has become the American language. Moreover, in light of the continuing problems faced by those charged with instructing American students in their language, we might be well advised to reconsider Webster's thoughts and to give his "seeds of improvement" the opportunity to develop. (pp. 12-21)

> *Bruce Southard, "Noah Webster: America's Forgotten Linguist," in* American Speech, *Vol. 54, No. 1, Spring, 1979, pp. 12-22.*

E. Jennifer Monaghan (essay date 1983)

[*Monaghan is an English-born American educator and educational historian who has written on literacy in the United States during the colonial and postrevolutionary eras. In the following excerpt from her* A Common Heritage: Noah Webster's Blue-Back Speller, *she examines the popular success of Webster's spelling book, part one*

of A Grammatical Institute, of the English Language, *and outlines the significance of the text's publication in successive revised editions.*]

There were surely two moments in the long life of [Webster's] spelling book when its fate hung in the balance. The first was when it had just arrived on the scene in 1783, and was faced with the task of wresting the public's loyalty and affection from its model and rival, Thomas Dilworth's *New Guide to the English Tongue.* The second was when Webster, resurfacing from his total immersion in his great dictionary, realized that his share of the textbook market had seriously eroded. His response was the creation of a dramatically different version of his spelling book, now to be called the ***Elementary Spelling Book;*** and it indicated that he himself considered this another time of crisis in the life of the speller.

If we look at the 1783 ***Grammatical Institute, of the English Language, Part I*** from the perspective of those who were seeing it for the first time, it is clear that Webster had no easy task ahead of him in persuading the public to accept it. All the discussions of the work that remain to us focus, interestingly, not on the fact that this was a book written by an American in the new American Republic (which was the approach that Webster himself would stress), but on its relationship to Dilworth's book. The controversies that surround it are not those of nationalism; instead, they center on two themes: the book's technical aspects (both content and methodology) and its unfamiliarity to the public. For the former, Webster defended the originality of his syllabic division and pointed to the merits of his arrangement of words. He deferred to public sentiment by reorganizing the work in later editions, so that the lessons appeared earlier. He also introduced the fables and illustrations that had been characteristic of Dilworth's book, and missed in Webster's. At the same time he excised any material that smacked of the frivolous. In terms of the work's unfamiliarity, Webster had to contend both with members of the public who were loyal to Dilworth as "the nurse of us all," and with school trustees who were "fearful of injuring the school" by introducing an unknown spelling book. In addition, he had to overcome the material disadvantage of being obliged to offer his book to the public at a much higher price than Dilworth's. For Dilworth's book was produced in huge editions by publishers all over the country who, not having to pay any royalties, "afford it very cheap."

Webster's frontal attack on these twin roadblocks to success was multifaceted. First, he had taken pains to produce a better product than Dilworth. This was an age which firmly believed that the function of an elementary reading book (which is precisely what the spelling book was) was to introduce children to the correspondences between letters and sounds. There was universal agreement among Webster's contemporaries that his key for indicating letter-sound correspondences was greatly superior to anything in Dilworth. In fact, anyone who tried to popularize a spelling book after Webster's also had to produce a work which was adequate in this respect. William Perry's speller [*The Only Sure Guide to the English Tongue*], for example, which Isaiah Thomas marketed in response to the challenge of Webster's, had a most complex and sophisticated method of indicating pronunciation. Second, Webster went to unusual lengths to overcome the disadvantage his book labored under as a newcomer, by mounting a publicity and public relations campaign that made his name, his books, and even his person, well known all over the country.

Webster had a third arrow in his quiver. With a plan for American education that was far more ambitious than just marketing a little spelling book, he placed his first work squarely in the mainstream of the American Revolution. In later life, he could never refer to it without somehow tying it to the end of the Revolutionary War. At the time, he introduced it as an exemplar of American independence: he called for cultural independence as the indispensable accompaniment of political independence. For the book was designed not merely to teach children to read, but to purify and unify the very language they spoke. Webster purposed to introduce a "federal language," and to "diffuse a uniformity and purity of *language*" throughout the new republic. (Here we must note . . . that whatever the objective likelihood was of a spelling book doing any such thing, the claim was considered not merely plausible, but axiomatic, by Webster's contemporaries.)

One of the most intriguing questions that arises from the birth and rapid rise to fame of the *Institute* (soon to be retitled, in 1787, the *American Spelling Book,* a much better name for the times) is how much each of these three factors—Webster's improvements in the technical aspects of the work, his publicizing it, and his insistence that it was an instrument for fostering a truly American language—contributed to the success of the book.

The length of time in which the speller's fate hung in the balance, it should be noted, was remarkably short. We may dub the speller an unequivocal success from the moment when Isaiah Thomas procured the rights to publish it in 1789. Given that Thomas already had two other spellers on the market, his purchase of the Webster license is undeniable testimony to the fact that the speller had already become part and parcel of the American consciousness, and a textbook publisher would do without it at his peril. (In fact, virtually every nationally known American publisher, including Mathew Carey, tried to get his hands on it.) This view is supported by comparing how the Webster speller fared in relation to Dilworth's: from 1792 on, Webster's sales increased in inverse proportion to Dilworth's, which underwent a steep decline. In all, the *American Spelling Book* reigned supreme for a total of some forty years, as even Lyman Cobb, its bitterest critic and author of a rival speller, had to admit. So the period for which we have to explain the meteoric rise of the speller is relatively brief—a time span of only six years or so, from 1783 to 1789.

When the spelling book first appeared, its success . . . was "better than he [Webster] had expected." And indeed its growth in sales was remarkable. The first edition of 5,000 copies was sold out in a few months; Webster was working on a second, revised edition in June of 1784, and he was able to claim that over 12,000 copies in all had been sold by January 1785, while the speller was then in its third edition. It would be a mistake, however, to assume that only at this point did Webster see that he had a money-spinner on his hands, and seek to exploit it by starting on his eighteen-month tour that May. . . . Everything points to his having brought the book to the attention of the public from the very first. The advertisements for the book date

from October 1783, and it was extensively advertised after January 1785. The nationwide tour, from May 1785 on, was not so much the start of a publicity campaign, as some have thought, as the climax to it.

Given the enthusiasm with which Webster promoted the work and the months of touring in which he used his lectures to bring himself and his books to the public eye, the cynic might be tempted to attribute the success of the spelling book to Webster's promotional efforts alone, and argue that its improvements over Dilworth or its claim to foster an American language were really immaterial to its success. This is not a proposition that can be accepted, however, for there is a "control group" in the form of Webster's other parts of the *Institute,* namely, his grammar and his reader. It should be borne in mind that Webster promoted all parts of his *Institute* at the same time, both during his tour of May 1785 and subsequently. Yet neither the grammar nor the reader succeeded, either in comparison to the speller, or more to the point, when compared with other grammars and readers. Webster's grammar was soon superseded by Lindley Murray's, and his reader was ousted by two main rivals, Caleb Bingham's *American Preceptor,* and Lindley Murray's *English Reader.*

The fate of Webster's [*An American Selection of Lessons in Reading and Speaking*] is particularly pertinent to this discussion. Unlike his spelling book, which had to wrestle with Dilworth, Webster's reader had the field entirely to itself at the time of its first publication in 1785. Readers as a type subsequently became a key text in every school system. (In fact, records of books in the New York State schools for the years 1827, 1830 and 1831 show that Lindley Murray's *English Reader* was the single most widely used book in the entire school system. No one spelling book was so popular.) So, if Webster's publicity efforts had been the only key to a book's success, the *American Selection* would surely have cornered the market, and we know it did not. It is therefore only reasonable to conclude that the Webster speller did not succeed solely because of its dextrous promotion.

The fate of *The Little Reader's Assistant* (1790) is also relevant. Although it was a book which was valuable in theory, because it was to bridge the gap between speller and reader, in practice it only ran to a few editions. Admittedly, Webster does not seem to have publicized it much, other than by advertising. But the real reason for its failure was surely not that he failed to promote it, but that it was too unconventional in both orthography and content. Respellings like *hed* and *nabor* were not acceptable, as later controversies over Webster's more unconventional spellings indicate; and its openly antislavery sentiments were undoubtedly considered unsuitable for a textbook. Webster's lack of success with *The Little Reader's Assistant* suggests that one of the reasons for his considerable success with his speller was that it was *not* unconventional: it resembled Dilworth's enough to be recognizable as an improved Dilworth, rather than a totally unfamiliar work. The changes that Webster made to his *New England Primer,* which restored the book to a version much closer to the original classic, also indicate that the public had conservative tastes in textbooks to which he was responding. Not for nothing have textbooks been dubbed "guardians of tradition."

The critical elements in the speller's initial success, then, were essentially three. First, there were the merits of the speller itself, which while adhering faithfully to the alphabet method, illuminated the relationship between letters and sounds with a clarity never achieved before in a work for children. Moreover, Webster improved and refined the work as time went on: he returned the lessons to their time-honored place after the tables; he created new tables and added additional words to existing ones; he excised any material that might be considered even faintly frivolous; and he kept an eagle's eye on the accuracy of the work, correcting misprints and misspellings.

The second element in the speller's success was Webster's skill in making it known to the public. He produced a work that was recognizable as an improved Dilworth (previously the most popular speller), and he went to extraordinary pains to publicize it. Third, in his introduction to his first edition, he linked his little book to the great experiment in American independence. Surely this was more of a factor than perhaps even his readers were aware of at the time. He spoke for a national language at a critical moment in American history when the public was predisposed to hear him.

The one aspect that we cannot credit for the success of the 1783 speller and its early revisions is Webster's own personal prestige. His early commercial success with his speller was not matched by a corresponding rise in his own popularity. In those early years he had been accused of plagiarism and sanctimony, and called pedantic, dull and arrogant; even his own friends urged "diffidence" upon him. If it seems that this view is based upon too great a reliance on stray comments issuing from prejudiced sources (such as Webster's enemy Samuel Campbell of New York), it is well to look at Webster's view of the matter. When his speller or other books were criticized, his immediate reaction was to attribute such attacks to his personal unpopularity, which he believed stemmed from his outspokenness on political matters and his spirited defense of the republic. So sure was he that "any doctrines I might advance, under the signature of my name, would not meet the consideration they might deserve," that he issued two books anonymously, and often withheld his name from his essays in the public press.

By the time Webster published his dictionary in 1828, however, almost a half-century had passed since his first appearance in print. And the public regard for him had undergone a substantial change. The brash young author had become the beloved patriot-intellectual, whose literary labors on behalf of his country were known to all. The fruits of his last quarter-century of labor, his *American Dictionary of the English Language,* were scorned by none. His *American Spelling Book* had become the most widely sold book in the nation, and most of those who admired the former had learned to read from the latter. In addition, Webster had buttressed his position as a leading figure in American education by producing a series of other textbooks.

It was well for Webster that he had an edge in this respect; for while he had been laboring over his dictionary, time had not stood still. By the time he was able, once again, to focus on his elementary book, he found to his dismay that it faced not one Dilworth as its rival, but literally dozens of other spelling books, most of them published after 1825.

As we know, Webster accused his publisher, Henry Hudson, of allowing the textbook market to slip from his grasp, and took the unprecedented step of introducing a brand new work to the public before the copyright to the old one had expired. In one sense, his criticisms of Hudson's guardianship were just. The growth of the sales of the speller was not what could be reasonably anticipated from its previous exploits. In addition, all the evidence Webster could gather from his sources also indicated that many school systems had forsaken his speller and adopted another in its place. In another sense, however, his accusations of Hudson were unjust. For the fact that Webster saw it necessary to produce a wholly revised book, so different from its predecessor that many thought (reasonably enough, as we know) that he had not written it himself, indicates that no matter what anyone had done to promote the old *American Spelling Book,* it would not have retained its hold on the public. Truth to tell, it looked thoroughly old-fashioned. The work that Webster produced to replace it, written (under Webster's close supervision) by a New York educator who was more in touch with contemporary taste than the septuagenarian Webster, was much more modern in flavor. Its overt religious content (but not its covert message) plummeted from forty-seven to ten per cent, and was a precursor of a general shift in the direction of secularity.

Not all the alterations Webster made to his old book, however, were to its advantage. The new book's initial lack of pictures, and its substitution of isolated sentences for any kind of connected prose, let alone a story or fable, alarmed even some of Webster's publishers. What is more, the book's typography looked strikingly different, not just from Webster's old book, but from anything else on the market. To appreciate how novel Webster's diacritical markings and new alphabetical characters appeared, it should be recalled that the American public was used to seeing a numerical marking system (whether in Webster's speller or another's); it had no experience with a modified alphabet; and, in all works which used the orthography of John Walker of England, it was accustomed to reading spellings like *centre, honour,* and *musick.*

By no means all of Webster's innovations proved acceptable. His new forms of the letters *c, s, t,* and *u* were doomed to extinction, and he was forced to retreat somewhat on his more extreme respellings, introduced into this edition for the first time. He also found it necessary to reintroduce some of the illustrated fables. On the credit side, Webster's major classes of orthographic reform survive to this day, and a diacritical marking system would become the standard way of indicating pronunciation in later school texts. Indeed, a true measure of their success, his orthography was copied and his "points" rapidly plagiarized by other authors. And Webster's classification of spelling words was now pretty well perfect. The great octosyllabic *incomprehensibility* would be the pinnacle of accomplishment in the rugged art of spelling. In addition, in this version Webster solved all those technical aspects of uniformity that had plagued him in his youth, for the new speller was now always printed from stereotyped plates.

The internal features of the 1829 speller, then, were less

unequivocally in its favor than those of its 1783 predecessor. And, paradoxically, Webster was faced once again with the difficulty of introducing an unfamiliar work to the public. For he was competing not only against the many rivals that had appeared since 1825, but against his own *American Spelling Book.* Men looked very carefully at this new edition to "see if Noah Webster had not injured the Spelling book by his alterations." In addition, Webster had to counter the parochialism of the west, where westerners favored western books. No wonder Webster turned to his tried-and-true methods of pushing his new book into the public eye, in order to win for it the affection and esteem enjoyed by his old.

If the *Elementary* was at a disadvantage in some respects, it was certainly not so in terms of Webster's promotional efforts. Indeed, nothing is better documented in this book than the zeal with which this septuagenarian plunged, once again, into the icy waters of textbook competition, in a mirror image of the efforts of his youth.

Nonetheless, it would again be unjust to ascribe the success of the *Elementary* to Webster's remarkable skill in promotion. For there were other books that he had written or edited and was "pushing." His Bible, for example, and his revised grammar and *Manual of Useful Studies*—these were all works that Webster promoted vigorously. Yet only his spelling book soared away in its sales until it seemed to have a life of its own, and [Webster's son] William, out in the west, was "embarrassed" by the demand for licenses to it.

It seems reasonable, then, to identify the reasons for the success of the 1829 spelling book as follows. If it was not considered undeniably superior to its rivals on all counts, its virtues outweighed its defects. Its key aspects—its system of points to indicate pronunciation and its major orthographical reforms—were generally adopted by later writers. It had as full a listing of polysyllabic words as could be found. It also had the advantage of Webster's skilled promotional efforts, which he expanded beyond the circle of his own friends and relatives, employing for the first time paid agents to promote and sell the work. Finally, it had the advantage of its author's reputation. Nothing, said Webster in 1830, had given him more pleasure, "than the respect and kindness manifested towards me in consequence of the use of my books. It convinces me that my fellow citizens consider me as their benefactor and the benefactor of my country." "Gratitude for past favors Rec^d from D^r W— Books" was the refrain that rang in Webster's ears. The name of Webster had reached mythic proportions. The new Webster speller, once it had passed inspection, was able to inherit all the affection and respect of the old. "I used this book 40 years ago," said the same old man who was afraid that Webster had injured his book by altering it, "& my sons have used it, & now my grandchildren shall have it." The Webster speller was a part of America itself.

It is ironic, of course, that this last Webster speller was not entirely Webster's own work. As we know, he had employed Aaron Ely to write for him. How much each man contributed to the book is not at all clear. Aaron Ely provided a small clue to the part he had played in its compilation when Lyman Cobb criticized the omission of words such as *bailiff* and *caitiff* from the *Elementary.* Ely's response was that these and other words ending in *-ff* "were

in the manuscript which I wrote, and they must be inserted in the next edition" of the speller. Webster said that he had "employed a person to write for me," but that every part of the *Elementary* and the 1830 school dictionary was "corrected, arranged, and the words marked for pronunciation, by my own hand." We realize that Webster cared not at all about content; in his view, the value of a spelling book rested on the twin rocks of orthography and pronunciation. Significantly, he took issue with other spelling books on these grounds alone. It seems therefore probable that he gave Ely general directions about the lists of spelling words and that Ely wrote the sentences. Webster certainly divided the words into syllables himself and added the diacritical marks for pronunciation.

It should not be thought that Webster was therefore dishonest in claiming the book as his own. As far as he was concerned, he had been responsible for the only elements in the book that really mattered—the form of the written language. In his cavalier disregard for meaning, he was in fact forever distancing himself from those who, even before the publication of the *Elementary Spelling Book,* were attacking the very foundations upon which every speller rested.

A spirit of reform was in the air in the 1820s; it held that the child's nature was not inherently sinful (as had been believed for so long), and could be trained to virtue. This new view of the child was ushering in new aims in education. A child should understand, even enjoy, his schooling, claimed the reformers. So the spelling book's use of the alphabet method, its long lists of words (all too many of which children had never heard before), and its inherent lack of interest were already under siege. When William Holmes McGuffey's carefully sequenced *Eclectic First* and *Second Readers* were published in 1836, they took the country by storm as the prototype of the reading text of the future. For the first time in the history of American reading instruction, children would have the chance to learn to read from simple stories about other children, lavishly illustrated, instead of from long lists of often meaningless words, which rarely reappeared in a context.

The man who emerges at the end of the saga of his spelling book is closer to Warfel's celebrationist portrait [see Further Reading entry dated 1936] than to Rollins' revisionist depiction. (pp. 196-205)

Certainly, it is not possible to accept Rollins' vision of Webster in his last years as a tired old man who, after 1840, retreated into a private world, ending his long journey in disillusionment, bitterness and despair [see Further Reading]. On the contrary, Webster's interest in the business aspects of his books (one, by the way, entirely overlooked in the "official" version of Webster's life offered us by his son-in-law Chauncey Goodrich [see Further Reading]) was a lifelong companion to his interest in language. We see Webster as the vigorous, determined and optimistic businessman until the very end.

Nor does Webster emerge as a man who wholly lost his faith either in the American people or in his ability to make a contribution to the Republic. At the end of his days, as at the beginning, Webster promoted, defined, respelled and cared deeply about the American language. "It is important that all the people of this country should follow one dictionary & Spelling book, that all may speak

& write alike. This is a matter of national importance," he told William late in his life.

If the spelling book failed to achieve the uniformity in the language spoken by Americans that Webster hoped for, it was not his personal failure, but the failure of a hope impossible of fulfilment, linguistically speaking. Nonetheless, whatever slight influence Webster did have on the spoken language must have been in the direction of "uniformity." With the written language he was on safer ground. His major spelling reforms, adopted by the McGuffey *Eclectic Readers* destined to replace his own book as America's most popular reading instructional text, became the standard American orthography and distinguish American from British spelling to this day.

In assessing Webster's contribution to education, we should note that many of his textbooks were in essence ahead of their time. His [*History of the United States*], for example, prefigured a work that would, much later, be a standard feature of the school curriculum. In contrast, his spelling book eventually fell behind the times. Webster had engaged in a vigorous dialectic on the subject of reading education all his life. As so often happens, however, when the moment for reassessment came Webster hardly knew what the discussion was about. A man of an earlier age, he was not intellectually prepared to entertain the argument that children should understand what they read. He confronted the issue of meaning in children's texts, and denied its importance. As a result, the success of the McGuffey *Eclectic Readers* was one of the few events within his lifetime whose significance he failed to grasp.

Had the spelling book not had a second string to its bow—which was, of course, that it could and did teach children to spell as well as to read—it might have fallen on hard times once the new McGuffey-style reading textbooks established themselves after 1836. As it was, the *Elementary Spelling Book* went soaring into the stratosphere, becoming the most widely published work written by one person (two, if you wish to give Aaron Ely his due) that the world has ever known. So this, indeed, was Webster's extraordinary contribution: for its first half-century, his spelling book taught America's children to read; for its second half-century, it taught them to spell. Moreover, there were half a million men and women who turned gratefully to the blue-back speller for reading instruction three-quarters of a century after Webster first compiled it. (pp. 206-08)

> *E. Jennifer Monaghan, in her* A Common Heritage: Noah Webster's Blue-Back Speller, *Archon Books, 1983, 304 p.*

Richard J. Moss (essay date 1984)

[*Moss is an American historian and educator who specializes in early American history. In the following excerpt, he elaborates on Webster's work as an editor and journalist during the 1780s and 1790s.*]

Webster's life as an author has very little unity to it. No long-term purpose or enduring commitment stands out as his grand passion. He wrote schoolbooks, political pamphlets, essays on language, dictionaries, and even dabbled in science. Never during his life was he able to focus all his energies on any one of his many interests. He was per-

haps, above all, a talented dilettante, never achieving real competence in anything he attempted. If we can trust the scholars who have tried to appraise his career, two areas of endeavor seem to dominate in his life—his schoolbooks and the dictionary. In most cases these two have been selected because they fit neatly with the simplistic notion that Webster was driven only by burning nationalism. Both the school texts and the dictionaries, some scholars claim, were sold to the public with flourishes of nationalistic rhetoric laced with Webster's obsession that Americans should learn from American books.

[However], another aspect of Webster's life . . . has been often underemphasized. Between 1787 and 1798 Webster was for the most part a journalist, exploring the role of newspapers, magazines, and popular nonfiction in the new republic. He entered this period as a twenty-nine-year-old full of energy and optimistic about America and Americans. He emerged in 1798, nearly forty, his optimism broken and moving quickly toward the pessimism and bitterness that characterized his later years. During this period he produced a year's run of a notable magazine: *The Prompter,* a charming and much-overlooked little volume; he also edited one of the major newspapers in New York and produced a major scientific work on the nature of disease and epidemics.

In the autumn of 1787 Webster gave up his teaching position in Philadelphia and moved to New York to seek the status and steady income that had eluded him for so long. The inspiration to found a magazine was not long in coming. In Philadelphia, Matthew Carey and Francis Hopkinson had established *The Columbian Magazine* and it had achieved something approximating success. In New Haven, Webster's Yale classmate, Josiah Meigs, was editing the *The New Haven Gazette* and *The Connecticut Magazine* that soon became an outlet for the satire of the Hartford Wits. New York City, Webster realized, was growing and would quickly come to dominate commerce and have a growing influence on American intellectual life—and it had no magazine.

After making a deal with Samuel Campbell, under which Webster sold the rights to his three schoolbooks for ready cash, he signed an agreement with Samuel Loudon to print a magazine. The venture lasted a year, finally dying from lack of subscribers and ready capital to support the magazine during its infancy. During its short life the *American Magazine* was too often a random assortment of short pieces hastily composed by Webster or borrowed from other American or British publications. For example, the first issue (December 1787) contained pieces called "Titus Blunt on Fashion" and "Anecdote of the Duke of Gordon," both probably written by Webster. It also featured a London review of John Adams's *Defence of the American Constitution.* Webster printed a considerable number of bad poems including "The Rare Adventures of Tom Brainless . . . " and "The Virgin's First Love." Some of this poetry was his own. The January 1788 issue began with the following effort by the editor entitled "Verses on the New Year":

> The circling Sun, bright Monarch of the day,
> Who rules the changes of this rolling sphere,
> With the mild influence of his favoring ray,
> From shades of night calls forth the opening Year.
> Propitious Year! O may thy light divine

Dispelt the clouds that this new world impend,
On infant States with peaceful lustre shine,
And bid their fame o'er all the world extend.

Hail, blest COLUMBIA! whose embattled meads
The crimson streams, of Heroes' blood have dy'd,
Here see bright turrets near their lofty heads,
And domes of slate adorn thy rising pride.

Thy noble sons, with generous ardor fir'd,
Shall gild the victories of their father's arms;
They blooming Fair, in innocence attir'd,
Shall deck thy glories with unnumber'd charms.

Now ARTS shall flourish in this Western clime,
And smiling COMMERCE triumph on the main,
The fields shall blossom in perpetual prime,
And fruit's luxuriant robe the verdant plain.

These are the prospects of thy golden days—
These the glad hopes that cheer each joyful face.
Fly swift thou Sun; diffuse thy peaceful rays,
And give these blessings to our fond embrace.

Webster would have been well advised to leave all the poetry to others. Politics and education were his strong suits.

The magazine also sought to be utilitarian, presenting pieces on the ingrafting of fruit trees and the proper way to construct a chimney. Politically, the *American Magazine* was staunchly Federalist. Webster, writing under the name Giles Hickory, criticized the antifederalist faction for wanting a Bill of Rights attached to the Constitution. The most interesting series in the magazine was Webster's essay on education that appeared in installments beginning with the first issue.

During his tenure as editor of the *American Magazine* Webster often tried his hand at literary criticism. His most notable review (July 1788) was of Timothy Dwight's *The Triumph of Infidelity;* a work that Webster clearly misunderstood. There was not much that he liked about the poem which he found a "jumble of unmeaning epithets . . . " and he criticized, particularly, the author, unknown to Webster, for his shabby treatment of the Chinese religion. The review was seriously flawed by Webster's inability to distinguish between the author's own views and those that Dwight put into the mouth of Satan or his henchmen. The review was so unfair that Dwight severed his relationship with Webster. Dwight was probably unfair in responding so violently; Webster's view of the poem was not vindictive, it was more the product of an overworked editor who did not have time to read carefully the long and difficult work and give it serious consideration.

As important as its contents was Webster's conception of what the magazine was to be. In the introduction to the first issue he explained to his readers what he was trying to do. The *American Magazine* was designed to be a national publication; it would concern itself with news from all sections of the country. Webster largely made good on this promise by presenting a section in each issue called "American Intelligence," composed of edited pieces from a wide range of American newspapers (there was also a section for "European Intelligence"). America, in the editor's view, needed such a national magazine because "while we allow foreign publications all their merit, it must be conceded that none of them can be wholly calculated for this country." Webster also set himself the difficult task of producing a magazine that would "gratify every class of reader—the Divine, the Philosopher, the Historian, the Statesman, the Moralist, the Poet, the Mer-

chant and the Laborer" [Introduction to *American Magazine* (December 1787)]. Special attention would also be given to female readers. In essence, Webster sought to create a national democratic magazine; one that would interest all sections of the country and all classes in society. He was, in the end, unable to achieve his noble goal. The result was a magazine that most often resembled a cut-and-paste effort by an inexperienced editor desperately short of copy.

When Webster realized that the magazine would not succeed, he made an attempt to secure more financial backing by taking in a number of partners from almost every state. He proposed that men such as Benjamin Rush, Jeremy Belknap, Joel Barlow, and James Madison become a set of proprietors who would invest in the magazine and collect original materials from their parts of the nation. When this plan failed, Webster gave up the magazine, left New York, and moved to Hartford. The *American Magazine* stands as one of the few attempts made during the 1780s and 1790s to issue a publication based on nationalistic and republican principles. Webster's failure to lure a significant audience at least suggests that the time had not yet come for such a magazine.

During most of Webster's life his work appeared regularly in newspapers. Often he wrote what amounted to letters to the editor, but he also used the papers as an outlet for other work. A prime example were the essays that eventually became one of his most popular books—*The Prompter.* Between December 1790 and June 1791 Webster published sixteen essays in the *Connecticut Courant,* later adding nine new pieces to make up the book. All the essays were in the manner of Franklin's [pseudonymous persona] Poor Richard. They feature short sentences, plain style, and use familiar situations to illustrate moral lessons. The best selections employ humor and simple stories to satirize common failings and vices. Webster also offered advice on manners, morals, and domestic economy. The book first appeared in a Hartford edition printed by Hudson and Goodwin in late 1791. It enjoyed widespread success in the United States and Great Britain. Between 1791 and 1850 *The Prompter* was reprinted some fifty times in various versions, and parts of the little volume were often pirated and used as newspaper filler copy. Until 1796, for reasons unknown, Webster did not acknowledge it as his work and his name did not begin to appear on the title page until 1798.

The Prompter has been unfairly overlooked by scholars who too often emphasize the dictionaries and schoolbooks. This little book revealed a great deal about Webster. In the first place, Webster confessed his own sense of the role he would like to play in society: the prompter, "the man who, in plays, sits behind the scenes, and looks over the rehearser, and with moderate voice, corrects him when wrong, or assists his recollection. . . . " Webster saw this role as "very necessary" and as one in which he could do "much good." This was more than an author's pose; it was a reflection of Webster's belief that although he was not cut out for public office, he was suited to act as judge of the morals and the behavior of "the numerous actors upon the great theater of life. . . . "

While there was a measure of presumption in this attitude, he carried it off in a subtle and inoffensive way. The prompter decided to put his advice to the people in a unique way. "He wanted to whip vice and folly out of the country—he thought of Hudibras and M'Fingal—and pondered well whether he should attempt the masterly style of those writings." But he found satire unsuitable and turned to the style "of sober moral writers, and the pompous flowing style of modern historians." This in turn Webster rejected because "one half of his readers would not understand him" and his purpose was to do "as much good as possible, by making men wiser and better." He finally settled on a style he called "good solid roast beef" because "it sits easily on the stomach." His final choice turned out to be a reasonably good imitation of Franklin's Poor Richard's plain style.

Using this style, Webster produced a series of essays full of utilitarian advice. The first piece, for example, tells the story of Jack Lounger and his problems with a fireplace. Jack, it seems, is too fond of his bellows; he piles coals and wood on the hearth and blasts away with a bellows. Jack manages to produce a small blaze that quickly dies and a room full of smoke. Billy Trim, on the other hand, "has attended more to the principles of nature" and carefully builds a fire so that natural air currents soon produce a bright, warm fire. The moral of the story is *common sense is money.*" The second essay (**"Green Wood Will Last Longer than Dry"**) was further advice on the crucial subject of fire-building.

Often the prompter's advice touched on subjects about which Webster clearly had firsthand experience. He strongly condemned the practice of dividing a small farm among the farmer's sons because they would not be able to live a decent life "on these mutilated farms." This advice no doubt reflected his father's experience in Connecticut. Webster's lack of success as a lawyer was probably the reason he believed, "let lawyers multiply till a famine of business come upon them, and then they will die like Egyptian frogs."

Advice and suggestions fly thick and fast; Webster considered no aspect of life as too small for comment. He often began with a simple aspect of daily life and worked his way to a larger lesson. Farmers who did not plan well were called "do-for-the-present-folks" and often, in his view, did "double their necessary labor." Failure to return tools to their proper place was, according to the prompter, not a small sin because it involved lost time when the tool was needed again:

> This time is lost, for it breaks in on some other business—the loss of this small portion of time appears trifling; but slovens and sluts incur such losses every day; and the loss of these little scraps of time determine a man's fortune. Let the Prompter make a little calculation—A farmer whose family expends one hundred pounds a year, if he can clear ten pounds a year, is a thriving man. In order to get his one hundred and ten pounds, suppose he labors ten hours a day: In this case, if he loses an *hour* every day, in repairing the carelessness of the day before, (and every sloven and slut loses more time than this, every day, for want of care and order) he loses a tenth part of his time—a *tenth* part of his income—this is a *eleven* pounds. Such a man cannot thrive. . . .

Such little sermons were more important than they first appear. The prompter was teaching time-thrift, a modern characteristic, largely unknown among rural people who adjusted their lives to the regular rhythms of nature. Webster was suggesting that the clock was more important to the American farmer who should put success and growth beyond mere self-sufficiency. The prompter was clearly a capitalist urging his readers to work hard, save, and expand: "If you have but a small piece of land, cultivate it well, make it produce as much as possible; and if you can get more than will maintain you from this little farm, lay out the surplus in buying more. If you cannot get more than a subsistence, it is time to think of lessening expenses, or selling out and buying new land."

Such expansive capitalistic attitudes were to have an important place in American history. The conservative habits of rural life left little room for speculation or growth. Franklin's Poor Richard and Webster's Prompter—advocates of saving, time-thrift, and gradual expansion—promoted America's change from a static agrarian society to a dynamic industrial nation. It would be wrong, however, to see Webster as having both feet in the modern age. His beliefs about thrift and saving owe as much to his Puritan ancestors as they do to his conception of the needs of a modern nation. Books such as *The Prompter* show Webster translating the seventeenth-century Protestant ethic into a usable formula for the nineteenth century.

Webster sought to instruct his fellow Americans on more than domestic economy. Several pieces, for example, discussed education of children. In these Webster revealed modern attitudes largely devoid of the Puritan emphasis on the innate evil of the young. Most of his comments assumed that if parents provided a just and loving environment for their children, all would turn out well. He sincerely believed that children would respond consistently to rational parents who dealt consistently with them. Good parents used punishment to correct faults, not simply to break their children's wills. *The Prompter* did not assume that children had an innate tendency to evil; instead, he maintained "that *nine* times out of *ten,* the bad conduct of children is owing to parents! Yet parents father most of it upon Adam and the devil."

As the prompter, Webster was, as usual, didactic and moralistic, but he pulled it off with a light and humorous touch that contrasted sharply with the heavy humorless approach he often adopted in his other writings. He was even capable of seeing that his views were necessarily subjective: he had the prompter claim, "And no way is so good as *mine.* The question is not, whether this or that is the *better* way, but whether it is *my* way or *your* way. Orthodoxy is *my* doxy, and heterodoxy is your doxy." The whole production was light and readable, the prompter's readers were preached at, but generally they never knew it.

Yet as we have seen, Webster changed a great deal during the 1790s. The popular protests against American neutrality and the Jay Treaty among other events had a profound impact on him. The excesses of the French Revolution seemed particularly significant to Webster, and the decade was topped by Jefferson's election. All of these influences turned Webster into a much more negative and frightened man. His political position became more conservative and his faith in the people's ability to participate in political affairs gradually declined.

The Prompter offers an excellent illustration of his metamorphosis. In 1803 Webster produced a revised edition of the little book that had been so popular for more than a decade. In addition to some minor changes in the original text, he added nineteen new essays, all of them radically different in style and content from his 1791 version. The titles of the new pieces reflected the change in Webster. The original essays often had coy and ambiguous titles; the new ones are straightforward and somber. They include **"The Counsels of Old Men Despised; or, the Revolt and Division of Empire," "Popular Discontent,"** and **"Inconstancy of the Populace."**

The new essays also showed a remarkable change in style. Webster cast aside Poor Richard's plain style in favor of a tone that most closely resembled sermonizing. Several times he used a story to illustrate his point, but instead of familiar tales of everyday life he employed biblical illustrations such as the history of the Jews and the story of Cain and Abel. The light satirical tone gave way to a straightforward didactic style. In **"The Counsels of Old Men Despised; or, the Revolt and Division of Empire,"** Webster bluntly stated his feeling that "the ruler shun the advice of proud and headstrong youth—and let the people shun their flatterers, as devils in human shape." The reader was bludgeoned with the moral as Webster added lectures and sermons to a book of fables and tales.

More important, the change in the 1803 edition of *The Prompter* provides a chance to gauge the transformation in Webster's thought. It is very important to realize that alterations in his ideas were almost always a matter of degree rather than kind. In 1791, for example, Webster believed that children could be properly trained if parents used mild and rational restraint. By 1803 he still was deeply interested in restraints, but he had profoundly altered his view about the nature and severity of the restraint needed. In the essay, **"Parental Indulgence,"** he employed the biblical story of David and Adonijah to show that mild treatment of a child will lead to disaster—Adonijah attempted to usurp David's throne. Webster thought the lesson was clear:

> This story is a fine satire on the modern system of education, which rejects the most salutary restraints, for checking the growth and expansion of the intellectual faculties, and making children bashful and clownish. This mode however has been adopted by honest people, who have not suspected that this is one of the means devised to undermine the foundations of civil order.

Most of the 1803 essays that touched on education were based on a new assumption. Webster had come to believe (given his experience in the decade just past) that children, indeed human beings in general, were more passionate and obstinate than he had thought in 1791. Put another way, he had come to appreciate more fully the innate evil in man. Essentially an optimist in the early 1790s, he had by 1803 grown sour about man's prospects. This change, for instance, took the form of an increased sense that human history was cyclical and that "the glory of nations is destined to fade before the incessant attacks of time and corruption." To Webster the course to steer was obvious; nations must turn away from sinful youth and let the affairs of state "be administered by elderly men, who have acquired wisdom by experience."

Offering older, more experienced men as a bulwark against the slide to corruption and decay was only a half-hearted hope. Just as often Webster was capable of total despair:

> No religion has been sufficient to control—no government or laws sufficient to restrain all the evil propensities of men. What then will men be, when freed from these restraints? Who is the projector of hardiness enough to risk the experiment and commit the destinies of a nation to the "self-government" of individuals?

Webster believed that America was in the process of launching just such an "experiment," and he was frightened. Still playing the part of prompter, he sought to warn his readers of the imminent dangers. In 1791 he had been a gentle prodder directing Americans toward lives of virtue; by 1803 the drama before him had changed, and the promptings sounded a great deal like a prophecy of doom.

In 1793 Webster returned to New York to launch, for the second time, a journalistic venture. As an ardent Federalist, Webster was chosen by members of the party to edit a newspaper in New York that would counter the rising tide of antifederalist criticism spread by partisan sheets like the *New York Journal.* To get the project off the ground, a group of Federalist leaders, including John Jay and Alexander Hamilton, each lent Webster (interest free) one hundred and fifty dollars. By late summer 1793 Webster had created a printing company, and by November he was in New York ready to publish. The first issue appeared 9 December 1793.

The original name was *The American Minerva, patroness of peace, commerce and the liberal arts.* In March 1794 the name was changed to *American Minerva, and the New York (Evening) Advertiser.* In May Webster announced the creation of *The Herald,* a country weekly that deleted most of the city-oriented advertising and condensed and reorganized the copy from the daily city editions. These were significant innovations and Webster was apparently among the first to employ them. It allowed him to sell twice copy that had been expensively typeset, and it expanded his circulation, carrying the news to people who usually had no newspaper. In 1797, after several more name changes, the two editions took the titles *Commercial Advertiser* and *Spectator.*

The venture was one of Webster's successes. After a slow start, circulation began to grow—as did advertising revenues—and he was able to pay off the loans that had allowed him to start the paper. The reasons for his rise are not hard to understand. Even in the 1790s most papers were still edited by glorified printers. Webster, with his college education, experience in journalism, and a reputation gained through his textbooks, was in an ideal position to publish a paper superior to most of his competition. This was part of an important change in American journalism. Papers were being edited rather than simply printed. Editors were becoming public figures. At about the same time Webster created the *Minerva,* other men with considerable talents were moving into journalism. Benjamin Franklin Bache, William Cobbett, and Philip Freneau, like Webster, were men of literary and intellectual skill who turned to journalism. They were editors who stamped their views and personalities on the papers they controlled. In the process they helped change American journalism from a world of news sheets to a world of news-papers.

Webster made his position as editor clear. He insisted upon his independence for, as he put it, "the complexion . . . of the paper has been given by myself, and I alone am responsible for the tenor of the *opinions* it contains." He stated the facts as he found them "without regard to party." "The National Government" had been "incorrupt and according to the spirit of the Constitution"—the *Minerva* defended its actions. While European powers battled, he defended American neutrality "because there has appeared no occasion for war, but great advantages in peace." Caught up in national and international disputes, he remained a true son of New England. Webster claimed that his principles were "those which prevail generally in the state which gave me birth and among the northern people."

The finest, and perhaps the best-known, example of his journalism was the so-called Curtius letters. This series of long editorials began in October 1794 when the *New York Journal* published a violent attack on John Jay and his conduct of the negotiations with England that sought to settle trade relations and the problem of Great Britain's continued presence in the American northwest. On 28 October a letter appeared in the *Minerva* defending Jay, and

Front page of the first issue of the American Minerva.

after nearly a year of increasingly bitter exchanges, the *Minerva* printed a series of twelve articles signed "Curtius" that sought to vindicate the Jay Treaty. They reappeared in the *Herald* and were widely reprinted in other Federalist papers.

These pieces would be out of place on today's editorial page. They were technical, densely reasoned, and overly long. Webster devoted a good deal of space to answering technical objections to the treaty. On the positive side he argued that America was in no position to compel England in any way. The treaty, in Webster's view, was the best deal available, given the realities Jay faced. In the end Webster called on the people to trust and pay deference to leaders like Jay and Washington: "Is there a shadow of reason to believe that men grown grey in the service of their country, whose patriotism and virtue were never suspected, have now in the evening of life . . . commenced to be traitors. . . . You have not been deceived."

The Curtius letters were important because they so often evoked the concept of deference. Webster, as a product of Connecticut, took it as an article of faith that leaders merited trust and deference from the people. Yet, ironically, Webster and the *Minerva* were involved in the process that was quickly undermining that deferential world. In the 1790s the idea of opposition to government rested on no very firm foundations, but they were being built. Newspapers began to criticize the actions of government and to do so in an increasingly partisan and violent way. Webster had, of course, been enlisted to counter just such criticism, and he never really accepted the legitimacy of opposition. In fact, he was so anxious about the inflammability of the public mind that he came to believe "that there must be something wrong in *principle* in opposition." To the end of his career as journalist he never understood that, as a partisan for the people in power, he helped to spawn partisan journalism in America. Since Webster's day most defenders of the government have come to see the partisanship in their actions. Webster never did. As a zealot, he saw himself defending truth and order against opposition and anarchy.

Webster left journalism for two reasons. Eventually, he was forced to sell his interest in the papers because he had incurred the wrath of Alexander Hamilton. Webster had supported Adams against Hamilton during the 1800 breakup of the Federalist Party, and Hamilton sought his revenge by financing a second Federalist paper (the *New York Evening Post*) in New York. Under this competitive pressure Webster sold his holdings and in 1803 washed his hands of the newspaper business. Long before that time his enthusiasm for the business had waned. In 1798 he had withdrawn from active participation in the paper's production, writing only the political columns. He was worn out; his wife recalled that "his labors were incessant . . . " and when he finally left journalism to return to New Haven, "he was in a critical condition, mentally and physically." He had marched off to New York in search of the rostrum from which he could lecture the American public; he withdrew convinced the people were well on their way to ruin.

During Webster's career as journalist he became involved in the raging controversy over the cause and treatment of epidemics. Most of America's major cities had suffered outbreaks of yellow fever during the 1790s. Noah, with a lifelong layman's interest in science, threw himself into the study of epidemics with the same energy that he exhibited in all his other endeavors.

American physicians offered two theories to explain the epidemics. One school, led by Dr. Benjamin Rush, believed that yellow fever was of local origin, arising out of unsanitary conditions; the other school, led by Dr. William Currie, believed the disease was imported. Webster set out to make his contribution to the debate.

He first tirelessly collected historical information on epidemic diseases. He wrote to his long list of contacts in the United States and abroad asking for any personal testimony they might give regarding yellow fever or other pestilential diseases. He questioned sailors and others who arrived in New York; he sent out circular letters to prominent figures; and, in time, he had amassed a huge file of data on epidemics. These data were first published in 1799 as a series of twenty-five letters that appeared in the press. The major product, however, was a two-volume work, *A Brief History of Epidemic and Pestilential Diseases* . . . printed by Hudson and Goodwin in New Haven in 1799.

The crux of this massive work was the notion that yellow fever was caused by the condition of the atmosphere. Webster believed that natural phenomena such as abnormally mild winters or hot damp summers were the primary causes of epidemics. The first volume of the work was given over to a correlation of such natural events as earthquakes, meteors, eclipses, and meteorological quirks with the outbreaks of epidemic diseases. Beginning with Moses, Webster carried his history up to 1799. In the second volume he essentially made the argument that his researches proved a connection between the quality of the air and the outbreak of disease.

Webster, of course, knew nothing of microorganisms and their role in epidemics. So, in a sense, he was combing a haystack that contained no needle. Without this knowledge Webster, nor any of his fellow workers in the area, could have identified the mosquito as the carrier of the contagion. In retrospect his labors seem almost pathetic. Yet they were part of the slow painful process of scientific discovery. Beyond that, his work in science illustrated several important qualities about Webster during the 1790s. He was trying almost desperately to be of service to his nation. Yellow fever was probably the most fundamental health problem faced by the new nation and he wanted to help solve it. Also he was a child of the Enlightenment. The pages of his work on diseases were illuminated by a faith in progress based on historical study and research. The Enlightenment mind may be nearly impossible to define, but it surely contained a firm belief that tomorrow could be materially better than yesterday. In his labors on epidemics Webster was living out that belief.

Webster spent most of the 1790s as a journalist. This portion of his life has been obscured by those years spent working, first on his schoolbooks, and then later, on the famous dictionary. As a newspaperman, he helped American journalism come of age, and he played a crucial part in the process that brought the editor out of the printshop and into a new role in politics. He produced, in *The Prompter,* perhaps his most readable and lovable book. His researches on yellow fever, that grew naturally out of his journalistic activities, were one of the major contributions by an American to epidemiology. By the end of the decade, however, there were clear signs that he was changing. His faith in the people was crumbling, his belief in progress was somewhat shaken—he had begun to grow bitter and disillusioned. (pp. 78-91)

Richard J. Moss, in his Noah Webster, *Twayne Publishers, 1984, 131 p.*

FURTHER READING

Allen, F. Sturges. *Noah Webster's Place among English Lexicographers.* Springfield, Mass.: G. & C. Merriam Co., 1909, 19 p.

> Transcription of a 1908 speech commemorating the 150th anniversary of Webster's birth. Allen offers "a brief sketch of his life and a general consideration of his lexicographic work."

Baugh, Albert C. "The English Language in America." In his *A History of the English Language,* pp. 406-66. New York: Appleton-Century-Crofts, 1957.

> Contains sections "Noah Webster and an American Language," "His Influence on American Spelling," and "His Influence on American Pronunciation."

Benton, Joel. "An Unwritten Chapter in Noah Webster's Life: Love and the Spelling-Book." *Magazine of American History* X, No. 1 (July 1883): 52-6.

> Describes Webster's brief residence in Sharon, Connecticut, in 1782, focusing on an early romantic interest of Webster's and his work on his first spelling text.

——. "The Webster Spelling-Book: Its Centennial Anniversary." *Magazine of American History* X, No. 4 (October 1883): 299-306.

> Elaborates on alterations to the fables and illustrations included in successive editions of part one of the *Grammatical Institute* during its first hundred years of publication.

Brooks, Van Wyck. *The Flowering of New England, 1816-1865,* pp. 66ff. New York: E. P. Dutton & Co., 1936.

> Discusses Webster's personality and lexicographic reforms in the context of the intellectual currents of Connecticut and New England during the early and mid-1800s.

Bynack, V. P. "Noah Webster's Linguistic Thought and the Idea of an American National Culture." *Journal of the History of Ideas* XLV, No. 1 (January-March 1984): 99-114.

> Outlines Webster's career, discussing the interrelationship of his political views, philosophical ideas, and his conception of a national culture based on a national language.

Cannon, Charles Dale. "Noah Webster's Influence on American English." *The University of Mississippi Studies in English* 13 (1972): 7-17.

> Examines "Webster's influence on spelling reform, his influence on lexicography, and his influence on the language deriving from patriotism."

Commager, Henry Steele. "Noah Webster, 1758-1958: 'Schoolmaster to America'." *Saturday Review,* New York XLI, No. 42 (18 October 1958): 10-12, 66-7.

Offers an overview of Webster's career and examines his motivations in developing a national language.

Downey, Charlotte. Introduction to *A Grammatical Institute of the English Language, Part II,* by Noah Webster, pp. v-xxii. 1800. Reprint. Delmar, N.Y.: Scholars' Facsimiles & Reprints, 1980.

Relates Webster's writings on grammar to those of earlier English grammarians and traces differences in the guidelines presented in successive editions of part two of the *Grammatical Institute.* The text proper offers a facsimile reproduction of an 1800 edition.

Ellis, Joseph J. "Noah Webster: The Connecticut Yankee as Nationalist." In his *After the Revolution: Profiles of Early American Culture,* pp. 161-212. London: W. W. Norton & Co., 1979.

Discusses Webster's life and writings, stressing his relationship to major intellectual and political currents of the late eighteenth century in the United States and France.

Evans, Bergen. "Noah Webster Had the Same Troubles." *The New York Times Magazine* (13 May 1962): 11, 77, 79, 80.

Describes the initial controversy surrounding the spelling reforms introduced by Webster in his *Compendious Dictionary* and *American Dictionary* in response to criticism of the third edition of *Webster's New International Dictionary.*

Ford, Emily Ellsworth Fowler. *Notes on the Life of Noah Webster.* 2 vols. Edited by Emily Ellsworth Ford Skeel. New York: Privately printed, 1912.

Major biography written by Webster's granddaughter and edited by his great-granddaughter which excerpts frequently from Webster's diary entries and written correspondence.

Friedman, Lawrence J. " 'The Rising Glory of America': Literature and Language in Post-Revolutionary Society." In his *Inventors of the Promised Land,* pp. 3-43. New York: Alfred A. Knopf, 1975.

Discusses Webster's dedication to creating an American national language, yet notes his limitations in relying on British linguistic authorities and in attributing a national character to New England regionalisms.

Friend, Joseph H. *The Development of American Lexicography, 1798-1864.* The Hague: Mouton, 1967, 129 p.

Comprises three sections: the first focusing on Webster's lexicographic precursors and on his *Compendious Dictionary;* the second closely analyzing technical aspects of the *American Dictionary;* and the third outlining the "war of the dictionaries," the competition between successive editions of dictionaries by Webster and Joseph E. Worcester in the mid-1800s.

Goodrich, Chauncey A. "Life and Writings of Noah Webster, LL.D." *The American Literary Magazine* II, No. 1 (January 1848): 5-32.

Presents biographical detail of Webster, praising "the life and labors . . . of one of the earliest and best known of American scholars."

Holmberg, Börje. "Noah Webster and American Pronunciation." *English Studies* 46 (1965): 118-29.

Compares and contrasts Webster's guidelines for spelling and pronunciation expressed in part one of the *Grammatical Institute,* the *American Dictionary,* and *Dissertations on the English Language* with those prevailing in British English.

King, Ethel. *The Rainbow in the Sky: Concerning Noah Webster and His Dictionary.* Brooklyn: Theo. Gaus' Sons, 1962, 95 p.

Provides noncritical biographical information.

Krapp, George Philip. *The English Language in America.* 2 vols. New York: Century Co., for the Modern Language Association of America, 1925.

Contains frequent reference to Webster's works, particularly part one of the *Grammatical Institute* and the *American Dictionary,* noting their relationship to the development of American English.

Laird, Charlton. "Etymology, Anglo-Saxon, and Noah Webster." *American Speech* XXI, No. 1 (February 1946): 3-15.

Focuses on Webster's use of Anglo-Saxon in his etymological work for the *American Dictionary,* questioning his fluency in the language and suggesting that he was "a mediocre student of Anglo-Saxon."

Leavitt, Robert Keith. *Noah's Ark, New England Yankees, and the Endless Quest.* Springfield, Mass.: G. & C. Merriam Co., 1947, 106 p.

Chronicles Webster's life and career, and traces the first hundred years of publication of Webster's *American Dictionary* by the G. & C. Merriam Company.

Lindblad, Karl-Erik. *Noah Webster's Pronunciation and Modern New England Speech.* Essays and Studies on American Language and Literature, edited by S. B. Liljegren, vol. XI. Cambridge, Mass.: Harvard University Press, 1954, 90 p.

Analyzes Webster's rules for the pronunciation of American English in his writings on language and relates them to the regional speech of New England and the general speech of the United States.

Malone, Kemp. "A Linguistic Patriot." *American Speech* 1, No. 1 (October 1925): 26-31.

Celebrates Webster's Americanization of English orthography and pronunciation as reflecting the "aggressive nationalistic spirit" of the early United States.

Marden, Philip S. "Another Great Lexicographer." In his *Detours: Passable but Unsafe,* pp. 58-69. Boston: Houghton Mifflin, 1926.

Reflects informally on the life and times of Webster and on the enduring lexicographic authority of his *American Dictionary.*

Mathews, M. M. "Noah Webster (1758-1843)." In his *The Beginnings of American English: Essays and Comments,* pp. 44-55. Chicago: University of Chicago Press, 1931.

Discusses Webster's writings on the subject of language and excerpts from relevant written correspondence: an 1809 letter to Thomas Dawes and a 1789 letter from Benjamin Franklin.

———. "The Nineteenth Century." In his *A Survey of English Dictionaries,* pp. 34-49. 1933. Reprint. New York: Russell & Russell, 1966.

Surveys major dictionaries appearing throughout the 1800s, including Webster's *Compendious Dictionary* and *American Dictionary.*

Morgan, John S. *Noah Webster.* New York: Mason/Charter, 1975, 216 p.

Details Webster's life and career, elaborating on his work as an educator, American nationalist, and lexicographer.

Peters, Robert K. Introduction to *A Collection of Essays and Fugitiv Writings on Moral, Historical, Political and Literary Subjects,* by Noah Webster, pp. iii-xi. 1790. Reprint. Delmar, N.Y.: Scholars' Facsimiles & Reprints, 1977.

Outlines Webster's writings prior to 1790 and judges his *Essays and Fugitiv Writings* "a capstone to this youthful, reform-minded period of his career."

Pyles, Thomas. "Noah Webster: Man and Symbol." In his *Words and Ways of American English,* pp. 93-124. New York: Random House, 1952.

Overviews Webster's life and focuses on the rules of spelling and pronunciation presented in his dictionaries and textbooks. Pyles deems Webster "one of the most influential commentators upon language who ever lived."

Read, Allen Walker. "Noah Webster as a Euphemist." *Dialect Notes* VI, Part VIII (1934): 385-91.

Discusses Webster's adaptation of the Bible as it demonstrates "his principal concern . . . in removing objectionable expressions, those words that 'cannot be uttered in families without disturbing devotion'."

Rollins, Richard M. *The Long Journey of Noah Webster.* Philadelphia: University of Pennsylvania Press, 1980, 195 p.

Elaborates on Webster's "long journey through a series of profound psychological, intellectual, religious, social, and political transformations."

Shoemaker, Ervin C. *Noah Webster: Pioneer of Learning.* New York: Columbia University Press, 1936, 347 p.

Provides extensive commentary on Webster's career and his significance as an American educator, with a substantial bibliography.

Smith, Gerald A. "Noah Webster's Conservatism." *American Speech* 25, No. 2 (May 1950): 101-04.

Reprints written correspondence between Webster and Horace Greeley in 1837 to question Webster's reputation as an American innovator of the English language.

Thompson, Everett E. "The Noah Webster Bicentennial, 1758-1958." *Word Study* XXXIII, No. 3 (February 1958): 1-8.

Outlines Webster's life and career, concluding with a description of his dictionary's continued publication by the G. & C. Merriam Company.

Wagenknecht, Edward. "The Man Behind the Dictionary." *The Virginia Quarterly Review* 5, No. 2 (April 1929): 246-58.

Focuses on Webster's personality and his views on diverse social, literary, and political issues of his era.

Warfel, Harry R. *Noah Webster: Schoolmaster to America.* New York: Macmillan Co., 1936, 460 p.

Details Webster's life, character, and the growth of his ideas and influence, in a seminal biography.

———. Introduction to *Sketches of American Policy,* by Noah Webster, edited by Harry R. Warfel, pp. i-iii. 1785. Reprint. New York: Scholars' Facsimiles & Reprints, 1937.

Discusses Webster's treatise as it expresses political ideas that foreshadowed the U.S. Constitution.

———. Introduction to *Dissertations on the English Language,* by Noah Webster, pp. iii-vi. 1789. Reprint. Gainesville, Fla.: Scholars' Facsimiles & Reprints, 1951.

Addresses Webster's concern with education in the United States and with the American form of the English language.

———. "Dictionaries and Linguistics." *College English* 22, No. 7 (April 1961): 473-78.

Contrasts the lexicographic work and linguistic theories of Webster and Samuel Johnson, focusing on "the metaphysics of language as they relate primarily to lexicography."

Whitehall, Harold. "The Development of the English Dictionary." In *Essays on Language and Usage,* edited by Leonard F. Dean and Kenneth G. Wilson, pp. 5-14. New York: Oxford University Press, 1959.

Examines briefly the "war of the dictionaries," describing the competition between the publishers of Webster's *American Dictionary* and Joseph E. Worcester's *Comprehensive Pronouncing, and Explanatory Dictionary of the English Language* (1830).

Nineteenth-Century
Literature Criticism

Cumulative Indexes
Volumes 1-30

This Index Includes References to Entries in These Gale Series

Contemporary Literary Criticism presents excerpts of criticism on the works of novelists, poets, dramatists, short story writers, scriptwriters, and other creative writers who are now living or who have died since 1960.

Twentieth-Century Literary Criticism contains critical excerpts by the most significant commentators on poets, novelists, short story writers, dramatists, and philosophers who died between 1900 and 1960.

Nineteenth-Century Literature Criticism offers significant passages from criticism on authors who died between 1800 and 1899.

Literature Criticism from 1400 to 1800 compiles significant passages from the most noteworthy criticism on authors of the fifteenth through the eighteenth centuries.

Classical and Medieval Literature Criticism offers excerpts of criticism on the works of world authors from classical antiquity through the fourteenth century.

Short Story Criticism combines excerpts of criticism on short fiction by writers of all eras and nationalities.

Poetry Criticism presents excerpts of criticism on the works of poets from all eras, movements, and nationalities.

Children's Literature Review includes excerpts from reviews, criticism, and commentary on works of authors and illustrators who create books for children.

Contemporary Authors Series encompasses five related series. *Contemporary Authors* provides biographical and bibliographical information on more than 97,000 writers of fiction and nonfiction. *Contemporary Authors New Revision Series* provides completely updated information on authors covered in *CA*. Only entries requiring significant change are revised for *CA New Revision Series*. *Contemporary Authors Permanent Series* consists of listings for deceased and inactive authors. *Contemporary Authors Autobiography Series* presents specially commissioned autobiographies by leading contemporary writers. *Contemporary Authors Bibliographical Series* contains primary and secondary bibliographies as well as analytical bibliographical essays by authorities on major modern authors.

Dictionary of Literary Biography encompasses three related series. *Dictionary of Literary Biography* furnishes illustrated overviews of authors' lives and works. *Dictionary of Literary Biography Documentary Series* illuminates the careers of major figures through a selection of literary documents, including letters, interviews, and photographs. *Dictionary of Literary Biography Yearbook* summarizes the past year's literary activity and includes updated entries on individual authors. A cumulative index to authors and articles is included in each new volume. *Concise Dictionary of Literary Biography,* a six-volume series, collects revised and updated sketches on major American authors that were originally presented in *Dictionary of Literary Biography.*

Something about the Author Series encompasses three related series. *Something about the Author* contains illustrated biographical sketches on authors and illustrators of juvenile and young adult literature from all eras. *Something about the Author Autobiography Series* presents specially commissioned autobiographies by prominent authors and illustrators of books for children and young adults. *Authors and Artists for Young Adults* provides high school and junior high school students with profiles of their favorite creative artists.

Yesterday's Authors of Books for Children contains heavily illustrated entries on children's writers who died before 1961. Complete in two volumes.

Literary Criticism Series
Cumulative Author Index

This index lists all author entries in the Gale Literary Criticism Series and includes cross-references to other Gale sources. References in the index are identified as follows:

Blackburn, Paul 1926-1971 . . . . . **CLC 9, 43**
See also CA 81-84; obituary CA 33-36R;
DLB 16; DLB-Y 81

Black Elk 1863-1950 . . . . **TCLC 33**

Blackmore, R(ichard) D(oddridge)
1825-1900 . . . . **TCLC 27**
See also CA 120; DLB 18

Blackmur, R(ichard) P(almer)
1904-1965 . . . . **CLC 2, 24**
See also CAP 1; CA 11-12;
obituary CA 25-28R; DLB 63

Blackwood, Algernon (Henry)
1869-1951 . . . . **TCLC 5**
See also CA 105

Blackwood, Caroline 1931- . . . . **CLC 6, 9**
See also CA 85-88; DLB 14

Blair, Eric Arthur 1903-1950
See Orwell, George
See also CA 104; SATA 29

Blais, Marie-Claire
1939- . . . . **CLC 2, 4, 6, 13, 22**
See also CAAS 4; CA 21-24R; DLB 53

Blaise, Clark 1940- . . . . **CLC 29**
See also CAAS 3; CANR 5; CA 53-56R;
DLB 53

Blake, Nicholas 1904-1972
See Day Lewis, C(ecil)

Blake, William 1757-1827 . . . . **NCLC 13**
See also SATA 30

Blasco Ibanez, Vicente
1867-1928 . . . . **TCLC 12**
See also CA 110

Blatty, William Peter 1928- . . . . **CLC 2**
See also CANR 9; CA 5-8R

Blessing, Lee 1949- . . . . **CLC 54**

Blish, James (Benjamin)
1921-1975 . . . . **CLC 14**
See also CANR 3; CA 1-4R;
obituary CA 57-60; DLB 8

Blixen, Karen (Christentze Dinesen)
1885-1962
See Dinesen, Isak
See also CAP 2; CA 25-28; SATA 44

Bloch, Robert (Albert) 1917- . . . . **CLC 33**
See also CANR 5; CA 5-8R; SATA 12;
DLB 44

Blok, Aleksandr (Aleksandrovich)
1880-1921 . . . . **TCLC 5**
See also CA 104

Bloom, Harold 1930- . . . . **CLC 24**
See also CA 13-16R; DLB 67

Blount, Roy (Alton), Jr. 1941- . . . . . **CLC 38**
See also CANR 10; CA 53-56

Bloy, Leon 1846-1917 . . . . **TCLC 22**
See also CA 121

Blume, Judy (Sussman Kitchens)
1938- . . . . **CLC 12, 30**
See also CLR 2, 15; CANR 13; CA 29-32R;
SATA 2, 31; DLB 52

Blunden, Edmund (Charles)
1896-1974 . . . . **CLC 2, 56**
See also CAP 2; CA 17-18;
obituary CA 45-48; DLB 20

Bly, Robert (Elwood)
1926- . . . . **CLC 1, 2, 5, 10, 15, 38**
See also CA 5-8R; DLB 5

Bochco, Steven 1944?- . . . . **CLC 35**

Bodker, Cecil 1927- . . . . **CLC 21**
See also CLR 23; CANR 13; CA 73-76;
SATA 14

Boell, Heinrich (Theodor) 1917-1985
See Boll, Heinrich
See also CANR 24; CA 21-24R;
obituary CA 116

Bogan, Louise 1897-1970 . . . . . **CLC 4, 39, 46**
See also CA 73-76; obituary CA 25-28R;
DLB 45

Bogarde, Dirk 1921- . . . . **CLC 19**
See also Van Den Bogarde, Derek (Jules
Gaspard Ulric) Niven
See also DLB 14

Bogosian, Eric 1953- . . . . **CLC 45**

Bograd, Larry 1953- . . . . **CLC 35**
See also CA 93-96; SATA 33

Bohl de Faber, Cecilia 1796-1877
See Caballero, Fernan

Boiardo, Matteo Maria 1441-1494 . . . . **LC 6**

Boileau-Despreaux, Nicolas
1636-1711 . . . . **LC 3**

Boland, Eavan (Aisling) 1944- . . . . . . **CLC 40**
See also DLB 40

Boll, Heinrich (Theodor)
1917-1985 . . . **CLC 2, 3, 6, 9, 11, 15, 27,
39**
See also Boell, Heinrich (Theodor)
See also DLB 69; DLB-Y 85

Bolt, Robert (Oxton) 1924- . . . . **CLC 14**
See also CA 17-20R; DLB 13

Bond, Edward 1934- . . . . **CLC 4, 6, 13, 23**
See also CA 25-28R; DLB 13

Bonham, Frank 1914- . . . . **CLC 12**
See also CANR 4; CA 9-12R; SAAS 3;
SATA 1, 49

Bonnefoy, Yves 1923- . . . . **CLC 9, 15, 58**
See also CA 85-88

Bontemps, Arna (Wendell)
1902-1973 . . . . **CLC 1, 18**
See also CLR 6; CANR 4; CA 1-4R;
obituary CA 41-44R; SATA 2, 44;
obituary SATA 24; DLB 48, 51

Booth, Martin 1944- . . . . **CLC 13**
See also CAAS 2; CA 93-96

Booth, Philip 1925- . . . . **CLC 23**
See also CANR 5; CA 5-8R; DLB-Y 82

Booth, Wayne C(layson) 1921- . . . . . . **CLC 24**
See also CAAS 5; CANR 3; CA 1-4R;
DLB 67

Borchert, Wolfgang 1921-1947 . . . . . **TCLC 5**
See also CA 104; DLB 69

Borges, Jorge Luis
1899-1986 . . . **CLC 1, 2, 3, 4, 6, 8, 9, 10,
13, 19, 44, 48; SSC 4**
See also CANR 19; CA 21-24R; DLB-Y 86

Borowski, Tadeusz 1922-1951 . . . . . . **TCLC 9**
See also CA 106

Borrow, George (Henry)
1803-1881 . . . . **NCLC 9**
See also DLB 21, 55

Bosschere, Jean de 1878-1953 . . . . . **TCLC 19**
See also CA 115

Boswell, James 1740-1795 . . . . **LC 4**

Bottoms, David 1949- . . . . **CLC 53**
See also CANR 22; CA 105; DLB-Y 83

Boucolon, Maryse 1937-
See Conde, Maryse
See also CA 110

Bourget, Paul (Charles Joseph)
1852-1935 . . . . **TCLC 12**
See also CA 107

Bourjaily, Vance (Nye) 1922- . . . **CLC 8, 62**
See also CAAS 1; CANR 2; CA 1-4R;
DLB 2

Bourne, Randolph S(illiman)
1886-1918 . . . . **TCLC 16**
See also CA 117; DLB 63

Bova, Ben(jamin William) 1932- . . . . **CLC 45**
See also CLR 3; CANR 11; CA 5-8R;
SATA 6; DLB-Y 81

Bowen, Elizabeth (Dorothea Cole)
1899-1973 . . . . . **CLC 1, 3, 6, 11, 15, 22;
SSC 3**
See also CAP 2; CA 17-18;
obituary CA 41-44R; DLB 15

Bowering, George 1935- . . . . **CLC 15, 47**
See also CANR 10; CA 21-24R; DLB 53

Bowering, Marilyn R(uthe) 1949- . . . **CLC 32**
See also CA 101

Bowers, Edgar 1924- . . . . **CLC 9**
See also CANR 24; CA 5-8R; DLB 5

Bowie, David 1947- . . . . **CLC 17**
See also Jones, David Robert

Bowles, Jane (Sydney) 1917-1973 . . . . **CLC 3**
See also CAP 2; CA 19-20;
obituary CA 41-44R

Bowles, Paul (Frederick)
1910- . . . . . . **CLC 1, 2, 19, 53; SSC 3**
See also CAAS 1; CANR 1, 19; CA 1-4R;
DLB 5, 6

Box, Edgar 1925-
See Vidal, Gore

Boyd, William 1952- . . . . **CLC 28, 53**
See also CA 114, 120

Boyle, Kay 1903- . . **CLC 1, 5, 19, 58; SSC 5**
See also CAAS 1; CA 13-16R; DLB 4, 9, 48

Boyle, Patrick 19??- . . . . **CLC 19**

Boyle, Thomas Coraghessan
1948- . . . . **CLC 36, 55**
See also CA 120; DLB-Y 86

Brackenridge, Hugh Henry
1748-1816 . . . . **NCLC 7**
See also DLB 11, 37

Bradbury, Edward P. 1939-
See Moorcock, Michael

Bradbury, Malcolm (Stanley)
1932- . . . . **CLC 32, 61**
See also CANR 1; CA 1-4R; DLB 14

Author Index

Colter, Cyrus 1910- .... **CLC 58**
See also CANR 10; CA 65-68; DLB 33

Colton, James 1923-
See Hansen, Joseph

Colum, Padraic 1881-1972........ **CLC 28**
See also CA 73-76; obituary CA 33-36R;
SATA 15; DLB 19

Colvin, James 1939-
See Moorcock, Michael

Colwin, Laurie 1945- .... **CLC 5, 13, 23**
See also CANR 20; CA 89-92; DLB-Y 80

Comfort, Alex(ander) 1920-........ **CLC 7**
See also CANR 1; CA 1-4R

Compton-Burnett, Ivy
1892-1969 .... **CLC 1, 3, 10, 15, 34**
See also CANR 4; CA 1-4R;
obituary CA 25-28R; DLB 36

Comstock, Anthony 1844-1915 .... **TCLC 13**
See also CA 110

Conde, Maryse 1937-............. **CLC 52**
See also Boucolon, Maryse

Condon, Richard (Thomas)
1915- .... **CLC 4, 6, 8, 10, 45**
See also CAAS 1; CANR 2, 23; CA 1-4R

Congreve, William 1670-1729 .... **LC 5**
See also DLB 39

Connell, Evan S(helby), Jr.
1924- .... **CLC 4, 6, 45**
See also CAAS 2; CANR 2; CA 1-4R;
DLB 2; DLB-Y 81

Connelly, Marc(us Cook)
1890-1980 .... **CLC 7**
See also CA 85-88; obituary CA 102;
obituary SATA 25; DLB 7; DLB-Y 80

Conner, Ralph 1860-1937........ **TCLC 31**

Conrad, Joseph
1857-1924 .... **TCLC 1, 6, 13, 25**
See also CA 104; SATA 27; DLB 10, 34

Conroy, Pat 1945-................ **CLC 30**
See also CANR 24; CA 85-88; DLB 6

Constant (de Rebecque), (Henri) Benjamin
1767-1830 .... **NCLC 6**

Cook, Michael 1933- .... **CLC 58**
See also CA 93-96; DLB 53

Cook, Robin 1940- .... **CLC 14**
See also CA 108, 111

Cooke, Elizabeth 1948- .... **CLC 55**

Cooke, John Esten 1830-1886..... **NCLC 5**
See also DLB 3

Cooney, Ray 19??- .... **CLC 62**

Cooper, J. California 19??- .... **CLC 56**
See also CA 125

Cooper, James Fenimore
1789-1851 .... **NCLC 1, 27**
See also SATA 19; DLB 3;
CDALB 1640-1865

Coover, Robert (Lowell)
1932- .... **CLC 3, 7, 15, 32, 46**
See also CANR 3; CA 45-48; DLB 2;
DLB-Y 81

Copeland, Stewart (Armstrong)
1952- .... **CLC 26**
See also The Police

Coppard, A(lfred) E(dgar)
1878-1957 .... **TCLC 5**
See also YABC 1; CA 114

Coppee, Francois 1842-1908 ...... **TCLC 25**

Coppola, Francis Ford 1939-....... **CLC 16**
See also CA 77-80; DLB 44

Corcoran, Barbara 1911-.......... **CLC 17**
See also CAAS 2; CANR 11; CA 21-24R;
SATA 3; DLB 52

Corman, Cid 1924- .... **CLC 9**
See also Corman, Sidney
See also CAAS 2; DLB 5

Corman, Sidney 1924-
See Corman, Cid
See also CA 85-88

Cormier, Robert (Edmund)
1925-..................... **CLC 12, 30**
See also CLR 12; CANR 5, 23; CA 1-4R;
SATA 10, 45; DLB 52

Corn, Alfred (Dewitt III) 1943-..... **CLC 33**
See also CA 104; DLB-Y 80

Cornwell, David (John Moore)
1931- .... **CLC 9, 15**
See also le Carre, John
See also CANR 13; CA 5-8R

Corso, (Nunzio) Gregory 1930-... **CLC 1, 11**
See also CA 5-8R; DLB 5, 16

Cortazar, Julio
1914-1984 ..... **CLC 2, 3, 5, 10, 13, 15,
33, 34; SSC 7**
See also CANR 12; CA 21-24R

Corvo, Baron 1860-1913
See Rolfe, Frederick (William Serafino
Austin Lewis Mary)

Cosic, Dobrica 1921- .... **CLC 14**
See also CA 122

Costain, Thomas B(ertram)
1885-1965 .... **CLC 30**
See also CA 5-8R; obituary CA 25-28R;
DLB 9

Costantini, Humberto 1924?-1987... **CLC 49**
See also obituary CA 122

Costello, Elvis 1955-.............. **CLC 21**

Cotter, Joseph Seamon, Sr.
1861-1949 .... **TCLC 28**
See also DLB 50

Couperus, Louis (Marie Anne)
1863-1923 .... **TCLC 15**
See also CA 115

Courtenay, Bryce 1933-........... **CLC 59**

Cousteau, Jacques-Yves 1910-..... **CLC 30**
See also CANR 15; CA 65-68; SATA 38

Coward, (Sir) Noel (Pierce)
1899-1973.........**CLC 1, 9, 29, 51**
See also CAP 2; CA 17-18;
obituary CA 41-44R; DLB 10

Cowley, Malcolm 1898-1989 .... **CLC 39**
See also CANR 3; CA 5-6R; DLB 4, 48;
DLB-Y 81

Cowper, William 1731-1800....... **NCLC 8**

Cox, William Trevor 1928- ...... **CLC 9, 14**
See also Trevor, William
See also CANR 4; CA 9-12R

Cozzens, James Gould
1903-1978 .... **CLC 1, 4, 11**
See also CANR 19; CA 9-12R;
obituary CA 81-84; DLB 9; DLB-Y 84;
DLB-DS 2; CDALB 1941-1968

Crabbe, George 1754-1832...... **NCLC 26**

Crace, Douglas 1944-............. **CLC 58**

Crane, (Harold) Hart
1899-1932 .... **TCLC 2, 5**
See also CA 104; DLB 4, 48

Crane, R(onald) S(almon)
1886-1967 .... **CLC 27**
See also CA 85-88; DLB 63

Crane, Stephen
1871-1900 ..... **TCLC 11, 17, 32; SSC 7**
See also YABC 2; CA 109; DLB 12, 54, 78;
CDALB 1865-1917

Craven, Margaret 1901-1980...... **CLC 17**
See also CA 103

Crawford, F(rancis) Marion
1854-1909 .... **TCLC 10**
See also CA 107; DLB 71

Crawford, Isabella Valancy
1850-1887 .... **NCLC 12**

Crayencour, Marguerite de 1903-1987
See Yourcenar, Marguerite

Creasey, John 1908-1973.......... **CLC 11**
See also CANR 8; CA 5-8R;
obituary CA 41-44R

Crebillon, Claude Prosper Jolyot de (fils)
1707-1777 .... **LC 1**

Creeley, Robert (White)
1926- ...... **CLC 1, 2, 4, 8, 11, 15, 36**
See also CANR 23; CA 1-4R; DLB 5, 16

Crews, Harry (Eugene)
1935-................ **CLC 6, 23, 49**
See also CANR 20; CA 25-28R; DLB 6

Crichton, (John) Michael
1942-.................... **CLC 2, 6, 54**
See also CANR 13; CA 25-28R; SATA 9;
DLB-Y 81

Crispin, Edmund 1921-1978....... **CLC 22**
See also Montgomery, Robert Bruce

Cristofer, Michael 1946- .... **CLC 28**
See also CA 110; DLB 7

Croce, Benedetto 1866-1952 ...... **TCLC 37**
See also CA 120

Crockett, David (Davy)
1786-1836 .... **NCLC 8**
See also DLB 3, 11

Croker, John Wilson 1780-1857 .. **NCLC 10**

Cronin, A(rchibald) J(oseph)
1896-1981 .... **CLC 32**
See also CANR 5; CA 1-4R;
obituary CA 102; obituary SATA 25, 47

Cross, Amanda 1926-
See Heilbrun, Carolyn G(old)

Crothers, Rachel 1878-1953...... **TCLC 19**
See also CA 113; DLB 7

Crowley, Aleister 1875-1947 ...... **TCLC 7**
See also CA 104

Crowley, John 1942-
See also CA 61-64; DLB-Y 82

Grabbe, Christian Dietrich
  1801-1836 .... NCLC 2

Grace, Patricia   1937-............. CLC 56

Gracian y Morales, Baltasar
  1601-1658 .... LC 15

Gracq, Julien   1910-........... CLC 11, 48
  See also Poirier, Louis

Grade, Chaim   1910-1982 .... CLC 10
  See also CA 93-96; obituary CA 107

Graham, Jorie   1951-............. CLC 48
  See also CA 111

Graham, R(obert) B(ontine) Cunninghame
  1852-1936 .... TCLC 19

Graham, W(illiam) S(ydney)
  1918-1986 .... CLC 29
  See also CA 73-76; obituary CA 118;
  DLB 20

Graham, Winston (Mawdsley)
  1910-...................... CLC 23
  See also CANR 2, 22; CA 49-52;
  obituary CA 118

Granville-Barker, Harley
  1877-1946 .... TCLC 2
  See also CA 104

Grass, Gunter (Wilhelm)
  1927- .. CLC 1, 2, 4, 6, 11, 15, 22, 32, 49
  See also CANR 20; CA 13-16R; DLB 75

Grau, Shirley Ann   1929- .... CLC 4, 9
  See also CANR 22; CA 89-92; DLB 2

Graves, Richard Perceval   1945- .... CLC 44
  See also CANR 9, 26; CA 65-68

Graves, Robert (von Ranke)
  1895-1985 ... CLC 1, 2, 6, 11, 39, 44, 45
  See also CANR 5; CA 5-8R;
  obituary CA 117; SATA 45; DLB 20;
  DLB-Y 85

Gray, Alasdair   1934- .... CLC 41
  See also CA 123

Gray, Amlin   1946- .... CLC 29

Gray, Francine du Plessix   1930-.... CLC 22
  See also CAAS 2; CANR 11; CA 61-64

Gray, John (Henry)   1866-1934 .... TCLC 19
  See also CA 119

Gray, Simon (James Holliday)
  1936-.................. CLC 9, 14, 36
  See also CAAS 3; CA 21-24R; DLB 13

Gray, Spalding   1941-............. CLC 49

Gray, Thomas   1716-1771........... LC 4

Grayson, Richard (A.)   1951-....... CLC 38
  See also CANR 14; CA 85-88

Greeley, Andrew M(oran)   1928-.... CLC 28
  See also CAAS 7; CANR 7; CA 5-8R

Green, Hannah   1932-......... CLC 3, 7, 30
  See also Greenberg, Joanne
  See also CA 73-76

Green, Henry   1905-1974 .... CLC 2, 13
  See also Yorke, Henry Vincent
  See also DLB 15

Green, Julien (Hartridge)   1900- .. CLC 3, 11
  See also CA 21-24R; DLB 4, 72

Green, Paul (Eliot)   1894-1981...... CLC 25
  See also CANR 3; CA 5-8R;
  obituary CA 103; DLB 7, 9; DLB-Y 81

Greenberg, Ivan   1908-1973
  See Rahv, Philip
  See also CA 85-88

Greenberg, Joanne (Goldenberg)
  1932-................... CLC 3, 7, 30
  See also Green, Hannah
  See also CANR 14; CA 5-8R; SATA 25

Greenberg, Richard   1959?- .... CLC 57

Greene, Bette   1934- .... CLC 30
  See also CLR 2; CANR 4; CA 53-56;
  SATA 8

Greene, Gael   19??- .... CLC 8
  See also CANR 10; CA 13-16R

Greene, Graham (Henry)
  1904- ..... CLC 1, 3, 6, 9, 14, 18, 27, 37
  See also CA 13-16R; SATA 20; DLB 13, 15;
  DLB-Y 85

Gregor, Arthur   1923-............. CLC 9
  See also CANR 11; CA 25-28R; SATA 36

Gregory, Lady (Isabella Augusta Persse)
  1852-1932 .... TCLC 1
  See also CA 104; DLB 10

Grendon, Stephen   1909-1971
  See Derleth, August (William)

Grenville, Kate   1950-............. CLC 61
  See also CA 118

Greve, Felix Paul Berthold Friedrich
  1879-1948
  See Grove, Frederick Philip
  See also CA 104

Grey, (Pearl) Zane   1872?-1939 ..... TCLC 6
  See also CA 104; DLB 9

Grieg, (Johan) Nordahl (Brun)
  1902-1943 .... TCLC 10
  See also CA 107

Grieve, C(hristopher) M(urray)   1892-1978
  See MacDiarmid, Hugh
  See also CA 5-8R; obituary CA 85-88

Griffin, Gerald   1803-1840 .... NCLC 7

Griffin, Peter   1942- .... CLC 39

Griffiths, Trevor   1935-......... CLC 13, 52
  See also CA 97-100; DLB 13

Grigson, Geoffrey (Edward Harvey)
  1905-1985 .... CLC 7, 39
  See also CANR 20; CA 25-28R;
  obituary CA 118; DLB 27

Grillparzer, Franz   1791-1872...... NCLC 1

Grimke, Charlotte L(ottie) Forten   1837-1914
  See Forten (Grimke), Charlotte L(ottie)
  See also CA 117, 124

Grimm, Jakob (Ludwig) Karl
  1785-1863 .... NCLC 3
  See also SATA 22

Grimm, Wilhelm Karl   1786-1859 .. NCLC 3
  See also SATA 22

Grimmelshausen, Johann Jakob Christoffel
  von   1621-1676 .... LC 6

Grindel, Eugene   1895-1952
  See also CA 104

Grossman, Vasily (Semenovich)
  1905-1964 .... CLC 41
  See also CA 124

Grove, Frederick Philip
  1879-1948 .... TCLC 4
  See also Greve, Felix Paul Berthold
  Friedrich

Grumbach, Doris (Isaac)
  1918-.................... CLC 13, 22
  See also CAAS 2; CANR 9; CA 5-8R

Grundtvig, Nicolai Frederik Severin
  1783-1872 .... NCLC 1

Grunwald, Lisa   1959-............. CLC 44
  See also CA 120

Guare, John   1938- .... CLC 8, 14, 29
  See also CANR 21; CA 73-76; DLB 7

Gudjonsson, Halldor Kiljan   1902-
  See Laxness, Halldor (Kiljan)
  See also CA 103

Guest, Barbara   1920-............. CLC 34
  See also CANR 11; CA 25-28R; DLB 5

Guest, Judith (Ann)   1936-....... CLC 8, 30
  See also CANR 15; CA 77-80

Guild, Nicholas M.   1944-.......... CLC 33
  See also CA 93-96

Guillen, Jorge   1893-1984 .... CLC 11
  See also CA 89-92; obituary CA 112

Guillen, Nicolas   1902-1989 .... CLC 48
  See also CA 116, 125

Guillevic, (Eugene)   1907-......... CLC 33
  See also CA 93-96

Guiraldes, Ricardo   1886-1927 ..... TCLC 39

Gunn, Bill   1934-1989 .... CLC 5
  See also Gunn, William Harrison
  See also DLB 38

Gunn, Thom(son William)
  1929-................. CLC 3, 6, 18, 32
  See also CANR 9; CA 17-20R; DLB 27

Gunn, William Harrison   1934-1989
  See Gunn, Bill
  See also CANR 12, 25; CA 13-16R

Gurney, A(lbert) R(amsdell), Jr.
  1930-................. CLC 32, 50, 54
  See also CA 77-80

Gurney, Ivor (Bertie)   1890-1937... TCLC 33

Gustafson, Ralph (Barker)   1909-.... CLC 36
  See also CANR 8; CA 21-24R

Guthrie, A(lfred) B(ertram), Jr.
  1901-...................... CLC 23
  See also CA 57-60; DLB 6

Guthrie, Woodrow Wilson   1912-1967
  See Guthrie, Woody
  See also CA 113; obituary CA 93-96

Guthrie, Woody   1912-1967 .... CLC 35
  See also Guthrie, Woodrow Wilson

Guy, Rosa (Cuthbert)   1928-..... CLC 26 13
  See also CANR 14; CA 17-20R; SATA 14;
  DLB 33

Haavikko, Paavo (Juhani)
  1931-.................... CLC 18, 34
  See also CA 106

Hacker, Marilyn   1942- .... CLC 5, 9, 23
  See also CA 77-80

Haggard, (Sir) H(enry) Rider
  1856-1925 .... TCLC 11
  See also CA 108; SATA 16; DLB 70

Author Index

Author Index

Kavanagh, Patrick (Joseph Gregory)
        1905-1967 .... CLC 22
        See also CA 123; obituary CA 25-28R;
        DLB 15, 20

Kawabata, Yasunari
        1899-1972 ....CLC 2, 5, 9, 18
        See also CA 93-96; obituary CA 33-36R

Kaye, M(ary) M(argaret) 1909?-.... CLC 28
        See also CANR 24; CA 89-92

Kaye, Mollie 1909?-
        See Kaye, M(ary) M(argaret)

Kaye-Smith, Sheila 1887-1956..... TCLC 20
        See also CA 118; DLB 36

Kazan, Elia 1909-.......... CLC 6, 16, 63
        See also CA 21-24R

Kazantzakis, Nikos
        1885?-1957............. TCLC 2, 5, 33
        See also CA 105

Kazin, Alfred 1915- .... CLC 34, 38
        See also CAAS 7; CANR 1; CA 1-4R

Keane, Mary Nesta (Skrine) 1904-
        See Keane, Molly
        See also CA 108, 114

Keane, Molly 1904- .... CLC 31
        See also Keane, Mary Nesta (Skrine)

Keates, Jonathan 19??-........... CLC 34

Keaton, Buster 1895-1966 .... CLC 20

Keaton, Joseph Francis 1895-1966
        See Keaton, Buster

Keats, John 1795-1821...... NCLC 8; PC 1

Keene, Donald 1922- .... CLC 34
        See also CANR 5; CA 1-4R

Keillor, Garrison 1942- .... CLC 40
        See also Keillor, Gary (Edward)
        See also CA 111; DLB 87

Keillor, Gary (Edward)
        See Keillor, Garrison
        See also CA 111, 117

Kell, Joseph 1917-
        See Burgess (Wilson, John) Anthony

Keller, Gottfried 1819-1890....... NCLC 2

Kellerman, Jonathan (S.) 1949-..... CLC 44
        See also CA 106

Kelley, William Melvin 1937-...... CLC 22
        See also CA 77-80; DLB 33

Kellogg, Marjorie 1922-........... CLC 2
        See also CA 81-84

Kelly, M. T. 1947- .... CLC 55
        See also CANR 19; CA 97-100

Kelman, James 1946-............. CLC 58

Kemal, Yashar 1922- .... CLC 14, 29
        See also CA 89-92

Kemble, Fanny 1809-1893 .... NCLC 18
        See also DLB 32

Kemelman, Harry 1908-........... CLC 2
        See also CANR 6; CA 9-12R; DLB 28

Kempe, Margery 1373?-1440? .... LC 6

Kempis, Thomas á 1380-1471 .... LC 11

Kendall, Henry 1839-1882....... NCLC 12

Keneally, Thomas (Michael)
        1935- ...... CLC 5, 8, 10, 14, 19, 27, 43
        See also CANR 10; CA 85-88

Kennedy, John Pendleton
        1795-1870 .... NCLC 2
        See also DLB 3

Kennedy, Joseph Charles 1929-...... CLC 8
        See also Kennedy, X. J.
        See also CANR 4; CA 1-4R; SATA 14

Kennedy, William (Joseph)
        1928-..........CLC 6, 28, 34, 53
        See also CANR 14; CA 85-88; DLB-Y 85;
        AAYA 1

Kennedy, X. J. 1929- .... CLC 8, 42
        See also Kennedy, Joseph Charles
        See also DLB 5

Kerouac, Jack
        1922-1969 .... CLC 1, 2, 3, 5, 14, 29, 61
        See also Kerouac, Jean-Louis Lebris de
        See also DLB 2, 16; DLB-DS 3;
        CDALB 1941-1968

Kerouac, Jean-Louis Lebris de 1922-1969
        See Kerouac, Jack
        See also CA 5-8R; obituary CA 25-28R;
        CDALB 1941-1968

Kerr, Jean 1923-................. CLC 22
        See also CANR 7; CA 5-8R

Kerr, M. E. 1927-............. CLC 12, 35
        See also Meaker, Marijane
        See also SAAS 1

Kerr, Robert 1970?- .... CLC 55, 59

Kerrigan, (Thomas) Anthony
        1918-.................... CLC 4, 6
        See also CANR 4; CA 49-52

Kesey, Ken (Elton)
        1935-.......... CLC 1, 3, 6, 11, 46
        See also CANR 22; CA 1-4R; DLB 2, 16

Kesselring, Joseph (Otto)
        1902-1967 .... CLC 45

Kessler, Jascha (Frederick) 1929-.... CLC 4
        See also CANR 8; CA 17-20R

Kettelkamp, Larry 1933-.......... CLC 12
        See also CANR 16; CA 29-32R; SAAS 3;
        SATA 2

Kherdian, David 1931-........... CLC 6, 9
        See also CAAS 2; CA 21-24R; SATA 16

Khlebnikov, Velimir (Vladimirovich)
        1885-1922 .... TCLC 20
        See also CA 117

Khodasevich, Vladislav (Felitsianovich)
        1886-1939 .... TCLC 15
        See also CA 115

Kielland, Alexander (Lange)
        1849-1906 .... TCLC 5
        See also CA 104

Kiely, Benedict 1919-.......... CLC 23, 43
        See also CANR 2; CA 1-4R; DLB 15

Kienzle, William X(avier) 1928- .... CLC 25
        See also CAAS 1; CANR 9; CA 93-96

Killens, John Oliver 1916-......... CLC 10
        See also CAAS 2; CANR 26; CA 77-80,
        123; DLB 33

Killigrew, Anne 1660-1685........... LC 4

Kincaid, Jamaica 1949?- .... CLC 43
        See also CA 125

King, Francis (Henry) 1923- ..... CLC 8, 53
        See also CANR 1; CA 1-4R; DLB 15

King, Stephen (Edwin)
        1947- .... CLC 12, 26, 37, 61
        See also CANR 1; CA 61-64; SATA 9, 55;
        DLB-Y 80

Kingman, (Mary) Lee 1919-........ CLC 17
        See also Natti, (Mary) Lee
        See also CA 5-8R; SAAS 3; SATA 1

Kingsley, Sidney 1906-............ CLC 44
        See also CA 85-88; DLB 7

Kingsolver, Barbara 1955-......... CLC 55

Kingston, Maxine Hong
        1940- .... CLC 12, 19, 58
        See also CANR 13; CA 69-72; SATA 53;
        DLB-Y 80

Kinnell, Galway
        1927-........... CLC 1, 2, 3, 5, 13, 29
        See also CANR 10; CA 9-12R; DLB 5;
        DLB-Y 87

Kinsella, Thomas 1928- ...... CLC 4, 19, 43
        See also CANR 15; CA 17-20R; DLB 27

Kinsella, W(illiam) P(atrick)
        1935-................... CLC 27, 43
        See also CAAS 7; CANR 21; CA 97-100

Kipling, (Joseph) Rudyard
        1865-1936 .... TCLC 8, 17; SSC 5
        See also YABC 2; CA 105, 120; DLB 19, 34

Kirkup, James 1918- .... CLC 1
        See also CAAS 4; CANR 2; CA 1-4R;
        SATA 12; DLB 27

Kirkwood, James 1930-1989 .... CLC 9
        See also CANR 6; CA 1-4R

Kis, Danilo 1935-1989 .... CLC 57
        See also CA 118, 129; brief entry CA 109

Kivi, Aleksis 1834-1872........ NCLC 30

Kizer, Carolyn (Ashley) 1925-... CLC 15, 39
        See also CAAS 5; CANR 24; CA 65-68;
        DLB 5

Klappert, Peter 1942-............. CLC 57
        See also CA 33-36R; DLB 5

Klausner, Amos 1939-
        See Oz, Amos

Klein, A(braham) M(oses)
        1909-1972 .... CLC 19
        See also CA 101; obituary CA 37-40R;
        DLB 68

Klein, Norma 1938-1989 .... CLC 30
        See also CLR 2; CANR 15; CA 41-44R;
        SAAS 1; SATA 7

Klein, T.E.D. 19??-.............. CLC 34
        See also CA 119

Kleist, Heinrich von 1777-1811.... NCLC 2

Klima, Ivan 1931-................ CLC 56
        See also CANR 17; CA 25-28R

Klimentev, Andrei Platonovich 1899-1951
        See Platonov, Andrei (Platonovich)
        See also CA 108

Klinger, Friedrich Maximilian von
        1752-1831 .... NCLC 1

Klopstock, Friedrich Gottlieb
        1724-1803 .... NCLC 11

Knebel, Fletcher 1911-........... CLC 14
        See also CAAS 3; CANR 1; CA 1-4R;
        SATA 36

McCauley, Stephen 19??-.......... **CLC 50**

McClure, Michael 1932- .... **CLC 6, 10**
See also CANR 17; CA 21-24R; DLB 16

McCorkle, Jill (Collins) 1958-..... **CLC 51**
See also CA 121; DLB-Y 87

McCourt, James 1941-.............. **CLC 5**
See also CA 57-60

McCoy, Horace 1897-1955 ...... **TCLC 28**
See also CA 108; DLB 9

McCrae, John 1872-1918........ **TCLC 12**
See also CA 109

McCullers, (Lula) Carson (Smith)
1917-1967 .... **CLC 1, 4, 10, 12, 48**
See also CANR 18; CA 5-8R;
obituary CA 25-28R; CABS 1; SATA 27;
DLB 2, 7; CDALB 1941-1968

McCullough, Colleen 1938?-....... **CLC 27**
See also CANR 17; CA 81-84

McElroy, Joseph (Prince)
1930- .... **CLC 5, 47**
See also CA 17-20R

McEwan, Ian (Russell) 1948- ...... **CLC 13**
See also CANR 14; CA 61-64; DLB 14

McFadden, David 1940-.......... **CLC 48**
See also CA 104; DLB 60

McGahern, John 1934-........ **CLC 5, 9, 48**
See also CA 17-20R; DLB 14

McGinley, Patrick 1937-.......... **CLC 41**
See also CA 120

McGinley, Phyllis 1905-1978 ...... **CLC 14**
See also CANR 19; CA 9-12R;
obituary CA 77-80; SATA 2, 44;
obituary SATA 24; DLB 11, 48

McGinniss, Joe 1942-............. **CLC 32**
See also CA 25-28R

McGivern, Maureen Daly 1921-
See Daly, Maureen
See also CA 9-12R

McGrath, Patrick 1950-.......... **CLC 55**

McGrath, Thomas 1916- .... **CLC 28, 59**
See also CANR 6; CA 9-12R, 130;
SATA 41

McGuane, Thomas (Francis III)
1939- .... **CLC 3, 7, 18**
See also CANR 5; CA 49-52; DLB 2;
DLB-Y 80

McGuckian, Medbh 1950-......... **CLC 48**
See also DLB 40

McHale, Tom 1941-1982........ **CLC 3, 5**
See also CA 77-80; obituary CA 106

McIlvanney, William 1936-........ **CLC 42**
See also CA 25-28R; DLB 14

McIlwraith, Maureen Mollie Hunter 1922-
See Hunter, Mollie
See also CA 29-32R; SATA 2

McInerney, Jay 1955- .... **CLC 34**
See also CA 116, 123

McIntyre, Vonda N(eel) 1948- ..... **CLC 18**
See also CANR 17; CA 81-84

McKay, Claude 1890-1948........ **TCLC 7**
See also CA 104; DLB 4, 45

McKuen, Rod 1933-............. **CLC 1, 3**
See also CA 41-44R

McLuhan, (Herbert) Marshall
1911-1980 .... **CLC 37**
See also CANR 12; CA 9-12R;
obituary CA 102

McManus, Declan Patrick 1955-
See Costello, Elvis

McMillan, Terry 1951- .... **CLC 50, 61**

McMurtry, Larry (Jeff)
1936- .... **CLC 2, 3, 7, 11, 27, 44**
See also CANR 19; CA 5-8R; DLB 2;
DLB-Y 80, 87

McNally, Terrence 1939-...... **CLC 4, 7, 41**
See also CANR 2; CA 45-48; DLB 7

McPhee, John 1931-.............. **CLC 36**
See also CANR 20; CA 65-68

McPherson, James Alan 1943-..... **CLC 19**
See also CANR 24; CA 25-28R; DLB 38

McPherson, William 1939- .... **CLC 34**
See also CA 57-60

McSweeney, Kerry 19??-.......... **CLC 34**

Mead, Margaret 1901-1978........ **CLC 37**
See also CANR 4; CA 1-4R;
obituary CA 81-84; SATA 20

Meaker, M. J. 1927-
See Kerr, M. E.; Meaker, Marijane

Meaker, Marijane 1927-
See Kerr, M. E.
See also CA 107; SATA 20

Medoff, Mark (Howard) 1940-... **CLC 6, 23**
See also CANR 5; CA 53-56; DLB 7

Megged, Aharon 1920-............ **CLC 9**
See also CANR 1; CA 49-52

Mehta, Ved (Parkash) 1934-....... **CLC 37**
See also CANR 2, 23; CA 1-4R

Mellor, John 1953?-
See The Clash

Meltzer, Milton 1915-......... **CLC 26 13**
See also CA 13-16R; SAAS 1; SATA 1, 50;
DLB 61

Melville, Herman
1819-1891 ...... **NCLC 3, 12, 29; SSC 1**
See also SATA 59; DLB 3, 74;
CDALB 1640-1865

Membreno, Alejandro 1972- .... **CLC 59**

Mencken, H(enry) L(ouis)
1880-1956 .... **TCLC 13**
See also CA 105; DLB 11, 29, 63

Mercer, David 1928-1980.......... **CLC 5**
See also CA 9-12R; obituary CA 102;
DLB 13

Meredith, George 1828-1909...... **TCLC 17**
See also CA 117; DLB 18, 35, 57

Meredith, William (Morris)
1919- .... **CLC 4, 13, 22, 55**
See also CANR 6; CA 9-12R; DLB 5

Merezhkovsky, Dmitri
1865-1941 .... **TCLC 29**

Merimee, Prosper
1803-1870 .... **NCLC 6; SSC 7**

Merkin, Daphne 1954-............ **CLC 44**
See also CANR 123

Merrill, James (Ingram)
1926- .... **CLC 2, 3, 6, 8, 13, 18, 34**
See also CANR 10; CA 13-16R; DLB 5;
DLB-Y 85

Merton, Thomas (James)
1915-1968 .... **CLC 1, 3, 11, 34**
See also CANR 22; CA 5-8R;
obituary CA 25-28R; DLB 48; DLB-Y 81

Merwin, W(illiam) S(tanley)
1927- .... **CLC 1, 2, 3, 5, 8, 13, 18, 45**
See also CANR 15; CA 13-16R; DLB 5

Metcalf, John 1938-.............. **CLC 37**
See also CA 113; DLB 60

Mew, Charlotte (Mary)
1870-1928 .... **TCLC 8**
See also CA 105; DLB 19

Mewshaw, Michael 1943-........... **CLC 9**
See also CANR 7; CA 53-56; DLB-Y 80

Meyer-Meyrink, Gustav 1868-1932
See Meyrink, Gustav
See also CA 117

Meyers, Jeffrey 1939- .... **CLC 39**
See also CA 73-76

Meynell, Alice (Christiana Gertrude
Thompson) 1847-1922 .... **TCLC 6**
See also CA 104; DLB 19

Meyrink, Gustav 1868-1932....... **TCLC 21**
See also Meyer-Meyrink, Gustav

Michaels, Leonard 1933-........ **CLC 6, 25**
See also CANR 21; CA 61-64

Michaux, Henri 1899-1984 ...... **CLC 8, 19**
See also CA 85-88; obituary CA 114

Michelangelo 1475-1564........... **LC 12**

Michener, James A(lbert)
1907- .... **CLC 1, 5, 11, 29, 60**
See also CANR 21; CA 5-8R; DLB 6

Mickiewicz, Adam 1798-1855 ..... **NCLC 3**

Middleton, Christopher 1926-...... **CLC 13**
See also CA 13-16R; DLB 40

Middleton, Stanley 1919-........ **CLC 7, 38**
See also CANR 21; CA 25-28R; DLB 14

Migueis, Jose Rodrigues 1901-..... **CLC 10**

Mikszath, Kalman 1847-1910 ..... **TCLC 31**

Miles, Josephine (Louise)
1911-1985 .... **CLC 1, 2, 14, 34, 39**
See also CANR 2; CA 1-4R;
obituary CA 116; DLB 48

Mill, John Stuart 1806-1873..... **NCLC 11**

Millar, Kenneth 1915-1983 .... **CLC 14**
See also Macdonald, Ross
See also CANR 16; CA 9-12R;
obituary CA 110; DLB 2; DLB-Y 83

Millay, Edna St. Vincent
1892-1950 .... **TCLC 4**
See also CA 104; DLB 45

Miller, Arthur
1915- .... **CLC 1, 2, 6, 10, 15, 26, 47**
See also CANR 2; CA 1-4R; DLB 7;
CDALB 1941-1968

Miller, Henry (Valentine)
1891-1980 .... **CLC 1, 2, 4, 9, 14, 43**
See also CA 9-12R; obituary CA 97-100;
DLB 4, 9; DLB-Y 80

Mott, Michael (Charles Alston)
1930- .... CLC 15, 34
See also CAAS 7; CANR 7; CA 5-8R

Mowat, Farley (McGill) 1921- ..... CLC 26
See also CLR 20; CANR 4; CA 1-4R;
SATA 3; DLB 68

Mphahlele, Es'kia 1919-
See Mphahlele, Ezekiel

Mphahlele, Ezekiel 1919-......... CLC 25
See also CA 81-84

Mqhayi, S(amuel) E(dward) K(rune Loliwe)
1875-1945 .... TCLC 25

Mrozek, Slawomir 1930-........ CLC 3, 13
See also CA 13-16R

Mtwa, Percy 19??-............... CLC 47

Mueller, Lisel 1924-.......... CLC 13, 51
See also CA 93-96

Muir, Edwin 1887-1959 .... TCLC 2
See also CA 104; DLB 20

Muir, John 1838-1914 .... TCLC 28

Mujica Lainez, Manuel
1910-1984 .... CLC 31
See also CA 81-84; obituary CA 112

Mukherjee, Bharati 1940-......... CLC 53
See also CA 107; DLB 60

Muldoon, Paul 1951- .... CLC 32
See also CA 113; DLB 40

Mulisch, Harry (Kurt Victor)
1927- .... CLC 42
See also CANR 6; CA 9-12R

Mull, Martin 1943-............... CLC 17
See also CA 105

Munford, Robert 1737?-1783........ LC 5
See also DLB 31

Munro, Alice (Laidlaw)
1931- ...... CLC 6, 10, 19, 50; SSC 3
See also CA 33-36R; SATA 29; DLB 53

Munro, H(ector) H(ugh) 1870-1916
See Saki
See also CA 104; DLB 34

Murasaki, Lady c. 11th century-... CMLC 1

Murdoch, (Jean) Iris
1919- ...... CLC 1, 2, 3, 4, 6, 8, 11, 15,
22, 31, 51
See also CANR 8; CA 13-16R; DLB 14

Murphy, Richard 1927-........... CLC 41
See also CA 29-32R; DLB 40

Murphy, Sylvia 19??-............. CLC 34

Murphy, Thomas (Bernard) 1935-... CLC 51
See also CA 101

Murray, Les(lie) A(llan) 1938- ..... CLC 40
See also CANR 11; CA 21-24R

Murry, John Middleton
1889-1957 .... TCLC 16
See also CA 118

Musgrave, Susan 1951- .... CLC 13, 54
See also CA 69-72

Musil, Robert (Edler von)
1880-1942 .... TCLC 12
See also CA 109

Musset, (Louis Charles) Alfred de
1810-1857 .... NCLC 7

Myers, Walter Dean 1937- .... CLC 35
See also CLR 4, 16; CANR 20; CA 33-36R;
SAAS 2; SATA 27, 41; DLB 33

Nabokov, Vladimir (Vladimirovich)
1899-1977 .... CLC 1, 2, 3, 6, 8, 11, 15,
23, 44, 46
See also CANR 20; CA 5-8R;
obituary CA 69-72; DLB 2; DLB-Y 80;
DLB-DS 3; CDALB 1941-1968

Nagy, Laszlo 1925-1978............ CLC 7
See also obituary CA 112

Naipaul, Shiva(dhar Srinivasa)
1945-1985 .... CLC 32, 39
See also CA 110, 112; obituary CA 116;
DLB-Y 85

Naipaul, V(idiadhar) S(urajprasad)
1932-.......... CLC 4, 7, 9, 13, 18, 37
See also CANR 1; CA 1-4R; DLB-Y 85

Nakos, Ioulia 1899?-
See Nakos, Lilika

Nakos, Lilika 1899?- .... CLC 29

Nakou, Lilika 1899?-
See Nakos, Lilika

Narayan, R(asipuram) K(rishnaswami)
1906- .... CLC 7, 28, 47
See also CA 81-84

Nash, (Frediric) Ogden 1902-1971 .. CLC 23
See also CAP 1; CA 13-14;
obituary CA 29-32R; SATA 2, 46;
DLB 11

Nathan, George Jean 1882-1958 ... TCLC 18
See also CA 114

Natsume, Kinnosuke 1867-1916
See Natsume, Soseki
See also CA 104

Natsume, Soseki 1867-1916..... TCLC 2, 10
See also Natsume, Kinnosuke

Natti, (Mary) Lee 1919-
See Kingman, (Mary) Lee
See also CANR 2; CA 7-8R

Naylor, Gloria 1950- .... CLC 28, 52
See also CANR 27; CA 107

Neff, Debra 1972-............... CLC 59

Neihardt, John G(neisenau)
1881-1973 .... CLC 32
See also CAP 1; CA 13-14; DLB 9, 54

Nekrasov, Nikolai Alekseevich
1821-1878 .... NCLC 11

Nelligan, Emile 1879-1941....... TCLC 14
See also CA 114

Nelson, Willie 1933-............. CLC 17
See also CA 107

Nemerov, Howard 1920- .... CLC 2, 6, 9, 36
See also CANR 1; CA 1-4R; CABS 2;
DLB 5, 6; DLB-Y 83

Neruda, Pablo
1904-1973 ..... CLC 1, 2, 5, 7, 9, 28, 62
See also CAP 2; CA 19-20;
obituary CA 45-48

Nerval, Gerard de 1808-1855...... NCLC 1

Nervo, (Jose) Amado (Ruiz de)
1870-1919 .... TCLC 11
See also CA 109

Neufeld, John (Arthur) 1938- ...... CLC 17
See also CANR 11; CA 25-28R; SAAS 3;
SATA 6

Neville, Emily Cheney 1919-....... CLC 12
See also CANR 3; CA 5-8R; SAAS 2;
SATA 1

Newbound, Bernard Slade 1930-
See Slade, Bernard
See also CA 81-84

Newby, P(ercy) H(oward)
1918-..................... CLC 2, 13
See also CA 5-8R; DLB 15

Newlove, Donald 1928-............ CLC 6
See also CANR 25; CA 29-32R

Newlove, John (Herbert) 1938-..... CLC 14
See also CANR 9, 25; CA 21-24R

Newman, Charles 1938-.......... CLC 2, 8
See also CA 21-24R

Newman, Edwin (Harold) 1919- .... CLC 14
See also CANR 5; CA 69-72

Newton, Suzanne 1936-........... CLC 35
See also CANR 14; CA 41-44R; SATA 5

Ngema, Mbongeni 1955- .... CLC 57

Ngugi, James (Thiong'o)
1938-................ CLC 3, 7, 13, 36
See also Ngugi wa Thiong'o; Wa Thiong'o,
Ngugi
See also CA 81-84

Ngugi wa Thiong'o 1938-... CLC 3, 7, 13, 36
See also Ngugi, James (Thiong'o); Wa
Thiong'o, Ngugi

Nichol, B(arrie) P(hillip) 1944-..... CLC 18
See also CA 53-56; DLB 53

Nichols, John (Treadwell) 1940-.... CLC 38
See also CAAS 2; CANR 6; CA 9-12R;
DLB-Y 82

Nichols, Peter (Richard) 1927-... CLC 5, 36
See also CA 104; DLB 13

Nicolas, F.R.E. 1927-
See Freeling, Nicolas

Niedecker, Lorine 1903-1970.... CLC 10, 42
See also CAP 2; CA 25-28; DLB 48

Nietzsche, Friedrich (Wilhelm)
1844-1900 .... TCLC 10, 18
See also CA 107

Nievo, Ippolito 1831-1861 .... NCLC 22

Nightingale, Anne Redmon 1943-
See Redmon (Nightingale), Anne
See also CA 103

Nin, Anais
1903-1977 ...... CLC 1, 4, 8, 11, 14, 60
See also CANR 22; CA 13-16R;
obituary CA 69-72; DLB 2, 4

Nissenson, Hugh 1933-.......... CLC 4, 9
See also CA 17-20R; DLB 28

Niven, Larry 1938-............... CLC 8
See also Niven, Laurence Van Cott
See also DLB 8

Niven, Laurence Van Cott 1938-
See Niven, Larry
See also CANR 14; CA 21-24R

Nixon, Agnes Eckhardt 1927-...... CLC 21
See also CA 110

Osceola 1885-1962
  See Dinesen, Isak; Blixen, Karen
    (Christentze Dinesen)

Oshima, Nagisa 1932- .... **CLC 20**
  See also CA 116

Oskison, John M. 1874-1947...... **TCLC 35**

Ossoli, Sarah Margaret (Fuller marchesa d')
    1810-1850
  See Fuller, (Sarah) Margaret
  See also SATA 25

Ostrovsky, Alexander
    1823-1886 .... **NCLC 30**

Otero, Blas de 1916- .... **CLC 11**
  See also CA 89-92

Owen, Wilfred (Edward Salter)
    1893-1918 .... **TCLC 5, 27**
  See also CA 104; DLB 20

Owens, Rochelle 1936-.......... **CLC 8**
  See also CAAS 2; CA 17-20R

Owl, Sebastian 1939-
  See Thompson, Hunter S(tockton)

Oz, Amos 1939- ... **CLC 5, 8, 11, 27, 33, 54**
  See also CA 53-56

Ozick, Cynthia 1928-...... **CLC 3, 7, 28, 62**
  See also CANR 28; CA 17-20R; DLB 28;
    DLB-Y 82

Ozu, Yasujiro 1903-1963......... **CLC 16**
  See also CA 112

Pa Chin 1904-.................. **CLC 18**
  See also Li Fei-kan

Pack, Robert 1929-.............. **CLC 13**
  See also CANR 3; CA 1-4R; DLB 5

Padgett, Lewis 1915-1958
  See Kuttner, Henry

Padilla, Heberto 1932-........... **CLC 38**
  See also CA 123

Page, Jimmy 1944-.............. **CLC 12**

Page, Louise 1955-.............. **CLC 40**

Page, P(atricia) K(athleen)
    1916-..................... **CLC 7, 18**
  See also CANR 4, 22; CA 53-56; DLB 68

Paget, Violet 1856-1935
  See Lee, Vernon
  See also CA 104

Palamas, Kostes 1859-1943 .... **TCLC 5**
  See also CA 105

Palazzeschi, Aldo 1885-1974...... **CLC 11**
  See also CA 89-92; obituary CA 53-56

Paley, Grace 1922-........... **CLC 4, 6, 37**
  See also CANR 13; CA 25-28R; DLB 28

Palin, Michael 1943- .... **CLC 21**
  See also Monty Python
  See also CA 107

Palma, Ricardo 1833-1919........ **TCLC 29**
  See also CANR 123

Pancake, Breece Dexter 1952-1979
  See Pancake, Breece D'J

Pancake, Breece D'J 1952-1979 .... **CLC 29**
  See also obituary CA 109

Papadiamantis, Alexandros
    1851-1911 .... **TCLC 29**

Papini, Giovanni 1881-1956...... **TCLC 22**
  See also CA 121

Paracelsus 1493-1541............. **LC 14**

Parini, Jay (Lee) 1948- .... **CLC 54**
  See also CA 97-100

Parker, Dorothy (Rothschild)
    1893-1967 .... **CLC 15; SSC 2**
  See also CAP 2; CA 19-20;
    obituary CA 25-28R; DLB 11, 45

Parker, Robert B(rown) 1932-..... **CLC 27**
  See also CANR 1, 26; CA 49-52

Parkin, Frank 1940-.............. **CLC 43**

Parkman, Francis 1823-1893..... **NCLC 12**
  See also DLB 1, 30

Parks, Gordon (Alexander Buchanan)
    1912-..................... **CLC 1, 16**
  See also CANR 26; CA 41-44R; SATA 8;
    DLB 33

Parnell, Thomas 1679-1718 .... **LC 3**

Parra, Nicanor 1914-............. **CLC 2**
  See also CA 85-88

Pasolini, Pier Paolo
    1922-1975 .... **CLC 20, 37**
  See also CA 93-96; obituary CA 61-64

Pastan, Linda (Olenik) 1932- ...... **CLC 27**
  See also CANR 18; CA 61-64; DLB 5

Pasternak, Boris
    1890-1960 .... **CLC 7, 10, 18, 63**
  See also CA 127; obituary CA 116

Patchen, Kenneth 1911-1972... **CLC 1, 2, 18**
  See also CANR 3; CA 1-4R;
    obituary CA 33-36R; DLB 16, 48

Pater, Walter (Horatio)
    1839-1894 .... **NCLC 7**
  See also DLB 57

Paterson, Andrew Barton
    1864-1941 .... **TCLC 32**

Paterson, Katherine (Womeldorf)
    1932-..................... **CLC 12, 30**
  See also CLR 7; CA 21-24R; SATA 13, 53;
    DLB 52

Patmore, Coventry Kersey Dighton
    1823-1896 .... **NCLC 9**
  See also DLB 35

Paton, Alan (Stewart)
    1903-1988 .... **CLC 4, 10, 25, 55**
  See also CANR 22; CAP 1; CA 15-16;
    obituary CA 125; SATA 11

Paulding, James Kirke 1778-1860.. **NCLC 2**
  See also DLB 3, 59, 74

Paulin, Tom 1949-............... **CLC 37**
  See also CA 123; DLB 40

Paustovsky, Konstantin (Georgievich)
    1892-1968 .... **CLC 40**
  See also CA 93-96; obituary CA 25-28R

Paustowsky, Konstantin (Georgievich)
    1892-1968
  See Paustovsky, Konstantin (Georgievich)

Pavese, Cesare 1908-1950 .... **TCLC 3**
  See also CA 104

Pavic, Milorad 1929-............. **CLC 60**

Payne, Alan 1932-
  See Jakes, John (William)

Paz, Octavio
    1914- ..... **CLC 3, 4, 6, 10, 19, 51; PC 1**
  See also CA 73-76

Peacock, Molly 1947-............ **CLC 60**
  See also CA 103

Peacock, Thomas Love
    1785-1886 .... **NCLC 22**

Peake, Mervyn 1911-1968...... **CLC 7, 54**
  See also CANR 3; CA 5-8R;
    obituary CA 25-28R; SATA 23; DLB 15

Pearce, (Ann) Philippa 1920-....... **CLC 21**
  See also Christie, (Ann) Philippa
  See also CLR 9; CA 5-8R; SATA 1

Pearl, Eric 1934-
  See Elman, Richard

Pearson, T(homas) R(eid) 1956- .... **CLC 39**
  See also CA 120

Peck, John 1941-................. **CLC 3**
  See also CANR 3; CA 49-52

Peck, Richard 1934-.............. **CLC 21**
  See also CLR 15; CANR 19; CA 85-88;
    SAAS 2; SATA 18

Peck, Robert Newton 1928-........ **CLC 17**
  See also CA 81-84; SAAS 1; SATA 21

Peckinpah, (David) Sam(uel)
    1925-1984 .... **CLC 20**
  See also CA 109; obituary CA 114

Pedersen, Knut 1859-1952
  See Hamsun, Knut
  See also CA 104, 109

Peguy, Charles (Pierre)
    1873-1914 .... **TCLC 10**
  See also CA 107

Pepys, Samuel 1633-1703........... **LC 11**

Percy, Walker
    1916- .... **CLC 2, 3, 6, 8, 14, 18, 47**
  See also CANR 1; CA 1-4R; DLB 2;
    DLB-Y 80

Perec, Georges 1936-1982 .... **CLC 56**

Pereda, Jose Maria de
    1833-1906 .... **TCLC 16**

Perelman, S(idney) J(oseph)
    1904-1979 ... **CLC 3, 5, 9, 15, 23, 44, 49**
  See also CANR 18; CA 73-76;
    obituary CA 89-92; DLB 11, 44

Peret, Benjamin 1899-1959 .... **TCLC 20**
  See also CA 117

Peretz, Isaac Leib 1852?-1915..... **TCLC 16**
  See also CA 109

Perez, Galdos Benito 1853-1920... **TCLC 27**
  See also CA 125

Perrault, Charles 1628-1703 .... **LC 2**
  See also SATA 25

Perse, St.-John 1887-1975.... **CLC 4, 11, 46**
  See also Leger, (Marie-Rene) Alexis
    Saint-Leger

Pesetsky, Bette 1932-............. **CLC 28**

Peshkov, Alexei Maximovich 1868-1936
  See Gorky, Maxim
  See also CA 105

Pessoa, Fernando (Antonio Nogueira)
    1888-1935 .... **TCLC 27**
  See also CA 125

Peterkin, Julia (Mood) 1880-1961... **CLC 31**
  See also CA 102; DLB 9

Peters, Joan K. 1945-............. **CLC 39**

Rohmer, Eric 1920- .... CLC 16
See also Scherer, Jean-Marie Maurice

Rohmer, Sax 1883-1959......... TCLC 28
See also Ward, Arthur Henry Sarsfield
See also CA 108; DLB 70

Roiphe, Anne (Richardson)
1935- .... CLC 3, 9
See also CA 89-92; DLB-Y 80

Rolfe, Frederick (William Serafino Austin
Lewis Mary) 1860-1913...... TCLC 12
See also CA 107; DLB 34

Rolland, Romain 1866-1944...... TCLC 23
See also CA 118

Rolvaag, O(le) E(dvart)
1876-1931 .... TCLC 17
See also CA 117; DLB 9

Romains, Jules 1885-1972......... CLC 7
See also CA 85-88

Romero, Jose Ruben 1890-1952 ... TCLC 14
See also CA 114

Ronsard, Pierre de 1524-1585....... LC 6

Rooke, Leon 1934-............ CLC 25, 34
See also CANR 23; CA 25-28R

Roper, William 1498-1578.......... LC 10

Rosa, Joao Guimaraes 1908-1967 ... CLC 23
See also obituary CA 89-92

Rosen, Richard (Dean) 1949-....... CLC 39
See also CA 77-80

Rosenberg, Isaac 1890-1918...... TCLC 12
See also CA 107; DLB 20

Rosenblatt, Joe 1933-............ CLC 15
See also Rosenblatt, Joseph

Rosenblatt, Joseph 1933-
See Rosenblatt, Joe
See also CA 89-92

Rosenfeld, Samuel 1896-1963
See Tzara, Tristan
See also obituary CA 89-92

Rosenthal, M(acha) L(ouis) 1917-... CLC 28
See also CAAS 6; CANR 4; CA 1-4R;
DLB 5

Ross, (James) Sinclair 1908-....... CLC 13
See also CA 73-76

Rossetti, Christina Georgina
1830-1894 .... NCLC 2
See also SATA 20; DLB 35

Rossetti, Dante Gabriel
1828-1882 .... NCLC 4
See also DLB 35

Rossetti, Gabriel Charles Dante 1828-1882
See Rossetti, Dante Gabriel

Rossner, Judith (Perelman)
1935-.................... CLC 6, 9, 29
See also CANR 18; CA 17-20R; DLB 6

Rostand, Edmond (Eugene Alexis)
1868-1918 .... TCLC 6, 37
See also CA 104, 126

Roth, Henry 1906-........... CLC 2, 6, 11
See also CAP 1; CA 11-12; DLB 28

Roth, Joseph 1894-1939......... TCLC 33

Roth, Philip (Milton)
1933-...... CLC 1, 2, 3, 4, 6, 9, 15, 22,
31, 47
See also CANR 1, 22; CA 1-4R; DLB 2, 28;
DLB-Y 82

Rothenberg, James 1931-.......... CLC 57

Rothenberg, Jerome 1931-......... CLC 6
See also CANR 1; CA 45-48; DLB 5

Roumain, Jacques 1907-1944..... TCLC 19
See also CA 117

Rourke, Constance (Mayfield)
1885-1941 .... TCLC 12
See also YABC 1; CA 107

Rousseau, Jean-Baptiste 1671-1741 ... LC 9

Rousseau, Jean-Jacques 1712-1778... LC 14

Roussel, Raymond 1877-1933 ..... TCLC 20
See also CA 117

Rovit, Earl (Herbert) 1927-......... CLC 7
See also CANR 12; CA 5-8R

Rowe, Nicholas 1674-1718.......... LC 8

Rowson, Susanna Haswell
1762-1824 .... NCLC 5
See also DLB 37

Roy, Gabrielle 1909-1983....... CLC 10, 14
See also CANR 5; CA 53-56;
obituary CA 110; DLB 68

Rozewicz, Tadeusz 1921-........ CLC 9, 23
See also CA 108

Ruark, Gibbons 1941- .... CLC 3
See also CANR 14; CA 33-36R

Rubens, Bernice 192?- .... CLC 19, 31
See also CA 25-28R; DLB 14

Rudkin, (James) David 1936- ...... CLC 14
See also CA 89-92; DLB 13

Rudnik, Raphael 1933-............ CLC 7
See also CA 29-32R

Ruiz, Jose Martinez 1874-1967
See Azorin

Rukeyser, Muriel
1913-1980 .... CLC 6, 10, 15, 27
See also CANR 26; CA 5-8R;
obituary CA 93-96; obituary SATA 22;
DLB 48

Rule, Jane (Vance) 1931-.......... CLC 27
See also CANR 12; CA 25-28R; DLB 60

Rulfo, Juan 1918-1986............. CLC 8
See also CANR 26; CA 85-88;
obituary CA 118

Runyon, (Alfred) Damon
1880-1946 .... TCLC 10
See also CA 107; DLB 11

Rush, Norman 1933-.............. CLC 44
See also CA 121, 126

Rushdie, (Ahmed) Salman
1947- .... CLC 23, 31, 55, 59
See also CA 108, 111

Rushforth, Peter (Scott) 1945- ..... CLC 19
See also CA 101

Ruskin, John 1819-1900......... TCLC 20
See also CA 114; SATA 24; DLB 55

Russ, Joanna 1937-.............. CLC 15
See also CANR 11; CA 25-28R; DLB 8

Russell, George William 1867-1935
See A. E.
See also CA 104

Russell, (Henry) Ken(neth Alfred)
1927-.................... CLC 16
See also CA 105

Russell, Willy 1947-............. CLC 60

Rutherford, Mark 1831-1913..... TCLC 25
See also CA 121; DLB 18

Ruyslinck, Ward 1929-........... CLC 14

Ryan, Cornelius (John) 1920-1974 ... CLC 7
See also CA 69-72; obituary CA 53-56

Rybakov, Anatoli 1911?- .... CLC 23, 53
See also CA 126

Ryder, Jonathan 1927-
See Ludlum, Robert

Ryga, George 1932- .... CLC 14
See also CA 101; obituary CA 124; DLB 60

Séviné, Marquise de Marie de
Rabutin-Chantal 1626-1696..... LC 11

Saba, Umberto 1883-1957 .... TCLC 33

Sabato, Ernesto 1911- .... CLC 10, 23
See also CA 97-100

Sachs, Marilyn (Stickle) 1927- ..... CLC 35
See also CLR 2; CANR 13; CA 17-20R;
SAAS 2; SATA 3, 52

Sachs, Nelly 1891-1970 .... CLC 14
See also CAP 2; CA 17-18;
obituary CA 25-28R

Sackler, Howard (Oliver)
1929-1982 .... CLC 14
See also CA 61-64; obituary CA 108; DLB 7

Sade, Donatien Alphonse Francois, Comte de
1740-1814 .... NCLC 3

Sadoff, Ira 1945-................. CLC 9
See also CANR 5, 21; CA 53-56

Safire, William 1929-............. CLC 10
See also CA 17-20R

Sagan, Carl (Edward) 1934-........ CLC 30
See also CANR 11; CA 25-28R

Sagan, Francoise
1935- .... CLC 3, 6, 9, 17, 36
See also Quoirez, Francoise
See also CANR 6

Sahgal, Nayantara (Pandit) 1927-... CLC 41
See also CANR 11; CA 9-12R

Saint, H(arry) F. 1941- .... CLC 50

Sainte-Beuve, Charles Augustin
1804-1869 .... NCLC 5

Sainte-Marie, Beverly 1941-1972?
See Sainte-Marie, Buffy
See also CA 107

Sainte-Marie, Buffy 1941-........ CLC 17
See also Sainte-Marie, Beverly

Saint-Exupery, Antoine (Jean Baptiste Marie
Roger) de 1900-1944 .... TCLC 2
See also CLR 10; CA 108; SATA 20;
DLB 72

Saintsbury, George 1845-1933..... TCLC 31
See also DLB 57

Sait Faik (Abasiyanik)
1906-1954 .... TCLC 23

Saki   1870-1916 . . . . TCLC 3
  See also Munro, H(ector) H(ugh)
  See also CA 104

Salama, Hannu   1936- . . . . CLC 18

Salamanca, J(ack) R(ichard)
  1922- . . . . CLC 4, 15
  See also CA 25-28R

Salinas, Pedro   1891-1951 . . . . TCLC 17
  See also CA 117

Salinger, J(erome) D(avid)
  1919- . . . . CLC 1, 3, 8, 12, 56; SSC 2
  See also CA 5-8R; DLB 2;
  CDALB 1941-1968

Salter, James   1925- . . . . CLC 7, 52, 59
  See also CA 73-76

Saltus, Edgar (Evertson)
  1855-1921 . . . . TCLC 8
  See also CA 105

Saltykov, Mikhail Evgrafovich
  1826-1889 . . . . NCLC 16

Samarakis, Antonis   1919- . . . . CLC 5
  See also CA 25-28R

Sanchez, Florencio   1875-1910 . . . . . TCLC 37

Sanchez, Luis Rafael   1936- . . . . CLC 23

Sanchez, Sonia   1934- . . . . CLC 5
  See also CA 33-36R; SATA 22; DLB 41

Sand, George   1804-1876 . . . . NCLC 2

Sandburg, Carl (August)
  1878-1967 . . . . CLC 1, 4, 10, 15, 35
  See also CA 5-8R; obituary CA 25-28R;
  SATA 8; DLB 17, 54; CDALB 1865-1917

Sandburg, Charles August   1878-1967
  See Sandburg, Carl (August)

Sanders, (James) Ed(ward)   1939- . . . CLC 53
  See also CANR 13; CA 15-16R, 103;
  DLB 16

Sanders, Lawrence   1920- . . . . CLC 41
  See also CA 81-84

Sandoz, Mari (Susette)   1896-1966 . . CLC 28
  See also CANR 17; CA 1-4R;
  obituary CA 25-28R; SATA 5; DLB 9

Saner, Reg(inald Anthony)   1931- . . . . CLC 9
  See also CA 65-68

Sannazaro, Jacopo   1456?-1530 . . . . LC 8

Sansom, William   1912-1976 . . . . . . CLC 2, 6
  See also CA 5-8R; obituary CA 65-68

Santiago, Danny   1911- . . . . CLC 33
  See also CA 125

Santmyer, Helen Hooven
  1895-1986 . . . . CLC 33
  See also CANR 15; CA 1-4R;
  obituary CA 118; DLB-Y 84

Santos, Bienvenido N(uqui)   1911- . . . CLC 22
  See also CANR 19; CA 101

Sappho   c. 6th-century B.C.- . . . . CMLC 3

Sarduy, Severo   1937- . . . . CLC 6
  See also CA 89-92

Sargeson, Frank   1903-1982 . . . . CLC 31
  See also CA 106, 25-28R; obituary CA 106

Sarmiento, Felix Ruben Garcia   1867-1916
  See Dario, Ruben
  See also CA 104

Saroyan, William
  1908-1981 . . . . . CLC 1, 8, 10, 29, 34, 56
  See also CA 5-8R; obituary CA 103;
  SATA 23; obituary SATA 24; DLB 7, 9;
  DLB-Y 81

Sarraute, Nathalie
  1902- . . . . CLC 1, 2, 4, 8, 10, 31
  See also CANR 23; CA 9-12R

Sarton, Eleanore Marie   1912-
  See Sarton, (Eleanor) May

Sarton, (Eleanor) May
  1912- . . . . CLC 4, 14, 49
  See also CANR 1; CA 1-4R; SATA 36;
  DLB 48; DLB-Y 81

Sartre, Jean-Paul (Charles Aymard)
  1905-1980 . . . CLC 1, 4, 7, 9, 13, 18, 24,
                              44, 50, 52
  See also CANR 21; CA 9-12R;
  obituary CA 97-100; DLB 72

Sassoon, Siegfried (Lorraine)
  1886-1967 . . . . CLC 36
  See also CA 104; obituary CA 25-28R;
  DLB 20

Saul, John (W. III)   1942- . . . . CLC 46
  See also CANR 16; CA 81-84

Saura, Carlos   1932- . . . . CLC 20
  See also CA 114

Sauser-Hall, Frederic-Louis   1887-1961
  See Cendrars, Blaise
  See also CA 102; obituary CA 93-96

Savage, Thomas   1915- . . . . CLC 40

Savan, Glenn   19??- . . . . CLC 50

Sayers, Dorothy L(eigh)
  1893-1957 . . . . TCLC 2, 15
  See also CA 104, 119; DLB 10, 36

Sayers, Valerie   19??- . . . . CLC 50

Sayles, John (Thomas)
  1950- . . . . CLC 7, 10, 14
  See also CA 57-60; DLB 44

Scammell, Michael   19??- . . . . CLC 34

Scannell, Vernon   1922- . . . . CLC 49
  See also CANR 8; CA 5-8R; DLB 27

Schaeffer, Susan Fromberg
  1941- . . . . CLC 6, 11, 22
  See also CANR 18; CA 49-52; SATA 22;
  DLB 28

Schell, Jonathan   1943- . . . . CLC 35
  See also CANR 12; CA 73-76

Schelling, Friedrich Wilhelm Joseph von
  1775-1854 . . . . NCLC 30
  See also DLB 90

Scherer, Jean-Marie Maurice   1920-
  See Rohmer, Eric
  See also CA 110

Schevill, James (Erwin)   1920- . . . . . . CLC 7
  See also CA 5-8R

Schisgal, Murray (Joseph)   1926- . . . . . CLC 6
  See also CA 21-24R

Schlee, Ann   1934- . . . . CLC 35
  See also CA 101; SATA 36, 44

Schlegel, August Wilhelm von
  1767-1845 . . . . NCLC 15

Schlegel, Johann Elias (von)
  1719?-1749 . . . . LC 5

Schmidt, Arno   1914-1979 . . . . CLC 56
  See also obituary CA 109; DLB 69

Schmitz, Ettore   1861-1928
  See Svevo, Italo
  See also CA 104, 122

Schnackenberg, Gjertrud   1953- . . . . . CLC 40
  See also CA 116

Schneider, Leonard Alfred   1925-1966
  See Bruce, Lenny
  See also CA 89-92

Schnitzler, Arthur   1862-1931 . . . . . . TCLC 4
  See also CA 104

Schorer, Mark   1908-1977 . . . . CLC 9
  See also CANR 7; CA 5-8R;
  obituary CA 73-76

Schrader, Paul (Joseph)   1946- . . . . . . CLC 26
  See also CA 37-40R; DLB 44

Schreiner (Cronwright), Olive (Emilie
  Albertina)   1855-1920 . . . . TCLC 9
  See also CA 105; DLB 18

Schulberg, Budd (Wilson)
  1914- . . . . CLC 7, 48
  See also CANR 19; CA 25-28R; DLB 6, 26,
  28; DLB-Y 81

Schulz, Bruno   1892-1942 . . . . TCLC 5
  See also CA 115, 123

Schulz, Charles M(onroe)   1922- . . . . CLC 12
  See also CANR 6; CA 9-12R; SATA 10

Schuyler, James (Marcus)
  1923- . . . . CLC 5, 23
  See also CA 101; DLB 5

Schwartz, Delmore
  1913-1966 . . . . CLC 2, 4, 10, 45
  See also CAP 2; CA 17-18;
  obituary CA 25-28R; DLB 28, 48

Schwartz, John Burnham   1925- . . . . CLC 59

Schwartz, Lynne Sharon   1939- . . . . . CLC 31
  See also CA 103

Schwarz-Bart, Andre   1928- . . . . CLC 2, 4
  See also CA 89-92

Schwarz-Bart, Simone   1938- . . . . CLC 7
  See also CA 97-100

Schwob, (Mayer Andre) Marcel
  1867-1905 . . . . TCLC 20
  See also CA 117

Sciascia, Leonardo
  1921-1989 . . . . CLC 8, 9, 41
  See also CA 85-88

Scoppettone, Sandra   1936- . . . . CLC 26
  See also CA 5-8R; SATA 9

Scorsese, Martin   1942- . . . . CLC 20
  See also CA 110, 114

Scotland, Jay   1932-
  See Jakes, John (William)

Scott, Duncan Campbell
  1862-1947 . . . . TCLC 6
  See also CA 104

Scott, Evelyn   1893-1963 . . . . CLC 43
  See also CA 104; obituary CA 112; DLB 9,
  48

Scott, F(rancis) R(eginald)
  1899-1985 . . . . CLC 22
  See also CA 101; obituary CA 114

Smith, Sara Mahala Redway 1900-1972
See Benson, Sally

Smith, Stevie 1902-1971.... **CLC 3, 8, 25, 44**
See also Smith, Florence Margaret
See also DLB 20

Smith, Wilbur (Addison) 1933-..... **CLC 33**
See also CANR 7; CA 13-16R

Smith, William Jay 1918-.......... **CLC 6**
See also CA 5-8R; SATA 2; DLB 5

Smolenskin, Peretz 1842-1885.... **NCLC 30**

Smollett, Tobias (George) 1721-1771 .. **LC 2**
See also DLB 39

Snodgrass, W(illiam) D(e Witt)
1926-............... **CLC 2, 6, 10, 18**
See also CANR 6; CA 1-4R; DLB 5

Snow, C(harles) P(ercy)
1905-1980 ...... **CLC 1, 4, 6, 9, 13, 19**
See also CA 5-8R; obituary CA 101;
DLB 15

Snyder, Gary (Sherman)
1930-............. **CLC 1, 2, 5, 9, 32**
See also CA 17-20R; DLB 5, 16

Snyder, Zilpha Keatley 1927-...... **CLC 17**
See also CA 9-12R; SAAS 2; SATA 1, 28

Sobol, Joshua 19??-.............. **CLC 60**

Soderberg. Hjalmar 1869-1941 .... **TCLC 39**

Sodergran, Edith 1892-1923...... **TCLC 31**

Sokolov, Raymond 1941-.......... **CLC 7**
See also CA 85-88

Sologub, Fyodor 1863-1927........ **TCLC 9**
See also Teternikov, Fyodor Kuzmich
See also CA 104

Solomos, Dionysios 1798-1857 ... **NCLC 15**

Solwoska, Mara 1929-
See French, Marilyn
See also CANR 3; CA 69-72

Solzhenitsyn, Aleksandr I(sayevich)
1918- ... **CLC 1, 2, 4, 7, 9, 10, 18, 26, 34**
See also CA 69-72

Somers, Jane 1919-
See Lessing, Doris (May)

Sommer, Scott 1951- .... **CLC 25**
See also CA 106

Sondheim, Stephen (Joshua)
1930- .... **CLC 30, 39**
See also CA 103

Sontag, Susan 1933-... **CLC 1, 2, 10, 13, 31**
See also CA 17-20R; DLB 2

Sophocles
c. 496? B.C.-c. 406? B.C...... **CMLC 2**

Sorrentino, Gilbert
1929- .... **CLC 3, 7, 14, 22, 40**
See also CANR 14; CA 77-80; DLB 5;
DLB-Y 80

Soto, Gary 1952-................. **CLC 32**
See also CA 119

Souster, (Holmes) Raymond
1921-..................... **CLC 5, 14**
See also CANR 13; CA 13-16R

Southern, Terry 1926- .... **CLC 7**
See also CANR 1; CA 1-4R; DLB 2

Southey, Robert 1774-1843 .... **NCLC 8**

Southworth, Emma Dorothy Eliza Nevitte
1819-1899 .... **NCLC 26**

Soyinka, Akinwande Oluwole 1934-
See Soyinka, Wole

Soyinka, Wole 1934- .. **CLC 3, 5, 14, 36, 44**
See also CA 13-16R; DLB-Y 86

Spackman, W(illiam) M(ode)
1905-...................... **CLC 46**
See also CA 81-84

Spacks, Barry 1931-.............. **CLC 14**
See also CA 29-32R

Spanidou, Irini 1946-............. **CLC 44**

Spark, Muriel (Sarah)
1918- .... **CLC 2, 3, 5, 8, 13, 18, 40**
See also CANR 12; CA 5-8R; DLB 15

Spencer, Elizabeth 1921-.......... **CLC 22**
See also CA 13-16R; SATA 14; DLB 6

Spencer, Scott 1945-.............. **CLC 30**
See also CA 113; DLB-Y 86

Spender, Stephen (Harold)
1909- .... **CLC 1, 2, 5, 10, 41**
See also CA 9-12R; DLB 20

Spengler, Oswald 1880-1936 ...... **TCLC 25**
See also CA 118

Spenser, Edmund 1552?-1599 .... **LC 5**

Spicer, Jack 1925-1965 .... **CLC 8, 18**
See also CA 85-88; DLB 5, 16

Spielberg, Peter 1929- .... **CLC 6**
See also CANR 4; CA 5-8R; DLB-Y 81

Spielberg, Steven 1947-........... **CLC 20**
See also CA 77-80; SATA 32

Spillane, Frank Morrison 1918-
See Spillane, Mickey
See also CA 25-28R

Spillane, Mickey 1918- .... **CLC 3, 13**
See also Spillane, Frank Morrison

Spinoza, Benedictus de 1632-1677 .... **LC 9**

Spinrad, Norman (Richard) 1940-... **CLC 46**
See also CANR 20; CA 37-40R; DLB 8

Spitteler, Carl (Friedrich Georg)
1845-1924 .... **TCLC 12**
See also CA 109

Spivack, Kathleen (Romola Drucker)
1938-...................... **CLC 6**
See also CA 49-52

Spoto, Donald 1941-.............. **CLC 39**
See also CANR 11; CA 65-68

Springsteen, Bruce 1949-.......... **CLC 17**
See also CA 111

Spurling, Hilary 1940-............. **CLC 34**
See also CANR 25; CA 104

Squires, (James) Radcliffe 1917-.... **CLC 51**
See also CANR 6, 21; CA 1-4R

Stael-Holstein, Anne Louise Germaine Necker,
Baronne de 1766-1817....... **NCLC 3**

Stafford, Jean 1915-1979...... **CLC 4, 7, 19**
See also CANR 3; CA 1-4R;
obituary CA 85-88; obituary SATA 22;
DLB 2

Stafford, William (Edgar)
1914- .... **CLC 4, 7, 29**
See also CAAS 3; CANR 5, 22; CA 5-8R;
DLB 5

Stannard, Martin 1947-.......... **CLC 44**

Stanton, Maura 1946- .... **CLC 9**
See also CANR 15; CA 89-92

Stapledon, (William) Olaf
1886-1950 .... **TCLC 22**
See also CA 111; DLB 15

Starbuck, George (Edwin) 1931-.... **CLC 53**
See also CANR 23; CA 21-22R

Stark, Richard 1933-
See Westlake, Donald E(dwin)

Stead, Christina (Ellen)
1902-1983 .... **CLC 2, 5, 8, 32**
See also CA 13-16R; obituary CA 109

Steele, Timothy (Reid) 1948-....... **CLC 45**
See also CANR 16; CA 93-96

Steffens, (Joseph) Lincoln
1866-1936 .... **TCLC 20**
See also CA 117; SAAS 1

Stegner, Wallace (Earle) 1909-... **CLC 9, 49**
See also CANR 1, 21; CA 1-4R; DLB 9

Stein, Gertrude 1874-1946... **TCLC 1, 6, 28**
See also CA 104; DLB 4, 54

Steinbeck, John (Ernst)
1902-1968 ..... **CLC 1, 5, 9, 13, 21, 34,
45, 59**
See also CANR 1; CA 1-4R;
obituary CA 25-28R; SATA 9; DLB 7, 9;
DLB-DS 2

Steinem, Gloria 1934-............. **CLC 63**
See also CANR 28; CA 53-56

Steiner, George 1929-............. **CLC 24**
See also CA 73-76

Steiner, Rudolf(us Josephus Laurentius)
1861-1925 .... **TCLC 13**
See also CA 107

Stendhal 1783-1842............. **NCLC 23**

Stephen, Leslie 1832-1904....... **TCLC 23**
See also CANR 9; CA 21-24R, 123;
DLB 57

Stephens, James 1882?-1950 .... **TCLC 4**
See also CA 104; DLB 19

Stephens, Reed
See Donaldson, Stephen R.

Steptoe, Lydia 1892-1982
See Barnes, Djuna

Sterling, George 1869-1926....... **TCLC 20**
See also CA 117; DLB 54

Stern, Gerald 1925-.............. **CLC 40**
See also CA 81-84

Stern, Richard G(ustave) 1928-... **CLC 4, 39**
See also CANR 1, 25; CA 1-4R

Sternberg, Jonas 1894-1969
See Sternberg, Josef von

Sternberg, Josef von 1894-1969..... **CLC 20**
See also CA 81-84

Sterne, Laurence 1713-1768.......... **LC 2**
See also DLB 39

Sternheim, (William Adolf) Carl
1878-1942 .... **TCLC 8**
See also CA 105

Stevens, Mark 19??-.............. **CLC 34**

Stevens, Wallace 1879-1955..... **TCLC 3, 12**
See also CA 104, 124; DLB 54

Transtromer, Tomas (Gosta)
1931- .... CLC 52
See also CA 117

Traven, B.   1890-1969 .... CLC 8, 11
See also CAP 2; CA 19-20;
obituary CA 25-28R; DLB 9, 56

Tremain, Rose   1943- .... CLC 42
See also CA 97-100; DLB 14

Tremblay, Michel   1942- .... CLC 29
See also CA 116; DLB 60

Trevanian   1925- .... CLC 29
See also CA 108

Trevor, William   1928- ..... CLC 7, 9, 14, 25
See also Cox, William Trevor
See also DLB 14

Trifonov, Yuri (Valentinovich)
1925-1981 .... CLC 45
See also obituary CA 103, 126

Trilling, Lionel   1905-1975 .... CLC 9, 11, 24
See also CANR 10; CA 9-12R;
obituary CA 61-64; DLB 28, 63

Trogdon, William   1939-
See Heat Moon, William Least
See also CA 115, 119

Trollope, Anthony   1815-1882 ..... NCLC 6
See also SATA 22; DLB 21, 57

Trollope, Frances   1780-1863 ..... NCLC 30
See also DLB 21

Trotsky, Leon (Davidovich)
1879-1940 .... TCLC 22
See also CA 118

Trotter (Cockburn), Catharine
1679-1749 .... LC 8

Trow, George W. S.   1943- .... CLC 52
See also CA 126

Troyat, Henri   1911- .... CLC 23
See also CANR 2; CA 45-48

Trudeau, G(arretson) B(eekman)   1948-
See Trudeau, Garry
See also CA 81-84; SATA 35

Trudeau, Garry   1948- .... CLC 12
See also Trudeau, G(arretson) B(eekman)

Truffaut, Francois   1932-1984 ...... CLC 20
See also CA 81-84; obituary CA 113

Trumbo, Dalton   1905-1976 .... CLC 19
See also CANR 10; CA 21-24R;
obituary CA 69-72; DLB 26

Trumbull, John   1750-1831 .... NCLC 30
See also DLB 31

Tryon, Thomas   1926- .... CLC 3, 11
See also CA 29-32R

Ts'ao Hsueh-ch'in   1715?-1763 .... LC 1

Tsushima Shuji   1909-1948
See Dazai Osamu
See also CA 107

Tsvetaeva (Efron), Marina (Ivanovna)
1892-1941 .... TCLC 7, 35
See also CA 104, 128

Tunis, John R(oberts)   1889-1975 ... CLC 12
See also CA 61-64; SATA 30, 37; DLB 22

Tuohy, Frank   1925- .... CLC 37
See also DLB 14

Tuohy, John Francis   1925-
See Tuohy, Frank
See also CANR 3; CA 5-8R

Turco, Lewis (Putnam)   1934- ... CLC 11, 63
See also CANR 24; CA 13-16R; DLB-Y 84

Turgenev, Ivan
1818-1883 .... NCLC 21; SSC 7

Turner, Frederick   1943- .... CLC 48
See also CANR 12; CA 73-76; DLB 40

Tutuola, Amos   1920- .... CLC 5, 14, 29
See also CA 9-12R

Twain, Mark
1835-1910 ... TCLC 6, 12, 19, 36; SSC 6
See also Clemens, Samuel Langhorne
See also YABC 2; DLB 11, 12, 23, 64, 74

Tyler, Anne
1941- .... CLC 7, 11, 18, 28, 44, 59
See also CANR 11; CA 9-12R; SATA 7;
DLB 6; DLB-Y 82

Tyler, Royall   1757-1826 .... NCLC 3
See also DLB 37

Tynan (Hinkson), Katharine
1861-1931 .... TCLC 3
See also CA 104

Tytell, John   1939- .... CLC 50
See also CA 29-32R

Tzara, Tristan   1896-1963 .... CLC 47
See also Rosenfeld, Samuel

Uhry, Alfred   1947?- .... CLC 55
See also CA 127

Unamuno (y Jugo), Miguel de
1864-1936 .... TCLC 2, 9
See also CA 104

Underwood, Miles   1909-1981
See Glassco, John

Undset, Sigrid   1882-1949 .... TCLC 3
See also CA 104

Ungaretti, Giuseppe
1888-1970 .... CLC 7, 11, 15
See also CAP 2; CA 19-20;
obituary CA 25-28R

Unger, Douglas   1952- .... CLC 34

Unger, Eva   1932-
See Figes, Eva

Updike, John (Hoyer)
1932- ...... CLC 1, 2, 3, 5, 7, 9, 13, 15,
23, 34, 43
See also CANR 4; CA 1-4R; CABS 2;
DLB 2, 5; DLB-Y 80, 82; DLB-DS 3

Urdang, Constance (Henriette)
1922- .... CLC 47
See also CANR 9, 24; CA 21-24R

Uris, Leon (Marcus)   1924- ...... CLC 7, 32
See also CANR 1; CA 1-4R; SATA 49

Ustinov, Peter (Alexander)   1921- .... CLC 1
See also CANR 25; CA 13-16R; DLB 13

Vaculik, Ludvik   1926- .... CLC 7
See also CA 53-56

Valenzuela, Luisa   1938- .... CLC 31
See also CA 101

Valera (y Acala-Galiano), Juan
1824-1905 .... TCLC 10
See also CA 106

Valery, Paul (Ambroise Toussaint Jules)
1871-1945 .... TCLC 4, 15
See also CA 104, 122

Valle-Inclan (y Montenegro), Ramon (Maria)
del   1866-1936 .... TCLC 5
See also CA 106

Vallejo, Cesar (Abraham)
1892-1938 .... TCLC 3
See also CA 105

Van Ash, Cay   1918- .... CLC 34

Vance, Jack   1916?- .... CLC 35
See also DLB 8

Vance, John Holbrook   1916?-
See Vance, Jack
See also CANR 17; CA 29-32R

Van Den Bogarde, Derek (Jules Gaspard
Ulric) Niven   1921-
See Bogarde, Dirk
See also CA 77-80

Vandenburgh, Jane   19??- .... CLC 59

Vanderhaeghe, Guy   1951- .... CLC 41
See also CA 113

Van der Post, Laurens (Jan)   1906- ... CLC 5
See also CA 5-8R

Van de Wetering, Janwillem
1931- .... CLC 47
See also CANR 4; CA 49-52

Van Dine, S. S.   1888-1939 .... TCLC 23

Van Doren, Carl (Clinton)
1885-1950 .... TCLC 18
See also CA 111

Van Doren, Mark   1894-1972 ..... CLC 6, 10
See also CANR 3; CA 1-4R;
obituary CA 37-40R; DLB 45

Van Druten, John (William)
1901-1957 .... TCLC 2
See also CA 104; DLB 10

Van Duyn, Mona   1921- .... CLC 3, 7, 63
See also CANR 7; CA 9-12R; DLB 5

Van Itallie, Jean-Claude   1936- ...... CLC 3
See also CAAS 2; CANR 1; CA 45-48;
DLB 7

Van Ostaijen, Paul   1896-1928 ..... TCLC 33

Van Peebles, Melvin   1932- ...... CLC 2, 20
See also CA 85-88

Vansittart, Peter   1920- .... CLC 42
See also CANR 3; CA 1-4R

Van Vechten, Carl   1880-1964 ...... CLC 33
See also obituary CA 89-92; DLB 4, 9, 51

Van Vogt, A(lfred) E(lton)   1912- ..... CLC 1
See also CA 21-24R; SATA 14; DLB 8

Varda, Agnes   1928- .... CLC 16
See also CA 116, 122

Vargas Llosa, (Jorge) Mario (Pedro)
1936- .... CLC 3, 6, 9, 10, 15, 31, 42
See also CANR 18; CA 73-76

Vassilikos, Vassilis   1933- .... CLC 4, 8
See also CA 81-84

Vaughn, Stephanie   19??- .... CLC 62

Vazov, Ivan   1850-1921 .... TCLC 25
See also CA 121

Waters, Roger 1944-
See Pink Floyd

Wa Thiong'o, Ngugi
1938- . . . . CLC 3, 7, 13, 36
See also Ngugi, James (Thiong'o); Ngugi wa
Thiong'o

Watkins, Paul 1964- . . . . CLC 55

Watkins, Vernon (Phillips)
1906-1967 . . . . CLC 43
See also CAP 1; CA 9-10;
obituary CA 25-28R; DLB 20

Waugh, Auberon (Alexander) 1939- . . CLC 7
See also CANR 6, 22; CA 45-48; DLB 14

Waugh, Evelyn (Arthur St. John)
1903-1966 . . . CLC 1, 3, 8, 13, 19, 27, 44
See also CANR 22; CA 85-88;
obituary CA 25-28R; DLB 15

Waugh, Harriet 1944- . . . . CLC 6
See also CANR 22; CA 85-88

Webb, Beatrice (Potter)
1858-1943 . . . . TCLC 22
See also CA 117

Webb, Charles (Richard) 1939- . . . . . . CLC 7
See also CA 25-28R

Webb, James H(enry), Jr. 1946- . . . . CLC 22
See also CA 81-84

Webb, Mary (Gladys Meredith)
1881-1927 . . . . TCLC 24
See also CA 123; DLB 34

Webb, Phyllis 1927- . . . . CLC 18
See also CANR 23; CA 104; DLB 53

Webb, Sidney (James)
1859-1947 . . . . TCLC 22
See also CA 117

Webber, Andrew Lloyd 1948- . . . . . . CLC 21

Weber, Lenora Mattingly
1895-1971 . . . . CLC 12
See also CAP 1; CA 19-20;
obituary CA 29-32R; SATA 2;
obituary SATA 26

Webster, Noah 1758-1843 . . . . NCLC 30
See also DLB 1, 37, 42, 43, 73

Wedekind, (Benjamin) Frank(lin)
1864-1918 . . . . TCLC 7
See also CA 104

Weidman, Jerome 1913- . . . . CLC 7
See also CANR 1; CA 1-4R; DLB 28

Weil, Simone 1909-1943 . . . . TCLC 23
See also CA 117

Weinstein, Nathan Wallenstein 1903?-1940
See West, Nathanael
See also CA 104

Weir, Peter 1944- . . . . CLC 20
See also CA 113, 123

Weiss, Peter (Ulrich)
1916-1982 . . . . CLC 3, 15, 51
See also CANR 3; CA 45-48;
obituary CA 106; DLB 69

Weiss, Theodore (Russell)
1916- . . . . CLC 3, 8, 14
See also CAAS 2; CA 9-12R; DLB 5

Welch, (Maurice) Denton
1915-1948 . . . . TCLC 22
See also CA 121

Welch, James 1940- . . . . CLC 6, 14, 52
See also CA 85-88

Weldon, Fay
1933- . . . . CLC 6, 9, 11, 19, 36, 59
See also CANR 16; CA 21-24R; DLB 14

Wellek, Rene 1903- . . . . CLC 28
See also CAAS 7; CANR 8; CA 5-8R;
DLB 63

Weller, Michael 1942- . . . . CLC 10, 53
See also CA 85-88

Weller, Paul 1958- . . . . CLC 26

Wellershoff, Dieter 1925- . . . . CLC 46
See also CANR 16; CA 89-92

Welles, (George) Orson
1915-1985 . . . . CLC 20
See also CA 93-96; obituary CA 117

Wellman, Manly Wade 1903-1986 . . CLC 49
See also CANR 6, 16; CA 1-4R;
obituary CA 118; SATA 6, 47

Wells, Carolyn 1862-1942 . . . . TCLC 35
See also CA 113; DLB 11

Wells, H(erbert) G(eorge)
1866-1946 . . . . . . TCLC 6, 12, 19; SSC 6
See also CA 110, 121; SATA 20; DLB 34,
70

Wells, Rosemary 1943- . . . . CLC 12
See also CLR 16; CA 85-88; SAAS 1;
SATA 18

Welty, Eudora (Alice)
1909- . . . . CLC 1, 2, 5, 14, 22, 33; SSC 1
See also CA 9-12R; CABS 1; DLB 2;
DLB-Y 87; CDALB 1941-1968

Wen I-to 1899-1946 . . . . TCLC 28

Werfel, Franz (V.) 1890-1945 . . . . . TCLC 8
See also CA 104

Wergeland, Henrik Arnold
1808-1845 . . . . NCLC 5

Wersba, Barbara 1932- . . . . CLC 30
See also CLR 3; CANR 16; CA 29-32R;
SAAS 2; SATA 1; DLB 52

Wertmuller, Lina 1928- . . . . CLC 16
See also CA 97-100

Wescott, Glenway 1901-1987 . . . . CLC 13
See also CANR 23; CA 13-16R;
obituary CA 121; DLB 4, 9

Wesker, Arnold 1932- . . . . CLC 3, 5, 42
See also CAAS 7; CANR 1; CA 1-4R;
DLB 13

Wesley, Richard (Errol) 1945- . . . . . . CLC 7
See also CA 57-60; DLB 38

Wessel, Johan Herman 1742-1785 . . . . LC 7

West, Anthony (Panther)
1914-1987 . . . . CLC 50
See also CANR 3, 19; CA 45-48; DLB 15

West, Jessamyn 1907-1984 . . . . . . CLC 7, 17
See also CA 9-12R; obituary CA 112;
obituary SATA 37; DLB 6; DLB-Y 84

West, Morris L(anglo) 1916- . . . . . CLC 6, 33
See also CA 5-8R; obituary CA 124

West, Nathanael 1903?-1940 . . . . TCLC 1, 14
See also Weinstein, Nathan Wallenstein
See also CA 125; DLB 4, 9, 28

West, Paul 1930- . . . . CLC 7, 14
See also CAAS 7; CANR 22; CA 13-16R;
DLB 14

West, Rebecca 1892-1983 . . CLC 7, 9, 31, 50
See also CANR 19; CA 5-8R;
obituary CA 109; DLB 36; DLB-Y 83

Westall, Robert (Atkinson) 1929- . . . CLC 17
See also CLR 13; CANR 18; CA 69-72;
SAAS 2; SATA 23

Westlake, Donald E(dwin)
1933- . . . . CLC 7, 33
See also CANR 16; CA 17-20R

Westmacott, Mary 1890-1976
See Christie, (Dame) Agatha (Mary
Clarissa)

Whalen, Philip 1923- . . . . CLC 6, 29
See also CANR 5; CA 9-12R; DLB 16

Wharton, Edith (Newbold Jones)
1862-1937 . . . . TCLC 3, 9, 27; SSC 6
See also CA 104; DLB 4, 9, 12, 78;
CDALB 1865-1917

Wharton, William 1925- . . . . CLC 18, 37
See also CA 93-96; DLB-Y 80

Wheatley (Peters), Phillis
1753?-1784 . . . . LC 3
See also DLB 31, 50; CDALB 1640-1865

Wheelock, John Hall 1886-1978 . . . . CLC 14
See also CANR 14; CA 13-16R;
obituary CA 77-80; DLB 45

Whelan, John 1900-
See O'Faolain, Sean

Whitaker, Rodney 1925-
See Trevanian

White, E(lwyn) B(rooks)
1899-1985 . . . . CLC 10, 34, 39
See also CLR 1; CANR 16; CA 13-16R;
obituary CA 116; SATA 2, 29;
obituary SATA 44; DLB 11, 22

White, Edmund III 1940- . . . . CLC 27
See also CANR 3, 19; CA 45-48

White, Patrick (Victor Martindale)
1912- . . . . CLC 3, 4, 5, 7, 9, 18
See also CA 81-84

White, T(erence) H(anbury)
1906-1964 . . . . CLC 30
See also CA 73-76; SATA 12

White, Terence de Vere 1912- . . . . . . CLC 49
See also CANR 3; CA 49-52

White, Walter (Francis)
1893-1955 . . . . TCLC 15
See also CA 115, 124; DLB 51

White, William Hale 1831-1913
See Rutherford, Mark
See also CA 121

Whitehead, E(dward) A(nthony)
1933- . . . . CLC 5
See also CA 65-68

Whitemore, Hugh 1936- . . . . CLC 37

Whitman, Sarah Helen
1803-1878 . . . . NCLC 19
See also DLB 1

Whitman, Walt 1819-1892 . . . . NCLC 4
See also SATA 20; DLB 3, 64;
CDALB 1640-1865

Literary Criticism Series
Cumulative Topic Index

This index lists all topic entries in the Gale Literary Criticism Series *Contemporary Literary Criticism, Literature Criticism from 1400 to 1800, Nineteenth-Century Literature Criticism,* and *Twentieth-Century Literary Criticism.*

Topic Index

NCLC Cumulative Nationality Index

Nationality Index

Title Index to Volume 30

Title Index